The Almanac of t.

THE ALMANAC OF THE Christian World

Edythe Draper, EDITOR
Helen Gorges, RESEARCH EDITOR
Kenneth Petersen, PROJECT EDITOR

Tyndale House Publishers, Inc.
Wheaton, Illinois

The 1993-1994 Almanac year runs from July 1, 1990 to December 31, 1991.

The purpose of *The Almanac of the Christian World* is to provide the Christian public with a resource book that covers all facets of the Christian world. It presents historical and contemporary information, products, and services of interest to evangelical Christians. The purpose of the Almanac is to inform, not to endorse.

The Scripture quotation in the epigraph is from *The Living Bible,* copyright © 1971 owned by assignment by KNT Charitable Trust. All rights reserved.

ISSN 1052-2670
ISBN 0-8423-1687-6

98 97 96 95 94 93
8   7   6   5   4   3   2

Some of us have been given special ability as apostles; to others he has given the gift of being able to preach well; some have special ability in winning people to Christ, helping them to trust him as their Savior; still others have a gift for caring for God's people as a shepherd does his sheep, leading and teaching them in the ways of God.

Why is it that he gives us these special abilities to do certain things best? It is that God's people will be equipped to do better work for him, building up the church, the body of Christ, to a position of strength and maturity; until finally we all believe alike about our salvation and about our Savior, God's Son, and all become full-grown in the Lord—yes, to the point of being filled full with Christ. . . .

We will lovingly follow the truth at all times—speaking truly, dealing truly, living truly—and so become more and more in every way like Christ who is the Head of his body, the Church. Under his direction, the whole body is fitted together perfectly, and each part in its own special way helps the other parts, so that the whole body is healthy and growing and full of love.

Ephesians 4:11-13, 15-16
The Living Bible

Contents

The Year in Review

THE YEAR IN REVIEW: JULY 1990 TO DECEMBER 1991

JULY 1990

➤NATIONAL

Church's influence on decline?—The church's influence on American society seems to be declining.

Four out of five American adults say they are "Christian," according to a study by the Barna Research Group, but only 38 percent of those studied believe the church is relevant for today.

Denominations act on women's issues— Delegates to the annual synod of the 314,000-member Christian Reformed Church vote 99 to 84 adopting a resolution giving churches discretion to utilize the gifts of women by placing them in offices of leadership.

But women in the denomination must still wait until at least 1992 before they can be ordained, due to church procedure for ratifying such a motion.

Meanwhile, delegates at the world conference of the Seventh-day Adventist Church strongly reject a proposal to allow ordination of women.

Mozart piece found at Christian school— An accounting manager for Eastern College in St. David's, Penn., gets a big surprise. She stumbles upon the long-sought originals of two of Wolfgang Amadeus Mozart's greatest piano works, Fantasia in C Minor and Sonata in C Minor.

The 14-page document containing the two musical works was donated to Eastern Seminary in 1950, where it remained unnoticed in a safe. The find by Judy DiBona, who herself plays the piano, is expected to earn the seminary between $930,000 and $1.4 million when auctioned.

Pro-abortion justice retires from Supreme Court—Pro-life advocates rejoice when Justice William Brennan retires from the Supreme Court, making way for President George Bush to appoint another pro-life judge to the bench.

Pro-life lobbyists say they have never been closer to overturning the 1973 *Roe v. Wade* decision, which legalized abortion. Although the views of Bush's nominee for the high court, David Souter, are not made clear during his confirmation hearings, pro-lifers say they only stand to gain by his confirmation. Pro-lifers say it would be hard for any nominee to be more liberal than Brennan was. "At the very worst, we'll be in the same position we're in right now," says Tom Glessner, executive director of the Christian Action Council. "At the very best, we'll get a vote to reverse Roe."

➤INTERNATIONAL

Western evangelists miss Communist target—Many Western evangelists, eager to make disciples in the newly open countries of Eastern Europe and the Soviet Union, are going to all the wrong places and teaching all the wrong ways.

There has been a massive influx of well-intentioned Western evangelists to the former Communist countries, where they often duplicate each other's efforts.

The evangelists often preach at larger churches in the larger cities, missing the smaller churches with greater needs. And the vast array of doctrinal opinions the Westerners bring are too much for the Soviets and Eastern Europeans to handle.

But Westerners are hitting the target in providing needed Bibles and Bible reference materials.

THE YEAR IN REVIEW: JULY 1990 TO DECEMBER 1991 cont.

China's students turn to Christ—Thousands of Chinese students and young professionals are turning to Christ in the wake of the 1989 Tiananmen Square massacre, when the Chinese Communist party killed hundreds of people rallying for democratic change.

Intellectuals are finding answers in Christianity. But at the same time, many new converts aren't comfortable in the house-church movement or in the churches of the state-backed Protestant Three-Self Patriotic movement. "The house churches and the Three-Self churches are having huge problems coping with a terrific influx of converts from the intelligentsia," says Lesley Francis, director of the China Program for Overseas Missionary Fellowship.

These new converts often view the Three-Self churches as offering merely surface religion, so they turn to the house churches, says Anthony Lambert, a leading evangelical scholar on the house-church movement. But when they turn to house churches, the intellectuals find cultural barriers between their urban perspective and the perspective of the house-church leaders, who are often rural peasants.

AUGUST 1990
➤NATIONAL

Neuhaus goes Catholic—Famous Lutheran theologian Richard John Neuhaus is formally received into the Roman Catholic Church by John Cardinal O'Connor of New York.

Neuhaus, an ardent defender of conservative theology, says his decision to leave the Evangelical Lutheran Church in America is a logical move based on his understanding of what the sixteenth century Lutheran Reformation was about.

Burger King boycotted—Christian Leaders for Responsible Television (CLeaR-TV) announces that its 1,600-member coalition is boycotting Burger King because it sponsors TV programs that are excessively violent and sexual in content.

How churches grow—In order for a church to grow these days, it must stop trying to be all things to all people and tailor programs to specific groups, says a report by the Barna Research Group of Glendale, California.

The report indicates that among churches that are increasing membership yearly at a rate of 10 percent or more, "church growth is not so much a magic formula as it is a series of creative and sensitive responses to a changing environment."

The report also says growing churches "refused to be enticed into areas of ministry in which they discerned no special calling. Instead, they concentrated on doing what they were called to do," such as focusing on teenagers, single adults, or the elderly. Ironically, growing churches don't set growth as their primary goal, but merely experience it as a by-product of their successful ministry.

➤INTERNATIONAL

Track stars wow Germans—Some of the world's top track stars speak to more than 8,000 fans, who stay after a track meet at West Berlin's Olympic Stadium to listen to the gospel message. The program is sponsored by Lay Witnesses for Christ, a Texas-based ministry that works with Olympic athletes.

Testimonies are given by Roger Kingdom, two-time Olympic gold medalist in the 110-meter hurdles, and Leroy Burrell, whose victory in the 1989 Goodwill Games earned him the title "world's fastest human."

During a similar program two days later at a track meet in Cologne, American superstar sprinter Carl Lewis gives his testimony to about 10,000 admirers. "It's hard for Americans to imagine Carl Lewis's popularity in Europe, because we are inundated with superstars," says Bob Carey of Lay Witnesses. "But when Carl began to speak, fans literally climbed over fences to stand closer to him."

Chaplains careful in Persian Gulf—With more than 100,000 U.S. troops on alert in the Persian Gulf, chaplains are dishing out spiritual help.

But in Saudi Arabia, where laws prohibit the exercise of any religion other than Islam, chaplains on the military bases are having to walk a careful line to avoid offending their host.

Clergy can't wear religious garb or crosses. And distribution of Bibles or any missionary activities are prohibited.

But more than 200 chaplains are finding ways to meet the needs of their military personnel, gingerly and diplomatically holding services on military grounds.

Baptists gather for world conference— More than 10,000 Baptists from 85 countries meet in Seoul for the sixteenth Baptist World Congress, including 177 pastors and laity from Eastern Europe and a delegation of 150 from the Soviet Union. At the meeting, which is held once every five years, about 10,000 Korean converts are baptized.

SEPTEMBER 1990
➤NATIONAL

Southern Baptist seminary goes conservative—Trustees of Southern Baptist Theological Seminary in Louisville, Kentucky, the oldest seminary in the Southern Baptist denomination, vote 36 to 14 requiring faculty to affirm a belief in the Bible as literally true.

X Rating replaced with NC-17—Christian leaders see a veiled motive when the Motion Picture Association of America decides to replace the "X" rating with a new rating called "NC-17."

The new rating ostensibly is meant to prevent children under the age of 17 from gaining entrance to see certain films, but the United States Catholic Conference and the National Council of Churches charge that the Motion Picture Association was "caving in to the commercial interests of those who are attempting to get sexually exploitive material into general theater release."

The first NC-17 movie, *Henry and June,* is boycotted and protested by some Christian groups, including delegations led by Ted Baehr, the publisher of *MovieGuide,* a Christian critique of the movies, and by Donald Wildmon of the American Family Association.

➤INTERNATIONAL

No more relief—Western relief officials are saying they will stop relief efforts to wartorn Sudan unless that nation's Islamic government quits confiscating grain that is bound for the impoverished in the rebel-controlled areas of the south.

While drought conditions have damaged the lives of about 5 million in the country's southern regions, the Islamic general who controls the Sudan's military says he has no plans to change his dealings with relief efforts.

Messianic Jews raise their voice—The Messianic Jewish Alliance of America begins a campaign to pressure Israeli authorities to give Messianic Jews automatic citizenship upon immigration to Israel.

The campaign's goal is to gather one million signatures on a petition. The petition would ask the Israeli Supreme Court and the *knesset* to reverse a 1989 decision that denied Messianic Jews automatic citizenship.

Soviets get religious freedom—After more than 60 years of antireligious regulations, the Soviet legislature passes a law forbidding government interference in religious activities and granting legal standing to the country's religious organizations.

The law also allows for religious instruction, charitable giving, and religious publications.

While the law makes matters formal, such freedoms have actually been enjoyed for a while under Mikhail Gorbachev's policies, say experts like Paul Steeves, director of Russian studies at Stetson University.

OCTOBER 1990
➤NATIONAL

Denominations fight drugs—On the same day that Washington, D.C., Mayor Marion Barry admits to drug use, about 60 denominational leaders gather in a local church in the nation's capital to declare their own war on drugs.

The consultation, called by the National Council of Churches, seeks to form concrete proposals to fight drug use in the church and in its parishes.

THE YEAR IN REVIEW: JULY 1990 TO DECEMBER 1991 cont.

Among their proposals: staging a major march in Washington, D.C., to raise consciousness about the drug problem; creating a nationwide teleconference broadcast via cable television on the "cocaine epidemic"; and forming a grass-roots advocacy program to sway public policy on drug issues.

Nude dancing case hits Supreme Court— The U.S. Supreme Court agrees to hear a case that examines whether public bars in Indiana can feature nude dancing. By taking the case, the justices offer hope for those fighting to ban nude dancing bars in that state.

An earlier ruling by a federal appeals court said Indiana's current public indecency law stops short of banning nude dancing in bars, which is practiced in some parts of the state. "Nonobscene nude dancing performed as entertainment is expression and as such is entitled to limited protection under the First Amendment," the federal court said.

End-times books sell—With the Persian Gulf crisis burning hot, Americans are turning to evangelical authors for advice and wisdom on biblical teachings about the end of the world.

Among those books burning up the shelves is Hal Lindsey's 1970 best-seller *The Late Great Planet Earth,* with sales up 80 percent, says a spokesman for Zondervan Publishing House.

Baylor football revival—An estimated 23 Baylor University football players commit their lives to the Lord after the team holds a prayer meeting for a critically ill teammate, says head coach Grant Teaff. The 19-year-old player had collapsed from kidney and liver failure during a practice for the Southern Baptist school's football team.

Conservative Episcopals meet—About 200 conservative Episcopals meet in Washington, D.C., to discuss how to stop a perceived tide of liberalism in their denomination. At a "summit" meeting, leaders of the Prayer Book Society, Episcopalians United, and the Episcopal Synod of America vow to oppose ordination of homosexuals and use of inclusive language in their denomination.

Two groups join NAE—The Conservative Baptist Association of America and the Salvation Army are accepted into membership of the National Association of Evangelicals (NAE), bringing the number of NAE member organizations to 48.

➤INTERNATIONAL

Romanian evangelicals gather—About 4,000 evangelicals gather in Romania's government palace for the first meeting of the general assembly of the Romanian Evangelical Alliance. During the meeting, an alliance delegation meets with Romanian president Ion Iliescu and asks him to broaden religious freedoms throughout the country.

German churches in limbo as nations reunite—As the countries of East and West Germany formally become one nation again, their churches still have unanswered questions.

The day reunification occurs—October 3—government officials suggest to Protestant and Roman Catholic church leaders that they ring their church bells in celebration. The Roman Catholics comply, but many Protestants don't.

It is a telling picture of the uncertainty that exists about how the church should respond to the state in the future.

Even more questions exist about how to unite traditional church denominations that have been separated for so long by a wall and doctrinal issues.

Bible societies join forces—About a dozen Bible-translation and distribution agencies gather for a first-ever meeting. The groups are concerned that the Bible is being read less and that distribution of the Scriptures is being neglected in missions. Among the groups meeting are the United Bible Societies, Open Doors, Wycliffe Bible Translators, the Bible League, the International Bible Society, and Living Bibles International.

South Africa's nonwhite churches join forces—The black and mixed-race branches of South Africa's Dutch Reformed Church join force, creating the Uniting Reformed Church in Southern Africa, one of the largest church bodies in southern Africa.

The new group, numbering 1.5 million members, is formed to repudiate apartheid. It forms despite strong opposition from the white branch of the Dutch Reformed Church.

NOVEMBER 1990

➤NATIONAL

Creationist scientist cries foul—Forrest Mims III is regarded as a skillful science writer. So it's not surprising when the prestigious *Scientific American* magazine asks him to write a regular column.

But the relationship soon begins to sour as Mims reveals he is a born-again Christian who believes in the biblical creation story versus Darwin's theory of evolution.

Mims announces he will seek arbitration to settle his differences with the magazine, which says it will no longer do business with him.

Church giving on rise—Charitable giving is on the rise, bolstered by the efforts of America's religious community, an Independent Sector/Gallup poll shows.

About 75 percent of Americans are contributing an average of $734 annually to charitable causes, a 20 percent upswing from two years ago.

Over half of those surveyed contribute to religious groups, and 80 percent of those affiliated with a religious group contribute to a charity.

CLeaR-TV ends boycott—Christian Leaders for Responsible Television (CLeaR-TV) announces it is ending a two-month boycott of Burger King after meeting twice with the fast-food company's executives.

CLeaR-TV leader Donald Wildmon says the company promised to "drastically" cut back on the amount of advertising during TV shows featuring sex and violence.

Moon group sues Moon—The Committee to Defend the United States Constitution, a group formed and funded by Sun Myung Moon in cooperation with several conservative Christian groups, announces that it is suing Moon for $122 million.

The group says Moon's Unification Church has "unlawfully, willfully, and knowingly engaged in a pattern of racketeering activity."

Bleak abortion facts—A new poll shows that the general public is confused about the facts surrounding abortion.

The poll by the Wirthlin Group shows that half of those surveyed think fewer than 500,000 abortions are performed annually, when the actual number is about 1.6 million.

Another poll by Gallup shows that the general public is divided pretty evenly when it comes to attitudes about abortion. About 33 percent say they are pro-life, 27 say they are pro-abortion, and 39 percent say they are "in the middle."

Urbana adds new, controversial flair—The music at Urbana 90 in late December gives folks plenty to talk about as the new year emerges. Gone are the familiar hymns; in their place, the 19,000 delegates (mostly college students) clap their hands to contemporary worship songs led by a band affiliated with the Vineyard Christian Fellowship movement.

Critics like New Age expert Dave Hunt complain about prayer times offered students for "emotional healing" through the laying on of hands.

But Urbana director Dan Harrison says the changes are needed to reflect the needs of the "twenty-something" generation, which must cope with its own emotional scars in order to be ready for the mission field.

Woman elected to head NCC—Joan Brown Campbell, 59, is elected as the first female general secretary of the National Council of Churches. Campbell is an ordained minister in the Christian Church (Disciples of Christ).

➤INTERNATIONAL

Marxists on ice—As the Cold War ends and communism crumbles throughout

THE YEAR IN REVIEW: JULY 1990 TO DECEMBER 1991 cont.

Eastern Europe, long-time supporters of liberation and Marxist theology are in a quandary.

"Those with a vision of a totally egalitarian society are a little shocked," Paul Albrecht, a veteran social activist and former World Council of Churches official, tells Religious News Service.

"I know young people who have given their lives in human struggle in South America and now they feel totally at a loss about how to proceed," Albrecht says.

Graham in China—Billy Graham takes his high-tech crusade team to Hong Kong, which is preparing to become a part of the People's Republic of China in 1997.

An estimated 100 million people from more than 30 countries hear his message.

"In some ways, I feel I am ready to go to heaven now," Graham says after the crusade. "I have seen the greatest crusade of my life, which I never dreamed I would see at my age." Graham turned 72 just before the crusade.

Filipinos commit to Christ—Nearly 73,000 Filipinos make first-time commitments to Christ and another 30,000 join churches as a result of Project Philip, a program sponsored by the Bible League.

The Bible distribution agency based in South Holland, Illinois, prints and ships 71,000 Bibles, 266,000 new Testaments, and 1.27 million evangelistic studies to the Philippines as part of the program.

Albanian Mass conducted—The first Mass since religion was banned in Albania in 1967 is conducted by the Roman Catholic Church, and about 30,000 people attend.

DECEMBER 1990
▶NATIONAL

The wrong Impressions?—Sparked by criticisms issued by James Dobson, the Impressions reading series, a 15-book curriculum for kindergarten through sixth grade used in 1,500 schools in 34 states, is under fire.

Many Christian parents say portions of certain books promote witchcraft, the occult, and other dark elements of life, and they want the books removed from classes.

But publisher Holt, Rinehart, and Winston of Canada, Ltd., defends their product as being valuable in stimulating creative thinking and learning among children.

The prison papers—Charles Colson's Prison Fellowship starts a newspaper designed especially for reading by inmates. The eight-page paper, called the *Inside Journal,* is edited by Craig Pruitt, a former businessman who served time in federal prison for tax fraud.

The paper features opinions and news about the U.S. Justice system from a prisoner's point of view, as well as information about surviving in prison and preparing to return to society.
▶INTERNATIONAL

Moscow's first Christmas Eve Mass—On the snowy night of Christmas Eve, a crowd gathers at St. Basil's Cathedral at Red Square to listen to the Soviet Navy Band play "O Come All Ye Faithful."

Russian Orthodox Patriarch Aleksi II conducts his first Christmas Eve Mass at Yelokhovsky's Cathedral. For the first time since the founding of the Soviet Union, the country publicly observes Christmas.

Christian pastor executed—An Assemblies of God pastor, Hoosein Soodmand, 55, is hanged in Iran after being tortured for two months.

The execution signals a new wave of repression aimed at Christian believers.

Portugal Protestants speak up—Portugal's public schools will begin teaching Protestant religion classes after a law dating back to 1926 is reversed. Under the new law, evangelicals will be allowed to teach religion in the public schools alongside Roman Catholics.

The law says that if 15 or more students in a class request it, any religion can be taught. Portugal's Commission for Evangelical

Action in Public Schools says it will provide the teachers for evangelical religion classes.

JANUARY 1991
➤NATIONAL

Graham and Bush pray prior to war—
Billy Graham and his wife, Ruth, spend the night at the White House with close personal friends George and Barbara Bush on January 16, the day Bush orders a strike on Iraq.

Bush stresses the importance of prayer in his decision-making process that led to war. Adds Graham, "No sane person wants war. At the same time, it has well been said that there is an ethical responsibility that goes with power, and sometimes it becomes necessary to fight the strong in order to protect the weak."

In the days ahead, the president invokes the just-war theory to justify the invasion by Desert Storm forces. He is backed by conservative religious leaders such as television broadcaster Pat Robertson, who says, "The U.S. has a job to do, and, as unpleasant and painful as it may seem, the sooner we get it over with, the better."

Other Christian leaders, including Myron Augsburger, president of the Christian College Coalition, urge continued negotiations instead of war. "The world needs to know that we are concerned about justice, not simply about oil and economic issues that meet our American interests," he says.

The National Council of Churches opposes the war.

A Gallup poll later indicates that 57 percent of Americans say their piety increased as the United Nation's January 15 deadline for Iraq to withdraw from Kuwait drew near. And 59 percent of Americans polled say they thought their prayers concerning the war were "very effective."

Homosexuality issues stir denominations—Meetings of special sexuality panels of United Methodists and Presbyterian Church (USA) create an uproar by proposing to relax their denominations' stand on homosexuality.

The United Methodist panel ultimately recommends dropping language from the denomination's book of discipline condemning homosexuality as "incompatible with Christian teaching."

Meanwhile, a Presbyterian report advocates ordaining homosexuals and urges acceptance of "any sexual relations in which there is genuine equality and mutual respect."

Utah makes strides against abortion—
Utah Governor Norman Bangerter (R) signs a bill that prohibits abortions, except in cases of rape, incest, or when a woman's life is in danger. But representatives from the National Right to Life Committee say that the bill's wording is too vague concerning when a woman's health is in danger, and they argue the bill could be construed to mean poor mental health as well as physical health might be cause for an abortion.

➤INTERNATIONAL

Revival in the desert—American soldiers are thrust into a life-and-death situation as they contemplate the possibility of an early January strike on Iraq; and with panoromic views of the Holy Land all around them, it's not surprising that hundreds of soldiers convert to Christianity.

Evangelical leads Guatemala—When Jorge Serrano Elias is sworn in as president of Guatemala on January 14, it is yet another sign of the rapidly growing influence of evangelicals in Latin America.Serrano becomes the first evangelical president of a Latin American country.

The 45-year-old Stanford-educated businessman wins by a two-to-one margin over newspaper publisher Jorge Carpio, marking the first time that a democratically elected president hands over power to an elected civilian successor.

U.S. evangelicals decry abortion pill—
Pro-lifers from the U. S. meet in France and Germany with manufacturers of the RU 486 abortion pill and tell them not to bring their product to the U.S. "I came away with a clear impression that [the manufacturers] understood the situation in the United States was very different from the situation in

THE YEAR IN REVIEW: JULY 1990 TO DECEMBER 1991 cont.

France," says Richard Land, executive director of the Southern Baptist Christian Life Coalition. Land's constituency, which included representatives from Concerned Women for America, Focus on the Family, the Lutheran Church-Missouri Synod, and the International Right to Life Foundation, insists that the majority of Americans don't want access to the abortion pill.

Costa Rica's evangelical centennial—First came the Roman Catholics. Then, 100 years ago, Protestants brought their strain of Christianity to Costa Rica.

That country's evangelicals celebrate their centennial of the proclamation of the gospel to Costa Ricans as more than 300,000 attend events corresponding with a Luis Palau crusade.

Soviet students follow Moon—Cult leader Sun Myung Moon of the Unification Church isn't far behind evangelicals seeking to win converts in the newly open Soviet Union, and may be ahead of some.

Moon wins permission from Soviet leader Mikhail Gorbachev to invite hundreds of Soviet students on "field trips" to the U.S. The students travel and attend classes on Moon's teachings; many convert to Moon's church.

Bible hailed as Czech treasure—Czechoslovakia's minister of education, Petr Vopenka, says in a speech to Czech students that the Bible is a cultural, literary, and ethical jewel. He urges students to study it and to seek God.

Palau wages Japanese crusade—Evangelist Luis Palau conducts his first-ever crusade in Japan, where an estimated 60,000 people hear the gospel. In Okinawa and Osaka, about 7,100 people make decisions for Christ, many in the form of first-time commitments. Less than 10 percent of Japan's population is Christian.

FEBRUARY 1991

►NATIONAL

Americans heaven-bound?—A Gallup poll indicates that 78 percent of Americans polled believe they are going to heaven. Although 60 percent of Americans polled believe in hell, only four percent think they are going there.

Florida churches torched—Parishioners in churches throughout Florida share a nightmare. An unidentified arsonist burns more than 10 churches during February and continuing into March. The crimes perplex law enforcement officials.

Deadly measles outbreak in faith-healing group—An outbreak of measles sends shock waves through two Philadelphia churches that forbid medical treatment and leads to the deaths of five children.

Members of the Faith Tabernacle Congregation and the First Century Gospel Church eventually are required by the city to have their children checked by doctors.

Home-schooling trend accelerates—Hundreds of thousands of parents concerned about the condition of public schools are beginning to hold school at home. In a matter of five years, the number of home-schooled children in the U.S. increases fivefold to 400,000. This compares with 10,000 to 15,000 home-schoolers in 1970.

►INTERNATIONAL

Desert Storm ends, relief work begins—As the Persian Gulf War ends, relief groups begin their work, with several Christian relief agencies leading the way.

Groups like World Vision, Samaritan's Purse, World Relief, Feed the Children, Mercy Corps International, and others, start sending teams to help with medical needs, food shortages, and lack of electricity.

Meanwhile, many of the same relief groups struggle to also meet the needs of about 27 million Africans on the verge of hunger or death due to local wars and droughts.

Egyptian Christians persecuted—While American troops were fighting alongside Egyptian soldiers in the Persian Gulf War to stop an oppressive Saddam Hussein, government officials in Egypt were persecuting three Egyptian Christians held in jail on trumped-up charges.

Mustafa Al-Sharkawi, 27, Mohammad Selam, 25, and Hassan Ismail, 21, are imprisoned though they say they have not broken any Egyptian law. The three reportedly suffer electric shocks, cigarette burns, and beatings.

Orthodox rift at World Council of Churches assembly—Enough is enough. So say leaders of the world's Orthodox faith concerning the perceived liberal leanings of the World Council of Churches (WCC) after the WCC's seventh assembly in Canberra, Australia, in late February.

Orthodox leaders say they are most concerned about a trend in WCC documents and statements away from declaring Jesus Christ as the world's Savior.

USSR sends mixed signals on religious freedom—Soviet leaders are straightforward: they need help.

So delegates from the Christian Legal Society, the Institute on Religion and Democracy, and the Catholic University Law School meet with Soviet educators, legal scholars, and politicians to discuss how Christian values can be linked to law, human rights, and democracy in the new USSR.

Western and Soviet leaders acknowledge the "moral vacuum" emerging in the Soviet Union. They say that while Soviet leader Mikhail Gorbachev's glasnost has opened the door for religious freedom, in some cases it has also paved the way for acts of religious intolerance. Religious freedom in the USSR and Eastern European countries is still very tenuous, these experts say.

Guerrillas attack Peruvian church—Thirty-three people are killed and seven wounded February 23 when Shining Path guerrillas attack an all-night prayer meeting at a small Pentecostal church in the Andean mountain village of Ccano.

The Shining Path, a communist revolutionary group, apparently decides to strike the congregation because some of its men have joined one of the many civil-defense militias formed by the Peruvian military.

MARCH 1991
➤NATIONAL

Bush admits ambiguity over religion—President George Bush is known for speaking ambiguously. But when he meets with a group of religious journalists, he is very straightforward about his faith: he says he is ambiguous about it.

Bush tells the group that he is a Christian, but he hasn't completely worked out how his faith relates to his public office.

"I've confessed to some religious leaders that I am still not too comfortable with what the role [of religion in government] ought to be," Bush says.

NAE chides Bush after war—The National Association of Evangelicals at their annual national meeting in St. Louis chides President George Bush for "thanking everyone but God" during his televised address before Congress on March 6 after the war ended.

Bush officials tell NAE officials that references of thanks to God had been cut out of the President's speech due to time constraints.

Christianity vs. the too-liberal arts?—John Frohnmayer, director of the National Endowment for the Arts (NEA), lashes out at Donald Wildmon, leader of the American Family Association (AFA), after Wildmon's group urges his supporters to voice outrage over NEA support of the movie *Poison*.

The movie, which received $25,000 from the NEA, contains pornographic scenes of a homosexual nature that Wildmon says disqualify it from getting taxpayers' money.

Frohnmayer says the movie is a serious work of art and that Wildmon has misled the public.

TV evangelist in amusement park controversy—Without a doubt, history repeats itself.

Morris Cerullo, the California television evangelist who in 1990 paid $52 million for Jim Bakker's South Carolina theme park, is sued by fellow stockholders, who claim Cerullo jeopardized the park's financial future.

THE YEAR IN REVIEW: JULY 1990 TO DECEMBER 1991 cont.

They say that Cerullo sold memberships to his television audience promising special privileges and putting the park in a financial bind.

The charges are similar to the ones that landed Bakker in jail. Bakker sold PTL memberships discount partnerships and was convicted for defrauding the public.

Supreme Court to consider school prayer—School prayer advocates can see early in 1991 that their day is coming.

The Supreme Court agrees to hear a pivotal school prayer case that experts say challenges the current, restrictive standards for allowing prayer in schools.

In the case, an eighth-grade girl and her parents sued a Rhode Island middle school claiming that a prayer said by a rabbi at a graduation ceremony violated separation of church and state.

The U.S. Justice Department filed an opposition to the family's claim, saying that the current test for whether a prayer violates separation of church and state is too restrictive.

First Presbyterian Houston stays PCUSA—The 3,400-member congregation of the First Presbyterian Church of Houston, Texas, votes 1,296 to 760 to stay in the Presbyterian Church (USA) (PCUSA), after several years of infighting over whether that denomination was turning too liberal.

Under a special agreement in 1983 during the merger of southern and northern Presbyterian churches, southern churches had until 1991 to pull out of the PCUSA.

Manuel Noriega accepts Christ?—A Baptist newspaper in Florida breaks the story that former Panamanian dictator Manuel Noriega says he has become a born-again Christian. Noriega says he made his decision in May of 1990 after two Texas evangelists witnessed several times to him in his prison in Dade County, Florida.

Operation Rescue strikes during Easter—Many liberals thought they had seen the last of Operation Rescue, which had been hit hard by several lawsuits. But during Easter of 1991, the abortion protest group comes back to life with a vengeance.

About 3,500 people risk arrest and about 2,000 people are arrested in 41 cities during the third National Days of Rescue held by Operation Rescue between March 25 and Easter Sunday.

Protestors block clinic entrances all around the country. Operation Rescue leaders say the effort proves that several years of legal opposition by Planned Parenthood and the National Organization for Women has not stopped their movement.

➤INTERNATIONAL

Kenyan missionary killed—Southern Baptist missionaries Lynda Bethea, 42, and her husband, Ralph, are traveling to a boarding school in northwest Kenya to meet their two older sons when robbers stop their car, kill Lynda, and injure Ralph.

The two had slowed their car when they saw a man sprawled across a rural road, but the man and three others attacked them.

Christians killed under Hussein's wrath—The Society for Threatened Peoples, a human rights group, charges that since 1968, Iraqi president Saddam Hussein has killed more than 20,000 Assyrian Christians, expelled 75,000, and destroyed nearly 100 churches.

The Society says Hussein has targeted for persecution the Assyrian Christians, who number an estimated 400,000 to 750,000 in northern Iraq, as well as the Kurds.

Liberia devastated after war—Missions and relief agencies returning to Liberia after a cease-fire is enacted say their worse-case scenarios have come true.

Officials report severe malnutrition among growing numbers of refugees after a war that killed an estimated 50,000 and displaced half of the country's 2.5 million population.

Pentecostalism on the rise—Pentecostal and charismatic churches worldwide claim 382 million members, or one in every five

Christians, according to the *International Bulletin of Missionary Research.*

Pentecostal and charismatic churches gain 19 million members per year, and they donate $34 million to Christian causes. Two of every three Pentecostals live in Third World nations.

Albania holds free election—Communists lose their stranglehold on Albania, a country where communism was once considered impenetrable.

In March elections, the Communists lose elections, although they maintain 60 percent of the parliamentary seats.

APRIL 1991

➤NATIONAL

Educational choice stirs debate—President George Bush fanned the flame of debate over whether the government should support religious schools by proposing a new education choice plan.

The Bush plan would allow parents to choose what school their child will attend, with the promise the child would be federally funded via vouchers. But many church-state separatists are upset because the plan would also fund children who choose private or religious schools over public schools.

Joseph Conn of Americans United for the Separation of Church and State leads opposition to the plan; but other lobby groups, like the National Association of Evangelicals, support it.

Americans favor Christianity—A new poll, billed as the largest ever of its kind, shows that 87 percent of Americans, or about 150 million people, claim to be Christians.

The poll by two researchers from the City University of New York shows that about 1.8 percent, or 3.1 million people, say they are Jewish; 500,000, or about .5 percent, say they are Muslim; about 1.2 million say they are agnostic; and about 13 million claim no religion.

The survey of 113,000 adult Americans shows an estimated 26 percent of Americans are Roman Catholic and about 60 percent are Protestant.

Court allows tract distribution—A person has the right to distribute religious literature on public property, according to a U.S. Court of Appeals in New York.

The court ruled that several street ministers had the right to distribute tracts outside the Nassau County Coliseum.

End-times Response—A survey by *Christianity Today* magazine reports that 20 percent of its readers considered the Persian Gulf War to be "a sign that biblical prophecy is being fulfilled and final events of world history will soon take place"; 42 percent say it was not; 38 percent say they weren't sure.

➤INTERNATIONAL

Carter decries China's human rights record—Former president Jimmy Carter in a speech to Chinese in Beijing calls on the government to reverse its policy of religious persecution.

Human rights violations in China continue to draw attention. The Puebla Institute, a Catholic human rights organization, reports that 77 Christian leaders are known to be in jail or facing house arrest.

Among those, 60 are Catholic leaders, including 20 bishops.

African Christian leader dies—Samuel Odunaike, long-time president of the Association of Evangelicals of Africa and Madagascar and chairman of the Nigeria Evangelical Fellowship, dies of pneumonia at age 57. At the time of his death, he is a top contender for the presidency of Nigeria.

British open airwaves to Christians—The British Parliament approves legislation allowing Christian broadcasters on the air. Previously, religious broadcasting was confined largely to a weekly, one-hour BBC show.

Christians persecuted by Hussein—Reports say that an estimated 500,000 Assyrian Christians, the descendants of a religious community at least 1,500 years old, were forced by Saddam Hussein's army to flee their homes in northern Iraq.

About 100,000 of those Assyrians are active in their faith, according to the Middle

THE YEAR IN REVIEW: JULY 1990 TO DECEMBER 1991 cont.

East Council of Churches. Many suffered dehydration and hunger when they were forced into the mountains. One report says 40 Assyrian men who tried to return to their villages were buried alive by the Iraqi army.

Catholic cardinals fear defections—Following a three-day meeting at the Vatican, Catholic cardinals say their church must defend against "defections" of Catholics to Protestant churches.

The cardinals express concern that more than 150 U.S. Catholics leave the church daily for Protestant churches.

MAY 1991

➤NATIONAL

Blacks have fastest-growing churches— Nine of the fifteen fastest-growing churches in the U.S. are predominantly black, according to a survey by church-growth expert John Vaughan.

The Word of Faith Center in Detroit, a predominantly black congregation with an estimated 3,500 members, shares the top spot on the list with Calvary Chapel of Albuquerque.

Many black "megachurches" are springing up, Vaughan says. Other black churches making the top fifteen: West Angeles Church of God in Christ, Los Angeles; Mount Ephraim Baptist Church, Atlanta; Bethel African Methodist Episcopal Church, Baltimore; Ben Hill United Methodist Church, Atlanta; Concord Baptist Church, Dallas; Bountiful Blessings, Memphis; New Saint Paul Tabernacle Church of God in Christ, Detroit.

Key abortion victories—In what many consider a glimpse of things to come, the Supreme Court renders a 5-to-4 decision upholding regulations that prevent government-subsidized clinics from counseling women to have an abortion.

Abortion opponents say the vote bodes well for eventually overturning *Roe v. Wade*. Gary Bauer of the Family Research Council, a conservative Washington, D.C., lobby, says the "ruling sends an important message to

family-planning providers who seek federal funds: if you seek taxpayer money, family planning—not abortion—should be your business, your only business."

Rachel Pine of the American Civil Liberties Union says her group can read the handwriting on the wall after the loss. "That frightens me for the future," she says.

Meanwhile, President Bush says he will veto a bill requiring all military medical facilities overseas to provide abortions at anytime during a pregnancy. Bush's statement is prompted when the proposed bill clears the U.S. House of Representatives.

Court ruling curtails professor's speech—In the past, whenever Phillip Bishop referred to his Christian faith in his University of Alabama classroom, he made sure his physical education students knew he was only stating his personal opinion.

If they wanted to talk more about spiritual matters, said Bishop, he would meet them after class.

But a federal appeals court rules that Bishop is out of line making such in-class comments to his students. The Eleventh Circuit U.S. Court of Appeals rules that the University of Alabama—and all other universities—have the right to regulate what their teachers say in class.

Recession hits Prison Fellowship, Southern Baptists—A recession is no respecter of persons, and many Christian ministries begin to feel the sting. Prison Fellowship, the 15-year-old ministry founded by Charles Colson, lays off 14 people in May after laying off 24 in February.

Meanwhile, foreign missions giving in the Southern Baptist Convention drops for the first time in 53 years, and support for the 125 ministry staffers at International Students, Inc. is down 5 to 7 percent.

Largest evangelistic mailing ever—Their message is simple: "Jesus is the solution to the world's problems," the booklet reads.

And an estimated 100,000 million Americans are targeted to read the booklet, produced and distributed by the Sycamore Church of Christ in Cookeville, Tennessee.

The 530-member church spearheads the campaign conceived by local millionaire businessman Horace Burks, who is seeking to raise $9 million to complete the mailing, touted as the largest ever in American history.

Moderate Baptists form group—Moderate Southern Baptists form their own organization—the Cooperative Baptist Fellowship—during a May meeting in Atlanta. "Our long denominational exile is over," says John Hewett, an Ashville, North Carolina, pastor the group elected as its first moderator.

The group denies it is a new denomination, though that is not ruled out as a future possibility. They pledge to finance their own missions and church education programs.

Crown jewel remains in Presbyterian Church USA—Members of Highland Park Presbyterian Church, a suburban Dallas church with about 8,100 members, vote 2,493 to 2,024 to leave the Presbyterian Church (USA) (PCUSA) for the more conservative Presbyterian Church in America (PCA). However, the two-thirds majority needed to switch denominations is not achieved, and the church remains in the PCUSA. But about 1,500 Highland Park attenders meet the following Sunday to start a new PCA church.

➤INTERNATIONAL

Relief groups taxed to limit—The spring of 1991 has ushered in more misery than relief agencies can handle.

Groups like World Vision struggle throughout the spring to meet the needs brought about by several disasters worldwide.

About 2 million Kurdish refugees have faced hunger and the cold fleeing from Saddam Hussein's army; earthquakes have left thousands needy in Costa Rica, Soviet Georgia, and Peru; and a devastating cyclone has killed over 200,000 and left 4 to 5 million homeless in Bangladesh.

World Vision workers killed—Norman Tattersall, 45, and José Chuquin, 45, were outside their World Vision Peru offices when a car came screeching by. Seconds later both men were lying on the ground after being sprayed with machine-gun fire from the fleeing car.

Tattersall, acting director of World Vision in Peru, dies instantly. Chuquin dies 11 days later.

Robert Seiple, World Vision's president, says the incident "was devastating," but, he adds, terrorists will not stop their work. "The work has to transcend the assassin's bullet. The work will go on," he says.

Muslims and Christians clash in Nigeria—Nigerians listen closely to Yahaya (translated "Chosen of God"), a 36-year-old Muslim leader. When in May Yahaya declares a holy war in northern Nigeria after being arrested by the Christian governor, the people respond by killing nearly 100 Christians and burning 24 churches.

Christians counter the attack, and as many as 500 Muslims and Christians are feared dead in the northern portion of the nation.

Ethiopian missionaries on alert—With rebel troops circling the capital of Addis Ababa, Ethiopia, many missionaries pack their bags and leave at the urging of U.S. officials.

The country's future appears dim since President Mengistu Haile Mariam has been forced to flee for his safety.

But even with the apparent danger, several hundred American missionaries choose not to leave.

Angola cease-fire welcome—Church leaders hold an ecumenical celebration over the May 31 cease-fire between Angola's government and rebel leaders. The country has endured 16 years of war.

The one-time marxist president, José Eduardo dos Santos signs the treaty with a U.S.-backed rebel group.

With the end of the war, the government is signaling a new openness to the church, allowing Christians to hold meetings in public buildings.

THE YEAR IN REVIEW: JULY 1990 TO DECEMBER 1991 cont.

JUNE 1991

➤NATIONAL

Conservative Southern Baptists reign— Conservatives dominate the agenda of the Southern Baptist Convention's (SBC) annual meeting in Atlanta, re-electing Morris Chapman as the SBC president and voting to cut off funds to the Baptist Joint Committee on Public Affairs, a Washington, D.C.-based group supported by several other Baptist denominations beside the SBC.

Convention delegates also send a strong message to mainline, liberal-leaning denominations that are considering loosening their stance on sexuality. A SBC resolution urges "all Christians to uphold the biblical standard of sexuality," which means abstaining from premarital sex, adultery, and homosexuality, among other things.

Seminary preserves all-male board— Westminster Theological Seminary in Philadelphia holds out against its accrediting agency's insistence that it appoint a female to its board of directors. And eventually the seminary prevails.

Westminster officials say it is against the school's convictions on biblical leadership to have female elders. And since only church elders can be board members, they refuse to budge to pressure by Middle States Association of Schools and Colleges to appoint women board members.

Middles States eventually relents to Westminster, saying the school has satisfied its concerns by appointing more females to lower-level leadership.

Nunchakus banned in L.A. police— No love has been lost between the L.A. Police Department and members of Operation Rescue, which claims L.A. cops have repeatedly used rough techniques including martial arts nunchakus to haul them from sit-in sites.

In response to a lawsuit by Operation Rescue, the L.A. Police Department announces it will no longer use the martial arts devices, which are two-foot-long sticks joined by a cord that is wrapped around the wrists and pulled tight to provoke pain.

It is no coincidence that the police department's decision to drop the painful devices comes just weeks after the much-publicized beating of motorist Rodney King by L.A. police.

Graham returns to Scotland— More than 250,000 people attend crusade meetings throughout Scotland led by evangelist Billy Graham, who calls on church leaders and youth to recapture the country's heritage as the home of John Knox, Presbyterianism, and the King James Bible.

"What we need in Scotland is young men and women to offer themselves as ministers, missionaries, and evangelists, people who have a gift from God," Graham says.

"Many of today's church leaders in Scotland trace their spiritual roots back to Graham's historic meetings in Glasgow in 1955," notes David McNee, chairman of Mission Scotland 1991. "Perhaps this mission will provide an infrastructure of new leadership in the future."

An average of 60 percent of those responding each night of Graham's 10-day crusade were under the age of 25.

NEA apologizes to Donald Wildmon— Antismut crusader Donald Wildmon of the American Family Association wins another battle when Julianne Ross Davis, counsel for the National Endowment for the Arts, is forced to apologize for inaccurate comments she made about Wildmon in a speech.

Wildmon had filed suit against Davis, who incorrectly stated that Wildmon favored the death penalty for homosexuals and the abolishment of all public schools.

U.S. House lifts abortion ban— The U.S. House of Representatives votes overwhelmingly to approve a bill that would lift the Bush administration's ban that prohibits public health centers from counseling women to have an abortion.

The House vote comes after the Supreme Court in May rules that the administration's ban was legal. The Senate's approval to lift the ban is still required.

Black Christians on rise—The rise in influence of the black church in America is signaled by two conferences held in June. About 350 pastors, youth workers, and Christian leaders join together for Chicago '91, sponsored by the Institute for Black Family Development. Keynote speaker Louis Sullivan, secretary of the U.S. Health and Human Services Department, says the black church needs to work with government and other community groups to help develop a "culture of character" in America.

Meanwhile, that same week about 150 black pastors meet in the nation's capital at a gathering sponsored by the Traditional Values Coalition of California, where Sullivan, President Bush, Housing and Urban Development Secretary Jack Kemp, and members of Congress speak.

Delegates there consider ways to get their laypeople more involved politically.

►INTERNATIONAL

Evangelists storm Eastern Europe and USSR—Scores of evangelists and western Christian groups stage crusades in former Communist countries this summer.

Two of the most prominent evangelists hold crusades in June: Luis Palau in Romania and John Guest in the USSR's Ukraine.

Palau reports 39,400 commitments to Christ, a 31-percent response rate, the highest ever recorded by LPEA. Despite cold and rain, about 125,000 people attend 11 stadium meetings held by Palau, who is also interviewed on television.

Guest concentrates on planting new churches in the Ukraine. "As an American evangelist, it is relatively easy to draw crowds and converts. The real work is follow-up," Guest says.

Bibles in the USSR—Once a complete impossibility, Soviet citizens now can shop in public for their own copy of the Scriptures.

A Bible center is opened in downtown Leningrad by the United Bible Society and gains the support of the Russian Orthodox Church.

The International Bible Society of Colorado Springs, teamed with other Bible distributors, has reached the halfway mark of distributing 4 million New Testaments in the USSR through a campaign called the "Moscow Project."

Christian Colleges play football in China—A 210,000-seat stadium sells out and 200 million others watch on via Chinese television as Evangel College, an Assemblies of God school in Springfield, Missouri, and Pacific Lutheran University of Tacoma, Washington, introduce the Chinese to American football.

JULY 1991
►NATIONAL

Thomas nominated—Little-known black conservative Clarence Thomas is nominated by President George Bush to fill the Supreme Court seat vacated by Thurgood Marshall.

Thomas, who was raised a Catholic and now attends a charismatic Episcopal church, receives the endorsement of many Washington, D.C.–based evangelical groups, who believe Thomas will vote a "profamily" line, including opposing abortion.

Gary Bauer, president of the Family Research Council, says there are hints Thomas would vote to overturn *Roe v. Wade* and thereby severely restrict abortion.

Habitat president reinstated—Millard Fuller is reinstated as president of Habitat for Humanity—a ministry that builds affordable homes for the poor—after resigning under protest of changes in his role with the group he founded.

President Jimmy Carter, an avid supporter of Fuller's, had expressed serious concern about Fuller's resignation.

Episcopalians hedge on sexuality issue—It isn't what Episcopalians do as much as what they fail to do at their general convention in Phoenix, Arizona.

The House of Bishops hedges on taking a stance on the hotly debated resolution that would have recognized homosexual relationships in the church.

Instead, they adopt a compromise resolution that affirms "that physical sexual expression is appropriate only within lifelong monogamous" marriage. That same

THE YEAR IN REVIEW: JULY 1990 TO DECEMBER 1991 cont.

resolution, however, admits there is disagreement among Episcopalians.

Environmental alert—Religious, scientific, and political leaders meet in New York to jointly express concern about the environment and to map out a course of action.

Among the evangelical leaders present are pastor Robert Schuller; Robert Seiple, president of World Vision, USA; and David McKenna, president of Asbury Theological Seminary. The meeting is at the urging of 34 reknowned scientists, who say, "Efforts to safeguard and cherish the environment need to be infused with a vision of the sacred."

Operation Rescue arrives in Wichita—They come to Wichita in mid-July with a modest goal of shutting down the city's three abortion clinics at least temporarily. When they arrive, Operation Rescue (OR) leaders find unprecedented support from local laypeople for their efforts.

Restaurants give OR workers food. Businesses offer their services for free. Says Randall Terry, OR's founder and leader, "I've never seen anything like it."

Evangelical Methodists meet—Good News, the unofficial evangelical arm of the United Methodists, meets in Washington, D.C., and calls on the denomination to stop opposing the appointment of ordained clergy to serve with the Missions Society for United Methodists, which is the missions agency backed by Good News.

"We believe that our missions society is an embarrassment to the [United Methodist denomination] general board because they know we are critical of their vague proclamation of Christ as Savior and Lord," says James Heidinger, executive secretary of Good News.

➤INTERNATIONAL

Graham trains USSR ministers—Even when the Iron Curtain was seemingly impenetrable, Billy Graham was traveling to the USSR to preach. And so, with most of the barriers to freedom of speech removed in Eastern Europe and the USSR, Graham

travels there to hold a megaconference to help train indigenous leaders in the USSR for evangelism.

About 5,000 ministers and Christian workers from 11 time zones attend Graham's School of Evangelism. It is the largest school Graham has ever held.

The meeting crosses denominational lines. Delegates are housed and fed by the Billy Graham Evangelistic Association at Moscow University.

Graham also visits personally with Mikhail Gorbachev and Boris Yeltsin.

First Albanian converts form church—Albanian Communist leaders swore for years that Christianity would never find its way into their country, but on July 1, 1991, it does.

A team of Christians including more than 100 missionaries from 12 evangelical organizations join together in what is called the Albanian Encouragement Project, the first organized Christian effort in Albania in 50 years.

They fill the main soccer stadium in Tirana for five nights. Bible smuggler Brother Andrew and others preach. Others do street evangelism. About 25,000 copies of the Gospels are passed out.

More than 100 people receive Christ, and two churches are founded. Missionaries report contact with a remnant of believers predating the formal ban of Christianity in 1940.

Orthodox signal NCC break—Disheartened by what they perceive as a growing liberalism in the National Council of Churches (NCC), the Greek Orthodox Church of North America announces it is suspending ties with the NCC pending further review.

"The Orthodox see the liberal leanings of our sister denominations, and I think it's come to the point where this has to be addressed," said Milton Efthimiou, ecumenical officer for the 1.9-million member Greek Orthodox Church.

Joan Campbell, NCC general secretary,

expresses disappointment and says they will work to resolve the matter.

New Canadian theological group forms— The Canadian Evangelical Theological Association is formed as a group of Canadian scholars break from the U.S.-based Evangelical Theological Society.

The group's new president, John Stackhouse, assistant professor of modern Christianity at Manitoba University, says the split was "amicable" and prompted by a desire for a "distinctly Canadian agenda and disposition toward theological education and reflection."

Egyptian Christians Freed—Three Egyptian Christian converts are released from a Cairo prison after being held and tortured for nearly ten months.

Sudan opens to gospel—Like many African countries, the Sudan has been hard for missionaries to penetrate in recent years due to warring factions. But with the end of the fighting, Sudanese officials open the door once again to religious and relief groups after formally expelling them in 1988.

AUGUST 1991
➤NATIONAL

Wichita's summer of mercy—Wichita's citizens have never seen anything like it. For that matter, neither has Randall Terry, who leads his Operation Rescue (OR) force into Wichita in July hoping to shut down three abortion clinics for a few weeks.

But by August, the movement is still gaining momentum. When it is all said and done, an estimated 2,500 arrests are made. "Rescuers" from all over the nation flock to Wichita to take their stand.

Terry and other OR leaders fight a battle of wits and words with federal judge Patrick Kelly, whose efforts to get tough with rescuers by enforcing stringent prison terms do little to squelch the protests. But they do get Kelly an interview on ABC's "Nightline."

Meanwhile, pastors from more than 80 evangelical churches in Wichita gather at one point for a day and night of prayer and fasting and emerge touting an agenda to take Wichita for Christ. It is a momentous occurrence since churches in Wichita seldom work together.

During the protests, OR officials claim that at least 27 women are dissuaded from aborting their babies.

On August 25, an estimated 30,000 people gather at the football stadium at Wichita State University for a pro-life rally, the largest ever in the state. Pat Robertson of the Christian Broadcasting Network speaks to the crowd.

Putting Jesus back in schools—Throughout the nation, public schools systems are opting for new textbooks that include thorough explanations of Christianity and Judaism, as well as other religions.

School officials say they are realizing that they have misapplied the Supreme Court's 1962 ruling, which prohibited prayer in schools. Though the ruling restricted only prayer, school officials for years backed away almost completely from the subject of religion in classrooms for fear of legal suits.

But the state of California and several other states as well are now asking for religion to be put back into textbooks, and publishers like Houghton Mifflin Company are responding.

Charles Haynes, executive director of George Mason University's First Liberty Institute, which is leading the new drive, says the new philosophy is called "natural inclusion," which means a teacher allows religion to be brought up in class wherever it naturally arises, as in history and social studies classes.

Catholic charismatic communities split— The Catholic charismatic renewal movement has been recently shaken as several key leaders admit misusing authority.

About one year ago, the Word of God community in Ann Arbor, Michigan, with about 3,000 members, split when founders Steve Clark and Ralph Martin chose to head in opposite directions.

Not too long after that, Martin and some other leaders asked forgiveness for abusing authority in the tightknit, communal group.

Clark, who now heads another group

THE YEAR IN REVIEW: JULY 1990 TO DECEMBER 1991 cont.

called Sword of the Spirit, continues using the methods Martin repented of.

Another similar group, the 350-member Servants of Christ in Steubenville, Ohio, was recently investigated by their Roman Catholic bishop, who found authority abuses existed there too.

Other groups also are scrutinized. But Catholic leaders say in the long run, the good in the communal groups will win out.

Taking from a trader—Several not-for-profit evangelical groups benefited from the benevolence of commodities trader Michael Douglas. But when he is convicted of swindling $30 million from investors, the money those Christian groups received from him is jeopardized.

Several creditors sue 15 charities, saying the money the charities were given by Douglas actually should go to pay off debts he owed them. The problem is that the charities already spent the money Douglas gave them, and they say it is unfair to make them pay it back.

Attorney Timothy Klenk, who represents nine of the charities, says that making the charities return the money would set bad precedent.

"Charities would have a hard time knowing that any gifts they have received wouldn't have to be returned," he says.

Among the charities named in the suit: Calvary Chapel of Chula Vista, California; Food for the Hungry, Inc.; Trinity College and Trinity Evangelical Divinity School of Deerfield, Illinois; and World Vision, Inc.

Christian schools make the grade—Students in Protestant schools test at least one year ahead of the national average. About 18,000 such schools now exist, and their enrollment has increased 149 percent since 1965.

Americans' beliefs—About 74 percent of Americans strongly agree that "there is only one true God, who is holy and perfect and who created the world and rules it today," according to a survey of 1,005 Americans by pollster George Barna.

About 64 percent of those polled either strongly agree or somewhat agree that "there is no such thing as absolute truth."

"The evidence continues to mount which suggests that while religion is important [to Americans], it is not central," says Barna of the survey. "People are more likely than ever to state that they do not have a high degree of confidence in religious institutions; to feel that being part of a local church is not a necessity; or to reject the idea that reading the Bible regularly will enhance their lives."

Americans also seem to be ambivalent about some of their beliefs, according to the report. For example, 62 percent of those surveyed say they are personally committed to Jesus Christ, but 64 percent say the term *born again* does not apply to them. And less than 50 percent strongly agree that the Bible is the written word of God and is totally accurate in all it teaches.

Denominational musings—At the Portland, Oregon, annual meeting of the Assemblies of God, something unusual happens. During a morning meeting, delegates break out into spontaneous prayer and praise, prompting General Superintendent G. Raymond Carlson to suspend an upcoming business meeting. The outburst is prompted after a report is given on the 1906 Azusa Street revival in Los Angeles.

Meanwhile, the Mennonite Church, based in Elkhart, Indiana, selects Donella Clemens of Souderton, Pennsylvania, as its first woman moderator during its annual meeting in Eugene, Oregon.

At its 103rd general conference, the Brethren Church adopts an abortion statement that says the issue at stake is "more than a question of the freedom of a women to control the reproductive functions of her own body." The statement also affirms that life begins at conception.

A Brethren resolution on AIDS says that the moral element cannot be overlooked when seeking remedies to AIDS and HIV, but that churches "must take the initiative and leadership in ministering to AIDS patients and to those infected with the virus."

Evolution battle in Christian Reformed Church—Evolution is a hotly contested issue among members of the Christian Reformed Church, and this summer's General Synod is expected to resolve the matter.

But instead, delegates produce ambiguity. A statement adopted says Adam and Eve are "the progenitors of the human race," but also states that several plausible interpretations of Genesis 1:1 exist and that the "present conflict between Christian faith and science over questions of origins cannot be easily resolved."

Parties at the convention on both sides of the issue claim victory.

National teen sex study halted—After the public expresses outrage over a planned study of teen sexual behavior, U.S. Health and Human Services Secretary Louis Sullivan cancels the project.

The $18 million survey would have asked children in grades 7 to 11 explicit questions about their sexual activity.

A coalition of conservative family groups, including the Family Research Council, Concerned Women for America, and the Christian Coalition, lead the oppostion to the study.

Christians affirm women's rights—More than 350 attend the annual meeting of Christians for Biblical Equality in Snow Mountain Ranch, Colorado.

Evangelical theologian Kenneth Kantzer, former dean of Trinity Evangelical Divinity School and chancellor of Trinity College, argues for equality of men and women before God, saying that Christians have always supported equal justice for all people.

The meeting reflects the growth of the group, which now has 24 chapters around the world, compared with only four when it was founded in 1989.

Student leaders gather at Wheaton College—Students from all over the world report that their ministries are growing, often amidst resistance, as delegates from more

than 100 countries gather for the World Assembly of the International Fellowship of Evangelical Students at Wheaton College, Wheaton, Illinois.

The makeup of the group is changing with the fall of communism, and new student groups are accepted for membership from Czechoslovakia, Hungary, Nepal, Belgium, Angola, Yugoslavia, and Poland.

➤INTERNATIONAL

Church resists failed USSR coup—Church leaders are among those pouring into the streets of Moscow in late August to resist a coup attempt against Mikhail Gorbachev.

Meanwhile, Christian workers from the West scramble to get out of the Soviet Union, but they encounter closed-down airports.

Evangelical delegations, like one led by Focus on the Family's James Dobson, delay traveling to the USSR.

And the Moscow Book Fair, a gathering of evangelical book publishers and distributers that was to be held in early September, has to be cancelled.

At the end of the failed coup, Kent Hill, executive director of the Institute on Religion and Democracy, says it's "another nail in the coffin of the antireligious policies of the past."

Charismatics gather in England—About 3,000 charismatics from both Protestant and Catholic backgrounds meet in Brighton, England, to map a strategy for seeing half the world's population converted by the year 2000.

Keep preaching in the Philippines—A proposal to ban street preaching without a permit in Manilla is overturned by the Philippines Commission on Human Rights.

Missionaries work India—About 6,500 indigenous missionaries now work in India, Bangladesh, Nepal, Myanmar, Pakistan, Bhutan, Thailand, and Tibet, and 4,000 churches were started last year in India alone, according to a Gospel for Asia report.

Missing: three World Vision workers—World Vision workers Luis Gutiérrez, 32, Marcial Sarmiento, 35, and Ciro Casaverde, 39, are traveling from a provincial town in

THE YEAR IN REVIEW: JULY 1990 TO DECEMBER 1991 cont.

Peru to their base office in Lima when they disappear. A local community leader traveling with them, Cayo Vargas, also vanishes.

Officials say their disappearances are not yet linked to the May 17 assassination of two other World Vision workers, but local church workers admit church leaders are probably being targeted by Maoist guerrillas in the Shining Path because of their perceived link to "Yankee imperialism."

SEPTEMBER 1991
➤NATIONAL

Public religion: right or wrong?—Are American Christians in danger of losing their religious freedom? In a poll of *Christianity Today* magazine readers, 42 percent say yes to the above question; and an additional 18 percent strongly affirm that religious freedoms are in danger.

An estimated 47 percent of those surveyed say they disagree, and 30 percent say they strongly disagree that prayers in public places "exert undue pressures on nonbelievers and members of minority religions."

And 72 percent agree that "the best way to guarantee religious freedom for Christians is to fight for religious freedom for all." Only 7 percent disagree with that assertion.

Deynekas form new ministry—After working for so many years in largely undercover efforts to minister in the Soviet Union, Peter and Anita Deyneka announce they are leaving the ministry Peter's father founded in 1934—Slavic Gospel Association.

They announce plans to form Peter Deyneka USSR Ministries, which will link "key Western organizations and individuals to Soviet churches and parachurch organizations for the purpose of nationwide evangelization."

Praising in the streets—More than 5,000. gather in St. Louis for a praise march from the Union Train Station to the old county courthouse. Young and old, black and white, nuns and fundamentalists all join in singing contemporary worship music written by Englishman Graham Kendricks.

The event is one of the first praise marches

in the United States, but in Great Britain similar marches are drawing 150,000 or more.

The leaders of the St. Louis event say marching is a fresh way for Christians from various denominations to express solidarity and to witness to their city. "We're not here to make a media statement," says St. Louis organizer Harry Schroeder. "Our hope is honestly to make an appeal to the Lord to move on our city."

Mainline church attendance drops; conservatives rise—The mainline churches are still losing members, according to a report in the *Yearbook of American & Canadian Churches 1991.*

The yearbook reports that the following churches lost members in the previous year: Presbyterian Church USA, down 1.5 percent to 2,866,482; United Church of Christ, down 1.1 percent to 1,625,969; Episcopal Church, down 0.9 percent to 2,433,413; United Methodist Church, down 0.8 percent, at 8,979,139; Assemblies of God, down 0.4 percent, at 2,137,890.

Those denominations reporting increases include: Presbyterian Church* in America, up 4.3 percent at 217,374; Roman Catholic Church, up 3.8 percent at 57,019,948; Christian and Missionary Alliance, up 2.4 percent at 265,863; Southern Baptist Convention, up 0.6 percent at 14,907,826; Lutheran Church–Missouri Synod, up 0.2 percent at 2,609,025.

Fewer doctors perform abortions—The "professional stigma" attached with performing abortions has contributed to the fact that fewer and fewer doctors are willing to perform the procedure.

A report by the National Abortion Federation says, "Young physicians in particular may be leery of the taint associated with abortion services, perceiving that involvement with abortion could adversely affect their careers."

The report also cites a 22-percent drop from 1976 to 1987 in the number of medical residency programs that train future doctors in how to perform first-trimester abortions.

Presbyterian fallout—When it is all said and done, 81 churches with about 25,500 members vote to leave the Presbyterian Church USA for either the younger Presbyterian Church in America or the Evangelical Presbyterian Church.

The departures come as part of an exit agreement eight years ago to placate those concerned over the merger of the southern and northern Presbyterian church branches.

Gorman defeats Swaggart—Former New Orleans Assemblies of God pastor Marvin Gorman had been promising to bring fellow pastor Jimmy Swaggart down after Swaggart exposed Gorman's extramarital affairs.

And he does.

Gorman wins a $10 million suit against Swaggart. The suit claims that Swaggart exagerated Gorman's extramarital affairs, spreading rumors and ruining Gorman's ministry.

The Assemblies of God denomination had originally been named as a defendant in the suit, but was dropped, leaving Swaggart to take most of the blame.

The ethics of Southern Baptist moderates—More signs of the makings of a future denomination appear when moderate Southern Baptists form their own ethics think tank and seminary.

The Baptist Center for Ethics will be separate from the Southern Baptist Convention's Christian Life Commission (CLC) and will be run by Robert Parham, who quits the CLC to move to the moderates' post.

Moderates also open the first round of classes at their newly formed Baptist Theological Seminary in Richmond, Virginia.

Pirates of the Dead Sea Scrolls—A professor of Hebrew and his graduate assistant pull off the archeological coup of the century.

Using a computer, they pirate a full copy of the Dead Sea Scrolls, portions of which had been hoarded by an elite group of scholars since their discovery almost a half century ago.

It is like piecing together a giant jigsaw puzzle. Ben-Zion Wacholder, a teacher at Hebrew Union College in Cincinnati, uses a concordance of the full scroll fragments, and along with his graduate assistant, Martin Abegg, creates a program that assembles all the missing pieces of the scrolls.

The announcement is cause for celebration for scholars worldwide who have been waiting for the opportunity to see the missing texts of the 237 scrolls and fragments found in desert caves around the Dead Sea.

Meanwhile, a member of the elite scroll oversight committee, Emile Puech, says in the *Chicago Tribune* they will sue to keep Wacholder from publishing the scrolls, as he intends to.

Methodists waver on sexuality—United Methodists appear to be in the same boat as their mainline Presbyterian friends. Their special study committee on homosexuality cannot agree on whether homosexuality is right or wrong, so they give their denomination's General Council of Ministries two versions of a sexuality report.

Eighteen members of the committee support a version that says homosexuals should no longer be condemned for their life-style.

The other version, supported by the study committee's remaining four members, says no evidence exists to alter the "previously held position" that condemns homosexuality.

New York loves Billy Graham—They pour into Central Park in the fashion often reserved for a pop concert by the likes of Simon and Garfunkel.

But this group of 250,000 people comes to hear Billy Graham, who preaches an old-fashioned, to-the-point evangelistic sermon to his listeners.

On this sunny September 22 event, touted as the largest single evangelistic happening in North American history, Catholics mingle with Protestants, and Graham's photo is front-page fodder for the *New York Times*.

Singers Sandi Patti, Johnny and June Cash, and a cappella group Take 6 perform. Other celebrities, including televison host Kathy Lee Gifford, speak.

Graham speaks twice, once on his thoughts about the Big Apple and then on the message of salvation.

New York Mayor David Dinkins calls the meeting the "largest multicultural revival meeting the world has ever seen."

THE YEAR IN REVIEW: JULY 1990 TO DECEMBER 1991 cont.

U.S. Senate puts clamps on obscene art— The Senate votes 68 to 28 to toughen standards for how the National Endowment for the Arts (NEA) uses tax dollars.

The Senate bill says the NEA can no longer use money to "promote, disseminate, or produce materials that depict or describe, in a patently offensive way, sexual or excretory activities or organs."

The bill is authored by Sen. Jesse Helms (R-N.C.), and is a reaction to earlier NEA funding to two artists who dealt in sexually explicit themes.

Flagpole prayer—About one million students meet at their high school flagpoles around the nation to pray on the morning of September 11.

The event is an outgrowth of a Texas event in 1990, in which about 45,000 students prayed for their teachers and fellow students at their schools' flagpoles.

➤INTERNATIONAL

Argentines form evangelical group—With their numbers rising throughout Argentina, evangelicals announce the formation of their own financial accountability group, called Asociacio'n Entidades Cristianas Auditadas.

The new group is patterned after the Evangelical Council for Financial Accountability in the U.S.

Some churches in Argentina are reporting 70,000 to 100,000 members.

Evangelizing former Communists—An estimated 170 delegates gather from all over Eastern Europe and the Soviet Union for the Lausanne Committee for World Evangelization in Budapest, Hungary. While there, they decry the techniques used by Western evangelists among their people.

Reports indicate that Western-style mass evangelism has been largely ineffective because of lack of follow-up.

Christians turn out in Israel—About 5,000 Christians from 75 countries show up for the twelfth-annual Christian Feast of Tabernacles in Israel. The crowd is gathered to express their support for Israel.

Zaire falls, missionaries flee—As an estimated 3,000 rebel soldiers loot Zaire's capital of Kinshasa, missionaries are forced to flee for their lives.

Missionary Aviation Fellowship reports that they incur millions in damages in a 48-hour period at the hands of the rebels.

YWAM takes gospel worldwide—Youth With A Mission becomes the first missions organization to lay stake to the claim of having worked in every country in the world, according to missions specialist David Barrett.

A YWAM crew of 30 finishes off the momentous task by sailing nine days in the South Pacific to Pitcairn Island, population 58, where they paint the island's only church.

OCTOBER 1991
➤NATIONAL

Judge Thomas and wife pray, attend church—The month of October is a living nightmare for Clarence Thomas and his wife, Virginia, as they endure Senate hearings concerning allegations by Oklahoma law professor Anita Hill that Thomas sexually harassed her.

But in the midst of the turmoil, they find solace in their relationship with the Lord. Virginia says they spend time together each day, turn up the volume on some Christian praise music, and pray.

The Sunday before Thomas is finally confirmed to the High Court, the two listen to a sermon at their church, Truro Episcopal, about being treated unfairly.

Back in Pin Point, Georgia, Thomas's family and friends hold prayer rallies throughout the confirmation process.

Friends and family of Anita Hill also pray for her. Her brother, Winston, pastors a church.

30th birthday for Christian Broadcasting Network—Pat Robertson's Christian Broadcasting Network celebrates its 30th anniversary in early October.

Robertson is joined by a host of leaders, including Campus Crusade's Bill Bright, German Pentecostal Evangelist Reinhard Bonnke, and Guatamalan

President Jorge Serrano, an evangelical.

The group also helps dedicate Robertson's new Founders Inn hotel and conference center.

Swaggart gets caught again— Televangelist Jimmy Swaggart gets caught with a prostitute again, this time as he picks her up in a car while visiting a friend in Indian Wells, California.

The 56-year-old is stopped by police who think he is driving drunk. Actually, Swaggart is swerving in his car trying to hide several pornographic magazines, after he sees the police car in his rearview mirror, according to the prostitute.

After the incident hits the press, Swaggart vacillates between saying he will step down from his Baton Rouge, Louisiana, church and ministry and saying that he will remain in the pulpit.

Roadside abortion protest—On October 6 an estimated 771,000 people at 373 locations in 42 states line major roadways holding posters saying "Abortion Kills Children."

The National Life Chain Sunday is an effort to provide a creative expression of oppositon to abortion, says Royce Dunn, the event's national director.

A second message, "Jesus Forgives and Heals," also is displayed.

➤INTERNATIONAL

Mid-East Christians seek peace—As U.S. Secretary of State James Baker corral Israelis and Palestinians into a historic peace conference in Spain, Western and Middle Eastern Christians gather for their own meeting in Cyprus.

They seek to iron out the wrinkles of misunderstanding that for so long have plagued cooperative efforts between the two groups.

One Middle Eastern leader calls the meeting "a new kind of Pentecost."

The meeting is sponsored by the Middle East Council of Churches and Evangelicals for Middle East Understanding and brings together about 90 Western Christian leaders with 60 of their Middle Eastern counterparts.

European Baptist seminary funding cut off—The only Baptist seminary in Europe is dealt a heavy blow when conservatives on the Southern Baptist Foreign Missions board voted to cut off about $365,000 in funding, which amounts to about 40 percent of the seminary's yearly budget.

The move is the latest example of a moderate-conservative battle among Southern Baptists.

Conservatives had felt that Ruschlikon Seminary in Ruschlikon, Switzerland, was leaning too far toward liberalism.

Yugoslavian conflict stirs churches— Churches and church groups can't escape the conflict between Serbs and Croatians in Yugoslavia.

The Home for Spiritual Rehabilitation, an evangelical youth center, is burned to the ground, and the Evangelical Theological Seminary is forced to temporarily relocate from Osijek to a site near the Austrian border.

Martyr in Haiti—Sylvio Claude, an outspoken evangelical leader, is burned to death by mobs supporting the ousted president, former Roman Catholic priest Jean-Bertrand Aristide.

Meanwhile, four other pastors are forced to flee Cap Haitien, Haiti's second-largest city, as mobs loot and burn houses there.

Though the American embassy urges missionaries to leave the country, many choose to remain and minister to the 6.5 million evangelicals there.

American and Soviet environmentalists gather—Convinced they need to learn from one another, about 200 environmentalists from the U.S., Canada, Great Britain, and the Soviet Union gather to meet on a boat that cruises from Moscow to St. Petersburg.

Scholars on the trip note that Russian Orthodoxy, with its penchant for mysticism, has much to say to Western evangelicals about appreciating God's creation.

Dead Sea Scroll controversy dies—After almost two decades of controversy, the Israel Antiquities Authority decides to open access to all the original fragments of the Dead Sea Scrolls, after an American Hebrew professor and his graduate assistant pirate a copy of the scrolls and promise to go public with it.

THE YEAR IN REVIEW: JULY 1990 TO DECEMBER 1991 cont.

NOVEMBER 1991

➤NATIONAL

Bush says he is fighting pornography— President George Bush comes out of the closet, announcing to a group of pornography opponents that he desires to publicly be linked with their cause.

"We've all heard the stories—innocent children drawn into the world of pornography, victimized by crimes whose consequences are beyond imagination. This horror must stop," says Bush to a national convention of the Religious Alliance Against Pornography, meeting in Washington, D.C.

Composed of Catholics, evangelicals, mainline Protestants, Mormons, and Jews, the group receives a promise from Bush that his administration is committed to prosecuting obscenity and child pornography crimes. "This will remain a priority," he says.

William Barr, recently nominated by Bush to fill the U.S. Attorney General's post vacated by Richard Thornburgh, assures the group he intends to continue his predecessor's active opposition to pornography.

Ollie North's book takes stores by storm—Former Marine Lieutenant Colonel Oliver North aims to set the record straight. With the aid of Christian publisher Zondervan Publishing House, North releases his book, *Under Fire,* which tells his version of the Iran-Contra affair. The book is an immediate best-seller.

The book's two-year development had remained top secret between North and officials of Zondervan and its parent company, Harper-Collins, in an effort to prevent a federal grand jury investigating North from subpoenaing material from it or stopping publication.

Ex-Klan member Duke claims Christian faith—In Louisiana, politics is theater, and the acting is at its most bizarre as former Ku Klux Klan Grand Wizard David Duke tries to convince voters that he is a born-again evangelical.

Duke, who eventually loses his bid to become governor to Edwin Edwards, is denounced by several Christian leaders throughout the state, including United Methodist Bishop William Oden, president of Louisiana's Interchurch Conference.

Schuller recovers from brain surgery— Robert Schuller, pastor of the Crystal Cathedral in Garden Grove, California, is back preaching in his pulpit after a six-week recovery from brain surgery.

Schuller, who injured his head while on a trip to the Netherlands, tells his church that prayer healed him. "It takes more than positive thinking to get through major surgery," he says.

Paige Patterson reinstated at Criswell College—Paige Patterson, a top leader of the conservative movement in the Southern Baptist Convention, is rehired in November as president of Criswell College, just a few weeks after the board of trustees fired him.

His reinstatement is linked to pressure placed on the board by top Southern Baptist conservatives including Adrian Rodgers, Charles Stanley, and Jerry Vines.

Disciples of Christ controversy—The general assembly of the Christian Church (Disciples of Christ) is hopping with controversy as a denomination renewal group, called Disciple Renewal, successfully stymies the election of liberal Michael Kinnamon as president.

The event marks a major setback for moderates and liberals in the denomination of 1.1 million.

In Kinnamon's place, the denomination elects a compromise candidate, William Nichols.

Conservative Episcopalians form ESA— Members of a conservative faction of the Episcopal Church vote to create their own "nongeographical diocese" to be ruled independently from the Episcopalian Church in the United States. The group, however, desires to remain under the Anglican Communion umbrella.

Members of the traditionalist Episcopal Synod of America (ESA) vote at a Fresno, California, meeting to form the new diocese.

"We have to choose where to stand, and we cannot stand upon the foundation built over the last two decades by our bishops and

General Convention," says an ESA statement. "That foundation is built upon sand. They have often acted against Scripture or allowed others to do so. They have consistently acted with no respect for the rest of the Anglican Communion."

Edmond Browning, presiding bishop of the Episcopal Church in the United States, denounces the move saying, "We are deeply troubled that the Synodical Council has taken the position that those who do not agree with them have rejected the authority of Scripture and the Creed and suppress and persecute biblical Christianity."

Russian Orthodox Aleksy II visits U.S.— The patriarch of the Russian Orthodox Church, Aleksy II, makes his first visit to the U.S.

While in New York, he meets with a group of Protestants, Catholics, Orthodox Christians, Jews, and Muslims, telling them tolerance is needed between Russian Orthodox Christians in the former Soviet Union and other believers.

Euthanasia defeated in Washington— Advocates of a Washington State initiative to legalize euthanasia are stunned when voters kill the proposal on November 5.

But euthanasia opponents from various Catholic and evangelical backgrounds say they aren't surprised, and that the proposal's defeat only serves to show they have power at the voting booth when they rally together.

➤INTERNATIONAL

Nigerian Muslims and Christians riot— Death estimates vary widely. As few as eight and as many as 300 are dead after riots break out between angry Muslims and Christians in Nigeria. At least 100 shops and residences are damaged as well.

The violence is apparently prompted when Nigerian officials grant German Pentecostal evangelist Reinhard Bonnke permission to hold a crusade in Kano, Nigeria, while denying approval for public meetings by a prominent Muslim leader.

The world is still hungry—More than half a billion people are still hungry worldwide, reports Bread for the World, a Washington, D.C., lobby group.

The bitter irony is that the world has never been in a better position to completely wipe out hunger, according to Bread for the World's president, David Beckmann.

Beckmann takes comfort that while the number of hungry has increased, the percentage is decreasing.

China's Christians persecuted—As many as 64 church leaders are under arrest in China, where government officials have stepped up resistance to Christians.

Several human rights groups speculate that recent invasions into house church services and other strong-arm tactics are prompted by the government's fear of the role religion played in the blossoming of new liberties in Eastern Europe and the Soviet Union.

Graham in Argentina—Evangelist Billy Graham and his team draw 45,000 to 83,500 into a soccer stadium in Buenos Aires between November 14 and 17. Meanwhile, his message is broadcast to an estimated 5 million throughout South America.

"Billy is the only one who could have brought us all together like this," says pastor Juan Terranova, touting a new unity among pastors and church groups in Argentina and drawing applause from the stadium crowd.

PrimeTime exposes three evangelists— "PrimeTime Live," an ABC network news magazine, airs a November 21 show that charges three Texas televangelists, Robert Tilton, W. V. Grant, and Larry Lea, with running scams.

PrimeTime's Diane Sawyer shows footage compiled during a four-month investigation.

The show charges that Lea lied to donors about his affiliation with a church being built in Poland. It also charges that he lied to donors, saying his family lost all they had when their Tulsa, Oklahoma, house burned. In fact, they still owned a large house in Texas.

The show claims Tilton takes in $80 million yearly from his television shows—in which he encourages viewers to call in and pledge money—and makes false promises to pray for their needs.

Grant, according to PrimeTime, conducts false healings and uses a Haitian orphanage

THE YEAR IN REVIEW: JULY 1990 TO DECEMBER 1991 cont.

as a front to raise money that is later allocated to other facets of his ministry.

Grant and Tilton denounced all charges. Lea initially dismissed the charges as well, but then later announced he was going off the air indefinitely to pray and seek God on the matter.

DECEMBER 1991

►NATIONAL

New kingdoms for the cults—When Kathleen Mickelsen's choir sang in one of Leningrad's largest music halls, her eyes kept meeting with a Russian woman's in the crowd. "I sang the songs as my testimony to her with all my heart," Mickelsen says.

Mickelsen's testimony? She's a Mormon.

Mickelsen's story, along with testimonies from other cult members, are cited in a *Christianity Today* magazine report that says missions run by cults are growing as fast—and sometimes even faster—than evangelical groups in Eastern Europe and the former Soviet Union.

The numbers are staggering. Jehovah's Witnesses report that more than 370,000 conventioneers attended meetings in the summer of 1991 in Czechoslovakia, Hungary, Yugoslavia, Poland, Romania, and the Soviet Union, and 18,293 converts were made.

The Mormon church is active in every Eastern European country and the former Soviet Union and is making government deals involving financial aid in exchange for property and the rights to proselytize.

Disciples of Sun Myung Moon are teaching in Moscow's most prestigious schools, and the Hare Krishna's can be seen regularly in Moscow's subway stations.

Cult-watching groups like Christian Research Institute say they are stepping up their efforts to send materials to churches in an effort to protect naive Eastern European and Soviet laypeople from being sucked into smooth-sounding cults.

Teens pray and read Bible—Three out of four American teenagers pray at least sometimes, and 44 percent read the Bible in private, says a recent Gallup poll.

The study says that young women are more likely to pray or read the Bible than their male counterparts; 86 percent of the 513 teens polled say they believe in the divinity of Jesus.

The survey also shows that as teens get older, they are less likely to believe in a loving God: 96 percent of teens under 16 stated such a belief, compared to 88 percent among 16- and 17-year-olds.

Senior pastors' salaries fair—Two out of three senior pastors feel they are fairly paid, but most part-time pastors feel underpaid, according to a nationwide study of about 4,000 churches conducted by *Christianity Today* and *Leadership* magazines.

The average annual total compensation (salary, housing, and benefits) for senior pastors is $45,515; for solo pastors, $32,163; and for part-time pastors, $14,442.

Church-state decisions—A convicted murderer, Karl Chambers, is set free by the Pennsylvania Supreme Court because the prosecutor in his case quoted from the Bible as he urged jurors to give the accused murderer the death penalty.

In another case, members of the Duncanville (Texas) High School junior varsity girls' basketball team win a victory over a legal challenge by the American Civil Liberties Union (ACLU).The ACLU challenged a practice by the girls' team of kneeling and praying at center court after each game. A judge said the team could continue the practice, as long as school officials do not encourage it or participate.

Falwell admits debt troubles—Jerry Falwell admits his Liberty University is running more than $60 million in debt and could be forced into bankruptcy after Kemper Securities reneges on a promise to finance $61 million in taxable bonds to bail the school out.

Falwell announces he has sued Kemper and that the settlement, should it go his way, could be for as much as $100 million. He says the school needs a $10 million miracle from donors to survive.

Split imminent in Christian Reformed Churches—Conservative churches in the 250,000-member Christian Reformed Church announce they intend to leave that denomination, citing liberal leanings on issues they consider key, such as the ordination of women.

The group takes the name Alliance of Reformed Churches and says that in future months they likely will consolidate into a denomination.

➤INTERNATIONAL

Evangelism's new hot spots—The hottest spots worldwide for doing evangelism in the nineties will be Latin America, China, and India, according to a newly released study by missions researcher Tom Houston of Oxford, England.

By A.D. 2000, Latin America should have 50 million new converts; India, 40 million; and China, 30 million.

Yugoslavian destruction—More than 380 church buildings and parishes have been destroyed during fighting in Croatia, according to U.S. Catholic bishops.

The Evangelical Theological Seminary and a Pentecostal church in Osijek, Croatia, are also reported hit during heavy fighting there.

Ethics in Soviet schools—Campus Crusade for Christ reports having trained more than 1,700 Soviet educators to teach ethics in the former USSR's elementary and high schools. Another 3,000 teachers will begin training soon.

With appreciation to *Christianity Today* and *Church Around the World.*

THE 1990s: WHAT TO EXPECT

No one knows for certain how the future will unfurl. But history and trends give us clues. Here are some things likely to surface within the church and society during the next decade.

Life-style
- Rapid changes; an era of flexibility
- Time will be most valued resource; more important than money or career
- Contradiction of behavior and values
- Speed addiction; pace of life will not slow down
- 24-hour consumer services; rush deliveries, while-you-wait, on-site services reflecting "I want it now" demand; personalized marketing appeals
- "Sunday" distinctives will fade
- More frequent, shorter vacations
- Air travel will double
- Cable TV primary source for entertainment; 60 percent of households will have cable by 1993; 100 percent by 2000
- VCRs in virtually every home.

Arts
- Shift from sports to arts as a leisure activity
- Churches will increasingly incorporate drama and other art forms into worship styles
- Resurgence of classical music to replace gradual decline of rock
- Compilation music recordings; two or more artists

Family
- Family concerns will become increasingly crucial
- Divorce, though declining due to fewer and delayed marriage commitments, will be more acceptable
- Stepfamilies will outnumber traditional families; continuing increase in single parent homes

THE 1990s: WHAT TO EXPECT cont.

- Increasing relocation of families; fewer roots, more insecurities
- Increase in teenage suicides along with changing family structures; is now third leading cause of death among teens
- Health care, a top family concern
- Home environment will be zealously protected
- Television/video will play a central role in family activities

Education
- Shortage of qualified teachers
- Christian day schools will prosper as parents demand moral values and public schools struggle to incorporate values and ethics into curriculum
- Home school growth hazy; some predict an estimated two to three million home-schoolers by 2000
- Video education: elementary, college, and graduate levels
- Shift to "hands on" training rather than academics
- Decrease in college enrollments
- High educational costs will force Christian colleges to close or merge; more co-op programs among colleges
- More older students and "second careerists" will enroll in graduate schools and seminaries
- Theological education by extension; more informal, convenient training programs, weekend college and seminary classes
- More demand for geriatrics, computer literacy, counseling, information management, and minorities programs
- More English-language schools internationally

Career
- Corporations increasingly large or small squeezing out mid-sized companies
- Entrepreneurial spirit will live on
- Home-based employment
- Flexible work hours; job-sharing
- Employee child care services
- Women and minorities will outpace traditional white male leadership
- More frequent career changes
- Women will break through to top executive status
- Authoritative, militant style will give way to inspiration/teacher/coach/facilitator style
- Earlier retirement

Technology
- Voice-recognition computers; PCs will be smaller and as powerful as 1989's supercomputers
- Home computer shopping
- "Carry with" pocket-sized, cellular telephones
- Built-in car phones
- Electronic mail
- "Smart cars" able to adjust speed limits, calculate locations
- "Smart houses" programmed to perform household functions: turn on bath water, open garage doors, instant alert to fire/police stations, remote control instructions to begin cooking dinner

Church Life
- Declining membership in mainline churches; increases among Evangelicals and Fundamentalists

- More cooperation between Evangelicals and Pentecostals; denominational distinctives will fade
- Baby boomers will return to church with their children
- Growth of megachurches; congregations averaging 500 or more will increase by 30 percent
- Telemarketing evangelism outreach
- Shift away from a "home church" toward attending two or more churches
- Sunday schools and youth activities forced to compete with high-quality, hi-tech entertainment
- Services-oriented outreach: counseling, bookstores, travel groups, financial planning, day care, retirement centers
- Increasing need for divorce recovery, single-parent, blended-family programs
- Less lay involvement; more team and professional leadership
- Worship styles will change; look for more variety, less structure
- Faster-pace church services
- More reflective theology; rejection of pat answers
- Increase in women leadership, ordinations; diffusion of traditional roles
- Shorter tenure for pastors, burnout more common

Evangelism
- Televangelism decline
- Search for spiritual values will intensify
- More personalized, life-style evangelism
- Crusade evangelism will become more upbeat, entertaining, fast-moving; less sermonizing, more focus on needs of specific age groups, as well as social, economic, and family concerns
- More use of telemarketing techniques
- AD 2000 focus will provide impetus for a variety of evangelistic activities

Media
- More newsletters; fewer magazines
- Two, maybe three, high-volume general Christian magazines; most successful magazines will be more specialized, focused
- "Quick reading" print products
- Music products will flourish; books decline
- High definition television; interactive TV programs, more channels on cable systems

Missions
- Two-thirds World countries will take lead in number of missionaries, increasing from 30,000 in 1988 to 160,0000 in 2000
- Growth of Christianity strongest in Latin America, China, Africa, Europe
- Increase in number of charismatic mission groups
- Increase among Americans in short-term missionary commitments, tentmakers and professionals, rather than career commitment
- Focus on urban centers; cities will grow to unprecedented populations in developing countries
- AD 2000 programs will become increasingly aggressive
- Unified European market, free trade will simplify evangelism outreach; English will move toward the universal language

Social/Political
- Issues of the decade will be environment, economy, drugs, AIDS, medical costs, family, education, population control, poverty

THE 1990s: WHAT TO EXPECT cont.

- Churches will become more involved in social issues; strengthening of New Evangelicalism stance
- AIDS epidemic; cases will increase from 700,000 to 6 million people worldwide by 2000. Total number infected may approach 20 million; greatest increase among newborns
- Soaring drug and alcohol abuse
- Ethics in surrogacy, biotechnology, and biomedical increasingly complex
- Continuing pressure to establish a "wall of separation." Madalyn Murray O'Hair's American Atheists group's agenda includes having "In God We Trust" stricken from currency, nativity scenes banished from all government property, religious symbols excised from city and state seals, and religious groups' tax-exempt status removed.

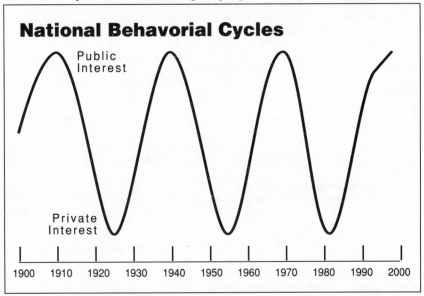

National Behavorial Cycles

Source: *America 2000* by George Barna and adapted from *Cycles of American History,* by Arthur Schlesinger, Jr., Houghton Mifflin Company, Boston, 1986.

NEWS HIGHLIGHTS OF THE 1980s

1980 Popular speaker **Bill Gothard** steps down as president of the successful **Institute in Basic Youth Conflicts,** largely as a result of the way he handled charges of sexual immorality involving his brother, Steve, a ministry executive. **Seventh-day Adventists** strip Adventist theologian Desmond Ford of his credentials for debunking church doctrine.

1981 After twenty-two years of forced inactivity, China grants **Three-Self Patriotic Movement** permission to hold a major convention, opening the door to greater religious freedom. Colombian guerrillas kill missionary **Chet Bitterman,** and **Sandra Day O'Connor** becomes the first female Supreme Court justice, to the dismay of most Evangelicals, who question her position on abortion.

1982 A federal judge in Little Rock, Arkansas, rules that **creationism** is religious in nature, and thus strikes down a state law mandating that creation be given equal time with evolution in public school classrooms. **Billy Graham** preaches for the first time in the Soviet Union and is criticized for allegedly overlooking religious persecution.

1983 Exiled Philippine leader **Benigno Aquino** is shot and killed in Manila. He had returned to the country because of his Christian faith, according to some who knew him. Billy Graham's **Amsterdam '83** gathers 4,000 itinerant evangelists from around the world for instruction and inspiration.

1984 Aggressive **political activism** is adopted by many conservative evangelicals, who play a major role in the re-election of Ronald Reagan. After fierce debate, Congress rejects the School Prayer Amendment, but as a compromise passes the **Equal Access Act,** allowing voluntary student religious groups to meet at school.

1985 Tensions in the Southern Baptist Convention headline the SBC's annual meeting in Dallas, at which conservative **Charles Stanley** is re-elected president and a peace committee is formed to study the SBC turmoil. Church groups and Christian relief agencies put millions of dollars into projects to ease the **African famine.**

1986 Pat Robertson all but formally announces his bid for the presidency. The attorney general announces a major effort to crack down on illegal **pornography.** Pro-life groups approve the appointment of **Antonin Scalia** to the Supreme Court, and the Dutch Reformed Church in South Africa denounces **apartheid** as unjust.

1987 Televangelists' troubles begin when **Oral Roberts** announces in January that God would call him home if he does not raise $8 million for medical mission scholarships. **Jim Bakker** resigns from PTL amid revelations of sexual impropriety, and **Robertson** makes his presidential candidacy official.

1988 Abortion opponents consider the election of **George Bush** an important victory. Amid hope brought by **glasnost** comes the celebration of 1,000 years of Christianity in the Soviet Union. **Jimmy Swaggart** is defrocked amid revelations of sexual scandal. Christians take to the streets as part of the **rescue movement** and to protest the movie *The Last Tempation of Christ*.

1989 The **Berlin wall** crumbles as political reform sweeps Eastern Europe. The **abortion** battle heats up throughout the country as the Supreme Court's decision in *Webster v. Missouri* gives states freedom to set their own agenda. Federal Judge Robert Potter sentences **Jim Bakker** to a forty-five-year prison term for fraud.

Source: December 15, 1989, issue of *Christianity Today* Magazine. Used by permission.

WHAT PEOPLE ARE SAYING: JULY 1990 TO DECEMBER 1991

"I need you." *President George Bush, in a brief message sent to Billy Graham. The message asked Graham and his wife, Ruth, to come to the White House on January 16, 1991, when President Bush made his announcement of war on television.*

"This war in the Gulf is not a Christian war, a Jewish war, or a Muslim war—it is a just war." *President George Bush, to the national meeting of the National Religious Broadcasters, drawing applause.*

"This is more like a revival than a war." *Baptist minister and chaplain Jeff Houston on the effect the Persian Gulf crisis had on soldiers.*

WHAT PEOPLE ARE SAYING: JULY 1990 TO DECEMBER 1991 cont.

"The primary reason for U.S. involvement in the Persian Gulf is to ensure the flow of unlimited cheap oil and not to protect Kuwait or Saudi Arabia from Iraqi aggression." *A statement from 1,700 U.S. Catholics, including 11 bishops, promising nonviolent protests if the U.S. goes to war with Iraq.*

"Our tears have become telescopes to heaven." *Billy Graham, during a talk to military families who lost a loved one in the Persian Gulf War.*

"I have received Christ as my Savior the 15th day of May of 1990 at 11 A.M." *Manuel Noriega about his conversion while in a Florida jail.*

"Something is very wrong. America isn't working." *Chuck Colson and Jack Eckerd in their 1991 book* Why America Doesn't Work, *noting that cultural and societal changes have caused Americans to lose their work ethic.*

"We're going to tell them that they don't have to wait until September. The Messiah has come," *said Jews for Jesus spokesman Bob Mendelsohn, concerning how his group will witness to a California sect of Hasidic Jews whose leader has said the Messiah would come by September 9, 1991.*

"It has been written that [the Pope] costs more than the Queen of England. Fortunately! Because the message he brings has a transcendental value," *retorted Pope John Paul II to a reporter who asks whether millions of dollars should be spent staging papal visits.*

"We thank you for sparing the lives of so many of our men and women who went to the Gulf. We pray for our enemies that a just peace may come to their troubled land. . . . We are not an arrogant nation, a gloating nation, for we know 'Blessed are the meek for they shall inherit the earth.'" *President George Bush in a prayer on April 7 at a special National Day of Thanksgiving service after the war.*

"I am still not too comfortable with what the role [of religion] ought to be [in government and public life]. I don't want to act like I'm holier than thou, or that I want to wear my faith or my religion on my sleeves, or than I'm the guy out there in the temple beating his breast and praying loudest. . . . And yet, I want to do what many that have gone before me have done, and that is to amplify as best one can that we are one nation under God," *answers President George Bush in April 1991 to a religious journalist's question about how his faith impacts his work as president.*

"I know of people in high positions in the evangelical church—pastors, denominational and parachurch leaders, publishers, best-selling authors—who are homosexual but who realize that to disclose this would ruin their careers." *Ralph Blair, of the New York City-based Evangelicals Concerned.*

"I've found Jesus. It's that simple. He's made the difference, and I'm glad I've found him while there's still time," *says Lee Atwater, the one-time cutthroat political strategist who masterminded George Bush's campaign to the White House. Atwater was diagnosed with brain cancer and made his comments after accepting Christ and repenting of some of his tough-handed tactics just months before he died.*

"We men and women were shaped by our Creator in a long process that links us wonderfully to the rest of creation. . . . Yet we seem to be rapidly losing a sense of what it means to be an image bearer to the Creator in a creation entrusted to our care." *Loren Wilkinson, et al., in* Earthkeeping in the '90s; Stewardship of Creation.

"There is a shortage of indigenous black leadership. The welfare system now substitutes for the family. So no longer is a family held responsible for its children, the government is." *John Perkins, founder of Voice of Calvary Ministries in Jackson, Mississippi, and Harambee Christian Family Center in Pasadena, California.*

"In rejecting the [majority report on sexuality] and affirming the current position on homosexuality, the general assembly was speaking the mind of the people. . . . If we accept homosexuals' interpretation of Scripture, what prevents us from accepting the adulterer's interpretation or from interpreting Scripture any way we want to?" *Robert Campbell of the Presbyterian Lay Committee, after the 203rd general assembly of the Presbyterian Church USA in June rejected a sexuality report that would have relaxed its stance on homosexuality.*

"I thank God that this group gave me the award. It lets me know that I have been somewhat effective." *Decency crusader Donald Wildmon on being given the "Jesse Helms Defamer of the Year" Award (for opposing homosexuality as an acceptable life-style) by the Gay and Lesbian Alliance Against Defamation.*

"'My grace is sufficient for you,' the Lord said to the apostle Paul. The average Christian in our culture cynically views that kind of counsel as simplistic, unsophisticated and naive. Can you imagine one of today's radio counselors simply telling a hurting caller that God's grace is enough to meet the need?" *John F. MacArthur, pastor of Grace Community Church in Sun Valley, California, in* Our Sufficiency in Christ.

"America's children . . . are being marinated in a popular culture that can pickle your brain." *Michael Medved, co-host of PBS television's "Sneak Previews," in a keynote address to the national conference of the Religious Alliance Against Pornography.*

"Every proposed action that would have represented progress to gay and lesbian people failed. But so did every proposed action that would have made us more fundamentalistic on sexuality." *Elisabet Hannon of Presbyterians for Lesbian and Gay Concerns, on the general assembly's rejection of the sexuality report.*

"We are going to use our first amendment rights to make them miserable." *Randall Terry, leader of Operation Rescue, during a May 29 Washington, D.C., press conference in which his group outlines plans for a new campaign that culminates in "The Summer of Mercy" in Wichita, Kansas.*

WHAT PEOPLE ARE SAYING: JULY 1990 TO DECEMBER 1991 cont.

"It is too early to say what will happen. . . . This could be looked at as a major turning point in church history in America, or it could be just a blip on the screen. Part of that depends on us." *Randall Terry on whether Operation Rescue's six-week-long protest in Wichita that garnered massive support from local churches could lead to a local or even national revival.*

"If you were to have suggested to some of these pastors five weeks ago that they would be saying and participating in some of the things they are today, they would have said, 'You are mad.'" *Wichita Mayor Robert Knight, an evangelical Christian, on the influence Operation Rescue's efforts had on local clergy.*

"They awakened a sleeping giant. For that, I am grateful." *Gene Williams, senior pastor of Wichita's First Church of the Nazarene, on the effect Operation Rescue had locally.*

"Where Christ is depicted as a drug addict or his crucifix is immersed in urine, the work magically becomes 'art' and is paid for by the National Endowment for the Arts with taxpayers' money. On the other hand, sincere religious expression is labeled unconstitutional and banished from the public square." *Robert Skolrood, director of the National Legal Foundation, expressing dismay over a Chicago federal appeals court ruling that 16 paintings depicting the life of Christ could not be displayed during Christmas in a public park in Ottawa, Illinois, while several artists whose work is considered sacrilegious by some are funded by the federal government.*

"The image of Christianity in America used to be that it was for a bunch of old ladies. Now athletes are being Christians. That is saying that it's cool to be a Christian." *Ralph Drollinger, director of Sports Outreach America, on the increasing number of professional athletes professing Christ.*

"Two thousand years ago, who would have put any money on Bethlehem?" *Mickey Maudlin on the assertion by some members of Kansas City Fellowship and the Vineyard that a new movement of prophecy in their midst may signal the last days.*

"Can we be good pastors to the rest of the church if we can't discipline ourselves? Are the bishops of this House capable of self-discipline?" *Retired Texas suffragan bishop Gordon Charlton, after the Episcopal House of Bishops refused at its July general convention to discipline two bishops who ordained gay clergy.*

"Morally, I was wrong sleeping with a lot of women. I wish it hadn't happened, but it did. All I can do is ask God's forgiveness and leave it in his hands. All I can do is pray a lot." *Magic Johnson, in December 1991, to ABC interviewer Connie Chung, redressing several comments he made about his former active and loose sex life.*

"If the scientific and religious communities could agree to work together for a decade, they could put the issue of the environment on the agenda in a way that it hasn't been so far, expecially in the evangelical community." *Ron Sider, executive director of Evangelicals for Social Action, after an unprecedented meeting of scientists and religious leaders in New York to discuss environmental concerns.*

"In the context of church growth, imitation is the quickest route to doom. Ministry by mimicry almost invariably results in deterioration, rather than growth." *Church marketing expert* **George Barna** *in* User Friendly Churches, *on the inability of many churches to reproduce megachurches simply by copycat techniques.*

"We exclude any preference according to one's attitude toward religion. The party respects feelings of believers, is for equality of all religions and professions, and is against one-sided privileges for any religious organization. The party thinks it inadmissible to use religion in political goals for instigating interethnic conflicts, religious intolerance, and hatred between believers of different religions, as well as between believers and nonbelievers." *A portion of the new party platform adopted by the Communist party led by* **Mikhail Gorbachev** *in August, less than a month before the failed coup attempt against Gorbachev.*

"Peculiar, how quickly government moves when white police officers beat a defenseless black man, but moves not at all when officers mistreat demonstrators who are not in accord with the liberal view of abortion." *Columnist* **Cal Thomas**, *a conservative Christian, on the difference in public reaction to videotaped L.A. police brutality against Operation Rescue protestors versus the April 1991 beating of Rodney King.*

"For the first time in their history, the church can look forward . . . and not worry about who is behind them." **Peter Deyneka, Jr.**, *of the newly formed Peter Deyneka USSR Ministries, on the impact the failed August coup against Mikhail Gorbachev had on churches.*

"The words of Jesus, 'Let him who is without sin cast the first stone,' are very appropriate today." *Senate Chaplain* **Richard Halverson**, *opening the Senate's proceedings on the day senators were to vote on whether to confirm embattled candidate Clarence Thomas for the Supreme Court.*

"Too often, what passes for a good marriage is a routine, pleasant arrangement that avoids loneliness and keeps things predictable and safe." **Dr. Larry Crabb** *in* Men & Women; Enjoying the Difference.

"In 1992, celebrations of the 500th anniversary of the arrival of Christopher Columbus in the 'New World' will be held. For the descendents of the survivors of the subsequent invasion, genocide, slavery, 'ecocide' and exploitation of the wealth of the land, a celebration is not an appropriate observance of this anniversary." *A resolution of the* **National Council of the Churches of Christ in the USA**.

"Many groups are exploiting the quincentenary for their particular causes, but I think we should look at history in its own context, and we should present both the good and the bad aspects of what happened. . . . Christianity is in a precarious position if we don't proceed in the spirit of Columbus, with his faith in God and his sense of mission." *Kay Brigham, author of two books on Christopher Columbus.*

"We're going to continue to do this, no matter what." *Philadelphia Eagle linebacker **Reggie White**, on the prayer circles conducted at center field after many pro-football games.*

"Derek: There. You got what you wanted. Ever since I was diagnosed as having cancer, you have done everything conceivable to precipitate my death. I was not alone in recognizing what you were doing. What you did, desertion and abandonment, and subsequent harassment of a dying woman, is so unspeakable, there are no words to describe the horror of it. Yet you know and others know too. You will have to live with this until you die. May you never, ever forget. Ann." *Ann Wickett Humphry, in an October, 1991, suicide note to her husband, Derek, with whom she cofounded the Hemlock Society, which favors euthanasia.*

FOCUS BOOK

Racing Toward 2001: The forces shaping America's religious future by Russell Chandler, award-winning journalist and religion writer for the *Los Angeles Times.* Published by Zondervan Publishing House and Harper San Francisco.

AWARDS: JULY 1990 TO DECEMBER 1991

The Knesset Speaker's Award—To the **International Christian Embassy in Jerusalem**, for protmoting goodwill in Israel, from the Israeli Knesset. It marks the first time the award has been given to a Christian institution in Israel.

International Platinum Award—To **Dan Johnson**, executive director of the McGee and Me! children's video series. The award was for the premiere episode, "The Big Lie." The McGee series is a joint venture of Tyndale House Publishers and Focus on the Family.

Decade of Growth Awards—To **five Bible colleges** that achieved the highest overall enrollment growth from 1980 to 1989: North Central Bible College (62.9%); American Baptist College (35.5%); Toccoa Falls College (31.9%); Briercrest Bible College (24.7%); and Pacific Christian College (24.5%). The awards were given by Christianity Today, Inc.

Festschrift: Perspectives on Theology in the Contemporary World—To **Bernard Ramm**, 74, by the National Association of Baptist Professors of Religion, for his pioneering work on the relation between science and Scripture.

Marian Pfister Anschutz "Back to the Family" Awards—To Housing and Urban Secretary **Jack Kemp**; Los Angeles teacher **Jaime Escalante**, who inspired the film *Stand and Deliver;* and **Robert Woodson**, the African-American who founded the National Center for Neighborhood Enterprise. The awards were given by the Family Research Council to recognize efforts to promote family values.

The 1990 Presidential End Hunger Award—To **Art Simon**, founder of Bread for the World, in recognition of his efforts to stop world hunger, by President George Bush.

The Priscilla and Aquila Award—To **George and Emily Walther**, who resigned from the board of a Christian marriage-enrichment ministry rather than compromise their convictions about mutual submission; and to **Alvin Schmidt**, who lost his teaching position at Concordia Theological Seminary in Fort Wayne, Indiana, when he refused to go along with that institution's views of limiting the role of women in ministry. The awards are given by Christians for Biblical Equality to recognize those that have "risked their necks" (Romans 16:3) for the sake of biblical feminism.

TRANSITIONS: JULY 1990 TO DECEMBER 1991

NAMED

Graeme Irvine, as president of World Vision International. Irvine served as acting president since January of 1989.

Robertson McQuilkin, as chancellor of Columbia Bible College and Seminary. McQuilkin served as president of the institution for 22 years before retiring to care for his wife.

John Orme, as executive director-designate of the Interdenominational Foreign Mission Association. Orme was a professor and chairman of the department of theology of the graduate school at Central American Theological Seminary in Guatemala and then served as pastor of Highland Park Baptist Church in Southfield, Michigan.

Eugene B. Habecker, as new president and chief executive officer of the Evangelical Council for Financial Accountability. He was president of Huntington College. He assumed his new post in June of 1991.

Philip Downer, as the new president of the Christian Business Men's Committee of USA. Downer, 43, was senior managing partner for an Atlanta law firm.

Thomas Graves, as the first permanent president of Baptist Theological Seminary in Richmond, Virginia, formed by Southern Baptist moderates of the Southern Baptist Alliance. Graves, 43, was pastor of Saint John's Baptist Church in Charlotte.

John Erickson, as general secretary of the United Bible Societies. Erickson is the vice president of the American Bible Society.

David Beckmann, 43, as president of Bread for the World. Beckmann is an economist and ordained pastor and succeeds Arthur Simon, who founded the group in 1974.

David Hope, as bishop of London, considered the third most-important post in the Church of England.

Dennis Kinlaw, as chancellor of Asbury College. Kinlaw served as the school's president for 18 years.

Edwin Blue, as president of Asbury College, to replace Dennis Kinlaw, who is named chancellor.

David Beckman, as president of Colorado Christian University, as of June 1, 1991. Beckman replaced Joe Wall, who became the school's chancellor.

John Zehr, the tenth president of Bethel College in North Newton, Kansas. Zehr had been professor of physiology and biophysics at the University of Illinois, Urbana.

Arthur Gay, as executive director of World Relief. Gay was senior minister at South Park Church in Park Ridge, Illinois.

John Bowling, as president of Olivet Nazarene University in Kankakee, Illinois. Bowling was pastor of College Church of the Nazarene in Bourbonnais, Illinois.

John Vawter, as the seventh president of Western Conservative Baptist Seminary in Portland, Oregon. Vawter was pastor of Wayzata Evangelical Free Church in Minneapolis.

TRANSITIONS: JULY 1990 TO DECEMBER 1991 cont.

Jack Fortin, 46, as the new chief of staff of World Vision. He worked 20 years previously with Young Life.

J. Raymond Tallman, as new general director of Arab World Ministries, effective January 1991. Until then, he continues as chairman of the Department of World Missions and Evangelism at Moody Bible Institute.

Michael Green, a professor of New Testament and evangelism at Regent College in Vancouver, by the archbishops of Canterbury and York, as one of two Anglicans to lead a new Anglican evangelistic effort.

Ray Sutton, as the new president of Philadelphia Theological Seminary, the 104-year-old Reformed Episcopal seminary. Sutton was a pastor in Texas.

James Didier, as the fourth president of Judson College, in Elgin, Illinois. Didier was Judson's dean of student affairs.

APPOINTED

Thomas H. Englund, as president of the Christian College Consortium. Englund was serving as vice president and dean of the college at Franklin Pierce College in Rindge, New Hampshire.

David Pickard, as new general director of Overseas Missionary Fellowship, replacing James Hudson Taylor III, who stepped down after 11 years.

Richard Walton, as new U.S. director of SEND International, replacing Charles Hufstetler, who served since 1987.

Clarence Reimer, as the new president and chief executive officer of the Evangelical Council for Financial Accountability.

Kenneth Keeler, as president of the Christian Service Brigade, succeeding Samuel Gray.

ELECTED

Agustin (Jun) Vencer, Jr., as international director-designate of World Evangelical Fellowship. Vencer, 43, a Filipino, will take over the job from David Howard on July 1, 1992.

Jane Dempsey Douglass, of Princeton Seminary, as president of the World Alliance of Reformed Churches, replacing Allan Boesak, who resigned following admitting an extramarital affair.

Gerald Gallimore, as president and chief executive officer of Youth for Christ International.

Johnny Miller, 46, as the new president of Columbia Bible College and Seminary, in Columbia, South Carolina. Miller was a New Testament professor there.

Wanda Franz, as the new president of the National Right to Life Committee. Franz, a professor of child development at West Virginia University, succeeds John Wilke, who decided not to seek the office again after 12 years at the helm.

Benjamin de Jesus, as the first executive director of the Alliance World Fellowship, composed of 41 autonomous church denominations in 41 nations and associated with the Christian and Missionary Alliance.

David Le Shana, as the fourth president of Western Evangelical Seminary, Portland, Oregon.

James Draper, as president of the Southern Baptist Convention Sunday School Board. He is a former president of the convention.

Metropolitan Bartholomeos, 51, as the new patriarch of the Eastern Orthodox Church.

INAUGURATED

James L. Edwards, as the fourth president of Anderson (Ind.) University.

RETIRED

James Franks, Sr., founder and former president of International Aid Inc.

RESIGNED

George C. Fuller, as president of Westminster Theological Seminary, effective in June of 1991.

Authur Borden, as president of the Evangelical Council for Financial Accountability, to accept a position with the American Bible Society.

Jerry Ballard, as executive director and chief executive officer of World Relief. During his 13-year tenure, the organization grew from a budget of $2 million per year to $20 million.

The board of directors of the U.S. Center for World Mission, following a long dispute over accountability and control of the organization with General Director Ralph Winter.

Haddon Robinson, at 60, after 12 years as president of Denver Theological Seminary, to become Harold John Ockenga Distinguished Professor of Preaching at Gordon-Conwell Theological Seminary.

Richard Gross, 60, as president of Gordon College, a position he held since 1976.

Sam Ericsson, as chief executive officer of the Washington, D.C.–based Christian Legal Society, to pursue other ministry opportunities.

DIED

Missiologist **Donald McGavran,** the father of the contemporary church-growth movement, on July 10, 1990, at the age of 92, at his California home. McGavran was a missionary to India who at age 67 accepted an invitation from Fuller Theological Seminary to launch its School of World Mission. There, McGavran virtually began the field of evangelical missiology and the now-popular church-growth movement.

W. Stanley Mooneyham, former president of World Vision, on June 3, 1990, of kidney failure in Los Angeles. He was 65. Mooneyham was World Vision's president from 1969 to 1982. Under his leadership, World Vision's budget grew about 600 percent and its staff tripled.

Wang Mingdao, a leader in the Chinese house-church movement, on July 28 at age 91, just before the Sunday morning service that regularly met in his home. In 1921, the same year the Chinese Communist party was founded, Wang preached his first sermon. From that point, he was a staunch opponent of communism. For years he was affiliated with China Inland Mission, now called Overseas Missionary Fellowship.

Malcolm Muggeridge, well-known British writer and social critic, on November 14, 1991, at the age of 87. He never recovered from a stroke suffered three years earlier.

Howard Long, 78, on July 31. Long, a successful businessman, was recognized as the catalyst for the translation of the New International Version of the Bible.

Philip Edgcumbe Hughes, 75, regarded as the leading evangelical Anglican theologian, of a heart attack.

Carl K. Becker, pioneer missionary physician, who served 45 years with Africa Inland Mission, at age 96. He worked extensively with lepers in Zaire.

Charles Troutman, Jr., on November 18, 1990, at age 76. Troutman was one of InterVarsity Christian Fellowship's founding pioneers.

William Sanford LaSor, professor emeritus of Old Testament at Fuller Theological Seminary, on January 11, 1991, in Altadena, California, at age 79, following heart surgery.

John Phillips "Jack" Odell, at 75, who for 37 years was a writer, announcer, and director for the radio broadcast "Unshackled."

James L. Cleveland, 59, known as the "King of Gospel." A native of Chicago's South Side, Cleveland taught Aretha Franklin to sing gospel music. He wrote more than 400 gospel songs.

Carl H. Lundquist, 74, president emeritus of Bethel College and Theological Seminary, in St. Paul, Minnesota, and former president of the Christian College Consortium; of cancer.

Robert C. Cook, 78, former president and chancellor of the King's College in Briarcliffe

TRANSITIONS: JULY 1990 TO DECEMBER 1991 cont.

Manor, New York, on March 11, 1991, after a five-month battle with leukemia. Cook helped found Youth for Christ International, and served as president of the National Association of Evangelicals and the National Religious Broadcasters.

James Collier, 62, who wrote and directed many movies for Billy Graham's Worldwide Pictures, including *The Hiding Place, Joni, The Prodigal,* and *For Pete's Sake.*

Former Astronaut **James Erwin,** 61, following a heart attack. Irwin, who walked on the moon during the Apollo 15 mission, led several expeditions to the mountains of Ararat in search of Noah's Ark.

Two-time Pulitzer Prize–winning **Vaughn "Shoes" Shoemaker,** who created the world-- renowned cartoon character John Q. Public. Shoemaker was a committed Christian and received an honorary doctor of letters from Wheaton College in 1945.

Paul Jewett, senior professor of systematic theology at Fuller Theological Seminary in Pasadena, California, at the age of 71, of cancer.

Patriarch Dimitrios I, head of the Greek Orthodox Church, and spiritual leader of the world's 300 million Eastern Orthodox Christians; of a heart attack.

Joseph Fletcher, 84, who made popular situation ethics. Fletcher at one time was an Episcopalian priest, but renounced his faith later in life.

KILLED

Sofia Sigfridsson, 18, of Sweden, and **Karen Goldsworthy,** 19, of New Zealand. The two youths, who were members of Operation Mobilization's ship, the *Doulos,* were visiting in August the Filipino port of Zamboanga with others from the ship, when an unknown assailant lobbed a grenade within their midst. Militant Muslims were suspected for the attack.

Five aviation students and an instructor from Trinity Western University, in Langely, British Colombia, Canada, when their two planes crashed in bad weather while flying home from a visit to Mission Aviation Fellowship's headquarters in Redlands, California. Those killed were: Teena Daly, Terry Townsend, Jeff Helzer, Danny Penner, Al Karim Merali, and instructor Graeme Seath.

John Speers, 32, shot by a unknown assailant while working with Christian Mission in Many Lands. Speers was working among Muslims in Manila, the Philippines.

Independent Baptist missionary **Clark Alan Jacobsen,** killed in August, 1990, amidst a civil war in Liberia. Jacobsen was arrested by government troops on August 17 and not seen again until his body was turned over to the U.S. embassy two days later.

Cnon Ezra Lawiri, a Sudan Bible translator, who was fatally shot on Good Friday 1991, after being caught in a crossfire between government forces and a rebel group. Archdeacon Bullen of the Episcopal Church of Sudan said that Lawiri's last words were, "I am not dying, but going home to the Father."

Nana Shaga, an Ethiopian church worker, who was stabbed to death while serving as an evangelist to the Omo River Valley tribespeople in southwestern Ethiopia.

OVERTURNED

Jim Bakker's 45-year prison sentence, by a U.S. Circuit Court of Appeals. Bakker's conviction on fraud and conspiracy charges was upheld, but it is ruled he must be resentenced because of prejudicial remarks made by the judge who initially sentenced him.

REDUCED

Jim Bakker's prison sentence, from 45 years to 18, making Bakker eligible for parole in 4 years.

FOUNDED

Crossway Books Ltd., the British counterpart of Good News Publishers' U.S. division.

MERGED

The Reformed Journal, published by the Christian Reformed Church, and *Perspectives,* a theological journal of the Reformed Church in America.

Last Days Ministries, founded by the late Christian singer Keith Green and his wife, Melody, with Youth With A Mission. The 80-member Last Days staff will continue to operate under their same name.

RENAMED

The Association of Evangelical Professors of Missions, to the Evangelical Missiological Society.

CHANGED

The name of Philadelphia's oldest seminary, from the Reformed Episcopal Seminary to Philadelphia Theological Seminary.

CEASED

Publication of *The Ecumenist,* a bimonthly ecumenical journal to about 5,500 intellectuals, that championed liberal views.

CELEBRATED

Trans World Radio's 30th year of broadcasting from Monte Carlo, Monaco.
The American Bible Society's 175th anniversary, on May 9, 1991.
InterVarsity Christian Fellowship's 50th year of ministry.
Campus Crusade's 40th year of ministry.

TOP 1991 NEWS STORIES: THREE PERSPECTIVES

How three different Christian authorities rank the top ten news stories of 1991:

Christianity Today Magazine News Staff	Religion Newswriters Association (about 150 newspaper journalists who cover religion)	Adult Sunday School Class of First United Methodist Church, Belzoni, MS
1. War in the Gulf. The conflict heightened not only interest in the end times, but also concern for peace in the Middle East.	1. The overwhelming rejection by Presbyterians (in the Presbyterian Church USA) of a report that promoted acceptance of homosexuality.	1. Fall of atheistic USSR and satellites.
2. Reforms in the USSR and Eastern Europe. Continued restructuring created new opportunities for believers.	2. The Christian blessing given Boris N. Yeltsin by Russian Orthodox Patriarch Aleksy II as Yeltsin was inaugurated president of the Russian federated republic. A related development was the influx of Western evangelistic and Bible distribution activities in the former Soviet Union made possible by a new climate of religious liberty.	2. Desert Storm influence on Muslim world.

3. Denominations address sexuality issues. Traditional standards of personal holiness were reconsidered and, by and large, upheld.

4. Euthanasia. Court cases, a suicide machine, a best-selling how-to-suicide book, and a state referendum put the issue high on the public agenda.

5. Religious liberty. Lower-court interpretations of a landmark Supreme Court decision eroded constitutional protections of religious practice, said church/state experts.

6. Operation Rescue in Wichita. The controversial movement once again claimed the national spotlight, fanning the already-hot abortion debate.

7. Southern Baptist moderates. After more than a decade of conservative victories in the Southern Baptist Convention, moderates formed their own fellowship.

8. Protestantism in Latin America. The changing religious landscape in this part of the world was highlighted by major visits from both Pope John Paul II and Billy Graham.

3. Scholars get free access to Dead Sea Scrolls, ending monopoly that has lasted for decades.

4. U.S. religious leaders raise questions about morality of U.S. military action in the Persian Gulf and fewer than half the Americans polled believe it met all six criteria defining a "just war."

5. Hundreds of antiabortion demonstrators, including clergy, arrested following demonstrations at clinics in Wichita, Kansas, and Fargo, North Dakota.

6. Southern Baptist fundamentalists tighten control of seminaries and agencies, but suffer major setback in Texas when moderates secure greater autonomy for Baylor University and get their candidates elected to the state convention's top posts. In other developments, moderates form Cooperative Baptist Fellowship and a new seminary, and European Baptists denounce a Southern Baptist Convention agency for cutting funds to a Swiss seminary regarded as too liberal.

7. Five Orthodox bodies suspend relations with National Council of Churches; Orthodox members of World Council of Churches threaten withdrawal. All object to alleged "liberal leanings" of some council members bodies.

8. The Episcopal Church's governing body approves compromise statement leaving church's stand on homosexual relationships ambiguous for at least another three years.

3. Recession: Effects on giving to church.

4. Revival of religion in USSR from the activity of the church underground in USSR.

5. Drug traffic—its effects.

6. Dead Sea Scrolls opened to public.

7. Reduction in armaments.

8. North and South Korea are talking.

9. Economic recession. Troubled times pinched Christian ministries and denominations, resulting in layoffs and cutbacks.

9. Pope John Paul II notes collapse of communism in Eastern Europe with encyclical that qualifies support of the market economy with caution about injustices. His letter commemorates the centenary of "Rerum Novarum," a landmark encyclical in Catholic social teaching. Later, the pope convenes a special synod of European bishops to seek a "new evangelization" of Europe.

9. Appointment of Clarence Thomas to Supreme Court.

10. Dead Sea Scrolls. After decades of frustration, scholars finally gained full access to the 2,000-year-old documents.

10. Clergy and religious bodies split on defeated proposal in Washington State that would have legalized doctor-assisted suicide. Earlier, the United Church of Christ became the first major mainline denomination to approve of active euthanasia.

10. Defeat of lottery proposal in Mississippi.

Reprinted from Christianity Today, *December 16, 1991*

Reprinted from Religious News Service, *December 27, 1991*

Declarations

THE LAUSANNE COVENANT
International Congress on World Evangelization,
Lausanne, Switzerland, July 1974

Introduction

We, members of the Church of Jesus Christ, from more than 150 nations, participants in the International Congress on World Evangelization at Lausanne, praise God for his great salvation and rejoice in the fellowship he has given us with himself and with each other. We are deeply stirred by what God is doing in our day, moved to penitence by our failures and challenged by the unfinished task of evangelization. We believe the gospel is God's good news for the whole world, and we are determined by his grace to obey Christ's commission to proclaim it to every person and to make disciples of every nation. We desire, therefore, to affirm our faith and our resolve, and to make public our covenant.

1. The Purpose of God

We affirm our belief in the one eternal God, Creator and Lord of the world, Father, Son and Holy Spirit, who governs all things according to the purpose of his will. He has been calling out from the world a people for himself, and sending his people back into the world to be his servants and his witnesses, for the extension of his kingdom, the building up of Christ's body, and the glory of his name. We confess with shame that we have often denied our calling and failed in our mission, by becoming conformed to the world or by withdrawing from it. Yet we rejoice that even when borne by earthen vessels the gospel is still a precious treasure. To the task of making that treasure known in the power of the Holy Spirit we desire to dedicate ourselves anew.

2. The Authority & Power of the Bible

We affirm the divine inspiration, truthfulness and authority of both Old and New Testament Scriptures in their entirety as the only written word of God, without error in all that it affirms, and the only infallible rule of faith and practice. We also affirm the power of God's Word to accomplish his purpose of salvation. The message of the Bible is addressed to all men and women. For God's revelation in Christ and in Scripture is unchangeable. Through it the Holy Spirit still speaks today. He illumines the minds of God's people in every culture to perceive its truth freshly through their own eyes and thus discloses to the whole Church ever more of the many-coloured wisdom of God.

3. The Uniqueness & Universality of Christ

We affirm that there is only one Saviour and only one gospel, although there is a wide diversity of evangelistic approaches. We recognise that everyone has some knowledge of God through his general revelation in nature. But we deny that this can save, for people suppress the truth by their unrighteousness. We also reject as derogatory to Christ and the gospel every kind of syncretism and dialogue which implies that Christ speaks equally through all religions and ideologies. Jesus Christ, being himself the only God-man, who gave himself as the only ransom for sinners, is the only mediator between God and people.

THE LAUSANNE COVENANT cont.

There is no other name by which we must be saved. All men and women are perishing because of sin, but God loves everyone, not wishing that any should perish but that all should repent. Yet those who reject Christ repudiate the joy of salvation and condemn themselves to eternal separation from God. To proclaim Jesus as "the Saviour of the world" is not to affirm that all people are either automatically or ultimately saved, still less to affirm that all religions offer salvation in Christ. Rather it is to proclaim God's love for a world of sinners and to invite everyone to respond to him as Saviour and Lord in the wholehearted personal commitment of repentance and faith. Jesus Christ has been exalted above every other name; we long for the day when every knee shall bow to him and every tongue shall confess him Lord.

4. The Nature of Evangelism

To evangelise is to spread the good news that Jesus Christ died for our sins and was raised from the dead according to the Scriptures, and that as the reigning Lord he now offers the forgiveness of sins and the liberating gift of the Spirit to all who repent and believe. Our Christian presence in the world is indispensable to evangelism, and so is that kind of dialogue whose purpose is to listen sensitively in order to understand. But evangelism itself is the proclamation of the historical, biblical Christ as Saviour and Lord, with a view to persuading people to come to him personally and so be reconciled to God. In issuing the gospel invitation we have no liberty to conceal the cost of discipleship. Jesus still calls all who would follow him to deny themselves, take up their cross, and identify themselves with his new community. The results of evangelism include obedience to Christ, incorporation into his Church and responsible service in the world.

5. Christian Social Responsibility

We affirm that God is both the Creator and the Judge of all. We therefore should share his concern for justice and reconciliation throughout human society and for the liberation of men and women from every kind of oppression. Because men and women are made in the image of God, every person, regardless of race, religion, colour, culture, class, sex or age, has an intrinsic dignity because of which he or she should be respected and served, not exploited. Here too we express penitence both for our neglect and for having sometimes regarded evangelism and social concern as mutually exclusive. Although reconciliation with other people is not reconciliation with God, nor is social action evangelism, nor is political liberation salvation, nevertheless we affirm that evangelism and socio-political involvement are both part of our Christian duty. For both are necessary expressions of our doctrines of God and man, our love for our neighbour and our obedience to Jesus Christ. The message of salvation implies also a message of judgment upon every form of alienation, oppression and discrimination, and we should not be afraid to denounce evil and injustice wherever they exist. When people receive Christ they are born again into his kingdom and must seek not only to exhibit but also to spread its righteousness in the midst of an unrighteous world. The salvation we claim should be transforming us in the totality of our personal and social responsibilities. Faith without works is dead.

6. The Church & Evangelism

We affirm that Christ sends his redeemed people into the world as the Father sent him, and that this calls for a similar deep and costly penetration of the world. We need to break out of our ecclesiastical ghettos and permeate non-Christian society. In the Church's mission of sacrificial service evangelism is primary. World evangelization requires the whole Church to take the whole gospel to the whole world. The Church is at the very centre of God's cosmic purpose and is his appointed means of spreading the gospel. But a church which preaches the cross must itself be marked by the cross. It becomes a stumbling block to evangelism when it betrays the gospel or lacks a living faith in God, a genuine love for people, or scrupulous honesty in all things including promotion and finance. The church is the community of God's people rather than an institution, and must not be identified with any particular culture, social or political system, or human ideology.

7. Cooperation in Evangelism
We affirm that the Church's visible unity in truth is God's purpose. Evangelism also summons us to unity, because our oneness strengthens our witness, just as our disunity undermines our gospel of reconciliation. We recognise, however, that organisational unity may take many forms and does not necessarily forward evangelism. Yet we who share the same biblical faith should be closely united in fellowship, work and witness. We confess that our testimony has sometimes been marred by sinful individualism and needless duplication. We pledge ourselves to seek a deeper unity in truth, worship, holiness and mission. We urge the development of regional and functional cooperation for the furtherance of the Church's mission, for strategic planning, for mutual encouragement, and for the sharing of resources and experience.

8. Churches in Evangelistic Partnership
We rejoice that a new missionary era has dawned. The dominant role of western missions is fast disappearing. God is raising up from the younger churches a great new resource for world evangelization, and is thus demonstrating that the responsibility to evangelise belongs to the whole body of Christ. All churches should therefore be asking God and themselves what they should be doing both to reach their own area and to send missionaries to other parts of the world. A reevaluation of our missionary responsibility and role should be continuous. Thus a growing partnership of churches will develop and the universal character of Christ's Church will be more clearly exhibited. We also thank God for agencies which labour in Bible translation, theological education, the mass media, Christian literature, evangelism, missions, church renewal and other specialist fields. They too should engage in constant self-examination to evaluate their effectiveness as part of the Church's mission.

9. The Urgency of the Evangelistic Task
More than 2,700 million people, which is more than two-thirds of all humanity, have yet to be evangelised. We are ashamed that so many have been neglected; it is a standing rebuke to us and to the whole Church. There is now, however, in many parts of the world an unprecedented receptivity to the Lord Jesus Christ. We are convinced that this is the time for churches and para-church agencies to pray earnestly for the salvation of the unreached and to launch new efforts to achieve world evangelization. A reduction of foreign missionaries and money in an evangelised country may sometimes be necessary to facilitate the national church's growth in self-reliance and to release resources for unevangelised areas. Missionaries should flow ever more freely from and to all six continents in a spirit of humble service. The goal should be, by all available means and at the earliest possible time, that every person will have the opportunity to hear, understand, and receive the good news. We cannot hope to attain this goal without sacrifice. All of us are shocked by the poverty of millions and disturbed by the injustices which cause it. Those of us who live in affluent circumstances accept our duty to develop a simple life-style in order to contribute more generously to both relief and evangelism.

10. Evangelism & Culture
The development of strategies for world evangelization calls for imaginative pioneering methods. Under God, the result will be the rise of churches deeply rooted in Christ and closely related to their culture. Culture must always be tested and judged by Scripture.

THE LAUSANNE COVENANT cont.

Because men and women are God's creatures, some of their culture is rich in beauty and goodness. Because they are fallen, all of it is tainted with sin and some of it is demonic. The gospel does not presuppose the superiority of any culture to another, but evaluates all cultures according to its own criteria of truth and righteousness, and insists on moral absolutes in every culture. Missions have all too frequently exported with the gospel an alien culture and churches have sometimes been in bondage to culture rather than to Scripture. Christ's evangelists must humbly seek to empty themselves of all but their personal authenticity in order to become the servants of others, and churches must seek to transform and enrich culture, all for the glory of God.

11. Education & Leadership

We confess that we have sometimes pursued church growth at the expense of church depth, and divorced evangelism from Christian nurture. We also acknowledge that some of our missions have been too slow to equip and encourage national leaders to assume their rightful responsibilities. Yet we are committed to indigenous principles, and long that every church will have national leaders who manifest a Christian style of leadership in terms not of domination but of service. We recognise that there is a great need to improve theological education, especially for church leaders. In every nation and culture there should be an effective training programme for pastors and laity in doctrine, discipleship, evangelism, nurture and service. Such training programmes should not rely on any stereotyped method-ology but should be developed by creative local initiatives according to biblical standards.

12. Spiritual Conflict

We believe that we are engaged in constant spiritual warfare with the principalities and powers of evil, who are seeking to overthrow the Church and frustrate its task of world evangelization. We know our need to equip ourselves with God's armour and to fight this battle with the spiritual weapons of truth and prayer. For we detect the activity of our enemy, not only in false ideologies outside the Church, but also inside it in false gospels which twist Scripture and put people in the place of God. We need both watchfulness and discernment to safeguard the biblical gospel. We acknowledge that we ourselves are not immune to worldliness of thought and action, that is, to a surrender to secularism. For example, although careful studies of church growth, both numerical and spiritual, are right and valuable, we have sometimes neglected them. At other times, desirous to ensure a response to the gospel, we have compromised our message, manipulated our hearers through pressure techniques, and become unduly preoccupied with statistics or even dishonest in our use of them. All this is worldly. The Church must be in the world; the world must not be in the Church.

13. Freedom & Persecution

It is the God-appointed duty of every government to secure conditions of peace, justice and liberty in which the Church may obey God, serve the Lord Christ, and preach the gospel without interference. We therefore pray for the leaders of the nations and call upon them to guarantee freedom of thought and conscience, and freedom to practise and propagate religion in accordance with the will of God and as set forth in The Universal Declaration of Human Rights. We also express our deep concern for all who have been unjustly imprisoned, and especially for those who are suffering for their testimony to the Lord Jesus. We promise to pray and work for their freedom. At the same time we refuse to be intimidated by their fate. God helping us, we too will seek to stand against injustice and to remain faithful to the gospel, whatever the cost. We do not forget the warnings of Jesus that persecution is inevitable.

14. The Power of the Holy Spirit

We believe in the power of the Holy Spirit. The Father sent his Spirit to bear witness to his Son; without his witness ours is futile. Conviction of sin, faith in Christ, new birth and Christian growth are all his work. Further, the Holy Spirit is a missionary spirit; thus evangelism should arise spontaneously from a Spirit-filled church. A church that is not a missionary church is contradicting itself and quenching the Spirit. Worldwide evangelization will become a realistic possibility only when the Spirit renews the Church in truth and wisdom, faith, holiness, love and power. We therefore call upon all Christians to pray for such a visitation of the sovereign Spirit of God that all his fruit may appear in all his people and that all his gifts may enrich the body of Christ. Only then will the whole Church become a fit instrument in his hands, that the whole earth may hear his voice.

15. The Return of Christ

We believe that Jesus Christ will return personally and visibly, in power and glory, to consummate his salvation and his judgment. This promise of his coming is a further spur to our evangelism, for we remember his words that the gospel must first be preached to all nations. We believe that the interim period between Christ's ascension and return is to be filled with the mission of the people of God, who have no liberty to stop before the end. We also remember his warning that false Christs and false prophets will arise as precursors of the final Antichrist. We therefore reject as a proud, self-confident dream the notion that people can ever build a utopia on earth. Our Christian confidence is that God will perfect his kingdom, and we look forward with eager anticipation to that day, and to the new heaven and earth in which righteousness will dwell and God will reign forever. Meanwhile, we rededicate ourselves to the service of Christ and of people in joyful submission to his authority over the whole of our lives.

Conclusion

Therefore, in the light of this our faith and our resolve, we enter into a solemn covenant with God and with each other, to pray, to plan and to work together for the evangelization of the whole world. We call upon others to join us. May God help us by his grace and for his glory to be faithful to this our covenant! Amen, Alleluia!

FOCUS QUOTE **If both economic and human compassion aren't seen in the lives of those of us who follow Jesus, and enormous number of the poor will never have convincing enough evidence to believe the good news of the Kingdom of God. The tragedy of many of our churches is that they contribute to this credibility gap.** —Tom Houston, International Director, Lausanne Committee for World Evangelization

---

LAUSANNE ADDRESS

Lausanne Committee for
World Evangelization
184A Cumnor Hill
Oxford OX2 9PJ
England

LAUSANNE SPONSORSHIPS

Since 1974 there have been numerous gatherings and publications sponsored by the Lausanne Committee for World Evangelization, or held in the unity of the Lausanne Covenant. What follows is a listing of the major congresses, consultations and publications that have been sponsored, singly or cooperatively, by the Lausanne Committee. More information on these events and resources can be obtained through the Lausanne Committee office.

International Congress on World Evangelization
Lausanne, Switzerland
July 1974
● Let the Earth Hear His Voice
  World Wide Publications; 1975
● The Lausanne Covenant: An Exposition and Commentary
  Lausanne Occasional Paper No. 3

Consultation on the Homogeneous Unit Principle
Pasadena, California, U.S.A.
June 1977
● The Pasadena Consultation,
  Lausanne Occasional Paper No. 1

Consultation on Gospel and Culture
Willowbank, Somerset Bridge, Bermuda
January 1978
● The Willowbank Report
  Lausanne Occasional Paper No. 2

Conference on Muslim Evangelization
Glen Eyrie, Colorado Springs, Colorado, U.S.A.
October 1978
● The Glen Eyrie Report
  Lausanne Occasional Paper No. 4
● The Gospel and Islam: A 1978 Compendium
  MARC; 1979

International Consultation on Simple Lifestyle
Hoddesdon, England
March 1980
● An Evangelical Commitment to Simple Lifestyle
  Lausanne Occasional Paper No. 20

Lausanne Consultation on World Evangelization
Pattaya, Thailand
July 1980
● Christian Witness to Refugees
  Lausanne Occasional Paper No. 5

● Christian Witness to the Chinese People
  Lausanne Occasional Paper No. 6
● Christian Witness to the Jewish People
  Lausanne Occasional Paper No. 7
● Christian Witness to Secularized People
  Lausanne Occasional Paper No. 8
● Christian Witness to Large Cities
  Lausanne Occasional Paper No. 9,
● Christian Witness to Nominal Christians Among Roman Catholics
  Lausanne Occasional Paper No. 10
● Christian Witness to New Religious Movements
  Lausanne Occasional Paper No. 11
● Christian Witness to Marxists
  Lausanne Occasional Paper No. 12
● Christian Witness to Muslims
  Lausanne Occasional Paper No. 13
● Christian Witness to Hindus
  Lausanne Occasional Paper No. 14
● Christian Witness to Buddhists
  Lausanne Occasional Paper No. 15
● Christian Witness to Traditional Religionists of Asia and Oceania
  Lausanne Occasional Paper No. 16
● Christian Witness to Traditional Religionists of Latin America and Caribbean
  Lausanne Occasional Paper No. 17
● Christian Witness to People of African Traditional Religions
  Lausanne Occasional Paper No. 18
● Christian Witness to Nominal Christians among the Orthodox
  Lausanne Occasional Paper No. 19
● Christian Witness to the Urban Poor
  Lausanne Occasional Paper No. 22
● Christian Witness to Nominal Christians among Protestants
  Lausanne Occasional Paper No. 23
● Cooperating in World Evangelization: A Handbook on Church/Para-Church Relationships
  Lausanne Occasional Paper No. 24

Consultation on the Relationship Between Evangelism and Social Responsibility
Grand Rapids, Michigan, U.S.A.
June 1982
- Evangelism and Social Responsibility, Lausanne Occasional Paper No. 21
- The Church in Response to Human Need,
Missions Advanced Research and Communication Center; 1983

International Prayer Assembly for World Evangelization
Seoul, Republic of Korea
June 1984
- Unleashing the Power of Prayer, Moody Press; 1989

Consultation on the Work of the Holy Spirit and Evangelization
Oslo, Norway
May 1985
- God the Evangelist
Eerdmans, Grand Rapids & Paternoster, Exeter; 1987

Young Leaders Conference—Singapore '87
Republic of Singapore
June 1987

Consultation on Conversion
Hong Kong
January 1988

- Turning to God
Eerdmans, Grand Rapids & Paternoster, Exeter; 1989

Younger Leaders Conference—Leadership '88
Washington, D.C., U.S.A.
June 1988
- Networking Directory
LCWE; 1988
- Joining Together in the Gospel: Four Studies from Philippians
LCWE; 1988

Lausanne II in Manila,
Second International Congress on World Evangelization
Manila, Philippines
July 1989
- The Challenge Before Us
World Wide Publications; 1989
- The Whole Gospel for the Whole World
Regal Books; 1989
- The Manila Manifesto: An Elaboration of the Lausanne Covenant Fifteen Years Later
LCWE; 1989

Continuing Publications:
- *World Evangelization* magazine
- World Evangelization Information Service

THE MANILA MANIFESTO

Lausanne II in Manila
Second International Congress on World Evangelization
Manila, Philippines, July 1989

Introduction
In July 1974 the International Congress on World Evangelization was held in Lausanne, Switzerland, and issued the Lausanne Covenant. Now in July 1989 over 3,000 of us from about 170 countries have met in Manila for the same purpose, and have issued the Manila Manifesto. We are grateful for the welcome we have received from our Filipino brothers and sisters.

During the 15 years which have elapsed between the two congresses some smaller consultations have been held on topics like Gospel and Culture, Evangelism and Social Responsibility, Simple Lifestyle, the Holy Spirit, and Conversion. These meetings and their reports have helped to develop the thinking of the Lausanne movement.

A "manifesto" is defined as a public declaration of convictions, intentions and motives. The Manila Manifesto takes up the two congress themes, "Proclaim Christ until he comes" and "Calling the Whole Church to take the Whole Gospel to the Whole World." Its first part

THE MANILA MANIFESTO cont.

is a series of 21 succinct affirmations. Its second part elaborates these in 12 sections, which are commended to churches, alongside the Lausanne Covenant, for study and action.

TWENTY-ONE AFFIRMATIONS

1. We affirm our continuing commitment to the Lausanne Covenant as the basis of our cooperation in the Lausanne movement.

2. We affirm that in the Scriptures of the Old and New Testaments God has given us an authoritative disclosure of his character and will, his redemptive acts and their meaning, and his mandate for mission.

3. We affirm that the biblical gospel is God's enduring message to our world, and we determine to defend, proclaim and embody it.

4. We affirm that human beings, though created in the image of God, are sinful and guilty, and lost without Christ, and that this truth is a necessary preliminary to the gospel.

5. We affirm that the Jesus of history and the Christ of glory are the same person, and that this Jesus Christ is absolutely unique, for he alone is God incarnate, our sin-bearer, the conqueror of death and the coming judge.

6. We affirm that on the cross Jesus Christ took our place, bore our sins and died for our death; and that for this reason alone God freely forgives those who are brought to repentance and faith.

7. We affirm that other religions and ideologies are not alternative paths to God, and that human spirituality, if unredeemed by Christ, leads not to God but to judgment, for Christ is the only way.

8. We affirm that we must demonstrate God's love visibly by caring for those who are deprived of justice, dignity, food and shelter.

9. We affirm that the proclamation of God's kingdom of justice and peace demands the denunciation of all injustice and oppression, both personal and structural; we will not shrink from this prophetic witness.

10. We affirm that the Holy Spirit's witness to Christ is indispensable to evangelism, and that without his supernatural work neither new birth nor new life is possible.

---

66 99 **We determine to go on seeking that unity in truth for which Christ prayed.**
FOCUS — Manila Manifesto
QUOTE

---

11. We affirm that spiritual warfare demands spiritual weapons, and that we must both preach the word in the power of the Spirit, and pray constantly that we may enter into Christ's victory over the principalities and powers of evil.

12. We affirm that God has committed to the whole church and every member of it the task of making Christ known throughout the world; we long to see all lay and ordained persons mobilized and trained for this task.

13. We affirm that we who claim to be members of the Body of Christ must transcend within our fellowship the barriers of race, gender and class.

14. We affirm that the gifts of the Spirit are distributed to all God's people, women and men, and that their partnership in evangelization must be welcomed for the common good.

15. We affirm that we who proclaim the gospel must exemplify it in a life of holiness and love; otherwise our testimony loses its credibility.

16. We affirm that every Christian congregation must turn itself outward to its local

community in evangelistic witness and compassionate service.

17. We affirm the urgent need for churches, mission agencies and other Christian organizations to cooperate in evangelism and social action, repudiating competition and avoiding duplication.

18. We affirm our duty to study the society in which we live, in order to understand its structures, values and needs, and so develop an appropriate strategy of mission.

19. We affirm that world evangelization is urgent and that the reaching of unreached peoples is possible. So we resolve during the last decade of the twentieth century to give ourselves to these tasks with fresh determination.

20. We affirm our solidarity with those who suffer for the gospel, and will seek to prepare ourselves for the same possibility. We will also work for religious and political freedom everywhere.

21. We affirm that God is calling the whole church to take the whole gospel to the whole world. So we determine to proclaim it faithfully, urgently and sacrificially, until he comes.

A. The Whole Gospel

The gospel is the good news of God's salvation from the powers of evil, the establishment of his eternal kingdom and his final victory over everything which defines his purpose. In his love God purposed to do this before the world began and effected his liberating plan over sin, death and judgment through the death of our Lord Jesus Christ. It is Christ who makes us free, and unites us in his redeemed fellowship.

1. OUR HUMAN PREDICAMENT

We are committed to preaching the whole gospel, that is, the biblical gospel in its fulness. In order to do so, we have to understand why human beings need it.

Men and women have an intrinsic dignity and worth, because they were created in God's likeness to know, love and serve him. But now through sin every part of their humanness has been distorted. Human beings have become self-centered, self-serving rebels, who do not love God or their neighbour as they should. In consequence, they are alienated both from their Creator and from the rest of his creation, which is the basic cause of the pain, disorientation and loneliness which so many people suffer today. Sin also frequently erupts in anti-social behavior, in violent exploitation of others, and in a depletion of the earth's resources of which God has made men and women his stewards. Humanity is guilty, without excuse, and on the broad road which leads to destruction.

Although God's image in human beings has been corrupted, they are still capable of loving relationships, noble deeds and beautiful art. Yet even the finest human achievement is fatally flawed and cannot possibly fit anybody to enter God's presence. Men and women are also spiritual beings, but spiritual practices and self-help techniques can at the most alleviate felt needs; they cannot address the solemn realities of sin, guilt and judgment. Neither human religion, nor human righteousness, nor socio-political programs can save people. Self-salvation of every kind is impossible. Left to themselves, human beings are lost forever.

So we repudiate false gospels which deny human sin, divine judgment, the deity and incarnation of Jesus Christ, and the necessity of the cross and the resurrection. We also reject half-gospels, which minimize sin and confuse God's grace with human self-effort. We confess that we ourselves have sometimes trivilized the gospel. But we determine in our evangelism to remember God's radical diagnosis and his equally radical remedy.

2. GOOD NEWS FOR TODAY

We rejoice that the living God did not abandon us to our lostness and despair. In his love he came after us in Jesus Christ to rescue and re-make us. So the good news focuses on the historic person of Jesus, who came proclaiming the kingdom of God and living a life of

THE MANILA MANIFESTO cont.

humble service, who died for us, becoming sin and a curse in our place, and whom God vindicated by raising him from the dead. To those who repent and believe in Christ, God grants a share in the new creation. He gives us new life, which includes the forgiveness of our sins and the indwelling, transforming power of his Spirit. He welcomes us into his new community, which consists of people of all races, nations and cultures. And he promises that one day we will enter his new world, in which evil will be abolished, nature will be redeemed, and God will reign for ever.

This good news must be boldly proclaimed, wherever possible, in church and public hall, on radio and television, and in the open air, because it is God's power for salvation and we are under obligation to make it known. In our preaching we must faithfully declare the truth which God has revealed in the Bible and struggle to relate it to our own context.

We also affirm that apologetics, namely "the defense and confirmation of the gospel," is integral to the biblical understanding of mission and essential for effective witness in the modern world. Paul "reasoned" with people out of the Scriptures, with a view to "persuading" them of the truth of the gospel. So must we. In fact, all Christians should be ready to give a reason for the hope that is in them.

We have again been confronted with Luke's emphasis that the gospel is good news for the poor and have asked ourselves what this means to the majority of the world's population who are destitute, suffering or oppressed. We have been reminded that the law, the prophets and the wisdom books, and the teaching and ministry of Jesus, all stress God's concern for the materially poor and our consequent duty to defend and care for them. Scripture also refers to the spiritually poor who look to God alone for mercy. The gospel comes as good news to both. The spiritually poor, who, whatever their economic circumstances, humble themselves before God, receive by faith the free gift of salvation. There is no other way for anybody to enter the Kingdom of God. The materially poor and powerless find in addition a new dignity as God's children, and the love of brothers and sisters who will struggle with them for their liberation from everything which demeans or oppresses them.

We repent of any neglect of God's truth in Scripture and determine both to proclaim and to defend it. We also repent where we have been indifferent to the plight of the poor, and where we have shown preference for the rich, and we determine to follow Jesus in preaching good news to all people by both word and deed.

3. THE UNIQUENESS OF JESUS CHRIST

We are called to proclaim Christ in an increasingly pluralistic world. There is a resurgence of old faiths and a rise of new ones. In the first century too there were "many gods and many lords." Yet the apostles boldly affirmed the uniqueness, indispensability and centrality of Christ. We must do the same.

Because men and women are made in God's image and see in the creation traces of its Creator, the religions which have arisen do sometimes contain elements of truth and beauty. They are not, however, alternative gospels. Because human beings are sinful, and because "the whole world is under the control of the evil one," even religious people are in need of Christ's redemption. We, therefore, have no warrant for saying that salvation can be found outside Christ or apart from an explicit acceptance of his work through faith.

It is sometimes held that in virtue of God's covenant with Abraham, Jewish people do not need to acknowledge Jesus as their Messiah. We affirm that they need him as much as anyone else, that it would be a form of anti-Semitism, as well as being disloyal to Christ, to depart from the New Testament pattern of taking the gospel to "the Jew first . . . ." We therefore reject the thesis that Jews have their own covenant which renders faith in Jesus unnecessary.

What unites us is our common convictions about Jesus Christ. We confess him as the eternal Son of God who became fully human while remaining fully divine, who was our substitute on the cross, bearing our sins and dying our death, exchanging his righteousness for our unrighteousness, who rose victorious in a transformed body, and who will return in glory to judge the world. He alone is the incarnate Son, the Saviour, the Lord and the Judge, and he alone, with the Father and the Spirit, is worthy of the worship, faith and obedience of all people. There is only one gospel because there is only one Christ, who because of his death and resurrection is himself the only way of salvation. We therefore reject both the relativism which regards all religions and spiritualities as equally valid approaches to God, and the syncretism which tries to mix faith in Christ with other faiths.

Moreover, since God has exalted Jesus to the highest place, in order that everybody should acknowledge him, this also is our desire. Compelled by Christ's love, we must obey Christ's Great Commission and love his lost sheep, but we are especially motivated by "jealousy" for his holy name, and we long to see him receive the honour and glory which are due to him.

In the past we have sometimes been guilty of adopting towards adherents of other faiths attitudes of ignorance, arrogance, disrespect and even hostility. We repent of this. We nevertheless are determined to bear a positive and uncompromising witness to the uniqueness of our Lord, in his life, death and resurrection, in all aspects of our evangelistic work including inter-faith dialogue.

❝ ❞

FOCUS QUOTE

We are ashamed of the suspicions and rivalries, the dogmatism over non-essentials, the power-struggles and empire-building which spoil our evangelistic witness. —Manila Manifesto

---

4. THE GOSPEL AND SOCIAL RESPONSIBILITY

The authentic gospel must become visible in the transformed lives of men and women. As we proclaim the love of God we must be involved in loving service, and as we preach the Kingdom of God we must be committed to its demands of justice and peace.

Evangelism is primary because our chief concern is with the gospel, that all people may have the opportunity to accept Jesus Christ as Lord and Savior. Yet Jesus not only proclaimed the Kingdom of God, he also demonstrated its arrival by works of mercy and power. We are called today to a similar integration of words and deeds. In a spirit of humility we are to preach and teach, minister to the sick, feed the hungry, care for prisoners, help the disadvantaged and handicapped, and deliver the oppressed. While we acknowledge the diversity of spiritual gifts, callings and contexts, we also affirm that good news and good works are inseparable.

The proclamation of God's kingdom necessarily demands the prophetic denunciation of all that is incompatible with it. Among the evils we deplore are destructive violence, including institutionalized violence, political corruption, all forms of exploitation of people and of the earth, the undermining of the family, abortion on demand, the drug traffic, and the abuse of human rights. In our concern for the poor, we are distressed by the burden of debt in the Two-Thirds World. We are also outraged by the inhuman conditions in which millions live, who bear God's image as we do.

Our continuing commitment to social action is not a confusion of the Kingdom of God with a Christianized society. It is, rather, a recognition that the biblical gospel has inescapable social implications. True mission should always be incarnational. It necessitates

THE MANILA MANIFESTO cont.

entering humbly into other people's worlds, identifying with their social reality, their sorrow and suffering, and their struggles for justice against oppressive powers. This cannot be done without personal sacrifices.

We repent that the narrowness of our concerns and vision has often kept us from proclaiming the lordship of Jesus Christ over all of life, private and public, local and global. We determine to obey his command "to seek first the Kingdom of God and his righteousness."

B. The Whole Church

The whole gospel has to be proclaimed by the whole church. All the people of God are called to share in the evangelistic task. Yet without the Holy Spirit of God all their endeavors will be fruitless.

5. GOD THE EVANGELIST

The Scriptures declare that God himself is the chief evangelist. For the Spirit of God is the Spirit of truth, love, holiness and power, and evangelism is impossible without him. It is he who anoints the messenger, confirms the word, prepares the hearer, convicts the sinful, enlightens the blind, gives life to the dead, enables us to repent and believe, unites us to the Body of Christ, assures us that we are God's children, leads us into Christlike character and service, and sends us out in our turn to be Christ's witnesses. In all this the Holy Spirit's main preoccupation is to glorify Jesus Christ by showing him to us and forming him in us.

All evangelism involves spiritual warfare with the principalities and powers of evil, in which only spiritual weapons can prevail, especially the Word and the Spirit, with prayer. We therefore call on all Christian people to be diligent in their prayers both for the renewal of the church and for the evangelization of the world.

Every true conversion involves a power encounter, in which the superior authority of Jesus Christ is demonstrated. There is no greater miracle than this, in which the believer is set free from the bondage of Satan and sin, fear and futility, darkness and death.

Although the miracles of Jesus were special, being signs of his Messiahship and anticipations of his perfect kingdom when all nature will be subject to him, we have no liberty to place limits on the power of the living Creator today. We reject both the skepticism which denies miracles and the presumption which demands them, both the timidity which shrinks from the fulness of the Spirit and the triumphalism which shrinks from the weakness in which Christ's power is made perfect.

We repent of all self-confident attempts either to evangelize in our own strength or to dictate to the Holy Spirit. We determine in the future not to "grieve" or "quench" the Spirit, but rather to seek to spread the good news "with power, with the Holy Spirit and with deep conviction."

6. THE HUMAN WITNESS

God the evangelist gives his people the privilege of being his "fellow-workers." For, although we cannot witness without him, he normally chooses to witness through us. He calls only some to be evangelists, missionaries or pastors, but he calls his whole church and every member of it to be his witnesses.

The privileged task of pastors and teachers is to lead God's people (laos) into maturity and to equip them for ministry. Pastors are not to monopolize ministries, but rather to multiply them, by encouraging others to use their gifts and by training disciples to make disciples. The domination of the laity by the clergy has been a great evil in the history of the church. It robs both laity and clergy of their God-intended roles, causes clergy breakdowns, weakens the church and hinders the spread of the gospel. More than that, it is fundamentally unbiblical. We therefore, who have for centuries insisted on "the priesthood of all believers" now also insist on the ministry of all believers.

We gratefully recognize that children and young people enrich the church's worship and outreach by their enthusiasm and faith. We need to train them in discipleship and evangelism, so that they may reach their own generation for Christ.

God created men and women as equal bearers of his image, accepts them equally in Christ and poured out his Spirit on all flesh, sons and daughters alike. In addition, because the Holy Spirit distributes his gifts to women as well as to men, they must be given opportunities to exercise their gifts. We celebrate their distinguished record in the history of missions and are convinced that God calls women to similar roles today. Even though we are not fully agreed what forms their leadership should take, we do agree about the partnership in world evangelization which God intends men and women to enjoy. Suitable training must therefore be made available to both.

Lay witness takes place, by women and men, not only through the local church (see Section 8), but through friendships, in the home and at work. Even those who are homeless or unemployed share in the calling to be witnesses.

Our first responsibility is to witness to those who are already our friends, relatives, neighbors, and colleagues. Home evangelism is also natural, both for married and for single people. Not only should a Christian home commend God's standards of marriage, sex and family, and provide a haven of love and peace to people who are hurting, but neighbours who would not enter a church usually feel comfortable in a home, even when the gospel is discussed.

Another context for lay witness is the workplace, for it is here that most Christians spend half their waking hours, and work is a divine calling. Christians can commend Christ by word of mouth, by their consistent industry, honesty and thoughtfulness, by their concern for justice in the workplace, and especially if others can see from the quality of their daily work that it is done to the glory of God.

We repent of our share in discouraging the ministry of the laity, especially of women and young people. We determine in the future to encourage all Christ's followers to take their place, rightfully and naturally, as his witnesses. For true evangelism comes from the overflow of a heart in love with Christ. That is why it belongs to all his people without exception.

7. THE INTEGRITY OF THE WITNESSES

Nothing commends the gospel more eloquently than a transformed life, and nothing brings it into disrepute so much as personal inconsistency. We are charged to behave in a manner that is worthy of the gospel of Christ, and even to "adorn" it, enhancing its beauty by holy lives. For the watching world rightly seeks evidence to substantiate the claims which Christ's disciples make for him. A strong evidence is our integrity.

Our proclamation that Christ died to bring us to God appeals to people who are spiritually thirsty, but they will not believe us if we give no evidence of knowing the living God ourselves, or if our public worship lacks reality and relevance.

Our message that Christ reconciles alienated people to each other rings true only if we are seen to love and forgive one another, to serve others in humility, and to reach out beyond our own community in compassionate, costly ministry to the needy.

Our challenge to others to deny themselves, take up their cross and follow Christ will be plausive only if we ourselves have evidently died to selfish ambition, dishonesty and covetousness, and are living a life of simplicity, contentment and generosity.

We deplore the failures in Christian consistency which we see in both Christians and churches: material greed, professional pride and rivalry, competition in Christian service, jealousy of younger leaders, missionary paternalism, the lack of mutual accountability, the loss of Christian standards of sexuality, and racial, social and sexual discrimination. All this

THE MANILA MANIFESTO cont.

is worldliness, allowing the prevailing culture to subvert the church instead of the church challenging and changing the culture. We are deeply ashamed of the times when, both as individuals and in our Christian communities, we have affirmed Christ in word and denied him in deed. Our inconsistency deprives our witness of credibility. We acknowledge our continuing struggles and failures. But we also determine by God's grace to develop integrity in ourselves and in the church.

8. THE LOCAL CHURCH

Every Christian congregation is a local expression of the Body of Christ and has the same responsibilities. It is both "a holy priesthood" to offer God the spiritual sacrifices of worship and "a holy nation" to spread abroad his excellences in witness. The church is thus both a worshipping and a witnessing community, gathered and scattered, called and sent. Worship and witness are inseparable.

We believe that the local church bears a primary responsibility for the spread of the gospel. Scripture suggests this in the progession that "our gospel came to you" and then "rang out from you." In this way, the gospel created the church which spreads the gospel which creates more churches in a continuous chain-reaction. Moreover, what Scripture teaches, strategy confirms. Each local church must evangelize the district in which it is situated, and has the resources to do so.

We recommend every congregation to carry out regular studies not only of its own membership and program but of its local community in all its particularity, in order to develop appropriate strategies for mission. Its members might decide to organize a visitation of their whole area, to penetrate for Christ a particular place where people assemble, to arrange a series of evangelistic meetings, lectures or concerts, to work with the poor to transform a local slum, or to plant a new church in a neighboring district or village. At the same time, they must not forget the church's global task. A church which sends out missionaries must not neglect its own locality, and a church which evangelizes its neighborhood must not ignore the rest of the world.

In all this each congregation and denomination should, where possible, work with others, seeking to turn any spirit of competition into one of cooperation. Churches should also work with para-church organizations, especially in evangelism, discipling and community service, for such agencies are part of the Body of Christ, and have valuable, specialist expertise from which the church can greatly benefit.

The church is intended by God to be a sign of his kingdom, that is, an indication of what human community looks like when it comes under his rule of righteousness and peace. As with individuals, so with churches, the gospel has to be embodied if it is to be communicated effectively. It is through our love for one another that the invisible God reveals himself today, especially when our fellowship is expressed in small groups, and when it transcends the barriers of race, rank, sex and age which divide other communities.

We deeply regret that many of our congregations are inward-looking, organized for maintenance rather than mission, or preoccupied with church-based activities at the expense of witness. We determine to turn our churches inside out, so that they may engage in continuous outreach, until the Lord adds to them daily those who are being saved.

9. COOPERATION IN EVANGELISM

Evangelism and unity are closely related in the New Testament. Jesus prayed that his people's oneness might reflect his own oneness with the Father, in order that the world might believe in him, and Paul exhorted the Philippians to "contend as one person for the faith of the gospel." In contrast to this biblical vision, we are ashamed of the suspicions and rivalries, the dogmatism over non-essentials, the power-struggles and empire-building which spoil our evangelistic witness. We affirm that co-operation in evangelism is indispensable, first because it is the will of God, but also because the gospel of reconciliation is discredited by our disunity, and because, if the task of world evangelization is ever to be accomplished, we must engage in it together.

"Cooperation" means finding unity in diversity. It involves people of different temperaments, gifts, callings and cultures, national churches and mission agencies, all ages and both sexes working together.

We are determined to put behind us once and for all, as a hangover from the colonial past, the simplistic distinction between First World sending and Two-Thirds World receiving countries. For the great new fact of our era is the internationalization of missions. Not only are a large majority of all evangelical Christians now non-western, but the number of Two-Thirds World missionaries will soon exceed those from the West. We believe that mission teams, which are diverse in composition but united in heart and mind, constitute a dramatic witness to the grace of God.

FOCUS FACT

In AD 1900 only 9 percent of the world's population lived in cities; in AD 2000 it is thought that more than 50 percent will do so. This worldwide move into the cities has been called "the greatest migration in human history." —Manila Manifesto

Our reference to "the whole church" is not a presumptuous claim that the universal church and the evangelical community are synonymous. For we recognize that there are many churches which are not part of the evangelical movement. Evangelical attitudes to the Roman Catholic and Orthodox Churches differ widely. Some evangelicals are praying, talking, studying Scripture and working with these churches. Others are strongly opposed to any form of dialogue or cooperation with them. All evangelicals are aware that serious theological differences between us remain. Where appropriate, and so long as biblical truth is not compromised, cooperation may be possible in such areas as Bible translation, the study of contemporary theological and ethical issues, social work and political action. We wish to make it clear, however, that common evangelism demands a common commitment to the biblical gospel.

Some of us are members of churches which belong to the World Council of Churches and believe that a positive yet critical participation in its work is our Christian duty. Others among us have no link with the World Council. All of us urge the World Council of Churches to adopt a consistent biblical understanding of evangelism.

We confess our own share of responsibility for the brokenness of the Body of Christ, which is a major stumbling-block to world evangelization. We determine to go on seeking that unity in truth for which Christ prayed. We are persuaded that the right way forward towards closer cooperation is frank and patient dialogue on the basis of the Bible, with all who share our concerns. To this we gladly commit ourselves.

C. The Whole World

The whole gospel has been entrusted to the whole church, in order that it may be made known to the whole world. It is necessary, therefore, for us to understand the world into which we are sent.

10. THE MODERN WORLD

Evangelism takes place in a context, not in a vacuum. The balance between gospel and context must be carefully maintained. We must understand the context in order to address

THE MANILA MANIFESTO cont.

it, but the context must not be allowed to distort the gospel.

In this connection we have become concerned about the impact of "modernity," which is an emerging world culture produced by industrialization with its technology and urbanization with its economic order. These factors combine to create an environment, which significantly shapes the way in which we see our world. In addition, secularism has devastated faith by making God and the supernatural meaningless; urbanization has dehumanized life for many; and the mass media have contributed to the devaluation of truth and authority, by replacing word with image. In combination, these consequences of modernity pervert the message which many preach and undermine their motivation for mission.

In AD 1900 only 9 percent of the world's population lived in cities; in AD 2000 it is thought that more than 50 percent will do so. This worldwide move into the cities has been called "the greatest migration in human history"; it constitutes a major challenge to Christian mission. On the one hand, city populations are extremely cosmopolitan, so that the nations come to our doorstep in the city. Can we develop global churches in which the gospel abolishes the barriers of ethnicity? On the other hand, many city dwellers are migrant poor who are also receptive to the gospel. Can the people of God be persuaded to re-locate into such urban poor communities, in order to serve the people and share in the transformation of the city?

Modernization brings blessings as well as dangers. By creating links of communication and commerce around the globe, it makes unprecedented openings for the gospel, crossing old frontiers and penetrating closed societies, whether traditional or totalitarian. The Christian media have a powerful influence both in sowing the seed of the gospel and in preparing the soil. The major missionary broadcasters are committed to a gospel witness by radio in every major language by the year AD 2000.

We confess that we have not struggled as we should to understand modernization. We have used its methods and techniques uncritically and so exposed ourselves to worldliness. But we determine in the future to take these challenges and opportunities seriously, to resist the secular pressures of modernity, to relate the lordship of Christ to the whole of modern culture, and thus to engage in mission in the modern world without worldliness in modern mission.

The great new fact of our era is the internationalization of missions. Not only are a large majority of all evangelical Christians now non-western, but the number of Two-Thirds World missionaries will soon exceed those from FOCUS **the West.** —Manila Manifesto
FACT

---

11. THE CHALLENGE OF AD 2000 AND BEYOND

The world population today is approaching 6 billion. One third of them nominally confess Christ. Of the remaining four billion half have heard of him and the other half have not. In the light of these figures, we evaluate our evangelistic task by considering four categories of people.

First, there is the potential missionary work force, the committed. In this century this category of Christian believers has grown from about 40 million in 1900 to about 500 million today, and at this moment is growing over twice as fast as any other major religions group.

Secondly, there are the uncommitted. They make a Christian profession (they have been baptized, attend church occasionally and even call themselves Christians), but the notion of a personal commitment to Christ is foreign to them. They are found in all churches throughout the world. They urgently need to be re-evangelized.

Thirdly, there are the unevangelized. These are people who have a minimal knowledge of the gospel, but have had no valid opportunity to respond to it. They are probably within reach of Christian people if only these will go to the next street, road, village or town to find them.

Fourthly, there are the unreached. These are the two billion who may never have heard of Jesus as Savior, and are not within reach of Christians of their own people. There are, in fact, some 2,000 peoples or nationalities in which there is not yet a vital, indigenous church movement. We find it helpful to think of them as belonging to smaller "people groups" which perceive themselves as having an affinity with each other (e.g. a common culture, language, home or occupation). The most effective messengers to reach them will be those believers who already belong to their culture and know their language. Otherwise, cross-cultural messengers of the gospel will need to go, leaving behind their own culture and sacrificially identifying with the people they long to reach for Christ.

There are now about 12,000 such unreached people groups within the 2,000 larger peoples, so that the task is not impossible. Yet at present only 7 percent of all missionaries are engaged in this kind of outreach, while the remaining 93 percent are working in the already evangelized half of the world. If this imbalance is to be redressed, a strategic redeployment of personnel will be necessary.

A distressing factor that affects each of the above categories is that of inaccessibility. Many countries do not grant visas to self-styled missionaries, who have no other qualification or contribution to offer. Such areas are not absolutely inaccessible, however. For our prayers can pass through every curtain, door and barrier. And Christian radio and television, audio and video cassettes, films and literature can also reach the otherwise unreachable. So can so-called "tent-makers" who like Paul earn their own living. They travel in the course of their profession (e.g. business people, university lecturers, technical specialists and language teachers), and use every opportunity to speak of Jesus Christ. They do not enter a country under false pretenses, for their work genuinely takes them there; it is simply that witness is an essential component of their Christian lifestyle, wherever they may happen to be.

We are deeply ashamed that nearly two millennia have passed since the death and resurrection of Jesus, and still two-thirds of the world's population have not yet acknowledged him. On the other hand, we are amazed at the mounting evidence of God's power even in the most unlikely places of the globe.

Now the year 2000 has become for many a challenging milestone. Can we commit ourselves to evangelize the world during the last decade of this millennium? There is nothing magical about the date, yet should we not do our best to reach this goal? Christ commands us to take the gospel to all peoples. The task is urgent. We are determined to obey him with joy and hope.

12. DIFFICULT SITUATIONS

Jesus plainly told his followers to expect opposition. "If they persecuted me," he said, "they will persecute you also." He even told them to rejoice over persecution, and reminded them that the condition of fruitfulness was death.

These predictions, that Christian suffering is inevitable and productive, have come true in every age, including our own. There have been many thousands of martyrs. Today the situation is much the same. We earnestly hope that *glasnost* and *perestroika* will lead to complete religious freedom in the Soviet Union and other Eastern block nations, and that Islamic and Hindu countries will become more open to the gospel. We deplore the recent brutal suppression of China's democratic movement, and we pray that it will not bring further suffering to the Christians. On the whole, however, it seems that ancient religions are becoming less tolerant, expatriates less welcome, and the world less friendly to the gospel.

THE MANILA MANIFESTO cont.

In this situation we wish to make three statements to governments which are reconsidering their attitude to Christian believers.

First, Christians are loyal citizens, who seek the welfare of their nation. They pray for its leaders and pay their taxes. Of course, those who have confessed Jesus as Lord cannot also call other authorities Lord, and if commanded to do so, or to do anything which God forbids, must disobey. But they are conscientious citizens. They also contribute to their country's well-being by the stability of their marriages and homes, their honesty in business, their hard work and their voluntary activity in the service of the handicapped and needy. Just governments have nothing to fear from Christians.

Secondly, Christians renounce unworthy methods of evangelism. Though the nature of our faith requires us to share the gospel with others, our practice is to make an open and honest statement of it, which leaves the hearers entirely free to make up their own minds about it. We wish to be sensitive to those of other faiths, and we reject any approach that seeks to force conversion on them.

Thirdly, Christians earnestly desire freedom of religion for all people, not just freedom for Christianity. In predominantly Christian countries, Christians are at the forefront of those who demand freedom for religious minorities. In predominantly non-Christian countries, therefore, Christians are asking for themselves no more than they demand for others in similar circumstances. The freedom to "profess, practise and propagate" religion, as defined in the Universal Declaration of Human Rights, could and should surely be a reciprocally granted right.

We greatly regret any unworthy witness of which followers of Jesus may have been guilty. We determine to give no unnecessary offence in anything, lest the name of Christ be dishonored. However, the offence of the cross we cannot avoid. For the sake of Christ crucified we pray that we may be ready, by his grace, to suffer and even to die. Martyrdom is a form of witness which Christ has promised especially to honor.

Conclusion: Proclaim Christ until He Comes

"Proclaim Christ until he comes." That has been the theme of Lausanne II. Of course we believe that Christ has come; he came when Augustus was Emperor of Rome. But one day, as we know from his promises, he will come again in unimaginable splendor to perfect his kingdom. We are commanded to watch and be ready. Meanwhile, the gap between his two comings is to be filled with the Christian missionary enterprise. We have been told to go to the ends of the earth with the gospel, and we have been promised that the end of the age will come only when we have done so. The two ends (of earth space and time) will concide. Until then he has pledged to be with us.

So the Christian mission is an urgent task. We do not know how long we have. We certainly have no time to waste. And in order to get on urgently with our responsibility, other qualities will be necessary, especially unity (we must evangelize together) and sacrifice (we must count and accept the cost). Our covenant at Lausanne was "to pray, to play and to work together for the evangelization of the whole world." Our manifesto at Manila is that the whole church is called to take the whole gospel to the whole world, proclaiming Christ until he comes, with all necessary urgency, unity and sacrifice.

MEN, WOMEN, AND BIBLICAL EQUALITY

The Bible teaches the full equality of men and women in creation and in redemption (Genesis 1:26-28, 2:23, 5:1, 2; 1 Corinthians 11:11, 12; Galatians 3:13, 28, 5:1).

The Bible teaches that God has revealed himself in the totality of Scripture, the authoritative Word of God (Matthew 5:18; John 10:35; 2 Timothy 3:16; 2 Peter 1:20, 21). We believe that Scripture is to be interpreted wholistically and thematically. We also recognize the necessity of making a distinction between inspiration and interpretation: Inspiration relates to the divine impulse and control whereby the whole canonical Scripture is the Word of God; interpretation relates to the human activity whereby we seek to apprehend revealed truth in harmony with the totality of Scripture and under the guidance of the Holy Spirit. To be truly biblical, Christians must continually examine their faith and practice under the searchlight of Scripture.

Biblical Truths

CREATION

1. The Bible teaches that both man and woman were created in God's image, had a direct relationship with God, and shared jointly the responsibilities of bearing and rearing children and having dominion over the created order (Genesis 1:26-28).

2. The Bible teaches that woman and man were created for full and equal partnership. The word "helper" (ezer), used to designate woman in Genesis 2:18, refers to God in most instances of Old Testament usage (e.g. 1 Samuel 7:12; Psalm 121:1, 2). Consequently the word conveys no implication whatsoever of female subordination or inferiority.

3. The Bible teaches that the forming of woman from man demonstrates the fundamental unity and equality of human beings (Genesis 2:21-23). In Genesis 2:18, 20 the word "suitable" (kenegdo) denotes equality and adequacy.

4. The Bible teaches that man and woman were co-participants in the Fall: Adam was no less culpable than Eve (Genesis 3:6; Romans 5:12-21; 1 Corinthians 15:21, 22).

5. The Bible teaches that the rulership of Adam over Eve resulted from the Fall and was therefore not a part of the original created order. Genesis 3:16 is a prediction of the effects of the Fall rather than a prescription of God's ideal order.

REDEMPTION

6. The Bible teaches that Jesus Christ came to redeem women as well as men. Through faith in Christ we all become children of God, one in Christ, and heirs to the blessings of salvation without reference to racial, social, or gender distinctives (John 1:12, 13; Romans 8:14-17; 2 Corinthians 5:17; Galatians 3:26-28).

COMMUNITY

7. The Bible teaches that at Pentecost the Holy Spirit came on men and women alike. Without distinction, the Holy Spirit indwells women and men, and sovereignly distributes gifts without preference as to gender (Acts 2:1-21; 1 Corinthians 12:7, 11, 14:31).

8. The Bible teaches that both women and men are called to develop their spiritual gifts and to use them as stewards of the grace of God (1 Peter 4:10, 11). Both men and women are divinely gifted and empowered to minister to the whole Body of Christ, under his authority (Acts 1:14, 18:6, 21:9; Romans 16:1-7, 12, 13, 15; Philippians 4:2, 3; Colossians 4:15; see also Mark 15:40, 41, 16:1-7; Luke 8:1-3; John 20:17, 18; compare also Old Testament examples: Judges 4:4-14, 5:7; 2 Chronicles 34:22-28; Proverbs 31:30, 31; Micah 6:4).

9. The Bible teaches that, in the New Testament economy, women as well as men exercise the prophetic, priestly and royal functions (Acts 2:17, 18, 21:9; 2 Corinthians 11:5; 1 Peter 2:9, 10; Revelation 1:6, 5:10). Therefore, the few isolated texts that appear to restrict the full redemptive freedom of women must not be interpreted simplistically and in contradiction to the rest of Scripture, but their interpretation must take into account their relation to the broader teaching of Scripture and their total context (1 Corinthians 11:2-16, 14:33-36; 1 Timothy 2:9-15).

10. The Bible defines the function of leadership as the empowerment of others for service rather than as the exercise of power over them (Matthew 20:25-28, 23:8; Mark 10:42-45; John 13:13-17; Galatians 5:13; 1 Peter 5:2, 3).

MEN, WOMEN, AND BIBLICAL EQUALITY cont.

FAMILY

11. The Bible teaches that husbands and wives are heirs together of the grace of life and that they are bound together in a relationship of mutual submission and responsibility (1 Corinthians 7:3-5; Ephesians 5:21; 1 Peter 3:1-7; Genesis 21:12). The husband's function as "head" is to be understood as self-giving love and service within this relationship of mutual submission (Ephesians 5:21-33; Colossians 3:19; 1 Peter 3:7).

12. The Bible teaches that both mothers and fathers are to exercise leadership in the nurture, training, discipline and teaching of their children (Exodus 20:12; Leviticus 19:3; Deuteronomy 6:6-9, 21:18-21, 27:16; Proverbs 1:8, 6:20; Ephesians 6:1-4; Colossians 3:20; 2 Timothy 1:5; see also Luke 2:51).

---

66 99 Nothing commends the gospel more eloquently than a transformed life, and nothing brings it into disrepute so much as personal inconsistency. We FOCUS are charged to behave in a manner that is worthy of the gospel of Christ, QUOTE and even to "adorn" it, enhancing its beauty by holy lives. For the watching world rightly seeks evidence to substantiate the claims which Christ's disciples make for him. A strong evidence is our integrity.—Manila Manifesto

---

Application

COMMUNITY

1. In the church, spiritual gifts of women and men are to be recognized, developed and used in serving and teaching ministries at all levels of involvement; as small group leaders, counselors, facilitators, administrators, ushers, communion servers, and board members, and in pastoral care, teaching, preaching, and worship.

In so doing, the church will honor God as the source of spiritual gifts. The church will also fulfill God's mandate of stewardship without the appalling loss to God's kingdom that results when half of the church's members are excluded from positions of responsibility.

2. In the church, public recognition is to be given to both women and men who exercise ministries of service and leadership.

In so doing, the church will model the unity and harmony that should characterize the community of believers. In a world fractured by discrimination and segregation, the church will dissociate itself from worldly or pagan devices designed to make women feel inferior for being female. It will help prevent their departure from the church or their rejection of the Christian faith.

FAMILY

3. In the Christian home, husband and wife are to defer to each other in seeking to fulfill each other's preferences, desires and aspirations. Neither spouse is to seek to dominate the other, but each is to act as servant of the other, in humility considering the other as better than oneself. In case of decisional deadlock, they should seek resolution through biblical methods of conflict resolution rather than by one spouse imposing a decision upon the other.

In so doing, husband and wife will help the Christian home stand against improper use of power and authority by spouses and will protect the home from wife and child abuse that sometimes tragically follows a hierarchical interpretation of the husband's "headship."

4. In the Christian home, spouses are to learn to share the responsibilities of leadership on the basis of gifts, expertise, and availability, with due regard for the partner most affected by the decision under consideration.

In so doing, spouses will learn to respect their competencies and their complementarity.

This will prevent one spouse from becoming the perennial loser, often forced to practice ingratiating or deceitful manipulation to protect self-esteem. By establishing their marriage on a partnership basis, the couple will protect it from joining the tide of dead or broken marriages resulting from marital inequities.

5. In the Christian home, couples who share a lifestyle characterized by the freedom they find in Christ will do so without experiencing feelings of guilt or resorting to hypocrisy. They are freed to emerge from an unbiblical "traditionalism" and can rejoice in their mutual accountability in Christ.

In so doing, they will openly express their obedience to Scripture, will model an example for other couples in quest of freedom in Christ, and will stand against patterns of domination and inequality sometimes imposed upon church and family.

We believe that biblical equality as reflected in this document is true to Scripture.

We stand united in our conviction that the Bible, in its totality, is the liberating Word that provides the most effective way for women and men to exercise the gifts distributed by the Holy Spirit and thus to serve God.

Gilbert Bilezikian
W. Ward Gasque
Stanley N. Gundry
Gretchen Gaebelein Hull
Catherine Clark Kroeger
Jo Anne Lyon
Roger Nicole

Source: Christians for Biblical Equality, Rosemount, MN.

THE DUPAGE DECLARATION:
A CALL TO BIBLICAL FIDELITY

Preamble

We evangelical renewal leaders from North American mainline churches gathered at Wheaton in DuPage County, Illinois, March 19, 20, 1990 express our concern for the church of Jesus Christ in its drift away from the evangelical faith. What is needed, we believe, is a genuine revival rooted in the Word of God. We therefore, present this declaration: *A Call to Biblical Fidelity.*

This declaration represents our understanding of theological and moral issues that are now in dispute in our churches. It is not intended to be an exhaustive list of church doctrines and concerns.

It is offered in the spirit of Christ, our Savior and Judge, who calls each of us to confess our complicity in private and public sin, "For it is time for judgment to begin with the family of God"(1 Peter 4:17, NIV; cf. 2 Timothy 4:1-5). We resolve to serve him with total fidelity and obedience to his Word.

Declaration

I

We affirm the Trinitarian name of God—Father, Son and Holy Spirit.

We deny that these designations are mere metaphors drawn from the cultural experience of the past and may therefore be replaced by new symbols reflecting the cultural ethos of today.

II

We affirm that God has revealed himself fully and decisively in Jesus Christ as attested in Holy Scripture.

We deny that there are other revelations in nature or history that fulfill or complete this one revelation of God.

III

We affirm that there is only one way to salvation—God's way to us in Jesus Christ, which is apprehended by faith alone through God's grace.

We deny that other religions are pathways to salvation, or that one can be in a right relationship with God apart from repentance and faith in Jesus Christ.

IV

We affirm that Jesus Christ is God incarnate in human flesh, fully human and fully divine, different from all other human beings in kind, not simply in degree.

We deny that Jesus Christ is essentially the flower of humanity, a spiritual master, a paradigm of what all human beings can become.

V

We affirm that Holy Scripture is the written Word of God, the uniquely inspired testimony to God's self-disclosure in the history of biblical Israel culminating in Jesus Christ. The scriptures of the Old and New Testaments take precedence over experience, tradition and reason and are therefore our infallible standard for faith and practice.

We deny that Holy Scripture is a merely human document that records the religious experiences of a past people, that it is only an aid in understanding our experiences in the present rather than a rule that is used by the Spirit of God to direct the people of God in every age.

VI

We affirm the biblical guidelines for human sexuality: chastity outside of marriage, lifelong fidelity and holiness in marriage, and celibacy for the sake of the kingdom.

We deny that premarital or extramarital relations, trial marriages, cohabitation outside of marriage, homosexual relations and so-called homosexual unions, can ever be in genuine accord with the will and purpose of God for his people.

VII

We affirm the sanctity of human life at every stage based on our creation in the image of God and our election by God for service in his kingdom.

We deny, for example, that the personal choice of either parent takes precedence over the right of the unborn child to life in the service of God's glory. We deplore the continuing traffic of abortion as the slaughter of innocents, which can only be an abomination in the sight of God.

VIII

We affirm that the mission of the church is to spread the good news of salvation by word and deed to a lost and despairing humanity. This mission to proclaim the atoning death and resurrection of Jesus Christ to all nations calls people of faith to discipleship and obedience in the pursuit of personal and social holiness. We further affirm that the fruit of the gospel proclamation is justice, mercy and peace.

We deny that the mission of the church is the self-development of exploited peoples or the political liberation of oppressed people.

We invite pastors and lay people from the Body of Christ to join us in affirming this declaration.

Persons or groups desiring to affirm this declaration by adding their names may contact: James V. Heidinger II, Good News, P.O. Box 150, Wilmore, KY 40390.

Original signatories of the DuPage Declaration:

Timothy Bayly Presbyterian Church (USA)	*Gerald M. Sanders* United Church of Christ	*Paul D. Johnston* Presbyterian Church (USA)
Richard M. Bowman Christian Church (Disciples of Christ)	*Armand L. Weller* United Church of Christ	*Brad Long* Presbyterian Church (USA)
J. Robert Campbell Presbyterian Church (USA)	*Waldo Werning* Lutheran	*Betty Moore* Presbyterian Church (USA)
David M. Higbee Independent Evangelical	*Parker Williamson* Presbyterian Church (USA)	*Kevin D. Ray* Christian Church (Disciples of Christ)
James Mark Kushiner Independent Evangelical	*Donald G. Bloesch* United Church of Christ	*Vernon Stoop, Jr.* United Church of Christ
Richard Lovelace Presbyterian Church (USA)	*Ray Bringham* Church of God, Anderson	*Matthew J. Welde* Presbyterian Church (USA)
Kevin Perrotta Roman Catholic	*James V. Heidinger II* United Methodist Church	*Todd Wetzel* Episcopal Church

FOCUS BOOKS

***Evangelical Renewal in the Mainline Churches,* Ronald H. Nash, editor.**
Discusses the status of evangelical renewal in eight of the most prominent mainline churches. Published by Crossway Books.

THE MOSCOW DECLARATION

We, the participants of the Lausanne Congress in Moscow, came together from all 15 Republics of the Soviet Union and 24 other countries in all continents of the world, representing many different confessions of the Church of Jesus Christ, which is His body. We affirm the common historic faith of Jesus Christ as outlined in the Lausanne Covenant.

We give thanks to God for the faithfulness and survival of the churches through the dark red night of atheistic rule in the USSR. We remember with reverence all who died, were bereaved, suffered imprisonment, cruelty, discrimination, separation, threats, and oppression.

We give thanks for the prayer of Christians in the rest of the world and their support in prayer, by radio, by visits, by the provision of Scriptures, literature, and other supplies.

We give thanks for the new day of openness and change, both in practice and in law, that gives freedom to preach the gospel.

We began to see the challenges that will fill our future as we endeavor to take the Good News of Jesus Christ to all the peoples of the Soviet Union.

We saw the challenge of scores of unreached peoples, particularly in Siberia, the Caucasus, and Central Asia, with few witnesses, no Scriptures, and very needy people.

We saw the challenge of our cities with their growing populations, plagued by loneliness, intimidated by violence, drawn into enslavement by drugs and sex and alcohol, and deprived of affection by the breakdown of the family.

We saw the challenge of the younger generation, both children and teenagers, and the need to build bridges of friendship and channels of Christian education to give them a start in life with the Savior who loves them.

We saw the challenges of communicating the gospel to university students and intellectuals and in the welter of different views with which they are confronted.

We saw the challenge of our prisons, hospitals, and other institutions for deprived, disabled, and mentally retarded people.

We saw the challenge of the aftermath of the Chernobyl disaster and the Armenian earthquake.

We saw the challenge of being the people of God to shine as lights at this juncture in the opening up and restructuring of the society and the economy.

---

66 99
FOCUS
QUOTE
"What we can give to our brothers and sisters in the Soviet Union is relatively easy for us to do. The inspiration and example that the Soviet believers give to us has been hammered out of their brutal and harsh history. The example of their faith in God and faithfulness to Him can be an unbelievable source of inspiration for the growth of God's Kingdom around the world."—Elmer M. Wilson, LCWE Director of Church Relations, after attending the Moscow Congress on Evangelization

---

We became aware of the ground we have to recover after over 70 years of captivity:

• In the need for leadership, lay and ordained, trained for the tasks of the new day.
• In the need for skills in writing, publishing, and broadcasting by radio and television.
• In the need for teachers and materials for Christian education.
• In the need for renewed cooperation with all who share a common faith after experiences that have driven us into isolation, mistrust, and suspicion.

We became aware also of the great resources we have:

• In the love of our heavenly Father.
• In the victory of Jesus Christ over the powers of darkness in His cross and resurrection.
• In the power of the Holy Spirit.
• In the Word of God in the Bible.
• In effectual prayer.
• In the gifts He has distributed to His people, both women and men, young and old.
• In the heritage we have inherited from our fathers and mothers in the faith.
• In the bonds of fellowship we have with the churches in the rest of the world.

In the light of all this:

We commit ourselves

To stay true to Christ in freedom and prosperity as we endeavored to do in restriction and poverty.

To uphold the whole gospel once for all delivered to us in the Holy Scriptures and proclaim it by word, demonstrate it in deeds, and model it in our attitudes and character in the church and in the world.

To stay together and show the wholeness of the body of Christ by our love and understanding and practical cooperation with all who in every place call on the name of our Lord Jesus Christ, both their Lord and ours.

Not to rest until the Good News is proclaimed and there is a viable church planted among every people in our country and every stratum in our society.

For this commitment we seek the help and blessing of God.

Izmailovo Congress Hall
October 26, 1990

The World in Review

STATUS OF THE CHRISTIAN WORLD

Year	1900	1970	1980	1992	2000
WORLD POPULATION					
1. Total population	1,619,886,800	3,610,034,400	4,373,917,500	5,480,851,000	6,251,055,000
2. Urban dwellers	232,694,900	1,354,237,000	1,797,479,000	2,386,947,000	2,916,501,000
3. Rural dwellers	1,387,191,900	2,255,797,400	2,576,438,500	3,093,904,000	3,334,554,000
4. Adult population	1,025,938,000	2,245,227,300	2,698,396,900	3,356,968,000	3,808,564,300
5. Literates	286,705,000	1,437,761,900	1,774,002,700	2,306,713,000	2,697,595,100
6. Nonliterates	739,233,000	807,465,400	924,394,200	1,050,255,000	1,110,969,200
WORLDWIDE EXPANSION OF CITIES					
7. Metropolises (over 100,000 population)	400	2,400	2,700	3,580	4,200
8. Megacities (over 1 million population)	20	161	227	350	433
WORLD POPULATION BY RELIGION					
9. Christians (total all kinds) (= World C)	558,056,300	1,216,579,400	1,432,686,500	1,833,022,000	2,130,000,000
10. Muslims	200,102,200	550,919,000	722,956,500	988,004,000	1,200,653,000
11. Nonreligious	2,923,300	543,065,300	715,901,400	897,520,000	1,021,888,400
12. Hindus	203,033,300	465,784,800	582,749,900	736,127,000	859,252,300
13. Buddhists	127,159,000	231,672,200	273,715,600	330,498,000	359,092,100
14. Atheists	225,600	165,288,500	195,119,400	238,968,000	262,447,600
15. New-Religionists	5,910,000	76,443,100	96,021,800	121,724,000	138,263,800
16. Tribal religionists	106,339,600	88,077,400	89,963,500	99,646,000	100,535,900
17. Sikhs	2,960,600	10,612,200	14,244,400	19,289,000	23,831,700
18. Jews	12,269,800	15,185,900	16,938,200	18,011,000	19,173,600
19. Non-Christians (= Worlds A and B)	1,061,830,500	2,393,455,000	2,941,231,000	3,647,828,000	4,121,055,000
GLOBAL CHRISTIANITY					
20. Total Christans as % of world (= World C)	34.4	33.7	32.8	33.4	34.1
21. Affiliated church members	521,563,200	1,131,809,600	1,323,389,700	1,692,466,000	1,967,000,000
22. Practicing Christians	469,259,800	884,021,800	1,018,355,300	1,243,235,000	1,377,000,000
23. Pentecostals/Charismatics	3,700,000	72,600,000	158,000,000	410,626,000	562,526,000
24. Crypto-Christians (secret believers)	3,572,400	55,699,700	70,395,000	143,069,000	176,208,000
25. Avg. Christian martyrs per yr	35,600	230,000	270,000	308,000	500,000
MEMBERSHIP BY ECCLESIASTICAL BLOC					
26. Anglicans	30,573,700	47,557,000	49,804,000	55,264,000	61,037,000
27. Catholics (non-Roman)	276,000	3,134,400	3,439,400	3,925,000	4,334,000
28. Marginal Protestants	927,600	10,830,200	14,077,500	19,441,000	24,106,000
29. Nonwhite indigenous Christians	7,743,100	58,702,000	82,181,100	155,879,000	204,100,000
30. Orthodox	115,897,700	143,402,500	160,737,900	183,577,000	199,819,000
31. Protestants	103,056,700	233,424,200	262,157,600	336,592,000	386,000,000
32. Roman Catholics	266,419,400	672,319,100	802,660,000	998,906,000	1,144,000,000
MEMBERSHIP BY GEOGRAPHICAL REGION					
33. Africa	8,756,400	115,924,200	164,571,000	249,626,000	323,914,900
34. East Asia	1,763,000	10,050,200	16,149,600	93,165,000	128,000,000
35. Europe	273,788,400	397,108,700	403,177,600	409,004,000	411,448,700
36. Latin America	60,025,100	262,027,800	340,978,600	461,057,000	555,486,000
37. Northern America	59,569,700	169,246,900	178,892,500	191,821,000	201,265,200
38. Oceania	4,311,400	14,669,400	16,160,600	18,819,000	21,361,500
39. South Asia	16,347,200	76,770,200	106,733,200	151,636,000	185,476,700
40. USSR	97,002,000	86,012,300	96,726,500	109,712,000	118,101,000

Year	1900	1970	1980	1992	2000
CHRISTIAN ORGANIZATIONS					
41. Service agencies	1,500	14,100	17,500	**21,600**	24,000
42. Foreign-mission sending agencies	600	2,200	3,100	**4,100**	4,800
43. Institutions	9,500	80,500	9,000	**99,900**	103,000
CHRISTIAN WORKERS					
44. Nationals (all denominations)	1,050,000	2,350,000	2,950,000	**4,038,000**	4,500,000
45. Pentecostal/Charismatic national workers	2,000	237,300	420,000	**974,000**	1,133,000
46. Aliens (foreign missionaries)	62,000	240,000	249,000	**295,000**	400,000
47. Pentecostal/Charismatic foreign missionaries	100	3,790	34,600	**102,000**	167,000
CHRISTIAN FINANCE (in US$, per year)					
48. Personal income of church members	270 billion	4,100 billion	5,878 billion	**9,696 billion**	12,700 billion
49. Personal income of Pentecostals/Charismatics	250,000,000	157 billion	395 billion	**1,114 billion**	1,550 billion
50. Giving to Christian causes	8 billion	70 billion	100.3 billion	**169 billion**	220 billion
51. Churches' income	7 billion	50 billion	64.5 billion	**86.7 billion**	100 billion
52. Parachurch and institutional income	1 billion	20 billion	35.8 billion	**82.7 billion**	120 billion
53. Ecclesiastical crime	300,000	5,000,000	30,000,000	**1.1 billion**	2 billion
54. Income of global foreign missions	200,000,000	3.0 billion	5.0 billion	**9.2 billion**	12 billion
55. Computers in Christian use (total numbers)	0	1,000	3,000,000	**111,200,000**	340,000,000
CHRISTIAN LITERATURE					
56. New commercial book titles per yr	2,200	17,100	18,800	**22,870**	25,000
57. New titles including devotional	3,100	52,000	60,000	**67,440**	75,000
58. Christian periodicals	3,500	23,000	22,500	**26,000**	35,000
59. New books/articles on evangelization per year	500	3,100	7,500	**12,000**	16,000
SCRIPTURE DISTRIBUTION (all sources)					
60. Bibles per year	5,452,600	25,000,000	36,800,000	**55,128,000**	70,000,000
61. New Testaments per year	7,300,000	45,000,000	57,500,000	**83,492,000**	110,000,000
CHRISTIAN BROADCASTING					
62. Christian radio/TV stations	0	1,230	1,450	**2,520**	4,000
63. Total monthly listeners/viewers	0	750,000,000	990,474,400	**1,525,696,000**	2,150,000,000
64. for Christian stations	0	150,000,000	291,810,500	**481,487,000**	600,000,000
65. for secular stations	0	650,000,000	834,068,900	**1,286,477,000**	1,810,000,000
CHRISTIAN URBAN MISSION					
66. Non-Christian megacities	5	65	95	**160**	202
67. New non-Christian urban dwellers per day	5,200	51,100	69,300	**107,000**	140,000
68. Urban Christians	159,600,000	660,800,000	844,600,000	**1,154,510,000**	1,393,700,000
69. Urban Christians as % of urban dwellers	68.6	48.8	47.0	**48.4**	47.8
70. Evangelized urban dwellers, %	72.0	80.0	83.0	**88.3**	91.0
WORLD EVANGELIZATION					
71. Unevangelized population (= World A)	788,159,000	1,391,956,000	1,380,576,000	**1,209,809,000**	1,038,819,000
72. Unevangelized as % of world	48.7	38.6	31.6	**22.2**	16.6
73. Unreached peoples (with no churches)	3,500	1,300	700	**400**	200
74. World evangelization plans since AD 30	250	510	620	**1,010**	1,400

David B. Barrett, World Evangelization database. Copyright © 1992 by the International Bulletin of Missionary Research. Reprinted by permission.

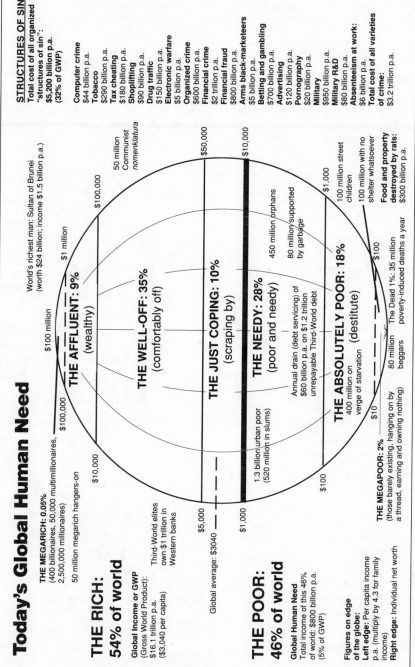

Today's Global Human Need

STRUCTURES OF SIN

Total cost of all organized "structures of sin":
$5,200 billion p.a. (32% of GWP)

Computer crime
$44 billion p.a.
Tobacco
$290 billion p.a.
Tax cheating
$180 billion p.a.
Shoplifting
$90 billion p.a.
Drug traffic
$150 billion p.a.
Electronic warfare
$5 billion p.a.
Organized crime
$600 billion p.a.
Financial crime
$2 trillion p.a.
Financial fraud
$800 billion p.a.
Arms black-marketeers
$5 billion p.a.
Betting and gambling
$700 billion p.a.
Advertising
$120 billion p.a.
Pornography
$20 billion p.a.
Military
$950 billion p.a.
Military R&D
$80 billion p.a.
Absenteeism at work:
$6 billion p.a.
Total cost of all varieties of crime:
$3.2 trillion p.a.

World's richest man: Sultan of Brunei (worth $24 billion; income $1.5 billion p.a.)

50 million Communist *nomenklatura*

$100,000

$50,000

$10,000

$1,000

$100

$10

$100 million

$1 million

THE AFFLUENT: 9% (wealthy)

THE WELL-OFF: 35% (comfortably off)

THE JUST COPING: 10% (scraping by)

THE NEEDY: 28% (poor and needy)

450 million orphans

80 million/supported by garbage

Annual drain (debt servicing) of $60 billion p.a. on $1.2 trillion unrepayable Third-World debt

THE ABSOLUTELY POOR: 18% (destitute)

100 million street children

100 million with no shelter whatsoever

Food and property destroyed by rats: $300 billion p.a.

The Dead 1%: 35 million poverty-induced deaths a year

400 million on verge of starvation

80 million beggars

THE MEGAPOOR: 2%
(those barely existing, hanging on by a thread, earning and owning nothing)

1.3 billion urban poor (520 million in slums)

Global average: $3040

THE RICH: 54% of world

Global Income or GWP (Gross World Product):
$16.1 trillion p.a.
($3,040 per capita)

Third-World elites own $1 trillion in Western banks

THE POOR: 46% of world

Global Human Need
Total income of this 46% of world: $800 billion p.a. (5% of GWP)

THE MEGARICH: 0.05%
(400 billionaires, 50,000 multimillionaires, 2,500,000 millionaires)

50 million megarich hangers-on

$100,000

$10,000

$5,000

$1,000

Figures on edge of the globe:
Left edge: Per capita income p.a. (multiply by 4.3 for family income)
Right edge: Individual net worth

Source: World Evangelization Database

Poverty, slums, disasters, deprivation, rights abuses, illness, disease, addiction:
Human need here focuses on the unfortunate victims involved (described by the detailed statistics). The globe on page 77 gives an overview. It is divided into 2 halves. The lower half depicts the world of the Poor (the so-called "lower classes") divided into 2 main slices (with a megapoor minislice) and into several population segments. The statistics detail today's global human need.

The upper half of the globe depicts the world of the Rich (the "middle and upper classes"), divided into 3 main slices (with a megarich minislice) and into several population segments. The figures shown attached to this upper half briefly outline the so-called "structures of sin."

All statistics refer primarily to the year 1990 (usually mid-1990). All monies are given in U.S. dollars. Note also that *p.a.* means "per annum", "per year", "a year", "each year", "every year." These terms are used alternately to provide variety. Note further that the same global totals throughout these diagrams may be given rounded to 1, 2, 3, or 4 significant figures (e.g., world population is 5.3 billion, or 5.292 million, etc.). Partial totals may not always add up to global totals or 100.0% because of rounding.

HUMANS ON THE GLOBE OF MID-1990
5,292,180,000 population
91,201,500 population increase p.a. (1.72% p.a.; 93% in developing countries)
Median age 24.2 years
141.6 million births a year (2.67% p.a.)
50.5 million deaths a year (0.96% p.a.)
Life expectancy at birth 62.3 years

BASIC RIGHTS: FOOD, WATER, SHELTER, CARE
1.8 billion undernourished
950 million hungry (inadequate food for active working life)
550 million severely malnourished
500 million suffering from iron-deficiency anemia
400 million on verge of starvation
10 million babies born malnourished p.a.
Infant mortality (deaths under 1 year old) 68 per 1000 live births
Maternal mortality 500,000 p.a.
15 million annual hunger-related deaths of under 5s
20 million starvation-related deaths p.a.
1.3 billion without safe water to drink
2.2 billion without adequate safe water supply
3.0 billion with unsafe water and bad sanitation
25,000 a day killed by dirty water
1.1 billion without adequate shelter
100 million with no shelter whatsoever
50 million cave dwellers
1.1 billion without money to buy food
1.3 billion with scarce firewood
60 million abandoned children and infants

300 million homeless/family-less children
100 million megacity street children
450 million orphans
520 million slum dwellers or shanty dwellers
New slum dwellers increase at 70 million p.a.
80 million supported by garbage collection/recycling
1.5 billion with no access to medical care
2.4 billion poor (46% of world)
1,273 million urban poor (1.1 billion in Third World)
952 million absolutely poor (in absolute poverty; 18%)
Poorest 20% of world gets 1.6% of GWP
Working-age population: 60 million more p.a.
Exploited child labor: 50 million
80 million beggars
90 million unemployed workers
600 million underemployed labor
1 billion urban part-time street vendors
Physical quality of life index (global average): 68%
50 countries with less calorie supply than essential (2,600 per capita per day)

SOCIOPOLITICAL RIGHTS
10 million stateless (with no nationality)
12 million deportees (persons expelled) p.a.
4 billion unprotected from human rights abuses
Human rights: 45% violated
14 million permanently unsettled refugees
25 million emigrants/immigrants p.a.
154 countries not controlled by popular votes
2.8 billion disenfranchised (no control by vote; 54% of world)
1,035 million illiterate/nonliterate adults (29%)
880 million orate (nonreader) adults unable to read or write (25%)
9 million more illiterate adults p.a.
250 million with language handicaps
3.7 billion without political freedom
1,307 million in religious countries
1,579 million in secular countries
1,488 million under atheistic regimes
400 million under oppressive regimes
70 million under racist regimes
2.5 billion women denied full rights and equality
1 billion victims of corruption
750 million uneducated (no past schooling)
1.5 billion school-age children (ages 5-19)
1.0 billion with little or no access to schools (67% of those eligible)
620 million school-agers not in schools
360 million with no access to schools (24%)
24 million children reach school age p.a.
41% without access to electricity
43% without telephone access
67% without radio or TV
100 million prisoners in 12-month period
4 million political prisoners
1 million prisoners due to religion
800,000 prisoners of conscience
2.6 billion denied freedom of religion
4.2 billion denied full political freedom and civil rights
2 billion in countries frequently employing torture
100,000 prisoners being tortured
130 million citizens killed by own governments since 1900

1,692,400 political executions,
1948–1977
40,000 executed by governments
each year
32 million slaves (bought and sold,
including bonded labor, involun-
tary servitude)
510 million victims of crime p.a.
850,000 murders a year
5 million child victims of pedophile
racketeers p.a.
22 million child-abuse incidents p.a.
200 million persons abused in childhood

FUNDAMENTAL FREEDOMS
3 billion denied freedom to travel in
own country
4 billion denied freedom to travel
abroad
3 billion denied freedom to assemble
3.5 billion denied freedom to teach
ideas

DISASTERS AND
DESERTIFICATION
1 million more desertification victims a year
10 million environmental refugees
850 million at risk through
desertification
1,500 major earthquakes, 1900–
1985, killing 1.8 million
80,000 earthquake victims (deaths)
a year
350 major floods, 1960–1981, killing 175,000
10,000 flood victims (deaths) a year
210 major cyclones, 1960–1981,
killing 536,000
250,000 environmental disaster victims p.a.
1 million poisoned by pesticides p.a.
625 million live in areas with unhealthy air
25,000 pollution deaths a day
1 million killed in man-made disasters p.a.
Traffic deaths 3 persons per 100 million vehicle miles

ILLNESS/DISEASE
42 million legally blind
28 million totally blind (nonsighted)
18 million with river blindness (85
million at risk)
320 million partially deaf (hearing-
impaired)
130 million severely deaf
20 million totally deaf
10 million dumb (deaf-mutes)
10 million with dracunculiasis
13 million leprosy sufferers (lepers)
60 million diabetics
400 million new malaria cases p.a.
2.8 billion live at risk of malaria
5 million malaria deaths p.a.
270 million with elephantiasis
200 million with schistosomiasis
(600 million at risk)
1 million a year bitten by venomous
snakes
40,000 deaths p.a. from venomous
snake bites
9 million with Parkinson's disease
10 million with tuberculosis (TB: 3
million deaths p.a.)
465 million iron-deficiency anemic
women
100 million with chemosensory
(taste and smell) disorders
3 million persons worldwide with artificial implants (pacemakers,
prostheses)
300,000 persons kept alive by artificial kidneys
50,000 organ transplants a year
3,000 heart transplants a year
60,000 awaiting organ donors
51 million psychotics
10 million schizophrenics
950 million psychoneurotics
300 million arthritics
900 million experiencing chronic
pain
1.6 billion disabled (handicapped)
340 million handicapped children
85 million severely handicapped
children
3 million dwarfs (little people)

2 billion sick/ill persons (30% children)
Labor absenteeism: $6 billion p.a.
2.8 million children die p.a. from
vaccine-preventable diseases
6 infectious diseases kill 4 million
unimmunized children p.a.
4 billion persons not immunized
5 million diarrheal deaths of children under 5 p.a.
4 million children die of pneumonia
p.a.
22 million prostitutes (9% male)
60 million AIDS carriers (growth
rate 100% p.a.)
3 million AIDS cases
400,000 AIDS-related deaths a year
401,000 suicides a year
650 million tobacco smokers
2.6 million tobacco-related deaths
p.a.
170 million alcoholics
55 million drug addicts (illicit drug
users)
Leading causes of 50.5 million
deaths p.a.:
Parasitic diseases 16.8 million
Circulatory diseases 13.3 million
Cancer 4.3 million
Perinatal diseases 3.3 million
Injury and poisoning 2.7 million
Cardiovascular disease 5 million
130 million severely mentally-
retarded
220,000 Downs-syndrome (mongol)
births p.a.
26 million epileptics
260,000 hemophiliacs (all males)
450,000 albinos (homozygous persons)
100 million albino-gene carriers

FINANCE
Money needed to provide those in
poverty with adequate food, water, education, health: $500 bil-
lion p.a.

**FOCUS
FACT**

- **One-third of all children in the developing world must drop out of school by age 10 to help support their families.**
- **100 million children are forced to work under hazardous, often fatal, conditions for meager wages.**
- **In Thailand 40,000 prostitutes are under age 14.**

—InterAction, American Council for Voluntary International Action

Today's Geopolitical-Religious Blocs

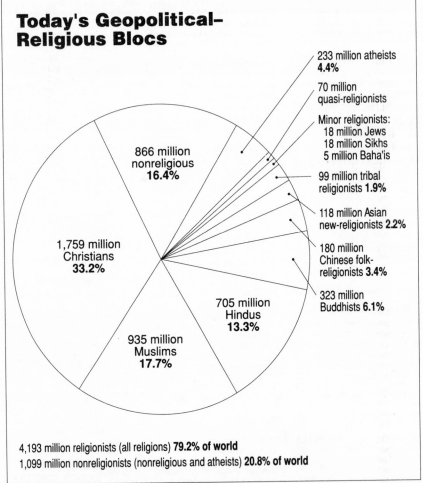

233 million atheists
4.4%

70 million
quasi-religionists

Minor religionists:
18 million Jews
18 million Sikhs
5 million Baha'is

99 million tribal
religionists **1.9%**

118 million Asian
new-religionists **2.2%**

180 million
Chinese folk-
religionists **3.4%**

323 million
Buddhists **6.1%**

866 million
nonreligious
16.4%

1,759 million
Christians
33.2%

705 million
Hindus
13.3%

935 million
Muslims
17.7%

4,193 million religionists (all religions) **79.2% of world**
1,099 million nonreligionists (nonreligious and atheists) **20.8% of world**

3 Worlds, 3 Megacontinents, 7 Continents, 9 Macro Regions, 25 Regions, 180 Nations, 251 Countries, 2,000 Provinces; With the Globe's 33 Major Religious and Antireligious Blocs

The statistics below enumerate the main varieties of political and religious segmentation of the world's population in use today. The various basic segments listed here can be grouped or regrouped in different ways depending on one's requirements. The pie chart shows the world's major religious blocs or segments.

Indented categories are part of (included in) preceding unindented categories. Figures in parentheses with a % sign are in all cases annual change (% increase, per year). All figures relate to the year 1990, usually to mid-1990, except for the Communist statistics which portray 1989 before the collapse of one-party Communism in Europe.

THE GLOBE IN MID-1990
5,292 million persons (1.72% p.a.)
13% in First (Western) world

33% in Second (Communist-related) world
54% in Third (Nonaligned) world
91 million more people a year

Land area: 135.8 million sq km

WORLDS DEVELOPMENT
More developed regions: 51 countries

Less developed regions: 200 countries

1.2 billion in more developed regions

4.0 billion in less developed regions

Least developed countries (LDCs): 41

370 million in least developed countries

GEOPOLITICAL WORLDS (1989)

Western world: 35 countries

Communist world: 30 countries

Third World: 186 countries

CONTINENTS AND REGIONS

3 megacontinents

7 continents

9 macro regions (continental areas)

25 regions

COUNTRIES

251 countries in world (21 under 1,000 population, 230 over)

180 sovereign nations (172 being UN members, including observer states)

71 nonsovereign countries (dependencies)

GOVERNMENT (1989)

82 multiparty democratic states

50 one-party states (30 Marxist)

28 military regimes

20 autocracies/dictatorships

71 dependencies/colonies (17 million population)

IDEOLOGY (1989)

108 religious countries

113 secular countries

30 atheistic countries

FREEDOM OR REPRESSION (adherence to UN Universal Declaration on Human Rights)

79 politically free countries

87 partially free politically

85 politically not free

ASSOCIATIONS OF COUNTRIES (number of member countries in each)

UN 172, FAO 158, GATT 96, IAEA 113, IBRD 151, ICAO 157, IDA 136, IFAD 142, IFC 133, ILO 150, IMF 151, IMO 131, ITU 162, UNESCO 158, UNIDO 144, UPU 168, WHO 166, WIPO 199, WMO 160, WTO 150.

PROVINCES

2,000 major civil divisions (MCDs)

MULTINATIONALS

10,500 transnational corporations (TNCs)

4,800 TNCs in association in Global T-Net

262 supranationals or intergovernmental organizations (IGOs)

3,500 international nongovernmental organizations (NGOs)

International electronic fund transfers $14 billion a day

International foreign exchange transactions p.a. $95 trillion

50 million internationals (persons living abroad)

WORLD COMMUNISM (situation in mid-1989)

122 Communist, Leninist, or Marxist parties (in 130 countries)

88.7 million Communist party members

16 Communist-ruled (Leninist) states (with 83 million party members)

30 Marxist-ruled (including Communist-ruled) states

12 international Communist front organizations with 1,400 affiliates (agencies)

1.7 billion persons under Marxist regimes

RELIGION

(30,000 religions, analyzable into 33 major religious and antireligious blocs)

ADHERENCE TO RELIGION IN 1990

4,193 million religionists (all religions) (annual increase 1.9% p.a.)

2,000 million popular-religionists

430 million New Age/occult/neo-Hindu cultists

720 million Christian popular-religionist-pietists

70 million quasi-religionists, including 6.9 million Freemasons (males)

1,099 million nonreligionists (2.8% p.a.)

866 million nonreligious (2.8% p.a.)

233 million atheists (1.7% p.a.)

ADHERENTS OF NON-CHRISTIAN RELIGIONS

2,434 million non-Christian religionists (annual increase 2.3% p.a.)

GREAT WORLD RELIGIONS

935 million Muslims (2.7% p.a.)

780 million Sunnis (2.7% p.a.)

145 million Shias (Shiites) (2.9% p.a.)

18 million Ismailis (3.4% p.a.)

10 million Admadis (4.2% p.a.)

705 million Hindus (2.3% p.a.)

493 million Vaishnavites (2.3% p.a.)

175 million Shaivites (2.3% p.a.)

20 million Saktists (2.2% p.a.)

12 million Neo-Hindus (3.3% p.a.)

4 million Reformed Hindus (2.5% p.a.)

323 million Buddhists (1.7% p.a.)

182 million Mahayana (1.7% p.a.)

122 million Theravada (1.7% p.a.)

19 million Tantrayana (Lamaists) (1.7% p.a.)

OTHER MAJOR RELIGIONS

180 million Chinese folk-religionists (0.8% p.a.)

118 million Asian New-Religionists (2.3% p.a.)

99 million tribal religionists (0.2% p.a.)

MINOR RELIGIONS

18 million Jews (1.1% p.a.)

18 million Sikhs (2.9% p.a.)

8 million non-Christian Spiritists (5.5% p.a.)

5 million Baha'is (3.6% p.a.)

3 million Shintoists (-1.7% p.a.)

3 million Jains (2.0% p.a.)

CHRISTIANS AND NON-CHRISTIANS

1,759 million Christians (2.2% p.a.)

3,533 million non-Christians (1.7% p.a.)

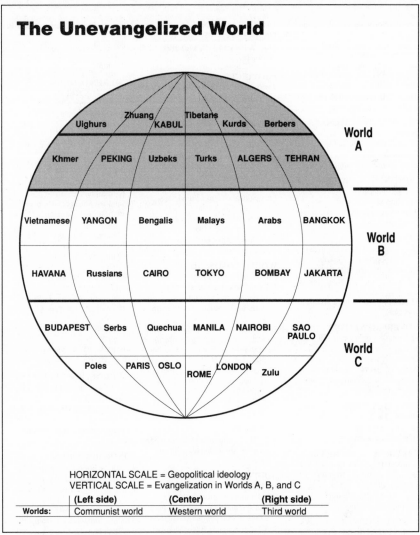

The Unevangelized World

HORIZONTAL SCALE = Geopolitical ideology
VERTICAL SCALE = Evangelization in Worlds A, B, and C

	(Left side)	(Center)	(Right side)
Worlds:	Communist world	Western world	Third world

In 3,030 major unevangelized population segments

The globe is divided here into some 15,000 distinct population segments, of 3 major varieties: ethnolinguistic peoples, metropolises (mother cities of over 100,000 population), and countries.

The 3 varieties of segment overlap because they are 3 different ways of dividing up the same one world. This segmented globe in turn can be subdivided into our 3 categories of world—Worlds A, B, and C. This superimposing on one schema (segments) on another (3 worlds) is done for purposes of illustration only, since most segments are composed each of a mixture of unevangelized persons, evangelized non-Christians, and Christians. For purpose of illustration also, we name a few segments below: a few megapeoples (in lower-case letters), and a few megacities (in capital letters), placing these segments where the majority of their individuals are located. In this schema, therefore, "evangelized non-Christian population segments," defined as segments with church members under 50%, are listed for convenience under World B; and "christianized population segments", defined as all segments with church members of 50% or over, are listed for convenience under World C.

The globe therefore gives a detailed representation of the nature of the unfinished Christian task. This task's main secular feature ought to be to rectify the grossly disproportionate spread of life's blessings—health, wealth, shelter, food, rights, justice—around the world. This disproportion is briefly sketched here in this series of global diagrams. From the Christian point of view, the major unfinished task is to spread the blessings of Christ throughout the segments of World A, the unevangelized world, here shown shaded gray for emphasis.

A. THE UNEVANGELIZED WORLD

1,253 million unevangelized persons (all being also unreached persons)

MACRO SEGMENTS
3,030 unevangelized population segments:
2,000 unreached peoples (1.0 billion population)
1,000 unevangelized metropolises
30 closed countries increasing by 2 a year including:
450 completely unreached peoples (with no churches)
150 unreached megapeoples
85 anti-Christian megacities

MICRO SEGMENTS
17,000 unreached people groups (minipeoples) in 1974, decreasing to 12,000 by 1990

50,000 unreached micropeoples
300,000 unreached sociopeoples

B. THE EVANGELIZED NON-CHRISTIAN WORLD

2,280 million evangelized non-Christians (of whom 0.5 billion are unreached, and 1.7 billion reached)

MACRO SEGMENTS
4,870 evangelized non-Christian population segments:
4,000 peoples
800 metropolises
76 countries (50 closed/restricted-access) including:
70 non-Christian megacities

MICRO SEGMENTS
150,000 micropeoples
700,000 sociopeoples

C. THE CHRISTIAN WORLD

1,759 million Christians (all reached)

MACRO SEGMENTS
7,100 christianized population segments:
5,500 peoples
1,450 metropolises
145 countries over 60% Christians (39 restricted-access, 10 closed) including:
167 mainly-Christian megacities
9,500 reached peoples (with own churches) in Worlds B and C

MICRO SEGMENTS
50,000 micropeoples
1 million sociopeoples
48,000 reached minipeoples, now coalesced into 12,000 agglomerated christianized minipeoples

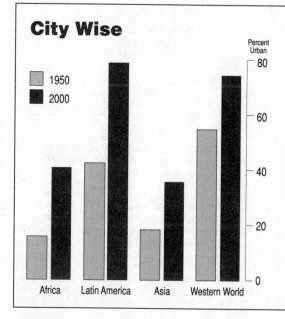

City Wise

1950
2000

Percent Urban
80
60
40
20
0

Africa Latin America Asia Western World

The urban population has doubled since 1950 in the more developed parts of the world. In the developing countries it has quadrupled. Overall the urban population has increased tenfold in the last 60 years, while the rural population has only doubled.

In the 1990s for the first time in the history of the world, more people will be living in cities than in villages or rural areas.

The United Nations expects that by A.D. 2000, 17 of the world's 20 largest cities will be in the Third World. In 1980 there were only 11. Mexico City and São Paulo, Brazil, are expected to top the list with about 25 million people each.

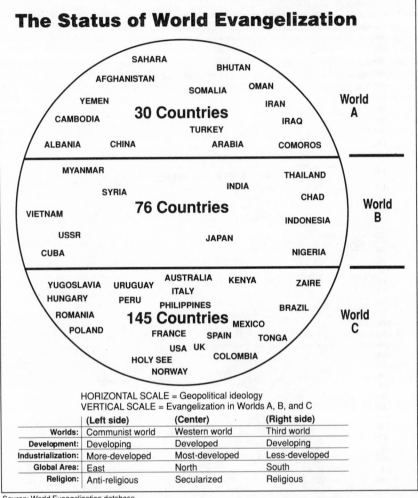

The Status of World Evangelization

	(Left side)	(Center)	(Right side)
Worlds:	Communist world	Western world	Third world
Development:	Developing	Developed	Developing
Industrialization:	More-developed	Most-developed	Less-developed
Global Area:	East	North	South
Religion:	Anti-religious	Secularized	Religious

Source: World Evangelization database

Today's globe is shown here as a detailed representation of the whole earth. It is divided on the criterion of demographic evangelization into 3 worlds each with distinct populations. These worlds, A, B, and C, are not geographically defined but are defined on the basis of response to the Christian faith. World C consists of all persons who individually are *Christians* anywhere across the globe. Worlds A and B consist of all persons, individually, who are non-Christians: World A those who in addition have never heard the gospel or heard of Jesus (the *unevangelized*), World B those who have heard the gospel (who have heard, with understanding about Christianity, Christ, and the gospel) but have not, or not yet, accepted it or become disciples of Christ (here termed *evangelized non-Christians*).

Onto this 3-world division, countries or metropolises or people do not easily fit because each is composed of a mixture of unevangelized persons, evangelized non-Christians and Christians. However, for purposes of illustration we add a few names of countries below, placing these population segments where the majority of their individuals are located. These countries are placed vertically according to a numerical scale of evangelization: most-evangelized countries at the bottom, least-evangelized at the top; also, on the left the Communist world (the whole Sino-Soviet bloc or sphere of influence, including Eastern Europe and other ex-Communist countries), the Third World on the right, the Western world inbetween. Note that to illustrate today's global mission, Worlds A and B do have Christian activities in their midst, and therefore have some Christian workers and some foreign missionaries present.

Note also that World C is not defined as precisely the same as "Christendom", "the Christian West" nor "the christianized world" nor does it include North America or Europe in their entirety. Non-Christians or atheists or agnostics in heavily-evangelized countries like the USA or Norway or Britain, for example, fall (on our definition) into World B.

A parallel but slightly differing definition of evangelization divides the world into 2 dichotomous categories of the state of being reached by the gospel: the *unreached world* (top half of the globe, covering World A and 0.5 billion persons in World B), and the *reached world* (bottom half of the globe, covering World C and 1.6 billion persons in World B). This expounds the concept of "individual evangelization" (persons who individually have received the opportunity to respond to the gospel if they wish to by joining a local church of their own culture), by contrast with "demographic evangelization" (families, groups, or people as a whole hearing and understanding the gospel).

THE GLOBE

THE HUMAN BACKDROP
5.3 billion persons
Land area 135.8 million sq km (11% arable)
Density 39 people per sq km
2,260 million urban dwellers
3,032 million rural dwellers
3,577 million adults (ages 15 and over) (67.6%)
1,011 million youth (ages 15-24) (19.1%)
704 million adolescents (teenagers, ages 13-19)
1,715 million children under 15 (32.4%)
630 million children under 15 (infants and babies; 11.9%)
487 million elderly (60 and over, 9.2%)
34 million elderly aged 80 or over
1,318 million women ages 15-49 (24.9%)
141.6 million births p.a. (388,000 a day)
190 live births per 1000 females
2,542 million literates (71% of adults)
1,035 million nonliterates (29% of adults)
Global income (GWP) US $16,100 billion p.a.
Growth of GWP 3.0% per year
Average income per person $3,040
Average family income $13,070
687 million telephones (95% direct-dial)
750 million TV sets

93 million computers

EVANGELIZATION
4.0 billion evangelized persons (4,039,623,000; 76.3% of world)
3.5 billion reached persons
1.8 billion unreached persons
1.3 billion unevangelized persons (23.7% of world)
Urban dwellers 88% evangelized
270 million unevangelized urbanites
364,000 newly-evangelized every day
500 million evangelized but unreached non-Christians
133 million newly-evangelized every year

CHURCH EXPANSION
Christians and churches exist in all 251 countries
38.7 million more Christians each year
35.7 million more church members each year
50,000 new churches each year

VERTICAL SCALE: Evangelization in Worlds A, B, C
(percentages "p.a." in parenthesis are annual rates)

A. THE UNEVANGELIZED WORLD
(30 countries each less than half evangelized, meaning E is 50% or less)
1,252,557,000 unevangelized persons (-0.1% p.a.)
23.7% of global population
5.0% of global income

3.0% of all telephones
3.0% of all TV sets
0.6% of all computers

B. THE EVANGELIZED NON-CHRISTIAN WORLD
(76 countries over half evangelized [E is greater than 50%] but with church members less than 60%)
2,280,845,000 evangelized non-Christians (4.5% p.a.)
500 million evangelized but unreached non-Christians
43.1% of global population
33% of global income
17.0% of all telephones
19.0% of all TV sets
11.4% of all computers

C. THE CHRISTIAN WORLD
(145 countries with church members 60% or over, all also having E 95% or over)
1,758,778,000 Christians (2.2% p.a.)
33.2% of global population
Christians receive, own and/or use:
62% of global income
80% of all telephones
78% of all TV sets
88% of all computers (56% of all being owned and operated by Christians)
Christians spend:
99.9% of Christian income on themselves
0.09% on the evangelized non-Christian world
0.01% on the unevangelized world

David B. Barrett and Todd M. Johnson. Copyright © 1990 by the Foreign Mission Board of the Southern Baptist Convention. Published by New Hope, Birmingham, AL. Reproduced with permission from *Our Globe and How to Reach It.*

 FOCUS QUOTE East Europeans are saying that while it took the Poles 10 years to achieve freedom, Hungary made it in 10 months, East Germany in 10 weeks, Czechoslovakia in 10 days, and Romania in 10 hours. But who really caused these things to come to pass? Who else but God? Who else could have done it?
—Thomas Wang in *AD2000 and Beyond* magazine, May–August 1990 issue.

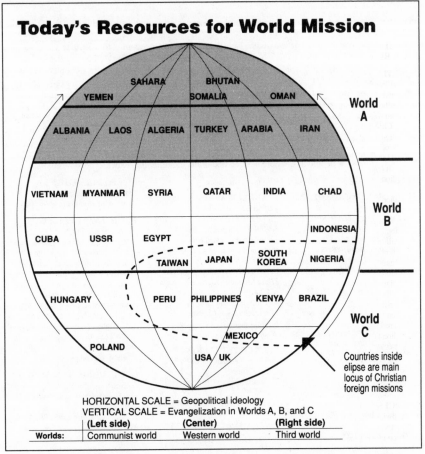

Today's Resources for World Mission

HORIZONTAL SCALE = Geopolitical ideology
VERTICAL SCALE = Evangelization in Worlds A, B, and C

Worlds:	(Left side) Communist world	(Center) Western world	(Right side) Third world

Countries inside elipse are main locus of Christian foreign missions

Churches, workers, institutions, agencies, media, literature, radio / TV, money, computers, networks, plans

This table enumerates the entire extent of global Christian resources of all kinds. Several of these are then shown as they are utilized today, divided among the 3 worlds, A, B, and C.

The present situation is that the vast bulk of these resources benefit only the Christian world. Even in foreign missions, 85% of personnel and money are devoted to Christian lands, such as missionaries from the U.S. to Brazil or Kenya or the Philippines (see inner ellipse in globe at bottom).

It is obvious that all segments of the earth have a right to their fair share of resources of all kinds. The least that Christians can do is to ensure that the resources which are under their own direct control—the spiritual resources catalogued below—get properly shared with all. To redress the present situation Christians will need to concentrate on World A far more, hence it is shown shaded gray and its segments are shown in bold on the globe. The faint lines of the other 2 worlds B and C suggest the far less significant share of global resources that these worlds should now be deliberately restricted to. The 2 thin arrows then show the new directions in which these ample resources need to be redirected or redeployed.

THE GLOBE
5.3 billion persons

GLOBAL CHRISTIAN RESOURCES IN 1990

CHRISTIAN PERSONS
1,759 million Christians (99.8% lay persons)
1,622 million professing Christians
137 million crypto-Christians (7.8% of all Christians)
135 million nominal Christians (7.7% of all Christians)
1,623,833,000 affiliated Christians (church members)
620 million Christian children under 15
230 million Christian infants under 5
1,095 million urban Christians (48.5% of all urbanites)
1.0 billion literate adult Christians
1,210 million practicing Christians
480 million weekly-worshipping Christians
900 million Christian regulars for Christian radio/TV
1,755 million lay persons (99.8% of all Christians)
25 million lay persons (lay Christians) residing abroad
120 million Christian pilgrims on move every year
250 million Christian foreign tourists a year
2,900 million Christian domestic tourists a year

INTERCESSION
36 worldwide intercessory networks (22 active)
20 million in full-time prayer ministry
10 million weekly prayer groups
170 million praying daily for world mission
2,100 religious institutes (orders, societies for the full-time religious life centered on prayer)
7,000 monasteries, ashrams, convents, abbeys, priories

ORGANIZATIONS
2.6 million worship centers (local churches)
23,500 distinct denominations
6,000 major councils of churches
3,970 foreign mission boards or societies
5,000 home mission boards, agencies, or societies
400 medical missions (foreign mission agencies)
21,000 parachurch or service agencies
400,000 base ecclesial communities (BECs)

INSTITUTIONS
99,200 major Christian/church-related institutions
500,000 minor Christian institutions
145,000 Christian primary/elementary schools
45,000 Christian secondary/high schools
300 million pupils
1,300 Christian universities and colleges
4,600 seminaries/theological colleges
4,500 Christian hospitals
29,500 Christian medical centers
50 million medical consultations a year (in Christian centers)
1,500 Christian-owned presses and publishers
350 ecumenical centers
950 church-related research centers

FINANCE
Christians by income: 58% rich (11% affluent, 37% well-off, 10% just coping), 42% poor (29% needy, 13% absolutely poor)
Church of the Rich: 942 million members
Church of the Affluent: 179 million members
Church of the Poor: 682 million members
Church of the Absolutely Poor: 211 million members
Personal income of Christians (church members) $8,950 billion p.a.
Personal income per capita of Christians, $5,510
Average Christian family income $19,280
Stewardship: giving per church member per week $1.85
Church/agency income $157 billion a year
Churches' Income $83.4 billion p.a.
Parachurch/institutional income $74.2 billion p.a.
$5 billion a year on new religious buildings (Christian)
Foreign missions giving per church member per week $0.10
Foreign missions $8.6 billion a year
Christian broadcasting (radio/TV) $5 billion p.a.

FULL-TIME PERSONNEL
950,000 ordained clergy, ministers, pastors, priests (5% women)
4,208,250 full-time Christian workers (36% women; 93% citizens)
1.5 million full-time women workers
50,000 ordained women clergy/ministers
470,000 monks including friars

1,045,000 nuns (sisters)
1 million professional theologians
20,000 professional missiologists
15 million Christian schoolteachers
1 million seminarians
30 million Christian students
100,000 TEE extension students in 120 countries
285,250 foreign missionaries
38,000 foreign missionaries from Third-World countries
800,000 home missionaries
3,923,000 national (citizen) workers
180,000 short-term foreign missionaries

LITERATURE AND PRINT MEDIA
22,400 new Christian book titles a year
100 million copies of new Christian books printed p.a.
11,000 books/articles on mission a year
3,000 new scholarly research books on Christian faith p.a.
13,000 major religious (Christian) libraries
23,800 religious (Christian) periodicals
51.4 million Bibles distributed a year
76.9 million New Testaments a year
1,430 million scriptures (all varieties) distributed p.a.
3 million Christian books printed p.a.
4 billion Christian tracts a year

ELECTRONIC MEDIA AND AUDIOVISUALS
2,160 Christian radio/TV stations
900 national/international Christian broadcasting agencies
100,000 full-time personnel in Christian broadcasting
3 billion a year view *Jesus* and other Christian films

MASS EVANGELISM
2,500 evangelistic mass campaigns a year
1,300 metropolises each year hold citywide evangelistic campaigns

COMPUTERS
54 million Christian-owned computers (worth $310 billion)
145 million Christian-owned screens/terminals
16,800 new Christian-owned computers a day
6,000 MIPS new Christian-purchased computer power a day
1.2 million electronic mail systems (95% secular)
450 secular commercial databases
5,000 secular electronic bulletin boards (BBS) active

200 million Christian computer users
50 million Christian computer professionals

**NETWORKS AND
GLOBAL PLANS**
4,000 Great Commission networks
56 Great Commission global networks
9 Great Commission global meganetworks
410 current global plans
260 current global plans making progress
78 global megaplans
33 global gigaplans
Plan expenditures $45 billion

**A. THE UNEVANGELIZED
WORLD**
Present cost of Christian foreign missions: $0.1 billion a year
30 restricted-access (closed) countries
3,000 foreign missionaries (1.0%)

No citywide evangelistic campaigns
30,000 full-time Christian workers
50,000 lay Christians residing abroad in closed countries
0.1% of all Christian literature
0.01% of all Christian radio/TV

**B. THE EVANGELIZED
NON-CHRISTIAN WORLD**
Per capita income of non-Christians: $1,350 p.a.
Present cost of Christian foreign missions: $1 billion a year
23,000 foreign missionaries (8.1%), 5,000 being in 50 restricted-access countries
200 cities per year have citywide evangelistic campaigns
200,000 full-time Christian workers, 50,000 being in 50 restricted-access countries
0.9% of all Christian literature
0.1% of all Christian radio/TV

C. THE CHRISTIAN WORLD
Present cost of home Christianity: $140 billion a year
Foreign missions to other Christian lands: $7.5 billion a year
259,250 foreign missionaries to other Christian lands (90.9%), 4,000 being in 39 restricted-access countries
1,100 cities per year have citywide evangelistic campaigns
4.0 million full-time Christian workers (95%) work in World C, including 200,000 in 39 restricted-access countries
500 million lay Christians live in 39 restricted-access heavily-Christian countries
99% of all Christian literature is consumed by World C
99.9% of all Christian radio/TV output is directed at World C

GROWTH IN PARACHURCH AGENCIES

Six Years of Parachurch Growth

1982	2,402
1984	2,989
1986	3,580
1988	4,074

Source: 1989 MARC Europe Handbook.

HISTORICAL PROFILE OF PARACHURCH GROWTH

More than 57 percent of today's parachurch agencies have been established in the last thirty years:

Pre-1900	19 percent
1900–1960	24 percent
1960–1990	57 percent

Source: 1989 MARC Europe Handbook.

FOCUS
FACT
Eastern College, affiliated with the American Baptist Convention, is the only church-related college in the U.S. to offer a M.S. or M.B.A. in economic development with a minor in missions and evangelism. Students choose an urban or global concentration. For information write to Eastern College, 10 Fairview Drive, St. David's, PA 19087-3696.

SEVEN MARKS OF AN AD 2000 MISSION

1. Be a networker.
2. Communicate why your mission makes a difference.
3. Celebrate diversity and distinctives within biblical norms. Learn to appreciate the mosaic that is the body of Christ.
4. Know who you are and constantly clarify your values. . . . Be characterized by intense activity interspersed with intense reflection.
5. Be motivational, but control-oriented. Commitment must be to personal growth, not organizational ascendancy.
6. Develop programs and products that make a difference. Get rid of the marginal programs.

7. **Reallocate:** Until you assign time, people, and money to it, you haven't got anything but a good intention.
Renew: More plans and visions within organizations fail because of their competition with established programs than for any other reason.
Recruit: Recruit to your vision.
Report: Report back exactly what happens.

Source: Rev. Paul McKaughan, executive director, Evangelical Foreign Missions Association. Condensed from *AD2000 and Beyond* magazine, May-August 1990 issue. See the Missions section of the *Almanac of the Christian World* for more information on the AD2000 movement.

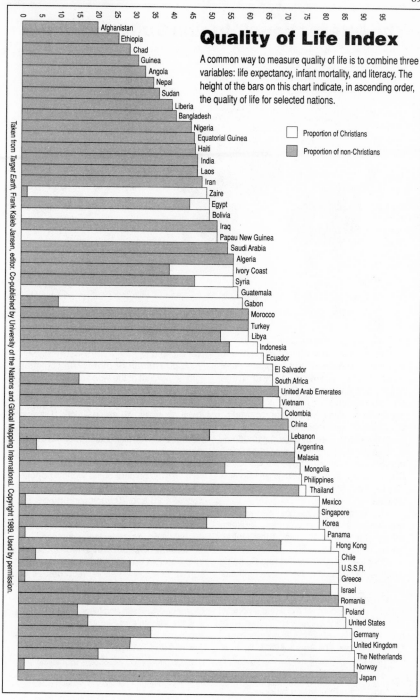

Quality of Life Index

A common way to measure quality of life is to combine three variables: life expectancy, infant mortality, and literacy. The height of the bars on this chart indicate, in ascending order, the quality of life for selected nations.

☐ Proportion of Christians

▨ Proportion of non-Christians

Afghanistan
Ethiopia
Chad
Guinea
Angola
Nepal
Sudan
Liberia
Bangladesh
Nigeria
Equatorial Guinea
Haiti
India
Laos
Iran
Zaire
Egypt
Bolivia
Iraq
Papau New Guinea
Saudi Arabia
Algeria
Ivory Coast
Syria
Guatemala
Gabon
Morocco
Turkey
Libya
Indonesia
Ecuador
El Salvador
South Africa
United Arab Emerates
Vietnam
Colombia
China
Lebanon
Argentina
Malasia
Mongolia
Philippines
Thailand
Mexico
Singapore
Korea
Panama
Hong Kong
Chile
U.S.S.R.
Greece
Israel
Romania
Poland
United States
Germany
United Kingdom
The Netherlands
Norway
Japan

The International Human Suffering Index

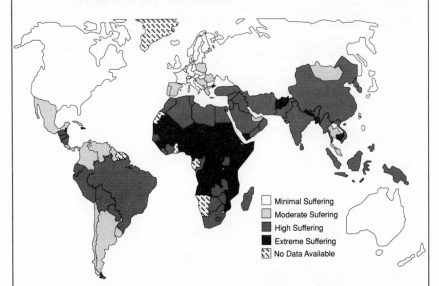

Minimal Suffering
Moderate Sufering
High Suffering
Extreme Suffering
No Data Available

By Sharon Camp and Joseph Speidel

The Human Suffering Index is compiled by adding 10 measures of human welfare related to economics, demography, health, and governance: **1)** income, **2)** inflation, **3)** demand for new jobs, **4)** urban population pressures, **5)** infant mortality, **6)** nutrition, **7)** clean water, **8)** energy use, **9)** adult literacy, and **10)** personal freedom.

Living conditions are worst in Mozambique, followed by Angola, Afghanistan, Chad, Mali, Ghana, Somalia, Niger, Burkina Faso, Central African Republic, Zaire, Benin, and Malawi.

The most comfortable countries to live in are Switzerland, West Germany, Luxembourg, the Netherlands, and the United States, in that order.

Countries rated in The Human Suffering Index were grouped in the following Quadrants:

Extreme Human Suffering: 30 countries with 11 percent of the world's population, or 519 million people, registered 75 or greater on The Human Suffering Index. Of these countries, 24 are in Africa; 6 are in

Asia. None is in Europe or the Western Hemisphere.

High Human Suffering: 44 countries with 58 percent of the world's population, or 2.85 billion people, registered between 50 and 74 on the Human Suffering Index. Of these countries, 16 are in Africa; 16 are in Asia; 11 are in Latin America; 1—Papua New Guinea—is in Oceania; none is in Europe.

Moderate Human Suffering: 29 countries with 10 percent of the world's population, or 491 million people, recorded an index between 25 and 49, indicating moderate levels of suffering. Of these countries, 10 are in Asia; 11 are in Latin America. Mauritius is the only African country in the category.

Minimal Human Suffering: 27 countries with 21 percent of the world's population, or one billion people, recorded 24 or lower on The Human Suffering Index. Of these countries, 20 are in Europe; 2 are in Oceania—Australia and New Zealand; 2 are in Asia—Japan and Singapore; 3 are in the Western Hemisphere —U.S., Canada, and Trinidad and Tobago.

Used by permission of Population Crisis Committee, 1120 19th Street, N.W., Washington, D.C. 20036.

Taken from *Target Earth*, Frank Kaleb Jansen, editor. Co-published by University of the Nations and Global Mapping International. Copyright © 1989. Used by permission.

ORGANIZATIONS TO HELP YOU RESPOND TO A SUFFERING WORLD

Bread for the World
802 Rhode Island Avenue, NE
Washington, DC 20018

Center for the Prevention of Sexual and Domestic Violence
1914 N. 34th Street, Suite 205
Seattle, WA 98103
206-634-1903

Child Sponsorship Program
Compassion
P.O. Box 7000
Colorado Springs, CO 80933

Christian Medical Dental Society
P.O. Box 830689
Richardson, TX 75083

EAPE (Evangelical Association for the Promotion of Education)
P.O. Box 238
St. Davids, PA 19087

Habitat for Humanity
Habitat and Church Streets
Americus, GA 31709

Literacy Volunteers of America
5795 Widewaters Parkway
Syracuse, NY 13214
315-445-8000

North American Association for Christians in Social Work
Eastern College
St. Davids, PA 19087

Prison Fellowship
P.O. Box 17434
Washington, DC 20041

Voice of Calvary Ministries
P.O. Box 10562
Jackson, MS 39209

World Concern
P.O. Box 33000
Seattle, WA 98133

World Relief
P.O. Box WRC
Wheaton, IL 60189

World Vision
919 W. Huntington Drive
Monrovia, CA 91016

Nations with Highest Inflation

Countries with the highest inflation rates in 1988, when the U.S. inflation rate was 4.4%.

- 1,722% Peru
- 980% Brazil
- 388% Argentina
- 243% Yugoslavia
- 86% Ecuador

Nations with Lowest Inflation

Industrialized nations with the highest inflation rates in 1988, when the U.S. inflation rate was 4.4%.

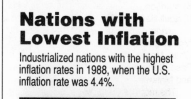

- 1.9% Australia, Luxembourg, Belgium and Switzerland
- 1.6% West Germany
- 1.2% The Netherlands
- 1.0% Japan

Source: International Labor Organization annual *Bulletin of Labor Statistics*.

Countries
of the World

Statistics . . . Peoples . . . Literacy . . . Economy . . . Politics . . . Religion

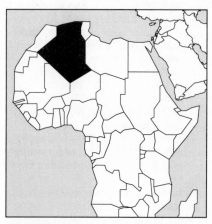

ALGERIA

Area 2,381,000 sq.km. Agriculturalized on the Mediterranean coast, in the Atlas mountains and oases. 80% in Sahara Desert.

Population 25,700,000. Annual growth 3.2%. People per sq.km. 11; 90% near the coast. About 1.7 million Algerians are migrants in Europe.

Peoples

Arab-Berber 70%. Speaking Arabic.

Berber (8 groups) 20%. Kabyle 2,700,000; Shawiya 1,100,000; Mzab (5 groups) 100,000; Tuareg 15,000.

European 0.8%. French 120,000; Russian 10,000, etc.

Literacy 38%. *Official language:* Arabic. French and, increasingly, English widely used. 25% speak one of the Berber dialects. *All languages* 15. *Bible translations* 1 Bible, 2 New Testaments, 5 portions.

Capital: Algiers 1,650,000. Urbanization 52%.

Economy: Heavily dependent on oil exports. Over 50% of work force is in agriculture, but its potential has not been effectively exploited. Income/person $2,760 (15% of USA).

Politics: French colony for 132 years. Independence in 1962 after a bitter war of liberation. The 28 year one-party rule of the National Liberation Front with its strong socialist policies is being threatened by the rise of Islamic fundamentalist parties. The likely future is an Islamic democratic government.

Religion: Since independence, the government has actively encouraged the development of an Islamic Arab socialist state. Proselytism is not allowed.

Muslim 99.5%. Increasing tendency to a more orthodox and radical expression of Ibadi Islam.

Christian 0.3%. Nominal 0.05%. Affiliated 0.25%.

Roman Catholic 0.24%. 53,000 adherents.

Orthodox 0.01%, 2,400 adherents.

Protestant 0.01%. 2,900 adherents; 1,100 members. 70% are expatriates.

Cross-cultural Christians witnessing in Algeria: 30 (1:750,000) in 5 agencies.

ARGENTINA

Area 2,777,000 sq.km. Latin America's second largest country with a great range of climate, rainfall and topography.

Population 31,900,000. Annual growth 1.4%. People per sq.km. 11.

Peoples

European 87%. A fusion of many nationalities, but largely Spanish, Italian and other East and West Europeans. Many minorities have retained a considerable degree of national identity.

Mestizo 10%. Largely Paraguayan, Bolivian and Chilean.

Amerindian 1.9%. Quechua 300,000; Mapuche 50,000; Lowland peoples (9) 208,000, mostly in the Chaco in the far north and Patagonia in the far south.

Literacy 93%. *Official language:* Spanish. *All languages* 21. *Bible translations* 1 Bible, 4 New Testaments, 6 portions.

Capital: Buenos Aires 11,400,000. Other major cities: Cordoba, 1,140,000; Rosario 1,000,000. Urbanization 82%.

Economy: Largely based on agriculture, but with much industry. There has been a steady, and at times catastrophic, fall in living standards this century. Once wealthy but now there is widespread poverty and unemployment. Hyperinflation has been the product of successive governments failing to curb overspending on a bloated bureaucracy and state/military-run industries. Income/person $2370 (13% of USA).

Politics: Independent from Spain in 1816. Peronist misrule, inflation and increasing leftist urban terrorism provoked the 1976 military takeover. The military government's incompetence, military adventurism and bad record on human rights led to the restoration of democratic rule in 1983. Successive democratic governments have been unable to contain the national economic crises.

Religion: Roman Catholicism is the official religion, but the new government has declared total freedom of conscience.

Nonreligious/Atheist 1.8%.

Jewish 2%. The fifth largest group of Jews in the world.

Muslim 0.2%. Mainly Palestinian and Lebanese.

Christian 95.5%. Affiliated 93.6%.

   Roman Catholic 86.5%. Practicing 63%. 26,500,000 adherents; 17,200,000 members. There are over 1.7 million baptized Catholics who have joined evangelical or other groups. After years of declining attendances and influence, there has been a reversal of this trend and much activity to win the youth.

   Orthodox (6 groups) 0.5%.

   Marginal groups 1.1%. Mormons 63,500 adherents; Jehovah's Witnesses, 56,500 adherents; New Apostolic 38,000 adherents.

   Protestant 5.5%. 1,680,000 adherents; 603,700 members. Denominations approximately 150. Largest adult members:

Seventh-Day Adventists 53,600
Assemblies of God 50,000
Vision de Futuro (?) 50,000
Brethren 40,000
Southern Baptist Convention 36,500
Christian Assemblies 36,000
Anglican 19,000
Evangelical 4.7% of population.

Missionaries to Argentina 590 (1:52,000 people) in 58 agencies. Missionaries from Argentina estimated 50.

AUSTRALIA

Area 7,687,000 sq.km. This island continent is largely grassland and desert in the interior but better watered in the east, southeast and southwest coastal regions, where most live in highly concentrated urban areas.

Population 16,800,000. Annual growth 1.6%. Immigration 0.8%. People per sq.km. 2.2.

Peoples

British origin 82.6%.

Other European 13%.

Middle Eastern 2%. Arab-speaking 250,000.

Asian 1.3%. Chinese, Vietnamese, Indian.

Australian Aborigine 1.1%. 172,000. (In 1780 approximately 300,000 speaking 260 languages.) About 50,000 are still nomadic.

Literacy 99%. *Official language:* English. Nearly 10% of the population do not use English as their first language. *All indigenous living languages* 121. *Bible translations* 1 Bible, 2 New Testaments, 28 portions.

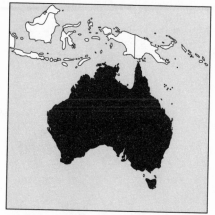

Capital: Canberra 260,000. Other cities: Sydney 3,500,000; Melbourne 3,000,000; Brisbane 1,160,000; Adelaide 1,000,000; Perth 980,000. Urbanization 86%.

Economy: Wealthy mixed economy based on industry, agriculture and mining, but world recession and severe droughts slowed the economy in the '80s. Income/person $10,900 (77% of USA).

Politics: Parliamentary democracy, independent of Britain in 1901.

Religion: A secular state with freedom of religion.

Nonreligious/Atheist, etc. 21.8%.

Muslim 1.5%. Predominantly Turks, Arabs and Yugoslavs.

Jewish 0.4%.

Chinese religions 0.3%.

Christian 76%. Affiliated 73.1%. Weekly church attendance is nearer 12% of the population.

  Roman Catholic 26.7%. 4,100,000 adherents; 2,860,000 members. High proportion of continental European nationalities.

  Orthodox 3.1%. Over 28 denominations mainly from Eastern Europe and Middle East.

  Marginal groups 1.1%. 182,000 adherents; 99,000 members. Over 54 cults. Largest (adherents): Jehovah's Witnesses 79,000; Mormons 47,000.

  Protestant 42%. A further 10% nominal Protestants. 6,630,000 adherents; 1,890,000 members. Denominations 150. Largest (adherents):

  Anglican Church 3,860,000
  Uniting Church 1,460,000
  Presbyterian Church (continuing) 213,000
  Baptist Union 204,000
  Lutheran Church 114,050
  Churches of Christ 92,000
  Salvation Army 75,000
  Methodist Church (continuing) 67,000
  Seventh-Day Adventist Church 54,000
  Assemblies of God 35,500
  Congregational Union 25,000
  Brethren 22,000

  Evangelical 17% of population.

Missionaries to Australia (cross-cultural) approximately 600 (1:26,000 people). Missionaries from within Australia 2,690 (1:2,460 Protestants) in 62 agencies.

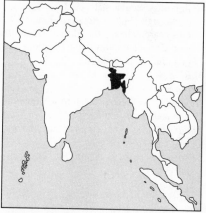

BANGLADESH

Area 144,000 sq.km. Occupying the delta and floodplains of the Ganges and Brahmaputra rivers, with high rainfall and frequent flooding.

Population 117,900,000. Annual growth 2.8%. People per sq.km. 819.

Peoples

Bengali 98%.

Bihari 1%. Mostly in refugee camps.

Tribal peoples 0.7%. 640,000 people in 28 tribes. Largest: Chakma 300,000.

Literacy 25%. *Official languages:* Bengali; English used widely. *All languages* 33. *Bible translations* 13 Bibles, 3 New Testaments, 8 portions.

Capital: Dhaka 5,300,000. Other cities: Chittagong 1,900,000. Urbanization 13%.

Economy: One of the world's poorest nations, suffering from gross overpopulation and periodic natural disasters such as devastating floods and cyclones. There seems little hope that the poverty of this unhappy land will ever be substantially alleviated. Income/person $160 (1% of USA).

Politics: Formerly East Pakistan; independent in 1971 after bitter civil war and defeat of Pakistan by Indian and Bangladesh forces. Corruption, instability, assassinations and 18 coups have marred the years since then. The military took over the government in 1982 but is unable to cope with the serious problems the country faces.

Religion: A secular state 1971-1988. Islam declared the State Religion in June 1988, thus marginalizing the Hindu, Buddhist and Christian minorities. Freedom for other religions has been promised.

Muslim 87%. Almost all are Sunni, a few Shi'a.

Hindu 11.7%. Decreasing through emigration and lower fertility.

Buddhist 0.6%. Mainly among the Chakma, Magh and Mru peoples.

Tribal religions 0.1%. Among the Garo, Santal, etc.

Christian 0.38%.

    Roman Catholic 0.18%. Practicing 59%. 190,000 adherents.

    Protestant 0.18%. 188,000 adherents; 72,600 members. Denominations 25. Largest (adult members):

    Baptist Union of Bangladesh (Baptist Missionary Society) 11,500

Garo Baptist Union 10,000

Bawm Evangelical Christian Church 9,600

All One in Christ Fellowship 7,100

Evangelical Lutheran Church 5,000

Church of Bangladesh (Anglican-Presbyterian) 4,400

Seventh-Day Adventist Church 4,200

Assemblies of God 2,400

Bangladesh Baptist Union 1,790

Evangelical 0.10% of population.

Missionaries to Bangladesh 440 (1:230,000 people) in 30 agencies.

BRAZIL

Area 8,512,000 sq.km. One half of the land surface and population of South America. The world's fifth largest country (36 times the size of the United Kingdom).

Population 150,300,000. Annual growth 2.0%. People per sq.km. 16.

Peoples: Brazil is a "melting pot" of the nations, with much intermarriage, so percentages given below are not meant to indicate rigid categories.

European 54%. Portuguese 15%, Italian 11%, Spanish 10%, German 3%.

African 11%. Descendants of slaves brought from West Africa and Angola.

Mixed race 33%. Mestizo and Mulatto.

Asian 1.5%. Japanese 1,000,000; Chinese 60,000; Arab, etc.

Amerindian 0.1%. In 1900 there were 500,000 in 230 tribes, but now there are less than 100,000 in 140 tribes and still decreasing through the encroachments of civilization, loss of land and disease.

Literacy 78%. *Official language:* Portuguese. *All languages* 152. *Bible Translations* 1 Bible, 18 New Testaments, 38 portions.

Capital: Brasilia 1,700,000. Other major cities: Sao Paulo 16,412,000; Rio de Janeiro 12,525,000; Recife 2,900,000; Porto Alegre 3,073,000; Belo Horizonte 3,785,000; Curitiba 2,827,000; Salvador 2,000,000; Fortaleza 1,900,000. Urbanization 71%.

Economy: Vast economic potential in the developing hinterland of the north and west, rapid growth and industrialization in the '60s and '70s in the south made Brazil one of the leading industrial and trading nations in the world. Lack of oil reserves, rampant inflation and crippling international debt has blunted growth and brought economic hardship to many. In 1989 the new government instituted stringent reforms and has greatly reduced the rate of inflation. Income/person $2,020 (11% of USA). Inflation in December 1989 alone 54%.

Politics: A republic with authoritarian military government since 1964. There was a return to a fully democratic government in 1985.

Religion: Complete freedom of religion.

Nonreligious/Atheist 1.4%. Secularism is on the increase in the middle and upper classes.

Buddhist 0.3%.

Muslim 0.1%.

Spiritist 30-35% (estimate). Probably 14% of all Brazilians are openly associated and more than 60% dabble in the various forms of spiritism of European, Amerindian, and especially African origin while still claiming to be Christian.

Christian 93%.
  Roman Catholic 73.1%. Practicing 12%. 101,000,000 adherents; 60,707,000 members. There are 18 million baptized Catholics who have joined evangelical or other groups.
  Other Catholic (2) 2%. 2,770,000 adherents.
  Marginal groups (58) 0.52%. 724,000 ad-

herents. Jehovah Witnesses 474,000 adherents; Mormons 161,800 adherents.
  Protestant 17.4%. 24,120,000 adherents; 10,377,000 members. Denominations 350. Largest (adult members):
  Assemblies of God 5,000,300
  Christian Congregation 1,253,000
  Baptist Convention (Southern Baptist Convention) 602,000
  Conference of Lutheran Churches 580,000
  Brazil for Christ 450,000
  Seventh-Day Adventist Church 403,000
  Cruzada Nacional (ICFG) 250,000
  Presbyterian Church 149,000
  Evangelical Lutheran Church 128,000
  Union of Evangelical Congregational Churches (Evangelical Union of South America) 115,000
  All other churches 1,445,000
  Evangelical 16% of population.
Missionaries to Brazil 2,600 (1:53,000 people) in 139 agencies.
Missionaries from within Brazil 840 (1:28,700 Protestants) in about 35 agencies.

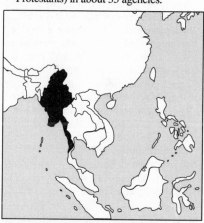

BURMA (Union of Myanmar)

Area 678,000 sq.km. Isolated from India, China and Thailand by a ring of mountains.

Population 41,700,000. Annual growth 2.3%. People per sq.km. 62.

Peoples

Bhama 65.1% and related *Mogh* (Arakanese) 5%.

Ethnic minorities (with their own states within Union) 24.1%. Karen 4,000,000; Shan 2,660,000; Kachin 860,000; Mon 720,000; Chin 720,000; Kayah 190,000.

Other ethnic minorities 2.2%. Palaung 266,000; Lisu 200,000; Wa 150,000; Lahu 100,000; Akha 60,000; Lushai (Mizo) 40,000; Naga 30,000, etc.

Immigrant minorities 3.6%. Chinese 750,000; Bangladeshi/Indian 300,000.

Literacy 78%. *Official language:* Burmese. *All languages* 90. *Bible translations* 12 Bibles, 10 New Testaments, 16 portions.

Capital: Yangon (Rangoon) 2,900,000. Other major city: Mandalay 725,000. Urbanization 24%.

Economy: Very poor due to years of unrest, inefficient socialism and excessive isolationist policies of the government. Huge illegal trade in opium breeds corruption at every level in the country. Some economic relaxations since 1980. Income/person $180 (1% of USA). Inflation 9.2%

Politics: The country has known little peace since the Japanese invasion in 1942. There has been much unrest and war since independence with constant ethnic and political revolts. One-party socialist republic since the 1962 military coup and almost total isolation of people and economy from international contacts. The prodemocracy movement was severely crushed and restricted in 1989, yet won a surprising victory in national elections in 1990. The military regime promises to relinquish power by 1992.

Religion: There is freedom of religion. Buddhism is no longer the state religion, but it still has great influence in governmental affairs.

Buddhist 87%. Shot through with animist practices. Mainly Burmese, Shan, Mon and many Arakanese.

Animist 2%. Many Buddhists are more animist than Buddhist. Karen and many smaller tribes

Muslim 3.6%. Bengali and Arakanese.

Hindu 0.9%. Indian.

Christian 5.9%. 95% from Animistic and 5% from Buddhist background; only 2% of Christians from Bhama majority.

Roman Catholic 1.2%. Practicing 63%. 442,000 adherents; 289,000 members.

Protestant 4.7%. 1,730,000 adherents; 668,000 members. Denominations 43. Largest (adult members):
Burma Baptist Convention 422,000
Assemblies of God 66,000
Church of Christ (Overseas Missionary Fellowship) 56,000
Anglican Church 20,000
Methodist Church (2) 20,000
Presbyterian Church 11,900
Evangelical 3.1% of population.

Missionaries to Burma 2. Missionaries from within Burma approximately 1,000 (1:1,700 Protestants).

CANADA

Area 9,980,000 sq.km. The world's second largest country. Much is cold arctic tundra or sparsely populated forest.

Population 26,500,000. Annual growth 0.8%, of this immigration 0.6%. 80% of population live within 150 km. of the 7,000 km. USA border. People per sq.km. 2.7.

Peoples: A mosaic of many nations and peoples often retaining much of their original culture.

British 42%. Majority in east, center and west.

French 29%. Majority in Quebec Province. Although Canada is officially bilingual with equal rights for all, the French minority includes a considerable separatist segment.

Other European 19%. German 1,560,000; Italian 830,000; Ukrainian 659,000; Dutch 490,000; Polish 366,000; Norwegian 195,000; Hungarian 146,000; Greek 140,000; Swedish 122,000; Yugoslav 122,000; Danish 98,000; Portuguese 98,000; Czech 73,000; Russian 70,000; Finnish 70,000; Belgian 50,000, etc.

Indigenous 5%. Amerindians (registered 340,000 in 61 tribes on reservations; non-registered 1,000,000), Eskimo 30,000.

Asian 3%. Indo-Pakistanis 350,000; Chinese 301,000; Vietnamese 90,000; Japanese 50,000; Korean 40,000.

Middle Eastern 1.1%. Mainly Arabic speaking.

African 0.8%. 200,000 North American, West Indian and African.

Latin American 0.8%. 200,000.

Literacy 99%. *Official languages:* English, French. *All indigenous languages* 70. *Bible translations* 2 Bibles, 2 New Testaments, 35 portions.

Capital: Ottawa 850,000. Major cities: Toronto 3,300,000; Montreal 3,300,000; Vancouver 1,350,000. Urbanization 76%.

Economy: One of the world's leading industrial nations. The USA is Canada's main trading partner. This interdependence moderates trends towards an economic nationalism. Income/person $15,080 (82% of USA).

Politics: Parliamentary and federal monarchy. Independent of Britain in 1867. Though the world's longest undefended border runs between Canada and the USA, Canada's own cultural and political identity leads to an independent line in foreign affairs to its NATO ally. Quebec separatism has become a dominant national issue.

Religion: Freedom of religion.

Nonreligious/Atheist 7.5%.

Muslim 1.5%. Pakistani, Arab, etc.

Jewish 1.4%. Some from North Africa and Commonwealth of Independent States (formerly the USSR).

Hindu 0.5%. Mostly Indian.

Sikh 0.2%.

Baha'i 0.2%

Animist 0.1%. Increasing again among Amerindians.

Christian 88%. Nominal 23.2%. Affiliated 64.8%.

Roman Catholic 39.6%. Practicing 40%. 10,060,000 adherents. Majority of French, Spanish, Italian, Portuguese, etc.

Orthodox 2.4%. 612,000 adherents. Denominations 31+. Mostly ethnic minorities of East European, Greek and Middle Eastern origin.

Marginal groups 2.3%. Over 34 cults. Largest (adult members): Mormons 90,000; Jehovah's Witnesses 77,003.

Protestant 20.6%. (A further 15% nominal.) 5,220,000 adherents; 2,880,000 members. Denominations 180. Largest (adult members):

United Church 983,000
Anglican Church 588,000
Pentecostal (30 groups) 266,000
Lutheran (8 groups) 223,000
Presbyterian (5 groups) 210,000
Baptist (11 groups) 205,000
Mennonite (12 groups) 64,000

Evangelical 6.5% of population.

Missionaries to Canada approximately 300 (mostly from the USA).

Missionaries from within Canada approximately 4,000 (1:1,300 Protestants) in over 50 agencies. Of these 420 serve in cross-cultural work in Canada.

CHINA

Area 9,561,000 sq.km. The third largest country in the world. Taiwan, Hong Kong and Macao are not included here.

Population 1,119,300,000. By far the largest nation in the world; 21% of world's population. Most live in the better-watered central and eastern coastal provinces. Annual growth 1.4%. People per sq.km. 117.

Peoples

Chinese (Han) 93%. Eight major languages and 600 dialects but one written language common to all. Putunghua (Mandarin) 748 million, Wu 90 million, Yueh (Cantonese) 54 million, Xiang (Hunanese) 53 million, Hakka 43 million, Minnan 32 million, Gan 26 million, Minpei 13 million.

Ethnic minorities 7%. 55 minorities officially recognized. Largest: Zhuang 14 million, Hui 7.6 million, Uighur 6.3 million, Yi 5.7 million, Hmong (Miao) 5.3 million, Manchu 4.5 million, Tibetan 4 million, Mongol 3.4 million, Bouyei-Tai 3.2 million, Tujia 3 million, Korean 1.8 million, Dong 1.5 million, Bai 1.2 million, Hani 1.1 million. Many smaller minorities live in the mountainous south and southwest.

Literacy 76%. *Official language:* Putunghua (Mandarin Chinese); local languages in the five Autonomous Regions. *All languages* 115. *Bible translations* 13 Bibles, 10 New Testaments, 23 portions.

Capital: Beijing (Peking) 9.2 million. Other cities: Shanghai 11.9 million, Tianjin 7.8 million, Chongqing 6.5 million, Guangzhou 5.6 million, Shenyang 5.1 million, Wuham 4.2 million, Nanjing 3.6 million. Thirty-eight other cities of over one million inhabitants. Urbanization 21%.

Economy: Socialist centralized economy, with considerable relaxations and economic development 1978-1989. The commune system has been dismantled and the peasants (nearly 80% of the population) allowed greater freedom to sell surplus crops. Small-scale private enterprises started in that period have been more and more restricted since the June 1989 clampdown. The economy is in crisis once more. Income/person $300 (2% of USA).

Politics: This great and ancient nation has regained its place of importance in the world after nearly two centuries of decline and humiliation at the hands of the Western powers and Japan. Since the final conquest of mainland China in 1949, the Communist Party has remoulded the nation along Marxist lines. The Cultural Revolution (1966–76) was the culmination of this policy. It caused immeasurable suffering and economic chaos. Intellectuals and religious believers were cruelly persecuted. The loss of life was enormous. After the death of Mao in 1976 the radical leftists were discredited and removed from power. A more pragmatic leadership initiated a series of economic, political and cultural reforms and developed links with other nations, but all within definite limits. The Communist party still maintains strict control over every aspect of life. In the latter half of 1983 a series of campaigns were initiated against crime, leftists, and "spiritual" pollution to counter growing corruption, dissident Western influences and revivals of religion. After a further period of relaxation, the student protest movement in Beijing in 1989 provoked a massacre in Tiananmen Square, repression of all protest, and a return to hard-line Marxist policies. The political situation remains tense and the aging leadership is unlikely to retain the status quo.

Religion: The elimination of all religious groups has always been the ultimate aim of the Marxist government. In the '50s the government engineered the infiltration, subversion and control of all organized Christianity. By 1958 this had been achieved through the Three-Self Patriotic movement among Protestants and the Catholic Patriotic Association among Catholics. During the Cultural Revolution even these front structures were moribund, and all religious activity was forced underground. In 1978 restrictions were eased and the Three-Self Patriotic movement and Catholic Patriotic Association resurrected as a means of regaining governmental control of the thousands of house churches. This has been only partially successful. Recent government policy has been to tolerate religious belief and allow worship under government supervision. There has been a marked increase in pressure and persecution for unregistered churches since June 1989.

All figures are estimates.

Atheist 12%. Communist party members nearly 40 million.

Nonreligious 50%(?). The atheistic education system ensures that most young people have no religious knowledge.

Chinese religions (Taoism, Buddhism, Confucianism) 28%(?).

Animist 2%. Among tribal peoples of the south, etc.

Muslim 2.4%. Ten national minorities are Muslim.

Christian 5%(?). The official estimate for all Christians is 6 million. House church and overseas researchers estimate 30 million to 50 million.

Roman Catholic 0.6%. Divided between the official CPA and those remaining loyal to the Vatican (over 50%). 6,600,000 adherents(?).

Marginal groups (3+) 0.1%. Various groups that are unitarian, "shouters," etc. 1,000,000 adherents(?).

Protestant 4.3%. 45,000,000 adherents, possibly subdivided thus:

Three-Self Patriotic movement 3,000,000 adherents

Three-Self Patriotic movement-related meeting points 9,000,000 adherents

Home meetings 33,000,000 adherents. Personnel in China-related ministries estimate 600 but working from other lands.

COLOMBIA

Area 1,139,000 sq.km. NW corner of South America. The fourth largest country in the continent. Mountains in west, plains and forests in east.

Population 31,800,000. Annual growth 2.0%. People per sq.km. 28. Only 3% live in the eastern half of the country.

Peoples

Spanish-speaking 97.4%. Approximate composition: Mestizo (Eurindian) 49%, Mu-

latto (Eurafrican) 21%, European 20%, African 7%.

Amerindians 1.6%. Approximately 100 tribes in about 10 language families. Largest: Guajiro 100,000; Paez 40,000; Catio 20,000; Guahibo 20,000.

Other 1%. Lebanese 120,000; Chinese 5,000, etc.

Literacy 84%. *Official language:* Spanish. *All languages* 75. *Bible translations* 1 Bible, 12 New Testaments, 29 portions.

Capital: Bogota 7 million. Other cities: Medellin 300,000, Cali 200,000, Barranquilla 1,500,000. Urbanization 67%.

Economy: Major export earners: coffee (legal) and cocaine (illegal). Income/person $1,220 (7% of USA). A great difference between incomes of rich and poor, but a growing middle class.

Politics: Independent from Spain in 1819. A democratic republic, but with several dictatorships and civil wars this century. The period of anarchy and civil war 1948–60 became known as "La Violencia," during which 300,000 died. The country is plagued by crime, Communist guerrilla movements, and narcotics terrorists. The latter became so powerful through intrigue, corruption and murder that the integrity of the State was threatened. In 1990 the presidential candidate most opposed to the drug barons was elected.

Religion: The Roman Catholic church is the state church and is accorded a privileged position. Since 1974 there has been considerable freedom for Evangelicals to evangelize, though policy towards foreign missions has been somewhat restrictive.

Nonreligious/Atheist 1.2%.
Tribal religions 1.1%.
Muslim 0.2%.
Baha'i 0.1%.
Christian 97.4%.
  Roman Catholic 93%. 27,250,000 adherents; 14,000,000 members.
  Marginal groups (8) 1.1%. 330,000 adherents; 114,000 members. Largest (adherents): Unitarian Pentecostals 190,000; Jehovah's Witnesses 96,400; Mormons 39,500.
  Protestant 3.1%. 900,000 adherents; 284,000 members. Denominations 97+.
  Largest (adult members):
  Seventh-Day Adventist Church 76,000
  International Church of Foursquare Gospel 35,000
  Christian Crusade Church 21,000
  Christian & Missionary Alliance 16,400
  Panamerican Mission 15,000
  Assemblies of God 11,500
  Amerindian churches (New Tribes Mission) 10,000
  Southern Baptist Convention 9,300
  Association of Evangelical Churches of East (The Evangelical Alliance Mission) 9,000
  Missionary Evangelical Union (Gospel Missionary Union) 7,900
  Evangelical 2.4% of population.
Missionaries to Colombia 1,150 (1:25,500 people) in 70 agencies. Missionaries from within Colombia approximately 40 (1:22,500 Protestants).

CZECHOSLOVAKIA
Area 128,000 sq.km. Landlocked state in central Europe.
Population 15,600,000. Annual growth 0.2%. People per sq.km. 121.
Peoples
Czech 62.5%. In center and west.
Slovak 29%. In east.
Other minorities 8.5%. Magyar (Hungarian) 620,000; Gypsy 385,000; Polish 80,000; German 77,000.

Literacy 99%. *Official languages:* Czech, Slovak. *All languages* 8. *Bible translations* 6 Bibles, 1 portion.
Capital: Prague 1,300,000. Urbanization 74%.

Economy: Highly industrialized and efficient before the Communist takeover. The efficient industrialized economy before World War II was devastated by both the war and four decades of Communist economics. The long and painful restoration of a free market has begun. Income/person $5,800 (31% of USA).
Politics: A federal republic of two nations—Czechs (Bohemia, Moravia and parts of Silesia) in the west and Slovaks in the east. Although a minority party, the Communists seized power in 1948. The liberalizing policies of the Dubcek Government (1966–68) were ended by the Russian invasion of 1968. The sudden and dramatic collapse of the hard-line Communist regime in November 1989 opened the way to free up the country's institutions and industry under the popular leadership of President Vaclav Havel. Yet the passage of a July 1991 law by the Federal Assembly allowing a national vote on the constitution split the Czech and Slovak national councils, threatening a national breakup.
Religion: After years of harsh control, repression, and persecution of Christians and churches during the Communist period,

religious freedom is flourishing. On July 4, 1991, the "Law on Freedom of Religion and the Churches" was passed, granting legal freedom to publish religious materials and teach biblical knowledge as a humanities course in the universities. Seminaries are training leadership. Christians can freely evangelize.

Nonreligious/Atheist 21.3%.

Jewish 0.1%. 4,000 left of the 360,000 in 1938.

Christian 78.6%.

Roman Catholic 68%. 10,540,000 adherents. Only 1 million attend church regularly.

Other Catholic 3.2%. 501,000 adherents. Mainly the Czech Hussite Church which broke away from Rome in 1920.

Orthodox 1.2%. 181,000 adherents.

Protestant 6%. 935,000 adherents; 570,000 members. Denominations 16. Largest (adult members):

Slovak Evangelical Lutheran Church 369,000

Slovak Reformed Church est. 130,000

Evangelical Church of Czech Brethren 200,000

United Methodist Church 10,000

Moravian Church 9,700

Seventh-Day Adventist Church 7,800

Church of Brethren (Congregational) 8,000

Brethren est. 5,400

Pentecostal Church (Assemblies of God) 4,600

Evangelical 2.1% of population.

Silerian Lutheran Church 46,000

EGYPT

Area 1,001,000 sq.km. 96% desert, and only 3% arable land along the banks of the Nile and around the Western Desert oases.

Population 56,300,000. Annual growth 2.8%. People per sq.km. 45; in fertile areas 1,875 people/sq.km. The rapid loss of cultivable land bodes ill for the future.

Peoples

Egyptian 86.4%. Speaking Arabic, but essentially the same people of ancient and biblical history.

Arab 6.3%. Lebanese, Sudanese, Yemeni, Palestinian, etc.

Nubian 3%. Mostly living in the southern part of the country.

Bedouin 2%. Many still nomadic in Sinai, etc.

Berber 2%. Most now Arabized, but a few still speaking a Berber dialect at the Siwa Oasis.

Other minorities 0.3%. Westerner, Armenian, Greek, etc.

Literacy 48%. *Official language:* Arabic. *All languages* 6. *Bible translations* 2 Bibles, 1 New Testament, 2 portions.

Capital: Cairo est. 12,000,000. Other major cities: Alexandria 3,162,000. Thirteen other cities with over 100,000 people. Rapid urbanization—now at 48%.

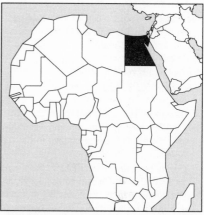

Economy: Poor, crippled by high birth rate and lack of agricultural land, but somewhat alleviated by USA aid and remittances from 1.8 million Egyptians resident abroad, but this number and source of income is rapidly diminishing. Income/person $710 (4% of USA).

Politics: President Sadat's diplomacy (1970–81) ended the dominance of the USSR (now the Commonwealth of Independent States) and won control of the valuable Suez Canal and Sinai oilfields from Israel as an outcome of the 1973 Yom Kippur War. The generally popular peace treaty with Israel in 1979 was bitterly opposed by many Arab nations and Muslim fundamentalists within the country and led to Egypt's isolation in the Middle East and Sadat's assassination. The present government of President Mubarak is cautiously introducing political liberizations and seeking rapprochement with other Arab states. The economic woes of the land are causing many to turn to fundamentalist Islamic political movements.

Religion: Islam is the state religion. Fundamentalist Muslims are pressing for the full Islamization of society. Christians are free to worship but not to openly evangelize Muslims. The 1981 clampdown on both Muslim fundamentalists and Christian leaders had its roots in tensions caused by enforced conversions to Islam and successful evangelism by Christians.

Muslim 82.4%. Cairo is the intellectual capital of Islam. Muslim fundamentalism has become a significant force over the last 10 years.

Nonreligious/Atheist 0.4%.

Christian 17.2%. Though officially only 6%. Gradual erosion of this percentage through high emigration to the West (130,000 in North America and Australia), lower birth rate, and pressures to convert to Islam.

>   *Coptic Orthodox Church* 15%. Practicing 83%. 7,600,000 adherents; 4,400,000 members. One of the ancient churches that has survived 1,300 years of Muslim Arab persecution and discrimination.
>
>   *Other Orthodox Churches* (5) 0.7%.
>
>   *Greek Orthodox* 350,000
>
>   *Roman Catholic* 0.33%. 155,000 adherents; 89,000 members. 7 groups and traditions.
>
>   *Protestant* 0.85%. 410,000 adherents; 154,000 members. Denominations 46. Largest (adult members):
>
>   Coptic Evangelical Church 88,000
>
>   Assemblies of God 13,000
>
>   Brethren (2 groups) 10,400
>
>   Free Methodist Church 9,000
>
>   *Protestant Evangelical* 0.69% of population, but possibly 3% if Orthodox included.

Missionaries to Egypt estimated 150 (1:322,000 people) in 27 agencies. Missionaries from Egypt 25 (1:16,400 Protestants) in 3 agencies.

ETHIOPIA

Area 1,222,000 sq.km. Fertile mountain plateau surrounded by the deserts of the Red Sea coast, and the Somali, Kenya and Sudan borders.

Population 50,800,000. Annual growth 2.1%. People per sq.km. 42.

Peoples: There are over 200 major dialects spoken, but the 1974 revolution has stimulated a greater sense of national identity in this diversity.

Semitic origin 36%. Amharas (4 groups) 8,840,000 in Central and Northern Highlands; Tigrinya 2,120,000 in Central Eritrea; Tigre 700,000 in Northern Eritrea; and Gurage (4) 1,000,000 in Southern Highlands. They originally came from Arabia, conquering and mixing with the local Hamitic peoples.

Cushitic 57%. Over 52 peoples in the east, center, and south.

>   *Oromo* 14,000,000 (Wolayta 3,400,000; Wallega 1,650,000; Arusi 1,050,000; Konso 400,000; and at least 14 other smaller groups.)
>
>   *Somali* 2,000,000—but about 500,000 are refugees in Somalia.
>
>   *Other significant peoples:* Sidamo 1,000,000; Hadiya 950,000; Kambalfa 460,000; Gideo 390,000; Kafa

230,000; Afar 200,000; Awiya
160,000; Boran 150,000; Beja 90,000;
Ari 60,000; She 50,000; Burji 30,000;
Bako 25,000; Banna 25,000.
Nilotic-Sudanic 6%. Twenty-two peoples
largely in south and west: Gumuz 250,000;
Berta 140,000; Murle 140,000; Anuak
130,000; Ma'en 130,000; Nuer 130,000;
Masengo 100,000; Nara 100,000; Tirma
50,000; Koma 43,000; Turkana 30,000;
Mabaan 7,000; etc., and Kunama (Eritrea)
200,000.
Falasha Jew 15,000. Black Jews who still
practice Old Testament animal sacrifices.
Foreign 0.8%. Arab 90,000; Eastern European; Westerner, etc.
Literacy 20%. *Official language:* Amharic,
65% of population are able to speak it. *All
languages* over 100. *Bible translations* 5
Bibles, 6 New Testaments, 10 portions.
Capital: Addis Ababa 1,845,000. Other major
city: Asmara 550,000. Urbanization 15%.
Economy: A semifeudal society radically
transformed by the changes and upheavals
following the 1974 revolution. The country's economy has been devastated by
drought, war, and ruinous Marxist
collectivisation attempts. In desperation
the government has opted to open up the
economy by drastic liberalizing reforms.
Terrible famines in 1984/85 and 1989/90
have caused the death of over one million
people.
Politics: The government of Emperor Haile
Selassie was overthrown in 1974 by the
army, but the Provisional Military Administrative Council did not gain full political
control until 1976. The Marxist-oriented
government has had to contend with six
separatist movements—the major ones
being in the Ogaden in the east and Eritrea
and Tigre Provinces in the north; bitter
fighting still continues. Economic necessity and world events have forced the government to renounce Marxism, and seek
more ties with the West. The isolation of
the government is such that its survival is
in doubt. The two most successful guerilla
movements in Eritrea and Tigre in the
north are strongly Marxist in ideology.

Religion: During the Marxist period 1974–
90, all religions were opposed and Chris-
tians especially subjected to much
persecution, and limitations. These pres-
sures are now reduced.
Nonreligious/Atheist 3%.
Tribal religions 10%. Mainly among the
peoples of the south and west.
Muslim 35%. Strong in the north (Tigre), east
(Afars), and southeast (Somalis and
Oromo groups).
Christian 52%. Majority among Amharas,
Tigre and many Oromo peoples of the
Highlands.
   Ethiopian Orthodox Church 41%.
   14,600,000 adherents; 8,600,000
   members.
   Roman Catholic 0.7%. 242,000 adherents;
   140,000 members.
   Protestant 10%. 3,580,000 adherents;
   1,700,000 members. Denominations 36.
   Largest (adherents):
   Kale Hiywot Church (KHC) 1,200,000
   Mekane Yesu Church (ECMY) 816,000
   Full Gospel Believers' Church 100,000
   Seventh-Day Adventist Church 35,000
   Assemblies of God 30,000
   Mulu Wengel Church 19,000
   Yihiywot Birhan Church 15,000
   Meseret Kristos Church 6,000
   Emmanuel Baptist Church 3,200
   Evangelical Church of Eritrea 2,500
   Evangelical 9.6% of population. There
   are also Orthodox Christians who are
   evangelical.
Missionaries to Ethiopia approximately 400
(1:89,000 people). Missionaries from within
Ethiopia approximately 50 (1:71,600).

FRANCE
Area 551,000 sq.km. The largest country in
Western Europe.
Population 56,300,000. Annual growth
0.4%. People per sq.km. 102.
Peoples
Indigenous 90.2%.
   French 79%.
   Minorities 10%. Alsatian 1,465,000;
   Breton 1,302,000; Flemish 380,000,
   Corsican 290,000; Basque 160,000.

Other minorities 2%. Jews 750,000; West Indian Antillean 230,000; Gypsy 160,000.

Foreign residents 9%.

North African/Middle Easterner 4%. Algerian 1,172,000; Moroccan 640,000; Tunisian 298,000; Turk 160,000; Irani 30,000.

European 3.2%. Portuguese 857,000; Italian 469,000; Spanish 430,000; Armenian 210,000; Polish 100,000; Yugoslavian 70,000.

Asian 1.2%. Vietnamese 250,000; Chinese 190,000; Laotian 100,000; Cambodian 70,000.

African 0.5%. Mostly from Francophone West Africa. Malian 20,000.

Literacy 98%. *Official language:* French.

Capital: Paris 10,413,000. The capital dominates the life of the country. Other major cities: Lyon 1,300,000; Marseille 1,230,000; Lille 1,100,000. Urbanization 79%.

Economy: Economic stability and growth gave the nation one of the highest standards of living in Europe. Oil price rises and world recession have bitten deep into those standards. Income/person $12,860 (70% of USA). Inflation 10%.

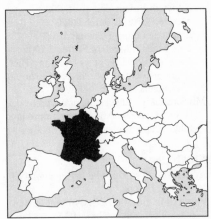

Politics: Democratic republic with strong executive presidency. A member of the European Community, and pressing for economic union within the EEC.

Religion: Secular state with freedom of religion.

Nonreligious/Atheist 16.0%. Many were baptized as Christians.

Muslim 4.6%. North African, African, Turk, etc.

Jewish 1.1%.

Christian 78%.

Roman Catholic 74%. Regular practicing 6%. 40,500,000 adherents; 29,800,000 members.

Other Catholic 0.2%. Over 73 small groups.

Orthodox groups (17) 0.8%.

Marginal groups 0.6%. Over 25 cults. Largest (adherents): Jehovah's Witnesses 166,100; Mormons 13,100.

Protestant 2%. 1,140,000 adherents; 655,000 members. Denominations 60 (also many independent congregations). Some of the largest (adult members):

Reformed Church 274,000
Lutheran Church (3 groups) 145,000
Assemblies of God 75,000
Reformed Church of Alsace & Lorraine 47,000
Gypsy Pentecostal Church 15,600
Free Pentecostal Church 8,000
Federation of Baptist Churches 3,800
Brethren 3,200

Evangelical 0.63% of population.

Missionaries to France 905 (1:60,000 people) in 80 agencies. Missionaries from France 373 (1:3,100 Protestants) in 32 agencies.

GERMANY

The Federal Republic of Germany and German Democratic Republic

Note: Statistics partly amalgamated, reflecting reunification.

Area 356,000 sq.km. (30% of which was the area of former East Germany). People per sq.km. 219.

Population 78,100,000 (of which 21% are of former East Germany). A further 3.5 million Germans live in Eastern Europe, Americas and Namibia.

Peoples

German 93%. Massive immigration from USSR and Eastern Europe Germans during 1989/90—possibly 300,000 over that period.

Other minorities 2%. Danes, Sorbs, Wends, etc.

Foreign 7% Migrant "guest workers" and their families from:

  S. European: Yugoslavs 613,000; Italians 565,000; Greeks 292,000; Spaniards 166,000; Portuguese 99,000.

  Middle Eastern/North African: Turks 1,552,000; Moroccans 44,000; Iranians 33,000; Tunisians 25,000, etc.

  Asian: Chinese 40,000; Tamils from Sri Lanka 30,000; Vietnamese 26,000; Pakistanis and Indians 16,000, Koreans 14,000; Indonesians 9,000; Japanese 6,000.

Literacy 99%. *Official language:* German.

Capital: Bonn (West) 515,000; East Berlin (East) 1,200,000. The new capital of the reunited Germany will probably be Berlin. Other major city complexes: Ruhr Area 8,850,000; Hamburg 2,810,000; Stuttgart 2,790,000, Frankfurt 2,680,000; Munich 2,310,000. Urbanization 85%.

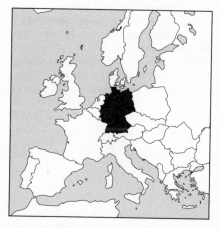

Economy: Highly industrialized and strong export-oriented economy with enormous trade surpluses. A leading member of the European Community and committed to the financial integration of the EC. Now facing the enormous cost of incorporating East Germany and rebuilding its shattered economy. The ecological disaster of Communist-run industries will take many de-

cades to rectify. Income/person: W - $14,460 (79% of USA); E - $6,000 (33% of USA).

Politics: Germany lost much of her eastern territories to the USSR and Poland at the end of World War II. The remaining third of the country was occupied by the Russians, who still maintain a large military presence. The collapse of the hard-line Honecker regime opened the way for democratic elections in the spring of 1990, rejection of Socialism and Marxism and a rapid move toward reunification with West Germany, which began with monetary reunification on July 1, 1990 and culminated with political reunification on October 3, 1990.

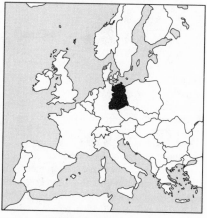

EAST GERMANY
(German Democratic Republic)

Religion: After 40 years of subtle pressures on the numerically strong Protestant church, there has been complete religious freedom since 1989.

Nonreligious/Atheist 38.7%.

Christian 61.5%. Nominal 16.4%. Affiliated 45.1%.

  Roman Catholic 7.4%. Practicing 20%. 1,250,000 adherents; 1,000,000 members.

  Marginal groups 0.87%. 147,000 adherents. New Apostolic 105,00 adherents, etc.

  Protestant 36.7%. 6,200,000 adherents; 4,910,000 members. Denominations 19. Eight regional churches in two major groups (adherents):

EKU (Lutheran/Reformed) 3,000,000
VELK (Lutheran) 2,900,000
Free Church (adult members):
Methodist Church 35,000
Free Church Union (Baptist) 22,000
Seventh-Day Adventist Church 10,000
Independent Lutheran 10,000
Reformed Church 8,400
Brethren 6,000
Evangelical 11% of population.

WEST GERMANY

Religion: Religious freedom, but close cooperation between the government and the Roman Catholic church and Protestant established churches, Evangelische Kirche in Deutschland, in religious education, radio, TV, church taxation through state channels, etc.
Nonreligious/Atheist 5%.
Muslim 3%. Almost entirely immigrant minorities.
Jewish 32,000 (564,000 in 1932 before the Nazi pogroms).
Christian 92%. Affiliated 86%. Only a minority of the population is involved in Christian activities.
   Roman Catholic 42%. 25,600,000 adherents; 19,700,000 members. 70% hardly ever attend church.
   Other Catholic groups (43) 0.1%.
   Orthodox Churches (13) 0.8%. 485,000 adherents. Greeks, East Europeans.
   Marginal groups (34) 1.5%. 892,000 adherents; 515,000 members. Largest

(adherents): New Apostolic Church 482,000; Jehovah's Witnesses (2 groups) 245,000; Mormons 27,500.
   Protestant (162 groups) 43%. 25,700,000 adherents; 6,670,000 members. There are two major groupings. *Evangelische Kirche in Deutschland (EKD)* 17 territorial or State churches. 24,500,000 adherents. Regular church attendance 1,400,000 (5.5% of those affiliated). *Free churches* 1,200,000 adherents; 420,000 members. Total weekly church attendance 700,000. Denominations 150. Largest (adult members):
Baptist Union 67,500
Independent Lutheran Church 37,000
Methodist Church 33,500
Brethren 32,000
Seventh-Day Adventist Church 25,000
Free Evangelical Church 24,000
Association of Free Pentecostal Churches 19,000
Mennonite Church (2) 15,800
Conservative Evangelical 7% of population.
Missionaries to Germany 680. Missionaries from Germany 2,686 (1:9,600 Protestants) in 62 agencies, including 311 short-term workers.

Berlin has long been a divided and depressing city, the western part being surrounded by the Communist-built "Wall of Shame." The euphoric dismantling of the Wall in 1989 and reunification of the city has brought a new hope and many opportunities for evangelism. Pray that the Christians may use them. Over 10% of the city is Turkish.

GHANA

Area 238,500 sq.km. Grasslands in north, farmland and forest in south. Center dominated by 520 km.-long Lake Volta.
Population 15,000,000. Annual growth 3.1%. People per sq.km. 63. Higher density in south.
Peoples: About 100 ethnic groups and 3 major language divisions.
Kwa 75%. 5 major subgroups in center and south.
   Akan (25 groups): Ashanti 1,900,000;

Fante 1,700,000; Brong 708,000, etc., most speak dialects of Twi.

Ewe (3) 1.9 million in southeast.

Ga-Adangme (4) 1.3 million around Accra.

Guan (13) 510,000 in center and north.

C. Togo (14) 125,000 on eastern border.

Gur 22%. 5 major sub-groups in north.

Mole-Dagbani (13). Dagomba 460,000; Dagari-Birifor 420,000; Frafra 400,000; Kusasi 256,000.

Gurma (5). Konkomba 450,000; Bimoba 68,000, etc.

Grusi (5). Sisaala 300,000; Kasena 78,000, etc.

Mande 0.9%. 2 small groups.

Foreign 2%.

Literacy 35%. *Official language:* English. *All languages* 60. *Bible translations* 4 Bibles, 9 New Testaments, 14 portions.

Capital: Accra 1,800,000. Other cities: Kumasi 800,000; Sekondi-Takoradi 255,000. Urbanization 32%.

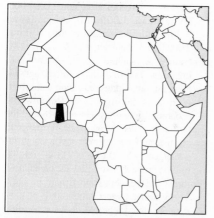

Economy: Slowly recovering from almost total collapse in 1982. Earlier government overspending, mismanagement and corruption reduced this once prosperous land to poverty. Main exports are cocoa, gold and timber. Living standards were reduced by uncontrolled inflation, periods of drought and enforced repatriation of Ghanaians from Nigeria 1983-85. Since 1984 Ghana has begun to recover and the shattered economic infrastructure slowly repaired. Income/person $390 (2% of USA).

Politics: Independent from Britain in 1957. Nkrumah's "socialist" experiment was a disaster from which the nation will take years to recover. There have been five military regimes and three short-lived civilian governments since Nkrumah's overthrow in 1966. The government has had close links with Libya and retained power despite early unpopularity and harshness of leftist elements to political opponents. The government has become more relaxed and pragmatic in international relations since 1984.

Religion: Secular state with religious freedom, but some members of the military government are hostile to Christianity and have sought to hamper the spread of the gospel.

African traditional religions 31%. Mainly among peoples on the northern border.

Muslim 17%. Sunni 9%, Ahmaddiya 8%. The majority among the Dagomba, Gonja and Wali; growing minority among other northern peoples.

Christian 52%. Nominal 5%. Affiliated 47%. Note that figures are very tentative for some denominations.

Roman Catholic 11.3%. Practicing 35%. 1,430,000 adherents; 758,000 members.

African marginal groups (700+) 12%. 1,500,000 adherents.

Foreign marginal groups (14) 1.2%. 157,000 adherents; 47,430 members. Largest: Jehovah's Witnesses 27,730 members.

Protestant 22.4%. Denominations 60+. 2,090,000 adherents; 1,000,000 members. Largest (adult members):
Methodist Church 186,966
Church of Pentecost 159,915
Presbyterian Church 132,860
Evangelical Presbyterian Church 76,400(?)
Anglican Church 64,000(?)
Seventh-Day Adventist Church 56,000
Apostolic Church 32,000(?)
Christ Apostolic Church 30,000(?)
Assemblies of God 20,000

Southern Baptist Convention 19,000
African Methodist Episcopal Zion 17,000
Evangelical 9% of population.
Missionaries to Ghana 380 (1:33,400
people) in 50 agencies. Missionaries from
within Ghana 25(?) (1:83,600 Protestants).

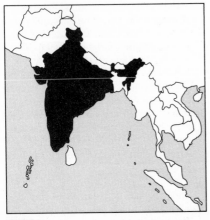

INDIA

Area 3,204,000 sq.km. 22 union states and 9
union territories. Geographically India
dominates South Asia and the Indian
Ocean.

Population 853,400,000. Annual growth
2.2%; 18.5 million increase every year.
People per sq.km. 266. Nearly 16% of the
world's population is Indian, living on
2.4% of the world's land surface.

Peoples: The great racial, ethnic, religious
and linguistic diversity makes a simple
subdivision of the population difficult.

Ethno-Linguistic:
  Indo-Aryan 72%. In Northern and Central
  India.
  Dravidian 25%. Majority in Southern In-
  dia.
  Sino-Tibetan 3%. Northern border and
  Northeast India.

Caste: A system that pervasively influences
every religion in India, to a lesser or
greater extent, but which is fundamental
to Hinduism. Caste discrimination is forbidden by the constitution, but it is socially important for over 80% of the
population.

Caste Hindus 64%. (Brahmin, Kshatriya,
  Vaisya, Sudra).
Harijan (Outcastes, Untouchables) 14%.
  Classified by the government as
  "Scheduled Castes."
Tribal peoples 7%. *Muslims* 12%. *Chris-
  tians* 3%, etc., are considered outside
  the caste structure. The former are clas-
  sified as "Scheduled Tribes."

Literacy 36%. *Official languages* 14; Hindi
31%, Telugu 8%, Tamil 7%, Urdu 5%, Gujarati
4.6%, Kannada 4%, Malayalam 4%, Oriya
4%, Punjabi 2.5%, Assamese 1.6%,
Kashmiri 0.5%. *Nationally used languages:*
Hindi and English; the latter being important
in education. *All languages* 1,658 (1971
census). 329 listed by Summer Institute of
Linguistics. Those with over 5,000 speakers
number 350. *Bible translations* 36 Bibles,
25 New Testaments, 54 portions. At least 13
New Testaments need a major revision.

Capital: Delhi 6,600,000. Other major cities:
Calcutta 10,200,000, Bombay 10,000,000,
Madras 6,900,000, Bangalore 4,000,000,
Hyderabad 3,000,000, Ahmedabad
3,000,000, Pune 2,000,000, Kanpur
2,000,000. Urbanization 23%.

Economy: Agriculture and industry are both
important. 74% of the labor force is agricultural, but rapid industrialization and urbanization is taking place. Remarkable
economic growth has been offset by the high
birth rate, illiteracy, prejudice, resistance to
change, and bureaucratic inefficiency. In-
come/person $300 (2% of USA). Yet 300
million probably live below the breadline.

Politics: Independent from Britain in 1947.
The world's largest functioning democracy. Troubled relations with surrounding
nations; two wars with Pakistan and one
with China. Internal tensions have arisen
because of regional, caste, and religious
loyalties that have sometimes broken out
into violence and rioting. The Sikh separatist movements in the Punjab and the
Muslim independence movement in
Kashmir have developed into virtual guerilla warfare and threaten the unity of the
country.

Religion: India is a secular state that grants

freedom to all religions to practice and propagate their faith. In practice there has been strong pressure from Hindu militants to prevent proselytization at a state and central level. Several states have discriminatory legislation against religious minorities, but the federal government has not followed this course. The 1989 elections brought in a new government coalition in which Hindu nationalist parties participate—a fact which could increase pressures on Christians and Muslims.

Hindu 82%. Figure somewhat raised by the automatic inclusion of many of the tribal animists. Hinduism is a social system and philosophy and readily absorbs elements of any religion with which it comes into contact. Popular Hinduism is idolatrous. Intellectual Hinduism is philosophical and mystical and has a growing appeal to Western countries. India suffers under its fatalism, castism, 200 million holy cows, 33 million gods, etc., to its economic and spiritual detriment.

Muslim 11.8% (Muslims claim 13%). A widespread minority, but a majority in Kashmir and Lakshadweep, and growing among Harijans.

Sikhs 1.92%. Majority in Punjab. Many in armed forces.

Tribal religions approximately 1.5%. Among scheduled tribes.

Buddhist 0.7%. A small minority in the land of its origin. Majority among Tibetans, several Northeastern tribes and growing among Harijans in Maharashtra.

Jain 0.47%.

Other religions and persuasions 0.4%. *Baha'i, Zoroastrian* 75,000; *Jews* 6,000.

Christian 2.61% officially (churches claim 3.6%). A great variation in percentages in the different states.

> *Roman Catholic* 1.55%. Strongest in the south and in Goa. Practicing 70%. 11,700,000 adherents.

> *Syrian Orthodox* 0.24%. 1,840,000 adherents. Predominantly in Kerala, southwest India; descended from churches planted by the Apostle Thomas in the first century.

Protestant 1.79%. More numerous in the south and northeast. 13,400,000 adherents; 5,480,000 members. Denominations 320+. Largest (adult members):
Church of South India (CSI) 600,000
United Lutheran Church 464,000
Council of Baptist Churches in N.E. 400,444
Methodist Church of South Asia 400,000
Salvation Army 400,000
Church of North India (CNI) 324,000
Mar Thoma Syrian Church 270,000
Presbyterian Church of N.E. 201,000
Telugu Baptist Churches 128,000
Seventh-Day Adventist Church 124,000
Independent Pentecostal Church of God 105,000
Baptist Convention of Northern areas 84,500
Christian Assemblies/Brethren 71,000
Church of God (Cleveland) 43,000
Assemblies (Bakht Singh) approximately 42,000

Evangelical 0.7% of population.

Missionaries to India 900 (1:850,000 people), with a rapid reduction in numbers. Missionaries from within India 4,200 in about 120 agencies. Not all are in cross-cultural ministries.

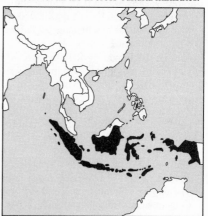

INDONESIA

Area 1,920,000 sq.km. 13,500 islands of which 3,000 are inhabited and cover 9,500,000 sq.km. of the Indian/Pacific Oceans, 27 provinces.

Population 188,300,000. The world's fifth most populous nation. Annual growth

2.0%. People per sq.km. 98; varying from Java's 700 to Irian Jaya's two.

Peoples. Major races:

Malay 94%. Seventeen languages with more than one million speakers of which the largest are: Javanese 42%, Sundanese 13.6%, Madurese 7%, Minangkabau 3.3%, Batak 2.9%, Sumatran Malay 2.9%, Bugis 2.8% Balinese 2.1%.

Chinese 4%. Many are becoming integrated into the Indonesian majority. Only 20% still use Chinese dialects. Scattered throughout the nation.

Irianese/Papuan peoples 1.2%. In Timor, Alor, Halmahera and Irian Jaya.

Other 0.8%. Arabs, Indians, Europeans, mixed race.

Literacy 64%; rising rapidly. *Official language:* Indonesian. Its increasing use is both unifying the nation and lessening the importance of smaller languages to the younger generation. *All languages 583;* 17 spoken by more than one million speakers; 238 spoken in Irian Jaya. *Bible translations* 8 Bibles, 21 New Testaments, 39 portions.

Capital: Jakarta 9,086,000. Other cities: Surabaya 3,054,000; Bandung 1,878,000; Medan 1,600,000; Semarang 1,056,000. Urbanization 24%.

Economy: Based on agriculture and oil. Enormous potential with impressive growth over the last 20 years. A rise in living standards is being slowed by overpopulation in Java, difficult communications by land and sea and cumbersome bureaucracy. Income/person $450 (2.5% of USA).

Politics: Independent from the Netherlands 1945–49 after 350 years of colonial rule. The abortive Communist coup in 1965 radically moderated the political orientation of the country. A strong presidential military-civilian government. President Suharto seeks to balance tendencies to religious extremisms and local secessionist nationalisms in this culturally diverse nation.

Religion: Monotheism and communal peace are the bases of the government ideology of "Pancasila." All are free to choose to follow Islam, Hinduism, Buddhism, or Christianity; but the numerical and political strength of Islam is frequently exercised to give it preferential treatment and limit Christian expansion. There are, therefore, some restrictions on open proselytism.

Muslim 78-80%. This figure needs to be qualified. 29% of the electorate voted in 1982 for parties that seek to make Indonesia an Islamic state. 43% could be defined as Quranic Muslims, living by many of Islam's tenets. A further 35% are statistical Muslims, who, though enumerated as Muslims for the census, are actually followers of the Javanese mystical religion that predates Islam, or else animists who have (to a lesser or greater extent) accepted some of the outward aspects of Islam. Islam is strongest in Sumatra, Java and in many coastal areas in the east.

Animist 5.1%. Discouraged by the government but strong among some peoples in Irian Jaya, East Timor, Sumba, and inland Sumatra, Kalimantan, Sulawesi, etc. Folk Islam followed by the majority is strongly influenced by animism.

Hindu 3.1%. Majority on Bali and among Tengger in East Java.

Buddhist/Chinese religions 1.22%. Mainly Chinese.

Nonreligious/Atheist 1.4%. Mainly Chinese and underground Communists.

Christian 11.2%. Church figures indicate 13.2%. A large number of known "sympathizers" would further increase this total.

Roman Catholic 3.5%. In the majority on Flores and East Timor. Practicing 74%. 4,900,000 adherents; 2,600,000 members.

Foreign and indigenous marginal groups 0.1%.

Protestant 9.7%. 16,100,000 adherents; 7,100,000 members.

Denominations 250+. Largest (adherents):

Regional Reformed Church (32) (Dutch and Swiss missions) 5,600,000
Pentecostal Church (72) 4,200,000
Lutheran Church (13)

(German and Scandinavian missions) 3,000,000

KINGMI (Christian & Missionary Alliance) 325,000

Seventh-Day Adventist Church 168,000

GIIJ (Unevangelized Fields Mission, Asia Pacific Christian Mission, RBMU International) 100,000

GMI (Methodist) 94,000

Churches related to WEC International-Indonesian

Missionary Fellowship 30,000

Churches related to The Evangelical Alliance Mission 20,000

Evangelical 4.3% of population.

Missionaries to Indonesia 700 (1:269,000 people)

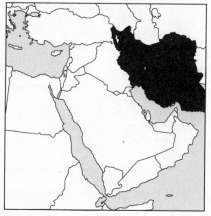

IRAN

Area 1,648,000 sq.km. A central desert ringed by mountains.

Population 55,700,000. Annual growth 3.4%. People per sq.km. 34.

Peoples: Over 45 peoples/tribes speaking at least 23 distinct languages. Many are small nomadic groups.

Indo-Iranic (22) 76.8%. Persian (speaking Farsi) 22,300,000, the dominant people. Kurds 3,800,000; also the related Luri-Bakhtiari peoples 3,400,000.

Turkic (18) 21%. Azerbaijani 7,600,000; Turkoman 710,000; Afshar 370,000; Qashqa'i 230,000, etc.

Arab (2) 1.5%. *Other* (5) 0.7%. Armenian 150,000 estimated; Assyrian 40,000 esti-

mated; Jews 50,000. Non-Muslim groups decreasing by emigration since the revolution.

Literacy 44%. *Official language:* Farsi. *All languages* 31. *Bible translations* 4 Bibles, 4 portions.

Capital: Tehran 6,700,000. Other cities: Rai 1,100,000, Qazvin 1,000,000, Isfahan 1,000,000, Mashad 1,000,000. Urbanization 50%.

Economy: Material progress under the Shah was reversed by the religious bigotry, national paranoia, and violence that followed the 1979 revolution. The eight-year Gulf War severely strained the oil-based economy. The diplomatic isolation of the country further prolongs the long economic recovery. Income/person $2,500 in 1982.

Politics: The progressive, West-leaning, but unpopular Shah was deposed in the Shi'ite Muslim Revolution, and a theocratic Islamic Republic formed in 1979. Regional loyalties and anarchy brought the country close to civil war and ruin. The invasion by Iraq in 1980 was the start of the bitter eight-year Gulf War. The casualties were high with over one million killed, 80% of which were Iranian. The death of the Ayatollah Khomeini in 1989 has only led to a slight moderation of the political extremes of the revolutionary period.

Religion: Shi'a Islam is the state religion. All deviations from Islam are liable to mean severe persecution. Other religious minorities tolerated.

Muslim 98%. Shi'a 91%, Sunni 7% (Kurds, Baluchis and Turkoman). Iran is the power house for exporting Shi'ite revolution to the Middle East and beyond.

Baha'i 0.8%. 340,000 followers of a Persian world religion founded in 1844. Severely persecuted as a heresy of Islam.

Parsi (Zoroastrian) 0.09%. 39,000 followers of Persia's ancient pre-Islamic religion.

Jewish 0.09%. 40,000 estimated. Farsi-speaking Jews, many of whom are descendants of those exiled to Persia at the time of Daniel.

Christian 0.4%.

Orthodox Churches (4) 0.34%. 153,000

adherents, 100,000 members. Largest (adherents):

Armenian Apostolic Church 140,000
Nestorian Church (Assyrians) 12,000
Roman Catholic 0.03%. 17,000 (3 different rites—Chaldean, Latin and Armenian.)
Protestant 0.02%. 8,700 adherents; 3,990 members. Denominations 20. Largest (adult members):
Evangelical Church (Presbyterian) 2,730
Pentecostal Church 1,800
Episcopal (Anglican) 1,200
Evangelical 0.02% of population.
Missionaries to Iran 0.

IRAQ

Area 435,000 sq.km. The site of the biblical Assyrian and Babylonian empires.

Population 18,800,000. Annual growth 3.8%. People per sq.km. 36.

Peoples: Ethnic and religious diversity is responsible for much of Iraq's agonizing recent history.

Arabs 77%. Almost all Muslim; Shi'a 54%, Sunni 23%. Migrant Egyptians 300,000.

Kurds 18%. Mostly Sunni Muslim, but 135,000 are Yezidis, followers of a syncretic form of Islam. The Kurds have been fighting intermittently for autonomy or independence in their northern mountains since 1919. The government took vengeful action on the dissident Kurds after the end of the Gulf War with heavy casualties being inflicted.

Other minorities 5%. Turkoman 386,000; Luri

230,000; Farsi 120,000; Assyrian 60,000; Romany 50,000; Armenian 40,000; Chaldean 35,000; Circassian 9,000.

Literacy 41%. *Official languages:* Arabic, Kurdish in Kurdish districts. *All languages* 18. *Bible translations* 3 Bibles, 1 New Testament, 1 portion.

Capital: Baghdad 6,492,000. Other city: Basra 1,000,000. Urbanization 76%.

Economy: Oil-based economy (since Genesis 11!); profits are used for industrialization. The war with Iran since 1980 has been a serious economic setback.

Politics: A violent revolution in 1958 overthrew the monarchy. The Baathist government has proved cruel in repression of both ethnic minorities and any potential dissent, and was responsible for attacking Iran and starting the Gulf War in 1980. The final months of the war in 1988 ended with moderate victories for Iraq. Iraq now perceives itself to be a regional superpower.

Religion: Islam is the state religion. Christians are tolerated but are occasionally discriminated against.

Muslim 95.8%. Of which 62% are Shi'a, 38% Sunni and 0.9% Yezidis.

Nonreligious/Atheist 0.5%.

Christian 3.4%.
   Roman Catholic (4 different rites) 2.6%. 410,000 adherents.
   Orthodox 0.7%. 110,000 adherents. Denominations 6.
   Protestant 0.02%. 4,200 adherents; 1,960 members. Denominations 12. Largest (adult members):
Arab Evangelical Church 585
Episcopal Church 180
Evangelical 0.02% of population.
Missionaries to Iraq 0.

ITALY

Area 301,000 sq.km. A long peninsula that dominates the central Mediterranean Sea.

Population 57,600,000. Annual growth 0%. People per sq.km. 192.

Peoples

Italian 95.2%. Deep cultural differences exist between the wealthier, and more radical northerners and the poorer, more conservative southerners.

Sardinian 2.2%. Speaking many Sard dialects.

Tyrolean 0.5%. In the northeast, speaking German.

Friulian/Ladin 0.8%. In the north.

Other European 0.5%. Albanian 260,000; French 70,000; British 25,000; Greek 15,000; Gypsy 12,000.

Middle Eastern 0.35%. Almost all Muslim.

Literacy 94%. *Official language:* Italian.

Capital: Rome 3,839,000. Other cities: Milan 6,940,000; Naples 4,116,000; Turin 2,171,000; Genoa 1,195,000; Florence 1,106,000. Urbanization 72%.

Economy: Highly centralized and inefficient government could have brought economic ruin had it not been for the drive of the private industrial sector and the initiative of the 'black' (illegal) economy. The north is very industrialized. Income/person $10,420 (57% of USA). Inflation 14%.

Politics: United as a single state in 1870. Republican democracy since 1946. Weak and unstable succession of 45 governments since the war but with an underlying social stability. National frustration was expressed in the '70s by anarchy, terrorism and increasing support for the Communist party, one of the largest and most democratic outside the Eastern Bloc.

Religion: Roman Catholicism ceased to be the state religion in 1984. All religions have equal freedom before the law.

Nonreligious/Atheist 18.3%. Almost all were baptized in the Catholic church.

Muslim 0.35%.

Jewish 39,000.

Christian 81.1%. Affiliated 80%.

Roman Catholic 78.9%. Practicing 15%. 45,300,000 adherents.

Orthodox 0.07%. 38,000 adherents.

Marginal groups 0.5%. 284,000 adherents. Over 6 cults. Largest (adherents): Jehovah's Witnesses 251,000; New Apostolic Church 20,000; Mormons 12,000.

Protestant 0.78%. 450,000 adherents; 300,000 members. Denominations 22 larger and 125 small groups. Largest (adult members):

Assemblies of God 190,000

Waldensian/Methodist Church 31,000

Brethren assemblies 15,000

Salvation Army 12,000

Lutheran Church 10,000

Seventh-Day Adventist Church 5,300

Baptist Union 4,250

Evangelical 0.6% of population.

Missionaries to Italy 420 (1:137,000 people) in 57 agencies. Missionaries from Italy approximately 20 (1:22,500 Protestants).

JAPAN

Area 372,300 sq.km. A 3,000 km. arc of four large islands (Honshu, Hokkaido, Shikoku, Kyushu) and 3,000 small islands in Northwest Pacific. Mountainous; only 13% can be cultivated.

Population 123,800,000. Annual growth

0.5%. People per sq.km. 332. Concentrated on the narrow coastal plains.

Peoples

Indigenous 99.3%. Japanese; Ainu 20,000 (19 dialects; dying language).

Foreign 0.7%. Korean 720,000; Chinese 55,000

Literacy 100%. *Official language:* Japanese. *Bible translations* 3 Bibles, 1 portion.

Capital: Tokyo. Major conurbations: Tokyo-Yokohama-Kawasaki 21,600,000, Osaka-Kobe 10,000,000, Fukuoko-Kita-Kyushu 3,100,000, Nagoya 2,200,000, Kyoto 1,500,000, Sapporo 1,500,000, Hiroshima 1,000,000. Urbanization 78%.

Economy: The world's most powerful export-oriented economy despite lack of oil and raw materials. Inflation 3%. Income/person $15,770 (86% of USA).

Politics: Stable democratic constitutional monarchy since 1947.

Religion: Freedom of religion is guaranteed to all by the constitution. In practice social and family pressures restrict that freedom. There has been a significant rise in officially approved Shinto practices since the death of Emperor Hirohito in 1989.

Nonreligious/Atheist 12.3%-60%. Many claim no personal religion but follow the customs of Japan's traditional religions.

Shinto/Buddhist 20-60% Polytheistic, ancestor-venerating Shintoism has been much modified by Confucianism and Buddhism. Many follow both Shinto and Buddhist teachings.

New religions (over 120) 23.5%. Most are Buddhist and some Shinto offshoots. Largest (adherents):
Sokka Gakkai 17,000,000
Risshokoseikai 5,500,000
Seichonoie 3,700,000

Christian 2%. Affiliated 1.3%. Many nominal and backsliding Christians.

Roman Catholic 0.34%. Practicing 34%. 405,000 adherents; 283,000 members.

Orthodox (2) 0.02%. Greek Orthodox 24,700 adherents.

Marginal groups (10+) 0.51%. 610,000 adherents; 430,000 members. Some claimed figures appear inflated! Largest (adherents): Unification Church

(Moonies) 270,000; Spirit of Jesus Church (Unitarian) 120,000; Jehovah's Witnesses 92,022; Mormons 71,000; Original Gospel Movement 47,000.

Protestant 0.44%. 534,000 adherents, 309,000 members. Denominations 120+. Largest (adherents):
United Church 192,000
Southern Baptist Convention 26,500
Presbyterian Church of Christ 12,300
Seventh-Day Adventist Church 11,500
Immanuel Church (Wesleyan Missionary) 10,500
NIKK (Japan Evangelistic Band) 10,200
Japan Holiness Church (OMS International) 9,720
Assemblies of God 9,000
NDKK (The Evangelical Alliance Mission) 7,100

Evangelical 0.23% of population.

Missionaries to Japan 2,570 (1:47,000 people) in 140 agencies. Missionaries from Japan 260 (300 Protestants) in 48 agencies.

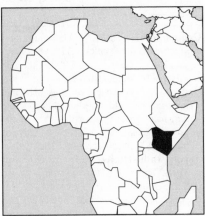

KENYA

Area 582,600 sq.km. Much of the north and east is desert. Most people live in the better watered plateaus of the south and west. Only 9.5% of the land is cultivated.

Population 25,100,000. Annual growth 4.1%. The highest natural incrase in the world. People per sq.km. 43.

Peoples: About 65 ethnic groups.

Bantu peoples 67%. Over 30 peoples:

Kikuyu 4,200,000; Luyia 2,200,000; Kamba 2,200,000; Gusii 1,200,000; Meru 1,100,000; Mijikenda (9 peoples) 969,000; Embu 250,000; Kuria 120,000; Mbere 100,000; Pokomo 60,000.

Nilotic peoples 29.5%. Over 16 peoples: Luo 2,900,000; Kalenjin (5 groups) 2,000,000; Maasai 280,000; Turkana 260,000; Samburu 100,000; Sabaot 95,000.

Cushitic peoples 2.6%. Two major groups: Somali (6) 430,000; Oromo-Boran (5) 130,000.

Other 0.9%. Asian 80,000; Arab 40,000; European 40,000.

Literacy 65%. *Official languages:* English, Swahili. *All languages* 55. *Bible translations* 14 Bibles, 5 New Testaments, 9 portions.

Capital: Nairobi 1,830,000. Other major city: Mombasa 520,000. Urbanization 19%.

Economy: Predominantly agricultural. Good growth following independence was not maintained after 1976 due to world recession, lack of oil, drought and a high population growth. Income/person $340 (2% of USA).

Politics: Independent from Britain in 1963. One-party republic. Relatively stable despite complex tribal divisions that make all political decisions a delicate balancing act.

Religion: Freedom of religion. Government very sympathetic to Christianity. Many Christians in high leadership positions, including the President.

African traditional religions 12.8%

Muslim 6%. Majority among coastal Swahili/Arab, Pokomo, Digo and Northeast desert Somali, Boran, etc.

Baha'i 1.1%.

Hindu/Sikh/Jain 0.3%.

Christian 80%. Nominal 15%. Affiliated 65%.

   Roman Catholic 20.5% (officially 29%). 4,143,000 adherents; 2,200,000 members.

   Orthodox Church 2.2% (officially 2.7%). Indigenous groups linked with Greek Orthodox and Coptic Churches.

Marginal groups 13% (officially 23%). 2,600,000 adherents; 1,200,000 members. Over 152 groups, some close to mainstream Christian doctrine, others very syncretic.

Protestant 29.3%. 5,925,000 adherents; 2,500,000 members. Denominations 60+. Largest (adult members):

Africa Inland Church 540,000
Anglican Church (CMS) 520,000
Presbyterian Church (CofS) 380,000
Pentecostal Assemblies of Canada 192,000
Seventh-Day Adventist Church 190,000
Pentecostal Evangelical Fellowship (Elim) 105,000
Full Gospel Churches (FFFM) 90,000
Methodist Church 80,000
Salvation Army 49,000
Southern Baptist Convention 27,000
Assemblies of God 25,000
African Gospel Church (WGM) 15,000

Evangelical 26.5% of population.

Missionaries to Kenya 1,850 (1:11,000 people) in about 100 agencies. Missionaries from within Kenya est. 100 (1:59,000 Protestants).

KOREA, NORTH

Area 121,000 sq.km. The larger part of the Korean peninsula, but climate more rigorous.

Population 23,000,000. Annual growth 2.4%. People per sq.km. 190. Two and a half million people died in the Korean War; 2 million more fled from the north to the south at that time.

Peoples

Korean 99.3%.

Chinese, Russian 0.7%.

Literacy 91%. *Official language:* Korean.

Capital: Pyongyang 1,501,000. Urbanization 64%.

Economy: Heavily industrialized and very centralized socialist economy. The revolutionary changes in the Communist world since 1989 have reinforced the isolationism of the present regime. Income/ person $620 (5% of USA).

Politics: Occupied by Japan 1910–45. On Russian insistence, Korea was partitioned after World War II. A Communist regime was installed in 1948 in the North. North Korea invaded South Korea in 1949. The Korean War dragged on until 1953. The large North Korean armed forces continue to threaten a second invasion. One of the most oppressive Communist regimes in the world. There are occasional hints of a reunification of the Koreas, but the fortified border between them is one of the most impenetrable in the world.

Religion: All religions have been harshly repressed. Many thousands of Christians were murdered during and after the Korean War. Religious affiliations are unknown, so the figures given are estimates.

Nonreligious/Atheist 60%.

Korean religions 39% (Buddhism, Animism, Confucianism, etc.)

Christian 1%.

KOREA, SOUTH

Area 98,500 sq.km. Southern half of Korean peninsula. Mountainous; only 22% is arable.

Population 43,700,000. Annual growth 1.3%. People per sq.km. 445.

Peoples

Korean 99.8%. An ancient and cultured nation.

Other 0.2%. United States military and Chinese (30,000).

Literacy 92%. *Official language:* Korean.

Capital: Seoul 10,028,000. Other major cities: Pusan 3,781,000; Taegu 1,848,000; Inchon 1,158,000. Urbanization 64%.

Economy: Rapid industrialization and growth since the Korean War. The economy has reached "take off" with high export earnings. The permanent state of confrontation and military preparedness before invasion threats from the North are a strain on the economy. Income/person $2,690 (15% of USA).

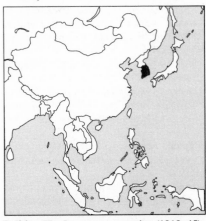

Politics: The Japanese occupation (1910–45), the Russian-imposed division of Korea (1945–48) and the Korean War in which the Communist North invaded the South (1950–53) have molded the attitudes and politics of South Korea. The military-civilian government allowed free elections in 1988 resulting in more democratic government.

Religion: There is complete religious freedom unless that freedom is used by religious leaders to attack government policies. The government has been favorable to Christianity, seeing this as an ideological bulwark against the Communist threat.

No professed religion 14%. Including secularists, nonreligious and many Shamanists (animist).

Buddhist 33%. Strong until 15th century, and with post-war resurgence.

Confucian 12%. Official religion until 1910. Both Buddhism and Confucianism have made a deep impact on Korean culture.

New religions 10.6%. Over 250 syncretic non-Christian religions, most of recent origin.

Muslim 0.1%. A growing movement among Koreans.

Christian 30%.

Roman Catholic 4.4%. Practicing 66%. 1,900,000 adherents; 1,060,000 members.

Foreign and indigenous marginal (at least 13 groups) 1.6%. 660,000 adherents; 220,000 members. Largest (adherents): Unification Church (Moonies) 500,000; Jehovah's Witnesses 77,428; Mormons 36,000.

Protestant 24%. 10,200,000 adherents; 4,370,000 members. Denominations 61. Largest (adherents):

Presbyterian Church in Korea (Haptong) 1,389,200

Presbyterian Church of Korea (Tonghap) 1,373,600

Methodist Church (4 groups) 1,007,600

Southern Baptist Convention (4 groups) 505,300

Full Gospel C. Church (Cho) 500,000

Korean Evangelical Church (OMS) (3 groups) 461,000

Christian Assemblies of God (6 groups) 293,200

Presbyterian Church in ROK 273,700

Koryo Presbyterian Church 250,800

Seventh-Day Adventist Church 134,500

Other Presbyterian (28 groups) 3,231,200

Evangelical 18% of population.

Missionaries to Korea 610 (1:70,000 people) in 60 agencies. Missionaries from Korea 360 (1:28,300 Protestants) in 17 sending agencies working in 37 countries. Just over half are cross-cultural missionaries.

MALAYSIA

Area 330,000 sq.km. Two distinct parts: Peninsular (West) Malaysia on the Kra peninsula of mainland Asia (PM), and East Malaysia (EM) consisting of the territories of Sarawak and Sabah on the northern third of the island of Borneo.

Population 17,800,000 (83% in PM). Annual growth 2.5%. People per sq.km. 54.

Peoples

Malay 48%. This figure includes some Muslim Orang Asli and all Indonesians (Javanese 136,000; Banjarese 45,000; Minangkabau 12,000, etc.). Predominantly rural, but influential in politics and civil service. A majority in PM only.

Chinese 36%. Speaking over 9 major dialects; majority Hokkien, Cantonese, Hakka and Teochew. Influential in commerce and business.

Indian 9%. Tamil 1,040,000; Punjabi 40,000; Malayali 36,000; Telugu 30,000, etc. Mainly poor estate workers or urban.

Orang Asli 7% ("Original People" tribal groups). In PM 75,000, EM 873,000 in about 80 tribes.

Literacy 59%. *Official language:* Malay. *All languages* 117. *Bible translations* 9 Bibles, 9 New Testaments, 12 portions.

Capital: Kuala Lumpur 1,397,000. Urbanization 35%. Chinese and Indian majority in urban areas.

Economy: Vigorous growth since independence through the development of oil, mining, agriculture and industry. Income/person $1,800 (10% of USA).

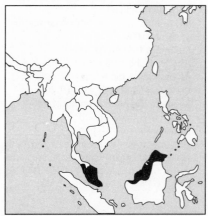

Politics: Independent from Britain in 1957 as the Federation of Malaya. Sabah and Sarawak joined to form the Federation of Malaysia in 1963. Recent years have been dominated by the efforts of the politically powerful Malays to extend their influence over the non-Malay half of the population in educational, economic and religious life. These have strained inter-ethnic relationships.

Religion: Sunni Islam is the official and favored religion in PM, and there is continual pressure to apply the same in EM where Islam is a minority. It is illegal to proselytize Muslims, but considerable effort is expended to induce animistic tribal people and Chinese to become Muslim.

Muslim 53%. Malays, some Indians and a few ethnic minorities in EM.

Buddhist and Chinese religions 28%.

Hindu 7%. Almost entirely Indian.

Animist 3%(?). Many tribal animists are classified as "Muslim."

Nonreligious/Atheist, other 3%.

Christian 7%. Affiliated 5%. The Church statistical situation is confusing and unclear for many denominations!

> *Roman Catholic* 2.9%. Practicing 60%. 460,000 adherents; 244,000 members. Mainly Chinese and Eurasian.
>
> *Marginal groups* (6+) 0.1%. 14,500 adherents.
>
> *Protestant* 2%. 320,000 adherents; 150,000 members. Denominations 48. Largest (adult members):
>
> S.I. Borneo (Overseas Missionary Fellowship) 50,000
> Methodist Church 40,000
> Anglican Church 20,000
> Assemblies of God 7,500
> Protestant Church of Sabah 7,200
> Southern Baptist Convention 4,700
> Christian Brethren 2,000
>
> *Evangelical* 1.2% of population.

Missionaries to Malaysia estimated 150, fairly rapid reduction in numbers. Missionaries from within Malaysia estimated 40 (1:8,000 Protestants) in 10 agencies.

MEXICO

Area 1,973,000 sq.km. Latin America's fourth largest country. Much of the country is arid or semi-arid; only 11% of the land is arable.

Population 88,800,000. Annual growth 2.4%. People per sq.km. 45. Massive illegal emigration to USA hardly alleviates the explosive population growth. Five million Mexicans live in the USA, increasing by 800,000 illegals per year.

Peoples

Spanish/Amerindian (Mestizo) 55%.

Amerindian 29%. 21.3% speaking Spanish only. Six million Indians still speak 236 languages. Major groupings: Aztec 4,800,000; Maya 2,700,000; Otomi 2,100,000; Zapotec 1,800,000; Mixtec 1,600,000; Totonac 240,000; Mazahua 160,000; Mazatec 160,000, etc.

Spanish and other European 15.3%.

African origin 0.5%. *Other* 0.2%.

Central American refugees 150,000.

Literacy 80%. *Official language:* Spanish, the world's largest Spanish-speaking nation. *All languages* 237. *Bible translations* 2 Bibles, 71 New Testaments, 41 portions.

Capital: Mexico City 18,535,000. Other cities: Guadalajara 3,483,000; Monterrey 2,622,000; Puebla 1,022,000. Urbanization 72%.

Economy: Mixed but very dependent on oil since 1975. Rapid population growth and overspending of new wealth led to massive international debts ($85 billion in 1985). The radical correctives imposed increased unemployment to 40% and inflation to 80% with a rise in urban and rural poverty. Recession and the lack of confidence in the economy have been checked by firm action by the government since 1989, with some visible improvement. Income/person $1,820 (10% of USA).

Politics: Independent from Spain in 1821.

Republic with what is virtually a one-party democracy since 1910. Pressures for more democratic multiparty politics led to a more open election in 1988.

Religion: Secular state with freedom of conscience and practice of religion, but with careful legal controls on Catholics, Protestants and others.

Nonreligious/Atheist 3.4%.

Jewish 0.1%, 57,000.

Baha'i 28,000.

Muslim 25,000.

Christian 96.4%. Nominal 4%. Affiliated 92.4%. Doubly affiliated 2.4%.

Roman Catholic 88% (officially 90.5%, but with many defections to other beliefs). 70,800,000 adherents; 37,500,000 members.

Marginal groups (16) 1%. Largest (adherents): Jehovah's Witnesses 388,000; Mormons 295,000.

Protestant 4%. 3,200,000 adherents; 1,300,000 members. Denominations 250. Largest (adult members):

Union of Ind. Evangelicals (Pentecostal) 270,000

Seventh-Day Adventist Church 210,000

Assemblies of God 120,000

Southern Baptist Convention 65,000

Presbyterian Church 53,000

Church of God (Cleveland) 29,000

Church of the Nazarene 21,700

Evangelical 3.1% of population.

Missionaries to Mexico 1,700 (1:47,000 people) in 84 agencies. Missionaries from Mexico approximately 98 (1:33,000 Protestants) in 3+ agencies.

MOROCCO

Area 447,000 sq.km. Northwest corner of Africa. A further 160,000 sq.km. of former Spanish Sahara claimed and occupied by Morocco in 1976. Fertile coastal areas, barren Atlas mountains inland and Sahara Desert to south and southeast.

Population 26,300,000. Annual growth 2.6%. People per sq.km. 59. Nearly one million Moroccans live and work in Europe.

Peoples

Arabic-speaking 65%. Culturally Arab, but predominantly Berber with Arab admixture.

Berber-speaking 34%. Three main languages: Shluh (speaking Shilha) 4,100,000 in south; Beraber (speaking Tamazight) 2,500,000 in center; Riff 1,360,000 in north. There are numerous tribal dialects and sub-dialects. Also Black Berber Haratine and Tuareg of the Sahara.

Other 1%. French 100,000; Spanish 20,000; Jewish 20,000, etc.

Literacy 24%. *Official language:* Arabic, French and English are widely used. *All languages* 5. *Bible translations* 1 Bible, 3 portions.

Capital: Rabat 1,212,000. Other cities: Casablanca 3,000,000; Marrakech 1,700,000; Fez 1,200,000. Urbanization 49%.

Economy: Mainly agricultural, but phosphate deposits in Morocco and the Sahara are large and important with 70% of world's proven reserves. The cost of the Sahara War has strained the economy. Income/person $620 (3% of USA).

Politics: Independent kingdom in 1956. Formerly French and Spanish protectorates. A limited democracy with an executive monarchy. The dominant political issue since 1974 has been the occupation of the Western Sahara and the subsequent warfare to retain it.

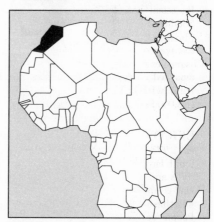

Religion: Islam is the state religion. The government is committed to the preservation of Islam as the religion of all Moroccans. Other religious groups are tolerated so long as they confine their ministry to expatriate communities.

Muslim 99.6%. Almost entirely Sunni.

Jewish 0.1%. 20,000 Sephardic Jews, the remnant of a large community that has emigrated to Israel.

Christian 0.27%. Foreign 97%. Moroccan 3%.
> *Roman Catholic* 0.25%. Practicing 10%. 60,000 adherents; 33,600 members. French, Spanish, etc. Only 500 Moroccans.
>
> *Protestant* 0.01%. 3,460 adherents; 1,780 members. About 60% Moroccan. Denominations 10. Largest (adherents):
> Indigenous fellowships 1,250
> French Reformed Church 1,000
> Anglican Church 800

Christian expatriates in Moroccan ministries inside and outside country approximately 100.

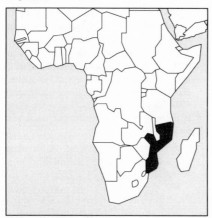

MOZAMBIQUE

Area 802,000 sq.km. Southeast African state with 2,800 km. coastline on the strategic Mozambique Channel.

Population 15,600,000. Annual growth 2.6%. People per sq.km. 19.

Peoples

African peoples 99%. *Northern peoples* 44%. Makua 4,300,000; Lomwe 1,200,000; Makonde 320,000; Yao 250,000.
> *Central peoples* 22%. Sena-Nyungwe 1,600,000; Shona-Ndua 1,100,000; Nyanja 350,000.

Southern peoples 33%. Tsonga (Shangaan) 1,600,000; Ronga (Tswa) 600,000; Chopi 800,000; Tonga 10,000.

Other 1%. Portuguese 30,000, Mixed race 30,000.

Literacy 24%. *Official language:* Portuguese. *All languages* 23. *Bible translations* 8 Bibles, 2 New Testaments, 6 portions.

Capital: Maputo 1,040,000. Urbanization 20%.

Economy: Subsistence economy despite fertile agricultural land and rich mineral deposits. Restrictive colonial exploitation, followed by overhasty application of Marxist economic theories, limited the development of resources and infrastructure. Drought, floods and widespread guerrilla warfare have further impoverished the country. It is possibly the poorest country in the world. Income/person $150 (0.7% of USA).

Politics: A Portuguese colony for 470 years. Independent in 1975 as a Marxist-Leninist state after a long and bitter war of independence. Widespread opposition to the central government's policies stimulated a dirty guerrilla war that has made chaos, a state of armed anarchy and starvation a way of life to most people. Over one million people have been killed or have died as a result. The government has openly abandoned its Marxist ideology.

Religion: Until 1982 government policy was "all-out war on the churches" and "destruction of religious superstitions." The collapse of the economy and desperate straits of the country have caused the government to declare freedom of religion.

Nonreligious/Atheist est. 5%.

Muslim 13%. The majority among the Yao in northwest and coastal Makonde and Makua.

African traditional religions 59.5%.

Christian 21%.
> *Roman Catholic* 13%. 1,562,000 adherents. The church suffered a serious decline after independence because of its links with the colonial regime.
>
> *Marginal groups* (100+) 0.4%. 56,000 adherents.

Protestant 6.4%. 890,000 adherents, 379,000 members. Denominations 30. Largest (adherents):

United Baptist (Africa Evangelical Fellowship, Scandinavian Baptist) 160,000
Pentecostal Assemblies of God 75,000
Presbyterian Church (Swiss Mission) 70,000
Anglican Church 65,000
United Methodist Church 60,000
Seventh-Day Adventist Church 57,000
Assemblies of God 35,000
Church of the New Covenant 25,000
Church of the Nazarene 22,000
Free Methodist Church 15,000
Evangelical 4.5% of population.
Missionaries to Mozambique estimated 100.

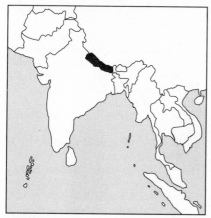

NEPAL

Area 141,000 sq.km. A mountain-ringed Himalayan state between China (Tibet) and India.

Population 19,200,000. Annual growth 2.5%. People per sq.km. 136. Very unevenly distributed. Most live on the overpopulated hills and in the Kathmandu valley; many are migrating to the lowland Terai in the south.

Peoples: Over 30 major ethnic groups; numerous smaller groups. Two main ethnic components, with considerable intermingling:

Indo-Aryan (from south and west) 79%. Nepali 8,800,000; Maithili 1,830,000; Bhojpuri 1,120,000; Tharu 686,000; Awadhi 438,000; Rajbansi 77,000; Dhanwar 14,000; also eight other languages.

Tibeto-Burman (from north and east) 20%. Thamang 768,000; Newari 630,000; Magar 400,000; Rai (21 dialects) 321,000; Gurung 238,000; Limbu 236,000; Sherpa 110,000; Sunwar 29,000; also 34 other languages.

Other 1%. Santali 29,000; Munda; Indian; European.

Literacy 20%. *Official language:* Nepali, the first language of 55% of the population. *All languages* 76. *Bible translations* 6 Bibles, 1 New Testament, 21 portions.

Capital: Kathmandu 430,000. Urbanization 6%.

Economy: An isolated subsistence economy. The difficult terrain and high population density in habitable regions, slow development of roads, agriculture and social projects. Main foreign exchange earners are tourism, agriculture and Gurkha soldiers. Heavily dependent on foreign aid. The economic confrontation with India in 1989-90 has had disastrous economic and ecological results on the already impoverished land. Income/person $160 (1% of USA) with 40% living below the poverty line (1% of USA).

Politics: Political isolation from the outside world ended in 1951. The strong executive powers invested in the king in the partyless government system was brought to an end through popular resistance in 1989/90. The aim is to have a multiparty democracy with a constitutional monarch.

Religion: The world's only Hindu kingdom. Hinduism is the state religion. Open Christian evangelism is illegal. On June 15, 1990, King Birendra granted amnesty to all religious prisoners. Christians continue to work with the government to incorporate religious freedom into the new constitution.

Hindu 89%. Much intertwined in Buddhism and a strong, underlying animism. A complex caste system exists despite its illegality since 1963.

Buddhist 7%. Lamaistic Buddhism is dominant among the Tibeto-Burman peoples. The Buddha was born in Nepal.

Muslim 3.5%. Predominantly in the Terai.

Christian 0.3%. Almost entirely Protestant Evangelicals.

Roman Catholic about 250 adherents.
Protestant 0.4%. 60,000 adherents; 40,000 members.

Missionaries to Nepal approximately 600 (1:26,700 people) in two large inter-mission fellowships and several independent agencies.

NETHERLANDS
Area 41,000 sq.km. Over 30% is below sea level.
Population 15,000,000. Annual growth 0.4%. People per sq.m. 365.
Peoples
Indigenous 91.2%. Dutch 12,800,000; Frisian 460,000; Gypsies 1,200.
Ex-colonial 4.1%. Dutch-Indonesian 320,000; Surinamese 260,000; South Molukkan 45,000; Antilles 33,000.
Immigrant communities 4.6%. Other European Economic Community countries 160,000; Turkish 150,000; North African 105,000; Chinese 45,000; Yugoslav 14,000.
Literacy 100%. *Official language:* Dutch (Nederlands).
Capital: Amsterdam 1,000,000. Other cities: The Hague (seat of government) 700,000; Rotterdam (the world's busiest seaport) 1,100,000. Urbanization 88%.

Economy: A strong industrial and trading economy. A member of the European Economic Community. Income/person $11,860 (64% of USA).
Politics: Stable democratic constitutional monarchy.
Religion: Complete freedom of religion, but

with a strong and steady secularization of society.
Nonreligious 28%. Also includes nominal Christians who have no affiliation to a church.
Muslim 2.1%. North African, Turk, Indonesian and some Surinamese.
Hindu 0.7%. Surinamese Asian and Sri Lankan Tamil.
Jewish 0.2%. Before World War II it was 1.4%.
Christian 69%. About half attend church.
Roman Catholic 39.2%. 5,650,000 adherents; 3,955,000 members. Predominantly in southern provinces.
Marginal groups 1%. 133,000 adherents; 82,000 members. Largest (adherents): Jehovah's Witnesses 46,700; Protestant Union (unitarian) 18,000; New Apostolic Church 12,500.
Protestant 28.7%. 4,130,000 adherents; 1,360,000 members. Predominant in north and center. Denominations approximately 150. Largest (adult members):
Reformed Church (NHK) 616,000
Reformed Church (GK) 480,050
Reformed Church (Liberated) (VGK) 60,850
Fellowship of Pentecostal Church & others 40,000
Christian Reformed Church (CRK) 38,500
Mennonite Church 26,300
Evangelical Lutheran Church 21,070
Netherlands Reformed Church (NRK) 17,600
Remonstrant Brotherhood 13,000
Baptist Union 12,000
Free Evangelical Church 7,450
Evangelical 8% of population.
Missionaries to Netherlands approximately 160. Missionaries from Netherlands 1,100 (1:3,800 Protestants) in over 75 agencies. Over 85% are evangelical.

NIGERIA
Area 924,000 sq. km. Tropical forest in south, merging into savannah in the north. Divided into 21 states to minimize the impact of ethnic loyalties on national politics.

Population est. 118,600,000. No reliable census since independence; the northern population is likely to be overestimated. Annual growth 2.9%. People per sq.km. 128. Africa's most populous state.

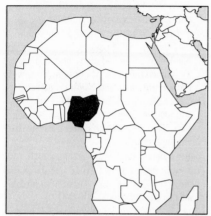

Peoples: Over 426 known. The major groups are: Yoruba 17.8%, Ibo 17.5%, Hausa 16.8%, Fulani 10.3%, Tiv 5.6%, Kanuri 4.7%.

Literacy 30%. *Official language:* English. *Trade languages:* Hausa in north and center, Yoruba in southwest, Ibo in southeast. *All languages* 408, though some say 510. *Bible translations* 15 Bibles, 33 New Testaments, 48 portions.

Capital: Lagos estimated 4-5 million, capital being transferred to Abuja in central Nigeria. Other major cities: Ibadan 4,000,000; Ado-Ekiti 1,400,000; Port Harcourt 500,000. Twenty-five cities of over 100,000 people. Urbanization 28%.

Economy: Rich in agricultural land and mineral resources. Vast oil wealth in the '70s raised educational and living standards, but also stimulated gross misuse of public funds. Grandiose prestige projects, spectacular corruption, incompetent management and neglect of agriculture were the result. The collapse of oil prices then quickened both the collapse of the economy and the fall of the corrupt civilian government in 1983. Solutions to Nigeria's economic woes are not yet in sight. Income/person $360 (2% of USA), but the cost of living is high.

Politics: Independent from Britain as a federal state in 1960. Colonial history further polarized the widely differing cultural, religious and educational systems between the Muslim feudal north and the traditional religion/Christian capitalist south. These differences underlie the tensions, coups and Biafra Civil War (1967–70), and attempts by the Muslim north to retain political control. The civilian government ousted in 1983 was predominantly Muslim, as was the military regime that followed. The latter found it difficult to cope with the economic crisis, and there was widespread disillusionment, which led to another coup in 1985. The new military government appears to be more vigorous in dealing with the inherent malaise in the structure and economy. The expressed intention is a handover to a civilian government in 1992.

Religion: Freedom of religion, but most postindependence governments giving preferential treatment to Islam. The Christian South and Middle Belt have become increasingly restive with Muslim gerrymandering to retain power. Statistics for religions and churches given below are nearly all estimates.

Muslim 36%. Muslims claim up to 60%, non-Muslims as low as 30%. Dominant in federal and military leadership until 1985, and in northern states.

Traditional religions 15%. The majority in numerous peoples in the Middle Belt, but influential in both Muslim peoples of north and west, and Christian peoples of the south.

Christian 49%. Nominal 18%. Affiliated 31%. Large numbers claim to be Catholic, Protestant, etc. but are not affiliated to any church. All statistics are approximate but given to indicate the growth of the church.

   Roman Catholic 6.6%. (12% claim to be Roman Catholic.) Practicing 40%. 6,040,000 adherents; 3,323,000 members.

   Indigenous marginal groups (800+) 5%. 4,560,000 adherents. A profusion of syncretistic denominations.

Foreign marginal groups (20+) 0.4%. Over 20 cults. Largest (adult members): Jehovah's Witnesses 113,360.

Protestant 19%. (28% would claim to be Protestant). 17,584,000 adherents; 5,800,000 members. Denominations 140+. Largest (adult members):

Anglican Church 1,000,000

Evangelical Churches of West Africa (Sudan Interior Mission) 650,000

TEKAN (The SUM Fellowship) est. 400,000

Nigerian Baptist Convention (Southern Baptist) 400,000

Christ Apostolic Church est. 400,000

Nigerian Christian Fellowship est. 350,000

Apostolic Church 320,000

Assemblies of God 275,000

Church of God Mission est. 250,000

Gospel Faith Mission est. 200,000

Methodist Church 160,000

Qua Iboe Church 83,000

Evangelical 14% of population.

Missionaries to Nigeria estimated 950 (1:96,000 people) in about 60 agencies. Missionaries from within Nigeria estimated 740 (1:23,500 Protestants) in about 10 agencies. About 60 of these are outside Nigeria.

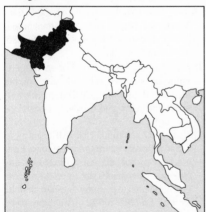

PAKISTAN

Area 804,000 sq.km. Arid mountains in the north and west. Sind desert in southwest. Vast irrigation schemes in the fertile Indus valley.

Population 113,600,000. Annual growth 2.9%. People per sq.km. 141. Over half the population lives in the Punjab.

Peoples

Punjabi 60%. Speaking Punjabi and Urdu. Their dominance is resented by other minorities. They live in the northern plains.

Sindhi 12%. Speaking Sindhi. In the south.

Pushtu-Afghan 15%. Speaking Pushtu and Dari. Numerous tribes and clans, and augmented by Afghan refugees. Majority in Northwest Frontier Province and North Baluchistan.

Baluch 3.5%. Speaking Baluchi. In the west and also in East Iran and South Afghanistan. The 800,000 Dravidian Brahui live among them.

Indian refugees (of 1947) 8%. Speaking Urdu.

Other minorities 1.5%. Tribal groups in the far north (27) 700,000; Tribal Mawari Bhil and Kohli (16 tribes) 700,000.

Literacy 18%. *Official languages:* Urdu, English. Urdu is becoming widely used by all. *All languages* 50. *Bible translations* 6 Bibles, 1 New Testament, 8 portions.

Capital: Islamabad 335,000. Other cities: Karachi est. 16,000,000; Lahore 3,600,000; Rawalpindi 2,000,000; Faisalabad 1,600,000; Peshawar 1,000,000. Urbanization 29%.

Economy: Predominantly agricultural. A large textile industry. Remittances from Pakistanis living and working in Europe, North America and Middle East are the largest source of foreign currency. The large army, and influx of millions of refugees from Afghanistan and Iran, have strained the country's resources. Income/person $390 (3% of USA).

Politics: Independent from Britain at the partition of India in 1947. Constant instability and three wars with India over Kashmir and East Pakistan. (The latter became independent as Bangladesh in 1971.) The military regime of President Zia ended with his death, and an elected government under Miss Benazir Bhutto came to power. Regional politics, ethnic violence and continued tensions with India have hindered all efforts to improve the social and economic life of the country.

Religion: Islamic republic, but continual tensions between fundamentalists and moderates have arisen over the avowed intent of the previous government to Islamize the structures of society. Minority religions are safeguarded in the constitution, but the situation is both delicate and unclear for non-Muslims.

Muslim 96.6%. Sunni 70%, Shi'a 27% (including the unorthodox Ismaili), Ahmaddiya 3%. The latter are not considered Muslims by the government and are persecuted, and many driven underground.

Hindu 1.6%. Tribal peoples of Sind and some Sindhis and Punjabis.

Christian 1.6%. Affiliated 1.5%.

  Roman Catholic 0.5%. Practicing 37%. 471,000 adherents; 254,000 members. Punjabis and also Goanese in Karachi.

  Protestant 1%. 974,000 adherents; 445,000 members. Denominations 44. Figures very approximate. Largest (adherents):
  Church of Pakistan 400,000
  United Presbyterian Church 250,000
  National Virgin Church (ex-Presbyterian) 52,000
  Salvation Army 50,000
  United Church in Pakistan (Lahore Church Council) 42,000
  National Methodist Church 32,000
  Association of Reformed Presbyterian Churches 25,000
  Full Gospel Assemblies (Swedish Free Mission) 12,000
  Pakistan Christian Fellowship (International Christian Fellowship) 2,600
  Indus Christian Fellowship (Conservative Baptist Foreign Missionary Society) 2,500
  International Missions (International Mission,Inc.) 2,500
  Evangelical Alliance Churches (The Evangelical Alliance Mission) 1,100
  Evangelical 0.2% of population.
Missionaries to Pakistan 680 (1:146,000 people) in about 40 agencies. Missionaries from within Pakistan estimated 10.

PERU

Area 1,285,000 sq.km. Andean state. Three zones—dry coastal plain in the west where most of the cities and industry are located, high plateau which is agricultural, and upper Amazon jungles in the east.

Population 21,900,000. Annual growth 2.1%. People per sq.km. 17.

Peoples

Spanish-speaking 45% (majority Mestizo, minority white and black).

Amerindian 54%. *Highland peoples*: Quechua 9,200,000; Aymara 1,000,000; *Lowland peoples* 330,000 speaking 41 languages.

Other minorities 1%. Japanese 65,000; Chinese 60,000; other European, etc.

Literacy 88%. *Official languages:* Spanish, Quechua. *All languages* 86. *Bible Translations* 2 Bible, 19 New Testaments, 24 portions.

Capital: Lima 5,627,000 including the port city of Callao. Other city: Arequipa 700,000. Urbanization 67%.

Economy: The combined effects of sudden climatic changes, world recession and destructive terrorism have brought the country to its knees and hindered necessary social and land reforms. The disastrous economic policies of the left-wing populist government has further devastated the country. Income/person $1,430 (8% of USA).

Politics: Fully independent from Spain in 1824. Return to democratic government since 1980, but a Maoist guerrilla movement has brought increasing instability and an atmosphere of fear through spectacular acts of terrorism. The socialist government elected in 1985 was unable to cope with the nation's problems. In 1990 a moderate government was elected.

Religion: Religious freedom guaranteed in 1978 constitution, but in practice the Catholic church still tends to be favored and exercises a decisive influence.

Nonreligious/Atheist 1%.

Animist 1%. Though at least 30% of nominal Catholics are in reality Christo-pagan.

Christian 98%. Affiliated 94%.

    Roman Catholic 89.1%. Practicing 20%. 17,400,000 adherents.

    Marginal groups (10) 0.86%. 167,000 adherents. Largest (adherents): Jehovah's Witnesses 75,080; Mormons 60,000.

    Protestant 3.6%. 692,000 adherents; 285,000 members. Denominations 85. Largest (adult members):

    Assemblies of God 97,000

    Seventh-Day Adventist Church 60,000

    Iglesia Evangelica Peruana (Evangelical Union of South America, SIM) 40,000

    Christian & Missionary Alliance 15,000

    Church of the Nazarene 12,400

    Southern Baptist Convention 8,500

    Church of God (Cleveland) 7,330

    Evangelical Churches of NE (RBMU International) 4,000

    Brethren 3,500

    Evangelical 3% of population.

Missionaries to Peru 890 (1:21,900 people) in 60 agencies. Missionaries from within Peru estimated 110 (1:6,300 Protestants).

PHILIPPINES

Area 300,000 sq.km. 73 provinces; 7,250 islands, of which over 700 are inhabited, the largest being Luzon (116,000 sq.km.) in the north and Mindanao (95,000 sq.km.) in the south.

Population 66,700,000. Annual growth 2.9%. People per sq.km. 222. Over 400,000 Filipinos working in 103 nations and on ships. About one million have emigrated to the USA.

Peoples

Malayo-Indonesian Filipinos 95%. Major languages: Cebuano 24.4%, Tagalog 23.8%, Ilocano 11.1%, Hiligaynon 10%, Bicol (many dialects) 7%, Waray 4.6%, Kapampangan 3.4%, Maranao 2.8%, Pangasinan 2.3%, Magindanao 2.2%, Tausug 1.5%, Samal 1%.

Tribal peoples 2.8%. In the more inaccessible mountainous areas of Luzon (46 tribes) 930,000; Mindanao (22 tribes) 490,000; Mindoro (6 tribes) 50,000; Palawan (6 tribes) 30,000.

Chinese 1%. Important in the commercial world.

Other 1%. USA citizens, Vietnamese, etc.

Literacy 88%. *Official languages:* Filipino (based on Tagalog), English. *All languages* 151. *Bible translations* 9 Bibles, 26 New Testaments, 55 portions.

Capital: Metro-Manila 10,000,000. Urbanization 37%.

Economy: A mixed agricultural and industrial economy. Serious economic difficulties have worsened under the combined impact of the oil crisis, decline of export income, widespread corruption, social and political unrest and a series of natural disasters. Loss of international confidence in the country's future since 1983 has caused hardship, with rising unemployment, 50% inflation rate and widespread poverty. Income/person $590 (3% of USA).

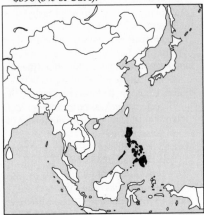

Politics: A Spanish colony from 1565 to 1898; hence the Catholic majority and many Spanish customs. Ruled by the USA until independence in 1946. Martial law imposed in 1971 to combat Communist subversion, and the country became virtually a one-party republic. Political manipulation, mismanagement and abuse of civil liberties stimulated antipathy to the government and led to its downfall in 1986. The government of Cory Aquino has proved relatively ineffective in controlling the economy or curbing the Communist guerillas, but has survived seven coup attempts. The Republic is a member of ASEAN and is an important ally of the USA.

Religion: Freedom of religion. Asia's only country with a Catholic majority.

Nonreligious/Atheist 1.5%.

Animist 1%. Many nominal Catholics are still animist at heart. Majority among many of the tribal peoples.

Muslim 8.4%. Sunni Islam. Almost all in Southwest Mindanao, Sulu Island and Palawan. Strong among the Magindanao, Maranao, Ilanon, Samal and Tausug; less strong, but in the majority among eight other peoples.

Christian 89.2%. Many Christo-pagan.

Roman Catholic 63.6%, though a further 12% were baptized Catholic, but have left the Church. 36,150,000 adherents; 19,240,000 members.

Indigenous Catholic groups 8%. 4,500,000 adherents; 2,600,000 members. Over 120 groups have broken away from Rome. Largest (adherents): Philippine Independent Church 4,200,000.

Indigenous marginal groups 6.1%. Over 280 groups. 3,433,000 adherents; 1,850,000 members. Largest (adherents): Iglesia ni Cristo 1,400,000.

Foreign marginal groups 0.7%. 388,000 adherents; 185,000 members. Most rapidly growing and largest (adherents): Jehovah's Witnesses 237,000; Mormons 76,000.

Protestant 10.7%. 6,010,000 adherents; 2,600,000 members. Denominations 140. Largest (adult members):

Seventh-Day Adventist Church 290,000
United Church 260,000
Christian & Missionary Alliance 185,000
United Methodist Church 166,000
Southern Baptist Convention 89,000
Assemblies of God 60,000

March of Faith 55,000
Convention of Philippino Baptist Churches 54,000
International Church of Foursquare Gospel 48,000
Evangelical Methodist Church 40,000
Episcopal Church 33,000
ABCOP (Overseas Missionary Fellowship, Send International) 16,000
Conservative Baptist Association 15,000
Evangelical 6.4% of population.

Missionaries to Philippines approximately 2,300 (1:24,700 people) in about 120 agencies. Missionaries from within the Philippines approximately 670 (1:9,000 Protestants) of which over 180 are serving in other lands.

POLAND

Area 313,000 sq.km. Poland has the misfortune of being sandwiched between Germany and the Commonwealth of Independent States (formerly the USSR).

Population 38,400,000. Annual growth .6%. People per sq.km. 122.

Peoples

Poles 96.6%. Over 10 million emigrants (65% in USA).

Minorities 3%. Ukrainian 256,000; Pomeranian 220,000; Byelorussian 220,000; German 73,000; Gypsy 70,000.

Military, etc. 0.4%.

Literacy 98%. *Official language:* Polish. *All languages* 7. *Bible translations* 4 Bibles, 1 portion.

Capital: Warsaw 1,770,000. Other major cities: Lodz 945,000, Cracow 800,000. Urbanization 61%.

Economy: The courage of the new government in radically tackling the chaos left by 45 years of Communist mismanagement is setting the land on the painful path to recovery. Income/person $1920 (10% of USA).

Politics: A well-remembered tragic history of wars and partition among powerful neighbors over the last 200 years. One quarter of the population died in World War II. The Soviet army imposed a Communist regime in 1945. Popular discontent caused gradual liberalizations during 1980–81. The Solidarity movement forced negotiations with the Communist regime in 1988/89 and in the subsequent partially democratic elections, came to power as part of an ambitious Communist/Solidarity coalition government in June 1989. This show of strength and resilience by Solidarity marks a watershed for Eastern Europe, and furthermore appears to have initiated dramatic changes of government in nearly every continent of the world. More recently, a jolting shift to a market economy and dissatisfaction with many of the effects thus far have tested Solidarity's cohesiveness. To be successful, the reforms will need to address cooperation of professionals and workers and form coalitions to ensure effective government.

Religion: The Roman Catholic church is too strong for the Communists to dominate or destroy, so there is more religious freedom than in any other Communist state. The Protestants have more freedom than for centuries because they are considered a counterbalance to the Roman Catholics.

Nonreligious/Atheist 10%.

Jewish 12,000 (3,500,000 in 1939).

Christian 89.8%
> *Roman Catholic* 87.3%. Practicing 65%. 32,800,000 adherents; 21,600,000 members.
> *Orthodox* 1.6%. 606,000 adherents; 375,000 members. Denominations 3.
> *Protestant* 0.45%. 171,000 adherents; 110,000 members. Denominations 24.

> Largest (adult members):
> Lutheran Church (German) 60,000
> United Evangelical Church 20,000
> Assemblies of God 8,500
> Baptist Union 4,200
> *Evangelical* 0.2% of population (0.5% including the members of Oasis).

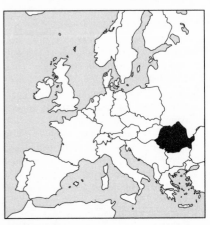

ROMANIA

Area 237,000 sq.km. Area is much reduced by Russian seizure of Bessarabia in 1940 (now the Moldavian Soviet Socialist Republic).

Population 23,300,000. Annual growth 0.5%. People per sq.km. 98.

Peoples

Romanian 84%. A Latin people descended from Romans settled in Dacia.

Hungarian 8.5%. In Transylvania.

Minorities 7.5%. Gypsy 700,000; German 300,000; Jew 106,000; Turk 100,000; Ukrainian 67,000; Serbian 65,000; etc.

Literacy 98%. *Official languages:* Romanian, Hungarian.

Capital: Bucharest 2,200,000. Urbanization 51%.

Economy: The Communist regime impoverished the country and brought its population to poverty and despair. The newly elected government is committed to set up a market economy, but social and economic dislocations are proving traumatic. Inflation has increased salaries and overall economic prices bringing the value of the currency (lci) to little use. There are no substantial material needs that can be purchased with the ballooned numbers. Income/person est. $1,988 (11% of USA).

Politics: The Russian-supported Communist coup in 1947 brought 43 years of tyranny and suffering to the country. The final collapse of Communism in December 1989 was sudden and violent. The May 1990 multiparty elections were neither peaceful nor acceptable to many, for many former Communists were elected as members of the National Salvation Front Party. Communications with the West are being strangled with a slow hold from gloves labeled as democracy. With quiet moves, the government is trying to pull Romania back to the old regime of Communism by falsely proving that democracy is failing.

Religion: Communist persecution of Christians was the most severe of any Eastern European country apart from Albania. There is a sense of freedom of religion that is promoted by the government. It is the freedom of speech and it ends at that, with no reform methods or desire to change.

Nonreligious/Atheist 14%.

Muslim 1.2%. Predominantly Turks, some Bulgars and Gypsies.

Jewish 0.5%. Steadily declining through emigration to Israel.

Christian 84.2%.

 Orthodox 67.4%; 15,400,000 adherents; 10,700,000 members. Denominations 6. Largest (adherents):

 Roman Catholic 5.5%. 1,244,000 adherents; 900,000 members.

 Marginal groups 0.3%. 66,000 adherents; 48,000 members.

 Protestant 11%. 2,500,000 adherents; 1,500,000 members. Denominations 14 legally acknowledged. Largest (adult members):

 Reformed Church 520,000

 Baptist Union 340,000(?)

 Church of God 230,000

 Assemblies of God 170,000

 Lutheran Church 94,500

 Brethren 63,000 (?)

 Seventh-Day Adventist Church 57,000

 Evangelical 7.8% of population (11% if the Lord's Army Christians are included).

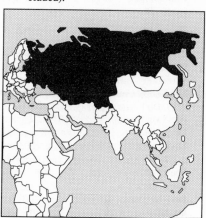

Russia and the Commonwealth of Independent States (formerly USSR)

[Editor's Note: Although Lithuania, Latvia, Estonia and Georgia are not part of the Commonwealth, statistical information has been retained for ready reference.]

Area 22,402,000 sq.km. The world's largest country; nearly 11,000 km. from east to west and 4,000 km. from north to south. The Commonwealth of Independent States straddles 11 time zones. 24% lies in Europe and 76% in Asia (Siberia).

Population 291,900,000. Annual growth 1.0 The Slavic population is almost static, but some groups, particularly the Turkic peoples of Central Asia, are growing at over 3%. Large areas are uninhabited. 25% of the population lives in Siberia. People per sq.km. 13.

Peoples: An extraordinary mosaic of peoples came under Russian domination over the past several centuries. There are approximately 154 ethnic groups.

Indo-European 78.2%.

 Slavic 72.8% (8 peoples). Russian 138,000,000; Ukrainian 43,000,000; Byelorussian 10,000,000; Polish 1,150,000.

 Baltic 1.6%. Lithuanian 3,020,000; Latvian 1,518,000.

 Iranian 1.3% (12 peoples). Tajik 3,400,000; Talysh 150,000; Kurdish 140,000.

Other 2.8%. Armenian 4,500,000; Romanian (Moldavian) 3,260,000; German 2,040,000; Ossetian 590,000; Greek 360,000; Gypsy (Jati, Romany) 337,000.

Altaic 16.5%.

Turkic 16% (24 peoples). Uzbek 15,000,000; Kazakh 7,800,000; Tatar 7,400,000; Azeri 6,500,000; Turkmen 2,430,000; Kirghiz 2,290,000; Chuvash 1,900,000; Bashkir 1,500,000; Karakalpak 350,000; Yakut 350,000; Crimean Turks 330,000; Uighur 250,000; Kumyk 226,000; Karachay 225,000; Tuvin 200,000; Gagauz 200,000.

Caucasian 2.5% (33 peoples). Georgian 3,900,000; Chechen 800,000; Avar 528,000; Karbardian 420,000; Lezgin 415,000; Dargin 310,000; Ingush 200,000; Adygey (Circassian) 120,000; Lak 110,000.

Finno-Ugric 1.7% (17 peoples). Mordvin 1,300,000; Estonian 1,100,000; Udmurt 770,000; Mari 670,000; Komi 500,000; Hungarian 180,000; Karelian 145,000.

Mongolian etc. 0.28% (12 peoples). Buryat 390,000; Kalmyk 160,000.

Jewish 0.7%. About 1,900,000, but some estimate the number at double this due to strong pressures by the authorities to Russify them.

Other 0.16%. Over 10 other Siberian peoples totalling 31,000; Chinese 55,000; Korean 400,000.

Literacy 99%. It was 25% before the revolution. *Official language:* Russian spoken as first language by 56% of the population. Local languages are officially recognized in the various independent states and autonomous regions. Sixty-five languages are recognized as literary languages for use in the media. *All languages* 138. *Bible translations* 25 Bibles, 5 New Testaments, 34 portions.

Capital: Minsk 1,589,000. Other major cities: Moscow 8,600,000; St. Petersburg 5,000,000; Kiev 2,500,000; Tashkent 2,100,000; Baku 1,700,000; Kharkov 1,600,000. There are 26 cities with populations over one million. Urbanization 66%.

Economy: The country is attempting to move away from a highly centralized socialist economy, with little private ownership. Officially sanctioned private enterprise has been shakily developing. If the economy can get going, private enterprise has a future. Vast mineral wealth as well as an extensive agricultural output make the country the world's leading producer of wheat, butter, iron ore etc. The extremes of climate and collectivized agriculture make for low and erratic production figures. Over 15% of the nation's resources are spent on the armed forces. Income/person $6,350 (45% of USA).

Politics: The USSR came into being following the Bolshevik revolution in 1917. The type of Marxism commonly attributed to the Soviet Union was adapted ideologically by Vladimir Lenin and translated bureaucratically by Josef Stalin. The monolithic governmental structure dominated until change back toward a capitalist system in the Soviet Union accelerated when Mikhail Gorbachev became General Secretary in March 1985. Through his policies of *glasnost* (openness) and *perestroika* (restructuring), Gorbachev attempted to rally all sectors of Soviet society to come to grips with problems facing the country. After the August 1991 coup attempt against Gorbachev failed, Marxism-Leninism collapsed. In September 1991 the old Soviet Parliament was replaced by a democratic parliament elected by the Republics. Gorbachev agreed to an alliance with Russia's president, Boris Yeltsin, giving Yeltsin considerable power leading to Yeltsin's declaring himself head of the Russian cabinet on November 7, 1991, and Gorbachev's subsequent resignation December 25, 1991. Ethnic conflicts in the central Asian republics as well as moves toward autonomy provide a sense of drama in a country already burdened with grave economic conditions. A multiparty system has been sanctioned in principle, and in practice most republics are working toward independence. Because of the complexity of this country's situation, lasting beneficial effects due to fundamental change in the economy or government are likely to involve profound social upheaval and will probably require several years or more to get established.

Religion: Religious opposition has been replaced by unrestricted freedom. The Russian Republic's education ministry is working on plans to introduce the Bible and classical texts with religious content into school curriculum. Churches have come out of hiding and are regaining the property and status they lost under Stalin. On October 1, 1990, the Soviet Parliament passed "The Law on the Freedom of Conscience." Yet nationalism has caused friction between evangelical and national churches. Pseudo-Christian cults, the occult, and Hindu beliefs are on the rise. Spiritual interest has surfaced in the CIS, but it shoots out in every direction.

Nonreligious/Atheist 52% and possibly up to 75%.

Muslim 18% ethnically; by profession around 12%; a large minority would claim to be atheist. Muslims are in the majority in six republics (Azerbaijan, Kazakhstan, Kirgizia, Tajikistan, Turkmenisten, and Uzbekistan), nine autonomous republics and four autonomous regions; 75% of Muslims live in Soviet Central Asia adjoining Iran, Afghanistan, and China. The majority are Sunni Muslim. The Azeri, Kurds, and Talysh are Shi'a. Official Islam is government controlled by spiritual directorates in four different regions. There is a strong fundamentalist underground Islamic movement.

Jewish 1.2%. Possibly over half are atheists. Two major groups: Western, and Eastern (Crimea, Georgia, and Central Asia). They have suffered much persecution over the past 15 years, especially the many who have applied for emigration to Israel.

Shamanist 0.1%. Many of the smaller tribal peoples of North Russia and Siberia are still animist—especially the Yakut, Chukchi, and also the Tungus and Samoyed peoples.

Buddhist 0.1%. The majority would not be practicing Buddhists. Mahayana Buddhism among the Buryats, Kalmyks, and Tuvinians. Some Koreans are also Buddhist. Officially recognized, but with a long history of repression by the Soviet authorities. Between 1933 and 1938 all 120 Buddhist monasteries were destroyed.

Christian 33%. Active adherents possibly 22%. Many are still baptized as children. Actual figures are only general estimates.

Orthodox 16.4%. 45,600,000 adherents (?). Over 43 national or breakaway denominations. Largest (adherents):
Russian Orthodox 37,000,000 (?)
Armenian Orthodox 3,000,000
Georgian Orthodox 2,500,000
Other Orthodox groups 2,700,000 (?)

Roman Catholic 3.2%. 9,000,000 adherents (?). Many Uniate Catholics have been compelled to be classified as Russian Orthodox.

Protestant 2.6%. 7,300,000 adherents; 2,800,000 members. Some officially sanctioned denominations, many unregistered groups, all totalling possibly 100. Largest (adherents):
UECB (registered) 250,000
Evangelical Lutheran Church of Latvia 350,000
Evangelical Lutheran Church of Estonia 250,000
Reformed Church of Transcarpathia 70,000
Other unregistered groups (?) 1,500,000

Evangelical 2.5% of population. Higher if evangelical Orthodox and Catholic included.

SOUTH AFRICA

Area 1,222,000 sq.km. This includes: 1. Walvis Bay (an enclave on Namibian coast 1,124 sq.km). 2. Four independent states: Transkei 45,000 sq.km., Bophuthatswana 40,000 sq.km., Ciskei 9,000 sq.km., and Venda 6,500 sq.km. These "TBVC" states are not internationally recognized so are not included here as part of South Africa.

Population 32,100,000. Annual growth 2.4% (White 1.2%, Black 2.8%). People per sq.

km. 27. TBVC states 5,100,000, National states ("Homelands") 7,100,000. 52% of the Black population lives in the ten enclave states created by the government.

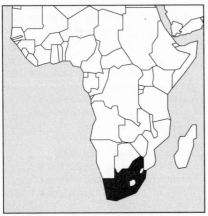

Peoples

Black 73%. *Nguni* (5) Zulu 6,600,000; Xhosa 5,900,000; Swazi 1,000,000; South Ndebele 477,000.

   Sotho (3) North Sotho/Pedi 2,800,000; East Sotho/Tswana 2,400,000; South Sotho 2,200,000; North Ndebele 340,000.

   Other (2) Tsonga/Shangaan 1,200,000, Venda 594,000.

White 15%. Afrikaners 2,700,000, English speaking 1,800,000. Portuguese 650,000; German 45,000; Greek 40,000.

Colored (Mixed race) 9%. Predominantly descendants of slaves with Black, Khoi-Khoi (Hottentot), European and Asian blood; 90% live in the Western Cape Province. The Cape Malays are considered part of this community.

Asian 3%. Indians 77% in Durban area of Natal, Chinese 11,000.

Literacy 89%. *National languages:* Afrikaans, English. The 10 national independent states also use their majority language as the official language. *All languages* 28. *Bible translations* 17 Bibles, 1 New Testament, 1 portion.

Capitals: Pretoria (administrative) 865,000; Cape Town (legislative) 1,740,000; Bloemfontein (judicial) 220,000. *Other major cities:* Johannesburg/Soweto 3,500,000

(6,600,000 live in the Witwatersrand and South Transvaal industrial complex); Durban 1,100,000; Port Elizabeth 680,000. Urbanization 56% (Asians 91%, Whites 89%, Coloreds 77%, Blacks 31%).

Economy: The richest and most industrialized country in Africa (25% of GNP, 40% of industrial output). The world's biggest exporter of nonpetroleum minerals—especially gold, platinum, chrome, diamonds, and coal. Lack of water and erratic rainfall could limit growth. World recession, drought, and worldwide opposition to the racial policies have further stimulated government overspending on the cumbersome administration of separate development (apartheid) and defense. Inflation and a severe decline in the economy since 1982 have been the result. Inflation 25% ('85). Income/person $2,450 (18% of USA). Whites, on average, earn three times that of Blacks.

Politics: The Union of South Africa was formed in 1910. A White minority parliamentary republic created in 1961. The constitution of 1984 instituted a strong presidency and a limited sharing of power with the Colored and Asian minorities, but created serious rifts in both the Afrikaner and other communities. The exclusion of Blacks (especially the urban population) from national politics and the compartmentalization of the races became major issues that dominated every aspect of national life. Changes were too fast for the fearful Whites and far too slow for the frustrated Blacks. The deteriorating security situation, adverse world publicity, and the economic crisis made more rapid changes essential. March 17, 1992 the "South African Referendum On Ending White Minority Rule" was presented to the voters. 68.6% voted yes, paving the way for the leadership to move toward a more equitable democratic process for all South Africans. The economic and strategic importance of South Africa is of international concern, both for surrounding Black states and the superpowers. The 10 national states are enclaves within South Africa. All are overpopulated and very dependent economically on South Africa.

They are the theoretical home for the 11 million Blacks in the White areas of South Africa (87% of the territory). Four have opted for political independence: Transkei 1976, Bophuthatswana 1977, Venda 1979, Ciskei 1981. All but Bophuthatswana are one-party states.

Religion: Freedom of religion. Official statistics omit the four independent states, which are here included:

African traditional religions approximately 20%. The more strongly so being Shangaan 49%, Venda 46%, Xhosa 25%, Zulu 25%.

Nonreligious/Atheist, etc. 5%.

Hindu 1.8%. Indians, mainly in Natal.

Muslim 1.1%. Cape Malays and Indians.

Jewish 0.42%. Over 130,000 mainly in Rand area of South Transvaal.

Christian 71.6%. Affiliated approximately 61% (including TBVC states). Church statistics below are based on 1980 government census which excludes TBVC states and are thus not affiliated figures as elsewhere. Numbers of Christians will also now be lower than indicated in 1980 for older, mainline denominations and higher for rapidly growing younger churches.

Roman Catholic 10.1%. 3,200,000 adherents. Growing among Blacks.

Orthodox 0.13%. Mostly Greeks.

African Independent Churches 22%. Over 3,700 groups. Largest (adherents):
Zion Christian Church 1,250,000
Nazarite Baptist Church approximately 500,000
St. John's Apostolic Faith Mission 400,000

Foreign marginal groups 0.5%. Largest (adherents): Jehovah's Witnesses 103,750; Mormons 9,000.

Protestant 40%. Approximately 12,800,000 adherents. Denominations probably 160. Largest (adherents of all races):
Nederduitse Gereformeeerde Kerk (Dutch Reformed) 3,478,000
Methodist Church 2,113,000
Church of the Province of South Africa (Anglican) 1,517,000
Lutheran Church 835,000
Presbyterian Church 499,000
Congregational Church (UCCSA) 407,000

Apostolic Faith Mission 303,000
Baptist Church 255,000
Full Gospel Church of God 169,000
Assemblies of God (various) 133,000
Church of England in South Africa 96,000
Other Pentecostal Churches 764,000
Evangelical 15% of population.

Missionaries to South Africa approximately 1,310 in over 80 agencies. Missionaries from within South Africa approximately 1,020, of which 240 serve outside South Africa (1:12,500 Protestants).

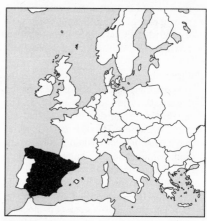

SPAIN

Area 505,000 sq.km. The major part of the Iberian peninsula, and including the Canary Islands off Northwest Africa, and the enclaves of Ceuta and Melilla on the North African coast.

Population 39,300,000. Annual growth 0.3%. People per sq.km. 78.

Peoples

Spanish 96%. Castilian 27,000,000; Catalan 6,900,000, Galician 3,200,000.

Basque 2.3%. Most in the four Atlantic provinces adjoining France. Many more Basques are being culturally absorbed into the Castilian majority. There is a strong separatist movement.

Gypsy 0.2%. Some claim that there may be 200,000.

Foreign 1%. German, French, Portuguese, British, Latin American, etc.

Literacy 93%. *Official language:* Castilian

Spanish. Regionally official: Basque, Catalan, Galician. Spanish is now the third most widely spoken language in the world. *All languages* 5. *Bible translations* 3 Bibles, 2 portions.

Capital: Madrid 4,000,000. Other major cities: Barcelona approximately 3,000,000; Valencia 1,000,000; Bilbao 1,000,000; Seville 1,000,000. Urbanization 91%.

Economy: The devastation caused by instability and the 1936–39 civil war impoverished the country. Steady growth through tourism and industry since 1968. Further radical changes are following Spain's entry into the EC in 1986. Income/person $6,010 (33% of USA). Unemployment 19%.

Politics: Spain's tumultuous past molds the present. The Muslim Moorish occupation lasted 700 years, ending in 1492. The worldwide Spanish Empire lasted for three centuries. The last two centuries have been ones of instability, civil wars, and dictatorships; the latter under General Franco lasted from 1939 to 1975. Constitutional monarchy since 1975, and a gradual democratization and liberalization since then. Parliamentary democracy with more autonomy being granted to regions—especially for the Catalans and Basques. The left-wing ETA Basque terrorist campaign for full independence has plagued Spain since 1961.

Religion: Severe discrimination against, and even open persecution of, non-Catholics followed Franco's victory in the civil war. Traditional Catholicism became dominant. Gradual easing of discriminatory laws culminated in religious freedom being guaranteed in the 1978 constitution.

Nonreligious/Atheist 4%. Rapid secularization with many baptized Catholics no longer linked to the church.

Christian 96%. Affiliated 94%.

  Roman Catholic 93.6%. Practicing 25%.

  Marginal groups 0.35%. 135,000 adherents; 57,000 members. Rapid growth. Largest (adult members): Jehovah's Witnesses 56,700; Mormons 7,200.

  Protestant 0.5%. 193,000 adherents; 63,700 members. Denominations 20. Largest (adult members):
Filadelfia Church (gypsies) 13,500
Brethren 12,000
Evangelical Baptist Union (Southern Baptist) 7,500
Seventh-Day Adventist Church 5,000
Federation of Independent Churches (The Evangelical Alliance Mission) 3,800
Assemblies of God 1,850
Evangelical 0.34% of population.
Missionaries to Spain 610 (1:63,400 people) in 88 agencies. Missionaries from Spain approximately 10 (1:19,300 Protestants).

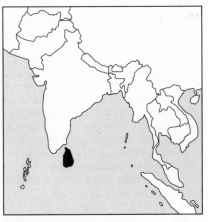

SRI LANKA

Area 65,600 sq.km. Large island 80 km. southeast of the southern tip of India.

Population 17,200,000. Annual growth 1.6%. People per sq.km. 264.

Peoples

Sinhalese 72%. An Aryan people; largely Buddhist. Many castes—unusual for Buddhist societies.

Tamil 20%. (Lanka Tamils residents for over 1,000 years, mainly in north and east) 1,770,000; Indian Tamils (imported laborers in 19th and 20th centuries; mainly in highland tea plantations). The majority are Hindu.

Moor 6%. Arab-Tamil descent 950,000, Tamil descent 28,000.

Burgher 0.3%. European-Asian descent. Once privileged; many emigrating to Australia. Nearly all live in Colombo.

Veddah: Only 140 left of the aboriginal people.

Literacy 90%. *Official language:* Sinhala. Tamil and English are recognized as national languages. *All languages* 5. *Bible translations* 3 Bibles.

Capital: Colombo 991,000. Urbanization 24%.

Economy: Agricultural with tea and rubber the most important export commodities. Increasing industrialization since 1977. Subsequent rapid progress has been marred by the impact of the communal violence. Inflation, the cost of living and foreign debt are soaring. Tourism and trade are adversely affected. Income/person $320 (2% of USA).

Politics: Independence gained in 1948, as a parliamentary democracy, after 450 years of successive colonial administrations by the Portuguese, Dutch, and British. Attempts to Sinhalize national life in 1956 and the attendant discrimination against ethnic and religious minorities provoked increasing communal violence and efforts by extremists to fight for an independent Tamil state in the north and east. The increasing scale of violence led to massacres, a massive refugee problem, and civil war. The Indian armed forces intervened in 1987 to suppress the Tamil Tiger guerilla movement with only partial success. The Indian peacekeeping force was asked by the government to leave in 1989. Renewed fighting betwen the government and Tamil Tigers continues.

Religion: Buddhism is the state religion and, as such, is protected and promoted. Although freedom for other religions is assured, there has been some discrimination against minority religions in taxation, employment, and education.

Buddhist 69.3%. Almost entirely of the Sinhala community. Resurgence since 1956, and actively seeking the conversion of Christians, and stimulating Buddhist missionary activity around the world.

Hindu 15.4%. Almost entirely Tamil.

Muslim 7.6% Moors and Malays.

Christian 7.4%. Affiliated 7%.

   Roman Catholic 6.3%. 1,030,000 adher-

ents; 577,000 members. Influential through a variety of social programs.

Protestant 0.75%. 124,000 adherents; 59,600 members. Denominations 30. Largest (adult adherents):

Church of Ceylon 48,800
Methodist Church 26,200
Salvation Army 5,500
Church of South India (Tamil) 5,300
Independent Indigenous Churches 5,000
Ceylon Pentecostal Mission 5,000
Assemblies of God 3,500
Baptist Union 3,200
Apostolic Church 3,100
Fellowship of Free Churches (Pentecostal) 2,500
Foursquare Gospel Church 1,750
Apostolic Church 1,250
Seventh-Day Adventist Church 1,000

Evangelical 0.2% of population.

Missionaries to Sri Lanka estimated 90 (10,182,000 people) in 20 agencies. Missionaries from within Sri Lanka estimated 12 (Ceylon Pentecostal Mission, which began in 1923 in Ceylon, has established churches in India, Malaysia, United Kingdom, France, Canada, USA, Mexico).

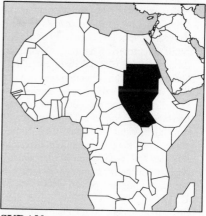

SUDAN

Area 2,506,000 sq.km. Africa's largest country. Desert in north, merging into tropical bush in south.

Population 25,300,000. Annual growth 2.8%. People per sq.km. 10. About 40% of the population is nomadic or seminomadic.

Peoples: Over 56 distinct ethnic groups, 597 subgroups. Many language families—Semitic, Cushitic, Nilotic, Nilo-Saharan, etc., too complex and unclear for breakdown here.

Sudanese Arab 51%. Predominant in center and north.

Other African peoples 49%.

Southern provinces 25%. Dinka 1,466,000; Nuer 800,000; Azande 360,000; Lotuko 200,000; Shilluk 190,000; Thuri 170,000; Toposa 160,000; Murle 70,000, etc.

North/northeastern peoples 8%. Beja 1,100,000; Nubians 450,000; Tigre 190,000.

Darfur 5%. Fur 400,000; Masalit 125,000; Zaghawa 120,000; Daju 80,000, Tama 60,000, etc.

West Africans 6%. Fulani 100,000, etc.

Kordofan peoples 5%. Nuba tribes (100 tribes speaking 37 languages) 900,000.

Refugees number 1-1.5 million. The majority from Ethiopia, many from Chad, some from Uganda. Just over half use Arabic as trade language.

Literacy 20%. *Official language:* Arabic, understood by 80% of the population. *All languages* 137. *Bible translations* 4 Bibles, 14 New Testaments, 10 portions.

Capital: Khartoum. Khartoum-Omdurman conurbation 2,258,000. Urbanization 21%.

Economy: Agricultural; cotton and peanuts being the major export commodities. The vast distances and inadequate transportation hinder development. The renewed civil war and the virtual collapse of the economy since 1983 have stopped big irrigation schemes and exploitation of southern oil deposits. Economic conditions in the south are tragic. Income/person $400 (3% of USA).

Politics: Independent from Britain and Egypt in 1956. Bitter fighting between Arab northerners and southern secessionists 1955–1972. After 12 years of uneasy peace, and a degree of autonomy for the south, fighting has broken out again. The erratic, and increasingly unstable, West-leaning government of President Nimeiry collapsed in 1985. Successive governments since then have been riven with religious differences on the national application of Islamic law, and thus unable to open peace negotiations with the southerners.

Religion: The strenuous efforts by Muslim northerners to impose Islam and Arab culture on the southerners has been one of the root causes for the present conflict. An Islamic republic—declared in 1983, with the imposition of Islamic sharia law on all citizens—provoked anger among non-Muslims and vociferous anti-Christian propaganda and actions by Muslim fundamentalists. Muslim efforts to Islamize the southerners have been both crude and forceful.

Muslim 74%. Sunni Islam, with several powerful Sufi religious orders, the largest being Ansar, the followers of the famous Mahdi. Almost the entire northern population is Muslim.

Traditional religions 15%. Predominantly among southern tribes, Nuba Mountain peoples and some Darfur peoples.

Nonreligious/Atheist 1.2%. Mainly urban intellectuals.

Christian 9.8%. Affiliated 9.1%. Most statistics are approximate.

Roman Catholic 5.2%. 1,100,000 adherents; 640,000 members.

Orthodox 0.8%. 170,000 adherents. Mainly Coptic in Nile Valley, and among Ethiopian refugees.

Protestant 3.1%. 650,000 adherents; 190,000 members. Denominations 11, largest (adherents):

Episcopal Church 520,000 (Anglican) (?)
Presbyterian Church 55,000 (?)
Sudanese Church of Christ (SUM) 40,000
Sudan Interior Church (Sudan Interior Mission) 9,000
Africa Inland Church (Africa Inland Mission) 4,000 (?)

Evangelical 1.6% of population.

Foreign Christian workers approximately 200 (1:110,000 people).

TAIWAN

Area 36,000 sq.km. A mountainous island

300 km. off coast of mainland China.
Population 20,200,000. Annual growth 1.1%.
People per sq.km. 561.

Peoples

Han Chinese 98% speaking three major languages.

Taiwanese (Hoklo, Minnan) 14,200,000. Over 300 years on Taiwan. Rural majority.

Hakka 2,100,000. About 200 years on Taiwan.

Mandarin 2,500,000. Refugees from mainland China 1945–50. Predominantly urban.

Malayo-Polynesian mountain peoples (11) 1.7%. Largest: Ami 104,000; Paiwan 53,000; Tayal 46,000; Bunun 32,000; Sediq 20,000.

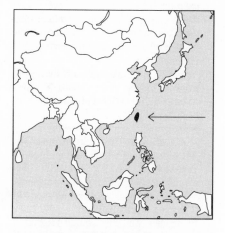

Literacy 90%. *Official language* and language of education: Mandarin. Hoklo is widely spoken. *All languages* 14. *Bible translations* 4 Bibles, 5 New Testaments, 1 portion.

Capital: Taipei 2,500,000. Major city: Kaoshiung 1,300,000. Urbanization 73%.

Economy: Rapid industrialization and economic growth to become one of the world's leading exporting states. Income/person $3,000 (21.3% of USA).

Politics: Under Japanese rule 1895–1945. After the fall of mainland China to the Communists in 1949, Taiwan became the refuge of the Nationalist Chinese government. A one-party republic dominated by mainlanders, but increasing Taiwanese participation

in economic and political life is lessening communal tensions. International political isolation of Taiwan led to the loss of UN membership in 1971. Both Chinese governments seek reunification on their own terms.

Religion: Secular state with freedom of religion. The strong anti-Communist stance of the government, and efforts to unify the country under one language, have placed it in conflict with some denominations— chiefly the large Presbyterian church, whose membership is predominantly Taiwanese.

Nonreligious/Atheist 20-30%. Many younger people are secular and abandon their family religions.

Chinese religions 60-70%. Blend of Confucianism, Taoism, and Buddhism, with strong emphasis on veneration of ancestors.

Muslim 0.5%. Postwar immigrant Hui.

Tribal religions 0.5%. Minority of mountain peoples.

Christian 5%.

Roman Catholic 1.4%. Practicing 50%. 275,000 adherents; 151,000 members.

Marginal groups 0.26%. 52,000 adherents; 35,000 members. Largest (adult members): True Jesus Church 27,300; Mormons 6,100.

Protestant 3.5%. 670,000 adherents; 347,000 members. Denominations 70, also numerous independent congregations. Largest (adult members):
Presbyterian Church of Taiwan 95,000
Assembly Hall (W. Nee) 48,000
Southern Baptist Convention 12,000
Seventh-Day Adventist Church 6,078
Taiwan Holiness Church (OMS International) 4,495
Taiwan Lutheran Church 4,239
Free Methodist Church 3,800
Methodist Church 3,000
Assemblies of God 2,700
Chinese Evangelical Lutheran Church 2,000

Evangelical 2.5% of population.

Missionaries to Taiwan 863 (1:22,000 people) in over 80 agencies. Missionaries from Taiwan 10 (1:67,000 Protestants). Many others have gone as "tentmaking" missionaries, or to pastor overseas Chinese congregations.

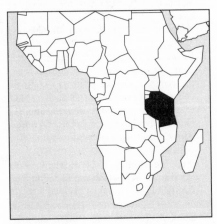

TANZANIA

Area 946,000 sq.km. Mainland Tanganyika and Zanzibar (two offshore islands) 2,650 sq.km.

Population 27,300,000. Zanzibar 728,000. Annual growth 3.6%. People per sq.km. 29.

Peoples: Over 126 distinct ethnic groups.

African peoples 99%. Tribalism has not been as divisive a force as in many lands. Major groups: Sukuma 2,820,000; Rufiji (4 groups) 1,950,000; Rukwa (3) 1,090,000; Makonde 890,000; Chagga 800,000.

Other 1%. Hutu refugees from Burundi, 100,000 (?); Indian 70,000 and decreasing, Westerners, etc.

Literacy 85%. *Official languages:* Swahili, English. The use of Swahili is so widespread, it is even replacing local languages in some areas. *All languages* 115. *Bible translations* 11 Bibles, 18 New Testaments, 15 portions.

Capital: Dar es Salaam 1,500,000. Capital designate. Dodoma. Urbanization 19%.

Economy: Agricultural subsistence economy. Inefficient, centralized bureaucracy and an overzealous nationalization of businesses and collectivization of rural communities into "ujamaa" villages have been detrimental. Lowered production,
and run-down industry and services, together with severe drought in the '80s have seriously reduced living standards. Income/person $220 (1% of USA).

Politics: Tanganyika gained independence from Britain in 1961, Zanzibar in 1963. The two countries united as a one-party federal socialist republic in 1964, though Zanzibar has retained a considerable degree of autonomy. The retirement of the respected President Nyerere may eventually lead to a shift away from his socialist dream. There is considerable pressure for change and liberalization in Zanzibar.

Religion: Religious freedom; the government encourages religious education in schools, though Islam is gaining in political influence.

Muslim 32.5%. The majority in Zanzibar (98%), along the coastal belt, and some peoples on the Mozambique border.

Traditional religions 19%.

Christian 47.7%. Nominal 12%. Affiliated 34%.

Roman Catholic 18.5%. 4,000,000 adherents; 2,200,000 members. Practicing 44%.

Orthodox 0.1%. 15,000 adherents.

Marginal groups 0.6%. 130,000 adherents. Predominantly African indigenous churches.

Protestant 14.8%. 3,200,000 adherents; 1,271,000 members. Denominations 30. Largest (adult members):

Evangelical Lutheran Church 436,000

Anglican Church 306,000

Africa Inland Church (African Inland Mission) 200,000

Moravian Church 79,500

Seventh-Day Adventist Church 53,000

Pentecostal Churches in Tanzania (ex-Swedish) 42,000

Tanzania Assemblies of God (AG) 18,000

Pentecostal Assemblies of Tanzania (Pentecostal Assemblies of Canada) 15,000

Brethren Assemblies 12,000

Evangelical 9% of population.

Missionaries to Tanzania approximately 660 (1:33,000 people) in about 60 agencies. Missionaries from within Tanzania approximately 10.

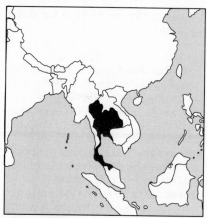

THAILAND

Area 514,000 sq.km. A fertile and well-watered land.

Population 56,600,000. Annual growth 1.7%. People per sq.km. 110.

Peoples: Four major peoples and numerous smaller groups.

Thai 80%. Four main groups. Central 19,000,000; Northern 6,000,000; Southern 4,000,000; Lao 12,500,000. The latter live in the northeast.

Chinese 12% or more. Thai-speaking 80%. A minority still use over six Chinese languages, mostly Chaochow.

Malay 3.2%. In the extreme south adjoining Malaysia.

Khmer 2.8%. Two main languages.

Tribal peoples 2%. Over 48 indigenous groups, most in the mountainous border regions. Six main groups: Mon-Khmer peoples (15 groups) 340,000; Karen (6) 280,000; Tai (9) 210,000; Miao-Yao (3) 156,000; Tibeto-Burman (10) 73,000; Austronesian (4) 8,000.

Refugees 1%. Kampucheans around 300,000; Laotians and Vietnamese 250,000; Burmese 15,000.

Literacy 84%. *Official language:* Thai. *All languages* 61. *Bible translations* 6 Bibles, 7 New Testaments, 10 portions.

Capital: Krung Thep (Bangkok) 6,043,000. Urbanization 17%.

Economy: Productive agricultural economy. Main exports are rice, pineapples, tapioca and rubber. The depletion of forest cover is worsening the cycle of droughts and floods. Rapid industrialization and development of mineral resources. The government is making a determined effort to eradicate the drug trafficking from the "Golden Triangle" in the far northwest of the country. Income/person $840 (5% of USA).

Politics: Never ruled by any Western power. Constitutional monarchy, with the popular king having a strong unifying and stabilizing role. The succession of stable governments, growth in the economy and the world collapse of Communism has boosted Thai importance and prospects.

Religion: Buddhism is the state religion, but there is freedom and all religions are seen as a bulwark against Communist ideology.

Buddhist 92%. Thai, Lao, Shan, some Chinese, etc. Much syncretism with spirit worship.

Muslim 4%. Malays and some Thai in the far south.

Chinese religions 1.6%. Many Chinese are included with the Buddhist figure.

Animist 1.4%. Among tribal peoples.

Christian 1%. Affiliated 0.72%.

Roman Catholic 0.4%. 212,000 adherents; 114,000 members. Stronger among Chinese and in Bangkok.

Protestant 0.31%. 167,000 adherents; 81,000 members. Denominations 33. Largest (adult members):

Church of Christ in Thailand (Presbyterian, Baptist, etc.) 35,000

Karen Baptist Convention 8,500

Seventh-Day Adventist Church 6,800

Lahu Church 4,000

Church Fellowships relating to Overseas Missionary Fellowship 3,200

Church Fellowships relating to WEC International 2,200

Gospel Church of Thailand (Christian & Missionary Alliance) 2,110

Thailand Baptist Churches Association (Southern Baptist) 2,100

Evangelical 0.2% of population.

Missionaries to Thailand approximately 1,030 (1:51,000 people) in 70 agencies. Missionaries from within Thailand approximately 14.

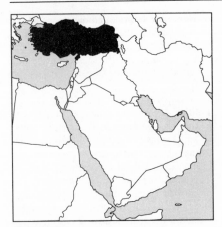

TURKEY

Area 781,000 sq.km. The country straddles two continents; 3% in Europe (Thrace), 97% in Asia (Anatolia), and controls the Bosphorus and the Dardanelles, the vital sea link between the Black Sea and Mediterranean. Its strategic position has made the area of prime importance throughout history.

Population 56,600,000. Annual growth 2.2%. People per sq.km. 73.

Peoples: There has been continued pressure on the ethnic minorities to conform to Turkish culture. Ethnic populations are therefore hard to assess.

Turks 80.2%. A Central Asian people that conquered and largely absorbed the indigenous peoples of the land from the eleventh century onward. The Turks are ethnically diverse, but culturally fairly homogenous. Distinctive subgroups: Azeri 530,000 in the east, Yoruk 320,000 on the west coast.

Kurds 16%. An Indo-Iranian people in southeast Anatolia, probably related to the ancient Medes. Their ethnic identity is denied by the Turks, and by 1990 there was a growing insurgency problem in the Kurdish area.

Arabs 1.4% in South Anatolia adjoining Syria.

Muslim minorities 1.1%. Adygey 130,000; Laz 92,000; Georgian 90,000; Serbo-Croat 61,000; Albanian 61,000; Bulgarian 27,000; Gypsy 20,000, all of whom are being rapidly absorbed into the Turkish majority.

Non-Muslim minorities 0.3%. Armenian 60,000; Assyrian 25,000; Greek 8,000. Rapid decline through emigration. There were 1,750,000 Armenians and 1,500,000 Greeks in Turkey in 1900.

Refugees 1%. Iranis 600,000; Central Asians possibly 50,000 from USSR and Afghanistan.

Literacy 62%. *Official language:* Turkish. *All languages* 29. *Bible translations* 7 Bibles, 2 New Testaments, 11 portions.

Capital: Ankara 2,300,000. Other major cities: Istanbul (Constantinople) 5,500,000; Izmir (Smyrna) 1,500,000; Adana 780,000; Bursa 620,000. Urbanization 53%. Rapid growth of cities with huge slum areas in which 65% of Ankara's population and 45% of Istanbul's live.

Economy: Political instability and social unrest together with world recession led to economic crises between 1973 and 1983. Steady recovery since then, but the land is only partially industrialized. Remittances from Turks in Europe are an important source of foreign exchange. Income/person $1,200 (7% of USA).

Politics: The Turkish Ottoman Empire once stretched across North Africa, Arabia, Western Asia, and Southeast Europe. Its demise and final fragmentation in World War I led to revolution and the formation of a republic in 1923. Periods of social disorder and military rule gave way to a democratic government in 1983, but with the military still retaining considerable power. Turkey is a member of NATO, but is in dispute with fellow-NATO member Greece for long-standing historic reasons and over territorial rights in the Aegean Sea and the division of Cyprus. Application has been made to join the EC.

Religion: Turkey's Ottoman Empire was for centuries the guardian of all the holy places of Islam and its chief protaganist. Since the sweeping reforms of the 1920s Turkey has officially been a secular state. In recent years Islam has become a more important political factor, making the lot of non-Muslim minorities more difficult despite the constitutional guarantee of religious freedom.

Muslim 99.5%. Sunni Muslims 85%. Alevi Shi'a 14% predominantly among Kurds. There are also Yezidis (a divergent syncretic sect) among the Kurds.

Christian 0.3%. Rapid decline. Almost entirely confined to national and foreign minorities.

Orthodox 0.23%. 120,000 adherents. Denominations 10. Largest (adherents): Armenian Orthodox Church 60,000; Greek Orthodox Church 23,000 (?); Syrian Orthodox Church 21,000.

Roman Catholic 0.02%. 15,000 adherents. Predominantly foreign residents and Assyrians.

Protestant 0.02%. 13,100 adherents; 4,500 members. Predominantly foreign residents and Armenians.

Evangelical only about 750 indigenous believers, mostly Armenian, Assyrian and Greek. Maybe 250 believers from a Muslim background.

Foreign Christians serving in Turkey approximately 100 (1:500,000 people).

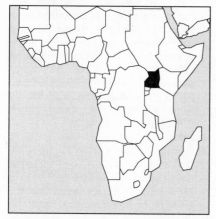

UGANDA

Area 236,000 sq.km. Much of the land is fertile and well watered. The climate is temperate in the highlands. Long known as the "Pearl of Africa."

NOTE: All following statistics are reasonable estimates; the anarchy and devastation since 1976 having been so great that accurate statistics are not available.

Population 17,600,000. Annual growth 3.4%. People per sq.km. 74. No one can estimate with accuracy the numbers who perished during Amin's dictatorship, and the subsequent civil wars, famines and tribal killings. Estimates vary from 800,000 to 2,000,000; 300,000 of these have been since 1981. Many more have fled into Kenya, Sudan and Zaire.

Peoples: Over 40 ethnic groups; three major divisions:

Bantu 65% (over 16 groups, mainly in west, southwest and south): Ganda 2,350,000; Ankole 1,200,000; Soga 1,175,000; Chiga 1,040,000; Toro-Nyoro 910,000; Nyaruanda 860,000; Luhya 400,000; Rundi 300,000; Konjo 250,000; Gwere 240,000, etc.

Nilotic 27% (12, mainly in the north and center): Teso 1,220,000; Lango 800,000; Acholi 630,000; Karamajong 300,000; Alur 280,000; Padhola 230,000; Kakwa 90,000, etc.

Sudanic 6.4% (over 10): Lugbara 544,000; Madi 176,000, etc.

Other 1.6%. Kenyans, etc.

Literacy 40%. *Official language:* English, spoken by about 10% of the population. *All languages* 43. *Bible translations* 16 Bibles, 3 New Testaments, 10 portions.

Capital: Kampala 500,000. Urbanization 14%.

Economy: The fertility of the soil could have provided a healthy economic future. The expulsion in 1972 of the Asian community, who had played such a vital role in the economy, and the chaos in the years following, have reduced the land to poverty. Many areas have been laid waste by marauding soldiers—especially in the West Nile District and Luwero Triangle northwest of Kampala. However by 1990 a slow recovery was under way. Income/person $560 (4% of USA).

Politics: Independence from Britain in 1962. An attempt at delicately balancing the political powers of the southern Bantu kingdoms and northern Nilotic peoples ended in

1967, when the northerner Milton Obote took complete control, favoring his own tribe, the Lango. Anarchy increased until Idi Amin seized power in 1971. The crazed dictatorship of Amin brutalized the country as the army pillaged and murdered with impunity. Amin's invasion of northwest Tanzania in 1978 provoked a vigorous response, and in 1979 Tanzanian and Ugandan exile troops deposed the military regime. Sadly, bitter tribal and political rivalries have continued with much bloodshed and civil war. The Museveni government is a military-civilian regime that has allowed a limited degree of democracy.

Religion: Under Amin there were restrictions and intense persecution of Christians (often for reasons of tribalism). For a time the Muslim minority was favored. There is now freedom of religion. Most figures below are rough estimates.

Traditional religions 12%. Throughout the country, but only in a majority in four or five northeastern peoples, the Karamajong, Pokot, etc.

Muslim 5%. Most live in the northwest, but there are some sprinkled all over the country. No group has a Muslim majority, but there are large minorities among the Kakwa, Madi, and Soga. Somewhat discredited since the fall of Amin.

Baha'i 2.8%.

Christian 80%. Nominal 9%, affiliated 71%.
   Roman Catholic 42.3%. 6,211,000 adherents; 3,540,000 members.
   Orthodox 0.14%. 20,000 adherents.
   African Indigenous Churches 0.9%. 130,000 adherents; 71,000 members.
   Protestant 27.6%. 4,068,000 adherents; 1,010,000 members. Largest (adherents):
   Anglican Church (CMS, Bible Churchman's Missionary Society, Africa Inland Mission) 3,700,000
   Pentecostal Assemblies of God 80,000 (?)
   Elim Pentecostal Fellowship 60,000 (?)
   Church of the Redeemed 50,000 (?)
   Baptist Union (Southern Baptist, Conservative Baptist Foreign Missionary Society) 30,000

Evangelicals 24.9% of population.
Missionaries to Uganda 190 (1:77,000 people) in 28 agencies. Missionaries from within Uganda 100 (?). Many are exiles serving the Lord in other lands.

UNITED KINGDOM

Area 244,000 sq.km. Two main islands: Britain and the northeast of Ireland. A union of four kingdoms: England 53%, Scotland 32.4%, Wales 8.5%, and Northern Ireland 5.8%. Also three small autonomous states that are dependencies of the British Crown: Isle of Man 588 sq.km. (island in the Irish Sea); Guernsey 78 sq.km. (five Channel Islands); Jersey 116 sq.km. (one Channel Island).

Population 57,400,000 of which England has 83.1%, Scotland 9.2%, Wales 5%, and Northern Ireland 2.7%. Annual growth 0.2%. People per sq.km. 235.

Peoples

Indigenous majorities 93%. English 76%, predominantly Anglo-Saxon; Scots 8%, Anglo-Saxon and Gaelic; Irish 5%, Gaelic and Scots (including immigrants into Britain from the Irish Republic); Welsh 4%, predominantly Celtic.

Indigenous minorities 0.9%. Jews 410,000; Gypsies 85,000.

Immigrant minorities 6%. *South Asians* 2.5%. Indian origin 700,000; Pakistani 250,000; Bangladeshi 200,000. Also refugees from East Africa 200,000. *West Indians* 1.9%. From many Caribbean countries; almost all are Blacks. *Other* 1.3%. Greeks 200,000; Italians 200,000; Arabs 150,000; Chinese 125,000; Africans 90,000; Turks, 55,000; Vietnamese 20,000.

Literacy 95%. *Official language:* English; in Wales both English and Welsh. English has become the primary language of 700 million in the world as well as the major language of international communication. *All languages* 7 indigenous, many more immigrant languages (at least 128 in London alone). *Bible translations* in indigenous languages 4 Bibles, 2 portions. There have been more translations of the Scriptures into English than into any other language.

Capital: London 10,100,000. Other major cities: Birmingham 2,800,000; Manchester 2,600,000; Bradford-Leeds 2,100,000; Glasgow 1,850,000; Liverpool 1,520,000; Newcastle-upon-Tyne 1,150,000. Urbanization 76%.

Economy: An industrialized economy—the world's first. Renewed economic growth in the '80s after years of decline through poor management, labor unrest, and the extent of public ownership in industry. The government has vigorously sought to rectify these with some success. Exploitation of North Sea oil has helped to stimulate recovery. The basic underlying ill-health of the economy is cause for concern. Income/person $10,430 (57% of USA).

Politics: Parliamentary, constitutional monarchy. The United Kingdom was formed in 1801 as a Union of Great Britain and Ireland. Southern Ireland formally seceded from the Union in 1921. The British Empire, which once covered one quarter of the world, has become 60 independent states, most being members of the British Commonwealth. Since 1945 the transition from a world power to a European state linked to its own continent has not been easy. The UK is a member of NATO and of the EC.

Religion: Complete religious freedom. The Church of England (Anglican) is recognized as the established church in England, and the Church of Scotland (Presbyterian) in Scotland. The Sovereign is recognized as the titular head of the Church of England.

Nonreligious/Atheist: 26%. Many nominal "Christians" are actually secularists.

Muslim 2.7%. The actual number of Muslims is disputed but·is between 1 and 1.5 million, predominantly South Asians, but also Arabs, Turks, etc.

Jewish 0.7%. Gradually declining.

Hindu 0.5%. *Sikh* 0.5%. Predominantly Indian.

Buddhist 0.2%. Chinese, etc.

Christian 69.4%. Nominal 20%. Affiliated 49.9%. Regular adult church attendance 11%; but with wide regional differences. See below:

Roman Catholic 9%. 5,100,000 adherents; 2,315,000 members. Predominantly lower class and many of Irish extraction. Highest percentage in northwest and London area.

Orthodox Churches 0.7%. 372,000 adherents; 125,000 members. Denominations 12. Predominantly Greek Cypriot, also many Eastern European refugee minorities.

Marginal 2.6%. 1,400,000 adherents; 348,000 members. Groups 14+. Largest (adult members): Jehovah's Witnesses 97,945; Mormons 67,000; Spiritualist 53,000; Scientology 45,000.

Protestant 48% including nominals. 31,200,000 adherents; 4,900,000 members. Many baptized Anglicans no longer attend church, hence the large adherent figure. Denominations 250+. Largest (adult members):

Anglican/Episcopal Church (8) 2,058,000

Presbyterian/United Reformed Church (14) 1,483,000

Methodist Church (6) 484,700

Baptist Church (10+) 226,000

All "house" churches 120,000

Other Pentecostal Churches (15+) 95,000

Other independent churches 85,000 (?)

West Indian Churches (numerous) 80,000

Brethren assemblies 65,000 (?)

Evangelical 7% of population.

Missionaries from within UK 5,800 (1:5,300

Protestants) in 102 agencies. Missionaries to UK estimated 580, increasingly so from the Third World and USA.

VENEZUELA

Area 912,000 sq.km., with a long Caribbean coastline. A further 230,000 sq.km. of Guyana to the east is claimed by Venezuela.

Population 19,600,000. Annual growth 2.4%. People per sq.km. 21.

Peoples

Spanish-speaking 96%. Approximate composition: Mestizo 64%, European 22%, African 10%. The large Italian community has been almost entirely absorbed into the majority.

Amerindian 2.8%. Over 30 tribes. Largest: Guajiro 50,000; Warao 15,000; Piaroa 12,000; Yanomano 10,000; Carib 10,000.

Other 1.2%. Arabs 100,000; Chinese 25,000; Jews 20,000, etc.

Literacy 86%. *Official language:* Spanish. *All languages* 37. *Bible translations* 1 Bible, 6 New Testaments, 11 portions.

Capital: Caracas 4,500,000. Other major cities: Maracaibo 1,050,000; Valencia 840,000; Barquisimeto 600,000. Urbanization 83%.

Economy: Oil has been the main foreign exchange earner, but the nation's prosperity was reduced by huge foreign debt and misuse of wealth, and in 1988/9 the economy went into severe recession. There is an unhealthy gap between the rich and the poor. Income/person $3,230 (18% of USA).

Politics: Independent from Spain in 1821. A succession of revolutions and harsh dictatorships ended in 1958. Since then there has been a stable democratic government. It is the first Latin American country to have a political party recognized as one founded by evangelicals on reformation principles.

Religion: Religious freedom is guaranteed in the constitution. The Catholic church regained official recognition in 1964 after years of strained Church-State relations, and has a pervasively influential position.

Nonreligious/Atheist 1.5%.

Muslim 0.4%. Predominantly Arab, but also an inflow of Iranis.

Animist and Spiritist 2.2%. Among tribal Amerindians and also the Spanish-speaking majority.

Christian 95.8%. Affiliated 93.5%.

Roman Catholic 90%. Practicing approximately 10%. 15,587,000 adherents.

Orthodox 0.09%. 16,000 adherents. Romanians, Greeks, Russians, Ukrainians etc., in 6 denominations.

Marginal groups 0.7%. 113,000 adherents; 35,400 members. Largest (adult members): Jehovah's Witnesses 25,300; Mormons 8,300.

Protestant 2.6%. 450,000 adherents; 187,000 members. Denominations 74 with many independent churches. Largest (adult members):

Seventh-Day Adventist Church 32,000

Assemblies of God 14,500

OVICE/AIEO (The Evangelical Alliance Mission/ORM) 13,100 (?)

Brethren 10,000 (?)

Southern Baptist Convention 8,300

The Native Church 7,500

International Church of Foursquare Gospel 4,000

Tribal Churches (New Tribes Mission) 3,800 (?)

Evangelicals 2.1% of population.

Missionaries to Venezuela 510 (1:34,000 people) in about 36 agencies. Missionaries from within Venezuela 12 (?).

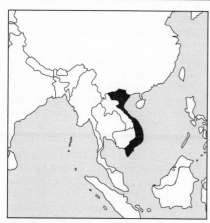

VIETNAM

Area 330,000 sq.km. Occupying the entire 2,000 km. eastern and southern coastline of Indochina.

Population 68,500,000. Annual growth 2.6%. People per sq.km. 208. Possibly 1,500,000 have fled Vietnam since 1975.

Peoples

Vietnamese 86%. Predominantly coastal people; large cultural differences between northern and southern Vietnamese.

Northern ethnic minorities 7.2%. Predominantly Sino-Tibetan; Thai-Tai (19 groups) 2,500,000; Muong 800,000; Hmong (Meo) 350,000; Yao 150,000; Nung 100,000.

Southern ethnic minorities 5.6%. About 40 different groups. Predominantly Austro-Asiatic and Austronesian (Malay) in Southern Highlands. Khmer 500,000; Cham 233,000; Jarai 200,000; Mnong 186,000; Koho 100,000; Hrey 100,000; Bru 70,000, etc.

Chinese 1%. About two-thirds fled to China and the West since 1975.

Literacy 55%. *Official language:* Vietnamese. *All languages* 62. *Bible translations* 2 Bibles, 11 New Testaments, 19 portions.

Capital: Hanoi 1,299,000. Other cities: Ho Chi Minh City (Saigon) 2,703,000, Danang 2,513,000. Urbanization 19%.

Economy: The destructive Vietnam wars have played havoc with the economy. High military expenditure, rigid socialist policies, and world isolation prevent much progress. Widespread hunger and poverty. There was some private enterprise and agriculture permitted in 1989.

Politics: Communist republic declared in North Vietnam in 1945. There has been continuous warfare since 1941, under the Japanese, against the French, South Vietnam, USA, and all surrounding lands. North Vietnam finally conquered the South in 1975, and Kampuchea in 1978-89. Vietnam's withdrawal from Kampuchea (Cambodia) in 1989 may end her diplomatic isolation. Worldwide rejection of Communism has scarcely affected Vietnam.

Religion: Government policy is the steady erosion of the influence of all religions in national affairs and control of all organized religious movements. Pressures on Christians continue to be severe. Statistics below are approximations.

Nonreligious/Atheist 22.5%.

Buddhist 54%. Numerous sects, and strongly permeated with Confucianism, animism and magic.

New religions 11%. Hoa Hao 1,800,000 (Buddhist offshoot), Cao Dai (Buddhist-Catholic syncretism) 3,600,000, etc.

Animist 4%. Minority ethnic groups.

Muslim 1%. Mainly Cham.

Christian 7.5%.

    Roman Catholic 7%. 4,200,000 adherents.

    Protestant 0.5%. 316,000 adherents; 106,000 members. Main groups (est. members):

    Evangelical Church (South) 80,000
    Evangelical Church (North) 10,000
    Other mountain churches 5,000
    Seventh-Day Adventist Church 3,600
    Baptist Church 1,900
    Evangelical 0.5% of population.

YUGOSLAVIA

Area 256,000 sq.km. A Balkan state bordering on the Adriatic Sea.

Population 23,800,000. Annual growth 0.6%. People per sq.km. 93.

Peoples

Serbo-Croatian-speaking 70%. Four distinct Slavic peoples: *Serbian* 39.4%. Predominant in center and east, and mainly Orthodox. *Croatian* 21%. Mainly in northwest and along Dalmatian coast. Predominantly Catholic. *Bosnian* 6%. Serbian Muslims, but officially considered an ethnic entity in the central republic of Bosnia. *Montenegrin* 2.6%. Mainly in the south coastal republic of Montenegro. *Slovene* 8%. A Slavic people in the northwestern republic of Slovenia.

Albanian 7.8%. Majority in the Kosovo region adjoining Albania and many in Montenegro and Macedonia. Mainly Muslim; descendants of the ancient Illyrians.

Macedonian 6%. A Slavic people related to the Bulgarians in the far southern republic of Macedonia. Predominantly Orthodox.

Hungarian 2%. A large minority in Vojvodina region. Many are Catholic or Reformed Protestant.

Other minorities 7.2%. Romany Gypsies, maybe 300,000; Rumelian Turks 125,000; Bulgarians 36,000; Ukranians 30,000, etc.

Literacy 90%. *Official languages:* Serbo-Croatian, Slovene, and Macedonian and, locally, six other languages. *All languages* 20. *Bible translations* 8 Bibles, 3 New Testaments, 3 portions.

Capital: Belgrade 1,600,000. Other major city: Zagreb 1,200,000. Urbanization 37%.

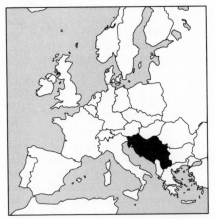

Economy: The world recession in 1979 exposed the inbuilt weaknesses of a bloated bureaucracy and excessive regionalization. There is a massive international debt, much unemployment and high inflation. The wide disparity in living standards between the wealthier north and poor south has further strained the fragile unity of the state. Croatia and Slovenia's desire for independence, war, and a UN and EEC boycott have all but shut down the economy. Average income/person $2,620 (19% of USA).

Politics: Modern Yugoslavia developed from fragments of the Austro-Hungarian and Turkish Ottoman Empire between 1878 and 1918. Communist republic formed in 1945, but nonaligned in world politics since President Tito's break with the USSR in 1948. Communism has not been so authoritarian as in other East European states. Yugoslavia is a federal socialist state consisting of six republics, two autonomous regions, three religions, eight major national groups and two alphabets! The fragmented and fierce nationalism of the various ethnic groups helped trigger World War I, provoked intense civil war in World War II, and is now creating ongoing internal conflicts. Since Tito's death a complex collective leadership and devolution of power to the constituent republics has hardly managed to keep the country together. Ineffective leadership in the face of civil war did little to contain the turmoil. Unless a diplomatic settlement is reached, Yugoslavia could become another Lebanon.

Religion: Atheism is actively promoted by the state in the education system. There is considerable religious freedom, and restrictions on churches' social and cultural ministries are virtually nonexistent since the collapse of Communism. Both indigenous and foreign missionary work is ongoing. Religion, however, is a badge of cultural identity, and evangelicals are attempting to ease the tensions.

Nonreligious/Atheist 18%. The Communist party has 2,200,000 members.

Muslim 11%. Bosnians, 80% of Albanians, Gypsies, Turks. Most are Sunni Muslims, a few are Shi'a. There are 2,250 functioning mosques.

Christian 71%. Affiliated 67%. Many are baptized, but do not attend church.
Orthodox 36.7%. 8,480,000 adherents Denominations 7. Mainly Serbians and Macedonians, a few Albanians.
Roman Catholic 29.7%. 6,680,000 adherents. Mainly Slovenes, Croats, Hungarians, and some Albanians.
Protestant 0.7%. 162,000 adherents; 96,000 members. Denominations approximately 40. Largest (adult members):
Lutheran Church (3) 42,000
Reformed Church (Hungarian) 20,000
Pentecostal Church (4) (?) 11,300
Seventh-Day Adventist Church 10,600
Baptist Church 3,650
Methodist Church (Macedonian & Hungarian) 1,850
Evangelicals 0.16% of population.
Foreign Christians serving Yugoslavians estimated 25. Missionaries from within Yugoslavia estimated 10.

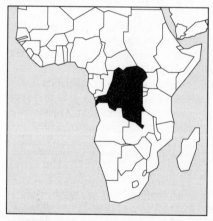

ZAIRE

Area 2,345,000 sq.km. Covering much of Central Africa's rain forest. The heavy rainfall and extensive river systems complicate communications.

Population 36,000,000. Annual growth 3.1%. People per sq.km. 15. Large areas are sparsely populated.

Peoples: An estimated 200 ethnic groups, and many more subgroups.

Bantu peoples 80%. Center and south. Over 32 peoples with more than 100,000. Largest: Luba group 6,173,000; Mongo group 5,600,000; Kongo 4,000,000; Bemba 1,700,000; Songe 800,000; Tetela 650,000; Chokwe 550,000; Bbadha 500,000.
Adamawa Eastern 10%. Northern borderlands. Three peoples with over 100,000 each are: Zande 1,500,000; Ngbaka 800,000; Ngbandi 250,000.
Sudanic 6.7%. Northeast corner. Two peoples with 100,000 and over. Mangbetu 500,000; Lugbara 100,000.
Nilotic 2%. One major people on Uganda border: Alur 700,000.
Pygmy 0.4%. Many small groups in the northern forests.
Other 0.7%. Foreigners, Westerners, other Africans, etc.

Literacy 45%. *Official language:* French. *Trade languages:* Lingala-Bangala in north and northwest, Swahili in east and south, Luba in center and Kongo-Tuba in west. *All languages* 192. *Bible translations* 20 Bibles, 12 New Testaments, 33 portions.

Capital: Kinshasa 4,200,000. Other major cities: Kananga 1,500,000; Lubumbashi 700,000; Kisangani 500,000. Urbanization 40%.

Economy: Vast mineral resources and agricultural potential. Postindependence chaos, widespread maladminstration and corruption have enriched the powerful elite, but impoverished the nation. The road system hardly functions, trade is reduced to a trickle, and profitable agricultural estates have reverted to forest. Africa's potentially most wealthy nation can no longer feed its own people, and is dependent on foreign aid. Some economies introduced since 1983 have brought slight improvements. Income/person $160 (1% of USA).

Politics: In 1960 Belgium hastily granted independence to an ill-prepared people, which led to eight years of violence, anarchy, and secessionist wars. A military coup in 1965 brought General Mobutu to national leadership as an autocratic president of a one-party state. A measure of peace and stability has been restored. The sheer size, ethnic complexity, and lack of communications in the country could imperil its future unity. In 1990 widespread antigovernment protests forced Mobutu to concede some form of multiparty political system in the future.

Religion: In 1972 the president decreed that only six organized religions were permitted to operate and own property: Catholic, one Protestant church (ECZ), Kimbanguist church, Orthodox, Muslim, and Jewish. The authenticity program of the government between 1971 and 1978 placed increasing controls and limitations on Christian institutions and activities. Economic and social disasters forced a dramatic reversal, so that by 1980 there was considerable religious freedom once more, though with a continued subtle pressure that equates Christian commitment with a denial of national heritage. Zaire's size and lack of statistics and communications prevent accuracy in many of the following figures—especially for the African Independent Churches.

Traditional religions 8-12%. Pockets of peoples and areas where the response to the gospel has been less.

Muslim 1.4%. Sunni Muslims predominantly in eastern towns.

Christian 88-92%. Practicing 62%.

    Roman Catholic 42%. 14,000,000 adherents; 8,100,000 members.

    African Indigenous Churches 15-19%. (?) Approximately 6,000,000 adherents. Kimbanguist Church 4,800,000 (?)

Protestant 28%. 9,270,000 adherents; 3,100,000 members. Almost all of the 83 Protestant churches are member communities of the Eglise du Christ au Zaire (ECZ). Most are evangelical, some more liberal, and others marginal in their theology. Some of the larger communities (adult members):

ECZ—Disciples of Christ 330,000 (?)
ECZ—Presbyterian 320,000
ECZ—CECA (Africa Inland Mission) 310,000
ECZ—Pentecostal (ZEM, UK) 151,000
ECZ—Baptist (Canadian Baptist Overseas Mission Board) 135,000
ECZ—Baptist (Baptist Missionary Society, UK) 120,000
ECZ—Methodist (UMC) 115,000
ECZ—CEAZ (Christian & Missionary Alliance) 98,374
ECZ—CECCA (WEC International) 78,000
ECZ—CADELU (RBMU International) 50,000
ECZ—CEHZ (Unevanglized Fields Mission) 49,000 (?)
ECZ—Assemblies of God (USA) 38,000
Anglican Church 72,000
Evangelical 17.6% of population.

Missionaries to Zaire 1,300 (1:25,500 people) in 85 agencies. Missionaries from within Zaire, very approximate 300.

Operation World by Patrick Johnstone. Copyright © 1986 by Patrick J. St. G. Johnstone. Published by Send the Light. Used by permission. Partial update as of February 1992.

Calendars &
Special Events

1993 CHURCH CALENDAR

JANUARY

1/Friday	New Year's Day
	Feast of the Holy Name of
	Our Lord Jesus Christ
	The Circumcision and the
	Name of Jesus
2/Saturday	
3/Sunday	Universal Week of Prayer
4/Monday	
5/Tuesday	
6/Wednesday	The Epiphany of Our Lord
	Jesus Christ
7/Thursday	
8/Friday	
9/Saturday	
10/Sunday	First Sunday after Epiphany
	Feast of the Baptism of Our Lord
	William Laud, Archbishop of
	Canterbury, 1645
11/Monday	
12/Tuesday	
13/Wednesday	Hilary, Bishop of Pointiers, 367
14/Thursday	
15/Friday	Martin Luther King Day
16/Saturday	
17/Sunday	Sanctity of Human Life Sunday
	Second Sunday after Epiphany
	Anthony, Abbot in Egypt, 356
18/Monday	Martin Luther King's Birthday
	Week of Prayer for Christian
	Unity begins
	The Confession of Saint Peter
	the Apostle
19/Tuesday	Wulfstan, Bishop of Worcester,
	1095
20/Wednesday	Fabian, Bishop and Martyr of
	Rome, 250
21/Thursday	Agnes, Martyr at Rome, 304
22/Friday	Vincent, Deacon of Saragossa,
	and Martyr, 304
23/Saturday	Phillips Brooks, Bishop of
	Massachusetts, 1893
24/Sunday	Ecumenical Sunday
	Third Sunday after Epiphany
25/Monday	The Conversion of Saint Paul
	the Apostle
26/Tuesday	Timothy and Titus, Com-
	panions of Saint Paul
27/Wednesday	John Chrysostom, Bishop of
	Constantinople, 407
28/Thursday	Thomas Aquinas, Priest and
	Friar, 1274
29/Friday	
30/Saturday	
31/Sunday	National Association of
	Evangelicals Sunday
	Fourth Sunday after Epiphany

FEBRUARY

1/Monday	
2/Tuesday	Groundhog Day
	The Presentation of Jesus in
	the Temple
	The Purification of Mary
3/Wednesday	Anskar, Archbishop of Hamburg,
	Missionary to Denmark
	and Sweden, 865
4/Thursday	Cornelius the Centurion
5/Friday	The Martyrs of Japan, 1597
6/Saturday	
7/Sunday	Fifth Sunday after Epiphany
8/Monday	
9/Tuesday	
10/Wednesday	
11/Thursday	
12/Friday	Lincoln's Birthday
13/Saturday	Absalom Jones, Priest, 1818
14/Sunday	St. Valentine's Day
	Sixth Sunday after Epiphany
	Cyril, Monk, and Methodius,
	Bishop, Missionaries to
	the Slavs, 869, 885
15/Monday	President's Day
	Thomas Bray, Priest and
	Missionary, 1730
16/Tuesday	
17/Wednesday	
18/Thursday	
19/Friday	

1993 CHURCH CALENDAR cont.

20/Saturday
21/Sunday   Brotherhood Week begins
                   Last Sunday after Epiphany
22/Monday   Washington's Birthday
23/Tuesday   Polycarp, Bishop and Martyr of
                   Smyrna, 156
24/Wednesday   Ash Wednesday, Lent begins
                   Saint Matthias the Apostle
25/Thursday
26/Friday
27/Saturday   George Herbert, Priest, 1633
28/Sunday

MARCH

1/Monday   David, Bishop of Menevia,
                   Wales, c. 544
2/Tuesday   Chad, Bishop of Lichfield, 672
3/Wednesday   John and Charles Wesley, Priests,
                   1791, 1788
4/Thursday
5/Friday   World Day of Prayer
6/Saturday
7/Sunday   Purim
                   Perpetua and her Companions,
                   Martyrs at Carthage, 202
8/Monday
9/Tuesday   Gregory, Bishop of Nyssa, c. 394
10/Wednesday
11/Thursday
12/Friday   Gregory the Great, Bishop of
                   Rome, 604
13/Saturday
14/Sunday
15/Monday
16/Tuesday
17/Wednesday   St. Patrick's Day
                   Patrick, Bishop and Missionary
                   of Ireland, 461
18/Thursday   Cyril, Bishop of Jerusalem, 386
19/Friday   Saint Joseph, husband of Mary
20/Saturday   Spring begins
                   Cuthbert, Bishop of Lindisfarne,
                   687
21/Sunday   Thomas Ken, Bishop of Bath and
                   Wells, 1711
22/Monday   James DeKoven, Priest, 1879
23/Tuesday   Gregory the Illuminator, Bishop
                   and Missionary of Arme-
                   nia, c. 332
24/Wednesday
25/Thursday   The Annunciation
26/Friday
27/Saturday   Charles Henry Brent, Bishop
                   of the Philippines, and of
                   western New York, 1929
28/Sunday

29/Monday   John Keble, Priest, 1866
30/Tuesday
31/Wednesday   John Donne, Priest, 1631

APRIL

1/Thursday   Frederick Denison Maurice,
                   Priest, 1872
2/Friday   James Lloyd Breck, Priest,
                   1876
3/Saturday   Richard, Bishop of Chichester,
                   1253
4/Sunday   Palm Sunday, Holy Week
                   begins
                   Daylight Savings Time begins
5/Monday
6/Tuesday
7/Wednesday
8/Thursday   Maundy Thursday
                   William Augustus Muhlenberg,
                   Priest, 1877
9/Friday   Good Friday
                   William Law, Priest, 1761
10/Saturday   Holy Saturday, Easter Eve
11/Sunday   Easter Sunday
                   George Augustus Selwyn,
                   First Missionary Bishop
                   of New Zealand, 1878
12/Monday
13/Tuesday
14/Wednesday
15/Thursday
16/Friday
17/Saturday
18/Sunday   First Day of Passover
19/Monday   Alphege, Archbishop of
                   Canterbury and Martyr,
                   1012
20/Tuesday
21/Wednesday   Anselm, Archbishop of
                   Canterbury, 1109
22/Thursday
23/Friday
24/Saturday
25/Sunday   Saint Mark the Evangelist
26/Monday
27/Tuesday
28/Wednesday
29/Thursday   Catherine of Siena, 1380
30/Friday

MAY

1/Saturday   Saint Philip and Saint James,
                   Apostles
2/Sunday   Arthanasius, Bishop of
                   Alexandria, 373
3/Monday

4/Tuesday	Monnica, Mother of Augustine of Hippo, 387
5/Wednesday	
6/Thursday	National Day of Prayer
7/Friday	May Fellowship Day
8/Saturday	Dame Julian of Norwich, c. 1417
9/Sunday	Mother's Day
	Rural Life Sunday
	Gregory of Nazianzus, Bishop of Constantinople, 389
10/Monday	
11/Tuesday	
12/Wednesday	
13/Thursday	
14/Friday	
15/Saturday	
16/Sunday	
17/Monday	
18/Tuesday	
19/Wednesday	Dunstan, Archbishop of Canterbury, 988
20/Thursday	Ascension Day
	Alcuin, Deacon, and Abbot of Tours, 804
21/Friday	
22/Saturday	
23/Sunday	
24/Monday	Jackson Kemper, First Missionary Bishop in the United States, 1870
25/Tuesday	Bede, the Venerable, Priest, and Monk of Jarrow, 735
26/Wednesday	Augustine, First Archbishop of Canterbury, 605
27/Thursday	
28/Friday	
29/Saturday	
30/Sunday	Memorial Day
	Pentecost, Whit Sunday
31/Monday	Memorial Day Observed
	The Visitation of the Blessed Virgin Mary

JUNE

1/Tuesday	Justin, Martyr at Rome, c. 167
2/Wednesday	The Martyrs of Lyons, 177
3/Thursday	The Martyrs of Uganda, 1886
4/Friday	
5/Saturday	Boniface, Archbishop of Mainz, Missionary to Germany, and Martyr, 754
6/Sunday	Holy Trinity Sunday
7/Monday	
8/Tuesday	
9/Wednesday	Columba, Abbot of Iona, 597
10/Thursday	Ephrem of Edessa, Syria, Deacon, 373
11/Friday	Saint Barnabas the Apostle
12/Saturday	

13/Sunday	
14/Monday	Flag Day
	Basil the Great, Bishop of Caesarea, 379
15/Tuesday	
16/Wednesday	Joseph Butler, Bishop of Durham, 1752
17/Thursday	
18/Friday	Bernard Mizeki, Catechist and Martyr in Rhodesia, 1896
19/Saturday	
20/Sunday	Father's Day
21/Monday	Summer begins
22/Tuesday	Alban, First Martyr of Britain, c. 304
23/Wednesday	
24/Thursday	The Nativity of Saint John the Baptist
25/Friday	
26/Saturday	
27/Sunday	
28/Monday	Irenaeus, Bishop of Lyons, c. 202
29/Tuesday	Saint Peter and Saint Paul, Apostles
30/Wednesday	

JULY

1/Thursday	Canada Day
2//Friday	The Visitation
3/Saturday	
4/Sunday	Independence Day
5/Monday	
6/Tuesday	
7/Wednesday	
8/Thursday	
9/Friday	
10/Saturday	
11/Sunday	Benedict of Nursia, Abbot of Monte Cassino, c. 540
12/Monday	
13/Tuesday	
14/Wednesday	
15/Thursday	
16/Friday	
17Saturday	William White, Bishop of Pennsylvania, 1836
18/Sunday	
19/Monday	
20/Tuesday	
21/Wednesday	
22/Thursday	Saint Mary Magdalene
23/Friday	
24/Saturday	Thomas à Kempis, Priest, 1471
25/Sunday	Saint James the Apostle
26/Monday	The Parents of the Blessed Virgin Mary
27/Tuesday	William Reed Huntington, Priest, 1909

1993 CHURCH CALENDAR cont.

28/Wednesday	
29/Thursday	Mary and Martha of Bethany
30/Friday	William Wilberforce, 1833
31/Saturday	Joseph of Arimathaea

AUGUST

1/Sunday	
2/Monday	
3/Tuesday	
4/Wednesday	
5/Thursday	
6/Friday	The Transfiguration of Our Lord Jesus Christ
7/Saturday	John Mason Neale, Priest, 1866
8/Sunday	Dominic, Priest and Friar, 1221
9/Monday	
10/Tuesday	Laurence, Deacon, and Martyr at Rome, 258
11/Wednesday	Clare, Abbess at Assisi, 1253
12/Thursday	
13/Friday	Jeremy Taylor, Bishop of Down, Connor, and Dromore, 1667
14/Saturday	
15/Sunday	Saint Mary the Virgin, Mother of Our Lord Jesus Christ
16/Monday	
17/Tuesday	
18/Wednesday	William Porcher DuBose, Priest, 1918
19/Thursday	
20/Friday	Bernard, Abbot of Clairvaux, 1153
21/Saturday	
22/Sunday	
23/Monday	
24/Tuesday	Saint Bartholomew the Apostle
25/Wednesday	Louis, King of France, 1270
26/Thursday	
27/Friday	
28/Saturday	Augustine, Bishop of Hippo, 430
29/Sunday	
30/Monday	
31/Tuesday	Aidan, Bishop of Lindisfarne, 651

SEPTEMBER

1/Wednesday	
2/Thursday	The Martyrs of New Guinea, 1942
3/Friday	
4/Saturday	
5/Sunday	
6/Monday	Labor Day
7/Tuesday	
8/Wednesday	

9/Thursday	
10/Friday	
11/Saturday	
12/Sunday	Grandparents Day
	John Henry Hobart, Bishop of New York, 1830
13/Monday	Cyprian, Bishop and Martyr of Carthage, 258
14/Tuesday	
15/Wednesday	
16/Thursday	First day of Rosh Hashanah
	Ninian, Bishop in Galloway, c. 430
17/Friday	
18/Saturday	Edward Bouverie Pusey, Priest, 1882
19/Sunday	Theodore of Tarsus, Archbishop of Canterbury, 690
20/Monday	John Coleridge Patteson, Bishop of Melanesia, and his Companions, Martyrs, 1871
21/Tuesday	Saint Matthew, Apostle and Evangelist
22/Wednesday	Autumn begins
23/Thursday	
24/Friday	
25/Saturday	Yom Kippur
	Sergius, Abbot of Holy Trinity, Moscow, 1392
26/Sunday	Lancelot Andrewes, Bishop of Winchester, 1626
27/Monday	
28/Tuesday	
29/Wednesday	Saint Michael and All Angels
30/Thursday	Jerome, Priest and Monk of Bethlehem, 420

OCTOBER

1/Friday	Remigius, Bishop of Rheims, c. 530
2/Saturday	
3/Sunday	World Communion Sunday
4/Monday	Children's Day
	Francis of Assisi, Friar, 1226
5/Tuesday	
6/Wednesday	William Tyndale, Priest, 1536
7/Thursday	
8/Friday	
9/Saturday	Robert Grosseteste, Bishop of Lincoln, 1253
10/Sunday	Laity Sunday
11/Monday	Columbus Day Observed
	Thanksgiving Day (Canada)
12/Tuesday	Columbus Day
13/Wednesday	
14/Thursday	

15/Friday	Samuel Isaac Joseph Schereschewsky, Bishop of Shanghai, 1906
16/Saturday	Hugh Latimer and Nicholas Ridley, Bishops, 1555, and Thomas Cranmer, Archbishop of Canterbury, 1556
17/Sunday	Ignatius, Bishop of Antioch, and Martyr, c. 115
18/Monday	Saint Luke the Evangelist
19/Tuesday	Henry Martyn, Priest and Missionary to India and Persia, 1812
20/Wednesday	
21/Thursday	
22/Friday	
23/Saturday	Saint James of Jerusalem, Brother of Our Lord Jesus Christ, and Martyr, c. 62
24/Sunday	
25/Monday	
26/Tuesday	Alfred the Great, King of the West Saxons, 899
27/Wednesday	
28/Thursday	Saint Simon and Saint Jude, Apostles
29/Friday	James Hannington, Bishop of Eastern Equatorial Africa, and his companions, Martyrs, 1885
30/Saturday	
31/Sunday	Hallowe'en Reformation Sunday Daylight Saving Time ends

NOVEMBER

1/Monday	All Saints Day
2/Tuesday	Election Day Commemoration of All Faithful Departed
3/Wednesday	Richard Hooker, Priest, 1600
4/Thursday	
5/Friday	World Community Day
6/Saturday	
7/Sunday	International Bible Sunday (Internation Bible Society) Willibrord, Archbishop of Utrecht, Missionary to Frisia, 739
8/Monday	
9/Tuesday	
10/Wednesday	Leo the Great, Bishop of Rome, 461
11/Thursday	Veteran's Day Martin, Bishop of Tours, 397
12/Friday	Charles Simeon, Priest, 1836
13/Saturday	
14/Sunday	Stewardship Day Consecration of Samuel Seabury, First American Bishop, 1784

15/Monday	
16/Tuesday	Margaret, Queen of Scotland, 1093
17/Wednesday	Hugh, Bishop of Lincoln, 1200
18/Thursday	Hilda, Abbess of Whitby, 680
19/Friday	Elizabeth, Princess of Hungary, 1231
20/Saturday	
21/Sunday	Thanksgiving Sunday Bible Sunday, National Bible Week begins (Laymen's National Bible Assoc., Inc.) Last Sunday after Pentecost Feast of Christ the King
22/Monday	
23/Tuesday	Clement, Bishop of Rome, c. 100
24/Wednesday	
25/Thursday	Thanksgiving Day
26/Friday	
27/Saturday	
28/Sunday	First Sunday of Advent
29/Monday	
30/Tuesday	Saint Andrew the Apostle

DECEMBER

1/Wednesday	Nicholas Ferrar, Deacon, 1637
2/Thursday	Channing Moore Williams, Missionary Bishop in China and Japan, 1910
3/Friday	
4/Saturday	John of Damascus, Priest, c. 760
5/Sunday	Second Sunday of Advent Clement of Alexandria, Priest, c. 210
6/Monday	Nicholas, Bishop of Myra, c. 342
7/Tuesday	Ambrose, Bishop of Milan, 397
8/Wednesday	
9/Thursday	First Day of Hanukkah
10/Friday	
11/Saturday	
12/Sunday	Third Sunday of Advent
13/Monday	
14/Tuesday	
15/Wednesday	
16/Thursday	
17/Friday	
18/Saturday	
19/Sunday	Fourth Sunday of Advent
20/Monday	
21/Tuesday	Winter begins Saint Thomas the Apostle
22/Wednesday	
23/Thursday	
24/Friday	
25/Saturday	Christmas Day

1993 CHURCH CALENDAR cont.

26/Sunday	Saint Stephen, Deacon and Martyr	28/Tuesday	The Holy Innocents
27/Monday	Saint John, Apostle and Evangelist	29/Wednesday	
		30/Thursday	
		31/Friday	

1994 CHURCH CALENDAR

JANUARY

1/Saturday	New Year's Day
	Feast of the Holy Name of Our Lord Jesus Christ
	The Circumcision and the Name of Jesus
2/Sunday	Universal Week of Prayer
3/Monday	
4/Tuesday	
5/Wednesday	
6/Thursday	The Epiphany of Our Lord Jesus Christ
7/Friday	
8/Saturday	
9/Sunday	First Sunday after Epiphany
	Feast of the Baptism of Our Lord
10/Monday	William Laud, Archbishop of Canterbury, 1645
11/Tuesday	
12/Wednesday	
13/Thursday	Hilary, Bishop of Pointiers, 367
14/Friday	
15/Saturday	Martin Luther King Day
16/Sunday	Sanctity of Human Life Sunday
	Second Sunday after Epiphany
17/Monday	Martin Luther King's Birthday
	Anthony, Abbot in Egypt, 356
18/Tuesday	Week of Prayer for Christian Unity begins
	The Confession of Saint Peter the Apostle
19/Wednesday	Wulfstan, Bishop of Worcester, 1095
20/Thursday	Fabian, Bishop and Martyr of Rome, 250
21/Friday	Agnes, Martyr at Rome, 304
22/Saturday	Vincent, Deacon of Saragossa, and Martyr, 304
23/Sunday	Ecumenical Sunday
	Third Sunday after Epiphany
	Phillips Brooks, Bishop of Massachusetts, 1893
24/Monday	
25/Tuesday	The Conversion of Saint Paul the Apostle
26/Wednesday	Timothy and Titus, Companions of Saint Paul

27/Thursday	John Chrysostom, Bishop of Constantinople, 407
28/Friday	Thomas Aquinas, Priest and Friar, 1274
29/Saturday	
30/Sunday	National Association of Evangelicals Sunday
	Fourth Sunday after Epiphany
31/Monday	

FEBRUARY

1/Tuesday	
2/Wednesday	Groundhog Day
	The Presentation of Jesus in the Temple
	The Purification of Mary
3/Thursday	Anskar, Archbishop of Hamburg, Missionary to Denmark and Sweden, 865
4/Friday	Cornelius the Centurion
5/Saturday	The Martyrs of Japan, 1597
6/Sunday	Fifth Sunday after Epiphany
7/Monday	
8/Tuesday	
9/Wednesday	
10/Thursday	
11/Friday	
12/Saturday	Lincoln's Birthday
13/Sunday	Last Sunday after Epiphany
	The Transfiguration of our Lord
	Absalom Jones, Priest, 1818
14/Monday	St. Valentine's Day
	Cyril, Monk, and Methodius, Bishop, Missionaries to the Slavs, 869, 885
15/Tuesday	Thomas Bray, Priest and Missionary, 1730
16/Wednesday	Ash Wednesday, Lent begins
17/Thursday	
18/Friday	
19/Saturday	
20/Sunday	Brotherhood Week begins
	First Sunday in Lent
21/Monday	President's Day
22/Tuesday	Washington's Birthday
23/Wednesday	Polycarp, Bishop and Martyr of Smyrna, 156

24/Thursday	Saint Matthias the Apostle
25/Friday	Purim
26/Saturday	
27/Sunday	Second Sunday in Lent
	George Herbert, Priest, 1633
28/Monday	

MARCH

1/Tuesday	David, Bishop of Menevia, Wales, c. 544
2/Wednesday	Chad, Bishop of Lichfield, 672
3/Thursday	John and Charles Wesley, Priests, 1791, 1788
4/Friday	World Day of Prayer
5/Saturday	
6/Sunday	Third Sunday in Lent
7/Monday	Perpetua and her Companions, Martyrs at Carthage, 202
8/Tuesday	
9/Wednesday	Gregory, Bishop of Nyssa, c. 394
10/Thursday	
11/Friday	
12/Saturday	Gregory the Great, Bishop of Rome, 604
13/Sunday	Fourth Sunday in Lent
14/Monday	
15/Tuesday	
16/Wednesday	
17/Thursday	St. Patrick's Day
	Patrick, Bishop and Missionary of Ireland, 461
18/Friday	Cyril, Bishop of Jerusalem, 386
19/Saturday	Saint Joseph, husband of Mary
20/Sunday	Spring begins
	Fifth Sunday in Lent
	Cuthbert, Bishop of Lindisfarne, 687
21/Monday	Thomas Ken, Bishop of Bath and Wells, 1711
22/Tuesday	James DeKoven, Priest, 1879
23/Wednesday	Gregory the Illuminator, Bishop and Missionary of Armenia, c. 332
24/Thursday	
25/Friday	The Annunciation
26/Saturday	
27/Sunday	Palm Sunday, Holy Week begins
	First Day of Passover
	Charles Henry Brent, Bishop of the Philippines, and of Western New York, 1929
28/Monday	
29/Tuesday	John Keble, Priest, 1866
30/Wednesday	
31/Thursday	Maundy Thursday
	John Donne, Priest, 1631

APRIL

1/Friday	Good Friday
	Frederick Denison Maurice, Priest, 1872
2/Saturday	Holy Saturday, Easter Eve
	James Lloyd Breck, Priest, 1876
3/Sunday	Easter Sunday
	Daylight Saving Time begins
	Richard, Bishop of Chichester, 1253
4/Monday	
5/Tuesday	
6/Wednesday	
7/Thursday	
8/Friday	William Augustus Muhlenberg, Priest, 1877
9/Saturday	William Law, Priest, 1761
10/Sunday	
11/Monday	George Augustus Selwyn, First Missionary Bishop of New Zealand, 1878
12/Tuesday	
13/Wednesday	
14/Thursday	
15/Friday	
16/Saturday	
17/Sunday	
18/Monday	
19/Tuesday	Alphege, Archbishop of Canterbury, and Martyr, 1012
20/Wednesday	
21/Thursday	Anselm, Archbishop of Canterbury, 1109
22/Friday	
23/Saturday	
24/Sunday	
25/Monday	Saint Mark the Evangelist
26/Tuesday	
27/Wednesday	
28/Thursday	
29/Friday	Catherine of Siena, 1380
30/Saturday	

MAY

1/Sunday	Saint Philip and Saint James, Apostles
2/Monday	Arthanasius, Bishop of Alexandria, 373
3/Tuesday	
4/Wednesday	Monnica, Mother of Augustine of Hippo, 387
5/Thursday	National Day of Prayer
6/Friday	May Fellowship Day
7/Saturday	
8/Sunday	Mother's Day
	Rural Life Sunday

1994 CHURCH CALENDAR cont.

8/Sunday	Dame Julian of Norwich, c. 1417
9/Monday	Gregory of Nazianzus, Bishop of Constantinople, 389
10/Tuesday	
11/Wednesday	
12/Thursday	
13/Friday	Ascension Day
14/Saturday	
15/Sunday	
16/Monday	
17/Tuesday	
18/Wednesday	
19/Thursday	Dunstan, Archbishop of Canterbury, 988
20/Friday	Alcuin, Deacon, and Abbot of Tours, 804
21/Saturday	
22/Sunday	Pentecost, Whit Sunday
23/Monday	
24/Tuesday	Jackson Kemper, First Missionary Bishop in the United States, 1870
25/Wednesday	Bede, the Venerable, Priest, and Monk of Jarrow, 735
26/Thursday	Augustine, First Archbishop of Canterbury, 605
27/Friday	
28/Saturday	
29/Sunday	Holy Trinity Sunday
30/Monday	Memorial Day
31/Tuesday	The Visitation of the Blessed Virgin Mary

J U N E

1/Wednesday	Justin, Martyr at Rome, c. 167
2/Thursday	The Martyrs of Lyons, 177
3/Friday	The Martyrs of Uganda, 1886
4/Saturday	
5/Sunday	Boniface, Archbishop of Mainz, Missionary to Germany, and Martyr, 754
6/Monday	
7/Tuesday	
8/Wednesday	
9/Thursday	Columba, Abbot of Iona, 597
10/Friday	Ephrem of Edessa, Syria, Deacon, 373
11/Saturday	Saint Barnabas the Apostle
12/Sunday	
13/Monday	
14/Tuesday	Flag Day Basil the Great, Bishop of Caesarea, 379
15/Wednesday	
16/Thursday	Joseph Butler, Bishop of Durham, 1752

17/Friday	
18/Saturday	Bernard Mizeki, Catechist and Martyr in Rhodesia, 1896
19/Sunday	Father's Day
20/Monday	
21/Tuesday	Summer begins
22/Wednesday	Alban, First Martyr of Britain, c. 304
23/Thursday	
24/Friday	The Nativity of Saint John the Baptist
25/Saturday	
26/Sunday	
27/Monday	
28/Tuesday	Irenaeus, Bishop of Lyons, c. 202
29/Wednesday	Saint Peter and Saint Paul, Apostles
30/Thursday	

J U L Y

1/Friday	Canada Day
2/Saturday	The Visitation
3/Sunday	
4/Monday	Independence Day
5/Tuesday	
6/Wednesday	
7/Thursday	
8/Friday	
9/Saturday	
10/Sunday	
11/Monday	Benedict of Nursia, Abbot of Monte Cassino, c. 540
12/Tuesday	
13/Wednesday	
14/Thursday	
15/Friday	
16/Saturday	
17Sunday	William White, Bishop of Pennsylvania, 1836
18/Monday	
19/Tuesday	
20/Wednesday	
21/Thursday	
22/Friday	Saint Mary Magdalene
23/Saturday	
24/Sunday	Thomas à Kempis, Priest, 1471
25/Monday	Saint James the Apostle
26/Tuesday	The Parents of the Blessed Virgin Mary
27/Wednesday	William Reed Huntington, Priest, 1909
28/Thursday	
29/Friday	Mary and Martha of Bethany
30/Saturday	William Wilberforce, 1833
31/Sunday	Joseph of Arimathaea

AUGUST

1/Monday	
2/Tuesday	
3/Wednesday	
4/Thursday	
5/Friday	
6/Saturday	The Transfiguration of Our Lord Jesus Christ
7/Sunday	John Mason Neale, Priest, 1866
8/Monday	Dominic, Priest and Friar, 1221
9/Tuesday	
10/Wednesday	Laurence, Deacon and Martyr at Rome, 258
11/Thursday	Clare, Abbess at Assisi, 1253
12/Friday	
13/Saturday	Jeremy Taylor, Bishop of Down, Connor, and Dromore, 1667
14/Sunday	
15/Monday	Saint Mary the Virgin, Mother of Our Lord Jesus Christ
16/Tuesday	
17/Wednesday	
18/Thursday	William Porcher DuBose, Priest, 1918
19/Friday	
20/Saturday	Bernard, Abbot of Clairvaux, 1153
21/Sunday	
22/Monday	
23/Tuesday	
24/Wednesday	Saint Bartholomew the Apostle
25/Thursday	Louis, King of France, 1270
26/Friday	
27/Saturday	
28/Sunday	Augustine, Bishop of Hippo, 430
29/Monday	
30/Tuesday	
31/Wednesday	Aidan, Bishop of Lindisfarne, 651

SEPTEMBER

1/Thursday	
2/Friday	The Martyrs of New Guinea, 1942
3/Saturday	
4/Sunday	
5/Monday	Labor Day
6/Tuesday	First Day of Rosh Hashanah
7/Wednesday	
8/Thursday	
9/Friday	
10/Saturday	
11/Sunday	Grandparent's Day
12/Monday	John Henry Hobart, Bishop of New York, 1830

13/Tuesday	Cyprian, Bishop and Martyr of Carthage, 258
14/Wednesday	Holy Cross Day
15/Thursday	Yom Kippur
16/Friday	Ninian, Bishop in Galloway, c. 430
17/Saturday	
18/Sunday	Edward Bouverie Pusey, Priest, 1882
19/Monday	Theodore of Tarsus, Archbishop of Canterbury, 690
20/Tuesday	John Coleridge Patteson, Bishop of Melanesia, and his Companions, Martyrs, 1871
21/Wednesday	Saint Matthew, Apostle and Evangelist
22/Thursday	
23/Friday	Autumn begins
24/Saturday	
25/Sunday	Sergius, Abbot of Holy Trinity, Moscow, 1392
26/Monday	Lancelot Andrewes, Bishop of Winchester, 1626
27/Tuesday	
28/Wednesday	
29/Thursday	Saint Michael and All Angels
30/Friday	Jerome, Priest, and Monk of Bethlehem, 420

OCTOBER

1/Saturday	Remigius, Bishop of Rheims, c. 530
2/Sunday	World Communion Sunday
3/Monday	Children's Day
4/Tuesday	Francis of Assisi, Friar, 1226
5/Wednesday	
6/Thursday	William Tyndale, Priest, 1536
7/Friday	
8/Saturday	
9/Sunday	Laity Sunday
	Robert Grosseteste, Bishop of Lincoln, 1253
10/Monday	Columbus Day Observed
	Thanksgiving Day (Canada)
11/Tuesday	
12/Wednesday	Columbus Day
13/Thursday	
14/Friday	
15/Saturday	Samuel Isaac Joseph Schereschewsky, Bishop of Shanghai, 1906
16/Sunday	Hugh Latimer and Nicholas Ridley, Bishops, 1555, and Thomas Cranmer, Archbishop of Canterbury, 1556
17/Monday	Ignatius, Bishop of Antioch, and Martyr, c. 115

1994 CHURCH CALENDAR cont.

18/Tuesday	Saint Luke the Evangelist
19/Wednesday	Henry Martyn, Priest and Missionary to India and Persia, 1812
20/Thursday	
21/Friday	
22/Saturday	
23/Sunday	Saint James of Jerusalem, Brother of Our Lord Jesus Christ, and Martyr, c. 62
24/Monday	
25/Tuesday	
26/Wednesday	Alfred the Great, King of the West Saxons, 899
27/Thursday	
28/Friday	Saint Simon and Saint Jude, Apostles
29/Saturday	James Hannington, Bishop of Eastern Equatorial Africa, and his Companions, Martyrs, 1885
30/Sunday	Daylight Saving Time ends Reformation Sunday
31/Monday	Hallowe'en Reformation Day

NOVEMBER

1/Tuesday	All Saints Day
2/Wednesday	Commemoration of All Faithful Departed
3/Thursday	Richard Hooker, Priest, 1600
4/Friday	World Community Day
5/Saturday	
6/Sunday	International Bible Sunday (Int'l Bible Society)
7/Monday	Willibrord, Archbishop of Utrecht, Missionary to Frisia, 739
8/Tuesday	Election Day
9/Wednesday	
10/Thursday	Leo the Great, Bishop of Rome, 461
11/Friday	Veterans Day Martin, Bishop of Tours, 397
12/Saturday	Charles Simeon, Priest, 1836
13/Sunday	Stewardship Day
14/Monday	Consecration of Samuel Seabury, First American Bishop, 1784
15/Tuesday	
16/Wednesday	Margaret, Queen of Scotland, 1093
17/Thursday	Hugh, Bishop of Lincoln, 1200
18/Friday	Hilda, Abbess of Whitby, 680
19/Saturday	Elizabeth, Princess of Hungary, 1231

20/Sunday	Bible Sunday, National Bible Week begins (Laymen's National Bible Assoc.) Thanksgiving Sunday
21/Monday	
22/Tuesday	
23/Wednesday	Clement, Bishop of Rome, c. 100
24/Thursday	Thanksgiving Day
25/Friday	
26/Saturday	
27/Sunday	First Sunday of Advent Feast of Christ the King
28/Monday	First Day of Hanukkah
29/Tuesday	
30/Wednesday	Saint Andrew the Apostle

DECEMBER

1/Thursday	Nicholas Ferrar, Deacon, 1637
2/Friday	Channing Moore Williams, Missionary Bishop in China and Japan, 1910
3/Saturday	
4/Sunday	Second Sunday of Advent John of Damascus, Priest, c. 760
5/Monday	Clement of Alexandria, Priest, c. 210
6/Tuesday	Nicholas, Bishop of Myra, c. 342
7/Wednesday	Ambrose, Bishop of Milan, 397
8/Thursday	
9/Friday	
10/Saturday	
11/Sunday	Third Sunday of Advent
12/Monday	
13/Tuesday	
14/Wednesday	
15/Thursday	
16/Friday	
17/Saturday	
18/Sunday	Fourth Sunday of Advent
19/Monday	
20/Tuesday	
21/Wednesday	Winter begins Saint Thomas the Apostle
22/Thursday	
23/Friday	
24/Saturday	
25/Sunday	Christmas Day
26/Monday	Saint Stephen, Deacon and Martyr
27/Tuesday	Saint John, Apostle and Evangelist
28/Wednesday	The Holy Innocents
29/Thursday	
30/Friday	
31/Saturday	

1993–1994 EVENTS CALENDAR

January 3-10, 1993
January 2-9, 1994
Universal Week of Prayer
Harry Genet, World Evangelical Fellowship, PO Box WEF, Wheaton, IL 60189 708-668-0440

January 5-8, 1993/Harbor Island, San Diego, CA
January 1994
Fellowship of Christian Educators Vocational Staff Conference
Jack L. Clark, The Fellowship of Christian Educators, ON345 Willow Road, Wheaton, IL 60187 708-665-4667

January 5-8, 1993
January 4-7, 1994
National Youth Leader's Convention
Dick Gibson, Christ in Youth, PO Box B, Joplin, MO 64802 417-781-2273

January 18-25, 1993
January 18-25, 1994
Week of Prayer for Christian Unity, sponsored by World Council of Churches and the Pontifical Council for Promoting Christian Unity
James T. Gardiner, Graymore Ecumenical Institute, 475 Riverside Drive, New York, NY 10115 212-870-2330

January 22-24, 1993
Missionfest
Neil Rempel Chairman, Missionfest '93, 606-228 Notre Dame Avenue, Winnipeg, MB R3B 1N7 Canada 204-667-0153, FAX: 204-668-0088

January 25-29, 1993/Washington, DC
January 24-28, 1994/Washington, DC
Federal Seminar for College Students
Don Brown, National Association of Evangelicals, 450 Gundersen Drive, Carol Stream, IL 60188 708-665-0500

January 31, 1993
January 30, 1994
National Association of Evangelicals Sunday
Don Brown, National Association of Evangelicals, 450 Gundersen Drive, Carol Stream, IL 60188 708-665-0500

January 1993/Garden Grove, CA
January 1994/Garden Grove, CA
Institute for Successful Church Leadership
Robert Schuller Institute, 12141 Lewis Street, Garden Grove, CA 92640 714-971-4133

February 13-16, 1993 (NRB 93)/Los Angeles, CA
January 1994 (NRB 94)/Washington, DC
Nat'l Religious Broadcasters Con. and Exposition
Nat'l Religious Broadcasters, 1777 Ashton Avenue, Manassos, VA 22110

February 15-18, 1993/Dallas, TX
February 1994
Christian Management Institute
Christian Management Association, PO Box 4638, Diamond Bar, CA 91765 714-861-8861

February 22-24, 1994/Newport Beach, CA
National Conference for Ministry Wives
Dr. Michael Duduit, Preaching Magazine, 1529 Cesery Blvd., Jacksonville, FL 32211 904-743-5994

February 22-24, 1994/Newport Beach, CA
National Conference on Preaching
Dr. Michael Duduit, Preaching Magazine, 1529 Cesery Blvd., Jacksonville, FL 32211 904-743-5994

March 5, 1993
March 4, 1994
World Day of Prayer
Don Brown, National Association of Evangelicals, 450 Gundersen Drive, Carol Stream, IL 60188 708-665-0500

March 6-9, 1993/Orlando, FL
March 1994
Nat'l Assoc. of Evangelicals Annual Conference
Don Brown, Nat'l Assoc. of Evangelicals, 450 Gundersen Drive, Carol Stream, IL 60188 708-665-0500

March through May 1993/Wheaton, IL
March through May 1994/Wheaton, IL
Sacred Arts Museum Exhibit, Billy Graham Ctr.
Billy Graham Center Museum, Wheaton College, Wheaton, IL 60187 708-752-5909

April 25-28, 1993/Hilton Head, SC
ECPA Seminar: The Changing Face of Evangelicalism
Doug Ross, Evangelical Christian Publishers Association, 3225 South Hardy Drive, Suite 101, Tempe, AZ 85282 602-966-3998

April 1994/Washington, DC
Washington Insight Seminar
Don Brown, Nat'l Assoc. of Evangelicals, 450 Gundersen Drive, Carol Stream, IL 60188 708-665-0500

May 4-6, 1993/Atlanta, GA
National Conference on Preaching
Dr. Michael Duduit, Preaching Magazine, 1529
   Cesery Blvd., Jacksonville, FL 32211 904-743-
   5994

May 4-6, 1993/Atlanta, GA
National Conference for Ministry Wives
Dr. Michael Duduit, Preaching Magazine, 1529
   Cesery Blvd., Jacksonville, FL 32211 904-743-
   5994

May 10-12, 1993/St. Paul, MN
Evangelical Press Association Convention
Gary Warner, Evangelical Press Assoc., PO Box
   4550, Overland Park, KS 66204 913-381-
   2017

May 17-23, 1993/Wheaton, IL
IFMA Missions Seminar
Conference Services, Wheaton College, Wheaton,
   IL 60187 708-752-5112

May 24-28, 1993/Wheaton, IL
Fellowship of Christian Air Line Personnel
Conference Services, Wheaton College, Wheaton,
   IL 60187 708-752-5112

June 1-6, 1993/Anaheim, CA
May 24-29, 1994/Columbus, OH
Christian and Missionary Alliance Gen. Council
Bobbie Reed, Christian and Missionary Alliance,
   PO Box 35000, Colorado Springs, CO 80935-
   3500 719-599-5999

June 1-3, 1993/Chicago, IL
May 31–June 2, 1994/Chicago, IL
Moody Pastor's Conference
Jim Jenks, Moody Bible Institute, 820 N. LaS-
   alle Blvd., Chicago, IL 60610-3284 312-329-
   4401

June 1-4, 1993/Wheaton, IL
Christian Writer's Institute
Conference Services, Wheaton College, Wheaton,
   IL 60187 708-752-5112

June 7-13, 1993/Wheaton, IL
June 6-12, 1994/Wheaton, IL
Pastoral Care Ministries Conference
Conference Services, Wheaton College, Wheaton,
   IL 60187 708-752-5112

June 7-9, 1993/Wheaton, IL
June 6-8, 1994/Wheaton, IL
Greater Europe Mission EUROCORPS Conf.
Conference Services, Wheaton College, Wheaton,
   IL 60187 708-752-5112

June 7-10, 1994/Wheaton, IL
Black Family Ministries Conference
Conference Services, Wheaton College, Wheaton,
   IL 60187 708-752-5112

June 13-25, 1994/Seoul, Korea
Global Consultation on World Evang. (GCOWE II)
AD 2000 Movement, PO Box 2139, San Gabriel, CA 91778 818-287-6981, FAX 818-
   287-6991

June 14-18, 1993/Wheaton, IL
June 13-17, 1994/Wheaton, IL
Billy Graham Evangelistic Association School of
   Evangelism
Conference Services, Wheaton College, Wheaton,
   IL 60187 708-752-5112

June 16-19, 1993/Grand Rapids, MI
National Leadership Conference on the Church
   and Disability
John Wern, Joni and Friends, PO Box 3333,
   Agoura Hills, CA 91301 818-707-5664

June 20-26, 1993/Wichita, KS
Evangelical Free Church of America Annual
   Conference
Evangelical Free Church of America, 901 E.
   78th Street, Minneapolis, MN 55420 612-
   854-1300

June 21-27, 1993/Wheaton, IL
June 22-26, 1994/Wheaton, IL
Billy Graham Center Institute of Evangelism Con-
   ference
Conference Services, Wheaton College, Wheaton,
   IL 60187 708-752-5112

June 23-26, 1993/Tulsa, OK
June 22-25, 1994/Tulsa, OK
High Praises Family Conference
Lisa Taylor, Carman Ministries, PO Box 701050,
   Tulsa, OK 74170 918-250-1529

June 26-30, 1993/Portland, OR
June 25-29, 1994/Denver, CO
Conservative Baptist Association of America
   National Meeting
CBA of America, PO Box 66, Wheaton, IL 60189
   708-653-5350

June 29–July 4, 1993/Des Moines, IA
June 30-26, 1994/Tacoma, WA
Baptist General Conference Annual Meeting
Calvin E. Fernlund, Baptist General Confer-
   ence, 2002 S. Arlington Heights Road, Ar-
   lington Heights, IL 60005 800-323-4215

June 1993/Cannon Beach, OR
All in the Family Retreat
John Wern, Joni and Friends, PO Box 3333,
   Agoura Hills, CA 91301 818-707-5664

June 1993/Hudson, FL
All in the Family Retreat
John Wern, Joni and Friends, PO Box 3333,
   Agoura Hills, CA 91301 818-707-5664

June through August 1993/Wheaton, IL
Afro-American Evangelicals Museum Exhibit, Billy Graham Center
Billy Graham Center Museum, Wheaton College, Wheaton, IL 60187 708-752-5909

July 10-15, 1993/Atlanta, GA
July 16-21, 1994/Washington, DC
Christian Booksellers Association Convention
Dorothy Hull, Christian Booksellers Association, PO Box 200, Colorado Springs, CO 80901-4000 719-576-7880

July 11-17, 1993/Wheaton, IL
Youth United Ministries Conference (Inner-City)
Conference Services, Wheaton College, Wheaton, IL 60187 708-752-5112

July 29–August 1, 1993/Wheaton, IL
Christians for Biblical Equality Conference
Conference Services, Wheaton College, Wheaton, IL 60187 708-752-5112

July 1993/Spruce Lake, PA
All in the Family Retreat
John Wern, Joni and Friends, PO Box 3333, Agoura Hills, CA 91301 818-707-5664

September 19-22, 1993/Denver, CO
September 18-21, 1994
Christian Stewardship Association Annual Conference
Christian Stewardship Association, PO Box 8, Wheaton, IL 60189 708-690-0016

September 29–October 2, 1993
Professional Association of Christian Educators
PACE, 805 N. Rockwell, 5 Plaza Square, Suite 222, Oklahoma City, OK 73132 405-841-1712

October 13-16, 1993/Garden Grove, CA
October 12-15, 1994/Garden Grove, CA
International Women's Conference
Robert Schuller Institute, 12141 Lewis Street, Garden Grove, CA 92640 714-971-4133

October 13-16, 1993
National Association of Professors of Christian Education
Dennis Williams, Denver Seminary, PO Box 10,000, Denver, CO 80210 303-761-2482

October 24-27, 1993/Palm Springs, CA
ECPA Seminar: Legal Challenges Facing Publishers Today
Doug Ross, Evangelical Christian Publishers Association, 3225 South Hardy Drive, Suite 101, Tempe, AZ 85282 602-966-3998

October 31–November 7, 1993
October 30–November 6, 1994
Pornography Awareness Week
Morality in Media, 475 Riverside Drive, Suite 239, New York, NY 10115 212-870-3222

November 1-7, 1993
October 31–November 6, 1994
National Religious Book Week
Doug Ross, Evangelical Christian Publishers Association, 3225 South Hardy Drive, Suite 101, Tempe, AZ 85282 602-966-3998

November 7, 1993
November 6, 1994
International Bible Sunday
International Bible Society, PO Box 62970, Colorado Springs, CO 80962 719-488-9200

November 21-28, 1993
November 20-27, 1994
National Bible Week
Laymen's National Bible Association, Inc., 475 Riverside Drive, Suite 439, New York, NY 10115-0122 212-408-1390

December 27-31, 1993/Champaign, IL
Urbana '93
InterVarsity Christian Fellowship, 6400 Schroeder Road, P.O. Box 7895, Madison, WI 53707-7895 608-274-7995

FOUR-YEAR CALENDAR OF MOVABLE HOLIDAYS

Year	Ash Wednesday	Easter	Pentecost	Labor Day	Election Day	Thanks-giving	1st Sunday Advent
1993	Feb 24	Apr 11	May 30	Sept 6	Nov 2	Nov 25	Nov 28
1994	Feb 16	Apr 3	May 22	Sept 5	Nov 8	Nov 24	Nov 27
1995	Mar 1	April 16	June 4	Sept 4	Nov 7	Nov 23	Dec 3
1996	Feb 21	Apr 7	May 26	Sept 2	Nov 5	Nov 28	Dec 1

1992 Calendar

JANUARY
S	M	T	W	T	F	S
			1	2	3	4
5	6	7	8	9	10	11
12	13	14	15	16	17	18
19	20	21	22	23	24	25
26	27	28	29	30	31	

FEBRUARY
S	M	T	W	T	F	S
						1
2	3	4	5	6	7	8
9	10	11	12	13	14	15
16	17	18	19	20	21	22
23	24	25	26	27	28	29

MARCH
S	M	T	W	T	F	S
1	2	3	4	5	6	7
8	9	10	11	12	13	14
15	16	17	18	19	20	21
22	23	24	25	26	27	28
29	30	31				

APRIL
S	M	T	W	T	F	S
			1	2	3	4
5	6	7	8	9	10	11
12	13	14	15	16	17	18
19	20	21	22	23	24	25
26	27	28	29	30		

MAY
S	M	T	W	T	F	S
					1	2
3	4	5	6	7	8	9
10	11	12	13	14	15	16
17	18	19	20	21	22	23
24	25	26	27	28	29	30
31						

JUNE
S	M	T	W	T	F	S
	1	2	3	4	5	6
7	8	9	10	11	12	13
14	15	16	17	18	19	20
21	22	23	24	25	26	27
28	29	30				

JULY
S	M	T	W	T	F	S
			1	2	3	4
5	6	7	8	9	10	11
12	13	14	15	16	17	18
19	20	21	22	23	24	25
26	27	28	29	30	31	

AUGUST
S	M	T	W	T	F	S
						1
2	3	4	5	6	7	8
9	10	11	12	13	14	15
16	17	18	19	20	21	22
23	24	25	26	27	28	29
30	31					

SEPTEMBER
S	M	T	W	T	F	S
		1	2	3	4	5
6	7	8	9	10	11	12
13	14	15	16	17	18	19
20	21	22	23	24	25	26
27	28	29	30			

OCTOBER
S	M	T	W	T	F	S
				1	2	3
4	5	6	7	8	9	10
11	12	13	14	15	16	17
18	19	20	21	22	23	24
25	26	27	28	29	30	31

NOVEMBER
S	M	T	W	T	F	S
1	2	3	4	5	6	7
8	9	10	11	12	13	14
15	16	17	18	19	20	21
22	23	24	25	26	27	28
29	30					

DECEMBER
S	M	T	W	T	F	S
		1	2	3	4	5
6	7	8	9	10	11	12
13	14	15	16	17	18	19
20	21	22	23	24	25	26
27	28	29	30	31		

1993 Calendar

JANUARY

S	M	T	W	T	F	S
					1	2
3	4	5	6	7	8	9
10	11	12	13	14	15	16
17	18	19	20	21	22	23
24	25	26	27	28	29	30
31						

FEBRUARY

S	M	T	W	T	F	S
	1	2	3	4	5	6
7	8	9	10	11	12	13
14	15	16	17	18	19	20
21	22	23	24	25	26	27
28						

MARCH

S	M	T	W	T	F	S
	1	2	3	4	5	6
7	8	9	10	11	12	13
14	15	16	17	18	19	20
21	22	23	24	25	26	27
28	29	30	31			

APRIL

S	M	T	W	T	F	S
				1	2	3
4	5	6	7	8	9	10
11	12	13	14	15	16	17
18	19	20	21	22	23	24
25	26	27	28	29	30	

MAY

S	M	T	W	T	F	S
						1
2	3	4	5	6	7	8
9	10	11	12	13	14	15
16	17	18	19	20	21	22
23	24	25	26	27	28	29
30	31					

JUNE

S	M	T	W	T	F	S
		1	2	3	4	5
6	7	8	9	10	11	12
13	14	15	16	17	18	19
20	21	22	23	24	25	26
27	28	29	30			

JULY

S	M	T	W	T	F	S
				1	2	3
4	5	6	7	8	9	10
11	12	13	14	15	16	17
18	19	20	21	22	23	24
25	26	27	28	29	30	31

AUGUST

S	M	T	W	T	F	S
1	2	3	4	5	6	7
8	9	10	11	12	13	14
15	16	17	18	19	20	21
22	23	24	25	26	27	28
29	30	31				

SEPTEMBER

S	M	T	W	T	F	S
			1	2	3	4
5	6	7	8	9	10	11
12	13	14	15	16	17	18
19	20	21	22	23	24	25
26	27	28	29	30		

OCTOBER

S	M	T	W	T	F	S
					1	2
3	4	5	6	7	8	9
10	11	12	13	14	15	16
17	18	19	20	21	22	23
24	25	26	27	28	29	30
31						

NOVEMBER

S	M	T	W	T	F	S
	1	2	3	4	5	6
7	8	9	10	11	12	13
14	15	16	17	18	19	20
21	22	23	24	25	26	27
28	29	30				

DECEMBER

S	M	T	W	T	F	S
			1	2	3	4
5	6	7	8	9	10	11
12	13	14	15	16	17	18
19	20	21	22	23	24	25
26	27	28	29	30	31	

1994 Calendar

JANUARY

S	M	T	W	T	F	S
						1
2	3	4	5	6	7	8
9	10	11	12	13	14	15
16	17	18	19	20	21	22
23	24	25	26	27	28	29
30	31					

FEBRUARY

S	M	T	W	T	F	S
		1	2	3	4	5
6	7	8	9	10	11	12
13	14	15	16	17	18	19
20	21	22	23	24	25	26
27	28					

MARCH

S	M	T	W	T	F	S
		1	2	3	4	5
6	7	8	9	10	11	12
13	14	15	16	17	18	19
20	21	22	23	24	25	26
27	28	29	30	31		

APRIL

S	M	T	W	T	F	S
					1	2
3	4	5	6	7	8	9
10	11	12	13	14	15	16
17	18	19	20	21	22	23
24	25	26	27	28	29	30

MAY

S	M	T	W	T	F	S
1	2	3	4	5	6	7
8	9	10	11	12	13	14
15	16	17	18	19	20	21
22	23	24	25	26	27	28
29	30	31				

JUNE

S	M	T	W	T	F	S
			1	2	3	4
5	6	7	8	9	10	11
12	13	14	15	16	17	18
19	20	21	22	23	24	25
26	27	28	29	30		

JULY

S	M	T	W	T	F	S
					1	2
3	4	5	6	7	8	9
10	11	12	13	14	15	16
17	18	19	20	21	22	23
24	25	26	27	28	29	30
31						

AUGUST

S	M	T	W	T	F	S
	1	2	3	4	5	6
7	8	9	10	11	12	13
14	15	16	17	18	19	20
21	22	23	24	25	26	27
28	29	30	31			

SEPTEMBER

S	M	T	W	T	F	S
				1	2	3
4	5	6	7	8	9	10
11	12	13	14	15	16	17
18	19	20	21	22	23	24
25	26	27	28	29	30	

OCTOBER

S	M	T	W	T	F	S
						1
2	3	4	5	6	7	8
9	10	11	12	13	14	15
16	17	18	19	20	21	22
23	24	25	26	27	28	29
30	31					

NOVEMBER

S	M	T	W	T	F	S
		1	2	3	4	5
6	7	8	9	10	11	12
13	14	15	16	17	18	19
20	21	22	23	24	25	26
27	28	29	30			

DECEMBER

S	M	T	W	T	F	S
				1	2	3
4	5	6	7	8	9	10
11	12	13	14	15	16	17
18	19	20	21	22	23	24
25	26	27	28	29	30	31

1995 Calendar

	JANUARY					
S	M	T	W	T	F	S
1	2	3	4	5	6	7
8	9	10	11	12	13	14
15	16	17	18	19	20	21
22	23	24	25	26	27	28
29	30	31				

	FEBRUARY					
S	M	T	W	T	F	S
			1	2	3	4
5	6	7	8	9	10	11
12	13	14	15	16	17	18
19	20	21	22	23	24	25
26	27	28				

	MARCH					
S	M	T	W	T	F	S
			1	2	3	4
5	6	7	8	9	10	11
12	13	14	15	16	17	18
19	20	21	22	23	24	25
26	27	28	29	30	31	

	APRIL					
S	M	T	W	T	F	S
						1
2	3	4	5	6	7	8
9	10	11	12	13	14	15
16	17	18	19	20	21	22
23	24	25	26	27	28	29
30						

	MAY					
S	M	T	W	T	F	S
	1	2	3	4	5	6
7	8	9	10	11	12	13
14	15	16	17	18	19	20
21	22	23	24	25	26	27
28	29	30	31			

	JUNE					
S	M	T	W	T	F	S
				1	2	3
4	5	6	7	8	9	10
11	12	13	14	15	16	17
18	19	20	21	22	23	24
25	26	27	28	29	30	

	JULY					
S	M	T	W	T	F	S
						1
2	3	4	5	6	7	8
9	10	11	12	13	14	15
16	17	18	19	20	21	22
23	24	25	26	27	28	29
30	31					

	AUGUST					
S	M	T	W	T	F	S
		1	2	3	4	5
6	7	8	9	10	11	12
13	14	15	16	17	18	19
20	21	22	23	24	25	26
27	28	29	30	31		

	SEPTEMBER					
S	M	T	W	T	F	S
					1	2
3	4	5	6	7	8	9
10	11	12	13	14	15	16
17	18	19	20	21	22	23
24	25	26	27	28	29	30

	OCTOBER					
S	M	T	W	T	F	S
1	2	3	4	5	6	7
8	9	10	11	12	13	14
15	16	17	18	19	20	21
22	23	24	25	26	27	28
29	30	31				

	NOVEMBER					
S	M	T	W	T	F	S
			1	2	3	4
5	6	7	8	9	10	11
12	13	14	15	16	17	18
19	20	21	22	23	24	25
26	27	28	29	30		

	DECEMBER					
S	M	T	W	T	F	S
					1	2
3	4	5	6	7	8	9
10	11	12	13	14	15	16
17	18	19	20	21	22	23
24	25	26	27	28	29	30
31						

1996 Calendar

JANUARY

S	M	T	W	T	F	S
	1	2	3	4	5	6
7	8	9	10	11	12	13
14	15	16	17	18	19	20
21	22	23	24	25	26	27
28	29	30	31			

FEBRUARY

S	M	T	W	T	F	S
				1	2	3
4	5	6	7	8	9	10
11	12	13	14	15	16	17
18	19	20	21	22	23	24
25	26	27	28	29		

MARCH

S	M	T	W	T	F	S
					1	2
3	4	5	6	7	8	9
10	11	12	13	14	15	16
17	18	19	20	21	22	23
24	25	26	27	28	29	30
31						

APRIL

S	M	T	W	T	F	S
	1	2	3	4	5	6
7	8	9	10	11	12	13
14	15	16	17	18	19	20
21	22	23	24	25	26	27
28	29	30				

MAY

S	M	T	W	T	F	S
			1	2	3	4
5	6	7	8	9	10	11
12	13	14	15	16	17	18
19	20	21	22	23	24	25
26	27	28	29	30	31	

JUNE

S	M	T	W	T	F	S
						1
2	3	4	5	6	7	8
9	10	11	12	13	14	15
16	17	18	19	20	21	22
23	24	25	26	27	28	29
30						

JULY

S	M	T	W	T	F	S
	1	2	3	4	5	6
7	8	9	10	11	12	13
14	15	16	17	18	19	20
21	22	23	24	25	26	27
28	29	30	31			

AUGUST

S	M	T	W	T	F	S
				1	2	3
4	5	6	7	8	9	10
11	12	13	14	15	16	17
18	19	20	21	22	23	24
25	26	27	28	29	30	31

SEPTEMBER

S	M	T	W	T	F	S
1	2	3	4	5	6	7
8	9	10	11	12	13	14
15	16	17	18	19	20	21
22	23	24	25	26	27	28
29	30					

OCTOBER

S	M	T	W	T	F	S
		1	2	3	4	5
6	7	8	9	10	11	12
13	14	15	16	17	18	19
20	21	22	23	24	25	26
27	28	29	30	31		

NOVEMBER

S	M	T	W	T	F	S
					1	2
3	4	5	6	7	8	9
10	11	12	13	14	15	16
17	18	19	20	21	22	23
24	25	26	27	28	29	30

DECEMBER

S	M	T	W	T	F	S
1	2	3	4	5	6	7
8	9	10	11	12	13	14
15	16	17	18	19	20	21
22	23	24	25	26	27	28
29	30	31				

1997 Calendar

JANUARY
S	M	T	W	T	F	S
			1	2	3	4
5	6	7	8	9	10	11
12	13	14	15	16	17	18
19	20	21	22	23	24	25
26	27	28	29	30	31	

FEBRUARY
S	M	T	W	T	F	S
						1
2	3	4	5	6	7	8
9	10	11	12	13	14	15
16	17	18	19	20	21	22
23	24	25	26	27	28	

MARCH
S	M	T	W	T	F	S
						1
2	3	4	5	6	7	8
9	10	11	12	13	14	15
16	17	18	19	20	21	22
23	24	25	26	27	28	29
30	31					

APRIL
S	M	T	W	T	F	S
		1	2	3	4	5
6	7	8	9	10	11	12
13	14	15	16	17	18	19
20	21	22	23	24	'25	26
27	28	29	30			

MAY
S	M	T	W	T	F	S
				1	2	3
4	5	6	7	8	9	10
11	12	13	14	15	16	17
18	19	20	21	22	23	24
25	26	27	28	29	30	31

JUNE
S	M	T	W	T	F	S
1	2	3	4	5	6	7
8	9	10	11	12	13	14
15	16	17	18	19	20	21
22	23	24	25	26	27	28
29	30					

JULY
S	M	T	W	T	F	S
		1	2	3	4	5
6	7	8	9	10	11	12
13	14	15	16	17	18	19
20	21	22	23	24	25	26
27	28	29	30	31		

AUGUST
S	M	T	W	T	F	S
					1	2
3	4	5	6	7	8	9
10	11	12	13	14	15	16
17	18	19	20	21	22	23
24	25	26	27	28	29	30
31						

SEPTEMBER
S	M	T	W	T	F	S
	1	2	3	4	5	6
7	8	9	10	11	12	13
14	15	16	17	18	19	20
21	22	23	24	25	26	27
28	29	30				

OCTOBER
S	M	T	W	T	F	S
			1	2	3	4
5	6	7	8	9	10	11
12	13	14	15	16	17	18
19	20	21	22	23	24	25
26	27	28	29	30	31	

NOVEMBER
S	M	T	W	T	F	S
						1
2	3	4	5	6	7	8
9	10	11	12	13	14	15
16	17	18	19	20	21	22
23	24	25	26	27	28	29
30						

DECEMBER
S	M	T	W	T	F	S
	1	2	3	4	5	6
7	8	9	10	11	12	13
14	15	16	17	18	19	20
21	22	23	24	25	26	27
28	29	30	31			

1998 Calendar

JANUARY
S	M	T	W	T	F	S
				1	2	3
4	5	6	7	8	9	10
11	12	13	14	15	16	17
18	19	20	21	22	23	24
25	26	27	28	29	30	31

FEBRUARY
S	M	T	W	T	F	S
1	2	3	4	5	6	7
8	9	10	11	12	13	14
15	16	17	18	19	20	21
22	23	24	25	26	27	28

MARCH
S	M	T	W	T	F	S
1	2	3	4	5	6	7
8	9	10	11	12	13	14
15	16	17	18	19	20	21
22	23	24	25	26	27	28
29	30	31				

APRIL
S	M	T	W	T	F	S
			1	2	3	4
5	6	7	8	9	10	11
12	13	14	15	16	17	18
19	20	21	22	23	24	25
26	27	28	29	30		

MAY
S	M	T	W	T	F	S
					1	2
3	4	5	6	7	8	9
10	11	12	13	14	15	16
17	18	19	20	21	22	23
24	25	26	27	28	29	30
31						

JUNE
S	M	T	W	T	F	S
	1	2	3	4	5	6
7	8	9	10	11	12	13
14	15	16	17	18	19	20
21	22	23	24	25	26	27
28	29	30				

JULY
S	M	T	W	T	F	S
			1	2	3	4
5	6	7	8	9	10	11
12	13	14	15	16	17	18
19	20	21	22	23	24	25
26	27	28	29	30	31	

AUGUST
S	M	T	W	T	F	S
						1
2	3	4	5	6	7	8
9	10	11	12	13	14	15
16	17	18	19	20	21	22
23	24	25	26	27	28	29
30	31					

SEPTEMBER
S	M	T	W	T	F	S
		1	2	3	4	5
6	7	8	9	10	11	12
13	14	15	16	17	18	19
20	21	22	23	24	25	26
27	28	29	30			

OCTOBER
S	M	T	W	T	F	S
				1	2	3
4	5	6	7	8	9	10
11	12	13	14	15	16	17
18	19	20	21	22	23	24
25	26	27	28	29	30	31

NOVEMBER
S	M	T	W	T	F	S
1	2	3	4	5	6	7
8	9	10	11	12	13	14
15	16	17	18	19	20	21
22	23	24	25	26	27	28
29	30					

DECEMBER
S	M	T	W	T	F	S
		1	2	3	4	5
6	7	8	9	10	11	12
13	14	15	16	17	18	19
20	21	22	23	24	25	26
27	28	29	30	31		

Ready-Reference Calendar

For ascertaining any day of the week for any given time from 1800 to 2050 inclusive.

Common Years, 1800 to 2050

Years	JAN	FEB	MAR	APR	MAY	JUN	JUL	AUG	SEP	OCT	NOV	DEC
1801 1829 1857 1885 1914 1942 1970 1998 2026 1807 1835 1863 1891 1925 1953 1981 2009 2037 1818 1846 1874 1903 1931 1959 1987 2015 2043	4	7	7	3	5	1	3	6	2	4	7	2
1802 1830 1858 1886 1915 1943 1971 1999 2027 1813 1841 1869 1897 1926 1954 1982 2010 2038 1819 1847 1875 1909 1937 1965 1993 2021 2049	5	1	1	4	6	2	4	7	3	5	1	3
1803 1831 1859 1887 1921 1949 1977 2005 2033 1814 1842 1870 1898 1927 1955 1983 2011 2039 1825 1853 1881 1910 1938 1966 1994 2022 2050	6	2	2	5	7	3	5	1	4	6	2	4
1805 1833 1861 1889 1907 1935 1963 1991 2019 2047 1811 1839 1867 1895 1918 1946 1974 2002 2030 1822 1850 1878 1901 1929 1957 1985 2013 2041	2	5	5	1	3	6	1	4	7	2	5	7
1800 1823 1851 1879 1913 1941 1969 1997 2025 1806 1834 1862 1890 1919 1947 1975 2003 2031 1817 1845 1873 1902 1930 1958 1986 2014 2042	3	6	6	2	4	7	2	5	1	3	6	1
1809 1837 1865 1893 1911 1939 1967 1995 2023 1815 1843 1871 1899 1922 1950 1978 2006 2034 1826 1854 1882 1905 1933 1961 1989 2017 2045	7	3	3	6	1	4	6	2	5	7	3	5
1810 1838 1866 1894 1917 1945 1973 2001 2029 1821 1849 1877 1900 1923 1951 1979 2007 2035 1827 1855 1883 1906 1934 1962 1990 2018 2046	1	4	4	7	2	5	7	3	6	1	4	6

Leap Year, 1804 to 2048

(FEB = 29)

Years	JAN	FEB	MAR	APR	MAY	JUN	JUL	AUG	SEP	OCT	NOV	DEC
1804 1832 1860 1888 1928 1956 1984 2012 2040	7	3	4	7	2	5	7	3	6	1	4	6
1808 1836 1864 1892 1904 1932 1960 1988 2016 2044	5	1	2	5	7	3	5	1	4	6	2	4
1812 1840 1868 1896 1908 1936 1964 1992 2020 2048	3	6	7	3	5	1	3	6	2	4	7	2
1816 1844 1872 1912 1940 1968 1996 2024	1	4	5	1	3	6	1	4	7	2	5	7
1820 1848 1876 1916 1944 1972 2000 2028	6	2	3	6	1	4	6	2	5	7	3	5
1824 1852 1880 1920 1948 1976 2004 2032	4	7	1	4	6	2	4	7	3	5	1	3
1828 1856 1884 1924 1952 1980 2008 2036	2	5	6	2	4	7	2	5	1	3	6	1

1	2	3	4	5	6	7
Monday 1	Tuesday 1	Wednesday . 1	Thursday 1	Friday 1	Saturday 1	SUNDAY 1
Tuesday 2	Wednesday . 2	Thursday 2	Friday 2	Saturday 2	SUNDAY 2	Monday 2
Wednesday . 3	Thursday 3	Friday 3	Saturday 3	SUNDAY 3	Monday 3	Tuesday 3
Thursday 4	Friday 4	Saturday 4	SUNDAY 4	Monday 4	Tuesday 4	Wednesday . 4
Friday 5	Saturday 5	SUNDAY 5	Monday 5	Tuesday 5	Wednesday . 5	Thursday 5
Saturday 6	SUNDAY 6	Monday 6	Tuesday 6	Wednesday . 6	Thursday 6	Friday 6
SUNDAY 7	Monday 7	Tuesday 7	Wednesday . 7	Thursday 7	Friday 7	Saturday 7
Monday 8	Tuesday 8	Wednesday . 8	Thursday 8	Friday 8	Saturday 8	SUNDAY 8
Tuesday 9	Wednesday . 9	Thursday 9	Friday 9	Saturday 9	SUNDAY 9	Monday 9
Wednesday 10	Thursday ... 10	Friday 10	Saturday ... 10	SUNDAY ... 10	Monday 10	Tuesday 10
Thursday ... 11	Friday 11	Saturday ... 11	SUNDAY ... 11	Monday 11	Tuesday 11	Wednesday 11
Friday 12	Saturday ... 12	SUNDAY ... 12	Monday 12	Tuesday 12	Wednesday 12	Thursday ... 12
Saturday ... 13	SUNDAY ... 13	Monday 13	Tuesday 13	Wednesday 13	Thursday ... 13	Friday 13
SUNDAY ... 14	Monday 14	Tuesday 14	Wednesday 14	Thursday ... 14	Friday 14	Saturday ... 14
Monday 15	Tuesday 15	Wednesday 15	Thursday ... 15	Friday 15	Saturday ... 15	SUNDAY ... 15
Tuesday 16	Wednesday 16	Thursday ... 16	Friday 16	Saturday ... 16	SUNDAY ... 16	Monday 16
Wednesday 17	Thursday ... 17	Friday 17	Saturday ... 17	SUNDAY ... 17	Monday 17	Tuesday 17
Thursday ... 18	Friday 18	Saturday ... 18	SUNDAY ... 18	Monday 18	Tuesday 18	Wednesday 18
Friday 19	Saturday ... 19	SUNDAY ... 19	Monday 19	Tuesday 19	Wednesday 19	Thursday ... 19
Saturday ... 20	SUNDAY ... 20	Monday 20	Tuesday 20	Wednesday 20	Thursday ... 20	Friday 20
SUNDAY ... 21	Monday 21	Tuesday 21	Wednesday 21	Thursday ... 21	Friday 21	Saturday ... 21
Monday 22	Tuesday 22	Wednesday 22	Thursday ... 22	Friday 22	Saturday ... 22	SUNDAY ... 22
Tuesday 23	Wednesday 23	Thursday ... 23	Friday 23	Saturday ... 23	SUNDAY ... 23	Monday 23
Wednesday 24	Thursday ... 24	Friday 24	Saturday ... 24	SUNDAY ... 24	Monday 24	Tuesday 24
Thursday ... 25	Friday 25	Saturday ... 25	SUNDAY ... 25	Monday 25	Tuesday 25	Wednesday 25
Friday 26	Saturday ... 26	SUNDAY ... 26	Monday 26	Tuesday 26	Wednesday 26	Thursday ... 26
Saturday ... 27	SUNDAY ... 27	Monday 27	Tuesday 27	Wednesday 27	Thursday ... 27	Friday 27
SUNDAY ... 28	Monday 28	Tuesday 28	Wednesday 28	Thursday ... 28	Friday 28	Saturday ... 28
Monday 29	Tuesday 29	Wednesday 29	Thursday ... 29	Friday 29	Saturday ... 29	SUNDAY ... 29
Tuesday 30	Wednesday 30	Thursday ... 30	Friday 30	Saturday ... 30	SUNDAY ... 30	Monday 30
Wednesday 31	Thursday ... 31	Friday 31	Saturday ... 31	SUNDAY ... 31	Monday 31	Tuesday 31

NOTE: To ascertain any day of the week, first look in the table for the year required. Then under the months find the figure that corresponds to the number below at the head of the columns of the days. **For example:** To know on what day of the week July 4, 1918, fell, look in the table of years for 1918, and in a parallel line under July is figure 1, which directs to column 1 where it will be seen that July 4 fell on Thursday.

Arts

PERFORMING GROUPS AVAILABLE FOR PERFORMANCES

Group/Affiliation	Address	Contact
Dance		
Ballet Magnificate School & Studios	4455 N. State, Jackson, MS 39206-5306	Jeff Bieber, Tour Director
Cadle, Michael	224 Taylor St., Jackson, MS 39216	
CrossCurrent Dance Theatre	5724 Vincent Ave. S., Minneapolis, MN 55410	Sharon Hinck, Artistic Director
Crystal Cathedral	12141 Lewis St., Garden Grove, CA 92669	Dorie Lee Mattson, Director of Dance
Dallas Ballet Center	5832 Abrams, Suite 103, Dallas, TX 75214	Brent & Judy Klopfenstein, Directors
Exaltation Dancers	c/o Briarwood Presbyterian, 2200 Briarwood Way, Birmingham, AL 35243	Barbara Barker, Director
Fiorino, Paul	PO Box 11040, Denver, CO 80211	
Henry, Valerie	PO Box 240, Devon, PA 19333	
Hosanna Sacred Dance	1318 S. Reisner St., Indianapolis, IN 46221	Kenneth Tolle, Artistic Director
Impact Productions	807 S. Xanthus Place, Tulsa, OK 74104	Andrea Jobe, Artistic Director
Kast & Company Liturgical Dancers	5320 S. University Ave., Chicago, IL 60615	Maggie Kast, Artistic Director
Mecholah Yachad	1202 Shelton Ave., Nashville, TN 37216	Rucele Consigny, Director
Praise His Name in the Dance	2327 Julianna Circle, Dallas, TX 75229	Judith Jenkins
Vine Dance Theatre, The	PO Box 6482, FDR Station, New York, NY 10150	Kathleen LaCamera, Artistic Director
Music		
A D/Proclaim	Anno Domini, Inc., 11570 San Jose Blvd., Suite 231, Jacksonville, FL 32223	John Bowers, Director
Basham, Glenn	1724 Crescent Ave., Fort Wayne, IN 46805	
Burleigh, Paul	759 Schadel Dr., Lancaster, OH 43130	
Campus Crusade for Christ Music Ministry	22912 Mill Creek Dr., #A, Laguna Hills, CA 92653	Janice Kaszycki, Associate Nat'l Director
Glise, Anthony	c/o 2703 Mitchell Ave., St. Joseph, MO 64507	
Halal Ministries	M611 Birch, Marshfield, WI 54449	James Washburn
Jones Marcia	22307 65th Ave. W., Mountlake Terrace, WA 98043	
Nash Productions	700 Paloma Ave., Oakland, CA 94610	Kenneth Nash
New Life Symphony	PO Box 434, Watertown, MA 02272	Derk Smid, President

Group/Affiliation	Address	Contact
New Sound, Inc.	PO Box 197, Merrimac, MA 01860	Dan Russell, Co-Director
Noel Paul Stookey with Bodyworks	c/o Neworld Media, Blue Hill Falls, ME 04615	Joyce Hall, Administrative Assistant
Northwestern College Music Dept.	101 7th St. SW, Orange City, IA 51041	Kimberly Utke Schouten, Music Dept. Chair
Quail Ministries	203 Brightwood Ave., Torrington, CT 06790	Michael Blanchard, Director of Ministry
Salt & Light Ministries	9306 Shiloh Rd., Richmond, VA 23237-3245	Jeffrey Smith, President
Singing Praise	806 Hopi Trail, Temple, TX 76504	Kay Coulter

Opera/Music Theatre

Group/Affiliation	Address	Contact
Christian Arts Incorporated	1755 W. End Ave., New Hyde Park, NY 11040	Derek deCambra, Artistic Director
New Life Drama Company	45 Walden St., #G1, Concord, MA 01742-2504	David MacAdam, Pastor
New Life Ministries Inc	11301 Penny Rd. #F, Apex, NC 27502-8158	Barry Hall, Associate Director
Refreshment Committee, The	801 Dayton Ave., St. Paul, MN 55104	Jeffrey Miller, Artistic Director
Towne & Country Players, Inc.	55 E. Main, PO Box 551, Norwalk, OH 44857	Ronn Koerper, Executive Director

Theatre

Group/Affiliation	Address	Contact
Acacia Theatre Company	924 E. Juneau Ave., #209, Milwaukee, WI 53202	Terese Hummel, Managing Director
After Dinner Players	2710 W. Alabama, Houston, TX 77098	Elizabeth Pentak-Aneill, Exec. Dir. Comm. Affairs
Andersen, Garold	Box 144, Guymon, OK 73942	
Anderson, Margaret	3-5 W. 122 St., PO Box 2449, New York, NY 10185	
Asbury College Theatre Arts	201 N. Lexington Ave., Wilmore, KY 40390	Sandra C. Harper, Dir. of Theatre Arts
California Baptist College	8431 Magnolia Ave., Riverside, CA 92504	Melodie Yocum, Communication Dept.
Captain Ken's Marionette Ministries	PO Box 441, Phoenixville, PA 19460-0441	Captain Ken, Reverend
Christ Community Church Drama Team	37W100 Bolcum Rd., St. Charles, IL 60175-6201	Pam Hiscock, Dir. of Communication
Christian Community Theater/ Christian Youth Theater	1591 Pioneer Way, El Cajon, CA 92020	Paul Russell, Artistic Director
Cloninger, Curt	PO Box 6811, Mobile, AL 36606	
Covenant Players	1741 Fiske Place, PO Box 2900, Oxnard, CA 93033	Bobbi Johnson-Tanner, Dir. of Administration
Dordt College Theatre Department	4th Ave., Sioux Center, IA 51250	Verne Meyer, Theatre Dept. Chair
Dramatic Word, The	PO Box 903, Salem, OR 97308	Art Obendorf, Booking Coordinator
Eastern Nazarene College Theatre	23 E. Elm Ave., Quincy, MA 02170	Rhonda Winderl, Chair, Communication
First Presbyterian Theater	300 W. Wayne St., Fort Wayne, IN 46802-3673	John Tolley, Drama Director
Frank Harvey Ministries	296 Carriage Lane, Lexington, KY 40502-4566	Frank Harvey
Friends of John Wesley, The	1716 1/4 Sierra Bonita, Pasadena, CA 91104	Roger Nelson, Director
Friends of the Groom	909 Center St., Milford, OH 45150-1305	Tom Long, Director
Greco, Christopher	1 Carolina Place #3, Jamaica Plain, MA 02130	

Group/Affiliation	Address	Contact
Hodgson, Karen	4227 Sheridan Ave. N., Minneapolis, MN 55412	
Inheritance Players	c/o Calvary Baptist Church, 123 W. 57th St., New York, NY 10019	Sydney Johnson, Director
InterMission "Thinkable Theatre"	CBN University Performing Arts, Virginia Beach. VA 23464	Darlene Graves, Artist-in-Residence
Iowa Christian Theater, Inc.	422 Heritage Rd., Cedar Falls, IA 50613	Jeff Hanson, Director
John Cochran Repertory Company	406 N. Raymond Ave., Pasadena, CA 91103-3705	Joyce Ericsson, Vice President
Lamb's Players Theatre	500 Plaza Blvd., PO Box 26, National City, CA 91951-0026	Robert Smyth, Artistic Director
Lamb's Theatre Company, Ltd.	130 W. 44th St., New York, NY 10036	Carolyn Rossi Copeland, Producing Director
Lion's Light Productions	3280 SW 170th #1704, Beaverton, OR 97006	Elizabeth Peters, Managing Director
Living Word Outdoor Drama, The	6010 College Hill Rd., PO Box 1481, Cambridge, OH 43725	Joyce Rice, General Manager
Macklin, Robert	4100 1/2 Los Feliz Blvd., Los Angeles, CA 90027	
Malone College Chancel Players	515 25th St. NW, Canton, OH 44709	Alan Hedges, Theatre Director
Master Arts Company	PO Box 9336, Grand Rapids, MI 49509	Priscilla McDonald, Exec. Director
Mullins, Don	PO Box 287, Westminster, MD 21157-0287	
Parable Players	c/o Church of the Ascension, 4729 Ellsworth Ave., Pittsburgh, PA 15213	Eileen Boarman, Artistic Director
Potters Cast	Green Acres Baptist Church 1612 Leo Lynn, Tyler, TX 75701	Ken Brumley, Singles Minister
Repertory Theatre at Christian Theological Seminary	1000 W 42nd St., Indianapolis, IN 46208	Dara Ciancio-Bunch, Office Manager
Rosenberg, Burt	PO Box 2242, Silver Spring, MD 20915	
South Jersey Black Theater Ensemble	Rd. #1 Lee Ave., Millville, NJ 08332	W. Wayne DeShields, Director
Spring Arbor College Readers Theatre	Spring Arbor College, Spring Arbor, MI 49283	Esther Lee Maddox, Assoc. Professor of Speech
St. Luke Productions	PO Box 761, Beaverton, OR 97075	Leonardo Defilippis, Producer/Director
Tapestry Theatre Company	PO Box 19844, Portland, OR 97280	Judy Urschel, Artistic Director
Taproot Theatre Company	204 N. 85th St., PO Box 31116, Seattle, WA 98103	Scott Nolte, Artistic Director
Team Ministry, The	13 Carey Lane, PO Box 100, Oxford, MA 01540	Vincent Rideout, Director
Vantage Theatre Ensemble	18305 NW Tara St., Beaverton, OR 97006	Terry Spivey, Artistic Director

Media Arts

Maranatha Productions, Inc.	PO Box 210, Dixon, IL 61021-0210	Bette Bluemker, Admin Assistant

Interdisciplinary

Bane, Randel	PO Box 412861, Kansas City, MO 64141	
Christian Performing Artists' Fellowship	10523 Main St., Suite 31, Fairfax, VA 22030	Patrick Kavanaugh, Executive Director
Josephson, Karen	305 Townsend Ave., New Haven, CT 06512	
Ricky Smith Mime Productions	PO Box 194, N. Chili, NY 14514	Liz Smith, Road Manager

Group/Affiliation	Address	Contact
Slack, Susanne	2360 Street de Ville, Atlanta, GA 30345	

Multidisciplinary

Because He Cares, Inc	1340 East Ave., PO Box 71, Akron, OH 44309-0071	Yvonne Brake, President
Belto, CCVI Michelle	618 Rockhill, San Antonio, TX 78209	
Fellowship of Artists for Cultural Evangelism	1605 Elizabeth St., Pasadena, CA 91104	Gene & Mary Lou Totten, Co-Directors
National Association of Pastoral Musicians	225 Sheridan St. NW, Washington, DC 20011	Thomas Wilson, Associate Director

Source: Christians in the Arts Networking, Inc., (CAN).

DRAMA RESOURCES

Agape Drama Press, Ltd., Box 1313, Englewood, CO 80110

Augsburg Publishing House, 426 S. Fifth Street, Minneapolis, MN 55415

Baker's Plays, 100 Chauncy St., Boston, MA 02111

Bethany Press, Box 179, St. Louis, MO 63166

Broadman Press, Baptist Convention Press, 127 Ninth Avenue N., Nashville, TN 37234

Christian Board of Publication, P.O. Box 179, St. Louis, MO 63166

Coach House Press, Inc., 53 W. Jackson Blvd., Chicago, IL 60604

Contemporary Drama Service, Box 7710-B5, Colorado Springs, CO 80933

Continental Ministries (Jeremiah People), P.O. Box 1996, Thousand Oaks, CA 91360

Creative Arts Productions, Box 7008, Santa Cruz, CA 95061

C.S.S. Publishing Company, 628 S. Main Street, Lima, OH 45804

Dramatic Publishing Co., 4150 N. Milwaukee Avenue, Chicago, IL 60641

Dramatists Play Service, 440 Park Avenue South, New York, NY 10016

Edna Means Dramatic Service, 610 Harmon Street, Tama, IA 52339

Eldridge Publishing Company, P.O. Drawer 216, Franklin, OH 45005

Friendship Press, P.O. Box 37844, Cincinnati, OH 45237

Hansen Drama Shop, 459 S. Seventh East, Salt Lake City, UT 84102

Heuer Publishing Company, Drawer 248, Cedar Rapids, IA 52406

Horizon Gate Productions, P.O. Box 1740, #52, La Mesa, CA 92401

I. E. Clark, Inc., P.O. Box 246, Schulenburg, TX 78956-0246

The Jeremiah People, Box 1996, Thousand Oaks, CA 91360 (Sketch books)

Judson Press, Valley Forge, PA 19481

Laudamus Press, 1821 Fourth St., NW, Ankeny, IA 50021

Lillenas Publishing Co., Box 419527, Kansas City, MO 64141

Lutheran Church Press, 2900 Queen Lane, Philadelphia, PA 19129

National Council of Church of Christ, Dept. of Worship and Arts, 475 Riverside Drive, New York, NY 10027

On Stage, P.O. Box 25365, Chicago, IL 60625-0365

Performance Publishing Company, 978 McLean Blvd. N., Elgin, IL 60120

Pioneer Drama Service, Inc., 2172 Colorado Blvd. S., P.O. Box 22555, Denver, CO 80222

Russell House, 522 E. Chase Avenue, Suite A, El Cajon, CA 92020

Ruth Vaughn, Inc., P.O. Box 1575, Bethany, OK 73008

Samuel French, Inc., 45 W. 25th Street, New York, NY 10010

Willow Creek Community Church, 67 E. Algonquin Road, South Barrington, IL 60010 (Sketch books)

Source: Steve Pederson, Drama Director, Willow Creek Community Church, South Barrington, IL and *Christian Drama.* Used by permission.

ARTS CONFERENCES

The following organizations sponsor annual conferences. Write directly to them for further information.

Cornerstone Festival, 4707 N. Malden, Chicago, IL 60640

February **Lillenas Drama Resources/Lillenas Publishing Company**, PO Box 419527, Kansas, MO 64141

June **Christians in Theatre Arts**, c/o Malone College, 515 25th Street NW, Canton, OH 44709

Christians in the Visual Arts, PO Box 10247, Arlington, VA 22210

July **Fellowship of Contemporary Christian Ministries**, 24-B N Belmont Avenue, PO Box 1337, Arlington Heights, IL 60006

Phoenix Power & Light Company, Inc., 609 Chapelgate Drive, PO Box 60, Odenton, MD 21113

August **Christian Artists Corporation**, PO Box 338950, Denver, CO 80233

October **Master Arts Company**, PO Box 9336, Grand Rapids, MI 49509

FOCUS FACT

Christians in the Arts Networking, Inc. exists to promote and encourage:
- **communication and fellowship among Christians involved in the arts**
- **bridges of understanding and trust between the church and the arts community, leading to spiritual maturity, unity, and usefulness**
- **development and maintenance of biblical standards for artists and their work**

—For information on how you can become involved write to: PO Box 1941, Cambridge, MA 02238-1941

ARTS ORGANIZATIONS

Archives of Modern Christian Art, 1500 Ralston Avenue, Belmont, CA 94002

Artists in Christian Testimony, 9521 A Business Center Drive, Cucamonga, CA 91730

Arts Group, Grace & Peace Fellowship, 5574 Delmar Street, St. Louis, MO 63112

Arts and Religion Forum, Washington Theological Consort, 487 Michigan Avenue NE, Washington, DC 20017

Associated Christian Ministries & Educational Services, Inc., PO Box 21593, Houston, TX 77226

Association Uniting Religion and Art, 302 Spencer Road, Devon, PA 19333

Catholic Fine Arts Society Inc./Catholic Artists of the 90s, Maria Regina Hall/Molloy College, 1000 Hempstead Avenue, Rockville Centre, NY 11570

Center for Liturgy and the Arts, 4327 Ravensworth Road #210, Annandale, VA 22003

Center for Perfomers & the Performing Arts, Inc., 484 W. 43rd Street, #42A, New York, NY 10036

Center for the Arts, Religion, and Education, c/o Pacific School of Religion, 1798 Scenic Avenue, Berkeley, CA 94709

Chicago Artists, 5255 N. Paulina, Chicago, IL 60640

Christian Architects' Fellowship, 115-25 84th Avenue, Kew Gardens, NY 11418

Christian Art League Ministry, 128 Westwood Drive, Visalia, CA 93277

Christian Visual Media International, 1713 E. Walnut Street, Pasadena, CA 91106

Christianity and Literature, Department of English, Seattle Pacific University, Seattle, WA 98119

Christians in Theatre Arts, c/o Malone College, 515 25th Street NW, Canton, OH 44709

Christians in the Arts Networking Inc., PO Box 1941, Cambridge, MA 02238-1941

Christians in the Visual Arts, PO Box 10247, Arlington, VA 22210
Eastbrook Artists' Group, 2844 N. Oakland Avenue, Milwaukee, WI 53211
Fellowship of Artists for Cultural Evangelism, 1605 Elizabeth Street, Pasadena, CA 91104
Fellowship of Contemporary Christian Ministries, 24-B N. Belmont Avenue, PO Box 1337, Arlington Heights, IL 60006
Foundation for Religion and the Arts, PO Box 6482, FDR Station, New York, NY 10150
Genesis Arts Phoenix. 2516 W. Curry Street, Chandler, AZ 85224
Grunewald Guild, 19003 River Road, Leavenworth, WA 98826
International Christian Cultural Center, 1300 Springwells, Fl 2, Detroit, MI 48209
International Christian Media Commission, PO Box 70632, Seattle, WA 98107-0632
Memphis Arts Group, 2167 Washington Avenue, Apt. 4, Memphis, TN 38104
National Association of Pastoral Musicians, 225 Sheridan Street NW, Washington, DC 20011
New York Arts Group, PO Box 489, Old Chelsea Station, New York, NY 10011-9998
North American Academy of Liturgy, Room 120, Huegli Hall, Valparaiso University, Valparaiso, IN 46383
Phoenix Power & Light Company Inc., 609 Chapelgate Drive, PO Box 60, Odenton, MD 21113
Professional Performing Artists' Fellowship, Marble Collegent, 1 W. 29th Street, New York, NY 10001
Tucson Christian Artists Fellowship, PO Box 755, Cartaro, AZ 85652-0755
United Church of Christ Fellowship in the Arts, Zion St. Paul UCC, General Delivery HCR 62, Hermann, MO 65041
Washington Arts Group, 2013 Q Street NW, Washington, DC 20009
Source: Christians in the Arts Networking, Inc. (CAN).

---

66 99
FOCUS
QUOTE Drama, narrative art, dance and mime are as old as our civilization. These are present ways of holding up—in a playful manner—a mirror to the audience's face, to make them think about themselves, about situations in life and about faith, without them having intended to do so. That's the real art of communication.
Christians shouldn't put themselves above the society in which they live. Jesus never did that. He was the best narrator of his time, and he used the best visual pictures to explain the Good News of God.—Geoffrey Stevenson in *Tema Info*, publication of The European Missionary Association

---

BOOKLIST: A TECHNICAL DRAMA REFERENCE LIBRARY

SCENERY DESIGN AND
    CONSTRUCTION
Scene Technology by Richard L. Arnold. Prentice-Hall
Scenography and Stage Technology by Willard Bellman. Thomas Crowell
Handbook of Technical Practice for the Performing Arts by Ned Bowman. Scenographic Media
Scenery for the Theatre by Harold Burris-Meyer and Edward Cole. Little, Brown, and Company
Stage Scenery by A. S. Gillette. Harper and Row, Publishers
Stage Scenery, Its Construction and Rigging by A. S. Gillette and J. Michael Gillette. Harper and Row, Publishers
Scene Design and Stage Lighting by W. Oren Parker and Harvey K. Smith. Holt, Rinehart and Winston
Designing and Painting for the Theatre by Lynn Pecktal. Holt, Rinehart and Winston

Essentials of Stage Scenery by Samuel Selden and Tom Rezzuto. Appleton-Century-Crofts

STAGE MANAGEMENT
The Stage Manager's Handbook by Bert Gruver. Drama Book Specialists
Stage Management: A Guidebook of Practical Techniques by Lawrence Stern. Allyn and Bacon

THE THEATRE FACILITY
Theatres and Auditoriums by Harold Burris-Meyer and Edward Cole. Reinhold
The Shapes of Our Theatre by Jo Meilziner. Clarkson N. Potter

MAKEUP
Stage Makeup by Herman Buchman. Watson-Guptill
Stage Makeup by Richard Corson. Prentice-Hall

LIGHTING
Lighting the Stage: Art and Practice by Willard F. Bellman. Crowell
Designing with Light by J. Michael Gillette. Mayfield
Scene Design and Stage Lighting by W. Oren Parker and Harvey K. Smith. Holt, Rinehart and Winston
Stage Lighting by Richard Pilbrow. Van Nostrand Reinhold
Essentials of Stage Lighting by H. D. Sellman. Appleton-Century-Crofts

SOUND
Sound in the Theatre by Harold Burris-Meyer, Vincent Mallory and Lewis Goodfriend. Theatre Arts Books
Stage Sound by David Collison. Drama Book Specialists

Source: Bill Jenkins in *Christian Drama*, February 1988 issue. Used by permission.

PRAISE HIS NAME, TWO, THREE, FOUR

Our church has seen several movements— the charismatic, the church-growth, and the small-group movements, to name a few. Still, we weren't prepared for the latest: the Movement movement.

It started innocently with a women's aerobics class, which was followed by some innocent swaying to praise choruses and fast-moving hymns. But it started to get out of hand when our intern from the seminary arrived, all excited about his class in "Theo-Kinetics." He proposed a Sunday morning dance troupe to "recapture the intuitive in worship." Then denominational headquarters, never wanting to be out of step (so to speak), issued a denominationwide study curriculum, "Motion and Mission."

But local congregations aren't always moving at the same speed as seminary professors and denominational hierarchs. After the worship-dance group's first Sunday-morning performance, the issue came to the board. Some favored the new expression, citing Jeremiah 31:13. Others ridiculed it as "discipleship in Danskin." It finally came to a motion (of course).

As expected, the board voted for a compromise between the progressives and conservatives. Worship dance is permissible, but for men only. That left our head ushers, Frank and Wilber, with the job of leading the men in an expressionistic interpretation of "All Hail the Power" as part of the call to worship. They resigned immediately.

Now we need a study from the seminary or headquarters on "Finding Ushers for Ministry."

Eutychus, *Christianity Today*, December 15, 1989

FOCUS BOOK

***State of the Arts—From Bezalel to Mapplethorpe* by Gene Edward Veith, Jr. Includes discussions of current trends and controversies. Speaks to all Christians, not just artists, who wish to learn about the arts.** Published by Crossway Books.

TOP 10 VIDEOS OF 1991

Rentals

1. *A Thief in the Night,* Mark IV Pictures
2. *A Distant Thunder,* Mark IV Pictures
3. *Image of the Beast,* Mark IV Pictures
4. *The Prodigal Planet,* Mark IV Pictures
5. *Hell's Bells—The Dangers of Rock 'n' Roll,* by Eric Holmberg, Reel to Real Ministries
6. *Do You Hear Me?!,* by Mike Warnke, Day-Spring (Word)
7. *Revival in the Land,* by Carman, Benson Videos
8. *McGee and Me! Take Me Out of the Ball Game,* Focus on the Family (Tyndale)
9. *Jesus,* Inspirational Media
10. *The Cross and the Switchblade,* Vanguard Video

Sales

1. *Adventures in Odyssey—The Knight Travellers,* Focus on the Family, WORDkids! (Word Publishing)
2. *McGee and Me! The Big Lie,* Focus on the Family (Tyndale)

3. *The Greatest Adventure Vol. 7, The Nativity,* Hanna-Barbera Productions (Sparrow)
4. *McGee and Me! Take Me Out of the Ball Game,* Focus on the Family (Tyndale)
5. *McGee and Me! 'Twas the Fight Before Christmas,* Focus on the Family (Tyndale)
6. *Revival in the Land,* by Carman, Benson Videos
7. *McGee and Me! Do the Bright Thing,* Focus on the Family (Tyndale)
8. *Kids Sing Praise,* Brentwood Kids Co. (Brentwood Music)
9. *Mother Goose Goes to the Zoo Video,* Brentwood Kids Co. (Brentwood Music)
10. *McGee and Me! Skate Expectations,* Focus on the Family (Tyndale)

This list is based on actual rentals and sales in Christian retail stores in the United States and Canada during 1991. All rights reserved. Copyright © 1992 CBA Service Corp. Reprinted by permission from the February 1992 issue of *Bookstore Journal,* official trade publication of the Christian Booksellers Association.

TOP 10 CHRISTIAN FILMS OF 1991

1. **Molder of Dreams,** Focus on the Family
2. **Future Tense,** Gospel Films
3. **Bamboo in Winter,** Gospel Films
4. **Geronimo,** Ed McDougal Films
5. **The Radicals,** Gateway Films
6. **Without Reservation,** Gospel Films
7. **On the Edge,** Side by Side Films
8. **A Man Called Norman,** Fiocus on the Family
9. **The Appointment,** Rich Christiano Films
10. **Love Is a Decision,** Zondervan Films

Source: Visual Media Center, Fresno Bible House, Fresno, CA

CROWN AWARDS

The Crown Awards are designed to recognize excellence in production and content of films and videos that are created to reflect Christian values in a secular world. Voting is done by CVMI (Christian Visual Media International) members, a trade organization made up of producers, distributors, directors, actors, and writers in the visual media.

Year Category	Film	Actor/Actress/ Director	Production Company
1977			
Best Actor	Sammy	Eric Buhr	Heartland Productions
Best Actress	All the King's Horses	Dee Wallace	Mark IV Pictures
Best Children's	Sammy		Heartland Productions
Best Documentary	World That Perished		Films for Christ
Best Film	All The King's Horses		Mark IV Pictures

Year Category	Film	Actor/Actress/Director	Production Company
Best Missionary	For All Men		Harvest Productions
Best Soul Winning	Senior Year		Ken Anderson Films
Outstanding Personality in the Film Industry		Ken Anderson	
Pioneer in Christian Film Production		Irwin Moon	
1978			
Best Actor	Pilgrim's Progress	Peter Thomas	Ken Anderson Films
Best Actress	Distant Thunder	Patty Dunning	Mark IV Pictures
Best Children's	Great Banana Pie Caper		Quadros Communications
Best Cinematography	Pilgrim's Progress	Max Anderson, Roger Boller	Ken Anderson Films
Best Director	Pilgrim's Progress	Ken Anderson	Ken Anderson Films
Best Documentary	Eldridge Cleaver		Gospel Films
Best Effects	Pilgrim's Progress		Ken Anderson Films
Best Film	Pilgrim's Progress		Ken Anderson Films
Best Historical	Megiddo		Cathedral Films
Best Missionary	Survivor No. 3		Moody Institute of Science
Best Musical Score	Pilgrim's Progress	Tim Simonec	Ken Anderson Films
Best Series	Faith for Today		Gateway Films
Best Soul Winning	Distant Thunder		Mark IV Pictures
Best Stewardship	Gift of Love		Christian Communications
Best Supporting Actor	The Prize	Chuck Woolery	Outreach Films
Best Supporting Actress	Distant Thunder	Sally Johnson	Mark IV Pictures
Best Youth	Nite Song		Heartland Productions
1979			
Best Actor	John Hus	Rod Colbin	Gateway Films
Best Actress	Crossfire	Jane Klint	Quadrus Communications
Best Biblical	Man from Tarsus		Harvest Productions
Best Children's	The Wacky Weirdos of Willoughby Castle		Quadrus Communications
Best Christian Living	Strike the Original Match		New Liberty Enterprises
Best Cinematography	Crossfire	Tim Dabner	Quadrus Communications
Best Director	Deceived	Mel White	Mel White Productions
Best Documentary	Deceived		Mel White Productions
Best Film of the Year	John Hus		Gateway Films
Best Musical Score	Christiana	Tim Simonec	Ken Anderson Films
Best Series	Focus on The Family		Word, Inc.
Best Soul Winning	Paradise Trail		Mark IV Pictures
Best Supporting Actor	John Hus	Regis Cordic	Quadrus Communications
Best Supporting Actress	Christiana	Tina Heath	Ken Anderson Films
Best Youth	Crossfire		Quadrus Communications
Outstanding Contribution to the Film Ministry		Mel White	
1980			
Best Actor	Ordinary Guy	Richard Foster	Day Star Productions
Best Actress	Heaven's Heroes	Heide Vaughn	Mark IV Pictures
Best Art Director	Stolen Watermelon	John Miller	Ken Anderson Films
Best Biblical	I, Paul		Gateway Films
Best Children's	Goosehill Gang/The Vanishing Schoolmate		Family Films
Best Cinematography	Sports Galaxy	Bob Cording	Omega Films
Best Direction	Heaven's Heroes	Don Thompson	Mark IV
Best Documentary	Assignment: Life		New Liberty Enterprises
Best Editing	Assignment: Life	Carrie Matrisciana	New Liberty Enterprises
Best Evangelistic	Heaven's Heroes		Mark IV Pictures
Best Film of the Year	Ordinary Guy		Day Star Productions
Best Film Series	Goosehill Gang		Family Films
Best Missionary	Telling Kelli		Harvest Productions
Best Musical Score	Music Box	Charles R. Johnson	White Lion Pictograph
Best Screen Play	Touch of the Master's Hand	Jimmy Murphy	Ken Anderson Films
Best Special Effects	Whitcomb's War	Timothy Doughton	Heartland Productions

Year Category	Film	Actor/Actress/Director	Production Company
Best Stewardship	Energy in a Twilight World		Moody Institute of Science
Best Supporting Actor	Heaven's Heroes	James O'Hagen	Mark IV Pictures
Best Supporting Actress	Whitcomb's War	Joanne Talarico	Heartland Productions
Best Youth	Super Christian		Gospel Films, Inc. (John Schmidt Prodctns)
Founder's Award		Harvey W. Marks, CFDA Exec. Sec.	
President's Award	The Spirit Controlled Temperment		Family Life Distributors
President's Award	Reflections of His Love		World Wide Pictures
1981			
Best Actor	Brother Enemy	William Wellman, Jr.	Heartland Productions
Best Actress	Early Warning	Delana Michaels	Missionary Enterprises
Best Biblical	Daring Daniel		Ken Anderson Films
Best Children's	Treehouse Ghosts		Family Films
Best Cinematography	Hudson Taylor	Heather Edmondson	Ken Anderson Films
Best Director	Hudson Taylor	Ken Anderson	Ken Anderson Films
Best Documentary	Some Through Fire		Ken Anderson Films
Best Editing	Football Fever	Bob Cording	Omega Films
Best Evangelistic	Brother Enemy		Heartland Productions
Best Film	Kevin Can Wait		John Schmidt Productions
Best Film Series	Marriage Enrichment		New Day Productions
Best Missionary	Hudson Taylor		Ken Anderson Films
Best Music	Kevin Can Wait	David Maddux	John Schmidt Productions
Best Screen Play	Kevin Can Wait	John Schmidt	John Schmidt Productions
Best Special Effects	Years of Beast	Dan Quick	Gospel Films
Best Supporting Actor	Kevin Can Wait	David Prince	John Schmidt Productions
Best Supporting Actress	Hudson Taylor	Marie Brady	Ken Anderson Films
Best Youth	Kevin Can Wait		John Schmidt Productions
Founder's Award		Leonard Skibitzke	
1982			
Information not available			
1983			
Information not available			
1984			
Best Actor	Never Ashamed	Timothy Elwell	Edward T. McDougal Films
Best Actress	Fanny Crosby	Wenda Shereos	Ken Anderson Films
Best Children's	Honesty		Gospel Films, Inc.
Best Children's	Sunshine Factory		Gospel Films, Inc.
Best Director	Fanny Crosby	Ken Anderson	Ken Anderson Films
Best Evangelistic	Never Ashamed		Edward T. McDougal Films
Best Film of the Year	Never Ashamed		Edward T. McDougal Films
Best Missionary	Mud, Sweat, Cheers		Ken Anderson Films
Best Series	Evidence for Faith		Word Films
Best Supporting Actor	Never Ashamed	Jon Jancovic	Edward T. McDougal Films
Best Supporting Actress	Fanny Crosby	Cathy Shipley	Ken Anderson Films
Best Youth	Never Ashamed		Edward T. McDougal Films
Founder's Award	The Healing		Heartland Productions
President's Award	Christian European		Visual Media Association
1985			
Best Actor	Fury to Freedom	Tom Salardi	Gospel Films, Inc.
Best Actress	Fury to Freedom	Joy Vogel	Gospel Films, Inc.
Best Children's	Hoomania		Gospel Films, Inc.
Best Cinematography	Journey of Life	Robert Miller and Don Valentine	
Best Director	Fury to Freedom	Eric Jacobson	Gospel Films, Inc.
Best Evangelistic	Fury to Freedom		Gospel Films, Inc.
Best Film of the Year	Fury to Freedom		Gospel Films, Inc.
Best Film Series	Love Is a Decision		Zondervan/Miller
Best Missionary	The Search		Harvest Films
Best Supporting Actor	Harley	Eli Cummings	Kuntz Brothers
Best Supporting Actress	Fractured Families	Tammy Taylor	Life Productions
Best Youth	They Lied to Us		Life Productions

Year Category	Film	Actor/Actress/ Director	Production Company
Founder's Award		John Schmidt	John Schmidt Productions
1986			
Best Actor	Wait of the World	Jim Schmidt	John Schmidt Productions
Best Actress	Consider It All Joy	Bonnie Hawley	Victory Int'l Productions
Best Children's	Badrock Valley Gang		Ken Anderson Films
Best Cinematography	Wait of the World	Jack Tankard and Roger Boller	John Schmidt Productions
Best Director	Wait of the World	John Schmidt	John Schmidt Productions
Best Evangelistic	Golden Dolphin		Ken Anderson Films
Best Film of the Year	Wait of the World		Gospel Films, Inc.
Best Film Series	Turn Your Heart toward Home		Word, Inc.
Best Missionary	The Calling		Gospel Films, Inc.
Best Supporting Actor	Wait of the World	Eddie Hailey	John Schmidt Productions
Best Supporting Actress	Wait of the World	Loren Cedar	John Schmidt Productions
Best Youth	Second Step		Ken Anderson Films
Founder's Award		Edward T. McDougal	Edward T. McDougal Films
President's Award		Kenneth Curtis	Gateway Films
1987			
Best Actor	Gold Through the Fire	Charles Harlan	Edward T. McDougal Films
Best Actress	Love Note	Sally Murphy	Ken Anderson Films
Best Children's	Bible Walk		Educational Evangelism/ Word, Inc.
Best Cinematog./Editing	Distinctively Human		Moody Institute of Science
Best Director	Gold Through the Fire	Edward T. McDougal	Edward T. McDougal Films
Best Documentary	A Winnable War		Focus on the Family
Best Evangelistic	Twice Pardoned		Focus on the Family
Best Film of the Year	Gold Through the Fire		Edward T. McDougal Films
Best Film Series	Twice Pardoned		Focus on the Family
Best Individual Non-Dramatic Presentation	Twice Pardoned	Harold Morris	Focus on the Family
Best Supporting Actor	Gold Through the Fire	Kris Wolff	Edward T. McDougal Films
Best Supporting Actress	Thin Ice	Alyson Davis	Gospel Films, Inc.
Best Youth	Love Note		Ken Anderson Films
Founder's Award		Wendell Moody	
President's Award		Heinz Fussle	
1988			
Best Cinematography	God's Outlaw	Mike Reed	Gateway Films
Best Evangelistic	Without Reservation		Gospel Films, Inc.
Best Film of the Year	A Man Called Norman		Focus on the Family
Best Film Series	The Homebuilders		Word Films
Best Individual Non-Dramatic Presentation	A Man Called Norman	Mike Adkins	Focus on the Family
Best Original Form Video-Children	Gerbert		E-Film and Video
Best Original Form Video-Dramatic	God's Outlaw		Gateway Films
Best Video of the Year	This Is the Day		Moody Institute of Science
Best Youth	Without Reservation		Gospel Films, Inc.
1989			
Best Actor	McGee & Me	Joseph Dammann	Focus on the Family
Best Actress	Next Time I Fall in Love	Samantha Mathis	
Best Children's	McGee & Me		Focus on the Family
Best Documentary	Molder of Dreams		Focus on the Family
Best Film of the Year	Molder of Dreams		Focus on the Family
Best Youth	On the Edge		Side by Side Films
Founder's Award		Ken Dymmel	
President's Award		Harvey & Freda Marks	
Best Video	Who Do You Listen To?		Gospel Films
1990			
Best Actor	Witnesses	Curt Cloninger	Gospel Films, Inc.
Best Actress	Wrestling with God	Allison Gregory	Gateway Films
Best Children's	Amazing Creation Room		Moody Institute of Science

Year Category	Film	Actor/Actress/ Director	Production Company
Best Cinematography	Future Tense	James Reid	Mars Hill Productions/ Gospel Films, Inc.
Best Director	Geronimo	Edward T. McDougal	Edward T. McDougal Films
Best Evangelistic	Future Tense		Mars HillProductions/ Gospel Films, Inc.
Best Film of the Year	Geronimo		Edward T. McDougal Films
Best Film or Video Series	Trial & Testimony of the Early Church		Gateway Films
Best Supporting Actor	Geronimo	Raufel Muhammad	Edward T. McDougal Films
Best Supporting Actress	Wrestling with God	Susan Seaforth Hayes	Gateway Films
Best Youth	Geronimo		Edward T. McDougal Films
Best Editing	Future Tense	Fred Carpenter & James Reid	Mars Hill Productions/ Gospel Films, Inc.
Best Video	Witnesses		Gospel Films, Inc.

ARTS MAGAZINES

II Chronicles Magazine, P.O. Box 42, Medford, OR 97501
Oregon Christian Arts Group. Arts, Semimonthly, 5,000 circ. $10.00/2 yrs

Christian Conjurer, 1705 Barbara Lane, Connersville, IN 47331
Fellowship of Christian Magicians, Inc. Drama, Digest, 6/year, $12.00 membership

Image: A Journal of the Arts and Religion, 526 Ziela Ave., Front Royal, VA 22630 703-635-9217

 That the arts can be corrupt does not mean that Christians should abandon them. On the contrary, it means that Christians dare not abandon them any FOCUS longer.—Gene Edward Veith, Jr., in *State of the Arts—from Bezalel to* QUOTE *Mapplethorpe.*

SACRED ARTS AWARDS

Co-Sponsored by First Presbyterian Church of Wheaton and Billy Graham Center Museum

Award	Year	Artist	Title
Best Collegiate Award	1980	Sarah Travis	Astral Dream
Best High School Award	1980	Greg McCallum	Baptismal Bowl
	1981	Andrew Ayers IV	Drawing
Best of Show	1985	Vivian Wright	Resurrection Triptych
	1986	R. Earl Cleveland	Prophecy
	1987	Vladislav Andrejev	Illuminated & Handwritten Gospel
	1988	James F. Darrow	Apostles' Creed
	1989	Michael Mallard	The Darkness of Excessive Light
	1990	Donald J. Forsythe	A Wise Virgin/A Foolish Virgin
	1991	Cheryl Agulnick	Response to a letter by Dietrich Bonhoeffer
Best Photograph	1985	Patricia Phelps Wheless	Aunt Margaret's Room
BGC Museum Purchase Award	1986	Joan Bohlig	Fully Interlocking Puzzle
	1987	David L. Gould	Untitled #099
	1988	Charles Rohrbacher	Mystical Supper

Award	Year	Artist	Title
BGC Museum Purchase Award (continued)		Chris Anderson	Historical Dislocations
		Forge Toro	Baby Christ in Glory
		Lynda L. Oren	Diptych
		Raymond N. Calvert	Missa III
	1989	Fred DelGuidice	Mercy Seat/Bread of Life
		Fred DelGuidice	No Mercy
		Kayano Umehara	Me and You
		Mark Ritchie	Celtic Cross
	1990	Guy Chase	Tablet for a New Law
		Vladimir P. Kozhemiakov	The Head
	1991	Gary Bergel	Lord of All-Syncopation I
		Cheryl Agulnick	Response to a letter by Dietrich Bonhoeffer
		Forge Toro	No Need for Sun or Moon
First Place	1982	Clara Harmelin von Tascha	Creation of Eve
	1983	Arlene Fitterer	Genesis
	1984	Community Presbyterian Church of Clarendon Hills	The Earth Is the Lord's and the Fullness Thereof
	1990	David Harmon	About Joel 2
	1991	Joel C. Sheesley	Eve in Suburbia
First Purchase Award	1980	Pat Koutny	Incarnation (Birth of Christianity)
	1981	Gregg Oakes	Paths of Life
High School Award	1982	Greg McCallum	Christ
	1983	Susan Eriksen	Blessed Be the Name of the Lord
Honorable Mention	1980	Jean Covert	This Do In Remembrance of Me
		Sue Jorden	Palm Sunday
	1981	Barbara Brien	Apocalypse 6:18
		Carol Friedle	The World Was Made by Him
		Clara Hamelin von Tascha	The Baptism
		Dorothy Turner	Bread and Wine
		Gregg Oakes	The Parable of the Farmer
		Jacqueline DeClute	Untitled
		Joseph Heyd	Jonah and the Whale
		Judith Hensel	Temptation of St. Anthony
		Lee Jens	Christ Among the Crowd
		Linda Nurmet	You Will Know Them
		Sister Richard Mehren	Corpus
		Thom Kapheim	Birth Rite
	1982	Alfred W. Heston	Christus
		Barbara Tribes	Then he opened their minds to understand the Scriptures—Luke 24:45
		Edward Dlugopolski	Entombment
		Edward Dlugopolski	Humann Esterrare
		Grover Boone	Trinity
		Janet Nisbett LaPage	And God Said, Let the Earth Be Filled with Living Creatures
		Judith & Liz Hoying Dioszegi	Pentecost Holy Spirit
		Mary Sabo	Untitled
		Sister Dorothy Bock	Fire Bread
		Sister Helena Steffens-Meier	Shekinah
		Sister Maureen McLain	St. Nicholas Church
		Thomas Holzaepfel	Three Days and Three Nights
	1983	Alex Elkind	And His Name Will Be Called Prince of Peace
		Frank Brun	Untitled Christ
		Kennet J. Hempel	Seven Wise and Seven Foolish
		Lou Ann Burkhardt	And They Shall Be Filled

Cheryl Agulnick
Response to a Letter by Dietrich Bonhoeffer (II)
Best of Show

Joel C. Sheesley
Eve in Suburbia
First Place

Award	*Year*	*Artist*	*Title*
Honorable Mention(continued)	1983		Louis E. RansomSmall Altar Cross
		Terry Groh	Untitled
		William C. Hill	The 19th Day of Daniel's Prayer
	1984	Dorothy Turner	Glory to God
		John A. Slavik	Shoe of a Fisherman
		Joseph Lipinski	Prophet IV
		Marilyn Kayton	Jacob's Coat
		Pat Koutny	Angels
		Peg Sindelar	Garden of Eden
		Thomas Manley	Jesus the Compassionate
		Tim Botts	Cicles
		William Lankton	Wings of Peace
	1985	Carmelo Gannello	Testimony Time
		Irene Elios	Jericho
		Jeff Thompson	Centerpiece
		John M. Bohlig	Wolf in Sheep's Clothing
		Joseph Heyd	Cloud/Moses/Sinai
		Ruth Meredith	Archangel Gabriel
	1986	Dhimitri Zonia	Adam and Eve
		Kay Wahlgren	Genesis
		Mary Hecht	Homage to Lipchitz: The Sacrifice
		Maureen Hubbard Cribbs	Ode to Psalm 24, Verses 1 & 2
		William Frederick	Chalice
	1987	Beva Farmer	Icon of Shadrach, Meshach, & Abednego
		Erica L. Schwartz	Christ and Lazarus
		Lynda L.Oren	Genesis Series
		Marvin Jarboe	Job
		William Frederick	Lectionary Cover
	1988	Cathie Boucher	Jesus Christ Our Lord
		Dan Spahn	Beatitude
		Donald Forsythe	In the Day of Judgment
		Jeff Thompson	Seven Stones
		Jonathan Blocher	Isaiah 41:10
		Lynda L. Oren	Servant's Basket
	1989	Arthur Geisert	Ark
		Bill Bippes	Untitled
		Don Schol	After Eden
		Jerry Dienes	The Temptation Diptych
		Kayano Umehara	Me and You
		Lewis Toby	Madonna
		Sandra Bowden	Sanctus
		William Weber	For the yolk I will give you is easy —Matthew 11:30
	1990	Aaron Benson	Revelation
		Laurence Conn	Christ and St. John on the Island of Patmos
		Karen Engelke	"For still the vision awaits its time"
		Edward Knippers	Lamentation (Angel at the Crucifixion)
		Irina Sukhanova-Oksengendler	Archangel Michael
		Forge Toro	Pray for the Peace of Jerusalem
	1991	Pat Doyle Mikrut	Blessed Are the Poor
		Mark Smothers	American Still Life
		David Kroft	A Prayer for Joshua
		Gary Bergel	Lord of All—Syncopation I
	1991	Barbara Taylor	Jacob's Ladder, or The Residue of Miracle

Jerry Dienes
Our Iniquities Testify Against Us
Second Place

Michael Mallard
Clowning Around the Throne of God
R. H. Love Award for Painting

Award	Year	Artist	Title
Honorable Mention(continued)	1991	Fred DelGuidice	Good Friday
Judge's Award	1989	Pat Groenenboom	Demons at the Entrance
McCormick Memorial Award	1985	Jonathan Flew	The Fisherman
	1986	Theresa Verdine	Altar to Unborn Children
	1987	Dhimitri Zonia	Genesis
	1988	Forge Toro	Baby Christ in Glory
	1989	Fred DelGuidice	No Mercy
Purchase Award—Photography	1986	Patricia Phelps Wheless	Meet Me in Heaven
R. H. Love Award	1990	Lynda Lowe Oren	Sparrow's Reliquary/Survivor's Reliquary
	1991	Michael Mallard	Clowning around the Throne of God
Second Place	1982	Gregg Oakes	Trinity at Gethsemane
	1983	Gregory Piro	Bible Cover
	1990	Lucinda Hubing	Worship
	1991	Jerry Dienes	Our Iniquities Testify against Us
Second Purchase Award	1980	Sarah Travis	Astral Dream
	1981	Mary Kingsbury Dowse	The Sleeping Church
Tenth Anniversary Award	1989	Arthur Geisert	Ark
Theme Prize (Celebration)	1984	Ruth Meredith	Noah's Ark
Theme Prize (Peace)	1983	Jacqueline Dodson	Peaceful Doves
Theme Prize (Pentecost)	1982	Dorothy Turner	Flame
		Dorothy Turner	Rainbow
Third Place	1982	Thomas Holzaepfel	Jonah and the Cross
	1990	Timothy Young	Acts 2:2
	1991	Nick Scalise	Members of the Group (Twelve Apostles)
Visitor's Choice Award	1982	Comm. Presbyterian Church/ Clarenden Hills	Antependia & Banners
	1983	Paul Higdon	To Guide Our Feet unto the Way of Heaven
	1984	Tim Botts	O Lord, What a Variety You Have Made
	1985	Carol Cameron	Aventine
	1986	Kay Wahlgren	Genesis
	1987	Lynda L. Oren	Genesis Series
	1988	Steven Rockwell	Easter
	1989	Mark Smothers	In the Twinkling of an Eye
	1990	Joseph DeVelasco	Satan Bound
	1991	Fred DelGuidice	Good Friday

Fred DelGuidice
Good Friday
Visitor's Choice Award

66 99
FOCUS QUOTE The creative men and women are in the church. Some express their art through music, the only art fully accepted by the church. But others sit quietly alone, waiting to be affirmed, encouraged, supported. They are waiting for the body of Christ to understand and find room for the novel, the film, and play, the master-piece ruminating within that could reach beyond the subculture and challenge the basic assumptions of our secular age and point the world toward ultimate truth.

Until the church goes beyond just lip service to encourage and invest some of her resources, her members, and even her own children in the pursuit of redeeming art, I fear the body of Christ will be left with only the shrill, small voice of reaction to art instead of the clear, powerful voice of the Creator of art.—Max McLean in *Christianity Today*, September 8, 1989 issue.

50 TOP CHRISTIAN SONGS OF 1991

1. "Place in This World" by Michael W. Smith, Reunion
2. "Home Free" by Wayne Watson, DaySpring
3. "Living Proof" by Newsong, DaySpring
4. "Jesus Answers" by Michele Wagner, Benson
5. "For the Sake of the Call" by Steven Curtis Chapman, Sparrow
6. "That's What Love Is For" by Amy Grant, Myrrh
7. "I'll Give You Peace" by Sandi Patti, Word
8. "No Better Place" by Steven Curtis Chapman, Sparrow
9. "Boy Like Me/Man Like You" by Rich Mullins, Reunion
10. "Mysterious Ways" by Kim Hill, Reunion
11. "Down on My Knees" by Susan Ashton, Sparrow
12. "Addictive Love" by BeBe & CeCe Winans, Sparrow
13. "All I Ever Wanted" by Margaret Becker
14. "Faithful Forever" by Michael Omartian, Myrrh
15. "Almighty" by Wayne Watson, DaySpring
16. "Blessed Are the Tears" by Bryan Duncan, Myrrh
17. "Be the One" by Al Denson, Benson
18. "The Me Nobody Knows" by Marilyn McCoo, Warner Alliance
19. "Nothing But Love" by Twila Paris, Star Song
20. "How Long Will Be Too Long" by Michael W. Smith, Reunion
21. "I Am Sure" by Deniece Williams, Sparrow
22. "Love Makes All the Difference" by Michele Pillar
23. "For Every Time" by Steve Camp, Sparrow
24. "Busy Man" by Steven Curtis Chapman, Sparrow
25. "Forgiven" by First Call, Myrrh
26. "For You" by Michael W. Smith, Reunion
27. "For All the World" by Sandi Patti, Word
28. "No One Knows My Heart" by Susan Ashton, Sparrow
29. "Couldn't We Stand" by 4 Him, Benson
30. "Wholehearted" by Newsong, DaySpring
31. "The Heartland" by Rob Frazier, Urgent
32. "Look Me in the Eye" by Margaret Becker, Sparrow
33. "Jesus Loves Ya" by Jon Gibson, Frontline
34. "Hope Set High" by Amy Grant, Myrrh
35. "A Man You Would Write About" by 4 Him, Benson
36. "I Love You with My Life" by Bryan Duncan, Myrrh
37. "Simple Heart" by Geoff Moore & The Distance, Forefront
38. "Since I Found You" by Mathew Ward, Live Oak
39. "Children of the Image" by Brian Becker, Benson
40. "Benediction" by Susan Ashton, Sparrow
41. "Solid as the Rock" by Michael English, Warner Alliance
42. "Desert Rose" by White Heart, Star Song
43. "Unexpected Friends" by Sandi Patti, Word
44. "Like a Wind" by Edin Adahl, Alarma
45. "Living in the Pages" by Bruce Carroll, Word
46. "The Same God" by Carman, Commissioned & the Christ Church Choir, Benson
47. "The Keeper" by Geoff Moore & The Distance, Forefront
48. "Always Here" by Eric Champion, Myrrh
49. "How Long" by Michael Card, Sparrow
50. "I'll Take You There" by BeBe & CeCe Winans, Sparrow

GOSPEL MUSIC FESTIVALS

Write directly to Festival offices for 1993/1994 performance dates

Music Florida Orlando, Fla. Contact: Kempke's Music, 2005 Tree Fork Lane, Suite 105, Longwood, FL 32750 407-831-0333

Hosanna '90 Grace Brethren Worship Center, Westerville, Ohio. Contact: Susan Zartman, 8225 Worthington, Galena Road, Westerville, OH 43081 614-431-8221

Christian Artists' Songship Dallas, Tex.; Anaheim, Calif.; Minneapolis, Minn. Contact: Christian Artists Corporation, P.O. Box 1984, Thousand Oaks, CA 91358 800-827-0099

Atlanta Fest Six Flags over Georgia, Atlanta, Ga. Contact: Tiley and Associates, P.O. Box 6271, Marietta, GA 30067 404-955-8669

Music Texas Ft. Worth, Tex. Contact: Kempke's Music, 2005 Tree Fork Lane, Suite 105, Longwood, FL 32750 407-831-0333

Creation Festival Agape Campground, Mt. Union, Pa. Contact: Come Alive Ministries, P.O. Box 86, Medford, NJ 08055 800-327-6921

Church Music in the Smokies Grand Hotel, Pigeon Forge, Tenn. Contact: J20& J Music, 234 N. Craft Highway, Chickasaw, AL 36611 800-456-4966

Jesus Northwest Clark County Fair, Vancouver, Wash. Contact: People's Church, P.O. Box 7718, Salem, OR 97303 503-393-1616

Kingdom '90 Youth Conference Contact: Regal Ventures, P.O. Box 1010, Kings Mountain, N.C. 28086 704-739-3838

National Quartet Convention Nashville, Tenn. Contact: National Quartet Convention, 54 Music Square West, Nashville, TN 37203 615-320-7000

Source: Gospel Music Association

20 BEST-SELLING CHRISTIAN RECORDS OF THE 80s

1. *Age to Age* by Amy Grant, Myrrh (Word)
2. *More Than Wonderful* by Sandi Patti, Impact (Benson)
3. *Hymns Just for You* by Sandi Patti, Helvering Productions (Benson)
4. *The Collection* by Amy Grant, Myrrh (Word)
5. *Morning Like This* by Sandi Patti, Word Records
6. *Songs from the Heart* by Sandi Patti, Impact (Benson)
7. *Straight Ahead* by Amy Grant, Myrrh (Word)
8. *Michael W. Smith Project* by Michael W. Smith, Reunion (Word)
9. *Unguarded* by Amy Grant, Myrrh (Word)
10. *Music Machine* by Candle, Birdwing (Sparrow)
11. *More Power to Ya* by Petra, Star Song

12. *Lead Me On* by Amy Grant, Myrrh (Word)
13. *For God and God Alone* by Steve Green, Sparrow Records
14. *Make His Praise Glorious* by Sandi Patti, Word Records
15. *Not of This World* by Petra, Star Song
16. *Heed the Call* by The Imperials, DaySpring (Word)
17. *Priority* by The Imperials, DaySpring (Word)
18. *Carman Live . . . Radically Saved!* by Carman, Benson Records
19. *Michael W. Smith 2* by Michael W. Smith, Reunion (Word)
20. *i 2 (EYE)* by Michael W. Smith, Reunion (Word)

This list was compiled from *Bookstore Journal's* music bestseller lists of the 1980s—not actual sales. Titles received 10 points for each No. 1 placement, nine points for each No. 2, etc. All rights reserved. Copyright © 1990 CBA Service Corp. From *Bookstore Journal,* Official Trade Publication of the Christian Booksellers Association. Reprinted by permission.

TOP 20 BEST-SELLING CHRISTIAN RECORDS/CDs OF 1991

1. *Heart in Motion,* by Amy Grant, Myrrh (Word)
2. *Go West Young Man,* by Michael W. Smith, Reunion (Word)
3. *Another Time . . . Another Place,* by Sandi Patti, Word Records
4. *For the Sake of the Call,* by Steven Curtis Chapman, Sparrow Records
5. *Addicted to Jesus,* by Carman, Benson Music Group
6. *Nu Thang,* by D.C. Talk, Yo!ForeFront (Benson)
7. *Beyond Belief,* by Petra, DaySpring (Word)
8. *Revival in the Land,* by Carman, Benson Music Group
9. *The Collection,* by Amy Grant, Myrrh (Word)
10. *Different Lifestyles,* by BeBe & CeCe Winans, Sparrow Records
11. *Shakin' the House,* by Carman, Commissioned & The Christ Church Choir, Benson Music Group
12. *We Believe,* by Steve Green, Sparrow Records
13. *Unseen Power,* by Petra, DaySpring (Word)
14. *Sleep Sound in Jesus,* by Michael Card, Sparrow Records
15. *Power House,* by White Heart, Star Song
16. *Another Child to Hold,* by Ray Boltz, Diadem (Spectra)
17. *Wakened by the Wind,* by Susan Ashton, Sparrow Records
18. *The Finest Moments,* by Sandi Patti, Word Records
19. *Home Free,* by Wayne Watson, Day-Spring (Word)
20. *i 2 (EYE),* by Michael W. Smith, Reunion (Word)

This list is based on actual sales in Christian retail stores in the United States and Canada during 1991. All rights reserved. Copyright © 1992 CBA Service Corp. and Spring Arbor Distributors. Distributed by Evangelical Christian Publishers Association. Reprinted by permission from the February 1992 issue of Bookstore Journal, official trade publication of the Christian Booksellers Association.

25 TOP CONTEMPORARY CHRISTIAN ALBUMS OF ALL TIME

1. *Only Visiting This Planet* by Larry Norman. Producer: Larry Norman. MGM/Verve 1972
2. *Slow Train Coming* by Bob Dylan. Producer: Jerry Wexler and Barry Beckett. Columbia 1979
3. *Welcome to Paradise* by Randy Stonehill. Producer: Larry Norman. Solid Rock 1976
4. *White Horse* by Michael Omartian. Producer: Michael Omartian. ABC/Dunhill 1974
5. *Age to Age* by Amy Grant. Producer: Brown Bannister. Myrrh 1982
6. *With Footnotes* by 2nd Chapter of Acts. Producer: Buck Herring. Myrrh 1974
7. *Love Song* by Love Song. Producer: Love Song and Freddie Piro. Good News 1972
8. *For Him Who Has Ears to Hear* by Keith Green. Producer: Bill Maxwell. Sparrow 1977
9. *Unguarded* by Amy Grant. Producer: Brown Bannister. Myrrh 1985
10. *Medals* by Russ Taff. Producer: Jack Joseph Puig and Russ Taff. Myrrh 1985
11. *Love Broke Through* by Phil Keaggy. Producer: Buck Herring. New Song 1976
12. *Victims of the Age* by Mark Heard. Producer: Mark Heard. Home Sweet Home 1982
13. *The Turning* by Leslie Phillips. Producer: T-Bone Burnett. Myrrh 1987
14. *Romeo Unchained* by Tonio K. Producer: Rick Neigher, Bob Rose, Howard Steele, T Bone Burnett. What? 1987
15. *October* by U2. Producer: Steve Lillywhite. Island 1981
16. *Truth Decay* by T Bone Burnett. Producer: Reggie Fisher. Takoma 1980

17. *The Joshua Tree* by U2. Producer: Daniel Lanois and Brian Eno. Island 1987
18. *Humans* by Bruce Cockburn. Producer: Eugene Martynec. Millenium 1980
19. *Shotgun Angel* by Daniel Amos. Producer: Jonathan David Brown. Maranatha! Music 1977
20. *Horrendous Disc* by Daniel Amos. Producer: Larry Norman. Solid Rock 1981
21. *Straight On* by DeGarmo & Key. Producer: Joe Hardy, Eddie DeGarmo, Dana Key. Lamb & Lion 1979
22. *Meltdown* by Steve Taylor. Producer: Jonathan David Brown. Sparrow 1985
23. *I Want to Be a Clone* by Steve Taylor. Producer: Jonathan David Brown. Sparrow 1984
24. *Awaiting Your Reply* by Resurrection Band. Producer: Resurrection Band. Star Song 1978
25. *Matters of the Heart* by Bob Bennett. Producer: Jonathan David Brown. Priority 1982

Source: This listing represents the opinions of writers and contributors to *Contemporary Christian Music* magazine, as of June 1988. Copyright © 1988 by CCM Publications, Inc. Used by permission.

DEVELOPMENT OF CHURCH MUSIC THROUGH THE CENTURIES
Gladys Christensen

Introduction

Period	Form	Characteristics	Example
Old Testament	Psalms	Hebrew poetry for temple worship. Responsorial usage allows people to respond with "Amen," "Hallelujah" or "His mercy endureth forever."	Psalm 136
		Antiphonal use involves two choruses alternately on psalm verse or half verse.	Psalm 142
New Testament	Canticles	Scriptural songs other than Psalms include: Magnificat, Benedictus	Luke 1
		Gloria in Excelsis, Nunc Dimittis,	Luke 2
		Agnus Dei	John 1
		Basis for Mass, Holy Communion, Morning and Evening Prayer services.	
Early Christian	Hymns	Free texts on scriptural themes include: Te Deum, Gloria Patri, Sanctus—Text expanded from "Holy, Holy, Holy."	Isaiah 6
	Chant	Monotone recitation of Scripture and liturgy by priest.	
		Plainsong—A single, undulating melodic line sung in unison. Text governs free rhythm.	
		Psalm tones—Melodic formulae for choir or soloist to sing the psalms.	
		Antiphon—A psalm portion that precedes and follows the entire psalm.	

Development of Choral Music

Period	Movement/ Form	Person/Contribution	Example
from 9th c.	ORGANUM	A *cantus firmus* (liturgical chant) accompanied by one or more additional voices at interval of 4th or 5th. Strict Style: Note against note	
	SEQUENCE/ TROPE	Practice of setting a free text to melismatic passage (syllabic)	

Period	Movement/ Form	Person/Contribution	Example
12th c.	MASS	**Leonin** writes earliest musical setting of mass.	
12–13th c.		**Perotin**. Development includes the upper voices moving more quickly than tenor.	
	MOTET	Given song in tenor is accompanied by upper parts singing own text (1250).	
14th c.	MASS	**Guillaume Machault**. First polyphonic (more than one voice) setting of ordinary (unchanging parts).	Messe de Notre Dame
15th c.	MASS, MOTET, HYMNS, ANTIPHONS	Development of polyphonic choral music and composition techniques by: **John Dunstable.** England **Johannes Okenghem.** Netherlands, Belgium, France **Josquin des Pres.** Belgium, Italy, France	
16th c.	MASS, MOTET, MAGNIFICAT	**Orlando Lassus** perfects the motet form; expressive settings.	Penitential Psalms (1565)
		Giovanni Perluigi (Palestrina) devotes entire life to church music; carries out reforms to preserve integrity of text.	
		Adrian Willaert. Venetian polychoral style (1550) places divided chorus in opposite galleries of St. Marks cathedral.	
	CONCERTATO STYLE	Instruments with voices or contrasting choral or instrumental groups. Andrea and Giovanni Gabrielli develop style.	
	ORATORIO	Opera on sacred text. Multimovement work utilizes chorus, solo or both. No action, scenery or costumes.	
		San Felippo dei Neri (c. 1550) institutes popular service in Oratory (Prayer chapel) Laude (devotional songs) provide basis for semidramatic work on sacred theme.	
c. 1600	MONODY	**Claudio Monteverdi.** Composition includes melodic writing in recitative style: a narrative text sung by solo voice with chordal accompaniment.	
16th c.	ENGLISH CHORAL MUSIC		
	ANTHEM	**Christopher Tye** writes the first English motet (c. 1550). Syllabic, more chordal, straightforward rhythm.	
		Thomas Tallis. A founder of English cathedral music. Latin masses and motets.	
		William Byrd develops the verse anthem to include choral and solo sections.	
		Latin masses and motets	

Period	Movement/ Form	Person/Contribution	Example
17th c.	CANTATA Italy	Smaller version of oratorio	
		Giacomo Carissimi. His cantatas establish older form consisting of two or more arias with recitative, no chorus.	
		Carissimi composes twelve oratorios on O.T. themes. Soloist carries out narrative. Music descriptive of text.	Jephte (c. 1650).
	VERSE ANTHEM		
	England	**Henry Purcell** adds instrumental sections to chorus and solo sections.	
	DRAMATIC CONCERTATO		
	Germany	**Heinrich Schutz.** Venetian influence: instruments with voices. Recitative is pictorial setting of text—perfect union of words and music in German. Continuo required. Not based on chorale or cantus.	Symphoniae Sacra (1629,-47,-50) The Seven Words of Christ on the Cross (1664) Passion Settings (1666)
17–18th c.	CHORALE CANTATA	**Dietrich Buxtehude** institutes evening concerts of sacred music during Advent. Writes chorale cantatas and motets for solo and chorus. Instrumental accompaniment.	Wachet Auf In Dulci Jubilo
		J. S. Bach. Cantatas for specific services include chorus, solo recitative, arias, duets. Instrumental accompaniment. Freely composed texts. Chorale tune harmonized at conclusion.	Magnificat, Passions, Mass, Motets (from 1723) Christmas Oratorio a series of cantatas (1733–34)
	ORATORIO		
	England	**George F. Handel.** Dramatic biblical text. Includes chorus, recitative, aria, duet, instrumental accompaniment.	Israel in Egypt (1738) Messiah (1741) Jephtha (1751)
		Anthem collections are high point of Baroque development.	
	CLASSIC-ROMANTIC DEVELOP-MENTS	Development of opera and symphony expands the resources of sacred choral composition.	
	MASS	**Haydn, Mozart, Beethoven, Schubert and Bruckner** compose concert settings of the mass.	
18th c.	Germany/ Austria	**Joseph Haydn.** New impetus to oratorio. Free text.	Seven Last Words (1785 orch) (1794 text) Creation (1798)

Period	Movement/ Form	Person/Contribution	Example
		Wolfgang A. Mozart	Solemn Vespers (1780)
			Requiem (Mass for Dead) (1791)
19th c.		**Ludwig van Beethoven**	Christ on the Mount of Olives (1803)
			Missa Solemnis (1818-23)
		Felix Mendelssohn	St. Paul (1836)
			Elijah (1846)
	France	**Hector Berlioz**	Requiem (1837)
			Te Deum (1848–49)
			L'Enfance du Christ (1854)
	Germany	**Johannes Brahms.** Musical settings of Scriptures on themes of comfort and eternal life.	A German Requiem (1857–1868)
	Austria	**Anton Bruckner**	Te Deum (1884)
	Italy	**Giuseppe Verdi**	Requiem Mass (1874)
	France	**Claude Debussy**	The Prodigal Son (1884)
		Gabriel Fauré	Requiem (1887)
		Cesar Franck	The Beatitudes (1870)
19–20th c.	England	**Charles Stanford**	
		Charles H. H. Parry. Anthems and service music of high quality set a new standard.	
	America	**Charles Ives.** Psalm settings	Psalm 67
20th c.	Representative Choral Works		
	France	**Arthur Honneger**	Symphonic Psalm King David (1923)
		Francis Poulenc	Gloria (1961)
	England	**Ralph Vaughan Williams**	Hodie (1954)
		William Walton	Belshazzar's Feast (1931)
		Benjamin Britten	A Ceremony of Carols (1942)
			Festival Te Deum (1945)
		Andrew Lloyd Webber	Requiem (1984)
		John Rutter. Carol Arrangements	Requiem (1978)

Period	Movement/ Form	Person/Contribution	Example
	America	**Igor Stravinsky**	Symphony of Psalms (1930) Mass (1948)
		Leo Sowerby	Forsaken of Man (1939)
		Randall Thompson	Peaceable Kingdom (1936)
		Leonard Bernstein	Chichester Psalms (1965)
		A theater piece including singers, players, dancers. Text added to traditional mass.	Mass (1972)
	Poland	**Krzysztof Penderecki**	Passion according to St. Luke (1965)

Development of Congregational Music

Period	Movement/ Form	Person/Contribution	Example
3rd c.	Greek and Latin Hymnody	**Clement of Alexandria** writes earliest extant hymn.	Shepherd of Tender Youth
4th c.		**Ambrose—Bishop of Milan** encourages congregational singing; writes hymns.	O Splendor of God's Glory
6th c.		**Gregory the Great—Rome.** Under his papal reign, the Schola Cantorum codifies chant and psalm tones. Writes hymns.	Father, We Praise Thee
8–13th c.		Period of rich development. Many hymns, translated to English, are still in use.	Come, Ye Faithful All Glory, Laud and Honor
13–15th c.	Carol	From carola—ring dance: a narrative dance song for any season.	In Dulci Jubilo (Christmas) O Sons and Daughters of the King (Easter)
		St. Francis of Assisi develops practice of singing Nativity songs around a manger scene (1223).	
16th c.	Metrical psalmody	The psalms in meter or verse	
	GERMAN REFORMATION	**Martin Luther** versifies psalms (1523). Translates Latin hymns to German. Encourages original hymns for congregational worship. Adapts music from quality folk songs and Latin chant.	Psalm 46 "God is our refuge and strength" becomes A Mighty Fortress or A Sure Stronghold Veni, Creator Spiritus becomes Komm, Gott Schopfer
	Chorale	German congregations sing hymns in unison.	
	GENEVAN REFORMATION		

Period	Movement/ Form	Person/Contribution	Example
		John Calvin begins to versify psalms (1539). Enlists poet Marot to continue the work in French. Publishes psalter in 1543. Bourgeois writes musical settings.	Psalms of David (1551) "Old Hundredth" tune set to Psalm 100
	English Psalmody	**Thomas Sternhold** revises his own versification modelled on Marot (1549).	
		John Hopkins enlarges psalter in 1562 to include all psalms. Printed with melodies. This is adopted as official psalter by those who flee to Geneva with Knox.	
	ANGLICAN REFORMA- TION Service Settings	**John Merbecke** sets service of Holy Communion in four-part harmony, one note for one syllable (1549).	Kyrie, Credo, Sanctus and Benedictus, Lord's Prayer, Agnus Dei, Gloria in Excelsis
	Anglican Chant	Method devised for singing psalms of canticles. Symbols indicate when to change pitch in verses of variable length.	
	NEW WORLD American Psalmody	Genevan and English psalters brought to America. Bay Psalm Book printed in America (1640).	
17th c.	ENGLAND English Hymnody	**Bishop Thomas Ken** desires that people praise God in own words—not only in psalms and canticles. Doxology is final stanza of his hymn.	All Praise to Thee, My God This Night (1674)
18th c.		**Isaac Watts** versifies psalms in freer translations than in previous psalters. Collection of original hymns	
		Hymns and Spiritual Songs (1707)	
		Examples for Psalms of David Imitated (1719)	Psalm 72 Jesus Shall Reign Psalm 90 O God, Our Help
		Charles Wesley writes hymns with freer texts based on psalms and N.T. themes. Publishes two major collections:	
		Foundery Collection (1742)	
		Hymns for the Use of the People Called Methodists (1780)	Contains original 18 stanzas of O for a Thousand Tongues
	AMERICA	Moravian missionary movement settles in Bethlehem, Pennsylvania (1741). Introduces classical music traditions and instrumentation.	
		William Billings publishes collection of psalms which include fuguing tunes.	New England Psalm Singer (1770) When Jesus Wept

Period	Movement/ Form	Person/Contribution	Example
19th c.	Gospel music	Outgrowth of Kentucky revival (1800)	
	White spirituals	Shape note hymns—System of teaching reading. Collections provide tunes in use today:	Southern Harmony (1835) contains tunes for Amazing Grace, What Wondrous Love
			The Sacred Harp (1844) tune "Beach Spring"
	ENGLAND OXFORD MOVEMENT	Return to Catholic traditions (1833) Emphasis on content and reverence in worship.	
		John Keble writes poetry for church year.	Sun of My Soul
		Many hymns from Greek or Latin are translated to poetic English by **Edward Caswall** and **John M. Neale**.	Jesus, the Very Thought of Thee
			All Glory, Laud and Honor
	REVIVAL MOVEMENTS		
	(England and America)	Musicians join evangelists: write gospel songs, sing, and direct singing (from 1873)	
		Ira D. Sankey with Dwight Moody	Composes tune: Hiding in Thee
		Phillip Bliss with Maj. Whittle	Tune: When Peace Like a River
		Homer Rodeheaver with Billy Sunday	Tune: Then Jesus Came
		Prolific writer **Fanny Crosby** writes 8000 gospel hymns.	To God Be the Glory, Blessed Assurance
20th c.	Evangelistic crusades	**Cliff Barrows** and **George Beverly Shea** with Billy Graham	
	Solo artist	**Ken Medema** composes and sings of social justice.	
20th c. trends	Hymnals	Inclusion of hymns, chant, chorales, spiritual songs from a wide variety of religious sources, ethnic and racial backgrounds. Themes include nature, environment, space, social concerns.	Earth and All Stars
			O Young and Fearless Prophet
		Gospel songs stress personal experience and conviction. Emphasis on the individual rather than institutional church. Exhortation to fellow-man.	I Am Thine, O Lord
		Folk songs: Songs in the common, pictorial language of the people, traced to racial or national origin.	What Wondrous Love (USA)

Period	Movement/ Form	Person/Contribution	*Example*
		Spirituals (Afro-American): Black folk songs about the tasks of day or a better day in heaven	Swing Low, Sweet Chariot
	Scripture songs	Literal Scripture passages set to simple, folklike melodies	
	Psalm singing	Renewed interest in recitation of psalms on musical tones	

Contemporary Popular Music

Period	Style	Performing Artist or Group/Contribution	*Example*
	Inspirational	Sandi Patti; Steve Green; Larnelle Harris; Evie Tornquist; Bill and Gloria Gaither. Lyrics tend to be praise-oriented.	Jesus, We Just Want to Thank You; We Shall Behold Him; He Touched Me; The Father Hath Provided
	Rock	Petra; Michael W. Smith; White Heart; Russ Taff; Rick Cua; Allies. Formula of two bars in blues or ballad style; both melody and harmony subject to beat. Development includes physical movement and high volume level. Ranges from "hard" to "soft." Lyrics often address social issues or personal morality and salvation.	Beat the System; I Can, I Will; The Devil Is a Liar
	Contemporary	Imperials; Amy Grant; Twila Paris; Michael Card; First Call. Softer sound than rock, often highlights solo singer with acoustic instrumentation. Lyrically, a combination of rock and inspirational forms.	Great Is the Lord; El Shaddai
	Southern Gospel	Hemphills; The Cathedrals; Florida Boys; Nelsons. Usually quartet harmonies, family groups. Lyrics often stress heavenly rewards and rely heavily on clever phrase turns.	He's Still Working on Me; When He Was on the Cross (You Were on His Mind); I'll Fly Away
	Traditional Black Gospel	Aretha Franklin; Shirley Caesar; Al Green. Spiritual and gospel songs, often sung by a choir, but with more emphasis on rhythm than church music or hymns.	One Lord, One Faith, One Baptism; Celebration; We Sing Praises
	Contemporary Black Gospel	The Winans; The Clark Sisters; Andrae Crouch. Combines elements of rock with rhythm and blues. Increasingly known as "Urban Contemporary."	Let My People Go; No Time to Lose; Give Me More Love in My Heart

About the author: Gladys Christensen taught for 35 years in the Wheaton College Conservatory of Music, Wheaton, Ilinois. She holds the Associate certificate of the American Guild of Organists. She has extensive experience as a church organist and accompanist for cantata and oratorio performances. Contemporary popular music information provided by John Styll, editor, *Contemporary Christian Music* magazine.

POPULAR MUSIC DEFINITIONS
Dave Hart

The world of popular music is becoming more complicated. Many people are getting lost in the sheer volume of classifications, subdivisions, terms, styles, genres, etc. It can literally boggle the mind. In an effort to sort through the musical mush, a brief list of modern musical terms and their definitions follow:

Acid Rock. A term used to describe the hard-edged electronic music created by "hippies" in the late 1960s and early 1970s. The music was supposed to reproduce the feelings and attitudes of the drug culture, particularly the psychedelic experiences of LSD (i.e., acid). It is sometimes still used today to refer to hard rock and heavy metal, but the term is generally considered old-fashioned and is rarely used by professional musicians or today's youth.

Blues. The mournful melodies of the African slaves became known as the blues sometime after the Civil War. During the 1920s and on into the 1940s, performers began to move from the rural clubs of the south (often known as road houses) to the clubs of the northern big cities like Chicago and Detroit. There it became a basic element in the development of big band jazz and other forms of popular music of the post–World War era. The sound was "rediscovered" in the early 1960s by young white musicians in America and Europe, becoming a major influence on the sound and direction of rock music.

Classical. Generally refers to vocal and instrumental compositions of 18th and 19th century Europe. Classical music includes operas, symphonies, chorales, sonatas, and chamber music. The many inspiring religious works of the period have led some people to believe that all classical music is of a Christian spiritual nature. However, many composers of this period were quite secular in their orientations, including some with notoriously immoral life-styles and others who used occult and mystical themes

to inspire the direction of their compositions.

Contemporary Christian Music (CCM). A generic term used to describe any popular music style with Christian lyrics and intent. CCM usually distinguishes itself from traditional church music forms such as classical music, church hymns, or gospel music. The bulk of CCM reflects pop music and adult contemporary styles, but includes rock, heavy metal, new wave, jazz, and improvisational/experimental styles as well. Generally the production quality, sound and look of contemporary Christian artists is on a par with secular artists, but with a Christian message or worldview.

Country Music. Derived from English and Irish folk music, which then developed into early American folk music, bluegrass, hillbilly mountain music, and country and western with its distinctive southern twang. In the 1940s it was combined with big band styles (including blues, jazz, even polkas) in what was known as Western swing. In the 1950s, it reflected the blues in honky-tonk music and later included a light rock feel known as rockabilly. By the 1970s country rock (played by rock musicians) and outlaw country (played by country artists) was essentially the same sound. The popularity of country during the Urban Cowboy craze of the late 1970s resulted in country music that was virtually indistinguishable from pop music and Top 40 radio. Lately there is a move to return to country roots with basic story- telling, Southern accents, and the twang of steel guitars.

Dance Music. A generic term for any popular music with enough rhythm and beat to get the toes tapping and the body moving. Rock and roll was always designed for dancing. Dance craze's came and went in the 1960s, most notably the Twist, one of the first popular dances that could be done without the necessity of a dance partner. For awhile everybody "boogied" especially to

POPULAR MUSIC DEFINITIONS cont.

the funky rhythms of black dance music in the early 1970s. Some of this music was reclaimed by white gays in what was to become known as disco.

As disco died, punks brought a violent form of body bashing known as slam dancing. But more commercial forms of New Wave brought back opportunities for couples to dance again. Black musicians dared to be different with break dancing, which included a lot of gymnastics and spinning on shoulders and heads. The Latin rhythms of Cuban, Mexican, and South American music introduced a spicy flavor to dancing called Salsa. The latest trend along those lines is called Lambada, which is unabashedly described as sex with your clothes on. Most of today's youth find their dance music in white pop, the current derivatives of New Wave music, and current versions of R & B, funk, and Rap/Hip Hop from the black music scene.

Disco. The dance club phenomenon of the mid-1970s was best exemplified in the 1977 film "Saturday Night Fever," featuring the music of the Bee Gees. Before that time, disco was stigmatized as music for blacks and gays. Many music critics of the time despised disco because it was coldly electronic and overproduced, with little real passion, warmth, or romance. Disco fever burned itself out by 1980, but dance music continued in the form of commercial New Wave and pop music.

Funk. A term applied to black dance music in the 1970s. It was characterized by a minimum of melody and a maximum of syncopated rhythms. The derivative word *funky* originally meant dirty or sexy. The word came to be applied to anything that was current and dynamic—synonymous with words like *groovy, hip,* and *happening.*

Fusion. The term simply means the merging of any two ideas. In music, it refers to combining two or more distinctive styles, such as a jazz-rock fusion, which combined brass horns with electric guitar. The 1970s also saw attempts at classical-rock fusion and funk-rock fusion. Some music critics

speculate that these ponderous styles of music and the electronic excesses of this era were so complex and sophisticated that they led to the severe decline in the music industry at that time. Since then music producers have tried to keep things simpler.

Gospel. Today the secular music industry refers to almost all modern Christian music as gospel music. But traditionally, the term refers to the sounds of the black church. It takes two basic forms. One is the plaintive spiritual that parallels blues and soul music in secular terms. The other form is the high energy call and response that so many black choirs are famous for. It is this sound that gave rise to rhythm and blues, and later, what we call rock and roll. In addition to Black Gospel, many people enjoy what they call Southern Gospel. This refers to music derived from country/western and American folk styles popular in white churches in the south, typically performed by quartets and family groups.

Heavy Metal. This style features bombastic power chords, screaming electric guitars, throat-wrenching vocals, and a demolition-derby approach to drumming. Devoted fans often treat heavy metal as a way of life. Today heavy metal can generally be divided into three basic categories. Each retains the extreme volume but may appeal to different audiences:

Black Metal. A demons-and-drama approach to rock music. This style combines the grossest images of a horror movie with loud, driving music to provide the ultimate in blood curdling entertainment. Magic, Satanism, mutilations, murder, and mayhem are reflected in their stage shows, lyrics, costumes and props. (Best examples: King Diamond, Slayer, W.A.S.P.)

Party/Glam Metal. Sex, drugs, and partying are the main themes. This music expresses the idea to live for today and don't think about tomorrow. It gives the impression that there is no price to pay for an irresponsible life-style. It is sometimes called glam metal (short for glamorous) because of the feminine makeup and brightly colored costumes, although many groups today have feigned that look. (Best examples: Bon Jovi, Def Leppard, Warrant, Skid Row.)

Thrash Metal. A synthesis of punk rhythms and the screaming electric guitars of heavy metal. Sometimes called speed metal or metal hardcore. Themes are best summed up as "67 ways to die," because so much of it focuses on anger, hatred, fatalism, gore, death, and a negative attitude toward authority. Fans participate in "moshing," which include the mosh pit (the heavy metal version of what punkers call slam dancing), headbanging (vigorous shaking of the head to the rhythm of the music), and stage-diving (a dangerous practice of throwing oneself from the stage into the crowd—sometimes they land on people, sometimes on the floor.) (Best examples: Metallica, Megadeth, Anthrax.)

Jazz. Originally a Creole Indian word for sex. It applies to many forms of improvisational music, both vocal and instrumental. The form started with a style in New Orleans that improvised on popular ragtime melodies. It came to be known as Dixieland Jazz. Big Bands were sometimes distinguished from popular orchestras by their experimental styles. These were variously referred to as swing (1930s), be-bop (1940s), and "cool," hard-bop, or modal playing (1950s). Progressive jazz represents the most experimental efforts to stretch the structure and form of popular music. Fifty years ago, jazz musicians were considered less than reputable, and the music was often forbidden in the church. Today's jazz stylings tend to be considered smooth and sophisticated and are more accepted in church circles than the angry, raw styles of rock music.

MTV. Music Television was an inevitable product of the advent of cable TV. Many predicted its early demise when it first aired in 1981. Instead it began to shape and influence music and our culture in a strong fashion. It often makes or breaks a new artist, and the music industry depends on music videos heavily to influence concert and record sales. MTV has also shaped fashions

and clothing styles. It has changed the way commercials are filmed and viewed, as well as influencing the pace and feel of movies and other TV programs.

New Age. A generic term for almost any kind of soft, light, improvisational jazz or instrumental music. Its gentle, soothing tones were designed to calm the nerves of Wall Street wizards and Yuppie jet-setters living in the fast lane. Light, airy instrumentals might also be accompanied by the sounds of nature such as ocean waves, bubbling brooks, soft rainfall, or gentle breezes. Some of this music is specifically designed to help those in the New Age movement to achieve meditative states, but much of it is just talented musicians exploring melodic jazz stylings.

New Wave. Also called new music, it is a wide-spread but almost meaningless musical term. It generally represents those who shifted from the raw, angry sounds of punk to the more commercial use of electronic synthesizers in performing music in the late 1970s. It was essentially pop music with the punk trappings of alienated lyrics and ultramodern fashions. Eventually, it became a catch-all phrase for any new musical scene that emerged after 1976 that wasn't strictly punk or heavy metal. Today this music is generally referred to as modern rock and tends to emphasize electronic synthesizers, hollow vocals, and an often bleak perspective of life. It may also be referred to as:

Alternative Music. A term that generally referred to new music and punk that was played on local college radio formats. This music was considered too abrasive, offensive, political, "underground," and elitist in the early to mid-1980s to get airplay on regular radio stations.

Dark Music. Refers to a somber dark style of new music characterized by eerie, haunting melodies, black clothing, and hopelessness. Themes of lost loves and death fantasies only serve to emphasize the dreary despair and a helpless resignation to a bleak future.

Gothic Rock. A more aggressive approach to the doom and gloom mentality of

POPULAR MUSIC DEFINITIONS cont.

dark music. The dark clothes and capes accent stark white faces and dark makeup, suggesting a New Wave Halloween party. The music may vary from somber to frantic and focus on themes of death and the occult. Like Black Metal, the musical performances are often accompanied by theatrical stage props to enhance the eerie horror movie atmosphere. There are entire clubs in Europe and America that cater to this scene.

Post-Modern. Also called post-punk or post-mod. It often reflects the political and social sensibilities of punk with more "accessible" or commercial music styles. This style usually gets airplay on radio and MTV.

Pop. Short for popular music. It represented a move from the more complex concert structures of opera and classical music to a focus on a single tune. Early pop hits in the 1930s were pushed by "drummers" (salesmen) of printed music and later popularized through the movies. Patriotic propaganda was pushed by pop tunes during World War II and the pop charts were developed during this time. Pop music became more accessible during the post-war era and the pop charts reflected the rise in record sales.

Pop music is sometimes contrasted to rock music in its emphasis on piano and keyboard arrangements and a focus on romantic themes, whereas rock emphasizes the electric guitar and more confrontational lyrics. But in general, pop music continues to be no better defined than whatever is popular on the radio and the Top 40 sales charts. Today those charts predominantly reflect the sales of CDs (compact discs) and cassette tapes, as vinyl records are becoming a thing of the past.

Punk Rock. Originated in England in the 1970s primarily as a protest against the music industry, which punks claimed had lost its revolutionary edge. The music is raw and angry, stressing the pounding rhythms rather than any kind of melodic form. The musicians were usually untrained and the music simple (three chords

and a drum), vocals were abrasive (shouting of obscenities and hatred), and rhythms were very fast (often a hundred or more beats a minute, give or take a few). Punk was never widely popular, although it did receive some sensational attention for awhile in the late 1970s.

Today punk has gone underground, which means that it is not part of the usual circles in the music industry. There are still punk bands and punk clubs, but most of the look and sound has been absorbed by the thrash metal scene. Punks are gaining some attention again in the form of Skinheads—a particular type of punk who shaves his head and tends to subscribe to white supremacy ideas.

Rap. Also known as hip hop and bass music. It originated on the streets of New York City with rappers speaking in rhymes over the back beat of a beat box. As stereo systems were added at dances, the sounds were enhanced by running the stereo needle quickly over records in a style called scratching. The songs usually reflect street life for blacks in the inner city, including boasting, sexual conquests (often in graphic detail), gang life, violence, and drugs. Rap is often fused with pop/dance styles in a form called house rap, where verses are rapped and the choruses are sung.

Reggae. Jamaican dance music, related to Afro-Caribbean styles like mento, calypso, and ska. The acoustic versions are generally pleasant because the rhythms duplicate the heartbeat. By the 1970s virtually all Reggae lyrics were influenced by Rastafarian beliefs. Among other things, Rastas think smoking marijuana ("de ganja") is a way to attain spiritual wisdom and believe that Haile Selassie, former emperor of Ethiopia, was Christ returned to earth.

Rock and Roll. Originally a blues term for sexual intercourse. Rock and roll was simply the white version of rhythm and blues. Early rock and roll in the mid-1950s was influenced by country music and folk as well as southern black music. After the British invasion of the mid-1960s, the music simply became known as rock. Drugs, sex, and rock and roll became the anthem of the younger generation in the 1960s. The music is more graphic and intense than ever with themes of passionate love, casual sex, rebellion toward authority, and seeking the endless party. Today there are also some messages of social responsibility, but that is countered with an increase in violence, references to the occult, and a good deal of macho sexism.

Rhythm and Blues. R & B is the black version of rock and roll. It is more energetic than the blues and covers a wider variety of topics in its lyrics. It was called "race music" for some time, but it gradually grew more respectable and evolved into soul, funk, disco, and other "black" music dance styles. It is largely derived from the gospel "shout" style and was essential in the development of rock and roll.

Source: Dave Hart is research analyst with Al Menconi Ministries. He is also a popular youth speaker nationally on the topic of the influence of rock music. And he is the pastor of Sanctuary, San Diego, a church that ministers to heavy metal fans. Reprinted with permission from Al Menconi Ministries. Dave is the associate editor of *Media Update,* the ministry's bimonthly publication that teaches parents and youth workers how to effectively deal with young people and their music. For a free sample copy, contact Menconi Ministries, P.O. Box 5008, San Marcos, CA 92069-1050, (619)591-4696.

INSTRUMENTS TEENS LIKE TO PLAY

1. Synthesizer/keyboards 34%
2. Woodwinds 32%
3. Acoustic piano 31%
4. Brass 21%
5. Guitar 13%

Source: American Music Conference, survey of 1,313 teens

FOCUS FACT Award for the most prolific hymn writer goes to Fanny Crosby (1820–1915), who wrote more than 8,000 hymns. Charles Wesley (1707–1788) is runner-up with 6,000 hymns to his credit.

MUSIC ORGANIZATIONS

American Choral Directors Association 2834 W. Kingsley Road, Garland, TX 75041

American Guild of Organists P.O. Box 26811, Richmond, VA 23261

Choral Conductors Guild 519 N. Halifax, Daytona Beach, FL 32018

Choristers Guild 2111 Samson Street, Philadelphia, PA 19103

Church Music Publishers Association P.O. Box 158992, Nashville, TN 37215

Contemporary Christian Music 1913 21st Avenue South, Nashville, TN 37212

Gospel Music Association P.O. Box 23201, Nashville, TN 37202

Hymn Society of America Texas Christian University, Fort Worth, TX 76129

Menconi Ministries P.O. Box 5008, San Marcos, CA 92069-1050

Music Educators National Association 1902 Association Drive, Reston, VA 22091

Music Publishers Association 110 E. 59th Street, New York, NY 10022

National Association of Schools of Music 11250 Roger Bacon Drive, Suite 21, Reston, VA 22091

National Music Publishers Association 205 E. 42nd Street, New York, NY 10017

Presbyterian Association of Musicians 1000 E. Moreland Street, Charlotte, NC 28204

Retail Sheet Music Dealers Association 1407 E. Harry, Wichita, KS 67211

Standing Commission on Church Music of the Episcopal Church 815 2nd Avenue, New York, NY 10017

AMERICA'S FAVORITE HYMNS

1. Amazing Grace
2. How Great Thou Art
3. In the Garden
4. The Old Rugged Cross
5. What a Friend We Have in Jesus
6. A Mighty Fortress
7. Blessed Assurance
8. He Lives
9. Victory in Jesus
10. Holy, Holy, Holy

"Amazing Grace"is the most popular hymn in America, according to a survey of 10,000 newspaper readers, ages 5 to 96, taken by George Plagenz , nationally syndicated religion columnist. Voters represent 32 denominations.

President and Mrs. Bush were among those who took part in the survey. Mrs. Bush chose "Nearer My God to Thee" as her favorite hymn. It ranked 19th in the poll.

President Bush chose "Eternal Father Strong to Save," which Mr. Plagenz said was "not among the leaders."

CAMPUS LIFE READERS' CHOICE MUSIC AWARDS

Campus Life magazine readers rate their favorite musicians and albums

1987

Best Female Artist	Amy Grant
Best Male Artist	Michael W. Smith
Best Band	Petra
Best Album	*Unguarded* by Amy Grant

1988

Best Female Artist	Amy Grant
Best Male Artist	Michael W. Smith
Best Band	Petra
Best Album	*The Joshua Tree* by U2

1989

Best Female Artist	Amy Grant
Best Male Artist	Michael W. Smith
Best Band	Petra
Best Album	*Lead Me On* by Amy Grant

1990

Best Female Artist	Amy Grant
Best Male Artist	Michael W. Smith
Best Band	Petra

1991

Best Female Artist	Amy Grant
Best Male Artist	Michael W. Smith
Best Band	Petra
Best Album	*Beyond Belief* by Petra

DOVE AWARDS

Sponsored by The Gospel Music Association, Dove Awards are voted on by approximately 2,000 professional and associate members of GMA, from all facets of the music industry: radio and record companies, promoters, artists, musicians, and songwriters.

Song of the Year

1970 **Jesus Is Coming Soon** R. E. Winsett; R. E. Winsett Music Company

1971 **The Night before Easter** Don Sumner/Dwayne Friend; Gospel Quartet Music Company

1972 No awards given

1973 **The Lighthouse** Ron Hinson; Journey Music

1974 **Why Me Lord?** Kris Kristofferson; Resasca Music

1975 **Because He Lives** Bill Gaither; Gaither Music Co.

1976 **One Day at a Time** Marijohn Wilkin/
Kris Kristofferson; Buckhorn Music
1977 **Statue of Liberty** Neil Enloe; Enloe
Music
1978 **Learning to Lean** John Stallings;
Heartwarming Music
1979 **Rise Again** Dallas Holm; Dimension
Music
1980 **He's Alive** Don Francisco; New Pax
Music
1981 **Praise the Lord** Brown Bannister/
Mike Hudson; Home Sweet Home
Music/Bug and Bear Music
1982 **We Shall Behold Him** Dottie Rambo;
John T. Benson Publishing
1983 **El Shaddai** Michael Card/John
Thompson; Whole Armour Publishing
1984 **More Than Wonderful** Lanny Wolfe;
Lanny Wolfe Music Co.
1985 **Upon This Rock** Gloria Gaither/Dony
McQuire; Gaither Music Co./It's-N-Me
Music/Lexicon Music
1986 **Via Dolorosa** Billy Sprague/Niles
Borop; Meadowgreen Music/Word
Music
1987 **How Excellent Is Thy Name** Dick
Tunney, Melodie Tunney & Paul
Smith; Word Music & Marquis III/
Laurel Press/Pamela Kay Music
1988 **In the Name of the Lord** Phil McHugh,
Gloria Gaither, Sandi Patti Helvering;
River Oaks Music/Sandi's Songs,
BMI/Gaither Music Co.
1989 **Friend of a Wounded Heart** Wayne
Watson and Claire Cloninger; Word
Music
1990 **Thank You** Ray Boltz; Gaither Music
1991 **Another Time, Another Place** Gary
Driskell; Word Records

Songwriter of the Year
1970 **Bill Gaither**
1971 **Bill Gaither**
1972 No awards given
1973 **Bill Gaither**
1974 **Bill Gaither**
1975 **Bill Gaither**
1976 **Bill Gaither**
1977 **Bill Gaither**
1978 **Bill Gaither**

1979 **Dallas Holm**
1980 **Don Francisco**
1981 **Gary Chapman**
1982 **Dottie Rambo**
1983 **Michael Card**
1984 **Lanny Wolfe**
1985 **Michael W. Smith**
1986 **Gloria Gaither**
1987 **Dick & Melodie Tunney**
1988 **Larnelle Harris**
1989 **Steven Curtis Chapman**
1990 **Steven Curtis Chapman**
1991 **Steven Curtis Chapman**

Male Vocalist of the Year
1970 **James Blackwood**
1971 **James Blackwood**
1972 No awards given
1973 **James Blackwood**
1974 **James Blackwood**
1975 **James Blackwood**
1976 **James Blackwood**
1977 **Johnny Cook**
1978 **James Blackwood**
1979 **Dallas Holm**
1980 **Dallas Holm**
1981 **Russ Taff**
1982 **Russ Taff**
1983 **Larnelle Harris**
1984 **Russ Taff**
1985 **Steve Green**
1986 **Larnelle Harris**
1987 **Steve Green**
1988 **Larnelle Harris**
1989 **Wayne Watson**
1990 **Steven Curtis Chapman**
1991 **Steven Curtis Chapman**

Female Vocalist of the Year
1970 **Vestal Goodman**
1971 **Ann Downing**
1972 No awards given
1973 **Sue Chenault**
1974 **Sue Chenault**
1975 **Sue Chenault Dodge**
1976 **Jeanne Johnson**
1977 **Joy McQuire**
1978 **Evie Tornquist**
1979 **Evie Tornquist**
1980 **Cynthia Clawson**
1981 **Cynthia Clawson**

DOVE AWARDS cont.

1982	**Sandi Patti**
1983	**Sandi Patti**
1984	**Sandi Patti**
1985	**Sandi Patti**
1986	**Sandi Patti**
1987	**Sandi Patti**
1988	**Sandi Patti**
1989	**Sandi Patti**
1990	**Sandi Patti**
1991	**Sandi Patti**

Male Group of the Year

1970	**Imperials**
1971	**Oak Ridge Boys**
1972	No awards given
1973	**Oak Ridge Boys**
1974	**Blackwood Brothers**
1975	**Blackwood Brothers**
1976	**Imperials**
1977	**Imperials**
1978	**Cathedral Quartet**
1979	**Imperials**
1980	**Imperials**

Mixed Group of the Year
(Category changed to "Group of the Year" in 1981)

1970	**Speer Family**
1971	**Speer Family**
1972	No awards given
1973	**Speer Family**
1974	**Speer Family**
1975	**Speer Family**
1976	**Speer Family**
1977	**Speer Family**
1978	**Speer Family**
1979	**Dallas Holm and Praise**
1980	**Bill Gaither Trio**

Group of the Year

1981	**Imperials**
1982	**Imperials**
1983	**Imperials**
1984	No award
1985	No award
1986	No award
1987	**First Call**
1988	**First Call**
1989	**Take 6**
1990	**BeBe and CeCe Winans**
1991	**Petra**

Album of the Year
Recording artist listed first, producer/producers listed second, record company third

1970	**It's Happening** Oak Ridge Boys; Bob MacKenzie; Heartwarming Music
1971	**Fill My Cup, Lord** Blackwood Brothers; Darol Rice; RCA Victor
1972	No awards given
1973	**Light** Oak Ridge Boys; Bob MacKenzie; Heartwarming Music
1974	**Street Gospel** Oak Ridge Boys; Bob MacKenzie; Heartwarming Music
1975	**Big and Live** Kingsman Quartet; Marvin Norcross; Canaan Records
1976	**I Just Feel Like Something Good Is about to Happen** Speer Family; Bob MacKenzie; Heartwarming Music

Rap Album of the Year

1991	**Nu Thang** D C Talk; Toby McKeenan/Mark Heimermann/Tommy Cathey, producers; Yo! Forefront Records

Rap Recorded Song of the Year

1991	**It's Time** The Winans; Marvin Winans/Carvin Winans/Teddy Riley/Bernard Bell, writers; Warner Alliance

Rock Album of the Year

1988	**Crack the Sky** Mylon LeFevre & Broken Heart; Joe Hardy & Mylon LeFevre, producers; Myrrh Records
1989	**Russ Taff** Russ Taff; Jack Joseph Puig; Myrrh Records
1990	**The Way Home** Russ Taff; Russ Taff and James Hollihan; Sparrow Records
1991	**Beyond Belief** Petra; John and Dino Elefante, producers; DaySpring Records

Rock Recorded Song of the Year

1989	**Won by One** Mylon and Broken Heart; Scott Allen, Trent Arganti, Kenneth Bentley, Ben Hewitt
1990	**The River Unbroken** Russ Taff; Darryl Brown and David Batteau; Myrrh Records
1991	**Beyond Belief** Petra; Bob Hartman; DaySpring Records

Contemporary Gospel Album of the Year
Recording artist listed first; producer/producers second; record company third

1977 **No Shortage** Imperials; Bob MacKenzie/Gary Paxton; Impact
1978 **Reba** Lady Reba Rambo Gardner; Phil Johnson; Greentree
1979 **Transformation** Cruse Family; Ken Harding; Canaan Records
1980 **All That Matters** Dallas Holm and Praise; Phil Johnson; Greentree
1981 **One More Song for You** Imperials; Michael Omartian; DaySpring Records
1982 **Priority** Imperials; Michael Omartian; DaySpring Records
1983 **Age to Age** Amy Grant; Brown Bannister; Myrrh Records
1984 **Side by Side** Imperials; Keith Thomas/Neal Joseph; DaySpring Records
1985 **Straight Ahead** Amy Grant; Brown Bannister, Myrrh Records
1986 **Medals** Russ Taff; Russ Taff/Jack Puig; Myrrh/Word Records
1987 **The Big Picture** Michael W. Smith; Michael W. Smith, John Potoker; Reunion Records
1988 **Watercolour Ponies** Wayne Watson; Wayne Watson & Paul Mills; DaySpring Records
1989 **Lead Me On** Amy Grant; Brown Bannister; Myrrh Records
1990 **Heaven** BeBe and CeCe Winans; Keith Thomas; Sparrow Records
1991 **Go West Young Man** Michael W. Smith; Michael W. Smith/Bryan Lenox; Reunion Records

Contemporary Recorded Song of the Year
1989 **His Eyes** Steven Curtis Chapman; Steven Curtis Chapman and James Isaac Elliott
1990 **Heaven** BeBe and CeCe Winans; Keith Thomas and Benjamin Winans; Sparrow Records
1991 **Another Time, Another Place** Sandi Patti; Gary Driskell; Word Records

Inspirational Album of the Year
Recording artist listed first; producer/producers listed second; record companies listed last

1977 **Jesus, We Just Want to Thank You** Bill Gaither Trio; Bob MacKenzie; Heartwarming Music
1978 **Ovation** Couriers; Jesse Peterson; Tempo
1979 **Pilgrim's Progress** Bill Gaither Trio; Bob MacKenzie/John W. Thompson; Impact Records
1980 **Special Delivery** Doug Oldham; Joe Huffman; Impact Records
1981 **You're Welcome Here** Cynthia Clawson; JEN Productions; Triangle
1982 **Joni's Song** Joni Earecksen; Kurt Kaiser; Word Records
1983 **Lift Up the Lord** Sandi Patti; Greg Nelson; Impact Records
1984 **More Than Wonderful** Sandi Patti; John Helvering, David Clydesdale/Greg Nelson/Sandi Patti Helvering; Impact Records
1985 **Songs from the Heart** Sandi Patti; Greg Nelson/Sandi Patti Helvering; Impact Records
1986 **I've Just Seen Jesus** Larnelle Harris; Greg Nelson; Impact/Benson Records
1987 **Morning Like This** Sandi Patti; Greg Nelson & Sandi Patti Helvering; Word Records
1988 **The Father Hath Provided** Larnelle Harris; Greg Nelson; Benson Records
1989 **Make His Praise Glorious** Sandi Patti; Greg Nelson and Sandi Patti; Word Records
1990 **The Mission** Steve Green; Greg Nelson; Sparrow Records
1991 **Another Time, Another Place** Sandi Patti; Sandi Patti Helvering/Greg Nelson; Word Records

Inspirational Recorded Song of the Year
1989 **In Heaven's Eyes** Sandi Patti; Phill McHugh
1990 **His Strength Is Perfect** Steven Curtis Chapman; Steven Curtis Chapman and Jerry Salley; Sparrow Records
1991 **Who Will Be Jesus** Bruce Carroll; Bruce Carroll and Aaron Wilburn; Word Records

DOVE AWARDS cont.

Traditional Album of the Year

Category changed to Southern Gospel with 18th annual. Includes Country, Folk and/or Bluegrass). Recording artist listed first, producer/producers listed second, record company listed third

1977 **Between the Cross & Heaven** Speer Family; Joe Huffman; Heartwarming Music

1978 **Then & Now** Cathedral Quartet; Ken Harding; Canaan Records

1979 **Kingsmen Live in Chattanooga** Kingsmen; Joe Huffman/Eldridge Fox; Heartwarming Music

1980 **From Out of the Past** Kingsmen; Joe Huffman/Eldridge Fox; Heartwarming Music

1981 **Workin'** Hemphills; Jerry Crutchfield; Heartwarming Music

1982 **One Step Closer** Rex Nelon Singers; Ken Harding; Canaan Records

1983 **Feeling At Home** Rex Nelon Singers; Ken Harding; Canaan Records

1984 **We Shall Behold the King** Rex Nelon Singers; Ken Harding; Canaan Records

1985 **The Best of and a Whole Lot More** Rex Nelon Singers; Ken Harding; Canaan Records

1986 **Excited** Hemphills; W. Hilton/T. Hemphill; Heartwarming Music

1987 **The Master Builder** The Cathedrals; William Gaither and Gary McSpadden; Riversong Records

Southern Gospel Album of the Year

1988 **Symphony of Praise** The Cathedrals; Lari Goss; Riversong Records

1989 **Goin' in Style** The Cathedrals; Lari Goss; Homeland Records

1990 **I Just Started Living** Cathedrals; Lari Goss; Homeland Records

1991 **Climbing Higher and Higher** The Cathedrals; Bill Gaither/Mark Trammell/Lari Goss; Homeland Records

Southern Gospel Recorded Song of the Year

1989 **Champions of Love** The Cathedrals; Phil Cross and Carolyn Cross

1990 **I Can See the Hand of God** Cathedrals; Steven Curtis Chapman, Jim Chapman III; Homeland Records

1991 **He Is There** The Talleys; Kirk Talley; Word Records

Country Gospel Album of the Year

1988 **An Evening Together** Steve & Annie Chapman; Ron Griffin & Steve Chapman; Star Song Records

1989 **Richest Man in Town** Bruce Carroll; Bubba Smith; New Canaan Records

1990 **Heirloom**; Heirloom; Michael Sykes and Trent Hemphill;Benson Records

1991 **Sojourner's Song** Buddy Greene; Bubba Smith; Word Records

Country Recorded Song of the Year

1989 **Above and Beyond** Bruce Carroll; Bruce Carroll and Paul Smith

1990 **'Tis So Sweet to Trust in Jesus** Amy Grant; Word Records

1991 **Seeing My Father in Me** Paul Overstreet; Taylor Dunn; Word Records/RCA Records

Contemporary Black Gospel Album of the Year

Recording artist listed first, producer/producers second, record company third

1981 **Give Me More Love in My Heart** Larnelle Harris; Howard McCrary/ Paul Johnson; Benson

1982 **Walter Hawkins & Family Live** Walter Hawkins Family; Walter Hawkins; Light Records

1983 **I'll Never Stop Loving You** Leon Patillo, Skip Konte; Myrrh Records

1984 **Come Together** Bobby Jones and New Life; Tony Brown, Myrrh Records

1985 **No Time to Lose** Andrae Crouch; Bill Maxwell; Light Records

1986 **Let My People Go** The Winans; Marvin Winans; Qwest Records

1987 **Heart & Soul** The Clark Sisters; Norbert Putnam and Twinkie Clark; Rejoice Records

1988 **Decisions** The Winans; Marvin Winans, Barry Hankerson, Carvin & Michael Winans; Qwest Records
1989 **Take 6** Take 6; Mark Kibble, Claude V. McKnight III, Mervyn E. Warren; Reunion Records
1990 **Will You Be Ready?** Commissioned Fred Hammand and Michael Brooks; Light Records
1991 **So Much 2 Say** Take 6; Mervyn Warren/Mark Kibble/Cedric Dent/ Alvin Chea/Claude B. McKnight/ David Thomas; Warner Alliance

Contemporary Black Gospel Recorded Song of the Year
1989 **If We Ever** Take 6
1990 **With My Whole Heart** BeBe and CeCe Winans; Patrick Henderson and Louis Brown III; Sparrow Records
1991 **I L-O-V-E U** Take 6; Mervyn Warren/Mark Kibble; Warner Records

Soul Album of the Year
Recording artist first, producer/producers second, record company third
1978 **This Is Another Day** Andrae Crouch and The Disciples; Bill Maxwell; Light Records
1979 **Live in London** Andrae Crouch and the Disciples; Bill Maxwell/Andrae Crouch; Light Records

Black Gospel Album of the Year
Recording artist listed first, producer/ producers second, record company third
1980 **Love Alive II** Walter Hawkins and the Love Center Choir; Walter Hawkins; Light Records

Traditional Black Gospel Album of the Year
Recording artist listed first, producer/ producers second, record company third
1981 **Incredible** Teddy Huffam and The Gems; Ken Harding; Canaan Records
1982 **Go** Shirley Caesar; Tony Brown/ Shirley Caesar; Myrrh Records
1983 **Precious Lord** Al Green; Al Green; Myrrh Records
1984 **We Sing Praises** Sandra Crouch; Sandra Crouch; Light Records

1985 **Sailin'** Shirley Caesar; Sanchez Harley/ Shirley Caesar/David Lehman; Myrrh Records
1986 **Celebration** Shirley Caesar; Dave Lehman/Shirley Caesar; Rejoice Records
1987 **Christmasing** Shirley Caesar; Norbert Putnam; Rejoice Records
1988 **One Lord, One Faith, One Baptism** Aretha Franklin; Aretha Franklin; Arista Records
1989 **Live . . . in Chicago** Shirley Caesar; Bubba Smith and Shirley Caesar; Rejoice Records
1990 **Saints in Praise** West Angeles Church of God in Christ Mass Choir; Patrick Henderson; Sparrow Records
1991 **Tramaine Hawkins Live** Tramaine Hawkins; Tramaine Hawkins/Lee Magid; Sparrow Records

Traditional Black Gospel Recorded Song of the Year
1989 **Hold My Mule** Shirley Caesar; Shirley Caesar Williams
1990 **Wonderful** Beau Williams; Virginia David and Theodore Fry; Light Records
1991 **The Potter's House** Tramaine Hawkins/Walter Hawkins; V. Michael McKay; Sparrow Records

Inspirational Black Gospel Album of the Year
Recording artist listed first, producer/ producers second, record company third
1981 **Rejoice** Shirley Caesar; Tony Brown/Ken Harding; Myrrh Records
1982 **Edwin Hawkins Live** Oakland Symphony Orchestra and Edwin Hawkins; Gil Askey; Myrrh Records
1983 **Touch Me Lord** Larnelle Harris; Greg Nelson; Impact Records

Instrumentalist of the Year
1970 **Dwayne Friend**
1971 **Dwayne Friend**
1972 No awards given
1973 **Tony Brown**
1974 **Henry Slaughter**
1975 **Henry Slaughter**
1976 **Henry Slaughter**

DOVE AWARDS cont.

1977 **Henry Slaughter**
1978 **Henry Slaughter**
1979 **Dino Kartsonakis**
1980 **Dino Kartsonakis**
1981 **Dino Kartsonakis**
1982 **Dino Kartsonakis**
1983 **Dino Kartsonakis**
1984 **Phil Driscoll**
1985 **Phil Driscoll**
1986 **Dino Kartsonakis**

Instrumental Album of the Year

1987 **Instrument of Praise** Phil Driscoll; Lari Goss, Phil Driscoll, Ken Pennel; Benson Records
1988 **The Wind & the Wheat** Phil Keaggy; Phil Keaggy, Tom Coomes; Colours (Maranatha! Music)
1989 **A Symphony Of Praise** Sandi Patti; David T. Clydesdale; Word Records
1990 **One of Several Possible Musiks** Kerry Livgren; Kerry Livgren; Sparrow Records
1991 **Come Before Him** Dick Tunney; Dick Tunney; Word Records

Worship and Praise Album of the Year

Recording artist listed first, producer second, record company third

1981 **The Lord's Prayer** Dony McGuire; Light Records
1982 **Exaltation** Ronn Huff
1983 **Light Eternal** Billy Ray Hearn; Birdwing Records
1984 **Celebrate the Joy** David T. Clydesdale; Impact Records
1985 **The Praise in Us** Neal Joseph; Myrrh Records
1986 **I've Just Seen Jesus** William J. Gaither/ Randy Vader; Gaither Music Records
1987 **Hymns** 2nd Chapter of Acts; Buck Herring; Live Oak Records
1988 **The Final Word** Michael Card; Norbert Putnam; Sparrow Records
1989 **Praise 10** Maranatha Singers Smitty Price and Tom Coomes; Maranatha Music Records
1990 **Our Hymns** Various Artists Word Records

1991 **Strong & Mighty Hands** Voices of Praise; John G. Elliot; Reunion Records

Musical Album of the Year

Recording artist listed first, creator second, record company third

1981 **The Messiah** Billy Ray Hearn; Irving Martin; Sparrow Records
1982 **The Love Story** Phil Brower/Don Wyrtzen; New Dawn Records
1983 **The Day He Wore My Crown** David T. Clydesdale; Impact Records
1984 **Dreamer** Cam Florida; Christian Artist Records
1985 **The Race Is On** Steve Taylor; Word Records
1986 **Come Celebrate Jesus** Neal Joseph/ Don Marsh; Word Records
1987 **A Mighty Fortress** Steve Green, Dwight Liles, Niles Borop, Creators; Sparrow Records
1988 **A Son! A Savior!** Various; Claire Cloninger, Gary Rhodes & Bob Krogstad; Word Music
1989 **In His Presence; The Risen King** Dick and Melodie Tunney; Dick and Melodie Tunney; Genevox Records
1990 **Friends Forever/Part 2** Billy Sprague; Jim Weber, Nan Gurley and Billy Sprague; Word/Meadowgreen Music
1991 **Handel's Young Messiah** Various; Paul Mills/Don Hart/Norman Miller; Word Records

Children's Music Album of the Year

Recording artist listed first, creator second, record company third

1981 **Very Best of the Very Best for Kids** Robert MacKenzie; Word Records
1982 **Kids under Construction** Bob MacKenzie/Ronn Huff; Paragon Records
1983 **Lullabies & Nursery Rhymes Vol. 1** Tony Salerno/Fletch Wiley; Birdwing Records
1984 **Music Machine II** Fletch Wiley/Tony Salerno/Ron Kreuger; Birdwing Records

1985 **Ten New Songs with Kids for Kids about Life** Ron W. Griffin; Word Records

1986 **Bullfrogs & Butterflies Part II** Tony Salerno; Birdwing Records

1987 **God Likes Kids** Joel & Labreeska Hemphill; Benson Records

1988 **Bullfrogs & Butterflies Part III** The Agapeland Singers & Candle; Tony Salerno; Sparrow Records

1989 **Wise Guys and Starry Skies** Kathie Hill; Sparrow Records

1990 **The Friendship Company** Sandi Patti; Sandi Patti; Word Records

1991 **Hide 'Em in Your Heart Songs** Steve Green; Frank & Betsy Hernandez; Sparrow Records

Artist of the Year

1981 **Imperials**
1982 **Sandi Patti**
1983 **Amy Grant**
1984 **Sandi Patti**
1985 **Sandi Patti**
1986 **Amy Grant**
1987 **Sandi Patti**
1988 **Sandi Patti**
1989 **Amy Grant**
1990 **Steven Curtis Chapman**
1991 **Steven Curtis Chapman**

Short Form Video of the Year

Title, Artist, Producer, Director

1987 **Famine in Their Land** The Nelons; Robert Deaton, George Flanigen; Word Record & Music Group

1988 **Stay for a While** Amy Grant; Marc Ball; Jack Cole, Scene Three Productions

1989 **Lead Me On** Amy Grant; Tina Silvey; Andrew Doucette

1990 **I Miss the Way** Michael W. Smith; Fire By Night Productions, Steve Yake

1991 **Revival in the Land** Carman; Stephen Yake; Stephen Yake; Video Impact

Long Form Video of the Year

Title, Artist, Producer, Director

1987 **Limelight** Steve Taylor; John Anneman, Steve Taylor; Sparrow Records

1988 **The Big Picture Tour Video** Michael W. Smith; Brian Shipley; Stephen Bowlby

1989 **Carman Live . . . Radically Saved** Carman; Cindy DuPree; George J. Flanigen IV and Robert Deaton

1990 **On Fire** Petra; FirstBorne Productions, Steve Yake, director

1991 **Revival in the Land** Carman; Stephen Yake; Stephen Yake; Video Impact

Contribution to Gospel Music by a Secular Artist

Recording artist listed first, producer/producers second, record company third

1976 **Sunday Morning with Charley Pride** Charley Pride; Jerry Bradley; RCA Records

1978 **Home Where I Belong** B. J. Thomas; Myrrh Records

1979 **First Class** The Boones; Chris Christian; Lamb & Lion

1980 **Slow Train Coming** Bob Dylan; Jerry Wexler-Barry Beckett; Columbia Records

1981 **With My Song** Debbie Boone; Brown Bannister; Lamb & Son

1982 **Amazing Grace** B. J. Thomas; Pete Drake; Myrrh Records

1983 **He Set My Life to Music** Barbara Mandrell; Tom Collins; MCA Records

1984 **Surrender** Debbie Boone; Brown Bannister; Lamb & Lion

1985 **You Were Loving Me** Lulu Roman Smith; Gary McSpadden; Canaan Records

1986 **No More Night** Glen Campbell; Glen Campbell/Ken Harding; Word Records

Horizon Award

1988 **BeBe & CeCe Winans**

Choral Collection Album of the Year

1989 **Sandi Patti Choral Praise** Sandi Patti; Greg Nelson; Word Music Records

1990 **The A Capella Collection** Greg Nelson Singers; Greg Nelson; Wordsong

DOVE AWARDS cont.

1991 **I Call You to Praise** Steve Green; Music Sculptors; Sparrow Records

Metal Album of the Year

1989 **In God We Trust** Stryper; Stryper and Michael Lloyd; Enigma Records
1990 **Triumphant Return** White Cross; Rex Carroll and Joey Powers; Pure Metal Records
1991 **Holy Soldier** Holy Soldier; Holy Soldier; David Zaffiro, producer; Myrrh Records

Metal Recorded Song of the Year

1989 **In God We Trust** Stryper; Stryper
1990 **In Your Face** Shout; Ken Tamplin; Frontline Records
1991 **Stranger** Holy Soldier; Holy Soldier/David Zaffiro; Myrrh Records

New Artist of the Year

1989 **Take 6**
1990 **David Mullen**
1991 **4 Him**

Impact Award

1990 **Sparrow Records**
1991 **Stephen Yake**

Grady Nutt Humor Award

1991 **Wendy Bagwell**

International Award

1990 **Phil and John, U.K.** Word
1991 **Adrian Snell**

Lifetime Achievement Award

1990 **How Great Thou Art** accepted by Hal Spencer
1991 **Maranatha Music**

Gospel Music Hall of Fame Inductees

Living

1970 "Pappy" Jim Waites
1971 Albert E. Brumley
1972 Le Roy Abernathy
1973 James Blackwood, Sr.
1974 Brock Speer
1975 Mosie Lister
1976 Eva Mae LeFevre
1977 George Beverly Shea
1978 Connor B. Hall
1979 John T. Benson, Jr., Ira Stanphill

1980 Thomas A. Dorsey
1981 William (Bill) Gaither
1982 Hovie Lister
1983 Ralph Carmichael
1984 John W. Peterson
1985 W. J. "Jake" Hess
1986 Cliff Barrows
1991 Bob Benson, Sr.

Deceased

1970 G. T. "Dad" Speer
1971 Lena Brock Speer, James D. Vaughan
1972 Denver Crumpler
1973 G. Keffer Vaughan
1974 Fanny Crosby
1975 George Bennard
1976 James "Big Chief" Wetherington
1977 Mahalia Jackson
1978 Ira Sanky
1979 Clarice Baxter
1980 John T. Benson, Sr.
1981 Marvin Norcross
1982 Cleavant Derricks
1983 Tim Spencer
1984 Urias LeFevre

In 1973 a special resolution was passed to induct the following persons into the Gospel Music Hall of Fame:

Deceased

J. R. Baxter, Jr.
E. M. Bartlett
John Daniel
Adger M. Pace
Homer Rodeheaver
A. J. Showalter
V. O. Stamps
Frank Stamps
W. B. Walbert
R. E. Winsett

In 1982 a special resolution was passed to induct the following persons into the Gospel Music Hall of Fame:

Deceased

Charles Gabriel
Haldor Lillenas
B. B. McKinney
Lowell Mason
John Newton

In 1984 a special resolution was passed to induct the following persons into the Gospel Music Hall of Fame:

Living
Rev. James Cleveland
John Wallace "Wally" Fowler
W. B. Nowlin
J. D. Sumner
P. J. Zondervan

Deceased
D. P. "Dad" Carter
Paul Heinecke
Lloyd Orrell
Clara Ward
Ethel Waters

In 1989 a special resolution was passed to induct J. G. Whitfield into the Gospel Music Hall of Fame.

GRAMMY AWARDS, RELIGIOUS CATEGORIES

Grammy winners are selected annually by the voting members of The Recording Academy, who number nearly 6000 creative contributors to the fields of recording. Their criteria for judging are artistic and/or technical excellence. Although Grammy winners were first selected in 1958, it was not until 1961 that a religious recording category was created.

Year	Category	Artist	Song/Album	Label
1961	Best Gospel or Other Religious Recording	Mahalia Jackson	Everytime I Feel the Spirit	Columbia
1962	Best Gospel or Other Religious Recording	Mahalia Jackson	Great Songs of Love and Faith	Columbia
1963	Best Gospel or Other Religious Recording (Musical)	Soeur Sourire (The Singing Nun)	Dominique	Philips
1964	Best Gospel or Other Religious Recording	Tennessee Ernie Ford	Great Gospel Songs	Capitol
1965	Best Gospel or Other Religious Recording (Musical)	George Beverly Shea & the Anita Kerr Singers	Southland Favorites	RCA
1966	Best Sacred Recording (Musical)	Porter Wagoner and the Blackwood Brothers	Grand Old Gospel	RCA
1967	Best Sacred Performance	Porter Wagoner and the Blackwood Brothers	More Grand Old Gospel	RCA
	Best Sacred Performance	Elvis Presley	How Great Thou Art	RCA
1968	Best Gospel Perf.	Happy Goodman Family	The Happy Gospel of the Happy Goodmans	Word
	Best Sacred Perf.	Jake Hess	Beautiful Isle of Somewhere	RCA
	Best Soul Gospel Perf.	Dottie Rambo	The Soul of Me	Heartwarming
1969	Best Gospel Perf.	Porter Wagoner and the Blackwood Brothers	In Gospel Country	RCA
	Best Sacred Perf.	Jake Hess	Ain't That Beautiful Singing	RCA
	Best Soul Gospel	Edwin Hawkins Singers	Oh Happy Day	Buddah
1970	Best Gospel Perf.	Oak Ridge Boys	Talk about the Good Times	Heart Warming
	Best Sacred Perf.	Jake Hess	Everything Is Beautiful	RCA
	Best Soul Gospel Perf.	Edwin Hawkins Singers	Every Man Wants to Be Free	Buddah
1971	Best Gospel Perf. (Other Than Soul Gospel)	Charley Pride	Let Me Live	RCA
	Best Sacred Perf.	Charley Pride	Did You Think to Pray	RCA
	Best Soul Gospel Perf.	Shirley Caesar	Put Your Hand in the Hand of the Man from Galilee	Hob
1972	Best Gospel Perf.	Blackwood Brothers	Love	RCA
1972	Best Inspir. Perf.	Elvis Presley	He Touched Me	RCA
	Best Soul Gospel Perf.	Aretha Franklin	Amazing Grace	Atlantic
1973	Best Gospel Perf.	Blackwood Brothers	Release Me (from My Sin) (Album)	Skylite
	Best Inspir. Perf.	Bill Gaither Trio	Let's Just Praise the Lord (Album)	Impact
	Best Soul Gospel Perf.	Dixie Hummingbirds	Loves Me Like a Rock (Single)	ABC
1974	Best Gospel Perf.	Oak Ridge Boys	The Baptism of Jesse Taylor (Single)	Columbia

GRAMMY AWARDS cont.

Year	Category	Artist	Song/Album	Label
	Best Inspir. Perf.	Elvis Presley	How Great Thou Art (Track)	RCA
	Best Soul Gospel Perf.	James Cleveland and the So. Calif. Comm. Choir	In the Ghetto (Album)	Savoy
1975	Best Gospel Perf.	Imperials	No Shortage (Album)	Impact
	Best Inspir. Perf.	The Bill Gaither Trio	Jesus, We Just Want to Thank You (Album)	Impact
	Best Soul Gospel Perf.	Andrae Crouch and the Disciples	Take Me Back (Album)	Light
1976	Best Gospel Perf.	Oak Ridge Boys	Where The Soul Never Dies (Single)	Columbia
1976	Best Inspir. Perf.	Gary S. Paxton	The Astonishing, Outrageous, Amazing, Incredible, Unbelievable, Different World of Gary S. Paxton (Album)	Newpax
	Best Soul Gospel Perf.	Mahalia Jackson	How I Got Over (Album)	Columbia
1977	Best Gospel Perf., Contemp./Inspir.	Imperials	Sail On (Album)	DaySpring/Word
	Best Gospel Perf., Tradtnl	Oak Ridge Boys	Just a Little Talk with Jesus (Track)	Rockland Road
	Best Inspir. Perf.	B.J. Thomas	Home Where I Belong (Album)	Myrrh/Word
	Best Soul Gospel Perf., Contemp.	Edwin Hawkins and the Edwin Hawkins Singers	Wonderful! (Album)	Birthright
	Best Soul Gospel Perf., Tradtnl	James Cleveland	James Cleveland Live at Carnegie Hall (Album)	Savoy
1978	Best Gospel Perf., Contemp./Inspir.	Larry Hart	What a Friend (Track)	Genesis
	Best Gospel Perf., Traditional	The Happy Goodman Family	Refreshing (Album)	Canaan
	Best Inspir. Perf.	B. J. Thomas	Happy Man (Album)	Myrrh
	Best Soul Gospel Perf., Contemp.	Andrae Crouch and the Disciples	Live in London (Album)	Light
	Best Soul Gospel Perf., Tradtnl	Mighty Clouds of Joy	Live and Direct (Album)	ABC
1979	Best Gospel Perf. Contemp./Inspir.	Imperials	Heed the Call (Album)	DaySpring
	Best Gospel Perf., Traditional	The Blackwood Brothers	Lift Up the Name of Jesus (Album)	Skylite
	Best Inspir. Perf.	B. J. Thomas	You Gave Me Love (When Nobody Gave Me a Prayer) (Album)	Myrrh
	Best Soul Gospel Perf., Contemp.	Andrae Crouch	I'll Be Thinking of You (Album)	Light
	Best Soul Gospel Perf., Tradtnl	Mighty Clouds of Joy	Changing Times (Album)	Epic
1980	Best Gospel Perf., Contemp./Inspir.	Reba Rambo, Dony McGuire, B. J. Thomas, Andrae Crouch, The Archers, Walter and Tramaine Hawkins, Cynthia Clawson	The Lord's Prayer (Album)	Light
	Best Gospel Perf., Traditional	Blackwood Brothers	We Come to Worship (Album)	Voice Box
	Best Inspir. Perf.	Debby Boone	With My Song I Will Praise Him (Album)	Lamb & Lion
	Best Soul Gospel Perf., Contemp.	Shirley Caesar	Rejoice (Album)	Myrrh
	Best Soul Gospel Perf., Tradtnl	James Cleveland and the Charles Fold Singers	Lord, Let Me Be an Instrmt (Album)	Savoy
1981	Best Gospel Perf. Contemp./Inspir.	Imperials	Priority (Album)	Dayspring/Word
	Best Gospel Perf., Traditional	J. D. Sumner, James Blackwood, Hovie Lister, Rosie Rozell, Jake Hess		The Masters V (Album) Skylite
	Best Inspir. Perf.	B. J. Thomas	Amazing Grace (Album)	Myrrh/Word

Year	Category	Artist	Work	Label
	Best Soul Gospel Perf., Contemp.	Andrae Crouch	Don't Give Up (Album)	W.B.
	Best Soul Gospel Perf., Tradtnl	Al Green	The Lord Will Make a Way (Album)	Hi-Myrrh/Word
1982	Best Gospel Perf., Contemp./Inspir.	Amy Grant	Age to Age (Album)	Myrrh/Word
	Best Gospel Perf., Traditional	Blackwood Brothers	I'm Following You (Album)	Voice Box
	Best Inspir. Perf.	Barbara Mandrell	He Set My Life to Music (Album)	Songbird/MCA
	Best Soul Gospel Perf., Contemp.	Al Green	Higher Plane (Album)	Myrrh/Word
	Best Soul Gospel Perf., Tradtnl	Al Green	Precious Lord (Album)	Myrrh/Word
1983	Best Gospel Perf., Duo/Group	Sandi Patti and Larnelle Harris	More Than Wonderful (Track)	Impact/Benson
	Best Gospel Perf., Female	Amy Grant	Ageless Medley (Single)	Myrrh/Word
	Best Gospel Perf., Male	Russ Taff	Walls of Glass (Album)	Myrrh/Word
	Best Inspir. Perf.	Donna Summer	He's a Rebel (Track)	Mercury/Polygram
	Best Soul Gospel Perf., Duo/Group	Bobby Jones with Barbara Mandrell	I'm So Glad I'm Standing Here Today (Track)	Myrrh/Word
	Best Soul Gospel Perf., Female	Sandra Crouch	We Sing Praises (Album)	Light/Lexicon
	Best Soul Gospel Perf., Male	Al Green	I'll Rise Again (Album)	Myrrh/Word
1984	Best Gospel Perf., Duo\Group	Debby Boone and Phil Driscoll	Keep the Flame Burning (from Debby Boone Surrender)	Lamb and Lion/Sparrow
	Best Gospel Perf., Female	Amy Grant	Angels (from Straight Ahead)	Myrrh/Word
	Best Gospel Perf., Male	Michael W. Smith	Michael W. Smith (Album)	Reunion/Word
	Best Inspir. Perf.	Donna Summer	Forgive Me (from Cats without Claws)	Geffen/Warner Brothers
	Best Soul Gospel Perf., Duo/Group	Shirley Caesar & Al Green	Sailin' on the Sea of Your Love (from Shirley Caesar Sailin)	Myrrh/Word
	Best Soul Gospel Perf., Female	Shirley Caesar	Sailin' (Album)	Myrrh/Word
	Best Soul Gospel Perf., Male	Andrae Crouch	Always Remember (from No Time to Lose)	Light/Lexicon
1985	Best Gospel Perf., Duo/Group	Larnelle Harris and Sandi Patti	I've Just Seen Jesus (from I've Just Seen Jesus)	Impact/Benson
	Best Gospel Perf., Female	Amy Grant	Unguarded (Album)	Myrrh/Word
	Best Gospel Perf., Male	Larnelle Harris	How Excellent Is Thy Name (from I've Just Seen Jesus)	Benson
	Best Inspir. Perf.	Jennifer Holliday	Come Sunday (from Say You Love Me)	Geffen
	Best Soul Gospel Perf., Duo/Group	The Winans	Tomorrow (Album)	Light
	Best Soul Gospel Perf., Female	Shirley Caesar	Martin (Single)	Rejoice/Word
	Best Soul Gospel Perf., Male	Marvin Winans	Bring Back the Days of Yea and Nay (from Tomorrow)	Light
1986	Best Gospel Perf. by a Duo, Group, Choir or Choirs	Sandi Patti and Deniece Williams	They Say (from So Glad I Know)	Sparrow
	Best Gospel Perf., Female	Sandi Patti	Morning Like This (Album)	Word
	Best Gospel Perf., Male	Philip Bailey	Triumph (Album)	Myrrh/Word
	Best Soul Gospel Perf. by a Duo, Group, Choir or Chorus	The Winans	Let My People Go (Album)	Qwest
	Best Soul Gospel Perf., Female	Deniece Williams	I Surrender All (from So Glad I Know)	Sparrow
	Best Soul Perf., Male	Al Green	Going Away (Single)	A&M
1987	Best Gospel Perf. by a Duo, Group, Choir or Chorus	Mylon LeFevre and Broken Heart	Crack the Sky (Album)	Myrrh/Word
	Best Gospel Perf., Female	Deniece Williams	I Believe In You (from Water Under the Bridge)	Columbia/CBS
	Best Gospel Perf., Male	Larnelle Harris	The Father Hath Provided (Album)	Benson
	Best Gospel Perf. by a Duo, Group, Choir or Chorus	The Winans and Anita Baker	Ain't No Need to Worry (Single)	Qwest
	Best Soul Gospel Perf., Female	Cece Winans	For Always (from Bebe and Cece Winans)	Sparrow
	Best Soul Gospel Perf., Male	Al Green	Everything's Gonna Be Alright (from Soul Survivor)	A&M

GRAMMY AWARDS cont.

Year	Category	Artist	Song/Album	Label
1988	Best Gospel Perf. by a Duo, Group, Choir or Chorus	The Winans	The Winans Live at Carnegie Hall	Qwest
	Best Gospel Perf., Female	Amy Grant	Lead Me On	A&M
	Best Gospel Perf., Male	Larnelle Harris	Christmas (Album)	Benson
	Best Soul Gospel Perf. by a Duo, Group, Choir or Chorus	Bebe Winans	Abundant Life (Track/Ron Winans Family and Friends Choir)	Selah
	Best Soul Gospel Perf., Female	Aretha Franklin	One Lord, One Faith, One Baptism	Arista
	Best Soul Gospel Perf., Male	Take 6	Take Six (Album)	Reprise
1989	Best Gospel Perf. by a Duo, Group, Choir or Chorus	Take 6	The Savior Is Waiting (Track/Our Hymns/Various Artists)	Word
	Best Gospel Perf., Female	Cece Winans	Don't Cry	Capitol
	Best Gospel Perf., Male	Bebe Winans	Meantime (Track/Heaven)	Capitol
1989	Best Soul Gospel Perf. by a Duo, Group, Choir or Chorus	Daniel Winans and Choir	Let Brotherly Love Continue	Rejoice
	Best Soul Gospel Perf., Male	Al Green	As Long as We're Together (Single)	A&M
1990	Best Rock/Contemporary Gospel Album	Petra	Beyond Belief	DaySpring Records
	Best Pop Gospel Album	Sandi Patti	Another Time . . . Another Place	Word Records
	Best Southern Gospel Album	Bruce Carroll	The Great Exchange	
	Best Traditional Soul Gospel Album	Tramaine Hawkins	Tramaine Hawkins Live	Sparrow Records
	Best Contemporary Soul Gospel Album	Take 6	So Much 2 Say	Warner Alliance
	Best Gospel Album by a Choir or Chorus	Rev. James Cleveland & the Southern Calif. Community Choir	Having Church	
1991	Best Rock/Contemporary Gospel Album	Russ Taff	Under Their Influence	Word Records
	Best Pop Gospel Album	Steven Curtis Chapman	For the Sake of the Call	Sparrow Records
	Best Southern Gospel Album	The Gaither Vocal Band	Homecoming	StarSong
	Best Traditional Soul Gospel Album	Mighty Clouds of Joy	Pray for Me	Word Records
	Best Contemporary Soul Gospel Album	BeBe & CeCe Winans	Different Lifestyles	Sparrow Records
	Best Gospel Album by a Choir or Chorus	Sounds of Blackness Gary Hines, choir director	The Evolution of Gospel	Perspective

STELLAR GOSPEL MUSIC AWARDS

Sponsor: Central City Productions

Year	Award	Artist
1986	Album of the Year—Contemporary	The Winans
	Album of the Year—Traditional	Shirley Caesar
	Best New Artist of the Year	Calvin Bridges
	Choir of the Year	Rev. Milton Brunson and the Thompson Community Singers
	Excellence Award for Gospel Performance by a Group—Contemporary	The Winans
	Excel. Award for Gospel Perf. by a Group—Traditional	The Williams Brothers
	Excel. Award for Single Gospel Artist/ Female Contemporary	Tramaine Hawkins
1986	Excel. Award for Single Gospel Artist/ Female Traditional	Shirley Caesar
	Excel. Award for Single Gospel Artist/ Male Contemporary	Walter Hawkins
	Excel. Award for Single Gospel Artist/Male Traditional	Howard Smith
	Most Notable Achievement Award	Andrae Crouch

1986	Producer of the Year	Andrae Crouch
	Producer of the Year	Sandra Crouch
	Significant Contributions to Gospel Music	Clara Ward
	Song of the Year	Sandra Crouch
1987	Album of the Year—Contemporary	Let My People Go by the Winans
	Album of the Year—Traditional	Celebration by Shirley Caesar
	Best New Artist of the Year	Calvin Bridges
	Choir of the Year	Rev. Milton Brunson and the Thompson Community Singers
	Excel. Award for Gospel Artist/Female Contemporary	Tramaine Hawkins
	Excel. Award for Gospel Perf. by a Group—Contemporary	The Winans
	Excel. Award for Gospel Perf. by a Group—Traditional	The Williams Brothers
	Excel. Award for Single Gospel Artist/Female Traditional	Shirley Caesar
	Excel. Award for Single Gospel Artist/Male Contemporary	Walter Hawkins
	Excel. Award for Single Gospel Artist/Male Traditional	Howard Smith
	For Significant Contributions to Gospel Music	Clara Ward
	Most Notable Achievement Award	Andrae Crouch
	Producer of the Year	Sandra Crouch and Andrae Crouch
	Song of the Year	Completely Yes by Sandra Crouch
1988	Album of the Year—Contemporary	Be Encouraged
	Album of the Year—Traditional	Rev. Milton Brunson
	Best Inspir. Soul Gospel Perf.	Aretha Franklin
	Best New Artist	Take 6
	Best Perf. by Group or Duo—Contemporary	Take 6
	Best Perf. by Group or Duo—Traditional	The Williams Brothers
	Best Solo Perf. by Female—Contemporary	Vanessa Bell Armstrong
	Best Solo Perf. by Female—Traditional	Shirley Caesar
	Best Solo Perf. by Male—Contemporary	Larnelle Harris
	Best Solo Perf. by Male—Traditional	Calvin Bridges
	Choir of the Year	New Jersey Mass Choir
	Song of the Year	William and Gloria Gaither
1989	Album of the Year—Contemporary	Bebe and Cece Winans
	Album of the Year—Traditional	The Mississippi Mass Choir
	Best Gospel Music Video	The Mississippi Mass Choir
	Best Inspirational Gospel Performance	Bebe and Cece Winans
	Best New Artist	The Mississippi Mass Choir
	Best Perf. by a Group or Duo—Contemporary	Bebe and Cece Winans
	Best Perf. by Group or Duo—Traditional	The Jackson Southernaires
	Best Solo Perf. by Female—Contemporary	Tramaine Hawkins
	Best Solo Perf. by Female—Traditional	Myrna Summers
	Best Solo Perf. by Male—Contemporary	Daryl Coley
	Best Solo Perf. by Male—Traditional	Rev. James Moore
	Choir of the Year	The Mississippi Mass Choir
	Song of the Year	Bebe and Cece Winans
1990	Album of the Year—Contemporary	The Winans
	Album of the Year—Traditional	John P. Kee and the New Life Community Choir
	Best Gospel Music Video	The Winans
	Best Urban Contemporary Gospel Performance	The Winans
	Best New Artist	Cathedral of Faith Choir

STELLAR AWARDS, cont.

1990	Best Perf. by a Group or Duo—Contemporary	The Winans
	Best Perf. by Group or Duo—Traditional	Willie Neal Johnson & The Gospel Keynotes
	Best Solo Perf. by Female—Contemporary	Helen Baylor
	Best Solo Perf. by Female—Traditional	Shirley Caesar
	Best Solo Perf. by Male—Contemporary	Richard Smallwood
	Best Solo Perf. by Male—Traditional	Rev. James Cleveland
	Choir of the Year—Contemporary	Milton Brunson and the Thompson Community Singers
	Choir of the Year—Traditional	John P. Kee and the New Life Community Choir
	Song of the Year	John P. Kee and the New Life Community Choir
1991	Album of the Year—Contemporary	Daryl Coley
	Album of the Year—Traditional	John P. Kee
	Best Gospel Music Video	The Mississippi Mass Choir
	Best Urban Contemporary Gospel Performance	BeBe and Cece Winans
	Best New Artist	Shun Pace Rhodes
	Best Perf. by a Group or Duo—Contemporary	Bebe and Cece Winans
	Best Perf. by Group or Duo—Traditional	The Williams Brothers
	Best Solo Perf. by Female—Contemporary	Yolanda Adams
	Best Solo Perf. by Female—Traditional	Tramaine Hawkins
	Best Solo Perf. by Male—Contemporary	Daryl Coley
	Best Solo Perf. by Male—Traditional	James Moore
	Choir of the Year—Contemporary	New Life Community Choir
	Choir of the Year—Traditional	Rev. Ernie Davis/Wilmington Chester Mass Choir
	Song of the Year	Rev. Ernie Davis/Wilmington Chester Mass Choir

Bible

TOP 10 BEST-SELLING BIBLES OF 1991

Study Bibles
1. *The NIV Student Bible*, Zondervan
2. *The NIV Study Bible*, Zondervan
3. *The Adventure Bible (NIV)*, Zondervan
4. *Women's Devotional Bible (NIV)*, Zondervan
5. *Serenity New Testament with Psalms and Proverbs (NKJV)*, Nelson
6. *Life Application Bible (NIV)*, Tyndale/Zondervan
7. *Life Application Bible (TLB)*, Tyndale
8. *The NIV Serendipity Bible*, Zondervan
9. *The New Open Bible (NKJV)*, Nelson
10. *Thompson Chain-Reference Bible (KJV)*, Kirkbride

General Versions and Translations
1. *New International Version,* various publishers
2. *King James Version,* various publishers
3. *New King James Version/The Bible,* Nelson
4. *The Living Bible,* Tyndale
5. *New Century Version,* Word
6. *New American Standard Bible,* various publishers
7. *Today's English Version/Good News Bible,* Nelson
8. *New American Bible (Catholic),* various publishers
9. *New Revised Standard Version,* various publishers
10. *The Amplified Bible,* Zondervan

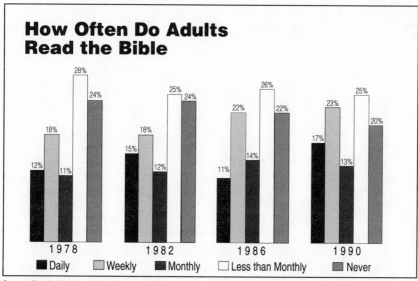

How Often Do Adults Read the Bible

	Daily	Weekly	Monthly	Less than Monthly	Never
1978	12%	18%	11%	28%	24%
1982	15%	18%	12%	25%	24%
1986	11%	22%	14%	26%	22%
1990	17%	23%	13%	25%	20%

Source: *The Role of the Bible in American Society* by George Gallup, Jr., and Robert Bezilla. Published by The Princeton Religion Research Center. Used by permission.

Best-Selling English Bibles in the USA since 1983

This chart is based on the sales statistics from Spring Arbor Distributors.

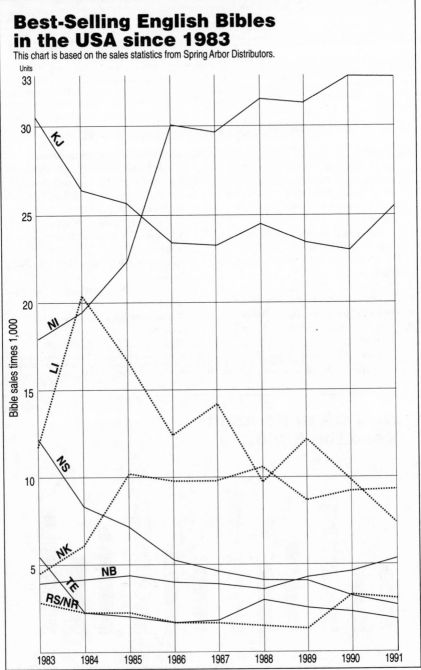

Taken from *Words About the Word* by John R. Kohlenberger III. Copyright © 1987 by John R. Kohlenberger. Used by permission of Zondervan Publishing House. Updated by ACW staff.

SPRING ARBOR DISTRIBUTORS BIBLE TRANSLATION TRENDS
(UNIT SALES in 1,000s)

Versions	Jul-Dec 1984	Jan-June 1985	Jul-Dec 1985	Jan-June 1986	Jul-Dec 1986	Jan-June 1987	Jul-Dec 1987	Jan-June 1988	Jul-Dec 1988	Jan-June 1989	Jul-Dec 1989	Jan-June 1990	Jul-Dec 1990	Jan-June 1991	Jul-Dec 1991
NI	19.5	22.6	22.3	22.9	30.0	30.9	29.8	31.6	31.9	31.9	31.5	30.1	33.3	32.3	34.1
KJ	26.5	26.2	25.4	25.2	23.5	23.8	23.4	23.1	24.6	22.7	23.6	24.2	23.0	25.4	25.4
NK	6.1	6.3	10.1	10.2	9.8	9.4	9.8	8.8	10.7	9.5	8.9	9.1	9.1	9.3	9.1
LI	20.4	18.4	16.7	14.7	12.5	14.0	14.1	12.6	9.9	12.0	12.2	11.9	9.9	7.7	7.1
NB	4.2	5.1	4.4	4.3	4.1	2.9	4.0	4.5	3.8	4.5	4.3	4.9	4.7	5.5	5.4
RS/NR	2.5	2.4	2.6	2.5	1.9	1.8	1.8	1.5	1.6	1.5	1.4	1.5	3.5	3.7	2.7
NS	8.4	7.8	7.3	6.6	5.3	4.8	4.7	4.0	4.2	3.8	4.1	3.2	3.2	2.9	2.9
TE	2.3	2.2	2.1	2.3	1.9	1.8	2.0	3.6	3.1	3.8	2.7	4.2	2.4	2.5	1.7
SP	0.0	.7	1.0	1.1	1.4	1.4	1.4	1.4	1.9	2.1	2.2	2.2	2.1	2.3	2.4
NC	0.0	0.0	0.0	0.0	1.3	1.5	2.0	2.2	2.6	2.1	2.7	2.2	2.9	2.2	2.5
AM	2.2	2.0	1.9	1.9	1.6	1.1	.9	1.3	1.2	1.3	1.3	1.4	1.4	1.4	1.5
PR	0.0	0.0	0.0	2.6	2.1	2.0	1.8	1.8	1.5	1.6	1.7	1.6	1.4	1.2	1.1
OE	0.0	0.0	0.0	1.2	1.0	1.4	1.5	1.4	1.1	1.1	1.1	1.4	1.3	1.2	1.3
FL	0.0	0.0	0.0	.9	.9	1.0	1.0	.9	.8	.8	.9	.9	.7	.9	1.0
IL	0.0	0.0	0.0	1.2	.5	.7	.6	.6	.5	.5	.5	.5	.4	.5	.5
NJ	1.3	1.2	1.4	1.2	1.1	1.2	1.2	.9	.7	.8	.6	.4	.5	.4	.4
CD	0.0	0.0	0.0	0.0	0.0	0.0	0.0	0.0	0.0	0.0	0.0	0.0	0.0	.3	.4
NE/RE	0.0	0.0	0.0	0.0	0.0	0.0	0.0	0.0	0.0	0.0	.3	.3	.2	.2	.1
CE	0.0	0.0	0.0	0.0	0.0	0.0	0.0	0.0	0.0	0.0	0.0	0.0	0.0	.1	.4

Key to Versions:

NI	New International Version	CD	Computer Software
KJ	King James Version	NE/RE	New English/Revised English
NK	New King James	CE	Contempory English
LI	Living Bible		
NB	New American Bible		
RS/NR	Revised Standard		
NS	New American Standard		
TE	Today's English		
SP	Spanish Bibles		
NC	New Century Version		
AM	Amplified Bible		
PR	Parallel Bibles		
OE	Other English Versions		
FL	Foreign Language		
IL	Interlinear Bibles		
NJ	New Jerusalem		

Notes on Bible Translation Trends from Spring Arbor Distributors:

—Spring Arbor does not claim to stock every Bible in print. We do, however, stock over 4,000 Bibles, testaments and Scripture portions.

—Our statistics honestly report unit sales we have experienced in our warehouse over a given period of time.

—Our statistics are affected by product availability, special promotions run by publishers and/or Spring Arbor, publisher advertising and other factors.

—We do not claim that our ranking speaks for all wholesalers or all markets into which Bibles are sold. It simply indicates the trends experienced by one major wholesaler.

HOW TO SELECT A BIBLE

Determine the textual content ("canon")
1. Old and New Testaments (most Protestants)
2. Old Testament and New Testament with Apocrypha (most Catholics)
3. Old Testament only (most Jewish)
4. New Testament only

Determine the needs
1. Determine reading level
   a. Age
   b. Education: secular and ecclesiastical
   c. Literacy or literary appreciation
   d. Familiarity with ecclesiastical vocabulary

2. Purpose
- a. Reading
  - 1) General study
  - 2) Devotional
  - 3) Public reading
- b. Detailed analysis: word study and diagramming
- c. Comparison: in general or within a congregation
- d. Communication: Preaching, teaching, writing
- e. Gift
- f. Conformity within a congregation

Determine the options

1. For children (through junior high)
2. For those with limited reading ability and little or no church background
3. For youth and adults with no reading difficulty but little or no church background
4. For youth and adults from a conservative church background
5. For youth and adults from a mainline or liberal church background
6. For youth and adults from a Catholic background
7. For youth and adults from a Jewish background
8. For those with an appreciation of literature and literary English
9. For those who want to do word and sentence analysis

Determine study features, if desired

1. Introductions and outlines
2. Cross references
3. Textual notes:
   - a. Simple explanations
   - b. Topical synthesis
   - c. Interpretive: note theological and/or critical preference
4. Concordance
5. Topical index
6. Dictionary
7. Maps
8. Illustrations and charts
9. Essays, articles, and other helps
10. Historical and harmony charts and outlines

Determine the layout (if there are options in the version)

1. Verse format or paragraph format
2. One-column or two-column
3. Type size and color (red-letter)
4. Trim size (book dimensions)

Determine the binding quality

1. Paperback and kivar (low cost)
   - a. For awards and other giveaways
   - b. For collecting translations for comparative study
   - c. For economic necessity
2. Cloth (economy and durability)
   - a. A permanent version
   - b. Can stand on a shelf
3. Imitation and bonded leather (economy)
   - a. A permanent version
   - b. Flexible

c. For economic necessity (vs. genuine leather)
4. Leather (durability and beauty)
   a. A permanent version
   b. Genuine leathers are most durable, but also most expensive

Taken from *Words About the Word* by John R. Kohlenberger III. Copyright © 1987 by John R. Kohlenberger. Used by permission of Zondervan Publishing House.

66 99 **The Bible is the constitution of Christianity.** —Billy Graham
FOCUS
QUOTE

HOW BIBLICALLY LITERATE ARE WE?

Many Americans are biblically illiterate. Recent surveys show that a large percentage could not correctly answer basic questions about the Bible.

Percent

Is the Book of Isaiah:
In the Old Testament 62
In the New Testament 10
Don't know 28

Is the expression "God helps those who help themselves" in the Bible?
Yes 41
No 31
Don't know 28

Is the Book of Jonah part of the Bible?
Yes 48
No 27
Don't know 25

Is the Book of Thomas part of the Bible?
Yes 21
No 52
Don't know 27

In what city was Jesus Christ born?
Bethlehem 61
Jerusalem 18
Nazareth 8
Named another city or area 2
Don't know 10

How many apostles were there?
Twelve 70
Incorrect number 14
Don't know 16

Barna Research Group, Glendale, CA.

Percent

Can you name five of the Ten Commandments?
All five correct 42
Four correct 21
Three correct 14
Two correct 8
One correct 2
Don't know 13

Gallup Survey for *Christianity Today.*

Will you tell me the names of the first four books of the New Testament of the Bible—that is, the four Gospels?
All four correct 46
Three correct 4
Two correct 2
One correct 2
None correct 3
Don't know 43

Who delivered the Sermon on the Mount?
Jesus 42
Incorrect answer 24
Don't know 34

Where was Jesus born?
Bethlehem 70
Incorrect answer 17
Don't know 13

Gallup Survey for the Robert H. Schuller Ministries.

How People View the Bible

Americans do not read the Bible much—even though they believe it is important to do so. Yet a majority believe the Bible is not too difficult to understand, is not outdated, and should be allowed in public libraries.

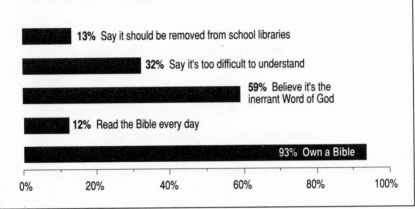

13% Say it should be removed from school libraries

32% Say it's too difficult to understand

59% Believe it's the inerrant Word of God

12% Read the Bible every day

93% Own a Bible

0%   20%   40%   60%   80%   100%

Barna Research Group, Glendale, Calif.

How People Interpret the Bible

The question of biblical inerrancy and authority has been debated for centuries and has never resulted in an absolute consensus of opinion on whether the Scriptures are historically reliable.

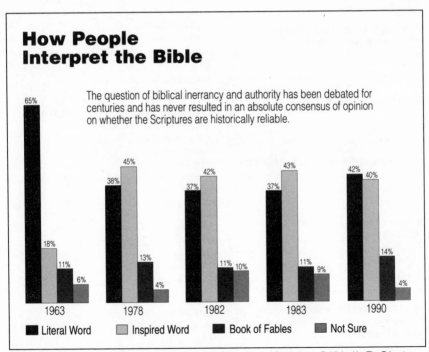

	1963	1978	1982	1983	1990
Literal Word	65%	38%	37%	37%	42%
Inspired Word	18%	45%	42%	43%	40%
Book of Fables	11%	13%	11%	11%	14%
Not Sure	6%	4%	10%	9%	4%

■ Literal Word   ▨ Inspired Word   ■ Book of Fables   ▨ Not Sure

Source: *The Role of the Bible in American Society.* By George Gallup, Jr., and Sarah Jones. Published by The Princeton Religion Research Center. Used by permission.

FREQUENCY OF BIBLE READING
by sex, age, region, education, income, religion

	Daily	Weekly	Monthly	Less than Monthly	Never
National	17%	23%	13%	25%	20%
Sex					
Male	13	21	15	25	25
Female	20	25	13	25	16
Age					
18–29 years	10	22	12	30	26
30–49 years	14	21	18	28	19
50 & older	25	27	9	17	19
Region					
East	14	16	12	24	33
Midwest	16	22	17	27	16
South	25	30	12	19	12
West	9	24	12	32	22
Education					
College graduates	15	22	14	27	18
College incomplete	17	26	10	28	19
High school grads.	16	21	15	24	23
Not H.S. grads	19	28	13	21	17
Income					
$50,000 & over	13	20	15	25	24
$30,000–$49,999	14	23	11	29	22
$20,000–29,999	17	25	14	20	24
Under $20,000	0	26	15	22	15
Religion					
Protestant	24	28	12	24	11
Catholic	7	16	18	27	30
None	4	7	8	31	42

Source: *The Role of the Bible in American Society,* by George Gallup, Jr., and Robert Begilla. Published by The Princeton Religion Research Center. Used by permission. Poll taken November 1990.

PEOPLE BELIEVE THE BIBLE BEST CURE FOR DEPRESSION

Eight in ten Americans (81%) report bouts with depression, which best-selling psychiatrist M. Scott Peck says often accompanies mental and spiritual growth needed to adapt successfully to life events.

While most turn to a hobby, television, reading, or music to overcome depression, spiritual activities—prayer, meditation, and Bible reading—are cited as the most effective means for dealing with depressive disorders.

Money and bills, job, family and health problems are most often causes of depression or discouragement, followed by general frustrations, problems with children, the state of the economy, world affairs, and one's social life.

Please tell me whether you frequently or occasionally do the following when you feel discouraged or depressed. (Based on the 81% who are ever depressed or discouraged.)

A—Percentage of those frequently or occasionally engaging in these activities
B—Percentage of those engaging in these activities who find them very or somewhat effective

	A	B
Spend more time alone, with a hobby, TV, reading, or listening to music	77	84
Seek out friends to talk with	68	90

	A	B
Seek out family members to talk with	66	88
Eat more/less	64	31
Spend more time in prayer, meditation or reading the Bible	48	94
Spend more time exercising	40	92
Shop more, spend money	31	47
Spend more hours at work	29	77
Seek out pastor, religious leader	27	87
Spend more time sleeping	26	59
Seek help from a doctor or professional counselor	14	71
Drink more alcohol	10	37
Rely more heavily on medication	6	58

Gallup Survey for the Christian Broadcasting Network, Inc. Taken from *100 Questions and Answers*. Published by Princeton Religion Research Center. Copyright © 1989 by George Gallup, Jr., and Sarah Jones. Used by permission.

❝ ❞ God walks in the Holy Scriptures, seeking men. —St. Ambrose

FOCUS
QUOTE

THE BIBLE TALKS ABOUT LIFE, RELATIONSHIPS, THE FUTURE

The Bible Talks about Life

Let him have all your worries and cares, for he is always thinking about you and watching everything that concerns you. *1 Peter 5:7*

AGITATION

"I am leaving you with a gift—peace of mind and heart! And the peace I give isn't fragile like the peace the world gives. So don't be troubled or afraid." *John 14:27*

Don't worry about anything; instead, pray about everything; tell God your needs and don't forget to thank him for his answers. If you do this you will experience God's peace, which is far more wonderful than the human mind can understand. His peace will keep your thoughts and hearts quiet and at rest as you trust in Christ Jesus. *Philippians 4:6, 7*

ANGER

If you are angry, don't sin by nursing your grudge. Don't let the sun go down with you still angry—get over it quickly; for when you are angry you give a mighty foothold to the devil. *Ephesians 4:26, 27*

Dear brothers, don't ever forget that it is best to listen much, speak little, and not become angry; for anger doesn't make us good, as God demands that we must be. *James 1:19, 20*

DEPRESSION

I waited patiently for God to help me; then he listened and heard my cry. He lifted me out of the pit of despair, out from the bog and the mire, and set my feet on a hard, firm path and steadied me as I walked along. He has given me a new song to sing, of praises to our God. *Psalm 40:1-3*

Yes, the Lord hears the good man when he calls to him for help, and saves him out of all his troubles. . . . The good man does not escape all troubles—he has them too. But the Lord helps him in each and every one. *Psalm 34:17, 19*

DISCOURAGEMENT

"Let not your heart be troubled. You are trusting God, now trust in me. There are many homes up there where my Father lives, and I am going to prepare them for your coming. When everything is ready, then I will come and get you, so that you can always be with me where I am." *John 14:1-3*

Be strong! Be courageous! Do not be afraid of them! For the Lord your God will be with you. He will neither fail you nor forsake you. *Deuteronomy 31:6*

ETERNAL LIFE

Jesus told her, "I am the one who raises the dead and gives them life again. Anyone who believes in me, even though he died like anyone else, shall live again. He is given eternal life for believing in me and shall never perish. Do you believes this, Martha?" *John 11:25, 26*

For we know that when this tent we live in now is taken down—when we die and leave these bodies—we will have wonderful new bodies in heaven, homes that will be ours forevermore, made for us by God himself, and not by human hands. How weary we grow of our present bodies. . . . We want to slip into our new bodies so that these dying bodies will, as it were, be swallowed up by everlasting life. This is what God has prepared for us and, as a guarantee, he has given us his Holy Spirit. *2 Corinthians 5:1, 2, 4, 5*

Yet what we suffer now is nothing compared to the glory he will give us later. *Romans 8:18*

FEAR

Fear not, for I am with you. Do not be dismayed. I am your God. I will strengthen you; I will help you; I will uphold you with my victorious right hand. *Isaiah 41:10*

He does not fear bad news, nor live in dread of what may happen. For he is settled in his mind that Jehovah will take care of him. That is why he is not afraid, but can calmly face his foes. *Psalm 112:7, 8*

You are my hiding place from every storm of life; you even keep me from getting into trouble! You surround me with songs of victory. *Psalm 32:7*

FRUSTRATION

You need to keep on patiently doing God's will if you want him to do for you all that he has promised. *Hebrews 10:36*

He will keep in perfect peace all those who trust in him, whose thoughts turn often to the Lord! Trust in the Lord God always,

for in the Lord Jehovah is your everlasting strength. *Isaiah 26:3, 4*

GUILT

But if we confess our sins to him, he can be depended on to forgive us and to cleanse us from every wrong. [And it is perfectly proper for God to do this for us because Christ died to wash away our sins.] *1 John 1:9*

I've blotted out your sins; they are gone like morning mist at noon! Oh, return to me, for I have paid the price to set you free. *Isaiah 44:22*

Come, let's talk this over! says the Lord; no matter how deep the stain of your sins, I can take it out and make you as clean as freshly fallen snow. Even if you are stained as red as crimson, I can make you white as wool. *Isaiah 1:18*

So overflowing is his kindness towards us that he took away all our sins through the blood of his Son, by whom we are saved. *Ephesians 1:7*

And I will be merciful to them in their wrongdoings, and I will remember their sins no more. *Hebrews 8:12*

IMPATIENCE

Rest in the Lord: wait patiently for him to act. Don't be envious of evil men who prosper. *Psalm 37:7*

Now as for you, dear brothers who are waiting for the Lord's return, be patient, like a farmer who waits until the autumn for his precious harvest to ripen. Yes, be patient. And take courage, for the coming of the Lord is near. *James 5:7, 8*

INSECURITY

What can we ever say to such wonderful things as these? If God is on our side, who can ever be against us? Since he did not spare even his own Son for us but gave him up for us all, won't he also surely give us everything else? *Romans 8:31, 32*

I am holding you by your right hand—I, the Lord your God—and I say to you, Don't be afraid; I am here to help you. *Isaiah 41:13*

That is why we can say without any doubt or fear, "The Lord is my Helper and I am not

THE BIBLE TALKS ABOUT LIFE, RELATIONSHIPS, THE FUTURE cont.

afraid of anything that mere man can do to me." *Hebrews 13:6*

INSULT

"Happy are those who are persecuted because they are good, for the Kingdom of Heaven is theirs. When you are reviled and persecuted and lied about because you are my followers—wonderful! Be happy about it! Be very glad! for a tremendous reward awaits you up in heaven. And remember, the ancient prophets were persecuted too. . . . But I say: Love your enemies! Pray for those who persecute you! In that way you will be acting as true sons of your Father in heaven. For he gives his sunlight to both the evil and the good, and sends rain on the just and on the unjust too." *Matthew 5:10-12, 44, 45*

JEALOUSY

And by all means don't brag about being wise and good if you are bitter and jealous and selfish; that is the worst sort of lie. For jealousy and selfishness are not God's kind of wisdom. Such things are earthly, unspiritual, inspired by the devil. For wherever there is jealousy or selfish ambition, there will be disorder and every other kind of evil. *James 3:14-16*

So do not be dismayed when evil men grow rich and build their lovely homes. For when they die they carry nothing with them! Their honors will not follow them. *Psalm 49:16, 17*

LONELINESS

I will lie down in peace and sleep, for though I am alone, O Lord, you will keep me safe. *Psalm 4:8*

For the mountains may depart and the hills disappear, but my kindness shall not leave you. My promise of peace for you will never be broken, says the Lord who has mercy upon you. *Isaiah 54:10*

"No, I will not abandon you or leave you as orphans in the storm—I will come to you." *John 14:18*

LOW SELF-ESTEEM

So God made man like his Maker. Like God did God make man; man and maid did

he make them. *Genesis 1:27*

"The second is: 'You must love others as much as yourself.' No other commandments are greater than these." *Mark 12:31*

As God's messenger I give each of you God's warning: Be honest in your estimate of yourselves, measuring your value by how much faith God has given you. Just as there are many parts to our bodies, so it is with Christ's body. We are all parts of it, and it takes every one of us to make it complete, for we each have different work to do. So we belong to each other, and each needs all the others. *Romans 12:3-5*

PAIN

"Father, Father," he said, "everything is possible for you. Take away this cup from me. Yet I want your will, not mine." *Mark 14:36*

These troubles and sufferings of ours are, after all, quite small and won't last very long. Yet this short time of distress will result in God's richest blessing upon us forever and ever! . . . I was given a physical condition which has been a thorn in my flesh, a messenger from Satan to hurt and bother me, and prick my pride. Three different times I begged God to make me well again. Each time he said, "No. But I am with you; that is all you need. My power shows up best in weak people." Now I am glad to boast about how weak I am; I am glad to be a living demonstration of Christ's power. Since I know it is all for Christ's good, I am quite happy about "the thorn," and about insults and hardships, persecutions and difficulties; for when I am weak, then I am strong—the less I have, the more I depend on him. *2 Corinthians 4:17; 12:7-10*

SICKNESS

Is anyone sick? He should call for the elders of the church and they should pray over him and pour a little oil upon him, calling on the Lord to heal him. And their prayer, if offered in faith, will heal him, for the Lord will make him well; and if his sickness was caused by some sin, the Lord will forgive him. *James 5:14, 15*

He nurses them when they are sick and soothes their pains and worries. *Psalm 41:3*

SUFFERING AND DEATH

And now, dear brothers, I want you to know what happens to a Christian when he dies so that when it happens, you will not be full of sorrow, as those are who have no hope. For since we believe that Jesus died and then came back to life again, we can also believe that when Jesus returns, God will bring back with him all the Christians who have died. *1 Thessalonians 4:13, 14*

The Lord is close to those whose hearts are breaking. *Psalm 34:18a*

But I am telling you this strange and wonderful secret: we shall not all die, but we shall all be given new bodies! It will all happen in a moment, in the twinkling of an eye, when the last trumpet is blown. For there will be a trumpet blast from the sky and all the Christians who have died will suddenly become alive, with new bodies that will never, never die; and then we who are still alive shall suddenly have new bodies too. For our earthly bodies, the ones we have now that can die, must be transformed into heavenly bodies that cannot perish but will live forever. When this happens, then at last this Scripture will come true— "Death is swallowed up in victory." O death, where then your victory? Where then your sting? *1 Corinthians 15:51-55*

TEMPTATION

But remember this—the wrong desires that come into your life aren't anything new and different. Many others have faced exactly the same problems before you. And no temptation is irresistible. You can trust God to keep the temptation from becoming so strong that you can't stand up against it, for he has promised this and will do what he says. He will show you how to escape temptation's power so that you can bear up patiently against it. *1 Corinthians 10:13*

Happy is the man who doesn't give in and do wrong when he is tempted, for afterwards he will get as his reward the crown of life that God has promised those who love him. And remember, when someone wants to do

wrong it is never God who is tempting him, for God never wants to do wrong and never tempts anyone else to do it. . . . So give yourselves humbly to God. Resist the devil and he will flee from you. *James 1:12, 13; 4:7*

For since he himself has now been through suffering and temptation, he knows what it is like when we suffer and are tempted, and he is wonderfully able to help us. *Hebrews 2:18*

WEARINESS

But they that wait upon the Lord shall renew their strength. They shall mount up with wings like eagles; they shall run and not be weary; they shall walk and not faint. *Isaiah 40:31*

"Come to me and I will give you rest—all of you who work so hard beneath a heavy yoke. Wear my yoke—for it fits perfectly—and let me teach you; for I am gentle and humble, and you shall find rest for your souls; for I give you only light burdens." *Matthew 11:28-30*

WORRY

He will keep in perfect peace all those who trust in him, whose thoughts turn often to the Lord! Trust in the Lord God always, for in the Lord Jehovah is your everlasting strength. *Isaiah 26:3, 4*

Let him have all your worries and cares, for he is always thinking about you and watching everything that concerns you. *1 Peter 5:7*

Then turning to his disciples he said, "Don't worry about whether you have enough food to eat or clothes to wear. For life consists of far more than food and clothes. And besides, what's the use of worrying? What good does it do? Will it add a single day to your life? Of course not! And if worry can't even do such little things as that, what's the use of worrying over bigger things? Look at the lilies! They don't toil and spin, and yet Solomon in all his glory was not robed as well as they are. And if God provides clothing for the flowers that are here today and gone tomorrow, don't you suppose that he will provide clothing for you, you doubters?" *Luke 12:22-28*

THE BIBLE TALKS ABOUT LIFE, RELATIONSHIPS, THE FUTURE cont.

The Bible Talks about Relationships

There are "friends" who pretend to be friends, but there is a friend who sticks closer than a brother. *Proverbs 18:24*

FRIENDS

Be with wise men and become wise. Be with evil men and become evil. *Proverbs 13:20*

Don't be selfish; don't live to make a good impression on others. Be humble, thinking of others as better than yourself. Don't just think about your own affairs, but be interested in others, too, and in what they are doing. *Philippians 2:3, 4*

INJUSTICE

Do what is right; then if men speak against you, calling you evil names, they will become ashamed of themselves for falsely accusing you when you have only done what is good. Remember, if God wants you to suffer, it is better to suffer for doing good than for doing wrong! Christ also suffered. He died once for the sins of all us guilty sinners, although he himself was innocent of any sin at any time, that he might bring us safely home to God. *1 Peter 3:16-18*

After you have suffered a little while, our God, who is full of kindness through Christ, will give you his eternal glory. He personally will come and pick you up, and set you firmly in place, and make you stronger than ever. To him be all power over all things forever and ever. Amen. *1 Peter 5:10, 11*

LOVE

"I have loved you even as the Father has loved me. Live within my love. When you obey me you are living in my love, just as I obey my Father and live in his love. I have told you this so that you will be filled with my joy. Yes, your cup of joy will overflow! I demand that you love each other as much as I love you. And here is how to measure it—the greatest love is shown when a person lays down his life for his friends; and you are my friends if you obey me. I no longer call you slaves, for a master doesn't confide in his slaves; now you are my friends, proved by the fact that I have told you everything the Father told me. You didn't choose me! I chose you! I appointed you to go and produce lovely fruit always, so that no matter what you ask for from the Father, using my name, he will give it to you." *John 15:9-16*

"For God loved the world so much that he gave his only Son so that anyone who believes in him shall not perish but have eternal life." *John 3:16*

God showed how much he loved us by sending his only Son into this wicked world to bring to us eternal life through his death. In this act we see what real love is: it is not our love for God, but his love for us when he sent his Son to satisfy God's anger against our sins. . . . We know how much God loves us because we have felt his love and because we believe him when he tells us that he loves us dearly. God is love, and anyone who lives in love is living with God and God is living in him. And as we live with Christ, our love grows more perfect and complete; so we will not be ashamed and embarrassed at the day of judgment, but can face him with confidence and joy, because he loves us and we love him too. . . . If anyone says "I love God," but keeps on hating his brother, he is a liar; for if he doesn't love his brother who is right there in front of him, how can he love God whom he has never seen? And God himself has said that one must love not only God, but his brother too. *1 John 4:9-21*

Love is very patient and kind, never jealous or envious, never boastful or proud, never haughty or selfish or rude. Love does not demand its own way. It is not irritable or touchy. It does not hold grudges and will hardly even notice when others do it wrong. It is never glad about injustice, but rejoices whenever truth wins out. If you love someone you will be loyal to him no matter what the cost. You will always believe in him, always expect the best of him, and always stand your ground in defending him. . . . There are three things that remain—faith, hope, and love—and the greatest of these is love. *1 Corinthians 13:4-7, 13*

MARRIAGE

Honor Christ by submitting to each other. You wives must submit to your husbands' leadership in the same way you submit to the Lord. . . . And you husbands, show the same kind of love to your wives as Christ showed to the Church when he died for her, to make her holy and clean, washed by baptism and God's Word; so that he could give her to himself as a glorious Church without a single spot or wrinkle or any other blemish, being holy and without a single fault. That is how husbands should treat their wives, loving them as parts of themselves. For since a man and his wife are now one, a man is really doing himself a favor and loving himself when he loves his wife. *Ephesians 5:21, 22, 25-28*

Wives, fit in with your husbands' plans; for then if they refuse to listen when you talk to them about the Lord, they will be won by your respectful, pure behavior. Your godly lives will speak to them better than any words. Don't be concerned about the outward beauty that depends on jewelry, or beautiful clothes, or hair arrangement. Be beautiful inside, in your hearts, with the lasting charm of a gentle and quiet spirit that is so precious to God. That kind of deep beauty was seen in the saintly women of old, who trusted God and fitted in with their husbands' plans. Sarah, for instance, obeyed her husband Abraham, honoring him as head of the house. And if you do the same, you will be following in her steps like good daughters and doing what is right; then you will not need to fear [offending your husbands]. You husbands must be careful of your wives, being thoughtful of their needs and honoring them as the weaker sex. Remember that you and your wife are partners in receiving God's blessings, and if you don't treat her as you should, your prayers will not get ready answers. *1 Peter 3:1-7*

A man should leave his father and mother, and be forever united to his wife. The two shall become one—no longer two, but one! And no man may divorce what God has joined together. Anyone who divorces his wife, except for fornication, and marries an-other, commits adultery. *Matthew 19:5, 9*

When a man divorces his wife to marry someone else, he commits adultery against her. And if a wife divorces her husband and remarries, she, too, commits adultery. *Mark 10:11, 12*

PARENTS AND CHILDREN

Children, obey your parents; this is the right thing to do because God has placed them in authority over you. Honor your father and mother. This is the first of God's Ten Commandments that ends with a promise. And this is the promise: that if you honor your father and mother, yours will be a long life, full of blessing. And now a word to you parents. Don't keep on scolding and nagging your children, making them angry and resentful. Rather, bring them up with the loving discipline the Lord himself approves, with suggestions and godly advice. *Ephesians 6:1-4*

The Bible Talks about the Future

Your words are a flashlight to light the path ahead of me and keep me from stumbling. *Psalm 119:105*

ASTROLOGY, HOROSCOPES, AND THE OCCULT

So why are you trying to find out the future by consulting witches and mediums? Don't listen to their whisperings and mutterings. Can the living find out the future from the dead? Why not ask your God? *Isaiah 8:19*

Call out the demon hordes you've worshiped all these years. Call on them to help you strike deep terror into many hearts again. You have advisors by the ton—your astrologers and stargazers, who try to tell you what the future holds. But they are as useless as dried grass burning in the fire. They cannot even deliver themselves! You'll get no help from them at all. Theirs is no fire to sit beside to make you warm! *Isaiah 47:12-14*

DIRECTION FOR LIFE

I will bless the Lord who counsels me; he gives me wisdom in the night. He tells me what to do. I am always thinking of the Lord; and because he is so near, I never need to stumble or to fall. *Psalm 16:7, 8*

THE BIBLE TALKS ABOUT LIFE, RELATIONSHIPS, THE FUTURE cont.

And if you leave God's paths and go astray, you will hear a Voice behind you say, "No, this is the way; walk here." *Isaiah 30:21*

He will teach the ways that are right and best to those who humbly turn to him. And when we obey him, every path he guides us on is fragrant with his lovingkindness and his truth. *Psalm 25:9, 10*

And remember, it is a message to obey, not just to listen to. So don't fool yourselves. For if a person just listens and doesn't obey, he is like a man looking at his face in a mirror; as soon as he walks away, he can't see himself any more or remember what he looks like. But if anyone keeps looking steadily into God's law for free men, he will not only remember it but he will do what it says, and God will greatly bless him in everything he does. *James 1:22-25*

MONEY MANAGEMENT

And it is he who will supply all your needs from his riches in glory, because of what Christ Jesus has done for us. *Philippians 4:19*

He who loves money shall never have enough. The foolishness of thinking that wealth brings happiness! *Ecclesiastes 5:10*

Do you want to be truly rich? You already are if you are happy and good. After all, we didn't bring any money with us when we came into the world, and we can't carry away a single penny when we die. So we should be well satisfied without money if we have enough food and clothing. But people who long to be rich soon begin to do all kinds of wrong things to get money, things that hurt them and make them evil-minded and finally send them to hell itself. For the love of money is the first step toward all kinds of sin. Some people have even turned away from God because of their love for it, and as a result have pierced themselves with many sorrows. *1 Timothy 6:6-10*

TRUST

Trust the Lord completely; don't ever trust yourself. In everything you do, put God first, and he will direct you and crown your efforts with success. *Proverbs 3:5, 6*

I know how to live on almost nothing or with everything. I have learned the secret of contentment in every situation, whether it be a full stomach or hunger, plenty or want; for I can do everything God asks me to with the help of Christ who gives me the strength and power. *Philippians 4:12, 13*

The Bible Talks about Faith

Faith comes from listening to this Good News—the Good News about Christ. *Romans 10:17*

BEING BORN AGAIN

Jesus replied, "With all the earnestness I possess I tell you this: Unless you are born again, you can never get into the Kingdom of God. . . . What I am telling you so earnestly is this: Unless one is born of water and the Spirit, he cannot enter the Kingdom of God. Men can only reproduce human life, but the Holy Spirit gives new life from heaven; so don't be surprised at my statement that you must be born again." *John 3:3, 5-7*

All honor to God, the God and Father of our Lord Jesus Christ; for it is his boundless mercy that has given us the privilege of being born again, so that we are now members of God's own family. *1 Peter 1:3*

The person who has been born into God's family does not make a practice of sinning, because now God's life is in him; so he can't keep on sinning, for this new life has been born into him and controls him—he has been *born again. 1 John 3:9*

FINDING GOD

"His purpose in all of this is that they should seek after God, and perhaps feel their way toward him and find him—though he is not far from any one of us. For in him we live and move and are! As one of your own poets says it, 'We are the sons of God.'" *Acts 17:27, 28*

For I know the plans I have for you, says the Lord. They are plans for good and not for evil, to give you a future and a hope. In those days when you pray, I will listen. You will find me when you seek me, if you look for me in earnest. *Jeremiah 29:11-13*

KNOWING GOD

How can we describe God? With what can we compare him? With an idol? . . . It is God who sits above the circle of the earth. (The people below must seem to him like grasshoppers!) He is the one who stretches out the heavens like a curtain and makes his tent from them. He dooms the great men of the world and brings them all to naught. They hardly get started, barely take root, when he blows on them and their work withers and the wind carries them off like straw. "With whom will you compare me? Who is my equal?" asks the Holy One. Look up into the heavens! Who created all these stars? As a shepherd leads his sheep, calling each by its pet name, and counts them to see that none are lost or strayed, so God does with stars and planets! *Isaiah 40:18, 22-26*

Dear friends, let us practice loving each other, for love comes from God and those who are loving and kind show that they are getting to know him better. But if a person isn't loving and kind, it shows that he doesn't know God—for God is love. *1 John 4:7, 8*

KNOWING JESUS CHRIST

Before anything else existed, there was Christ, with God. He has always been alive and is himself God. He created everything there is—nothing exists that he didn't make. Eternal life is in him, and this life gives light to all mankind. His life is the light that shines through the darkness—and the darkness can never extinguish it. God sent John the Baptist as a witness to the fact that Jesus Christ is the true Light. John himself was not the Light; he was only a witness to identify it. Later on, the one who is the true Light arrived to shine on everyone coming into the world. But although he made the world, the world didn't recognize him when he came. Even in his

own land and among his own people, the Jews, he was not accepted. Only a few would welcome and receive him. But to all who received him he gave the right to become children of God. All they needed to do was to trust him to save them. All those who believe this are reborn!—not a physical rebirth resulting from human passion or plan—but from the will of God. And Christ became a human being and lived here on earth among us and was full of loving forgiveness and truth. And some of us have seen his glory—the glory of the only Son of the heavenly Father! *John 1:1-14*

Christ is the exact likeness of the unseen God. He existed before God made anything at all, and, in fact, Christ himself is the Creator who made everything in heaven and earth, the things we can see and the things we can't; the spirit world with its kings and kingdoms, its rulers and authorities; all were made by Christ for his own use and glory. He was before all else began and it is his power that holds everything together. He is the Head of the body made up of his people—that is, his Church—which he began; and he is the Leader of all those who arise from the dead, so that he is first in everything; for God wanted all of himself to be in his Son. . . . You were dead in sins, and your sinful desires were not yet cut away. Then he gave you a share in the very life of Christ, for he forgave all your sins, and blotted out the charges proved against you, the list of his commandments which you had not obeyed. He took this list of sins and destroyed it by nailing it to Christ's cross. *Colossians 1:15-19; 2:13, 14*

God's Son shines out with God's glory, and all that God's Son is and does marks him as God. He regulates the universe by the mighty power of his command. He is the one who died to cleanse us and clear our record of all sin, and then sat down in highest honor

66 99 The Bible is meant to be bread for our daily use; not just cake for special occasions.
FOCUS QUOTE

THE BIBLE TALKS ABOUT LIFE, RELATIONSHIPS, THE FUTURE cont.

beside the great God of heaven.... but of his Son he says, "Your kingdom, O God, will last forever and ever; its commands are always just and right." *Hebrews 1:3, 8*

KNOWING THE HOLY SPIRIT

He has put his brand upon us—his mark of ownership—and given us his Holy Spirit in our hearts as guarantee that we belong to him and as the first installment of all that he is going to give us. *2 Corinthians 1:22*

But you are not like that. You are controlled by your new nature if you have the Spirit of God living in you. (And remember that if anyone doesn't have the Spirit of Christ living in him, he is not a Christian at all.) Yet, even though Christ lives within you, your body will die because of sin; but your spirit will live, for Christ has pardoned it. And if the Spirit of God, who raised up Jesus from the dead, lives in you, he will make your dying bodies live again after you die, by means of this same Holy Spirit living within you. *Romans 8:9-11*

"If you love me, obey me; and I will ask the Father and he will give you another Comforter, and he will never leave you. He is the Holy Spirit, the Spirit who leads into all truth. The world at large cannot receive him, for it isn't looking for him and doesn't recognize him. But you do, for he lives with you now and some day shall be in you.... But when the Father sends the Comforter instead of me—and by the Comforter I mean the Holy Spirit—he will teach you much, as well as remind you of everything I myself have told you." *John 14:15-17, 26*

PRAYER

Admit your faults to one another and pray for each other so that you may be healed. The earnest prayer of a righteous man has great power and wonderful results. *James 5:16*

"But if you stay in me and obey my commands, you may ask any request you like, and it will be granted!" *John 15:7*

"Ask, and you will be given what you ask for. Seek, and you will find. Knock, and the door will be opened. For everyone who asks, receives. Anyone who seeks, finds. If only you will knock, the door will open." *Matthew 7:7, 8*

If we confess our sins to him, he can be depended on to forgive us and to cleanse us from every wrong. *1 John 1:9*

HOW MUCH TIME TO READ THE BIBLE?

How much time does it take to read from Genesis to Revelation? If you would read the Bible at standard pulpit speed (slow enough to be heard and understood), the reading time would be seventy-eight hours. If you would break that down into minutes and divide it into 365 days, you could read the entire Bible, cover to cover, in only twelve minutes a day. Is this really too much time to spend reading about God?

❝❞ FOCUS QUOTE A Bible that's falling apart probably belongs to someone who isn't. Christian Johnson

---

❝❞ FOCUS QUOTE Trying to absorb the depths of the Bible is like trying to mop up the ocean floor with a sponge.

 FOCUS BOOK *Thirty Days to Understanding the Bible* by Max E. Anders. Helpful overview that covers major people, events, and geography in just 15 minutes a day. Published by Wolgemuth & Hyatt.

BIBLE READING GUIDES

These guides are designed so you can cut out the reading guide you prefer
and place in your Bible for ready reference.

Topically

God's Power
Jan 1 Ex 7:14-24
2 Ex 8:1-19
3 Jb 9:1-12
4 Ps 66:1-7
5 Is 44:18-28
6 Jer 10:12-16
7 Ez 17:11-24

Sustainer
8 Hb 3:1-15
9 Gn 45:4-15
10 1 Kgs 17:1-16
11 1 Kgs 19:1-8
12 Ez 34:11-16, 25-31
13 Mt 6:25-34
14 Acts 17:22-28

Master of All
15 Col 1:15-19
16 Dt 2:16-25
17 1 Sm 2:1-10
18 Jb 12:13-25
19 Jb 26
20 Jb 37
21 Is 41:1-10

Our Victory
22 Mt 8
23 Dt 7:17-26
24 Dt 20:1-4
25 Ps 27
26 Ps 28
27 Is 33:13-22
28 Is 41:8-16

Our Deliverer
29 1 Cor 15:51-58
30 Jgs 6:11-18
31 2 Chr 20:5-17
Feb 1 Ps 40:1-5
2 Is 11:10-16
3 Is 51:1-11
4 Acts 12:1-17

Accessible
5 Acts 16:25-40
6 Is 55:1-9
7 Mt 28:16-20
8 Lk 11:5-13
9 Eph 2:11-22
10 Heb 4:12-16
11 Heb 10:11-25

Our Conqueror
12 Jas 5:13-18
13 Is 31:1-5
14 Is 49:22-26
15 Jer 51:27-33
16 Na 1:7-15
17 Na 2
18 Zec 9:9-17

**Our Help in
Spiritual Warfare**
19 Rom 7:13-25
20 Ps 18:31-50
21 Rom 6:15-23
22 Rom 8:26-39
23 2 Cor 10:1-12
24 Eph 6:10-20
25 2 Tm 1:3-14

Redeems Israel
26 2 Tm 2:1-19
27 Is 43:14-21
28 Is 49:-7
Mar 1 Is 60:5-22
2 Jl 3:9-21
3 Am 9:5-15
4 Zep 3:6-13

Reconciles
5 Zec 12:1–3:1
6 Jb 33:19-33
7 Hos 2:14-23
8 Zec 13
9 Gal 3:23-4:7
10 Col 1:21-29
11 Heb 9:11-22
12 Heb 9:11-22

Restores
13 Ez 37:15-28
14 Hos 14
15 Jl 2:18-32
16 Zep 3:9-20
17 Zec 8
18 Lk 15:11-24
19 Acts 26:1-23

**Our Response in
Humility**
20 Ps 131
21 Mk 9:33-37; 10:13-16
22 Lk 18:9-14
23 Rom 12:3-13
24 1 Cor 1:18-31

25 Phil 3:1-11
26 1 Pt 5:1-11

God's Love
27 Ps 107:1-3, 17-22
28 Ps 136:1-3, 23-26
29 Mt 18:10-14
30 Jn 10:1-18
31 Jn 12:20-36
Apr 1 Rom 5:1-11
2 Eph 4:25-5:2

Our Substitute
3 Ps 22
4 Is 53
5 Rom 15:1-13
6 2 Cor 5:11-21
7 Gal 3:10-14
8 Heb 2:9-18
9 1 Pt 2:18-25

Our Salvation
10 Is 12:1-6
11 Is 61
12 Lk 15:1-10
13 Lk 19:1-10
14 Acts 4:1-12
15 Acts 28:2-31
16 Eph 1:3-14

**Blessings in Path
of Life**
17 Dt 7:6-11
18 Ps 18:20-24
19 Ps 19:7-14
20 Ps 92:5-15
21 Is 26:7-15
22 Is 58:6-14
23 Mal 3:6-12

Eternal Life
24 Ps 23
25 Jn 6:25-40
26 Jn 6:50-69
27 Jn 17:1-5
28 1 Thes 4:13-18
29 1 Jn 5:6-12
30 Rv 22

Kingdom of God
May1 Ps 145
2 Mt 18:21-35
3 Mt 20:1-16
4 Mt 25:1-13

5 Mt 25:14-30
6 Mk 4:1-20
7 Lk 14:16-24

Great Hope
8 Ps 16
9 Ps 130
10 Jer 17:5-18
11 Jn 14:1-7
12 1 Cor 15:12-28
13 Heb 6:9-20
14 1 Pt 1:3-12

God's Sovereignty
15 Jb 36:22-33
16 Ps 47
17 Is 60:1-9
18 Jer 27
19 Jer 51:15-24
20 Dn 4:10-37
21 Rv 19:5-16

God's Uniqueness
22 Dt 10:12-22
23 Dt 32:34-43
24 Ps 148
25 Is 40:12-26
26 Is 44:1-8
27 Is 45:14-25
28 Jer 10:1-10

A Jealous God
29 Ex 20:1-7
30 Ex 34:11-17
31 Dt 4:15-24
Jun 1 Dt 29:16-29
2 Is 31
3 Ez 23:22-35
4 Mt 10:34-42

**Penitence
Required**
5 Ps 52
6 Ez 18:21-32
7 Dn 9:3-19
8 Hos 14
9 Mt 3:7-10
10 Lk 13:1-9
11 Acts 2:22-42

God's Patience
12 Ps 86
13 Ps 103:6-14
14 Is 30:15-26

15 Jer 15:15-21
16 Jl 2:12-19
17 Rom 2:1-11
18 2 Pt 3:8-18

Source of Rest
19 Ps 4
20 Ps 116
21 Prv 3:21-27
22 Is 28:5-13
23 Mt 11:25-30
24 2 Thes 1:5-12
25 Heb 4:1-11

God of Mercy
26 Nm 21:4-9
27 Dt 4:25-31
28 Jer 31:15-20
29 Jon 4
30 Rom 9:14-26
Jul 1 Rom 11:17-32
2 1 Tm 1:12-17

God of Grace
3 Is 54
4 Mi 7:8-20
5 Acts 11:1-18
6 Rom 3:21-26
7 Rom 5:12-21
8 Eph 1:3-14
9 Ti 2:11-14

Eternal God
10 Gn 21:25-34
11 Ex 3:7-17
12 Ps 102:23-28
13 Is 48:9-13
14 1 Tm 6:11-16
15 Heb 1:1-12
16 Rv 1:4-8, 12-18

Wise God
17 Jb 28:12-28
18 Ps 104:24-35
19 Prv 120:33
20 Prv 3:13-26
21 Prv 8:22-36
22 Dn 2:17-23
23 1 Cor 2:6-16

God of Great Glory
24 Ex 24:9-18
25 1 Kgs 8:1-13
26 Ps 24:1-11
27 Is 30:29-33
28 Ez 1:15-28
29 Rv 4
30 Rv 15

Worthy of Worship
31 Dt 6:4-17
Aug 1 1 Chron. 16:7-36
2 Ps 135
3 Ps 149
4 Ps 150
5 Lk 4:1-13

6 Jn 4:5-24

Our Love for God
7 Dt 30:1-10
8 Ps 31:19-24
9 Ps 63:1-8
10 Mk 12:28-34
11 Lk 7:36-50
12 1 Jn 5:1-5
13 Rv 2:1-7

Our Love for Mankind
14 Mt 25:31-46
15 Lk 10:25-37
16 Jn 15:12-15
17 Rom 12:9-21
18 1 Cor 8
19 1 Cor 13
20 1 Jn 4:7-21

Love Shown in Obedience
21 Lv 26:3-13
22 Jos 22:1-6
23 Is 56:1-8
24 Jn 14:12-24
25 Jn 15:1-11
26 Rom 13:1-4
27 2 Cor 6:14–7:1

God's Forgiveness
28 Ps 32:1-7
29 Ps 130
30 Jer 31:23-34
31 Jer 33:1-11
Sep 1 Ez 36:22-36
2 Mi 7:9-2
3 Col 2:8-15

God's Fatherhood
4 Ps 68:1-10
5 Jer 3:19-25
6 Hos 11
7 Mt 7:7-12
8 Jn 5:19-29
9 Gal 4:1-7
10 Heb 12:1-11

God's Faithfulness
11 Gn 7:1-5; 8:1-22
12 Gn 45:1-8
13 Neh 9:5-15
14 Ps 147:7-20
15 Is 49:5-13
16 Lk 12:22-34
17 Jn 14:15-31

God's Protection
18 Ex 15:1-13
19 Ps 62:1-8
20 Ps 91
21 Is 43:1-7
22 Jn 17:15-26
23 Acts 23:16-30
24 2 Tm 4:16-22

Salvation Through Faith
25 Jn 3:14-18
26 Acts 13:26-39
27 Rom 1:8-17
28 Rom 4:1-15
29 Gal 3:21-29
30 Eph 2:1-10
Oct 1 Heb 7:15-25

Live by Faith
2 1 Sm 17:31-49
3 Ps 40:1-10
4 Prv 3:1-8
5 Rom 4:16-25
6 Gal 3:1-9
7 Heb 11:1-16
8 Heb 11:17-40

Result of Faith: Contentment
9 Ps 34:1-10
10 Ps 37:8-19
11 1 Cor 7:17-24
12 2 Cor 12:1-10
13 Phil 4:4-13
14 1 Tm 6:3-10
15 Heb 12:28–13:8

Result of Faith: Meekness
16 Mt 5:38-48
17 Eph 4:1-16
18 Col 3:12-17
19 1 Thes 5:12-22
20 2 Tm 2:20-26
21 Ti 3:1-11
22 Jas 3:13-18

Gives Us Joy
23 Ps 126
24 Is 12:1-6
25 Lk 6:17-23
26 2 Cor 6:1-10
27 Phil 4:1-4
28 Jas 1:1-8
29 1 Pt 1:3-9

Makes Us Patient
30 Ps 37:1-9
31 Lam 3:19-27
Nov 1 2 Cor 4:7-18
2 1 Thes 1
3 2 Tm 2:1-7
4 Jas 5:7-11
5 2 Pt 1:1-11

Fills Us with Thanksgiving
6 Ps 33:1-6, 18-22
7 Ps 71
8 Ps 136:1-3, 23-26
9 Ps 138
10 2 Cor 9:6-15
11 Phil 1:3-11
12 Col 2:1-7

Gives Us Courage
13 Jos 1:1-9
14 Dn 3:1-18
15 Jn 16:16-24
16 Acts 5:17-42
17 2 Cor 5:1-10
18 Phil 1:15-30
19 1 Pt 4:7-14

Motivates Us to Discipline
20 Ps 119:33-40
21 Mt 16:24-28
22 1 Cor 8:1-13
23 1 Cor 9:19-27
24 1 Cor 10:23-32
25 Phil 3:7-16
26 2 Thes 3:6-15

Call to Perseverance
27 Hos 12:2-9
28 Mt 24:3-14
29 2 Cor 4:7-18
30 Gal 6:1-10
Dec 1 1 Tm 6:11-21
2 2 Tm 4:1-18
3 Rv 3

Purity of Heart
4 Ps 82
5 Prv 2
6 Ez 18:1-9
7 Mi 6:1-8
8 Mal 3:13-38
9 Jas 4:1-10
10 1 Pt 3:1-7

The New Man
11 Ps 24:1-6
12 Ps 40:6-12
13 Is 1:10-20
14 Mal 3:1-5
15 Mt 5:27-42
16 1 Cor 10:1-15
17 1 Pt 1:13-25

Christlikeness
18 Ez 11:14-21
19 Jn 3:1-8, 19-21
20 Rom 8:1-8
21 Gal 5:16-23
22 Phil 3:17-21
23 Col 3:7-17
24 1 Pt 2:1-10
25 Ps 1
26 Jn 13:1-17
27 Rom 6:1-14
28 Rom 7:1-12
29 2 Cor 3:4-18
30 Eph 4:17-32
31 1 Jn 3

NAE © 1983

Source: National Association of Evangelicals. Used by permission.

Chronologically

Jan 1	Gn 1-5
2	Gn 6-11
3	Gn 12-16
4	Gn 17-22
5	Jb 1-7
6	Jb 8-14
7	Jb 15-18
8	Jb 19-24
9	Jb 25-31
10	Jb 32-37
11	Jb 38-42
12	Gn 23-28
13	Gn 29-33
14	Gn 34-38
15	Gn 39-45
16	Gn 46-50
17	Ex 1-5
18	Ex 6-10
19	Ex 11-14
20	Ex 15-19
21	Ex 20-25
22	Ex 26-31
23	Ex 32-36
24	Ex 37-40
25	Ps 90
26	Lv 1-6
27	Lv 7-12
28	Lv 13-17
29	Lv 18-23
30	Lv 24-27
31	Nm 1-6
Feb 1	Nm 7-11
2	Nm 12-16
3	Nm 17-21
4	Nm 22-26
5	Nm 27-31
6	Nm 32-36
7	Dt 1-4
8	Dt 5-9
9	Dt 10-15
10	Dt 16-22
11	Dt 23-28
12	Dt 29-34
13	Ps 91
14	Jos 1-6
15	Jos 7-12
16	Jos 13-18
17	Jos 19-24
18	Jgs 1-5
19	Jgs 6-12
20	Jgs 13-16
21	Jgs 17-21
22	Ruth 1-4
23	1 Sm 1:1-16:13
24	Ps 23
25	1 Sm 16:14-19:11
26	Ps 59
27	1 Sm 19:12-21:15
28	Ps 34, 56
Mar 1	1 Sm 22:1-2
2	Ps 57, 142
3	1 Sm 22:3-23
4	Ps 52
5	1 Sm 23:1-29
6	Ps 54, 63
7	1 Sm 24-31
8	2 Sm 1-7
9	Ps 30
10	2 Sm 8:1-14
11	Ps 60
12	2 Sm 8:15-12:14
13	Ps 51, 32
14	2 Sm 12:15-15:37
15	Ps 3, 69
16	2 Sm 16:1-20:26
17	Ps 64, 70
18	2 Sm 21:1-22:51
19	Ps 18
20	2 Sm 23-24
21	Ps 4
22	Ps 5
23	Ps 6
24	Ps 7
25	Ps 8
26	Ps 9
27	Ps 11
28	Ps 12
29	Ps 13
30	Ps 14
31	Ps 15
Apr 1	Ps 16
2	Ps 17
3	Ps 19
4	Ps 20
5	Ps 21
6	Ps 22
7	Ps 24
8	Ps 25
9	Ps 26
10	Ps 27
11	Ps 28
12	Ps 29
13	Ps 31
14	Ps 35
15	Ps 36
16	Ps 37
17	Ps 38
18	Ps 39
19	Ps 40
20	Ps 41
21	Ps 53
22	Ps 55
23	Ps 58
24	Ps 61
25	Ps 62
26	Ps 65
27	Ps 68
28	Ps 72
29	Ps 86
30	Ps 101
May 1	Ps 103
2	Ps 108
3	Ps 109
4	Ps 110
5	Ps 138
6	Ps 139
7	Ps 140
8	Ps 141
9	Ps 143
10	Ps 144
11	Ps 145
12	1 Kgs 1-4
13	Prv 1-5
14	Prv 6-10
15	Prv 11-15
16	Prv 16-20
17	Prv 21-26
18	Prv 27-31
19	Sg 1-4
20	Sg 5-8
21	1 Kgs 5-11
22	Eccl 1-4
23	Eccl 5-9
24	Eccl 10-12
25	1 Kgs 12-16
26	1 Kgs 17-22
27	2 Kgs 1-5
28	2 Kgs 6-10
29	2 Kgs 11-14:25
30	Jon 1-4
31	2 Kgs 14:26-29
Jun 1	Am 1-9
2	2 Kgs 15-20
3	2 Kgs 21-25
4	Ps 1
5	Ps 2
6	Ps 10
7	Ps 33
8	Ps 43
9	Ps 66
10	Ps 67
11	Ps 71
12	Ps 89
13	Ps 92
14	Ps 93
15	Ps 94
16	Ps 95
17	Ps 96
18	Ps 97
19	Ps 98
20	Ps 99
21	Ps 100
22	Ps 102
23	Ps 104
24	Ps 105
25	Ps 106
26	Ps 111
27	Ps 112
28	Ps 113
29	Ps 114
30	Ps 115
Jul 1	Ps 116
2	Ps 117
3	Ps 118
4	Ps 119
5	Ps 120
6	Ps 121
7	Ps 122
8	Ps 123
9	Ps 124
10	Ps 125
11	Ps 127
12	Ps 128
13	Ps 129
14	Ps 130
15	Ps 131
16	Ps 132
17	Ps 133
18	Ps 134
19	Ps 135
20	Ps 136
21	Ps 146
22	Ps 147
23	Ps 148
24	Ps 149
25	Ps 150
26	1 Chr 1-5
27	1 Chr 6-10
28	1 Chr 11-16
29	Ps 42
30	Ps 44
31	Ps 45
Aug 1	Ps 46
2	Ps 47
3	Ps 48
4	Ps 49
5	Ps 50
6	Ps 73
7	Ps 74
8	Ps 75
9	Ps 76
10	Ps 77
11	Ps 78
12	Ps 79
13	Ps 80
14	Ps 81
15	Ps 82
16	Ps 83
17	Ps 84
18	Ps 85
19	Ps 87
20	Ps 88
21	1 Chr 21-23
22	1 Chr 24-29
23	2 Chr 1-4
24	2 Chr 5-9
25	2 Chr 10-16
26	2 Chr 17-21
27	Ob
28	2 Chr 22
29	Jl 1-3
30	2 Chr 23:1-26:8
31	Is 1-5
Sep 1	2 Chr 26:9-23
2	Is 6
3	2 Chr 27-32
4	Is 7-11
5	Is 12-16
6	Is 17-21
7	Is 22-26
8	Is 27-31
9	Is 32-37
10	Is 38-42
11	Is 43-47
12	Is 48-52
13	Is 53-58
14	Is 59-66
15	Hos 1-5
16	Hos 6-10
17	Hos 11-14
18	Mi 1-4
19	Mi 5-7
20	Na 1-3
21	2 Chr 33-34
22	Zep 1-3
23	2 Chr 35
24	Hb 1-3
25	Jer 1-5
26	Jer 6-10
27	Jer 11-17
28	Jer 18-23
29	Jer 24-28
30	Jer 29-34
Oct 1	Jer 35-39
2	Jer 40-45
3	Jer 46-49
4	Jer 50-52
5	Lam 1-5
6	2 Chr 36:1-8
7	Dn 1-6
8	Dn 7-12
9	2 Chr 36:9-21
10	Ps 137
11	Ez 1-6
12	Ez 7-12
13	Ez 13-19
14	Ez 20-24
15	Ez 25-31
16	Ez 32-37
17	Ez 38-43
18	Ez 44-48
19	Est 1-5
20	Est 6-10
21	2 Chr 36:22-23
22	Ezr 1:1-5:1
23	Hg 1-2
24	Zec 1-5
25	Zec 6-9
26	Zec 10-14
27	Ps 107, 126
28	Ezr 5:2-10:44
29	Neh 1-7
30	Neh 8-13
31	Mal 1-4
Nov 1	Mt 1-4
2	Mt 5-9
3	Mt 10-13
4	Mt 14-16
5	Mk 1-4
6	Mk 5-9
7	Mk 10-13
8	Mk 14-16
9	Lk 1-4
10	Lk 5-9
11	Lk 10-14
12	Lk 15-19
13	Lk 20-24
14	Jn 1-4
15	Jn 5-9
16	Jn 10-14
17	Jn 15-18
18	Jn 19-21
19	Acts 1-4
20	Acts 5-10
21	Acts 11-14
22	Jas 1-5
23	Acts 15
24	Gal 1-6
25	Acts 16
26	Phil 1-4
27	Acts 17:1-10
28	1 Thes 1-5
29	2 Thes 1-3
30	Acts 17:11-18:11
Dec 1	1 Cor 1-5
2	1 Cor 6-11
3	1 Cor 12-16
4	2 Cor 1-4
5	2 Cor 5-9
6	2 Cor 10-13
7	Acts 18:12-20:1
8	Eph 1-6
9	Rom 1-5
10	Rom 6-11
11	Rom 12-16
12	Acts 20-23
13	Acts 24-28
14	Col 1-4
15	Heb 1-4
16	Heb 5-10
17	Heb 11-13
18	Ti 1-3
19	Phlm
20	1 Tm 1-6
21	2 Tm 1-4
22	1 Pt 1-5
23	2 Pt 1-3
24	1 Jn 1-5
25	2 Jn
26	3 Jn
27	Jude
28	Rv 1-6
29	Rv 7-12
30	Rv 13-17
31	Rv 18-22

A. B. Davis

Weekly Psalms

Jan 1 Ps 1-3
2 Jn 1:1-18
3 Gn 1-4
4 Gn 5-8
5 Gn 9-12
6 Gn 13-16
7 Gn 17-19
8 Ps 4-7
9 Gn 20-22
10 Jb 1-4
11 Jb 5-8
12 Jb 9-12
13 Jb 13-16
14 Jb 17-20
15 Ps 8-11
16 Jb 21-24
17 Jb 25-28
18 Jb 29-32
19 Jb 33-36
20 Jb 37-39
21 Jb 40-42
22 Ps 12-14
23 Gn 23-26
24 Gn 27-30
25 Gn 31-34
26 Gn 35-38
27 Gn 39-42
28 Gn 43-46
29 Ps 15-17
30 Gn 47-50
31 Ex 1-3
Feb 1 Ex 4-6
2 Ex 7-9
3 Ex 10-12
4 Ex 13-15
5 Ps 18-20
6 Ex 16-18
7 Ex 19-21
8 Ex 22-24
9 Ex 25-27
10 Ex 26-30
11 Ex 31-33
12 Ps 21-23
13 Ex 34-37
14 Ex 38-40
15 Lv 1-3
16 Lv 4-6
17 Lv 7-9
18 Lv 10-12
19 Ps 24-26
20 Lv 13-15
21 Lv 16-18
22 Lv 19-21
23 Lv 22-24
24 Lv 25-27
25 Nm 1-3
26 Ps 27-29
27 Nm 4-6
28 Nm 7-10
Mar 1 Nm 11-12
2 Nm 13-15
3 Nm 16-18
4 Nm 19-21
5 Ps 30-32
6 Nm 22-24
7 Nm 25-27
8 Nm 28-30
9 Nm 31-33
10 Nm 34-36
11 Dt 1-3
12 Ps 33-35
13 Dt 4-6
14 Dt 7-9
15 Dt 10-12
16 Dt 13-15

17 Dt 16-18
18 Dt 19-21
19 Ps 36-38
20 Dt 22-24
21 Dt 25-27
22 Dt 28-30
23 Dt 31-34
24 Jos 1-3
25 Jos 4-6
26 Ps 39-41
27 Jos 7-9
28 Jos 10-12
29 Jos 13-15
30 Jos 16-18
31 Jos 19-21
Apr 1 Jos 22-24
2 Ps 42-44
3 Jgs 1-3
4 Jgs 4-6
5 Jgs 7-9
6 Jgs 10-12
7 Jgs 13-15
8 Jgs 16-18
9 Ps 45-47
10 Jgs 19-21
11 Ru 1-4
12 1 Sm 1-3
13 1 Sm 4-6
14 1 Sm 7-9
15 1 Sm 10-13
16 Ps 48-50
17 1 Sm 14-16
18 1 Sm 17-19
19 1 Sm 20-22
20 1 Sm 23-25
21 1 Sm 26-28
22 1 Sm 29-31
23 Ps 51-53
24 2 Sm 1-3
25 2 Sm 4-6
26 2 Sm 7-9
27 2 Sm 10-12
28 2 Sm 13-15
29 2 Sm 16-18
30 Ps 54-56
May 1 2 Sm 19-21
2 2 Sm 22-24
3 1 Kgs 1-4
4 Prv 1-3
5 Prv 4-6
6 Prv 7-9
7 Ps 57-59
8 Prv 10-12
9 Prv 13-15
10 Prv 16-18
11 Prv 19-21
12 Prv 22-24
13 Prv 25-27
14 Ps 60-62
15 Prv 28-31
16 Sg 1-4
17 Sg 5-8
18 1 Kgs 5-7
19 1 Kgs 8-11
20 Eccl 1-4
21 Ps 63-6
22 Eccl 5-8
23 Eccl 9-12
24 1 Kgs 12-14
25 1 Kgs 15-17
26 1 Kgs 18-20
27 1 Kgs 21-22; 2 Kgs 1
28 Ps 66-68
29 2 Kgs 2-4
30 2 Kgs 5-7

31 2 Kgs 8-10
Jun 1 2 Kgs 11:1-14:25
2 Jon
3 2 Kgs 14:26-29; Am 1-3
4 Ps 69-71
5 Am 4-6
6 Am 7-9
7 2 Kgs 15-17
8 2 Kgs 18-21
9 2 Kgs 22-25
10 1 Chr 1-3
11 Ps 72-74
12 1 Chr 4-6
13 1 Chr 7-9
14 1 Chr 10-12
15 1 Chr 13-16
16 1 Chr 17-19
17 1 Chr 20-22
18 Ps 75-77
19 1 Chr 23-25
20 1 Chorn. 26-29
21 2 Chr 1-3
22 2 Chr 4-8
23 2 Chr 7-9
24 2 Chr 10-12
25 Ps 78-80
26 2 Chr 13-15
27 2 Chr 16-18
28 2 Chr 19-22
29 Jl 1-3; Ob
30 2 Chr 23:1-26:8
Jul 1 Is 1-3
2 Ps 81-83
3 Is 4:6; 2 Chr 26:9-23
4 2 Chr 27-29
5 2 Chr 30-32
6 Is 7-9
7 Is 10-12
8 Is 13-15
9 Ps 84-86
10 Is 16-18
11 Is 19-21
12 Is 22-24
13 Is 25-27
14 Is 28-30
15 Is 31-33
16 Ps 87-90
17 Is 34-36
18 Is 37-39
19 Is 40-42
20 Is 43-45
21 Is 46-48
22 Is 49-51
23 Ps 91-93
24 Is 52-54
25 Is 56-57
26 Is 58-60
27 Is 61-63
28 Is 64-66
29 Hos 1-3
30 Ps 94-96
31 Hos 4-6
Aug 1 Hos 7-9
2 Hos 10-12
3 Hos 13-14; Mi 1
4 Mi 2-4
5 Mi 5-7
6 Ps 97-99
7 Na 1-3
8 2 Chr 33-34; Zep 1
9 Zep 2-3; 2 Chr 35
10 Heb 1-3
11 Jer 1-3
12 Jer 4-6
13 Ps 100-102

14 Jer 11-12, 26
15 Jer 7-9
16 Jer 10, 14-15
17 Jer 16-18
18 Jer 19-20, 35
19 Jer 25, 36, 45
20 Ps 103-105
21 Jer 46-49
22 Jer 13, 22-23
23 Jer 24, 27-28
24 Jer 29, 50-51
25 Jer 30-33
26 Jer 21, 34, 37
27 Ps 106-108
28 Jer 38-39, 52
29 Jer 40-42
30 Jer 43-44; Lam 1
31 Lam 2-5
Sep 1 2 Chr 36:1-8, Dn 1-3
2 Dn 4-6
3 Ps 109-111
4 Dn 7-9
5 Dn 10-12
6 2 Chr 36:9-21, Ez 1-3
7 Ez 4-6
8 Ez 7-9
9 Ez 10-12
10 Ps 112-114
11 Ez 13-16
12 Ez 17-20
13 Ez 21-24
14 Ez 25-28
15 Ez 29-32
16 Ez 33-36
17 Ps 115-117
18 Ez 37-40
19 Ez 41-44
20 Ez 45-48
21 2 Chr 36:22-23;
Ezr 1-3
22 Ezr 4; Hg 1-2
23 Zec 1-3
24 Ps 118-119:16
25 Zec 4-6
26 Zec 7-9
27 Zec 10-12
28 Zec 13-14
29 Ezr 5-7
30 Ezr 8-10
Oct 1 Ps 119:17-72
2 Est 1-3
3 Est 4-6
4 Est 7-10
5 Neh 1-3
6 Neh 4-6
7 Neh 7-9
8 Ps 119:73-120
9 Neh 10-13
10 Mal
11 Mt 1-3
12 Mt 4-7
13 Mt 8-10
14 Mt 11-13
15 Ps 119:121-176
16 Mt 14-16
17 Mt 17-19
18 Mt 20-22
19 Mt 23-25
20 Mt 26-28
21 Mk 1-4
22 Ps 120-122
23 Mk 5-8
24 Mk 9-12
25 Mk 13-16
26 Lk 1-4

27 Lk 5-8
28 Lk 9-12
29 Ps 123-125
30 Lk 13-16
31 Lk 17-20
Nov 1 Lk 21-24
2 Jn 1-3
3 Jn 4-6
4 Jn 7-9
5 Ps 126-128
6 Jn 10-12
7 Jn 13-15
8 Jn 16-18
9 Jn 19-21
10 Acts 1-4
11 Acts 5:1-8:3
12 Ps 129-131
13 Acts 8:4-11:18
14 Acts 11:19-14:28
15 Jas
16 Gal
17 Acts 15-17:10
18 Phil
19 Ps 132-134
20 1 Thes
21 2 Thes, Acts
17:11-18:11
22 1 Cor 1-3
23 1 Cor 4-7
24 1 Cor 8:1-11:1
25 1 Cor 11:2-14:40
26 Ps 135-137
27 1 Cor 15-16
28 2 Cor 1-5
29 2 Cor 6-9
30 2 Cor 10-13
Dec 1 Acts 18:12-19:41;
Eph 1-2
2 Eph 3-6
3 Ps 138-140
4 Rom 1-3
5 Rom 4-6
6 Rom 7-9
7 Rom 10-12
8 Rom 13-1
9 Acts 20-226
10 Ps 141-143
11 Acts 23-25
12 Acts 26-28
13 Col
14 Heb 1-4
15 Heb 5-8
16 Heb 9-11
17 Ps 144-146
18 Heb 12-13; Ti
19 Phlm
20 1 Tm, 2 Tm
21 1 Pt
22 1 Jn
23 2 Pt; 2, 3 Jn; Jude
24 Ps 147-148
25 Rv 1-3
26 Rv 4-7
27 Rv 8-10
28 Rv 11-14
29 Rv 15-18
30 Rv 19-22
31 Ps 149-150

NAE © 1989

Source: National Association of Evangelicals. Used by permission.

CLASSIC DEVOTIONAL BOOKS

Recommended by Robert Kregel, Chairman of the Board, Kregel Publications.

Listed below are some of the finest classic devotionals and biographies in print. Unless otherwise indicated, each title is published by several publishers.

Beyond Humiliation, by J. Gregory Mantle, Bethany House Publishers

The Christian's Secret of a Happy Life, by Hannah Whitehall Smith

God's Best Secrets, by Andrew Murray, Zondervan Publishing House

The Greatest Thing in the World, by Henry Drummond

He That Is Spiritual, by Lewis Sperry Chafer, Zondervan

Hinds' Feet on High Places, by Hannah Hurnard

How to Live a Victorious Life, by an Unknown Christian, Zondervan

The Kneeling Christian, by an Unknown Christian, Zondervan

The Knowledge of the Holy, by A. W. Tozer, Harper & Row, Publishers

Memoirs and Remains of Robert Murray Mc-Cheyne, by Andrew Bonar, Banner of Truth

Morning and Evening, by Charles Spurgeon, Zondervan and Henrickson Publishers

My Utmost for His Highest, by Oswald Chambers

Our Lord Prays for His Own, by Marcus Rainsford, Kregel Publications

Pilgrim's Progress, by John Bunyan

The Pursuit of God, by A. W. Tozer, Christian Publications

A Serious Call to a Devout and Holy Life, by William Law

Spiritual Leadership, by J. Oswald Sanders, Moody Press

The Spiritual Man, by Watchman Nee, Christian Fellowship Publishers

With Christ in the School of Prayer, by Andrew Murray

Bookstore Journal, Official Trade Publication of the Christian Booksellers Association. Copyright © 1990. Reprinted by permission.

❝❞ FOCUS QUOTE Whatever truth you have chosen, read only a small portion of it, endeavoring to taste and digest it, to extract the essence and substance thereof, and proceed no farther while any savor or relish remains in the passage. When this subsides, take up your book again and proceed as before, seldom reading more than half a page at a time. For it is not the quantity you read, but the manner of reading that yields the profit.—Madame Guyon (1646-1717)

BIBLE SOFTWARE PROGRAMS

For further information on these programs contact Mark Rice. Hermeneutika Company, P.O. Box 98563, Seattle, WA 98198. Phone: 206-824-9673; FAX: 206-824-7160.

1200 various machine-readable Bible Translations in most languages, United Bible Societies: Translation Department, Attn: Harold Scanlin, 1865 Broadway, New York, NY 10023

"Ask God" Expert System Bible Software, Business Solutions, 15395 SE 30th Place, Suite 310, Bellevue, WA 98007, 206-644-2015

"Atari Bible Concordance" Bible Study Software, SpiritWare, 15th Avenue Bible Church, 15211 15th Ave., NE, Seattle, WA, 98155, 206-685-1854

"Bible Library" on CD-ROM Software, Ellis Enterprises, Inc., 4205 McAuley Blvd., Suite 315, Oklahoma City, OK 73120, 405-749-0273

"Bible Scholar" Bible Research Software, Scholar Systems, Inc., 2313 Overland, Boise, ID 83705, FAX 208-336-3844, 208-343-6262

"Bible Search" Bible Study Software, SOGWAP Company, 115 Bellmont Road, Decatur, IN 46733, 219-724-3900

"Bible Word" Greek NT, LXX, Hebrew OT Bible Research Software; "On-Line Bible" Research Software, Hermeneutika Computer-Aided Bible Research Software Company, P.O. Box 98563, Seattle, WA 98198, 206-824-WORD, 206-824-7673, 206-824-3927, FAX 206-824-7160

"BibleQ" Game with 1200 Questions & Answers; "Daily Bread" TSR Software program with "Verse of the Day" at bootup, SmithSoft, 557 Plantation Road, Pelican Lake, WI 54463, 715-487-5484

"BookMaster" Bible Study Software, Koala-T Software/BookMaster Bible, 3255 Wing Street, Suite 220, San Diego, CA 92110, 800-642-1144

"CDWord Interactive Bible Library" CD-ROM Bible Research Software, CDWord Library, Inc., Two Lincoln Centre, 5420 LBJ Freeway LB7, Dallas, TX 75240-6215, 214-770-2414

"Christian Marriage Analysis," "Christian Personality Profile," & "Stress & Coping Strength" Christian Counseling Software, Wellness Publications, Inc., P.O. Box 2397, Holland, MI 49422-2397, 616-396-5477

"CompuBible" Bible Research Software, NASSCO, P.O. Box 65600, Lubbock, TX 79464, 800-288-2044, 806-791-5138

"EB-2000" Selectronics Electronic Handheld/Pocket Bible Hardware, Chapel Hill Marketing, Inc., 1506 E. Franklin St., The Center, Suite 100, Chapel Hill, NC 27514, 919-933-7674

"EveryWord" KJV and TEV Bible Scripture Study Software, ECHO Microtek, P.O. Box 1088, Orem, UT 84057, 801-226-7800, 801-226-7897

"FindIT Bible" Study Software (many translations: English, French, Spanish, et al.), Murray & Gillespie Computer Solutions, 90 Nolan Court, Unit 22, Markham, Ontario L3R 4L9, Canada, FAX 416-477-8506, 416-477-0260

"Folio KJV" Bible Study Software based upon "Folio Views" Software, InfoBasix Corporation, 9587 S. Grandview Dr., Sandy, UT 84092, 801-944-8716

"Franklin KJV or RSV" Handheld/Pocket Electronic Bible Hardware, Franklin Computer Corporation, 122 Burrs Road, Mt. Holly, NJ 08060, Sales Dept: 609-261-4800, FAX 609-261-1631

"GodSpeed" Bible Research Software, Kingdom Age Software, 3368 Governor Dr., Suite F-197, San Diego, CA 92122, 619-586-1082

"GramCord Scholar," Greek NT Grammatical Research Software plus Greek & Hebrew Multilingual Word Processor Software, GramCord Institute, 2065 Half Day Road, Deerfield, IL 60015, 312-223-3242

Greek, Hebrew, English Bible Texts (ASCII) on disk, University of Pennsylvania Computer Center for Analysis of Texts (CCAT/CATSS), Attn: Dr. Robert Kraft, Box 36, College Hall, Philadelphia, PA 19104-6303, 215-898-1597

Greek Literature from Homer through AD600 on CD-ROM (over 600 MB of data), Dr. Theodore F. Brunner, TLG Project—Thesaurus Linguae Graecae, 156 Humanities Hall, University of California, Irvine, Irvine, CA 92717, 714-856-7031, 714-856-6404

"Greek MemCards" & "Hebrew Mem-Cards" Biblical Vocabulary Learning Software, Memorization Technology, P.O. Box 60788, Palo Alto, CA 94306, 415-857-9220

"HyperBible," Thompson Chain Reference HyperText Bible Software, Beacon Technology, Inc., 5369 Camden Ave., Suite 230, San Jose, CA 95124, 800-777-1841, 408-723-4884

HyperCard "BibleStack" Bible Software (Mac), Holy Mountain Software, 2775 Fountain Circle, Sarasota, FL 34235, 813-951-0246

"Interlinear Text" Bible/Text Processing Software for Linguistic Translation Work & TextBase Management, SIL/Wycliffe: IT & IT Formatter SIL—Academic Computing, 7500 W. Camp, Wisdom Road, Dallas, TX 75236, 214-709-2418, 214-296-3105

Jewish Culture Software including Biblical Hebrew Vocabulary Software, Davka Corporation, 845 N. Michigan Ave., Suite 843, Chicago, IL 60611, 800-621-8227, 312-944-4070

"LaserGreek," "LaserHebrew," Fonts for over 200 other Languages in Postscript, Macintosh, Linguist's Software, Inc., P.O. Box 580, Edmunds, WA 98020-0580, 206-775-1130

"LBase" Biblical/General Text Linguistic Database/TextBase Management & Search/Display Software (including Greek & Hebrew & Coptic Fonts) plus: CD-ROM accessing Software, Silver Mountain Software, Attn: John Baima, 7246 Cloverglen Drive, Dallas, TX 75249, 214-709-8987

"**Lexegete" Lectionary Sermon Exegetical Helps Software,** Tischrede Software, P.O. Box 9594, North Dartmouth, MA 02747, 617-994-7907

"**Master Search Bible" Research Library on CD-ROM with Accessing Software,** TriStar Publishing, P.O. Box 7515, Fort Washington, PA 19034, 800-872-2828, 800-29BIBLE

"**MegaWord Gold" & "MegaWord Silver" Bible Research Software,** Paraclete Software, 1000 E. 14th Street, Suite 425, Plano, TX 75074, 214-578-8185, 800-825-6342

"**Multi-Lingual Scholar" Business/Academic Multilingual Word Processing Software,** Gamma Productions, Inc., 710 Wilshire Blvd, Suite 609, Santa Monica, CA 90401, FAX 213-395-4214, 213-394-8622

"**NASB Computer Bible" Study Software,** Foundation Press Publications, Inc., 1121 N. Kraemer Place, P.O. Box 6439, Anaheim, CA 92806, 714-630-6450

"**NIV On-Line Bible" Research Software,** ROCKware Publishing, 57 Bater Road, Coldwater, MI 49036, 517-369-6035

"**NIV PC" Bible Research Software & "MacBible" Bible Research Software & "ScriptureFonts" Greek & Hebrew Fonts for WordPerfect,** Zondervan Corporation, 1415 Lake Drive, SE, Grand Rapids, MI 49506, 616-698-6900, 800-727-3060

"**On-Line Bible" Bible Research Software,** Timnathserah, Inc., R.R. 2, West Montrose, Ontario, N0B 2V0, Canada, 519-664-2266

"**Panoplia: The Full Armour of God,"** Christian Bible Games Software, Choice Software, P.O. Box 620535, Littleton, CO 80123, 303-763-8950.

"**PassageWay" Bible Study Software,** PassageWay Bible, P. O. Box 3789, Pensacola, FL 32526, 904-456-1595

"**Pastor's Story File & Parables," "Auto-Illustrator," 3700 indexed stories with cross-references + Subscription Software,** Saratoga Press, 14200 Victor Place, Saratoga, CA 95070, 408-867-4211

"**PC Study Bible" Bible Research Software,** BibleSoft, 22014 7th Ave., S. Seattle, WA 98198, 206-824-0656

"**PHI Demonstration CD-ROM": including CCAT Greek, Hebrew, English Bible texts on CD-ROM,** Packard Humanities Institute, 300 Second Street, Los Altos, CA 94022, 415-948-0150

"**QuickVerse" Bible Software, "Membership Plus" Church Organization Software,** Parsons Technology, 375 Collins Road, NE, Cedar Rapids, IA 52402, FAX 319-395-0217, 800-369-5000

"**SeedMaster" Bible Research Software,** White Harvest Software, Inc., P.O. Box 97153, Raleigh, NC 27624-7153

"**WORD Processor," "VerseSearch" Bible Research Software,** Bible Research Systems, 2013 Wells Branch Parkway, #304, Austin, TX 78728, 512-251-7541

"**WordSearch" Bible Study Software & "InfoSearch" Sermon Illustration & Current Christian Abstracts & Music Hymnal DataBase Management & Quarterly Subscription Software,** NavPress, P.O. Box 6000, Colorado Springs, CO 80934, 800-888-9898, 719-598-1212

Source: Hermeneutika Company, Computer-Aided Bible Research Software, over 400 Products, Mail Order, Discount Software for Bible Research, Bible Study, Writing, Education. Compiled by Mark Rice.

COMPUTER MAGAZINES TO KEEP YOU INFORMED ON BIBLICAL SOFTWARE

Christian Computing Magazine
P.O. Box 227
Versailles, MO 65084
314-378-6566

Church Bytes
562 Brightleaf Square, #9
905 West Main St.
Durham, NC 27701

FOCUS FACT A list of colleges offering Bible correspondence courses appears in the Education section of *The Almanac of the Christian World,* page 448.

Growth in Scripture Translation and Publication since 1800

The numerals indicate the cumulative number of Bibles, Testaments, and Scripture portions published by the end of each decade.

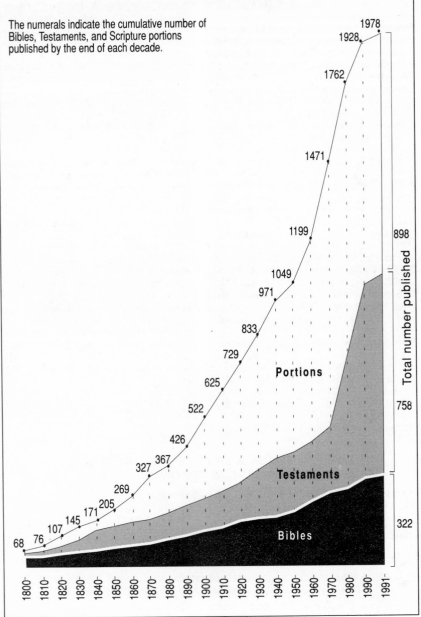

THE BIBLE IN WORLD LANGUAGES

Translation and Distribution Statistics

	Portions	Testaments	Complete Bibles	Total
Africa	226	219	121	566
Asia	225	166	99	490
Australia/New Zealand/Pacific Islands	157	138	26	321
Europe	103	25	59	187
North America	43	20	7	70
Caribbean/Latin America	142	190	9	341
Constructed Languages	2	0	1	3
Total	898	758	322	1978

United Bible Societies

WHERE TO OBTAIN BIBLES IN VARIOUS LANGUAGES

American Bible Society, 1865 Broadway, New York NY 10023

Bibles for India, 4221 Richmond NW, Grand Rapids, MI 49504

Bibles for the World, Inc., 116 N. Schmale Rd., Carol Stream, IL 60188

Bible Literature International, P.O. Box 477, Columbus, OH 43216

Christian Literature and Bible Center, 1006 Oak Cliff Dr., Toccoa, GA 30577

Christian Literature Crusade, PO Box 1449, Fort Washington, PA 19034

Christian Literature International, P.O. Box 777, Canby, OR 97013

Gideons International, 2900 Lebanon Rd., Nashville, TN 37214

International Bible Society, 1820 Jet Stream Dr., Colorado Springs, CO 80921-3696

Multi-Language Media, P.O. Box 548, Waynesboro, GA 30830

The Bible League, 16801 Van Dam Rd., South Holland, IL 60473

World Literature Crusade, 20232 Sunburst Ave., Chatsworth, CA 91311

World Missionary Press, P.O. Box 120, New Paris, IN 46553

❝❞ **The Bible is a stream wherein the elephant may swim and the lamb may wade.** —Pope Gregory the Great

FOCUS QUOTE

GUTENBERG BIBLE CENSUS

The Gutenberg Bible, printed in 1456 by Johann Gutenberg, is believed to be the first Bible printed with movable type. There are 48 known copies of the Gutenberg Bible in existence today. This list comes from the Pierpont Morgan Library, New York City. Copies are arranged roughly according to the quantity of sheets in first setting each contains. Copies printed on vellum precede those printed on paper.

In 1978, University of Texas at Austin purchased a Gutenberg Bible for $2.4 million (#30 on list). In December 1987, Maruzen Book Co., Tokyo, purchased a copy for $5.4 million (#39 on list).

Vellum Copies

1. Bibliotheque Nationale, Paris, France

2. Henry E. Huntington Library, San Marino, Calif.
3. Deutsches Buch-und Schrift Museum der Deutschen Bucherei, Leipzig, Germany
4. Landesbibliothek, Fulda, Germany
5. Karl-Marx Universitatsbibliothek, Leipzig, Germany
6. Universitatsbibliothek, Gottingen, Germany
7. Staatsbibliothek Preussischer Kulturbesitz, Berlin, Germany
8. Library of Congress, Washington, D.C.
9. Pierpont Morgan Library, New York, N.Y.
10. British Library (Grenville), London, England
11. Biblioteca Apostolica Vaticana (Barberini Collection), Vatican Library, Italy
12. Lambeth Palace Library, London, England

Paper Copies

13. Bayerische Staatsbibliothek, Munich, Germany
14. Stadt-und Universitatsbibliothek, Frankfurt-am-Main, Germany
15. Hofbibliothek, Aschaffenburg, Germany
16. Gutenberg Museum, Mainz, Germany
17. Wurttembergische Landesbibliothek, Stuttgart, Germany
18. Gabriel Wells (bookseller), New York, N.Y.
19. Karl-Marx Universitatsbibliothek, Leipzig, Germany
20. Bibliotheque Mazarine, Paris, France
21. Eton College Library, Eton, England
22. Bodleian Library, Oxford, England
23. The John Rylands Library, Manchester, England
24. Harvard College Library, Cambridge, Mass.
25. Biblioteka Seminarium Duchownego, Pelplin, Poland
26. The Scheide Library, Princeton, N.J.
27. British Library (George III), London, England
28. Pierpont Morgan Library, New York, N.Y.
29. Osterreichische Nationalbibliothek, Vienna, Austria
30. University of Texas Library, Austin, Tex.
31. Bibliotheca Bodmeriana, Cologny, Switzerland
32. Biblioteca Nacional, Lisbon, Portugal
33. University Library, Cambridge, England
34. Yale University Library, New Haven, Conn.
35. Biblioteca Publica Provincial, Burgos, Spain
36. New York Public Library, New York, N.Y.
37. National Library of Scotland, Edinburgh, Scotland
38. Pierpont Morgan Library, New York, N.Y.
39. Maruzen Book Company, Tokyo, Japan
40. Biblioteca Apostolica Vaticana (DeRossi Collection), Vatican Library, Italy
41. Stadtbibliothek, Trier, Germany
42. Landesbibliothek, Kassel, Germany
43. Bibliotheque Municipale, St. Omer, France
44. Bibliotheque Nationale, Paris, France
45a* Bibliotheque Universitaire, Mons, Belgium
45b* Indiana University Library, Bloomington, Ind.
46. Gutenberg Museum, Mainz, Germany
47. Kongelige Bibliotek, Copenhagen, Denmark
48. Biblioteca Universitaria, Seville, Spain

*The Mons partial Vol. I, the Bloomington New Testament, some large fragments of Vol. I owned since the last century by the Counts Von Seilern, ten leaves added to the Scheide copy and a number of separate leaves now scattered were once parts of a single copy, according to Paul Needham.

A rare-book collector met a guy who said he'd just thrown out an old Bible that had been packed away for generations. "Somebody named Guten-something had printed it," the man explained.

"Not Gutenberg!" gasped the book lover. "You've just thrown away one of the most famous books ever printed. One copy recently sold at an auction for over $4 million!"

The other man was still unmoved. "My copy wouldn't have brought a dime," he said. "Some guy named Martin Luther scribbled notes all over it."

Tal D. Bonham, *The Treasury of Clean Jokes.* Published by Broadman.

ENGLISH BIBLE VERSIONS THROUGH 19TH CENTURY
J. H. Skilton

Date AD	Version (italics = Catholic Version)	Translator
ANGLO-SAXON VERSIONS		
Late 7th cent.	English verse (oral)	Caedmon
	John's Gospel, + ?	Bede
	Psalms; entire Bible?	Aldhelm (640-709)
	Anglo-Saxon Psalter glosses	
Late 9th cent.	Ten Commandments	Alfred the Great (849-901)
	Ex. 21-23	
	Acts 15	
	Scripture refs. in Gregory's "De Cura Pastorali"	
c.950	Anglo-Saxon gloss of the Lindisfarne Gospels	
	Anglo-Saxon gloss of the Rushworth Gospels	
11th cent.	Parts of the OT	Aelfric
	Four Gospels into continuous English text	
MIDDLE ENGLISH VERSIONS		
c.1300	Metric Psalter	
	Prose Psalter	Richard Rolle of Hampole c.1380-1383
	Wyclif Bible	Nicholas of Hereford and Wyclif (?)
	Revision of Wyclif's Bible	John Purvey
SIXTEENTH-CENTURY VERSIONS		
1525/6	NT	William Tyndale
1530	Pentateuch	Tyndale
1531	Jonah	Tyndale
	Isaiah	George Joye
1534	OT selections	Tyndale
	NT revision	
	Psalms	Joye
	Lamentations	
	Jeremiah	
	Song of Moses at the Red Sea	
	Revision (unauthorized) of Tyndale's NT	
1535	NT revision	Tyndale
	First complete Bible in English	Miles Coverdale
1537	The Matthew Bible	John Rogers? ('Thomas Matthew')
1538	Parallel English-Latin NT (Vulgate)	Coverdale
1539	Revision of the Matthew Bible	Richard Taverner
	The Great Bible	Coverdale, for Thomas Cromwell
1540	2nd edition of the Great Bible	Preface by Archbp. Cranmer
1545	Revised Primer ("Primer of Henry VIII")	

1557	Geneva NT	William Whittingham
1560	Geneva Bible	Various (including Whittingham)
1568	The Bishops' Bible	Matthew Parker and others
1572	Revised folio edition of the Bishops' Bible	
1582	*Rheims NT*	*Gregory Martin, William Allen and others*

SEVENTEENTH-CENTURY VERSIONS

1609–1610	*Douay OT*	*Gregory Martin and others*
1611	Authorized (King James) Version	Fifty-four translators
1613	Revision of AV	
1616–1623	Pentateuch	Henry Ainsworth
	Song of Solomon	
	Psalms	

EIGHTEENTH-CENTURY VERSIONS

1718–1719	*NT*	*Cornelius Nary*
1729	Greek and English NT	William Mace
1730	NT	*Robert Witham*
1738	*Fifth edition of Rheims NT*	
1745	The Primitive NT	William Whiston
1749–1772	*Two rev. of Douay OT, five rev. of Rheims NT*	*Richard Challoner*
1755	Revision of AV	John Wesley
1764	NT	Richard Wynne
	Bible	Anthony Purver
1768	Liberal translation of the NT	E. Harwood
1770	NT	John Worsley
1783–1810	*Revisions of Rheims and Douay texts*	*Bernard MacMahon*

NINETEENTH-CENTURY VERSIONS

1822	Paul's Epistles	Thomas Belsham (Unitarian)
1832	Paul's Epistles	Charles Eyre (Unitarian)
1833	NT	Rodolphus Dickinson
1840	NT	Samuel Sharpe (Unitarian)
1849–1860	*Annotated revision of Douay-Rheims text*	*Bishop Francis Patrick Kenrick*
1855	Gospels	Andrew Norton
1858	NT	Leicester Ambrose Sawyer
1862	OT & NT	Robert Young
1863	Gospels	G. W. Braineld
1869	NT	Henry Alford
	OT & NT	Robert Ainslie
1871	NT	J. N. Darby
1872	NT	J. B. Rotherham
1875	NT	Samuel Davidson
1881	Revised version of the AV NT	British & American companies
1882	Romans	Ferrar Fenton
1883	Paul's Epistles	Fenton
1885	RV complete Bible	British & American companies
1890	Bible	J. N. Darby
1895	Current English NT	Fenton

The People's Study Bible: The Living Bible Harold Lindsell, Ph.D., D.D., General Editor, Tyndale House Publishers, Inc., Wheaton, IL, ©1986: pp. 1823-1826. From *New Bible Dictionary;* used by permission of InterVarsity Press.

20TH-CENTURY ENGLISH BIBLE VERSIONS

The translations are arranged under the date the entire Bible was published. Earlier parts of the translation are listed under this date. If only the New Testament has been translated, it is, of course, listed under its date. If no complete New Testament or Old Testament exists, then the date of the first portion is used. The compilers are aware that there may be other translations not listed, especially those of individual books, particularly the Psalms. Annotations are included for those that the compilers were able to examine. Reference is made to the appropriate chapter when that translation has been treated in the book. Reprints of pre-twentieth-century Bibles are not included in the list.

The compilers were especially indebted to the following two works in putting together this bibliography: Margaret T. Hills, editor, *The English Bible in America: A Bibliography of Editions of the Bible and the New Testament Published in America, 1777–1957* (New York: The American Bible Society and the New York Public Library, 1961). A. S. Herbert, *Historical Catalogue of Printed Editions of the English Bible, 1525–1961* (London: The British and Foreign Bible Society; New York: The American Bible Society, 1968).

1900 **Hayman's Epistles** The Epistles of the New Testament. An attempt to present them in current and popular idiom by Henry Hayman. London: A. and C. Black.

1901 **The American Standard Version** The Holy Bible containing the Old and New Testaments translated out of the Original Languages. The Version set forth A.D. 1677, compared with the most ancient authorities and revised A.D. 1881–1885. Newly edited by the American Revision Committee. A.D. 1901 Standard Edition, New York: Thomas Nelson and Sons.

1901 **Modern American Bible** The New Testament; The Books of the Bible in Modern American Form and Phrase with Notes and Introduction by Frank Schell Ballantine. New York: Thomas Whittaker, 1899–1901
Part I: S. Mark (1899?). Part II: S. Matthew, S. Peter, S. Jude, and S. James (1899?). Part III: S. Luke (Gospel-Acts) (1899?). Part IV: S. Paul (including Hebrews) (1901?). Part V: S. John (Gospel, Letters, Revelation) (1901?). Based on Textus Receptus and later Greek Texts. Preceded this by translation of the Four Gospels (Good News—The Four Gospels in a Modern American Dress, 1897). Revised 1909.

1901 **Moffatt's Historical New Testament** The Historical New Testament; A New Translation, by James Moffat. Edinburgh: T. & T. Clark.
The books are chronologically arranged. A different translation from Moffat's later translation.

1901 **Way's Epistles** The letters of St. Paul to Seven Churches and Three Friends. Translated by Arthur S. Way. London: The Macmillan Company.
Arthur S. Way, a classical scholar, translated the Letters of St. Paul, the first edition of which appeared in 1901 and a second thoroughly revised edition, which included Hebrews, was published in 1906 and reprinted in 1951.

1901 **Young People's Bible** or, the Scriptures Corrected, Explained, and Simplified, by Harriet Newell Jones, with Introduction by Rev. Malcolm MacGregor. Philadelphia: American Book and Bible House.

1902 **Emphasized Bible (Rotherham)** a new translation designed to set forth the exact meaning, the proper terminology, and the graphic style of the sacred originals; arranged to show at a glance narrative, speech, parallelism, and logical analysis, also to enable the student readily to distinguish the several divine names; and emphasized throughout

20TH-CENTURY ENGLISH BIBLE VERSIONS cont.

after the idioms of the Hebrew and Greek tongues. By Joseph Bryant Rotherham.

Old Testament (1902), New York, Chicago, Toronto: Fleming H. Revell Company, 3 vols. Vol I: Genesis-Ruth. Vol. II: 1 Samuel-Psalms. Vol. III: Proverbs-Malachi.

New Testament (1897), is rewritten edition of the version first printed in 1872 and reissued in a revised form in 1878. Gospel according to Matthew (1868). Greek text of Tregelles. In 1916, published four volumes in one.

1902? **Godbey's New Testament** Translation of the New Testament from the original Greek. By Rev. W. B. Godbey. Cincinnati: M. W. Knapp, Office of God's Revivalist.

Based on Tischendorf's edition of the Codex Sinaiticus. Dedicated to "The Holiness People of all lands."

1902 **Twentieth Century New Testament.** A translation into Modern English. Made from the original Greek. New York: Fleming H. Revell Company.

Part I: The Five Historial Books (undated, 1898?). Part II: Paul's Letters to the Churches (1900). Part III: The Pastoral, Personal and General Letters, and the Revelation (1901). Based on Westcott and Hort's Greek text.

One-volume edition (revised) in 1904. Reprinted frequently.

1903 **Fenton's Bible** The Holy Bible in Modern English, containing the complete sacred Scriptures of the Old and New Testaments, translated into English direct from the original Hebrew, Chaldee, and Greek, by Ferrar Fenton.

1882, Romans; 1884, Epistles; 1895, New Testament; 1903, whole Bible. New Testament and four parts of Old Testament.

First edition of New Testament in Modern English 1895, revised 1900. Vol. I: Pentateuch, 1901? Vol. II: Joshua–II Kings, 1902? Vol. III: Isaiah, Jeremiah, Ezekiel, Minor Prophets, Prophets, 1902?

Ferrar Fenton was a London businessman who devoted some twenty years of his life to fulfill a pledge of making the Scriptures intelligible "through the use of modern English." This work by an amateur was popular for a time, but "its erroneous and inaccurate renderings have rather damaged its earlier favor" (Price).

1903 **Weymouth's New Testament** The New Testament in Modern Speech. An Idiomatic Translation into Every Day English from the text of The Resultant Greek Testament by Richard Francis Weymouth.

The text was revised in the 1924 edition by the Rev. S. W. Green, the Rev. Prof. A. J. D. Farrer, and the Rev. Prof. H. T. Andrews, and again in 1929 by the Rev. Prof. James Alexander Robertson.

1904 **Worrell's New Testament** The New Testament Revised and Translated by A. S. Worrell, with Notes and Instructions designed to aid the earnest Reader in obtaining a clear Understanding of the Doctrines, Ordinances and primitive Assemblies as revealed in these Scriptures. Louisville, Ky: A. S. Worrell.

Based on the Greek text underlying the ERV and on Westcott and Hort as modified by Scrivener and others. "Baptize" is translated "immerse"; "church" is "assembly" or "congregation." Claims great fidelity to the Greek. "To handle the tenses carelessly," writes the translator, "is to trifle with the word of God. . . . It is the business of the translator to translate with scrupulous exactness." Contains some textual variants, alternate renderings and explanatory notes.

1905 **Lloyd's New Testament** The Corrected English New Testament. A Revision of the "Authorized" Version (By Nestle's Resultant Text). Prepared with the Assistance of

Eminent Scholars and Issued by Samuel Lloyd, a Life Governor of the British and Foreign Bible Society as His Memorial of the Society's Centenary, 1904. London: Samuel Bagster & Sons, Ltd.

The corrections are of two kinds: (1) the removal of textual defects in the underlying Greek and (2) a modernization of the English. Because of the large extent to which the Authorized Version had failed, Lloyd proposed that the Bible Society produce a new revision as a memorial to its centenary. When this was not accepted, he, with the cooperation of a number of biblical scholars, independently produced this version of the New Testament as an illustration of the kind of revision needed. He attempted "to show the possibility of popularizing without demeaning the Sacred Scriptures and of correcting without defacing the Version so worthily beloved."

1906 **Forster** St. John's Gospel, Epistles, and Revelation, translated by Henry Langstaff Forster. Adelaide: Hunkin, Ellis and King.

The Revelation (1903). Tasmania: Henry Langstaff Forster.

1907 **Bourne's Gospels** The Fourfold Portrait of the Heavenly King, translated by "Interpreter" i.e., A. E. Bourne. London: E. Stock.

A new translation of the Gospels.

1907 **Moulton's Modern Reader's Bible** The Books of the Bible with Three Books of the Apocrypha presented in Modern Literary Form; edited with Introductions and Notes, by Richard G. Moulton. New York: The Macmillan Company.

1908 **Rutherford's Epistles** Paul's Epistles to the Thessalonians and to the Corinthians. A New Translation by W. G. Rutherford, London.

1909 **The Bible in Modern English** The Bible in Modern English. A Rendering from the Originals by an American, making use of the best scholarship and the latest research at home and abroad. Perkiomen, Pa.

---

66 99
FOCUS
QUOTE
A little from God is better than a great deal from men. What is from men is uncertain, and is often lost and tumbled over and over by men; but what is from God is fixed as a nail in a sure place. —John Bunyan

---

1909 **Weaver New Testament** New Testament in Modern Historical and Literary Form for the church, the school and the home, embracing the life of Jesus Christ in the words of Matthew, Mark, Luke, and John, and the Church of the Apostles according to the Acts, the Epistles and Revelation, historically harmonized. Translated by S. Townsend Weaver. Philadelphia: University Literature Extension.

1910 **Cunard's** The first judgment of the Christians by the Spirit, Alpha and Omega. An Authorized Revision of St. Matthew and the History of this Planet, from the First Strata to the End. Written for the Spirit at Command by F. W. Cunard. Liverpool: Cunard & Sons.

1912 **Improved Bible Union Version** The Holy Bible containing the Old and New Testaments. An Improved Edition (Based in Part on the Bible Union Version). Philadelphia: American Baptist Publication Society.

20TH-CENTURY ENGLISH BIBLE VERSIONS cont.

The Bible Union Version was an "immersion" version begun in the middle of the nineteenth century, but of which the Old Testament was never fully completed. The New Testament of that version used "immersion" for "baptism." The Improved Version has "baptism (immersion)," "baptize (immerse)," and "baptized (immersed)." The poetic portions of the Old Testament, including those of the prophets, are printed in poetic form.

1914 **Numeric New Testament** The New Testament from the Greek text as established by Bible Numerics. Edited by Ivan Panin. New Haven: Bible Numerics Company.
Based on the number value of the Greek and Hebrew letters. Awkward in many places. Second edition, 1935 and reprinted several times.

1914 **Cunnington's New Testament** The New Covenant, commonly called the New Testament of our Lord and Saviour Jesus Christ. A revision of the version of A.D. 1611 by E. E. Cunnington. London: G. Routledge & Sons.
Other editions appeared, e.g., in 1919 by T. Foster Unwin, London, under the title The Adelphi New Testament; and in 1926 with the title The Western New Testament.

1916 **McFadyen** The Psalms in Modern Speech and Rhythmical Form by John Edgar McFadyen. London: James Clarke & Company.
The Wisdom Books, also Lamentations and the Song of Songs, in Modern Speech and Rhythmical form by John Edgar McFadyen, 1917. Isaiah in Modern Speech, 1918. Jeremiah in Modern Speech, 1919.

1917 **Jewish Publication Society Bible** The Holy Scriptures According to the Masoretic Text. A New Translation with the Aid of Previous Versions and with Constant Consultation of Jewish Authorities. Philadelphia: The Jewish Publication Society.
Jewish Publication Society Version. Psalms, 1903.

1918 **Anderson New Testament** The New Testament. Translated from the Sinaitic Manuscript Discovered by Constantine Tischendorf at Mount Sinai, by H. T. Anderson. Cincinnati: The Standard Publishing Company.

1919 **The Messages of the Bible** The Messages of the Bible, edited by Frank K. Sanders and Charles F. Kent. 12 vols. New York: Charles Scribner's Sons, 1898-1919.
Brief introductions of each book and free rendering in paraphrase.

FOCUS
QUOTE

One of the many divine qualities of the Bible is this: that it does not yield its secrets to the irreverent and censorious. —J. I. Packer

---

1921 **Pym** Mark's Account of Jesus. Cambridge: W. Heffer and Sons. "Common Speech" by T. W. Pym.

1921 **Shorter Bible** The Shorter Bible, translated and arranged by Charles Foster Kent with the Collaboration of Charles Cutler Torrey, Henry A. Sherman, Frederick Harris, Ethel Cutler. New York: Charles Scribner's Sons.
New Testament, 1918. Old Testament, 1921. About two-thirds of the Old Testament and one-third of the New Testament are omitted.

1922 **Plainer Bible** A Plainer Bible for Plain People in Plain America (New Testament), from the original Greek by Chaplain [Frank Schell] Ballentine. Jersey City, N.J.: Plainer Bible Press.

See 1901, Modern American Bible.

1923 **Riverside New Testament** The Riverside New Testament; a translation from the original Greek into the English of today, by William G. Ballantine. Boston: Houghton, Mifflin.

An eclectic rendering of Nestle's Greek text by William G. Ballantine, a former President of Oberlin College, who confesses his indebtedness to other versions, such as Weymouth's, Moffatt's and The Twentieth Century New Testament. Produced in a very readable form with an index, this version was first published in 1923, and revised in 1934.

1923 **Robertson** A Translation of Luke's Gospel with Grammatical Notes by A. T. Robertson. New York: George H. Doran Company.

---

66 99 The Scriptures teach us the best way of living, the noblest way of suffering, and the most comfortable way of dying. —John Flavel
FOCUS
QUOTE

1924 **Labor Determinative Version** The New Covenant: a Mutual Arrangement or Testament for a true civilization founded upon brotherly labor, following the Greek title which is usually rendered the New Testament, translated out of the Greek as a Labor Determinative Version, and diligently compared with former translations herein revised for the recovery of Biblical labor standards. Jackson, Michigan: Home of the American Labor Determinative Revision Committee.

1924 **Montgomery's Centenary Translation** Centenary Translation of the New Testament in Modern English. Translated by Helen Barrett Montgomery. Philadelphia: Judson Press. 2 vols.

In commemoration of the centenary of the American Baptist Publication Society, Mrs. Helen Barrett Montgomery of Rochester, N.Y., and a graduate of Wellesley College, published this translation. Many of her colloquial paragraph and chapter headings are striking, such as "Play the Game," "A 'Close-up' of Sin," "Paul's Swan Song" and "Orchestrate Your Virtues."

1925 **Askwith's Psalms** The Psalms Books IV and V. Rendered into English in Rhythm Consonant with that of the Original Hebrew by E. H. Askwith. London: M. Hopkinson and Company.

1925 **People's New Covenant** The People's New Covenant. Translated from the Metaphysical — Standpoint by Arthur E. Overbury. Monrovia, Calif.: Arthur E. Overbury.

This version is based on the premise of Scientific Statement of Being, as given in *Science and Health* by Mary Baker Eddy.

1925 **Children's Bible** The Children's Bible. Selections from the Old and New Testaments. Translated and arranged by Henry A. Gherman and Charles Foster Kent. New York: Charles Scribner's Sons.

A translation in readable, simple English of selections from the Old Testament and New Testament. Includes not only narratives, but poetic and didactic selections.

1926 **Moffatt** A New Translation of The Bible, Containing the Old and New Testaments, by James Moffatt. New York and London: Harper and Brothers.

20TH-CENTURY ENGLISH BIBLE VERSIONS cont.

New Testament, 1913. New edition, revised, 1917. Old Testament, 1924-25, in 2 vols. Vol. I: Genesis-Esther (1924). Vol. II: Job-Malachi (1925). Revision of complete Bible in 1935.

1927 **Kent's Student's Old Testament** The Student's Old Testament Logically and Chronologically Arranged and translated by Charles Foster Kent. New York: Charles Scribner's Sons, 1904-27.

Six vols. I: Narratives of the Beginnings of Hebrew History from the Creation to the Establishment of the Hebrew Kingdom, 1904. II: Israel's Historical and Biographical Narratives from the Establishment of the Hebrew Kingdom to the End of the Maccabean Struggle, 1905. III: The Sermons, Epistles, and Apocalypses of Israel's Prophets from the Beginning of the Assyrian Period to the End of the Maccabean Struggle, 1910. IV: Israel's Laws and Legal Precedents from the Days of Moses to the Closing of the Legal Canon, 1907. V: The Songs, Hymns, and Prayers of the Old Testament, 1914. VI: Proverbs and Didactic Poems, 1927.

1927 **Smith-Goodspeed** The Bible. An American Translation. The Old Testament Translated by J. M. Powis Smith and a Group of Scholars. The New Testament Translated by Edgar J. Goodspeed. Chicago: The University of Chicago Press.

Revised, 1935. The New Testament, An American Translation, 1923. The Old Testament, An American Translation, 1927. The Apocrypha, An American Translation, 1938. Reprinted, with Apocrypha included, 1939.

1927 **Christian's Bible** New Testament. Strasburg, Pa.: George N. Le Fevre.

A translation from the Greek, chiefly from B and Aleph. Not simply a translation of the Words, but under the guidance of the Holy Ghost, His thoughts as recorded. George Le Fevre is considered the translator as well as publisher.

1928 **Czarnomska Version** The Authentic Literature of Israel freed from the Disarrangements, Expansions, and Comments of Early Native Editors, edited with an introduction by Elizabeth Czarnomska. New York: The Macmillan Company, 1924-28.

1928 **Spiritualist's Matthew** The Good Message according to Matthew. For the use of Christian Spiritualists, an entirely new and accurate translation edited by J. W. Potter. London: Society of Communion.

1929 **Gowen's Psalms** The Psalms; or, the Book of Praises. A New Transcription and Translation arranged Strophically and Metrically from a critically constructed text, with introduction, textual notes, and glossary by Herbert H. Gowen. London: Mowbray.

1930 **Loux's Mark** Mark: To Every Man His Work, His Pay, His Rest. Translated by DuBois H. Loux. Jackson, Mich.: Privately printed.

1931 **Wales's Psalms** The Psalms. A Revised Translations, by Frank H. Wales. London: Oxford University Press.

1932 **Chaplain Ballentine** Our God and Godhealth, our Healer. Godhealth's Messenger and Godhealth's Message of Life and Light and Love and Law, the wisdom of the ages: translated from the original Greek, reinterpreted in the thought-forms, language, and idioms of America today, and arranged for reading with sustained interest from beginning to end as a modern novel, by Chaplain [Frank Schell] Ballentine. Collegeville, Pa.: The Craigie Publishing Company.

1932 **Kleist's Memoirs of St. Peter** The Memoirs of St. Peter, or the Gospel according to

St. Mark, translated into English sense-lines. By James A. Kleist, S. J. Milwaukee: Bruce Publishing Company.

—   Translated into sense-lines, which it is maintained is the form that resembles the original itself.

1933 **Torrey's Four Gospels** The Four Gospels, a New Translation by Charles Cutler Torrey. New York and London: Harper and Brothers.

⟶   Its purpose is to show that the Gospels of Matthew, Mark, and John were composed in Aramaic.

1934 **Royds's Epistles and Gospels** The Epistles and Gospels for the Sundays & chief holy days of the Christian year. A new translation by Thomas Fletcher Royds. Oxford: Basil Blackwell.

New Testament into modern English: "such English as intelligent village schoolchildren can understand without much explaining of long words." Nestle Greek text. Not continuous text. Good straightforward translation.

1934 **Old Testament in Colloquial English** The Books of the Old Testament in Colloquial English, 1920–34.

Listed in E. H. Robertson's *The New Translations of the Bible.*

❝❞ **He who hath heard the Word of God can bear his silences.** —St. Ignatius

FOCUS
QUOTE

1934 **Wade** The Documents of the New Testament. Translated and Historically Arranged with Critical Introduction by G. W. Wade. London: Thomas Murby & Company. Copies of Mark, Luke, and John issued separately in 1936.

Claims to be "an accurate, yet not literal" translation. Avoids ambiguity by presenting what the translator judges to be the most probable meaning. Literary relationships are indicated in the Synoptics, Acts, and 2 Peter–Jude. Westcott and Hort text.

1935 **Westminster Version** The Westminster Version of the Sacred Scriptures, general editor, Cuthbert Lattey. Introductions and commentaries with translation.

New Testament, 1935. Smaller edition in 1948, translations with brief introductions by Father Lattey.

New Testament in parts from 1913–35, edited by Cuthbert Lattey and J. Keating. Malachi, 1934—Lattey. Ruth, 1935—Lattey. Nahum and Habakkuk, 1937—Bevenot. Jonah, 1938—T. E. Bird. Psalms 1–41, 1939—Lattey. Psalms, 1944—Lattey. Daniel, 1948—Lattey. Obadiah, Micah, Zephaniah, Haggai, Zechariah, 1953—Sebastian Bullough.

An excellent translation by English Roman Catholic scholars under the editorship of Cuthbert Lattey, S.J., based on the original texts in both Testaments. An independent venture; not an "official" translation.

1937 **Cornish's St. Paul from the Trenches** Translated by Gerald Warre Cornish. Two epistles of Corinthians, part of Ephesians.

For the story behind this expanded version see F. F. Bruce, *The English Bible,* New and Revised Edition, p. 22 (New York: Oxford Press).

1937 **Greber's New Testament** The New Testament. A New Translation and Explanation Based on The Oldest Manuscripts, by Johannes Greber. New York: John Felsberg, Inc.

20TH-CENTURY ENGLISH BIBLE VERSIONS cont.

The English translation was made by a professional translator and corrected by a committee of American clergymen. A somewhat eccentric translation. It is based mainly on Codex Bezae, but at times the translator has given a version with no MS authority. Originally published in German but subsequently translated into English. Translator is a former Roman Catholic priest who came to believe in communication with the world of divine spirits.

1937 **Martin's New Testament** The New Testament critically reconstructed and retranslated, by William Wallace Martin. Nashville, Tenn.: Parthenon Press.

Epistles in 2 vols. Part I: Press of Marshall and Bruce Company, Nashville, 1929. Part II: Press of the Methodist Episcopal Church, Nashville, 1930.

The twenty-one canonical Epistles have been reconstructed into thirty-six, including as authors Apollos, Barnabas, and John, son of Zebedee (as the writer of the Epistle of James).

The Psalms Complete: Their Prayers, their Collects, their Praises, in three Books. Separated, arranged, and translated by William Wallace Martin. Nashville, Tenn.: Marshall & Bruce Company.

The Book of Job in Two Versions: A Judean Version, an Ephramaean Version; and The Book of Ecclesiastes. Nashville, Tenn.: Methodist Publishing House. Isaian Prophecies. Nashville, Tenn.: Parthenon Press.

Jeremiah–Ezekiel Prophecies. Nashville, Tenn.: Parthenon Press.

The Book of Genesis Complete. The Ephramaean Version . . .Judean Version. Nashville, Tenn.: Parthenon Press.

Twelve Minor Prophets. Nashville, Tenn.: Parthenon Press.

1937 **Spencer's New Testament** The New Testament of Our Lord and Saviour Jesus Christ; translated into English from the original Greek by the Very Rev. Francis Aloysius Spencer, O.P.; edited by Charles J. Callan, O.P., and John A. McHugh, O.P. New York: The Macmillan Company.

After publishing a new translation of the Gospels from the Latin in 1898, Father Francis Aloysius Spencer was moved to attempt a new translation from the Greek. The four Gospels were published in 1901 and the rest of the NT finished with notes shortly before Spencer's death in 1913. The whole NT, however, was not published until 1937, under the editorship of Charles J. Callan and John A. McHugh, and has been reprinted several times since. The words of Christ are printed in italics, quotations from the OT are put in small capitals, and Vulgate readings that differ from the Greek are given in brackets or footnotes.

1937 **Williams's New Testament** The New Testament; a translation in the language of the people, by Charles B. Williams. Boston: Bruce Humphries. Slightly revised edition, Chicago: Moody Press, 1950. Verse numbers inserted in the text. Westcott and Hort Greek text.

A Greek professor from Union University (Jackson, Tenn.), Charles B. Williams's aim was to reproduce as far as possible the exact shades of meaning in the Greek tenses. To do this requires the use of auxiliaries and the like in English and can result in overtranslation and in the use of language that is hardly the "language of the people."

1938 **Book of Books** A Translation of the New Testament Complete and Unabridged. London: R.T.S. The Lutterworth Press, The United Society for Christian Literature. R. Mercer Wilson, General Secretary, The United Society for Christian Literature translated this NT to celebrate the centenary of the *Annotated Para-*

graph Bible, which he follows in the arrangement of his text, and the fourth centenary of the setting up of the English Bible in the churches. Rather straightforward simple translation.

1938 **Buttenweiser's Psalms** The Psalms. Chronologically Treated with a New Translation by Moses Buttenweiser, Prof. Emeritus of Biblical Exegesis, Hebrew Union College. Chicago: The University of Chicago Press.

1938 **Clementson's New Testament** The New Testament. A Translation by Edgar Lewis Clementson. Pittsburgh: The Evangelization Society of the Pittsburgh Bible Institute.

1939 **Oesterley Psalms** The Psalms. Translated with Text-Critical and Exegetical Notes by W. O. C. Oesterley. London: S.P.C.K.; New York: The Macmillan Company. 2 vols.

1940 **Dakes's Gospels** Christ Jesus: The Authentic Story of the Founder of Christianity as told by Matthew, Mark, Luke and John in the Four Gospels. Translated from the original Greek by John A. Dakes. Chicago: Avalon Publishing Company.

Dakes was a Greek businessman who felt "that a translation made by a Greek who had learned the original language of the Gospels in the schools of Greece might prove helpful." Certain Greek words are transliterated, such as *petros* and *petra* in Matthew 16:18, *ecclesia, aeonian,* and *Logos.* A glossary appears at the back of the book.

1940 **St. Mark in Current English** By Mary L. Matheson. Melbourne: National Council of Religious Education of Australia.

1944 **Callan's Psalms** The Psalms. Translated from the Latin Psalter, in the Light of the Hebrew, of the Septuagint and Peshitta Versions, and of the Psalterium Juxta Hebraeos of St. Jerome. With Introductions, Critical Notes, and Spiritual Reflections by Charles J. Callan. New York: Joseph F. Wagner.

---

66 99
FOCUS QUOTE
The amazing wealth of the Bible is precisely what makes it a difficult book to study. —Paul Tournier

---

1944 **Wand's New Testament Letters** The New Testament Letters, prefaced and paraphrased by J. W. C. Wand. Brisbane, Australia. Revised edition published in England, 1946.

Romans–Jude. According to the Introduction, the work "may be called either a free translation or a close paraphrase." "I have tried," says Bishop Wand, "to put the Epistles into the kind of language a Bishop might use in writing a monthly letter for his diocesan magazine."

1945 **Stringfellow's New Testament** New Testament. A Translation, Harmony and Annotations by Erwin Edward Stringfellow. . . . Planographed by John S. Swift Company, Inc.
Vol. I: The Gospels (1943). Vol. II: Acts–Revelation (1945). Dubuque, Iowa: Wm. C. Brown Company
Westcott and Hort text.

1946 **Lenski** The Interpretation of [the New Testament] . . . R. C. H. Lenski. Columbus, Ohio: Lutheran Book Concern, 1931–46.
Twelve vols. Commentary with independent translation by a noted Lutheran scholar.

20TH-CENTURY ENGLISH BIBLE VERSIONS cont.

1947 Eerdmans's Psalms The Hebrew Books of Psalms by B. D. Eerdmans. Oudtestamentliche Studien, IV. Leiden: E. J. Brill.

1947 Swann's New Testament The New Testament. Translated from the Greek text of Westcott and Hort. By Rev. George Swann, Louisville, Ky.: Pentecostal Publishing Company. 2nd ed., 1949.
Third ed.

1948 Letchworth New Testament The New Testament. Letchworth Version in Modern English, by T. F. Ford and R. E. Ford. Letchworth, Herts: Letchworth Printer, Ltd.
A translation of the TR Greek text into current English, mainly using words of Anglo-Saxon origin, and free from colloquialisms and slang expressions. Seeks to maintain in modern dress the simple, dignified style of writing associated with the classical English versions.

1949 Basic Bible Containing the Old and New Testaments in Basic English. Cambridge: The University Press and Evans Bros. New York: Dutton.
The New Testament in Basic English, 1940. Whole Bible, 1949. Selections, 1933; Micah and Habakkuk, 1934; Mark, 1945; John, 1938.
Basic English is a system of simplified English with a primary vocabulary of 850 words devised by C. K. Ogden as an international auxiliary language and as an aid in learning English. In 1940 a committee under the direction of S. H. Hooke of the University of London produuced an independent translation of the New Testament, using the 850 words in the primary vocabulary of Basic English to which 50 special Bible words and 100 others were added.

1949 Leslie's Psalms The Psalms. Translated and Interpreted in the Light of Hebrew Life and Worship by Elmer A. Leslie. New York and Nashville: Abingdon-Cokesbury Press.

1951 Authentic Version The New Testament. Plattsburg, Mo.: Brotherhood Authentic Bible Society.
Anonymous translator: "Believing that I have been given divine authority through the Holy Spirit to bring the true translation of the original Greek text, and that which has been given me through the inspiration of the Holy Spirit, I have diligently and carefully compared with the original Greek text by the use of the best Greek dictionaries and former translations, some out of the Greek and some Latin: and find that what the Spirit has given me is according to the Original Greek." Modern speech version.

1951 Vernon's Mark The Gospel of St. Mark: A New Translation in Simple English, translated by Edward Vernon.
For the average intelligent child of twelve years old and upwards.

1952 New Testament in Plain English The New Testament; a new translation in plain English by Charles Kingsley Williams. London: S.P.C.K., Longmans, Green and Company. The Life of Our Lord Jesus Christ according to St. Luke, together with some passages from the other Gospels, newly done into very simple English from the Greek of The Revised Version, 1933. Matthew, 1934.
"Plain English" is a simplified form of the English language based on a list of 1,500 "fundamental and common words that make up ordinary English speech," plus some 160 or 170 others that are explained in a glossary at the end of the volume. The translation is based on Souter's Greek Text (Oxford Press, 1910).

1952 **Penguin Bible (Rieu)** The Four Gospels, a New Translation from the Greek by E. V. Rieu. London and Melbourne: Penguin Books.

Acts of the Apostles by Saint Luke, by C. H. Rieu, son of E. V. Rieu.

E. V. Rieu justifies his translation on the basis that it is from the literary standpoint more in harmony with the Greek Gospels than the KJV, whose translators "mistook ⏤ fidelity to the idiom of the Greek for fidelity to its meaning" and "felt the sanctity and importance of the original so keenly that the use of normal language would have seemed a kind of sacrilege." Accurate and readable.

1952 **Revised Standard Version** The Holy Bible, being the Version Set Forth A.D. 1611. Revised 1881 and 1901 and Revised 1952. New York, Toronto, Edinburgh: Thomas Nelson and Sons.

New Testament, 1946. Old Testament with Complete Bible, 1952. Apocrypha, 1957.

---

66 99
FOCUS
QUOTE

I am sorry for men who do not read the Bible every day. I wonder why they deprive themselves of the strength and the pleasure. —Woodrow Wilson

---

1954 **Kissane's Psalms** The Books of Psalms. Translated from a Critically Revised Hebrew Text with a Commentary by Monsignor Edward J. Kissane. Dublin: Brown and Nolan, Ltd. Vol. I, 1953; Vol. II, 1954.

1954 **Kleist and Lilly's New Testament** The New Testament rendered from the original Greek with Explanatory Notes. Milwaukee: Bruce Publishing Company.

The Four Gospels translated by James A. Kleist, S.J., and the Acts to Revelation by Joseph L. Lilly, C. M. Made from 1943 Bover Greek Text into modern popular English. An independent modern American translation.

1954 **Kleist and Lynam's Psalms** The Psalms in Rhythmic Prose. By James A. Kleist, S.J., and Thomas James Lynam, S.J. Milwaukee: Bruce Publishing Company.

Based on Latin text of the Pontifical Biblical Institute, Rome.

1954 **Moore's New Testament** A New, Independent, Individual Translation from the Greek, by George Albert Moore, Colonel, U.S.A. Chevy Chase, MD.: The Country Dollar Press.

Based on Souter's 1950 Greek text. Gospels issued separately in 1953.

1955 **Fides Translation (Psalms)** The Psalms. Introduction and Notes by Mary Perkins Ryan. Chicago: Fides Publishers Association.

Made in accordance with the new Roman Psalter.

1955 **Knox** The Holy Bible; a translation from the Latin Vulgate in the light of the Hebrew and Greek originals. Authorized by the hierarchy of England and Wales and the hierarchy of Scotland. Translated by Monsignor Knox. London: Burns and Oates.

Old Testament. New York: Sheed and Ward, 1948-50, 2 vols. Vol. I: Genesis-Esther. Vol. II: Job-Maccabees.

New Testament. Newly Translated from the Vulgate Latin at the Request of their Lordships, the Archbishops of England Wales. New York: Sheed & Ward, British Trial Edition, 1944.

20TH-CENTURY ENGLISH BIBLE VERSIONS cont.

1955 **Schonfield's Authentic New Testament** The Authentic New Testament, edited and translated from the Greek for the general reader by Hugh J. Schonfield. London: D. Dobson.

—   This is a work of high quality by the distinguished Jewish Scholar, Dr. Hugh J. Schonfield, who approaches these documents "as if they had recently been recovered from a cave in Palestine or beneath the sands of Egypt, and had never previously been given to the public." Much helpful information on the Jewish references in the New Testament is given in the Notes and Introduction.

1956 **Laubach's Inspired Letters** The Inspired Letters in Clearest English. Prepared by Frank C. Laubach. New York: Thomas Nelson and Sons.

Romans–Jude. Written in short, clear sentences with a limited vocabulary of about two thousand words, this translation is intended as a preparation for the reading of the RSV for beginning students of English. The Gospels and Acts, the translator feels, are simple enough in the RSV. By the world's leader in the fight against illiteracy.

1957 **Concordant Version** International Edition. The Sacred Scriptures. An Idiomatic, Consistent, Emphasized Version. Los Angeles: Concordant Publishing concern.

Old Testament—Half title: Concordant Version of the Hebrew Scriptures. In a Beginning, commonly called "Genesis."

—   [The New Testament] Concordant Version, 1919-26. One-volume reprint, 1931.

This version is based on the belief that "every word in the original should have its own English equivalent." It is said to aim "at truth and accuracy rather than literary elegance." It shows the eccentricities "of a self-taught and opinionated 'one man' translator who has certain peculiar views to proclaim yet is 'reverent, careful, and thorough.' "

1957 **Lamsa's** The Holy Bible from ancient Eastern manuscripts. Containing the Old and New Testaments, translated from the Peshitta, the authorized Bible of the church of the East, by George M. Lamsa. Philadelphia: A. J. Holman Company.

The Four Gospels according to the Eastern Version, 1933.

The Book of Psalms according to the Eastern Version, 1939.

The New Testament, 1940.

—   George M. Lamsa's translation purports to be produced "from original Aramaic sources." Lamsa's original claims for his work are generally questioned. The Peshitta is not to be identified with the "original Aramaic." Lamsa also adapted some questionable renderings such as "rope" for "camel" in Matthew 19:24, et al.

1958 **Hudson** The Pauline Epistles: Their Meanings and Message. Introduction, Translation, Marginal Analysis, and Paraphrase by James T. Hudson. London: James Clarke & Company, Ltd.

—   "New translation with the missing steps in Paul's thought supplied in brackets." Omits Hebrews.

1958 **Meissner's Gospels** New Testament Gospels, a Modern Translation by Lawrence Meissner. Portland, Oreg.

All the verses, 40 percent fewer words.

1958 **Phillips's New Testament** New Testament in Modern English. New York: The Macmillan Company letters to Young Churches; a translation of the New Testament Epistles, by J. B. Phillips; with an introduction by C. S. Lewis, 1951. A corrected edition, 1957. First published in England, 1947. The Gospels, translated into modern English by J.

B. Phillips, c. 1951. First published in 1952. The Young Church in Action; a Translation of the Acts of the Apostles by J. B. Phillips, 1955. Book of Revelation, 1957. Gospels, a corrected edition, 1958. Four Prophets: Amos, Hosea, First Isaiah, Micah; a modern translation from the Hebrew, by J. B. Phillips, 1963. Second revised edition of the New Testament, 1973.

1958 **Tomanek's New Testament** The New Testament of Our Lord and Savior Jesus
— Anointed, by James L. Tomanek. Pocatello, Ida.: Arrowhead Press.

1959 **Cressman** St. Mark. Toronto: Full Gospel Publishing House. Mark, 2d ed., 1960. John, American Bible Society, 1962. Simplified English for Liberians by Annie Cressman of the Assemblies of God Mission.

1959 **Modern Language Bible (Berkeley)** The Holy Bible, the Berkeley Version in Modern English, containing the Old and New Testaments. Translated afresh from the original languages and diligently compared with previous translations, with numerous helpful nondoctrinal notes to aid the understanding of the reader. Gerrit Verkuyl, editor-in-chief and translator of the New Testament section. Grand Rapids: Zondervan Publishing House.
Berkeley Version of the New Testament, 1945. Berkeley, Calif.: James J. Gillick & Company. Grand Rapids: Zondervan Publishing House, 1950, 1953.

1960 **The Children's "King James"** The Children's "King James" Bible: New Testament. Jay Green is responsible for the wording; "Peter" Palmer for the stories. Evansville, Ind.: Modern Bible Translations.
— Not KJV of 1611, but a modern version using the same text the KJ translation used.

1961 **New World Translation—Jehovah's Witnesses** New World Translation of the Holy Scriptures, rendered from the original languages by the New World Bible Translation Committee. Revised. Brooklyn: Watchtower Bible and Tract Society of New York.
The New World Translation of the Christian Greek Scriptures, 1950.
— Based on Westcott and Hort, supplemented by Nestle, Bover, Merk.
New World Translation of the Hebrew Scriptures, 1953–60. Issued in five vols. Genesis–Ruth, 1953; 1 Samuel–Esther, 1955; Job–Song of Solomon, 1957; Isaiah–Lamentations, 1958; Ezekiel–Malachi, 1960. Based on 3d ed. Kittel, 1951.

FOCUS QUOTE **Nobody ever outgrows Scripture; the book widens and deepens with our years.** —Charles Haddon Spurgeon

---

1961 **Noli's Greek Orthodox New Testament** The New Testament of our Lord and Savior Jesus Christ. Translated into English from the approved Greek text of the Church of
— Constantinople and the Church of Greece, by Fan S. Noli. Boston: Albanian Orthodox Church in America.

1961 **One Way** One Way: The Jesus People New Testament. A Translation in Modern English. Pasadena, Calif.: Compass Press.
This is the same as Norlie's The New Testament in Modern English, 1951.

1961 **Simplified New Testament (Norlie)** Simplified New Testament in Plain English for Today's Reader. A New Translation from the Greek by Olaf M. Norlie. With the Psalms for Today, a new translation in current English by R. K. Harrison. Grand Rapids: Zondervan Publishing House.

20TH-CENTURY ENGLISH BIBLE VERSIONS cont.

— Dr. Olaf M. Norlie of St. Olaf College designed this translation particularly for teenagers. It is rendered in plain, lucid, and straightforward English.

An earlier translation of Norlie was published by the author in 1951 in Northfield, Minn., with the title: The New Testament . . . in Modern English translated from the original Greek and supplied with an outline by Olaf Morgan Norlie. Still earlier, in 1943, a translation of the Gospel of John was published in mimeographed form in San Antonio, Tex., by the Life Builders Press.

1961 **Wuest's Expanded New Testament** Expanded Translation of the Greek New Testament by Kenneth S. Wuest. Grand Rapids: Wm. B. Eerdmans Publishing Company.

Vol. 1: Gospels (1956). Vol. 2: Acts through Ephesians (1958). Vol. 3: Philippians through Revelation (1959).

— Kenneth S. Wuest endeavors to reproduce for the English readers the nuances of the Greek text, both philologically and theologically. Bible scholars may feel that he at times overtranslates and finds shades of meaning not actually in the Greek text. He — does for all parts of speech what Williams does for verbs.

1962 **Children's Version** The Children's Version of the Holy Bible. New York: McGraw Hill.

Printed in large, Caledonia type for easy reading. The text is arranged in paragraphs, though the verse numbers are retained in small type interspersed through the text. Difficult words, names, and places are diacritically marked and some are phonetically pronounced. The text is a simplification and modernization of the KJV. The preface is by Jay P. Green.

1963 **Gelineau's Psalms** The Psalms: A New Translation. Translated from the Hebrew and arranged for Singing to the Psalmody of Joseph Gelineau. Philadelphia: The Westminster Press.

1963 **The Holy Name Bible** The Holy Name Bible containing the Holy Name Version of the Old and New Testaments. Revised by A. B. Traina. Irvington, N.J.: The Scripture Research Association, Inc.

— The New Testament of our Messiah and Saviour Yahshua. Sacred Name Version, 1950.

This translation is understood to have been made by A. B. Traina and reprinted at — his expense. The version attempts to restore Semitic proper names to their Aramaic or Hebrew form and to clear up difficulties in the text in the light of possible Semitic background.

1964 **Anchor Bible** Anchor Bible, edited by William F. Albright and David N. Freedman. Individual translators for books. Garden City, N.J.: Doubleday & Company.

1964 **Hadas's Psalms** The Book of Psalms for the Modern Reader: A New Translation by Gershon Hadas. New York: Jonathan David.

1965 **Amplified Bible** The Amplified Bible, containing the Amplified Old Testament and the Amplified New Testament. Grand Rapids: Zondervan Publishing House.

The Amplified New Testament. Zondervan Publishing House, 1958–65. Old Testament: Part I (1964), Genesis–Esther; Part II (1962), Job–Malachi. Zondervan Publishing House. Translation by Frances E. Siwert.

1965 **Bruce's Expanded Paraphrase** An Expanded Paraphrase of the Epistles of Paul. Printed in parallel with the Revised Version, with fuller references by Drs. Scrivener, Moulton & Greenup, by F. F. Bruce. Exeter: Paternoster Press.

American edition has title: The Letters of Paul: Expanded Paraphrase.

This paraphrase is designed, as Bruce states, "to make the course of Paul's argument as clear as possible." The "expanded paraphrase" is printed alongside the Revised Version of 1881, "for the convenience and interest of readers who may care to compare and contrast two renderings produced on directly opposite principles."

1966 **The Bible in Simplified English** Listen . . . The Lord is Speaking: The Bible in Simplified English. Collegeville, Minn.: The Liturgical Press.

The authorized English edition of the Katholische Schulbibel, which is an abridged selection of biblical passages rearranged to provide a chronological history of the biblical period. The poetic books, duplicated historical material, and Epistles are not included. Written in simple English, this is intended for beginners in the study of the Bible.

---

66 99 In this little Book is contained all the wisdom of the world. —George
FOCUS Heinrich Ewald
QUOTE

1966 **Burke** God Is for Real, Man: Interpretations of Bible Passages and Stories as Told by Some of God's Bad-tempered Angels with Busted Haloes to Carl F. Burke. New York: Association Press.

1969 edition entitled God Is Beautiful, Man.

— Free treatment of selected Bible passages in American downtown slang by young people of the inner city.

1966 **Jerusalem Bible** General editor, Alexander Jones. Garden City, New York, and London: Doubleday and Darton, Longman and Todd.

1966 **Living Scriptures** The Living Scriptures, a New Translation in the King James Tradition. Edited by Jay P. Green. Marshatton, Del.: National Foundation for Christian American Bible Society. New York: The Macmillan Company.

1967 **Dale's New World** New World: The Heart of the New Testament in Plain English, by Alan T. Dale. London: Oxford University Press, c. 1967, 1968.

1967 **Liverpool Vernacular Gospels** The Gospels in Scouse, translated by Dick Williams and Frank Shaw. Revised edition, London: White Lion Publishers, 1977.

"A rollicking, carefree interpretaion of some Gospel passages in the Liverpool vernacular."

1968 **Cotton Patch Version** The Cotton Patch Version of Paul's Epistles, by Clarence Jordan. New York: Association Press.

The Cotton Patch version of Luke and Acts, 1969. The Cotton Patch Version of Matthew and John, 1970. First eight chapters of John only. The Cotton Patch Version of Hebrews and the General Epistles, 1973.

A local dialect version rather than merely an English version. Intended for the South, especially the area around Atlanta. This version goes to the limit of the spectrum in translating ideas and substitutes local place names for biblical ones. Based on Nestle-Aland, 23rd ed., 1957. By the founder of an interracial farming community in Americus, Georgia, with a Ph.D. in Greek from Southern Baptist Theological Seminary.

1968 **Hanson's Psalms in Modern Speech** The Psalms in Modern Speech for Public and Private Use, by Richard S. Hanson. Philadelphia: Fortress Press.

20TH-CENTURY ENGLISH BIBLE VERSIONS cont.

3 vols. Vol. 1: Psalms 1–41. Vol. 2: Psalms 42–89. Vol. 3: Psalms 90–150.

A fresh poetic rendering of "the Hymnbook of Ancient Israel," with special attention to its liturgical usage. Contains an informative "Introduction," introductory notes to many of the Psalms, and footnotes explaining deviations from previous translations.

1968 **Restoration of Original Name New Testament** The New Testament of Our Master and
— Saviour Yahvahshua the Messiah (commonly called Jesus Christ): Restoration of Original Name New Testament. Junction City, Oreg.: Missionary Dispensary Bible Research.

Rotherham's version but with changes made principally by returning to the Hebrew form of God's name and by replacing Lord and God in the New Testament by
— YAHVAH or, for the latter, Elohim when it is used with God.

1969 **Barclay's New Testament** The New Testament: a new translation by William Barclay. London, Cleveland: Collins.

Gospels and Acts, 1968. Letters and The Revelation, 1969.

1969 **Children's New Testament** Translated by Gleason H. Ledyard. Waco, Tex.: Word Books.

1970 **King James II New Testament** Translated by Jay P. Green. Byron Center, Mich.: Associated Publishers.

1970 **The Mercier New Testament** The Mercier New Testament: A Version of the New Testament in Modern English. Part I: Matthew, Mark, Luke, John. Prepared by Kevin Condon. Cork: Mercier Press. (Identical with The Alba House New Testament.)

A fresh Catholic translation from the Greek in plain, simple, modern English. Patterned after the German Das Neue Testament fur Menschen unserer Zeit (1964). Not meant to compete with the standard English versions, but to lead to a greater appreciation and use of them. Illustrated by a hundred carefully selected photographs.

1970 **New American Bible** Translated from the original languages, with the critical use of all the ancient sources, by members of the Catholic Biblical Association of America. New York: P. J. Kenedy.
—   The New Testament of Our Lord and Savior Jesus Christ translated from the Latin Vulgate. A revision of the Challoner-Rheims Version edited by Catholic Scholars under the patronage of the episcopal committee of the Confraternity of Christian Doctrine. Paterson, N.J.: St. Anthony Guild Press, 1941. (The NT in the NAB is a new translation from the Greek text.)

Genesis, 1948; Vol. I (Genesis–Ruth), 1952; Vol. III (Sapiential or Wisdom Books), 1955; Vol. IV (Prophetic Books), 1961; Vol. II (Samuel–Maccabees), 1969.

1970 **New English Bible** The New English Bible with the Apocrypha. Oxford University Press and Cambridge University Press.

New Testament, 1961; 2d ed., 1970. The Old Testament and Apocrypha, 1970.

1971 **Blackwelder's Exegetical Translation** Letters from Paul. An Exegetical Translation by Boyce W. Blackwelder. Anderson, Ind.: Warner Press.

Based on Nestle's 4th ed., 1904. At times reads more like a condensed commentary
— than a translation. Sacrifices literary quality for exegetical values. Uses brackets in place of italics to indicate words or expressions that are added to complete the meaning of the Greek. Does not include Hebrews. By the chairman of the Department of NT at Anderson College, Anderson, Ind.

1971 **The Living Bible** The Living Bible, Paraphrased. Wheaton, Ill.: Tyndale House.
Living History of Israel, a paraphrase of Joshua, Judges, 1 and 2 Samuel, 1 and 2 Kings, 1 and 2 Chronicles, Ezra, and Nehemiah, 1970. Living Prophecies: the Minor Prophets paraphrased with Daniel and the Revelation, 1965, 1967. Living New Testament Paraphrased, 1967. Living Letters: the Paraphrased Epistles, c. 1962, 1967.

1971 **New American Standard Bible** Carol Stream, Ill.: Creation House.
New Testament Pilot ed., La Habra, Calif. Produced and published by the Lockman Foundation, 1963.

1972 **The Bible in Living English** Translated by Stephen T. Byington. Brooklyn, N.Y.: Watchtower Bible and Tract Society of New York, Inc.

1973 **A Child's Bible** A Child's Bible in Colour: The Old Testament, rewritten for children by Anne Edwards. The New Testament, rewritten for children by Shirley Steen. London and New York: Pan Books and Paulist Press.

1973 **Common Bible** Common Bible: The Holy Bible; Revised Standard Version, containing the Old and New Testament with Apocrypha/Deuterocanonical Books. New York: William Collins Sons.

1973 **New International Version** The Holy Bible, New International Version: The New Testament. Grand Rapids: Zondervan Bible Publishers.

❝❞ FOCUS QUOTE I read my Bible to know what people ought to do, and my newspaper to know what they are doing. —Cardinal John Henry Newman

---

1973 **The Psalms** The Psalms: An Exploratory Translation by Mother Maus [Lydia Gysi]. New Pagnell, Bucks.: Green Orthodox Monastery of the Assumption.

1973 **The Translator's New Testament** The Translator's New Testament. London: The British and Foreign Bible Society.
Under the direction of W. D. McHardy a team of thirty-five Bible scholars and eighteen missionary linguists prepared this translation in order "to make available, to those translators of the New Testament into their own mother tongue who depend on English for access to the sources of biblical scholarship, such help as is necessary for the making of effective translations in the languages of today." Includes Notes and a Glossary. Based on the United Bible Societies" Greek Text, 1966.

1973 **The Better Version of the New Testament** The Better Version of the New Testament based on the Greek text according to eminent scholars and according to certain fundamental principles and rules of biblical interpretation, by Chester Estes. Muscle Shoals, Ala.

1974 **Klingensmith New Testament** The New Testament in Everyday English, by Don J. Klingensmith, Fargo, N. Dak.: Kayes Inc.
A translation of the "simple Greek" into the simple words of everyday English. Leaves out chapter and verse divisions. In the Gospels the Pharisees are the Orthodox, the Sadducees are Liberals, scribes are scholars, disciples are students, hypocrites are stage players, Gehenna is a junkyard, and repentance is a change of thinking.

1975 **The Word Made Fresh** A paraphrase of selected portions of the Bible by Andrew Edington. 3 vols. Atlanta: John Knox.

20TH-CENTURY ENGLISH BIBLE VERSIONS cont.

1976 **Train Up a Child** Train Up a Child. Pt 1, Genesis, paraphrased for children by Ben Nutt. Chicago: Adams Press.

1976 **Concise Jewish Bible** Edited and translated by Philip Birnbaum. New York: Sanhe-
— drin Press.

1976 **Beck's: An American Translation** The Holy Bible in the Language of Today, An American Translation by William F. Beck. Stylistic alterations and other changes dictated by the latest MS evidence made by Elmer B. Smick and Erich H. Kiehl. Nashville: Hollman Bible Publishers.

The New Testament in the Language of Today, St. Louis: Concordia Publishing House, 1963.

A refreshing translation by a Lutheran scholar in simple, precise English. It is printed in readable type with orderly paragraphing and lively headings. OT quotations are printed in italics. Makes an attempt to date the events of the NT. In John 8:57 it follows P75 and a few other MSS in its translation "and Abraham has seen you?" "Grace" (*charis*) is usually translated as "love," and "justify" as "make righteous." Contains approximately twenty-five textual notes in the NT. A numbered list of OT references is given at the close of each book.

1976 **Good News Bible** The Bible in Today's English Version, New York: The American Bible Society, 1976.

Good News for Modern Man. The New Testament in Today's English Version. New York: American Bible Society, 1966, 1971, 1976.

Psalms for Modern Man, 1970. Job for Modern Man, 1971. Wisdom for Modern Man (Proverbs & Ecclesiastes), 1972.

1976 **Renaissance New Testament** The Renaissance New Testament, by Randolph O. Yeager. Bowling Green, Ky.: Renaissance Press.

Contents, v. 1. Matthew I-VIII.

1976 **New Life Testament** The New Life Testament. Translated by Gleason H. Ledyard. Canby, Oreg.: Christian Literature International.

1976 **The Gospel Jesus** The Gospel Jesus: The Story in Modern English by Ronald Cox. Nole Plaza, Ind.: Our Sunday Visitor.

1977 **The Song of Songs** The Song of Songs: Love poems from the Bible, translated from the original Hebrew by Marcia Falk. 1st ed. New York: Harcourt Brace Jovanovich.

1977 **The Psalms** The Psalms translated [from the Hebrew] by Peter Levi, with an introduction by Nicholas de Lange. Harmondsworth: Penguin.

1977 **The Gospels in Scouse** The Gospels in Scouse by Dick Williams and Frank Shaw, illustrated by Derek Alden, introduction by David Sheppard. Rev. ed. London: White Lion Publishers.

1977 **Marrow Gospels** The Four Gospels; newly translated from the Greek. Luton, England: White Crescent Press.

For the most part uses the Greek text of The British and Foreign Bible Society.

1977 **The Psalms** The Psalms, a New Translation for Worship prepared by David L. Frost and a panel of Hebrew and Biblical Scholars. London: Collins Liturgical.

1977 **Christian Counselor's New Testament** The Christian Counselor's New Testament; a new translation in everyday English with notations . . . by Jay E. Adams. Grand Rapids: Baker Book House, 1977. NT in Everyday English, 1979.

1977 **The Holy Bible for Children** The Holy Bible for Children: A Simplified Version of the Old and New Testaments edited by Allan Hart Johsmann. Illustrations and maps by Don Kueker. St. Louis: Concordia.
A simplified retelling of selected portions of the books of the Bible.

1978 **The Holy Name Bible** The Holy Name Bible, containing the Holy Name Version of — the Old and New Testaments. Brandywine, Md.

 All things desirable to men are contained in the Bible.
—Abraham Lincoln
FOCUS
QUOTE

1978 **The New International Version** The Holy Bible, New International Version, Grand Rapids: Zondervan Bible Publishers.
The Holy Bible, New International Version: The New Testament, Grand Rapids: Zondervan Bible Publishers.

1978 **New Testament for the Deaf** The New Testament: English Version for the Deaf, translated from the Greek Text. Grand Rapids: Baker Book House.

1979 **The Psalms** The Psalms: A New Translation by Bonaventure Zerr. New York: Paulist Press.

1979 **Ephesians** Ephesians by R. Paul Caudill. Nashville: Broadman Press.

1979 **Lattimore's Gospels and Revelation** The Four Gospels and the Revelation. Newly translated from the Greek by Richmond Lattimore. New York: Farrar, Straus and Giroux.

1979 **Sasson's Ruth** Ruth: A New Translation with a Philological Commentary and a Formalist Folklorist Interpretation by Jack M. Sasson. Johns Hopkins University Near Eastern Studies. Baltimore: Johns Hopkins University Press.

1979 **Mitchell's Job** Into the Whirlwind: A Translation of the Book of Job, by Stephen Mitchell. Garden City, N.J.: Doubleday.

1982 **New Jewish Version** The Writings, Kethubim: The third section of A New Translation of the Holy Scriptures according to the Masoretic Text. Philadelphia: The Jewish Publication Society of America.
The Torah: The Five Books of Moses, the first section, 1962. 2nd rev. ed., 1973. The Five Megilloth and Jonah; a new translation. Introductions by H. L. Ginsberg, with drawings by Ismar David, 1969. Psalms 1972, Isaiah 1973, Jeremiah 1974.
The Prophets, Nevi'im. Second section of a new translation, 1978.

1982 **The New King James** Holy Bible. The New King James Version, Nashville, Camden, New York: Thomas Nelson Publishers, 1979.
The New King James Bible New Testament, Nashville, Camden, New York: Thomas Nelson Publishers.

20TH-CENTURY ENGLISH BIBLE VERSIONS cont.

1982 **The Reader's Digest Bible** The Reader's Digest Bible condensed from the Revised Standard Version, Old and New Testament, Pleasantville, N.Y.: The Reader's Digest Association.

1983 **First Corinthians** First Corinthians: a translation with notes by R. Paul Caudill. Nashville: Broadman Press.

1983 **In the Beginning** In the Beginning: A New Translation of the Book of Genesis. Edited and translated by Everett Fox. New York: Schocken.

1983 **International Children's Version: New Testament** Sweet Publishing.

1983 **New Testament in Scots** New Testament in Scots, edited and translated by William L.
? Lorimer. Edinburgh, Southside: Canongate.

1984 **The Five Scrolls** Herbert Bronstein and Albert Friedlander, eds. New York:
? CCAR.

1984 **New Testament into Everyday American English** Julian G. Anderson, ed. Naples, Fla.: Julian G. Anderson

1984 **The New World Translation** The New World Translation of the Holy Scriptures with
— references, rendered from the original languages, by the New World Bible Translation Committee, revised. Watchtower Bible and Tract Society of New York, International Bible Students Association.
  Revised edition of New World Translation published in 1981.

1984 **The Psalms** The Psalms: A New Translation for Prayer and Worship translated by Gary Chamberlain. Nashville: Upper Room.

1984 **The Psalter** The Psalter. Monks of the Brotherhood of Saint Francis, ed. Cambridge, N.Y.: New Skete Monastery.

1984 **The Word** The Word: New Century Version, NT. Translated by the World Bible Translation Center.

1985 **New Jerusalem Bible** Henry Wansbrough, ed. London: Darton, Longman and Todd and Garden City, N.Y.: Doubleday and Company.
  A revision of the New Jerusalem Bible published in 1966.

1985 **One Gospel** Taken literally from the four gospels in the Authorized KJV by the Bible compiled by R. Lewis Pryor. Jefferson, N.C.: McFarland.

1985 **The Original New Testament** by Hugh J. Schonfield. New York: Harper and Row.

1985 **The Psalms** Translated by Peter Levi, with an introduction by Nicholas de Lange. New York: Penguin Books.

1985 **Tanakh** A Translation of the Holy Scriptures according to the Traditional Hebrew Text.
⌒ Philadelphia: Jewish Publication Society. Was called the New Jewish Version before the complete Hebrew Scripture was published.
  Published in three stages: The Torah, 1962; The Prophets (Nevi'im), 1978; and The Writings (Kethuvim), 1982. Brought together in 1985 as the complete English Tanakh (Torah, Nevi'im, Kethuvim).
  Some parts of these three sections were published separately: The Five Megillot and Jonah, 1969; Psalms, 1973; Isaiah, 1973; Jeremiah, 1974; Job, 1980.

1986 **The Navarre Bible** St. Mark, 1986; St. John, 1987. Houston: Lumen Christi.

1986 **New American Bible New Testament** Revised edition. Collegeville, Minn.: Liturgical Press.

—→ Revision of the NAB New Testament published in 1970.

1986 **The Psalms** A new version by Roy Koeblitz. Palm.

1987 **The Holy Bible** English version for the deaf; translated from the original languages.
? Grand Rapids: Baker Book House.

1988 **The Book of Isaiah** A New Translation with Interpretive Keys from the Book of Mormon, by Avraham Giliadi. Salt Lake City, Utah: Deseret Book.

---

66 99
FOCUS QUOTE The Bible—banned, burned, beloved. More widely read, more frequently attacked than any other book in history. Generations of intellectuals have attempted to discredit it; dictators of every age have outlawed it and executed those who read it. Yet soldiers carry it into battle believing it more powerful than their weapons. Fragments of it smuggled into solitary prison cells have transformed ruthless killers into gentle saints.—Charles Colson

---

1988 **Christian Community Bible** Translated, presented and commented for the Christian
? communities of the Philippines and the Third World, and for those who seek God. 2d ed. Quezon City: Claretian Publications; Makati: Saint Paul Publications; Manila: Divine Word Publications.

1988 **New Testament** McCord's New Testament translation of the everlasting Gospel; translated by Hugo McCord. Freed-Hardeman College.

1988 **New Century** The Everyday Bible: New Testament. Minneapolis: World Wide Publishers.

1988 **God's Word to the Nations** The New Testament. Ed. Phillip B. Giessler. Luther Bible Society Revision Committee Staff. Cleveland: Biblion Publishers.

1988 **The Holy Gospel of John** A New Translation by P. Levi. Wilton, Conn.: Morehouse-Barlow.

1989 **God's New Covenant** A New Testament Translation. Translated from the Greek by Heinz W. Cassirer. Grand Rapids: Eerdmans.

1989 **Revised English Bible with the Apocrypha** Oxford and Cambridge: Oxford University Press and Cambridge University Press.
A revision of the New English Bible published in 1970.

1989 **Jewish New Testment** A Translation That Expresses Its Jewishness. Translated by
— David H. Stern. Jerusalem: Jewish New Testament Publications.

1989 **New Revised Standard Version Bible** Revision of The Revised Standard Version of 1952. Division of Christian Education of the National Council of the Churches of Christ in the United States of America.

1991 **Contemporary English Version: New Testament** New York: American Bible Society.

THE STORY OF THE BIBLE

"Behind and beneath the Bible, above and beyond the Bible, is the God of the Bible."

The Bible is God's written revelation of his will to men.

Its central theme is salvation through Jesus Christ.

The word *Bible* comes from the Greek word *biblos,* which means "book."

The Bible contains sixty-six books, written by forty authors, covering a period of approximately sixteen hundred years. The authors were kings and princes, poets and philosophers, prophets and statesmen. Some were learned in all the arts of the times and others were unschooled fishermen. Other books soon are out of date, but this Book spans the centuries.

The Old Testament was written mostly in Hebrew (a few short passages in Aramaic). About a hundred years (or more) before the Christian Era the entire Old Testament was translated into the Greek language. The New Testament was written in Greek.

The word *testament* means "covenant" or "agreement." The Old Testament is the covenant God made with man about his salvation before Christ came. The New Testament is the agreement God made with man about his salvation after Christ came.

In the Old Testament we find the covenant of law. In the New Testament we find the covenant of grace, which came through Jesus Christ. One led into the other (Galatians 3:17-25).

The Old commences what the New completes.

The Old gathers around Sinai—the New around Calvary.

The Old is associated with Moses—the New with Christ (John 1:17).

The Old Testament begins with God (Genesis 1:1). The New Testament begins with Christ (Matthew 1:1).

From Adam to Abraham we have the history of the human race. From Abraham to Christ we have the history of the chosen race. From Christ on we have the history of the church.

Interesting Facts

OLD TESTAMENT BOOKS

Law—five
History—twelve
Poetry—six
Prophecy—sixteen (Major, four; Minor, twelve)

NEW TESTAMENT BOOKS

The New Testament was written to reveal to us the character and teaching of Jesus Christ, the mediator of the New Covenant, by at least eight men, four of whom—Matthew, John, Peter, and Paul—were apostles; two—Mark and Luke—were companions of the apostles; and two—James and Jude—were brothers of Jesus. The books were written at various times during the second half of the first century.

The books in the New Testament may be grouped this way:

Gospels—four
History—one
Prophecy—one
Letters—twenty-one (Pauline, thirteen; General, eight)

The major themes of the New Testament are God, man, sin, redemption, justification, sanctification, glorification. In two words—*grace, glory.* In one word—*Jesus.*

OLD TESTAMENT—PRINCIPAL FACTS

1. Creation (Genesis 1:1–2:3)
2. Fall of man (Genesis 3)
3. Flood (Genesis 6–9)
4. Babel (Genesis 11:1-9)
5. Call of Abraham (Genesis 11:10–12:3)
6. Descent into Egypt (Genesis 46–47)

66 99
FOCUS QUOTE
The Bible was never intended to be a book for scholars and specialists only. From the very beginning it was intended to be everybody's book, and that is what it continues to be. —F. F. Bruce

7. Plagues (Exodus 7–12)
8. Passover and Exodus (Exodus 12)
9. Giving of the Law (Exodus 19–24)
10. Wilderness wanderings (Numbers 13–14)
11. Conquest of the Promised Land (Joshua 11)
12. Dark ages of the chosen people (Judges)
13. Anointing of Saul as king (1 Samuel 9:27–10:1)
14. Golden age of Israel under David and Solomon, united kingdom (2 Samuel 5:4-5; 1 Kings 10:6-8)
15. The divided kingdom—Israel and Judah (1 Kings 12:26-33)
16. The Captivity (2 Kings 17; 25)
17. The Return (Ezra)

NEW TESTAMENT—PRINCIPAL FACTS
1. Early life of Christ
2. Ministry of Christ
3. Church in Jerusalem
4. Church extending to the Gentiles
5. Church in all the world

How to Study the Bible

Many say, "The Bible is so great. I don't know where to begin and don't know how to go on." This is often said quite earnestly and sincerely. And it is true that, unless we have some method, we will surely lose the very best results, even though we may spend much time with the Book.

G. Campbell Morgan once stated, "The Bible can be read from Genesis 1 to Revelation 22 at pulpit rate in seventy-eight hours." A lawyer challenged him on that. Morgan told him to go on and try it before he challenged. The lawyer went home and read the Bible in less than eighty hours.

Do you want to read the Bible through? Leave eighty hours for it. Plot out that time. How much time can you give each day? How many days a week? This is a highly practical proposition and should be seized by the very busiest. We are all busy and must take time for it. Unless we do, we will never come into any worthy knowledge of the Word, for it is impossible from pulpit ministry to get that knowledge of the Word that is possible and is indeed needful. The Bible reveals the will of God so as to lead man into it. Each book has a direct teaching. Find out what it is and shape your life by it.

Remember, the books of the Bible were given to us by forty different men over a period of about sixteen hundred years. All these are brought together and are called "the Book." We can begin at Genesis and read on through to the end. There is no jar. We can pass from one style of literature to another as easily as though we were reading a story written by one hand and produced by one life, and indeed we have here a story produced by one Mind (2 Peter 1:21), though not written by one hand.

While divine, the Bible is human. The thought is divine and the revelation is divine, but the expression of the communication is human. *It was the Holy Spirit* [divine element] *within these godly men* [human element] *who gave them true messages from God* (2 Peter 1:21).

So we have here a book unlike all others. The Book—a divine revelation, a progressive revelation, a revelation of God to man communicated through men—moves on smoothly from its beginnings to its great end. In Genesis we have beginnings, in Revelation we have endings, and from Exodus to Jude we see how God carried out his purpose.

The Old Testament is the foundation; the New Testament is the superstructure. A foundation is of no value unless a building is built upon it. A building is impossible unless there is a foundation. So the Old Testament and New Testament are essential to one another. As Augustine said:
The New is in the Old contained,
The Old is in the New explained.

One Book, One History, One Story

The Bible is one book, one history, one story, his story. Behind ten thousand events stands God, the builder of history, the maker of the ages. Eternity bounds one side, eternity bounds the other side, and time is in between: Genesis—origins, Revelation—endings, and all the way between, God is working things out. You can go down into the minutest detail everywhere and see that there is one great purpose moving through the ages: the eternal design of the Almighty God to redeem a wrecked and ruined world.

The Bible is one book, and you cannot take it in pieces and expect to comprehend the magnificence of divine revelation. Don't suppose reading little scraps can ever be enough—we would scorn reading any other book, even the lightest novel, in this fashion. God has taken pains to give a progressive revelation, and we should take pains to read it from beginning to end. We must see it in its completeness, doing deep and consecutive work on the Bible itself. We must get back to the Book.

---

66 99
FOCUS QUOTE
It is not possible ever to exhaust the mind of the Scriptures. It is a well that has no bottom. —St. John Chrysostom

---

The Bible is not a book of texts—it is a story, a revelation, to be begun and pursued and ended as we start and continue other books. Don't divide it into short devotional paragraphs and think you have understood its messages. It may be excusable for someone who can hardly read to open the Bible and take whatever his eyes light upon as the message of God. Many people do that, but the Bible shouldn't be misused in that manner. We must come to it in a commonsense fashion. Believe that every book is about something, and read and reread until you find out what that something is.

First read the Book, not books about the Book, such as the commentaries. They will come in good time, perhaps, but give the Book a chance to speak for itself and to make its own impression, to bear its own testimony.

The Word of God is alive, and every part is necessary to the perfection of the whole. We don't say that every part is equally important. If you were to ask me whether I would give up my finger or my eye, of course I would part with my finger. So with the Word of God. All is necessary to make a perfect whole, but some portions are more precious than others. You can't take away the Song of Solomon and have a perfect revelation. No one says the Song of Solomon is comparable with John's Gospel, but both are parts of an organism, and that organism is not complete if any part is missing.

Christ, the Living Word

The Old Testament is an account of a nation (the Jewish nation). The New Testament is an account of a Man (the Son of man). The nation was founded and nurtured by God in order to bring this man into the world (see Genesis 12:1-3).

God himself became a man so that we might know what to think of when we think of God (John 1:14; 14:9). His appearance on the earth is the central event of all history. The Old Testament sets the stage for it. The New Testament describes it.

As a man, Christ lived the most perfect life ever known. He was kind, tender, gentle, patient, and sympathetic. He loved people. He worked marvelous miracles to feed the hungry. Crowds—weary, pain-ridden, and heartsick—came to him, and he gave them rest (Matthew 11:28-30). It is said that if all the deeds of kindness that he did were written, the world could not contain the books (John 21:25).

Then he died—to take away the sin of the world and to become the Savior of mankind.

Then he rose from the dead. He is alive today. He is not merely a historical character but a living Person—the most important fact of history and the most vital force in the world today. And he promises eternal life to all who come to him.

The whole Bible is built around the story of Christ and his promise of everlasting life. It was written only so that we would believe and understand, know and love, and follow him.

Apart from any theory of inspiration or any theory of how the Bible books came to their present form or how much the text may have suffered in passing through the hands of editors and copyists or what is historical and what may be poetical—assume that the Bible is just what it appears to be. Accept the books as we have them in our Bible as units. Study them to know their contents. You will find there is a unity of thought that indicates that one Mind inspired the writing of the whole series of books, that it bears on its face the stamp of its Author, that it is in every sense the *Word of God*.

Source: *What the Bible Is All About,* Living Bible Edition, Henrietta C. Mears, Copyright © 1953, 1954, 1960, 1966, 1983 by Gospel Light Publications. Living Bible edition copyright © 1987 by Tyndale House Publishers, Inc. Used by permission.

OVERVIEW OF THE BOOKS OF THE BIBLE

THE OLD TESTAMENT
The first five books of the Bible tell the origins of the Jewish race and culture.

Genesis: The book of beginnings describes creation, the first rebellions against God, and God's choosing of Abraham and his offspring.

Exodus: God rescued the Israelites from slavery in Egypt and led them to the Sinai Desert. There, he gave Moses the laws to govern the new nation.

Leviticus: God set up laws for the Israelites, mostly regarding holiness and worship.

Numbers: Because of their rebellion and disobedience, the Israelites had to wander in a wilderness for 40 years before entering the promised land.

Deuteronomy: Just before his death, Moses made three emotional farewell speeches, recapping history and warning the Israelites against further mistakes.

HISTORY BOOKS
The next twelve books continue the history of the Israelites: they moved into the land of Canaan and established a kingdom that lasted almost 500 years.

Joshua: After Moses' death, Joshua commanded the armies that conquered much of the territory in the promised land.

Judges: The new nation fell into a series of dismal failures. God raised up leaders called "judges."

Ruth: This story of love and loyalty between two widows shines out brightly in an otherwise dark period.

1 Samuel: Samuel became a transition leader between the time of the judges and that of the kings. He appointed Israel's first king, Saul. After his own failure, Saul tried violently to prevent God's king-elect David from taking the throne.

2 Samuel: David, "a man after God's own heart," brought the nation together. But after committing adultery and murder, he was haunted by family and national crises.

1 Kings: Solomon succeeded David, with mixed success. At his death, a civil war tore apart the nation. Successive kings were mostly bad, and the prophet Elijah had dramatic confrontations with King Ahab.

2 Kings: This book continues the record of the rulers of the divided kingdom. None of the Northern kings followed God consistently, and so Israel was finally destroyed by an invader. The South, Judah, lasted much longer, but finally Babylon conquered Judah and deported its citizens.

1 Chronicles: The book opens with the most complete genealogical record in the Bible, then adds many incidents from the life of David (often the same as those in 2 Samuel).

2 Chronicles: Often paralleling the books of Kings, this book records the history of the rulers of Judah, emphasizing the good kings.

Ezra: After being held captive in Babylon for decades, the Jews were allowed to return to their homeland. Ezra, a priest, emerged from one of the first waves of refugees.

Nehemiah: Nehemiah returned from the Babylonian captivity after the temple had been rebuilt. He concentrated on restoring the protective wall around Jerusalem and joined Ezra in leading a religious revival.

Esther: This story is set among captive Jews in Persia. A courageous Jewish queen foiled a plan to exterminate her people.

BOOKS OF POETRY
Almost one-third of the Old Testament was originally written in poetry. These books concentrate on questions about pain, God, life, and love.

Job: The best man of his day suffered the greatest personal tragedy. The entire book deals with the question, "Why?"

Psalms: These prayers and hymns cover the full range of human emotion; together, they represent a personal journal of how to relate to God. Some were also used in public worship services.

OVERVIEW OF THE BOOKS OF THE BIBLE cont.

Proverbs: The proverbs offer advice on every imaginable area of life. The style of wise living described here leads to a fulfilled life.

Ecclesiastes: A life without God, 'under the sun,' leads to meaninglessness and despair, says the Teacher in a strikingly modern book.

Song of Songs: This beautiful poem celebrates romantic and physical love.

BOOKS OF THE PROPHETS

During the years when kings ruled Israel and Judah, God spoke through prophets. Though some prophets did predict future events, their primary role was to call God's people back to him.

Isaiah: The most eloquent of the prophets, Isaiah analyzed the failures of all the nations around him and pointed to a future Messiah who would bring peace.

Jeremiah: Jeremiah led an emotionally tortured life, yet held to his stern message. He spoke to Judah in the last decades before Babylon destroyed the nation.

Lamentations: All Jeremiah's warnings about Jerusalem came true, and Lamentations records five poems of sorrow for the fallen city.

Ezekiel: Ezekiel spoke to the Jews who were captive in Babylon. He often used dramatic stories and "enacted parables" to make his points.

Daniel: A captive in Babylon, Daniel rose to the office of prime minister. Despite intense political pressure, he lived a model life of integrity and left highly symbolic prophecies about the future.

Hosea: By marrying a loose-living wife, Hosea lived out his message: that Israel had committed spiritual adultery against God.

Joel: Beginning with a recent catastrophe in Judah (a locust plague), Joel foretold God's judgment on Judah.

Amos: A country boy, Amos preached to Israel at the height of its prosperity. His grim warnings focused on materialism.

Obadiah: Obadiah warned Edom, a nation bordering Judah.

Jonah: Jonah reluctantly went to Nineveh and found Israel's enemies responsive to God's message.

Micah: Micah exposed corruption in every level of society, but closed with a promise of forgiveness and restoration.

Nahum: Long after Jonah had stirred Nineveh to repentance, Nahum foretold the mighty city's total destruction.

Habakkuk: Habakkuk addressed his book to God, not people. In a frank dialogue with God, he discussed problems of suffering and justice.

Zephaniah: Zephaniah focused on the coming day of the Lord, which would purge Judah, resulting in a remnant used to bless the entire world.

Haggai: After returning from the Babylonian captivity, the Jews began rebuilding the temple of God. But before long they set aside that task to work on their own homes. Haggai reminded them to put God first.

Zechariah: Writing around the same time as Haggai, Zechariah also urged the Jews to work on the temple. He used a more uplifting approach, describing how the temple would point to the coming Messiah.

Malachi: The last Old Testament prophet, Malachi faced a nation that had grown indifferent. He sought to stir them from apathy.

THE NEW TESTAMENT

History Books The word *gospel* means "good news." Almost half the New Testament consists of four accounts of the life of Jesus and good news he brought to earth. Each of these four books, or Gospels, has a different focus and a different audience; taken together, they give a complete picture of Jesus' life and teaching. About a third of their pages are devoted to the events of his last week on earth, including the Crucifixion and Resurrection.

Acts continues the history into the period after Jesus left earth.

Matthew: Written to a Jewish audience, this Gospel links the Old and New Testaments. It presents Jesus as the Messiah and King promised in the Old Testament. Matthew emphasizes Jesus' authority and power.

Mark: Mark probably had pragmatic Roman readers in mind. His Gospel stresses action and gives a straightforward, blow-by-blow account of Jesus' work on earth.

Luke: A doctor, Luke was also a fine writer. His Gospel provides many details of human interest, especially in Jesus' treatment of the poor and needy. A joyful tone characterizes Luke's book.

John: John has a different, more reflective style than the other Gospels. Its author selected seven signs that point to Jesus as the Son of God and wove together everything else to underscore that point.

Acts: Acts tells what happened to Jesus' followers after he left them. Peter and Paul soon emerged as leaders of the rapidly spreading church.

THE LETTERS

The young church was nourished by apostles who set down their beliefs and messages in a series of letters. The first 13 such letters (Romans through Philemon) were written by the apostle Paul, who led the advance of Christianity to non-Jewish people.

Paul's Letters:

Romans: Written for a sophisticated audience, Romans sets forth theology in a logical, organized form.

1 Corinthians: A very practical book, 1 Corinthians takes up the problems of a tumultuous church in Corinth: marriage, factions, immorality, public worship, and lawsuits.

2 Corinthians: Paul wrote this follow-up letter to defend himself against a rebellion led by certain false apostles.

Galatians: A short version of the message of Romans, this book addresses legalism. It shows how Christ came to bring freedom, not bondage to a set of laws.

Ephesians: Although written in jail, this letter is Paul's most optimistic and encouraging. It tells of the advantages a believer has in Christ.

Philippians: The church at Philippi ranked among Paul's favorites. This friendly letter stresses that joy can be found in any situation.

Colossians: Written to oppose certain cults, Colossians tells how faith in Christ is complete. Nothing needs to be added to what Christ did.

1 Thessalonians: Composed early in Paul's ministry, this letter gives a capsule history of one church, as well as Paul's direct advice about specific problems.

2 Thessalonians: Stronger in tone than his first letter to the Thessalonians, the sequel goes over the same topics, especially the church's questions about Christ' second coming.

1 Timothy: As Paul neared the end of his life, he chose young men such as Timothy to carry on his work. His two letters to Timothy form a leadership manual for a young pastor.

2 Timothy: Written just before Paul's death, 2 Timothy offers Paul's final words to his young assistant.

Titus: Titus was left in Crete, a notoriously difficult place to nurture a church. Paul's letter gave practical advice on how to go about it.

Philemon: Paul urged Philemon, owner of runaway slave Onesimus, to forgive his slave and accept him as a brother in Christ.

OTHER LETTERS

Hebrews: No one knows who wrote Hebrews, but it probably first went to Christians in danger of slipping back into Judaism. It interprets the Old Testament, explaining many Jewish practices as symbols that prepared the way for Christ.

James: James, a man of action, emphasized the right kind of behavior for a believer. Someone who calls himself a Christian ought to act like it, James believed, and his letter spells out the specifics.

1 Peter: Early Christians often met violent opposition, and Peter's letter comforted and encouraged Christians who were being persecuted for their faith.

2 Peter: In contrast to Peter's first letter, this one focused on problems that sprang up from the inside. It warns against false teachers.

1 John: John could fill simple words—light, love, life—with deep meaning, and in this

OVERVIEW OF THE BOOKS OF THE BIBLE cont.

letter, he elegantly explains basic truths about the Christian life.

2 John: Warning against false teachers, John counseled churches on how to respond to them.

3 John: Balancing 2 John, this companion letter mentions the need to be hospitable to true teachers.

Jude: Jude gave a brief but fiery expose of heretics.

Revelation: A book of visions and symbols, Revelation is the only New Testament book that concentrates on prophecy. It completes the story, begun in Genesis, of the cosmic battle between good and evil being waged on earth. It ends with a picture of a new heaven and new earth.

Taken from *The Student Bible*, New International Version. Copyright © 1986 by the Zondervan Corporation. Used by permission.

A CHRONOLOGY OF OLD AND NEW TESTAMENT EVENTS

Old Testament (B.C.)

2166	Abram born
2091	Abram enters Canaan
2066	Isaac born
2006	Jacob and Esau born
1991	Abraham dies
1929	Jacob flees to Haran
1915	Joseph born
1898	Joseph sold into slavery
1886	Isaac dies
1885	Joseph begins to rule in Egypt
1876	Jacob's family comes to Egypt
1859	Jacob dies
1805	Joseph dies
1526	Moses born
1446	Exodus from Egypt
1406	Israel enters Canaan
1375-1050	Judges' rule
1367-1327	Othniel
1309-1229	Ehud
1209-1169	Deborah
1162-1122	Gideon
1105	Samuel born
1078-1072	Jepthath
1075-1055	Samson

United Kingdom

1050-1010	Saul's rule
1010-970	David's rule
970-930	Solomon's rule

Divided Kingdoms

JUDAH (KINGS/PROPHETS)

930-913	Rehoboam
910-869	Asa
872-848	Jehoshaphat
855-840	Obadiah
853-841	Jehoram
841-835	Athaliah
835-796	Joash
810-750	Joel
792-740	Azzariah (Uzziah)
750-735	Jotham
742-687	Micah
740-681	Isaiah
735-715	Ahaz
715-686	Hezekiah
697-642	Manasseh
664-612	Nahum
640-609	Zephaniah
640-609	Josiah
627-586	Jeremiah
609-598	Jehoiakim
605-589	Habakkuk
597	Jehoiachin
597-586	Zedekiah
c.587	Obadiah
586	Fall of Jerusalem

ISRAEL (KINGS/PROPHETS)

930-909	Jeroboam I
909-908	Nadab
908-886	Baasha
886-885	Elah
885	Zimri, Timri
885-874	Omri
875-848	Elijah
874-853	Ahab
852-841	Joram

848-797 .... Elisha
841-814 .... Jehu
814-798 ....Jehoahaz
798-782 .... Jehoash
793-753 ....Jeroboam II
785-775 .... Jonah
760-750 .... Amos
753-752 .... Zechariah
752 ....Shallum
752-742 .... Menahem
752-732 .... Pekah
750-715 .... Hosea
732-722 .... Hoshea
722 .... Fall of Northern Kingdom

CAPTIVITY

586 .... Babylonian Captivity

Prophets in exile:
605-530 .... Daniel
593-571 ....Ezekiel

Recovery

538 ... First group returns with Zerubbabel
537 .... Rebuilding of temple begins
520 ....Haggai
520-480 .... Zechariah
516 .... Rebuilding of temple finished
458 ...... Second group returns with Ezra
445 ...... Nehemiah comes to Jerusalem, begins first governorship
440-430 .... Malachi
433 .. Nehemiah begins second governorship
432-6 B.C. .... Between the Testaments

New Testament Events

6/5 B.C. .... Christ's birth
A.D. 6/7 .... Jesus in the temple
26 ....John the baptist begins his ministry
26/27 .... Christ is baptized, begins his ministry

30 .... Christ is crucified, resurrected, and enthroned
30 .... Pentecost
34/35 .... Paul's conversion
44 .... James, the apostle, is martyred
46-48 ..... Paul's first missionary journey
49/50 .... Jerusalem council
50-52 .. Paul's second missionary journey
53-57 .... Paul's third missionary journey
59-62 ......Paul's imprisonment in Rome
67 .... Paul's second imprisonment
65-67 .... Peter martyred
68 .... Paul martyred
90-95 .... John exiled
c.100 .... John dies

New Testament Books

45-50 ....James
49 or 56 ....Galatians
50's .... Mark
50, 51 .... 1 & 2 Thessalonians
55, 56 .... 1 & 2 Corinthians
56/57 .... Romans
60 .... Luke
60's .... Matthew
60/61 .... Colossians, Philemon, Ephesians
61/62 .... Philippians
63 .... 1 Timothy
63 .... 1 Peter
64-68 .... Hebrews
64-72 ....Acts
65 .... Titus
65-67 .... 2 Peter
67 .... 2 Timothy
70-80 .... Jude
85-90 .... John, Epistles of John
95 ....Revelation

The People's Study Bible: The Living Bible Harold Lindsell, Ph.D., D.D., General Editor, Tyndale House Publishers, Inc., Wheaton, IL, © 1986: pp. 1823-1826. From *New Bible Dictionary*; used by permission of InterVarsity Press.

IMPORTANT BIBLE WORDS

Certain words and ideas are found over and over again in the Bible because they refer to significant concepts that governed the lives of God's people. These words have come down through the centuries as aspects of church life and thought and, today also, reflect the essence of what Christians believe.

The entries here are the most important words found in the Bible and in Christian theology.

Adoption The process through which a person who does not belong to a given family is formally brought into it and made a full,

IMPORTANT BIBLE WORDS cont.

legal family member with the rights and responsibilities of that position. The practice of adoption was not common among the Jews, but was more widespread in the Greek and Roman world. The apostle Paul used the term to illustrate the truth that believers have been given the status of "sonship" in the heavenly family; they can call God "Father" (Romans 8:15; Galatians 4:6). Adoption makes it clear that our sonship is conferred on us, in distinction from Christ's, which is inherent.

Apostle "Someone who is sent," often "a messenger." In the New Testament the word refers particularly to twelve apostles whom Jesus selected to be with him and whom he sent out to preach and to cast out demons (Mark 3:14-15). Other individuals than the Twelve bore that title—for example, Paul and Barnabas (Acts 14:14). Apostles were important figures in the early church (1 Corinthians 12:28). They were appointed by Christ, not by men (Galatians 1:1), and they gave authoritative witness to what God had done in Christ (Acts 1:22).

Assurance Certainty of salvation, because of the promises of God and the effectiveness of Christ's atonement (1 John 5:13). The word does not occur often in the Bible, but the idea is more frequent. It is basic that people do not deserve their salvation because of their own efforts; that would leave them always uncertain, never knowing whether they had been good enough. But Christ did all that was needed, and we can rely on his perfect work. Further, believers have evidence of God's power in their lives (1 John 2:3-5; 3:19-21). Our assurance rests on the certainty that what God has begun he will complete (Philippians 1:6).

Atonement Literally "at-one-ment," the making at one of those who have been separated. The word is used of Christ's dying to bring God and sinners together. Sin had separated them (Isaiah 59:2) and made them enemies (Colossians 1:21); it was thus a very serious matter. A many-sided act was required to remove that sin; words like *redemption* and *reconciliation* bring out significant aspects of Christ's saving work. Whatever had to be done about sin, Christ's death did, and thus opened up salvation for sinners.

Christ English form of a Greek word meaning "anointed"; "Messiah" is the English form of the Hebrew word with the same meaning. In Old Testament days God anointed people for special service, especially the king (2 Samuel 1:14; 23:1) and the priest (Leviticus 4:3). Eventually the understanding developed that an outstanding "anointed one" would appear, who would do God's will in a very special way (Daniel 9:25-26). This great One is often referred to without the use of the term *anointed* (Isaiah 9:6-7; 11:1-9). The New Testament shows that Jesus was this chosen One, God's Messiah (John 4:25-26; cf. Matthew 23:10; Mark 9:41).

Conversion The decisive act in which a sinner turns away from sin in genuine repentance and accepts the salvation that Christ offers. The imagery in conversion is that of turning. A person is going along a road and realizes that he or she is on the wrong track. They will never reach the destination if they continue in that direction. So the person "turns," or "is converted." He or she ceases to go in the wrong direction and begins going in the right one. Conversion changes the direction of one's course of life from the wrong way to the right way, the way that God wants.

Covenant A solemn agreement, such as the pact between Jacob and Laban (Genesis 31:44). God's love and grace are shown in his readiness to make covenants with people. When God promised Noah that he would not again destroy the world with a flood, he made a covenant with him (Genesis 6:18; 9:9-17). A very important covenant existed between God and Israel (Exodus 24:1-8), which is pictured in the book of Hebrews as the "old covenant." When the people repeatedly broke that covenant, God promised a new covenant based on forgiveness and the writing of his law on people's hearts (Jeremiah 31:31-34). Jesus inaugurated this new covenant with his blood (Mark 14:24; 1 Corinthians 11:25).

Disciple In Bible times, a student. Whereas a student today studies a subject (law, architecture, or whatever), a disciple in olden days learned from a teacher. Attachment to a specific teacher was the essence of discipleship. The Pharisees and John the Baptist had disciples (Mark 2:18). The Jews saw themselves as disciples of Moses (John 9:28). The term is used often in the Gospels and Acts of the followers of Jesus. They learned from him and attached themselves wholeheartedly to him. It meant putting Christ before family and possessions. It meant taking up the cross (Luke 14:26-33). Today, too, to be a disciple of Jesus means total commitment.

---

66 99
FOCUS
QUOTE
I know the Bible is inspired because it finds me at a greater depth of my being than any other book. —Samuel Taylor Coleridge

---

Doctrine "Teaching"; used of the content rather than the act of teaching. The Greek word may be used of the doctrines of men (Matthew 15:9), but, more important, refers to the teaching of Jesus (Matthew 7:28) and later the teaching of his followers. "My teaching," Jesus said, "is not my own. It comes from him who sent me" (John 7:16; i.e., it is from God). The word was used of Christian doctrine (Acts 2:42), to which believers are to be wholeheartedly committed (Romans 6:17). It is important to "continue" in the doctrine (2 John 9) and to be able both to teach it and to refute those who oppose it (Titus 1:9).

Election Chosen by God. The idea of election goes back to Abraham (Genesis 12:1-3). God chose to make a nation of that patriarch's descendants. He chose Israel to be his people. He worked his purposes out through that one nation and in due course sent his Messiah as a Jew. After that, God continued to choose, or elect, people in accordance with his purpose (Romans 9:11), grace (Romans 11:5), love (1 Thessalonians 1:4), and foreknowledge (1 Peter 1:2). The "elect" can rely on God's concern for them (Luke 18:7) and on their sure salvation (Romans 8:33). They are to live lives befitting their status (Colossians 3:12-14). Mystery is inherent in the concept of election, because we also know that God desires the salvation of all persons (1 Timothy 2:4).

Expiation See *Propitiation*

Faith Relying on what God has done rather than on one's own efforts. In the Old Testament, *faith* is rarely mentioned. The word *trust* is used frequently, and verbs like *believe* and *rely* are used to express the right attitude to God. The classic example is Abraham, whose faith was reckoned as righteousness (Genesis 15:6). At the heart of the Christian message is the story of the cross: Christ's dying to bring salvation. Faith is an attitude of trust in which a believer receives God's good gift of salvation (Acts 16:30-31) and lives in that awareness thereafter (Galatians 2:20; cf. Hebrews 11:l).

Gospel "Good News." Our word *gospel* comes from two Old English words. There is no good news like the good news that God sent his Son to die on a cross to get rid of our sins. 1 Corinthians 15:1-11 summarizes the good news or gospel, that the apostle Paul preached. The term emphasizes the truth that salvation is entirely of grace. From its use for the central Christian message, the word came to be used as the title of each of the four books (Matthew, Mark, Luke, John) that tell the story of Jesus' life and atoning death.

Grace God's unmerited favor. The Greek words for *joy* and *grace* are related; grace causes joy. In the Christian understanding, nothing brings joy like the good news of what God has done in Christ to bring us

IMPORTANT BIBLE WORDS cont.

salvation. Salvation by grace is "through faith—and this not from yourselves, it is the gift of God—not by works. . ." (Ephesians 2:8-9). God's grace also brings about qualities of conduct in the believer (2 Corinthians 9:8; 12:9; Ephesians 4:7). The word *grace* came to be used as a kind of prayer ("grace to you") in Christian greetings at the beginning and end of some of the New Testament letters (2 Corinthians 1:2; 13:14).

Heaven The abode of God (1 Kings 8:30) and of the angels (Mark 13:32); believers will be there in due course (1 Peter 1:4). The New Testament uses striking imagery to bring out the wonder and loveliness of heaven (gates of pearl and a street of gold—Revelations 21:21). Heaven means eternal joy in the presence of God.

Hell The abode of Satan and his angels (Matthew 25:41), described in the Bible with the imagery of eternal fire, outer darkness, being lost, perishing, and the like. It is impossible to envisage a state that can be described in so many different ways. Clearly it is horrible and is to be avoided at all costs (Mark 9:43).

Incarnation Literally, "en-flesh-ment" (Latin *carnis*— "flesh"); the doctrine that the Son of God became human (John 1:14). Jesus did not play at becoming a man but took on our flesh with all its problems and weaknesses. Incarnation, in the Christian understanding, means that Christ was both God and human.

Justification Legal term meaning "acquittal," a declaration that someone is in the right. Sinners are in the wrong before God. They have broken his laws, they deserve punishment, but on the cross Christ took their place. Now, when they put their trust in Christ, they are declared to be in the right, acquitted, justified. The cross shows God to be just, not simply in the fact that he forgives, but in the way he forgives. To pass over sins would show mercy, but it would not show justice. Forgiveness by the way of the cross shows both (Romans 3:25-26).

Kingdom of God An expression first used by Jesus, although the idea that God reigns is everywhere in the Old Testament. The coming of the kingdom of God was the most frequent topic in the teaching of Jesus (Mark 1:15). It expresses the truth that God is a great God who does what he wills in human affairs. Specifically he wills to save people through the life, death, resurrection, and ascension of Jesus. In one sense the kingdom of God is a present reality. People enter it now (Matthew 21:31). In another sense it is future (Matthew 16:28). God's control is plain in both aspects, and in the end his sovereign will be perfectly done (1 Corinthians 15:28).

Last Judgment The evaluation of all humankind on the basis of works at Christ's return (Matthew 25:31-32). The wicked will be condemned because of their evil deeds. Salvation is by grace and through faith (Ephesians 2:8); the last judgment will test what believers have done with their lives (1 Corinthians 3:13-15). Some will be rewarded (Luke 19:16-19). Thus, although our salvation depends on what Christ has done, our eternal reward is related to the use we have made of God's gifts to us.

Love God's benevolent concern for humankind. All religions have some idea of the importance of love. Christian theology stresses the importance of love because God has revealed that he is love (1 John 4:8, 16). Love is both what God is and what he has done; God always acts in love. Love is a transitive reality—that is, it requires an object. In the Bible, love is described as personal (between persons) and selfless (desiring the best for others). Christians see God's love in sending his Son to die on the cross to save sinners (Romans 5:8; John 3:16; 1 John 4:10). Christians are to be known by the fact that they love God and others (John 13:34-35). Their love is not to be like the love the world has (Luke 6:32, 35). Love is best seen in actions and in most cases is to be identified with what we do—in our compassion and commitment to those around us, regardless of the object's virtue (1 John 4:19). Our loving attitudes and behavior are to reflect God's love. Jesus said that only two commands are needed to govern our lives: love of God and love of neighbor. If such love is demonstrated, all the law and prophets are fulfilled.

Messiah See *Christ*.

❝❞ FOCUS QUOTE Every Christian must refer always and everywhere to the Scriptures for all his choices, becoming like a child before it, seeking in it the most effective remedy against all his various weaknesses, and not daring to take a step without being illuminated by the divine rays of those words. —Pope John Paul II

Predestination God's sovereign working out of his purposes in the affairs of nations and in individual lives. God predestines those who are saved (Romans 8:28-29; Ephesians 1:4-5). He does not stand on the sidelines, a helpless spectator (so to speak) until we, with our repentance and conversion, give him permission to do something. Unless our names were written "in the book of life from the creation of the world" (Revelation 17:8) we would not even make the motion of turning from sin. Predestination means that our salvation, from first to last, is God's work. See also *Election*.

Propitiation/Expiation Offering whatever will turn away anger; paying the penalty. Propitiation has to do with persons, expiation with things. Sin arouses the wrath of God; if people are to be forgiven, something must be done about his anger. Jesus' death on the cross brought about a process of propitiation; it was the means by which divine anger was averted from sinners.

Redemption Originally, the payment of a price to secure the release of a prisoner of war. The word came to be used also of the release of a slave, and sometimes of a person under sentence of death (Exodus 21:28-30). Redemption always means the payment of a price to secure release. People who sin become slaves of sin (John 8:34); they cannot free themselves from that slavery. Christ's death on the cross was the payment of a ransom price (Mark 10:45) by which sinners are set free. Now that they are redeemed they must live as free people (1 Corinthians 6:19-20; Galatians 5:1).

Regeneration Being reborn; the subject of Jesus' discourse with Nicodemus in John 3 (cf. Titus 3:5). This word is not found often in Scripture, but the idea is important. Regeneration is seen to be the work of the Holy Spirit (John 3:5-8). The "natural man" always thinks of salvation (however understood) as resting in one's own hands, but Jesus taught that it is necessary for a divine work to take place if anyone is to be saved. Sinners must be reborn spiritually.

Remnant Something remaining. In the Old Testament some passages refer to total destruction of a nation (e.g., the Babylonians in Jeremiah 50:26). When God brings judgment on his people, however, he does not destroy the faithful with the wicked, but leaves a remnant (Ezekiel 6:8; Micah 2:12). The concept of a remnant stood for that part of the nation who were faithful even though most people rejected the ways of God (Isaiah 4:2-4. The fact of the existence of a remnant is said to be due to God himself (Isaiah 1:9; Zephaniah 3:12). The remnant, then, is the real people of God, a concept we also find in the New Testament, "a remnant chosen by grace" (Romans 11:5).

Repentance Sorrowing over and forsaking sin, a wholehearted turning away from all that is evil. This is more than regret or remorse, attitudes that point to sorrow over sin but no more. Repentance was looked for in Old Testament times (Ezekiel 14:6; 18:30). It was the first item in the preaching of John the Baptist (Matthew 3:1-2), Jesus

IMPORTANT BIBLE WORDS cont.

(Matthew 4:17), and the apostles (Mark 6:12; cf. Acts 2:38). Beyond repentance, faith is needed. But repentance is indispensable. Sin must be forsaken decisively.

Resurrection The raising and transformation of a person who has died. Resuscitation means the bringing back of people to this life after they have left it, for example, the raising of the son of the widow of Nain (Luke 7:11-15) or of Lazarus (John 11). Resurrection is more than that. Jesus rose on the third day after he died, but his new body was transformed. It was not subject to the limitations of his former early life (Luke 24:16, 31; John 20:19). Jesus' resurrection, following his atoning death, is central to the Christian faith (1 Corinthians 15:14-19). Believers, too, will be resurrected (1 Thessalonians 4:16; 1 Corinthians 15:42-57).

Revelation Uncovering, making plain what was not known before. The word may be used of something God makes known during a church service (1 Corinthians 14:26), but more usually it has to do with something on a larger scale, like God's righteousness, wrath (Romans 1:17-18), or righteous judgment (Romans 2:5). It may be used to describe a book (Revelation 1:1). God reveals things through the Spirit (1 Corinthians 2:10). The gospel is not something people have made up but has been revealed by Christ (Galatians 1:11-12). The fullness of revelation awaits the return of Christ (2 Thessalonians 1:7; 1 Peter 1:13).

Righteousness Right standing, specifically before God. Among the Greeks, righteousness was an ethical virtue. Among the Hebrews it was a legal concept; the righteous man was the one who got the verdict of acceptability when tried at the bar of God's justice. Christ's death took away our sins and made it possible for sinners to have "the righteousness of God," i.e., right standing before God (Romans 1:16-17; 3:22; 5:17). That gift of righteousness is to be followed by upright living (Romans 6:13-14).

Salvation Deliverance of various kinds, for example, deliverance from the enemy (Exodus 14:13). In the Bible it is God who brings salvation from temporal as well as spiritual ills. Thus in the Gospels, referring to his miraculous healings, Jesus sometimes says, "Your faith has saved you," meaning "healed you" (Luke 18:42 KJV). Characteristically, the term refers to salvation from sin (Romans 1:16; 1 Thessalonians 5:9). Salvation means the decisive defeat of sin on the cross, but also victory over evil in a believer's daily life. Its full content will be realized only in the life to come (Hebrews 9:28; 1 Peter 1:5).

Sanctification The process of developing holiness. God said to Israel, "Be holy, because I am holy" (Leviticus 11:44-45). Because God wants us to become like him, it is necessary that his people be a special kind of people, holy men and women. The basic idea in sanctification is "being set apart for God; those thus set apart live in a way that is pleasing to God. They have no power of their own to do that, but God enables them (2 Corinthians 3:17-18). Sanctification is not an option. God requires it of all his people (1 Thessalonians 4:3).

Second Coming Christ's return at the end of the world to establish God's kingdom (1 Corinthians 15:23-25). The New Testament does not use this expression; it refers simply to "the coming" (*parousia*), also called a "reveal(ing)" of Jesus (1 Corinthians 1:7), or an "appearing" (Titus 2:13). There is dispute about the relationship of Christ's second coming to the thousand years, or millennium (Revelation 20:4), but none as to the fact that it will be God's decisive and indispensable intervention. Christ's coming to destroy all evil will be the culmination of his redemptive work.

Sin Anything that fails to conform to the law of God. Evil is a complex phenomenon in the Scriptures. The idea of sin is conveyed by a variety of expressions with meanings like missing the mark, rebelling, going astray, transgressing, stumbling, etc. Basically "sin is lawlessness" (1 John 3:4), referring to an inward attitude as well as to the breaking of written commandments. All people commit sin (1 Kings 8:46; Romans 3:23). To deny that we have sinned is to make God a liar (1 John 1:10); all his dealings with humanity are on the basis that we are sinners. But the blood of Jesus cleanses from all sin (1 John 1:7).

Sovereignty Term used to describe the fact that God is the supreme ruler of everything. God created the world and all that is in it. He sustains the entire created order in existence. He guides the affairs of human beings and nations. He providentially interacts with all that takes place. He works for the good of the world and finally will bring all things to a satisfactory conclusion. Because he is God, he has the absolute right to work his will. Sometimes sovereignty is misunderstood to mean that God forces his will on people and that we are not free to choose. That is false. God's sovereignty includes the free choices of human beings. What makes God's sovereignty effective is that his will is ultimately done—sometimes along with, sometimes in spite of, our free choices.

Spiritual Gifts Special gifts of the Spirit (*charismata*; e.g., Romans 12:6-8; 1 Corinthians 12:4-11, 28-31). There is some dispute as to whether these gifts were all meant as permanent endowments of the Christian church or as gifts only for its early days. In modern times, charismatics claim to exercise particular gifts, especially "tongues," "healing," and "prophecy." Other believers emphasize the fruit of the Spirit more than spiritual gifts (Galatians 5:22-23).

Tithe Word meaning "tenth," used of the offering of a tenth for religious purposes. Abraham gave a tenth to Melchizedek, the priest-king (Genesis 14:18-20). The Israelites were required to give a tithe to the Levites (Numbers 18:21, 24), and the Levites in turn were to give a tithe of the tithe to the priests (Numbers 18:25-28).

The tithe was taken from things like grain, fruits, and animals (Leviticus 27:30-32). There is no command to tithe in the New Testament (cf. 1 Corinthians 16:2), but many Christians believe that the concept is a useful guide in their giving.

Tongues Speaking in a language one has not learned. Luke wrote of a gift of tongues on the day of Pentecost (Acts 2:4-6), when everybody understood what was being said. Elsewhere we read of the Spirit's enabling people to speak in words that neither they nor anyone else understood unless they had another gift, that of interpretation (1 Corinthians 12:10, 28). The possessor of the gift of tongues used it to speak about God, but edified nobody but himself, Paul said (1 Corinthians 14:2-4). His mind was not active (1 Corinthians 14:14). Paul did not forbid the use of the gift, however; he spoke in tongues himself (1 Corinthians 14:18). But he regulated its use (1 Corinthians 14:27-28) and saw edification as a more important consideration (1 Corinthians 14:4-5).

Wrath of God In Scripture, God's strong and vigorous opposition to everything evil. There is a Greek verb that can be used both of anger and of the swelling of buds as the sap rises. It points to the kind of anger that results from a settled and consistent disposition, and not to a losing of one's temper. God's wrath is like that, rather than like human anger on a grand scale. With us, wrath always has elements of passion, lack of self-control, and irrationality. The wrath of God does not.

Reprinted from "Glossary of Important Biblical Words" by Leon Morris in *The Shaw Pocket Bible Handbook*, ed. Walter A. Elwell. Copyright © 1984 by Harold Shaw Publishers, Wheaton, Ill. Used by permission.

66 99
FOCUS
QUOTE
The New Testament holds up a strong light by which a man can read even the small print of his soul. —John A. Hutton

EVERYDAY PHRASES IN THE BIBLE

Identify the book and, if possible, the chapter and verse where these commonly used phrases originated.

1. The skin of my teeth.
2. Wolf in sheep's clothing.
3. Salt of the earth.
4. Holier than thou.
5. Woe is me!
6. Can a leopard change his spots?
7. A drop in a bucket.
8. Eat, drink, and be merry.
9. Pride goeth before a fall.
10. Give up the ghost.
11. Spare the rod and spoil the child.
12. My brother's keeper.
13. Fat of the land.
14. A lamb for the slaughter.
15. The blind leading the blind.

ANSWERS
1. "I am escaped with the skin of my teeth" (Job 19:20).
2. "Beware of false prophets, which come to you in sheep's clothing, but inwardly they are ravening wolves" (Matthew 7:15).
3. "Ye are the salt of the earth" (Matthew 5:13).
4. "I am holier than thou" (Isaiah 65:5).
5. "Woe is me! for I am undone" (Isaiah 6:5).
6. "Can the Ethiopian change his skin, or the leopard his spots?" (Jeremiah 13:23).
7. "Behold, the nations are as a drop of a bucket, and are counted as the small dust of the balance" (Isaiah 40:15).
8. "A man hath no better thing under the sun, than to eat, and to drink and to be merry" (Ecclesiastes 8:15).
9. "Pride goeth before destruction, and an haughty spirit before a fall" (Proverbs 16:18).
10. "But man dieth, and wasteth away; yea, man giveth up the ghost, and where is he?" (Job 14:10).
11. "He that spareth the rod hateth his son" (Proverbs 13:24).
12. "Am I my brother's keeper?" (Genesis 4:9).
13. "And he shall eat the fat of the land" (Genesis 45:18).
14. "He is brought as a lamb to the slaughter" (Isaiah 53:7).
15. "If a blind man leads a blind man, both will fall into a pit" (Matthew 15:14).

Taken from *The Complete Book of Bible Trivia.* Copyright © 1988 by J. Stephen Lang. Published by Tyndale House Publishers. Used by permission.

WHO DID WHAT FIRST?

1. Who had the first birthday party in the Bible?
2. Where was the first beauty contest in the Bible, and who won?
3. Who was the first Christian martyr?
4. What is the first dream mentioned in the Bible?
5. What is the first war mentioned in the Bible?
6. Who was the first drunk?
7. Where was the first piggy bank?
8. Who was the first person to fall asleep during a sermon?
9. What is the first commandment in the Bible?
10. What is the first purchase of land in the Bible?
11. What was the first instance of book burning?
12. What was the first military coup in Israel?
13. Who used the first pseudonym?
14. Who built the first city?
15. Who was the first hunter?
16. Who was the first murderer?
17. What is the first book of the Bible named after a woman?
18. Who is the first prophet mentioned in the Bible?
19. Where did Jesus work his first miracle?
20. What was the first of the ten plagues of Egypt?
21. Who was the first king of Israel?
22. Who were the first foreign missionaries?
23. Who was the first shepherdess?
24. Who was the first single man to be exiled?

25. Who was the first judge of Israel?
26. Who was the first disciple chosen by Jesus?
27. Who wore the first bridal veil?
28. Who told the first lie?
29. Who was the first priest mentioned in Scripture?
30. Who wore the first ring?
31. What was the first city called?
32. What was the first animal out of the ark?
33. Where were the disciples first called Christians?
34. Who took the first census of the Hebrews?
35. Who was the first shepherd?
36. Who were the first exiles?
37. Who were the first twins?
38. Who constructed the first altar?
39. Who built the first Jerusalem temple?
40. Who planted the first garden?
41. Who was the first metal craftsman?
42. Who was the first farmer?
43. Who was the first polygamist?
44. What is the first commandment with a promise attached to it?
45. Who was the first apostle to be martyred?
46. Who was the first child mentioned in the Bible?
47. Who was the first daughter mentioned by name?
48. What is the first color mentioned in the Bible?
49. Who planted the first vineyard?

ANSWERS

1. Pharaoh, at the time Joseph was in Egypt (Genesis 40:20)
2. The one at the court of Persian ruler Ahasuerus. The winner was Esther (Esther 2).
3. Stephen (Acts 6:7—8:2)
4. The dream of Abimelech, in which he was told to return Sarah to Abraham (Genesis 20:3-8)
5. The war of the kings of the north, led by Chedorlaomer, king of Elam (Genesis 14)
6. Noah, who planted a vineyard after leaving the ark (Genesis 9:21)
7. In the temple at Jerusalem. It was a chest, ordered by King Joash, who had a hole bored in the lid to keep priests from stealing funds (2 Kings 12)
8. Eutychus, who dozed off and fell out of a window during Paul's sermon (Acts 20:9)
9. "Be fruitful and multiply" (Genesis 1:28)
10. Abraham bought the Cave of Machpelah as a tomb for Sarah (Genesis 23:3-20)
11. Jeremiah's scroll, sent to King Jehoiakim, was burnt piece by piece as it was being read to the king (Jeremiah 36:21-23)
12. Absalom led an attempt to overthrow his father, David (2 Samuel 15–18)
13. Esther, whose real name was Hadassah (Esther 2:7)
14. Cain (Genesis 4:17)
15. Nimrod (Genesis 10:9)
16. Cain (Genesis 4:8)
17. Ruth.
18. Abraham (Genesis 20:7)
19. Cana (John 2:1-11)
20. The river turns to blood (Exodus 7:14-24)
21. Saul (1 Samuel 10:1)
22. Paul and Barnabas (Acts 13)
23. Rachel (Genesis 29:9)
24. Cain (Genesis 4:12)
25. Othniel (Judges 3:9)
26. Simon Peter (John 1:42)
27. Rebekah (Genesis 24:65)
28. The serpent (Genesis 3:4)
29. Melchizedek (Genesis 14:18)
30. Pharaoh (Genesis 41:42)
31. Enoch, named after Cain's son (Genesis 4:17)
32. The raven (Genesis 8:7)
33. The raven (Genesis 8:7)
34. The priest Eleazar (Numbers 26:1-2)
35. Abel (Genesis 4:2)
36. Adam and Eve, driven from the garden (Genesis 3:24)
37. Jacob and Esau (Genesis 25:23-26)
38. Noah (Genesis 8:20)
39. Solomon (1 Kings 6)
40. God (Genesis 2:8)
41. Tubal-cain (Genesis 4:22)
42. Cain (Genesis 4:2)
43. Lamech (Genesis 4:19)
44. "Honor your father and mother" (Deuteronomy 5:16; Ephesians 6:2-3) The promise is that the person will have a long life if he honors his parents.
45. James (Acts 12:1,2)
46. Cain (Genesis 4:1)
47. Naamah, daughter of Lamech (Genesis 4:22)
48. Green—"I have given every green herb" (Genesis 1:30)
49. Noah (Genesis 9:20)

FOCUS QUOTE The Holy Scriptures tell us what we could never learn any other way: they tell us what we are, who we are, how we got here, why we are here and what we are required to do while we remain here. —A. W. Tozer

WHAT JONAH FELT LIKE

They picked up Jonah and threw him overboard into the raging sea—and the storm stopped! . . . Now the Lord had arranged for a great fish to swallow Jonah. And Jonah was inside the fish three days and three nights. Jonah 1:15, 17 TLB

In February 1891, the ship *Star of the East* was off the Falkland Islands when the crew spotted an 80-foot sperm whale. Two rowboats filled with crewmen were launched to capture the monster. Closing in, one harpooner let go his weapon and shafted the whale, which lashed out, almost overturning the boats. Returning to the ship with their dead whale, the crewmen realized one sailor, James Bartley, was missing. It was decided he had been tossed overboard in the fight and had drowned.

Six hours later the crewmen began removing the blubber from the dead beast. By midnight the task was still unfinished, and the sailors went to bed. In the morning, they resumed their job. Then the unexpected happened. According to M. de Parville, editor of the *Journal des Debats,* writing in Paris in 1914, "Suddenly the sailors were started by something in the stomach which gave spasmodic signs of life. Inside was found the missing sailor, James Bartley, doubled up and unconscious. He was placed on deck and treated to a bath of seawater which soon revived him, but his mind was not clear and he was placed in the captain's quarters." Recovering, Bartley recalled being hit by the whale's tail and that he had been "encompassed by great darkness, and he felt he was slipping along a smooth passage that seemed to move and carry him forward. His hands came in contact with a yielding, slimy substance, which seemed to shrink from his touch. He could easily breathe, but the heat was terrible. It seemed to open the pores of his skin and draw out his vitality. The next he remembered he was in the captain's cabin."

Except for the fact that his face, neck, and hands had been bleached white, Bartley—like Jonah—survived the belly of the monster.

The People's Almanac by David Wallechinsky and Irving Wallace. Published by Doubleday & Company, Inc. Copyright © 1975.

DISTINCTIVE BIBLE PERSONALITIES

1. Earliest:	**Adam**	world's first human being	Gen. 2:7
2. Oldest:	**Methuselah**	son of Enoch, who lived to be 969	Gen. 5:27
3. Strongest:	**Samson**	carnal Nazarite whom God used to deliver Israel from the Philistines	Judg. 14:6; 15:5
4. Wisest:	**Solomon**	king of Israel and son of David	1 Kings 3:12
5. Richest:	**Solomon**		1 Kings 10:23
6. Tallest:	**Goliath**	over nine feet tall, killed in battle by David	1 Sam. 17:4
7. Shortest:	**Zacchaeus**	who climbed a sycamore tree to see Jesus	Luke 19:3-4
8. Fattest:	**Eglon**	Moabite king killed by the judge Ehud	Judg. 3:17
9. Meekest:	**Moses**	Israel's great lawgiver and author of Scripture's first five books	Num. 12:3
10. Cruelest:	**Manasseh**	who shed blood from one end of Judah to the other but later repented	2 Chr. 33:1-13
11. Fastest:	**Asahel**	described in Scripture as "light of foot as a wild roe"	2 Sam. 2:18

12. Greatest of the prophets:	**John the Baptist**	forerunner of Christ	Matt. 11:11
13. Guiltiest:	**Judas**	who betrayed the Savior for 30 pieces of silver	Matt. 27:3-5
14. Proudest:	**Nebuchadnezzar**	Babylonian king who destroyed Jerusalem and was later humbled by God himself	Dan. 4
15. Most Beautiful:	**Esther**	Jewish queen who saved her people from the first holocaust attempt in history	Esther 2:7
16. Most Traveled:	**Paul**	the great theologian and missionary	Acts 13:4; 15:36; 18:23
17. Most Sorrowful:	**Jeremiah**	persecuted by his own countrymen for preaching on sin and who saw his beloved Jerusalem destroyed	Jer. 9:1; Lam. 1:12
18. Most Persecuted:	**Job**	attacked by Satan, totally misunderstood by his wife, and criticized by his friends	Job 1–2
19. Most Lovestruck:	**Jacob**	who agreed to work seven years for the hand of Rachel	Gen. 29:18-20
20. Most Frightened:	**Belshazzar**	whose knees knocked as the handwriting on the wall appeared	Dan. 5:6
21. Most Rash:	**Jephthah**	who vowed to offer a special sacrifice if God would allow him to win a battle. The sacrifice turned out to be his daughter	Judg. 11:30
22. Most Doubtful:	**Thomas**	who said he could not believe in Christ's resurrection until he saw and touched the Savior	John 11:16; 20:24-29

Taken from *Willmington's Book of Bible Lists.* Copyright © 1987 by H. L. Willmington. Published by Tyndale House Publishers. Used by permission.

FOCUS QUOTE

It ain't those parts of the Bible that I can't understand that bother me; it is the parts that I do understand. —Mark Twain

---

WHAT IS GOD LIKE?

23 Facts about God

1. God is self-existent . . . . Exod. 3:13-14
2. God is self-sufficient . . . . Ps. 50:10-12
3. God is eternal . . . . Deut. 33:27; Ps. 90:2
4. God is infinite . . . . 1 Kings 8:22-27; Jer. 23:24
5. God is omnipresent . . . . Ps. 139:7-12
6. God is omnipotent . . . . Gen. 18:14; Rev. 19:6
7. God is omniscient . . . . Ps. 139:2-6; Isa. 40:13-14
8. God is wise . . . . Prov. 3:19; 1 Tim. 1:17
9. God is immutable . . . . Heb. 1:10-12; 13:8
10. God is sovereign . . . . Isa. 46:9-11

11. God is incomprehensible .... Job 11:7-19; Rom. 11:33
12. God is holy .... Lev. 19:2; 1 Pet. 1:15
13. God is righteous and just .... Ps. 119:137
14. God is true .... John 17:3; Titus 1:1-2
15. God is faithful .... Deut. 7:9; Ps. 89:1-2
16. God is light .... James 1:17; 1 John 1:5
17. God is good .... Ps. 107:8
18. God is merciful .... Ps. 103:8-17
19. God is gracious .... Ps. 111:4; 1 Pet. 5:10
20. God is love .... John 3:16; Rom. 5:8
21. God is spirit .... John 4:24
22. God is one .... Deut. 6:4-5; Isa. 44:6-8
23. God is a Trinity .... Matt. 28:19; 2 Cor. 13:14

QUESTIONS PEOPLE WOULD LIKE TO ASK GOD

Suppose you could ask God any *three* questions on this list. What would they be?

	National %
Will there ever be lasting world peace?	37
How can I be a better person?	33
What does the future hold for me and my family?	31
Will there ever be a cure for all diseases?	28
Why is there suffering in the world?	28
Is there life after death?	26
What is heaven like?	22
Will man ever love his fellowman?	21
Why is there evil in the world?	16
When will the world end?	16
Why was man created?	10
Don't know/Don't believe in God	8

Note: Percentages add to more than 100% due to multiple responses.

QUESTIONS GOD ASKS PEOPLE

Whom did God ask:

1. "How long will this people provoke me?" (Hint: a leader.)
2. "Whom shall I send, and who will go for us?" (Hint: a prophet.)
3. "Have I any pleasure at all that the wicked should die?" (Hint: a prophet.)
4. "Doest thou well to be angry?" (Hint: a reluctant prophet.)
5. "Who told thee that thou wast naked?"
6. "Why is thy countenance fallen? If thou doest well, shalt thou not be accepted?" (Hint: a farmer.)
7. "How long wilt thou mourn for Saul, seeing I have rejected him from reigning over Israel?" (Hint: a judge and prophet.)
8. "I am the Lord, the God of all flesh; is there anything too hard for me?" (Hint: a prophet.)
9. "Son of man, can these bones live?" (Hint: a prophet.)
10. "Who is this that darkeneth counsel by words without knowledge?" (Hint: a righteous man.)
11. "Who hath made man's mouth?" (Hint: a leader.)
12. "What is this that thou hast done?" (Hint: a woman.)
13. "Shall the clay say to him that fashioneth it, What makest thou?" (Hint: a foreign king.)
14. "Shall seven years of famine come unto thee in thy land? Or wilt thou flee three months before thine enemies?" (Hint: a king.)
15. "Shall I not spare Nineveh, that great city?" (Hint: a prophet.)

16. "Hast thou an arm like God? Or canst thou thunder with a voice like him?" (Hint: a righteous man.)
17. "Why is this people of Jerusalem slidden back by a perpetual backsliding?" (Hint: a prophet.)
18. "Have I not commanded thee? Be strong and of good courage; be not afraid." (Hint: a conqueror.)
19. "Is anything too hard for the Lord?" (Hint: a patriarch.)
20. "Hast thou killed, and also taken possession?" (Hint: a king.)

ANSWERS
1. Moses (Numbers 14:11)
2. Isaiah (6:8)
3. Ezekiel (18:23)
4. Jonah (4:9)
5. Adam (Genesis 3:11)
6. Cain (Genesis 4:6-7)
7. Samuel (1 Samuel 16:1)
8. Jeremiah (32:26-27)
9. Ezekiel (37:3)
10. Job (38:2)
11. Moses (Exodus 4:11)
12. Eve (Genesis 3:13)
13. Cyrus (Isaiah 45:1-9)
14. David (2 Samuel 24:13)
15. Jonah (4:11)
16. Job (40:9)
17. Jeremiah (8:4-12)
18. Joshua (1:1, 9)
19. Abraham (Genesis 18:13)
20. Ahab (1 Kings 21:19)

Taken from *The Complete Book of Bible Trivia.* Copyright © 1988 by J. Stephen Lang. Published by Tyndale House Publishers. Used by permission.

100 BEST-SELLING REFERENCE BOOKS

This list was compiled from information supplied by publishers. The first sales figure shown for each entry is the number of copies sold during 1991; the second figure is the total number sold in the title's history with the publisher.

Although the books are ranked according to the total sold in the past year, not all publishers granted permission for sales totals to be published. Unreleased or unavailable figures are designated by "n.a.," but the books are ranked in their proper position.

1. **Halley's Bible Handbook** H. H. Halley, Zondervan © 1965. n.a. This book provides a concise Bible commentary, archaeological facts, maps, and a record of church history.
2. **The New Strong's Exhaustive Concordance of the Bible** James Strong, Nelson © 1990. n.a. Designed for laypeople, this concordance lists words not included in the popular edition.
3. **Major Bible Themes** Lewis Chafer and John Walvoord, Zondervan © 1991. n.a. The authors explore the Bible's significant themes and topics.
4. **The Mother's Topical Bible** Mike Murdock, Honor Books © 1988. n.a. This volume offers more than 1,700 Scriptures on more than 93 topics.
5. **Vine's Expository Dictionary of Biblical Words,** revised W. E. Vine, et al., Nelson © 1985. n.a. This edition includes a modern typeface and two-column format. It's keyed to *Strong's Exhaustive Concordance* and other references.
6. **With the Word** Warren Wiersbe, Nelson © 1991. n.a. In this devotional commentary, Wiersbe discusses basic truths of the entire Bible.
7. **Holman Bible Dictionary** Trent Butler, general editor, Holman © 1991. n.a. This 1,486-page work offers more than 600 color illustrations, maps, charts, and articles by nearly 300 contributors.
8. **How to Read the Bible for All Its Worth** Gordon Fee and Douglas Stuart, Zondervan © 1982. n.a. This book helps readers understand the Bible's messages and purposes.
9. **What the Bible Is All About** Henrietta Mears, Regal © 1953, 1983. n.a. Emphasizing themes, this book gives an overview of the Bible.
10. **Matthew Henry's Commentary on the Whole Bible** Matthew Henry, Zondervan © 1961. n.a. Henry's classic devotional commentary has been condensed to one volume.
11. **The New Unger's Bible Dictionary** Merrill Unger, et al., Moody © 1966. 21,995 / 79,493 This volume offers 6,779 articles

100 BEST-SELLING REFERENCE BOOKS cont.

and more than 500 photos featuring biblical persons, places, and objects.

12. **The Prophecy Knowledge Handbook** John Walvoord, Victor © 1990. 19,945 / 41,746 Walvoord covers prophecy from Genesis to Revelation, including various interpretations.

13. **What the Bible Is All About for Young Explorers** Frances Blankenbaker, Regal © 1986. n.a. This Bible overview for kids includes time lines and a Bible dictionary.

14. **The New Strong's Concordance of the Bible,** concise ed., James Strong, Nelson © 1985. n.a. This conveniently sized commentary offers many features of the *New Strong's Exhaustive Concordance.*

15. **The Practical Bible Dictionary and Concordance** Barbour © 1985. 17,261 / 371,158 This volume includes a concise Bible dictionary, a concordance, a section of Bible facts and figures, and a course on how to begin regular Bible study.

16. **Nuevo Diccionario Bíblico Ilustrado** Samuel Vila and Santiago Escuain, Editorial CLIE © 1985. 17,123 / 95,000 This illustrated Bible dictionary is designed for Spanish Bible students.

17. **Strong's Exhaustive Concordance of the Bible** James Strong, World Bible © 1986. n.a. This edition of the century-old reference offers larger type, Christ's words in red, and Hebrew-Greek keying.

18. **The New Compact Bible Dictionary** T. Alton Bryant, editor, Zondervan © 1967. n.a. This volume provides concise definitions of people, places, objects, and events.

19. **Learn New Testament Greek** John Dobson, Baker © 1989. n.a. This 52-lesson plan concentrates on Greek vocabulary and forms common in the New Testament.

20. **Nelson's Illustrated Bible Dictionary** Herbert Lockyer, Sr., editor, Nelson © 1986. n.a. With 5,500 entries based on the NKJV text, this volume also offers maps, charts, photos, and tables of information.

21. **Smith's Bible Dictionary** William Smith, Nelson © 1986. n.a. These editions contain special articles on biblical topics, illustrations, and maps.

22. **Bible Knowledge Commentary—New Testament** John Walvoord and Roy Zuck, Victor © 1983. 13,598 / 223,725 This verse-by-verse exposition is based on the New International Version.

23. **Talk Thru the Bible,** Vol. 1. Bruce Wilkinson and Kenneth Boa, Nelson © 1983. n.a. Part of a five-volume series, this book is designed for lay Bible readers and clergy. Introductory sections and detailed outlines precede discussions of each book, and the text is discussed verse-by-verse.

24. **The Expositor's Bible Commentary,** Vol. 5. Frank Gaebelein, editor, Zondervan © 1989. n.a. This volume includes commentary on Psalms, Proverbs, Ecclesiastes, and Song of Songs.

25. **Philippians, Colossians, Philemon** (The New American Commentary) Richard Melick, Jr., Broadman © 1991. n.a. Based on the NIV text, this commentary is designed for pastors, students, and Bible study teachers.

26. **Harper's Bible Dictionary** Paul Achtemeier, Harper © 1985. 12,756 / 135,108 Prepared by 179 members of the Society of Biblical Literature, this volume contains 3,700 entries, outlines of all the books of the Bible, and color maps and photographs.

27. **The NRSV Concordance,** Unabridged. John Kohlenberger III, Zondervan © 1991. n.a. This concordance includes the apocryphal/deuterocanonical books.

28. **Zondervan Pictorial Bible Dictionary** J. D. Douglas and Merrill Tenney, general editors, Zondervan © 1988. n.a. With more than 5,000 entries and 700 illustrations, this volume includes monographs on biblical topics.

29. **Meredith's Book of Bible Lists** Joel Meredith, Bethany © 1980. 12,260 / 174,928 This collection of Bible facts is presented in list form.

30. **The Teen's Topical Bible** Mike Murdock, Honor Books © 1989. n.a.

This volume offers more than 2,200 Scriptures on more than 80 topics.

31. **Smith's Bible Dictionary** William Smith, Barbour © 1987. 11,986 / 68,513 This volume defines and explains thousands of significant biblical words.

32. **Mark** (The New American Commentary) James Brooks, Broadman © 1991. n.a. Based on the NIV text, this commentary relates all discussion to Mark's central theological theme.

33. **Bible Knowledge Commentary—Old Testament** John Walvoord and Roy Zuck, Victor © 1985. 11,744 / 178,895 This verse-by-verse exposition is based on the New International Version.

34. **The Compact Survey of the Bible** John Balchin, editor, Bethany © 1987. 11,532 / 66,719 This concise overview of the Bible offers insight on key themes and suggests applications.

35. **Revell Bible Dictionary** Lawrence Richards, Revell © 1990. 11,073 / 59,587 This readable reference features more than 2,000 entries, descriptions of 3,300 Bible people and 1,400 places, illustrations, and outlines of Bible books.

36. **Nelson's New Compact Illustrated Bible Dictionary** Laurence Urdang, Nelson © 1978. n.a. Urdang describes biblical places, names, events, and books.

37. **Complete Works of Josephus** Flavius Josephus, Kregel © 1960. n.a. Translated by William Whiston, this account of Jewish culture and history includes illustrations and other Bible-study aids.

38. **The 365-Day Devotional Commentary** Lawrence Richards, Victor © 1990. 10,198 / 21,711 Each day's reading includes a core passage, a personal application, and a quote from a well-known Christian.

39. **An Encyclopedia of Bible Difficulties** Gleason Archer, Zondervan © 1982. n.a. Archer addresses in canonical order the biblical questions and problems that are raised against the doctrine of inerrancy.

40. **Cruden's Concordance** Alexander Cruden, Barbour © 1987. 10,121 / 55,815 This title includes more than 200,000 entries.

41. **Romans 1-8** ("MacArthur New Testament Commentary" series) John MacArthur, Moody © 1991. 10,052 / n.a. MacArthur's commentary includes illustrations and exegesis with practical applications designed for pastors and laypeople.

42. **The Teacher's Commentary** Lawrence Richards, Victor © 1987. 9,680 / 72,753 Including maps and charts, this volume helps teachers explain and apply every portion of Scripture.

❝❞ FOCUS QUOTE The most learned, acute, and diligent student cannot, in the longest life, obtain an entire knowledge of the Bible. The more deeply he works the mine, the richer he finds the ore.
—Sir Walter Scott

---

43. **Willmington's Book of Bible Lists** Harold Willmington, Tyndale © 1987. 9,542 / 53,539 Willmington's Bible information is arranged in groups, categories, and lists.

44. **Gospel Parallels,** 4th ed., Burton Throckmorton, Nelson © 1979. n.a. This book provides a thorough study of the first three Gospels by comparing corresponding passages in adjacent columns.

45. **The New International Dictionary of the Bible** J. D. Douglas and Merrill Tenney, general editor, Zondervan © 1987. n.a. This reference includes more than 5,000 entries and 700 pictures and maps.

46. **Bible Knowledge Commentary,** 2 vols., John Walvoord and Roy Zuck, Victor © 1985. 8,795 / 36,859 This set contains a volume each for the Old and New Testaments. Verse-by-verse exposition is based on the NIV.

100 BEST-SELLING REFERENCE BOOKS cont.

47. **A Survey of the New Testament,** revised, Robert Gundry, Zondervan © 1982. n.a. This book is designed to acquaint readers with the Bible through articles that introduce and analyze the material.

48. **Strong's Exhaustive Concordance** James Strong, Baker © 1979. n.a. Unabridged, this edition includes Strong's numbering system and every relevant feature of the original work.

49. **The Zondervan Expository Dictionary of Bible Words** Lawrence Richards, Zondervan © 1985. n.a. This book is designed to help Bible students read their English translations with an understanding of the words' original meanings.

50. **Thompson Chain-Reference Bible Companion** Howard Hanke, Kirkbride © 1989. 8,000 / 18,000 This handbook explores issues of continuity and unity between the Old and New Testaments.

51. **The NIV Exhaustive Concordance** Edward Goodrick and John Kohlenberger III, Zondervan © 1990. n.a. This exhaustive concordance lists every word in the NIV Bible and its references.

52. **Bible Questions and Answers** Nelson © 1987. n.a. The 6,000 questions and answers in this book are organized under the topics history, poetry, prophecy, Gospels, acts of the Apostles, and Epistles.

53. **The International Bible Commentary** F. F. Bruce, editor, Zondervan © 1986. n.a. This volume offers an analytical look at the NIV Bible by 43 scholars.

54. **Things to Come** J. Dwight Pentecost, Zondervan © 1958. n.a. This encyclopedic reference covers eschatology and biblical prophecy, including methods of interpretation.

55. **Romans,** revised (Tyndale New Testament Commentary) F. F. Bruce, Eerdmans © 1985. n.a. Designed for serious lay readers, this commentary discusses date and authorship and provides interpretive notes.

56. **Christian Theology** Millard Erickson, Baker © 1986. n.a. This unabridged one-volume work of systematic theology is designed for evangelical pastors, students, and teachers.

57. **Josephus: The Essential Writings** Paul Maier, Kregel © 1988. n.a. This slightly condensed version includes photos, illustrations, an index, and other references.

58. **Strong's Comprehensive Concordance of the Bible** James Strong, World Bible public domain n.a. This 1,425-page concordance features Strong's numbering system and eliminates minor articles, including *and, a,* and *the.*

59. **Old Testament Survey** William LaSor, David Hubbard, and Frederick Bush, Eerdmans © 1982. n.a. For college and seminary-level students, this volume is subtitled "The Message, Form and Background of the Old Testament."

60. **John** (Tyndale New Testament Commentary) R.V.G. Tasker, Eerdmans © 1960. n.a. This exegetical commentary provides readers tools for interpretation and explanation.

61. **New Bible Dictionary** J. D. Douglas, editor, Tyndale © 1982. 6,854 / 137,746 Approximately 2,000 entries discuss the Bible's books, people, key words, and major doctrines. Also featured are Israel's history and culture.

62. **Eerdmans Handbook to the Bible,** revised, David & Pat Alexander, editors, Eerdmans © 1983. n.a. Prepared by biblical scholars, this illustrated book answers Bible questions with text, maps, charts, and photos.

63. **Acts,** revised (Tyndale New Testament Commentary) I. Howard Marshall, Eerdmans © 1980. n.a. Exegetical in nature, this commentary provides readers an inexpensive resource that is neither too technical nor too brief.

64. **Believer's Bible Commentary: New Testament** William MacDonald, Nelson © 1980. n.a. Designed for Bible students from all walks of life, this commentary

discusses controversial issues from a theologically conservative viewpoint.

65. **The NIV Compact Dictionary of the Bible** J. D. Douglas and Merrill Tenney, editors, Zondervan © 1989. n.a. An abridgment of the *New International Dictionary of the Bible,* this work features more than 300 illustrations.

66. **The Father's Topical Bible** Mike Murdock, Honor Books © 1988. n.a. This volume offers more than 1,800 Scriptures on more than 90 topics.

67. **Harper's Bible Commentary** James Mays, editor, Harper © 1988. 6,426 / 64,757 This fully illustrated volume helps readers understand the Old and New Testaments and Apocrypha.

68. **Willmington's Guide to the Bible** H. L. Willmington, Tyndale © 1981. 6,349 / 179,142 Written in lay language, this volume includes an archaeological handbook, theological manual, and an illustrated Bible encyclopedia.

69. **The Bible Dictionary** James Boyd, Barbour © 1991. 6,293 / 6,293 This illustrated reference features information on all people, places, and things in the Bible.

70. **Unger's Bible Handbook** Merrill Unger, Moody © 1967. 6,200 / n.a. This companion to Bible study offers an encyclopedia of information.

71. **The Businessman's Topical Bible** Mike Murdock, Honor Books © 1988. n.a. This volume offers more than 1,500 Scriptures on more than 90 topics.

72. **Revelation,** revised (Tyndale New Testament Commentary), Leon Morris, Eerdmans © 1987. n.a. This commentary is designed to arrive at the full, clear meaning of biblical text.

73. **The Harper Concise Atlas of the Bible** James Pritchard, Harper © 1991. 5,960 / 5,960 Illustrated with more than 250 maps, site reconstructions, and color photographs, this work places biblical history in its geographic settings.

74. **Matthew,** revised (Tyndale New Testament Commentary), R. T. France, Eerdmans © 1986. n.a. This exegesis is

designed to arrive at the full and clear meaning of the biblical text.

75. **A Harmony of Samuel, Kings, and Chronicles** William Crockett, Baker © 1985. n.a. The complete texts of these historical books are printed in columns, organized so readers can compare corresponding texts. The book also contains a complete list of other parallel Scripture.

76. **Cruden's Compact Concordance** Alexander Cruden, Zondervan © 1968. n.a. This is slightly abridged from the complete volume.

77. **Young's Compact Bible Dictionary** G. Douglas Young, Tyndale © 1989. 5,663 / 34,803 This revision includes nearly 7,000 entries; hundreds of maps, charts, and theological terms; and recent archaeological findings.

> **66 99**
> **FOCUS QUOTE** The Bible's eclipse would plunge the world into chaos, its extinction would be the epitaph of history.

78. **New Testament Fulfillment of Old Testament Prophecies** Abram Kenneth Abraham, Barbour © 1988. 5,505 / 19,439 This book offers many proofs that Jesus is the Messiah.

79. **The New Topical Textbook** Barbour © 1988. 5,393 / 24,703 This book offers thousands of topically arranged Scripture passages and R. A. Torrey's "Methods of Bible Study."

80. **Hebrews,** revised (Tyndale New Testament Commentary), Donald Guthrie, Eerdmans © 1983. n.a. Designed for the serious reader, this exegetical commentary attempts to be neither too technical nor too brief.

81. **A Survey of the Old Testament** Andrew Hill and John Walton, Zondervan © 1991. n.a. This college-level text focuses on the purpose, message, and literary structure of each Old Testament book.

82. **Thru the Bible with J. Vernon McGee,**

100 BEST-SELLING REFERENCE BOOKS cont.

Vol. 4, J. Vernon McGee, Nelson © 1983. n.a. This conservative commentary covers Matthew through Romans.

83. **1 Corinthians,** revised (Tyndale New Testament Commentary), Leon Morris, Eerdmans © 1986. n.a. Morris offers readers an inexpensive resource that discusses the text's full meaning.

84. **Thru the Bible with J. Vernon McGee,** Vol. 5, J. Vernon McGee, Nelson © 1983. n.a. This conservative commentary covers 1 Corinthians through Revelation.

85. **All about the Bible** Sydney Collett, Barbour © 1989. 5,067 / 12,202 This volume discusses the Bible's origin, inspiration, and alleged errors and contradictions.

86. **Chronological Charts of the Old Testament** John Walton, Zondervan © 1978. n.a. Walton arranges and organizes portions of Scripture that are sometimes difficult to harmonize chronologically.

87. **New Twentieth-Century Encyclopedia of Religious Knowledge** J. D. Douglas, editor, Baker © 1991. n.a. This update of a 1955 work includes more than 2,000 articles by 250 contributors on the 20th-century context of faith and life.

88. **Christianity through the Centuries** Earle Cairns, Zondervan © 1954, 1981. n.a. This history covers the Western church from 5 B.C. to the present, with text, charts, maps, and illustrations.

89. **People and Places in the Bible** John Farrar, Barbour © 1987. 4,821 / 37,407 Short definitions are given for names of biblical characters and locations.

90. **Thru the Bible with J. Vernon McGee,** Vol. 2, J. Vernon McGee, Nelson © 1983. n.a. This conservative commentary covers Joshua through Psalms.

91. **Thru the Bible with J. Vernon McGee,** Vol. 1, J. Vernon McGee, Nelson © 1983. n.a. This conservative commentary covers Genesis through Deuteronomy.

92. **James,** revised (Tyndale New Testament Commentary), Douglas Moo, Eerdmans © 1986. n.a. Designed for serious lay readers, this commentary discusses date and authorship and provides interpretive notes.

93. **Pocket Interlinear New Testament** Jay Green, editor, Baker © 1989. n.a. This reference uses interlinear and margin translations and Strong's numbering system above each word to help Bible students understand the text's original meaning.

94. **Thru the Bible with J. Vernon McGee,** Vol. 3, J. Vernon McGee, Nelson © 1983. n.a. This conservative commentary covers Proverbs through Malachi.

95. **Bible Manners and Customs** Barbour © 1991. 4,436 / 4,436 This volume offers a detailed view of life in Bible times, an evaluation of Scripture's figurative language, and a discussion of the relationship between divinity and humanity.

96. **The Letters of John,** revised (Tyndale New Testament Commentary), John Stott, Eerdmans © 1988. n.a. Part of a 20-volume series, this commentary provides readers easily accessible exegesis.

97. **1 Peter,** revised (Tyndale New Testament Commentary), Wayne Grudem, Eerdmans © 1988. n.a. This 192-page commentary provides readers an inexpensive resource that comprises sound discussions, notes, and other Bible-study tools.

98. **Chronological and Background Charts of the New Testament** Wayne House, Zondervan © 1981. n.a. House illustrates all aspects of the chronology, historical background, and criticism of the New Testament.

99. **International Children's Bible Dictionary** Lynn Waller, Word © 1988. n.a. Cross-referenced with the *International Children's Bible* and other versions, this volume explains words, phrases, and Bible events.

100. **2 Peter and Jude,** revised (Tyndale New Testament Commentary), Michael Green, Eerdmans © 1987. n.a. Designed for serious lay readers, this 208-page commentary discusses date and authorship and provides interpretive notes.

Bookstore Journal, Official Trade Publication of the Christian Booksellers Association. Copyright © 1992. Reprinted by permission.

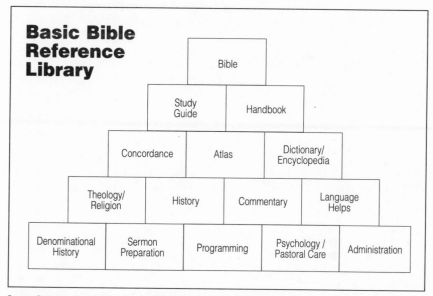

Basic Bible Reference Library

Bible

Study Guide | Handbook

Concordance | Atlas | Dictionary/ Encyclopedia

Theology/ Religion | History | Commentary | Language Helps

Denominational History | Sermon Preparation | Programming | Psychology / Pastoral Care | Administration

THE GOLDEN RULE

Do not that to thy neighbor that thou wouldst not suffer from him. *Pittacus of Lesbos* (650–570 B.C.)

Never do to others what you would not like them to do to you. *Confucius* (550–478 B.C.)

We should behave to friends as we would wish friends to behave to us. *Aristotle* (384–322 B.C.)

What is hateful to you, do not to your fellowmen. That is the entire law; all the rest is commentary. *Talmud* (Judaism)

Do for others what you want them to do for you. *Jesus Christ in Matthew 7:12* (Christianity)

Hurt not others in ways that you yourself would find hurtful. *Dana-Varga* (Buddhism)

This is the sum of duty; do naught unto others which would cause you pain if done to you. *Mahabharata* (Brahmanism)

Regard your neighbor's gain as your own gain and your neighbor's loss as your own loss. *T'ai Shang Kan Ying P'ien* (Taoism)

That nature alone is good which refains from doing unto another whatsoever is not good for itself. *Dadistan-i-dinik* (Zoroastrianism)

No one of you is a believer until he desires for his brother that which he desires for himself. *Sunnah* (Islam)

Do not do unto others as you would that they should do unto you. Their tastes may not be the same. *George Bernard Shaw*

When we and ours have it in our power to do for you and yours what you and yours have done for us and ours, then we and ours will do for you and yours what you and yours have done for us and ours. *Old English Toast*

Every man takes care that his neighbor does not cheat him. But a day comes when he begins to care that he does not cheat his neighbor. Then all goes well. *Ralph Waldo Emerson*

We have committed the Golden Rule to memory; let us now commit it to life. *Edwin Markham*

Church History

100 MOST IMPORTANT EVENTS IN CHURCH HISTORY

Rank	Event	Year
1	Council of Nicea	325
2	Luther posts "Ninety-five Theses"	1517
3	East-West split	1054
4	Vatican II opens	1962
5	Augustine converted	386
6	Bible printed by Gutenberg	1455
7	Council of Trent begins	1545
8	Chalcedon and Leo the Great	451
9	Thomas Aquinas completes *Summa Theologica*	1272
10	Calvin's *Institutes*, 1st edition published	1536
11	Edict of Milan	313
12	Jerome completes Vulgate	406
13	King James Bible published	1611
14	Diet of Worms	1521
15	The Great Schism	1378
16	Henry VIII and Act of Supremacy	1534
17	Benedict's monastic *Rule*	540
18	Athanasius letter establishes 27 books of NT canon	367
19	Great Awakening begins	1735
20	Destruction of Jerusalem by Titus	70
21	Crusades launched by Pope Urban II's speech	1095
22	Anabaptist movement begun	1525
23	Martin Luther King, Jr., leads march on Washington	1963
24	Christianization of Russia	988
25	John and Charles Wesley converted	1738
26	Paris and Oxford founded	c.1150
27	Charlemagne crowned Holy Roman Emperor	800
28	Westminster Confession	1647
29	Passage of Bill of Rights	1789
30	Gregory the Great elected Pope	590
31	Gorbachev becomes General Secretary of Communist Party of USSR	1985
32	Augsburg Confession	1530
33	First Vatican Council meets	1869
34	Wycliffe supervises English Bible translation	c.1380
35	Karl Barth writes *Epistle to the Romans*	1919
36	*Book of Common Prayer* released	1549
37	World Council of Churches organized	1948
38	Zwingli called as people's priest at Zurich Minster	1518
39	Fourth Lateran Council held under Innocent III	1215

Rank	Event	Year
40	Wilberforce leads abolition of slave trade	1807
41	Origen begins writing	c.215-220
42	Treaties of Westphalia	1648
43	Edict of Nantes	1598
44	Tyndale's New Testament published	1525
45	Monastery at Cluny founded	910
46	Hus burned at the stake	1415
47	Peter and Paul executed	c.65
48	Francis renounces wealth	1208
49	Cyril and Methodius' mission to Slavs	864
50	Colloquy at Marburg	1529
51	Donatist Schism begins	312
52	Patrick begins mission to Ireland	432
53	Bernard founds monastery at Clairvaux	1115
54	Athanasius becomes bishop of Alexandria	328
55	Syllabus of Errors issued by Pope Pius IX	1864
56	Tertullian begins writing	196
57	International Missionary Conference, Edinburgh	1910
58	Anthony takes up life of solitude	269
59	Establishment of Spanish Inquisition	1478
60	William Carey sails for India	1793
61	Battle of Tours	732
62	Waldensian movement begins	1175
63	British and Foreign Bible Society formed	1804
64	Chinese church grows despite Cultural Revolution	1965
65	Bultmann calls for demythologization of NT	1941
66	Justin Martyr's *First Apology* dedicated	c.150-155
67	*Fundamentals* published	1929
68	Synod of Dort	1618
69	Public churches begin to be built	c.230
70	Kierkegaard writes *Attack on Christendom*	1854
71	Boniface sets out as missionary	716
72	Bede's *Ecclesiastical History* published	731
73	John Knox's final return to Scotland	1559
74	St. Bartholomew's Day Massacre	1572
75	Bunyan writes *The Pilgrim's Progress*	1678
76	Anselm becomes Archbishop of Canterbury	1093
77	Chrysostom consecrated bishop of Constantinople	398
78	First trial of Galileo	1616
79	John Keble's Sermon initiates Oxford Movement	1833
80	Columba establishes mission community on Iona	563
81	Xavier begins mission to Japan	1549
82	Mayflower Covenant drafted	1620
83	Bonhoeffer executed	1945
84	Synod of Whitby	664
85	Roger Williams establishes Providence, RI	1636
86	Francis Asbury assumes leadership of USA Methodist congregations	1772
87	Azusa Street revival breaks out	1906
88	Whitefield converted	1735

Rank	Event	Year
89	Richard Allen elected bishop of the new AME church	1816
90	John Smyth baptizes self and other Christians	1609
91	Charismatic renewal advances in USA	1960
92	William & Catherine Booth found Salvation Army	1878
93	Los Angeles Crusade catapults Billy Graham	1949
94	Irenaeus appointed bishop of Lyons	177
95	Ambrose prevails in "sit in" confrontation	385
96	D.L. Moody's conversion	1855
97	Finney leads revival in Rochester	1830
98	Student Volunteer Movement begins	1886
99	Niebuhr's *Nature and Destiny of Man,* Volume 1	1941
100	Medellin Conference	1968

Source: *Christian History Magazine,* Fall 1990. Copyright 1990. Christianity Today, Inc. Used by permission.

CHRONOLOGY OF SIGNIFICANT PLANS TO EVANGELIZE THE WORLD FROM AD 30 TO 1990

1st Century

AD 30 Jesus begins public ministry, starts on his immediate plan to win the world.

31 Jesus chooses Twelve Apostles, unfolds his master plan of personal evangelism, gives them power and authority, commissions them to go initially only to Israelites (Matthew 10:1-6); later commissions Mission of the 70 disciples to evangelize the 70 Gentile nations (Luke 10:1).

33 Jesus' Great Commission given by the Risen Lord as his final plan and as spiritual counterpart of Genesis 1:28 with 2 components of evangelizing and discipling: "Go forth to every part of the world (in Greek, *cosmos*), and proclaim the Good News to the whole creation" (Mark 16:15, NEB); "Go to all peoples everywhere and make them my disciples" (Matthew 28:19, GNB).
   Jesus as Risen Lord and later Ascended King gives Great Commission in a number of different forms at different times during the 40 days to different groups, including individuals, emphasizing the 7 mandates: Receive! Go! Witness! Proclaim! Disciple! Baptize! Train!

34 Apostles (the Twelve plus others) begin evangelizing Jews widely: several remain in Jerusalem for a decade or two, several travel outside, but most continue to evangelize only Jews until AD 38 (Peter), 43 (Paul), and after AD 50 (others).

35 Proliferation of "signs and wonders" among early believers (listed 9 times in Acts); miracles and healings at this time an everyday occurrence and an essential part of proclamation of the gospel; "power evangelism" thus one of the normal kinds of evangelism in the Early Church.

36 Martyrdom of Stephen the protomartyr; Jewish persecution of Early Church, especially of Hellenistic Christians; gospel spreads rapidly through persecution and martyrdom.

38 After 5-year period of hesitation and partial obedience to Christ's Great Commission, first Gentiles are deliberately evangelized by the Twelve Apostles.
   Commission to evangelize pagan Gentiles as Gentiles first forced on consciousness of Jewish church, through baptism by Peter of Cornelius, a God-fearer but not a Jewish proselyte (Acts 10:1-48).

c.38 Twelve Apostles, after 5 years' uncertainty, scatter across globe spreading the gospel, from Ethiopia (Matthew), to Armenia (Bartholomew) to India (Thomas); all martyred over subsequent 60 years.

CHRONOLOGY OF WORLD EVANGELIZATION FROM AD 30 TO 1990 cont.

46   Paul's 1st missionary journey (45-48), with Barnabas: Antioch, Cyprus, Pamphilia, Pisidia, Lycaonia; develops strategy of urban evangelization and urban ministry, moving from city to city or town to town.

61   Paul writes: "The Good News which has reached you is spreading all over the world" (Colossians 1:6, Jerusalem Bible); "The Good News, which you have heard, has been preached to the whole human race" (Colossians 1:23; Greek "to all creation under the sky").

65   Prophecies of John the Divine: "I saw another angel flying high in the air, with an eternal message of Good News to announce to the peoples of the earth, to every race, tribe, language and nation" (Revelation 14:6-11, GNB).

66   Evangelist Luke concludes his 2-volume narrative (Luke-Acts): The worlds of empire and Judaism have now been evangelized, the gospel is now known to all peoples throughout them, and the Great Commission there largely completed.

2nd Century

c.100   Christianity predominantly urban, based in Roman cities, spreading from city to city along trade routes; later missions to Armenia, Ethiopia, China (under Nestorians) all center on capital cities.

c.130   Christianity spreads principally and normally, though not exclusively, through (as prevailing strategy) the planting of churches which then serve as missionary communities to evangelize their areas by continuing to attract and enlist converts; most converts are reached through casual contacts, witnessing a martyrdom, hospitality and care of strangers, et alia.

c.140   Hermas writes: "The Son of God . . . has been preached to the ends of the earth" (*Shepherd of Hermas*).

c.150   Justin Martyr (c100-165) founds disciple-training school over a house in Rome, documents current "signs and wonders"(exorcisms, healings, and prophesyings), and writes: "The first Apostles, twelve in number, in the power of God went out and proclaimed Christ to every race of men"; and "There is not one single race of men, whether barbarians, or Greeks, or whatever they may be called, nomads, or vagrants, or herdsmen dwelling in tents, among whom prayers and giving of thanks are not offered through the name of the Crucified Jesus"; teaches that all orthodox Christians believe in a resurrection of the flesh and in a millennial reign in the New Jerusalem; martyred at Rome.

156   Phrygia: rise of Montanism under new convert Montanus (c120-c175), a puritanical, prophetic, charismatic, millennial, apocalyptic movement claiming to be a new age of the Holy Spirit; 206, Tertullian joins; 230, movement excommunicated by Synod of Iconium; continues underground until c880.

c.180   Irenaeus bishop of Lyons (c120-203) documents recent charismata (exorcisms, visions, prophecies), and teaches that Antichrist will be a Jew of the tribe of Dan, also Christ will inaugurate a literal millennium of 1,000 years.

197   Tertullian (c160-222) documents recent healings and exorcisms, also writes: "Christ commanded them to go and teach all nations. Immediately, therefore, so did the apostles"; "The blood of the martyrs is seed"; and "There is no nation indeed which is not Christian"; 206, joins Montanist movement.

3rd Century

c.205   First known Christian scholar and apologist Clement of Alexandria (c155-215) deals with problem of how to relate Christian faith to Greek philosophy and culture, writes: "The whole world, with Athens and Greece, has already become the domain of the Word."

c.220	Origen (c185-254) writes: "The gospel of Jesus Christ has been preached in all creation under heaven, to Greeks and barbarians, to wise and foolish. . . . It is impossible to see any race of men which has avoided accepting the teaching of Jesus"; "The divine goodness of Our Lord and Saviour is equally diffused among the Britons, the Africans, and other nations of the world"; and "The preaching of the gospel through the whole Oikumene (whole inhabited earth) shows that the church is receiving divine support"; but also "Many people, not only barbarians, but even in the Empire, have not yet heard the word of Christ"; and "The gospel has not yet been preached to all nations, since it has not reached the Chinese or the Ethiopians beyond the river, and only small parts of the more remote and barbarous tribes"; 248, in *Contra Celsum* foresees possibility of conversion of entire world.
249	Seven missionary bishops sent to peoples of Gaul by Cornelius of Rome: Gatien (Tours), Trophime (Arles), Paul (Narbonne), Saturnin (Toulouse), Denis (Paris), Martial (Limoges), Austremoine (Clermont); many others also strategically located and sent in all directions.
c.270	Rise of monasticism in Egypt, as direct challenge to lifestyle of the rich: (1) eremitical (Anthony of Egypt, c251-356), (2) cenobitic (Pachomius, c287-346); widespread over next 2 centuries, with many documented healings, exorcisms, miracles, signs and wonders; Egyptian monks travel widely, evangelizing in Europe, Britain, Ireland, et alia.

4th Century

303	10th and last imperial Roman persecution, under Diocletian; aimed at clergy and bishops, with substantial defections; destruction of all church buildings and Scriptures ordered; 500,000 Christians killed or executed in witness under total persecution.
308	Church of the Martyrs with 29 bishops in Egypt organized by bishop Meletius (died 325) of Lycopolis, in opposition to leniency towards lapsi favored by Peter I Ieromartyros (Seal of Martyrs) patriarch of Alexandria who is himself martyred in 311; ideal of martyrdom as major factor in evangelizing the world spreads; Meletian sect is approved by Arians, lasts until c520.
c.310	Eusebius of Caesarea (c265-339) writes apologetic works: "Praeparatio evangelica" (refuting paganism), "Demonstratio evangelica" (fulfilment of Hebrew prophecy in Christ); 314, completes his *Ecclesiastical History,* and *Martyrs of Palestine*; writes "The doctrine of the Saviour has irradiated the whole Oikumene (whole inhabited earth)"; 325, at Council of Nicea expounds Matthew 28:19.
313	Constantine at Milan issues *Edict of Toleration* legalizing Christianity throughout Roman empire; 323, becomes sole emperor, attempts to spread gospel by law and authority.
325	Council of Nicea I (1st Ecumenical Council): council makes political province the basic unit for church's larger divisions, brings church's jurisdictional areas into line with secular dioceses and provinces of Roman empire, in order better to witness.
347	Cyril bishop of Jerusalem (310-386) teaches that Antichrist will be a magician who takes over Roman empire, claims to be Christ, deceives Jews by rebuilding Temple, persecutes Christians, then is slain at Second Advent by the Son of God.
c.360	8-volume *Apostolic Constitutions*, a Syrian collection of ecclesiastical law, makes frequent allusions to Great Commission of Jesus in Matthew 28:19-20.
374	A layman, Ambrose of Milan (c339-397), acclaimed bishop by crowds; in his writings, documents current healings and glossalalia; later teaches Second Coming of Christ will be preceded by destruction of Rome and appearance of Antichrist on Earth.

CHRONOLOGY OF WORLD EVANGELIZATION FROM AD 30 TO 1990 cont.

378   Jerome (c345-419) writes: "From India to Britain, all nations resound with the death
           and resurrection of Christ"; estimates 1.9 million Christians to have been martyred
           since AD 33 (out of 120 million Christians, i.e. 1.6% or 1 in 60); documents numerous
    —   current "signs and wonders" (healings, exorcisms, miracles).

392   Ascetic writer John Cassian (c360-435) enters Bethlehem monastery; 415, founds mon-
           astery in Marseilles; promotes spread of monasticism in West; much evangelization
           due to these itinerant evangelistic monks.

398   John Chrysostom (c344-407) appointed patriarch of Constantinople, founds training
           school for native Gothic evangelists; writes, "'Go and make disciples of all nations' was
    —   not said for the Apostles only, but for us also"; teaches that final Antichrist under direct
           inspiration of Satan will appear immediately before Second Advent of Christ in AD 430.

5th Century

c.410   — Episcopate in Proconsular Africa, Numidia and Mauretania expands to 768 bishops; to-
           tal episcopate across North Africa, including Egypt and Donatists, numbers 1,200 bish-
           ops; Honoratus at Lerins monastery trains succession of notable missionary bishops,
           sent across world for Christ.

426   Augustine (354-430) bishop of Hippo completes in 13 years his treatise *The City of God*
           (De Civitate Dei), against background of Visigoth invasion of Rome; propounds allegori-
    —   cal millennialism, but also teaches that future final Antichrist will arise as Nero Redivi-
    —   vus; opposes emerging theory of cessation of charismatic gifts, as overreaction to
           excesses of Montanism, et alia, with the teaching that miracles and charismata ended
    ?   with the Apostolic age; documents numerous recent miracles, exorcisms, healings, and
           resuscitations.

428   French apologist Prosper Tiro (c390-463) defends Augustine of Hippo, writes treatise
           De Vocatione Omnium Gentium envisaging conversion of all barbarians to Christ,
           whose grace extends everywhere: "Nulla pars mundi ab Evangelio vacat Christi."

499   — Task of translating Jesus' message into Greek and Latin cultures virtually completed,
           after 16 generations.

6th Century

c.510   Irish Peregrini or Exultantes Christi (unorganized wandering hermits and preachers
           using pugilatores scotorum [Irish writing-tablets] as their major piece of equipment)
           embark on peregrinatio pro Christi amore as missionary pilgrims for Christ, begin to
           migrate across Europe for next 400 years, to the Alps, Germany, Danube, Italy, also to
           Orkneys, Faeroes, Iceland, converting much of Europe in one of great missionary feats
           of all time.

535   Cosmas Indicopleustes, Nestorian merchant missionary over most of world, retires to
           monastery and in 547 completes his global survey *Topographia Christiana* in 12 books.

c.550   Nestorian monasticism organized and reformed by Abraham of Kashkar (501-586); nu-
           merous monasteries and missions begun, with special concern for physical and spiri-
           tual needs of people; through persecution, spreads across Asia to Yemen, South India,
           Ceylon, Samarkand, China.

594   Roman Pope Gregory the Great (540-604) publishes *Dialogues* describing contempo-
    —   rary Christian miracles, visions, prophecies, supernatural awareness, and other spiri-
           tual gifts; places detailed planning of organized missions to all heathen among his
           major objectives, in view of imminence of Last Judgment.

7th Century

635   China (then richest and most civilized nation on Earth): first missionary (Alopen, a
         Nestorian bishop from Syria) reaches Thailand and then Tang Chinese capital Ch'ang-an
         (Hsian), translates Scriptures for emperor Tai-tsung; Nestorianism influential till sup-
         pressed for a time in 845.

8th Century

c.700   End of Patristic Age, during which Greek Fathers and Latin Fathers have all expounded
         the words *euangelizo, euangelizesthai, euangelismos, evangelizare, evangelizatio,*
         evangelizator, et alia.

720   Anglo-Saxon translations of John's Gospel by historian and theologian Bede (Baeda,
         c673-735), monk at Jarrow on Tyne; Bede predicts fall of Colosseum will be followed
         by that of Rome and then also of the whole world.

c.780   Forced baptism of Saxon race by Charlemagne; 4,500 executed in one day for resisting,
         thousands more deported.

10th Century

962   Holy Roman Empire founded by Otto I (912-973), king of Germany, crowned by Pope
         John XII; seen as embodiment of rule of Christ on Earth; 10 million by AD 1000, 16 mil-
         lion by AD 1200, 29 million by 1800; finally abolished in 1806.

11th Century

1000   Millennial year preceded by widespread terrors; followed by 150 years of vast increase
         in pilgrimages to Holy Land, with widespread continuing belief in imminent end of
         world with final king of the Franks leading all faithful to Jerusalem to await Second
         Coming of Christ.
            Catholic Apostolic Church of the East (East Syrian or Nestorian church) is by now
         the most extensive in world, with 250 dioceses across Asia and 12 million adherents;
         expansion of Nestorianism in Tenduc, country of Keraits with Karakorum as capital,
         home of legendary ruler Prester John.

1090   College of Cardinals established in Rome by reforms of Pope Urban II (c1042-1099), to
         expand rule of Christ across the Earth.

1095   Military expeditions by Western Christians against Muslim powers to liberate Holy
         Land, launched by Pope Urban II, known as Crusades: 1st 1095-99 (People's Cru-
         sade); 2nd 1147-49; 3rd 1189-93 (Richard the Lion-Heart); 4th 1202-04; 5th 1212-21
         (Children's Crusade); 6th 1228-29; 7th 1248-54; 8th 1270-72 (Prince Edward of En-
         gland).

12th Century

c.1180   Joachim of Fiore (c1130-1202), Italian Cistercian abbot and mystic, divides all history
         into three 40-generation ages or periods (Old Testament, New Testament, future age),
         writes *Vaticini del Vangelo Eterno* (Prophecies of the Eternal Gospel) and *Expositio in*
         Apocalypsim describing imminent crisis of evil, apocalyptic symbols of Antichrist, and
         his 3rd or Final Age of the Spirit (Love) coming by 1260 after Age of the Father (Law),
         and Age of the Son (Grace), for spiritual men through pilgrimage and great tribulation
         in a spiritualized Johannine Church replacing carnal Petrine Church; Joachimism
         spreads widely over next 3 centuries.

CHRONOLOGY OF WORLD EVANGELIZATION FROM AD 30 TO 1990 cont.

c.1190   Rise of demand for vernacular versions of Scriptures, illustrated by *Historia Scholastica*, a narrative of biblical history, by 12th-century scholar Petrus Comestor (c1100-1180); poetical and prose versions now available in Old French (Provençal, Vaudois), Italian, Spanish.

13th Century

1209   Francis of Assisi (1182-1226) founds traveling preachers (Franciscans), largest of the mendicant orders (OFM); widespread healings, signs and miracles reported; 1270, missionaries in almost every part of the known world; by 1400, missions from Lapland to Congo and Azores to China; soon reaches a medieval peak of 60,000 Franciscans by 1400, 77,000 by 1768, falling to 14,000 by 1900, rising to 40,000 by 1970.

1215   Dominic (1170-1221) founds Order of Preachers (OP, Dominicans) in southern France for "Propagation of the Faith through Preaching," "accepting our Lord's command, Go ye into all the world"; soon reaches a peak of 12,000 Dominicans, falling to 7,055 by 1983; other orders of mendicant friars arise including in 1256 Augustinians (OSA).

1221   First of many papal mission encyclicals on foreign missionary affairs: Bull of Honorius III, "Ne si secus" to the 13 metropolitans of the Catholic church, asking them to send out missionaries.

c.1250   Height of the Catholic church's political power in Europe, taken for granted by most Christians as God's instrument for spreading the rule of Christ around the world.

c.1260   Italy and Europe: greatest period of religious art begins, and lasts 400 years, with as central theme Christ's passion and crucifixion; all art—paintings, drawings, tapestries, stained-glass windows, sculpture, architecture—now regarded as major method of teaching and evangelizing illiterate populations.

1266   Mongol ruler Kublai Khan (1215-1294) requests Roman pope: "Send me 100 men skilled in your religion . . . and so I shall be baptized, and then all my barons and great men, and then their subjects. And so there will be more Christians here than there are in your parts"; 2 Dominicans sent, but turn back; then 1278, pope sends 5 Franciscans; greatest missed opportunity in Christian history.

14th Century

1349   Apogee of East Syrian or Nestorian expansion across Asia, geographically more extensive and more prosperous than ever before or since; 25 metropolitans (each with 6-12 suffragan bishops) in 250 dioceses in China, India, Kashgar, Samarkand, Turkestan, et alia, with total of over 15 million Christians; a mighty organization with missionary enterprise unsurpassed in Christian history.

1399   Catalan Dominican wandering preacher Vincent Ferrer (c1350-1419) reevangelizes and transforms Christendom throughout Europe; brings Jews to dialogues, converts 25,000 across Europe; preaches 6,000 apocalyptic sermons each 3 hours long, with glossolalia, healings, miracles widely reported; writes of future coming of Antichrist, predicts world will end after 2537 more years in AD 3936 (based on number of verses in Book of Psalms).

15th Century

c.1400   Societas Peregrinantium pro Christo founded by Franciscans.

1420   Taborites, extreme militant wing of Bohemian Hussites at Tabor south of Prague, founded as strict biblicists under their bishop Nicholas of Pelhrimov, seek to establish Kingdom of God by force of arms and military campaigns including destruction of churches; finally defeated at Lipany in 1434, Tabor captured 1452.

1431   Council of Basle (17th Ecumenical Council): question of papal supremacy, and the
Hussite heresy; edict orders all Jews to attend Christian sermons.

1450   Invention of printing (typography and the printing press) by Johannes Gutenberg
(c1395-1468) at Mainz, Germany, in order to disseminate the Holy Scriptures across
the world; 1455, inventor ruined financially by lawsuit; in 6 languages by 1478; by
1500, more than 100 printed editions of the Bible produced.

1455   German mystic Thomas à Kempis (c1380-1471) writes *The Imitation of Christ;* a major
influence on evangelization.

1493   Pope issues Demarcation Bull "Inter Caetera," giving Portugal authority over Africa,
much of Asia and later Brazil; Spain given authority over rest of world west of a north-
south line 345 miles west of the Azores.

16th Century

1500   Total of saints and martyrs who are known by name, formally recognized or canonized
by the churches, now numbers over 10,000; from 1500-1903, Rome recognizes 113
further canonizations and 547 beatifications; total by 1985, known by name, for all confessions: 50,000 (0.1% of grand total all martyrs by 1985, known and unknown); total
effect on world evangelization has been incalculable.

1517   Leonardo da Vinci (1452-1519), greatest genius ever, artist, scientist, engineer, inventor (submarine, tanks, aircraft, parachute, helicopter, anatomy, "Last Supper," etc.), produces "Visions of the End of the World" or "Deluge," depicting with overpowering
pictorial imagination the primal forces that rule nature.

c.1520   Martin Luther (1483-1546) writes: "The gospel will always be preached. . . . It has gone
out throughout the length and the breadth of the world. . . . It is made known farther
and farther, to those who have not heard it before," and "The gospel preached by the
Apostles in various languages, sounds forth even now till the end of time"; teaches that
institution of papacy, and hence every pope (without singling individuals out), is Antichrist; expects Advent of Christ in 1558.

1523   Spanish monarch orders Cortes to enforce mass conversion of Amerindians across
New World; in Mexico, Franciscans baptize over a million in 7 years, with at times
14,000 a day; by 1536, 6 million Amerindians baptized in 17 years in Mexico alone;
c1550, 800,000 Peruvian Amerindians confirmed by one archbishop of Lima.
               Ignatius Loyola (1491-1556) works in Palestine for conversion of Muslims; 1534,
founds Society of Jesus, with missions around world (Japan by 1549); 1556, Society
becomes leading missionary order with 1,000 Jesuits; peaks at 36,038 by 1965, falls to
25,550 in 1983 in 200 countries; official scope "Defense and Propagation of the Faith
through Preaching."

1528   Berne Disputation, with its *10 Theses,* brings Reformation to city of Berne; Anabaptists
insist that Great Commission applies to everyone who confesses Christ's name.

1530   Luther and Calvin teach that Great Commission (Mark 16:15) was work of 1st-century
Apostles only and expired with them.

1534   Anabaptist refugees from persecution seize city of Munster, found Kingdom of a Thousand Years, eject unbelievers, establish New Jerusalem; 1534 city captured, King John
of Leiden executed; the major 16th-century millenarian outburst.

1536   Sculptor and painter Michelangelo Buonarroti (1475-1564) completes vast painting
"The Last Judgment" in Sistine Chapel, Vatican, a powerful fresco of the Day of Wrath
inspired by Dante and medieval hymn "Dies irae."

CHRONOLOGY OF WORLD EVANGELIZATION FROM AD 30 TO 1990 cont.

1547   Nostradamus (Michel de Notredame, 1503-1566), astrologer and physician, makes extensive prophecies from 1547, first published as *The Centuries* in 1555; condemned by Roman Index in 1781; the most widely read seer of the Renaissance, in print continuously ever since, with vast literature of commentaries; end of world predicted for 1666, or 1734, 1886, 1943, 2000, 2038, or 3797.

c.1547   Anabaptists view Great Commission as binding on all church members.

1559   Anabaptists the only Reformed grouping to deliberately work for and obey Jesus' Great Commission, especially through Hutterian Brethren's itinerant evangelism.

1568   Commission of cardinals instituted in Rome by Pius V for foreign missions in East Indies, for Italo-Greeks, and for Protestant lands of Europe; 1573, congregation for conversion of infidels formed.

1580   Discalced (Reformed) Carmelite Sisters become a separate order; by 1983, 11,649 cloistered contemplative nuns in 727 monasteries; serving evangelization of the world in name of Christ by prayer and works of charity.

1584   Jesuit priest Alonso Sanchez drafts evangelistic scheme for invasion and military conquest of China; others plan for forcible baptism of all peoples of the world.

1588   Anglican parish priest Hadrian Saravia (1531-1613) becomes one of first non-Roman advocates of foreign missions, stressing binding validity of Matthew 28:19: "The command to preach the gospel to the Gentiles pertained not only to the age of the apostles, but to all future times to the end of the world."
            Consistorial Congregation erected in Rome, responsible for all matters concerning all Catholic bishops and dioceses across world except Eastern-rite and missionary jurisdictions; includes Pontifical Commission for Migration and Tourism; 1967, renamed Sacred Congregation for Bishops.

1589   Russian Orthodox patriarchate instituted ('The Third Rome'); 1700, Peter the Great orders christianization of Siberia, 1721 abolishes patriarchate, rules church directly; as state church, its missions expand across Europe, Central Asia, Persia, Siberia, 1685 China, 1743 Kamchatka, 1784 Alaska, 1861 Mongolia, 1861 Japan, 1898 Korea, by means of traders, merchants, colonists, soldiers, diplomats, exiles, settlers (1 million Russians in Siberia from 1700-1783), monks, bishops, missionaries; 1826, best epoch of Russian Orthodox missions begins; 1870, Orthodox Missionary Society founded by metropolitan of Moscow, I. Veniaminov (1797-1879), in 55 Russian dioceses; whole mission enterprise destroyed in 1917 Revolution.

17th Century

c.1600   Episcopi Vagantes (Wandering Bishops, or Bishops-at-Large, in 15 disputed or contested lines of apostolic succession) begin to multiply across Europe; 1866, Julius Ferrette as bishop of Iona begins their modern era; by 1975, 760 bishops-at-large lead 280 distinct autocephalous Catholic churches/denominations with 10,285,000 adherents in 80 countries; each proposes grandiose plan for reunion of Christendom and conversion of world, calling on Rome, Constantinople, Canterbury, and Geneva to abandon their global pretensions and join each's new ecclesiastical body.

c.1610   Dominican historian Tomas Malvenda (1566-1628) translates Hebrew Old Testament into Latin, writes treatise on coming of Antichrist.

1613   Major missionary work by Discalced Carmelite monk of Spain, Thomas a Jesu (1564-1627), *De procuranda salute omnium gentium*, urges and envisages conversion of entire world to Christ.

1622   Sacred Congregation for the Propagation of the Faith (Propaganda, meaning dissemina-
            tion or progressive plantation) founded by Pope Gregory XV (1554-1623); 1967, re-
            named by Pope Paul VI as SC for the Evangelization of Peoples.

1627   English biblical scholar Joseph Mede (1586-1638), a premillennialist, writes
            Apocalyptica: Key of the Revelation; formulates theory of progressive millennialism
            (later termed postmillennialism): Christ will only return at close of man-made millen-
            nium on Earth.

1648   Spanish Jesuit Ildefonso de Flores (1590-1660) calculates total Christian martyrs of all
            epochs to date at 11 million; major impact of martyrdom on world evangelization recog-
            nized; his estimate agrees closely with later survey done in 1980-1990.

1656   Calvinist and Puritan statesman Oliver Cromwell (1599-1658), protector of Common-
            wealth of England, Scotland and Ireland from 1653-1658, allows Jews prohibited since
            1290 to return to England, in order to hasten Christ's Second Coming.

1657   Quint (Fifth) Monarchy Men (named from Daniel 2:44; after empires of Assyria, Persia,
            Greece, Rome, the Fifth is at hand as the Millennium), a Puritan sect, propose abolish-
            ing established church in England to bring about Parousia; 1657 and 1661, rise in
            armed revolt against Cromwell, but crushed.

1667   English poet John Milton (1608-1674) in his *Paradise Lost* draws attention to the Chris-
            tian goal "To Evangelize the Nations."

1680   Founding in Rheims of Christian Brothers (FSC) to teach Christian doctrine to the poor
            and working classes across the world; by 1976, 12,641 lay brothers; by 1983, declines
            to 9,348.

1698   First 2 non-Roman missionary societies formed, by Church of England: Society for Pro-
            moting Christian Knowledge (SPCK), and (1701) Society for the Propagation of the Gos-
            pel in Foreign Parts (SPG); goal of world evangelization claimed, but in practice they
            work largely in British sphere of influence.

18th Century

1700   Evangelistic campaigns in Germany of Ernst Christoph Hochmann von Hochenau (1670-
            1721), major separatist Pietist/Lutheran mystic of his time, converted 1693. Regarding
            the conversion of the Jews as the sign of Christ's impending return, he engaged briefly
            in Jewish missionary work.

1703   Spiritans (CSSp, Holy Ghost Fathers) founded for "Evangelizzazione degli infedeli"; by
            1983, 857 houses with 3,671 missionaries.

1705   Origin of Danish-Halle Mission (Lutheran), forerunner of Protestant missionary socie-
            ties; first workers include Protestant pioneers to Tranquebar (India): Bartholomew
            Ziegenbalg (1682-1719), Heinrich Plutschau (1677-1747) and Christian Schwartz
            (1726-1798).

1710   Canstein House printing press, Halle (Germany) with first Bible society (Cansteinische
            Bibelanstalt) founded by Count Karl von Canstein: 3 million Bibles and NTs printed in 80
            years.

1725   The Great Awakening, revival in New England (USA) spreading throughout the Thirteen
            Colonies; begun under T.J. Frelinghuysen in New Jersey; mass conversions of
            dechristianized European populations in North America, led by revivalist Jonathan Ed-
            wards (1703-1758), who expounds progressive millennialism (later called postmillenni-
            alism), envisaging establishment of Christ's millennial kingdom on Earth around year
            1990, with Second Advent at close of millennium; Edwards calls for "concerts of
            prayer" for world revival; Awakening lasts until 1770.

CHRONOLOGY OF WORLD EVANGELIZATION FROM AD 30 TO 1990 cont.

1732   Moravian missions land in St Thomas, West Indies; 1733, Greenland; 1736, among
            Samoyeds of Archangelsk; 1787, Society of the United Brethren for Propagating the
            Gospel among the Heathen, formed in Pennsylvania, USA; 1732-1862, Moravians send
            abroad 2,000 missionaries.

1774   United Society of Believers in Christ's Second Appearing (Shakers) founded in
            Niskeyuna, NY (USA) by Ann Lee and pilgrims from England as millennial messianic
            sect in New World, based on celibacy.

1780   Deutsche Christentumsgesellschaft (Christendom Society)begun in Germany to build
            kingdom of God on an ecumenical basis; 1815, members found Evangelische
            Missionsgesellschaft in Basel (Basel Mission).

1782   Concerts of Prayer (for revival and world mission), as envisaged by Jonathan Edwards,
            begin and spread in Britain, then from 1790 in USA; basis for subsequent worldwide
            missionary advance.

1783   Native Baptist Church, first Jamaican Afro-Christian movement, begun by ex-slave,
            George Lisle; plays a significant political role 80 years later; precursor of later End-time
            pentecostal renewal across world.

1785   Evangelical awakenings (revivals) throughout Wales under Howel Harris (1714-1773)
            and others: 1785 Brynengan, 1786 Trecastle, 1791 Bala, 1805 Aberystwyth, 1810
            Llangeitho, 1817 Beddgelert, 1821 Denbighshire, 1822 Anglesey, 1828
            Carmarthenshire, 1832 Caernarvonshire, 1840 Merionethshire, 1849 South Wales, et
            alia.

1787   English Baptist minister Andrew Fuller (1754-1815) writes *The Gospel of Christ Worthy
            of All Acceptation* and over 128 other titles, urges obedience to the Great Commission.

1792   William Carey (1761-1834) publishes first statistical global survey of Christian world
            mission: *An Enquiry Into the Obligations of Christians, to Use Means for the Conver-
            sion of the Heathens,* accurately enumerating populations and Christians on all conti-
            nents in world's first statistical survey (world population 731 million: 57%
            pagan/Hindu/Buddhist, 18% Muslim, 14% RC, 6% Protestant, 4% Orthodox, 1% Jew-
            ish); 1793, sails for India under Particular Baptist Society for Propagating the Gospel
            Among the Heathen (formed 1792); at Serampore, initiates modern era of Protestant
            world missions, serves without home leave for 41 years in Bengal, translates and prints
            Bible in 35 languages.

1795   London Missionary Society begun; founders' "vision of a world covered by missionary
            centres that would reach out and link up until there was no place where the gospel was
            not preached."

19th Century

1800   Widespread evangelistic camp meetings begin in USA; Kentucky Revival awakening,
            with crowds of up to 25,000, sweeps over Kentucky, Tennessee, and the Carolinas.

1802   Massachusetts Baptist Mission Society formed "for the evangelization of frontier com-
            munities."

1804   British & Foreign Bible Society (BFBS) founded, in London, with vision of providing
            Scriptures to whole world.

1806   USA: Haystack Prayer Meeting at Williams College, MA, launches North America for-
            eign missions, to preach the gospel to all nations; 1810, these students form Society of
            Inquiry on the Subject of Missions; soon after, ABCFM is formed.

1810   W. Carey conceives idea of regional ecumenical missionary conferences around globe;
            nothing results until 1825 Bombay and 1854 New York.

Congregationalists in Massachusetts, USA, organize American Board of Commissioners for Foreign Missions (ABCFM) "to devise, adopt and prosecute ways and means for propagating the gospel among those who are destitute of the knowledge of Christianity"; by 1880, 1,200 missionaries overseas; 1961, renamed United Church Board for World Ministries, "to serve Christ in the world"; 1985, 229 foreign missionaries in 54 countries.

1814   Society of Jesus reestablished by Pope Pius VII (1742-1823) after 40 years' ban, with renewed interest in global mission and evangelization.

1815   Italian priest Caspar Del Bufalo (1786-1837) founds Missioners of the Most Precious Blood, with "his goal for his missioners the evangelization of the world" through charitable works.

1818   *The Conversion of the World: or the Claims of 600 Millions, and the Ability and Duty of the Churches Respecting Them:* book by G. Hall & S. Newell (ABCFM, India); proposal to convert heathen millions across world by sending 30,000 Protestant missionaries from USA and Europe in 21 years, at cost of US$4 from each Protestant and Anglican communicant in Christendom.

1819   Missionary Society of Methodist Episcopal Church organized; 1939 constitution states "The supreme aim of missions is to make the Lord Jesus Christ known to all peoples in all lands as their divine Saviour"; 1940, 1964, reorganized as Board of Global Ministries, United Methodist Church; 1974, 839 foreign missionaries (9.5% non-USA); 1985, 516 foreign missionaries in 50 countries.

1824   USA: beginnings of interdenominational city-wide cooperative evangelism; spreads to cities across world.

1825   Bombay Missionary Union (Anglicans, Congregationalists, Presbyterians, et alii) formed; first interdenominational regional conferences of missionaries 1855 in India, 1872 Japan, 1873 first all-India decennial conference, 1877 China, c1885 Mexico, et alia.

1826   Glasgow City Mission founded by David Nasmiths, secretary of 23 Christian societies, first of 50 city missions begun in Britain's largest cities (Bristol, Chester, Edinburgh, Glasgow, Leeds, Liverpool, 1832 London, York, et alia); also 1833 New York City Mission, Boston, Brooklyn, etc.; also 1848 Hamburg, 1874 Berlin, and 70 other German cities by 1899.

1827   J.N. Darby (1800-1882), Anglican clergyman, joins Christian Brethren movement in Dublin; propounds dogma of total premillennial apostasy and ruin of Christendom (the major churches); later develops "dispensationalism," a new variety of futurist premillennialism, dividing biblical and later history into 7 eras or dispensations.

1828   Karl Gutzlaff (1803-1851), a Lutheran, begins work in Indonesia, Siam, southern China, Hong Kong; 1844, attempts to evangelize China in one generation through 300 evangelists.

1829   Christian Brethren begin foreign missions as A.N. Groves and party go out to Baghdad, then later to India; much later, loosely organized as Christian Missions in Many Lands; by 1965, 1,200 foreign missionaries in 55 countries.

1830   USA: widespread campaigns through professional evangelists Andrew, Barnes, Burchard, Baker, Caughey, Griffith, Inskip, Knapp, Maffit, Swan.
        Joseph Smith (1805-1844) at Fayette, NY (USA), has visions of incurable corruption of Christendom, and of divine restoration of Christ's church, which lead to establishment of Church of Jesus Christ of Latter-day Saints (Mormons); 1844, murdered by mob; movement migrates to Utah as headquarters of the coming millennial kingdom; subsequently evolves into massive heterodox organization unrelated to the rest of global Christianity, governed since 1844 by a Council of the Twelve Apostles; by 1988, its world mission includes 34,750 foreign missionaries (1- or 2-year termers) working in over 82 countries with annual mission budget of over US$550 million.

CHRONOLOGY OF WORLD EVANGELIZATION FROM AD 30 TO 1990 cont.

1831 Seminary president J.H. Rice calls Presbyterian Church in the US "a Missionary Society, the object of which is to aid in the conversion of the world."

1837 Board of Foreign Missions, Presbyterian Church in the USA established "to aid in the conversion of the world . . . every member of this church is a member for life of said society and bound to do all in his power for the accomplishment of this object"; 1958, becomes Commission on Ecumenical Mission and Relations, for which "The supreme and controlling aim of the Christian Mission to the world is to make the Lord Jesus Christ known to all men . . . in which Christians of all lands share in evangelizing the world and permeating all of life with the spirit and truth of Christ." ABCFM mission strategist Rufus Anderson (1796-1880) restores apostolic model for mission; in essay "The Time for the World's Conversion Come," first published in 1837 journal, argues that the churches are now, for the first time ever in history (as a result of rise of voluntary mission societies), adequately organized to complete the conversion of the world.

1841 CMS general secretary Henry Venn (1796-1873) requires all missionaries to complete annual questionnaires recording church growth statistics, as a means of monitoring progress in world evangelization; propounds "three-self" goal of mission that local churches must become self-supporting, self-governing, self-propagating.

1844 First Young Men's Christian Association (YMCA) founded, by Evangelicals in London; 1855, World Alliance of YMCAs founded in Paris (France), with headquarters in Geneva, emphasizing "extension of His Kingdom"; world vision, lay witness to Christ, global missionary thrust; 1894, World YWCA for women; subsequently, concerns broaden; 1988, 6.5 million men members in 74 National YMCA Movements and in 16 other countries; and 5 million women members.

1845 Southern Baptist Convention, largest USA Baptist denomination, comes into being in reaction against ABFMS refusing to accept slave-owners as missionaries; based from its origin on global mission, it founds Board of Domestic Missions (later, Home Mission Board) and Foreign Mission Board, beginning work in China, then 1846 Liberia and 1850 Nigeria; by 1988, has 7,000 full-time professional missionaries at home and abroad.

1846 Beginnings of world conciliarism: Evangelical Alliance formed in London by 800 Christians representing 52 confessions, to further unity among Evangelicals worldwide; national alliances then formed in Britain and Canada (1846), Sweden and Germany (1847), India (1849), Turkey (1855), USA (1867); and international conferences held in London 1851, Paris 1855, Berlin 1857, Geneva 1861, Amsterdam 1867, New York 1873, Basel 1879, Copenhagen 1884, Florence 1891, London 1896 and the final one in 1907; 1912, title officially changed to World's Evangelical Alliance (WEA).

1850 British Quaker millionaire and missions philanthropist Robert Arthington (1823-1900) donates millions to missionary societies and accumulates vast store of information on frontier evangelization of all peoples in world; 1900, his will expounds global strategy of (a) do a world survey of unreached peoples, (b) supply these peoples with translations of Luke, John and Acts, (c) teach 10 people in each tribe to read the gospel, (d) visit each tribe until a church emerges, (e) that tribe evangelizes the next, while (f) missionaries move on to regions beyond; Arthington is later followed by long series of eccentric millionaire philanthropist-strategists in Europe and USA.

1854 First Union Missionary Convention, in New York, USA, guided by Alexander Duff (1806-1878): "To what extent are we authorized by the Word of God to expect the conversion of the world to Christ?"; similar conference held in London, England; 1867, Duff appointed to first chair of evangelism and evangelical theology at New College, Edinburgh.

Foreign Mission Committee, Canada Presbyterian Synod, inaugurated; 1962, becomes Board of World Mission, United Church of Canada, "committed by its very nature to a global mission."

c.1855   Russian surge of world mission: Orthodox missiologist N.I. Ilminsky (1821-1891) works out scientific basis for missionary work; vast missionary expansion; 1870-1917, Orthodox Missionary Society organized (St Petersburg, Russia); 1917, its world mission is destroyed by Bolshevik Revolution.

1857   USA: evangelist D.L. Moody (1837-1899), a Congregationalist, evolves organized mass evangelism in Chicago; during his lifetime estimated to have had individual evangelistic personal dealings with 750,000 persons; perfects methods of preparation and publicity in cooperative city campaigns, use of theaters and tents, finance committees; other evangelists R.A. Torrey (1856-1928), Billy Sunday (1862-1925), Robert P. Wilder (1863-1938); beginnings of large-scale lay-centered evangelism.

1858   Sermons on evangelization increase: 1858 J. Parker publishes "The duty of the present generation of Christians to evangelize the world," New York; 1866 C. Dickson publishes "The duty of the Church to evangelize the World," Presbyterian Church of the USA, New York.

1859   Founding of Society of St Francis de Sales (Salesians of Don Bosco, SDB), a religious congregation dedicated to Christian education of youth across world; by 1975, 18,426 men in 1,524 houses; by 1983, 16,982 in 1,466 houses; also 17,269 Salesian Sisters (FMA).

1860   Earl of Shaftesbury, British evangelical social reformer (A.A. Cooper, 1801-1885), states: "Those who hold the truth have the means enough, knowledge enough, and opportunity enough, to evangelize the globe fifty times over."

1861   USA: Woman's Union Missionary Society of America for Heathen Lands (WUMSA) formed in New York as pioneer women's sending society, with 40 other women's societies arising later.

1862   Founding of Congregation of Immaculate Heart of Mary (Scheutists, CICM) with as goal "Evangelizzazione dei popoli"; by 1983, 1,507 members in 53 houses; over the years many Scheutist missionaries have been martyred.

1863   Universal Catholic Church (later renamed New Apostolic Church) founded in Germany by excommunicated German prophet H. Geyer of Catholic Apostolic Church (UK), emphasizing a successional apostolate subject to a chief apostle with quasi-papal powers, and the gifts of the Holy Spirit including prophecy, tongues, miraculous healing, sacraments, hierarchy of 48 living Apostles; by 1988, has 1.7 million members worldwide (mainly Germans) in 45 countries; cooperates with no other church.

1865   Christian Revival Association (1878, renamed Salvation Army) founded by Methodist evangelist William Booth in England for urban social outreach and street evangelism; 1985, 4,226,900 Salvationists in 75 countries, with vast social service and evangelistic activities and institutions; overriding first agenda defined in 1987 by SA general as "To emphasize the supremacy of evangelism in fulfilling of the Lord's great commission. . . . To work to the end that every man and woman and child has the opportunity to hear the good news of the gospel."

1867   Beginnings of confessional conciliarism: Archbishop of Canterbury C.T. Longley (1794-1868) convenes first decennial Lambeth Conference of all bishops of Anglican Communion (London), with 76 bishops present; 1875, origin of World Alliance of Reformed Churches and 1876 World Methodist Council; by 1983, grand total of 45 world confessional councils are in existence, representing all major Christian traditions, and all with own approaches to world mission.
        Founding of Combonians (MCCI/FSCI/MFSC) with as goal "Evangelizzazione dei popoli, non ancora o non sufficientemente evangelizzati"; by 1983, 1,938 missionaries.

CHRONOLOGY OF WORLD EVANGELIZATION FROM AD 30 TO 1990 cont.

1869   Anglican Broad Church Evangelical, F.W. Farrar, later dean of Canterbury, describes Europeans as God's chosen evangelizers: "The Aryan should advance farther and farther to . . . the evangelization of the whole habitable globe."

1870   Rise of first megaministry (reaching over 1% of world per annum, i.e. 14 million people a year): BFBS, ABS and other Bible societies' distribution reaches 38,000 scriptures a day.

     Pan-Orthodox world missions emerge: Orthodox Missionary Society organized in Russia by metropolitan of Moscow, I.Veniaminov (1797-1879); branches in 55 Russian dioceses; rapid missionary expansion; by 1900, Russians form largest single Christian ethnolinguistic people in whole world; 1917, Bolsheviks destroy Russian world missions; 1959, Pan-Orthodox world mission reorganized based on Athens (Greece).

     Churches of Christ (Non-Instrumental), schism from Disciples of Christ, organize in USA; by 1985, they sent out 982 foreign missionaries in 74 countries, with related churches in total of 141 countries.

1872   Salesian Sisters (FMA) founded, in Italy, for world mission by prayer and works of charity; by 1983, 17,269 nuns, in 60 countries.

1873   East London Institute for Home and Foreign Missions formed (UK); 1900, renamed Regions Beyond Missionary Union invoking Apostle Paul's world vision (2 Corinthians 10:16); by 1985, 103 North American missionaries in 5 countries, 58 British in 5 countries, with total 200 missionaries of all nationalities.

1877   Shanghai, China: 1st General Foreign Missions conference, with 473 missionaries from 20 Protestant societies; states, "We want China emancipated from the thraldom of sin in this generation"; probable origin, among field missionaries, of Watchword "The Evangelization of the World in This Generation"; similar conferences in 1890 and 1907.

1880   Circulation of Watchcry (Watchword) on various Protestant mission fields becomes crystallized in 1885 article by A.T. Pierson entitled "A plan to evangelize the world," published in his journal *The Missionary Review of the World after 20 Years of Reflection*; Pierson calls for "an ecumenical council solely to plan a world-wide campaign and proclaim the good tidings to every living soul in the shortest time."

1881   United Society of Christian Endeavor formed in USA; 1895, World's Christian Endeavor Union organized (38,000 societies across world, with 2,225,000 members); 1927, International Society of Christian Endeavor; by 1965, 3 million members in 85 Protestant denominations in 80 countries; by 1987, 2 million in 78 nations.

1884   A.O. Van Lennep publishes statistical survey *The Growth of Christianity during Nineteen Centuries* (New York), blaming inadequate growth on lack of giving (in USA, annual per capita expenditure on alcohol is $49.70 but on foreign missions only $0.05); concludes, "When Christ's Church shall be as lavish in its outlay of men and money as the world is, the conversion of Nations will not long be postponed."

1885   At D.L. Moody's Northfield Convention for lay workers, A.T. Pierson chairs committee to "divide the world according to a comity agreement" and then pursue "the immediate occupation and evangelization of every destitute district of the earth's population," so that "the entire current population of the earth would hear the gospel by the year 1900"; Moody prepares in 3 days "An Appeal to Disciples Everywhere," claiming task could be completed even if only 10 million active Christians participated.

1886   1st International Christian Student Conference, Mount Hermon, MA, USA addressed by D.L. Moody, A.T. Pierson, et alii; 251 attenders.

1887   Christian and Missionary Alliance organized in USA; 1975, Alliance World Fellowship founded, in 51 nations; by 1985, 874 USA foreign missionaries in 50 countries.

1888   Student Volunteer Movement for Foreign Missions organized with 2,200 initial volunteers, based on Watchword "The Evangelization of the World in This Generation"; 1892, Student Volunteer Missionary Union (SVMU) begun in Britain; by 1945, as a result of SVM, a total of 25,000 university graduates have gone overseas as foreign missionaries.
One By One Band started in London by T. Hogben as "a worldwide fellowship devoted wholly to winning men to Christ," based on Hogben's book *God's Plan for Soul Winning.*

1889   Japan: 500 Japanese students at Student Conference send telegram to SVM Conference, Northfield (USA), urging "Make Jesus King."
SVM chairman John R. Mott writes to sister Hattie that the task of world evangelization will be accomplished by the dawn of the 20th century.

1890   Scandinavian Alliance Mission of North America founded for worldwide evangelism and church planting; 1949, renamed TEAM (The Evangelical Alliance Mission); 1985, 929 USA missionaries in 25 countries.

1893   Sudan Interior Mission begun as Africa Industrial Mission in order to evangelize the world's largest single totally unevangelized area with no resident missionary among 90 million people (Africa's 4,000-mile Sahel and Sudan); 1982, renamed SIM International, expands to Latin America; 1985, 654 missionaries in 15 countries.

1895   Association of Pentecostal Churches in America (1919, renamed Church of the Nazarene) formed, 1897 begins foreign missions; by 1987, World Mission Division has 617 foreign missionaries in 84 countries, with two AD 2000 programs: Thrust to the Cities ("maximizing holiness evangelism in key cities") and Two Million Adherents by 1995.
World Student Christian Association/Federation (WSCF) emerges from Vadstena Castle meeting, Sweden, begun by SCMs around world whose "aim was to claim students—the future leaders of their nations—for Christ and for the evangelization of the world"; after 1914, non-evangelistic interests predominate (leadership, social issues, universities, Christian presence, etc.); 1987, over 3 million members and participants.

1897   4th Lambeth Conference; 194 Anglican bishops present; first of 14 resolutions on foreign missions passed: "We recommend that prompt and continuous efforts be made to arouse the Church to . . . the fulfilment of our Lord's great commission to evangelize all nations."
House of Laymen, Province of Canterbury (Church of England) resolves: "In view of the Great Commission to evangelize the world, its long and serious neglect . . . the whole Church needs rousing on this question."
Encyclical letter "On the Holy Spirit" issued by Pope Leo XIII, directing attention to the 7-fold gifts of the Spirit (Isaiah 11) and promoting universal novena (9-day cycle of prayer) to Holy Spirit before Pentecost Sunday each year; millions influenced.
Arabia, and the world, "could easily be evangelized within the next 30 years if it were not for the wicked selfishness of Christians"—Samuel Zwemer, Apostle to Islam (1867-1952).

1899   Gideons International begun, for free distribution of Bibles; by 1965, active in 75 countries rising to 133 by 1985 and 137 by 1988, with 30,000 overseas members; 1987, 24 million Bibles distributed, with grand total 400 million placed over 89 years.
At end of "Golden Age of Jewish Missions" (19th century), over 200,000 Jews have been baptized as Protestants, and similar numbers as Roman Catholics; 650 Protestant missionaries minister to Jews at 213 mission stations across world; many believe future conversion of the Jews could ensure completion of world evangelization.

20th Century

1900   New York Ecumenical Missionary Conference: 2,500 members, 200,000 attenders; delegates from 162 mission boards; 500 speakers, huge public meetings; formation of an international missionary committee (to complete world missionary task) canvassed, urged, then unanimously adopted only to fizzle out soon after.

CHRONOLOGY OF WORLD EVANGELIZATION FROM AD 30 TO 1990 cont.

Methodist layman John R. Mott publishes classic, *The Evangelization of the World in This Generation;* many Christian strategists envisage winning of entire world to Christ during 20th century, then seen as certain to be "the Christian century."

Origins of Pentecostalism in USA: British-Israelite holiness preacher Charles F. Parham (1873-1929, Methodist) opens Bethel Bible School near Topeka, Kansas, with 40 students; 1901, they receive baptism of Holy Spirit; 1903 revival spreads through Kansas, 1905 Houston, 1906 to Los Angeles and thence across world (1906 Norway, 1907 Chile, 1908 China, 1909 Korea, 1910 Brazil, and so on).

Total of all Christian denominations begins to rise steeply as Christianity spreads across world, from only 92 in AD 1000, to 150 in AD 1500, to 510 in AD 1800, to 1,900 by AD 1900; then by 1985 to 22,000; proliferation seen by many in 1900 as a sure guarantee that world will soon become evangelized.

1901	Latter-Rain teaching: after 1,800 years of apparent cessation of large-scale charismata and 100 years of expectancy and teaching in USA on gifts of the Spirit, "restoration of all things" begins with Spirit-baptism and glossolalia, as pentecostal power is restored to the church; thousands of seekers travel to revival centers in USA, Europe, Asia, South America; expounded in D.W. Myland, *The Latter Rain Pentecost* (1910).
	Founding of Consolata Missionary Fathers (IMC), in Turin, specifically for "Evangelizzazione degli infedeli"; by 1983, 1,008 foreign missionaries in 248 houses.
1902	Young People's Missionary Education Movement (1911, title shortened to MEM) founded by 15 USA denominational boards, YMCA and SVMU, to enlist missionaries outside college world.
	4th International Convention, Student Volunteer Movement for Foreign Missions, in Toronto, Canada, produces 691-page report World-wide Evangelization, the Urgent Business of the Church.
1903	All Nations Flag Church (Church of God of Prophecy) founded, 1911 begins work overseas (Bahamas); by 1985, links with 69 countries.
1904	Welsh revival through ministry of Evan Roberts (1878-1951) in Glamorganshire, Anglesey, Caernarvonshire, with 100,000 converts in Wales in 6 months; short-lived (1904-1906), but literally sweeps the world; worldwide publicity from the press; leads into worldwide Pentecostal movement including 1905 Switzerland and Germany, 1907 England.
1905	National conciliarism begins: 1905 Fédération Protestante de France, 1908 Federal Council of the Churches of Christ in North America (1950 NCCCUSA), 1922 National Christian Council of China, 1922 Aliança Evangélica de Angola, et alia, up to 550 nationwide councils by 1983, all in theory committed to world mission.
1906	Proliferation of world mission atlases, both Protestant (1906, 1910, 1925, 1938) and RC (1906, 1913, 1929), with statistics listed by mission societies or RC dioceses rather than by denominations and countries.
	C.F. Parham teaches that missionaries need only to receive the baptism with the Holy Ghost and can then, through the gift of glossolalia, be immediately understood in native languages to the farthest corners of the world; but Pentecostal missionaries abroad try this only to report failure.
	1st General Conference of Missionaries to the World of Islam, convened through Reformed missionary S.M. Zwemer, held in Cairo, Egypt.
	Laymen's Missionary Movement (LMM) launched as foreign missions auxiliary agency via SVM and 17 major North American Protestant denominations; uses large city-wide conferences, crusade dinners, business methods, publicity etc; by 1916, one million men have attended its 3,000 conferences, quadrupling USA Protestant mission giving.

1907   Laymen's Missionary Movement of Southern Baptists formed by 200 laymen "for mobilized laymen to evangelize our world in our lifetime," asserting that "Southern Baptists are able financially and otherwise to conquer the world for Christ"; 1927, renamed Baptist Brotherhood of the South; 1938, goal of "A Million Men for Christ"; 1950, Brotherhood Commission of SBC; 1987, enrollment 572,987 including 235,687 boys under 18 years.

1910   World Missionary Conference, Edinburgh, Scotland (previously called 3rd Ecumenical Missionary Conference until 1908 change); 1,355 delegates; beginning of 20th-century ecumenical movement; report of Commission I is entitled Carrying the Gospel to All the Non-Christian World, stating, "The Church is confronted today with a literally worldwide opportunity to make Christ known," and including survey "Unoccupied sections of the world."

                 Reunion of Christendom through organic union of denominations set forth as goal by bishop C.H. Brent (1862-1929) of Protestant Episcopal Church in the USA, as essential stage to conversion of world.

                 Men and Religion Forward Movement (MRFM, 1910-12) advances LMM concerns into a global social gospel organization, but includes nationwide evangelism, social-evangelism crusades, home and foreign missions, business ethics, detailed research on 70 cities, and every kind of Christian endeavor; reaches 1,492,646 persons in 60 USA towns through 7,062 meetings; 1913, carried worldwide by touring party.

                 Church of God (Cleveland) "initiates efforts at world evangelism," begins World Missions in Bahamas, Egypt and Cuba; by 1985, 109 foreign missionaries with churches in 98 countries; 1987, elaborate plan Decade of Destiny announced for every year 1988-1999.

1912   First attempt by a mission body to reach systematically every home in an entire nation: 1912-17 in Japan, Oriental Missionary Society reaches its 10,300,000 homes; later extended to other countries, then to world.

1913   English missionary C.T. Studd (1862-1931), deeply impressed by report Carrying the Gospel, founds Christ's Etceteras (later renamed Worldwide Evangelization Crusade) to focus on evangelizing "the remaining unevangelized parts (peoples) of the world."

                 United Missionary Campaigns across USA under LMM, Foreign Missions Conference of North America, and Home Missions Council of USA; 695 Protestant interdenominational conferences held by 1916.

1915   Elim Foursquare Gospel Alliance and Revival Party begun in Britain by Pentecostal healer G. Jeffreys (1889-1962); 1935, founds World Revival Crusade.

1917   True Jesus Church (Chen Ye-Su Chiao Hui) begun in Peking, a charismatic schism ex Apostolic Faith Movement; by 1975, a Chinese world mission with missionaries serving in Hong Kong, India, Indonesia, Japan, Korea, Malaysia, Singapore and USA.

                 Interdenominational Foreign Mission Association of North America (IFMA) founded "to make possible a united testimony concerning the existing need for a speedy and complete evangelization of the world," organized by SAGM, CIM, CAM, AIM, SIM, SAIM, WUMSA and later other Protestant missions of fundamentalist stance: 1967, 44 member missions with 8,500 missionaries in over 100 countries; 1979, 49 agencies with over 9,000 in over 115 countries; 1985, 103 nondenominational agencies in USA and Canada with over 11,000 foreign missionaries (over 8,000 from North America).

1918   Worldwide Evangelism, a vision of Pentecostal evangelist Aimee S. McPherson (1890-1944), who then in 1922 broadcasts first radio sermon, and in 1923 founds Angelus Temple, Los Angeles, and the International Church of the Foursquare Gospel.

                 USA Methodists launch Christian Crusade for World Democracy, to further Protestant missionary expansion.

CHRONOLOGY OF WORLD EVANGELIZATION FROM AD 30 TO 1990 cont.

USA Presbyterian executives believe the War experience justifies "Protestant Christianity in launching a united drive for world evangelism."

Interchurch World Movement of North America (IWM) launched to seek "complete evangelization of all life" and "conquest of the world for Christ" in one massive "forward movement"; vast support from entire range of 34 major USA denominations and 85% all USA Protestant missions; 1919, motto "The giving of the whole Gospel to the whole world by the whole church"; aims to include virtually all church-related activity; 1920, World Survey Conference, Atlantic City (NJ) with 1,700 church leaders produces massive 2-volume *World Survey* books, with plan proposing evangelization of world within 3 years; 1920, member denominations raise its $336,777,572 budget but refuse to release it; in 7-day period, IWM collapses in financial fiasco and bankruptcy.

1919	International Missionary Council (IMC) launched (directly succeeding Continuation Committee of 1910 World Missionary Conference, Edinburgh) with preliminary conference in Crans, Switzerland, then in 1921 (1-6 October) formally constituted and founded at Lake Mohonk, NY (USA); 2nd meeting in Oxford, England, in 1923.
1920	Interchurch World Movement, before its own disintegration, proposes (1) a federal "United Churches of Christ in America," and (2) a global "League of Denominations" (parallel to League of Nations); both proposals fizzle out.
	Ecumenical Patriarchate of Constantinople issues encyclical addressed to "all the Churches of Christ" calling for formation of a "League of Churches."
	Catholic missiologist P. Charles (1883-1954) of Louvain identifies goal of mission as the founding or planting of the visible church in all lands and in all cultural groups (Charles, *Etudes missiologiques,* 1956).
	Mennonite Central Committee begun in Akron, PA (USA); many varieties of development services; by 1985, 527 foreign missionaries in 50 countries, based on long Anabaptist/Mennonite centrality of the Great Commission.
	General Council of Cooperating Baptist Missions of North America organized; first vision to evangelize Africa extended in 1924 to Venezuela, then to worldwide outreach; 1953, renamed Baptist Mid-Missions; 1965, 725 USA missionaries in 27 countries; 1985, 636 missionaries in 32 countries.
1921	Institute of Social and Religious Research, New York, organized under J.R. Mott to carry on IWM's socioreligious scientific surveys; lasts until 1934.
	Oxford Group formed in Britain (1921-38), later renamed Moral Re-Armament (MRA); as evangelical renewal centering on personal devotion to Christ, the 4 Absolutes, personal evangelism, and "drawing-room evangelism," spreads rapidly through major denominations and across world; by 1950 no longer solely christocentric, embracing renewal among Buddhists, Hindus, et alii.
	General Council of the Assemblies of God USA appoints committee on worldwide cooperation for "the calling of a conference for the formation of an ecumenical union of Pentecostal believers for the more perfect and rapid evangelization of the world"; committee proves unable to meet and the effort collapses by 1923.
	Origins of global electronic church: first broadcast of a church worship service (Calvary Episcopal Church, Pittsburgh, USA), first Baptist broadcast, 1922 first Pentecostal broadcast (Aimee S. McPherson); by 1988, regular listeners/viewers for Christian programs number 1.2 billion (24% of the world).
1923	BBC (Britain) commences radio broadcasting, including daily Christian programs; in USA, 10 churches now operate radio stations; by 1928, 60 stations, falling by 1933 to 30; in 1936, BBC commences religious television.
c.1923	Million Testaments Campaigns founded in Philadelphia, USA, by journalist G.T.B. Davis, for scripture distribution in needy areas including China, Latin America, and the Jewish world.

1924 USA: White ministers all withdraw from interracial Pentecostal Assemblies of the World (Unitarian Pentecostals) to form a separate white denomination, explaining that "the mixture of races prevents the effective evangelization of the world"; becomes The Pentecostal Church, Incorporated.

United Pentecostal Church International begun in USA; by 1985, Foreign Missions Division has 212 foreign missionaries in 50 countries.

1926 Lighthouse of International Foursquare Evangelism (LIFE Bible College) begun by Aimee S. McPherson in Los Angeles, USA, for training in world mission and evangelism.

1927 1st World Conference on Faith and Order, Lausanne; over 400 delegates from 90 churches (Roman Catholics being forbidden by pope).

Association of Baptists for Evangelism in the Orient (ABEO) formed; 1939, name changed to ABWE (WE = World Evangelism); 1985, 462 missionaries in 21 countries.

1928 World Fundamental Baptist Missionary Fellowship (later, World Baptist Fellowship Mission) founded in Texas; its "purpose is to help to fulfill the Great Commission by the evangelization of the world" through indigenous Baptist churches; 1985, 126 missionaries in 23 countries.

1929 Congregationalist missionary Frank C. Laubach (1884-1970) begins "Each one teach one" method in Philippines, develops literacy primers for 300 languages worldwide; 1950, publishes *Literacy as Evangelism.*

1930 Movement for World Evangelization (Mildmay Movement) begun in London to generate converts worldwide as "God's key representatives" in the entire global range of secular worlds, leading to world evangelization within one generation; begins with world survey, with on-the-spot surveys of every mission field on Earth, publishes *World Dominion;* 1955, begins annual Christian Holiday Crusade at Filey (UK); gradually abandons original global plan in order to supply evangelists and ministerial conferences for Britain, later for Portugal, Spain, India, Australia, New Zealand, et alia.

Formation of World Council for Life and Work, replacing Continuation Committee of 1925 Stockholm Conference.

"The Lutheran Hour" broadcast over station WHK in Cleveland, Ohio, begun by LCMS; 1931, heard by 5 million a week, 1943 15 million, 1965 30 million in 120 countries over more than 1,000 radio stations; 1940, foreign broadcasting now named Bringing Christ to the Nations; 1945, worldwide to 20 million a week; 1975, broadcast in over 50 languages, heard by 22 million a week; 1987, 40 million regular listeners in 34 languages around world.

International Missions (originally The India Mission) founded in USA by B. Davidson, "dedicated to the propagation of the gospel in obedience to the Great Commission, the ultimate goal being the establishing of self-supporting and self-propagating New Testament churches in all fields"; 1985, 159 missionaries in 12 countries.

Foundation Farthest Out begun as "a world-belt of prayer around the world"; renamed Association of Camps Farthest Out (CFO International, USA) as "one of the vital instruments that God is using to establish the Kingdom of God on the Earth"; 1988, prayer camps in 85 countries.

1931 Unevangelized Fields Mission (UFM) founded in London, UK; 1980, renamed UFM International; 1985, 338 missionaries in 12 countries.

Radio Vatican inaugurated in Rome by Pius XI (1857-1939); entrusted to Jesuits; daily announcement motto "Laudetur Jesus Christus" (Praised be Jesus Christ); 1975, broadcasts to 157 countries in 32 languages for 16 hours a day; 1982, John Paul II inaugurates Vatican Television; 1987, in 35 languages.

World-Wide Prayer & Missionary Union founded (Chicago), serving 50 evangelical missions agencies.

CHRONOLOGY OF WORLD EVANGELIZATION FROM AD 30 TO 1990 cont.

1932   Conference of Bible Societies, London, discusses ways and means of international co-operation to bring the Scriptures to the whole world.

1933   Pentecostal preacher W.M. Branham (1909-1965) offends mainline Pentecostal denominations by prophesying that 1906-1977 is the Laodicean Church Age, followed immediately by mass apostasy, Second Advent of Christ, and the Millennium in 1977; Branhamites (followers) claim him as Last Prophet with messianic attributes.
            Origin of the Navigators, a one-by-one disciple-making agency based on multiplication theory/process "to contribute to the fulfillment of the Great Commission"; 1985, 191 overseas personnel in 30 countries.

1934   W. Cameron Townsend begins Wycliffe Bible Translators for Scripture translation by professional linguists, with overseas work under name Summer Institute of Linguistics (SIL); 1959, slogan "Two Thousand Tongues To Go" coined; by 1985, 3,022 translators serving overseas in 55 countries, aiming to translate Scriptures into every remaining tribal language on Earth.
            First Youth for Christ rally in Brantford, Ontario, under Paul Guiness; 1944, YFC International begun, first in USA cities, as a worldwide evangelistic movement "specializing in aggressive teen-age evangelism"; 1948, first of 12 annual world congresses of evangelism (Switzerland, Tokyo, Caracas, Mexico City, Sao Paulo, et alia); in 95 nations by 1987, now attempting to identify 600 Pacesetters to raise up a worldwide youth prayer movement.

1935   World Revival Crusade founded by Pentecostal leader G. Jeffreys.
            World Intercessors (Prayer Circle Department of Oriental Missionary Society) begun as worldwide prayer movement for world evangelization; over 2,000 prayer groups by 1968; 1987, over 40,000 participants (600 groups in USA alone); World Intercession School of Prayer (6 lessons); prayer seminars; 90,000 receive magazine *Prayer and Praise Guide.*

1936   Student Foreign Missions Fellowship (SFMF) begun by IVCF (USA); 1946, begins triennial mass conventions with "Complete Christ's Commission" and 1948 Urbana series with over 17,000 attenders each time.

1937   Child Evangelism Fellowship founded, based on belief that "before Christ's return a mighty work among children will encircle the globe"; by 1985, 160 foreign missionaries in 60 countries.

1938   4th World Missionary Conference/Meeting of International Missionary Council, Tambaram, Madras, India; 471 delegates from 69 countries; report states: "We summon the Churches to unite in the supreme work of world evangelization until the kingdoms of this world become the Kingdom of our Lord."
            Gospel Recordings (Language Recordings International) founded: "the aim of the work is to produce gospel records in every known language and dialect" in order to spread the gospel throughout the world; by 1967, recordings made in 3,400 languages and dialects, rising by 1988 to over 4,300.
            World Home Bible League founded in Chicago with as objective "the placement of a Bible in every Bibleless home, so that people can be won for Jesus Christ"; 1965, in 30 countries with over 4 million Scriptures distributed; 1985, in over 70 countries.

1939   Conference of Bible Societies, Woudschoten (Netherlands), proposes a World Council of Bible Societies.
            World-wide Signs Following Evangelism, Inc., begun under United Fundamentalist Church (Los Angeles, USA).

1941   Brazil: emergence, as a new theory of evangelization, of idea of grassroots or base ecclesial communities (comunidades eclesiais de base, BECs or CEBes); 1963 formally established, with the Catholic Church standing with the poor; fully developed after 1968 Medellin and 1979 Puebla conferences.

Origin of large-scale international multilingual Bible correspondence course organizations: Emmaus Bible School founded in Toronto, Canada; by 1966, courses mushroom worldwide, especially in closed countries (Morocco 110,000 enrollments).

1942 Ling Liang World-Wide Evangelistic Mission founded in Shanghai, China "to send Chinese missionaries to the uttermost part of the world"; 1965, in 10 countries.

New Tribes Mission begun in USA to evangelize unreached tribes across the world; by 1985, 1,438 USA missionaries in 18 countries; 1988, 2,500 missionaries working in 160 tribes, "with 2,500 tribes still to be reached."

Committee on World Literacy and Christian Literature (Lit-Lit) organized by F.C. Laubach's World Literacy Committee, and Committee for Christian Literature, Foreign Missions Conference of North America (25 major boards and agencies); work in over 60 countries.

1943 USA: National Religious Broadcasters of North America formed, as official broadcasting arm of National Association of Evangelicals, with 50 organizations growing by 1979 to over 800; by 1986, annual convention attracts 4,000.

Global Outreach Mission founded (Buffalo, NY); by 1985, 114 foreign missionaries in 13 countries.

Conservative Baptist Foreign Mission Society formed in Wheaton, IL (USA); by 1985, 525 missionaries in 25 countries, based on Great Commission imperative.

1944 Dutch East Indies sees rise of Third-World missionaries: Chinese evangelist John Sung trains 5,000 3-man evangelistic teams who make major impact across country; 1969, Japanese and Pakistani evangelistic teams; 1975, Asian Evangelists Commission (AEC)conducts crusades in Palembang, Medan and other cities.

1945 Evangelical Foreign Missions Association organized in USA: "We recognize our responsibility under the Great Commission to give all men everywhere the privilege of hearing and receiving the message of salvation . . . present an urgent call to more effectively evangelize the unreached of our generation"; by 1987, 83 member agencies sending out 13,343 missionaries (11,593 from North America, 1,726 being 1-2 year short-termers).

Massive surge of new Christian parachurch agencies or multinationals independent of the churches, increasing by 1980 to 17,500 distinct and separate agencies, with multifold ministries; great majority articulate commitment to Great Commission.

Norwegian missiologist O.G. Myklebust proposes creation of an International Institute of Scientific Missionary Research, with an association and conferences devoted to global mission; ignored until IAMS formed in 1970.

1946 Series of massive student conferences in North America: 1st IVSFM Conference, Toronto, on "Complete Christ's Commission" with 575 participants; 1948, 1st Urbana Conference, 1,400 students; steady rise in numbers to 17,112 by 1976 ("Declare His Glory among the Nations"), and 18,145 by 1984 ("Faithful in Christ Jesus").

Conference of Bible Societies, Haywards Heath (UK), creates United Bible Societies (UBS) as federation and fellowship of 13 autonomous Bible societies from Europe and North America; expands rapidly by 1986 to 70 member societies and 30 national offices, working in 180 countries; UBS becomes "a worldwide fellowship whose aim is to reach every person with the Bible or some part of it in a language he can understand and at a price he can afford."

World Literature Crusade (WLC) begins in Canada for radio outreach, then expands to systematic tract distribution through Every Home Crusades in 103 countries, with goal of reaching every home on Earth by 1970; results by 1985 in 1.42 billion gospel messages handed out producing 14.5 million documented written responses for Christ.

Egede Institute of Missionary Study & Research, in Oslo, founded to promote scholarly research in the world mission of the church.

CHRONOLOGY OF WORLD EVANGELIZATION FROM AD 30 TO 1990 cont.

Asociación Misionera Evangélica Nacional (AMEN, National Evangelical Missionary Association) begun as home mission in Peru; 1979, reorganized (with Methodist personnel) as a Third-World home and foreign missionary society with a global vision, renamed Asociación Misionera Evangélica a las Naciones; thousands of young Peruvians trained; missions in 20 countries including UK, France and Spanish North Africa (Melilla).

1947   5th Meeting of International Missionary Council, Whitby, Toronto, Canada; 112 delegates from 40 countries; upholds "the evangelization of the world in this generation," coins term "expectant evangelism."

Lutheran World Federation (LWF) founded, with first purpose stated as "To bear united witness before the world to the Gospel of Jesus Christ as the power of God for salvation"; 1st Assembly, at Lund, Sweden; 1949, LWF Commission on World Missions formed, meets at Oxford (UK).

Fuller Theological Seminary founded by C.E. Fuller in Pasadena, CA (USA), as part of his expressed desire "to see the world evangelized in this generation."

World Revival Prayer League (National Christian Women's Prayer League) founded, based on Tokyo, Japan.

Oral Roberts Evangelistic Association founded (Tulsa, OK, USA), with own foreign missions program: 1953, begins Pentecostal television preaching; becomes massive ministry with worldwide healing crusades, Oral Roberts University, City of Faith, Charismatic Bible Ministries.

1948   1st World Congress on World Evangelization (also termed 1st World Congress on Evangelism) convened by YFCI (with Billy Graham) in Beatenberg, Switzerland (August), first of long annual series: 1949, 2nd World Congress in Cannes, France; 1950, 3rd in Brussels; 1951, 4th in Winona Lake, IN (USA); 1952, 5th in Belfast; 1953, 6th in Tokyo (1,200 delegates from 24 countries: workshops, crusades, teams into 43 of Japan's 44 prefectures, 4,000 commitments to Christ); 1955 Sao Paulo (Brazil), 1956 Caracas (Venezuela), 1957 Copenhagen; 1959 Madras (India), also Tokyo, also Mexico City, 1960 Bristol (UK), then series discontinued; culminating in 1966 Berlin Congress.

World Council of Churches (WCC) inaugurated in 1st Assembly at Amsterdam by 147 churches from 44 countries; theme "Man's disorder and God's design"; 351 delegates and 238 alternates, but no RC observers; "We intend to stay together" (22 August–4 September); 7th function of WCC is stated as "To support the churches in their task of evangelization."

International Council of Christian Churches (ICCC) founded (anti-ecumenical, fundamentalist); 1st Congress at Amsterdam as rival to WCC; 150 persons from 29 countries (August); later plenary congresses every 3 or 4 years; 1948-1984, 98 major ICCC conferences held; 1983 plenary with 4,000 delegates from 93 nations and 399 denominations with (1988) 4.7 million members.

Christian Crusade (Christian Echoes National Ministry, USA) organized as anticommunist mission, moves to Tulsa, OK; heard over 400 radio stations, 10 TV stations; 1953, launches ICCC Bible Balloon project, sending over 1 million Scripture portions into communist Eastern Europe by means of hydrogen-filled balloons; also other missions across world.

Latter Rain Revival (New Order of the Latter Rain) erupts among classical Pentecostals in Saskatchewan, Canada, spreads rapidly to Europe, USA, and across world; emphasis on laying on of hands with prophecy, government by order of living apostles; begins Global Missions Broadcast; from 1965, merges into Charismatic Movement.

1949   T.L. Osborn Evangelistic Association established (also termed Association for Native Evangelism), for mass evangelism utilizing citizen Christian workers in overseas countries; 1965, in over 40 countries, having reached over 20,000 unevangelized areas.

World Gospel Crusades (Every Creature Crusade) founded with as its purpose "the evangelization of the world through the mass media of communication—literature distribution, Scripture distribution, correspondence courses, radio, TV, united evangelistic campaigns"; by 1965, in 60 nations; by 1986, only 4 overseas workers left, in 2 countries.

Survey Application Trust (London) produces 5-yearly survey, World Christian handbook (1949, 1952, 1957, 1962, 1968) edited by K.G. Grubb (1900-1980), with church membership statistics compiled and totaled for first time by denomination and country.

Cursillos de Cristianidad (short courses) movement begun in Spain by RC bishop J. Hervas; short 3-day retreats to renew personal faith of Catholics; 1950s spreads to Latin America, then to USA, 1961 Britain, then globally; many leaders later become first Catholic charismatics.

1950   USA: beginnings of evangelistic association evangelism (Billy Graham Evangelistic Association, et alia); by 1976 Billy Graham has preached face-to-face to 50,780,505 across world, in 229 crusades, with 1,526,729 inquirers (decisions or converts: 3.0% of attenders), and to 104,390,133 by end of 1984.

Help Open Paths to Evangelize (HOPE Bible Mission) founded in USA "to take the gospel to unevangelized areas"; bimonthly news sheet *His Millions.*

World Vision founded (Monrovia, CA, USA) for relief and development, emergency aid, pastors' conferences; emphasis on using research, new technology, new systems, new tools, new media, "using a computer to help evangelize the world . . . to reach the world for Christ in this generation" (vice president T.W. Engstrom, 1966 Berlin Congress on Evangelism); 1988, works in over 80 countries with over 4,400 staff (mainly nationals) on 4,254 projects.

USA: evangelistic broadcasting spreads: 1950, Billy Graham begins on ABC radio, and 1951 on TV; 1953, Rex Humbard telecasts weekly, 1958 opens 5,000-seat Cathedral of Tomorrow (Akron, OH).

"Hour of Decision" radio program with Billy Graham begins over 150 stations; 1951, 20 million listeners (200,000 letters received per year); by 1978, 900 radio/TV stations worldwide, and a million letters per year (with 70 million viewers in USA).

Full Gospel Business Men's Fellowship International (FGBMFI) founded in USA as an end-time ministry by dairy magnate D. Shakarian after a vision of the people of every continent; preachers and women excluded; grows rapidly by 1970 to 300,000 members in 700 chapters worldwide, and by 1986 to 700,000 regular attenders worldwide in 3,000 chapters (1,715 in USA) in 95 countries including USSR, Czechoslovakia, Saudi Arabia, and other closed countries.

Baptist Bible Fellowship International founded as fundamentalist mission, with (by 1985) 620 foreign missionaries in 58 countries.

Missionaries of Charity (1950 Sisters, 1963 Brothers) begun in Calcutta by Mother Teresa, one of world's greatest Catholic evangelists, to minister in the name of Jesus to the poor, destitute, sick, and dying; by 1986, 2,500 sisters, 600 novices, and 344 religious houses in 77 countries including Cuba, Nicaragua, and most closed countries, with attempts to open in China and USSR; global aim "worldwide evangelization bringing Jesus to the poorest of the poor."

World-Wide Missions International organized by 35 churches in Nigeria; 1965, 1,100 workers in over 70 nations, with magazine circulation (World-Wide Missions) of 800,000; 1985, decline to 15 USA missionaries in 31 countries.

1951   1st World Congress of the Lay Apostolate, in Rome, aiming to mobilize laity (99.8% of all Christians) for outreach to the world; subsequent congresses in Rome in 1957, 1967, 1975.

1952   Worldwide Revival Movement inaugurated in Ireland by W.E. Allen and Revival Publishing Company (Lisburn) to promote theme "Revival is the key to world evangelization."

CHRONOLOGY OF WORLD EVANGELIZATION FROM AD 30 TO 1990 cont.

World Wide Pictures established by BGEA; 1953, classic movie *Mr. Texas;* by 1984, over 100 films produced and distributed, with 28,000 showings a year; viewed by over 50 million persons with 1.5 million decisions for Christ; some dubbed in 17 languages (100 prints circulate in Japan in Japanese).

1953   Worldwide Evangelization Crusade begins work on Java, founds Batu Bible School, results in indigenous Indonesian Missionary Fellowship (organized 1961), with its own plan for world evangelization with 206 personnel by 1980.

World Committee for Christian Broadcasting (WCCB) constituted in Britain, then International Committee for Christian Broadcasting (ICCB); 1961, founds World Association for Christian Broadcasting (WACB), 1968 merges with Coordinating Committee for Christian Broadcasting (CCCB) to form World Association for Christian Communication (WACC).

Congress of Catholic Action, in Chimbote (Peru), one of roots of liberation theology; this new approach to man and God, primarily from Latin America, leads to mushrooming of BECs (base ecclesial communities), new ministries, and above all to new approaches to evangelization.

1954   2nd Assembly of World Council of Churches, in Evanston, IL, USA: "Christ the Hope of the World"; 502 delegates; report states, "To evangelize is to participate in Christ's life and ministry to the world."

WCC official survey, Evangelism: the Mission of the Church to Those outside Her Life, notes "an almost chaotic confusion as to the meaning and scope of evangelism"; surveys the future and suggests: "The drama of missions and evangelism may, indeed, under God's rule over time and history be only in its infancy."

MAP International begun as interdenominational evangelical service agency providing medical assistance to 82 countries by 1985.

World Missionary Evangelism begun as nondenominational service agency (Dallas, TX, USA) in 14 countries.

New Life League World Missionary Society begun (Waco, TX, USA), "winning the world for Christ through the published word"; Restoration Baptist; missionary printing presses, radio, mass media, literature, in 50 countries (including printing Bibles for China).

1955   World Conference on Missionary Radio (WCMR) begun in USA; 1963, joins with National Religious Broadcasters of North America (NRB) to form International Christian Broadcasters (ICB), which disbands in 1968.

Midnight Call Missionary Work (L'Appel de Minuit) founded in Zurich, Switzerland, "to extend the redemptive message of the gospel into unreached parts of the world."

1956   USA: charismatic (neo-pentecostal) renewal begins among Episcopal and Protestant churches, first being at Trinity Episcopal Church, Wheaton, IL; rapidly increases to 10% of all clergy and 1 million laity by 1970, and to 1.6 million active Spirit-baptized charismatics by 1980; over these decades, vast new proliferation of "signs, wonders and healings" arises worldwide accompanying expansion of charismatic movement.

DWME of WCC begins publication of regular series, *A Monthly ILtter about Evangelism;* in subsequent 33 years covers every conceivable aspect of evangelism and world evangelization.

Catholic bishop L.-J. Suenens publishes *The Gospel to Every Creature;* considerable influence on Vatican Council II.

1957   Global Conquest program (Assemblies of God USA) prepared as a "new strategy for world evangelization," for "the rapid evangelization of the world before the return of Christ," with detailed 3-year goals especially focusing on large cities; name changed in 1967 to Good News Crusades; 1968, Council on Evangelism with its Statement of Purpose makes major impact.

Nights of Prayer for World-Wide Revival (NPWR) launched in London by Anglican layman and CMS missionary to India, G.S. Ingram (c1881-1969); continues till his death.

Send the Light (later termed Operation Mobilization) incorporated in USA, Mexico, then in over 50 countries; an interdenominational youth agency sending short-term mission workers abroad for evangelism and literature distribution.

Conference of World Confessional Groups founded, in Geneva, supported by 7 WCFs: BWA, FWCC, ICC, LWF, WCCC, WMC, WPA (WARC); 1968, RCC joins; 1968, name changed to Conference of World Confessional Families; 1979, renamed Conference of Christian World Communions; 1985, 29th Conference meets in Windsor, UK, with 20 WCFs/CWCs; now meeting annually; agreed positions on world mission emerge.

1958	Bibles For The World (BFTW) begun by Hmar believer from Northwest India in order "to mail a Bible to every telephone subscriber in the world by 1985"; BFTW is "committed to mail one billion Bibles to one billion families on planet earth"; by 1986 "It is the stated goal of BFTW to mail a book-size copy of the New Testament, in the language of the people, to a billion homes" using telephone directories; NTs mailed 1971-1982 total to 6,444,628; 1987, averages 1,500,000 a year.
1959	Southern Baptists in USA develop long-term emphasis on "Sharing Christ around the World"/"Sharing Christ with the Whole World" (Baptist Jubilee Advance, 1959-1964, jointly with 20 other USA Baptist groups); 1970 SB Convention approves concept and phrase "Bold Mission," and Home Mission Board develops it in 1974 "Sharing Christ's Bold Mission"; 1974 SB Convention in Dallas authorizes Foreign Mission Board and Home Mission Board to plan "Bold new strategies" for last 25 years of century; 1976 FMB develops "Total Missions Thrust: Global Discipleship: Foreign Missions looks toward AD 2000" and 1976 "Bold New Thrusts in Foreign Missions 1976-2000"; 1976 "Bold Mission Thrust—Acts 1.8," 1977 "by the year 2000" added; 1977 BMT adopted by many state conventions and associations.

First nationwide Evangelism-in-Depth campaign organized, in Nicaragua (125 local churches, 65,000 homes visited, 126,000 attenders in 14 local crusades, 2,604 professions of faith, 500 prayer cells formed); on successful conclusion, Latin America Mission sponsors similar campaigns in 11 other Latin American countries by 1971 (1961 Costa Rica, 1962 Guatemala, 1964 Venezuela, 1965 Bolivia and Dominican Republic, 1967 Peru, 1968 Colombia, 1970 Ecuador and Haiti, 1971 Mexico and Paraguay); spreads to other parts of world, including Tokyo 1980 and Mexico 1986 (Evangelismo a Fondo); but after 1975 fades out as a movement because largely accepted and incorporated into church programs.

Worldwide Missionary Society (Sekai Senkyo Kyokai) founded in Yokohama, Japan, to send Japanese missionaries to all foreign countries; mainly in India.

1960	IFMA Congress on World Missions, Chicago, USA; closing statement reads: "We declare the need for a total mobilization of all the resources . . . so that the total evangelization of the world may be achieved in this generation"; resurgence among Conservative Evangelicals of the Watchword "The Evangelization of the World in this Generation"; congress report by J.O. Percy entitled *Facing the unfinished task*.

Baptist International Missions founded as fundamentalist missions body, with (by 1985) 593 foreign missionaries in 53 countries.

World Missionary Assistance Plan (World MAP) founded (California, USA) as interdenominational, evangelical, charismatic service agency; inaugurates Leadership Spiritual Renewal Seminars "to create spiritual renewal among all the world's church leadership to bring change within all nations, hence worldwide evangelization, to be completed by the year 2000"; by 1987, claims 60% of that goal has been completed.

CHRONOLOGY OF WORLD EVANGELIZATION FROM AD 30 TO 1990 cont.

IVP editor/director J.T. Bayly writes satirical novel *The Gospel Blimp,* about an agency, International Gospel Blimps, Inc., who operate an airship towing sign "One Billion Unreached"; ends in disaster; archetype of attempts to evangelize by depersonalized technology without personal contact with unevangelized populations.

Youth With A Mission (YWAM) begins as evangelical-charismatic sending agency, expanding as outgrowth of the Jesus Movement in USA; at first, little church consciousness; 1977, outfits 10,000-ton evangelistic ship m.v. *Anastasis* for discipleship and mercy ministries; by 1983, the world's largest evangelistic agency with 14,000 short-term young people sent overseas each year, in 56 countries; by 1987, 50,000; goal to field 100,000 a year by AD 2000.

1961
World Missionary Press begun (New Paris, IN, USA) as nondenominational agency distributing Scripture booklets in 214 languages in 179 countries.

2nd World Survey of Unreached Areas (Areas of the World Unreached by the Gospel): L.G. Brierley publishes section 4, The challenge of the unachieved, and other WEC survey volumes describing "The 19 Point Programme to Reach the Unreached"; also survey articles in WEC's magazine *World Wide*; in introduction quoting WEC founder C.T. Studd, Brierley states: "Unless some new heroic effort is made by God's people entailing great sacrifices, great faith and desperate courage, the evangelization of the whole world in this and several future generations is a patent impossibility."

1st Pan-Orthodox Conference, Rhodes (Greece); agreement to move towards a future Great & Holy Council of the Orthodox Church; subsequent conferences 1963, 1964, 1968, 1976.

World Evangelism founded in USA by Pentecostal evangelist Morris Cerullo; 1967, World Evangelism Society of Great Britain.

3rd Assembly of WCC, in New Delhi, India; Russian and other Orthodox Churches join WCC; integration of WCC and IMC, latter emerging as Division of World Mission and Evangelism (DWME and CWME) whose report states, "Two-thirds of the human race are without the knowledge of Christ as the light of the world"; report on "Christian witness" states "All disciples stand under the Great Commission of the One Lord."

Joint Action for Mission (JAM) promulgated by International Missionary Council, then by DWME/WCC as "a plan of ecumenical mission," local or global, "recommended by CWME to be followed in all six continents"; but meets resistance from confessional and institutional structures of churches and missionary agencies, and soon peters out.

First religious TV station opened, in USA: WYAH (M.G. Robertson, in Tidewater, VA), later Christian Broadcasting Network; by 1980, almost every major metropolitan center in USA has its own religious TV station; by 1987, CBN World Outreach involves "sharing the love of Jesus in more than 85 nations."

6th International Student Missionary Convention, Urbana, IL, USA; 5,027 attenders; "The world must be evangelized in one decade" (Billy Graham); "We can evangelize the world in this decade. It is possible" (Clyde Taylor, NAE).

World Association for Christian Broadcasting (WACB) founded, becoming by 1968 the WACC.

World Radio Missionary Fellowship inaugurates HCJB-TV (Quito, Ecuador) as pioneer missionary telecaster; 1985, 218 overseas personnel in 8 countries.

Swiss Protestant scholar Karl Barth (1886-1968) writes: "The Great Commission is truly the most genuine utterance of the risen Jesus"; widespread resurgence of interest by theologians in Commission's significance and interpretation.

African/Independent Lutheran Church (Loyalist Religion) founded in Maragoli (Kenya) as Luhya indigenous body; 1980, renamed Third World Missions Federation, with aim to promote world evangelization by Third-Worlders.

1962
Haggai Institute for Advanced Leadership Training begins courses in Singapore as a service agency training Christian leaders in national and world evangelization, with 5,100 Third-World alumni in 99 nations by 1987, and a goal of 10,000 by AD 2000.

1963	International Christian Broadcasters (ICB) formed by USA Evangelicals; 1967, meets in Concordia, Milwaukee; but fades out by 1968, displaced by NRB (USA).

7th UBS Council Meeting, Hakone (Japan), with 27 member societies, launches plan "God's Word for a New Age," agrees to publish Bible selections, sets global goal of Scripture distribution: a Bible in every literate Christian home, an NT for every literate Christian, a portion for every literate adult, Scripture outreach to every nonliterate, and a selection for every soul on earth.

New Life For All (NLFA) begins as 10-year campaign in Nigeria, spreads across African countries.

Methodist professor of evangelism R.E. Coleman writes a classic, *The Master Plan of Evangelism,* expounding evangelistic message and methodology of Jesus, God's strategy of world conquest, long-range goals, based on training Twelve Apostles "to go with the Gospel to the whole world," "to win the world for Christ."

1964   Missiologist D.A. McGavran begins *Church growth bulletin;* 1979, renamed *Global church growth,* stated to be "the only worldwide missiological magazine dedicated exclusively to the Great Commission Mission," whose purpose "is to report from the Church Growth perspective, what God is doing in world evangelization and to share effective strategies, insights and resources."

Evangelical missions quarterly (EMQ) founded by IFMA/EFMA, operated by EMIS, "dedicated in obedience to the command of Jesus Christ to the proclamation of the gospel of the Son of God to the whole world"; over next 25 years, all material relates directly or indirectly to world evangelization.

1965   Oriental Orthodox Churches Conference, in Addis Ababa: first conference of heads of Armenian, Coptic, Ethiopian, Syrian, and Malabar churches; "The Church's role is to convey the message of salvation to the world . . . Christ's command 'Go into all the world and preach the Gospel' . . . should be its central concern, its main preoccupation."

World Evangelization Research Centre begun in Nairobi, Kenya, by CMS missionary D.B. Barrett for ecumenical-interdenominational-scholarly research; also termed CSWE (Centre for the Study of World Evangelization).

Emphasis on evangelizing tribes and peoples leads to 7-year DWME/AACC Unreached Peoples research project throughout Africa sponsored by 1965 consultation on "The Evangelisation of West Africa Today" at Yaoundé, Cameroon.

1966   Evangelical Congress on "The Church's Worldwide Mission," Wheaton, IL, USA, sponsored by both IFMA and EFMA; 938 delegates from 71 countries agree to Wheaton Declaration, holding local church chiefly responsible for ongoing mission and evangelism: "We covenant together . . . for the evangelization of the world in this generation, so help us God!"

World Congress on Evangelism, Berlin: "One race, one gospel, one task"; 1,200 delegates from over 100 countries; from now on, strategic plans and conferences for countrywide and world evangelization proliferate; closing Statement states "Evangelism is the proclamation of the Gospel."

1st Assembly of Pacific Conference of Churches, in Lifou, Loyalty Islands (New Caledonia), on theme "Go Ye . . ."

Missions Advanced Research and Communication Center (MARC) founded by World Vision (E.R. Dayton) in Los Angeles with the express goal of "making available and understandable the tools of technology which can aid the Church in giving every man an opportunity to say yes to Jesus Christ."

Release the World for Christ begun as Greek Orthodox agency based in Houston, TX, USA, holding evangelistic crusades overseas (India, Thailand).

1967   International Correspondence Institute founded by Assemblies of God USA as Bible courses arm of Good News Crusades, with accumulative enrollment of 5,077,014 in 164 nations by 1987, with 280,810 recorded decisions for Christ (5.5%).

CHRONOLOGY OF WORLD EVANGELIZATION FROM AD 30 TO 1990 cont.

South Korea: massive evangelistic campaigns held: 1965, 17-denomination 80th an-niversary of Protestantism (20,000 professions of faith); 1967, Crusade for World Re-vival (30,000 attenders a night), linked with organization CWR begun in 1965 in Britain; 1973, Seoul crusade (3,210,000 attenders, 275,000 enquirers); 1974, EXPLO 74 train-ing conference on evangelism and discipleship (323,419 workers from 78 countries); 1977, National Evangelization Crusade; 1978 Here's Life Korea; 1980, 16.5 million at-tend 4-day World Evangelization Crusade, in Seoul; et alia.

1968
4th Assembly of WCC, in Uppsala, Sweden: "Behold, I make all things new"; 2,741 par-ticipants (704 delegates, 750 press); report states, "Our part in evangelism might be de-scribed as bringing about the occasions for men's response to Jesus Christ"; but also there is "widespread defeatism in the churches about the work of evangelism and world mission" (D.T. Niles).

World Association for Christian Communication (WACC) founded as merger of WCCB, WACB, and CCCB; works in 60 countries.

Association for World Evangelism (AWE) founded in Portland, Oregon (USA); nonde-nominational; 1985, 8 workers in France and Switzerland.

African Independent Churches Service (AICS) proposed by D.B. Barrett as service agency to assist Africa's 5,000 indigenous denominations in order to help them to mobi-lize the world's 85 million non-white indigenous Christians in 7,000 denominations in a global plan to evangelize the world; 1976, Egyptian Orthodox bishop A. Markos launches scheme (Organization of African Instituted [Indigenous] Churches, OAIC) based in Nairobi, Kenya, with vast activities, conferences, TEE, et alia; by 1987 a major force but with its global goal abandoned.

1969
Pentecostal evangelist Jimmy L. Swaggart begins USA radio ministry "Camp Meeting Hour," then in 1972 television ministry; by 1987, Jimmy Swaggart Ministries air tele-casts over 3,200 TV stations in 15 languages viewed by 510 million in 145 countries weekly, raising donations of $150 million a year, and claim "the medium of television is the most expedient method of spreading the gospel the world has ever known. It is God's directive that the Great Commission be carried out by this means"; 1988, partial collapse due to sex scandal.

World Evangelism Foundation founded (Texas, USA) by Baptist missionaries to mobi-lize Southern Baptist laypersons to spread Partnership Evangelism; by 1988, over 7,000 persons from USA have held 200 major evangelistic campaigns in 40 countries, with 200,000 decisions for Christ.

1970
5th Assembly, Lutheran World Federation (LWF), Evian (France), on theme "Sent into the World"; new Commission on Church Cooperation (CCC) formed centered on evan-gelism, meets 1971 Tokyo, 1972 Kecskemet (Hungary), 1973 Santiago (Chile), 1974 Lund, 1975 Adelaide, 1976 Saskatoon, 1978 Montreux, 1979 Singapore, 1981 Chicago, 1982 Stavanger.

9th International Student Missionary Convention, Urbana, IL, USA, on theme "World Evangelism: Why? How? Who?"; 12,304 attenders.

Popular books on premillennial eschatology (an interpretation held by 41% of all Evangelicals, and countless others) sell 31 million copies over 15 years, especially H. Lindsay's 9-title series beginning with *The Late Great Planet Earth;* these however all dismiss human responsibility for global mission and world evangelization after only miniscule passing mention (less than 1% of text). "AD 2000: 350 million Christians in Africa" published in IRM by D.B. Barrett, on Third-World progress towards world evan-gelization.

Frankfurt Declaration on Mission, promulgated by 14 Conservative Evangelical Lu-theran theologians in Germany.

12th Baptist World Congress, Tokyo, launches 5-year evangelistic program "World Mission of Reconciliation Through Jesus Christ"; officially gets under way in 1973, with campaigns across world.

OM purchases 2,500-ton evangelistic ship m.v. Logos for UK §80,000 to visit large-city ports in difficult countries around world, with literature evangelism, book sales, missionary conferences; 110 crew, total 1,500 crew from 1970-88; 20 million persons exposed to gospel through related shore teams, 7 million visitors aboard buying literature in 107 different countries; 1988, ship (now valued at §1 million) runs aground and is lost off Tierra del Fuego; 1977, sister ship m.v. *Doulos* (6,000 tons) begins travels, reaching 600 visitors per conference.

1971   Final Advance of Scripture Translation (FAST) launched with WBT/SIL cooperation as computerized closure vision to finally complete remaining task of translating Bible into every language; main purpose to galvanize denominational Bible translating agencies (Baptist, Pentecostal, Catholic, et alia), but finally terminates in 1983 despite over 5,000 languages still remaining untranslated.

International Crusades begun in Dallas, Texas, as agency coordinating Southern Baptist 2-week Partnership Crusades overseas; goal: "To see one million people pray to receive Christ by the turn of the century using partnership evangelism."

Conference on Church-Mission Relationships in Creative Tension, held at Green Lake, WI (USA), with 400 attenders, under aegis of EMIS and sponsored by IFMA/EFMA: "We affirm the continuing worldwide mandate upon the worldwide church to fulfill the Great Commission of Jesus Christ."

1972   International Catholic Charismatic Renewal Office (ICCRO) founded as International Communications Office in Ann Arbor, MI (USA); first 2 International Leaders Conferences (1973, 1975) held there; 1976, office transferred to Brussels; 1981 relocates as ICCRO in Rome, organizes 5 worldwide leaders' conferences (4 in Rome, 1 in Dublin), 1985 relocates in Vatican "moving to the heart of the Church," by 1988 representing 63.5 million Catholic pentecostals in over 160 countries.

Consultation on the Gospel and Frontier Peoples, Chicago (December), sponsored by NCCCUSA and North American boards; detailed survey presented by D.B. Barrett entitled "Frontier situations for evangelisation in Africa, 1972: a survey report," tabulating data, documenting and mapping situation of 213 Muslim peoples, 411 peoples responsive to Christianity, and 236 unevangelized peoples.

Great Commission Prayer Crusade launched by Campus Crusade for Christ International; leadership by women; a few conferences held (Dallas 1976, 1984 International Prayer Assembly, Seoul).

World Conference and Assembly of CWME/WCC, Bangkok, Thailand (3rd Meeting of CWME): "Salvation Today"; moratorium on foreign missions and missionaries proposed by younger churches, widely accepted 1972-80; report states, "Each generation must evangelize its own generation" (29 December 1972-8 January 1973).

1973   Mission to the World (agency of Presbyterian Church in America) launched; 1987, 500 missionaries in 40 countries, church planting in 12 countries; stress on taking its appropriate part in Great Commission; goals include evangelizing 25 world-class cities by 1993.

Korea: 1st Annual Summer Institute of World Mission (SIWM) in Seoul; by 14th Institute in 1986, some 1,000 students have been trained at East-West Center for overseas service, with goal of 10,000 Asian foreign missionaries by AD 2000.

Globe Missionary Evangelism begun (Pensacola, Florida), with 65 foreign missionaries in 15 countries (by 1985).

All-Asia Missions Consultation, Seoul, Korea; formation of Asia Missions Association (AMA); 1975 Inaugural Convention publishes "Seoul Declaration on Christian Mission."

Urbana 73: 10th Inter-Varsity Missionary Convention, Urbana, on theme "Jesus Christ: Lord of the Universe, Hope of the World"; 14,158 attend (December); similar number each successive year up to Urbana 87 and Urbana 90 in 1990.

CHRONOLOGY OF WORLD EVANGELIZATION FROM AD 30 TO 1990 cont.

Trinity Broadcasting Network launched, in southern California, as Pentecostal television station "to get the gospel to every living human being on planet Earth" before Jesus comes; by 1986, TBN owns 55 TV stations in USA with 26 affiliates, also stations in Guatemala, St Kitts-Nevis, Italy, Ciskei.

World Film Crusade founded in Florida, USA (later known as World Thrust Films, or World Mission Crusade); 1985, Brother John publishes *Winning the World: a proposal on how to win the world for Christ now . . . in our generation*; 1987; further plan announced under name World Mission Teams.

Pentecostal missions executive D.A. Womack writes *Breaking the stained-glass barrier* urging church "to abandon its sanctuaries of security and return to the evangelistic strategy of the Apostle Paul (the Ephesian Method of spontaneous lay evangelism)"; proposes mathematical formula measuring evangelization.

1974   Operation World, a prayer survey, published by P.J. Johnstone (Dorothea Mission, and WEC; subsequent editions 1978, 1980, 1986), emphasizing world evangelization through daily intercession, centrality of local churches, and the call to "mobilize the churches of the whole world to finish the task."

International Congress on World Evangelization (ICOWE), Lausanne, Switzerland, on "Let the Earth Hear His Voice"; 2,700 delegates, from 150 countries, 4,000 total (50% from Third World); produces Lausanne Covenant stating: "Evangelism itself is the proclamation of the historical, biblical Christ" (July); results by 1980 in vast, amorphous, network known as Lausanne Movement directed by LCWE (Lausanne Committee for World Evangelization).

EXPLO-74 in Seoul, Korea: 2nd Training Congress on Evangelism (Campus Crusade for Christ); 323,419 residents for one week, evening meetings 800,000 daily, with one rally drawing a new world record of 1.5 million (90% responding to invitation to commitment to Christ); biggest Christian conference in history to date (August).

"Sharing Christ's Bold Mission," theme developed by Southern Baptist Home Mission Board, extended to worldwide application.

Philippines: DAWN (Discipling A Whole Nation) conference; 75 leaders of 4,000 Evangelical churches plan to have 50,000 churches planted by AD 2000, one in every barrio in the country (November); 1985, National Church Growth Strategy Congress with 300 leaders of 12,000 Evangelical churches reaffirms this goal (19-22 February); after 1981 it becomes a world plan, with motto "389 People can change the World: you can be one of them," involving 25 countries by 1987, with goal to begin by AD 2000 a DAWN project in every country of the world, with slogan "7 Million More Churches by 2000 AD."

Presbyterian Order for World Evangelism begun (later under USCWM, Pasadena, CA), as denominational support agency.

1975   Full Gospel World Mission Association established (1 April) in Seoul, Korea, as sending body supporting 8 overseas churches and 22 Korean missionaries; by 1985, 143 missionaries in 21 countries.

5th Assembly of WCC, in Nairobi, Kenya: "Jesus Christ frees and unites," 2,085 participants (850 delegates, 600 press); report on "Confessing Christ today" states, "We are commissioned to proclaim the Gospel of Christ to the ends of the earth."

13th Baptist World Congress (BWA), Stockholm, on theme "New People for a New World—Through Christ"; 9,936 delegates from 92 countries.

Associates for World Evangelization (AWE) begun for students associated with USCWM.

New Life International begun as evangelical charismatic service agency involved in TEE, literature, research; 1984, renamed Total World Evangelization Vision (Fresno, CA, USA), in 8 countries.

Genesis Project is begun to produce whole Bible on film, word for word; 33-year project envisaged, covering OT/NT with 300 films as the New Media Bible, to be dubbed in 27 languages; by 1986, 33 films emerge, but only Genesis and Luke completed; major achievement the *Jesus* film with CCCI.

World Evangelical Fellowship Missions Commission inaugurated in Seoul, Korea, dedicated to development of the non-Western missionary movement (Third World missions), utilizing a network of agencies and Evangelical fellowships across the world.

1976   Southern Baptist Convention USA, meeting in Norfolk, VA, adopts resolution and plan for remainder of century to implement world evangelization through strategy Bold Mission Thrust: "To enable every person in the world to have opportunity to hear and to respond to the gospel of Christ by the year 2000"; at 1988 midpoint, Foreign Mission Board reaffirms this intention.

Gabriel Olasoji World Evangelism (GOWE) founded in Ibadan (Nigeria) with motto "Reaching the Unreached" based on Mark 16:15; by 1988, power evangelism and mass crusades in 25 nations.

Pasadena, CA, USA: founding of US Center for World Mission, restricted to Conservative Evangelicals.

LCWE Strategy Working Group (SWG) formed; meets every year or two, works on plural strategies and tactics rather than any single overall strategy.

Australia: Congress on World Missions and Evangelism (May).

AMEN (American Military Evangelizing Nations) formed, by USA denomination Churches of Christ, for lay evangelism by US armed forces around world.

Church Growth International Seminars begun in Seoul by P. Yonggi Cho; by 1986, 70,000 pastors and leaders from 30 countries have attended; at 10th Seminar in 1986, goal of world evangelization announced with specific plan to win 10 million Japanese to Christ by AD 2000.

1st Chinese Congress on World Evangelization (CCOWE), Hong Kong, on "Vision and Mission," with 1,600 participants from over 20 countries (August); CCCOWE (Chinese Coordination Centre of World Evangelism) set up in Hong Kong (October).

EFMA mission executives meet and tally the number of people groups in the unreached category which their agencies alone are in touch with, or are planning to reach by 1990; total estimated at 6,000 people groups.

Lausanne Intercession Advisory Group formed after ICOWE I; organizes conferences, annual day of prayer for world evangelization (Pentecost Sunday).

Habitat for Humanity International founded (USA) "to eliminate poverty housing throughout the world in the name of Jesus Christ, seeking to glorify Him and to spread His Gospel throughout the earth"; 1988, builds 2,000 houses in 300 cities; goal by 1996, to build in 2,000 North American cities and in 60 other countries.

Fellowship of World Christians (FOW) begun by USCWM for students (mostly ex-AWE) concerned for world evangelization; rallies; defunct by 1978; 1985, name taken over by different group (World Literature Crusade) offering 100 people a year two-week mission encounters in Mexico, Haiti, et alia.

1977   1st Conference on the Charismatic Renewal in the Christian Churches; ecumenical, at last embracing all pentecostal traditions; on theme "Jesus is Lord"; in Kansas City, USA; 59,000 present (July); but after this ecumenical climax, charismatic conferences revert to monodenominational or monoconfessional status (15,000 Lutheran charismatics each year in Minneapolis, 10,000 RCs in Notre Dame, et alii).

World Conference on Audio-Visuals and Evangelization, Munich (November).

Here's Life, World (saturation and total mobilization evangelization campaign), organized by Campus Crusade for Christ, bankrolled by History's Hundred (100 USA billionaires), launched in 100 countries, on every continent, with announced goal "to fulfil the Great Commission in the whole world by the end of 1980."

1978   World Mission 1978-1981 begun as World Methodist Council's 4-year plan of global evangelism.

International Conference on the Charismatic Renewal in the Catholic Church, in Dublin: "You shall be My Witnesses"; 15,000 participants, led by L.-J. Suenens cardinal primate of Belgium (June).

CHRONOLOGY OF WORLD EVANGELIZATION FROM AD 30 TO 1990 cont.

1st Norwegian Congress on World Evangelization (related to LCWE), followed about every 2 years by Danvik National Conferences on Evangelization, with 140 church leaders, held in Drammen (Norway) in 1980, 1981, 1982, 1984, 1986.

Attempt by MARC (USA) to set up an information network for world evangelization entitled SHARE (Systems, Hardware and Research for Evangelization); scheme founders by 1985 due to inability to obtain original field data.

Great Commission Strategy Resource Network (GCSRN) launched by CCCI "to finish the task of reaching by 1980 those who have not yet heard the gospel," based on 5 functions: (1) information gathering and distribution, (2) resource reference, (3) research, (4) vision rooms, (5) international communication system; but peters out until by 1987 is reduced to computer hardware maintenance.

1979 Anglican renewal agency SOMA (Sharing of Ministries Abroad) founded, "dedicated to fostering Renewal in the Holy Spirit world wide so as to enable and equip the Church to fulfil the Great Commission of Jesus Christ, to proclaim the Kingdom of God and minister in the power of the Holy Spirit"; holds international conferences 1981 Singapore, 1983 Nairobi, 1984 Fiji; by 1987, its work in 50 countries covers 26 of the 31 Anglican Provinces worldwide.

Foursquare Missions International announces plan to begin work among 100 unreached peoples; by 1985, has 83 foreign missionaries with related churches in 47 countries (International Church of the Foursquare Gospel).

Over 10,000 pilgrims attend International Charismatic Pilgrimage to Lourdes on shrine's 100th anniversary (July).

12th Pentecostal World Conference, in Vancouver, Canada: "The Holy Spirit in the Last Days" (October).

Canadian Congress on World Evangelization.

International Mission Congress (FABC and SC Propaganda), in Manila, on "Towards a New Age in Mission: the Good News of the Kingdom to the Peoples of Asia" (2-7 December).

Jesus film produced by The Jesus Project, Campus Crusade for Christ, filmed in Palestine in 1979; by 1986, is circulating dubbed in 106 languages; annual viewers then total 275 million, decisions for Christ reach 33 million (12%); 1988, goal announced for 5,000 teams with copies dubbed in 271 languages of over a million speakers each by 1993 plus 1,000 other strategic languages and dialects by 1998 with 5 million viewers a night; also that, by AD 2000, 6 billion people shall have seen it of whom 600 to 1,500 million pray to receive Christ.

Evangelist Billy Graham (at IVCF Urbana conference) and USA Evangelical foreign mission leaders issue call for "120,000 missionaries by the year 2000" in order to reach unreached peoples and establish "A church for every people by AD 2000."

USA: Angel-I/Angel-II/Angel-III Project to blanket Earth with gospel broadcasts proposed by NRB and WEF: 3 satellites in geostationary orbit filling roles of 3 angels of Revelation 14:6-11, each covering a third of Earth's surface, fulfilling Matthew 24:14 "for a witness unto all nations"; by 1983, author realizes project has been "committeed to death," so proposal passes into oblivion, though use of satellites for USA Christian TV grows.

TV evangelist J. Bakker of PTL Ministries announces plan to start PTL missions throughout the world; funds raised but plan fizzles out within a year; 1987, Ministries collapse in financial and sex scandal.

Lutherans for World Evangelization begun in Pasadena, CA (USA), as research and information service.

Caleb Project begun by USCWM to tap potential of students and young adults committed to world mission, undertaking field research among unreached peoples; 1986, merges with Joshua Projects.

1980 LCWE International Consultation on Simple Life-Style, Hoddesden, UK (March), on how adoption of biblical life-styles could accomplish world mission.

Stuttgart Congress on World Evangelization, Germany (April).

A large African indigenous charismatic church, World Evangelical Crusaders in Christ Ministries (Benin City, Nigeria), begins Operation World Begin From Here; other AIC denominations across Africa also advance similar global plans.

1st World Missionary Conference on Mission and Evangelism (4th Meeting of CWME/WCC), in Melbourne, Australia, with title "Your Kingdom come" and theme "Good News to the Poor"; 650 delegates representing 300 churches from 100 countries; "The proclamation of the Gospel to the whole world remains an urgent obligation of all Christians" (12-24 May).

LCWE Consultation on World Evangelization (COWE) in Pattaya, Bangkok: "How shall they hear?"; 875 delegates from 87 countries; 17 miniconsultations (16-27 June).

USA: 8th Annual Meeting, American Society of Missiology (ASM), in Wheaton, IL, on theme "World Evangelization Today: Convergence or Divergence?" (22-24 August).

10th United Bible Societies Council Meeting, Chiang Mai (Thailand), with 68 member societies, on theme "God's Word: open for all" (September); over last 80 years, annual circulation of complete Bibles in all languages has risen from 5.4 million in 1900 to 36.8 million by 1980; UBS plan for decade to provide by 1990 common Bible translations in every language with over 1 million literates.

World Evangelization Crusade (Here's Life, Korea), Seoul; 16,500,000 attendances, including largest single meeting in Christian history to date (2.7 million).

United States Festival of World Evangelization; 50,000 participants (September).

Third Wave of 20th-century Renewal in the Holy Spirit begins in 40 major Evangelical churches, emphasizing power evangelism, power encounters, power healing, et alia.

1981   Christian broadcasting expands from origin in 1921 to global force heard or seen regularly by 23% of world's population.

USA: new generation of charismatic TV evangelists arises, including Oral Roberts (who began Pentecostal TV preaching in 1953) and son Richard, Pat Robertson, Rex Humbard, Jimmy Swaggart, Kenneth Copeland, Paul Crouch, Jim Bakker, et alia.

Evangelize the World by Computer Dialing: a scheme, proposed by several agencies, involving continous automatic dialing through world's telephone directories and giving recorded messages to whoever replies.

2nd Chinese Congress on World Evangelization (CCOWE), on "Life and Ministry," with over 1,500 church leaders, Singapore (June).

World Evangelization Strategy Work Group begun, formed by Baptist World Alliance; numerous meetings, papers; publishes *World Evangelization Now!;* presses idea of a Baptist Fund for World Evangelization (to support Third-World missionaries); 1988, BWA General Council announces "Vision 2000: Jesus Christ for All People" as "a vision for encouraging world evangelization by the year 2000 AD."

14th World Methodist Conference meets in Hawaii, endorses WMC's World Evangelism Committee's Continuing Plan for the Mission to the 80s (Decade of Evangelism), also known since 1971 inception as World Evangelism.

Mission to Unreached Peoples (USA) begun under original name Gooddeeds.

Dominion Video Satellite (Dominion Network) incorporated in Florida (USA) to provide Christian radio/TV programs over DBS system (direct broadcast satellites), based on Great Commission, DBS as the angel of Revelation 14:6, 30-inch portable dish receivers, and bypassing of secular control over TV.

1982   Project 223 begun by YWAM, "to establish a vital permanent ministry in every country on Earth," in 2 stages: (1) trailblazing, sending teams on evangelistic trips, one team to each of the world's 223 countries, involving initially 15,000 short-termers (2 weeks to 1 year) each year; completed in 1988 with No. 222 (Pitcairn Islands) and No. 223 (Svalbard & Jan Mayen Islands); also Project 300 to reach the 300 world-class megacities, with YWAM presence in 69 by 1988; and (2) pioneering (permanent

CHRONOLOGY OF WORLD EVANGELIZATION FROM AD 30 TO 1990 cont.

residence) in 90 countries by 1988; with AD 2000 goal of 100,000 workers, aiming to fulfill the Great Commission in 25 years by AD 2011; 1988, among many new Projects introduced in Target 2000: Great Commission Torch Run, begun in Jerusalem on Easter Sunday, to involve 1 million runners.

1st ICFG Global Leadership Conference (Los Angeles) launches "Harvest Vision: 1990," a plan produced by Foursquare Missions International to reach 160 hidden people groups, enter 76 new countries, and total 2.1 million ICFG members, all by 1990.

5th Conference, International Association for Mission Studies (IAMS), Bangalore, India, on theme "Christ's Mission to the Multitudes: Salvation, Suffering and Struggle" (4-9 January); IAMS exists "for the scholarly study of Christian witness and its impact in the world."

Publication of World Christian encyclopedia: a comparative survey of churches and religions in the modern world, AD 1900-2000, designed deliberately as global survey to document world evangelization, the unfinished task, and rise of a global evangelization movement.

LCWE Chicago Consultation on Terminology concerning Unreached Peoples; subsequently, clear distinction drawn between (a) "ethnolinguistic peoples" (being legitimate targets of church-planting efforts to establish beachheads with as goal in each a viable organized church fellowship able to evangelize its own culture), and (b) "bridges" or "bridge people groups" (smaller social or functional groupings affording opportunities for evangelism without church planting) (25-26 March).

World Satellite Evangelism (motto "Using Mass Media to Reach the Unreached of the World for Christ") begun in Tulsa, OK, (USA) "mobilizing media to reach every person in every home with the gospel" especially in closed countries; forms a global media task force in 50 nations, starting Christian universities and other centers.

1st Korean World Mission Congress, in Pasadena, CA (USA), with 300 delegates from Korean churches on 5 continents, "to unite Koreans worldwide for the Great Commission of Christ" and "to establish a Korean World Mission Coordinating Center" (17-30 May).

Major document Mission and Evangelism: an Ecumenical Affirmation produced in Geneva by CWME and officially promulgated by Central Committee of WCC (July).

Institute for World Evangelism established in Atlanta, GA (USA), as major long-range achievement of World Evangelism Committee, World Methodist Council; its 1987 3rd biennial International Seminar, Atlanta, on theme "The Holy Spirit and World Evangelization" draws over 100 delegates from 33 countries; authentic Wesleyan evangelism, with 2-fold witness to personal salvation and social redemption, given a new credibility and acceptance in Methodism worldwide.

IFMA Frontier Peoples Committee formed; attempts to survey constituency of 96 IFMA member mission agencies in USA and Canada, but little substantial results; 1988, 71st IFMA Annual Meeting in Hamilton (Ontario) takes as its theme "Countdown 2000" (12-15 September).

EFMA Missions Consultation on "The Challenge of Our Task," in Colorado Springs, CO, USA (27-30 September), based on World Christian encyclopedia; 1989, EFMA Mission Executives Retreat on "Evangelizing the World by AD 2000," in Colorado Springs (25-28 September).

1983   World Baptist Congress on Urban Evangelism, in Niteroi, Brazil (26 June-3 July).

Lengthy document "A global strategy for world evangelization by AD 2000: list of 105 steps or stages or aspects" produced for Southern Baptist Foreign Mission Board by WERC (Nairobi).

1st International Conference for Itinerant Evangelists, Amsterdam; theme "Do the Work of an Evangelist"; 3,800 evangelists from 132 nations (July).

6th Assembly of WCC in Vancouver, Canada, on theme "Jesus Christ the Life of the World"; 900 delegates (300 being women) from 310 member denominations, 850 journalists, 15,000 attenders at opening service (24 July–10 August).

Global Mapping Project started on USCWM campus, to assist churches with data and maps, with as objective "Visualizing the Task of World Evangelization."

Lumen 2000 launched as Catholic global television evangelism agency, based in Dallas (USA) and Vatican City, "to preach the gospel of Jesus to the uttermost parts of the Earth, spreading the love of Jesus around the globe"; 1986, in 50 countries.

Committee on the Holy Spirit & Frontier Missions (CHSFM) begun in conjunction with USCWM to involve charismatics in frontier missions among hidden peoples; defunct by 1985.

L.E. Keyes writes *The last age of missions: a survey of Third World mission societies,* describing world evangelization by 5,000 missionaries in over 400 Third-World locally-supported societies and boards (especially from Brazil); since 1940, movement has mushroomed, with AD 2000 projection of 100,000 non-Western missionaries from 1,000 non-Western mission agencies.

New Focus Incorporated founded (San Bernardino, CA) as "a Great Commission ministry committed to sports media strategies to reach the whole world with the gospel by the year 2000"; geared especially to TV specials at Olympics in 1988 in Korea, 1992 in Barcelona (Spain), 1996, and 2000.

1984

LCWE International Prayer Assembly for World Evangelization, Seoul, Korea (June); title, "Seeking God's Face for a Movement of Prayer for the World"; 3,200 participants from 69 nations.

Ethnic Chinese Congress on World Evangelization (ECCOWE), in Honolulu, with 144 delegates (5-12 July).

Over 30 national and 8 regional LCWE conferences on world evangelization, plus intensive prayer, commitment and planning, are organized for 5-year period leading into 1989 ICOWE II.

7th Assembly, Lutheran World Federation (LWF) in Budapest, Hungary, on "In Christ—hope for the world"; 12,000 attenders (22 July-5 August).

STEP (Strategy to Every People) Programme introduced by WEC International, calling for "800 for the 80s" (800 new WEC workers for the 1980s), evangelizing 45 new peoples through resident teams; original name "Worldwide Evangelization Crusade" now changed to "Worldwide Evangelization for Christ" because 90% of new goals are among Muslim peoples.

Venezuelan Baptist Convention launches plan named Baptist World Discipleship Movement.

Costa Rica: interdenominational missions society begun by 14 denominations, 1986 formalized as Federación Misionera Evangélica Costarricense (FEDEMEC), launches campaign "Unidos en Cristo Evangelizando las Naciones" specifically "From Costa Rica to the Uttermost Parts of the Earth," aiming to mobilize 10,000 world prayer missionaries and to send out 500 missionaries to 25 unreached peoples by AD 2000.

1985

"Mission 2000" scheme proposed by missiologists D.A. McGavran and R.D. Winter, aiming to plant a church in each of world's unreached peoples by AD 2000 through formation of 100,000 local church mission fellowships in Western countries.

Korea: massive increase in number of Protestant and Catholic Korean missionaries sent abroad since first Protestant in 1912; by 1973, 620 serving abroad in 30 countries (270 Protestants, 250 Korean indigenous, 90 Roman Catholics), rising by 1987 to 511 Protestants in 89 Korean mission agencies (increased from 47 agencies in 1982) in 47 nations; 1985, Protestant churches announce world evangelization plans calling for 10,000 Korean missionaries abroad by AD 2000 with at least one working in every country of the world.

Youth Congress on World Evangelization, Stuttgart, Germany (February).

Interchurch Consultation on Future Trends in Christian World Mission, Maryknoll, NY, on research methodology, sociopolitical issues, and unfinished tasks of world evangelization (15-17 February).

CHRONOLOGY OF WORLD EVANGELIZATION FROM AD 30 TO 1990 cont.

LCWE/WEF Consultation on the Work of the Holy Spirit and Evangelization, in Oslo, Norway; over 70 participants from 30 countries (May); results in published book *God the Evangelist.*

1st Global Evangelization Strategy Consultation, Ridgecrest, NC (USA), with 70 participants from Baptist churches across world associated with Southern Baptist Convention; results inter alia in publication of "The AD 2000 Series" (25-28 June).

World Conference of Baptist Evangelists, Bolivar, MO (USA): "Strategies of evangelism to win world cities" (July).

6th All-Christian Peace Assembly (ACPA), convened by Christian Peace Conference (CPC), in Prague, on theme "God calls: choose life; the hour is late!"; 800 participants from 90 countries (2-9 July).

5th West Malaysia Chinese Congress on World Evangelization, sponsored by CCCOWE, in Port Dickson (5-9 August).

International Consultation on Missions (ICOM) convened in Jos, Nigeria, by NEMA (Nigeria Evangelical Missions Association) and WEF, on theme "Mobilizing Indigenous Missions for the Final Harvest"; 83 mission executives, mainly Nigerians (11 August).

Global Simultaneous Evangelistic Missions launched in Indonesia, Nigeria and other countries by World Methodist Council; thousands of local mission outreach campaigns planned across world.

Asia Committee for World Evangelization, Hong Kong (3-6 September).

God's Global Envoys—Nonresidential Missionaries for World Evangelization, an overall plan evolved by WERC/FMB, Richmond, VA, USA, envisaging cooperation of entire spectrum of all Christians of all traditions whether like-minded or not; based on 3 elements: (a) segmentization of unevangelized world into 3,000 distinct segments (peoples, cities, countries), (b) matching-up of segments with one professional missionary each, and (c) nonresidential mission and ministry through computerized research and networking; 1985, first descriptions published in print (May).

Project "The World by 2000" announced by 3 major Christian broadcasting agencies, FEBC, HCJB/World Radio Missionary Fellowship, TWR (and later ELWA-SIM): to complete by AD 2000 giving everyone on Earth the opportunity to hear the gospel of Christ by radio (September); 1987, target modified to be (1) all major trade languages with over 1 million speakers each by AD 2000, then (2) all minor trade languages, then later (3) the world's 6,500 "heart" languages.

World Ambassadors, a plan of Maranatha Christian Ministries to evangelize the world through conversions among the 200,000 international non-Christian students from 170 nations (65 closed to missionaries) who are resident in the USA; slogan "Reaching international students to reach the world" by returning home to plant churches; goal to train 15,000 such leaders each year.

World Consultation on Evangelism, Lake Junaluska (USA), sponsored by World Evangelism (World Methodist Council) (September); 5-year evangelism plan for 1987–1991 adopted.

1st Venezuelan Congress of World Missions, Maracay, aiming to appoint 500 missionaries by 1987 (15-19 October).

CWME Orthodox Advisory Group meets in Sofia (Bulgaria) on 1,100th anniversary of death of Methodius, issues call to rectify Orthodoxy's failure to fulfill Jesus' Great Commission and "to reach out to the unreached" (21-26 October).

Global Network of Centers for World Mission formed, based on 30 research and study centers; 1986, issues Singapore Statement (27 June); 1988, holds its 1st World Meeting, in Singapore (1-9 November).

Amsterdam Prayer Conference for World Evangelization, sponsored by LCWE, YWAM, et alia (November).

EXPLO-85 global Christian training teleconference organized in 95 locations in 55 countries simultaneously by Campus Crusade for Christ (CCCI), using satellite video relays (6 uplinks, several thousand downlinks), training 550,000 Christian workers from 100 countries worldwide in prayer, evangelism and discipleship, with 4 telecasts reaching 60 million (27-31 December).

Association of International Mission Services (AIMS) begun, to serve Charismatic Renewal, with slogan "Unity in the Spirit for World Evangelization"; 75 member agencies.

1986   "Reaching the World's Cities by AD 2000," a plan of Assemblies of God (USA), Division of Foreign Missions, with "declared objective to help evangelize every city on the face of the earth."

Consultation on Evangelizing World Class Cities, Moody Bible Institute, Chicago (14-17 March).

Worldwide Student NetWork launched by CCCI (USA) with goal of evangelizing by AD 2000 all the world's 30,000 tertiary-level universities and colleges (3,000 top universities, 8,000 university colleges, 19,000 vocational or professional colleges) with 60 million students, generating parallel surge from the campus to the entire world.

International Prophetic Ministry Convention, Mount Carmel (Israel) and Jerusalem; 30 modern prophets and 5,000 attenders, at Easter (Christians of all confessions).

1st General Assembly, Latin American Evangelical Confraternity (CONELA, founded 1982, with 225 member denominations, councils, associations and agencies), in Maracaibo, Venezuela; topic, challenge to evangelize Latin America and the world, with "millions of Latin American missionaries sent to the Muslim world and other regions where they are needed" (M. Ortiz, president); 95 delegates and over 1,000 attenders (22-25 April).

USA: International Conference for Equipping Evangelists (charismatic) in Sacramento, CA, "training thousands of evangelists to equip millions of Christians to reach billions of unbelievers" (5-9 May).

8th General Assembly, World Evangelical Fellowship, in Singapore, on "Renew the Church—Reach the World," with 250 delegates from 50 WEF member alliances and fellowships (22-27 June).

2nd International Conference for Itinerant Evangelists (ICIE), Amsterdam; 8,000 evangelists from 150 countries (12-21 July).

3rd Chinese Congress on World Evangelization (CCOWE '86) sponsored by CCCOWE, held in Taipei (Taiwan), on theme "Renewal, Breakthrough and Growth"; 1,900 Chinese church leaders from over 20 countries (6-13 August); CCCOWE produces 6-volume survey in Chinese (2 volumes in English) of whole Chinese diaspora across world.

4th Triennial Convention, Asia Missions Association (AMA), in Pasadena, CA, USA, on "Thy Will be done on Earth" (6-12 October); Asians abroad as foreign missionaries reported as 10,210, with AD 2000 total expected to be 67,000.

Good News World (Operation World/Mass Scripture Distribution), a global plan announced by Southern Baptist Sunday School Board, Nashville (TN), as: "Purpose: To place Scriptures in the hands of everyone in the world in 1994 to prepare for worldwide revival in 1995."

"Toward 2000," a program of Issachar Frontier Missions Research (Seattle, USA), specializing in witness in closed countries; publishes *Strategic Times journal.*

Mandate '86, 1st Annual Mid-West Student Missions Conference, "to reach the world's unreached," organized in Illinois (USA) with 800 students by IVCF-related students, supported by CCCI, AoG, SBC, IVCF et alia, with 9 related regional meetings; also Mission Advance 86 (Hamilton, Canada, 850 students); 1987, numerous student-run conferences—Mandate '87 (in Muncie, IN; 1,200 students, 23-25 January), Harvest (in Minneapolis, 6-8 February), Vision, Proclaim, Go (Global Outreach), GAP (Global Awareness Project).

USA: Presbyterian Church announces Decade of Evangelism for 1990-2000.

North American Leaders Congress on the Holy Spirit and World Evangelization (RC/Protestant charismatic renewal), New Orleans, with over 7,500 pastors and leaders, also 4,000 other attenders (October); vast numbers of regional and denominational conferences and seminars proliferate.

CHRONOLOGY OF WORLD EVANGELIZATION FROM AD 30 TO 1990 cont.

US Society for Frontier Missiology founded in Colorado Springs; 1987, 2nd Annual Meeting in Orlando, Florida (USA) discusses AD 2000 closure and countdown thinking; 86 mission leaders from 46 North American agencies (25-26 September).

Intercontinental Broadcasting Network (IBN) begun in Virginia Beach, USA, by independent charismatics linking up with European counterparts.

Global Strategy Group formed to coordinate planning for Southern Baptist Foreign Mission Board (December).

K.P. Yohannan (founder, Gospel For Asia) writes *The coming revolution in world missions,* describing a coming Third Wave of mission, namely a massive movement producing one million evangelists from thousands of native missionary movements in India, Asia, and across the world.

Missiologist J.H. Kane writes *Wanted: World Christians* (these being essential for world evangelization), holding as key "A World Christian is one who recognizes his own personal responsiblity for world missions."

Televised Evangelism for All, a project proposed by Christian Broadcasting Network vice-president N. Van Hamm: 6 million 10-inch flat liquid-screen printed-circuit solar-cell television units, costing $1 each, dumped out of aircraft across world, glide to Earth over unevangelized peoples, pretuned to 18-language transmissions over 3 or 4 geostationary satellites.

1987   John Paul II announces new Office in Rome, "Evangelization 2000," initially confined to Catholics, with news service New Evangelization 2000, and later to lead into ecumenical 1990-2000 Decade of Evangelization; comprising retreats, biggest public rally ever, 3-satellite global telecasts, global homilies, conscientization teams, mass video cassette distribution, with as aim to win 1.5 billion new Christians "as a present for Jesus on his 2,000th birthday."

44th Annual Convention & Exposition, National Religious Broadcasters (USA), Washington, with over 4,000 broadcasters, on theme "Communicating Christ to the Nations" (31 January-4 February).

Consultation on World Evangelization, Singapore, with 31 global charismatic renewal leaders (RC/Lutheran/SOMA-Anglican, et alii) (9-12 February).

International Conference of Evangelical Bible Societies (ICEBS) founded "to evangelize and disciple all nations through the placement of God's word," with 10 member agencies: ASGM, BLI, EHC, IBS, LBI, OD, PTL, WGC, WHBL, WMP.

National Charismatic Leaders' Conference (North American Renewal Service Committee, NARSC), related to global Charismatic Renewal in mainline denominations (300 million Christians, fielding 74,000 foreign missionaries), meets in Glencoe, MO (USA), appoints World Evangelization Strategy Committee with AD 2000 goal in mind (4-8 May).

World Literature Crusade changes name to Every Home for Christ, proclaims goal "to systematically place 2 gospel booklets in every home in the world, one country at a time, by AD 2000"; 40% of world's homes reached since 1946; 1986, 21,969,676 pieces of literature distributed, producing 178,509 written responses (0.8%); 1957–86, tracts distributed total 1,462,406,418, with 14,605,937 responses (1.0%).

Proposal "Countdown to the Year 2000" circulated by USCWM founder R.D. Winter, with statistics and graphics urging the engaging (entering) and reaching (discipling) by mission agencies of 1,500 new unreached peoples every year until 17,000 have been reached by AD 2000.

Global-Village Evangelism (based on Marshall McLuhan's description of the world as now a "global village") launched by Bibles For The World as "a revolutionary new concept in missions which places the local church in the center of the world mission program."

Singapore '87 LCWE International Younger Leaders' Conference on world evangelization; 300 younger Evangelical leaders from 67 countries (1-10 June).

North American General Congress on the Holy Spirit and World Evangelization, in New Orleans (successor to 1977 Kansas City ecumenical charismatic rally); over 50,000 participants (RC/Protestant charismatic renewal), 51% RCs; theme "Power Evangelism" (22-26 July); launches magazine *AD 2000 Together* with front page motto "To Bring the Majority of the Human Race to Jesus Christ by the End of the Century."

Dominion Network (satellites to homes) launched into orbit by Community Satellite Corporation, USA, utilizing DBS (direct broadcast satellites).

Global Share Network announced by Global Mapping International (USA) as a missions mapping database.

T. Yamamori writes *God's new envoys: a bold strategy for penetrating closed countries,* presenting a detailed plan describing the strategic work Christian lay tentmakers in secular work can perform in world evangelization; chapter 6 entitled "The Basic Battle Plan" calls for 100,000 such persons in 77 closed countries.

Research project "The Future of the Christian World Mission" begun under auspices of American Society of Missiology, majoring on scenarios for the future of world evangelization.

Mission World '89 (International Satellite Mission) announced by Billy Graham Evangelistic Association, to originate from a major global city (Seoul) and to be beamed by satellite to hundreds of other cities across the world; but whole plan suddenly cancelled 5 months later and replaced by scaled-down London crusade in 1989 with relays across England only.

Global Broadcasting System (GBS) launched for Christian radio and TV broadcasting to any place on Earth through "Top Hat" system of super-pressure platform network of 800 high-tech balloons at 120,000 feet altitude covering whole world.

Adopt-a-People, a proposal to link North American churches and mission agencies with specific unreached people groups, begun by USCWM.

Christian Communication Technology (CCT) formed to develop AVCAPI (computer/laser reading system for illiterates) with goal: "By the year 2000, CCT will teach every capable and willing man, woman and child on earth to read the Bible in their own language."

Worldwide Prayer Crusade launched from Vatican City by Evangelization 2000 office, geared to Decade of Universal Evangelization 1990-2000; sudden, unexpected, and massive enthusiastic response from contemplatives, convents, and monasteries worldwide.

Project 2000 begun by Partnership International, formerly Christian Nationals Evangelism Commission (CNEC, begun 1943), now in 50 countries; project pledges "to help establish an evangelistic growing church in each of the 17,000 unreached people groups of the world by the year 2000," "to help strengthen 400 ministries under 80 different indigenous national organizations."

Destiny '87 Conference (Here's Life, Black America); 1,700 Black Americans gather in Atlanta, GA, to affirm "a growing number of black Christians believe it is their destiny to play a major role in world evangelization."

New Life 2000 announced as closure project by Campus Crusade for Christ/Here's Life, World—"The comprehensive global strategy to take the gospel to every culture on every continent by the year 2000; to present the gospel message to 6.5 billion people; to see 1 billion people receive Jesus Christ as Lord and Savior; to establish 10,000 New Life Bible study groups; to establish 1 million new churches; to provide 5,000 teams showing the *Jesus* film 100 times a year to 1,000 people per night (yielding 10% to 25% salvation decisions a night); to establish 15,000 prayer movements by 1995, in every city over 50,000 and all university campuses."

Interdenominational Global Missions Conference (Dallas I) convened (17-18 September) by Southern Baptist FMB president R.K. Parks, with 20 mission agencies present; agreement on (1) prayer and fasting every Pentecost weekend up to AD 2000 as "focused intercession for global evangelization," and (2) sharing data, plans and strategies; 1988, Dallas II (February), followed by teleconferences.

CHRONOLOGY OF WORLD EVANGELIZATION FROM AD 30 TO 1990 cont.

Status Report on the Great Commission published by World Mission Teams (formerly World Mission Crusade), Florida, as open letter addressed "To All Pastors of All Christian Churches" setting out logistics and finances of how to evangelize the world by means of "the fourth dimension in evangelism" (1st = personal witness, 2nd = printing, 3rd = broadcasting, 4th = motion picture evangelism).

Decade of Harvest inaugurated by Assemblies of God (USA), as denominational program to reach all persons on Earth by AD 2000; coordination by Total Church Evangelism Strategy Committee, renamed in 1987 Harvest Task Force (for work within USA); 1988 (July), world conference of AoG-related churches overseas to plan strategy.

Ibadan, Nigeria: Consultation between All Africa Baptist Fellowship and Overseas Mission Bodies (October); produces Ibadan Declaration, on Great Commission and "mutual sharing in the holistic evangelisation of the world."

2nd Asia Leadership Congress on World Evangelization (ALCOWE or ALCOE II), under LCWE/ALCOWE auspices, in Singapore, on theme "Witnessing for Christ through the Local Church" (20-28 October).

1st Ibero-American Missions Congress (Congreso Misionero Ibero-Americano, COMIBAM '87), in Sao Paulo (Brazil), with 3,500 Evangelical representatives (70% pentecostal/charismatic) from across Latin America, and preceded by series of national missions consultations in 23 countries; goal of world evangelization, with 10,000 new Latin American foreign missionary vocations generated (23-28 November).

Church of God (Cleveland, TN), with work in 98 countries, launches "Decade of Destiny for Church of God World Missions," with a different continent targeted for each year from 1990 to 2000.

Advance Ministries: Reaching the Unreached, a mission-sending agency serving the USA's 60,000 independent charismatic churches, begun with Mennonite support.

World Evangelism World Plan 1987-1991 launched at Jamaica meeting after 15th World Methodist Conference (Nairobi, July 1986, 3,000 delegates) on theme "Christ Jesus: God's 'Yes' for the World": 1988 Aldersgate Year, Open-Air Preachings, 1989 World Conference on Physical & Spiritual Poverty, 1990 4th International Christian Youth Conference, 1991 Conference on World Evangelization followed by 16th World Methodist Conference in Singapore.

1988   Conferences on evangelization: since 1945, some 5,510 conferences on mission and evangelism (at international, continental, regional or national level) have been held, via 5 groupings: 1,050 by Roman Catholic agencies; 1,100 by Ecumenical Movement agencies; 2,100 by Protestant and Anglican mission agencies; 840 by Evangelical mission agencies; and 420 by Charismatic Renewal agencies.

2nd All-India Congress on Missions and Evangelism (AICOME '88), sponsored by indigenous-mission body India Missions Association, IMA (with 300 member agencies), in Pune, India; 350 participants (4-8 January); global total of organized Third-World mission agencies now 500.

World Evangelization Database (segmentizing world into 250 countries, 11,000 ethnolinguistic peoples, 15,000 languages, 3,300 metropolises, et alia), first begun in 1962 as computer knowledge base, is finally brought online globally by WERC/FMB to assist mission agencies to match up nonresidential missionaries with entire unevangelized world; operated by massive computerized AI network, the World Evangelization Expert System (WEES).

Literature on evangelization: on narrower definition, titles strictly on "evangelize," "evangelism" or "evangelization" total 400 new books and articles every year; on broader definition, titles on evangelization and synonyms total 10,000 a year.

World Prayer Force inaugurated in Saint Petersburg, FL (USA), aiming to enroll 165 million Christians (10% of world total) promising to pray daily for world evangelization.

Inter-Agency Consultation for Resources and Information on Reaching the Unreached (Dallas II), held in Irving, TX (USA), by 28 denominations and agencies (9-11 February); followed by sharing of online databases and a series of Great Commission electronic teleconferences, with all mission executives and leaders participating from own headquarters.

Evangelistic citywide mass campaigns: several hundred organized multidenominational campaigns (under Billy Graham, Luis Palau, et alii), and some 3,000 denominational campaigns, are held in 1,300 metropolises and cities across the world each year; also hundreds of megameetings (over 100,000 attenders) under Christ For All Nations and numerous other charismatic agencies, using slogan "The Great Commission to Each Generation."

Singapore II Consultation on World Evangelization, with 65 global charismatic renewal leaders organized as CUWE, Charismatics United for World Evangelization with the new watchword "The whole church, bringing a whole Christ, to the whole world!," "to consider the distinctive contribution that the charismatic renewal could make in spreading the Christian gospel in the years leading up to AD 2000" (February).

Consultation to inaugurate Third World Missions Advance (TWMA), convened by AMA/IMF/EMS/COMIBAM; 35 Third-World leaders meet in Portland, OR, USA (9-13 May); International Mutual Fund created; TWMA aims to represent the hundreds of new missions agencies, with potential of fielding 100,000 Third-World missionaries by AD 2000.

Explosive growth of charismatic, evangelical and fundamentalist "video churches," video denominations and video mission agencies; vast rash of house-church networks begins to spread in all countries with large denominations.

Leadership '88, an LCWE conference in Washington, DC, for 2,200 emerging leaders, to "equip them to take aggressive action to fulfill the Great Commission," to "strategize to join together for world evangelization" and "to form new networks for completing the task of world evangelization" (27 June-1 July).

North American African World Missions Congress (Initiative '88) to implement global evangelization, organized by Nigerians after 1986 formation of North American Commission of African Christians; theme "African Initiatives in World Missions: a Strategic Gathering for a New Decade"; 1,500 Africans from over 30 African countries, living in North America, present in Chicago (13-17 July).

7th General Congress, International Association for Mission Studies (IAMS), in Rome, on theme "Christian Mission towards the Third Millennium: the Gospel of Hope" (29 June-5 July).

International Evangelical Bible Consultation/Conference (sponsored by LCWE, BGEA et al), in Amman, Jordan, stressing biblical position on justice and human rights.

World Wesleyan Conference on Witness and Evangelism, sponsored by World Methodist Council, on 250th anniversary of John Wesley's conversion.

'88 World Evangelization Crusade, Korea, led by charismatics (Methodists, Presbyterians) and pentecostals.

1989   Global Consultation on World Evangelization by AD 2000 and Beyond, convened in Singapore by a group including LCWE/COMIBAM/FMB-SBC/YWAM, inviting 2 representatives of each of the 78 major current megaplans for world evangelization, "open to all leaders of Great Commission groups within the worldwide body of Christ" (5-8 January).

2nd World Consultation on Frontier Missions (WCFM).

2nd World Conference on Mission and Evangelism (5th Meeting of CWME/WCC, Commission on World Mission and Evangelism), San Antonio, TX (USA); 600 attenders, mostly church nominees; theme "Your Will be Done: Mission in Christ's Way"; distributes pan-Orthodox missionary icon widely (22 May-1 June).

World Evangelization Conference on Liberation Theology and Personal Salvation (sponsored by World Methodist Council), in Latin America.

CHRONOLOGY OF WORLD EVANGELIZATION FROM AD 30 TO 1990 cont.

Lausanne II, or 2nd International Congress on World Evangelization (ICOWE II) convened by Lausanne Committee (LCWE), in Manila; congress theme, "Proclaim Christ Until He Comes"; attended by 6,000 evangelizers (11-20 July).

15th Pentecostal World Conference, in Singapore, on theme "Behold the Glory of the Lord"; over 6,000 delegates from 100 countries, 30,000 attenders (27 September–1 October).

Consultation on Dimensions of Christian Martyrdom, dealing with effects of martyrdom on upbuilding and evangelistic growth of whole church; total martyrs since AD 33 estimated at 40,500,000 (0.5% of all Christians ever), with current rate of 320,000 each year.

Jerusalem Charismatic Leaders Meeting (Pentecost 89)convened for 120 Renewal leaders worldwide, dealing with power intercession, power evangelism, world evangelization; in Jerusalem over Pentecost weekend (7-14 May).

1990   Vast increases in all types of evangelization and of evangelistic activity: virtually all major Christian denominations and agencies announce programs leading up to AD 2000.

Decade of Universal Evangelization (also termed Worldwide Decade of Evangelization) inaugurated by John Paul II and other world Christian leaders, calling all Christians to a decade of mission, with as aims (a) to unite all Christians and all churches by AD 2000, and (b) to bring the total of Christ's disciples to over 50% of world (3.1 billion) by AD 2000.

Round the World Prayer Event, organized by World Evangelism (World Methodist Council), to inaugurate evangelism in decade of 1990s.

Peace Council/Convocation of Christians: World Convocation on Justice, Peace, and the Integrity of Creation (JPIC), a worldwide ecumenical event, convened by RCC, WCC et alia, to oppose injustice, war and environmental destruction.

USA: Joint IFMA/EFMA Conference convenes, after 1988 IFMA conference on "Countdown 2000" and 1989 EFMA conference on "Evangelizing the World by AD 2000"; approves specific allotments for 1995 schedule for reaching all peoples on Earth with gospel.

World Congress on the Holy Spirit and World Evangelization, in Indianapolis, on "Power Evangelism"; over 60,000 attenders (Catholic/Protestant charismatic renewal).

EXPLO '90 global Christian 5-day training teleconference organized in all major countries by Campus Crusade for Christ (expanded version of EXPLO-85); also their *Jesus* film becomes after 10 years translated into world's 280 languages each with over 1 million mother-tongue speakers, and is being shown to 10 million persons every night, of whom 2 million become converts or enquirers each night.

Asia Regional Missions Congress on AD 2000 and Beyond (LCWE/TWMA/AMA/et alia).

Africa Regional Missions Congress on AD 2000 and Beyond (LCWE/TWMA/EMS/ et alia).

AD 2000 National Consultations proliferate, planned each for one country during the period 1990-1999 by LCWE/TWMA/et alia.

1991   Global Congress of Charismatic Leaders for World Evangelization, in Brighton (UK), to usher in decade of evangelization before AD 2000; 10,000 renewal leaders (8-14 July).

7th Assembly, World Council of Churches (WCC), in Canberra, Australia, with delegates from 350 member denominations; call to global commitment; ongoing programs include the Ecumenical Decade (1988-1998) for Churches in Solidarity with Women (launched at Easter 1988).

4th Chinese Congress on World Evangelization, CCOWE '91 (sponsored by CCCOWE/LCWE), in Hong Kong.

Sudden growth and mushrooming worldwide of youth churches completely outside control by denominations: loosely organized churches begun and run by charismatic under-25s, meeting at lunchtimes in hotels, theaters, cinemas, shops, warehouses, anywhere; huge growth of converts.

Conference on World Evangelization organized in Singapore by World Methodist Council.

AD 2000 Regional Consultations sponsored by LCWE/TWMA/et alia begin in earnest: 1991 North America; 1991 Europe; 1991 Middle East & North Africa; 1993 Asia; 1993 Latin America; 1993 Africa.

After 30 years' preparation since 1961 1st Pan-Orthodox Conference (on island of Rhodes), Great & Holy Council of the Orthodox Church convenes in Greece as first fully recognized ecumenical council of the entire church since 7th Ecumenical Council (Council of Nicaea II, last one recognized by Eastern Orthodox) in AD 787; statement promulgated on Orthodoxy's mission to the world; mission icon distributed.

Possible future scenarios with plans

1994   Final decade of 20th century proves to be greatest decade in Christian history for signs and wonders, miracles, conversions, evangelism and evangelization: greatest sign or wonder being Christians loving one another and gathering in unity everywhere.

1999   World-level conference convened by Evangelicals with a representative from every people group on Earth, in last-minute attempt to complete evangelization of panta ta ethne by AD 2000.

Catholics begin preparations to celebrate Jubilee Year of AD 2000, in the Holy Year series, with pope to telecast on 25 December 2000 to 6 billion viewers via network of satellites.

2000   Celebration 2000, a massive global event on the part of all Great Commission Christians, in myriads of locations; already by 1988 being planned in detail.

Respect for Christ: person of Christ now widely known and respected throughout world, by all world religions, even among atheists and agnostics; also his teachings and his gospel (but not his church) are understood and valued, though not accepted or implemented, almost universally.

Entire world finally reached with Christian gospel for first time in history, in the sense that everyone everywhere has heard or hears the gospel in depth with understanding and has access to Scripture, churches, missions, Christians, Christian broadcasting (with 4,000 Christian radio and TV stations worldwide), movies, literature, and other means of grace.

Global church-planting goal completed: at least one fellowship or church or congregation or nucleus of disciples has been planted as an ongoing indigenous witness in each of the world's 11,500 ethnolinguistic peoples and 4,000 metropolises of over 100,000 population.

2004   Massive pentecostal-charismatic latter-rain revival sweeps across whole of Asia due to power evangelism with signs and wonders, with 150 million converts in Korea, Japan, China, Viet Nam, Thailand, Malaysia, Indonesia, Burma, Cambodia, India, Sri Lanka and Pakistan.

2006   Declining Euroamerican denominations in Western world spark off itinerant tourist churches, groupings of believers ceaselessly travelling and witnessing around the Earth; Latin Americans independently form itinerant pilgrim churches which multiply phenomenally across world.

2008   Global church research project to determine which major events or situations in past history of evangelization should be changed by messages or messengers sent from today, as soon as science invents method of tachyonic time travel and alteration of the past; preference for rectifying the great missed opportunities of Christian history (as with China in 1266, 1644, 1843).

CHRONOLOGY OF WORLD EVANGELIZATION FROM AD 30 TO 1990 cont.

2009   Total global charismatic worship of Christ introduced, in which at a fixed time each Sunday one billion living believers across world are holographically present visibly at same location; the ultimate in inspiration and evangelistic converting power.

2011   Religious pilgrims become a major force in world, over 400 million religious zealots (50% being Christians) constantly on move from shrine to shrine and country to country, ignoring secular and state restrictions; Christian pilgrims form a vast unorganized network of continuously itinerant pilgrim churches.

2027   Christian broadcasting (overt and clandestine) utilizes vast range of 3,000 major languages, programs of every type; reputation for truth results in 90% of world as regular audience; but dangerously exposed to disinformation tactics and terrorism.

c.2030   Church of the future plays dynamic part in the evolution of mankind, bringing the world to final perfection in Point Omega (Teilhard de Chardin).

2030   Conversion of China to Christianity through multitude of Chinese house-church evangelists and witnesses, resulting in 1.5 billion zealous, charismatic, nondenominational Christians, who then launch their own global mission without reference to Western or Eastern churches and missions, or to historic Christianity, or to the 1,200 previously proposed world evangelization plans.

2045   Global Bible distribution reaches optimal maximum level of 10 billion Scriptures per year (whole Bibles, NTs, portions, selections), in languages understood by whole world's population; but highly susceptible both to antichristian terrorism and also to world government edicts.

2050   Christianity now dominated worldwide by Third-World indigenous pentecostal-charismatic bodies, spreading like wildfire through unorganized self-replicating media churches.

2080   Spread of Christianity throughout Chinese and Arab races generates vast missionary zeal to point where both launch independent schemes for total world evangelization and conversion.

2090   Church of the Martyrs: on one scenario, ruthless 80-year persecution by world government reaches climax, decimates global Christianity, reduces churches to a tiny minority, then liquidates all churches, which thus follow their Master to final execution and martyrdom.

Biblical end-time scenarios

(The remaining 10 schemas below represent biblical end-time visions often quoted or used as justification for world evangelization plans throughout history. No suggested future dates of any kind can be proposed for these visions.)

Revivals and rapid church growth with mass acceptance of gospel in some parts of the world, with mass rejection of gospel in others: millions converted in last great global spiritual revival; worldwide signs and wonders accompany proclamation of the gospel in every land.

Failure of the church to evangelize the world, part remaining still unevangelized until the Tribulation (Matthew 10:23b).

The Four Horsemen of the Apocalypse (opening of the first 4 Seals), white, red, black, pale: (1) war/conquest/deception/false religions/cults/pseudo-messiah/antichrist, (2) slaughter, (3) famine, (4) death [or (1) missionary preaching of the gospel, (2) civil war/bloodshed, (3) famine/hunger/disease/poverty, (4) terror/pestilence/death/destruction; 25% of world slaughtered] (Matthew 24:7, Revelation 6:1-8).

Sufferings of the church multiplied as it prophesies and witnesses to the world (Revelation 10:9-11).

Great Commission of Christ fulfilled in the sense that universal preaching of the gospel to all nations (world evangelization, discipling of the peoples) has been finally accomplished by the church militant on Earth, with disciples and witnesses found in every race and population and people and language (Matthew 24:14, 28:19-20).

Penultimate direct supernatural work of the Holy Spirit in proclamation, evangelization and conversions throughout world as Church Age draws to its close (Acts 2:16-17).

The 144,000 converted Israelites become End-time evangelists who reach world's last unreached people groups and so complete task of world evangelization (Revelation 7:4-8).

Last supernatural proclamation from heaven of Everlasting Gospel of love in all its fullness to every nation, and kindred, and tongue, and people, either to convert or to seal doom of mankind; last appeal and announcement of final chance for repentance and salvation, imminent end of Age of Grace with following judgment upon wicked in climax of Great Tribulation (Rev 14:6-7, being Revelation's 4th group of 7 visions; Lk 16:31).

Universal spread and acceptance of the Kingdom of God (as envisaged by Irenaeus in AD 180); gradual conversion of vast numbers to Christ.

The Two Witnesses (Olive Trees, Lampstands: Moses and Elijah, Law and Prophecy; Joshua and Zerubbabel the anointed religious and civil leaders; the witness-bearing two-sevenths of the universal church about to be martyred), after 42 months or 3½ years (literal or figurative) of preaching the gospel and opposing New Age philosophy, complete their task of world evangelization through bearing witness to claims of Christ, are slain by Antichrist symbolizing near-obliteration of the church, in 3rd Persecution; but then are raised from dead, symbolizing final global revival of faith in Christ with millions converted (Zecheriah 4:11-14, Revelation 11:3-14).

Seven Hundred Plans to Evangelize the World by David B. Barrett and James W. Reapsome. ©1988 by Foreign Mission Board of the Southern Baptist Convention. Published by New Hope, Birmingham, AL. Used by permission.

FOCUS FACT

From the time of Nero (A.D. 64) until the conversion of Emperor Constantine and the Edict of Milan (A.D. 313), whereby Christianity was made legal, the Christian faith was officially regarded as a *religio prava*, an evil or depraved religion.

Source: *Glimpses*, published by Christian History Institlute.

---

20 SIGNIFICANT CHURCH HISTORY LEADERS
Selected by Dr. Earle E. Cairns, author and historian

Justin Martyr (c.100–165). Christian apologist. Born of pagan parents in Samaria, he was converted about 132. A few years later he went to Rome and stoutly declared his Christian faith to the highest in the land, trying to show how it went beyond even the noblest aspects of Greek philosophy. Finally, with some fellow believers, he was denounced as a Christian and subversive and was condemned to be beheaded. Justin is held to have been the first Christian apologist to bring together the claims of faith and reason. His *First Apology* (c.155) and *Dialogue with Trypho* (c.160) both emphasize that Christians are the inheritors, the heirs of Israel and its promises.

Constantine the Great (c.274/280–337). First Christian emperor of Rome. Brought up at the court of Diocletian, he became Western emperor after a military victory near Rome in 312, which he attributed to the God of the Christians. The Edict of Milan in 313 decreed full toleration and other advantages for Christians, including the restitution of confiscated property. In 325, by now

TWENTY SIGNIFICANT CHURCH HISTORY LEADERS cont.

sole emperor of East and West, Constantine summoned the Council of Nicea to settle the Arian controversy. He presided at the opening sessions. The result was a victory for orthodoxy, but Constantine had no theological discernment and was soon thereafter swayed by bishops of Arian tendencies. In 330 he established a new capital in the East, which he called Constantinople.

Athanasius (c.293–373). Bishop of Alexandria. Although only a deacon at the Council of Nicea, it was there he became the chief defender of orthodox Christianity against Arianism. Bishop of his native Alexandria from 328, his determination to uphold the true doctrine of God involved him in exhausting controversies with highly placed Arians in church and state. He was banished several times, returning finally only about six years before his death. By his faithful ministry, steadfast character, significant writings, and zeal for God's truth, he contributed much toward the triumph of orthodoxy at the Council of Constantinople eight years after his death.

> **❝❞ FOCUS QUOTE**
> He became what we are that he might make us what he is.
> —Athanasius

Augustine of Hippo (354–430). Bishop of Hippo (modern Annaba, Algeria). Born and educated in North Africa, he became a teacher of rhetoric, a profession continued when he went to Milan in 384. Influenced by that city's bishop, Ambrose, he forsook Manichaeism for Christianity. While visiting Hippo in 391 he was reluctantly ordained, and in 395 he was consecrated as successor to Bishop Valerius. He defended Christianity against attacks by Manichees, Donatists, pagans, and Pelagians, and showed himself a faithful pastor, preacher, administrator, and encourager of monasticism. Augustine is often called the greatest thinker in Christian

antiquity. His writings include *The Confessions* (c.399) and *The City of God* (c.413–427). His *Confessions* is considered to be the first instance of Christian spiritual autobiography. His basic understanding of theology was that "I believe in order that I may understand"—*"credo ut intelligam."*

Innocent III (1160–1216). Pope from 1198. One of the greatest of medieval popes, he defended his office ably against the claims of emperors and other rulers. He supported the Fourth Crusade, encouraged the beginnings of the Franciscan and Dominican orders, summoned the Lateran Council of 1215, and launched a campaign in France against the Albigensians. He was a shrewd organizer and statesman, and under him the Papal States were expanded.

Francis of Assisi (1182–1226). Founder of the Franciscans. Son of a prosperous merchant, he turned in 1205 to a life of prayer and poverty, renouncing his worldly possessions. He began to preach in 1208, and in 1209 he received papal approval for the establishing of his order. Francis resigned the leadership in 1223, disliking internal disputes about administration. He spent his last three years in solitude and prayer and in occasional writing. He is the first known stigmatist; he received the stigmata in 1224 while praying on Monte La Verna. He composed the *Canticle of the Sun* and the very familiar prayer beginning, *"Make me an instrument of thy peace."*

John Wycliffe (c. 1329–1384). English Reformer. Priest and Oxford philosopher, he became widely known during his last ten years, when he was rector of Lutterworth in Leicestershire. Critical of the church's acquisitive attitude to property, he began to question other things publicly. Right thinking and right living were almost identical for Wycliffe. He instituted "simple" itinerant priests to supplement church services by religious instruction in the vernacular. They were helped by an English translation of the Bible and by Wycliffe's tracts and sermons.

His proclamation of a simple gospel, though unwelcomed in England until the 16th century, greatly influenced Jan Hus. Wycliffe has been called the "morning star of the Reformation."

> **66 99**
> **FOCUS**
> **QUOTE**
> My conscience is captive to the Word of God. . . . Here I stand, I can do no other.
> —Martin Luther at Worms

Martin Luther (1483–1546). Leader of the Reformation in Germany. Son of a Saxon miner, he graduated in arts at Erfurt, then in 1505 forsook further studies in law to become an Augustinian. He was ordained in 1507, and from 1508 taught theology at Wittenberg. There his lectures began to reflect his growing belief that justification by faith rather than by works expressed the church's true faith. He grew increasingly uneasy about the sale of papal indulgences as a means of boosting church revenue, but his demand for a theological examination of the practice brought only a trial for heresy. Others who saw the need for reforms in Roman Catholicism gathered around him and protested that the gospel of Jesus Christ had become obscured in the church by worldly accretions. Excommunicated by the pope and outlawed by the emperor, Luther nonetheless found powerful protectors and sympathizers, and soon the cause of the Reformation was irreversible. Luther rejected on one hand various kinds of religious extremists within protestantism, and on the other such humanists as Erasmus, who sought reform from within the old church. Luther's fear of anarchy led him to side with authority against the Peasants' Revolt in 1525, an action that alienated some of the common people. And he differed also with the Swiss Reformer Ulrich Zwingli over the meaning of the Lord's Supper. Luther was a prolific writer, issuing pamphlets to combat the evils of the time and doctrinal works that would set Protestantism on a sound theological foundation. His greatness can be seen,

suggests one scholar, in that more books have been written about him than about anyone else in history except Jesus of Nazareth.

Ulrich Zwingli (1484–1531). Swiss Reformer. An admirer of Erasmus, he became chief preacher at Zurich's Great Munster (1518), where his New Testament lectures marked the beginning of the Swiss Reformation. He attacked Roman Catholic doctrine and practice; defeated its supporters in public debate; and supported by the civil authorities, suppressed the Mass, celebrated the Lord's Supper after a Reformed manner, and established ecclesiastical independence. Zwingli's view of the Eucharist as purely symbolic estranged him from Luther and made a united protestantism impossible. The Reformation divided Switzerland, and in the ensuing civil war, Zwingli was killed while serving as chaplain and standard-bearer with the Protestant forces.

> **66 99**
> **FOCUS**
> **QUOTE**
> There is no work better than another to please God; to pour water, to wash dishes, to be a cobbler, or an apostle: all is one. —William Tyndale

William Tyndale (c.1495–1536). English biblical translator and martyr. Educated at Oxford and Cambridge and ordained about 1521, he studied further under Luther at Wittenberg and completed his New Testament translation at Worms in 1526. Copies were smuggled into England, and his life was thereafter in danger. He continually revised that work, translated also parts of the Old Testament and wrote *Obedience of a Christian Man* (1528). Tyndale followed Luther on the authority of Scripture and on justification by faith but tended toward the sacramental views of Zwingli. Possibly at Henry VIII's instigation, he was betrayed to the imperial authorities and strangled and burned at the stake near Brussels. His translations formed the bases of the Authorized and Revised Versions of the Bible.

TWENTY SIGNIFICANT CHURCH HISTORY LEADERS cont.

Menno Simons (1496–1551). Early Mennonite leader. Ordained as a Roman Catholic priest in the Netherlands in 1524, he had misgivings about the church's teaching on infant baptism and the Eucharist and in 1536 he left the church and became prominent in the Anabaptist movement. Hunted and with a price on his head, he moved from place to place debating, encouraging, and writing extensively (he established a printing press). Each of his many works reflects his aim in the preface, quoting 1 Corinthians 3:11: "No other foundation can any one lay than that which is laid, which is Jesus Christ."

Conrad Grebel (c.1498–1526). Founder of the Swiss Brethren Movement, also called Anabaptist. Having broken with Zwingli in 1524, Grebel organized the Brethren as an independent Anabaptist church in Zurich. An able humanist and biblical scholar, he defied the city council's ban on his activities, and performed the first adult baptism in modern history. He served two prison terms, totaling six months, before his early death.

66 99
FOCUS QUOTE
God thrust me into the fray.
—John Calvin after the publication of *Institutes.*

John Calvin (1509–1564). French Protestant reformer. Born in Picardy, he studied theology in Paris and law at Orleans and Bourges, during which time he came under protestant influence. He broke with Roman Catholicism in 1533 after a conversion experience in which he felt called to restore the church to its original purity. Forced to leave Paris because of rising feelings against protestantism, he settled in Basel and in 1536 published the *Institutes of the Christian Religion* in Latin. His studious inclinations were disrupted when, on a visit to Geneva in 1536, he unwillingly agreed to become William Farel's colleague in organizing the Reformation there. Appointed preacher and professor of theology, he excluded the unworthy from Communion and proposed other reforms. The result was the expulsion of Calvin and Farel from the city in 1538. In Strasbourg for the next three years he got to know Martin Bucer and Philip Melanchthon, and he published a commentary on Romans. Welcomed back to Geneva in 1541, he established a regime with a strong Old Testament emphasis that gave the supreme council under Calvin wide powers over the private lives of citizens. Adultery, blasphemy, and heresy were punishable by death. Calvin and Calvinism controlled church and state. Calvin preached regularly, introduced congregational singing into the Reformed church services, and gave lectures that brought students from near and far. His Bible commentaries are still hailed as classics. He was also a champion of the Huguenots, welcomed protestant refugees from Mary Tudor's England, trained John Knox for his leadership of the Scottish Reformation, and counseled protestants in other lands. Calvin believed that virtue should be practiced for its own sake, regardless of future rewards and punishments.

George Fox (1624–1691). Founder of the Society of Friends, or Quakers. Apprenticed to a shoemaker, he left his Leicestershire home in 1643 to seek religious enlightenment. After painful experiences he spoke of having found One who spoke to his condition, and in 1646 he came to reply on the "inner light of the living Christ." He forsook church attendance, rejected outward sacraments and paid clergy, and taught that truth is to be found primarily in God's voice speaking to the soul. So emerged the "Friends of Truth." Fox taught the priesthood of all believers and urged a simple lifestyle on his colleagues, who later included William Penn. He established a base at Swarthmore Hall in northwest England but traveled widely at home and abroad. Eight times he saw the inside of prisons, serving terms totaling six years. He fought prison conditions and other social evils and sought to establish religious toleration in an intolerant age. Fox could show a mean spirit on occasion toward opponents, but he was a true pacifist, whose use of group silence was a brake on impetuous conduct.

Philip Jacob Spener (1635–1705). German pastor and founder of Pietism. Influenced by Johann Arndt and Richard Baxter and distressed by the lack of personal content in the theology of his day, he set out to reform Lutheranism from within. For individuals, he stressed the local church and instituted small group sessions (*collegia pietatis*) that encouraged fellowship, Bible study, the priesthood of all believers, right behavior, piety, devotion, and love instead of argument. For the church in Germany, he called for spiritual preaching and for the reform of theological education, an emphasis that resulted in the founding of the University at Halle (1694), where dogmatics was deemphasized and personal piety was stressed. And for the church at large, Spener emphasized missions and evangelism. Spener's influence was enormous in the church, and some see the roots of the later romanticism here.

66 99 FOCUS QUOTE God buries his workmen but carries on his work. —Charles Wesley

Count von Nikolaus Ludwig Zinzendorf (1700–1760). Founder of the Moravian church. Born in Dresden and raised in Pietist circles, he studied law at Wittenberg and in 1721 entered Saxon government service. Herrnhut, the famous Christian community, emerged from his giving of refuge to a group of Bohemian refugees on his estate. He left government service in 1727 and was ordained as a Lutheran pastor in 1734 and as bishop of the Unitas Fratrum in 1737. From Herrnhut, Zinzendorf sent his missionaries to many countries; John Wesley was only one from other traditions who found his heart strangely warmed through contact with the Moravians. Zinzendorf himself traveled ex-

tensively, notably in America, and spent five years ministering in England. It is hard to overestimate his contribution to the modern missionary movement.

66 99 FOCUS QUOTE Lord, let me not live to be useless. —John Wesley

Charles Wesley (1707–1788). Methodist hymn writer. Eighteenth child of a Lincolnshire rector, he graduated from Oxford, where he was a member of the Holy Club and was ordained in 1735. Three years later he experienced an evangelical conversion and became a revivalist preacher, often in company with his brother John. He traveled little after 1756 but preached in Bristol and (from 1771) London. He produced several thousand hymns, many of which are still regularly sung. They include "Love Divine, All Loves Excelling," "Lo! He Comes, With Clouds Descending," "Jesus, Lover of My Soul," and "Hark! The Herald Angels Sing."

John Wesley (1703–1791). Founder of Methodism. Fifteenth child of Samuel and Susanna Wesley, he was educated at Oxford and ordained in the Church of England but did not experience conversion until 1738. Soon afterwards, he embarked on his great task: "To reform the nation, particularly the church, and to spread scriptural holiness over the land." Before he died he had preached more than 40,000 sermons and covered nearly 250,000 miles. He encountered opposition from hostile mobs, uncooperative clergy, and other Evangelicals who disliked his Arminian theology, and he unwillingly fathered a breakaway church. When he died, however, one secular magazine hailed him as "One of the few characters who outlived enmity and prejudice."

William Booth (1829–1912). Founder of the Salvation Army. Born in Nottingham and converted in 1844, he was a Methodist preacher; but chafing under denominational restrictions, he left in 1861 to pursue

TWENTY SIGNIFICANT CHURCH HISTORY LEADERS cont.

independent evangelistic work that led him to London's East End. Out of his "Christian Mission" there developed the Salvation Army (1878). Booth was a tireless fighter against such things as squalid slums, uncaring authority, abused children, drink, forced labor conditions, internal dissension, and unfounded charges, but chiefly against the devil and all his works. His book *In Darkest England—and the Way Out* (1890) became a best seller. He traveled 5 million miles and preached nearly 60,000 sermons. Forty thousand people attended his funeral in London.

Washington Gladden (1836–1918). American Congregational pastor. He served churches in Massachusetts, New York, and Ohio, and liked to speak of a practical gospel that had liberated him from "the bondage of an immoral theology." He wrote twelve books and was a leader in formulating and popularizing the so-called social gospel. He was also the author of the well-known hymn "O Master, Let Me Walk With Thee."

Source: Taken from *The Concise Dictionary of the Christian Tradition* by J. D. Douglas, Walter A. Elwell, and Peter Toon. Copyright 1989 by J. D. Douglas, Walter A. Elwell, and Peter Toon. Used by permission of Zondervan Publishing House.

THE PENDULUM EFFECT IN CHURCH HISTORY

Montanism A 2nd-century Christian heresy. It originated in Montanus, a Christian who, in a Phrygian village about 156, fell into a trance and reportedly began to "prophesy under the influence of the Spirit." Two young women also prophesied, and the movement quickly spread through Asia Minor. Montanus claimed to have a new and final revelation, foretold the return of Christ and the establishment of the New Jerusalem on a Phrygian plain, encouraged fasting, and welcomed persecution. The Asia Minor bishops finally excommunicated the Montanists about 177, but the sect survived until the 6th century (remnants of it into the 9th century). Tertullian was its most famous adherent.

Gnosticism (Gk. *gnosis*, "knowledge") Salvation through special knowledge. The word covers a wide variety of 1st- and 2d-century teachings, some of which may be called Christian Gnosticism. All have the essential ingredient that salvation is by enlightenment and by possession of special knowledge. Famous teachers were Valentinus (2d century), Basilides (2d century), and Marcion (d. 160). Christian authors who attacked Gnosticism as being pagan in origin and for misusing the Bible were Irenaeus (d. 200), Tertullian (d. 225),

and Hippolytus (d. 236). Modern knowledge of Gnosticism has been greatly supplemented by archaeological findings, notably at Nag-Hammadi in 1945.

Monasticism A way of Christian life involving asceticism, self-denial, and obedience to a superior, followed in whole or partial seclusion from the secular world. Usually it is according to a fixed rule of life and under lifelong vows of poverty, chastity, and obedience. The purpose is to seek God and to gain perfection; this pursuit may involve service to human beings or commitment to a life of prayer.

Christian monasticism began in Egypt and was introduced into the West in the 4th century. A rule was provided by St. Benedict (480–543) that was used as the basis of many communities of monks and nuns. In the East the great center of monasticism has been Mount Athos in Greece. Protestants have criticized monasticism on the basis that it encourages the idea of salvation by works and that it elevates the idea of celibacy over that of the married state.

Scholasticism (Lat. *schola*, "place of learning") The system and method of philosophy and theology developed in the academic centers of medieval Europe. It has a technical (scholastic) language and method. Much material was derived from the early fathers, especially Augustine of Hippo, and it made use of the philosophy of Aristotle. The most famous exponent of scholasticism was Thomas Aquinas (1225–1274). As protestant theologians of the late 16th and 17th centuries used a technical method and vocabulary to produce protestant doctrine, what they produced in their learned tomes is often called "Protestant scholasticism."

Mysticism The experience in which the believer arrives at a special union of love with God. It transcends knowledge of God achieved through the normal powers of mind

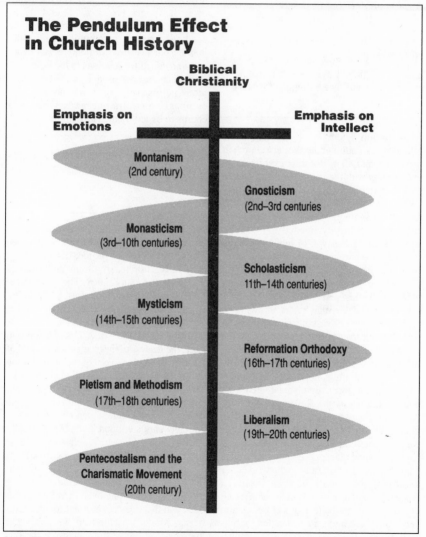

The Pendulum Effect in Church History

Biblical Christianity

Emphasis on Emotions — **Emphasis on Intellect**

Montanism (2nd century)

Gnosticism (2nd–3rd centuries

Monasticism (3rd–10th centuries)

Scholasticism 11th–14th centuries)

Mysticism (14th–15th centuries)

Reformation Orthodoxy (16th–17th centuries)

Pietism and Methodism (17th–18th centuries)

Liberalism (19th–20th centuries)

Pentecostalism and the Charismatic Movement (20th century)

and reason. There is a loss of the sense of time with great feelings of joy and exultation. God is felt to be extremely near. It is fellowship with God known through the embrace of a unifying love. To know what mysticism is requires a personal knowledge of mystical experience or the reading of books by those known as mystics (e.g., Teresa of Avila, John of the Cross, Julian of Norwich, and Eckhart). A classic treatment of the subject is found in *Mysticism* (1911) by Evelyn Underhill.

---

66 99
FOCUS
QUOTE
Lord, open the King of England's eyes. —William Tyndale while burning at the stake

---

Reformation A term chiefly applied to the religious revolution in the Western church in the 16th century. The Reformation originated in Germany with the inability of Roman Catholicism to cope with Martin Luther's protest against the sale of indulgences in 1517. This shortsightedness on the part of long-entrenched authority opened the door to demand for the renewal of biblically based Christianity—primitive purity in doctrine, worship, and organization. Progress was helped in those early years by political squabbling between Charles V and the papacy and several influential German rulers throwing in their lot with the Protestants. The movement was introduced into Switzerland by Ulrich Zwingli and continued by John Calvin. It was Calvinism that spread more readily to other parts of Europe, notably to the Netherlands and Scotland. Calvinism fathered what became known as the Reformed churches. Alongside the two main groupings—respectively following Luther and Calvin and becoming Protestant state churches (or national churches)—and often opposed to and by them were the extreme Protestants who worked for a radical Reformation; they included Anabaptists, Mennonites, and Separatists, all of whom rejected the idea of a close relation between church and state and called for religious liberty. The two great doctrinal emphases of the Reformation as confessed by the

Protestants were the final authority of the Bible in matters of faith and conduct (the formal principle) and the doctrine of justification by faith (the material principle). The Counter-Reformation was Roman Catholicism's belated reaction to the Reformation.

Pietism A renewal movement among German Lutherans that began in the 17th century. In origin it is associated with the names of P. J. Spener (1635–1705) and A. H. Francke (1663–1727). It emphasized the need for genuine communion with God, pointed out that dead orthodoxy was of no use, and called for missions to the heathen.

Pietism is also used in a wider sense, often pejoratively, to designate an overemphasis on religious experience and claims to be led by the Holy Spirit.

---

66 99
FOCUS
QUOTE
Sour godliness is the devil's religion. —John Wesley

Methodism The teaching, organization, and discipline of those denominations that see themselves following the idea of Christianity originally supplied by John and Charles Wesley in the 18th century. The word *Methodists* came into use in Oxford in the 1720s as a description of a group of serious-minded young men who were methodical in their devotions and good works. Out of this group came the leaders of the evangelical revival of the 18th century, and out of the revival came the societies of the people called Methodists. They have spread to many countries and, because of divisions, comprise various Methodist and Holiness denominations—of which twenty are found in the U.S. Virtually all Methodist bodies are Arminian in doctrine (the exception is the Welsh Methodists [Presbyterians who are Calvinist]). The World Methodist Council has delegates from over forty countries representing over 45 million members, and this does not account for all Methodists. Modern Methodism worship varies from a strong liturgical emphasis on the one side to an emphasis on freedom on the other.

This in turn reflects the origins of Methodism—converts from the Church of England made by Church of England priests (therefore liturgical) and the pursuit of "scriptural holiness" and the fullness of the Spirit by the membership of the societies (therefore freedom). In terms of church polity it is connectional.

Liberalism A form of theology that flourished in the Western church from the mid-19th to the early 20th century. Found primarily in Protestantism, it also had supporters in Roman Catholicism. The key themes were freedom and progress—freedom from old dogmas and freedom to investigate new ideas, progress in collaboration with the new confident sciences. Important thinkers who set the stage for this type of theology were F.D.E. Schleiermacher (1768–1834) and Albrecht Ritschl (1822–1889). The result was a theology that had few points of contact left with the traditional view of the Bible and Christian faith. Two world wars and the massive influence of Karl Barth caused the demise of the old liberal theology as a major movement. It still lives on in a new dress in modern forms of theology that deny the deity of Jesus Christ and allow belief only in what is said to be rational.

Pentecostalism Either a movement in which the gifts of the Holy Spirit are said to be experienced or several denominations that emphasize the possession and exercise of the gifts of the Spirit. The name arises since the Spirit (and thus the gifts of the Spirit) were first given to the church at the Feast of Pentecost (Acts 2). As a movement in modern times it began with the Topeka Revival of 1901 and the Azusa Street Revival of Los Angeles in 1906, with claims to certain gifts of the Spirit, especially speaking in tongues. Similar events took place in other places, and thus the movement to encourage prayer for

and receipt of the gifts began. It occurred outside the mainline denominations and churches and led ultimately to the formation of various new groups—Assemblies of God, Pentecostal Assemblies of the World, Pentecostal Church of God, and United Pentecostal Church International. These denominations, with others, have continued; but since World War II a new form of the Pentecostal movement has arisen and has deeply affected most of the traditional churches and denominations. It is known as the charismatic movement or Neo-Pentecostalism and is best described as a renewal movement in which the gifts of the Spirit are emphasized in the context of each church being seen as a body of Christ.

Charismatic Movement Contemporary religious phenomenon that embodies a renewed emphasis on the person and work of the Holy Spirit. Beginning in the late 1950s and early 1960s non-Pentecostal Christians, many from the mainline denominations, began experiencing Pentecostal visitations that included speaking in tongues, divine healings, prophecies, and various physical phenomena such as prostrations and fainting, in a way reminiscent of the great awakenings of the past. It created a vast unrest and rethinking on the part of traditional non-Pentecostal Christians, including the Roman Catholics, of what place such gifts and experiences ought to play in the Christian life. Voluminous literature and over one hundred official denominational documents have discussed its value pro and con with the general feeling (although not universally held) that one ought not to bridle the Holy Spirit, who "blows where he will," but still one must "test the spirits" to see if they are of God.

Dictionary of Christianity in America edited by Daniel G. Reid, Robert D. Linder, Bruce L. Shelley & Harry S. Stout. This unprecedented 1306-page volume covers the breadth of individuals, denominations, organizations, traditions, movements, events, and ideas that have shaped American Christianity—from Christopher Columbus to the Crystal Cathedral. Published by InterVarsity Press.

FOCUS BOOK

TEST YOUR CHURCH HISTORY IQ

1. Polycarp was:
   (a) A Roman emperor who ordered persecution of Christians
   (b) A Christian bishop burned at the stake for his faith
   (c) A region of North Africa known for its fierce persecution of Christians
   (d) Parrot food made from fish

2. This young noblewoman, along with her slave-girl, Felicitas, was martyred for her faith in Carthage about A.D. 200 Who was she?
   (a) Priscilla
   (b) Perpetua
   (c) Patagonia
   (d) Polynesia

3. In the early 300s a Roman emperor became a Christian, suddenly reversing a policy of persecution against Christians. Who was he?
   (a) Caligula
   (b) Constantine
   (c) Augustine
   (d) Ovaltine

4. Though he had little formal education, this fifth-century Christian is credited with taking the gospel to Ireland. Who was he?
   (a) St. Augustine
   (b) St. Patrick
   (c) St. Dublin
   (d) Sgt. O'Malley

5. This group of Christians fled persecution and settled on an estate in Germany, which they called Herrnhut. In the 1700s they pioneered a mission movement in the Americas. Who were they?
   (a) the Mohicans
   (b) the Calvinists
   (c) the Moravians
   (d) the Beatles

6. This Bohemian preacher was one of the first Protestant reformers, predating Martin Luther by more than a century. He was burned at the stake for his beliefs.
   (a) Savonarola
   (b) Francis of Assisi
   (c) John Hus
   (d) John Calvin

7. Joan of Arc was a young woman who claimed to see heavenly visions and led French troops in battle against the British. How did she die?
   (a) Pneumonia
   (b) Burned at the stake
   (c) Firing squad
   (d) Boredom

8. Just because a government leader is a Christian doesn't mean he's a good leader, as one reformer pointed out, saying that, as far as leaders were concerned, "Better a wise Turk than a Christian donkey." Who said this?
   (a) Francis of Assisi
   (b) Martin Luther
   (c) John Calvin
   (d) Calvin Klein

9. This shoemaker shook British Christians out of missions lethargy and sailed to India as a missionary. He said, "Expect great things from God; attempt great things for God." Who was he?
   (a) Hudson Taylor
   (b) William Carey
   (c) Thom McAn
   (d) William Wilberforce

10. This young missionary was killed in 1956, along with four others, in an effort to take the gospel to the Auca Indians of Ecuador. His widow went on to become a popular speaker and author.
   (a) Francis Schaeffer
   (b) Frank ten Boom
   (c) Jim Elliot
   (d) Peter Marshall

Answers: 1.b 2.b 3.b 4.b 5.c 6.c 7.b 8.b 9.b 10.c

Source: *Glimpses,* published by Christian History Institute. Copyright © 1989. Used by permission.

❝❞
FOCUS
QUOTE
How shall we labor with any effect to build up the church if we have no thorough knowledge of her history, or fail to apprehend it from the proper point of observation? History is, and must ever continue to be, next to God's Word, the richest foundation of wisdom and the surest guide to all successful practical activity. —Philip Schaff, German Reformed church historian (1819-1893)

FOCUS
BOOK
30 Days to Understanding Church History by Max E. Anders and Judith A. Lunsford. A good overview of the ebb and flow of 2000 years of church history. Takes only 15 minutes of your time each day for a month. Published by Wolgemuth & Hyatt.

Church Life

100 LARGEST CHURCHES IN AMERICA

1990 Worship Attendance

ATT.	CHURCH	CITY, STATE	AFF.	PASTOR
20000	First Baptist Church	Hammond, IN	IB	Dr. Jack Hyles
13003	Willow Creek Community	S. Barrington, IL	IND	Pastor Bill Hybels
12000	Calvary Chapel	Santa Ana, CA	CALC	Pastor Church Smith
10543	First Assembly of God	Phoenix, AZ	AG	Dr. Tommy J. Barnett
9175	Mt. Paran Church of God	Atlanta, GA	COGC	Dr. Paul Walker
8476	Second Baptist Church	Houston, TX	SBC	Dr. H. Edwin Young
8250	Calvary Chapel	Downy, CA	CALC	Rev. Jeff Johnson
8212	Deliverance Evangelistic	Philadelphia, PA	INDC	Rev. Benjamin Smith
8000	Grace Community Church	Sun Valley, CA	BIB	Dr. John MacArthur
8000	Harvest Fellowship	Riverside, CA	CALC	Pastor Greg Laurie
7800	First Baptist Church	Jacksonville, FL	SBC	Drs. Lindsey Jr./Vines
7625	First Baptist Church	Dallas, TX	SBC	Dr. W. A. Criswell
7500	W. Angeles Church of God	Los Angeles, CA	COGIC	Dr. Charles E. Blake
7400	Chapel Hill Harvester	Decatur, GA	INDC	Bishop Earl Paulk
7123	Calvary Church	Santa Ana, CA	IND	Dr. David Hocking
7001	Bellevue Baptist Church	Cordova, TN	SBC	Dr. Adrian Rogers
7000	Lakewood Church	Houston, TX	INDC	Dr. John Osteen
6621	Crystal Cathedral	Garden Grove, CA	RCA	Dr. Robert Schuller
6500	Pleasant Grove M. Baptist	Houston, TX	NBC/USA	Dr. Charles Jackson
6200	Overlake Christian	Kirkland, WA	ICC	Dr. Bob Moorehead
6150	First Baptist Church	Houston, TX	SBC	Dr. John Bisagno
6000	Elmbrook Church	Waukesha, WI	IND	Dr. Stuart Briscoe
6000	Beaverton Foursquare Church	Beaverton, OR	FSQ	Dr. Ron Mehl
6000	Crenshaw Christian Center	Los Angeles, CA	INDC	Dr. Fred K.C. Price
6000	Calvary Chapel	W. Covina, CA	CALC	Pastor Raul Ries
5900	Capital Christian Center	Sacramento, CA	AG	Dr. Glen D. Cole
5800	New Hope Community	Portland, OR	INDC	Rev. Dale E. Galloway
5800	Peachtree Presbyterian	Atlanta, GA	PCUSA	Dr. Frank Harrington
5787	Mt. Olivet Lutheran	Minneapolis, MN	ELCA	Dr. Paul M. Youngdahl
5700	Calvary Chapel	Albuquerque, NM	CALC	Pastor Skip Heitzig
5666	Southeast Christian	Louisville, KY	ICC	Dr. Robert L. Russell
5645	Chapel in University Park	Akron, OH	IND	Rev. Knute Larson
5500	Horizon Fellowship	San Diego, CA	CALC	Pastor Mike McIntosh
5345	Church on the Way	Van Nuys, CA	FSQ	Dr. Jack Hayford
5210	Full Gospel Tabernacle	Orchard Park, NY	AG	Dr. Tommy Reid
5200	Trinity Baptist Church	San Antonio, TX	SBC	Dr. Buckner Fanning
5160	Young Nak Presbyterian	Los Angeles, CA	KPCA	Rev. Hee Min Park
5048	Oriental Mission Church	Los Angeles, CA	IND	Dr. Byung H. Lee
5000	Brentwood Baptist Church	Houston, TX	SBC	Dr. Joe S. Ratliff
5000	Bethany World Prayer Center	Baker, LA	INDC	Rev. Larry Stockstill
5000	Hartford Memorial Baptist	Detroit, MI	PNB	Dr. Charles Adams
5000	South Coast Community Ch	Newport Beach, CA	INDC	Rev. Bob Shank

Att.	Name	City, ST	Affil.	Pastor
5000	World Harvest Church	Columbus, OH	INDC	Rev. Rod Parsley
4800	Mt. Ephraim Baptist	Atlanta, GA	NBC	Rev. R. L. White
4700	First Assembly of God	Tacoma, WA	AG	Dr. Fulton W. Buntain
4700	Word of Faith Center	Detroit, MI	INDC	Rev. Keith Butler
4680	First Baptist Church	Atlanta, GA	SBC	Dr. Charles Stanley
4600	Vineyard Christian Fellowship	Wheatridge, CO	INDC	Pastor Tom Stipe
4500	Roswell Street Baptist	Marietta, GA	SBC	Dr. Nelson Price
4500	People's Church	Fresno, CA	AG	Dr. George L. Johnson
4500	Crossroads Cathedral	Oklahoma City, OK	AG	Dr. Daniel T. Sheaffer
4500	Church of the Open Door	Crystal MN, MN	CMA	Rev. David Johnson
4500	Emmanuel Faith Comm Ch	Escondido, CA	IND	Dr. Richard Strauss
4452	Washington National COG	Ft. Washington, MD	COGC	Dr. T. L. Lowery
4400	Bethel AME Church	Baltimore, MD	AME	Rev. Frank M. Reid III
4390	Boston Church of Christ	Woburn, MA	CC	Randy McKean
4390	Church of Christ	Boston, MA	CC	Rev. Al Baird
4300	Christian Life Center	Stockton, CA	UP	Dr. Kenneth F. Haney
4200	Trinity Baptist Church	Jacksonville, FL	IB	Dr. Bob Gray
4200	Christian Faith Center	Seattle, WA	IND	Pastor Casey Treat
4200	Faith Fellowship Outreach	Edison, NJ	INDC	Dr. David DeMola
4120	First Baptist Church	Milford, OH	SBC	Pastor Charles Keen
4120	Prestonwood Baptist	Dallas, TX	SBC	Dr. Jack Graham
4100	First Baptist Church	Jackson, MS	SBC	Dr. Frank Pollard
4079	Central Church	Memphis, TN	IND	Dr. James Latimer
4050	Victory Christian Center	Tulsa, OK	INDC	Rev. Billy Joe Daugherty
4000	Coral Ridge Presbyterian	Ft. Lauderdale, FL	PCA	Dr. James Kennedy
4000	Sweetwater Church-Valley	Glendale, AZ	INDC	Rev. Glen Foster
4000	First Baptist Church	Euless, TX	SBC	Dr. Jimmy Draper*
3897	Cornerstone Church	San Antonio, TX	INDC	Dr. John C. Hagee
3883	San Jacinto Baptist Church	Amarillo, TX	SBC	Dr. Stan Coffey
3879	Eastside Foursquare Church	Kirkland, WA	FSQ	Rev. Doug Murren
3875	Windsor Village U. Meth Ch	Houston, TX	UMC	Dr. Kirbyjon H. Caldwell
3843	First Baptist Church	Orlando, FL	SBC	Dr. Jim Henry
3823	Saddleback Community	Mission Viejo, CA	SBC	Rev. Rick Warren
3768	Valley Cathedral	Phoenix, AZ	INDC	Dr. Donald Price
3750	Faith Tabernacle	Oklahoma City, OK	AG	Dr. Coy R. Barker
3750	Loveland Missionary Baptist	Fontana, CA	SBC	Dr. Charles Singleton
3750	Evangel Christian Center	Louisville, KY	AG	Rev. Bob Rodgers
3747	First Assembly of God	Grand Rapids, MI	AG	Rev. Wayne M. Benson, Sr.
3679	Rolling Hills Covenant Church	Rolling Hls Estate, CA	ECOV	Rev. Gordon E. Kirk*
3540	First Presbyterian Church	Mt. Clemens, MI	PCUSA	Dr. Robert W. Battles, Jr.
3527	Frazer Memorial UMC	Montgomery, AL	UMC	Rev. John Mathison
3510	Madison Church of Christ	Madison, TN	CC	Dr. Steve Flatt
3500	Full Faith Church of Love	Shawnee, KS	INDC	Rev. Ernie Gruen
3500	Templo Calvario	Santa Ana, CA	AG	Rev. Daniel de Leon
3500	Miss. Blvd. Christian Church	Memphis, TN	DIS	Pastor Alvin O. Jackson
3500	Allen Temple Baptist Church	Oakland, CA	ABC	Dr. J. Alfred Smith, Jr.
3500	Akron Baptist Temple	Akron, OH	IB	Dr. Charles Billington
3500	Xenos Christian Fellowship	Columbus, OH	INDC	Rev. Dennis McCallum
3500	Chapel on N. Forrest Road	Williamsville, NY	INDC	Dr. James W. Andrews
3500	Concord Baptist Church	Dallas, TX	NBCA	Rev. E.K. Bailey
3500	Applegate Christian Center	Jacksonville, OR	CALC	Pastor John Courson
3400	Champion Forest Baptist	Houston, TX	SBC	Dr. O. Damon Shook
3384	Cherry Hills Community	Englewood, CO	EP	Dr. J.M. Dixon
3384	Cherry Creek Presbyterian Ch	Englewood, CO	EP	Rev. Mark A. Brewer
3374	Scottsdale Bible Church	Scottsdale, AZ	IND	Rev. Darryl DelHousaye

Att.	Name	City, ST	Affil.	Pastor
3350	Higher Dimensions Center	Tulsa, OK	INDC	Dr. Carlton Pearson
3329	Menlo Park Presbyterian	Menlo Park, CA	PCUSA	Rev. Walt Gerber
3315	Lake Avenue Congregational	Pasadena, CA	CCCC	Rev. Jerry Johnson

* No longer pastor at this church.

The information listed above excludes churches that prefer not to share their growth data.

100 LARGEST SUNDAY SCHOOLS IN AMERICA

1991 Sunday School Attendance

ATT.	CHURCH	CITY, STATE	AFF.	PASTOR
20000*	First Baptist Church	Hammond, IN	IB	Dr. Jack Hyles
10543	First Assembly of God ***	Phoenix, AZ	AG	Dr. Tommy J. Barnett
9336	Metro Assembly of God ***	Brooklyn, NY	AG	Rev. Bill Wilson
9000	Harvest Christian Fellowship	Riverside, CA	CALC	Pastor Greg Laurie
7629	Willow Creek Community Ch	S. Barrington, IL	IND	Pastor Bill Hybels
7558	First Baptist Church ***	Dallas, TX	SBC	Joel C. Gregory
6654	First Baptist Church	Jacksonville, FL	SBC	Drs. Lindsey Jr./Jerry Vines
6004*	University Presbyterian	Seattle, WA	PCUSA	Rev. Earl Palmer
5583	Second Baptist Church	Houston, TX	SBC	Dr. H. Edwin Young
5210	Capital Christian Center	Sacramento, CA	AG	Dr. Glen D. Cole
5176	Bellevue Baptist Church	Cordova, TN	SBC	Dr. Adrian Rogers
4820	First Baptist Church	Houston, TX	SBC	Dr. John Bisagno
4675	First Assembly of God	Tacoma, WA	AG	Dr. Fulton W. Buntain
4500*	Crossroads Cathedral	Oklahoma City, OK	AG	Dr. Daniel T. Sheaffer
4486	First Assembly of God	Grand Rapids, MI	AG	Rev. Wayne M. Benson, Sr.
4250	Trinity Baptist Church	Jacksonville, FL	IB	Dr. Bob Gray
4205	Prestonwood Baptist Church	Dallas, TX	SBC	Dr. Jack Graham
3750**	New Life Church	Philadelphia, PA	AG	Rev. Tony McCreary
3700**	Grace Community Church	Sun Valley, Ca	BIB	Dr. John MacArthur
3601	First Baptist Church	Orlando, FL	SBC	Dr. Jim Henry
3500**	Calvary Church	Santa Ana, CA	IND	Dr. David Hocking
3327	First Baptist Church	Atlanta, GA	SBC	Dr. Charles Stanley
3190	Chapel in University Park	Akron, OH	IND	Rev. Knute Larson
3060	Hyde Park Baptist Church	Austin, TX	SBC	Dr. Ralph M. Smith
3007	First Baptist Church	Midland, TX	SBC	Dr. James C. Denison
3000	Skyline Wesleyan Church	Lemon Grove, CA	WES	Dr. John Maxwell
2900**	Peachtree Presbyterian Ch	Atlanta, GA	PCUSA	Dr. Frank Harrington
2896	Green Acres Baptist Church	Tyler, TX	SBC	Dr. David O. Dykes
2819	First Baptist Church	Arlington, TX	SBC	Dr. Charles R. Wade
2800*	Happy Church	Denver, CO	AG	Rev. Wallace R. Hickey
2794	First Baptist Church	Euless, TX	SBC	Dr. Jimmy Draper ****
2771	Central Church	Memphis, TN	IND	Dr. James Latimer
2722	Ward Evangelical Presbyterian	Livonia, MI	EP	Dr. Bartlett L. Hess
2714	Mt. Paran Church of God	Atlanta, GA	COGC	Dr. Paul L. Walker
2684	Champion Forest Baptist Ch	Houston, TX	SBC	Dr. O. Damon Shook
2674	Templo Calvario Assembly	Santa Ana, CA	AG	Rev. Daniel de Leon
2651	First Baptist Church	Springdale, AR	SBC	Dr. Ronnie Floyd
2588*	Grace Presbyterian Church	Peoria, IL	PCUSA	Rev. Bruce Dunn
2569	First Baptist Church	Jackson, MS	SBC	Dr. Frank Pollard
2550**	Highland Park Presbyterian Ch	Dallas, TX	PCUSA	Dr. B. Clayton Bell
2536	Sagemont Baptist Church	Houston, TX	SBC	Dr. John Morgan
2529**	Assembly of God	Pace, FL	AG	Rev. Glyn Lowery, Jr.
2504**	Southeast Christian Center	Louisville, KY	ICC	Dr. Robert L. Russell

Att.	Name	City, ST	Affil.	Pastor
2500	Young Nak Presbyterian Ch	Los Angeles, CA	KPCA	Rev. Hee Min Park
2500	Park Cities Baptist Church	Dallas, TX	SBC	Dr. James L. Pleitz
2466**	Lake Avenue Cong Church	Pasadena, CA	CCCC	Dr. Gordon Kirk
2374	Saddleback Valley Comm Ch	Mission Viejo, CA	SBC	Rev. Richard D. Warren
2360	Madison Church of Christ	Madison, TN	CC	Dr. Steve Flatt
2359	Shades Mt. Baptist Church	Birmingham, AL	SBC	Dr. Charles Carter
2323	Graceland Baptist Church	New Albany, IN	SBC	Rev. Steve Marcum
2320	Lakeview Temple	Indianapolis, IN	AG	Rev. Thomas Paino
2316	Roswell Street Baptist Church	Marietta, GA	SBC	Dr. Nelson Price
2300*	Washington National COG	Ft. Washington, MD	COGC	Dr. T.L. Lowery
2291	Wheaton Bible Church	Wheaton, IL	BIB	Dr. David Krental
2263	First Southern Baptist Church	Del City, OK	SBC	Dr. Tom Elliff
2258	Highview Baptist Church	Louisville, KY	SBC	Rev. William Hancock
2255	First Baptist Church	Amarillo, TX	SBC	Dr. Ben Loring
2237	Casas Adobes Baptist Church	Tucson, AZ	SBC	Rev. Roger Barrier, Jr.
2229	Rehobeth Baptist Church	Tucker, GA	SBC	Dr. Richard G. Lee
2225	Grace Community Church	Tempe, AZ	BIB	Dr. Larry Finch
2225*	First Presbyterian Church	Flint, MI	PCUSA	Dr. William N. Jackson
2218	Frazer Memorial U. Meth Ch	Montgomery, AL	UMC	Rev. John Mathison
2200	Briarwood Presbyterian Ch	Birmingham, AL	PCUSA	Dr. Frank Barker
2183	Mount Hope Church	Lansing, MI	AG	David R. Williams
2170	Travis Avenue Baptist Church	Ft. Worth, TX	SBC	Interim Pastor
2170	Trinity Baptist Church	San Antonio, TX	SBC	Dr. Buckner Fanning
2169	First Baptist Church	Pasadena, TX	SBC	Dr. Charles Redmond
2117	First Baptist Church	Jonesboro, GA	SBC	Dr. Charles Carter
2109	Full Gospel Tabernacle	Orchard Park, NY	AG	Rev. Thomas F. Reid
2098	Hickory Grove Baptist Church	Charlotte, NC	SBC	Dr. Joe B. Brown
2096	People's Church	Fresno, CA	AG	Dr. George L. Johnson
2090	Metro Assembly of God	Cleveland, OH	AG	Rev. James W. Davidson
2082	Menlo Park Presbyterian Ch	Menlo Park, CA	PCUSA	Rev. Walt Gerber
2069	Cottage Hill Baptist Church	Mobile, AL	SBC	Dr. Fred Wolfe
2048	Calvary Temple	Irving, TX	AG	Rev. J. Don George
2047	Hoffmantown Baptist Church	Albuquerque, NM	SBC	Dr. Charles Lowery
2046	First Baptist Church	W. Palm Beach, FL	SBC	Dr. Keith Thomas
2045	Eastside Baptist Church	Marietta, GA	SBC	Dr. Clark Hutchinson
2044	First Baptist Church	Roanoke, VA	SBC	Dr. Charles Fuller
2042	First Baptist Church	Norfolk, VA	SBC	Dr. Kenneth S. Hemphill
2000	First Presbyterian	Greensboro, NC	PCUSA	Dr. Jerold Shetler
2000	Iglesia Puerta Del Cielo	El Paso, TX	AG	Rev. Marco A. Aquire
1996*	Myers Park Presbyterian	Charlotte, NC	PCUSA	Rev. Timothy Croft
1984	Calvary Baptist Church	Winston-Salem, NC	SBC	Dr. Mark Corts
1981	Braeswood Assembly of God	Houston, TX	AG	Pastor Earl J. Banning
1980	First Baptist Church	Carrollton, TX	SBC	Dr. Wayne Allen
1971	Whitesburg Baptist Church	Huntsville, AL	SBC	Rev. Jimmy E. Jackson
1960*	Trinity United Presbyterian Ch	Santa Ana, CA	PCUSA	Rev. George Munzing
1945	Community Church of Joy	Glendale, AZ	ELCA	Walt P. Kallestad
1936	Dawson Memorial Baptist Ch	Birmingham, AL	SBC	Rev. Gary Fenton
1920**	Calvary Church	Charlotte, NC	IND	Rev. Ross s. Rhoads
1900**	Los Gatos Christian Church	Los Gatos, CA	ICC	Dr. Daniel Henderson
1900**	First Presbyterian Church	Jackson, MS	PCUSA	Dr. James Baird
1886	Germantown Baptist Church	Germantown, TN	SBC	Dr. Ken Story
1870*	Coral Ridge Presbyterian Ch	Ft. Lauderdale, FL	PCA	Dr. James Kennedy
1840	Trinity Life Center	Las Vegas, NV	AG	Rev. Richard M. Guerra
1832	First Baptist Church	Lubbock, TX	SBC	Dr. Hayes Wicker
1824	Eastwood Baptist Church	Tulsa, OK	SBC	Rev. Ruffin Snow

Att.	Name	City, ST	Affil.	Pastor
1815	First Church of the Nazarene	Bethany, OK	NAZ	Dr. Melvin McCullough
1800	First Presbyterian Church	Colorado Springs, CO	PCUSA	Dr. John H. Stevens
1800**	First Presbyterian Church	Orlando, FL	PCUSA	Dr. J. Howard Edington
1800	Metro Assembly of God	Atlanta, GA	AG	Karen D. Bennett
1800*	Grace Presbyterian Church	Houston, TX	PCUSA	Dr. David G. McKechnie

* 1989 Attendance.
** 1990 Attendance.
*** Includes off-campus Sunday School.
**** No longer pastor at this church.
The information listed above excludes churches that prefer not to share their growth data.
Copyright © 1992. Dr. John N. Vaughan. All Internationl rights reserved. Address: Southwest Baptist University, 1601 S. Springfield, Bolivar, MO 65613. Phone: (417) 326-1773 Fax: (417) 326-1783. Correspondence welcome.

100 FASTEST GROWING CHURCHES IN AMERICA

1989-1990 Fastest-Growing Churches

No.	89-90 Gain	'89 Wor.	'90 Wor.	Church	City, ST	Aff.	Pastor
1	3250	1550	4800	World Changers	College Park, GA	INDC	Rev. Creflo Dollar
2	2500	4000	6500	Pleasant Grove M. Bapt Ch	Houston, TX	NBC-USA	Dr. Charles Jackson
	2500	5000	7500	W. Angeles COGC	Los Angeles, CA	COGIC	Bishop Charles E. Blake
3	2104	4897	7001	Bellevue Baptist Church	Cordova, TN	SBC	Dr. Adrian Rogers
4	2000	2500	4500	Church of the Open Door	Crystal, MN	CMA	Rev. David Johnson
5	1527	2348	3875	Windsor Village U. Meth Ch	Houston, TX	UMC	Dr. Kirbyjon H. Caldwell
6	1409	265	1674	Los Angeles Ch of Christ	Santa Monica, CA	CC	Kip McKean & Marty Fuqua
7	1300	1700	3000	Times Square Church	Manhattan, NY	INDC	Rev. David Wilkerson
	1300	4500	5800	Peachtree Presbyterian Ch	Atlanta, GA	PCUSA	Dr. W. Frank Harrington
	1300	1500	2800	Riverbend Baptist Church	Austin, TX	SBC	Dr. Gerald Mann
8	1200	2000	3200	Calvary Chapel	Ontario, CA	CALC	Pastor David Rosales
	1200	3500	4700	Word of Faith Center	Detroit, MI	INDC	Rev. Keith Butler
9	1183	2700	3883	San Jacinto Baptist Ch	Amarillo, TX	SBC	Dr. Stan Coffey
	1183	5438	6621	Crystal Cathedral	Garden Grove, CA	RCA	Dr. Robert Schuller
10	1123	6000	7123	Calvary Church	Santa Ana, CA	IND	Dr. David Hocking
11	1080	11923	13003	Willow Creek Comm Ch	S. Barrington, IL	IND	Rev. Bill Hybels
12	1019	2136	3155	Calvary Christian Center	Sacramento, CA	INDC	Dr. Phillip Goudeaux
13	1000	6000	7000	Lakewood Church	Houston, TX	INDC	Dr. John Osteen
	1000	3000	4000	Sweetwater Church-Valley	Glendale, AZ	INDC	Rev. Glen Foster
	1000	5000	6000	Calvary Chapel	W. Covina, CA	CALC	Raul Ries
14	990	1210	2200	Parkway Christ Fellowship	Birmingham, AL	INDC	Rev. Mark Correll
15	969	5181	6150	First Baptist Church	Houston, TX	SBC	Dr. John Bisagno
16	900	1200	2100	Heritage Christian Center	Denver, CO	INDC	Rev. Dennis Leonard
17	885	7327	8212	Deliverance Evang Ch	Philadelphia, PA	INDC	Dr. Benjamin Smith
18	884	2500	3384	Cherry Creek Presby Ch	Englewood, CO	EP	Rev. Mark A. Brewer
19	848	4200	5048	Oriental Mission Church	Los Angeles, CA	KPCA	Dr. Byung H. Lee
20	800	4000	4800	Mt. Ephriam Baptist Ch	Atlanta, GA	NBC	Rev. R. L. White
	800	2300	3100	New St. Paul Tabernacle	Detroit, MI	COGIC	Bishop P. A. Brooks
	800	2100	2900	First Baptist Church	Merritt Island, FL	SBC	Larry L. Thompson
	800	2000	2800	New Life Church	Colorado Springs, CO	INDC	Rev. Ted Haggard
21	774	1226	2000	Lover's Lane U Meth Ch	Dallas, TX	UMC	Dr. Donald R. Benton
22	750	5000	5750	World Harvest Church	Columbus, OH	INDC	Rev. Rod Parsley
23	728	610	1338	Indiana Avenue Baptist Ch	Lubbock, TX	SBC	Rev. Jon D. Randles
24	700	2000	2700	Family Christian Center	Griffith, IN	INDC	Rev. Steve Munsey
	700	1300	2000	Korean Presby Ref Ch	Los Angeles, CA	CRC	Dr. John Eui-Whan Kim
	700	2200	2900	East Hill Foursquare Ch	Gresham, OR	FSQ	Dr. Ted Roberts
	700	3600	4300	Christian Life Center	Stockton, CA	UP	Rev. Kenneth F. Haney
	700	2800	3500	Applegate Chr Fellowship	Jacksonville, OR	CALC	Pastor Jon Courson
	700	2800	3500	Mississippi Blvd. Chr Ch	Memphis, TN	DIS	Pastor Alvin O. Jackson
	700	2000	2700	Belmont Church	Nashville, TN	CC	Dr. Don Finto
	700	4500	5200	Trinity Baptist Church	San Antonio, TX	SBC	Dr. Buckner Fanning
25	680	1000	1680	Vineyard Chr Fellowship	Cincinnati, OH	IND	Rev. Steve Sjogren
26	678	2292	2970	New York City Chof Christ	New York, NY	CC	Steve Johnson

No.	88-89 Gain	'88 Wor.	'89 Wor.	Church	City	State	Affil.Pastor
27	650	2600	3250	Trinity Church	Lubbock, TX	INDC	Rev. Randall Ross
28	647	3503	4150	Saddleback Valley Comm Ch	Mission Viejo, CA	SBC	Pastor Rick Warren
29	636	5030	5666	Southeast Christian Ch	Louisville, KY	ICC	Robert L. Russell
30	623	1727	2350	San Diego Ch of Christ	San Diego, CA	CC	Pastor Dave Weger
31	610	90	700	Victory Baptist Church	Richardson, TX	SBC	Darrell L. Gilyard
32	608	1292	1900	Community Baptist Ch	Alta Loma, CA	GCB	Dr. Robert V. Acker
33	600	3600	4200	Christian Faith Center	Seattle, WA	IND	Pastor Casey Treat
	600	1600	2200	First Baptist Church	Snellville, GA	SBC	Dr. James Merritt
	600	3600	4200	Faith Fellowship Ministries	Edison, NJ	INDC	Dr. David T. Demola
	600	1200	1800	Calvary Chapel of Phil	Feasterville, PA	INDC	Rev. Joe Focht
	600	2100	2700	Alamo City Baptist Ch	San Antonio, TX	SBC	Dr. David C. Walker
	600	2750	3350	Higher Dimension Ev Ctr	Tulsa, OK	INDC	Rev. Carlton Pearson
	600	3279	3879	Eastside Foursquare Ch	Kirkland, WA	FSQ	Rev. Doug Murren
34	590	1700	2290	Trinity Fellowship	Amarillo, TX	INDC	Rev. Jimmy Evans
35	585	900	1485	First Baptist Church	Albuquerque, NM	SBC	Rev. Joe McKinney
36	578	1857	2435	College Avenue Baptist Ch	San Diego, CA	BGC	Dr. Gerald Sheveland
37	570	1390	1960	Christ Church	Nashville, TN	INDC	Dr. L.H. Hardwick, Jr.
38	564	1750	2314	Central Church of God	Charlotte, NC	COGC	Rev. H. Loran Livingston
39	550	3200	3750	Evangel Christian Life Ctr	Louisville, KY	AG	Rev. Bob Rodgers
	550	1400	1950	Cedar Springs Presby Ch	Knoxville, TN	PCA	Rev. John M. Wood
	550	1950	2500	Metropolitan Baptist Ch	Houston, TX	SBC	Dr. Curtis Dodd
40	540	1560	2100	Harvest Church	Mt. Rainier, MD	INDC	Dr. James Thompson
41	539	1750	2289	Evangelical Free Church	Hershey, PA	EFC	Rev. David V. Martin
42	530*	7095	7625*	First Baptist Church	Dallas, TX	SBC	Dr. Joel C. Gregory
43	525	1700	2225	Calvary Baptist Church	Winston-Salem, NC	SBC	Dr. C. Mark Corts
44	523	1835	2358	Chicago Church of Christ	Berkeley, IL	CC	** Ron Drabot
45	500	2000	2500	First Assembly of God	Shreveport, LA	AG	Rev. Rodney Duron
	500	850	1350	New Life Chr Fellowship	Jacksonville, FL	INDC	Rev. Paul Zink
	500	3000	3500	Allen Temple Baptist Ch	Oakland, CA	ABC	Dr. J. Alfred Smith, Jr.
	500	2500	3000	Metro Vineyard Fellowship	Kansas City, MO	INDC	Pastor Mike Sullivan
	500	2000	2500	Castle Hills First BaptCh	San Antonio, TX	SBC	Dr. George H. Harris
	500	800	1300	Northland Community Ch	Longwood, FL	IND	Dr. Joel C. Hunter
	500	1700	2200	Oak Cliff Bible Fellowship Ch	Dallas, TX	IND	Rev. Anthony Evans
	500	4500	5000	Brentwood Baptist Ch	Houston, TX	SBC	Dr. Joe S. Ratliff
	500	4100	4600	Vineyard Chr Fellowship	Wheat Ridge, CO	INDC	Pastor Tom Stipe
	500	2700	3200	Hickory Grove Baptist Ch	Charlotte, NC	SBC	Dr. Joe B. Brown
	500	600	1100	Believer's Chapel	Cicero, NY	INDC	Rev. Paul Wagner
	500	4000	4500	Roswell Street Baptist Ch	Marietta, GA	SBC	Dr. Nelson Price
	500	3000	3500	Xenos Chr Fellowship	Columbus, OH	INDC	Dennis McCallum
	500	1500	2000	Brooklyn Tabernacle Ctr	Brooklyn, NY	IND	Bishop James S. Copeland
	500	2100	2600	The Church at Rocky Peak	Chatsworth, CA	IND	Dr. David Miller
	500*	2700	3200*	Green Acres Baptist Ch	Tyler, TX	SBC	David O. Dykes
	500	2500	3000	Dawson Memorial Bapt Ch	Birmingham, AL	SBC	Dr. Gary Fenton
	500	2500	3000	Calvary Temple	Denver, CO	INDC	Dr. Charles E. Blair
	500	1200	1700	Fellowship Bible Ch N	Plano, TX	IND	Rev. Gene Getz
	500	500	1000	Berendo St. Baptist Ch	Los Angeles, CA	SBC	Sung Kun Park
	500	2100	2600	Arlington Christian Center	Arlington, TX	INDC	Rev. James Hester
	500	1200	1700	Bread of Life Church	Houston, TX	INDC	Rev. Dusty Kemp
	500	3550	4050	Victory Christian Center	Tulsa, OK	INDC	Rev. Billy Joe Daugherty
	500	1000	1500	Grace United Presby Ch	Houston, TX	PCUSA	Dr. David G. McKechnie
46	488	1212	1700	Christ Memorial Ref Ch	Holland, MI	CRC	Dr. Timothy Brown
47	478	2372	2850	Calvary Church	Charlotte, NC	IND	Dr. Ross S. Rhoads
48	470	480	950	Hunter St. Baptist Church	Birmingham, AL	SBC	Rev. Buddy Gray
49	457	1019	1476	Life Christian Center	St. Louis, MO	INDC	Rev. Rick Shelton
50	450	1350	1800	Calvary Baptist Temple	Savannah, GA	SBC	Dr. Len B. Turner
	450	2850	3300	Sunshine Ministry Center	Grand Rapids, MI	CRC	Rev. Lewis Vander Meer

* Includes missions.
** Pastor now serves as pastor of another congregation.
The information listed above excludes churches that prefer not to share their growth data.

24 MEGAREASONS FOR THE MEGACHURCH PHENOMENON

1. Gradual disappearance of denominationally loyal churchgoers born before 1930 who preferred the intimacy and spontaneity of life in a small congregation.
2. Growing number of people who commute 3 to 40 miles to work and find it easy to commute 5 to 20 miles to church.
3. Improvement in the quality and safety of highways.
4. Convenient off-street parking.
5. Higher-quality physical facilities, preaching, music, nurseries, teaching, and youth ministries.
6. Freedom to ignore denominational labels and shop for a church that meets needs.
7. Rapid increase in exodus of people born since 1945 from Roman Catholic churches into evangelical and charismatic Protestant congregations.
8. Most Americans born after 1940 grew up in a world of big institutions.
9. Capability to design and staff range of specialized ministries.
10. The power of the critical mass—the 26-year-old looking for a spouse is more likely to be successful in a singles ministry that includes 1,200 people than in a group of 9 singles.
11. Shift in priorities in many denominations from people and needs to institutions and tradition.
12. Focus on attendance in megachurches contrasted with emphasis on membership in long-established congregations.
13. More persuasive public relations and advertising program in megachurches.
14. Sensitivity and responsiveness to "the market" as opposed to smaller congregations driven by tradition.
15. Refusal by municipalities to grant permission to long-established congregations to increase off-street parking or physical facilities because of complaints from the neighbors.
16. Decision by a growing proportion of the 3 to 7 million Americans who attend two churches every week in order to have their religious needs met to switch to "one-stop shopping" at a megachurch.
17. Search by millions of people born in the 1942-67 era for a Christ-centered church that offers Bible-centered preaching and teaching.
18. Capability of the larger churches to offer a broad range of choices for worship and ministry.
19. Inability of the vast majority of Protestant churches in the late 1960s to welcome the Jesus People.
20. Greater preference for a faster pace for corporate worship.
21. Shift toward the theological Left by many pastors, while most of the churchgoers born since 1955 are theologically more conservative than their parents.
22. Satisfaction by members to learn that 20 to 35 percent of their contributions are allocated to missions, benevolences, and community outreach compared to the 10 to 16 percent typical of smaller congregations.
23. Inability or unwillingness of majority of long-established churches to accommodate that growing number of self-identified charismatic Christians who seek a church with a prayer-and-praise service.
24. Trend in American society toward larger institutions.

Source: Lyle E. Schaller in *Christianity Today* magazine, March 5, 1990 issue. Used by permission.

50 LARGEST CHURCHES IN THE WORLD

1991 Worship Attendance

ATT.	CHURCH	CITY, STATE, COUNTRY	PASTOR
600,000	Yoido Full Gospel Church	Seoul, KOREA	Dr. Cho, Paul Yonggi
105,000	Nambu Full Gospel Church	Anyang, KOREA	Cho, Yong Mok

Att.	Church	City, State, Country	Pastor
99,000	Jotabeche M. Pentecostal Ch	Santiago, CHILE	Jose Javier Vasquez
80,000	Vision de Futuro	Sante Fe, ARGENTINA	Omar Cabrera
70,000	Miracles of Jesus Church	Buenos Aires, ARGENTINA	Hector Jimenez
70,000	Deeper Christian Life Ministry	Lagos, NIGERIA	William Kumuyi
56,000	Kum Ran Methodist Church	Seoul, KOREA	Kim, Hong Do
50,000	Elim Church	San Salvador, EL SALVADOR	Sergio Solorzano
47,887	Soong Eui Methodist Church	Seoul, KOREA	Lee, Ho Moon
42,000	Ju-an Presbyterian Church	Seoul, KOREA	Na, Kyum-Il
30,000	Sung Rak Baptist Church	Seoul, KOREA	Kim, Ki Dong
30,000	Kwang Lim Methodist Church	Seoul, KOREA	Kim, Sun Do
28,000	Young Nak Presbyterian Church	Seoul, KOREA	Lim, Young-soo
25,000	Bethel Church of God	Surabaya, INDONESIA	Dr. Abraham A. Tanusaputra
23,000	Hyesung Presbyterian Church	Seoul, KOREA	Yoo, Bok Jong
22,500	The So-mang Presbyterian Ch	Seoul, KOREA	Kwak, Sun Hee
20,000	First Baptist Church	Hammond, IN, USA	Dr. Jack Hyles
20,000	Miracle Center	Benin City, NIGERIA	Dr. Benson Idahosa
20,000	Centro Evangelical	San Salvador, EL SALVADOR	Hector Bojorquez
19,720	Ju-An Presbyterian Church	Seoul, KOREA	Pastor Kyum Il Na
19,000	Myungseong Presbyterian Ch	Seoul, KOREA	Kim, Sam Hwan
17,000	Kang Nam Full Gospel Church	Seoul, KOREA	Kim, Sung Kwang
15,867	Cathedral of Praise	Manila, PHILIPPINES	David Sumrall
15,000	Assembly of God	Campo de Sao Custovos, BRASIL	Notulu Barro Ferreira
14,000	Assembly of God Central	Culaba, Mato Grosso, BRAZIL	Sebastiao Rodriguez
13,003	Willow Creek Community Church	S. Barrington, IL, USA	Pastor Bill Hybels
13,000	Suyoungro Presbyterian Church	Pusan, KOREA	Chung, Pil Do
12,500	Masan Church of Resurrection	Masan, KOREA	Lee, Tae Hwa
12,000	Assembly of God Central	Belem, Para, BRAZIL	Armino Gouvela
12,000	Calvary Chapel	Santa Ana, CA, USA	Pastor Church Smith
12,000	San Hae Won Resurrection Ch	Kyong Nam, KOREA	Lee, Tai Hwa
12,000	The Hankook Jerusalem Church	Incheon, KOREA	Lee, Cho Seok
11,000	Assembly of God	Manaus, Amazonas, BRAZIL	Samuel Camara
10,543	First Assembly of God	Phoenix, AZ, USA	Dr. Tommy J. Barnett
10,500	Deeper Christian Life Ministry	Ibadan, NIGERIA	Isaiah Lawson
10,500	Kang Nam Joong Ang Baptist	Seoul, KOREA	Kim, Choong Ki
10,500	Bible Baptist Church	Cebu City, PHILIPPINES	Dr. Armie F. Jesilva
10,000	St. Mark's Cathedral	Cairo, EGYPT	Pope Shenouda II
10,000	Jesus is Lord Fellowship	Manila, PHILIPPINES	Eddie Villanueva
10,000	Incheon Full Gospel Church	Incheon, KOREA	Choi, Sung Kyu
10,000	Seobu Presbyterian Church	Pusan, KOREA	Lee, Jae Soon
10,000	Assembly of God Belenzinho	Sao Paulo, BRAZIL	Jose W. B. Da Costa
10,000	Assembly of God Central	Curitiba, Parana, BRAZIL	Jose Pimentel de Carvallo
9,500	Sa-rang Presbyterian Church	Seoul, KOREA	Ok, Han-Hum
9,175	Mt. Paran Church of God	Atlanta, GA, USA	Dr. Paul Walker
9,000	Calvary Church	Seoul, KOREA	Park, Cho-Choon
9,000	Taegu Full Gospel Church	Taegu, KOREA	Ko, Suk Hwan
9,000	Manmin Jungang Evang. Holiness	Seoul, KOREA	Lee, Jae Rok
9,000	Assembly of God Central	Recife, Pemambuco, BRAZIL	Jose Leoncio Da Silva
8,800	Deeper Christian Life Ministry	Kaduna, NIGERIA	Christopher Anasado

The information listed above excludes churches that prefer not to share their growth data.
Note: Most of the Latin America churches reflect both main church and satellite centers attendance. For information, additions, or corrections contact: Dr. John Vaughan, Southwest Baptist University, 1601 S. Springfield, Bolivar, MO 65613, USA. Telephone (417)326-1773. FAX (417)326-1783. International Copyright © 1992, Dr. John N. Vaughan. All rights reserved. Appreciation is expressed to U.S. denominations and churches and to the following people whose research assisted in portions of this research: Korea: Rev. Sang-sik Ham; USA: Dr. Peter Wagner, Dr. Vinson Synan.

HOW TO FIND A CHURCH THAT'S RIGHT FOR YOU

For each element enter a number from 1 to 10 in the space provided. A "1" indicates the church is totally inadequate for your needs in that area; a "10" suggests the church provides exactly what you are looking for.

When you are evaluating the relative appeal of churches, take into account how important each of the measured characteristics is in your own decision. There is no sense attending a church that is great in all the areas you don't care about, but flounders when it comes to the things you feel are most important—regardless of what the mathematics of this evaluation system indicate.

Evaluation Criteria

A. Spiritual beliefs about:
____God
____Jesus Christ
____the Holy Spirit
____communion
____the Bible
____sin, Satan
____salvation
____sacraments
____purpose of life
____the role of women
____baptism
____spiritual gifts
____social issues

B. Worship experience:
____sermons
____music
____service contents
____style of worship
____participation
____tone of worship
____prayer
____attitude toward worship

C. Leadership:
____sense of vision
____active laity
____opportunities to lead
____enough leaders
____discernible priorities
____knowledge of the Bible
____commitment to the Bible

D. People:
____friendly
____people your age
____committed
____involved with each other

____accepting of differences
____people you know are there
____congregational unity

E. Special programs:
____adult Sunday school
____youth program
____missions activity
____Bible study groups
____women's programs
____sports program
____community outreach
____evangelism
____prayer
____social events
____discipleship
____issues seminars
____entertainment events
____counseling

F. Opportunity for service:
____match members' gift with needs
____multiple opportunities
____appealing opportunities
____laity ownership or programs
____express gratitude for service
____time commitments expected

G. Structure:
____easy to meet people
____people involved
____ministers accessible
____well-organized
____method of government
____focus on people, not programs

____support groups
____in touch with community
____communications tools

H. Size:
____membership
____youth program

I. Location:
____security of area
____distance from home
____part of community

J. Facilities and equipment:
____condition of buildings
____sufficient space
____adequate parking
____athletic facilities
____classroom space
____library
____sound equipment
____video equipment

K. Affiliations:
____denomination
____community associations
____national coalitions

L. Follow-up by church:
____contacted
____reasons for their interest
____introductory class

George Barna in *How to Find* Your *Church.* Published by World Wide Publications. Copyright © 1989. Used by permission.

MAJOR DENOMINATIONAL GROUPS

by Robert Charles Walton

Group	Origins	Form of Government	Major Creedal Documents	Sacraments or Ordinances
Roman Catholic	Trace origins to Peter as first Pope; 451—primacy of Bishop of Rome formally recognized	Episcopal	Ecumenical creeds such as Nicea (325), Constantinople (381), and Chalcedon (451)	Infant baptism, penance, confirmation, Eucharist, marriage, ordination, extreme unction; (convey grace)
Orthodox	1054—Leo IX & Michael Cerularius finalized split developed over centuries; 1970—Orthodox Church of America	Episcopal	Ecumenical creeds of seven ecumenical councils prior to 787	Baptism by trine immersion, confirmation, Eucharist, penance, ordination, marriage, anointing of sick; (convey grace)
Lutheran	1517—Martin Luther posts 95 Theses in Wittenberg, Germany; break complete by 1520; 1748—Mohlenberg forms ministerium of PA	Incorporates both Episcopal and Congregational elements	1530—Augsburg Confession; 1577— Formula of Concord	Infant baptism, Lord's Supper (consubstantiation); (convey grace)
Reformed	16th century in Switzerland (Zwingli, Calvin), France (Huguenots), Germany, Hungary, Netherlands	Modified Presbyterian	1558— Gallican Confession; 1561—Belgic Confession; 1563—Heidelberg Catechism; 1566—2nd Helvetic Confession; 1619—Canons of Synod of Dordt	Infant baptism, Lord's Supper; (symbolic)
Anabaptist	1525—Conrad Grebel, Felix Manz in Zurich; later in Germany and Netherlands (Menno Simons); 1683—First Mennonites in PA Congregational		1527—Schleitheim Confession; generally anti-creedal	Believer's baptism (often by effusion), Lord's Supper (symbolic)
Episcopal	1534—Henry VIII repudiates papal authority; 1789—Protestant Episcopal church formed in Philadelphia, PA	Episcopal	Thirty-nine Articles (1563)	Infant baptism, Holy Communion, others; (convey grace)

Relationship to State	Other Emphases and Distinctives	Major Representatives in the United States (over 250,000 members)	Group
Vatican City is a sovereign state, and church is established by concordates with many nations	Pope as Vicar of Christ, apostolic succession, transubstantiation, authority of tradition (popes, councils, church fathers, Canon Laws) elaborate ritual, clerical celibacy, veneration of Mary & saints	Roman Catholic church	Roman Catholic
Affiliated with state in various nations of Eastern Europe and Middle East	Celibacy of monks and bishops only; Holy Spirit proceeds only from God the Father; elaborate ritual; veneration of icons	Orthodox Church in America; Greek archdiocese of North and South America	Orthodox
Close ties at one time in Germany and Scandinavia	Justification by faith; liturgical worship	Evangelical Lutheran Church of America; Lutheran Church, Missouri synod; Wisconsin Evangelical Lutheran synod	Lutheran
Close ties at one time in Switzerland, Netherlands	Calvinistic; simple worship emphasizing sermon	Reformed Church in America; Christian Reformed church; United Church of Christ (merger of various Congregational, Reformed, and Lutheran bodies)	Reformed
Oppose all church-state ties	Strict church discipline; simple lifestyle; pacifism; often practice foot washing; separation from world	None over 250,000 (American Anabaptists include Mennonites, Amish, and Hutterites)	Anabaptist
Established in England	*Book of Common Prayer* used in worship; archbishop of Canterbury recognized as head of Anglican communion; "Middle Way" between Catholics and Protestants	Episcopal church	Episcopal

Group	Origins	Form of Government	Major Creedal Documents	Sacraments or Ordinances
Presbyterian	1560—John Knox in Scotland; 1706—Francis Makemie forms Philadelphia Presbytery	Presbyterian	1648—Westminster Confession of Faith	Infant baptism, Lord's Supper (spiritual presence)
Baptist	16th Century Anabaptist; 1609—John Smyth, England, General Baptists; 1638—Eng. Particular Baptists; 1638—Roger Williams, Providence, R.I.	Congregational	1689—London Confession; 1742—Philadelphia Confession; 1832— New Hampshire Confession; generally noncreedal	Believer's baptism by immersion, Lord's Supper (symbolic)
Methodist	John Wesley in England; 1784—Asbury & Coke, Baltimore, Md.—Methodist Episcopal church; 1795—Methodist church in England	Episcopal	1739—Articles of Religion; generally noncreedal	Infant or believer's baptism by sprinkling, pouring, or immersion, Lord's Supper
Christian Church Disciples of Christ	Barton Stone, Ky.; Thomas & Alexander Campbell, Pa.; organized 1832	Congregational	Anticreedal	Believer's baptism by immersion, Lord's Supper (weekly)
Pentecostal	1901—Charles F. Parham, Topeka, Kans.; 1906—William J. Seymour, Azusa St. Revival	Mostly Congregational (some groups Episcopal)	Generally noncreedal	Believer's baptism by immersion, Lord's Supper

FOCUS BOOKS

***Dictionary of Pentecostal and Charismatic Movements,* edited by Stanley M. Burgess and Gary B. McGee. Winner of the 1990 Critic's Choice Award.** Published by Gospel Publishing House.

***Spreading the Flame* by Edward K. Pousson. Charts the worldwide independent charismatic missionary movement.** Published by Zondervan Publishing House.

Relationship to State	Other Emphases and Distinctives	Major Representatives in the United States (over 250,000 members)	Group
Established in Scotland	Calvinistic; plurality of elders; simple worship emphasizing sermon	Presbyterian Church, U.S.A.	Presbyterian
Emphasize separation of church and state	Autonomy of local church; freedom of conscience; simple worship emphasizing sermon	Southern Baptist Convention; American Baptist Convention; American Baptist Association; National Baptist Convention, U.S.A.; National Baptist Convention of America; National Primitive Baptist Association, U.S.A.; Conservative Baptist Association; General Association of Regular Baptists	Baptist
No church-state ties	Arminian; perfectionist; organization grew from Wesley's Methodist societies; emphasize social action	United Methodist church; African Methodist Episcopal church; Christian Methodist Episcopal church; Church of the Nazarene	Methodist
No church-state ties	Baptism necessary for salvation; return to New Testament Christianity; freedom of biblical interpretation; autonomy of local church; some groups reject instrumental music	Christian church (Disciples of Christ)	Christian church Disciples of Christ
No church-state ties	Holy Spirit baptism; speaking in tongues; divine healing; Arminian; perfectionist	Assemblies of God; Pentecostal Church of God in America; United Pentecostal Church International; Church of God (Cleveland, Tenn.); Church of God in Christ	Pentecostal

Robert Charles Watson is chairman, Bible Department, The Christian Academy, Media, Pa.

UNITED STATES DENOMINATIONAL STATISTICS

The following four pages provide current and noncurrent statistics for United States religious bodies, listed alphabetically. Current statistics are defined as those gathered and reported for 1990 and 1989. Those bodies having current statistics, and the statistics themselves, are shown in boldface type. Noncurrent statistics are those for 1988 or earlier. They appear in lightface type. No statistics for "Full, Communicant, or Confirmed members," "Number of Sunday or Sabbath Schools," and "Total Enrollment" are reported for bodies having noncurrent statistics.

Religious Body	Year Reported	No. of Churches	Inclusive Member-ship	Full, Commu-nicant or Confirmed Members	No. of Pastors Serving Parishes	Total No. of Clergy	No. of Sunday or Sabbath Schools	Total Enroll-ment
Advent Christian Church	1989	346	25,400	25,400	279	479	344	17,700
African Methodist Episcopal Church	1981	6,200	2,210,000		6,050	6,550		
African Methodist Episcopal Zion Ch.	1987	6,060	1,220,260		6,300	6,698		
Alaska Moravian Church	1987	23	5,159		11	15		
Albanian Orthodox Archdiocese in Am.	1978	16	40,000		18	25		
Albanian Orthodox Diocese of Am.	1990	2	714	714	1	3	2	58
Allegheny Wesleyan Meth. Connection (Orig. Allegheny Conf.)	1989	124	2,306	2,168	96	202	123	7,416
Amana Church Society	1990	1	450	400	N.R.	N.R.	1	44
American Baptist Association	1986	1,705	250,000		1,740	1,760		
American Baptist Churches in USA	1989	5,833	1,548,573	1,548,573	5,390	8,242	N.R.	308,335
American Carpatho-Russian Orthodox Greek Catholic Church	1990	71	20,000	20,000	79	92	71	1,650
American Rescue Workers	1984	20	2,700		35	53		
The Anglican Orthodox Church	1983	40	6,000		8	8		
The Antiochian Orthodox Christian Archdiocese of North America	1989	160	350,000	350,000	250	325	160	5,700
Apostolic Catholic Assyrian Church of the East, N. Am. Diocese	1989	22	120,000	120,000	92	109	22	1,050
Apostolic Christian Church (Nazarene)	1985	48	2,799		178	178		
Apostolic Christian Churches of Am.	1989	80	11,450	11,300	300	340	80	7,000
Apostolic Faith Mission of Portland, Oreg.	1989	50	4,100	4,100	76	86	50	6,600
Apostolic Faith Mission Church of God	1989	18	6,200	4,700	27	32	18	1,570
Apostolic Lutheran Church of Am.	1989	53	7,582	3,351	29	34	42	2,263
Apostolic Overcoming Holy Ch. of God	1988	177	12,479		127	130		
Armenian Apostolic Church of Am.	1990	30	180,000	30,000	24	29	17	450
Armenian Church of Am., Diocese of	1979	66	450,000		45	61		
Assemblies of God	1989	11,192	2,137,890	1,266,982	16,028	30,471	10,814	1,365,734
Assemblies of God, International Fellowship (Independent/Not Affiliated)	1962	136	N.R.		136	367		
Associate Reformed Presbyterian Church, General Synod	1989	182	38,274	32,600	162	245	170	16,732
Baptist Bible Fellowship, International	1986	3,449	1,405,900		3,400	4,500		
Baptist General Conference	1990	792	133,742	133,742	1,200	1,700	792	78,453
Baptist Missionary Assoc. of Am.	1989	1,339	229,315	229,315	1,350	2,648	1,335	97,613
Beachy Amish Mennonite Church	1989	99	6,872	6,872	376	376	99	N.R.
Berean Fundamental Church	1989	52	5,231	2,673	35	38	52	3,905
The Bible Church of Christ	1990	6	6,500	4,800	8	51	6	697
Bible Way Church of Our Lord Jesus Christ, World Wide, Inc.	1970	350	30,000		350	350		
Brethren Church (Ashland, Ohio)	1989	126	13,155	13,155	92	176	126	6,898
Brethren in Christ Church	1989	189	17,240	16,842	186	239	164	12,730
Buddhist Churches of America	1989	67	19,441	19,421	65	107	67	N.R.
Bulgarian Eastern Orthodox Church (Diocese of N. & S. Am./Australia)	1971	13	86,000		N.R.	11		
Christ Catholic Church	1989	12	1,394	1,146	10	11		
Christadelphians	1964	850	15,800					
The Christian and Missionary Alliance	1989	1,829	265,863	134,336	1,766	2,370	1,638	189,491
Christian Brethren (a.k.a. Plymouth Brethren)	1984	1,150	98,000		N.R.	500		
Christian Catholic Church (Evangelical Protestant)	1990	6	2,500	2,500	10	19	6	1,000
Christian Church (Disciples of Christ)	1989	4,113	1,052,271	690,115	3,895	6,897	4,113	318,730
Christian Church of N. Am., Gen. Council	1985	104	13,500		107	169		
Christian Churches and Churches of Christ	1988	5,579	1,070,616		5,525	6,596		
The Christian Congregation	1989	1,454	108,881	108,881	1,452	1,457	1,308	47,617
Christian Methodist Episcopal Church	1983	2,340	718,922		2,340	2,650		
Christian Nation Church, USA	1989	5	200	200	4	23	5	270
Christian Reformed Church in N. Am.	1989	712	225,699	145,308	624	1,099	N.R.	N.R.
Christian Union	1984	114	6,000		80	114		
Church of Christ	1972	32	2,400		169	188		
Church of Daniel's Band	1951	4	200		4	10		
The Church of God	1978	2,035	75,890		1,910	2,737		
Church of God (Anderson, Ind.)	1989	2,338	199,786	199,786	2,170	3,410	2,188	176,113
Church of God by Faith	1973	106	4,500		125	150		
Church of God (Cleveland, Tenn.)	1989	5,763	582,203	582,203	6,207	7,544	5,436	509,250
Church of God Gen. Conf. (Oregon, Ill.)	1990	88	5,718	4,399	66	87	88	3,334

Religious Body	Year Reported	No. of Churches	Inclusive Membership	Full, Communicant or Confirmed Members	No. of Pastors Serving Parishes	Total No. of Clergy	No. of Sunday or Sabbath Schools	Total Enrollment
The Church of God in Christ	1982	9,982	3,709,661		9,204	10,426		
The Church of God in Christ, Int'l	1982	300	200,000		700	1,600		
Church of God in Christ (Mennonite)	**1989**	**70**	**9,389**	**9,389**	**N.R.**	**N.R.**	**71**	**N.R.**
The Church of God of Prophecy	**1990**	**2,119**	**73,430**	**73,430**	**4,262**	**6,772**	**2,267**	**85,578**
The Church of God of the Mountain Assembly	**1990**	**104**	**4,238**	**3,826**	**67**	**129**	**104**	**5,500**
Church of God (Seventh Day), Denver	**1990**	**140**	**5,000**	**5,000**	**88**	**123**	**N.R.**	**N.R.**
Church of God (which He purchased with His own blood)	**1990**	**9**	**800**	**800**	**16**	**20**	**8**	**N.R.**
Church of Illumination	1983	4	9,000		60	60		
The Church of Jesus Christ (Bickertonites)	**1989**	**63**	**2,707**	**2,466**	**183**	**262**	**63**	**2,231**
The Church of Jesus Christ of Latter-Day Saints	**1989**	**9,049**	**4,175,400**	**3,630,400**	**27,147**	**30,960**	**9,049**	**3,329,000**
Church of Our Lord Jesus Christ of the Apostolic Faith	1954	155	45,000		150	185		
Church of the Brethren	**1989**	**1,102**	**149,681**	**149,681**	**1,911**	**2,436**	**N.R.**	**N.R.**
Church of the Living God (C.W.F.F.)	1985	170	42,000		N.R.	170		
Church of the Luth. Brethren of Am.	**1989**	**114**	**12,625**	**7,540**	**110**	**195**	**114**	**10,494**
Church of the Lutheran Confession	**1989**	**69**	**8,738**	**6,371**	**56**	**77**	**64**	**1,416**
Church of the Nazarene	**1989**	**5,158**	**561,253**	**558,664**	**4,313**	**9,138**	**4,990**	**864,703**
Churches of Christ	**1989**	**13,375**	**1,626,000**	**1,278,000**	**N.R.**	**N.R.**	**N.R.**	**N.R.**
Churches of Christ in Christian Union	**1989**	**250**	**9,674**	**9,674**	**151**	**317**	**250**	**13,561**
Churches of God, Gen. Conf.	**1989**	**350**	**33,909**	**33,909**	**305**	**500**	**346**	**27,253**
Community Churches, Int'l Council of	**1990**	**210**	**250,000**	**250,000**	**N.R.**	**350**	**N.R.**	**N.R.**
Congregational Christian Churches, Nat'l Assoc. of	**1990**	**400**	**90,000**	**90,000**	**400**	**450**	**N.R.**	**N.R.**
Congregational Holiness Church	1981	174	8,347		176	488		
Conservative Baptist Assoc. of Am.	**1989**	**1,126**	**210,000**	**210,000**	**1,126**	**1,324**	**N.R.**	**N.R.**
Conservative Congregational Christian Conference	**1989**	**180**	**28,413**	**28,413**	**271**	**457**	**164**	**12,094**
Coptic Orthodox Church	**1990**	**42**	**165,000**	**150,000**	**49**	**49**	**N.R.**	**6,600**
Cumberland Presbyterian Church	**1989**	**743**	**90,906**	**84,866**	**590**	**717**	**743**	**41,009**
Duck River (and Kindred) Assoc. of Baptists	1975	85	8,632		148	148		
Elim Fellowship	1983	36	N.R.		144	185		
The Episcopal Church	**1989**	**7,372**	**2,433,413**	**1,714,122**	**8,122**	**14,831**	**N.R.**	**555,887**
The Estonian Evang. Lutheran Ch.	**1989**	**24**	**7,298**	**7,298**	**17**	**19**	**N.R.**	**N.R.**
Ethical Culture Movement	1988	21	3,212		19	43		
Evangelical Church	**1989**	**185**	**16,113**	**16,113**	**232**	**342**	**185**	**17,611**
Evangelical Congregational Church	**1989**	**155**	**34,779**	**24,606**	**122**	**199**	**153**	**17,461**
The Evangelical Covenant Church	**1989**	**592**	**89,014**	**89,014**	**821**	**1,264**	**515**	**72,866**
Evangelical Free Church of America	**1990**	**1,040**	**165,000**	**165,000**	**N.R.**	**1,795**	**N.R.**	**N.R.**
Evangelical Friends Alliance	1982	217	24,095		192	483		
Evangelical Lutheran Church in Am.	**1989**	**11,067**	**5,238,798**	**3,909,302**	**10,125**	**17,246**	**9,810**	**1,155,276**
Evangelical Luterhan Synod	**1989**	**125**	**21,544**	**15,740**	**108**	**144**	**112**	**3,794**
Evangelical Mennonite Church	**1990**	**26**	**4,026**	**4,026**	**34**	**52**	**26**	**4,471**
Evangelical Methodist Church	1987	130	8,282		151	238		
Evangelical Presbyterian Church	**1990**	**160**	**54,781**	**50,987**	**217**	**280**	**160**	**29,500**
Fellowship of Evang. Bible Churches	1988	14	1,925		18	47		
Fellowship of Fundamental Bible Churches	1984	31	1,840		31	52		
The Fire-Baptized Holiness Church (Wesleyan)	1958	53	988		N.R.	N.R.		
Free Christian Zion Church of Christ	1956	742	22,260		321	420		
Free Lutheran Congregations, The Association of	1988	193	26,870		114	139		
Free Methodist Church of North America	**1989**	**1,066**	**75,869**	**59,754**	**N.R.**	**1,790**	**N.R.**	**97,642**
Free Will Baptists, National Association of	**1989**	**2,517**	**204,489**	**204,489**	**2,800**	**2,900**	**2,517**	**159,944**
Friends General Conference	1987	505	31,690					
Friends United Meeting	**1989**	**543**	**54,155**	**47,228**	**300**	**582**	**459**	**23,413**
Full Gospel Assemblies, Int'l	1984	150	3,800		122	399		
Full Gospel Fellowship of Churches and Ministers, Int'l	1985	450	65,000		850	850		
Fundamental Methodist Church, Inc.	1987	13	733		14	21		
General Association of Regular Baptist Churches	**1989**	**1,582**	**216,468**	**216,468**	**N.R.**	**N.R.**	**N.R.**	**N.R.**
General Baptists (Gen. Assoc. of)	**1989**	**872**	**73,738**	**73,738**	**N.R.**	**1,477**	**N.R.**	**N.R.**

Religious Body	Year Reported	No. of Churches	Inclusive Membership	Full, Communicant or Confirmed Members	No. of Pastors Serving Parishes	Total No. of Clergy	No. of Sunday or Sabbath Schools	Total Enrollment
General Church of the New Jerusalem	1971	33	2,143		17	31		
General Conference of Mennonite Brethren Churches	1986	128	17,065		N.R.	N.R.		
General Conference of the Evangelical Baptist Church, Inc.	1952	31	2,200		22	37		
General Convention, The Swedenborgian Church	1988	50	2,423		45	54		
General Six Principle Baptists	1970	7	175		4	7		
Grace Brethren Churches, Fellowship of	**1989**	**319**	**39,481**	**39,481**	**N.R.**	**653**	**319**	**29,513**
Grace Gospel Fellowship	**1990**	**50**	**4,500**	**2,500**	**68**	**120**	**50**	**N.R.**
Greek Orthodox Archdiocese of North and South America	1977	535	1,950,000		610	655		
The Holiness Church of God, Inc.	1968	28	927		25	36		
Holy Ukrainian Autocephalic Ch. in Exile	1965	10	4,800		15	24		
House of God, which is the Church of the Living God, the Pillar and Ground of the Truth, Inc.	1956	107	2,350		80	120		
Hungarian Reformed Church in Am.	**1989**	**27**	**9,780**	**7,280**	**29**	**32**	**14**	**N.R.**
Hutterian Brethren	1987	77	3,988		N.R.	N.R.		
Independent Fundamental Churches of America	**1990**	**705**	**73,809**	**73,809**	**820**	**1,516**	**705**	**71,368**
International Church of the Foursquare Gospel	**1989**	**1,404**	**203,060**	**197,881**	**N.R.**	**5,179**	**983**	**41,974**
International Pent. Church of Christ	**1990**	**77**	**2,914**	**2,577**	**126**	**126**	**76**	**3,808**
Jehovah's Witnesses	**1989**	**9,141**	**825,570**	**825,570**				
Jews*	**1989**	**3,416**	**5,944,000**	**3,750,000**	**N.R.**	**6,500**	**N.R.**	**N.R.**
Kodesh Church of Immanuel	1980	5	326		2	28		
Korean Presbyterian Church in Am., General Assembly of the	1986	180	24,000		200	225		
Latvian Evangelical Lutheran Church in America, The	**1989**	**56**	**12,865**	**11,697**	**31**	**46**	**20**	**N.R.**
Liberal Catholic Church—Province of the United States of America	1987	34	2,800		64	127		
Liberty Baptist Fellowship	1987	510	200,000		150	N.R.		
The Lutheran Church—Missouri Synod	**1989**	**5,990**	**2,609,025**	**1,961,114**	**5,339**	**8,271**	**5,715**	**660,229**
Lutheran Churches, The Am. Assoc. of	1988	78	15,150		63	80		
Mennonite Church	**1989**	**1,034**	**92,517**	**92,517**	**1,504**	**2,545**	**N.R.**	**N.R.**
Mennonite Church, The Gen. Conf.	**1989**	**220**	**33,982**	**33,982**	**210**	**392**	**220**	**15,307**
Metropolitan Church Association, Inc.	1958	15	443		13	62		
Metropolitan Community Churches, Universal Fellowship of	**1989**	**195**	**22,296**	**11,806**	**N.R.**	**271**	**N.R.**	**N.R.**
The Missionary Church	**1989**	**292**	**26,881**	**26,881**	**276**	**509**	**282**	**N.R.**
Moravian Church in Am.—N. Prov.	**1989**	**100**	**31,248**	**23,802**	**88**	**167**	**97**	**6,742**
Moravian Church in Am.—S. Prov.	**1989**	**55**	**21,341**	**17,208**	**54**	**89**	**55**	**8,597**
National Baptist Convention of America	1956	11,398	2,668,799		7,598	28,574		
National Baptist Convention, USA, Inc.	1958	26,000	5,500,000		26,000	27,500		
National Primitive Baptist Con., Inc.	1975	616	250,000		460	636		
National Spiritualist Assoc.of Churches	**1990**	**120**	**3,406**	**3,406**	**186**	**218**	**49**	**478**
Netherlands Reformed Congregations	**1989**	**15**	**5,169**	**2,769**	**5**	**6**	**N.R.**	**N.R.**
New Apostolic Church of N. Am.	**1989**	**497**	**37,201**	**37,201**	**742**	**828**	**N.R.**	**2,256**
North American Baptist Conf.	**1989**	**276**	**42,629**	**42,269**	**286**	**433**	**267**	**22,602**
North Am. Old Roman Catholic Church	1986	133	62,611		109	150		
North Am. Old Roman Catholic Church (Archdiocese of New York)	1988	5	615		6	9		
Old German Baptist Brethren	**1989**	**55**	**5,435**	**5,435**	**236**	**236**	**N.R.**	**N.R.**
Old Order Amish Church	**1989**	**785**	**70,650**	**70,650**	**3,140**	**3,140**	**N.R.**	**N.R.**
Old Order (Wisler) Mennonite Church	1980	36	9,731		N.R.	N.R.		
Open Bible Standard Churches, Inc.	**1990**	**330**	**46,000**	**42,000**	**968**	**968**	**285**	**25,000**
The (Original) Church of God	1971	70	20,000		50	124		
Orthodox Church in America	1978	440	1,000,000		457	531		
The Orthodox Presbyterian Church	1987	188	19,094		160	334		
Pent. Assemblies of the World, Inc.	1960	550	4,500		450	600		
Pentecostal Church of God, Inc.	**1989**	**1,165**	**90,870**	**39,590**	**N.R.**	**1,603**	**N.R.**	**N.R.**
Pent. Fire-Baptized Holiness Ch.	1969	41	545		80	80		
The Pent. Free Will Bapt. Ch., Inc.	**1990**	**141**	**11,757**	**11,757**	**163**	**228**	**141**	**11,734**
Pentecostal Holiness church, Int'l	**1989**	**1,475**	**119,073**	**119,073**	**1,583**	**2,095**	**1,385**	**132,727**

*Inclusive membership represents estimates of the total number of Jews seen as an ethnic, social, and religious community. Full membership is the number of Jews estimated to be associated with synagogues and temples of the Orthodox, Conservative, and Reform branches by officials of the congregational organizations of these three groups.

Religious Body	Year Reported	No. of Churches	Inclusive Membership	Full, Communicant or Confirmed Members	No. of Pastors Serving Parishes	Total No. of Clergy	No. of Sunday or Sabbath Schools	Total Enrollment
Pillar of Fire	1949	61	5,100		N.R.	N.R.		
Polish National Catholic Church of Am.	1960	162	282,411		141	141		
Presbyterian Church in America	**1989**	**1,100**	**217,374**	**174,134**	**1,193**	**1,949**	**N.R.**	**109,216**
Presbyterian Church (USA)	**1989**	**11,469**	**2,886,482**	**2,886,482**	**10,410**	**20,078**	**N.R.**	**1,099,211**
Primitive Advent Christian Church	**1990**	**9**	**350**	**350**	**99**	**8**	**351**	
Primitive Baptists	1960	1,000	72,000		N.R.	N.R.		
Primitive Methodist Church, USA	**1989**	**85**	**8,244**	**5,779**	**54**	**84**	**85**	**4,898**
Progressive Nat'l Baptist Con., Inc.	1967	655	521,692		N.R.	863		
The Protestant Conference (Lutheran)	**1989**	**9**	**1,065**	**790**	**8**	**8**	**6**	**154**
Protestant Reformed Churches in Am.	1980	21	4,544		19	31		
Reformed Church in America	**1989**	**928**	**330,650**	**198,832**	**863**	**1,727**	**N.R.**	**99,464**
Reformed Church in the U.S.	1985	34	3,778		28	34		
Reformed Episcopal Church	**1990**	**83**	**6,565**	**5,882**	**88**	**147**	**72**	**2,938**
Reformed Mennonite Church	1970	12	500		18	21		
Reformed Methodist Union Episcopal Church	1983	18	3,800		24	33		
Reformed Presbyterian Church of North America	1988	68	5,174		59	127		
Reformed Zion Union Apostolic Church	1965	50	16,000		28	N.R.		
Religious Society of Friends (Cons.)	1984	28	1,744		N.R.	17		
Religious Society of Friends (Unaffiliated Meetings)	1980	112	6,386		N.R.	N.R.		
Reorganized Church of Jesus Christ of Latter Day Saints	**1989**	**1,048**	**190,183**	**190,183**	**16,182**	**16,912**	**N.R.**	**N.R.**
The Roman Catholic Church	**1989**	**23,500**	**57,019,948**	**N.R.**	**34,553**	**53,111**	**N.R.**	**7,106,653**
The Romanian Orthodox Episcopate of America	**1989**	**37**	**65,000**	**65,000**	**37**	**81**	**30**	**1,800**
Russian Orthodox Church in the USA, Patriarchal Parishes	1985	38	9,780		37	45		
The Salvation Army	**1989**	**1,122**	**445,566**	**130,551**	**2,656**	**5,184**	**1,139**	**113,977**
The Schwenkfelder Church	**1989**	**5**	**2,461**	**2,461**	**8**	**10**	**5**	**799**
Second Cumberland Presbyterian Church in the U.S.	1959	1212	30,000		121	125		
Separate Baptists in Christ	1988	101	10,000		101	165		
Serbian Eastern Orthodox Church in the USA and Canada	1986	68	67,000		60	82		
Seventh-Day Adventist Church	**1989**	**4,193**	**701,781**	**701,781**	**2,305**	**4,493**	**4,222**	**466,753**
Seventh Day Baptist Gen. Conf.	**1990**	**86**	**5,200**	**5,200**	**48**	**77**	**86**	**N.R.**
Social Brethren	1975	40	1,784		47	47		
Southern Baptist Convention	**1989**	**37,739**	**14,907,826**	**14,907,826**	**37,500**	**64,100**	**36,322**	**7,931,112**
The Southern Methodist Church	**1990**	**137**	**7,572**	**7,572**	**105**	**128**	**N.R.**	**N.R.**
Sovereign Grace Baptists	1988	275	2,600		260	275		
Syrian Orthodox Ch. of Antioch (Archdiocese of the USA and Canada)	1988	28	30,000		20	25		
Triumph the Church and Kingdom of God in Christ (International)	1972	475	54,307		860	1,375		
True (Old Calendar) Orthodox Church of Greece (Synod of Metropolitan Cyprian), Am. Exarchate	**1990**	**8**	**1,300**	**1,300**	**6**	**12**	**N.R.**	**N.R.**
Ukrainian Orthodox Ch. in the USA	1966	107	87,745		107	131		
Ukrainian Orthodox Church of Am. (Ecumenical Patriarchate)	1986	27	5,000		36	37		
Unitarian Universalist Association	**1989**	**1,010**	**182,211**	**182,211**	**1,181**	**1,252**	**N.R.**	**46,345**
United Brethren in Christ	**1989**	**252**	**25,462**	**25,462**	**320**	**382**	**252**	**14,410**
United Christian Church	1987	12	420		8	11		
United Church of Christ	**1989**	**6,388**	**1,625,969**	**1,625,969**	**5,614**	**9,870**	**N.R.**	**433,980**
United Holy Church of America	1960	470	28,890		379	400		
The United Methodist Church	1988	37,514	8,979,139		20,844	38,303		
United Pentecostal Church, Int'l	**1990**	**3,592**	**500,000**	**500,000**	**N.R.**	**7,447**	**N.R.**	**N.R.**
United Zion Church	1987	13	850		19	20		
Unity of the Brethren	**1989**	**26**	**4,336**	**2,764**	**20**	**26**	**21**	**1,357**
Vedanta Society	1988	13	2,500		14	14		
Volunteers of America	1978	607	36,634		704	704		
The Wesleyan Church	**1989**	**1,650**	**110,027**	**101,879**	**1,848**	**3,076**	**N.R.**	**179,360**
Wisconsin Evang. Lutheran Synod	**1989**	**1,198**	**419,312**	**317,117**	**1,144**	**1,573**	**1,169**	**49,320**
World Confessional Lutheran Assoc.	1987	12	1,530		18	27		

From *Yearbook of American and Canadian Churches,* 1991 edited by Constant H. Jacquet, Jr., and Alice M. Jones. Copyright © 1991 The National Council of The Churches of Christ in the USA. Reprinted by permission of Abingdon Press.

MAJOR DENOMINATIONS

American Baptist Assoc., 4605 N. State Line Ave., Texarkana, TX 75503 214-792-2783

American Baptist Churches in the USA, PO Box 851 Valley Forge, PA 19482 215-768-2000 FAX: 215-768-2275

Assemblies of God, 1445 Boonville Ave., Springfield, MO 65802 417-862-2781 FAX: 417-862-8558

Assemblies of God Int'l Fellowship, 8504 Commerce Ave., San Diego, CA 92121 619-530-1727 FAX: 619-530-1543

Baptist Bible Fellowship Int'l, 720 E. Kearney St., Springfield, MO 65803 417-862-5001 FAX: 417-865-0794

Baptist General Conference, 2002 S. Arlington Heights Road, Arlington Heights, IL 60005 708-228-0200 FAX: 708-228-5376

Christian and Missionary Alliance, PO Box 35000, Colorado Springs, CO 80935 719-599-5999 FAX: 719-593-8692

Christian Brethren (Plymouth Brethren), 218 W. Willow, Wheaton, IL 60187 708-653-6573 FAX: 708-653-6573

Christian Church (Disciples of Christ), 222 S. Downey Ave., PO Box 1986, Indianapolis, IN 46206 317-353-1491 FAX: 317-359-7546

Christian Reformed Church in North America, 2850 Kalamazoo Ave. SE, Grand Rapids, MI 49560 616-246-0744 FAX: 616-246-0834

Church of God, PO Box 13036, 1207 Willow Brook, Huntsville, AL 35802 205-881-9629

Church of God (Anderson, Ind.), Box 2420, Anderson, IN 46018 317-642-0256

Church of God (Cleveland, Tenn.), PO Box 2430, Cleveland, TN 37320 615-472-3361 FAX: 615-478-7052

Church of God in Christ, 272 S. Main St., Memphis, TN 38103 901-578-3800

Church of God of Prophecy, PO Box 2910, Cleveland, TN 37320 615-479-8511

Church of the Brethren, 1451 Dundee Ave., Elgin, IL 60120 708-742-5100 FAX: 708-742-6103

Church of the Nazarene, 6401 The Paseo, Kansas City, MO 64131 816-333-7000 FAX: 816-333-1748

Churches of God, Gen. Conf., 900 S. Arlington Ave., Room 200, Harrisburg, PA 17109 717-652-0255

Community Churches, Int'l Council of, 7808 College Dr., 2 SE, Palos Heights, IL 60463 708-361-2600

Conservative Baptist Assoc. of America, 25W560 Geneva Road, Box 66, Wheaton, IL 60189 708-653-5350

Conservative Congregational Christian Conf., 7582 Currell Blvd., Suite 108, St. Paul, MN 55124

Cumberland Presbyterian Church, 1978 Union Ave. Memphis, TN 38104 901-276-4572 FAX: 901-276-4578

Episcopal Church, The, 815 Second Ave., New York NY 10017 212-867-8400

Evangelical Congregational Church, 100 W. Park Ave., PO Box 186, Myerstown, PA 17067 717-866-7383

Evangelical Covenant Church, The, 5101 N. Francisco Ave., Chicago, IL 60625 312-784-3000

Evangelical Free Church of America, The, 901 E. 78th St., Bloomington, MN 55320 612-866-3343 FAX: 612-866-7539

Evangelical Lutheran Church in America, 8765 W. Higgins Road, Chicago, IL 60631 312-380-2700

Evangelical Presbyterian Church, 26049 Five Mile Road, Detroit, MI 48239 313-532-9555

Fellowship of Evangelical Bible Churches, 5800 S. 14th St., Omaha, NE 68107 402-731-4780

Fellowship of Fundamental Bible Churches, PO Box 43 Glassboro NJ 08028

Free Methodist Church of North Am., 770 N. High School Road, Indianapolis, IN 46214 317-244-3660 FAX: 317-244-1247

Free Will Baptists, National Assoc. of, 1134 Murfreesboro Road, Nashville, TN 37217 615-361-1010 FAX: 615-367-5769

Friends General Conference, 1216 Arch St., 2B, Philadelphia, PA 19107 215-561-1700

Friends United Meeting, 101 Quaker Hill Dr., Richmond, IN 47374 317-962-7573 FAX: 317-966-1293

Full Gospel Fellowship of Churches and Ministers Int'l, 4325 Ledbetter Dr., Dallas, TX 75233 241-339-1200

General Assoc. of Regular Baptist Churches, 1300 N. Meacham Road, Schaumburg, IL 60173 708-843-1600 FAX: 708-843-3757

General Baptists, General Assoc. of, 100 Stinson Dr., Poplar Bluff, MO 63901 314-785-7746 FAX: 314-686-5198

Grace Brethren Churches, Fellowship of, PO Box 386, Winona Lake, IN 46590 219-267-5566

Independent Fundamental Churches of America, 3520 Fairlanes, Grandville, MI 49468 616-531-1840

Int'l Church of the Foursquare Gospel, 1910 W. Sunset Blvd., Suite 610, Los Angeles, CA 90026 213-484-2400

Lutheran Church—Missouri Synod, 1333 S. Kirkwood Road, St. Louis, MO 63122

Lutheran Churches, The American Assoc. of, 10800 Lyndale Ave. S., Suite 124, Minneapolis, MN 55420

Mennonite Church, 421 S. Second St., Suite 600, Elkart, IN 46516 219-294-7131

Mennonite Church, The General Conference, 722 Main, Newton, KS 67114 316-283-5100 FAX: 316-283-0454

Missionary Church, The, 3901 S. Wayne Ave., Ft. Wayne, IN 46807 219-456-4502 FAX: 219-456-4903

Moravian Church in America, 1021 Center St., PO Box 1245, Bethlehem, PA 18016 215-867-7566 FAX: 215-866-9223

National Baptist Convention, USA, 1620 Whites Creek Pike, Nashville, TN 37207 615-228-6292 FAX: 615-226-5935

New Apostolic Church of North America, 3753 N. Troy St., Chicago, IL 60618

North American Baptist Conference, 1 S. 210 Summit Ave., Oakbrook Terrace, IL 60181 708-495-2000 FAX: 708-495-3301

Open Bible Standard Churches, Inc., 2020 Bell Ave., Des Moines, IA 50315 515-288-6761 FAX: 515-288-6764

Orthodox Presbyterian Church, 7401 Old York Road, Philadelphia, PA 19126 215-635-0700

Pentecostal Church of God, 4901 Pennsylvania, PO Box 850, Joplin, MO 64802

Pentecostal Holiness Church, Int'l, PO Box 12609, Oklahoma City, OK 73157 405-787-7110 FAX: 405-789-3957

Presbyterian Church in America, 1852 Century Pl., Atlanta, GA 30345 404-320-3366 FAX: 404-320-7964

Presbyterian Church (USA), 100 Witherspoon St., Louisville, KY 40202 502-569-5360 FAX: 502-569-5018

Reformed Church in Am., 475 Riverside Dr., New York, NY 10115 212-870-2841 FAX: 212-870-2499

Salvation Army, The, 799 Bloomfield Ave., Verona, NJ 07044 201-239-0606 FAX: 201-239-8441

Southern Baptist Convention, 901 Commerce, Suite 750, Nashville, TN 37203 615-244-2355

United Brethren in Christ, 302 Lake St., Huntington, IN 46750 219-356-2312

United Church of Christ, 700 Prospect Ave., E. Cleveland, OH 44115 216-736-2100

United Methodist Church, The, PO Box 320, Nashville, TN 37202 615-742-5470

United Pentecostal Church Int'l, 8855 Dunn Road, Hazelwood, MO 63042 314-837-7300 FAX: 314-837-4503

Wesleyan Church, The, PO Box 50434, Indianapolis, IN 46250 317-842-0444

Wisconsin Evangelical Lutheran Synod, 2929 N. Mayfair Road, Wauwatosa, WI 53222 414-771-9357 FAX: 414-771-3708

24 LARGEST U.S. PROTESTANT DENOMINATIONS IN 1989
(by membership)

Southern Baptist Convention	14,907,826	Wisconsin Evang. Lutheran Synod	419,312
United Methodist Church	8,979,139	Reformed Church in America	330,650
Evangelical Lutheran Church in Am.	5,238,798	Christian and Missionary Alliance	265,863
Presbyterian Church (USA)	2,886,482	Church of God (Anderson, Ind.)	199,786
Lutheran Church—Missouri Synod	2,609,025	Church of the Brethren	149,681
Episcopal Church	2,433,413	Baptist General Conference	133,742
Assemblies of God	2,137,890	Mennonite Church	92,517
United Church of Christ	1,625,969	Cumberland Presbyterian Church	90,906
Christian Church (Disciples of Christ)	1,052,271	Evangelical Covenant Church of Am.	89,014
Seventh-day Adventist Church	701,781	Free Methodist Church of N. Am.	75,869
Church of God (Cleveland, Tenn.)	582,203	North American Baptist Conference	42,629
Church of the Nazarene	561,253		
Salvation Army	445,566		

Source: 1991 *Yearbook of American and Canadian Churches.*

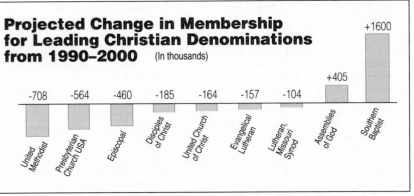

Projected Change in Membership for Leading Christian Denominations from 1990–2000 (In thousands)

-708	-564	-460	-185	-164	-157	-104	+405	+1600
United Methodist	Presbyterian Church USA	Episcopal	Disciples of Christ	United Church of Christ	Evangelical Lutheran	Lutheran, Missouri Synod	Assemblies of God	Southern Baptist

Source: George Barna in *The Frog in the Kettle*. Copyright © 1990. Published by Regal Books. Used by permission.

BABY BOOMERS AND THE CHURCH

Increasingly, baby boomers are attending church. Research shows that 42.8% of older baby boomers (those born 1946–1958) regularly attend. Predictions are that the church of the 1990s will see a boom in church attendance as baby boomers mature, settle down, and raise their families.

	Boomer men	Boomer women
Importance of religion		
Very important	39%	58%
Fairly important	42	31
Not very important	18	11
Importance next 5 years		
More important	61	66
Same	25	20
Less important	13	12
Time you will spend on religious activities next 5 years		
More time	37	44
Same amount	55	52
Less time	7	3
Church member?		
Yes	61	69
No	39	31
Nonmembers expecting to join next 5 years		
Yes	38	39
No	55	57
Not sure	7	4
Want children to receive religious education		
Yes	73	78
No	17	15
Not sure/not applicable	10	7

Source: *Emerging Trends*, June 1991 issue. Published by the Princeton Religion Research Center. Results of telephone interviews with 477 randomly selected adults, ages 26-45, February 21-24, 1991.

10 CHARACTERISTICS OF CHURCHES APPEALING TO BABY BOOMERS

1. They are open to a spiritual experience.
2. Their Bible teaching stresses practical living.
3. They place a healthy emphasis on relationships.
4. They have fewer titles and less formality.
5. They understand the new family in America.
6. They share their faith by what they say and do.
7. They recognize the ability of women.
8. They place an emphasis on worship.
9. They have a high tolerance for diversity.
10. They are action-oriented.

Source: Jack Simms in *The Baby Boomerang* by Doug Murren. Published by Regal Books.

FOCUS BOOK

The Baby Boomerang by Doug Murren. A book that will help your church understand and appeal to the Baby Boomers. Published by Regal Books.

WHERE HAVE THE BABY BOOMERS COME FROM?

	Born around 1946	Born around 1958
TV series	"Father Knows Best"	"The Partridge Family"
Kiddie show	"Howdy Doody"	"Romper Room"
Toy	Mr. Potato Head (with a real potato)	Mr. Potato Head (the all-plastic version)
Runner-up toy	The Hula Hoop	G.I. Joe
Goopy stuff	Garden-variety mud	Play-Doh
Singing family	The Everly Brothers	The Jackson Five
Teen dance step	The Mashed Potato	The Bump
Transportation	Scooters	Skateboards
Monsters	Godzilla, King Kong	"The Munsters"
Cartoon	"Mighty Mouse"	"The Flintstones"
Comic-book heroes	Superman	Batman
Sports heroes	Jackie Robinson	Hank Aaron
Female role model	Annette Funicello of the Mouseketeers	Stefanie Powers as April Dancer in "The Girl from U.N.C.L.E."
Most significant childhood memory	Air-raid drills	No cartoons after JFK was shot
Adult activity	Choosing a commune	Choosing a personal financial planner

USA Weekend, 19-21 August 1988 and *Baby Boomers and the Future of World Missions* by Dr. James F. Engel and Jerry D. Jones. Copyright © 1989. Used by permission.

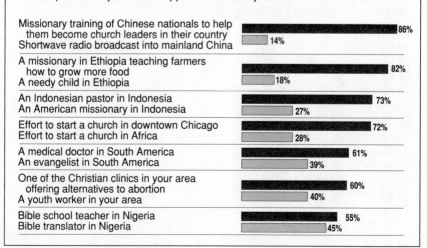

What Are Their Ministry Interests?

Chicago-area evangelical baby boomers were asked to make a choice between a series of ministry opportunities. Below are seven pairs of ministry opportunities. Imagine that you had the resources to financially support any of them. Which one in each pair would you rather support on a monthly basis?

Missionary training of Chinese nationals to help them become church leaders in their country	86%
Shortwave radio broadcast into mainland China	14%
A missionary in Ethiopia teaching farmers how to grow more food	82%
A needy child in Ethiopia	18%
An Indonesian pastor in Indonesia	73%
An American missionary in Indonesia	27%
Effort to start a church in downtown Chicago	72%
Effort to start a church in Africa	28%
A medical doctor in South America	61%
An evangelist in South America	39%
One of the Christian clinics in your area offering alternatives to abortion	60%
A youth worker in your area	40%
Bible school teacher in Nigeria	55%
Bible translator in Nigeria	45%

Baby Boomers and the Future of World Missions by Dr. James F. Engle and Jerry D. Jones. Copyright © 1989. Used by permission.

Frequency of Church Attendance

In a typical month, among those who call themselves "Christian"

- 23% None
- 40% Four or More Times
- 12% Twice
- 12% Once
- 11% Three Times
- 1% Don't Know/Varies

Source: Barna Research Group, Glendale, CA., May 1991

REASONS FOR GOING TO CHURCH MORE FREQUENTLY

(Based on those now going more frequently than five years ago)

For our children	18%
Now have stronger faith, belief	18
Worship as a family	11
I am older, maturer, wiser	10
I like going, makes me feel good	10
Because of the current world situation	6
The fellowship	5
Gives guidance, inner peace, need it	4
Have become more involved	4
Have greater need now	4
Now have more time	4
Need its support	3
Got back in the habit, returned	2
I have reformed	2
Now work for the church	2
Spiritual reasons, prayer	2
Suffered a loss of a loved one	2
Survived a life-threatening incident	2
Other	5

Source: *Emerging Trends*, June 1991 issue. Published by The Princeton Religion Research Center.

Church Attendance by Generations

Depression Era Babies (born in 1930s)				War Babies (born in 1939–45)			Older Baby Boomers (born in 1946–58)		Younger Boomers & Young Adults (born in 1958–70)
48%	46%	40%	38%	34%	30%	35%	42%	33%	28%
20s	30s	40s	50s	20s	30s	40s	20s	30s	20s

Each generation's church attendance, at various ages, is represented.

Sources: The Gallup Poll and National Research Council

How Church Size Affects Teenagers

Comparison of teens in churches with fewer than 100 people to teens in churches with 100 or more people

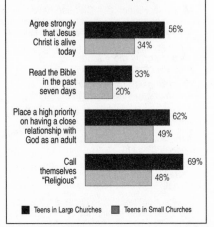

	Teens in Large Churches	Teens in Small Churches
Agree strongly that Jesus Christ is alive today	56%	34%
Read the Bible in the past seven days	33%	20%
Place a high priority on having a close relationship with God as an adult	62%	49%
Call themselves "Religious"	69%	48%

■ Teens in Large Churches ■ Teens in Small Churches

Sources: The Barna Research Group. Based on interviews nationwide with a representative sample of 710 Americans between the ages of 13-18.

REASONS FOR GOING TO CHURCH LESS FREQUENTLY

Have no time, too busy	19%
Conflicts with work, study schedule	14
Disagree with policies, teachings	8
Doesn't meet my needs	7
Not sure	7
Illness	6
Too commercial, money hungry	5
Atheist, nonbeliever	4
Hypocrisy, bigotry, close-minded	4
Move around too much, new to community	4
Boring, no interest	3
Don't like organized religion	3
Life-style has changed	3
Stopped going when left parents' home	3
Too far to travel	3
Too lazy	3
Other	9

Source: *Emerging Trends*, June 1991 issue. Published by The Princeton Religion Research Center.

CHRISTIAN EDUCATION PERIODICALS

Christian Education Today
P.O. Box 15337, Denver, CO 80215

Christian Education Journal
P.O. Box 650, Glen Ellyn, IL 60138

Current Christian Abstracts Periodical
P.O. Box 7596, Columbia, MO 65205

PERCENTAGE OF ADULTS WHO RATE THE FOLLOWING ASPECTS OF THEIR CHURCH EXCELLENT

Friendliness of the congregation	46%
Concern and care by pastor and staff	45%
Preaching	44%
Music in the worship services	44%
Buildings and facilities	43%
Management of the church, in general	35%
Programs for young children	32%
Quality of teaching in the classes	28%
Programs for teens	24%

Source: George Barna in *What Americans Believe*. Coyright © 1991. Published by Regal Books. Used by permission.

CHRISTIAN EDUCATION ASSOCIATIONS

Association of Professors and Researchers in Religious Education 1100 E. 55th Street, Chicago, IL 60615

Christian Education Association P.O. Box 4532, Huntsville, AL 35802

Evangelical Teacher Training Association P.O. Box 327, Wheaton, IL 60189

Fellowship of Christian Educators 0N345 Willow Road, Wheaton, IL 60187

International Christian Education Association 24200 Woodward Avenue, Pleasant Ridge, MI 48069

National Christian Education Association 302 Lake Street, Huntington, IN 46750

Professional Association of Christian Education (PACE) 8405 N. Rockwell, Suite 222, Oklahoma City, OK 73162

Religious Education Association 409 Prospect Street, New Haven, CT 06511-2177

FOCUS QUOTE 66 99 The holiest moment of the church service is the moment when God's people—strengthened by preaching and sacrament—go out of the church door into the world to be the church.—Ernest Southcott

WHY TEENAGERS DROP OUT OF CHURCH

Most people who drop out of church do so between the ages of 16-19. Six main reasons include:
1. Part-time jobs conflict with church life.
2. They think church is irrelevant.
3. They feel they don't fit in.
4. Challenging church training programs usually cease or taper off at this age.
5. Church activities are boring.
6. They are going through a time of questioning and doubting.

Source: "Why High Schoolers Drop Out of Church," *Group* magazine, March 1991 issue.

WHAT CHRISTIANS BELIEVE: THE APOSTLES' CREED

The Apostles' Creed is a concise statement of faith that has been adopted or used over the centuries by virtually every branch of Christendom. Quite possibly this creed came into being in Rome about AD 150. Although it was believed to state correctly the apostles' faith, the possibility that any apostle had any part in composing it is unlikely. We use it here as a summary of Christian doctrine, explaining it clause by clause, so that readers will be able to see what believers of every description have believed from the beginning of the church.

The Apostles' Creed
In the words of this creed Christians confess: *I believe in God the Father almighty, maker of heaven and earth, and in Jesus Christ, his only Son, our Lord, who was conceived by the Holy Ghost, born of the virgin Mary, suffered under Pontius Pilate, was crucified, dead, and buried; he descended into hell. The third day he rose again from the dead. He ascended into heaven, and sitteth on the right hand of God the Father almighty. From thence he shall come to judge the quick and the dead. I believe in the Holy Ghost, the holy catholic church, the communion of saints, the forgiveness of sins, the resurrection of the body, and the life everlasting.*

I believe in God the Father almighty, maker of heaven and earth
That statement describes God as Christians know him. The word *Father* summarizes all that Christ had said about God's loving, providing, caring, forgiving, and answering of prayer. In his inmost nature, God is like a good father toward all people, though not all live as his children (Luke 15:11-32; John 1:12).

Almighty means that God is supreme over all, acting in total freedom within the limits he sets for himself—his own character—and the responsible freedom he has given to human-kind. That means that God is supreme in history and will in the end outwit evil and get his own way. Because God is fatherly love, love is the ultimate power in the world.

The phrase *maker of heaven and earth* points to God as originator, fashioner, and sustainer of all that is. To him belong all things and all creatures. To believe in God is to worship, trust, pray, obey him, enjoy his world, and esteem everything in it with a sense of responsibility and care (Matthew 6:25-33; Romans 11:33-36; 1 Timothy 1:17).

And in Jesus Christ, his only Son, our Lord
Here the foundations of Christian faith are laid in history—not in experiences or vision or emotion, but in Jesus of Nazareth, a first-century Jew, the Jesus of the Gospels. *Jesus* is the Greek form of *Joshua*, meaning "God saves," or "Savior" (Matthew 1:21).

The title *Christ,* meaning "anointed," signifies one sent on divine mission (John 17:18; 20:21; 1 John 4:14), but especially the expected king who was to restore the Davidic monarchy, rule in God's name, and establish God's kingdom. That hope was nourished by numerous prophecies (Deuteronomy 18:15; 2 Samuel 7:16; Psalms 2; 110; Isaiah 9:2-7; Micah 5:2; Zechariah 9:9; Malachi 3:1-4) and was in part fulfilled by Jesus (Matthew 20:29–21:11; 22:41-45). But Jesus adopted from Ezekiel (2:1, etc.) and Daniel (7:13) the ambiguous title *Son of man* and reinterpreted Messiahship by other prophecies: those of the Servant of God who would suffer to achieve God's will (Isaiah 42:1-4; 52:13–53:12; Matthew 12:17-21; Luke 4:16-21; Acts 8:30-35; 1 Peter 2:21-25).

In calling Jesus God's *only Son* the church underlines Christ's uniqueness in history. Others are children of God by divine favor, through Christ, by rebirth (John 1:12-13; 3:3, 5) and adoption (Galatians 4:4-5). Jesus is Son of God, in likeness and in essential nature, originally, eternally, and by right (Matthew 21:37; John 3:16-18; Romans 1:4; Hebrews 1:1-3). He is, among all the religious heroes of humanity, the only divine Savior (Acts 4:12).

He is *our Lord,* Lord of mind (Philippians 2:5), of conscience (Romans 13:14), of will

(2 Corinthians 10:5), of relationships (Romans 14:3-4; 1 Corinthians 7:39), of Scripture (Matthew 5:21-22), of the church (Colossians 1:18), of life and death (Romans 14:7-9). To believe in Jesus is to trust only and completely in him as Savior, to serve and follow him as Lord out of gratitude, admiration, and love.

Who was conceived by the Holy Ghost, born of the virgin Mary

In these words the creed asserts the central miracle of Christianity, the incarnation of God in Christ (Luke 1:35). Jesus was not produced by time and circumstances (though he was divinely prepared for). He came (John 13:3), intervening in human affairs by God's initiative, as one given (John 3:16) and sent (John 6:57). His origin and nature were divine (John 1:1). Yet he was born of a woman (Galatians 4:4), was truly human, grew, was tempted, asked questions, prayed, and was weary, hungry, sorrowful, suffering, rejected, and mortal (John 1:14; Philippians 2:6-7; Hebrews 2:5-18; 1 John 4:2).

In the words *born of the virgin,* Christ's divine origin is again stressed. He was born "not of the will of man" (see Matthew 1:18-25). (To many early Christians who were convinced that the original sin was transmitted through human fathers, Christ's virgin birth also resolved the problem of how Christ could be truly human and sinless.) The name of Mary in the creed reminds Christians of the true place of this pious Jewess as mother of the Lord. To believe these things about Jesus is to wonder at his perfect humanity and strive to be conformed to his likeness.

Suffered under Pontius Pilate, was crucified, dead, and buried; he descended into hell

Here we have a fivefold insistence that Jesus really died. Here are listed the date, judicial circumstances, cruel manner, obvious physical consequence, and inescapable spiritual consequence that he descended, not into the place of fire and torment popularly understood as hell, but into hades, the abode of departed spirits (Luke 23:43; and the puzzling 1 Peter 3:18-20; see Acts 2:27, 31). So the creed answered charges that Christ did not truly die, but swooned, was rescued, escaped because, some asserted, a son of God could never die.

It need not surprise us that nothing is said about why Jesus died. The creed was recited at baptism, where the convert accepted Christ's death on his or her behalf and died with Christ to sin, self, and the world (Romans 6:1-23; Galatians 2:20; 6:14). It was also recited at the Lord's Supper, where Christ's blood of the new covenant between God and human-kind was clearly and repeatedly set forth. Jesus died as the Lamb of God bearing away the sins of the world, the righteous for the unrighteous to bring us to God. He offered expiation for sin, redeeming humankind (John 1:29; 1 Peter 3:18; 1 John 4:10; Romans 3:24-25; 2 Corinthians 5:18-21). In so doing, he demonstrated God's love for sinful men and women (1 John 4:9-10). To believe that is to live gratefully, pardoned, and at peace.

The third day he rose again from the dead

That assertion offers another dated historical fact. Jesus did not merely survive or pass through death; he rose (or, as Scripture often insists, God raised him "out from among the dead" (Acts 2:32; 1 Corinthians 15:15; 1 Peter 1:21). The central facts are that Christ conquered death and is alive forevermore, a living, present Savior. Here we have a second reason for Christ's uniqueness: he has risen from the dead. He returned from death as the same Christ, yet different, glorified. Far from the disciples' expecting the event, their hopes creating the conviction that it had happened, they were astonished, unbelieving, and afraid. At first they did not recognize him. Paul recited the evidence (1 Corinthians 15). Later the Gospels record the remembered details with much of the wonder and confusion of the experience still in their stories.

The risen Christ is the focus of the Christian's daily faith. His resurrection confirms who he is (Romans 1:4), that God accepted his sacrifice (Romans 4:25), and that all who are in Christ will also someday rise (1 Corinthians 15:20-23). Those holding such a faith live in Christ's company, sure of everlasting life, unafraid of death.

WHAT CHRISTIANS BELIEVE: THE APOSTLES' CREED cont.

He ascended into heaven, and sitteth on the right hand of God the Father almighty
Here we have the church's declaration that Jesus was at last fully vindicated, crowned, in the sense of sharing God's throne, and victorious. The Jewish messianic prophecies of kingship were fulfilled beyond anything the prophets foresaw. The ascension of Christ is beautifully described in Luke 24:50-51, more fully in Acts 1:9-11 and dramatically (as the homecoming of a victorious Roman general) in Ephesians 4:7-10. Arguments about the meaning of *up and down* are somewhat childish. Christ passed into the eternal sphere of God's immediate presence in victory and glory. Remembering that these are human words for divine realities, how else can human language express such ideas except in three-dimensional terms?

To believe in Christ's ascension is to know that we have a friend at court interceding for us (Romans 8:34). It is to be drawn upward in aspiration and hope to things above (Colossians 3:1-3). It is to be reminded that the author and perfecter of our faith has himself gone all the way before us, through struggle and suffering to glory (Hebrews 12:1-3).

From thence he shall come to judge the quick and the dead
Christian faith has a forward look, too. Christ's story is not ended. Just as Jesus promised to be with us always (Matthew 28:20), so he promised to return (Matthew 24:30; 25:31; John 14:3), thus consummating our spiritual fellowship with him in his manifestation in power and glory. The early church eagerly expected his return (Acts 1:10-11; Philippians 3:20-21; 1 Thessalonians 1:10; 2:19; 2 Timothy 4:8). First Thessalonians 4:16 attempts to describe his coming. Usually that truth is expressed in metaphors, such as lightning (Matthew 24:27), the secret thief (Matthew 24:43; 1 Thessalonians 5:2), the arriving bridegroom (Matthew 25:6), the returning master (Matthew 24:46; 25:19). The time has been fixed by God but is unknown to us (Matthew 24:36, 42, 44; Acts 1:7), and even to Christ himself (Matthew 24:36). That point is emphatically made.

At Christ's coming, Christians will be changed into his likeness, bodily (1 Corinthians 15:51-52; Philippians 3:20-21) and spiritually (1 John 3:2). To believe this is to be vigilant, faithful in service, lest he should come suddenly and find us asleep (Mark 13:35-37).

A second purpose of Christ's coming is for judgment of the living (*quick*) and the dead (John 5:22; Acts 17:31). Jesus himself said he will judge accordingly as people have served him in serving others (Matthew 25:31-46), that is, by the supreme law of love for God and neighbor. Such judgment will be universal (Romans 2:5-11, 16; 14:10). But Christians need fear no condemnation, for they have passed from death to life (Romans 8:1, 38-39; John 5:24). Yet we Christians must all appear before the judgment seat of Christ for assessment of our service (2 Corinthians 5:10; Romans 14:10-12).

Christian belief in divine judgment is therefore not self-righteous nor vengeful, but is instead a deep confidence in the moral constitution of the world—that truth and right are eternal and will triumph. In the end, God is king. To believe that fact is to live humbly and reverently, with enduring certainty that our struggle and sacrifice will prove worthwhile.

Completing its statement about Jesus, the creed seems to take a fresh breath before drawing very large conclusions from what God has done in Christ.

I believe in the Holy Ghost
Ghost is the old word for "disembodied spirit." In the Old Testament the invisible power of God at work in the world is called his *breath*. The same word also means "spirit": God's personal activity, manifest only by its effects. Jesus was conceived by God's Spirit (Luke 1:35), anointed by the Spirit in baptism (Luke 3:22), and endowed by the Spirit for his ministry (Luke 4:18). At the end he promised the same Spirit to the disciples (Luke 24:49; John 14:16-17, 26; 16:7-15; Acts 1:8).

Pentecost is the record of the Spirit's coming on the church (Acts 2). At first, the spectacular effects—equipping and empowering Christians especially for communication and for healing—impressed onlookers (Acts 2:1-4; 3:1-10; 1 Corinthians 12:4-11). Later, as the Spirit was recognized more clearly as the Spirit of Jesus (Acts 16:7; 2 Corinthians 3:17), the deeper effects in Christian character were more highly valued. That especially meant love (Galatians 5:22-23; 1 Corinthians 13; 2 Corinthians 3:18). The Spirit teaches, leads into truth, convicts, shows things to come. One might say that the Spirit replaces Jesus.

The church experiences the Spirit as the Spirit of truth, purity (holiness), power, and progress. All Christians are born of the Spirit (John 3:5) and possessed of the Spirit (Romans 8:9; 1 Corinthians 12:13). Regrettably, not all live in full enjoyment of his ministry and gifts. To believe in the Spirit is to open all the windows of one's soul in surrender and trust to his coming in.

The holy catholic church, the communion of saints

The Spirit of Jesus is not an abstract idea but is embodied in the living church, the body of Christ (1 Corinthians 12:12-27), which Christ purchased (Acts 20:28), loves and cherishes (Ephesians 5:22-30), and indwells (1 Corinthians 3:16; Ephesians 3:16-17). Despite its faults the church is rightly called holy, a people set apart for Christ. Because there is only one body of Christ through the whole world and all time it is rightly called *catholic*, although several sections of the church have adopted that title as meaning orthodox or true. Christianity is corporate as well as individual. It creates a kingdom, a family of God, a band of disciples bound together by a law of love.

Differences of tradition, government, and culture do not destroy our essential oneness in Christ. The communion of saints extends from the church militant on earth to include the church triumphant in heaven. When we believe in Christ, we identify with some convenient local outcropping of the church. We love it, are loyal to it, serve it, yet we cherish fellowship with all who acknowledge Christ as Lord. We emphasize things that unite us; we are honest and tolerant about things that divide us.

The forgiveness of sins

Fatalists, some psychologists, and remorseful, guilt-ridden souls find it hard to believe that forgiveness is possible. What's done is done, they say. Physical and social consequences of wrongdoing are indeed sometimes permanent. Restitution for wrongdoing is part of penitence; the Christian convert should never expect to be let off from doing what can be made right, or from receiving what is deserved from wrongdoing. At times it happens that we do escape the consequences of our sin. Other times we must receive help from God to bear whatever the undesirable results.

Forgiveness is essentially a changed relationship with God. It is being accepted, reconciled (2 Corinthians 5:18-21), loved, trusted—with all concealment ended, sin confessed and put away. God forgives, initially, for Jesus' sake (Ephesians 4:32), then cleanses (1 John 1:7) and strengthens (Ephesians 3:16), enabling us to overcome temptation (Romans 6:6-7, 12-14). The catalyst of forgiveness is penitence, confession, and faith (Acts 2:37-38; 1 John 1:9). The fruit of forgiveness is a healing peace (Romans 5:1) and a spirit of forgiving toward others (Matthew 6:12, 14-15; 18:23-35).

The resurrection of the body, and the life everlasting

Christian belief in eternal life rests in part on humankind's almost universal intuition of the indestructible nature of the human spirit. It rests on the promises and resurrection of Christ. It rests on our present experience of fellowship with the eternal God, who will not allow the soul he made, loves, and has redeemed, to be extinguished. (Psalms 16:10-11 and 73:23-26 lay a foundation for Matthew 22:31-32; Romans 8:38-39; Philippians 1:21, 23; John 10:27-29).

As an unborn child cannot imagine the world that awaits it after birth, so our imagination now fails to picture the life to come. Our personality will endure. "Because I live," Jesus said, "you also will live." "I will raise him [the one who believes in Christ] at the last day" (John 14:19; 6:39-40, 44, 54).

WHAT CHRISTIANS BELIEVE: THE APOSTLES' CREED cont.

Hebrew thought resisted the widespread dividing-up of the human being into body and spirit. Each person is an embodied spirit. Disembodied we are naked (2 Corinthians 5:1-4), less than human. Immortality, therefore, involves a resurrection body. But the gospel resurrection-stories and the writings of the apostle Paul insist on our continuing identity amid that change (1 Corinthians 15:36-53; Philippians 3:20-21). The immortal soul inherits a body transformed to be appropriate for its new life, imperishable, glorious, powerful, spiritual (1 Corinthians 15:42-44). To believe this adds realism to our thoughts of eternal life and profound sacredness to our present body (1 Corinthians 6:13-14; Romans 8:10-11, 23).

Reprinted from "What Christians Believe" by R. E. O. White in *The Shaw Pocket Bible Handbook,* ed. Walter A. Elwell. Copyright © 1984 by Harold Shaw Publishers, Wheaton, IL. Used by permission.

MAJOR THEOLOGICAL SCHOOLS OF THOUGHT

Orthodoxy (Gk. *orthos,* right; *doksa,* opinion). Used in several ways: (1) of the teaching of the ecumenical councils from Nicea to Chalcedon on the doctrines of the Trinity and Person of Christ; (2) of the worship, doctrine, and organization of the so-called Orthodox churches that submit to the teaching of the seven ecumenical councils; (3) by North American Evangelicals to describe basic evangelical doctrine, which adds to the Trinity and Person of Christ views about the Atonement, the Bible, and personal faith.

Calvinism The teaching of John Calvin (1509–1564) or of one of his successors or followers. Calvin's own theology is summarized in his *Institutes of the Christian Religion.* It represents an attempt to expound the meaning of Scripture in the light of the experience of the church before and during the Reformation. Thus, aspects of traditional theology are retained (e.g., the doctrine of the Trinity and the person of Christ) and other aspects are renewed and restated (i.e., the new emphasis on justification by faith). Calvinism was developed by his successors as they were in debate with Roman Catholics, Lutherans, and among themselves. Classic expositions of developed Calvinism are found in the Canons of the Synod of Dort (1618) and the Westminster Confession of Faith (1647). This may be described as Reformed orthodoxy, High Calvinism, or simply Calvinism.

Arminianism The approach to the doctrines of God and his salvation that had its origin with Jacobus Arminius (1560–1609), a Dutch theologian. The doctrines of Arminius were articulated in the conviction that the teaching of the successors of John Calvin (1509–1564) in the Calvinist churches was developing in an unsatisfying and unbiblical way. The doctrines were set forth in the Remonstrance (1610). This document taught that God eternally elected in Christ all who will believe in Christ, that Christ died for every person, that each believer must be regenerated by the Holy Spirit, that it is possible to resist the grace of God, and therefore that the possibility of falling completely from grace must be seriously entertained. The orthodox Calvinists responded to these articles by their own five articles produced at the Synod of Dort (1618–1619). Arminianism is used also of two English theological movements. First, that associated with Archbishop Laud in the 1620s and 1630s; and second, that taught by John Wesley, the founder of the Methodist church. Methodist teaching is often called Arminianism.

Evangelical A word with several meanings. (1) When used in Germany, it usually refers to the Lutheran state church. (2) In the Church of England it refers to a party, or school (often called "Low Church"), who trace their origins to the "Evangelical Revival" of the 18th century. (3) In a general context it refers to a particular conservative Protestant form of Christianity that especially emphasizes the inspiration and authority of the Bible and the need for personal conversion to God.

Liberalism A form of theology that flourished in the Western church from the mid-19th to the early 20th century. Found primarily in Protestantism, it also had supporters in Roman Catholicism. The key themes were freedom and progress—freedom from old dogmas and freedom to investigate new ideas, progress in collaboration with the new confident sciences. Important thinkers who set the stage for this type of theology were F. D. E. Schleiermacher (1768–1834) and Albrecht Ritschl (1822–1889). The result was a theology that had few points of contact left with the traditional view of the Bible and Christian faith. Two world wars and the massive influence of Karl Barth caused the demise of the old liberal theology as a major movement. It still lives on in a new dress in modern forms of theology that deny the deity of Jesus Christ and allow belief only in what is said to be rational.

Pentecostalism Either a movement in which the gifts of the Holy Spirit are said to be experienced or several denominations that emphasize the possession and exercise of the gifts of the Spirit. The name arises since the Spirit (and thus the gifts of the Spirit) were first given to the church at the Feast of Pentecost (Acts 2). As a movement in modern times it began with the Topeka Revival of 1901 and the Azusa Street Revival of Los Angeles in 1906, with claims to certain gifts of the Spirit, especially speaking in tongues. Similar events took place in other places, and thus the movement to encourage prayer for and receipt of the gifts began. It occurred outside the mainline denominations and churches and led ultimately to the formation of various new groups—Assemblies of God, Pentecostal Assemblies of the World, Pentecostal Church of God, and United Pentecostal Church International. These denominations, with others, have continued; but since World War II a new form of the Pentecostal movement has arisen and has deeply affected most of the traditional churches and denominations. It is known as the Charismatic movement or Neo-Pentecostalism and is best described as a renewal movement in which the gifts of the Spirit are emphasized in the context of each church being seen as a body of Christ.

Ecumenism (Gk. *oikumene,* "the whole inhabited world"). With the modern concern for Christian unity, ecumenical has the meaning of "working for unity and reunification." Ecumenism is everything involved in this process—ethos, methods, and activities. The origin of the ecumenical movement is usually taken as the 1910 Edinburgh Missionary Conference. The World Council of Churches was formed in 1948 and is now the focal point of this work for unity. Since much of the evangelical Christianity in the world remained outside the movement, it is not as yet truly ecumenical (covering all the world).

Fundamentalism A term coined around 1920 to describe conservative Evangelicalism, found particularly in the U.S. Taking its name from a series of booklets entitled *The Fundamentals* (1910–1915), it is an attempt to preserve traditional Protestant doctrines and values—especially the belief in the inerrancy and literal interpretation of Scripture—from the eroding effects of rationalism and modernism.

Neoorthodoxy A type of Protestant and Reformed theology of the 20th century, the name of Karl Barth (Barthianism) is especially associated with it. It is neo (new) in that it opposes the dominant Liberalism of the day; it is orthodox in that it attempts to recover the major theological themes of the Reformation and the Patristic period. This approach involves the use of higher critical methods in the interpretation of the Bible. They do not regard the Scripture to be inerrant but believe that God speaks through Scripture and his Son to obligate humankind to obedience and faithfulness to God.

Charismatic/Neo-Pentecostalism Contemporary religious phenomenon that embodies a renewed emphasis on the person and work of the Holy Spirit. Beginning in the late 1950s and early 1960s non-Pentecostal Christians, many from the mainline denominations, began experiencing Pentecostal visitations that included speaking in tongues, divine healings, prophecies, and various physical phenomena such as prostrations and fainting, in a way reminiscent of the great awakenings of the past. It created a vast unrest and rethinking on the part of traditional non-Pentecostal Christians, including the Roman Catholics, of what place such gifts and experiences ought to play in the Christian life. Voluminous literature and over one hundred official denominational documents have discussed its value pro and con with the general feeling (although not universally held) that one ought not to bridle the Holy Spirit, who "blows where he will," but still one must "test the spirits" to see if they are of God.

New Evangelicalism Term used in the U.S. to describe the modified form of traditional, conservative Evangelicalism (or Fundamentalism) that manifests a greater emphasis on social concern and responsibility. Basic doctrines are not changed, but they are related to concern for the external as well as internal lives of human beings. The idea of holistic salvation represents a further development.

Taken from *The Concise Dictionary of the Christian Tradition* by J. D. Douglas, Walter A. Elwell, and Peter Toon. Copyright © 1989 by J. D. Douglas, Walter A. Elwell, and Peter Toon. Used by permission of Zondervan Publishing House.

WHAT WE SING, WHAT WE MEAN
Duane Shinn

What We Sing	*What We Mean*
I Surrender All	I Surrender Some
There Shall Be Showers of Blessing	There Shall Be Sprinkles of Blessings
Fill My Cup, Lord	Fill My Spoon, Lord
Oh, How I Love Jesus	Oh, How I Like Jesus
He's Everything to Me	He's Quite a Bit to Me
I Love to Tell the Story	I Love to Talk about Telling the Story
Take My Life and Let It Be	Take My Life Then Let Me Be
It Is No Secret What God Can Do	It Is My Secret What God Can Do
There Is Sunshine in My Soul Today	There Is Scattered Cloudiness in My Soul Today
We Are One in the Spirit	We Are One in the Bond of Our Denomination
Onward Christian Soldiers	Onward Christian Reserves
Where He Leads Me I Will Follow	Where He Leads Me I Will Consider Following
Just As I Am	Just As I Pretend to Be
Stand Up, Stand Up for Jesus	Stand Up, Stand Up (but Keep Your Arms Down) for Jesus
When the Saints Go Marching In	When the Saints Go Sneaking In

Reprinted with permission from The Door, issue #105. 1224 Greenfield Dr., El Cajon, CA 92021.

STRANGE CHURCH NAMES

- Country Club Christian Church/from Michael Smith, Liberty, MO
- Ralph Lutheran
- Looney Valley Lutheran
- Big Canoe Lutheran/from Rev. Anthony G. Boder (and the *1988 Yearbook of the Evangelical Lutheran Church in America*), Brooklyn Center, MN
- Happy Church/from Mike LaTorra, Arvada, CA
- Dolly Pond Church of God in Grasshopper Settlement
- Mitchell Chapel Church of the Fire Baptized Holiness Church of God of the Americas
- African Casteroil Dead Church
- Catholic Church of South Africa King George Win the War/from Craig Meyer (from A.C. Griders book *Reminiscences*), Madison, WI
- First United Church of Kane/from Peter deVries, Templeton, PA
- Light Pink Baptist Church/from Bob Korth, Cincinnati, OH
- The Church of the Big Hole [Note: Important to watch your step!]/from Kurt Boyum, Fairmont, MN

Reprinted with permission from *The Door*, issue #105. 1224 Greenfield Dr., El Cajon, CA 92021

LITTLE-KNOWN LAWS CONCERNING
THE CHURCH AND THE SABBATH

In Gilman, Connecticut, it's strictly against the law to slurp your soup on Sunday. Anyone caught slurping soup in public on the Sabbath is subject to arrest and a fine of $5.00.

Young girls are never allowed to walk a tightrope in Wheeler, Mississippi, with one exception: they may walk a tightrope if it's inside a church.

It's against the law in Blackwater, Kentucky, to tickle a woman under her chin with a feather duster while she is attending a church service. To do so can bring a $10.00 fine and one day in the local jail.

Lingerie cannot be hung on a backyard clothesline on Sunday in Toomsboro, Georgia, unless the undies are carefully hidden from view by a screen or fence.

A woman weighing over two hundred pounds cannot ride a horse anywhere in public on Sunday in Opal, Wyoming.

Logandale, Nevada, won't allow anyone to fly over a large body of water on the Sabbath unless they carry food in the plane. In addition, eating snake meat on Sunday is prohibited.

No one can eat unshelled, roasted peanuts while attending church in Idanha, Oregon; nor can churchgoing Christians eat watermelon on the Sabbath.

In Colebrook, Pennsylvania, a city ordinance makes it illegal to give a cigarette to a female at any time while church services are being held.

Within the city limits of Studley, Virginia, there is a local law which prohibits swinging a yo-yo anywhere in public on the Sabbath, and especially in church or during Sunday School.

In Slaughter, Louisiana, no turtle races are allowed on the Sabbath, nor are turtle races allowed within 100 yards of a local church at any time.

No citizen is allowed to dress up in any red-colored garment and then attend a church service in Leecreek, Arkansas.

A local ordinance in Snowhill, Alabama, prohibits fishermen from chewing tobacco on Sunday without the written permission of a local physician.

All citizens of Bagdad, Florida, are outlawed from dipping snuff while on the grounds of any local church. Neither are they allowed to smoke a pipe or a cigar on the Sabbath. (Nothing is mentioned about cigarettes in this law.)

In Leona, Kansas, no female wearing a nightgown—sheer or otherwise—can be rescued by a fireman on the Sabbath. This law specifically states that a woman of any age must always get fully dressed before she can be legally assisted by firemen during a Sunday fire.

A local ordinance in Honey Creek, Iowa, prohibits anyone other than a policeman from carrying a slingshot to church on the Sabbath.

The law in the community of Garysburg, North Carolina, allows the shooting of whales from an airplane on the Sabbath. However, no other animals, including birds, can be hunted in this manner, nor can fish be shot while church is in progress.

It's against the law in Maizie, Kentucky, to drive a car down a public street on Sunday while a dog or cat sits between the driver and the passenger. This law mentions nothing about having the pet on either party's lap.

Robert W. Pelton. Reprinted with permission from *The Door*, issue #89, 1224 Greenfield Dr., El Cajon, CA 92021.

SERMONS ACTUALLY PREACHED

- Do I Have to Wear a Bun in My Hair? (Matthew 5:28)/from Rev. San Warfield, Cincinnati, Ohio
- Groan! Groan! That's Okay: God Is Molding You Today/Joel Osborn, Madison, Wis.
- Up to Your Neck in Whale Puke/Rev. Paul "Bud" D. Pratt, Flint, Mich.
- The Sermon I Won't Preach/Pastor Michael Loomis, Buffalo, N.Y.
- God's Word: Why Hell Is Like Heaven (Luke 16:19-31)/Brad Whitlock, Raleigh, N.C.
- The Problem of Denial: Do You Really Love God or Are There Roosters in Your Life?/Marcia Hirst, Bakersfield, Calif.
- You Won't Get Quaker Oats by Sowing Wild Oats/Dean McIntyre, Clovis, N.M.
- We Didn't Know Who You Was/Kay Freyer, Mequon, Wis.
- Hypotasso/Pastor Michael Loomis, Buffalo, N.Y.
- Peanut and the Purdy Girl/Donna Hildebrand, Medford, Oreg.

Reprinted with permission from *The Door,* issue #91, 1224 Greenfield Dr., El Cajon, CA 92021

A BENCH? A PEW? AREN'T THEY ALL BENCHES?

In Colonial America, benches in the front of the church were purchased by upper class members for their exclusive use. To these, were given a distinctive name to set them apart: pew.

Gradually, the practice faded out giving way to the assertion of some church leaders that "all the church is for all the people." Rather than downgrade the pew to the bench, the bench was upgraded to the pew. And so we have our present day pew.

SEEN ON CHURCH BULLETIN BOARDS

- The competition is fierce, but we're still open for business.
- Last chance to pray before entering the freeway.
- God so loved the world that he didn't send a committee.
- Keep off the grass. This means thou.
- Come to church Sunday. If you have no sins, bring someone who has.
- Join our sit-in demonstration every Sunday.
- Come in and pray today. Beat the Christmas rush.
- If you have troubles, come in and tell us about them. If you have none, come in and tell us how you do it.
- The Lord loves a cheerful giver. He also accepts from a grouch.
- Everyone occupies some kind of pulpit and preaches some kind of sermon every day.
- All new sermons, no reruns.

QUESTIONS NOT TO ASK!

Before, during, or after church:
- You asleep?
- Now what's the matter?
- Have I kept you waiting?
- You don't remember me, do you?
- Will you promise not to get mad if I ask you something?

Jane Goodsell, Press Associates in the February 1990 issue of *Reader's Digest.*

DO YOU KNOW THE DIFFERENCE?

Reverend: From the Latin *reverendus* meaning "worthy of respect." The British began the custom of calling their minister "Reverend"—an indicator of respect for him and his leadership.

Pastor: Comes from the Latin word for shepherd and *pascere* which means "to feed." The Bible speaks of Christ as the Shepherd feeding his flock and ministers as "shepherds of the flock."

Parson: In the demanding hardships of Colonial American life, few had time for educational pursuits. And so the local minister often became the resource person for information. Before long, people began to refer to him as the "town person." Spoken with the heavy New England accent, the phrase was sometimes misunderstood and grad-

ually turned into the "town parson" as it made its way across the country.

Vicar: From the Latin *vicarius* meaning "substitute." Ministers are referred to as substitutes or representatives of Christ on earth.

Evangelist: From the Greek *euangelion* and Latin *evangelium,* meaning "good news." Traveling ministers brought good news to the people to whom they ministered and so became known as evangelists.

NATIONAL ASSOCIATION OF EVANGELICALS AWARDS

LAYPERSON-OF-THE-YEAR AWARD
The Layperson-of-the-Year is chosen based on: Christian character and commitment; tangible relationship with NAE, including agreement with the NAE statement of faith; lay leadership in evangelical activity and thought; strategic support of evangelical work in general; public recognition of his/her work in a leadership capacity.

1961	Kenneth Keyes, Highlands, N.C.	1977	Paul Steiner, Ft. Wayne, Ind.
1962	Carl Gundersen, Des Plaines, Ill.	1978	Floyd Robertson, Annandale, Va.
1963	Herbert Taylor, Chicago, Ill.	1979	Walter Meloon, Orlando, Fla.
1964	John Anderson, Rockford, Ill.	1980	Abner Haldeman, Upland, Calif.
1965	Stephen Paine, Houghton, N.Y.	1981	Everett Koop, Philadelphia, Pa.
1966	Robert VanKampen, Santa Barbara, Calif.	1982	James Dobson, Arcadia, Calif.
		1983	Charles Colson, Washington, D.C.
1967	Bill Jones, Los Angeles, Calif.	1984	William Armstrong (R-CO), Washington, D.C.
1968	John Broger, Falls Church, Va.		
1969	George Wilson, Minneapolis, Minn.	1985	Joni Eareckson Tada, Woodland Hills, Calif.
1970	Ted Engstrom, Monrovia, Calif.		
1971	Seth Rohrer, Elkhart, Ind.	1986	Stanley Tam, Lima, Ohio
1972	Frank D. Nicodem, Mt. Prospect, Ill.	1987	Daniel Coats (R-IN), Ft. Wayne, Ind.
1973	George Willms, Newton, Kans.	1988	Orville & Ruth Merillat, Adrian, Mich.
1974	Everett Graffam, King of Prussia, Pa.	1989	Tony Hall, Dayton, Ohio
1975	Lester Gerig, Ft. Wayne, Ind.	1990	Donald Duff, Ft. Wayne, Ind.
1976	Jack Frizen, Wheaton, Ill.	1991	John Ashcroft, Jefferson City, Mo.

J. ELWIN WRIGHT AWARD
The J. Elwin Wright award is chosen based on: faithfulness in advancing evangelical cooperation on both a national and international level throughout a productive career; initiated and been instrumental in implementing plans of action which have contributed to the cause of increasing evangelical cooperation; contributed, through speaking and/or writing, ideas and strategies that have strengthened the evangelical movement; inspired and motivated others to join in the cause of evangelical unity.

1989 Dr. Oswald Hoffman
1990 Dr. Carl F. H. Henry
1991 Jerry Ballard

JAMES DeFOREST MURCH AWARD

The James DeForest Murch award is chosen based on: performance of editorial functions for a denominational magazine or other evangelical publication throughout a productive career; attained and maintained a high degree of excellence of editorial skills as evidenced by the quality of the periodicals produced; provided leadership and promoted integrity in evangelical publishing; stimulated and motivated readers through personal and editorial writing.

1989 Dr. O. W. Polen
1990 Forrest J. Boyd
1991 James Reapsome

MUSTARD SEED AWARD

Sponsored by LOVE INC., a division of World Vision. Recognizes the church with the most enterprising outreach to the poor. Criteria for the award are based on the program's innovativeness, use of volunteers, demonstrated results, long-term focus, sound management, and capacity to be duplicated or adapted by other churches.

Year	Program	Church
1989	Noon Day Ministry	First Baptist Church, Albuquerque, N.M.
1990	Highway City	Northwest Baptist Church, Fresno, Calif.

Education

CHURCH-RELATED ELEMENTARY AND HIGH SCHOOLS

Accredited schools with an enrollment of 100 or more.
Boarding facilities indicated by !. Special education indicated by &.

State/School	City	Affiliation	Grades/Enrollment
Alabama			
Kingwood Christian Schl	Alabaster	Assembly of God	P-12 / 380
Faith Christian Schl	Anniston	Presbyterian	K-8 / 105
Central Park Christian Schls	Birmingham	Baptist	P-12 / 336
Parkway Christian Academy	Birmingham		P-12 / 606
Shades Mountain Christian Schls	Birmingham	Independent	P-12 / 592&
Tuscaloosa Christian Schl	Cottondale	Baptist	K-12 / 241
Grace Baptist Church Schls	Decatur	Baptist	P-12 / 223
Northside Methodist Academy	Dothan	Methodist	P-12 / 486
Florence Christian Academy	Florence	Free Will Baptist	K-12 / 160
Tabernacle Christian Schl	Gardendale	Baptist	P-12 / 243
Liberty Christian Academy	Guin	Free Will Baptist	P-12 / 176
Bethel Baptist Schl	Hartselle	Baptist	P-12 / 179
Brooklane Baptist Academy	Hueytown	Baptist	K-12 / 236
Triana Village Baptist Schl	Huntsville	Baptist	P-12 / 223
Chilton Christian Academy	Jemison	Baptist	K-12 / 113
Faith Academy	Mobile	Life Church of Mobile	P-12 / 444&
Greystone Christian Schl	Mobile	Greystone Bible Church	P-12 / 247
Calvary Christian Academy	Montgomery	Baptist	K-12 / 250
Trinity Christian Schl	Opelika	Presbyterian	K-8 / 173
Trinity Christian Academy	Oxford	Baptist	P-12 / 411
Dale County Christian Schl	Ozark	Baptist	K-12 / 126
Shelby Christian Schl	Pelham	Baptist	1-12 / 116
Bible Methodist Schl	Pell City	Methodist	K-12 / 166
Grace Baptist Schl	Prattville	Baptist	K-12 / 212
Magnolia Springs Christian Schl	Theodore	Baptist	P-12 / 231
West End Christian Schl	Tuscaloosa	Baptist	P-12 / 392
Alaska			
Abbott Loop Christian Schl	Anchorage	Abbott Loop Christian Cntr	K-12 / 284&
Anchorage Christian Schl	Anchorage	Baptist	K-12 / 468
Grace Christian Schl	Anchorage	Brethren	K-12 / 296
Muldoon Christian Schl	Anchorage	Muldoon Community Assembly	K-12 / 134
Far North Christian Schl	Fairbanks	Far North Missionary Fellowship	K-12 / 116
Juneau Christian Schl	Juneau	Bethel Christian Cntr	P-8 / 158
Valley Baptist Academy	Juneau	Baptist	P-8 / 103
Kodiak Christian Schl	Kodiak		P-8 / 100
North Pole Christian Schl	North Pole		P-12 / 148
Valley Christian Schl	Palmer	Baptist	P-12 / 102
Arizona			
Glendale Baptist Schls	Glendale	Glendale Bible Church	K-12 / 100
Northwest Christian Academy	Glendale	Sweetwater Church	P-12 / 486
Eastside Christian Schls, Inc.	Mesa		P-8 / 170
Redeemer Christian Schl	Mesa	Church of The Redeemer	K-8 / 207
Southwest Indian Schl	Peoria	World Gospel Mission	7-12 / 103!

State/School	City	Affiliation	Grades/Enrollment
Christian Challenge Academy	Phoenix	Phoenix Christian Assembly	P-8 / 123
Fountainhead Christian Academy	Phoenix	Fountainhead Christian Comm Chrch	P-12 / 140
Grace Christian Schl	Phoenix	Brethren	K-10 / 403
Light & Life Christian Schl	Phoenix	Free Methodist	P-8 / 220
Mexican Gospel Mission Evangelical Schl	Phoenix	The Evangelical Church	K-12 / 157
Northwest Community Christian Schl	Phoenix		P-12 / 776
Paradise Valley Christian	Phoenix		P-8 / 192
Phoenix Christian Grade Schl	Phoenix	Reformed	K-8 / 171
Phoenix Christian High Schl	Phoenix	Independent	9-12 / 260
Scottsdale Christian Academy	Phoenix		P-12 / 587
Valley Cathedral Christian Schl	Phoenix	The Valley Cathedral	P-8 / 291
Western Christian Schl	Phoenix	Evangelical	K-8 / 161
Christian Academy of Prescott	Prescott	Baptist	P-8 / 145
Twin Wells Indian Schl	Sun Valley	Native American Ministries	1-9 / 148!&
Immanuel Mission Schl	Teec Nos Pos		K-12 / 103
Grace Community Christian Schl	Tempe	Grace Comm Church of the Valley	K-8 / 458
Tri-City Christian Academy	Tempe	Baptist	K-12 / 419
Valley Christian High Schl	Tempe		9-12 / 196
Grace Christian Schls	Tucson	Grace Chapel	P-8 / 408
Palo Verde Christian Schl	Tucson	Baptist	K-12 / 280
Tucson Christian Schl	Tucson	Baptist	P-12 / 197
Hilltop Christian Schl	Window Rock	Western Indian Ministries	P-8 / 171

Arkansas

Westside Christian Learning Cntr	El Dorado	Baptist	P-11 / 294
Calvary Christian Schl	Forest City		P-12 / 200
Fort Smith Christian Schl	Fort Smith	Baptist	K-12 / 247
Arkansas Baptist High Schl	Little Rock	Baptist	9-12 / 150&
Cloverdale Christian Academy	Little Rock	Assembly of God	K-8 / 178
Heritage Christian Schl	Little Rock	Baptist	K-12 / 148
Southwest Christian Academy	Little Rock		P-8 / 140
Walnut Valley Christian Academy	Little Rock	Bible Church of Little Rock	K-8 / 334&
Abundant Life Schls	North Little Rock	Baptist	P-12 / 390
New Life Christian Schl	Pine Bluff	Baptist	P-11 / 188
Shiloh Christian Schl	Springdale	Baptist	K-12 / 450

California

Sahag-Mesrob Armenian Christian Schl	Altadena		1-8 / 152
Discovery Christian Schls	Anaheim	Independent	P-8 / 353
Trinity Lutheran Christian Schl	Anaheim	Lutheran	P-8 / 186
Apple Valley Christian Schl	Apple Valley	Baptist	P-12 / 372&
Arcadia Christian Schl	Arcadia		P-8 / 371
Christian Schl of Arcata	Arcata	Baptist	K-8 / 140
Coastal Christian Schl	Arroyo Grande		K-12 / 255
North County Christian Schl	Atascadero	Independent	K-12 / 282
Forest Lake Christian Schl	Auburn		P-12 / 381
Light & Life Christian Schl	Azusa	Free Methodist	P-8 / 300&
Heritage Academy	Bakersfield	Heritage Bible Church	P-8 / 590
Stockdale Christian Schls	Bakersfield	Assembly of God	P-8 / 586&
Baldwin Park Christian Schl	Baldwin Park	Baptist	P-10 / 287
Barstow Christian Schl	Barstow	Free Methodist	P-8 / 223&
Cherry Valley Brethren Schls	Beaumont	Brethren	P-8 / 193
Bell Gardens Christian Schl	Bell Gardens	Full Gospel	K-8 / 178
Christian Schl of the Desert	Bermuda Dunes		K-12 / 329
Bloomington Christian Schl	Bloomington	Nazarene	P-12 / 418
Christian Church Schl	Camarillo	Camarillo Christian Church	P-12 / 509&
West Valley Christian Schl	Canoga Park	West Valley Christian Church	K-12 / 309&
Santa Clarita Christian Schl	Canyon Country	Baptist	K-9 / 238&
Dana Point Christian Schl	Capistrano Beach	Calvary Chapel	K-8 / 210
Peninsula Christian Schl	Carson		K-8 / 137

State/School	City	Affiliation	Grades/Enrollment
Redwood Christian Schl	Castro Valley		K-12 / 904&
Covenant Christian Schl	Chula Vista		K-10 / 110
Western Christian Schl	Claremont		K-8 / 180
Colton Christian Schl	Colton	Assembly of God	P-12 / 221
Calvary Christian Academy	Compton	Calvary Immanuel COGIC	K-9 / 109
Tower of Faith Christian Academy	Compton	Tower of Faith Evangelistic Chrch	P-8 / 136
Concord Christian Schl	Concord	Full Gospel	P-8 / 340
Kings Valley Grade Schl	Concord	Concord Christian Cntr	K-8 / 275
Tabernacle Baptist Schl	Concord	Baptist	P-8 / 402
Ygnacio Valley Christian Schl	Concord	Independent	K-8 / 171
Corona Christian Schl	Corona	Corona Christian Cntr	P-12 / 138
Crossroads Christian Schl	Corona	Crossroads Christian Church	K-9 / 320
Newport Christian Schls	Corona Del Mar	Covenant Community Church	P-12 / 198
Western Christian Schl	Covina		7-12 / 447
San Francisco Christian Schl	Daly City	Baptist	K-12 / 258
San Ramon Valley Christian Academy	Danville	Presbyterian	K-8 / 201
Calvary Chapel Christian Schl	Downey	Calvary Chapel of Downey	P-9 / 453
Valley Christian Cntr Schl	Dublin	Valley Christian Cntr	P-12 / 758
Christian Unified Schls of San Diego	El Cajon	Baptist	P-12 / 1132&
El Monte Christian Schl	El Monte	Wesleyan	P-8 / 210
El Sobrante Christian Schl	El Sobrante	Assembly of God	K-8 / 341
Encinitas Christian Schl	Encinitas	North County Fellowship	K-8 / 100
Escondido Christian Schl	Escondido	Foursquare	P-8 / 531
Light & Life Christian Schl	Escondido	Free Methodist	P-8 / 400
Freedom Christian Schl	Fair Oaks	Open Bible Church	K-12 / 103
Ambassador Baptist Schls	Fontana	Baptist	P-12 / 500
First Southern Baptist Christian Schl	Fountain Valley	Baptist	P-8 / 516
Christian Community Schls	Fremont	Fremont Community	P-8 / 507
Fremont Christian Schl	Fremont	Assembly of God	K-12 / 867
Fresno Christian Schls	Fresno		K-12 / 685&
Eastside Christian Elementary Schl	Fullerton	Eastside Christian	P-8 / 429
Calvary Baptist Elementary Schl	Gardena		K-8 / 421
Gardena Valley Christian Schl	Gardena	Assembly of God	K-8 / 375
Foothill Christian Schls	Glendora	Foothill Christian Cntr	P-8 / 536
Hillcrest Christian Schl	Granada Hills		K-9 / 411&
Hacienda Christian Schl	Hacienda Heights	Nazarene	P-8 / 165
Harbor Christian Schls	Harbor City	Foursquare	P-12 / 250&
Acacia Baptist Schl	Hawthorne	Baptist	K-8 / 197
American Heritage Christian Schl	Hayward	Baptist	K-12 / 148
Hayward Christian Schl	Hayward	Assembly of God	K-8 / 140
Baptist Christian Schl	Hemet	Baptist	P-12 / 437
Hesperia Christian Schl	Hesperia	Hesperia Community	P-12 / 566
New Life Christian Schl	Hesperia	Foursquare	P-8 / 341
Liberty Christian Schl	Huntington Beach	Baptist	1-12 / 428
Faith Academy	Imperial	Assembly of God	P-9 / 136
Celeste Scott Christian Schl	Inglewood	Ladies of Song	P-10 / 300
Christ-Centered Childrens University	Inglewood	Apostolic	K-9 / 175
Inglewood Christian Schl	Inglewood	First Christian Church	K-8 / 335
Liberty Christian Academy	Irvine	Baptist	P-8 / 157
Whittier Christian High Schl	La Habra		9-12 / 750
La Mesa Christian Schl	La Mesa	Baptist	K-8 / 128
Brethren Elementary & Junior High Schls	La Mirada	Brethren	K-8 / 309
Lindsey Schls	La Mirada		P-8 / 154
Calvary Baptist Schl	La Verne	Baptist	P-12 / 263
Mission Hills Christian Schls	Laguna Hills	Mission Hills Christian Cntr	K-8 / 190
Christian Cntr Schl	Lakeport	Lakeport Christian Cntr	P-9 / 109
Antelope Valley Christian Schl	Lancaster	Independent	P-12 / 250
Bethel Christian Academy	Lancaster	Baptist	P-12 / 584
Lancaster Christian Schl	Lancaster	Nazarene	K-8 / 169
Landmark Christian Schl	Lancaster	Baptist	P-12 / 131
Kings Christian Schl	Lemoore	Nondenominational	K-12 / 209

State/School	City	Affiliation	Grades/Enrollment
Mokelumne River Schl	Lodi		K-8 / 161
At The Cross Christian Schl	Long Beach	Calvary Chapel Paramount	K-12 / 158
Bethany Baptist Schl	Long Beach	Baptist	K-9 / 304
East L A Light & Life Christian Schl	Los Angeles	Free Methodist	K-9 / 166
First Church of God Christian Schl	Los Angeles	Church of God	K-8 / 347
Miracle Baptist Christian Schl	Los Angeles	Baptist	K-9 / 244
Pacific Christian High Schl	Los Angeles		7-12 / 123
Sycamore Grove Schl	Los Angeles	Pillar of Fire Church	K-8 / 144
West Angeles Christian Academy	Los Angeles	Church of God	K-8 / 240
Westminster Academy	Los Angeles	Independent	K-8 / 214
Los Gatos Christian Schl	Los Gatos	Los Gatos Christian Church	K-8 / 425&
Manteca Christian Schl	Manteca	Assembly of God	P-8 / 228
Merced Christian Schl	Merced	Baptist	K-8 / 140
Bethany Christian Academy	Midway City	Bethany Bible Fellowship	K-8 / 269&
Milpitas Christian Schl	Milpitas		P-8 / 665
Calvary Temple Christian Schl	Modesto		P-8 / 181
Modesto Christian Schl	Modesto	Neighborhood Church	K-12 / 549&
Orangeburg Christian Schl	Modesto	Baptist	P-8 / 130
Montebello Baptist Schl	Montebello	Baptist	K-8 / 284&
Southbay Christian Schl	Mountain View	Southbay Christian Cntr	P-12 / 468
Southport Christian Academy	National City	Southport Christian Cntr	K-12 / 145
Baptist Christian Schls	Norwalk	Baptist	K-12 / 132
Grace Christian Schl	Norwalk	Evangelical Free	P-12 / 281
Nazarene Christian Schl	Norwalk	Nazarene	P-9 / 413
Norwalk Christian Schl	Norwalk	Norwalk Assembly	P-8 / 295
Trinity Lutheran Schl	Norwalk	Lutheran	P-8 / 238
Christian Life Schl	Novato	Assembly of God	P-10 / 327
Calvary Christian Schl	Ontario	Calvary Church	P-9 / 324
Crystal Cathedral Academy	Orange	Crystal Cathedral	K-8 / 160
Independence Christian Schl	Orange	Orange Villa Bible Church	K-8 / 181&
Southern California Christian Schl	Orange		7-12 / 303&
Valley Christian Academy	Orcutt	Baptist	K-12 / 363
Alma Heights Christian Academy	Pacifica	Pillar of Fire Church	K-11 / 205
Country Christian Schl	Palo Cedro	Little Country Church	P-8 / 296
Paradise Christian Schl	Paradise	Baptist	K-10 / 114
Brethren Jr/Sr High Schl	Paramount	Greater Lng Bch Chrstn Schls, Inc.	7-12 / 490
Gethsemane Baptist Schl	Paramount	Baptist	K-12 / 259
Pasadena Christian Schl	Pasadena		K-8 / 525
Temple Christian Schls	Perris	Baptist	P-12 / 410
Community Christian Schls	Pine Grove	Community Church of Pine Grove	P-9 / 223
Christian Cntr Schl	Pittsburg	Assembly of God	P-12 / 403
Hueneme Christian Schl	Port Hueneme	Baptist	P-8 / 390
Cornerstone Christian Schl	Poway	Grace Trinity Church	K-8 / 150
Grace Baptist Schls	Redding	Baptist	K-12 / 361
North Valley Christian Schl	Redding	Baptist	P-12 / 295
Calvary Chapel Christian Schl of Redlands	Redlands	Calvary Chapel	K-10 / 203
Coast Christian Schl	Redondo Beach	Calvary Church	P-12 / 750
Deep Valley Christian Schl	Redwood Valley		P-8 / 108
Immanuel High Schl	Reedley	Mennonite Brethren	9-12 / 235
Immanuel Christian Schl	Ridgecrest	Southern Baptist	K-12 / 194
Riverside Christian High Schl	Riverside	Interdenominational	P-12 / 408
Capital Christian Schl	Sacramento		P-12 / 977
Citadel Baptist Schl	Sacramento	Baptist	K-12 / 107
Colonial Christian Academy	Sacramento	Baptist	P-12 / 204
Liberty Towers Christian Schl	Sacramento	Nazarene	K-8 / 213
Southpointe Christian Schl	Sacramento		K-8 / 105
Trinity Christian Schls	Sacramento	Trinity Church	P-8 / 435
Salinas Christian Schls	Salinas	Assembly of God	P-8 / 337
Winham Street Christian Academy	Salinas		K-12 / 123
Arrowhead Christian Academy	San Bernardino		7-12 / 130

State/School	City	Affiliation	Grades/ Enrollment
New Life Christian Academy	San Bernardino	New Life Fellowship	K-12 / 125
Valley Christian Schl	San Bernardino	Nazarene	P-8 / 295
Highland Christian Schls	San Bruno	Church of The Highlands	P-8 / 727
Alpha Beacon Christian Schl	San Carlos	Independent	P-12 / 255
Clairemont Christian Schl	San Diego	Clairemont First Assembly	K-12 / 249&
Horizon Christian Schl	San Diego	Horizon Christian Fellowship	K-8 / 270&
Midway Baptist Schls	San Diego	Baptist	K-12 / 395
Mira Mesa Christian Schl	San Diego	Chapel of The Rock	K-8 / 104
Voice of Pentecost Christian Schl	San Francisco		K-12 / 113
San Gabriel Christian Schl	San Gabriel	San Gabriel Union Church	K-8 / 631&
Christian Community Academy	San Jose	Christian Community Church	K-12 / 270
Liberty Baptist Schl	San Jose	Baptist	K-12 / 471
Valley Christian Schls	San Jose		K-12 / 867&
Capistrano Valley Christian Schls	San Juan Capistrano	Baptist	P-12 / 900&
Calvary Church Christian Schl	Santa Ana		K-8 / 495
Santa Barbara Christian Schl	Santa Barbara		K-8 / 275
North Valley Baptist Schls	Santa Clara	Baptist	K-12 / 131
John H. Jenkins Christian Academy/ Preschool	Santa Paula	Baptist	P-12 / 200
Rincon Valley Christian Schl	Santa Rosa	Santa Rosa Bible Church	P-12 / 314
Santa Rosa Christian Schl	Santa Rosa		K-9 / 271
Bible Missionary Fellowship Christian Schl	Santee	Baptist	K-12 / 151
Carlton Hills Christian Elementary Schl	Santee	Lutheran	K-8 / 149
Baymonte Christian Schls	Scotts Valley		K-12 / 188&
Maranatha High Schl	Sierra Madre		9-12 / 452
Grace Brethren Schl	Simi Valley	Brethren	P-9 / 492&
Santa Fe Christian Community Schl	Solana Beach		K-12 / 478
Santa Ynez Valley Christian Academy	Solvang		K-8 / 120
Brookside Christian High Schl	Stockton		7-12 / 180
Calvary Christian Academy	Stockton	Baptist	K-12 / 136
Northside Christian Academy	Stockton	Free Will Baptist	K-8 / 135
Sierra Christian Schl	Stockton		K-8 / 124
Stockton Christian Schls	Stockton	Christian Life Cntr	K-12 / 250
Grace Community Church Schls	Sun Valley		K-12 / 495&
Village Christian Schls	Sun Valley	Village Church	K-12 / 1821
Calvary Academy	Susanville	Baptist	1-12 / 116
The Linfield Schl	Temecula	Independent	K-12 / 401
First Baptist Academy	Thousand Oaks	Baptist	P-8 / 264
Hillcrest Christian Schl	Thousand Oaks	Hillcrest Christian Cntr	P-12 / 309
Mother Lode Christian Schl	Tuolumne		K-12 / 228
Turlock Christian Schls	Turlock		K-12 / 362
Colonial Bible Church Schl	Tustin	Colonial Bible Church	P-8 / 241
Vacaville Christian Academy	Vacaville	Independent	P-8 / 226
North Hills Christian Schl	Vallejo	Baptist	P-12 / 471
College Heights Christian Schl	Ventura	Baptist	K-8 / 250
Temple Christian Schl	Ventura	Baptist	K-8 / 140
Victor Valley Christian Schls	Victorville	Assembly of God	P-12 / 428
Tri-City Christian Schl	Vista	Baptist	P-12 / 713&
Christian Chapel Schls	Walnut	Christian Chapel	P-8 / 635
Berean Christian High Schl	Walnut Creek	Regular Baptist	9-12 / 300
Walnut Creek Christian Academy	Walnut Creek	Baptist	K-8 / 250
Woodlands Chr Schl/Contra Costa Chr High	Walnut Creek		P-12 / 304
North Kern Christian	Wasco	Wasco Bible Church	P-8 / 104&
Monte Vista Christian Schl	Watsonville		6-12 / 615!&
South Hills Academy	West Covina	Baptist	K-8 / 640
West Covina Christian Schl	West Covina	Baptist	K-8 / 500&
Westminster Christian Schl	Westminster	Christ Church	P-8 / 301
Bethany Christian Schl	Whittier	Baptist	K-8 / 414
Whittier Christian Schls	Whittier	Calvary Baptist Church	P-8 / 1052&
Pacific Harbor Christian Schl	Wilmington		P-9 / 369

State/School	City	Affiliation	Grades/Enrollment
Wilmington Christian Schl	Wilmington	Assembly of God	K-12 / 381
Woodland Christian Schls	Woodland	Baptist	K-9 / 450&
Friends Christian Schl	Yorba Linda	Friends	P-8 / 1252
Faith Christian Schls	Yuba City	Independent	K-12 / 331
Grace Christian Academy	Yuba City	Baptist	P-8 / 107

Colorado

Maranatha Christian Cntr	Arvada		P-12 / 643
Colorado Springs Christian Schl	Colorado Springs		P-12 / 813&
Evangelical Christian Academy	Colorado Springs	Presbyterian	P-10 / 340
Springs of Life Christian Schl	Colorado Springs	Full Gospel	K-8 / 130
Beth Eden Baptist Schl	Denver	Baptist	K-12 / 254
Colorado Christian Schl	Denver	Calvary Temple	P-8 / 248&
Silver State Baptist Schl	Denver	Baptist	K-12 / 451
Heritage Christian Schl	Fort Collins		P-12 / 198&
Faith Baptist Schl	Longmont	Baptist	K-12 / 337
Colorado West Christian Schl	Montrose	Reformed Presbyterian	P-12 / 142

Connecticut

West Woods Christian Academy	Hamden	West Woods Bible Chapel	K-12 / 149
Cornerstone Christian Schl	Manchester	Nazarene	K-11 / 179
Fellowship Baptist Schls	Middlestown	Baptist	P-12 / 129
Emmanuel Christian Academy	Newington	Baptist	K-12 / 245
North Stonington Christian Academy	North Stonington	Baptist	P-12 / 187
Wildwood Christian Schl	Norwich	C&MA	P-8 / 158
Central Christian Academy	Southington	Baptist	K-12 / 187
Christian Heritage Schl	Trumbull		K-12 / 355
Heritage Christian Academy	Wallingford	Baptist	K-12 / 147
Baptist Bible Academy	Waterford	Baptist	K-12 / 126
Hartford Christian Academy	West Hartford	Baptist	K-12 / 186

Delaware

Capitol Baptist Schl	Dover	Baptist	P-12 / 166
Christian Tabernacle Academy	Lincoln		K-12 / 141
New Castle Baptist Academy	New Castle	Baptist	P-12 / 671
Concord Christian Academy	Wilmington	Baptist	K-12 / 153

Florida

Altamonte Christian Schl	Altamonte Springs	Baptist	P-12 / 304
Christian Day Schl	Belle Glade	Baptist	K-12 / 331
Boca Raton Christian Schl	Boca Raton	Bibletown Community Church	K-8 / 209
Brandon Heights Christian Schl	Brandon	Baptist	K-10 / 213
Grace Christian Schl	Brandon	Grace Community Church	P-12 / 301
Tampa Bay Christian Schl	Brandon		P-12 / 129
Brunswick Christian Academy	Brunswick	Baptist	K-12 / 311
Lakeside Christian Schl	Clearwater		P-12 / 288&
Skycrest Christian Schl	Clearwater	Baptist	P-8 / 412
DeLand Christian Schl	DeLand	Nazarene	K-12 / 104
Deltona Christian Schl	Deltona	Baptist	P-12 / 129
Heritage Christian Academy	Englewood	Baptist	K-12 / 138
New Testament Christian Schl	Floral City	Baptist	P-12 / 146
Grace Brethren Christian Schl	Fort Lauderale	Brethren	K-8 / 166
Evangelical Christian Schl	Fort Myers	Baptist	P-12 / 505
Riverside Christian Schl	Fort Myers	Baptist	K-12 / 110
Sonshine Christian Academy	Fort Myers	Evangelistic Cntr	P-12 / 130
Fort Walton Christian Schl	Fort Walton Beach	Baptist	P-12 / 113
Countryside Christian Schl	Gainesville	Baptist	K-12 / 108
Heritage Christian Schl	Gainesville	Baptist	P-12 / 240
Landmark Christian Schl	Haines City	Baptist	P-12 / 358
Gadsden Christian Academy	Havana	Baptist	P-12 / 352
Dade Christian Schl	Hialeah	Baptist	P-12 / 1375
First Baptist Schl	Hialeah	Baptist	P-12 / 316

State/School	City	Affiliation	Grades/ Enrollment
Hobe Sound Bible Academy	Hobe	Florida Evangelistic Association	K-12 / 227
Hollywood Christian Schl	Hollywood	Baptist	K-12 / 1042
Sheridan Hills Christian Schl	Hollywood	Baptist	K-12 / 385
South Dade Baptist Church Schl	Homestead	Baptist	K-10 / 159
Grace Christian Schls of Pasco	Hudson	Grace Bible Church	P-12 / 215
Glendale Christian Schl	Indian River	Baptist	K-8 / 113
Island Christian Schl	Islamorada	Island Community Church	P-12 / 293
First Coast Christian Schl	Jacksonville	Baptist	K-12 / 157
Grace Christian Academy	Jacksonville	Grace Bible Church	K-9 / 284
Harvest Christian Academy	Jacksonville	Baptist	P-12 / 136
San Pablo Christian Learning Cntr & Schl	Jacksonville	Baptist	P-12 / 158
Southern Baptist Academy	Jacksonville	Baptist	P-11 / 541
Trinity Christian Academy	Jacksonville	Baptist	P-12 / 1544
University Christian Schl	Jacksonville	Baptist	P-12 / 738
Victory Christian Academy	Jacksonville	Baptist	P-12 / 602
Word of Life Schls	Jacksonville		P-12 / 139
Jupiter Christian Schl	Jupiter	Baptist	K-12 / 295
Heritage Christian Schl	Kissimmee	Baptist	K-12 / 185
Lake Park Baptist Schl	Lake Park	Baptist	P-8 / 320
Evangel Christian Schl	Lakeland	Carpenters Home Church	P-12 / 440
Lakeland Christian Schl	Lakeland		K-12 / 722&
Temple Christian Schl	Lakeland	Baptist	P-12 / 307
Central Pinellas Christian Schl	Largo	Baptist	K-12 / 198
Harvest Temple Christian Schl	Largo		P-12 / 221
Merritt Island Christian Schl	Merritt Island	Baptist	P-12 / 304
Cutler Ridge Christian Academy	Miami	Baptist	K-12 / 259
Florida Christian Schl	Miami	Baptist	P-12 / 561
King's Christian Schl	Miami	Southwest Community Church	K-9 / 217
Miami Christian Schl	Miami	Independent	P-12 / 365
Northwest Christian Academy	Miami	Baptist	P-12 / 549
Westwood Christian Schl	Miami	Baptist	P-12 / 1041
Santa Rosa Christian Schl	Milton	Grace Fellowship Church	P-12 / 183
Florida Bible Christian Schl	Miramar	Florida Bible Church	K-12 / 338
Grace Community Day Care and Schl	Naples	Grace Community Church	K-12 / 134
Rocky Bayou Christian Schl	Niceville	Baptist	P-12 / 309
Oak Griner Christian Schl	Ocala	Baptist	K-8 / 175
Ocala Christian Academy	Ocala	Baptist	K-12 / 640
Grace Christian Schls	Okeechobee	Brethren	P-12 / 175
Community Christian Schl	Oneco	Baptist	P-12 / 380
Azalea Park Baptist Church	Orlando	Baptist	P-8 / 146
Downey Christian Schl	Orlando	Downey Memorial Church	P-12 / 274
Eastland Christian Schl	Orlando	Baptist	K-12 / 189
Edgewood Ranch Academy	Orlando	Edgewood Ranch Foundation, Inc.	7-12 / 105
Faith Christian Academy	Orlando	Assembly of God	K-8 / 151
Orlando Christian Schl	Orlando	Baptist	K-12 / 213
Pine Hills Christian Academy	Orlando	Baptist	P-12 / 409
The Master's Academy	Orlando	Baptist	K-12 / 400
Calvary Christian Academy	Ormond Beach	Assembly of God	K-12 / 250
Panama City Christian Schl	Panama City	Baptist	P-12 / 486
East Hill Christian Schl	Pensacola		P-10 / 382
Pensacola Christian Schl	Pensacola	Baptist	P-12 / 1937
First Baptist Christian Schl	Pinellas Park	Baptist	P-12 / 173
Pinellas Park Christian Schl	Pinellas Park	Baptist	P-12 / 195
Ambassador Christian Academy	Plantation	Baptist	P-12 / 117
Highlands Christian Academy	Pompano Beach	Baptist	K-12 / 486
Community Christian Schl	Port Charlotte	Baptist	P-8 / 288
Port Charlotte Christian Schl	Port Charlotte	Assembly of God	P-12 / 115
Faith Christian Schl	Port Saint Joe	Faith Bible Church	P-9 / 114
Princeton Christian Schl	Princeton	Nazarene	K-12 / 283
Providence Christian Schl	Riverview	Baptist	P-12 / 414
Greater Bethel Christian Schl	Riviera Beach	Primitive Baptist	P-12 / 189

State/School	City	Affiliation	Grades/Enrollment
Ruskin Christian Schl	Ruskin	Baptist	P-12 / 162
Trinity Chapel Christian Schl	Saint Augustine		P-12 / 148&
Keswick Christian Schl	Saint Petersburg	Moody Bible Institute	P-12 / 679
Northside Christian Schl	Saint Petersburg	Baptist	P-12 / 766
Faith Christian Schl	Sarasota	Assembly of God	P-8 / 261
West Florida Christian Schl	Sarasota	Baptist	P-12 / 137
Community Christian Schl	Seminole	Community Bible Church	K-11 / 236
Warner Christian Academy	South Daytona	Church of God	P-12 / 581
First Baptist Christian Schl	Stuart	Baptist	P-8 / 205
North Florida Christian Schl	Tallahassee	Baptist	P-12 / 1286
Citrus Park Christian Schl	Tampa	Baptist	K-9 / 298
Faith Outreach Christian Schl	Tampa		K-12 / 108
Tampa Baptist Academy	Tampa	Baptist	P-12 / 465
Tampa Christian Academy	Tampa	Northwest Christian Church	K-9 / 351
Temple Heights Christian Schl	Tampa	Baptist	P-12 / 713
West Gate Christian Schl	Tampa	Baptist	P-12 / 143
Park Avenue Baptist Schl	Titusville	Baptist	P-8 / 278
Berean Christian Schl	West Palm Beach	Baptist	K-12 / 345
First Baptist Christian Schl	West Palm Beach	Baptist	P-8 / 260
Summit Christian Schl	West Palm Beach	Baptist	P-12 / 415
The King's Academy	West Palm Beach	Baptist	K-12 / 1163
Calvary Baptist Christian Schl	Winter Garden	Baptist	K-12 / 272
First Baptist Church Schl	Winter Garden	Baptist	K-12 / 232
Haven Christian Academy	Winter Haven	Baptist	P-12 / 148
Nassau Christian Academy	Yulee	Baptist	P-12 / 147

Georgia

State/School	City	Affiliation	Grades/Enrollment
Byne Memorial Baptist Schl	Albany	Baptist	K-12 / 513
Athens Christian Schl	Athens	Baptist	K-12 / 681
Prince Avenue Baptist Christian Schl	Athens	Baptist	K-12 / 170
De Kalb Christian Academy	Atlanta	C&MA	K-12 / 529
Curtis Baptist Schl	Augusta	Baptist	7-12 / 121
Southgate Christian Schl	Augusta	Baptist	K-12 / 319
Forrest Hills Christian Schl	Avondale Estates	Baptist	K-12 / 299
Old Suwanee Christian Schl	Buford	Baptist	K-9 / 117
Mt. Pisgah Christian Schl	College Park	Baptist	K-12 / 159
Calvary Christian Schl	Columbus	Baptist	K-8 / 201
Christian Heritage Academy	Columbus	Baptist	1-12 / 256
Grace Christian Schl	Columbus	Baptist	K-12 / 251
Philadelphia Christian Schl	Conyers	Baptist	K-12 / 239
Tabernacle Christian Schl	Covington	Baptist	K-12 / 117
Green Pastures Christian Academy	Decatur		P-12 / 244
Buford Highway Christian Schl	Doraville	Baptist	K-8 / 109
King's Way Christian Schl	Douglasville	Baptist	K-12 / 194
Chalecdon Christian Schl	Dunwoody	Reformed Presbyterian	P-12 / 115
Colonial Hills Christian Schl	East Point	Baptist	K-12 / 310
Fayette Christian Schl	Fayetteville	Baptist	K-12 / 410
Forest Park Christian Schl	Forest Park	Baptist	K-12 / 161
Lake City Christian Schl	Forest Park	Baptist	K-12 / 282
Glennville Christian Academy	Glennville	Free Will Baptist	K-12 / 173
Calvary Baptist Schl	Hampton	Baptist	K-12 / 111
North Cobb Christian Schl	Kennesaw	Nondenominational	K-8 / 240
Shiloh Hills Christian Schl	Kennesaw	Baptist	K-12 / 521
Northeast Atlanta Christian Schl	Lawrenceville	Baptist	K-12 / 240
Lithia Christian Academy	Lithia Springs		P-12 / 134
Central Fellowship Christian Academy	Macon	Baptist	K-12 / 492
Gilead Christian Academy	Macon	Baptist	K-12 / 454
Progressive Christian Academy	Macon	Baptist	P-8 / 494
Eastside Baptist Christian Schl	Marietta	Baptist	K-9 / 296
Augusta Christian Schls	Martinez		P-12 / 641
Clayton Christian Schl	Morrow		P-8 / 401

State/School	City	Affiliation	Grades/Enrollment
Maranatha Christian Academy	Oakwood	Baptist	K-12 / 264
Bible Baptist Christian Schl	Riverdale	Baptist	K-10 / 172
Pineland Christian Academy	Savannah	Baptist	K-12 / 169
Smyrna Christian Academy	Smyrna	Baptist	K-12 / 240
New Hope Christian Academy	St. Marys	Baptist	K-12 / 182
Mt. Vernon Christian Schl	Stockbridge	Baptist	K-12 / 319
Stone Mountain Christian Schl	Stone Mountain	Baptist	K-12 / 447
Lowndes Christian Academy	Valdosta	Baptist	K-12 / 170
Open Bible Christian Schl	Valdosta	Baptist	K-12 / 233
Warner Robins Christian Academy	Warner Robins	Baptist	K-12 / 177
Southside Christian Schl	Waycross	Baptist	K-1 / 222
Hope Christian Academy	Winder	Baptist	K-12 / 174

Hawaii

State/School	City	Affiliation	Grades/Enrollment
Kaahumanuhou Christian Schl	Kahului	Assembly of God	P-12 / 104
Kailua Church Christian Schl	Kailua		P-12 / 137&
Koolau Baptist Church Academy	Kaneohe	Baptist	K-12 / 134
Windward Nazarene Academy	Kaneohe	Nazarene	P-8 / 197
Hanalani Schls	Mililani	Baptist	K-12 / 492
Doris Todd Memorial Christian Schls	Paia	Berean Mission, Inc.	P-8 / 143
Lanakila Baptist Schls	Waipahu	Baptist	K-12 / 324

Idaho

State/School	City	Affiliation	Grades/Enrollment
Cole Christian Schl	Boise	Cole Community Church	P-9 / 321
Valley Christian Schl	Lewiston	Valley Christian Cntr	P-12 / 127
Nampa Christian Schls	Nampa	Interdenominational	K-12 / 265&
Twin Falls Christian Academy	Twin Falls	Baptist	P-12 / 118

Illinois

State/School	City	Affiliation	Grades/Enrollment
Mississippi Valley Christian Schl	Alton	Baptist	K-12 / 214
Aurora Christian Schl	Aurora		P-12 / 900
Covenant Christian Schl	Aurora	Living Waters Fellowship	K-8 / 114
Beardstown Christian Academy	Beardstown	First Christian Church	P-8 / 105
Calvary Baptist Christian Schl	Belvidere	Baptist	K-12 / 109
Bethany Christian Schl	Berwyn	Bethany Tabernacle	P-12 / 330
East Park Baptist Academy	Boody	Baptist	K-12 / 135
Judah Christian Schl	Champaign		K-12 / 254
Midwestern Christian Academy	Chicago	Midwest Bible Church	P-8 / 200
Northwest Christian Schl	Chicago	Independent	K-8 / 132
Ravenswood Baptist Schl	Chicago	Baptist	P-12 / 224
Decatur Christian Schl	Decatur	Baptist	1-10 / 142
Brentwood Baptist Academy	Des Plaines	Baptist	P-12 / 153
Marquette Manor Baptist Academy	Downers Grove	Baptist	P-12 / 372
Christian Fellowship Schl	Duquoin	Christian Fellowship Church	P-12 / 181
Bethany Christian Academy	Galesburg	Baptist	K-12 / 124
Faith Baptist Christian Schl	Groveland	Baptist	K-12 / 197
Quentin Road Christian Schl	Hawthorn Woods	Quentin Road Bible Church	P-12 / 268
Homewood Christian Academy	Homewood	Full Gospel	K-12 / 242
Ridgewood Baptist Academy	Joliet	Baptist	K-11 / 225
Grace Baptist Academy	Kankakee	Baptist	P-12 / 208
La Salle - Peru Christian Schl	La Salle	Baptist	K-12 / 157
Medinah Christian Schl	Medinah	Baptist	P-8 / 245
Calvary Christian Schl	Naperville	Calvary Temple Church	K-8 / 212
Calvary Baptist Academy	Normal	Baptist	K-12 / 366
Christian Heritage Academy	Northbrook		P-8 / 128
South Side Baptist Schl	Oak Lawn	Baptist	P-12 / 218
Stone Church Christian Academy	Palos Heights	Stone Church	K-8 / 173
Peoria Christian Schl	Peoria		P-12 / 475
Bible Baptist Schl	Quincy	Baptist	P-12 / 143
Berean Baptist Christian	Rockford	Baptist	P-12 / 264
Family Christian Fellowship Academy	Rockford		K-12 / 130
North Love Christian Schl	Rockford	Baptist	K-12 / 175

State/School	City	Affiliation	Grades/Enrollment
Rockford Baptist Schls	Rockford	Baptist	K-12 / 196
Rockford Christian Elementary	Rockford		P-8 / 445
Bible Baptist Christian Academy	Romeoville	Baptist	K-12 / 163
Schaumburg Christian Schl	Schaumburg	Baptist	P-12 / 653
Somonauk Baptist Schls	Somonauk	Baptist	K-12 / 102
Calvary Academy	South Holland		K-12 / 234
Christian Elementary Schl	Springfield	West Side Christian Church	K-8 / 275
Twin City Nazarene Schl	Sterling	Nazarene	K-12 / 159
Lake County Baptist Schl	Waukegan	Baptist	K-12 / 168
Wheaton Christian High Schl	West Chicago		9-12 / 215
Wheaton Christian Grammar Schl	Wheaton	Wheaton Soc for Chrstn Instr	K-8 / 450
Waukegan Christian Schl	Zion		K-12 / 252

Indiana

State/School	City	Affiliation	Grades/Enrollment
Indiana Christian Academy	Anderson	Baptist	P-12 / 290
Liberty Christian Schl	Anderson	Independent	P-12 / 323
Faith Christian Academy	Auburn	Baptist	K-12 / 134
Faith Christian Academy	Berne	Baptist	P-12 / 116
Bethesda Christian Schls	Brownsburg	Baptist	K-12 / 297
Temple Christian Schl	Connersville	Baptist	K-12 / 143
Faith Heritage Christian Schl	Evansville	Baptist	K-12 / 128
Blackhawk Christian Schl	Fort Wayne	Baptist	K-12 / 365
Calumet Baptist Schls, Inc.	Griffith	Regular Baptist	P-12 / 289
Heritage Christian Schls	Hammond	Assembly of God	P-12 / 189
Baptist Academy	Indianapolis	Baptist	P-12 / 200
Colonial Christian Schl	Indianapolis	Baptist	K-12 / 329
Eagledale Christian Schl	Indianapolis	Baptist	K-12 / 196
Heritage Christian Schl	Indianapolis		K-12 / 844&
Suburban Baptist Schls	Indianapolis	Baptist	P-12 / 287
Kokomo Christian Schl	Kokomo	Baptist	P-12 / 247
Lowell Baptist Schl	Lowell	Baptist	K-12 / 154
Chapel Heights Academy	Marion	Baptist	K-12 / 142
Lakeview Christian Schl	Marion	Wesleyan	P-12 / 330
Tabernacle Christian Schl	Martinsville	Baptist	K-12 / 155
First Baptist Christian	Mishawaka	Baptist	P-8 / 161
Heritage Hall Christian Schl	Muncie	Baptist	P-12 / 339
United Christian Schl	Nappanee		1-12 / 108
Grace Baptist Christian Schl	Plymouth	Baptist	K-12 / 110
Portage Christian Schls	Portage	Dunes Christian Educators, Inc.	P-12 / 170
Bethel Christian Schl	Princeton	Bethel Memorial Church	K-8 / 103
Christian Cntr Schl	South Bend	Christian Cntr Cathedral of Praise	K-12 / 242
Terre Haute Baptist Schl	Terre Haute	Baptist	K-12 / 169
South Haven Christian Schl	Valparaiso	South Haven Christian Church	K-12 / 126
Emmanuel Christian Schl	Wabash	Free Will Baptist	P-8 / 122

Iowa

State/School	City	Affiliation	Grades/Enrollment
Cedar Rapids Christian Schl	Cedar Rapids	Baptist	P-12 / 122
Cedar Valley Christian Schl	Cedar Rapids	Cedar Valley Bible Church	P-9 / 162
Quint City Baptist Schl	Davenport	Baptist	K-12 / 107
Des Moines Christian Schl	Des Moines		P-12 / 765&
Community Christian Schls	Fort Dodge	Evangelical Free	P-12 / 129
Morningside Christian Schl	Sioux City	Billy Sunday Memorial Tabernacle	K-12 / 233
Walnut Ridge Baptist Academy	Waterloo	Baptist	K-12 / 321

Kansas

State/School	City	Affiliation	Grades/Enrollment
Central Christian Schl	Hutchinson		P-12 / 308
Muncie Christian Schl	Kansas City		P-12 / 167
Oak Grove Baptist Schl	Kansas City	Baptist	K-12 / 199
Newton Bible Christian Schl	Newton	Newton Bible Church	K-8 / 141
Berean Christian Schl	Olathe	Berean Fundamental Church	K-12 / 145
Kansas City Christian Schl	Prairie Village		K-12 / 495
Maranatha Academy-West Campus	Shawnee		K-12 / 412

State/School	City	Affiliation	Grades/ Enrollment
Shawnee Mission Christian Schl	Shawnee Mission	Baptist	K-12 / 114
Cair Paravel Latin Schl	Topeka		K-12 / 225

Kentucky

State/School	City	Affiliation	Grades/ Enrollment
Christian Fellowship Schl	Benton	Christian Fellowship Church	K-12 / 175
Anchored Christian Schl	Bowling Green	Baptist	K-12 / 135
Calvary Christian Schl	Covington	Baptist	K-12 / 388
Assembly Christian Schl	Lexington	Assembly of God	K-12 / 131&
Lexington Christian Schl	Lexington		P-12 / 286
Riverside Christian Schl	Lost Creek	Brethren	K-12 / 122
Alliance Christian Academy	Louisville	C&MA	P-8 / 163
Evangel Schls	Louisville	Evangel Tabernacle	K-12 / 243
Highview Baptist Schl	Louisville	Baptist	P-12 / 770
Northside Christian Schl	Louisville	Baptist	K-12 / 139

Louisiana

State/School	City	Affiliation	Grades/ Enrollment
Mt. Olive Christian Schl	Athens	Baptist	K-12 / 115
Family Christian Academy	Baton Rouge		P-12 / 519&
Parkview Baptist Schl	Baton Rouge		K-12 / 1147
Northlake Christian Schls	Covington		K-12 / 423
Northside Christian Schl	Crowley	Assembly of God	P-12 / 186
Family Life Christian Academy	Lafayette		K-8 / 107
Westbank Cathedral Academy	Marrero		K-8 / 208
Word of Faith Academy	New Orleans		K-12 / 245
Riverside Christian Academy	River Ridge	Baptist	P-12 / 229&
Claiborne Christian Schl	West Monroe	Family Worship Cntr	P-12 / 227

Maine

State/School	City	Affiliation	Grades/ Enrollment
Bangor Baptist Schls	Bangor	Baptist	K-12 / 136
Kennebunk Christian Academy	Kennebunk	Advent Christian Church	K-12 / 130
Eastgate Christian Schl	New Gloucester	Eastgate Christian Fellowship	K-9 / 111
Temple Academy	Waterville	Calvary Temple	K-12 / 145
Windham Assembly Christian Academy	Windham	Assembly of God	P-12 / 122

Maryland

State/School	City	Affiliation	Grades/ Enrollment
Annapolis Area Christian Schl	Annapolis		K-12 / 625&
Arlington Baptist Schl	Baltimore	Baptist	P-12 / 743
Baltimore Christian Academy	Baltimore	Assembly of God	P-12 / 275
Faith Bible Church Academy	Baltimore	Faith Bible Church	K-12 / 103
Grace Christian Schl	Bowie	Baptist	K-8 / 219
Camp Springs Christian Schl	Camp Springs	Camp Springs Community Church	P-12 / 392
Victory Christian Schl	Charlotte Hall	Baptist	1-12 / 120
Independent Baptist Academy	Clinton	Independent Baptist	K-12 / 153
Wesleyan Christian Schl	Denton	Wesleyan Methodist	K-11 / 119
Elkton Christian Schl	Elkton	Baptist	K-12 / 250
Maranatha Baptist Church Academy	Elkton	Baptist	K-12 / 103
Frederick Christian Academy	Frederick	Baptist	K-12 / 278
Granite Baptist Church Schl	Glen Burnie	Baptist	K-12 / 244
Heritage Academy	Hagerstown	Baptist	K-12 / 282
Lanham Christian Schl	Lanham	Brethren	P-12 / 324
Puritan Christian Schl	Laytonsville	Orthodox Presbyterian	K-12 / 123
Lexington Park Christian Schl	Lexington Park		1-8 / 151
Mount Airy Full Gospel Christian Schl	Mount Airy	Full Gospel Church	P-12 / 160
Odenton Christian Schl	Odenton	Baptist	K-12 / 307
Liberty Christian Schl	Owings Mills	Reformed Presbyterian	P-8 / 208&
Harford Christian Schl	Street	Evangelical Methodist	K-12 / 597
Bethel Christian Schl	Suitland	Baptist	P-8 / 314
Capitol Christian Academy	Upper Marlboro	Baptist	K-12 / 483
Clinton Christian Schl	Upper Marlboro	Baptist	N-12 / 563
Riverdale Baptist Schl	Upper Marlboro	Baptist	K-12 / 1019
Carroll Christian Academy	Westminster	Church of the Open Door	K-12 / 389
Holly Grove Christian Schl	Westover	Mennonite	P-8 / 135

State/School	City	Affiliation	Grades/Enrollment
Massachusetts			
Brockton Christian Elementary	Brockton	Baptist	K-8 / 168
First Baptist Christian Academy	East Longmeadow	Baptist	P-8 / 110
Christian Schl of Greater Fall River	Fall River	Independent	P-8 / 196
Lexington Christian Academy	Lexington	Independent	7-12 / 213&
Twin City Christian Schls	Lunenburg	Baptist	K-12 / 313
North Shore Christian Schl	Lynn		P-8 / 210&
New Testament Christian Schl	Norton	Baptist	K-12 / 183
Faith Baptist Christian Academy	Palmer	Baptist	K-12 / 111
Parkway Christian Academy	Revere	Parkway Christian Cntr	P-8 / 230
Dayspring Christian Academy	South Attleboro	Assembly of God	P-8 / 228&
Fair Haven Christian Schl	South Hamilton	Fair Haven Chapel, Essex	K-8 / 115
Trinity Schl of Cape Cod	South Yarmouth		P-8 / 192
Pioneer Valley Christian Schl	Springfield		P-12 / 272&
Springfield Christian Schl	Springfield	Glorious Gospel Church	P-12 / 217
New England Baptist Academy	West Bridgewater	Baptist	K-12 / 200
Michigan			
Berean Baptist Academy	Adrian	Baptist	K-12 / 128
Lenawee Christian Schl	Adrian	Independent	P-12 / 633&
Oakland Christian Schl	Auburn Hills		K-12 / 618
Metro Baptist Schls	Belleville	Baptist	K-12 / 147
Northern Michigan Christian Academy	Burt Lake	Northern Michigan Bible Church	K-12 / 142
Heritage Christian Schl	Cadillac		P-12 / 113
Plymouth Christian Academy	Canton	Baptist	P-12 / 448
Springfield Christian Academy	Clarkston	Baptist	K-12 / 419
Faith Baptist Schls	Davison	Baptist	K-12 / 335
Faith Christian Schl	Fruitport	Baptist	K-12 / 126
Harbor Light Christian Schl	Harbor Springs	Harbor Light Chapel	K-12 / 118
Saint Matthew Lutheran Schl	Holt	Lutheran	P-12 / 146&
Hidden Springs Christian Schl	Howell	Hidden Springs Retreat Cntr	K-12 / 125&
Freedom Baptist Academy	Hudsonville		K-12 / 350
Jackson Baptist Elementary Schls	Jackson	Baptist	K-12 / 392
Howardsville Christian Schl	Marcellus	Howardsville Gospel Chapel	K-12 / 147
Mount Pleasant Baptist Academy	Mount Pleasant	Baptist	P-12 / 146
Calvary Baptist Academy	Muskegon	Baptist	K-10 / 150
North Branch Wesleyan Academy	North Branch	Wesleyan	P-12 / 296
Oxford Christian Academy	Oxford	Baptist	K-12 / 220
North Hills Christian Schl	Port Huron	Nazarene	P-12 / 128
Rochester Hills Christian Schl	Rochester	Baptist	K-12 / 264
Oakfield Baptist Academy	Rockford	Baptist	P-12 / 143
Calvary Christian Schl	Roseville	Baptist	K-12 / 276
Community Baptist Christian Schl	Saginaw	Baptist	K-12 / 200
Zoe Christian Academy	Saint Clair Shores	New Life Fellowship of Believers	K-8 / 194
Saline Christian Schl	Saline	Assembly of God	P-12 / 271
Sturgis Christian Schl	Sturgis	Nazarene	K-12 / 115
Light And Life Christian Schl	Taylor	Free Methodist	K-8 / 164
State Line Christian Schl	Temperance	Baptist	K-12 / 353
Bethany Christian Schl	Troy	Baptist	K-12 / 450
Juniata Christian Schl	Vassar	Baptist	K-12 / 287
Macomb Christian Schl	Warren	Baptist	P-11 / 333
Grace Christian Schl	Watervliet	Grace Christian Education Assoc	K-12 / 247
Tri-Unity Christian Schls	Wyoming		K-12 / 628
Calvary Christian Academy	Ypsilanti	Baptist	K-12 / 360
Minnesota			
Meadow Creek Christian Schl	Andover	Meadow Creek Church	P-12 / 520
Lake Region Christian Schl	Baxter	Baptist	K-12 / 160
Bethany Academy	Bloomington	Bethany Missionary Church	K-12 / 155&
Chisago Lakes Baptist Academy	Chisago City	Baptist	K-12 / 176
Chapel Hill Academy	Deephaven		K-10 / 135

State/School	City	Affiliation	Grades/Enrollment
Beaver River Christian Schl	Duluth	Fredenberg Chrstn Ed Assoc	K-12 / 155
Maranatha Christian Academy	Edina	Cathedral of Praise	K-12 / 286
Christian Life Church Schls	Farmington	Christian Life Church	K-12 / 170
Hillcrest Lutheran Academy	Fergus Falls	Lutheran Brethren	9-12 / 116
Woodcrest Baptist Academy	Fridley	Baptist	K-12 / 209
Fourth Baptist Christian Schl	Minneapolis	Baptist	K-12 / 594
Northside Christian Schl	Minneapolis		K-9 / 203
Powderhorn Christian Schl	Minneapolis	Nondenominational	K-8 / 120&
Park Christian Schl	Moorhead		K-8 / 200
Owatonna Christian Schl	Owatonna	Baptist	K-12 / 283
Victory Christian Academy	Rochester	Baptist	K-12 / 128
First Baptist Church Schls	Rosemount	Baptist	K-12 / 269
Faith Baptist Christian Schl	St. Paul	Baptist	K-8 / 182
Temple Baptist Schls	St. Paul	Baptist	K-12 / 104
New Life Christian Schl	Woodbury	Baptist	P-12 / 355&

Mississippi

Amory Christian Academy	Amory	Free Will Baptist	K-12 / 131
Temple Christian Academy	Gulfport	Baptist	1-12 / 112
C M & I High Schl	Jackson	Holiness	P-12 / 326
Southern Baptist Educational Cntr	Olive Branch	Baptist	P-12 / 703&

Missouri

Eagle Heights Christian Schl	Avondale	Baptist	K-11 / 196
First Baptist Academy	Belton	Baptist	P-12 / 163
Pisgah Christian Schl	Excelsior Springs	Baptist	P-12 / 158
Twin City Christian Academy	Festus	Baptist	K-12 / 293
Faith Christian Schl	Florissant	Baptist	K-12 / 187
Gray Summit Christian Schl	Gray Summit	Baptist	K-12 / 108
Harrisonville Church Schl	Harrisonville	Mennonite	K-8 / 134
Englewood Christian Schl	Independence	Assembly of God	P-12 / 423
New Hope Christian Schl	Independence	Baptist	K-12 / 140
Blue Ridge Christian Schl	Kansas City	Blue Ridge Bible Church	K-12 / 458&
Northland Cathedral Academy	Kansas City	Assembly of God	K-8 / 112
Tri-City Christian Schl	Kansas City	Baptist	P-12 / 625
Southern Missouri Christian Schls, Inc.	Poplar Bluffs	Assembly of God	K-12 / 123
Kingdom Christian Academy	Saint Ann	Independent	P-10 / 192
Saint Joseph Christian Schl	Saint Joseph		K-12 / 111
Christian Schls of Springfield	Springfield	Baptist	P-12 / 298
New Covenant Academy	Springfield	Independent	K-11 / 153
Cornerstone Christian Academy	St. Clair	Baptist	K-12 / 165
Wesleyan Christian Schl	Warrenton	Wesleyan	K-12 / 140

Montana

Emmanuel Christian Schl	Great Falls	Emmanuel Church	K-12 / 102

Nebraska

Nebraska Christian Schls	Central City		K-12 / 157!
Lincoln Christian Schls	Lincoln		K-12 / 346
Parkview Christian Schl	Lincoln	Baptist	K-12 / 117
Bellevue Christian Academy & High Schl	Omaha	Assembly of God	1-12 / 428
Omaha Christian Academy	Omaha	Nondenominational	K-9 / 130

New Hampshire

Good Shepherd Schl	Barrington		P-8 / 124
Faith Christian Cntr	Bedford		K-12 / 174
Concord Christian Schl	Concord	Baptist	K-12 / 253
Dublin Christian Academy	Dublin	Baptist	K-12 / 169
Faith Christian Academy	Gilford	Baptist	P-8 / 180
Bethel Christian Schl	Hudson	Baptist	K-8 / 132
Tabernacle Christian Schls	Hudson	Baptist	P-12 / 168

State/School	City	Affiliation	Grades/Enrollment
Laconia Christian Schl	Laconia	Laconia Christian Fellowship	K-12 / 183
Southeastern N.H. Christian Academy	Somersworth	Baptist	K-12 / 218

New Jersey

State/School	City	Affiliation	Grades/Enrollment
Central Jersey Christian Schls	Asbury Park		K-12 / 178
Brookdale Christian Schl	Bloomfield	Baptist	P-8 / 240
Cape May County Christian Schl	Cape May Court Hse	Faith Fellowship Chapel	K-12 / 178
Bethel Baptist Christian Schl	Cherry Hill	Baptist	K-8 / 239
Crossroads Christian Academy	Clinton	Baptist	P-8 / 222
American Christian Schl	Flanders	Baptist	P-8 / 107
Heritage Christian Schls	Garfield	Baptist	P-12 / 130
Hackensack Christian Schl	Hackensack	Baptist	P-12 / 314
Baptist High Schl	Haddon Heights	Baptist	6-12 / 154
The Kings Christian Schl	Haddon Heights		K-12 / 812&
Faith Christian Schl	Hamilton Square	Baptist	P-8 / 377
Hawthorne Christian Academy	Hawthorne	Hawthorne Gospel	K-12 / 368&
North Jersey Christian Academy	Linden	Calvary Tabernacle	K-12 / 114&
Lighthouse Christian Academy	Manahawkin	Baptist	K-8 / 143
Maranatha Baptist Schl Ministry	Millville	Baptist	K-12 / 100
Bethel Christian Academy	Newark	Assembly of God	K-8 / 184
Parsippany Christian Schl	Parsippany	Baptist	P-12 / 257
Madison Avenue Baptist Academy	Paterson	Baptist	K-12 / 156
Park Bible Academy	Pennsville	Baptist	K-12 / 110
Phillipsburg Christian Academy	Phillipsburg	The Fellowship Church	P-8 / 117
Timothy Christian Schl	Piscataway		K-12 / 465
Gloucester Christian Schl	Pitman	Bethel Community Church	K-12 / 272
Bethel Christian Schl	Port Republic		P-12 / 182
Ringwood Christian Schl	Ringwood	Baptist	P-8 / 183
New Life Christian Schl	South Plainfield	New Life Gospel Church	K-10 / 409
Ambassador Christian Academy	Tom River	Baptist	P-12 / 266
Mercer Christian Academy	Trenton		K-12 / 171
Victory Christian Schl	Williamstown	Baptist	P-12 / 368
Zarephath Christian Schl	Zarephath	Pillar of Fire	K-12 / 107

New Mexico

State/School	City	Affiliation	Grades/Enrollment
Community Christian Schl	Alamogordo	Christ Community Church	P-10 / 170&
Evangel Temple Academy	Albuquerque	Evangel Temple	P-12 / 218
Victory Christian Schl	Albuquerque	Alameda Bible Church	K-12 / 115
Brethren Navajo Missionry & Brding Schl	Counselor	Brethren	K-12 / 117!
Mesilla Valley Christian Schls	Las Cruces	Independent	K-12 / 304
Gateway Christian Schl	Roswell	Baptist	P-12 / 142
Temple Baptist Christian Schl	Santa Fe	Baptist	P-12 / 102

Nevada

State/School	City	Affiliation	Grades/Enrollment
Christian Cntr Schls	Boulder City	Foursquare	P-8 / 100
Trinity Christian Schl	Las Vegas	Trinity Temple	P-12 / 443

New York

State/School	City	Affiliation	Grades/Enrollment
Perth Bible Christian Academy	Amsterdam	Perth Bible Church	P-12 / 212
Glad Tidings Academy	Bronx		P-8 / 288
Bethel Christian Learning Cntr	Cambria Heights	New Greater Bethel Church	1-10 / 101
Upton Lake Christian Schl	Clinton Corners	Evangelical Free	K-12 / 111
Upper Room Christian Schl	Dix Hills		P-12 / 314
Elmira Christian Academy	Elmira		K-12 / 107
Levant Christian Schl	Falconer	Wesleyan	P-12 / 205
Good Shepherd Schl	Kingston	Morning Star Christian Fellowship	P-8 / 122&
Latham Christian Academy	Latham	Baptist	P-12 / 225
Lima Christian Schl	Lima	Baptist	K-12 / 174&
Loudonville Christian Schl	Loudonville	Loudonville Community Church	P-8 / 223
Harmony Christian Schl	Middletown	Baptist	P-9 / 175
Manhattan Christian Academy	New York	Manhattan Bible Church	K-12 / 250
Valley Heights Christian Academy	Norwich	Baptist	P-12 / 111

State/School	City	Affiliation	Grades/ Enrollment
Christian Learning Cntr	Painted Post		P-11 / 110
Lakeshore Christian Schl	Plattsburgh	Baptist	K-12 / 100
Tabernacle Christian Academy	Poughkeepsie	Baptist	1-12 / 106
Northern Dutchess Christian Schl	Rhinebeck	Baptist	P-8 / 116
Living Water Christian Schl	Riverhead		P-12 / 131
Northstar Christian Academy	Rochester	Baptist	K-12 / 490
Mountainside Christian Academy	Schroon Lake	Mountainside Bible Chapel	K-12 / 134
Schenectady Christian Schl	Scotia	Presbyterian	K-12 / 357
Faith Heritage	Syracuse	Interdenominational	K-12 / 600
Tioga Cntr Christian Schl	Tioga Cntr	Baptist	P-12 / 105
West Seneca Christian Schl	West Seneca	Baptist	K-12 / 343
Yonkers Christian Academy	Yonkers		P-8 / 114

North Carolina

Asheville Christian Academy	Asheville		K-12 / 208
Rhema Christian Schl	Asheville	Assembly of God	K-9 / 120
Charlotte Christian Schl	Charlotte		K-12 / 630
Hilltop Christian Schl	Fuquay-Varina	Baptist	K-12 / 124
Vandalia Christian Schl	Greensboro	Baptist	K-12 / 442
Greenville Christian Academy	Greenville	Baptist	K-12 / 398
Wesleyan Education Cntr	High Point	Wesleyan	P-12 / 811&
Sheets Memorial Christian Schl	Lexington	Baptist	P-12 / 285
Bible Baptist Christian Schl	Matthews	Baptist	K-12 / 335
The Gramercy Schl	Newport	Faith Evangelical Bible Church	K-8 / 124
Friendship Christian Schls	Raleigh	Baptist	P-12 / 457
Wake Christian Academy	Raleigh	Baptist	K-12 / 621
Community Baptist Schls	Reidsville	Baptist	P-8 / 175
Rockwell Christian Schl	Rockwell	Baptist	K-8 / 154
Roxboro Christian Academy	Roxboro	Independent	P-12 / 164
North Hills Christian Schl	Salisbury	North Hills Church	P-12 / 254
Calvary Christian Schl	Southern Pines	Calvary Memorial Church	K-12 / 117
Carolina Christian Academy	Thomasville		K-12 / 154
Columbus Christian Academy	Whiteville	Missionary Alliance Church	K-12 / 105
Wilmington Christian Academy	Wilmington	Baptist	K-12 / 560
Salem Baptist Christian Schl	Winston Salem	Baptist	1-8 / 198

North Dakota

Shema Christian Schl	Grand Forks	Shema Christian Schl / Inc.	K-8 / 103
Shiloh Christian Schl	Mandan	Independent	K-12 / 251
Our Redeemers Christian Schl	Minot	Lutheran Brethren	P-8 / 106

Ohio

Ashland Christian Schl	Ashland	Brethren	P-8 / 300
Ashtabula Christian Life Academy	Ashtabula	Assembly of God	K-12 / 173
Heritage Christian Schl	Brooklyn	Baptist	K-12 / 343
Wayside Christian Schl	Bucyrus	Wayside Chapel	K-12 / 132
Geauga Christian Schl	Burton	Assembly of God	K-12 / 145
World Harvest Christian Academy	Canal Winchester	World Harvest Church	P-10 / 258
Heritage Christian Schl	Canton		P-12 / 442
Central Baptist Schls	Cincinnati	Baptist	K-12 / 243
Norwood Baptist Christian Schl	Cincinnati	Baptist	K-12 / 225&
Baptist Christian Schl	Cleveland	Baptist	7-12 / 102
Westside Baptist Christian Schl	Cleveland		K-8 / 120
Columbus Christian Schl	Columbus	The Redeemers Church	K-12 / 146&
Liberty Christian Academy	Columbus	Independent	1-12 / 302
Maranatha Christian Schl	Columbus	Baptist	K-12 / 341
Sonshine Christian Academy	Columbus		P-12 / 202
Cuyahoga Valley Christian Academy	Cuyahoga Falls		7-12 / 450
Dayton Christian Schls, Inc.	Dayton	Independent	K-12 / 1860&
Temple Christian Schl	Dayton	Baptist	K-12 / 156
Delaware Christian Schl	Delaware	Delaware Bible	K-12 / 228
East Liverpool Christian Schl	East Liverpool	Independent	P-12 / 185

State/School	City	Affiliation	Grades/Enrollment
Open Door Christian Schl, Inc.	Elyria	Church of the Open Door	P-12 / 625&
The Kings Academy-Upper Schl	Elyria	Christ The King Community	4-12 / 180
Tri-County Christian Schls	Fairfield	Assembly of God	K-12 / 543&
Heritage Christian Schl	Findlay	Baptist	K-12 / 250
Evangel Christian Academy	Gahanna	Assembly of God	P-8 / 255&
Ohio Valley Christian Schl	Gallipolis	Baptist	K-12 / 202
Faith Christian Schl	Greenville	Baptist	P-12 / 151
Hamilton Christian Schl	Hamilton	Baptist	P-12 / 185
Lake Cntr Christian Schl	Hartville	Mennonite	K-8 / 210&
Licking County Christian Academy	Heath	Baptist	K-12 / 279
Valley Christian Schls	Kettering	Christ Life Sanctuary	P-8 / 155
Lima Christian Academy	Lima	Calvary Bible Church	K-12 / 102
Temple Christian Schl	Lima	Baptist	K-12 / 375
North Coast Christian Academy	Lorain	Church On The North Coast	1-8 / 106
Mansfield Christian Schl	Mansfield	Independent	K-12 / 638
Temple Christian Schl	Mansfield	Baptist	K-12 / 259
Marietta Christian Schl	Marietta	Marietta Bible Cntr Church	K-12 / 123
First Baptist Christian Schl	Medina	Baptist	P-12 / 322
Middletown Christian Schl	Middletown	Baptist	K-12 / 388
Christian Cntr Schls	Parma	Foursquare	K-12 / 240
Parma Heights Christian Academy	Parma Heights	Baptist	K-8 / 159
Ridgeville Christian Schls, Inc.	Springboro	Ridgeville Community Church	P-12 / 355
Cathedral Christian Schl	Sylvania	Cathedral of Praise	K-12 / 105
Toledo Christian Schls	Toledo	Nondenominational	K-12 / 706
Troy Christian Schls	Troy	Baptist	K-8 / 226
Warren Christian Schl	Warren	Assembly of God	K-12 / 169
Dailyville Christian Schl	Waverly	Baptist	P-10 / 117
Christ The King Christian Schl	Westerville	Lutheran	K-10 / 191
Northside Christian Schl	Westerville	Calvary Bible Church	K-12 / 242
Willo Hill Christian Schl	Willoughby	Baptist	K-12 / 329
Grace Brethren Christian Schl	Worthington		P-12 / 1071
Xenia Christian Day Schl	Xenia	Baptist	K-12 / 169
Xenia Nazarene Christian Schl	Xenia	Nazarene	P-8 / 260
Calvary Christian Academy	Youngstown	Pentecostal	K-12 / 216
Youngstown Christian Schl	Youngstown	Assembly of God	P-12 / 300
Zanesville Christian Schl	Zanesville	Maranatha Bible Church	K-12 / 173

Oklahoma

Tulsa Emmanuel Christian Schl	Broken Arrow		K-12 / 108
Christian Heritage Academy	Del City	Baptist	P-12 / 536
Mid-Del Christian Schl	Del City	Assembly of God	P-12 / 334
Oklahoma Christian Schls	Edmond	Independent	P-12 / 459
Oklahoma Bible Academy	Enid		7-12 / 124
Cookson Hills Christian Schl	Kansas	Christian & Church of Christ	1-12 / 120!&
Star Christian Schl of Fine Arts	Moore	Independent	K-10 / 105
Community Christian Schl	Norman	Independent	P-11 / 211
The Master's Schl	Norman	Baptist	P-8 / 117
Britton Christian Academy	Oklahoma City	Independent	P-12 / 142
Grace Christian Academy	Oklahoma City	Assembly of God	K-12 / 347
Life Christian Schl	Oklahoma City	Life Christian Cntr	P-12 / 484
Liberty Academy	Shawnee	Baptist	P-12 / 396
Evangelistic Temple Schl	Tulsa		P-8 / 180
Tulsa Christian Schls	Tulsa	Baptist	K-12 / 650

Oregon

Faith Bible Christian Schl	Aloha	Faith Bible Church	P-12 / 286
Hope Christian Schl	Aloha	Living Hope Fellowship	K-9 / 179
Morning Star Christian Schl	Bend	Neighborhood Church	K-10 / 145
Damascus Christian Schl	Boring		K-12 / 222
Canyonville Bible Academy	Canyonville		K-12 / 105!
Santiam Christian Schls, Inc.	Corvallis		6-12 / 137

State/School	City	Affiliation	Grades/Enrollment
Eugene Christian Schls	Eugene	Nondenominational	P-12 / 202
Willamette Christian Schl	Eugene	Willamette Christian Cntr	P-8 / 290
Grace Christian Schl	Gladstone	Assembly of God	K-9 / 189
Pleasant Valley Christian Schl	Grants Pass	Pleasant Valley Vineyard	P-8 / 110
Bethlehem Christian Schl	Lake Oswego	Baptist	P-8 / 244
East Linn Christian Academy	Lebanon	Nondenominational	K-12 / 290
Grace Christian Schl	Medford	Baptist	P-8 / 416
Kingsview Christian Schl	North Bend	Nazarene	K-8 / 182
Portland Christian Schls	Portland		K-12 / 717
Temple Christian Schl	Portland	Bible Temple	K-12 / 359&
West Hills Christian Schl	Portland	Nondenominational	K-8 / 230
Douglas County Christian Schls	Roseburg		P-11 / 215
Umpqua Valley Christian Schls	Roseburg	Foursquare	K-12 / 121

Pennsylvania

Lehigh Christian Academy	Allentown		P-8 / 160
Eden Christian Academy	Allison Park	Independent	P-10 / 337&
Centre County Christian Academy	Bellefonte	Baptist	P-12 / 176
Belleville Mennonite Schl	Belleville		P-12 / 252&
Bethlehem Christian Day Schl	Bethlehem		K-8 / 170
Bloomsburg Christian Schl	Bloomsburg	Baptist	K-12 / 251
Cumberland Valley Christian Schl	Chambersburg	The Open Door Church	K-12 / 317
Shalom Christian Academy	Chambersburg		K-12 / 372
Calvary Baptist Academy	Clymer	Baptist	K-12 / 102
Blair City Christian Schl	Duncansville	Foot of Ten Indpndnt Bible Chrch	K-12 / 301
Mt. Calvary Christian Schl	Elizabethtown	Mt. Calvary Church	K-12 / 313
Bethel Christian Schl of Erie	Eria	Baptist	K-12 / 236
South Hills Christian Schl	Finleyville	Baptist	K-12 / 225
Open Door Christian Academy	Fort Washington	Church of The Open Door	P-8 / 196
High Point Baptist Academy	Geigertown	Baptist	K-12 / 436
Johnstown Christian Schl	Hollsopple		K-12 / 268&
Mt. View Christian Schl	Hummelstown	Mt. View Bible Church	K-12 / 212
Canaan Christian Academy	Lake Ariel	Canaan Bible Chapel	K-12 / 188
Lancaster Christian Schl	Lancaster		P-12 / 396
Living Word Academy	Lancaster	The Worship Cntr	K-12 / 411
New Danville Mennonite Schl	Lancaster	Mennonite	K-8 / 221
Chapel Christian Academy	Limerick	Limerick Chapel	K-12 / 384
Lititz Christian Schl	Lititz	Brethren	P-8 / 259
Wilson Christian Academy	McKeesport	Wilson Foundation	P-12 / 137
Calvary Baptist Christian Academy	Meadville	Baptist	P-12 / 178
The Christian Academy	Media		P-12 / 830
Conestoga Christian Schl	Morgantown		K-12 / 250
Twin Valley Bible Academy	Morgantown	Twin Valley Bible Chapel	K-12 / 161
Mt. Carmel Christian Schl	Mt. Pleasant	Mt. Carmel Community Church	K-12 / 194
Grace Christian Schl	Myerstown	Brethren	P-12 / 193
Delaware County Christian Schl	Newton Square	Independent	K-12 / 835&
Penn Christian Academy	Norristown	Nondenominational	1-8 / 194
Calvary Temple Christian Academy	Philadelphia		P-8 / 259
Cedar Grove Academy	Philadelphia		P-12 / 735&
Christ Independent Baptist Academy	Philadelphia	Baptist	K-12 / 111
Timothy Academy	Philadelphia	Baptist	P-8 / 301
North Hills Christian Schl	Pittsburgh	Baptist	K-12 / 173
Plumstead Christian Schl	Plumsteadville		6-12 / 336
Ebenezer Faith Christian Schl	Plymouth	Baptist	K-12 / 127
Portersville Christian Schl	Portersville	C&MA	P-12 / 227
Red Lion Christian Schl	Red Lion	Red Lion Bible Church	P-12 / 199
Beaver Valley Christian Academy	Rochester		K-12 / 116&
Faith Christian Schl	Roseto		P-12 / 319
Faith Christian Schl	Roslyn	Faith Community Church	P-9 / 173
Upper Bucks Christian Schl	Sellersville	Baptist	P-12 / 641
Sharon Christian Academy	Sharon	Baptist	P-12 / 143

State/School	City	Affiliation	Grades/ Enrollment
Locust Grove Mennonite Schl	Smoketown		K-8 / 457
Somerset Alliance Comm Christian Schl	Somerset	C&MA	K-8 / 105
Watsontown Christian Academy	Watsontown	C&MA	/ 152
Canyon Christian Academy	Wellsboro	Baptist	K-12 / 117
West Chester Christian Schl	West Chester	Baptist	K-12 / 371
Christian Schl of York	York		K-12 / 670&
West Side Christian Schl	York	Baptist	K-12 / 127

Rhode Island

Barrington Christian Academy	Barrington	Baptist	K-8 / 148
West Bay Christian Academy	North Kingstown		K-8 / 143
First Baptist Christian Schl	Warwick	Baptist	K-12 / 315

South Carolina

Oakwood Christian Schl	Anderson	Baptist	K-12 / 512
Calvary Christian Schl	Belton	Baptist	K-12 / 135
Beaufort Christian Schl	Burton	Baptist	K-12 / 126
Northside Christian Schl	Charleston Heights	Baptist	K-12 / 642
Grace Christian Schl	Columbia	Baptist	K-12 / 512
Easley Christian Schl	Easley	Baptist	K-12 / 174
Landmark Christian Academy	Easley	Baptist	K-12 / 105
Florence Christian Schls	Florence	Baptist	K-12 / 615
Maranatha Christian Schl	Florence	Free Will Baptist	1-12 / 212
Heritage Christian Schl	Gaffney	Baptist	K-12 / 199
Hampton Park Christian Schl	Greenville	Baptist	K-12 / 510
Mitchell Road Christian Academy	Greenville	Presbyterian	P-8 / 284&
Southside Christian Schl	Greenville	Baptist	K-12 / 741
Emmanuel Baptist Schl	Hartsville	Baptist	K-12 / 241
Hilton Head Christian Academy	Hilton Head Island	Baptist	K-12 / 142
Faith Christian Schl	Laurens	Baptist	P-12 / 120
St. Paul's Christian Schl	Leesville	Methodist	K-12 / 174
Calvary Christian Schl	Myrtle Beach	Calvary Bible Church	K-12 / 398
Ferndale Baptist Schl	North Charleston	Baptist	K-12 / 436
Garden City Christian Schl	Orangeburg	Baptist	K-12 / 328
Orangeburg Christian Schl	Orangeburg	Baptist	K-12 / 188
New Covenant Christian Schl	Pageland	Baptist	K-11 / 172
Trinity Christian Schl	Rock Hill	Trinity Bible Church	K-12 / 361
Westgate Christian Schl	Spartanburg	Baptist	K-12 / 215
Sumter Christian Schl	Sumter	Sumter Bible Church	K-12 / 475
Temple Baptist Christian Schl	Sumter	Baptist	P-12 / 189
The Academy of Arts	Taylors	Baptist	K-12 / 152

South Dakota

James Valley Christian Schl	Huron	Interdenominational	K-12 / 132
Sunshine Bible Academy	Miller		K-12 / 122!

Tennessee

Lighthouse Christian Schl	Antioch	Baptist	K-12 / 380
Fairview Christian Academy	Athens	Baptist	K-12 / 108
Tri-Cities Christian Schl	Blountville	Baptist	P-12 / 878
Calvary Christian Schl	Chattanooga	Baptist	P-12 / 179
Grace Baptist Academy	Chattanooga	Baptist	K-11 / 629
Tennessee Temple Academy	Chattanooga	Baptist	K-12 / 631
Bible Baptist Academy	Clarksville	Baptist	K-12 / 122
College Heights Christian Academy	Gallatin	Baptist	K-9 / 204
Hendersonville Christian Academy	Hendersonville	Baptist	K-12 / 198
Berean Academy	Hixson	Baptist	K-12 / 191
Hamill Road Christian Schl	Hixson	Baptist	K-8 / 160
Trinity Christian Academy	Jackson		K-9 / 146
Cedar View Christian Schl	Kingsport	Methodist	K-12 / 188
Kingsport Christian Schls	Kingsport	Baptist	K-12 / 241
Calvary Baptist Schl	Kingston	Baptist	K-12 / 252

State/School	City	Affiliation	Grades/Enrollment
Christian Academy of Knoxville	Knoxville	Independent	K-12 / 381
Knoxville Baptist Christian Schls	Knoxville	Baptist	K-12 / 305
Madison Nazarene Christian Academy	Madison	Nazarene	K-12 / 148
Metropolitan Baptist Schl	Madison	Baptist	K-12 / 248
Central Baptist Schl	Memphis	Baptist	K-12 / 227
Evangelical Christian Schls	Memphis	Interdenominational	K-12 / 1426
Macon Road Baptist Schl	Memphis	Baptist	K-12 / 252
Randall Christian Academy	Memphis	Free Will Baptist	K-12 / 186
Thrifthaven Baptist Schls	Memphis	Baptist	K-12 / 296
Word of Faith Christian Academy	Memphis		P-10 / 154
Mount Juliet Christian Academy	Mount Juliet	Baptist	1-12 / 217&
Franklin Road Christian Schl	Murfreesboro	Baptist	K-12 / 306
Christ Presbyterian Academy	Nashville	Presbyterian	K-9 / 364&
Woodbine Christian Academy	Nashville	Free Will Baptist	K-12 / 202
Faith Christian Academy	Oliver Springs		K-12 / 100
Pleasant View Christian Schl	Pleasant View	Baptist	K-12 / 345
Temple Baptist Schl	Powell	Baptist	K-12 / 261
Harrison Chilhowee Baptist Academy	Seymour	Baptist	8-12 / 122!
Volunteer Christian Academy	Sparta	Baptist	K-12 / 105
South Haven Christian Academy	Springfield	Baptist	K-12 / 107

Texas

State/School	City	Affiliation	Grades/Enrollment
Trinity Christian Academy	Addison		K-12 / 902
Living Stones Christian Schl	Alvin		K-12 / 260
Amarillo Christian Cntr Academy	Amarillo		K-12 / 100
Bible Heritage Schl	Amarillo		P-12 / 144
San Jacinto Christian Academy	Amarillo	Baptist	P-10 / 220
West Texas Christian Schl	Amarillo	Baptist	K-9 / 125
Bethel Christian Schl	Arlington	Assembly of God	P-12 / 175
Pantego Christian Academy	Arlington	Pantego Bible Church	P-9 / 374&
Texas Christian Academy	Arlington	Baptist	K-12 / 321
Central Christian Schl	Austin	Assembly of God	K-12 / 159&
Nazarene Christian Schl	Austin	Nazarene	K-8 / 100
Baytown Christian Academy	Baytown	Alliance Bible Church	P-12 / 199
Cathedral In The Pines Christian Schl	Beaumont		K-8 / 350
Bellaire Christian Academy	Bellaire	Baptist	K-11 / 208
First Baptist Schl	Brownsville	Southern Baptist	P-8 / 287
Bracken Christian Schl	Bulverde	Independent	P-8 / 112
Trinity Christian Schl	Cedar Hill		P-12 / 524
Cornerstone Christian Schl	Cedar Park	Baptist	P-8 / 118
Hilltop Baptist Academy	Cedar Park	Baptist	P-12 / 182
Covenant Christian Academy	Colleyville	Presbyterian	P-9 / 109
Covenant Christian Schl	Conroe	Conroe Bible Church	P-8 / 157&
Lifestyle Christian Schl	Conroe	Assembly of God	K-12 / 199
People's Baptist Church Schl	Corpus Christi	Baptist	K-12 / 130
Corsicana Christian Academy	Corsicana	Independent	K-12 / 102
Brandon Street Christian Academy	Dallas	Foursquare	P-12 / 151
First Baptist Academy	Dallas	Baptist	K-12 / 682
First Baptist Academy East Campus	Dallas	Baptist	K-8 / 157
Life Christian Schl of Dallas	Dallas	Assembly of God	P-12 / 183
Metropolitan Christian Schl	Dallas	Metropolitan Tabernacle	P-8 / 278
Tyler Street Christian Academy	Dallas	United Methodist	P-12 / 470
Liberty Christian Schl	Denton		K-12 / 299&
Brook Hollow Christian Schl	DeSoto	Baptist	K-12 / 198
Christway Academy	Duncanville		K-12 / 194
Northeast Christian Academy	El Paso	Baptist	K-12 / 212
The Oaks	Euless	Covenant	1-8 / 112
Lexington Academy	Farmers Branch	Word of Faith World Outreach Cntr	P-12 / 225
Castleberry Baptist Christian Schl	Fort Worth	Baptist	K-12 / 131
Christian Temple Schl	Fort Worth		K-12 / 135
Lake Country Christian Schl	Fort Worth	Baptist	K-12 / 315

State/School	City	Affiliation	Grades/Enrollment
Meadowbrook Christian Schl	Fort Worth	Bethel Temple	P-10 / 291
Seminary South Assembly Day Schl	Fort Worth		P-8 / 174
Temple Christian Schl	Fort Worth	Baptist	K-12 / 524
Westridge Christian Schl	Fort Worth	Baptist	K-8 / 211
Garland Christian Academy	Garland	Baptist	K-12 / 668
Evangel Temple Christian	Grand Prairie	Assembly of God	P-12 / 323
Shady Grove Christian Academy	Grand Prairie	Shady Grove Church	K-12 / 233
Greenville Christian Schl	Greenville		K-12 / 242
Central Christian Academy	Houston	Independent	K-12 / 101
Greenwood Village Christian Schl	Houston	Baptist	K-12 / 232
North Houston Christian Schls	Houston	Baptist	K-12 / 186
San Jacinto Christian Schl	Houston	Baptist	P-12 / 185
Sweetwater Christian Schl	Houston	Assembly of God	K-12 / 410
Berean Christian Schl of Humble	Humble	Baptist	P-9 / 168
Irving Christian Academy	Irving	Baptist	K-12 / 237
Vineyard Christian Schl	Jacksonville	The Vineyard Church	P-8 / 109
Grace Christian Academy	Killeen	Grace Christian Cntr	K-10 / 134
Brazosport Christian Schl	Lake Jackson		P-9 / 185
Eaglemount Christian Schl	Lewisville	Eaglemount Family Ministries	P-10 / 107
Grace Christian Schls	Longview	Brethren	K-8 / 190
Trinity Christian Schls	Lubbock	Trinity Church	P-10 / 523&
Angelina Christian Schl	Lufkin	Assembly of God	P-9 / 208
Community Christian Schl	Orange	Community Church	K-12 / 306
Fountain Gate Christian Schls	Plano	Fountain Gate Ministries	P-8 / 145
Canyon Creek Christian Academy	Richardson	Baptist	K-12 / 230
Church On The Rock Christian Schl	Rockwall	Church On The Rock	P-9 / 456
Castle Hills First Baptist Schl	San Antonio	Baptist	P-12 / 520
New Covenant Faith Academy	San Antonio	New Covenant Fellowship Church	P-8 / 109
Rainbow Hills Baptist Schl	San Antonio	Baptist	P-11 / 198
San Antonio Christian Schls	San Antonio	Independent	K-12 / 630&
Sunnybrook Christian Academy	San Antonio	Temple of Praise	P-12 / 197
Trinity Church Education	San Antonio	Trinity Church	K-8 / 170
Glad Tidings Christian Schl	Sherman	Assembly of God	K-12 / 164
Faith Lutheran Church Schl	Sugar Land	Lutheran	P-8 / 205
Northside Assembly, Inc.	Texarkana	Northside Assembly	K-12 / 256
Concordia Lutheran High Schl	Tomball	Lutheran	9-12 / 125
Christian Heritage Schl	Tyler	Youth With A Mission	P-12 / 183

Utah

Intermountain Christian Schl	Salt Lake City	Evangelical Free	P-12 / 253

Vermont

Websterville Baptist Christian Schl	Websterville	Baptist	K-12 / 142
Trinity Baptist Schls	Williston	Baptist	K-12 / 112

Virginia

Engleside Christian Schl	Alexandria	Baptist	K-12 / 210
Dayspring Christian Fellowship	Blacksburg		P-12 / 109
Gateway Christian Academy	Blacksburg	Baptist	K-12 / 112
Great Hope Baptist Schl	Chesapeake	Baptist	K-12 / 142
Greenbrier Christian Academy	Chesapeake		K-12 / 610
Stonebridge Schl	Chesapeake		P-8 / 182
Richmond Christian Schl	Chesterfield	Baptist	K-12 / 400&
Culpeper Christian Schl	Culpeper	Independent	K-8 / 115
Evangel Christian Schl	Dale City	Baptist	K-12 / 225
Southall Christian Schl	Danville	Baptist	K-12 / 168
Valley Baptist Christian Schl	Edinburg	Baptist	K-12 / 133
Bethlehem Baptist Christian Academy	Fairfax	Baptist	P-12 / 463
Fairfax Baptist Temple Academy	Fairfax	Baptist	K-12 / 278
Timberlake Christian Schl	Forest	Baptist	K-12 / 399
Faith Baptist Schls	Fredericksburg	Baptist	K-12 / 220
Fredericksburg Christian Schl	Fredericksburg		P-10 / 468

State/School	City	Affiliation	Grades/Enrollment
Gloucester Christian Academy	Gloucester	Lighthouse Worship Cntr	P-11 / 101
Bethel Christian Schl	Hampton	Baptist	P-12 / 269
Hampton Christian High Schl	Hampton	Covenant	7-12 / 162&
West End Christian Schl	Hopewell	Presbyterian	P-12 / 234
Mt. Carmel Christian Academy	Luray	Baptist	K-12 / 187
Lynchburg Christian Academy	Lynchburg	Baptist	P-12 / 961&
Emmanuel Christian Schl	Manassas	Baptist	P-12 / 491
Fresta Valley Christian Schl	Marshall		P-12 / 170
Martinsville Christian Schl	Martinsville	Baptist	K-12 / 126
Denbigh Baptist Christian Schl	Newport News	Baptist	K-12 / 234
Bayview Christian Schl	Norfolk	Baptist	P-9 / 109
Norfolk Christian Schls	Norfolk	Tabernacle Church of Norfolk	P-12 / 861&
Alliance Christian Schls	Portsmouth	C&MA	K-12 / 263
Central Baptist Church Schl	Portsmouth	Baptist	K-12 / 171
Commonwealth Christian Schl	Richmond	Baptist	K-12 / 200
Landmark Christian Schl	Richmond	Baptist	K-12 / 347
Roanoke Valley Christian Schls	Roanoke	Baptist	K-12 / 539&
Christian Heritage Academy	Rocky Mount	Independent	K-12 / 106
Berean Christian Academy	Salem	Baptist	K-12 / 210
Immanuel Christian Schl	Springfield	Immanuel Bible Church	K-8 / 212
Word of Life Christian Academy	Springfield	Assembly of God	P-12 / 299
Stanleytown Baptist Academy	Stanleytown	Baptist	K-12 / 105
Grace Christian Schl	Staunton	Community Fellowship Church	K-9 / 108
Shenandoah Valley Christian Academy	Stephens City	Baptist	K-12 / 160
Faith Christian Schl	Sterling	Faith Bible Church	P-8 / 216&
Atlantic Shores Christian Schl	Virginia Beach	Baptist	P-12 / 495
Tabernacle Baptist Schls	Virginia Beach	Baptist	K-12 / 285
Williamsburg Christian Academy	Williamsburg	Williamsburg New Testament Church	P-12 / 145
Rosedale Christian Academy	Winchester	Baptist	K-12 / 145
Heritage Christian Schl	Woodbridge	Baptist	K-11 / 158
Woodbridge Christian Schl	Woodbridge		K-10 / 148

Washington

Arlington Christian Schl	Arlington	Independent	K-12 / 194
El-Shaddai High Schl	Auburn	Christian Enterprises	7-12 / 160
Neighborhood Christian Schl	Bellevue	Assembly of God	P-8 / 175
Heritage Christian Schl	Bothell	Baptist	P-9 / 461
Bremerton Christian Schl	Bremerton		K-12 / 222
Centralia Christian Schl	Centralia	First Christian Church	P-8 / 246
Silver Lake Christian Schl	Everett	Silver Lake Chapel	P-8 / 140
Columbia Heights Christian Academy	Longview	Assembly of God	K-12 / 183
Snohomish County Christian Schl	Lynwood	Independent	P-12 / 482
Grace Academy	Marysville	Baptist	P-12 / 234
Viewcrest Christian Schl	Mount Vernon	Assembly of God	P-12 / 129
Mountlake Christian Schl	Mountlake Terrace		P-12 / 133&
Evergreen Christian Schl	Olympia	Evergreen Christian Church	P-10 / 269
Christ the King Academy	Poulsbo	Christ Memorial Church	K-8 / 150
Redmond Christian Schl	Redmond		P-11 / 175
Crista Schls	Seattle	Crista Ministries	P-12 / 1166
Seattle Christian Schl	Seattle		K-12 / 567
Valley Christian Schl	Spokane	Valley Fourth Memorial	K-12 / 176
Kings Way Christian Schl	Vancouver	Church of God	K-8 / 163
Valley Assembly Schl	Veradale	Assembly of God	P-12 / 116
Liberty Christian Schl	Walla Walla		K-8 / 106
West Side Christian Schl	Yakima	Baptist	K-12 / 240

West Virginia

Cross Lanes Christian Schl	Charleston	Cross Lanes Bible Church	K-12 / 267
Fair Haven Christian Schl	Charleston	Baptist	K-12 / 120
Emmanuel Christian Schl	Clarksburg	Baptist	K-12 / 129

State/School	City	Affiliation	Grades/Enrollment
Elk Valley Christian Schl	Elkview	Baptist	K-12 / 139
Calvary Christian Schl	Fairmont	Baptist	K-12 / 100
Grace Christian Schl	Huntington	Grace Gospel Church	K-12 / 234
Mid-America Christian Schl	Huntington	Baptist	K-9 / 108
Mingo Christian Schl	Lenore	Baptist	K-12 / 197
Faith Christian Academy, Inc.	Martinsburg	Independent	P-12 / 164
Martinsburg Christian Academy	Martinsburg	Baptist	K-12 / 147
Alliance Christian Schl	Morgantown	Alliance Ministries, Inc.	P-9 / 181
Mercer Christian Academy	Princeton	Baptist	K-12 / 284
Greater Beckley Christian Schls	Prosperity	Baptist	K-12 / 173
Rainelle Christian Academy	Rainelle	Baptist	K-12 / 173
Teays Valley Christian	Scott Depot	Scott Depot Christ Fellowship	K-12 / 236
New Life Christian Academy	Summersville		P-12 / 105

Wisconsin
Green Bay Christian Schl	Green Bay	Interdenominational	K-8 / 221
Christian Life Schl	Kenosha	Assembly of God	K-12 / 304&
Faith Christian Schl	La Crosse	Baptist	P-12 / 110&
Calvary Baptist Schl	Menomonee Falls	Baptist	K-12 / 163
Falls Baptist Academy	Menomonee Falls	Baptist	K-8 / 107
Heritage Christian Schls, Inc.	Milwaukee	Independent	K-12 / 853
Oshkosh Community Christian Schl	Oshkosh	Independent	P-9 / 127
Good Shepherd Christian Academy	River Falls	Communion of Saints	K-12 / 111
Maranatha Academy, Inc.	Superior	Interdenominational	K-12 / 109
Union Grove Christian Schl	Union Grove	Baptist	P-12 / 138
Waukesha Christian Academy	Waukesha	Baptist	K-10 / 126
Calvary Life Academy	West Bend	Assembly of God	P-12 / 130
Faith Christian Schl	Williams Bay		K-12 / 185

Wyoming
Heritage Christian Schl	Gillette		P-12 / 118

Puerto Rico
Colegio Bautista De Levittown	Levittown	Baptist	P-12 / 435

Alberta, Canada
Glenmore Christian Academy	Calgary	C&MA	P-9 / 413
Heritage Christian Schls	Calgary		K-12 / 520
Covenant Community Training Cntr	Edmonton	Peoples Church	P-12 / 135
Meadowlark Christian Schl	Edmonton	Baptist	K-9 / 103
Millwoods Christian Schl	Edmonton	Calvary Community Church	K-12 / 243
Fort Saskatchewan Christian Schl	Fort Saskatchewan	C&MA	K-9 / 100
Grande Prairie Christian Schl	Grande Prairie		K-9 / 145&
Cornerstone Christian Schl	Medicine Hat		K-12 / 132
Olds Koinonia Christian Schl	Olds		K-12 / 115
Strathcona Christian Academy	Sherwood Park	C&MA	P-12 / 629
Prairie General Education Schls	Three Hills	Prarie Bible Institute	K-12 / 608!

Ontario, Canada
KRT Christian Schl	Brampton	Kennedy Road Tabernacle	P-10 / 472
Park Avenue Academy	Burlington	Park Avenue Church	P-8 / 171
Stouffville Christian	Claremont		P-10 / 180&
Niagara Christian College	Fort Erie	Brethren in Christ	7-12 / 190!
Crestwicke Christian Academy	Guelph	Baptist	P-8 / 163
Scarborough Christian Schl	Miliken		K-12 / 217
Newmarket & District Christian Academy	Newmarket	Grace Church	K-8 / 229
Oakville Christian Schl	Oakville		P-11 / 203&
Grace Christian Academy	Peterborough	Grace Christian Ministries, Inc.	K-8 / 121
Pickering Christian Schl	Pickering		P-8 / 120
Faith Christian Academy	Saint Thomas	Baptist	P-8 / 118&
Peoples Christian Schls	Willowdale		K-12 / 685

What Kids Want to Be When They Grow Up

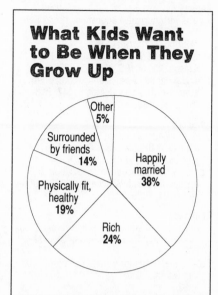

- Other 5%
- Surrounded by friends 14%
- Happily married 38%
- Physically fit, healthy 19%
- Rich 24%

Source: Sesame Place Kids' Poll of 450 kids, ages 5-12

How Kids Picture the 1990s

- Other 3%
- Black President 16%
- A Female U.S. President 39%
- Commercial Space Flight 20%
- Fall of Communism 22%

Source: The Newlin Company Inc. poll of 1,000 children

FOCUS FACT The largest Christian elementary/high school in the world? Liceo Cristiano in San Salvador, El Salvador, founded in 1963 by the Assemblies of God, has an enrollment of more than 19,000 students through grade 12.

HOME SCHOOL SUPPORT ORGANIZATIONS

Alabama
Alabama Home Educators, Inc., PO Box 160091, Mobile, 36616, 1984

Alaska
Alaska Private & Home Educators Association, PO Box 70, Talkeetna, 99676, 907-733-2482, 1987

Arizona
Arizona Families for Home Education, PO Box 4661, Scottsdale, 85261, 602-948-7310, 1982

Christian Home Educators of Arizona, 3015 S. Evergreen Road, Tempe, 85282, 602-897-7688, 1990

Arkansas
Arkansas Christian Home Education Association, PO Box 501, Little Rock, 72203, 501-834-7729, 1981

California
Christian Home Educators Association of California, PO Box 28644, Santa Ana, 92799-8644, 715-537-5121, 1982

Colorado
Colorado Home Schooling Network, 7490 W. Apache, Sedalia, 80135, 303-688-4136, 1981

Homes Offering Meaningful Education (HOME), 1015 S. Gaylord, #226, Denver, 80209, 303-777-1082, 1985

Connecticut
Connecticut Home Schoolers Association, Box 464, Chester, 06412, 203-526-5005, 1983

Education Association of Christian Homeschoolers, Box 446, Broad Brook, 06106

Emanuel Homestead Home Education Resource Center, PO Box 355, S. Woodstock, 06267, 203-974-2416

Delaware
Tri-State Home School Network, Box 7193, Newark, 19714, 303-368-4217, 1987

Florida
Florida at Home, 7615 Clubhouse Estates Drive, Orlando, 32819, 407-422-5357, 1986
Florida Parent-Educators Association, 9245 Woodrun Road, Pensacola, 32514, 904-477-9642, 1984

Georgia
Georgians for Freedom in Education, 5986 Randy Lane, Ellenwood, 30049, 404-832-1910, 1983

Hawaii
Christian Homeschoolers of Hawaii, 91-824 Oama Street, Ewa Beach, 96706, 808-689-6398, 1986
Hilo Home School Association, PO Box 469, Mt. View, 96771, 808-968-8434, 1989

Idaho
Idaho Home Educators, Box 4022, Boise, 83711-4022, 1982

Illinois
Illinois Christian Home Educators, PO Box 261, Zion, 60099, 1984

Indiana
Indiana Association of Home Educators, PO Box 17135, Indianapolis, 46217, 317-782-3397, 1983

Iowa
Iowa Home Educators' Association, PO Box 213, Des Moines, 50301, 1983

Kansas
Kansas for Alternative Education, 19985 Renner Road, Spring Hill, 66083, 913-686-2310, 1984
Kansas Home Educators, 3201 Berry Road, Kansas City, 66106, 913-722-2386
Teaching Parents Association, 100 E. 109th Street North, Valley Center, 67147, 316-755-2159, 1980

Kentucky
Kentucky Christian Home Schooling Association, 1301 Bridget Drive, Fairdale, 40118, 502-363-5104, 1985
Kentucky Home Education Association, 580 Ruckerville Road, Winchester, 40391, 606-744-6404, 1989

Louisiana
Christian Home Educator's Fellowship, PO Box 14421, Baton Rouge, 70898-4421, 504-642-2059, 1985
Louisiana Citizens for Home Education, 3403 Van Buren, Baker, 70714, 504-755-5472, 1982

Maine
Christian Homeschool Association of Maine, PO Box 5496, Augusta, 04332, 207-872-2015, 1985
Guardians of Education for Maine, HC Route 68, Box 124, Cushing, 04563, 207-254-6336, 1978
Maine Homeschool Association, PO Box 3283, Auburn, 04240, 207-777-1700, 1988

Maryland
Maryland Association of Christian Home Education Organizations, PO Box 1041, Emmitsburg, 21727, 301-662-0022, 1984
Maryland Home Education Association, 9085 Flamepool Way, Columbia, 21045, 301-730-0073, 1980

FOCUS FACT A California sex education curriculum titled "Intelligent Choice of Sexual Lifestyle" advises seventh graders to set a "purely personal standard of sexual behavior" for themselves. A sex education curriculum for an *elementary* school system in the same state specifies that children will "develop an understanding of homosexuality," view films, act out homosexual roles, and take a test on what they have learned. So ten-year-olds get gold stars if they do well in homosexual role-play. Every area of education has been infected by this value-neutral philosophy. This is not only tragic but ironic, since at one time the pursuit of virtue was the specific goal of education. "If you ask what is the good of education," said Plato, "the answer is easy—that education makes good men, and that good men act nobly."
—Charles Colson in *Against the Night*, published by Servant Publications.

Massachusetts
Massachusetts Home Learning Association, PO Box 1976, Lenox, 01240, 413-637-2169, 1987
Massachusetts Home Schooling Association of Parent Educators, 15 Ohio Street, Wilmington, 01887, 508-658-8970

Michigan
Christians United to Reclaim Education, PO Box 71050, Madison Heights, 48071-0050, 1985,
Information Network for Christian Homes, 4150 Ambrose N.E., Grand Rapids, 49505, 616-364-4438, 1984

---

66 99 **Many great leaders of the past were home-schooled,**
FOCUS **including John Quincy Adams,**
QUOTE **William Penn, Abraham Lincoln, Thomas Edison, Woodrow Wilson, Franklin D. Roosevelt, General George Patton, and General Douglas MacArthur.**

Historical evidence indicates that prior to the introduction of public education and compulsory school attendance laws, Americans were probably the most literate people in the world.

Source: *Home Education: Is It Working?* Published by Home Oriented Private Education for Texas

---

Minnesota
Minnesota Association of Christian Home Educators, Box 188, Anoka, 55303, 612-753-2370, 1984
TEACH Institute and Accrediting Association, 4350 Lakeland Avenue North, Robbinsdale, 55422, 612-535-5514, 1983

Mississippi
Mississippi Home Schoolers, Box 2067, Starkville, 39759, 601-324-2668, 1983

Missouri
Families for Home Education, 21709 E. Old Atherton Road, Independence, 64058, 816-796-0978

Montana
Grapevine, 1702 Highway 83 North, Seeley Lake, 59868, 406-754-2481, 1986
Home Schoolers of Montana, Box 40, Billings, 59101, 406-248-6762, 1982

Montana Coalition of Home Educators, PO Box 654, Helena, 59624, 406-357-2893, 1988

Nebraska
Nebraska Home Educators Association, 5000 Grand View Lane, Lincoln, 68521, 402-476-9925, 1986

Nevada
Home Schools United—Vegas Valley, PO Box 26811, Las Vegas, 89126, 702-870-9566, 1983
Nevada Home Schools—Northern Division, Box 21323, Reno, 89515, 702-323-0566, 1985
Silver State Education Advocates, 2516 Janelle Drive, Sparks, 89431, 702-356-7058, 1989

New Hampshire
Christian Home Educators of New Hampshire, Box 1653, Hillsboro, 03244
New Hampshire Home Educators Association, 9 Mizoras Drive, Nashua, 03062, 1983

New Jersey
Education Network of Christian Home Schoolers of New Jersey, 65 Middlesex Road, Matawan, 07747, 201-583-7128, 1989
New Jersey Unschoolers Network, 2 Smith Street, Farmingdale, 07727, 201-938-2473, 1977

New Mexico
National Association for the Legal Support of Alternative Schools, PO Box 28223, Santa Fe, 87501, 505-471-6938
New Mexico Christian Home Educators, 5749 Paradise N.W., Albuquerque, 87114, 505-897-1772, 1984
New Mexico Family Educators, PO Box 13383, Albuquerque, 87192, 505-892-5783, 1982

New York
Home Schoolers Exchange, RD 1, Box 172E, East Chatham, 12060, 518-392-4277, 1984
Loving Education at Home, PO Box 332, Syracuse, 13205, 518-377-6019, 1983

North Carolina
North Carolinians for Home Education, 204 N. Person Street, Raleigh, 27601, 919-834-6243, 1983
North Dakota Home School Association, PO Box 539, Turtle Lake, 52575, 701-448-9193, 1984

Ohio

Christian Home Educators of Ohio, PO Box 9083, Canton, 44711, 216-673-7272, 1983

Oklahoma

Coalition of Christian Home Educators of Oklahoma, PO Box 471032, Tulsa, 74147-1032, 918-455-6284, 1984

Oregon

Oregon Christian Home Educators' Association Network, 2515 NE 37th, Portland, 97212, 503-288-1285, 1986

Parents' Education Association, PO Box 1482, Beaverton, 97075, 1983

Pennsylvania

Parent Educators of Pennsylvania, RD 2, Box 141, Wrightsville, 17368, 717-252-0286, 1985

Pennsylvania Homeschoolers, RD 2, Box 11, Kittanning, 16201, 412-783-6512, 1981

Rhode Island

Parent Educators of Rhode Island, PO Box 782, Glendale, 02826, 1984

Rhode Island Guild of Home Teachers, 272 Pequot Avenue, Warwick, 02886, 401-737-2264

South Carolina

South Carolina Home Educators Association, PO Box 33, Goose Creek, 29445, 803-761-3076, 1989

South Dakota

South Dakota Home School Association, 1606 South 4th Avenue, Sioux Falls, 57105, 605-334-2213, 1983

Western Dakota Christian Home Schools, Box 528, Black Hawk, 55718-0528, 605-787-5928, 1983

Tennessee

National Coalition of Alternative Community Schools, 58 Schoolhouse Road, Summertown, 38483, 615-964-3670, 1976

Tennessee Home Education Association, 3677 Richbriar Court, Nashville, 37211, 615-834-3529, 1984

Texas

Family Educators Alliance of South Texas, 1400 N. Flores, San Antonio, 78212, 1989

Hearth & Home Ministries, Inc., PO Box 835105, Richardson, 75083, 214-231-9838, 1984

Home Oriented Private Education for Texas, PO Box 43887, Austin, 78745, 512-280-4673, 1986

Southeast Texas Home School Association, 5620 FM 1960 W. Box 354, Houston, 77069-4202, 713-586-8897, 1984

Utah

Utah Christian Home Schooling, 3190 South 4140 West, West Valley City, 84120, 1985

Vermont

Vermont Home Schoolers Association, Spruce Knob Road, Middletown Springs, 05757, 802-235-2620, 1985

Vermont Homeschoolers Association, RFD, Wells, 05774, 198

Virginia

Home Educators Association of Virginia, PO Box 1810, Front Royal, 22630-1810, 703-635-9322, 1984

Home School Legal Defense Association, Paeonian Springs, 22129, 703-882-3838, 1983

National Center for Home Education, PO Box 125, Hwy 9 at Route 781, Paeonian Springs, 22129, 703-882-4770, 1990

Washington

Family Learning Organization of Washington, PO Box 7256, Spokane, 99207-0256, 509-467-2552, 1983

 FOCUS FACT **Statistical analysis of more than 80 studies indicates that a pupil taught individually achieves on the average 30 percentile points higher on norm-referenced standard achievement tests than a pupil taught in a conventional classroom of 25 or more students.**

Source: *Home Education: Is It Working?* Published by Home Oriented Private Education for Texas

---

Homeschooler's Support Association, 23335 269th Avenue SE, Maple Valley, 98038

National Homeschool Association, PO Box 58746, Seattle, 98138-1746, 206-1544, 1988

Washington Association of Teaching Christian Homes (WATCH), PO Box 554, Colville, 99114, 509-684-3270, 1989

Washington Homeschool Organization (WHO), PO Box 938, Maple Valley, 98038, 206-432-3935, 1986

West Virginia

West Virginia Home Education Association, PO Box 266, Glenville, 26351, 304-462-8296, 1986

West Virginians for Religious Training, PO Box 7504, Charleston, 25356, 304-776-1948, 1982

Wisconsin

Wisconsin Parents' Association, Inc., PO Box 2502, Madison, 53701, 1983

Wyoming

Homeschoolers of Wyoming, PO Box 2197, Mills, 82644, 307-235-4928, 1988

Source: *The Big Book of Home Learning, Volume 1, Getting Started* by Mary Pride. Published by Crossway Books. Copyright © 1990. Used by permission of Good News Publishers/Crossway Books, Wheaton, IL 60187

FOCUS FACT Estimates range from 250,000 students to 1,000,000 students who are being taught at home. Even at the minimum estimate of 250,000 students there are more home schoolers nationally than there are public school students in 16 states! The maximum estimate of one million home schoolers living in one area would represent the 12th largest state in student enrollment.

The Home School Court Report Spring 1990 issue.

HOME SCHOOL GOVERNMENT INFORMATION

Alabama Private Schools Unit, Room 348, State Office Bldg., Montgomery, 36103, 205-261-2910

Alaska Centralized Correspondence Study, Department of Education, PO Box GA, Juneau, 99811-0544, 907-789-2835

Arizona Department of Ed., 1535 W. Jefferson St., Phoenix, 85007, 602-542-3759

Arkansas Dept. of Education, Room 404-B, #4 State Capitol Mall, Little Rock, 72201, 501-682-4252

California Alternative Education Unit, Dept. of Education, PO Box 944272, Sacramento, 94244-2720, 916-322-1048

Colorado State Office of Education, 201 E. Colfax Avenue, Denver, 80203, 303-866-6678

Connecticut State Department of Education, PO Box 2219, Hartford, 06145, 203-566-5458

Delaware Dept. of Public Instruction, PO Box 1402, Dover, 19903, 302-736-4629

Florida Dept. of Education, Administrator of Student Services, Tallahassee, 32301, 904-488-8974

Georgia State Dept. of Education, 1661 Twin Towers East, Atlanta, 30334, 404-656-2446

Hawaii Dept. of Education, PO Box 2360, Honolulu, 96804, 808-548-6095

Idaho Dept. of Education, Len B. Jordan Office Bldg., Boise, 83720, 208-334-2165

Illinois Board of Ed., S-284, 100 N. First Street, Springfield, 62777, 217-782-3950

Indiana Dept. of Education, Room 229, State House, Indianapolis, 46204-2798, 317-232-6614

Iowa Dept. of Education, Grimes State Office Bldg., Des Moines, 50319-0146, 515-281-5295

Kansas Board of Education, Topeka, 66603, 913-296-3142

Kentucky Dept. of Ed., Capital Plaza Tower, Frankfort, 40601, 502-564-2116

Louisiana Dept. of Education, PO Box 94064, Baton Rouge, 70804, 504-342-3473

Maine Dept. of Educational and Cultural Services, Augusta, 04333, 207-784-2094

Maryland State Dept. of Education, 200 W. Baltimore Street, Baltimore, 21201-2595, 301-333-2433

Massachusetts Dept. of Education, 1385 Hancock Street, Quincy, 02169,

Michigan Dept. of Education, PO Box 30008, Lansing, 48909, 517-373-3324

Minnesota Dept. of Education, Room 710, Capitol Square Bldg., 550 Cedar Street, St. Paul, 55101, 612-296-6595

Mississippi State Dept. of Education, PO Box 771, Suite 301, Jackson, 39205, 601-359-3598

Missouri Dept. of Elementary & Secondary Education, PO Box 480, Jefferson City, 65102, 314-751-7602

Montana Office of Public Inst., Room 106, Capitol Station, Helena, 59620, 406-444-4402

Nebraska State Dept. of Ed., 301 Centennial Mall South, Lincoln, 68509, 402-471-2783

Nevada State Dept. of Education, Basic Education Branch, 400 West King Street, Carson City, 89710, 702-687-3136

New Hampshire Division of Standards and Certification, 101 Pleasant Street, Concord, 03301, 603-271-3453

New Jersey Non-Public School Services, 225 West State Street, CN 500, Trenton, 08625, 609-292-5161

New Mexico Dept. of Education, Instructional Support, Education Building, Santa Fe, 87501-2786, 505-827-6515

New York State Education Dept., Room 475 BBA, Albany, 12234, 518-474-4948

North Carolina Division of Non-Public Education, 116 Wet Jones Street, Raleigh, 27603-8001, 919-733-4276

North Dakota Dept. of Public Instruction, State Capitol, 600 East Blvd., Bismarck, 58505, 701-224-2295

Ohio Dept. of Education, Columbus, 43215, 614-466-2761

Oklahoma State Dept. of Education, Oklahoma City, 73105, 405-521-3333

Oregon State Dept. of Ed., 700 Pringle Parkway SE, Salem, 97310, 503-378-3702

Pennsylvania Dept. of Education, Advisory Services, 333 Market Street, Harrisburg, 17126, 717-783-3750

Rhode Island Dept. of Ed., 22 Hayes Street, Providence, 02908, 401-277-2031

South Carolina Dept. of Education, Columbia, 29201, 803-734-8500

South Dakota State Division of Education, Kneip Office Bldg., 700 Governors Drive, Pierre, 57501-2293, 605-773-4662

Tennessee Home Schools, Dept. of Education, 542 Cordell Hull Building, Nashville, 37219, 615-741-2963

Texas Education Agency, 1701 N. Congress, Austin, 78701, 512-463-9734

Utah State Ofc. of Education, 250 E. 500 S., Salt Lake City, 84111, 801-533-6040

Vermont Home Study, Independent School Consultant, State Office Building, 120 State Street, Montpelier, 05602, 802-828-3124

Virginia Dept. of Education, PO Box 6A, Richmond, 23216

Washington Office of Private Education, Old Capitol Building, FG-11, Olympia, 98504, 206-753-256

West Virginia Office of Accreditation, Capitol Complex, B-346, Charleston, 25305, 304-348-3788

Wisconsin Dept. of Public Instruction, 125 S. Webster Street, PO Box 7841, Madison, 53707, 606-266-5761

Wyoming State Dept. of Ed., Hathaway Building, Cheyenne, 82002, 307-777-6213

Books Children Love: A Guide to the Best Children's Literature by Elizabeth Wilson. Resource book to the best children's literature covering a broad range of reading matter, secular and Christian. Published by Crossway Books.

FOCUS
BOOK

HOME SCHOOL EDUCATIONAL ORGANIZATIONS

A Beka Correspondence School/A Beka
Video Home School
PO Box 18000, Pensacola, FL, 32523-9160,
800-874-2352

Advanced Training Institute of America
Box One, Oak Brook, IL, 60521, 708-323-9800

Alpha Omega Publications
PO Box 3153, Tempe, AZ, 85281, 800-821-4443

Alta Vista Home School Curriculum
PO Box 222, Medina, WA, 98039, 206-454-7691

Associated Christian Schools Curriculum
PO Box 27115, Indianapolis, IN, 46227,
317-881-7132

Bob Jones University Press
Greenville, SC, 29614, 800-845-5731

Christian Liberty Academy Satellite Schools
502 Euclid Avenue, Arlington Heights, IL,
60004, 708-259-8736

Christian Light Education
PO Box 1126, Harrisonburg, VA, 22801,
703-424-0750

Christian Schools International
3350 E. Paris Avenue SE, Grand Rapids,
MI, 49508, 800-635-8288

Creative Christian Education
PO Box K, Angwin, CA, 94508, 707-695-3004

Hewitt Research Foundation
PO Box 9, Washougal, WA, 98671, 206-835-8708

Home Study International
6940 Carroll Avenue, Takoma Park, MD,
20913, 202-722-6570

International Institute
PO Box 99, Park Ridge, IL, 60068

Lindenwood Academy
PO Box 3405, Fort Smith, AR, 72913-3405,
501-782-6277

McGuffey Academy
1000 E. Huron, Milford, MI, 48042, 800-521-4350

Rod and Staff Publishers
Crockett, KY, 41413, 606-522-4348

Summit Christian Academy
PO Box 802041, Dallas, TX, 75380, 214-991-2096

Sycamore Tree
2179 Meyer Place, Costa Mesa, CA, 92627,
714-650-4466

SECONDARY CORRESPONDENCE SCHOOLS

American School
850 E. 58th Street, Chicago, IL 60637, 312-947-3300

Arizona, University of
Correspondence/Independent Study, 1955
East Sixth Street, Tucson AZ 85719, 602-621-1896

Arkansas, University of
Department of Independent Study, #2 University
Center, Fayetteville AR 72701, 501-575-3647

Citizens' High School
5575 Peachtree Road, Atlanta, GA 30341, 404-455-8258

Colorado at Boulder, University of,
Division of Continuing Education, Box 178,
Boulder CO 80309-0178, 303-331-2801

Florida, University of
Dept. of Independent Study, 1223 NW 22nd Avenue, Gainesville FL 32611, 904-392-1711

Granton Institute of Technology
263 Adelaide Street West, Toronto, ON M5H
1Y3, 416-977-3929

Hadley School for the Blind
700 Elm Street, Winnetka, IL 60093, 708-446-8111

Home Study International
6940 Carroll Avenue, Takoma Park, MD
20912, 202-722-6570

ICS Newport/Pacific High School
Oak Street and Pawnee Avenue, Scranton, PA
18509, 717-342-7701

Idaho, University of
Correspondence Study in Idaho, CEB-116, Moscow ID 83843-4171, 208-885-6641

Indiana University
Independent Study Program, School of Continuing Studies, Owen Hall, Bloomington IN 47405, 812-855-3693

Kansas, University of
Lawrence, KS 66045, 913-864-4440

Kentucky, University, Eastern
Division of Extended Programs, Coates 27A, Richmond KY 40475-0931, 606-622-2003

Learning and Evaluation Center
479 Drinker Street, PO Box 616, Bloomsburg, PA 17815, 717-784-5220

Massachusetts Dept. of Education
Correspondence Instruction, 1385 Hancock Street, Quincy MA 02169, 617-770-7582

Minnesota, University of
Department of Independent Study, 45 Westbrook Hall, 77 Pleasant Street SE, Minneapolis MN 55455, 612-624-0000

Mississippi State University
Continuing Education, PO Drawer 5245, Mississippi State MS 39762, 601-325-2649

Missouri, University of
Center for Independent Study, 136 Clark Hall, Columbia MO 65211, 314-882-2491

Nebraska, University of
Independent Study, 269 Nebraska Center, Lincoln NE 68583-0900, 402-472-1926

North Dakota State University
Division of Independent Study, State University Station, Box 5036, Fargo ND 58104-5036, 701-237-7182

Oklahoma, University of
Independent Study Department, 1700 Asp, Norman OK 73037, 405-325-1921

Oregon State System of Higher Education
Independent Study, PO Box 1633, Portland OR 97207, 503-464-4865

South Dakota, University of
Independent Study Division, 414 E. Clark, Vermillion SD 57069, 605-677-6108

Tennessee, University of
Dept. of Independent Study, 420 Communications Bldg., Knoxville TN 37996-0300, 615-974-5134

Texas Tech University
Division of Continuing Education, PO Box 4110, Lubbock TX 79409, 806-828-6392

Texas, University of, at Austin
EIMC Independent Learning, PO Box 7700, Austin TX 78713-7700, 512-471-7716

Utah State University
Independent Study, UMC 5000, Logan UT 84322-5000, 801-750-2328

Washington State University
Independent Study Program, 202 Van Doren Hall, Pullman WA 99164-5220, 509-335-3557

Wisconsin, University of
Extension, Independent Study, 432 North Lake Street, Madison WI 53706, 608-263-2055

Wyoming, University of
Correspondence Study Department, PO Box 3294, University Station, Laramie WY 82071, 307-742-5631

Source: *The Home School Manual* by Theodore E. Wade, Jr. Copyright © 1988 and 1990. Published by Gazelle Publications, 5580 Stanley Drive, Auburn, CA 95603. Used by permission.

HOME SCHOOL MAGAZINES

Christian Educator, The Christian Liberty Academy Satellite Schools, 203 E. McDonald Road, Prospect Heights, IL 60070 708-259-8736.

Creative Learning Magazine PO Box 37568, San Antonio, TX 78237. Learning activities around a monthly theme.

Home Education Magazine PO Box 1083, Tonasket, WA 98855 509-684-9855. Articles and "kids' pages" with a wide variety of interests. $24 for 6 issues.

Home Free CBN Publishing, CBN Center, Virginia Beach, VA 23463 804-424-7777. Sent to Home Free Club members. The $29.95 yearly membership fee includes discounts on other home school materials.

Home School Digest Wisdom Publications, PO Box 3154, LaVale, MD 21502 301-759-3218. $10 for four quarterly issues.

Home School Gazette PO Box 359, Burtonsville, MD 20866 301-421-1473. Features articles submitted by children.

Hostex News PO Box 2241, Santa Fe, NM 87504-2241. Stories, poems, drawings, pen pals, for and by home study students. Provides opportunity for kids to get into print. $10 for 8 issues.

KidsArt News PO Box 274, Mt. Shasta, CA 96067 916-926-5076. A 16-page quarterly magazine with art activities for children. $8 per year.

Parent Scene PO Box 2222, Redlands, CA 92373 714-792-2412. Newsletter sent without charge by Dr. Kay Kuzma, seminar speaker, mother and founder of the family ministry and radio program, "Parent Scene."

Teaching Home, The PO Box 20219, Portland, OR 97220-0219 502-253-9633. Magazine for Christian home school families. Affiliated support organizations in 22 states consider TTH their official journal and furnish material to include in center inserts for copies for their territories.

Source: *The Home School Manual* by Theodore E. Wade, Jr. Copyright © 1988 and 1990. Published by Gazelle Publications, 5580 Stanley Drive, Auburn, CA 95603. Used by permission.

FOCUS BOOK *Discovering Your Child's Design* **by Ralph Mattson and Thom Black. Helps you discover and build on the specific gifts God has already provided to your children.** Published by D. C. Cook Publishing Company.

BOOKLIST: HOME SCHOOLING

The Big Book of Home Learning, Volume 1, Getting Started by Mary Pride. Puts you in touch with the books, catalogs, magazines, supplies and organizations that can help your child's educational success. Published by Crossway Books, 1300 Crescent St., Wheaton, IL 60187 $15.

The Christian Home School by Gregg Harris. Beginner's book on home schooling. Answers commonly asked questions, defuses common objections, provides tips on how to make home schooling work. Published by Christian Life Workshops, 182 SE Kane, Gresham, OR 97080 $13.95.

For the Children's Sake by Susan Schaeffer Macaulay. Explains how to make education a "wonderful, life-enriching, joyous" experience. Draws heavily on the philosophy of 19th century British educator Charlotte Mason. Published by Crossway Books, 1300 Crescent St., Wheaton, IL 60187 $7.95.

Home School Burnout by Raymond S. Moore and Dorothy N. Moore. Addresses home schooling burnout: what it is, what causes it and how to cure it. Includes encouraging examples of successful home school parents. Published by Wolgemuth & Hyatt, Publishers, Inc., 1749 Mallory Lane, Suite 110, Brentwood, TN 37027 $14.95.

Home School Manual, The by Theodore E. Wade. Guide dealing with all aspects of home schooling. Published by Gazelle Publications, 5580 Stanley Drive, Auburn, CA 95603

Survivor's Guide to Home Schooling by Luanne Shackelford and Susan White. Amusing book answers all the questions other books avoid, like how in the world you're going to get the laundry done while home schooling six kids. Published by Crossway Books, 1300 Crescent St., Wheaton, IL 60187 $8.95.

RELIGIOUS TRAINING FOR CHILDREN STRONGLY FAVORED

Question: Would you want your child to receive religious instruction?

	Yes / %	No / %	No opinion / %
NATIONAL	86	7	7
Men	83	9	6
Women	88	6	6
Whites	86	8	6
Blacks	87	7	6
Hispanics	80	10	10
Protestants	90	5	5
Catholics	91	4	5
Churched	96	2	2
Unchurched	73	14	13
Respondents with children 4-18	90	6	4

Source: *100 Questions and Answers: Religion in America* by George Gallup, Jr., and Sarah Jones. Published by Princeton Religion Research Center. Copyright 1989. Used by permission.

INTERNATIONAL SCHOOLS

AUSTRALIA

Address:	Australian Christian Academy 319 S. Pine Rd., P.O. Box 10, Strathpine 4500 QLD Australia
Affiliation:	Australian Christian Academy
Type:	National
Grades:	1-12
Enrollment:	756

Address:	Fountain Centre Christian School Box 101, Booleroo Centre SA 5482 Australia
Affiliation:	Booleroo Ministry Centre
Type:	National
Grades:	1-12
Enrollment:	25

Address:	Pacific Hills Christian School Locked Bag No. 3, Round Corner 2158, NSW Australia
Affiliation:	Christian Brethren Schools Ltd.
Type:	National

AUSTRIA

Address:	Vienna Christian School Postfach 277, A-1050, Vienna Austria
Affiliation:	MultiMission
Type:	Missionary
Grades:	1-10
Enrollment:	50

BAHAMAS

Address:	Kingsway Academy N4378, Nassau Bahamas
Affiliation:	Independent
Type:	National
Grades:	K-12
Enrollment:	654

Address:	Windermere High School Box 63, Governor's Harbour, Eleuthera Bahamas
Affiliation:	Gospel Missionary Union
Type:	National
Grades:	9-12
Enrollment:	93
Notes:	Boarding Facilities

BELGIUM

Address:	International Christian Academy Chaussee de Waterloo 36, 1640 Rhode St., Genese Belgium
Affiliation:	Assemblies of God
Type:	Missionary
Grades:	K-6
Enrollment:	16

BOLIVIA

Address:	Carachipampa Christian School Cajon 736, Cochabamba Bolivia

Affiliation:	SIM International
Type:	Missionary
Grades:	K-12
Enrollment:	146

Address:	Santa Cruz Christian Learning Center
	Cajon 4049, Santa Cruz
	Bolivia
Affiliation:	Multi-Mission
Type:	Missionary
Grades:	P-12
Enrollment:	127
Notes:	Special Education

BRAZIL

Address:	Academia Crista de Boa Viagem
	Rua Ribeiro de Brito, 700 Boa
	Viagem, 50,000 Recife, PE
	Brazil
Affiliation:	Boa Viagem Presbyterian
Type:	National
Grades:	P-4
Enrollment:	90

Address:	Amazon Valley Academy
	CP 3030 Agencia Independencia,
	Belem Para 66,041
	Brazil
Affiliation:	UFM International, Inc.
Type:	Missionary
Grades:	1-12
Enrollment:	110
Notes:	Boarding Facilities/Special Education

Address:	Fortaleza Academy
	Caixa Postal 1691, Fortaleza
	CE 60,151
	Brazil
Affiliation:	Baptist Mid-Missions
Type:	Missionary
Grades:	1-12
Enrollment:	68
Notes:	Boarding Facilities

Address:	New Tribes Mission School
	Caixa Postal 1421, Manaus
	69,062, Amazonas
	Brazil
Affiliation:	New Tribes Mission
Type:	Missionary
Grades:	K-12
Enrollment:	86

Address:	Pan American Christian Academy
	Caixa Postal 12,491, 04798
	Sao Paulo
	Brazil
Affiliation:	Missionary
Type:	Special Education
Grades:	K-12
Enrollment:	276

BRITISH WEST INDIES

Address:	Grand Turk Christian Academy
	P.O. Box 14, Grand Turk,
	Turks & Caicos
	British West Indies
Affiliation:	Bible Baptist Church
Type:	National
Grades:	K-6
Enrollment:	195

Address:	Triple C School
	P.O. Box 498, Grand Cayman
	British West Indies
Affiliation:	Church of God
Type:	National
Grades:	K-12
Enrollment:	253
Notes:	Special Education

COLOMBIA

Address:	El Camino Academy
	Apartado Aereo 101241, Bogota 10
	Colombia
Affiliation:	Independent
Type:	Missionary
Grades:	K-12
Enrollment:	71

Address:	New Tribes Mission School
	A.A. 23-53, Villavicencio Meta
	Colombia
Affiliation:	New Tribes Mission
Type:	Missionary
Grades:	1-12
Enrollment:	48
Notes:	Boarding Facilities

DOMINICAN REPUBLIC

Address:	Caribe-Vista School
	c/o 1000 South 350 East, Marion, IN
	46953
	USA
Affiliation:	New Horizons Youth Ministries
Type:	Missionary
Grades:	7-12
Enrollment:	36
Notes:	Boarding Facilities/Special Education

Address:	Colegio Cristiano Logos
	Apartado 2647, Santo Domingo
	Dominican Republic
Affiliation:	Iglesia Biblica del Senor Jesucristo
Type:	National
Grades:	P-7
Enrollment:	197

Address:	Santiago Christian School
	Apartado 62, Santiago
	Dominican Republic
Affiliation:	Missionary
Type:	P-12
Grades:	309
Enrollment:	Special Education

INTERNATIONAL SCHOOLS cont.

ECUADOR

Address:	Alliance Academy
	Casilla 6186, Quito
	Ecuador
Affiliation:	C&MA
Type:	Missionary
Grades:	K-12
Enrollment:	485
Notes:	Boarding Facilities/Special Education

Address:	Nate Saint Memorial School
	Shell, Pastaza
	Ecuador
Affiliation:	HCJB
Type:	Missionary
Grades:	K-8
Enrollment:	24

EL SALVADOR

Address:	Liceo Cristiano
	Apartado 989, San Salvador
	El Salvador
Affiliation:	Assemblies of God
Type:	National
Grades:	P-12
Enrollment:	19,017

ETHIOPIA

Address:	Bingham Academy
	Box 4937, Addis Ababa
	Ethiopia
Affiliation:	SIM International
Type:	Missionary
Grades:	1-8
Enrollment:	141
Notes:	Boarding Facilities

FED REPUBLIC OF GERMANY

Address:	Black Forest Academy
	Postfach 1109, 7842 Kandern 1
	Fed Republic of Germany
Affiliation:	Janz Team Ministries
Type:	Missionary
Grades:	1-12
Enrollment:	200
Notes:	Boarding Facilities/Special Education

Address:	Trinity Christian School
	Neckarplatt 3, 6800 Mannheim 51
	Fed Republic of Germany
Affiliation:	Overseas Christian Servicemen's Center
Type:	Missionary
Grades:	K-12
Enrollment:	46

FED STATES OF MICRONESIA

Address:	Berea Christian School

	P.O. Box 9, Moen, Truk 96942
	Fed States of Micronesia
Affiliation:	Independent
Type:	National
Grades:	K-12
Enrollment:	588

Address:	Nukuno Christian Elementary
	P.O. Box 174, Moen, Truk 96942
	Fed States of Micronesia
Affiliation:	Nukuno Protestant Church
Type:	National
Grades:	K-8
Enrollment:	179

GUAM

Address:	Evangelical Christian Academy
	P.O. Box 23998, GMF 96921
	Guam
Affiliation:	Chalan Pago Evangelical Church
Type:	National
Grades:	P-12
Enrollment:	124

Address:	Harvest Christian Academy
	P.O. Box 23189, GMF 96921
	Guam
Affiliation:	Harvest Baptist Church
Type:	National
Grades:	P-12
Enrollment:	770

Address:	Trinity Christian School
	P.O. Box 11343, Yigo 96929
	Guam
Affiliation:	First Assembly of God
Type:	National
Grades:	K-8
Enrollment:	281

GUATEMALA

Address:	Christian Academy of Guatemala
	Apartado 25-B, 01903, Guatemala City
	Guatemala
Type:	Missionary
Grades:	K-12
Enrollment:	157

Address:	Inter-American School
	Apartado 24, Quexaltenango 09902
	Guatemala
Affiliation:	Assn. of North Am. Missionary Parents
Type:	Missionary
Grades:	P-12
Enrollment:	134

HAITI

Address:	Cowman School
	M.F.I.-Haiti, Box 15665,
	West Palm Beach, FL 33406 USA

Affiliation: OMS International
Type: Missionary
Grades: K-8
Enrollment: 30

Address: Quisqueya Christian School
M.F.I.-Haiti, Box 15665,
West Palm Beach, FL 33406
USA
Affiliation: Independent
Type: Missionary
Grades: P-12
Enrollment: 281
Notes: Special Education

HONDURAS

Address: Academia Los Pinares
Apartado 143-C, Tegucigalpa DC
Honduras
Affiliation: Multi-Mission
Type: Missionary
Grades: P-12
Enrollment: 454

INDONESIA

Address: Bandung Alliance School
J1 Gunung Agung 14,
Bandung 40141, Java
Indonesia
Affiliation: C&MA
Type: Missionary
Grades: 1-6
Enrollment: 40

Address: Hillcrest International School
Tromol Pos 4, Sentani 99000,
Irian Jaya
Indonesia
Affiliation: Multi-Mission
Type: Missionary
Grades: 9-12
Enrollment: 25
Notes: Boarding Facilities

Address: Sentani International School
Kotak Pos 239, Sentani, Irian Jaya
99352
Indonesia
Affiliation: C&MA
Type: Missionary
Grades: 1-8
Enrollment: 100
Notes: Boarding Facilities

Address: Wesley International School
Kotak Pos 88, Malang 65101 East Java
Indonesia
Affiliation: OMS International
Type: Missionary
Grades: K-7
Enrollment: 32

JAPAN

Address: Christian Academy in Japan
1-2-14 Shinkawa Cho, Higashi
Kurume Shi, Tokyo 203
Japan
Affiliation: Multi-Mission
Type: Missionary
Grades: K-12
Enrollment: 285
Notes: Boarding Facilities

Address: Kansai Christian School
951 Tawaraguchi Cho, Ikoma Shi,
Nara Ken 630-02
Japan
Affiliation: Multi-Mission
Type: Missionary
Grades: 1-12
Enrollment: 40

Address: Neighborhood School
P.O. Box 4, Okinawa City 904, Okinawa
Japan
Affiliation: Assemblies of God
Type: National
Grades: P-12
Enrollment: 260

Address: Okinawa Christian School
P.O. Box 42, Urasoe City,
Okinawa 901-21
Japan
Affiliation: Okinawa Christian School Assoc.
Type: Missionary
Grades: P-12
Enrollment: 308

KENYA

Address: Hannah Hunter Cole Memorial School
Box 53435, Nairobi
Kenya
Affiliation: Conservative Bapt. Foreign Mission
Type: Missionary
Grades: K-8
Enrollment: 13

Address: Rift Valley Academy
P.O. Box 80, Kijabe
Kenya
Affiliation: Africa Inland Mission
Type: Missionary
Grades: K-12
Enrollment: 480
Notes: Boarding Facilities

Address: Rosslyn Academy
P.O. Box 14146, Nairobi
Kenya
Affiliation: Assemblies of God, Baptist, Mennonites
Type: Missionary
Grades: K-10
Enrollment: 218
Notes: Special Education

INTERNATIONAL SCHOOLS cont.

KOREA

Address:	Korea Christian Academy
	0-Jung Dong, Taejon 300-210
	Korea
Affiliation:	Southern Baptist, Southern Presbyterian
Type:	Missionary
Grades:	K-12
Enrollment:	75

Address:	Liberty Christian School
	P.O. Box 23, Uijongbu 480-600
	Korea
Affiliation:	Liberty Mission of Korea
Type:	Missionary
Grades:	P-12
Enrollment:	271

LIBERIA

Address:	Barnes Foundation School
	P.O. Box 2029, Monrovia
	Liberia
Affiliation:	
Type:	National
Grades:	P-9
Enrollment:	119

Address:	ELWA Academy
	P.O. Box 192, Monrovia
	Liberia
Affiliation:	SIM International
Type:	Missionary
Grades:	P-8
Enrollment:	170

Address:	West Africa Christian High School
	P.O. Box 37, Monrovia
	Liberia
Affiliation:	SIM Intl & Assemblies of God
Type:	Missionary
Grades:	9-11
Enrollment:	25

MALAYSIA

Address:	Dalat School
	Tanjong Bungah, 11200 Penang
	Malaysia
Affiliation:	C&MA
Type:	Missionary
Grades:	1-12
Enrollment:	194
Notes:	Boarding Facilities

MEXICO

Address:	Colegio Emaus
	Apartado Postal 991, Hermosillo, Sonora
	Mexico
Affiliation:	Emmaus Evangelical Fellowship
Type:	National

Grades:	K-12
Enrollment:	165

Address:	Puebla Christian School
	Apartado 511, 72000 Puebla, Puebla
	Mexico
Affiliation:	CAM Intl & UFM Intl
Type:	Missionary
Grades:	1-9
Enrollment:	36
Notes:	Special Education

NEW ZEALAND

Address:	Hebron Christian College
	P.O. Box 77-105, Mt. Albert, Auckland 3
	New Zealand
Affiliation:	Auckland Christian Fellowship
Type:	National
Grades:	K-12
Enrollment:	166

NIGER

Address:	Sahel Academy
	B.P. 10065, Niamey
	Niger
Affiliation:	SIM Francophone
Type:	Missionary
Grades:	1-9
Enrollment:	29
Notes:	Boarding Facilities

NIGERIA

Address:	Good Shepherd Christian Academy
	P.M.B. 100 Akot Anta P.A., Ukanafun,
	Akwa Ibom State
	Nigeria
Affiliation:	Independent
Type:	National
Grades:	P-5
Enrollment:	60
Notes:	Boarding Facilities/Special Education

NORTHERN MARIANA ISLANDS

Address:	Grace Christian Academy
	Navy Hill 643 C.K., Saipan, MP 96950
	Northern Mariana Islands
Affiliation:	Saipan First Assemblies of God
Type:	National
Grades:	K-12
Enrollment:	154

PAKISTAN

Address:	Murree Christian School
	P.O. Jhika Gali, Murree Hills
	Pakistan

Affiliation:	Multi-Mission
Type:	Missionary
Grades:	K-12
Enrollment:	170
Notes:	Boarding Facilities

PALAU, REPUBLIC OF

Address:	Bethania High School
	Koror, W. Caroline Islands 96940
	Republic of Palau
Affiliation:	Palau Evang. Church & Liebenzell Mission
Type:	National
Grades:	0-12
Enrollment:	89
Notes:	Boarding Facilities

PANAMA

Address:	Hogar Misionero
	Chame
	Panama
Affiliation:	New Tribes Mission
Type:	Missionary
Grades:	1-12
Enrollment:	27
Notes:	Boarding Facilities

PAPUA NEW GUINEA

Address:	Aiyura International Primary School
	Box 407, Ukarumpa Via Lae
	Papua New Guinea
Affiliation:	Summer Inst. of Linguistics
Type:	Missionary
Grades:	K-6
Enrollment:	290
Address:	New Tribes Mission School
	P.O. Box 1079, Goroka
	Papua New Guinea
Affiliation:	New Tribes Mission
Type:	Missionary
Grades:	K-12
Enrollment:	144
Notes:	Boarding Facilities

PARAGUAY

Address:	Asuncion Christian Academy
	Casilla 1562, Asuncion
	Paraguay
Affiliation:	Multi-Mission
Type:	Missionary
Grades:	P-12
Enrollment:	191

PHILIPPINES

Address:	Faith Academy
	P.O. Box 820, 1299 Makati
	Philippines
Affiliation:	Multi-Mission

Type:	Missionary
Grades:	K-12
Enrollment:	638
Notes:	Boarding Facilities/Special Education
Address:	Grace Christian High School
	P.O. Box 2712, Manila
	Philippines
Type:	National
Grades:	P-12
Enrollment:	5001

PORTUGAL

Address:	Greater Lisbon Christian Academy
	Rua Marechal Carmona, 27,
	Loures 2670
	Portugal
Affiliation:	Assn of Baptists for World Evangelism
Type:	Missionary
Grades:	K-12
Enrollment:	35
Address:	InterNational
	Avenida de Sintra Lote #1, Cascais 2750
	Portugal
Affiliation:	Independent
Type:	Missionary
Grades:	P-7
Enrollment:	37

PUERTO RICO

Address:	Academia Menonita
	Collins Esq Asomante, Caparra Heights
	00920
	Puerto Rico
Affiliation:	Mennonite Church
Type:	National
Grades:	P-12
Enrollment:	695
Address:	Carib Christian School
	P.O. Box 470, Ramey Stn., Aguadilla
	00604
	Puerto Rico
Affiliation:	Borinquen Baptist Church
Type:	National
Grades:	P-9
Enrollment:	470
Address:	Wesleyan Academy
	Box 1489, Guaynabo 00657
	Puerto Rico
Affiliation:	Wesleyan Church Corp.
Type:	National
Grades:	P-12
Enrollment:	800

SENEGAL

Address:	Dakar Academy
	B.P. 3189, Dakar
	Senegal
Affiliation:	Multi-Mission
Type:	Missionary

INTERNATIONAL SCHOOLS cont.

Grades: K-10
Enrollment: 95
Notes: Boarding Facilities

SIERRA LEONE

Address: Kabala Rupp Memorial School
Box 28, Kabala Via Freetown
Sierra Leone
Affiliation: Multi-Mission
Type: Missionary
Grades: 1-9
Enrollment: 23
Notes: Boarding Facilities

SPAIN

Address: Evangelical Christian Academy
Calle Talia 26, 28022 Madrid
Spain
Affiliation: Multi-Mission
Type: Missionary
Grades: K-12
Enrollment: 45

TAIWAN R.O.C.

Address: Morrison Academy - Taipei
Ting Chou Lu 705, P.O. Box 30-134,
Taipei 10098
Taiwan R.O.C.
Affiliation: Morrison Christian Assn.
Type: Missionary
Grades: K-8

Address: Morrison Academy - Kaohsiung
400 Hsin Hsing Lane, Kao Tan, Jen Wu
District, Kaohsiung 81405
Taiwan R.O.C.
Affiliation: Morrison Christian Assn.
Type: Missionary
Grades: K-8

Address: Morrison Academy - Taichung
Box 27-24, Taichung 40098
Taiwan R.O.C.
Affiliation: Morrison Christian Assn.
Type: Missionary
Grades: K-12
Notes: Boarding Facilities/Special Education

Address: Morrison Academy - Taitung
P.O. Box 90, Taitung 95099
Taiwan R.O.C.
Affiliation: Morrison Christian Assn.
Type: Missionary
Grades: K-8

TONGA

Address: Lavengamalie Christian School
P.O. Box 367, Nuku'alofa
Tonga
Affiliation: Tokaikolo Christian Fellowship
Type: National
Grades: P-12
Enrollment: 1300

VENEZUELA

Address: Christiansen Academy
Apartado 75, San Cristobal, Tachira
Venezuela
Affiliation: Evangelical Alliance Mission
Type: Missionary
Grades: 1-12
Enrollment: 85
Notes: Boarding Facilities/Special Education

Address: Colegio American de Aragua
Apartado 530, Maracay, Aragua 2101A
Venezuela
Affiliation: Evangelical Free Church of America
Type: Missionary
Grades: K-8
Enrollment: 27

VIRGIN ISLANDS

Address: School of the Good Shepherd
P.O. Box 1069, Kingshill, Saint Croix 00851
Virgin Islands
Affiliation:
Type: National
Grades: P-8
Enrollment: 151

Address: St. Croix Christian Academy
P.O. Box 712, Christiansted 00821
Virgin Islands
Affiliation: First Assembly of God
Type: National
Grades: P-5
Enrollment: 195

WEST AFRICA

Address: International Christian Academy
BP 1171, Bouake 01, Cote d'Ivoire
West Africa
Affiliation: Multi-Mission
Type: Missionary
Grades: 1-12
Enrollment: 202
Notes: Boarding Facilities

Address:	Vavoua International School
	BP 131, Vavoua,
	Cote d'Ivoire
	West Africa
Affiliation:	WEC International
Type:	Missionary
Grades:	1-12
Enrollment:	47
Notes:	Boarding Facilities

ZAMBIA

Address:	Sakeji School
	P.O. Box 20, Ikelenge, Via Kitwe
	Zambia
Affiliation:	Brethren Missions
Type:	Missionary
Grades:	1-9
Enrollment:	99
Notes:	Boarding Facilities

Source: Association of Christian Schools International, LaHabra, CA. Used by permission.

FOCUS BOOK

Choosing Your Child's School **by David W. Smith. Compares public, private. Christian and home schooling. Shows the positives and negatives of each.** Published by Zondervan Publishing House.

HOW TO FIND MORE SCHOOL INFORMATION

For information regarding additional Christian schools write:
- Christian Schools International, 3350 E. Paris Ave, S.E., P.O. Box 8709, Grand Rapids, MI 49518-8709
- American Association of Christian Schools, Box 1088, Fairfax, VA 22030
- Association of Christian Schools International, P.O. Box 4097, Whittier, CA 90607

For information regarding schools affiliated with Lutheran churches write:
- Wisconsin Evangelical Lutheran Synod, 2929 Mayfair Road, Milwaukee, WI 53222 (386 schools)
- The Lutheran Church—Missouri Synod, 1333 S. Kirkwood Road, St. Louis, MO 63122-7295 (1099 schools)
- Evangelical Lutheran Church in America, 8765 W. Higgins Road, Chicago, IL 60631-4194 (154 schools)

THE TEN LARGEST CHURCH-RELATED ELEMENTARY/HIGH SCHOOLS IN THE U.S.

School	Address	Affiliation	Grades	Enroll
1. Pensacola Christian School	Pensacola, FL	Baptist	P-12	1937
2. Dayton Christian Schools Inc.	Dayton, OH	Independent	K-12	1860
3. Village Christian Schools	Sun Valley, CA	Village Church	K-12	1821
4. Trinity Christian Academy	Jacksonville, FL	Baptist	P-12	1544
5. Evangelical Christian Schools	Memphis, TN	Interdenominational	K-12	1426
6. Dade Christian School	Hialeah, FL	Baptist	P-12	1375
7. North Florida Christian School	Tallahassee, FL	Baptist	P-12	1286
8. Friends Christian School	Yorba Linda, CA	Friends	P-8	1252
9. Crista Schools	Seattle, WA	Crista Ministries	P-12	1166
10. The King's Academy	West Palm Beach, FL	Baptist	K-12	1163

The Voices of Tomorrow

At an annual meeting of the National Association of Student Councils, USA TODAY asked the high school student leaders about their attitudes and their hopes for the future. Among their replies:

When looking for a college, cost is uppermost in students' minds:

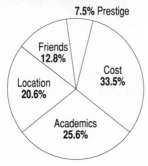

Looking to the future, marriage is slightly more important than career:

The biggest influence on their lives?

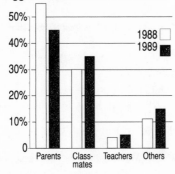

What's most important in a job?

Personality is the most important attribute in a spouse:

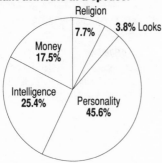

Main concern for the world's future is the environment:

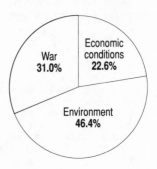

Source: USA TODAY poll of 703 high school student leaders

AMERICANS WANT RELIGION IN SCHOOLS

Question: Here are some sample questions about the Bible, including both Old and New Testaments. Please tell me whether you would or would not object to the public schools . . .

	Would not object %	Would object %	No opinion %
Teaching about the major religions of the world	79	16	5
Using the Bible in literature, history, and social studies classes	75	20	5
Making facilities available after school hours for use by student organizations	74	21	5
Offering elective courses in Bible studies	75	20	5

Source: *100 Questions and Answers: Religion in America* by George Gallup, Jr., and Sarah Jones. Published by Princeton Religion Research Center. Copyright 1989. Used by permission.

HOW MANY TEENS CAN NAME THE TEN COMMANDMENTS?

Commandments Named:	All teenagers %	Regular churchgoers %	Non-regular %
Don't steal	68	73	63
Don't commit adultery	61	69	54
Don't murder	59	67	52
Don't covet	37	45	30
Honor father and mother	34	45	24
Don't bear false witness	29	36	22
Don't take God's name in vain	28	33	24
Don't have other gods	25	35	15
Keep Sabbath Day	16	24	9
Don't worship idols	10	13	7

Source: Gallup Poll, *Emerging Trends*.

CHURCH-RELATED COLLEGES AND UNIVERSITIES

Entrance difficulty rating, as determined by the schools themselves: 1—30% acceptance rate; 2—60% acceptance rate; 3—85% acceptance rate; 4—95% acceptance rate; 5—100% acceptance rate.

School	City, ST	Affiliation	Enroll	Tuition / Board	Diff./Type
United States					
Adrian College	Adrian, MI	United Methodist	1207	$8096 / $2545	3 / LA
Agnes Scott College	Decatur, GA	Presbyterian—Women's college	591	$10450 / $4180	2 / LA

School	City, ST	Affiliation	Enroll	Tuition / Board	Diff./Type
Alaska Bible College	Glennallen, AK	Nondenominational	70	$2060 / $3200	5 / BC
Alaska Pacific University	Anchorage, AK	United Methodist	809	$6330 / $3870	3 / LA
Albion College	Albion, MI	Methodist	1700	$9222 / $3682	3 / LA
Albright College	Reading, PA	United Methodist	1306	$11956 / $3620	2 / LA
Alderson-Broaddus College	Philippi, WV	Baptist	759	$7336 / $2490	3 / LA
Allegheny College	Meadville, PA	United Methodist	1956	$14000 / $3890	3 / LA
Alma College	Alma, MI	Presbyterian	1241	$9852 / $3626	3 / LA
American Baptist College	Nashville, TN	Baptist	167	$1805 / $1884	/ BC
American Indian Bible College	Phoenix, AZ	Assemblies of God	99	$2530 / $2340	5 / BC
American University	Washington, DC	Methodist	10153	$12100 / $5100	3 / LA
Anderson University	Anderson, IN	Church of God	2115	$7330 / $2610	3 / LA
Appalachian Bible College	Bradley, WV	Baptist	186	$3390 / $2600	4 / BC
Arizona College of the Bible	Phoenix, AZ	Independent	130	$3790 / $1420 (Room)	4 / BC
Arkansas Baptist College	Little Rock, AR	Baptist	268	$1670 / $2200	5 / BC
Arkansas College	Batesville, AR	Presbyterian	831	$5330 / $2660	3 / LA
Arlington Baptist College	Arlington, TX	Baptist	182	$2350 / $2350	5 / BC
Asbury College	Wilmore, KY	Nondenominational	1082	$6734 / $2271	3 / LA
Ashland University	Ashland, OH	Brethren	4391	$8632 / $3568	3 / LA
Atlanta Christian College	East Point, GA	Independent	180	$3208 / $2200	4 / LA
Atlantic Christian College	Wilson, NC	Christian Church (Dscpls of Christ)	1434	$5700 / $2570	3 / LA
Augsburg College	Minneapolis, MN	Lutheran	2702	$8835 / $3328	3 / LA
Augustana College	Rock Island, IL	Lutheran	2267	$10308 / $3492	3 / LA
Augustana College	Sioux Falls, SD	Evangelical Lutheran Church in Amer	2004	$8640 / $2650	3 / LA
Austin College	Sherman, TX	Presbyterian	1227	$8735 / $3498	3 / LA
Averett College	Danville, VA	Baptist	1216	$7900 / $4100	3 / LA
Azusa Pacific University	Azusa, CA	Interdenominational	2933	$7740 / $3400	3 / LA
Baker University	Baldwin City, KS	United Methodist	1,121	$5995 / $2990	3 / LA
Baldwin-Wallace College	Berea, OH	Methodist	4713	$9225 / $3675	3 / LA
Baptist Bible College	Springfield, MO	Baptist	815	$1490 / $2190	5 / BC
Baptist Bible College of Pennsylvania	Clarks Summit, PA	Baptist	620	$4979 / $2971	4 / BC
Baptist College at Charleston	Charleston, SC	Baptist	2051	$5832 / $2902	3 / LA
Barber-Scotia College	Concord, SC	Presbyterian Church (USA)	383	$3000 / $2487	5 / LA
Bartlesville Wesleyan College	Bartlesville, OK	Wesleyan	465	$4495 / $3600	4 / LA
Bay Ridge Christian College*	Kendleton, TX	Church of God	45	N/A / N/A	N/A / BC
Baylor University	Waco, TX	Baptist	11774	$5620 / $3485	3 / LA
Beaver College	Glenside, PA	Presbyterian Church (USA)	2294	$9210 / $4225	3 / LA
Belhaven College	Jackson, MS	Presbyterian	721	$5850 / $2100	3 / LA
Belmont College	Nashville, TN	Baptist	2706	$5250 / $2650	3 / LA
Benedict College	Columbia, SC	Baptist	1616	$4571 / $2280	5 / LA
Bennett College	Greensboro, NC	United Methodist	572	$5230 / $2250	3 / LA
Berean College	Springfield, MO	Assemblies of God	685	(cred)$59 / N/A	5 / LA
Bethany Bible College	Scotts Valley, CA	Assemblies of God	465	$5725 / $3000	4 / LA
Bethany College	Bethany, WV	Christian Church (Dscpls of Christ)	825	$9700 / $3630	3 / LA
Bethany College	Lindsborg, KS	Lutheran	736	$6067 / $2912	3 / LA
Bethel College	McKenzie, TN	Cumberland Presbyterian	536	$4100 / $2350	4 / LA
Bethel College	Mishawaka, IN	Missionary Church	585	$6410 / $2500	4 / LA
Bethel College	North Newton, KS	General Conference Mennonite	605	$6182 / $2800	3 / LA
Bethel College	St. Paul, MN	Baptist General Conference	1832	$9250 / $3380	3 / LA
Bethune-Cookman College	Daytona Beach, FL	Methodist	2145	$4134 / $2545	4 / LA
Biola University	La Mirada, CA	Nondenominational	2566	$9172 / $3820	3 / LA
Birmingham-Southern College	Birmingham, AL	Methodist	1937	$8435 / $3280	3 / LA

School	City, ST	Affiliation	Enroll	Tuition / Board	Diff./Type
Blackburn College	Carlinville, IL	Presbyterian	486	$7420 / $3300	3 / LA
Bloomfield College	Bloomfield, NJ	Presbyterian	1605	$7050 / $3500	4 / LA
Blue Mountain College	Blue Mountain, MS	Southern Baptist	355	$3120 / $1940	4 / LA
Bluefield College	Bluefield, VA	Baptist	435	$5020 / $3320	3 / LA
Bluffton College	Bluffton, OH	Mennonite	625	$7065 / $2901	3 / LA
Bob Jones University	Greenville, SC	Independent	4367	$3340 / $3060	2 / LA
Boise Bible College	Boise, ID	Nondenominational	65	$2826 / $2450	5 / BC
Brewton-Parker College	Mt. Vernon, GA	Southern Baptist	1804	$3150 / $2130	5 / LA
Bridgewater College	Bridgewater, VA	Church of the Brethren	985	$8520 / $3960	3 / LA
Bryan College	Dayton, TN	Interdenominational	551	$5270 / $3200	3 / LA
Buena Vista College	Storm Lake, IA	Presbyterian	1045	$8953 / $2794	3 / LA
California Baptist College	Riverside, CA	Southern Baptist	673	$5410 / $3130	4 / LA
California Lutheran University	Thousand Oaks, CA	Lutheran	2853	$8730 / $4000	3 / LA
Calvary Bible College	Kansas City, MO	Independent	317	$3500 / $2440	5 / BC
Calvin College	Grand Rapids, MI	Christian Reformed	4325	$6790 / $2860	3 / LA
Campbell University	Buies Creek, NC	Baptist	4820	$6386 / $2515	3 / LA
Campbellsville College	Campbellsville, KY	Baptist	642	$4500 / $2760	3 / LA
Capital University	Columbus, OH	Evangelical Lutheran Church in Amer	3008	$9530 / $3330	3 / LA
Carroll College	Waukesha, WI	Presbyterian	1478	$9360 / $3070	3 / LA
Carson-Newman College	Jefferson City, TN	Southern Baptist	2017	$6100 / $2580	3 / LA
Carthage College	Kenosha, WI	Lutheran Church in America	2002	$9400 / $3350	3 / LA
Catawba College	Salisbury, NC	United Church of Christ	1044	$7300 / $3500	3 / LA
Cedar Crest College	Allentown, PA	United Church of Christ	962	$9680 / $4180	3 / LA
Cedarville College	Cedarville, OH	Baptist	1942	$5238 / $3255	3 / LA
Centenary College	Hackettstown, NJ	Methodist	820	$9550 / $4575	3 / LA
Centenary College of Louisiana	Shreveport, LA	Methodist	1033	$6180 / $2910	3 / LA
Central Baptist College	Conway, AR	Baptist	183	$2040 / $1700	4 / BC
Central Bible College	Springfield, MO	Assemblies of God	972	$3120 / $2600	4 / BC
Central Christian College of the Bible	Moberly, MO	Christian Churches/ Churches of Christ	73	$2280 / $2000	5 / BC
Central College*	McPherson, KS	Free Methodist	275	$5200 / $2700	N/A / LA
Central Indian Bible College*	Mobridge, SD	Assemblies of God	55	N/A / N/A	N/A / BC
Central Methodist College	Fayette, MO	Methodist	754	$6160 / $2950	3 / LA
Central University of Iowa	Pella, IA	Reformed Church in America	1751	$8725 / $3172	3 / LA
Central Wesleyan College	Central, SC	Wesleyan	439	$6500 / $2820	4 / LA
Centre College	Danville, KY	Presbyterian	855	$8568 / $3355	2 / LA
Chapman College	Orange, CA	Christian Church (Dscpls of Christ)	2221	$11910 / $4640	3 / LA
Christ College Irvine	Irvine, CA	Lutheran Church— Missouri Synod	569	$7995 / $2310	3 / LA
Christian Heritage College	El Cajon, CA	Baptist	340	$6240 / $3100	3 / LA
Cincinnati Bible College	Cincinnati, OH	Church of Christ	614	$3366 / $2826	5 / LA
Circleville Bible College	Circleville, OH	Churches of Christ	148	$2960 / $2580	4 / BC
Claflin College	Orangeburg, SC	United Methodist	850	$4118 / $1890	4 / LA
Clear Creek Baptist Bible College	Pineville, KY	Southern Baptist	153	$1780 / $2000	5 / BC
Clearwater Christian College	Clearwater, FL	Nondenominational	310	$3600 / $3000	4 / LA
Coe College	Cedar Rapids, IA	Presbyterian	1217	$9430 / $3600	3 / LA
College of Idaho	Caldwell, ID	Presbyterian	1189	$8550 / $2300	3 / LA
College of Wooster	Wooster, OH	Presbyterian	1787	$11,570/3660	3 / LA
Colorado Christian University	Lakewood, CO	Interdenominational	781	$4380 / $1980	3 / LA
Columbia Bible College	Columbia, SC	Independent	938	$4265 / $2445	3 / BC
Columbia College	Columbia, MO	Christian Church (Dscpls of Christ)	704	$6498 / $2935	4 / LA
Columbia College	Columbia, SC	United Methodist	1173	$7600 / $2890	3 / LA
Concordia College	Ann Arbor, MI	Lutheran Church— Missouri Synod	416	$6326 / $3290	3 / LA
Concordia College	Moorhead, MN	Lutheran	2884	$8125 / $2525	3 / LA
Concordia University	River Forest, IL	Lutheran Church— Missouri Synod	1275	$6896 / $3363	3 / LA

School	City, ST	Affiliation	Enroll	Tuition / Board	Diff./Type
Concordia College	St. Paul, MN	Lutheran Church—Missouri Synod	1128	$7800 / $2850	4 / LA
Concordia College	Bronxville, NY	Lutheran	416	$7540 / $3900	3 / LA
Concordia College	Portland, OR	Lutheran Church—Missouri Synod	555	$7050 / $2800	4 / LA
Concordia Lutheran College	Austin, TX	Lutheran Church	607	$5960 / $3000	4 / LA
Concordia Univ., Wisconsin	Mequon, WI	Wisconsin Synod	1480	$6700 / 3100	3 / LA
Concordia Lutheran Theological Seminary	St. Catharines, ON	Lutheran Church—Missouri Synod	42	N/A / N/A	N/A / LA
Concordia Teachers College	Seward, NE	Lutheran Church—Missouri Synod	810	$5750 / $2500	3 / LA
Cornell College	Mount Vernon, IA	Methodist	1147	$9980 / $3510	3 / LA
Covenant College	Lookout Mountain, GA	Presbyterian Church in America	580	$7550 / $3250	3 / LA
Crichton College	Memphis, TN	Independent	348	$3900 / $1350	4 / LA
Criswell College Studies	Dallas, TX	Southern Baptist	379	$2680 / N/A	5 / BC
Culver-Stockton College	Canton, MO	Christian Church (Dscpls of Christ)	1067	$6160 / $2340	3 / LA
Cumberland College	Williamsburg, KY	Southern Baptist	1881	$3980 / $2476	4 / LA
Dakota Wesleyan University	Mitchell, SD	United Methodist	640	$5700 / $2500	3 / LA
Dallas Baptist University	Dallas, TX	Southern Baptist	2269	$4620 / $2923	3 / LA
Dallas Christian College	Dallas, TX	Christian Churches/Churches of Christ	92	$2203 / $2590	4 / LA
Dana College	Blair, NE	Evangelical Lutheran Church in Amer	486	$6420 / $2520	3 / LA
Davidson College	Davidson, NC	Presbyterian	1400	$11327 / $3567	2 / LA
Davis & Elkins College	Elkins, WV	Presbyterian	856	$6853 / $3512	4 / LA
Deaconess College of Nursing	St. Louis, MO	United Church of Christ	197	$5000 / $2000	3 / LA
Defiance College, The	Defiance, OH	United Church of Christ	1006	$7184 / $3040	3 / LA
Depauw University	Greencastle, IN	United Methodist	2415	$10550 / $3860	3 / LA
Doane College	Crete, NE	United Church of Christ	671	$7250 / $2325	3 / LA
Dordt College	Sioux Center, IA	Christian Reformed	1038	$6400 / $2240	3 / LA
Dr. Martin Luther College	New Ulm, MN	Wisconsin Evangelical Lutheran Synod	443	$3132 / $1650	5 / LA
Drew University	Madison, NJ	United Methodist	2289	$13992 / $4376	2 / LA
Drury College	Springfield, MO	Christian Church (Dscpls of Christ)	1395	$6950 / $2740	3 / LA
Duke University	Durham, NC	United Methodist	10376	$14123 / $5066	1 / LA
Earlham College	Richmond, IN	Friends	1267	$11610 / $3393	3 / LA
East Coast Bible College	Charlotte, NC	Church of God	273	$2790 / $1850	4 / BC
East Texas Baptist University	Marshall, TX	Baptist	811	$4050 / $2752	3 / LA
Eastern College	St. Davids, PA	American Baptist	1282	$8720 / $3470	3 / LA
Eastern Mennonite College	Harrisonburg, VA	Mennonite	969	$6895 / $3080	3 / LA
Eastern Nazarene College	Quincy, MA	Nazarene	912	$7020 / $3100	3 / LA
Eckerd College	St. Petersburg, FL	Presbyterian	1351	$10895 / $3030	3 / LA
Edward Waters College	Jacksonville, FL	African Methodist Episcopal	686	$3000 / $3540	N/A / LA
Elizabethtown College	Elizabeth, PA	Church of the Brethren	1878	$10700 / $3750	2 / LA
Elmhurst College	Elmhurst, IL	United Church of Christ	3007	$7276 / $2850	3 / LA
Elon College	Elon, NC	United Church of Christ	3368	$6170 / $3150	3 / LA
Emmanuel Coll Schl of Christian Minist	Franklin Springs, GA	Pentecostal Holiness	38	$3360 / $2490	5 / BC
Emmaus Bible College	Dubuque, IA	Nondenominational	178	$1700 / $3580	5 / BC
Emory & Henry College	Emory, VA	United Methodist	853	$6800 / $3700	3 / LA
Emory University	Atlanta, GA	Methodist	9398	$13700 / $4300	2 / LA
Erskine College	Due West, SC	Associate Reformed Presbyterian	514	$8760 / $3105	3 / LA
Eugene Bible College	Eugene, OR	Open Bible Standard Church	118	$3192 / $2250	4 / BC
Eureka College	Eureka, IL	Christian Church (Dscpls of Christ)	438	$7775 / $2920	3 / LA

School	City, ST	Affiliation	Enroll	Tuition / Board	Diff./Type
Evangel College	Springfield, MO	Assemblies of God	1525	$5278 / $2730	3 / LA
Faith Baptist Bible College	Ankeny, IA	Regular Baptist	299	$3514 / $2494	5 / BC
Ferrum College	Ferrum, VA	Methodist	1238	$6500 / $3000	3 / LA
Fisk University	Nashville, TN	United Church of Christ	891	$4665 / $2285	3 / LA
Fla. Bapt. Theological College	Graceville, FL	Southern Baptist	386	$1254 / (rm only)$900	5 / BC
Florida Bible College	Kissimmee, FL	Independent	131	$2740 / $1700	5 / BC
Florida Christian College	Kissimmee, FL	Christian Churches/ Churches of Christ	127	$3140 / $1466	4 / BC
Florida Southern College	Lakeland, FL	United Methodist	1955	$6080 / $3870	3 / LA
Fort Wayne Bible College*	Fort Wayne, IN	Missionary Church	385	N/A / N/A	N/A / BC
Franklin College of Indiana	Franklin, IN	American Baptist	801	$7700 / $2825	3 / LA
Free Will Baptist Bible College	Nashville, TN	Free Will Baptist	269	$2770 / $2560	5 / LA
Fresno Pacific College	Fresno, CA	Mennonite Brethren	1364	$6780 / $3010	3 / LA
Friends Bible College	Haviland, KS	Friends	104	$5975 / $2500	5 / BC
Friends University	Wichita, KS	Friends	1287	$6575 / $2400	3 / LA
Furman University	Greenville, SC	Baptist	2794	$9874 / $3632	2 / LA
Gardner-Webb College	Boiling Springs, NC	Baptist	2189	$5770 / $3200	3 / LA
Geneva College	Beaver Falls, PA	Reformed Presbyterian	1308	$6670 / $3250	3 / LA
George Fox College	Newberg, OR	Friends	944	$8135 / $3400	3 / LA
Georgetown College	Georgetown, KY	Baptist	1562	$5266 / $3150	3 / LA
Gettysburg College	Gettysburg, PA	Evangelical Lutheran Church in Amer	1950	$13625 / $3160	2 / LA
God's Bible School & College	Cincinnati, OH	Interdenominational	210	$2525 / $2090	4 / BC
Gordon College	Wenham, MA	Interdenominational	1216	$10700 / $3406	3 / LA
Goshen College	Goshen, IN	Mennonite	1152	$7205 / $3105	3 / LA
Grace Bible College	Grand Rapids, MI	Grace Gospel Fellowship	113	$3355 / $2400	4 / BC
Grace College	Winona Lake, IN	Brethren	738	$6550 / $3200	3 / LA
Grace College of the Bible	Omaha, NE	Independent	312	$3392 / $2140	3 / BC
Grand Canyon University	Phoenix, AZ	Southern Baptist	1842	$4928 / $2280	3 / LA
Grand Rapids Baptist College	Grand Rapids, MI	Baptist	902	$4846 / $3330	4 / LA
Grand Rapids Schl of the Bible and Music*	Grand Rapids, MI	Independent	185	N/A / N/A	N/A / BC
Grand View College	Des Moines, IA	Evangelical Lutheran Church in Amer	1407	$6740 / $2720	4 / LA
Great Lakes Bible College	Lansing, MI	Independent	132	$3390 / $2460	4 / BC
Greensboro College	Greensboro, NC	United Methodist	1078	$6000 / $3000	3 / LA
Greenville College	Greenville, IL	Free Methodist	743	$7761 / $3300	3 / LA
Grove City College	Grove City, PA	Presbyterian	2125	$4390 / $2390	3 / LA
Guilford College	Greensboro, NC	Friends	1155	$9540 / $3922	3 / LA
Gustavus Adolphus College	St. Peter, MN	Evangelical Lutheran Church in Amer	2349	$11000 / $2750	2 / LA
Hamline University	St. Paul, MN	United Methodist	2235	$10865 / $3809	3 / LA
Hampden-Sydney College	Hampden-Sydney, VA	Presbyterian	944	$11117 / $3741	2 / LA
Hannibal-LaGrange College	Hannibal, MO	Southern Baptist	995	$4300 / $1900	5 / LA
Hanover College	Hanover, IN	Presbyterian	1072	$5750 / $2540	3 / LA
Hardin-Simmons University	Abilene, TX	Baptist	1863	$4930 / $2410	3 / LA
Hastings College	Hastings, NE	Presbyterian	953	$6990 / $2610	3 / LA
Heidelberg College	Tiffin, OH	United Church of Christ	1303	$10100 / $3220	3 / LA
Hendrix College	Conway, AR	United Methodist	1029	$6653 / $2595	3 / LA
Hesston College*	Hesston, KS	Mennonite	550	$5200 / $3000	N/A / LA
High Point College	High Point, NC	United Methodist	2023	$6085 / $2985	3 / LA
Hillsdale Free Will Baptist College	Moore, OK	Free Will Baptist	135	$2355 / $2540	5 / LA
Hiram College	Hiram, OH	Christian Church (Dscpls of Christ)	930	$11116 / $3531	3 / LA
Hobart College	Geneva, NY	Episcopal	1105	$15346 / $4899	2 / LA
Hobe Sound Bible College	Hobe Sound, FL	Nondenominational	182	$3100 / $2215	5 / BC
Hood College	Frederick, MD	United Church of Christ	1976	$10780 / $5345	3 / LA
Hope College	Holland, MI	Reformed Church in America	2770	$9426 / $3610	3 / LA

School	City, ST	Affiliation	Enroll	Tuition / Board	Diff./Type
Houghton College	Houghton, NY	Wesleyan	1164	$8123 / $3044	3 / LA
Houston Baptist University	Houston, TX	Baptist	2243	$4720 / $2595	3 / LA
Howard Payne University	Brownwood, TX	Southern Baptist	1283	$3950 / $2420	4 / LA
Huntingdon College	Montgomery, AL	United Methodist	838	$5160 / $2900	3 / LA
Huntington College	Huntington, IN	United Brethren in Christ	611	$7370 / $3010	3 / LA
Illinois College	Jacksonville, IL	Interdenominational	813	$5000 / $2900	3 / LA
Illinois Wesleyan University	Bloomington, IL	United Methodist	1749	$10085 / $3475	2 / LA
Independent Baptist College*	Dallas, TX	Baptist	35	N/A / N/A	N/A / BC
Indiana Wesleyan University	Marion, IN	Wesleyan	1068	$6420 / $2930	3 / LA
International Bible College	Florence, AL	Churches of Christ	131	$1889 / $700 (Room)	5 / BC
Iowa Wesleyan College	Mt. Pleasant, IA	United Methodist	803	$6500 / $2750	3 / LA
Jamestown College	Jamestown, ND	Presbyterian	841	$6420 / $2980	3 / LA
Jarvis Christian College	Hawkins, TX	Christian Church (Dscpls of Christ)	543	$3631 / $2712	4 / LA
John Brown University	Siloam Springs, AR	Nondenominational	930	$4980 / $2860	3 / LA
John Wesley College	High Point, NC	Interdenominational	60	$3740 / $1200	4 / BC
Johnson Bible College	Knoxville, TN	Christian Churches/ Churches of Christ	434	$3050 / $3275	4 / BC
Jordan College*	Cedar Springs, MI	Nondenominational	2280	$4165 / N/A	4 / LA
Judson College	Elgin, IL	Baptist	522	$7040 / $3590	3 / LA
Judson College	Marion, AL	Baptist	420	$3930 / $2390	3 / LA
Kansas City College & Bible School	Overland Park, KS	Church of God	81	$2495 / $2353	4 / BC
Kansas Wesleyan University	Salina, KS	United Methodist	761	$6220 / $2900	3 / LA
Kendall College	Evanston, IL	United Methodist	400	$6051 / $3777	3 / LA
Kentucky Christian College	Grayson, KY	Christian Churches/ Churches of Christ	479	$3028 / $2760	4 / BC
Kentucky Mountain Bible* Institute	Vancleve, KY	Holiness	45	N/A / N/A	5 / BC
Kentucky Wesleyan College	Owensboro, KY	Methodist	850	$5600 / $3100	3 / LA
King College	Bristol, TN	Presbyterian Church (USA)	588	$5900 / $3050	3 / LA
King's College	Briarcliff Manor, NY	Nondenominational	513	$7515 / $3520	3 / LA
Knoxville College	Knoxville, TN	Presbyterian	1225	$4890 / $3400	5 / LA
Lafayette College	Easton, PA	Presbyterian Church (USA)	1993	$14000 / $4600	2 / LA
LaGrange College	LaGrange, GA	United Methodist	964	$4975 / $3315	3 / LA
Lakeland College	Sheboygan, WI	United Church of Christ	1766	$7445 / $3100	3 / LA
Lambuth College	Jackson, TN	United Methodist	804	$4200 / $2800	3 / LA
Lancaster Bible College	Lancaster, PA	Nondenominational	289	$5720 / $2690	4 / BC
Lane College	Jackson, TN	Christian Methodist Episcopal	525	$4000 / $2242	4 / LA
Lebanon Valley College	Annville, PA	United Methodist	1303	$10650 / $4240	3 / LA
Lee College	Cleveland, TN	Church of God	1535	$4013 / $2700	4 / LA
Lees-McRae College	Banner Elk, NC	Presbyterian Church (USA)	833	$5000 / $2700	4 / LA
Lemoyne-Owen College	Memphis, TN	Independent	1130	$3600 / N/A	5 / LA
Lenoir-Rhyne College	Hickory, NC	Lutheran	1853	$8060 / $3300	3 / LA
LeTourneau University	Longview, TX	Nondenominational	773	$6802 / $3680	3 / LA
Liberty University	Lynchburg, VA	Baptist	16605	$4750 / $3400	4 / LA
LIFE Bible College	Los Angeles, CA	Church of Foursquare Gospel	370	$3670 / $2325	5 / LA
Lincoln Christian College	Lincoln, IL	Christian Churches/ Churches of Christ	357	$3610 / $2410	4 / BC
Lindenwood College	St. Charles, MO	Presbyterian	2105	$7680 / $3900	3 / LA
Lindsey Wilson College	Columbia, KY	United Methodist	1153	$4832 / $2980	5 / LA
Linfield College	McMinnville, OR	American Baptist	1312	$9490 / $3050	3 / LA
Livingstone College	Salisbury, NC	African Methodist Episcopal Zion	558	$3774 / $2468	4 / LA
Louisiana College	Pineville, LA	Southern Baptist	1242	$3860 / $2532	3 / LA

School	City, ST	Affiliation	Enroll	Tuition / Board	Diff./Type
Lubbock Christian University	Lubbock, TX	Church of Christ	1075	$5180 / $2330	5 / LA
Luther College	Decorah, IA	Evangelical Lutheran Church in Amer	2299	$9750 / $3100	3 / LA
Lutheran Bible Institute of Seattle	Issaquah, WA	Lutheran	138	$2410 / $3085	4 / BC
Lycoming College	Williamsport, PA	United Methodist	1204	$10200 / $3650	3 / LA
Lynchburg College	Lynchburg, VA	Christian Church (Dscpls of Christ)	2559	$8800 / $4300	3 / LA
Macalester College	St. Paul, MN	Presbyterian	1855	$11542 / $3500	2 / LA
MacMurray College	Jacksonville, IL	United Methodist	620	$7650 / $3170	3 / LA
Magnolia Bible College	Kosciusko, MS	Churches of Christ	53	$2400 / $1100	5 / BC
Malone College	Canton, OH	Evangelical Friends	1457	$6744 / $2800	3 / LA
Manchester College	North Manchester, IN	Church of the Brethren	1100	$7260 / $2810	3 / LA
Manhattan Christian College	Manhattan, KS	Christian Churches/ Churches of Christ	206	$3010 / $2320	5 / BC
Manna Bible Institute*	Philadelphia, PA	Independent	50	N/A / N/A	N/A / BC
Maranatha Baptist Bible College	Watertown, WI	Baptist	477	$3150 / $2470	5 / BC
Mars Hill College	Mars Hill, NC	Baptist	1344	$5650 / $2700	4 / LA
Mary Baldwin College	Staunton, VA	Presb Church (USA)/ Women's College	684	$8050 / $5550	3 / LA
Maryville College	Maryville, TN	Presbyterian	787	$7750 / $3550	3 / LA
Master's College	Newhall, CA	Nondenominational	1008	$6450 / $3690	3 / LA
McKendree College	Lebanon, IL	United Methodist	1098	$6331 / $2980	3 / LA
McMurry University	Abilene, TX	United Methodist	1720	$4950 / $2270	3 / LA
McPherson College	McPherson, KS	Church of the Brethren	462	$5930 / $2960	3 / LA
Mercer University	Macon, GA	Baptist	3985	$5895 / $3375	3 / LA
Mercer University Atlanta	Atlanta, GA	Baptist	1300	$5895 / N/A	3 / LA
Meredith College	Raleigh, NC	Baptist	2212	$4910 / $2470	3 / LA
Messiah College	Grantham, PA	Brethren in Christ	2280	$8070 / $3990	3 / LA
Methodist College	Fayetteville, NC	United Methodist	1447	$6650 / $2850	4 / LA
Miami Christian College	Miami, FL	Nondenominational	180	$4480 / $2880	3 / BC
Mid-America Bible College	Oklahoma City, OK	Church of God	236	$4118 / $2440	4 / BC
Mid-Continent Baptist Bible College	Mayfield, KY	Baptist	109	$1550 / $1312	5 / BC
MidAmerica Nazarene College	Olathe, KS	Nazarene	1189	$5090 / $2990	5 / LA
Midland Lutheran College	Fremont, NE	Lutheran	935	$7590 / $2400	3 / LA
Midway College	Midway, KY	Christian Church (Dscpls of Christ)	522	$4700 / $3250	4 / LA
Miles College	Birmingham, AL	Christian Methodist Episcopal	620	$3700 / $2300	N/A / LA
Milligan College	Milligan College, TN	Independent	760	$5742 / $2606	3 / LA
Millikin University	Decatur, IL	Presbyterian (USA)	1805	$9256 / $3544	3 / LA
Millsaps College	Jackson, MS	United Methodist	1443	$8196 / $3080	3 / LA
Minnesota Bible College	Rochester, MN	Christian Churches/ Churches of Christ	100	$2910 / $1050 (Room)	4 / BC
Mississippi College	Clinton, MS	Southern Baptist	4221	$4432 / $2260	3 / LA
Missouri Baptist College	St. Louis, MO	Southern Baptist	1032	$5030 / $2300	4 / LA
Missouri Valley College	Marshall, MO	Presbyterian	1177	$7479 / $4356	3 / LA
Mobile College	Mobile, AL	Baptist	1190	$4350 / $2892	4 / LA
Monmouth College	Monmouth, IL	Presbyterian	672	$10635 / $3000	3 / LA
Montreat-Anderson College	Montreat, NC	Presbyterian	414	$5250 / $3000	4 / LA
Moody Bible Institute	Chicago, IL	Independent	1507	$650 / $3600	3 / BC
Moravian College	Bethlehem, PA	Moravian	1785	$11660 / $3780	3 / LA
Morningside College	Sioux City, IA	United Methodist	1240	$8466 / $2830	3 / LA
Morris Brown College	Atlanta, GA	African Methodist Episcopal	1805	$6040 / $3250	3 / LA
Morris College	Sumter, SC	Baptist	796	$3540 / $2255	5 / LA
Mount Olive College	Mount Olive, NC	Free Will Baptist	996	$5500 / $2550	4 / LA
Mount Union College	Alliance, OH	United Methodist	1359	$10680 / $3100	3 / LA

School	City, ST	Affiliation	Enroll	Tuition / Board	Diff./Type
Mount Vernon Nazarene College	Mount Vernon, OH	Nazarene	1061	$5490 / $2840	3 / LA
Muhlenberg College	Allentown, PA	Lutheran	1630	$14100 / $3935	2 / LA
Multnomah School of the Bible	Portland, OR	Interdenominational	659	$4650 / $2600	4 / BC
Muskingum College	New Concord, OH	Presbyterian Church (USA)	1122	$10325 / $3080	3 / LA
Nazarene Bible College*	Colorado Springs, CO	Nazarene	520	N/A / N/A	N/A / BC
Nebraska Christian College	Norfolk, NE	Christian Churches/ Churches of Christ	129	$2290 / $3010	4 / BC
Nebraska Wesleyan University	Lincoln, NE	United Methodist	1607	$7188 / $2570	3 / LA
Newberry College	Newberry, SC	Lutheran	701	$6600 / $2600	3 / LA
North Carolina Wesleyan College	Rocky Mount, NC	United Methodist	1475	$6400 / $3100	3 / LA
North Central Bible College	Minneapolis, MN	Assemblies of God	1174	$4420 / $2810	5 / BC
North Central College	Naperville, IL	United Methodist	2555	$9186 / $3528	3 / LA
North Park College	Chicago, IL	Evangelical Covenant	1098	$9930 / $3765	3 / LA
Northeastern Bible College*	Essex Fells, NJ	Nondenominational	200	$5400 / $2800	3 / BC
Northland College	Ashland, WI	United Church of Christ	721	$7510 / $3240	3 / LA
Northwest Christian College	Eugene, OR	Interdenominational	216	$5270 / $3072	4 / LA
Northwest College of the Assemblies of God	Kirkland, WA	Assemblies of God	695	$5150 / $2300	4 / LA
Northwest Nazarene College	Nampa, ID	Nazarene	1133	$6510 / $2490	3 / LA
Northwestern College	Orange City, IA	Reformed Church in America	1064	$7400 / $2700	3 / LA
Northwestern College	St. Paul, MN	Interdenominational	1036	$7575 / $2520	3 / LA
Northwestern College	Watertown, WI	Wisconsin Evangelical Lutheran (Men's College)	218	$2915 / $1580	3 / LA
Nyack College	Nyack, NY	C&MA	814	$6380 / $3080	4 / BC
Oak Hills Bible College	Bemidji, MN	Independent	112	$3330 / $2280	4 / BC
Oakland City College	Oakland City, IN	General Baptist	648	$6146 / $2480	5 / LA
Ohio Northern University	Ada, OH	United Methodist	2595	$10845 / $3195	3 / LA
Ohio Wesleyan University	Delaware, OH	United Methodist	1966	$12328 / $4526	2 / LA
Oklahoma Baptist University	Shawnee, OK	Baptist	2173	$3826 / $2450	3 / LA
Oklahoma City University	Oklahoma City, OK	Methodist	3778	$4558 / $3060	3 / LA
Olivet College	Olivet, MI	Congregational Christian Church	766	$6860 / $2715	3 / LA
Olivet Nazarene University	Kankakee, IL	Nazarene	1875	$5548 / $3078	4 / LA
Oral Roberts University	Tulsa, OK	Nondenominational	4170	$5595 / $3660	3 / LA
Ottawa University	Ottawa, KS	American Baptist	525	$5600 / $2760	3 / LA
Otterbein College	Westerville, OH	United Methodist	2315	$9261 / $3414	3 / LA
Ouachita Baptist University	Arkadelphia, AR	Baptist	1316	$4410 / $2000	3 / LA
Ozark Christian College	Joplin, MO	Christian Church (Dscpls of Christ)	535	$2080 / $1990	5 / BC
Pacific Christian College	Fullerton, CA	Nondenominational	535	$4350 / $3000	3 / LA
Pacific Coast Bapt. Bible College	San Dimas, CA	Baptist	N/A	N/A / N/A	N/A / BC
Pacific Lutheran University	Tacoma, WN	Evangelical Lutheran	3855	$10449 / $3780	3 / LA
Paine College	Augusta, GA	Methodist	580	$4950 / $2585	4 / LA
Palm Beach Atlantic College	West Palm Beach, FL	Southern Baptist	1375	$4960 / $2650	3 / LA
Patten College	Oakland, CA	Interdenominational	333	$3310 / $3508	4 / LA
Paul Quinn College	Waco, TX	African Methodist Episcopal	517	$2900 / $2750	5 / LA
Pfeiffer College	Misenheimer, NC	United Methodist	905	$6620 / $2960	3 / LA
Philadelphia College of Bible	Langhorne, PA	Nondenominational	578	$5870 / $3400	3 / BC
Philander Smith College	Little Rock, AR	United Methodist	620	$2150 / $1150	5 / LA
Phillips University	Enid, OK	Christian Church (Dscpls of Christ)	1005	$7627 / $2462	3 / LA
Piedmont Bible College	Winston-Salem, NC	Baptist	276	$2890 / $2100	5 / BC
Piedmont College	Demorest, GA	Congregational Christian Church	529	$2736 / $2680	4 / LA

School	City, ST	Affiliation	Enroll	Tuition / Board	Diff./Type
Pikeville College	Pikeville, KY	Presbyterian Church (USA)	915	$3900 / $2350	5 / LA
Pillsbury Baptist Bible College	Owatonna, MN	Baptist	411	$3250 / $2296	5 / LA
Point Loma Nazarene College	San Diego, CA	Nazarene	2221	$7221 / $3390	4 / LA
Practical Bible Training School*	Johnson City, NY	Independent	160	N/A / N/A	N/A / BC
Presbyterian College	Clinton, SC	Presbyterian	1146	$9458 / $3024	3 / LA
Puget Sound Christian College	Edmonds, WA	Christian Church/ Churches of Christ	82	$3915 / $2700	5 / LA
Queens College	Charlotte, NC	Presbyterian	1573	$8300 / $4200	3 / LA
Randolph-Macon College	Ashland, VA	United Methodist	1120	$9280 / $3945	3 / LA
Randolph-Macon Woman's College	Lynchburg, VA	Methodist	750	$10860 / $4750	3 / LA
Reformed Bible College	Grand Rapids, MI	Independent	193	$4320 / $2500	5 / BC
Regent University*	Virginia Beach, VA	Interdenominational	850	$2900 / N/A	N/A / LA
Rhodes College	Memphis, TN	Presbyterian	1386	$11628 / $4282	2 / LA
Roanoke Bible College	Elizabeth City, NC	Independent Christian	112	$2000 / $2060	4 / BC
Roanoke College	Salem, VA	Evangelical Lutheran Church in Amer	1696	$9400 / $3600	3 / LA
Roberts Wesleyan College	Rochester, NY	Free Methodist	824	$8082 / $2826	3 / LA
Rocky Mountain College	Billings, MT	Interdenominational	705	$5800 / $2883	3 / LA
Rust College	Holly Springs, MS	United Methodist	925	$3000 / $1500	3 / LA
Saint Augustine's College	Raleigh, NC	Episcopal	1885	$4150 / $2950	4 / LA
Saint Paul's College	Lawrenceville, VA	Episcopal	736	$4288 / $2855	4 / LA
Salem College	Winston-Salem, NC	Moravian	886	$9075 / $5600	3 / LA
Samford University	Birmingham, AL	Baptist	4159	$5500 / $2754	3 / LA
San Jose Christian College	San Jose, CA	Independent	184	$4806 / $2460	5 / BC
Schreiner College	Kerrville, TX	Presbyterian	618	$6700 / $4300	3 / LA
Seattle Pacific University	Seattle, WA	Free Methodist	3435	$9000 / $3432	3 / LA
Sheldon Jackson College	Sitka, AK	Presbyterian	290	$5390 / $4100	5 / LA
Shenandoah College and Conservatory	Winchester, VA	United Methodist	1016	$7400 / $3500	3 / LA
Shorter College	Rome, GA	Baptist	883	$5000 / $3070	3 / LA
Simpson College	Indianola, IA	Methodist	1737	$8985 / $3100	3 / LA
Simpson College	Redding, CA	C&MA	206	$5672 / $3300	4 / BC
Sioux Falls College	Sioux Falls, SD	American Baptist	962	$6210 / $2575	3 / LA
Southeastern Baptist College	Laurel, MS	Baptist	62	$2220 / $1700	5 / BC
Southeastern Bible College	Birmingham, AL	Nondenominational	141	$3470 / $2576	3 / BC
Southeastern Coll of the Assemblies of God	Lakeland, FL	Assemblies of God	1130	$2805 / $2360	5 / BC
Southern Baptist College	Walnut Ridge, AR	Southern Baptist	517	$2706 / $1812	4 / LA
Southern California College	Costa Mesa, CA	Assemblies of God	898	$6360 / $3100	3 / LA
Southern Methodist University	Dallas, TX	United Methodist	8924	$9880 / $4498	3 / LA
Southern Nazarene University	Bethany, OK	Nazarene	1402	$3696 / $2822	5 / LA
Southwest Baptist University	Bolivar, MO	Southern Baptist	2920	$5785 / $2210	5 / LA
Southwestern Assemblies of God College	Waxahachie, TX	Assemblies of God	701	$3390 / $2512	5 / BC
Southwestern Coll of Christian Ministr	Bethany, OK	Pentecostal Holiness	97	$3139 / $2270	4 / BC
Southwestern College	Phoenix, AZ	Conservative Baptist	126	$4320 / $1960	4 / BC
Southwestern College	Winfield, KS	United Methodist	649	$4152 / $2484	3 / LA
Southwestern University	Georgetown, TX	Methodist	1219	$7600 / $3994	2 / LA
Spring Arbor College	Spring Arbor, MI	Free Methodist	807	$7246 / $2783	4 / LA
St. Andrews Presbyterian College	Laurinburg, NC	Presbyterian	794	$7650 / $3445	3 / LA
St. Louis Christian College	Florissant, MO	Independent Christian	143	$2870 / $1915	4 / LA
St. Olaf College	Northfield, MN	Lutheran	3132	$11200 / $3100	2 / LA
St. Paul Bible College	St. Bonifacius, MN	C&MA	560	$5850 / $3016	4 / BC
Sterling College	Sterling, KS	Presbyterian	457	$6250 / $2800	4 / LA
Stetson University	DeLand, FL	Baptist	3090	$9285 / $3670	3 / LA
Stillman College*	Tuscaloosa, AL	Presbyterian	750	$3550 / $2440	3 / LA
Summit Christian College	Fort Wayne, IN	Missionary Church	371	$5420 / $2610	4 / LA
Susquehanna University	Selinsgrove, PA	Lutheran	1529	$13120 / $3850	3 / LA

School	City, ST	Affiliation	Enroll	Tuition / Board	Diff./Type
Tabor College	Hillsboro, KS	Mennonite Brethren	436	$5590 / $2750	3 / LA
Tarkio College	Tarkio, MO	Presbyterian	553	$6760 / $3200	3 / LA
Taylor University	Upland, IN	Independent	1708	$8183 / $3142	3 / LA
Teikyo Westmar University	LeMars, IA	Methodist	566	$7493 / $2948	4 / LA
Tennessee Temple University	Chattanooga, TN	Baptist	1130	$3870 / $3064	4 / LA
Tennessee Wesleyan College	Athens, TN	United Methodist	605	$4614 / $2876	4 / LA
Texas Christian University	Fort Worth, TX	Christian Church (Dscpls of Christ)	6725	$7096 / $2580	3 / LA
Texas College	Tyler, TX	Methodist Episcopal	441	$3150 / $2430	5 / LA
Texas Lutheran College	Seguin, TX	Evangelical Lutheran Church in Amer	1015	$5300 / $2940	3 / LA
Texas Wesleyan University	Fort Worth, TX	United Methodist	1561	$5200 / $3180	3 / LA
Thiel College	Greenville, PA	Evangelical Lutheran Church in Amer	918	$7830 / $3800	3 / LA
Toccoa Falls College	Toccoa Falls, GA	C&MA	795	$4130 / $2750	3 / BC
Transylvania University	Lexington, KY	Christian Church (Dscpls of Christ)	1076	$8906 / $3748	3 / LA
Trevecca Nazarene College	Nashville, TN	Nazarene	1436	$4775 / $2450	5 / LA
Trinity Bible College	Ellendale, ND	Assemblies of God	410	$3848 / $2988	5 / BC
Trinity Christian College	Palos Heights, IL	Christian Reformed	534	$6890 / $2910	3 / LA
Trinity College	Deerfield, IL	Evangelical Free	849	$8130 / $3690	3 / LA
Trinity College of Florida*	Holiday, FL	Independent	125	N/A / N/A	N/A / BC
Trinity University	San Antonio, TX	Presbyterian	2573	$9676 / $4050	2 / LA
Tusculum College	Greenville, TN	Presbyterian	642	$5544 / $3000	3 / LA
Union College	Barbourville, KY	United Methodist	1050	$5020 / $2320	3 / LA
Union University	Jackson, TN	Southern Baptist	1730	$3900 / $2030	3 / LA
United Wesleyan College*	Allentown, PA	Wesleyan	165	$5200 / $2700	5 / BC
University of Dubuque	Dubuque, IA	Presbyterian	1126	$7945 / $2850	3 / LA
University of Evansville	Evansville, IN	United Methodist	3290	$8600 / $3320	3 / LA
University of Findlay	Findlay, OH	Church of God	1799	$7375 / $3186	3 / LA
University of Indianapolis	Indianapolis, IN	United Methodist	3119	$7590 / $3050	3 / LA
University of Mary Hardin-Baylor	Belton, TX	Southern Baptist	1762	$4380 / $2600	4 / LA
University of Puget Sound	Tacoma, WA	Methodist	3303	$11420 / $3800	2 / LA
University of Richmond	Richmond, VA	Baptist	4909	$10850 / $2765	2 / LA
University of the Nations*	Kailu-Kona, HI	Interdenominational	1450	$5800 / $2850	N/A / LA
University of The Ozarks	Clarksville, AR	Presbyterian	796	$3010 / $2160	3 / LA
University of the South	Sewanee, TN	Episcopal	1075	$12720 / $3010	2 / LA
University of Tulsa	Tulsa, OK	Presbyterian	4318	$7450 / $3100	3 / LA
Upsala College	East Orange, NJ	Evangelical Lutheran Church in Amer	990	$8850 / $3940	3 / LA
Ursinus College	Collegeville, PA	United Church of Christ	1100	$11520 / $4250	2 / LA
Valley Forge Christian College	Phoenixville, PA	Assemblies of God	529	$3076 / $2524	4 / BC
Valparaiso University	Valparaiso, IN	Lutheran Church— Missouri Synod	3858	$9070 / $2700	3 / LA
Vennard College	University Park, IA	Interdenominational	153	$3869 / $2050	4 / BC
Virginia Intermont College	Bristol, VA	Baptist	521	$5980 / $3620	4 / LA
Virginia Union University	Richmond, VA	Baptist	1200	$5840 / $3010	4 / LA
Virginia Wesleyan College	Norfolk, VA	United Methodist	1280	$7400 / $3900	3 / LA
Voorhees College	Denmark, SC	Episcopal	590	$5672 / $2522	4 / LA
Wake Forest University	Winston-Salem, NC	Baptist	5337	$9700 / $2470	2 / LA
Warner Pacific College	Portland, OR	Church of God	450	$7044 / $3188	3 / LA
Warner Southern College	Lake Wales, FL	Church of God	423	$4850 / $2740	4 / LA
Warren Wilson College	Swannanoa, NC.	Presbyterian Church (USA)	523	$7550 / $812	3 / LA
Wartburg College	Waverly, IA	Lutheran	1456	$8860 / $2960	3 / LA
Washington Bible College	Lanham, MD	Nondenominational	315	$4978 / $3070	3 / BC
Wayland Baptist University	Plainview, TX	Baptist	2052	$3670 / $2390	4 / LA
Waynesburg College	Waynesburg, PA	Presbyterian Church (USA)	1155	$6706 / $2860	3 / LA
Wesley College	Dover, DE	United Methodist	1200	$6475 / $3675	3 / LA
Wesley College	Florence , MS	Independent	50	$1600 / $2000	5 / LA

School	City, ST	Affiliation	Enroll	Tuition / Board	Diff./Type
Wesleyan College	Macon, GA	Methodist Women's College	522	$7490 / $3850	3 / LA
West Coast Christian College	Fresno, CA	Church of God	160	N/A / N/A	N/A / LA
W. Virginia Wesleyan College	Buckhannon, WV	United Methodist	1571	$10930 / $3000	3 / LA
Western Baptist College	Salem, OR	Baptist	358	$6225 / $2943	4 / BC
Westminster College	Fulton, MO	Presbyterian	734	$7700 / $3300	3 / LA
Westminster College	New Wilmington, PA	Presbyterian Church (USA)	1554	$9550 / $2730	3 / LA
Westmont College	Santa Barbara, CA	Independent	1256	$11530 / $4650	3 / LA
Wheaton College	Wheaton, IL	Nondenominational	2548	$8836 / $3640	2 / LA
Whitworth College	Spokane, WA	Presbyterian	1788	$9090 / $3425	3 / LA
Wilberforce University	Wilberforce, OH	African Meth. Episcopal	779	$6092 / $3170	4 / LA
Wiley College	Marshall, TX	United Methodist	406	$3946 / $2544	5 / LA
Willamette University	Salem, OR	United Methodist	2223	$9980 / $3550	2 / LA
William Carey College	Hattiesburg, MS	Southern Baptist	1600	$4352 / $2120	4 / LA
William Jewell College	Liberty, MO	Baptist	1400	$7450 / $2530	3 / LA
William Penn College	Oskaloosa, IA	Friends	671	$7800 / $2320	3 / LA
William Tyndale College	Farmington Hills, MI	Independent	383	$4410 / $3060	4 / LA
William Woods College	Fulton, MO	Christian Church (Dscpls of Christ)	750	$7400 / $3200	3 / LA
Wilmington College	Wilmington, OH	Friends	890	$7660 / $2900	3 / LA
Wilson College	Chambersburg, PA	Presbyterian	792	$10076 / $4530	3 / LA
Wingate College	Wingate, NC	Baptist	1690	$5070 / $2550	3 / LA
Wisconsin Lutheran College	Milwaukee, WI	Wisconsin Evangelical Lutheran	273	$6360 / $3000	3 / LA
Wittenberg University	Springfield, OH	Evangelical Lutheran Church in Amer	2340	$12,747 / $3843	3 / LA
Wofford College	Spartanburg, SC	United Methodist	1121	$8085 / $3700	3 / LA

Canadian

School	City, ST	Affiliation	Enroll	Tuition / Board	Diff./Type
Aldersgate College	Moose Jaw, SK	Free Methodist	47	$3150 / $2290	5 / LA
Bethany Bible College	Sussex, NB	Wesleyan	165	$2750 / $2650	4 / BC
Briercrest Bible College	Caronport, SK	Interdenominational	870	$2519 / $2270	3 / BC
Canadian Bible College	Regina, SK	C&MA	415	$3191 / $3000	5 / BC
Catherine Booth Bible College*	Winnipeg, MB	Salvation Army	60	N/A / N/A	N/A / BC
Central Baptist Bible College*	Toronto, ON	Baptist	65	N/A / N/A	N/A / BC
Central Pentecostal College	Saskatoon, SK	Pentecostal	75	$1880 / $2600	5 / BC
College of Emmanuel and St. Chad	Saskatoon, SK	Episcopal	46	$1220 / $3045	5 / LA
Columbia Bible College*	Clearbrook, BC	Mennonite	220	N/A / N/A	N/A /
Eastern Pentecostal Bible College*	Peterborough, ON	Pentecostal	500	N/A / N/A	N/A / BC
Emmanuel Bible College	Kitchener, ON	Missionary Church	211	2596 / 2600	3 / BC
Hillcrest Christian College	Medicine Hat, AB	Congregational	75	$2420 / $2200	4 / BC
King's College*	Edmonton, AB	Nondenominational	295	$2785 / $1155	3 / LA
London Baptist Bible College*	London, ON	Baptist	160	N/A / N/A	N/A / BC
Mennonite Brethren Bible College	Winnipeg, MB	Mennonite Brethren	85	$1800 / $2550	5 / BC
North American Baptist College*	Edmonton, AB	North American Baptist	220	$1900 / $2800	3 / BC
Northwest Baptist Theological College*	Vancouver, BC	Baptist	160	N/A / N/A	N/A / BC
Northwest Bible College*	Edmonton, AB	Pentecostal	140	N/A / N/A	N/A / BC
Ontario Bible College	Willowdale, ON	Independent	343	$2786 / $3124	3 / BC
Redeemer College	Ancaster, ON	Interdenominational	373	$6043 / $2958	N/A / LA
Steinbach Bible College*	Steinbach, MB	Mennonite	80	N/A / N/A	N/A / BC
Trinity Western University	Langley, BC	Evangelical Free	1300	$5525 / $3760	3 / LA
Western Pentecostal Bible College	Clayburn, BC	Pentecostal Assemblies	224	$2297 / $2760	4 / BC
Winnipeg Bible College	Otterburne, MB	Nondenominational	307	$3240 / $2710	5 / BC

Source: *Peterson's Guide to Four-Year Colleges, 1991* © 1990 Peterson's Guides Inc. Used by permission. * Indicates college not listed in *Peterson's Guide to Four-Year Colleges.*

COLLEGES AND UNIVERSITIES THAT OFFER CORRESPONDENCE AND/OR VIDEO COURSES

Baptist Bible College
628 E. Kearney
Springfield, MO 65803

Briercrest Bible College
Caronport, SK
S0H 0S0

Central Bible College
3000 N. Grant
Springfield, MO 65803

Cincinnati Bible College
2700 Glenway Avenue
Cincinnati, OH 45204

Columbia Bible College
P.O. Box 3122
Columbia, SC 29230

Emmaus Bible College
2570 Asbury Road
Dubuque, IA 52001

Eugene Bible College
2155 Bailey Hill Road
Eugene, OR 97405

Evangel College
Springfield, MO 65802

Fort Wayne Bible College
1025 W. Rudisill Blvd.
Ft. Wayne, IN 46807

Johnson Bible College
7900 Johnson Drive
Knoxville, TN 37998

Kentucky Christian
College
617 N. Carol Malone Blvd.
Grayson, KY 41143

LIFE Bible College
1100 Glendale Blvd.
Los Angeles, CA 90026

Mid-America Bible
College
3500 S.W. 119th Street
Oklahoma City, OK 73170

Moody Bible Institute
820 N. LaSalle Drive
Chicago, IL 60610

North Central Bible College
910 Elliot Avenue South
Minneapolis, MN 55404

Ontario Bible College
25 Ballyconnor Ct.
Willowdale, ON M2M 4B3

Philadelphia College of
Bible
Langhorne Manor
Langhorne, PA 19047

Reformed Bible College
1869 Robinson Road
Grand Rapids, MI 49506

Regent University
CBN Center
1000 Centerville Turnpike
Virginia Beach, VA 23464

Seattle Pacific University
W 3307 Third Avenue
Seattle, WA 98119

Southeastern Bible College
2901 Pawnee Avenue
Birmingham, AL 35256

Southeastern College of
Assemblies of God
1000 Longfellow Blvd.
Lakeland, FL 33801

Southwestern Assemblies
of God College
1200 Sycamore
Waxahachie, TX 75156

Tennessee Temple
University
1815 Union Avenue
Chattanooga, TN 37404

Trinity Bible College
50 South Sixth Avenue
Ellendale, ND 58436

Valley Forge Christian
College
Charlestown Road
Phoenixville, PA 19460

Washington Bible College
6511 Princess Garden Pkwy
Lanham, MD 20706

Westminster Theological
Seminary
Box 27009
Philadelphia, PA 19118

66 99
FOCUS
QUOTE

The highest service may be prepared for and done in the humblest surroundings. In silence, in waiting, in obscure, unnoticed offices, in years of uneventful, unrecorded duties, the Son of God grew and waxed strong.
—Inscription in the Stanford University Chapel.

MOST SELECTIVE CHURCH-RELATED COLLEGES

With the exception of Duke, the following schools have been listed by *Peterson's Guide* with an entrance difficulty of 2, which indicates a 60 percent acceptance rate. Duke is the only religious-based school that carries a rating of 1, which indicates a 30 percent acceptance rate.

School	City ST	Affiliation
Agnes Scott College	Decatur, GA	Presbyterian—Women's
Albright College	Reading, PA	United Methodist
Bob Jones University	Greenville, SC	Independent
Centre College	Danville, KY	Presbyterian
Davidson College	Davidson, NC	Presbyterian
Drew University	Madison, NJ	United Methodist
Duke University	Durham, NC	United Methodist
Elizabethtown College	Elizabeth, PA	Church of the Brethren
Emory University	Atlanta, GA	Methodist
Furman University	Greenville, SC	Baptist
Gettysburg College	Gettysburg, PA	Evang. Lutheran Church in Am.
Gustavus Adolphus College	St. Peter, MN	Evang. Lutheran Church in Am.
Hampden-Sydney College	Hampden-Sydney, VA	Presbyterian
Hobart College	Geneva, NY	Episcopal
Illinois Wesleyan University	Bloomington, IL	United Methodist
Lafayette College	Easton, PA	Presbyterian Church (USA)
Macalester College	St. Paul, MN	Presbyterian
Muhlenberg College	Allentown, PA	Lutheran
Ohio Wesleyan University	Delaware, OH	United Methodist
Rhodes College	Memphis, TN	Presbyterian
Southwestern University	Georgetown, TX	Methodist
St. Olaf College	Northfield, MN	Lutheran
Trinity University	San Antonio, TX	Presbyterian
University of Puget Sound	Tacoma, WA	Methodist
University of Richmond	Richmond, VA	Baptist
University of the South	Sewanee, TN	Episcopal
Ursinus College	Collegeville, PA	United Church of Christ
Wake Forest University	Winston-Salem, NC	Baptist
Wheaton College	Wheaton, IL	Nondenominational

FIFTEEN LARGEST CHURCH-RELATED COLLEGES/UNIVERSITIES

School	City ST	Affiliation	Enrollment
Liberty University	Lynchburg, VA	Baptist	16605
Baylor University	Waco, TX	Baptist	11774
Duke University	Durham, NC	United Methodist	10376
American University	Washington, DC	Methodist	10153
Emory University	Atlanta, GA	Methodist	9398
Southern Methodist University	Dallas, TX	United Methodist	8924
Texas Christian University	Fort Worth, TX	Christian Church	6725
Wake Forest University	Winston-Salem, NC	Baptist	5337
University of Richmond	Richmond, VA	Baptist	4909
Campbell University	Buies Creek, NC	Baptist	4820
Baldwin-Wallace College	Berea, OH	Methodist	4713

Ashland University	Ashland, OH	Brethren	4391
Bob Jones University	Greenville, SC	Independent	4367
Calvin College	Grand Rapids, MI	Christian Reformed	4325
University of Tulsa	Tulsa, OK	Presbyterian	4318

FOCUS FACT

Five of the nine colonial colleges in America were established as a result of the First Great Awakening: Dartmouth College; Princeton University; Rutgers University; University of Pennsylvania; and Brown University.

TWENTY MOST EXPENSIVE CHURCH-RELATED COLLEGES

	Tuition	School	City ST	Affiliation
1.	$15346	Hobart College	Geneva, NY	Episcopal
2.	$14123	Duke University	Durham, NC	United Methodist
3.	$14100	Muhlenberg College	Allentown, PA	Lutheran
4.	$14000	Allegheny College	Meadville, PA	United Methodist
5.	$14000	Lafayette College	Easton, PA	Presbyterian
6.	$13992	Drew University	Madison, NJ	United Methodist
7.	$13700	Emory University	Atlanta, GA	Methodist
8.	$13625	Gettysburg College	Gettysburg, PA	Evangelical Lutheran
9.	$13120	Susquehanna University	Selinsgrove, PA	Lutheran
10.	$12747	Wittenberg University	Springfield, OH	Evangelical Lutheran
11.	$12720	University of the South	Sewanee, TN	Episcopal
12.	$12328	Ohio Wesleyan University	Delaware, OH	United Methodist
13.	$12100	American University	Washington, DC	Methodist
14.	$11956	Albright College	Reading, PA	United Methodist
15.	$11910	Chapman College	Orange, CA	Christian Church
16.	$11660	Moravian College	Bethlehem, PA	Moravian
17.	$11628	Rhodes College	Memphis, TN	Presbyterian
18.	$11610	Earlham College	Richmond, IN	Friends
19.	$11570	College of Wooster	Wooster, OH	Presbyterian
20.	$11542	Macalester College	St. Paul, MN	Presbyterian

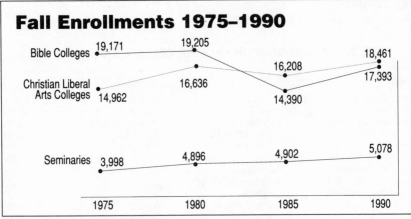

Fall Enrollments 1975–1990

Source: Christianity Today, September 16, 1991 issue.

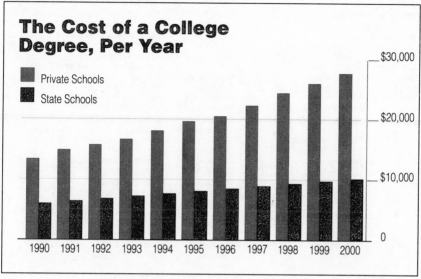

The Cost of a College Degree, Per Year

■ Private Schools

▓ State Schools

(Years: 1990 1991 1992 1993 1994 1995 1996 1997 1998 1999 2000)
(Scale: $30,000 / $20,000 / $10,000 / 0)

Source: *The Frog in the Kettle,* by George Barna. Published by Regal Books. Copyright © 1990. Used by permission.

❝❞
FOCUS
QUOTE

Five Things I Wish They Had Told Me When I Graduated:
1. It's OK to be human.
2. It's lonely to lead.
3. It is necessary to fail.
4. It is hardest at home.
5. It is essential to serve.

Source: Outline of Charles R. Swindoll message at the 1991 Wheaton College undergraduate commencement address.

SEMINARIES AND GRADUATE SCHOOLS

School	City, ST	Affiliation	Enroll
United States			
Alliance Theological Seminary	Nyack, NY	C&MA	280
American Baptist Seminary of the West	Berkeley, CA	American Baptist	93
American Baptist Theological Seminary	Nashville, TN	Baptist	170
Anderson University School of Theology	Anderson, IN	Church of God	
Andover Newton Theological School	Newton Centre, MA	United Church of Christ/Amer Baptist	395
Asbury Theological Seminary	Wilmore, KY	Interdenominational	794
Ashland Theological Seminary	Ashland, OH	Brethren	423
Assemblies of God Theological Seminary	Springfield, MO	Assemblies of God	285
Austin Presbyterian Theological Seminary	Austin, TX	Presbyterian Church (USA)	255
Azusa Pacific University Graduate School of Theology	Azusa, CA	Wesleyan	108
Bangor Theological Seminary	Bangor, ME	United Church of Christ	102
Baptist Missionary Association Theological Seminary	Jacksonville, TX	Baptist Missionary Association	76
Beeson Divinity School	Birmingham, AL	Southern Baptist	90

School	City, ST	Affiliation	Enroll
Berkeley Divinity School	New Haven, CT	Episcopal	N/A
Bethany Theological Seminary	Oak Brook, IL	Church of the Brethren	130
Bethel Theological Seminary	St. Paul, MN	Baptist General Conference	514
Biblical Theological Seminary	Hatfield, PA	Nondenominational	190
Boston University School of Theology	Boston, MA	United Methodist	513
Brite Divinity School	Fort Worth, TX	Christian Church (Disciples of Christ)	206
Calvin Theological Seminary	Grand Rapids, MI	Christian Reformed	230
Candler School of Theology	Atlanta, GA	United Methodist	769
Capital Bible Seminary	Lantham, MD	Interdenominational	185
Central Baptist Theological Seminary	Kansas City, KS	American Baptist	140
Chicago Theological Seminary	Chicago, IL	United Church of Christ	176
Christian Theological Seminary	Indianapolis, IN	Christian Church (Disciples of Christ)	338
Church Divinity School of the Pacific	Berkeley, CA	Episcopal	108
Church of God School of Theology	Cleveland, TN	Church of God	177
Cincinnati Bible Seminary	Cincinnati, OH	Christian Churches & Churches of Christ	289
Claremont School of Theology	Claremont, CA	United Methodist	265
Colgate Rochester Div Schl/Crozer Theol Seminary	Rochester, NY	American Baptist	208
Columbia Biblical Seminary & Grad School of Missions	Columbia, SC	Nondenominational	420
Columbia Theological Seminary	Decatur, GA	Presbyterian Church (USA)	547
Concordia Seminary	St. Louis, MO	Lutheran—Missouri Synod	555
Concordia Theological Seminary	Fort Wayne, IN	Lutheran Church—Missouri Synod	530
Covenant Theological Seminary	St. Louis, MO	Presbyterian	158
Dallas Theological Seminary	Dallas, TX	Nondenominational	1350
Denver Conservative Baptist Seminary	Denver, CO	Conservative Baptist	489
Denver Seminary	Denver, CO	Conservative Baptist	
Drew University Theological School	Madison, NJ	United Methodist	600
Duke University Divinity School	Durham, NC	United Methodist	443
Eastern Baptist Theological Seminary	Philadelphia, PA	American Baptist	382
Eastern Mennonite Seminary	Harrisonburg, VA	Mennonite	101
Eden Theological Seminary	St. Louis, MO	United Church of Christ	172
Emmanuel School of Religion	Johnson City, TN	Christian Churches & Churches of Christ	139
Episcopal Divinity School	Cambridge, MA	Episcopal	117
Episcopal Theological Seminary of the Southwest	Austin, TX	Episcopal	67
Erskine Theological Seminary	Due West, SC	Presbyterian	189
Evangelical School of Theology	Myerstown, PA	Evangelical Congregational	72
Faith Baptist Seminary	Ankeny, IA	Baptist	
Fuller Theological Seminary	Pasadena, CA	Interdenominational	2670
Garrett-Evangelical Theological Seminary	Evanston, IL	United Methodist	351
General Theological Seminary	New York, NY	Episcopal	161
Golden Gate Baptist Theological Seminary	Mill Valley, CA	Southern Baptist	910
Gordon-Conwell Theological Seminary	South Hamilton, MA	Interdenominational	721
Graduate Theological Union	Berkeley, CA	Interdenominational	374
Grand Rapids Baptist Seminary	Grand Rapids, MI	Baptist	
Harding Graduate School of Religion	Memphis, TN	Churches of Christ	183
Hartford Seminary	Hartford, CT	Interdenominational	161
Harvard University Divinity School	Cambridge, MA	Nondenominational	470
Hood Theological Seminary	Salisbury, NC	A.M.E. Zion	35
Houston Graduate School of Theology	Houston, TX	Friends	122
Howard University Divinity School	Washington, DC	Nondenominational	191
Iliff School of Theology	Denver, CO	United Methodist	332
Interdenominational Theological Center	Atlanta, GA	Interdenominational	264
Lancaster Theological Seminary	Lancaster, PA	United Church of Christ	233
Lexington Theological Seminary	Lexington, KY	Christian Church (Disciples of Christ)	167
Liberty Baptist Theological Seminary	Lynchburg, VA	Baptist	253
Lincoln Christian Seminary	Lincoln, IL	Christian Churches & Churches of Christ	178
Louisville Presbyterian Theological Seminary	Louisville, KY	Presbyterian Church (USA)	187
Luther Northwestern Theological Seminary	St. Paul, MN	Lutheran-ELCA	723
Luther Rice Seminary	Jacksonville, FL	Baptist	3100
Lutheran School of Theology at Chicago	Chicago, IL	Lutheran-ELCA	309
Lutheran Theological Seminary at Gettysburg	Gettysburg, PA	Lutheran-ELCA	282

School	City, ST	Affiliation	Enroll
Lutheran Theological Seminary at Philadelphia	Philadelphia, PA	Lutheran-ELCA	262
Lutheran Theological Southern Seminary	Columbia, SC	Lutheran-ELCA	159
Master's Seminary	Sun Valley, CA	Interdenominational	677
McCormick Theological Seminary	Chicago, IL	Presbyterian Church (USA)	556
Memphis Theological Seminary	Memphis, TN	Presbyterian	135
Mennonite Biblical Seminary	Elkhart, IN	Mennonite	122
Mennonite Brethren Biblical Seminary	Fresno, CA	Mennonite Brethren	122
Methodist Theological School in Ohio	Delaware, OH	United Methodist	239
Midwestern Baptist Theological Seminary	Kansas City, MO	Southern Baptist	513
Moody Graduate School	Chicago, IL	Interdenominational	400
Moravian Theological Seminary	Bethlehem, PA	Moravian	58
Multnomah Graduate School	Portland, OR	Interdenominational	170
Nashotah House	Nashotah, WI	Episcopal	69
Nazarene Theological Seminary	Kansas City, MO	Nazarene	444
New Brunswick Theological Seminary	New Brunswick, NJ	Reformed Church in America	139
New Orleans Baptist Theological Seminary	New Orleans, LA	Southern Baptist	2113
New York Theological Seminary	New York, NY	Interdenominational	280
North American Baptist Seminary	Sioux Falls, SD	North American Baptist	134
North Park Theological Seminary	Chicago, IL	Evangelical Covenant	138
Northern Baptist Theological Seminary	Lombard, IL	American Baptist	181
Oral Roberts University School of Theology	Tulsa, OK	Interdenominational	413
Pacific Lutheran Theological Seminary	Berkeley, CA	Lutheran-ELCA	129
Pacific School of Religion	Berkeley, CA	Interdenominational	206
Payne Theological Seminary	Wilberforce, OH	A.M.E.	15
Perkins School of Theol of Southern Methodist Univ	Dallas, TX	United Methodist	444
Phillips Graduate Seminary	Enid, OK	Christian Church (Disciples of Christ)	131
Pittsburgh Theological Seminary	Pittsburgh, PA	Presbyterian Church (USA)	450
Presbyterian School of Christian Education	Richmond, VA	Presbyterian Church (USA)	113
Princeton Theological Seminary	Princeton, NJ	Presbyterian Church (USA)	798
Protestant Episcopal Theological Seminary in Virginia	Alexandria, VA	Episcopal	222
Reformed Episcopal Seminary	Philadelphia, PA	Reformed Episcopal	45
Reformed Presbyterian Theological Seminary	Pittsburgh, PA	Reformed Presbyterian	80
Reformed Theological Seminary	Jackson, MS	Reformed	336
Reformed Theological Seminary	Orlando, FL	Reformed	120
Saint Paul School of Theology	Kansas City, MO	United Methodist	258
San Francisco Theological Seminary	San Anselmo, CA	Presbyterian Church (USA)	791
Seabury-Western Theological Seminary	Evanston, IL	Episcopal	87
Shaw Divinity School	Raleigh, NC	Baptist	102
Southeastern Baptist Theological Seminary	Wake Forest, NC	Southern Baptist	1003
Southern Baptist Theological Seminary	Louisville, KY	Southern Baptist	2232
Southwestern Baptist Theological Seminary	Fort Worth, TX	Southern Baptist	4001
Talbot School of Theology	La Mirada, CA	Interdenominational	511
Trinity Episcopal School for Ministry	Ambridge, PA	Episcopal	108
Trinity Evangelical Divinity School	Deerfield, IL	Evangelical Free	1094
Trinity Lutheran Seminary	Columbus, OH	Lutheran-ELCA	249
Union Theological Seminary	New York, NY	Interdenominational	403
Union Theological Seminary in Virginia	Richmond, VA	Presbyterian Church (USA)	225
United Theological Seminary	Dayton, OH	United Methodist	338
United Theological Seminary of the Twin Cities	New Brighton, MN	United Church of Christ	204
University of Chicago Divinity School	Chicago, IL	Interdenominational	273
University of Dubuque Theological Seminary	Dubuque, IA	Presbyterian Church (USA)	194
University of the South School of Theology	Sewanee, TN	Episcopal	157
Vanderbilt University Divinity School	Nashville, TN	Interdenominational	271
Virginia Union University School of Theology	Richmond, VA	Baptist	124
Wartburg Theological Seminary	Dubuque, IA	Lutheran-ELCA	230
Wesley Biblical Seminary	Jackson, MS	Interdenominational	95
Wesley Theological Seminary	Washington, DC	United Methodist	363
Western Conservative Baptist Seminary	Portland, OR	Baptist	480
Western Evangelical Seminary	Portland, OR	Interdenominational	157
Western Theological Seminary	Holland, MI	Reformed Church in America	166
Westminster Theological Seminary	Philadelphia, PA	Independent	538
Wheaton College Graduate School	Wheaton, IL	Interdenominational	300

School	City, ST	Affiliation	Enroll
Winebrenner Theological Seminary	Findlay, OH	Churches of God	43
Yale University Divinity School	New Haven, CT	Interdenominational	455

Canadian

Acadia Divinity School	Wolfville, NS	Baptist	120
Atlantic School of Theology	Halifax, NS	Interdenominational	123
Canadian Theological Seminary	Regina, SK	C&MA	153
Concordia Lutheran Seminary	St. Catharines, ON	Lutheran/Missouri Synod	42
Edmonton Baptist Seminary	Edmonton, AB	North American Baptist	60
Emmanuel College of Victoria University	Toronto, ON	United Church of Canada	241
Huron College Faculty of Theology	London, ON	Anglican	56
Joint Board of Theological Colleges	Montreal, PQ	Interdenominational	18
Knox College	Toronto, ON	Presbyterian	137
Lutheran Theological Seminary	Saskatoon, SK	Lutheran-ELCIC	111
McGill University Faculty of Religious Studies	Montreal, PQ	Interdenominational	145
McMaster Divinity College	Hamilton, ON	Baptist	145
Ontario Theological Seminary	Willowdale, ON	Interdenominational	371
Queen's Theological College	Kingston, ON	United Church	88
Regent College	Vancouver, BC	Interdenominational	362
St. Andrew's College	Saskatoon, SK	United Church of Canada	54
St. Stephen's College	Edmonton, AB	United Church of Canada	82
Toronto School of Theology	Toronto, ON	Interdenominational	
Trinity College Faculty of Divinity	Toronto, ON	Anglican	135
University of Winnipeg Faculty of Theology	Winnipeg, MB	United	116
Vancouver School of Theology	Vancouver, BC	Interdenominational	111
Waterloo Lutheran Seminary	Waterloo, ON	Lutheran-ELCIC	133
Winnipeg Theological Seminary	Otterburne, MB	Interdenominational	208
Wycliffe College	Toronto, ON	Anglican	141

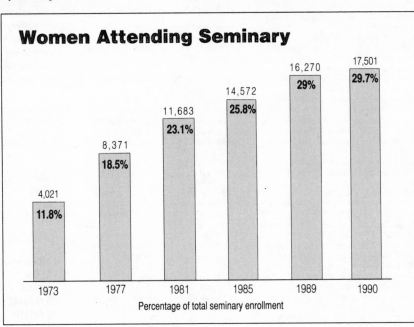

Women Attending Seminary

4,021	8,371	11,683	14,572	16,270	17,501
11.8%	18.5%	23.1%	25.8%	29%	29.7%
1973	1977	1981	1985	1989	1990

Percentage of total seminary enrollment

Source: Association of Theological Schools

INFORMATIVE BOOKS TO HELP YOU FIND
THE RIGHT EDUCATIONAL INSTITUTION

Peterson's Four Year Colleges In addition to profiles on over 1,900 institutions, a complete majors directory, an entrance difficulty directory, and a full listing of cost level, this 2,700-page book contains nearly 800 in-depth descriptions written by admissions directors about their own colleges.

Consider a Christian College Answers questions that students and their families ask when they are interested in pursuing postsecondary education at a Christian college. Provides information on the 78 member schools of the Christian College Coalition.

Peterson's College Money Handbook Full account of costs and details on financial aid packages and merit scholarships at more than 1,700 accredited U.S. four-year colleges. Features an overview of the financial aid process, a financial aid glossary, and a worksheet for calculating the expected family contribution, plus over 90 directories of non-need scholarships by type, athletic scholarships by sport, and money-saving options.

The ISS Directory of Overseas Schools Guide to 500 overseas schools. Profiles include tuition and fees, description of facilities and programs, and breakdown of nationalities of staff and students and accreditation source.

Financial Resources for International Study Listing of financial aid awards for U.S. citizens who study abroad. Covers over 600 grants of at least $500.

Peterson's Guide to Independent Secondary Schools Guide to nearly 1,400 accredited day schools, boarding schools, and schools serving students with special needs. Contains directories that identify schools by type, religious affiliation, and financial aid offerings.

The Independent Study Catalog The National University Continuing Education Association's guide to independent study through correspondence instruction for people who want to study without the restriction of regular class attendance. Lists 10,000 correspondence courses at the high school, college, and graduate levels.

1992 Summer Employment Directory of the United States Lists 50,000 summer jobs for students and teachers with businesses, expeditions, resorts, summer camps, theaters, and the government. Includes a job category index to help users locate specific types of positions.

For more information on these books write to Peterson's Guides, P.O. Box 2123, Princeton, NJ 08543-2123 or call 1-800-EDU-DATA.

❝❞ FOCUS QUOTE Who among the evangelicals can stand up to the great secular or naturalistic or atheistic scholars on their own terms of scholarship and research? Who among the evanglical scholars is quoted as a normative source by the greatest secular authorities on history or philosophy or psychology or sociology or politics?—Charles Malik

---

❝❞ FOCUS QUOTE So far as the university is concerned, I have no patience with piety alone—I want the most rigorous intellectual training, I want the perfection of the mind; equally, I have no patience with reason alone—I want the salvation of the soul, I want the fear of the Lord, I want at least neutrality with respect to the knowledge of Jesus Christ. . . . The greatest danger besetting American evangelical Christianity is the danger of anti-intellectualism.—Charles Malik

BELIEFS AND BEHAVIOR OF COLLEGE STUDENTS

Believe in God 89%
Believe in divinity of Jesus Christ 77%
Member of a church or synagoue 67%
Religious beliefs very important 55%
Denominational preference:
       Protestant 49%
       Roman Catholic 29%
       Jewish 4%
       Other 94%
Attend religious services weekly 34%
Religious commitment stronger since entering college 27%
Religious commitment weaker since entering college 23%
Read the Bible at least weekly 24%
Describe as born-again or evangelical Christian 23%
Member of campus religious group 12%
Favorably impressed by New Age movement 6%
Professed agnostic or atheist 6%
Some chance of joining religious cult group 2%

Source: The Gallup Organization Poll of 1,227 adults, age 18 and older, conducted October 12-15, 1989.

66 99 We are not only endowed with a soul and a will to be saved but also with a
reason to be sharpened and satisfied. . . . It is neither a shame nor a sin to
FOCUS discipline and cultivate our reason to the utmost; it is a necessity, it is a
QUOTE duty, it is an honor to do so.
    The greatest danger besetting American evangelical Christianity is the
danger of anti-intellectualism. The mind as to its greatest and deepest reaches is not
cared for enough. This cannot take place apart from profound immersion for a period of
years in the history of thought and spirit. People are in a hurry to get out of the university and start earning money or serving the church or preaching the gospel. They have
no idea of the infinite value of spending years of leisure in conversing with the greatest
minds and souls of the past, and thereby ripening and sharpening and enlarging their
powers of thinking. The result is that the arena of creative thinking is abdicated and
vacated to the enemy.—Charles Malik

Evangelism

15 SIGNIFICANT EVANGELISTS THROUGHOUT HISTORY
Daniel Moul

Gilbert Tennent (1703-1764). The First Great Awakening began in the 1720s, largely through the efforts of the Presbyterian Minister Gilbert Tennent and the Dutch Reformed Minister Theodorous Jabobus Frelinghuysen. Both encouraged personal experiences of redemption, calling people to repentance through pastoral counseling and sermons.

Tennent trained for the ministry in a simple "log college" run by his father and located next to his home. His ministry began in New Brunswick, New Jersey, where he met Frelinghuysen. Revivals began in both churches by 1729, and by 1740 the Great Awakening was at its zenith. George Whitefield considered Tennent "a son of thunder." He said of Tennent, "Hypocrites must either soon be converted or enraged at his preaching," and "He is deeply sensible of the deadness and formality of the Christian church in these parts, and has given noble testimonies against it."

Tennent travelled through Massachusetts and Connecticut on a preaching tour, enjoying great success. In Boston, one pastor reported that in the course of three months, 600 people visited him "concerned for their souls."

Jonathan Edwards (1703-1758). One of the greatest theologians America has produced, Jonathan Edwards played a prominent role in the Great Awakening. His famous sermon, "Sinners in the Hands of an Angry God," helped spark revival in his town of Northampton, Massachusetts. As people witnessed the changes in church-goers' lives, revival spread to the surrounding communities. Edwards described and defended the awakening in his book, *A Faithful Narrative of the Surprising Work of God in the Conversion of Many Hundred Souls in Northampton and the Neighboring Towns.*

Thousands were converted through his sermons, which he would read without emotional hype. His strength in preaching centered in his careful exposition of the Scriptures, intellectual rigor, focus on Christ, and call to personal piety and holy affection.

A graduate of Yale and a Presbyterian minister for twenty-two years of one of the largest and wealthiest churches in Massachusetts, he also served as a missionary to the Mohican Indians before assuming the presidency of the College of New Jersey (now Princeton University). He died from a smallpox vaccine shortly after taking office.

George Whitefield's voice was so loud and clear he could be heard by more than 20,000 people at one time.

FOCUS
FACT

George Whitefield (1714-1770). While studying at Oxford, George Whitefield received a book from Charles Wesley. Through it, he explained, "God showed me that I must be born again, or be damned." Ordained in the Anglican church, Whitefield drew large crowds

SIGNIFICANT EVANGELISTS THROUGHOUT HISTORY cont.

wherever he spoke. His "vulgar style" of preaching in the everyday language of his audience drew criticism from some fellow ministers. After he was denied the pulpits in some churches, he, along with the Wesleys, pioneered evangelistic preaching in fields and marketplaces.

Originally coming to Georgia to establish the first orphanage in America, Whitefield traveled throughout the colonies. He was well-known for his dramatic style and strong voice, which satisfied audiences of more than 20,000 at one time. His energy and enthusiasm were contagious, and he became one of driving forces of the Great Awakening.

During his tours he preached an average of forty hours each week. Over the thirty-three years of his ministry, he preached around 18,000 sermons and established schools, orphanages, and religious societies. His goal in ministry was "to awaken a drowsy world, to rouse them out of their formality, as well as profaneness, to put them upon seeking a present and great salvation." He died during a preaching tour in Rhode Island.

Francis Asbury (1745-1816). America's greatest Methodist leader, Francis Asbury oversaw the tremendous growth of the Methodist church from less than 3000 in 1775 to around 60,000 by 1790. As the first bishop of the American Methodist Church, he was instrumental in forming the church into a mature organization whose influence extended throughout the frontier.

---

66 99
FOCUS
QUOTE
Go into every kitchen and shop; address all, aged and young, on the salvation of their souls. —Francis Asbury on his conviction that preachers should be "out and about"

Asbury promoted revival camp meetings and circuit-riding preachers as key strategies for evangelizing the young nation. He wrote, "I pray God that there may be twenty camp meetings in a week, and wonderful seasons of the Lord in every direction." His preachers were known for their diligence; in bad weather people would say, "There is nothing out today but crows and Methodist preachers."

Asbury modeled the commitment of the Methodist preachers. Although often ill, he rode 4000 to 6000 miles each year. In all, he traveled over 300,000 miles by horseback, wrote 50,000 letters, and ordained 4000 preachers.

Richard Allen (1760-1831). Born into slavery, Richard Allen was converted through the ministry of a Methodist circuit rider in Delaware at age seventeen. Allen's change of character and genuine faith prompted his master, Mr. Stokeley, to open his house for meetings of prayer and preaching. After Stokeley became a Christian he made it possible for his slaves to purchase their freedom. For the next five years Allen worked odd jobs to save money and became an itinerant preacher, traveling with leading Methodist preachers of the day.

He visited Philadelphia to preach in 1786 and decided to stay, becoming a member of St. George's Methodist and working among the blacks of the city. He wrote, "I soon saw a large field open in seeking and instructing my African brethren, who had been a long forgotten people, and few of them attended public worship."

As the number of black worshipers increased at St. George's, segregated seating was enforced. Allen determined that a separate church for blacks was necessary, and finally one Sunday after especially humiliating treatment, a group of blacks left St. George's Church, promising never to go back.

Bishop Francis Asbury dedicated Bethel, the first black Methodist church, in 1799, and ordained Allen as the pastor. In 1816, after years of tension over matters of jurisdiction, black pastors met in Philadelphia to organize the African Methodist Episcopal Church. Allen was elected as the first bishop and continued serving as pastor of Bethel A.M.E. Church. His organizing abilities enabled the young denomination to grow, increasing sevenfold during his years of oversight.

A man of action and energy, Allen was committed to improving the lot for Africans in America. Along with overseeing a successful series of businesses, he was heavily involved in civic affairs. In his ministry he called people to repentance and eternal life, but also to physical liberation through self-help, education, moral reform, and through attacking the vices of dishonesty and drunkenness.

Charles Grandison Finney (1792-1875). Charles Finney left his promising law career in 1821 after receiving "a retainer from the Lord to plead his cause," and in so doing initiated a new era of revivalism. While Jonathan Edwards and George Whitefield had focussed on God's work in converting sinners, Finney focussed on the role of the evangelist and the sinners in securing their salvation. He wrote, "A revival of religion is not a miracle. It is not a miracle, or dependent on a miracle, in any sense . . . a revival is the result of the right use of the appropriate means."

These means, or "New Measures," included praying for sinners by name, permitting women to pray in the meetings, holding meetings for weeks at a time, establishing the anxious bench for those wanting to repent, and reasoning with the audience like a lawyer with a jury.

Finney was criticized by eminent church leaders including Lyman Beecher and Asahel Nettleton. He responded with published arguments and repeated success in his evangelistic meetings.

He expected that a changed heart would be reflected in a changed life, and he repeatedly spoke out against alcohol and slavery. After pastoring the Broadway Tabernacle (built especially for him), Finney taught theology at the newly-formed Oberlin College. Later he became president of the college, opening its doors to blacks and women.

He continued to hold evangelistic meetings throughout the midwest and northeast. He spoke at Whitefield's Tabernacle in London; the inquiry room filled with 1600 people. Literally hundreds of thousands of people converted to Christ as a result of his ministry, including many who were highly educated and who appreciated his lawyerly arguments and conversational sermons.

---

66 99
FOCUS QUOTE
I look upon this world as a wrecked vessel. God has given me a lifeboat and said to me, "Moody, save all you can." —D. L. Moody

---

Dwight Lyman Moody (1837-1899). D. L. Moody was the leading evangelist of his day. Born in Massachusetts, he moved to Boston before finishing school and found a job as a shoe clerk. While there, his Sunday school teacher led him to Christ. After he moved to Chicago and established a successful shoe business, he established a Sunday school in North Market Hall which grew to a weekly attendance of 1500.

When he was 23, Moody left his shoe business, began working with the Young Men's Christian Association, and developed his evangelistic, fund-raising, and organizational skills.

In 1873 he and soloist Ira Sankey traveled to England to hold evangelistic meetings. Though poorly educated, Moody preached sincere, simple sermons that drew large crowds. When the pair returned to America they were national sensations and quickly became the most influential evangelists in the nation.

SIGNIFICANT EVANGELISTS THROUGHOUT HISTORY cont.

Moody carefully organized and publicized his meetings in major cities throughout America. Stressing the importance of the local church, he devised a new strategy. He divided the city into sections, and held meetings in a centrally-located church in each section. Volunteers from each section publicized the meetings and assisted in them. Moody wrote, "The plan of holding meetings in the tabernacle centralizes the interest and possibly draws out larger crowds, but the churches are the places to do effective work." In the course of his ministry Moody traveled at least 1 million miles and preached to more than 100 million people.

Moody established a number of educational institutions, including Northfield Seminary for girls, Mount Hermon School for boys, and the Chicago Bible Institute (now Moody Bible Institute). In addition, Moody was actively involved in a number of rescue missions and other expressions of Christian social compassion.

Summer student conferences held near his home in Massachusetts grew into the Student Volunteer Movement, through which thousands of students dedicated their lives to missions. SVM's motto reflected Moody's own desire: "the evangelization of the world in this generation."

Moody's message addressed the "Three R's:" Ruin by Sin, Redemption by Christ, and Regeneration by the Holy Ghost. Instead of employing the sensationalism of Finney, Moody won his audiences with sentimental stories that focused on a loving, father God who wishes to bring lost people back into relationship with himself.

Sam Jones (1847-1906). Called the "Moody of the South," Sam Jones was born into a family of Methodist circuit riders in Alabama. Jones began drinking to blunt the pain of recurrent ulcers; as a result he ruined his law practice and drove away his wife. He finally quit drinking after his dying father asked Jones to meet him in heaven. One week later he became a Christian and soon began preaching.

Jones became a Methodist circuit rider in North Carolina and became known for his logical sermons and exceptional speaking ability. Through the early 1880s he preached in urban centers throughout the South, and, following a campaign in Brooklyn in 1885, he preached in every major city in America.

Nashville became the center for his ministry. In 1885 he began preaching in a tent holding 3000, and by 1892 10,000 converts had joined churches in the area. A wealthy businessman converted through his ministry wanted a permanent building for Jones and built the Union Gospel Tabernacle, later home to the Grand Ole Opry.

Jones spoke bluntly in simple language using wit and stories in a style similar to Will Rogers. His message was aimed first to rouse church members to a dynamic faith and then to call the unsaved to commitment. He spoke out against gambling, evolution, and liquor, and insisted that Christians lead a life of moral excellence.

J. Wilbur Chapman (1859-1918). Chapman assisted D. L. Moody during the 1893 World's Fair in Chicago, and worked a year with B. Fay Mills, a classmate and friend. Mills pioneered Simultaneous Evangelistic Campaigns in which simultaneous evangelistic meetings occurred throughout a whole city.

Chapman refined Mill's approach, and soloist Charles Alexander joined him between 1908 and 1918. Special attention was given to share the gospel with shut-ins, the elderly, men on skid row, and others who would not come to the main meetings.

A long Philadelphia campaign in 1908 recorded 1.4 million attenders. In Boston in 1909, more than 30 assistant evangelists and 1000 personal workers reaped 7,000 decisions among the 720,000 attenders. After the Boston meetings the success of the simultaneous meetings waned, and the Chapman–Alexander team returned to more traditional evangelistic meetings both in the U.S. and around the world.

Amanda Berry Smith (1837-1915). Born a slave, Amanda Smith became an internation-ally-known evangelist. She gave her life to Christ at thirteen at a Methodist Episcopal church in Pennsylvania and dedicated her life to God's service at eighteen. After her husband and youngest child died, she gave herself to evangelistic work among blacks in New York.

Her gift for speaking was recognized by her friends, who encouraged her to speak at a holiness camp meeting attended primarily by whites. A warm reception there led to more invitations, and she became a regular speaker at holiness meetings.

She spoke at a Keswick conference and a number of evangelistic meetings throughout England, traveled to India to work as a visiting evangelist, then to Liberia in West Africa for seven years. She returned to America and preached throughout the east.

In addition to her evangelist work, she organized women's temperance groups and groups for children. She retired near Chicago and poured herself and her savings into an orphanage for black children.

Billy Sunday (1862-1935). Billy Sunday captured America's mood during the pre-World War I era and was probably America's most flamboyant evangelist. Born in a log cabin and raised in Iowa, Sunday first reached national prominence as a professional baseball player. Known for his speed, he stole 96 bases in 100 games. He played for Chicago, Pittsburgh, and Philadelphia.

While in Chicago he was converted at Pacific Garden Mission, attended a Presbyterian church, and married Helen A. Thompson, who attended there. In 1891 he left Philadelphia and a salary of $500.00 per month to work with the YMCA in Chicago at $83.33 per month. With the YMCA, Sunday held prayer meetings, distributed tracts in bars, and led meetings on the street.

From 1893 to 1895 he worked as an advance man for J. Wilbur Chapman, from whom Sunday learned the art of holding evangelistic meetings. When Chapman settled into a pastorate in 1895, Sunday was asked to hold evangelistic campaigns. Chapman lent Sunday his sermons to get him started.

Ordained in the Presbyterian Church in 1903, even though his theological education was weak, Sunday continued his evangelistic campaigns in small towns. As the reputation of the "Baseball Evangelist" grew, Sunday received national media attention and moved his meetings to larger cities. From 1912 to 1918, Sunday was one of the most popular preachers in America. Magazines and newspapers printed transcripts of his sermons and "box scores" recording the number of converts.

For each city campaign, Sunday and his team arrived weeks in advance to build support, develop local volunteer committees, and build a wooden tabernacle for the meetings. Sawdust covered the wooden floors to keep down the noise, and those who converted to Christ during the meetings were said to have "hit the sawdust trail."

Sunday was known for his wild gestures and one-line zingers. He raised chairs over his head and imitated drunkards when preaching against liquor. His one-liners include, "Going to church don't make a man a Christian any more than going to a stable makes a man a horse," and "the bars of the Church are so low that any old hog with two or three suits of clothes and a bank roll can crawl through." Sunday became a chief spokesman for national morality and decency. He preached hard and often against alcohol, saying "I'm trying to make America so dry that a man must be primed before he can spit."

His popularity declined quickly after the war. A change in the national mood, questions of impropriety in the publishing of a book, and an unwillingness to submit to financial accountability all contributed to his decline from public prominence. His ministry contin-ued, however, and he died while preaching in Mishawaka, Indiana, in 1935.

W. J. Seymour (d. 1923). Charles F. Parham, a non-denominational evangelist originally from Iowa, opened Bible schools first in Topeka, Kansas, and then in Houston, Texas. His students

SIGNIFICANT EVANGELISTS THROUGHOUT HISTORY cont.

studied the Scriptures in late 1900 and determined that speaking in tongues was the biblical evidence for the baptism of the Holy Spirit, an event separate from conversion or sanctification. Mrs. N. O. LaBerge first spoke in tongues in early 1901 and the Pentecostal movement was born.

W. J. Seymour, a black hotel waiter in Houston, carried the message to Los Angeles as an associate pastor. After being locked out of the church for his views, a small group moved their meeting to an old building on Azusa Street.

Word of the Azusa Street revival spread widely; people came from all across the country. Often speaking in tongues for the first time, visitors returned home with their hearts on fire, bringing Pentecostalism with them.

Seymour presided over the Azusa Street meetings and three years of continuous revival. Pentecostal revival spread around the world, and by 1960 10 million people held Pentecostal convictions. Today, Pentecostal denominations are among the fastest-growing churches in the world.

Mel Trotter (1870-1960). Wounded by his dysfunctional family, Mel Trotter, then an alcoholic, visited the Pacific Garden Mission in Chicago the night he had planned to commit suicide. He gave his life to Christ, and his new faith transformed his life.

In a short time Trotter moved to Grand Rapids to establish a new rescue mission, then helped start sixty more. These missions provided basic food and shelter along with evangelistic activities.

Speaking in tough street slang and familiar with the pain of the slums, Trotter communicated the love of Christ in a powerful way. He wrote, "The only way you can get men to Christ is by love, and you have got to love them into the kingdom of God. A rescue mission without love wouldn't amount to anything."

During World War I Trotter preached to soldiers at bases around America. He recorded 15,000 conversions during a year and a half of ministry. He assisted Billy Sunday after the war and held his own evangelistic campaigns as well.

Evangeline Booth (1865-1950). Eva's family life centered around the Salvation Army, a young organization started by her father, William. Her parents modeled compassion for the less fortunate, piety, and personal religious commitment. She often played at preaching with her brothers and sisters while growing up, and at fifteen she began her work with the Army, selling the *War Cry* on the streets of London. At seventeen she received her own Salvation Army post.

She preached, sang, and played guitar in public houses and run-down halls, gaining the nickname, "White Angel of the Slums." Her natural peacemaking abilities and common sense were often employed in the service of the Army. When hot spots arose, General Booth said, "Send Eva."

For this reason Eva first came to America. Now calling herself Evangeline, she patched up a potential defection of the American branch of the Salvation Army and later became commander of the quickly growing U.S. forces. Under her able leadership the Salvation Army developed rescue homes for "fallen women," help for unwed mothers, convicts, and the unemployed. After the San Francisco earthquake of 1906, Evangeline established the disaster relief arm of the Army.

She spoke in support of the prohibition movement and her public lectures were well attended. She was a good speaker and musician. Some of her hymns are still in the Salvation Army songbook.

For the Salvation Army's service to American soldiers in World War I, Evangeline was awarded the Distinguished Service Medal in 1919. She demonstrated her commitment to the United States by becoming a citizen in 1923.

Eleven years later she left America with "a pang," returning to England in order to take the leadership of the worldwide Salvation Army. A hard worker, Evangeline drove herself at a crushing pace for weeks on end, then retreated for periods of complete rest. After her retirement in 1939 she returned to her home in the U.S. and died at age eighty-five.

Billy Graham (b. 1918). Billy Graham's early years included milking chores on his parents dairy farm in Charlotte, North Carolina, and a love for baseball. At sixteen Graham was converted at the Charlotte revival meetings of Mordecai Ham. He studied at a small Florida Bible college (now Trinity College), and began preaching with the encouragement of the college's dean. Graham had prepared four sermon outlines in advance, but when he preached for the first time, he sped through all four outlines in just eight minutes.

V. Raymond Edman, president of Wheaton College (Illinois), encouraged young Graham to complete his studies at Wheaton. There he met his future wife, Ruth Bell, and took the pastorate of the Gospel Tabernacle, located only a few blocks from campus.

After pastoring the First Baptist Church of Western Springs, Illinois, 1943-1945, Graham accepted Torrey Johnson's invitation to become a Youth for Christ evangelist. During the following two years he traveled 200,000 miles to participate in meetings in 47 states.

From 1947 to 1952 Graham served as president of Northwestern Schools in Minneapolis and continued his evangelistic ministry.

He was catapulted into national prominence during the Los Angeles meetings of 1949. Originally planned for three weeks, the public response to the gospel was so great that the meetings were extended first one week, then another, then another—lasting eight weeks in all. The Hearst newspapers covered the meetings and brought Graham national attention.

The Hour of Decision radio broadcast began in 1950 and by 1984 had a listening audience estimated at 20 million. Schools of Evangelism were established to train pastors in evangelism, starting in 1962. In 1967 Graham used closed circuit television for the first time.

In the course of his ministry Billy Graham has traveled to 84 countries and every state in the U.S. He has preached the gospel in person to more than 100 million people around the world. His characteristic humility has remained unchanged through the years, as has his message: lasting peace and the solutions to the problems of the world today can be found only in the personal transformation which comes through turning to Christ and being born again.

Prayer and extensive preparations mark each city-wide crusade. Churches work together in common purpose; local lay people learn to share their faith through Christian Life and Witness classes, and Schools of Evangelism train pastors; thousands of counselors receive training; choirs of several thousand voices are organized. Extensive use of the media and invitations by thousands of believers bring the unconverted to the meetings, which often set attendance records wherever the meetings are held.

Graham's ministry has played a significant role in shaping the modern ethos of evangelicalism. In 1966 he helped found *Christianity Today*, a national magazine designed to help pastors and educated lay persons. The Billy Graham Evangelistic Association helped sponsor the World Congress on Evangelism in Berlin and the Lausanne Conference in 1974. This second conference brought together over 2,400 people from 150 countries. The Lausanne Covenant, which emerged from the meetings, has become the basis for Christian cooperative evangelism around the world. Two special international conferences for evangelists were held in Amsterdam in 1983 and 1986.

Billy Graham has played a unique role as the major figure in Protestant Christianity worldwide. His integrity and commitment to evangelism have enabled Christians of various theological traditions to work in unprecedented cooperation, and converts from the ministry of the BGEA are serving Christ and his church around the world.

About the author: Daniel Moul is Research and Technical Resources Coordinator, Institute of Evangelism, Billy Graham Center.

A table of 788 plans, proposals, visions, goals, programs, organizations, slogans, mottoes, publications, events, statements or attempts, all related specifically to implementing world evangelization. Titles in italics refer to published books or to journals. In a sense, this listing is only symbolic. Other plans exist, unknown and unheralded. New plans are surfacing weekly.

Most of the global plans listed are described in further detail in historical context in "Chronology of Significant Plans to Evangelize the World from AD 30—1990" under Church History.

The meanings of the 16 columns are as follows. Evaluations shown by code values chosen for particular plans are not evaluations of the sponsoring bodies or events themselves, but are evaluations of the relevance and significance of the plans vis-a-vis world evangelization.

Column

1. No: Reference number in this listing.
2. Year of origin.
3. Brief name for plan.
4. Author: Name of author, sponsor or most prominent individual.
5. Init: Initials or acronym for plan or for its originating church, agency, or organization (parentheses give alternative or additional names; hyphens elaborate entities within wide organizations; slashes separate cooperating agencies or organizations).
6. Type: Code indicates level from absence of human plans to massively-detailed master plans.
   1. a vision or view or scenario of the end-time with God's plan for world evangelization
   2. a one-time challenge to Christians to evangelize the world
   3. published sermon or letter
   4. printed document, book, survey, publication
   5. pledge, declaration
   6. unorganized movement or campaign
   7. statement of purpose by an organization or board
   8. announcement of plan with no details worked out
   9. serious plan with some details, procedures
   10. well worked-out scheme with considerable detail and strategy
   11. massively-detailed plan detailing logistics, personnel, finances, schedules
7. Min: Main type of outreach ministry proposed by the sponsor of the plan.
   1. no human activity proposed or required, God will do it by supernatural means
   2. no human activity proposed except repentance and nurture of one's personal life
   3. prayer, worship, monastic life, revivals
   4. survey, research, communication
   5. presence, lifestyle, martyrdom, lay apostolate
   6. broadcasting, film, video, audio, hi-tech
   7. preaching, evangelism
   8. power evangelism with signs and wonders, healing, miracles
   9. converting, discipling
   10. church planting, baptizing
   11. forcible baptism and church rule
   12. military conquest with forcible baptism and church rule
   13. training, leadership, networking, administration
   14. literature, Scripture distribution, literacy, art
8. Origin: Where this plan originated. The name given is that of the country at the time of origin, which in several early cases differs from its current name in 1991.
9. Tradition: Affiliation. Note a distinction between two often-confused terms: *Nondenominational* refers to plans developed independently of existing major denominations; whereas *interdenominational* is reserved for those plans in whose evolution a number of denominations have been involved, exercise control and receive a degree of accountability. By contrast a denominational label (Methodist, Baptist, Lutheran, etc.) usually implies a firmer degree of control and accountability.
10. Coop: Degree of cooperation with other agencies.
    1. none
    2. minimal
    3. partial; other like-minded traditions may participate if they wish
    4. general; cooperation of all like-minded traditions needed, wanted and assumed
    5. essential; cooperation of like-minded traditions indispensable
    6. total; plan envisages cooperation of entire spectrum of Christians of all traditions, like-minded and otherwise
11. P: Literature about the plan.
    1. nothing written except incidental reference
    2. briefly written up in published form
    3. published article, encyclical, message
    4. published book, books
    5. printed publicity materials
    6. detailed plans printed for private use
    7. detailed plans published as a book or books
12. Dline: Year of closure or date when end-time envisaged. Dash means no date proposed.
13. Reso: Total resources of mission-related personnel and finances employed for implementing this plan. The term *worker-year* is similar to *man-year* or *man-hour* and gives a rough estimate of the scale of work and resources involved, assuming on average a plan lasts 10 years.
    1. negligible; less than 1 worker-year (one individual's work only)
    2. minimal; 1-10 worker-years (a few individuals)
    3. limited; 10-100 worker-years (a small team, under $10,000/year)
    4. modest; 100-1,000 worker-years (from 10-100 workers, $10,000-100,000 a year)
    5. sizeable; 1,000-10,000 worker-years (from 100-1,000 workers, $100,000 to $10 million a year)
    6. massive; over 10,000 worker-years (over 1,000 workers, $10 million to $100 million a year)
    7. gigantic; over 50,000 worker-years (over 5,000 workers, $100 million a year or $1 billion over one decade)
14. Unev: Percentage of the world's population at year of plan's origin that was unaware of Christianity.
15. Ratio: Ratio of total unevangelized persons in world divided by total Christians in world when plan originated. This ratio is a measure of the relative difficulty of the unfinished task.
16. Status: Status as a global plan to implement world evangelization as of 1988. This variable refers to the current status of the plan, not necessarily the same as the current status of its sponsor.
    1. fizzled out, abandoned without reaching stated goal
    2. defunct; little or insufficient interest shown
    3. defunct; completion of task claimed
    4. implemented but goal not, or not yet, achieved
    5. still alive, but plan clearly fizzling out
    6. still alive, but plan in decline
    7. still alive, but static
    8. still alive, but with original goals abandoned, scaled down, redefined or otherwise igored
    9. alive and making progress toward goals
    10. alive and being massively implemented

No. 1	Year 2	Brief name for plan 3	Author 4	Init 5	Type 6	Min 7	Origin 8	Tradition 9	Coop 10	P 11	Dline 12	Reso 13	Unev 14	Ratio 15	Status 16
1	AD 30	"The Kingdom of God has arrived"	Jesus of Nazareth	-	1	8	Palestine	-	5	3	-		99.9	-	9
2	31	The Twelve Apostles as personal evangelists	Jesus the Rabbi	-	8	8	Palestine	-	5	3	-		99.9	-	3
3	31	Mission to Israel	Jesus the Messiah	-	8	8	Palestine	-	5	3	-		99.9	-	3
4	31	Mission of the Seventy	Jesus the Son of Man	-	8	8	Palestine	-	5	3	-		99.9	-	1
5	32	Lightning spread to all nations	Jesus the Returning Judge	-	8	8	Palestine	-	5	3	-		99.9	-	1
6	33	Great Commission–1	The Risen Lord	-	0	8	Palestine	Apostolic	5	3	-	3	99.9	42550.0	1
7	33	Great Commission–2	The Ascended King	-	1	8	Palestine	Apostolic	5	3	-	4	99.8	42550.0	9
8	34	Mission of the Twelve to the Jewish Diaspora	The Twelve Apostles	-	5	8	Palestine	Apostolic	5	3	70	4	99.4	17020.0	9
9	35	Power Evangelism, with Signs and Wonders	The Twelve Apostles	-	5	8	Palestine	Apostolic	5	3	-	3	99.4	6481.0	1
10	36	Martyrdom: witness unto death	Stephen the Protomartyr	-	7	8	Palestine	Apostolic	5	3	-	2	99.0	-	3
11	38	Evangelization of the first Gentiles	The Twelve Apostles	-	0	5	Palestine	Apostolic	5	3	-	1	98.6	5594.0	3
12	38	Peter's mission to the Gentiles	Apostle Peter	-	5	8	Palestine	Apostolic	5	3	-	2	97.7	4157.0	3
13	c38	Worldwide witness of the Twelve	The Twelve Apostles	-	5	5	Palestine	Apostolic	5	3	-	1	97.7	4157.0	3
14	46	Paul's urban mission from city to city	Apostle Paul	-	8	5	Syria	Apostolic	5	3	-	2	94.4	944.0	1
15	61	Preaching to all Creation	Apostle Paul	-	6	8	Greece	Apostolic	5	3	-	2	88.2	294.0	3
16	65	Worldwide Proclamation by Three Angels	John the Divine	-	0	8	Asia Minor	Apostolic	5	3	-	0	86.5	288.3	2
17	66	A History of the Great Commission (Luke–Acts)	Luke the Physician	-	3	8	Italy	Apostolic	5	3	-	0	86.1	287.0	9
18	c85	*Epistle of Barnabas*	Barnabas	-	3	1	Cyprus	Apostolic	3	2	2000	0	78.2	156.4	9
19	94	"Entire Roman Empire has been evangelized"	Clement of Rome	-	3	8	Italy	Catholic	5	2	-	1	74.5	149.0	2
20	96	Foreordained martyrdom	John the Divine	-	0	5	Asia Minor	Apostolic	5	2	-	3	73.7	122.8	0
21	c100	Evangelization via cities and trade routes	Ignatius of Antioch	-	0	8	Syria	Catholic	3	1	-	3	72.0	120.0	2
22	c130	Church-planting and conversions through casual contacts	Telesphorus	-	5	10	Italy	Catholic	3	1	-	3	70.8	47.2	9
23	c140	*Shepherd of Hermas*	Hermas	-	3	7	Italy	Catholic	3	3	-	3	70.4	39.1	8
24	c150	Disciple-training school proclaiming Christ to every race	Justin Martyr	-	7	13	Italy	Catholic	3	3	-	3	70.0	35.0	2
25	156	New Age of the Holy Spirit	Montanus	-	0	1	Asia Minor	Montanist	0	2	-	0	69.8	31.7	8
26	c180	Antichrist, Christ, and Millennium	Irenaeus of Lyons	-	0	0	France	Catholic	0	2	-	0	68.8	23.7	2
27	197	"The blood of the martyrs is seed"	Tertullian	-	7	0	Tunisia	Montanist	1	3	-	1	68.1	20.0	0
28	c205	Apologetics relating gospel to pagan philosophy and culture	Clement of Alexandria	-	7	3	Egypt	Orthodox	3	2	-	3	67.4	17.9	2
29	c220	Reaching unreached populations throughout the Oikumene	Origen	-	2	7	Egypt	Orthodox	3	3	-	3	67.4	13.8	9
30	249	Missionary bishops strategically located across world	Cornelius of Rome	-	9	0	France	Catholic	0	3	-	5	66.5	9.6	9
31	c270	Eremitical monasticism challenging lifestyle of the rich	Anthony	-	5	5	Egypt	Orthodox	2	2	-	4	65.9	7.9	8
32	303	Witness under total persecution	Peter I Seal of Martyrs	-	0	2	Egypt	Orthodox	0	3	-	5	64.9	6.1	8
33	308	Church of the Martyrs	Meletius of Lycopolis	-	0	0	Egypt	Orthodox	0	3	-	5	64.7	5.8	8
34	c310	*Demonstratio Evangelica*	Eusebius of Caesarea	-	3	1	Palestine	Orthodox	3	3	-	2	64.7	5.8	0
35	313	State establishment of Christianity as outreach plan	Constantine	-	10	12	Byzantium	Orthodox	3	3	-	5	64.6	5.6	2
36	c320	Itinerant evangelization by Cenobitic monasticism	Pachomius	-	8	2	Egypt	Orthodox	2	3	-	5	64.5	5.4	8
37	325	Ecumenical councils plan Christian presence	Eusebius of Caesarea	-	10	13	Palestine	Orthodox	2	3	-	5	64.5	5.1	8
38	347	"Antichrist will persecute Christians"	Cyril of Jerusalem	-	3	0	Palestine	Orthodox	0	3	-	0	64.0	4.4	0
39	c360	*Apostolic Constitutions*	Dionysius Exiguus	-	3	7	Syria	Orthodox	2	3	-	1	62.6	4.1	0
40	374	Signs, Healings, and Glossolalia	Ambrose of Milan	-	2	2	Italy	Catholic	1	2	-	5	62.0	3.8	0
41	378	Signs, Wonders, and Martyrs	Jerome	-	0	8	Palestine	Catholic	0	2	-	5	61.9	3.7	2
42	378	"Antichrist has been born"	Martin of Tours	-	0	0	France	Catholic	0	2	-	0	61.9	3.7	0
43	392	Western monasticism with itinerant evangelization	John Cassian	-	5	2	Palestine	Catholic	2	3	-	5	61.3	3.4	8
44	398	Constantinople Schl of Evangelists for Great Commission	John Chrysostom	-	8	13	Byzantium	Orthodox	3	3	430	3	61.1	3.3	0

No.	Year	Brief name for plan	Author	Init	Type	Min	Origin	Tradition	Coop	P	Dline	Reso	Unev	Ratio	Status
1	2 / 3		4	5	6	7	8	9	10	11	12	13	14	15	16
45	c410	Universal episcopate as plan for world mission	Innocent I	-	10	10	Algeria	Catholic	0	0	-	5	60.7	3.2	8
46	417	*Historia Adversus Paganos*	Paulus Orosius	-	0	10	Spain	Catholic	3	3	-	5	60.5	3.2	0
47	426	*The City of God*	Augustine of Hippo	-	3	8	Tunisia	Catholic	4	3	-	1	60.2	3.1	0
48	428	*De Vocatione Omnium Gentium*	Prosper Tiro	-	0	7	France	Catholic	3	3	-	-	60.2	3.1	0
49	499	Cultural translation of Jesus' message	Symmachus	-	5	14	Greece	Orthodox	3	3	-	4	58.0	2.6	3
50	510	Irish Peregrini: Missionary Pilgrims for Christ	Columbanus	-	5	8	Ireland	Celtic	2	1	-	4	58.3	2.6	0
51	535	*Topographia Christiana*	Cosmas Indicopleustes	-	3	3	Egypt	Nestorian	1	3	-	2	59.0	2.6	0
52	c550	Nestorian monasticism sends mission across Asia	Abraham of Kashkar	-	5	2	Persia	Nestorian	0	1	-	5	59.5	2.6	0
53	594	"The Last Judgment demands missions to all heathen"	Gregory the Great	-	2	7	Italy	Catholic	0	3	-	1	60.8	2.5	0
54	635	Nestorian world missions	Alopen	-	9	7	Syria	Nestorian	0	3	-	5	62.4	2.6	0
55	c700	Patristic Age: Greek and Latin Fathers expound *evangelizo*	Theodotus of Ancyra	-	3	3	Greece	Catholic	2	3	-	4	65.0	2.7	0
56	720	Fall of Colosseum, Rome, and the World	Bede	-	0	0	England	Anglican	2	3	-	5	65.8	2.8	0
57	780	Nestorian strategy of metropolitan sees worldwide	Timothy I	-	10	0	Persia	Nestorian	3	1	-	5	68.2	3.0	0
58	c780	Forcible baptism of whole races begun	Charlemagne	-	8	11	Germany	Catholic	0	2	-	5	68.2	3.0	0
59	960	Imminent End of the World	Bernard of Thuringia	-	0	0	Germany	Catholic	0	3	992	2	74.2	3.7	0
60	962	Holy Roman Empire as Rule of Christ on Earth	John XII	-	10	11	Germany	Catholic	0	3	-	5	74.2	3.7	0
61	992	Coming of Antichrist into World	Adso of Montier-en-Der	-	0	5	France	Catholic	0	1	1000	2	74.8	4.0	0
62	999	Advent travel to Jerusalem	Gregory V	-	5	5	Palestine	Catholic	1	3	1000	3	75.0	4.0	0
63	1000	Mass millennial pilgrimage to await Advent	Sylvester II	-	10	5	Palestine	Catholic	0	3	1000	5	75.0	4.0	8
64	1000	Global spread of Catholic Apostolic Church of the East	Ishoyab IV	-	6	13	Syria	Nestorian	0	5	-	5	74.6	4.0	8
65	1090	College of Cardinals to expand Rule of Christ	Urban II	-	10	12	Vatican	Roman Catholic	0	3	-	5	74.5	4.0	0
66	1095	Crusades for the Defense of Christianity	Urban II	-	0	0	Italy	Roman Catholic	0	3	-	3	74.5	4.0	8
67	1139	*Prophecy of the Popes*	Malachy O'Morgain	-	0	0	Ireland	Roman Catholic	0	1	2000	1	74.3	3.9	8
68	1179	Imminent major catastrophe in AD 1186	John of Toledo	-	0	0	Spain	Roman Catholic	0	3	1186	-	74.1	3.8	9
69	c1180	Final Age of the Spirit	Joachim of Fiore	-	0	0	Italy	Roman Catholic	0	3	1260	2	74.1	3.8	9
70	c1190	Vernacular scriptures: *Historia Scholastica*	Petrus Comestor	-	5	14	France	Roman Catholic	1	3	-	2	74.1	3.8	9
71	1209	Order of Friars: mendicant orders of travelling preachers	Francis of Assisi	OFM	10	8	Italy	Roman Catholic	1	3	-	2	74.1	3.8	9
72	1215	Order of Preachers: "Propagation of the Faith through Preaching"	Dominic	OP	10	7	France	Roman Catholic	1	5	-	6	73.9	3.7	9
73	1221	Bull "Ne Si Secus" to the 13 Catholic Metropolitans	Honorius III	-	2	13	Vatican	Roman Catholic	0	5	-	6	73.9	3.7	9
74	c1250	Church's temporal power as God's instrument for mission	Innocent IV	-	10	11	Italy	Roman Catholic	0	2	-	2	73.8	3.6	3
75	c1250	Popular preachers warn of Coming of Antichrist	Berthold von Regensburg	OFM	0	0	Germany	Roman Catholic	0	3	1260	5	73.5	3.4	5
76	1254	Imminent Third Age of the Holy Spirit	Gerard of Borgo San Domino	OFM	0	0	Italy	Roman Catholic	1	1	-	2	73.5	3.4	0
77	c1260	Religious art: painting, stained glass, sculpture	Duccio de Buoninsegna	-	0	1	Italy	Roman Catholic	1	3	1260	0	73.5	3.4	0
78	1266	"Send me 100 men"	Kublai Khan	-	0	14	Mongolia	Roman Catholic	1	3	-	5	73.4	3.3	8
79	c1280	Congregation of Friars Pilgrims for Christ Among the Gentiles	William of Tripoli	OP	1	9	France	Roman Catholic	0	1	-	2	73.3	3.3	0
80	1288	*Notitia Seculi*	Alexander of Roes	-	8	7	Germany	Roman Catholic	0	2	-	4	73.2	3.2	0
81	1290	*The Coming of Antichrist*	Arnold of Villanova	-	0	1	Spain	Roman Catholic	0	3	-	0	73.1	3.1	0
82	1305	*Liber de Fine*: Preaching plus Military Force	Ramon Lull	OFM	1	12	Algeria	Roman Catholic	0	3	1500	1	73.1	3.1	0
83	1315	*The Final Coming of Antichrist*	Hugh of Newcastle	OFM	0	10	France	Roman Catholic	0	3	-	0	72.7	3.0	0
84	1349	East Syrian/Nestorian apogee	Yabalaha III	-	10	0	Syria	Nestorian	0	3	-	5	72.7	3.0	0
85	c1350	Revelation of Antichrist in AD 2000	St John of the Cleft Rock	-	0	1	Italy	Roman Catholic	0	0	2000	0	72.0	3.0	0
86	1399	Wandering preachers proliferate across world	Vincent Ferrer	OP	2	8	Spain	Roman Catholic	0	1	3936	3	73.0	3.0	9

No. 1	Year 2	Brief name for plan 3	Author 4	Init 5	Type 6	Min 7	Origin 8	Tradition 9	Coop 10	P 11	Dline 12	Reso 13	Unev 14	Ratio 15	Status 16
87	c1400	Societas Peregrinantium pro Christo	William of Casale	OFM	8	7	Italy	Roman Catholic	0	2	-	4	73.0	3.0	0
88	1420	Taborite Kingdom of God	Nicholas of Pelhrimov	-	9	12	Bohemia	Hussite	0	1	-	5	74.2	3.2	0
89	1431	Council of Basle orders non-Christians to attend sermons	Eugenius IV	·	2	11	Vatican	Roman Catholic	1	5	-	4	74.9	3.3	0
90	1450	Dissemination of Scriptures by typography and printing	Johannes Gutenberg	-	9	14	Germany	Roman Catholic	1	5	-	5	76.0	3.5	8
91	1455	*The Imitation of Christ*	Thomas à Kempis	-	3	5	Germany	Roman Catholic	0	3	-	1	76.3	3.6	6
92	1490	Reforming beggar-monks itinerate evangelizing	Wolfgang Capito	-	5	7	Germany	Roman Catholic	0	1	-	3	78.4	4.0	0
93	1493	"Inter Caetera"	Alexander VI	-	2	11	Vatican	Roman Catholic	0	3	-	1	78.6	4.1	0
94	1499	3-story Rhine ark	Johannes Stoeffler	-	0	1	Germany	Roman Catholic	0	1	1524	2	78.9	4.1	0
95	1500	World missions via Spanish/Portuguese imperialism	Alexander VI	-	10	11	Vatican	Roman Catholic	0	5	-	5	79.0	4.2	0
96	1500	End-time predictions	Bartolomeo di Saluzzo	-	0	1	Italy	Roman Catholic	0	1	-	5	79.0	4.2	0
97	1500	Saints and martyrs as evangelizing witnesses	George Novi of Sophia	-	5	5	Italy	Roman Catholic	1	3	-	3	79.0	4.2	8
98	1517	"Visions of the End of the World"	Leonardo da Vinci	-	0	14	Italy	Roman Catholic	2	3	-	1	78.7	4.1	6
99	c1520	Completion of the Task by the Twelve Apostles	Martin Luther	-	0	0	Germany	Lutheran	2	3	1558	5	78.6	4.1	2
100	1523	Conquistadores enforce mass baptism across New World	Charles V	-	10	12	Mexico	Roman Catholic	0	3	-	0	78.5	4.1	0
101	1523	Conversion of Islam and the Whole World to Christ (Jesuits)	Ignatius Loyola	SJ	10	9	Palestine	Roman Catholic	0	6	-	6	78.5	4.1	9
102	1523	Astrologers' prediction of End of World in 1524	Paracelsus (von Hohenheim)	-	0	1	Switzerland	Roman Catholic	0	1	1524	1	78.5	4.1	0
103	1528	Berne Disputation and its Ten Theses	Ulrich Zwingli	-	2	12	Switzerland	Reformed	2	1	1524	4	78.4	4.1	0
104	1530	Melchiorites and the New Jerusalem	Melchior Hofmann	-	9	0	Netherlands	Anabaptist	0	1	1533	5	78.4	4.1	0
105	1530	Cessation of Apostolic Commission	John Calvin	-	0	12	Switzerland	Reformed	2	1	-	0	78.4	4.1	2
106	1534	New Zion and the Kingdom of a Thousand Years	John of Leiden	-	9	14	Germany	Anabaptist	0	1	-	5	78.3	4.1	0
107	1536	"The Last Judgment" inspired by hymn "Dies Irae"	Michelangelo Buonarroti	-	0	14	Italy	Roman Catholic	2	3	2000	4	78.3	4.1	6
108	1547	*The Centuries* with detailed future prophecies	Michel de Nostradamus	-	1	14	France	Roman Catholic	0	3	-	3	78.1	4.1	9
109	c1547	Anabaptist view of the Great Commission	Michael Sattler	-	0	7	Germany	Anabaptist	2	3	-	1	78.1	4.1	9
110	c1550	Numerology of Apocalypse and End of World in 1666	J.H. Bullinger	-	0	0	Switzerland	Reformed	2	1	1666	1	78.0	4.1	0
111	1559	Hutterian Brethren's itinerate evangelism	Jakob Hutter	-	5	8	Moravia	Anabaptist	0	3	-	3	77.8	4.1	9
112	1568	Commission of Cardinals begun for foreign missions	Pius V	-	6	13	Vatican	Roman Catholic	0	5	-	2	77.6	4.1	9
113	1573	Congregation for Conversion of Infidels	Gregory XIII	-	6	13	Vatican	Roman Catholic	0	3	-	2	77.5	4.1	0
114	1580	Discalced Carmelite Sisters: evangelization by prayer	Theresa of Avila	-	10	0	Spain	Roman Catholic	0	5	-	5	77.4	4.1	9
115	1584	Evangelistic military conquest	Alonso Sanchez	SJ	9	12	Spain	Roman Catholic	0	3	-	0	77.3	4.1	0
116	1588	Binding validity of Great Commission	Hadrian Saravia	-	2	0	England	Anglican	3	2	-	1	77.2	4.1	9
117	1588	Consistorial Congregation (Sacred Congregtn for Bishops)	Sixtus V	-	10	13	Vatican	Roman Catholic	0	5	-	6	77.2	4.1	0
118	1589	Russian Orthodox state-supported missions	Peter the Great	ROC	10	10	Russia	Eastern Orthodox	0	5	-	4	77.2	4.1	0
119	1594	Logarithms and the Apocalypse, and Number of the Beast	John Napier	-	0	10	Scotland	Presbyterian	0	3	-	1	77.1	4.1	9
120	1600	Bruno's Magico-Religious System	Giordano Bruno	-	0	1	Italy	Roman Catholic	0	3	-	1	77.0	4.1	0
121	c1600	Episcopi Vagantes with plans for Reunion of Christendom	Julius Ferrette	-	5	2	Italy	Old Catholic	0	3	-	4	77.0	4.1	5
122	1610	The Coming of Antichrist	Tomas Malvenda	OP	3	9	Spain	Roman Catholic	1	1	-	1	76.7	4.0	0
123	1613	*De Procuranda Salute Omnium Gentium*	Thomas a Jesu	-	0	9	Spain	Roman Catholic	3	3	-	1	76.6	3.9	3
124	1620	Mission preaching restricted to Twelve Apostles	Johann Gerhard	-	0	7	Germany	Lutheran	0	3	-	6	76.3	3.9	2
125	1622	Propaganda Fide: Spreading the Faith to the World	Gregory XV	-	10	0	Vatican	Roman Catholic	0	6	-	6	76.3	3.8	9
126	1627	Progressive Millennialism before Return of Christ	Joseph Mede	-	0	1	England	Anglican	2	3	-	1	76.1	3.8	4
127	1648	Eleven Million Martyrs	Ildefonso de Flores	SJ	0	5	Spain	Roman Catholic	1	3	-	5	75.4	3.6	8
128	1656	Return of the Jews	Oliver Cromwell	-	0	1	England	Anglican	0	1	-	5	75.2	3.5	0
129	1657	Fifth Monarchy Men	Thomas Venner	-	0	0	England	Anglican	0	1	c1660	2	75.2	3.5	0
130	1658	Antichrist as Parody of Christ	Bartholomaus Holtzhauser	-	0	0	Germany	Roman Catholic	0	0	-	0	75.2	3.5	0

No. 1	Year 2	Brief name for plan 3	Author 4	Init 5	Type 6	Min 7	Origin 8	Tradition 9	Coop 10	P 11	Dline 12	Reso 13	Unev 14	Ratio 15	Status 16
131	c1660	Millennium centered on church in Peru	G. Tenorio	OFM	0	1	Peru	Roman Catholic	.	3	-	0	75.2	3.5	0
132	1663	Missionary Work among Unevangelized Peoples	Justinian von Welz	-	3	7	Germany	Lutheran	2	3	-	2	75.2	3.5	1
133	1667	"To Evangelize the Nations" (*Paradise Lost*)	John Milton	-	2	7	Britain	Anglican	3	3	-	1	75.1	3.5	5
134	1680	Christian Brothers: evangelization by schools	J.-B. de La Salle	FSC	10	13	France	Roman Catholic	0	5	-	5	75.0	3.4	5
135	1693	Knights of the Apocalypse	Innocent XII	-	7	12	Italy	Roman Catholic	0	1	-	2	74.9	3.4	9
136	1698	Society for Promoting Christian Knowledge	Thomas Bray	SPCK/SPG	9	9	Britain	Anglican	2	5	-	4	74.8	3.4	0
137	1700	Missions to Jews	E.C.H. von Hochenau	-	7	7	Germany	Lutheran	0	0	-	2	74.8	3.4	7
138	1703	Spiritans: "Evangelizzazione degli infedeli"	C.F. Poullart des Places	CSSp	10	7	France	Roman Catholic	0	5	-	5	74.8	3.4	1
139	1705	Danish-Halle Mission	B. Ziegenbalg	-	9	7	Denmark	Lutheran	2	5	-	4	74.7	3.3	9
140	1710	Canstein Bible Society	K.H. von Canstein	-	10	7	Germany	Lutheran	2	5	-	4	74.7	3.3	7
141	1725	Great Awakening and Progressive Millennialism	Jonathan Edwards	-	8	14	NorthAm	Congregationalist	2	3	1990	3	74.5	3.3	3
142	1730	End of the World by Deluge	William Whiston	-	1	1	Britain	Anglican	0	1	1736	4	74.4	3.4	0
143	1732	Society for Propagating the Gospel among the Heathen	N.L. von Zinzendorf	-	9	8	Germany	Moravian	2	5	-	4	74.4	3.4	8
144	1770	Tribulation and Antichrist in AD 2000	Jeanne Le Rocher	-	0	0	France	Roman Catholic	0	0	2000	0	73.6	3.3	0
145	1774	United Society of Believers in Christ's Second Appearing	Ann Lee	-	9	7	Germany	Quaker	2	1	-	2	73.5	3.3	0
146	1780	Christendom Society and Basel Mission	C.G. Blumhardt	DCG/EMB	9	7	Germany	Evangelical	2	5	-	4	73.4	3.2	7
147	1782	Concerts of Prayer (for revival and world mission)	Jonathan Edwards	-	9	2	Britain	Evangelical	0	5	-	3	73.3	3.2	3
148	1783	Revival pentecostalism among Black slaves	George Lisle	-	5	8	Jamaica	Baptist	1	1	-	3	73.3	3.2	9
149	1785	Evangelical awakenings throughout Wales	Howel Harris	-	5	8	Wales	Anglican	1	1	-	3	73.2	3.2	9
150	1787	*The Gospel of Christ Worthy of All Acceptation*	Andrew Fuller	-	3	7	Britain	Baptist	2	3	-	0	73.2	3.2	5
151	1792	*Obligations of Christians for Conversion of the Heathens*	William Carey	BMS	3	3	Britain	Baptist	2	2	-	4	73.0	3.2	7
152	1795	London Missionary Society	William Ellis	LMS	9	3	Britain	Congregationalist	2	1	-	2	72.9	3.2	1
153	1800	Revival camp meetings sweep across large populations	James McGready	-	5	8	USA	Methodist	2	1	-	4	72.8	3.2	4
154	1802	Massachusetts Baptist Mission Society	Hezekiah Smith	MBMS	7	7	USA	Baptist	1	1	-	2	72.4	3.1	1
155	1804	Foreign-language Bible Societies: BFBS, ABS, et alia	Thomas Charles	BFBS	10	14	Britain	Interdenominational	2	5	-	5	72.0	3.1	9
156	1805	*Le Dernier Homme*: first modern End-of-the-World novel	J.-B. Cousin de Grainville	-	0	1	France	Roman Catholic	0	3	-	1	71.8	3.1	0
157	1806	Society of Inquiry on the Subject of Missions	Adoniram Judson	-	8	2	USA	Baptist	3	2	-	2	71.6	3.1	0
158	1810	Ecumenical missionary conferences	William Carey	BMS	8	13	India	Baptist	3	1	-	0	70.7	3.0	1
159	1810	American Board of Commissioners for Foreign Missions	S. Newell	ABCFM(UCBWM)	10	9	USA	Congregationalist	2	5	-	5	70.7	3.0	7
160	1811	*Dissertation on Antichrist*	Ethan Smith	-	0	4	USA	Evangelical	0	5	1866	1	70.5	3.0	0
161	1814	Reestablished Jesuit missions	Pius VII	SJ	10	4	Italy	Roman Catholic	0	5	-	4	69.9	3.0	9
162	1815	"The Duty and Reward of Evangelizing the Heathen"	H. Bardwell	-	2	9	USA	Evangelical	3	3	-	0	69.7	3.0	0
163	1815	Missions of the Most Precious Blood	Caspar Del Bufalo	-	9	4	Italy	Roman Catholic	0	3	-	4	69.7	3.0	8
164	1815	*The Spirit of British Missions*	G. Hall & S. Newell	CMS	2	7	Britain	Anglican	2	3	-	0	69.7	2.9	1
165	1818	*The Conversion of the World: or the Claims of 600 Millions*	Josiah Pratt	ABCFM	3	9	India	Congregationalist	2	1	-	1	69.0	2.9	0
166	1819	Missionary Society of the Methodist Episcopal Church	N. Bangs	BGM	10	7	USA	Methodist	2	5	-	6	68.8	2.9	9
167	c1820	Lucifer Unchained by 1940	Catherine Emmerich	-	0	0	Germany	Roman Catholic	0	0	c1980	0	68.6	2.9	0
168	1823	"The Conversion of the World"	Josiah Pratt	CMS	2	9	Britain	Anglican	2	3	-	5	67.9	2.8	8
169	1824	Interdenominational citywide cooperative evangelism	A.F. Schauffler	-	10	7	USA	Interdenominational	2	1	-	0	67.7	2.8	0
170	1825	Bombay Missionary Union	William Carey	-	6	7	India	Interdenominational	3	3	-	5	67.5	2.8	8
171	1826	Glasgow City Mission and 200 other city missions	David Nasmiths	BMU	6	7	Britain	Interdenominational	2	1	-	4	67.3	2.6	5
172	1827	Premillennial apostasy of Christendom: Dispensationalism	J.N. Darby	LCM/NYCM/&c	0	7	Britain	Nondenominational	2	3	-	1	67.0	2.7	0
173	1828	Evangelizing in One Generation through Native Evangelists	Karl F.A. Gutzlaff	-	8	0	China	Lutheran	2	0	-	4	66.8	2.7	0
174	1829	Christian Brethren (Christian Missions in Many Lands)	A.N. Groves	CMML	5	5	Britain	Brethren	0	1	-	4	66.6	2.7	8
175	1830	Evangelistic campaigns through professional evangelists	Evangelist Andrew	-	9	7	USA	Interdenominational	1	1	-	5	66.4	2.7	3

No. 1	Year 2 3	Brief name for plan	Author 4	Init 5	Type 6	Min 7	Origin 8	Tradition 9	Coop 10	P 11	Dline 12	Reso 13	Unev 14	Ratio 15	Status 16
176	1830	Church of Jesus Christ of Latter-day Saints	Joseph Smith	CJCLdS	10	5	USA	Mormon	0	5	-	6	66.4	2.7	9
177	1831	Presbyterian Church in the United States	J.H. Rice	PCUS	10	7	USA	Presbyterian	1	5	-	5	66.1	2.6	7
178	1832	Catholic Apostolic Church	Edward Irving	CAC	10	0	Britain	Catholic Apostolic	0	4	c1840	5	65.9	2.6	4
179	1836	Appeal from Missionaries at the Sandwich Islands	William Richards	ABCFM	2	7	Hawaii	Congregationalist	2	3	-	4	65.0	2.5	0
180	1836	Thoughts on Evangelizing the World	T.S. Skinner	-	3	7	USA	Evangelical	2	2	-	5	65.0	2.5	0
181	1837	Board of Foreign Missions, Presbytm Church in the USA	J.C. Lowrie	BFM(COEMAR)	10	7	USA	Presbyterian	3	3	-	0	64.8	2.5	7
182	1837	The Time for the World's Conversion Come	Rufus Anderson	ABCFM	2	9	USA	Congregationalist	3	3	-	5	64.8	2.5	0
183	184i	Church growth statistics: monitoring world evangelization	Henry Venn	CMS	8	0	Britain	Anglican	2	5	-	3	63.9	2.4	8
184	1842	Predictions of the End of the World	John Dee	-	0	0	Britain	Anglican	0	0	1842	6	63.7	2.4	0
185	1844	Seventh-day Adventists	William Miller	SDA	0	0	USA	Adventist	1	5	1844	2	63.2	2.4	9
186	1844	Christadelphians (Brothers of Christ)	John Thomas	-	0	0	USA	Christadelphian	0	3	-	5	63.2	2.4	4
187	1844	World Alliance of YMCAs/World YWCA	George Williams	YMCA/YWCA	6	13	Switzerland	Evangelical	3	3	-	5	63.2	2.4	7
188	1845	Southern Baptist Convention	James B. Taylor	SBC-FMB	10	0	USA	Baptist	1	5	-	6	63.0	2.4	8
189	1846	Evangelical Alliance and world conciliarism	P. Schaff	EA	0	13	Germany	Reformed	0	3	-	2	62.8	2.3	8
190	1850	Pyramidology and the future of Christianity	John Taylor	-	0	0	Britain	Anglican	0	3	2001	2	61.9	2.3	1
191	1850	"Antichrist will not delay his coming"	Bertine Bouquillon	-	9	7	France	Roman Catholic	0	0	-	4	61.9	2.3	3
192	1850	Millionaire philanthropist-strategists	Robert Arthington	-	9	7	Britain	Quaker	0	0	-	4	61.9	2.3	3
193	1854	First Union Missionary Convention	Alexander Duff	-	4	13	Britain	Presbyterian	2	2	-	0	60.8	2.2	0
194	1854	Foreign Mission Committee, Canada Presbyterian Synod	J. Geddie	CPS/BWM-UCC	10	9	Canada	Presbyterian	0	2	-	4	60.8	2.2	7
195	c1855	Russian Orthodox scientific basis for missions	N.I. Ilminsky	ROC	3	7	Russia	Eastern Orthodox	1	3	-	0	60.6	2.2	0
196	1857	Organized large-scale lay-centered mass evangelism	D.L. Moody	-	10	10	USA	Congregationalist	2	2	-	5	60.6	2.2	8
197	1858	"The Duty of the present generation to evangelize the World"	J. Parker	-	7	7	USA	Evangelical	0	4	-	5	60.1	2.1	0
198	1859	Liverpool Conference on Missions	Earl of Shaftesbury	-	4	13	Britain	Anglican	3	3	-	5	60.1	2.1	8
199	1860	Salesians: Christian education of youth across world	John Bosco	SDB	10	10	Italy	Roman Catholic	3	5	-	5	59.8	2.1	9
200	1860	Reorganized Church of Jesus Christ of Latter Day Saints	Joseph Smith II	RCJCLDS	6	7	USA	Mormon	0	3	-	4	59.5	2.1	8
201	1861	Women's mission societies	Francis Mason	WUMSA	9	7	USA	Congregationalist	2	5	-	5	59.3	2.0	4
202	1862	Scheutists: "Evangelizzazione dei popoli"	Theophile Verbist	CICM	10	7	Belgium	Roman Catholic	0	5	-	6	59.3	2.0	9
203	1863	New Apostolic Church	H. Geyer	NAK(NAC)	9	1	Germany	Catholic Apostolic	0	1	-	0	59.0	2.0	8
204	1865	Christian Revival Association	William Booth	SA	8	8	Britain	Salvationist	3	3	-	5	58.7	2.0	9
205	1866	"The Duty of the Church to evangelize the World"	C. Dickson	PCUSA	2	7	Britain	Presbyterian	3	3	-	0	58.5	1.9	0
206	1867	Confessional conciliarism: Lambeth Conference of Bishops	C.T. Longley	CofE	9	13	Britain	Anglican	3	3	-	5	57.9	1.9	8
207	1867	Combonians: "Evangelizzazione dei popoli"	Daniele Comboni	MCCI/FSCI/MFSC	10	7	Italy	Roman Catholic	0	5	-	5	57.7	1.9	8
208	1869	Aryan Race as God's Chosen Evangelizers	F.W. Farrar	-	2	7	Britain	Anglican	0	0	-	5	57.4	1.9	0
209	1870	Megaministries (each reaching 1% of the world per year)	Charles Jackson	BFBS/ABS/NBS	10	14	Britain	Interdenominational	3	6	-	5	57.4	1.9	8
210	1870	Pan-Orthodox world missions	I. Veniaminov	ROC/OMS	10	9	Russia	Eastern Orthodox	1	3	-	5	56.9	1.9	8
211	1870	Churches of Christ (Non-Instrumental)	A. Campbell	CC	10	5	USA	Disciples	0	3	-	5	56.9	1.9	7
212	1870	Watch Tower Bible & Tract Society	Charles T. Russell	WTBTS-IBSA	10	9	USA	Witnesses	0	6	1874	6	56.6	1.9	9
213	1871	"Apostolic Missions: the Gospel for Every Creature"	Joseph Angus	BMS	2	7	Britain	Baptist	1	5	-	5	56.6	1.9	0
214	1872	Salesian Sisters: evangelization by works of charity	John Bosco	FMA	10	4	Italy	Roman Catholic	0	5	-	4	56.6	1.8	9
215	1873	Regions Beyond Missionary Union	H.G. Guinness	RBMU	8	7	Britain	Nondenominational	0	0	-	4	56.4	1.8	9
216	1874	Signs of the Times	James White	SDA	8	0	USA	Adventist	0	3	-	5	56.1	1.8	8
217	1875	Verbites: "Evangelizzazione dei Popoli"	Arnold Janssen	SVD	10	7	Netherlands	Roman Catholic	0	5	-	5	55.8	1.8	8
218	1876	Watchcry	A.T. Pierson	PCUSA	1	3	USA	Presbyterian	3	2	-	5	55.6	1.8	9
219	1877	Shanghai Watchword	-	-	4	3	China	Interdenominational	3	2	-	2	55.3	1.8	0
220	1880	"A plan to evangelize the World," The Missionary Review	A.T. Pierson	-	3	3	USA	Presbyterian	3	2	-	5	54.0	1.7	0
221	1881	World's Christian Endeavor Union	Francis E. Clark	USCE	9	13	USA	Interdenominational	2	3	-	5	53.7	1.7	5

No. 1	Year 2	Brief name for plan 3	Author 4	Init 5	Type 6	Min 7	Origin 8	Tradition 9	Coop 10	P 11	Dline 12	Reso 13	Unev 14	Ratio 15	Status 16
222	1884	*The Christian Century*	C.C. Morrison	-	3	14	USA	Nondenominational	3	3	2000	3	52.9	1.6	5
223	1884	"No conversion of Nations without adequate outlay"	A.O. Van Lennep	-	3	3	USA	Ecumenical	3	3	-	2	52.9	1.6	0
224	1885	Ecumenical Council: "An Appeal to Disciples Everywhere"	D.L. Moody	-	2	3	USA	Congregationalist	3	3	1900	2	52.7	1.6	0
225	1886	1st International Christian Student Conference	D.L. Moody	-	4	13	USA	Interdenominational	2	3	1900	2	52.4	1.6	9
226	1887	Christian & Missionary Alliance	A.B. Simpson	C&MA	9	7	USA	Holiness	3	5	-	2	52.1	1.6	9
227	1888	Student Volunteer Movement for Foreign Missions	R.P. Wilder	SVMFM/SVMU	9	13	USA	Interdenominational	3	3	1900	5	51.9	1.6	9
228	1888	The Great Controversy	Ellen G. White	SDA	3	1	USA	Adventist	0	3	-	3	51.9	1.6	0
229	1888	One By One Band: God's Plan for Soul Winning	T. Hogben	-	8	5	USA	Nondenominational	1	3	-	3	51.9	1.6	0
230	1889	Make Jesus King	R.P. Wilder	-	1	7	Britain	Interdenominational	3	1	-	2	51.6	1.6	0
231	1889	SVMFM closure prediction: World Evangelization by 1900	John R. Mott	SVMFM	0	9	USA	Methodist	3	3	1900	5	51.6	1.6	1
232	1890	Scandinavian/Evangelical Alliance Mission	F. Franson	TEAM	9	9	USA	Nondenominational	2	4	1900	5	51.3	1.6	9
233	1891	*The Encyclopedia of Missions: Historical, Statistical*	H.O. Dwight	-	3	3	USA	Ecumenical	2	5	-	5	51.0	1.6	3
234	1893	Africa Industrial Mission/SIM International	Walter Gowans	SIM	8	7	Canada	Nondenominational	2	3	-	5	50.6	1.5	0
235	1894	*Methods of the Evangelization of the Non-Christian World*	R.N. Cust	BFBS	3	3	Britain	Anglican	3	3	-	1	50.3	1.5	0
236	1895	Make Colleges In All Lands Centers of Evangelization	L.D. Wishard	-	3	13	USA	Ecumenical	3	3	-	5	50.0	1.5	9
237	1895	Assoc of Pentecostal Churches in America (Nazarene)	P.F. Bresee	-	6	8	USA	Holiness	3	6	-	5	50.0	1.5	9
238	1895	World Student Christian Federation	John R. Mott	APCA-CoN	8	13	Sweden	Ecumenical	3	3	-	5	50.0	1.5	7
239	1896	Liverpool Students Conference	R.P. Wilder	WSCF	3	13	Britain	Interdenominational	3	3	-	2	49.8	1.5	9
240	1897	4th Lambeth Conference: resolution on Great Commission	Frederick Temple	-	4	13	Britain	Anglican	3	3	-	3	49.5	1.5	0
241	1897	Canterbury House of Laymen: resolution on Great Commission	Eugene Stock	CMS	4	13	Britain	Anglican	3	3	-	3	49.5	1.5	0
242	1897	"Selfishness of Christians is the only hindrance"	S.M. Zwemer	RCA	1	5	Arabia	Reformed	0	1	-	0	49.5	1.5	0
243	1897	Encyclical "On the Holy Spirit"	Leo XIII	-	2	14	Vatican	Roman Catholic	1	1	-	3	49.5	1.5	9
244	1899	Gideons International	J. Nicholson	-	9	7	USA	Nondenominational	2	5	-	5	49.0	1.4	9
245	1899	Golden Age of Jewish Missions	Leopold Cohn	-	5	3	Germany	Interdenominational	3	3	-	4	49.0	1.4	8
246	1900	New York Ecumenical Missionary Conference	J.S. Dennis	-	4	3	USA	Ecumenical	4	3	-	1	49.0	1.4	0
247	1900	*The Evangelization of the World in This Generation*	John R. Mott	SVMFM	3	8	USA	Ecumenical	1	3	1925	5	48.7	1.4	0
248	1900	Pentecostalism (First Wave, Renewal in the Holy Spirit)	C.F. Parham	-	5	10	USA	Pentecostal	0	3	-	5	48.7	1.4	8
249	1900	Spread of denominationalism across world	Cosmo Gordon Lang	-	5	8	USA	Interdenominational	0	1	-	5	48.7	1.4	3
250	1901	Latter Rain restoration	D.W. Myland	-	7	7	USA	Pentecostal	3	5	-	5	48.7	1.4	8
251	1901	Consolata Fathers: "Evangelizzazione degli infedeli"	G. Allamano	IMC	10	13	Italy	Roman Catholic	3	6	-	5	48.6	1.4	8
252	1902	Missionary Education Movement	C.G. Trumbull	MEM	10	3	USA	Interdenominational	4	3	-	5	48.6	1.4	0
253	1902	*Centennial Survey of Foreign Missions*	J.S. Dennis	APM	3	7	USA	Presbyterian	0	6	-	3	48.5	1.4	0
254	1902	World-wide Evangelization the Urgent Business of the Church	T. Jays	SVMFM	4	8	Canada	Interdenominational	0	3	-	4	48.5	1.4	0
255	1903	All Nations Flag Church/Church of God of Prophecy	A.J. Tomlinson	CGP	9	8	USA	Pentecostal	2	3	-	4	48.3	1.4	8
256	1904	Welsh Revival	Evan Roberts	-	5	1	Wales	Methodist	0	3	-	4	48.2	1.4	0
257	1904	Premillennialism's theory that world is already evangelized	W.E. Blackstone	-	0	13	USA	Fundamentalist	4	2	-	5	48.2	1.4	2
258	1905	National conciliarism as basis for world mission	John R. Mott	-	6	3	France	Reformed	3	3	-	2	48.1	1.4	8
259	1906	World mission atlases and surveys	H.P. Beach	-	3	3	USA	Ecumenical	3	3	-	2	48.0	1.4	6
260	1906	Glossolalia to accomplish world evangelization	C.F. Parham	-	0	7	USA	Pentecostal	0	1	-	3	48.0	1.4	0
261	1906	1st Gen. Conference of Missionaries to the World of Islam	S.M. Zwemer	RCA	4	7	Egypt	Reformed	1	4	-	5	48.0	1.4	0
262	1906	Laymen's Missionary Movement	J.B. Sleman	LMM	10	5	USA	Interdenominational	4	3	-	4	48.0	1.4	0
263	1907	*Lord of the World*	R.H. Benson	-	3	1	Britain	Roman Catholic	1	5	c2020	4	47.9	1.4	8
264	1907	Laymen's Missionary Movement of Southern Baptists	Joshua Levering	LMMSB/SBC	8	13	USA	Baptist	5	3	-	4	47.9	1.4	8
265	1908	*The Unfinished Task of the Christian Church*	J.L. Barton	-	3	3	Britain	Ecumenical	4	3	-	1	47.7	1.4	0

No. 1	Year 2	Brief name for plan 3	Author 4	Init 5	Type 6	Min 7	Origin 8	Tradition 9	Coop 10	P 11	Dline 12	Reso 13	Unev 14	Ratio 15	Status 16
266	1910	"Unoccupied sections of the world"/World Missionary Conference	John R. Mott	WMC	3	3	Britain	Ecumenical	4	3	-	4	47.5	1.3	3
267	1910	Reunion of Christendom (Episcopal Church in the USA)	C.H. Brent	-	8	13	USA	Anglican	4	3	-	4	47.5	1.3	4
268	1910	Vision of coming of Antichrist	Pius X	OFM	0	1	Vatican	Roman Catholic	0	2	-	4	47.5	1.3	0
269	1910	Can the World Be Won For Christ?	N. Maclean	-	3	9	Britain	Ecumenical	0	2	-	1	47.5	1.3	0
270	1910	Men and Religion Forward Movement	John R. Mott	MRFM	10	13	USA	Interdenominational	3	4	-	5	47.5	1.3	0
271	1910	Church of God (Cleveland) World Missions	R.M. Evans	CoGWM	10	8	USA	Pentecostal	0	5	-	5	47.5	1.3	9
272	1910	God's Missionary Plan for the World	J.W. Bashford	-	3	3	Britain	Ecumenical	3	3	-	4	47.5	1.3	0
273	1911	Unoccupied Mission Fields	S.M. Zwemer	RCA	3	3	USA	Reformed	3	3	-	1	47.4	1.3	0
274	1912	International Review of Missions	J.H. Oldham	IRM	3	3	Britain	Ecumenical	4	2	-	3	47.2	1.3	7
275	1912	Reaching Every Home	C.E. Cowman	OMS	8	7	Japan	Holiness	2	2	-	3	47.2	1.3	3
276	1913	Christ's Etceteras (Worldwide Evangelization Crusade)	C.T. Studd	WEC	9	7	Britain	Nondenominational	0	5	-	5	47.1	1.3	9
277	1913	United Missionary Campaigns	John R. Mott	LMM/FMCNA/HMC	10	7	USA	Ecumenical	3	4	-	4	47.1	1.3	0
278	1914	Encyclical concerning the Last Age	Benedict XV	-	10	7	Vatican	Roman Catholic	3	4	1914	4	47.1	1.3	0
279	1914	Church Peace Union	John R. Mott	CPU/WAIF	7	2	USA	Ecumenical	2	2	-	2	47.0	1.3	0
280	1914	Inauguration of Kingdom of God on Earth	Charles T. Russell	WTBTS-IBSA	10	4	USA	Witnesses	0	6	1914	5	47.0	1.3	5
281	1915	Elim Foursquare Gospel Alliance	G. Jeffreys	-	8	5	Britain	Pentecostal	0	2	-	3	46.9	1.3	0
282	1916	World Dominion Movement: surveys of unevangelized regions	S.J.W. Clark	SAT(WDM)	9	8	Britain	Ecumenical	3	4	-	3	46.9	1.3	0
283	1916	The World and the Gospel	J.H. Oldham	IRM/IMC	9	3	Britain	Ecumenical	3	5	-	1	46.7	1.3	0
284	1917	True Jesus Church	Paul Wei	TJC	3	4	China	Pentecostal	0	5	-	3	46.7	1.3	9
285	1917	Interdenominational Foreign Mission Association	H.W. Frost	IFMA	9	8	USA	Fundamentalist	2	5	-	6	46.6	1.3	9
286	1918	Worldwide Evangelism	Aimee S. McPherson	ICFG	10	13	USA	Pentecostal	0	3	-	5	46.6	1.3	9
287	1918	Christian Crusade for World Democracy	John R. Mott	CCWD	10	8	USA	Methodist	1	3	-	2	46.4	1.3	0
288	1918	United Drive for World Evangelism	R.E. Speer	-	9	4	USA	Presbyterian	1	0	-	0	46.4	1.3	0
289	1918	Interchurch World Movement of North Am., World Survey	S.E. Taylor	IWM(IWMNA)	7	13	USA	Ecumenical	3	6	1922	5	46.4	1.3	0
290	1919	International Missionary Council	A.L. Warnshuis	IMC	10	13	Switzerland	Ecumenical	3	2	-	4	46.3	1.3	0
291	1920	League of Denominations	S.E. Taylor	IWM (IWMNA)	9	13	USA	Ecumenical	4	2	-	0	46.2	1.3	1
292	1920	League of Churches of Christ	Meletios IV Metaxakis	-	7	13	Turkey	Eastern Orthodox	4	2	-	0	46.2	1.3	1
293	1920	Planting of church in all cultures	P. Charles	-	8	10	Belgium	Roman Catholic	1	5	-	4	46.2	1.3	3
294	1920	Mennonite Central Committee	J.A. Lapp	MCC	8	4	USA	Mennonite	1	2	-	5	46.2	1.3	8
295	1920	General Council of Co-operating Baptist Missions	W.C. Haas	BMM	8	7	USA	Baptist	0	5	-	4	46.2	1.3	6
296	1921	Institute of Social and Religious Research	John R. Mott	-	8	3	USA	Ecumenical	3	3	-	5	46.0	1.3	0
297	1921	Oxford Group (Moral Re-Armament)	F.N.D. Buchman	MRA	5	5	Britain	Interdenominational	2	3	-	3	46.0	1.3	4
298	1921	Ecumenical Union of Pentecostal Believers	F.A. Hale	AoG-USA	7	13	USA	Pentecostal	2	3	-	5	46.0	1.3	0
299	1921	Electric or electronic church	Aimee S. McPherson	ICFG	10	6	USA	Pentecostal	1	6	-	5	46.0	1.3	8
300	1922	1st International Missionary Congress	Benedict XV	IMC	4	7	Vatican	Roman Catholic	1	6	c1930	1	45.9	1.3	0
301	1922	"Miserando Redemptor"	Pius XI	-	2	2	Italy	Roman Catholic	0	5	-	5	45.9	1.3	0
302	1922	Catholic Action: "Ubi arcano"	Pius XI	-	2	5	Vatican	Roman Catholic	2	6	-	6	45.8	1.3	5
303	1923	Daily radio and television church services	George V	BBC(UK)	10	6	Britain	Nondenominational	0	6	-	2	45.8	1.3	6
304	1923	Evangelism in the Modern World	E.A. French	-	3	7	Britain	Methodist	2	3	-	3	45.8	1.3	0
305	c1923	Million Testaments Campaigns	G.T.B. Davis	-	8	14	USA	Nondenominational	1	3	-	3	45.6	1.3	0
306	1924	Global White leadership in world evangelization	R.E. McAlister	PAW/PCI	7	13	USA	Pentecostal	0	5	-	5	45.6	1.3	0
307	1924	United Pentecostal Church International	J.G. Schepe	UPCI-FMD	10	8	USA	Pentecostal	0	5	-	5	45.6	1.3	9
308	1925	Universal Christian Conference on Life and Work	N. Söderblom	-	4	4	Sweden	Ecumenical	4	3	-	4	45.5	1.3	0

No. 1	Year 2	Brief name for plan 3	Author 4	Init 5	Type 6	Min 7	Origin 8	Tradition 9	Coop 10	P 11	Dline 12	Reso 13	Unev 14	Ratio 15	Status 16
309	1925	*World Missionary Atlas*	H.P. Beach	ISRR/IMC	3	3	USA	Ecumenical	3	3		3	45.5	1.3	0
310	1926	*The Unfinished Task of Foreign Missions*	R.E. Speer	-	3	3	USA	Presbyterian	4	3		1	45.3	1.3	0
311	1926	Lighthouse of International Foursquare Evangelism	Aimee S. McPherson	LIFE-ICFG	8	13	USA	Pentecostal	0	4		4	45.3	1.3	8
312	1927	1st World Conference on Faith and Order	V.S. Azariah	-	4	4	Switzerland	Ecumenical	4	3		4	45.2	1.3	0
313	1927	Association of Baptists for World Evangelism	R.C. Thomas	ABWE	9	7	USA	Baptist	0	2		4	45.2	1.3	8
314	1927	*The Future of Christianity*	G.H. Williams	-	3	3	Britain	Anglican	3	3		1	45.2	1.3	0
315	1928	*The Unfinished Evangelistic Task*	C.H. Fahs	IMC	3	3	Britain	Ecumenical	4	4		4	45.1	1.3	0
316	1928	World Fundamental Baptist Missionary Fellowship	J.F. Norris	WFBMF(WBFM)	8	10	USA	Fundamentalist	0	3		4	45.1	1.3	9
317	1929	Each One Teach One	F.C. Laubach	-	8	14	Philippines	Congregationalist	4	4		4	44.9	1.3	0
318	1930	Movement for World Evangeliztn/Christian Holiday Crusade	Thomas Cochrane	MWE-CHC	8	7	Britain	Nondenominational	1	4		5	44.8	1.3	5
319	1930	World Council for Life and Work	William Temple	-	4	4	Britain	Ecumenical	4	3		3	44.8	1.3	0
320	1930	Voice of Prophecy	H.M.S. Richards	SDA	0	6	USA	Adventist	2	5		5	44.8	1.3	9
321	1930	Bringing Christ to the Nations (The Lutheran Hour)	W.A. Maier	LCMS	10	10	USA	Lutheran	2	5		5	44.8	1.3	8
322	1930	International Missions	B. Davidson	IM	9	10	USA	Nondenominational	0	4		4	44.8	1.3	8
323	1930	Association of Camps Farthest Out	Glenn Clark	CFO	8	2	USA	Charismatic	2	5		5	44.6	1.3	0
324	1931	Unevangelized Fields Mission	E.J. Pudney	UFM	9	7	Britain	Interdenominational	0	5		5	44.6	1.3	9
325	1931	Laudetur Jesus Christus (Radio Vatican)	Pius XI	SJ	10	6	Vatican	Roman Catholic	0	4		4	44.6	1.3	9
326	1931	World-Wide Prayer & Missionary Union	D. Dimilch	WWPMU	8	2	USA	Interdenominational	2	4		4	44.5	1.3	5
327	1932	Conference of Bible Societies	Eric M. North	ABS/BFBS	0	14	Britain	Ecumenical	4	4		4	44.4	1.3	3
328	1933	Laodicean Church Age with Millennium in 1977	W.M. Branham	-	0	0	USA	Pentecostal	2	4	1977	4	44.4	1.3	8
329	1933	The Navigators	Dawson Trotman	-	9	9	USA	Nondenominational	2	3		1	44.4	1.3	0
330	1934	*Jesus Christ and World Evangelization*	Alexander McLeish	WDM	3	3	Britain	Ecumenical	2	3		2	44.2	1.3	8
331	1934	Evangelize to a Finish to Bring Back the King	A.B. Buxton	IVMF-IVF	4	7	Britain	Interdenominational	0	3		3	44.2	1.3	0
332	1934	Biblical Research Society	D.L. Cooper	BRS	10	14	USA	Messianic Jewish	4	3		2	44.2	1.3	0
333	1934	Two Thousand Tongues To Go	W.C. Townsend	WBT-SIL	9	14	USA	Interdenominational	1	5		5	44.2	1.3	9
334	1934	Youth For Christ International	Torrey Johnson	YFCI	9	7	Canada	Interdenominational	4	5		5	44.1	1.3	5
335	1935	World Revival Crusade	G. Jeffreys	WRC	8	8	Britain	Pentecostal	0	3		3	44.1	1.3	8
336	c1935	World Intercessors	Alice Huff	OMS(IAMS)	0	2	USA	Holiness	1	2		5	44.1	1.3	3
337	1936	Student Foreign Missions Fellowship	R.C. McQuilkin	SFMF-IVCF	9	13	USA	Interdenominational	2	3		5	43.9	1.3	0
338	1936	*Awaiting the Light; Unevangelized Areas of the World*	J.G.K. Harman	IVMF	3	3	Britain	Interdenominational	2	3		1	43.9	1.3	7
339	1936	Holy Spirit Assoc for Unification of World Christianity	Sun Myung Moon	HSAUWC	10	13	Korea	Presbyterian	0	5		5	43.9	1.3	8
340	1937	Child Evangelism Fellowship	J.I. Overmoltzer	CEF	3	7	USA	Nondenominational	1	3		3	43.8	1.3	3
341	1938	*Evangelism for the World Today* (125 opinions)	John R. Mott	IMC	3	3	USA	Ecumenical	3	2		1	43.7	1.3	3
342	1938	"Unoccupied fields." *Interpretative Statistical Survey*	J.I. Parker	IMC	4	3	Britain	Ecumenical	3	2		3	43.7	1.3	3
343	1938	4th World Missionary Conference	William Paton	IMC	9	7	India	Ecumenical	4	5		3	43.7	1.3	3
344	1938	Gospel Recordings International	Joy Ridderhof	GRI	9	6	USA	Nondenominational	0	3		3	43.7	1.3	0
345	1938	World Home Bible League	W.A. Chapman	WHBL	8	14	USA	Nondenominational	2	4		4	43.7	1.3	8
346	1939	World Council of Bible Societies	Hendrik Kraemer	BFBS/ABS/NBS	4	3	Netherlands	Ecumenical	4	4		4	43.5	1.3	0
347	1939	"The Unfinished Evangelistic Task"	Alexander McLeish	IMC/WDM	3	14	India	Ecumenical	3	2		0	43.5	1.3	8
348	1939	"Sunday schools and world evangelism"	A. Black	IRM	7	8	Britain	Ecumenical	3	2		3	43.5	1.3	0
349	1939	World-Wide Signs Following Evangelism	L.R.M. Kopp	UFC	8	4	USA	Messianic Jewish	0	5		2	43.5	1.3	0
350	1941	Base ecclesia communities	Helder Camara	CEBes(BECs)	8	7	Brazil	Roman Catholic	1	5		1	43.2	1.3	9
351	1941	The Battle of World Evangelization	A.T. Houghton	IVF/BCMS	9	14	Burma	Anglican	2	2		4	43.2	1.3	0
352	1941	International multilingual Bible correspondence courses	Oswald J. Smith	EBS-BCC	9	7	Canada	Nondenominational	2	5		4	43.2	1.3	0
353	1942	1st World Survey of Unreached Areas: "The Black Spots Survey"	L.G. Brierley	WEC	3	3	Britain	Nondenominational	0	5		2	43.2	1.3	1

No. 1	Year 2	Brief name for plan 3	Author 4	Init 5	Type 6	Min 7	Origin 8	Tradition 9	Coop 10	P 11	Dline 12	Reso 13	Unev 14	Ratio 15	Status 16
354	1942	Ling Liang World-Wide Evangelistic Mission	T.S.K. Dzao	NTM	8	7	China	Nondenominational	0	3	-	3	43.1	1.3	5
355	1942	New Tribes Mission	P.W. Fleming	FMCNA	9	7	USA	Fundamentalist	1	4	-	5	43.1	1.3	9
356	1942	Committee on World Literacy & Christn Literature (Lit-Lit)	F.C. Laubach	NRB	8	14	USA	Ecumenical	3	3	-	2	43.1	1.3	0
357	1943	National Religious Broadcasters	W.W. Ayer		10	6	USA	Nondenominational	2	5	-	5	43.0	1.2	7
358	1943	*"Into All the World": the Great Commission*	S.M. Zwemer		3	3	USA	Reformed	2	3	-	4	43.0	1.2	0
359	1943	Global Outreach Mission	J.O. Blackwood	GOM	8	7	USA	Nondenominational	1	4	-	4	43.0	1.2	8
360	1943	Conservative Baptist Foreign Mission Society	Vincent Brushwyler	CBFMS	7	10	USA	Baptist	1	4	-	5	43.0	1.2	8
361	1944	Third-World missionaries begin international evangelizing	John Sung	AEC	5	8	Indonesia	Interdenominational	2	1	-	5	42.8	1.2	8
362	1945	Evangelical Foreign Missions Association	Clyde W. Taylor	EFMA/NAE	8	13	USA	Interdenominational	2	4	-	6	42.7	1.2	8
363	1945	Parachurch agencies support Great Commission ministries	Herman C. Rutgers	NBS/ABS	10	13	Netherlands	Interdenominational	2	5	-	5	42.7	1.2	8
364	1945	International Institute of Scientific Missionary Research	O.G. Myklebust	IISMR	8	3	Norway	Lutheran	4	1	-	0	42.7	1.2	1
365	1946	"Complete Christ's Commission" and IVSFM conferences	Clyde W. Taylor	IVSFM/SFMF	9	13	USA	Interdenominational	4	2	-	4	42.6	1.2	9
366	1946	United Bible Societies	J.R. Temple	UBS/BFBS	10	14	Britain	Ecumenical	4	3	1970	6	42.6	1.2	0
367	1946	World Literature Crusade	J. McAlister	WLC-EHC	10	14	Canada	Nondenominational	2	5	-	4	42.6	1.2	8
368	1946	*Into All the World: a Statement on Evangelism*	V.C. Alexander		3	3	Scotland	Presbyterian	1	3	-	2	42.6	1.2	5
369	1946	Egede Institute of Missionary Study and Research	O.G. Myklebust	EIMSR	8	3	Norway	Lutheran	3	3	-	2	42.6	1.2	0
370	1946	Asociación Misionera Evangélica a las Naciones	Obed Alvarez	AMEN	8	7	Peru	Methodist	2	3	-	4	42.6	1.2	5
371	1947	Whitby IMC Meeting: "Expectant Evangelism"	C.W. Ranson	IMC	4	7	Britain	Ecumenical	4	3	-	4	42.4	1.2	8
372	1947	Commission on World Missions, Lutheran World Federatn	Hanns Lilje	CWM-LWF	4	7	Sweden	Lutheran	2	3	-	4	42.4	1.2	7
373	1947	*Euntes Docete*	J. Saraiva Martins	PUU	3	14	Vatican	Roman Catholic	1	2	-	1	42.4	1.2	6
374	1947	*We Can If We Will: The Challenge of World Evangelism*	R.V. DeLong		3	14	USA	Holiness	2	2	-	3	42.4	1.2	0
375	1947	Fuller Theological Seminary	C.E. Fuller		1	13	USA	Conservative Evang	2	5	-	4	42.4	1.2	8
376	1947	World Revival Prayer League	Margaret K. Ross		6	8	Japan	Nondenominational	2	1	-	4	42.4	1.2	0
377	1947	Oral Roberts Evangelistic Association	Oral Roberts	OREA/ORU/CBM	9	2	USA	Pentecostal	1	4	-	6	42.4	1.2	9
378	1948	10 World Congresses on World Evangelization	Torrey Johnson	YFCI	4	8	Switzerland	Nondenominational	2	3	-	4	42.3	1.2	9
379	1948	World Council of Churches, 7th Function	W.A. Visser 't Hooft	WCC	6	4	Netherlands	Ecumenical	3	6	-	5	42.3	1.2	9
380	1948	International Council of Christian Churches	C. McIntire	ICC	6	13	USA	Fundamentalist	6	0	-	5	42.3	1.2	5
381	1948	Christian Crusade/ICCC Bible Balloon Project	B.J. Hargis	CENM/ICCC	7	7	USA	Fundamentalist	0	4	-	4	42.3	1.2	0
382	1948	*Set a Watchman: a World Survey*	F.C. Maddox	IVF	3	3	China	Interdenominational	2	2	-	3	42.3	1.2	0
383	1948	New Order of the Latter Rain: Global Missions Broadcast	George Hawtin	NOLR	5	8	Canada	Pentecostal	0	3	-	4	42.3	1.2	3
384	1949	WCC Study "The Evangelization of Man in Modern Mass Society"	J.C. Hoekendijk	WCC	3	3	Switzerland	Ecumenical	4	3	-	2	42.1	1.2	0
385	1949	Association for Native Evangelism	T.L. Osborn		8	8	USA	Pentecostal	0	4	-	3	42.1	1.2	8
386	1949	World Gospel Crusades/Every Creature Crusade	C.E. Cowman	WGC/OMS	9	14	USA	Holiness	1	4	-	2	42.1	1.2	4
387	1949	*World Christian Handbk (1949, 1952, 1957, 1962, 1968)*	K.G. Grubb	WCH/WDM	3	3	Britain	Ecumenical	4	3	-	2	42.1	1.2	0
388	1949	Cursillos de Cristianidad	J. Hervas		10	13	Spain	Roman Catholic	1	3	-	2	42.1	1.2	7
389	1950	Billy Graham Evangelistic Association	Billy Graham	BGEA	7	7	USA	Nondenominational	2	6	-	5	42.0	1.2	9
390	1950	Help Open Paths to Evangelize (HOPE)	G.F. Gudladt	HOPE	8	7	USA	Fundamentalist	6	2	-	6	42.0	1.2	0
391	1950	World Vision International	Bob Pierce	WV-WVI	3	8	USA	Nondenominational	2	4	-	3	42.0	1.2	9
392	1950	*Literacy as Evangelism/World Literacy Evangelism*	F.C. Laubach	WLE	1	14	Philippines	Ecumenical	1	3	-	5	42.0	1.2	3
393	1950	Evangelistic broadcasting/Cathedral of Tomorrow	Rex Humbard		7	6	USA	Pentecostal	4	5	-	4	42.0	1.2	3
394	1950	Hour of Decision	Billy Graham	BGEA	7	6	USA	Baptist	1	5	-	5	42.0	1.2	8
395	1950	Full Gospel Businessmen's Fellowship International	D. Shakarian	FGBFI	1	13	USA	Pentecostal	2	5	-	5	42.0	1.2	9
396	1950	Baptist Bible Fellowship International	F. Donnelson	BBFI	6	6	USA	Baptist	0	3	-	3	42.0	1.2	8
397	1950	Missionaries of Charity	Mother Teresa	MC	6	4	India	Roman Catholic	2	3	-	5	42.0	1.2	9
398	1950	World-Wide Missions International	Basil Miller	WWM	6	7	Nigeria	Fundamentalist	0	1	-	4	42.0	1.2	5

No. 1	Year 2	Brief name for plan 3	Author 4	Init 5	Type 6	Min 7	Origin 8	Tradition 9	Coop 10	P 11	Dline 12	Reso 13	Unev 14	Ratio 15	Status 16
399	1951	1st World Congress of the Lay Apostolate	Pius XII		1	5	Italy	Roman Catholic	0	3	-	1	41.8	1.2	8
400	1952	*Christ's Hope of the Kingdom*	Alexander McLeish	WDM	3	3	Britain	Ecumenical	3	3	-	3	41.7	1.2	0
401	1952	"Trends in world evangelism"	E.J. Homrighausen	WCH-SAT	3	3	Britain	Ecumenical	3	2	-	1	41.7	1.2	0
402	1952	"The Great Commission for Anabaptists"	F.H. Littell		3	7	USA	Methodist	3	3	-	0	41.7	1.2	0
403	1952	Worldwide Revival Movement	W.E. Allen		3	2	Ireland	Nondenominational	3	3	-	2	41.7	1.2	0
404	1952	World Wide Pictures	Billy Graham	WWP-BGEA	10	8	USA	Evangelical	0	5	-	4	41.7	1.2	9
405	1953	Indonesian Missionary Fellowship	Petrus Octavianus	WEC/IMF	8	6	Indonesia	Evangelical	0	5	-	4	41.7	1.2	8
406	1953	World Committee for Christian Broadcasting	Edwin Robertson	WCCB/BBC/ICCB	1	7	Britain	Nondenominational	2	1	-	0	41.5	1.2	0
407	1953	World Evangelization in Our Time"	D.B. Barrett	CMS/BFBS	3	6	Britain	Anglican	5	5	-	2	41.5	1.2	1
408	1953	Congress of Catholic Action: Liberation Theology	G. Gutierrez	CA/CEBes	3	4	Peru	Roman Catholic	1	5	-	5	41.5	1.2	8
409	1954	"Christ the Hope of the World"	W.A. Visser t' Hooft	WCC	4	4	Switzerland	Ecumenical	4	6	-	4	41.3	1.2	3
410	1954	WCC Survey "Evangelism: the mission of the Church"	J.C. Hoekendijk	WCC	4	13	Switzerland	Ecumenical	4	3	-	3	41.3	1.2	0
411	1954	MAP International	L.E. Dixon	MAP	6	4	USA	Nondenominational	2	2	-	5	41.3	1.2	6
412	1954	Schemes for future evangelization	J.E. Rattenbury	MCGB	3	3	Britain	Methodist	1	3	-	0	41.3	1.2	0
413	1954	*The Bible in World Evangelism*	A.M. Chirgwin	UBS/BFBS	3	14	Britain	Ecumenical	4	1	-	3	41.3	1.2	0
414	1954	World Missionary Evangelism	J.E. Douglas	WME	6	4	USA	Nondenominational	1	1	-	1	41.3	1.2	5
415	1954	New Life League World Missionary Society	F.D. Jarvis	NLL	6	14	USA	Baptist	0	4	-	3	41.3	1.2	8
416	1955	World Conference on Missionary Radio	C.W. Jones	WCMR	4	6	USA	Nondenominational	1	1	-	2	41.1	1.2	0
417	1955	Midnight Call Missionary Work	W. Malgo		7	7	Switzerland	Evangelical	1	2	-	3	41.1	1.2	8
418	1955	*A Survey of World Missions*	J.C. Thiessen	-	3	3	USA	Conservative Evang	2	3	-	3	41.1	1.2	0
419	1956	Charismatic Movement (Second Wave, Renewal in the Holy Spirit)	R. Winkler	-	5	2	USA	Charismatic	3	5	-	5	41.0	1.2	8
420	1956	*A Monthly Letter About Evangelism*	D.T. Niles	DWME-WCC	3	14	Switzerland	Ecumenical	4	2	-	3	41.0	1.2	7
421	1956	*The Gospel to Every Creature*	L.-J. Suenens		3	14	Belgium	Roman Catholic	3	3	-	2	41.0	1.2	0
422	1956	*Mission Fields Today: A Brief World Survey*	A.J. Dain	IVF	3	3	Britain	Anglican	3	3	-	1	41.0	1.2	0
423	1957	*World Evangelism Today*	D.T. Niles	WCC	3	3	Switzerland	Ecumenical	4	3	1960	2	40.8	1.2	0
424	1957	Global Conquest	J.P. Hogan	AoG(USA)	8	8	USA	Pentecostal	2	0	-	4	40.8	1.2	8
425	1957	Nights of Prayer for World-wide Revival	George S. Ingram	CMS	7	2	India	Anglican	0	2	-	1	40.8	1.2	0
426	1957	Easter Day Encyclical	Pius XII		0	1	Vatican	Roman Catholic	1	2	c1965	2	40.8	1.2	0
427	1957	*The Unfinished Task*	S.C. Neill	WCC/CMS	3	3	Ireland	Anglican	4	5	-	1	40.8	1.2	9
428	1957	Operation Mobilization/Send The Light	George Verwer	OM-STL	10	5	USA	Nondenominational	2	5	-	5	40.8	1.2	9
429	1957	Conference of World Confessional Groups	B.B. Beach	WCFs/CWCs	6	13	Switzerland	Ecumenical	4	1	-	4	40.8	1.2	5
430	1958	Ecumenical Mission to the World	Alan Walker	ACC	2	4	Australia	Methodist	3	0	-	1	40.6	1.2	5
431	1958	*Porefthendes* (Go Ye)	A. Yannoulatos	SYNDESMOS	4	14	Greece	Eastern Orthodox	3	4	-	2	40.6	1.2	0
432	1958	Bibles For The World	Rochunga Pudaite	BFTW	8	14	India	Conservative Evang	2	4	-	3	40.6	1.2	6
433	1958	*Bilan du Monde: Encyclopédie Catholique du Monde Chrétien*	Jean Frisque	FERES	3	3	Belgium	Roman Catholic	2	3	-	2	40.6	1.2	0
434	1959	Sharing Christ with the Whole World	Baker J. Cauthen	SBC	6	7	USA	Baptist	0	3	-	5	40.5	1.2	3
435	1959	Evangelism-in-Depth	R.K. Strachan	EiD	10	5	Nicaragua	Interdenominational	3	3	-	5	40.5	1.2	6
436	1959	Prophecies of the final Antichrist	P.I. Rissaut		0	0	Palestine	Roman Catholic	0	1	2004	0	40.5	1.2	0
437	1959	Worldwide Missionary Society	David Tsutada		7	7	Japan	Nondenominational	1	1	-	2	40.5	1.2	0
438	1960	*Facing the Unfinished Task*	J.O. Percy	IFMA	4	4	USA	Fundamentalist	0	4	-	4	40.3	1.2	0
439	1960	Baptist International Missions	D. Sisk	BIM	6	7	USA	Baptist	0	4	-	4	40.3	1.2	8
440	1960	World MAP (World Missionary Assistance Plan)	R. Mahoney	WMAP	8	13	USA	Pentecostal	3	3	2000	3	40.3	1.2	5
441	1960	*The Gospel Blimp*: "One Billion Unreached"	Joseph T. Bayly	IVCF-IVP	3	14	USA	Nondenominational	2	3	-	1	40.3	1.2	0
442	1960	Youth With A Mission	Loren Cunningham	YWAM/AoG	10	8	USA	Pentecostal	3	5	-	6	40.3	1.2	9

No.	Year	Brief name for plan	Author	Init	Type	Min	Origin	Tradition	Coop	P	Dline	Reso	Unev	Ratio	Status
1	2	3	4	5	6	7	8	9	10	11	12	13	14	15	16
443	1961	World Missionary Press	W. Goodman	WMP	8	14	USA	Nondenominational	0	1	-	3	40.1	1.2	1
444	1961	2nd World Survey: "19 Point Programme to Reach the Unreached"	L.G. Brierley	-	9	7	Britain	Nondenominational	2	5	-	3	40.1	1.2	8
445	1961	1st Pan-Orthodox Conference	Athenagoras I	WEC	6	5	Greece	Eastern Orthodox	1	3	-	2	40.1	1.2	5
446	1961	World Evangelism	Morris Cerullo	WE(MCWE)	7	8	USA	Pentecostal	3	1	-	3	40.1	1.2	9
447	1961	Commission on World Mission and Evangelism	D.T. Niles	DWME-CWME	7	7	India	Ecumenical	3	2	-	5	40.1	1.2	0
448	1961	Joint Action for Mission	Lesslie Newbigin	JAM-WCC	7	4	Switzerland	Ecumenical	1	5	-	9	40.1	1.2	9
449	1961	Christian Broadcasting Network/CBN World Outreach	M.G. Robertson	WYAH(CBN)	6	6	USA	Charismatic	2	3	-	2	40.1	1.2	0
450	1961	6th International Student Missionary Convention	Clyde W. Taylor	IVCF-SFMF	4	13	USA	Interdenominational	1	1	1971	2	40.1	1.2	8
451	1961	World Association for Christian Broadcasting	Edwin Robertson	WACB/WCCB/BBC	6	6	Kenya	Ecumenical	1	4	-	4	40.1	1.2	1
452	1961	World Radio Missionary Fellowship: HCJB-TV	C.W. Jones	HCJB-TV/WRMF	6	6	Ecuador	Nondenominational	3	1	-	0	40.1	1.2	4
453	1961	Theological centrality of the Great Commission	Karl Barth	-	1	3	Switzerland	Reformed	2	0	-	1	40.1	1.2	0
454	1961	Third World Missions Federation	Elam Angali	TWMF	7	7	Kenya	Lutheran	2	6	-	5	40.1	1.2	6
455	1962	Vatican Council II (21st Ecumenical Council)	John XXIII	-	10	7	Vatican	Roman Catholic	3	3	-	0	40.0	1.2	0
456	1962	Presence evangelizatn: *The Missionary Nature of the Church*	J. Blauw	NMC	3	5	Kenya	Ecumenical	0	4	-	3	40.0	1.2	0
457	1962	Haggai Institute for Advanced Leadership Training	John Haggai	HIALT	8	10	Netherlands	Nondenominational	2	3	-	4	40.0	1.2	0
458	1962	Catholic prophecies of Antichrist	G. Barberini	-	0	0	Singapore	Roman Catholic	2	1	-	2	40.0	1.2	0
459	1963	Witness in Six Continents	Lesslie Newbigin	CWME-WCC	7	5	Palestine	Ecumenical	1	2	-	2	39.8	1.2	0
460	1963	International Christian Broadcasters	C.W. Jones	ICB	7	6	Mexico	Nondenominational	3	2	-	5	39.8	1.2	4
461	1963	"Pacem in Terris"	John XXIII	-	3	3	USA	Roman Catholic	2	3	-	5	39.8	1.2	0
462	1963	"God's Word for a New Age"	Olivier Beguin	UBS	9	14	Vatican	Ecumenical	1	1	-	2	39.8	1.2	0
463	1963	New Life For All	W. Bellamy	NLFA	9	14	Japan	Interdenominational	3	2	-	5	39.8	1.2	0
464	1963	Jesus' strategy for the world: *The Master Plan of Evangelism*	Robert E. Coleman	-	9	9	Nigeria	Methodist	3	3	-	5	39.8	1.2	4
465	1964	"Lumen Gentium" and "Ad Gentes"	Paul VI	-	9	5	USA	Roman Catholic	3	3	-	2	39.6	1.2	3
466	1964	Each One Teach and Win One	F.C. Laubach	ICG-SWM	3	7	Vatican	Congregationalist	2	3	-	4	39.6	1.2	7
467	1964	*Global Church Growth*	D.A. McGavran	-	8	8	USA	Interdenominational	2	3	-	3	39.6	1.2	4
468	1964	Secretariat for Non-Christians	Sergio Pignedoli	-	8	10	Vatican	Roman Catholic	2	3	-	3	39.6	1.2	5
469	1964	*Evangelical Missions Quarterly*	James W. Reapsome	EMQ/EMIS	3	4	USA	Evangelical	1	2	-	3	39.6	1.2	6
470	1965	Oriental Orthodox Churches Conference	Kyrillos VI	OOCC	6	5	Ethiopia	Oriental Orthodox	2	3	-	3	39.5	1.2	8
471	1965	World Evangelization Research Centre	D.B. Barrett	WERC/CSWE	8	8	Kenya	Anglican	3	3	-	1	39.5	1.2	7
472	1965	Unreached Peoples emphasis	V.E.W. Hayward	IRM/AACC/WERC	8	3	Cameroon	Ecumenical	3	3	-	3	39.5	1.2	6
473	1965	Secretariat for Non-Believers	Franz König	-	6	4	Vatican	Roman Catholic	5	3	-	4	39.5	1.2	6
474	1965	"Decree on the Apostolate of the Laity"	Paul VI	-	3	5	Vatican	Roman Catholic	3	3	-	2	39.5	1.2	8
475	1966	Wheaton Declaration: "The Church's Worldwide Mission"	Clyde W. Taylor	EFMA/IFMA	4	7	USA	Conservative Evang	3	3	-	3	39.3	1.2	8
476	1966	World Congress on Evangelism	Billy Graham	BGEA/CT	7	7	Germany	Interdenominational	3	3	-	3	39.3	1.2	0
477	1966	Pacific Conference of Churches: "Go Ye . . ."	Baiteke Nabetari	PCC	7	7	New Caledonia	Ecumenical	3	3	-	3	39.3	1.2	0
478	1966	Missions Advanced Research and Communication Center	E.R. Dayton	MARC-WVI	8	3	USA	Nondenominational	3	1	-	2	39.3	1.2	0
479	1966	Release the World for Christ	C. Panos	GOC	1	7	Greece	Eastern Orthodox	2	1	2000	4	39.3	1.2	5
480	1967	Sacred Congregation for the Evangelization of Peoples	Sergio Pignedoli	SCEP-RCC	10	3	Vatican	Roman Catholic	2	6	-	2	39.1	1.2	4
481	1967	International Correspondence Institute	G. Flattery	AoG(USA)-ICI	9	14	Belgium	Pentecostal	2	6	-	6	39.1	1.2	9
482	1967	Crusade for World Revival	P. Yonggi Cho	CWR	1	1	Korea	Pentecostal	1	4	-	3	39.1	1.2	8
483	1967	Council of the Laity (Pontificium Consilium pro Laicis)	Maurice Roy	-	6	5	Vatican	Roman Catholic	4	1	-	3	39.1	1.2	8
484	1967	*Encyclopedia of Modern Christian Missions*	B.L. Goddard	-	3	5	USA	Nondenominational	4	3	-	2	39.1	1.2	6
485	1968	"Behold I make all things new"	N. Goodall	WCC	5	7	Sweden	Ecumenical	3	3	-	3	38.9	1.2	0

No. 1	Year 2,3	Brief name for plan	Author 4	Init 5	Type 6	Min 7	Origin 8	Tradition 9	Coop 10	P 11	Dline 12	Reso 13	Unev 14	Ratio 15	Status 16
486	1968	Total World Evangelization	J.F. Shepherd	-	3	7	USA	Evangelical	2	2	-	0	38.9	1.2	0
487	1968	World Association for Christian Communication	Edwin Robertson	WACC/WACB	6	6	Britain	Ecumenical	3	6	-	4	38.9	1.2	3
488	1968	Anglican Consultative Council	J.W.A. Howe	ACC	6	13	Britain	Anglican	2	3	-	4	38.9	1.2	7
489	1968	"A strategy for world evangelism"	E.L. Copeland	SBC-FMB	3	3	USA	Baptist	2	2	-	0	38.9	1.2	0
490	1968	Association for World Evangelism	F. Reddington	AWE	7	17	USA	Nondenominational	2	0	-	5	38.9	1.2	2
491	1968	African Independent Churches Service	D.B. Barrett	AICS/CMS/COC	9	13	Kenya	Ecumenical	5	5	-	6	38.8	1.2	7
492	1969	Jimmy Swaggart Ministries	Jimmy L. Swaggart	JSM-AoG	10	6	USA	Pentecostal	5	4	-	5	38.8	1.2	9
493	1969	"Peace on Earth" International Assemblies	Nathan H. Knorr	IBSA-JWs	10	5	Denmark	Witnesses	0	6	1975	8	38.8	1.2	8
494	1969	World Evangelism Foundation	W.H. Jackson	WEF/FMB-SBC	9	9	USA	Baptist	0	4	-	4	38.8	1.2	8
495	1970	Commission on Church Cooperation	J.A. Scherer	CCC-LWF	6	7	USA	Lutheran	2	2	-	3	38.6	1.2	6
496	1970	9th International Student Missionary Convention	Clyde W. Taylor	-	4	13	USA	Interdenominational	2	4	-	3	38.6	1.2	2
497	1970	The Late Great Planet Earth	H. Lindsay	-	0	1	USA	Fundamentalist	0	3	-	0	38.6	1.2	8
498	1970	"AD 2000: 350 million Christians in Africa"	D.B. Barrett	IRM/CMS/SWM	8	3	Kenya	Anglican	5	5	2000	2	38.6	1.2	7
499	1970	Frankfurt Declaration on Mission	P. Beyerhaus	-	8	7	Germany	Conservative Evang	2	1	-	1	38.6	1.2	0
500	1970	World Mission of Reconciliation through Jesus Christ	Robert S. Denny	BWA	4	7	USA	Baptist	3	3	-	2	38.6	1.2	2
501	1970	"Strategy for world evangelism: are we too late?"	C.F.H. Henry	CT/WVI	3	1	USA	Conservative Evang	2	2	-	2	38.6	1.2	0
502	1970	Missionary Message to the World	Paul VI	-	1	7	Samoa	Roman Catholic	2	3	-	2	38.6	1.2	0
503	1970	Saturation Evangelism	G.W. Peters	-	3	7	USA	Conservative Evang	3	3	-	1	38.6	1.2	4
504	1970	m.v. Logos and literature evangelism	George Miley	OM	9	14	Britain	Nondenominational	0	5	-	0	38.6	1.2	0
505	1971	"Issues in World Evangelism"	J.R.W. Stott	IVP	3	7	Britain	Anglican	3	3	-	3	37.9	1.2	5
506	1971	Final Advance of Scripture Translation	A. Bergstedt	FAST/SIL	8	14	USA	Nondenominational	1	1	2000	4	37.9	1.2	5
507	1971	International Crusades	B.W. Mieth	IC	7	7	USA	Baptist	3	4	-	3	37.9	1.2	0
508	1971	Conference on Church-Mission Relationships	James W. Reapsome	EMIS	4	4	USA	Conservative Evang	2	3	-	3	37.9	1.2	0
509	1971	World Evangelization Strategy Consultation	P. Rees	-	4	3	USA	Nondenominational	2	0	-	1	37.9	1.2	5
510	1971	Evangelical Alliance Commission on World Mission	A.M. Derham	EAGB	3	7	Britain	Evangelical	3	3	-	2	37.9	1.2	8
511	1972	International Catholic Charismatic Renewal	Ralph Martin	ICCRO	5	2	USA	Roman Catholic	3	3	-	6	37.2	1.1	9
512	1972	"World evangelisation"/World Pentecost	Donald Gee	WPC	2	8	Britain	Pentecostal	2	2	-	7	37.2	1.1	0
513	1972	Consultation on the Gospel and Frontier Peoples	R. Pierce Beaver	-	4	3	USA	Interdenominational	3	3	-	3	37.2	1.1	0
514	1972	The Explo Story: a Plan to Change the World	G. Eshleman	CCCI	3	7	USA	Interdenominational	3	3	-	2	37.2	1.1	9
515	1972	MIAMSI (Rome)	G. Benelli	MIAMSI	6	5	Italy	Roman Catholic	1	1	-	2	37.2	1.1	0
516	1972	Koinonia/Look/The Frontiersman	L.G. Brierley	WEC-IRO	3	14	Brazil	Nondenominational	3	2	-	2	37.2	1.1	8
517	1972	Great Commission Prayer Crusade	Vonette Bright	GCPC-CCCI	4	2	USA	Nondenominational	3	4	-	3	37.2	1.1	5
518	1972	Salvation Today	John G. Gatu	CWME-WCC	4	4	Thailand	Ecumenical	3	2	1980	1	37.2	1.1	0
519	1972	Mission to The World	Paul E. McKaughan	PCA-MTW	4	10	USA	Presbyterian	2	4	-	4	37.2	1.1	8
520	1973	Summer Institute of World Mission	P. Yongqi Cho	SIWM	8	8	Korea	Presbyterian	2	3	-	4	36.5	1.1	8
521	1973	Globe Missionary Evangelism	K. Sumrall	GME	8	8	USA	Charismatic	2	1	-	4	36.5	1.1	6
522	1973	Seoul Declaration on Christian Mission	David J. Cho	AMA	4	4	Korea	Evangelical	3	4	-	2	36.5	1.1	0
523	1973	10th Inter-Varsity Missionary Convention	J.E. Kyle	IVCF-SFMF	1	7	USA	Interdenominational	3	3	-	5	36.5	1.1	0
524	1973	Trinity Broadcasting Network	Paul F. Crouch	TBN	7	6	USA	Pentecostal	1	4	-	6	36.5	1.1	9
525	1973	World Film Crusade/Winning the World for Christ	Brother John	WFC-WTF-WMC	7	6	USA	Nondenominational	3	4	-	6	36.5	1.1	9
526	1973	Ephesian Method: Breaking the Stained-glass Barrier	David A. Womack	AoG	9	8	USA	Pentecostal	2	3	-	5	36.5	1.1	3
527	1973	Confessing Christ Today	A. Yannoulatos	-	6	6	Romania	Eastern Orthodox	3	3	-	5	35.8	1.1	3
528	1973	Operation World: a Guide to Praying for the World	Patrick J. Johnstone	DM/STL/OM	3	2	Zimbabwe	Conservative Evang	2	3	-	4	35.8	1.1	3
529	1974	Lausanne Committee for World Evangelization	G. Osei-Mensah	ICOWE-LCWE	6	13	Switzerland	Conservative Evang	3	5	-	5	35.8	1.1	9
530	1974	EXPLO-74 (2nd Training Conference on Evangelism)	Joon Gon Kim	CCCI	8	13	Korea	Nondenominational	2	3	-	4	35.8	1.1	3
531	1974	Holy Year Jubilee	Paul VI	-	1	7	Vatican	Roman Catholic	0	3	-	5	35.8	1.1	0

No. 1	Year 2	Brief name for plan 3	Author 4	Init 5	Type 6	Min 7	Origin 8	Tradition 9	Coop 10	P 11	Dline 12	Reso 13	Unev 14	Ratio 15	Status 16
532	1974	Sharing Christ's Bold Mission	Baker J. Cauthen	FMB-SBC	8	7	USA	Baptist	0	3	-	5	35.8	1.1	0
533	1974	3rd Synod of Bishops: "The Evangelization of the Modern World"	Wladyslaw Rubin	SB-RCC	4	4	Vatican	Roman Catholic	1	3	-	6	35.8	1.1	9
534	1974	World Mission 1975 (World Methodist Mission)	Alan Walker	WMC	8	7	Israel	Methodist	1	1	-	4	35.8	1.1	0
535	1974	Mission Renewal Teams	B. Goheen	IVCF	7	7	USA	Nondenominational	2	0	-	5	35.8	1.1	0
536	1974	Reaching the Unreached	E.C. Pentecost	MARC-WVI	7	3	USA	Conservative Evang	2	3	-	1	35.8	1.1	0
537	1974	Discipling A Whole Nation	J. Montgomery	DAWN	9	9	Philippines	Nondenominational	3	4	-	3	35.8	1.1	8
538	1974	Religious and the Evangelization of the World	J. Cloutier	CRC-CCC	7	2	Canada	Roman Catholic	2	3	-	2	35.8	1.1	0
539	1974	World Evangelism and the Word of God	A.P. Johnston	-	3	7	USA	Fundamentalist	2	2	-	1	35.8	1.1	4
540	1974	Presbyterian Order for World Evangelization	Roberta Winter	POWE	6	3	USA	Presbyterian	2	1	-	3	35.8	1.1	0
541	c1974	Missão Antioquia	Jonatan Santos	MA/WEC	8	8	Brazil	Nondenominational	0	3	-	3	35.8	1.1	8
542	1975	Full Gospel World Mission Association	P. Yonggi Cho	FGWMA/AoG	8	8	Korea	Pentecostal	0	3	-	4	35.1	1.1	9
543	1975	World Conference on the Holy Spirit	M. Benhayim	-	1	7	Israel	Pentecostal	1	4	-	2	35.1	1.1	0
544	1975	"Jesus Christ Frees and Unites"	Philip Potter	WCC	4	4	Kenya	Ecumenical	3	4	-	5	35.1	1.1	3
545	1975	"New People for a New World—Through Christ"	Robert S. Denny	BWA	1	4	Sweden	Anglican	2	3	-	5	35.1	1.1	3
546	1975	World evangelization communication strategy	J.F. Engel	-	3	3	USA	Baptist	2	3	-	5	35.1	1.1	0
547	1975	Total Missions Thrust: Global Discipleship	Baker J. Cauthen	FMB-SBC	9	9	USA	Evangelical	1	6	-	2	35.1	1.1	0
548	1975	Project Look Up	J. Wiebe	PLU/ICB	8	6	USA	Evangelical	0	4	-	5	35.1	1.1	0
549	1975	Associates for World Evangelization	Bruce Graham	AWE	4	7	USA	Evangelical	2	0	-	3	35.1	1.1	0
550	1975	International Missionary Congress	Agnelo Rossi	IMC-RCC	4	7	Italy	Roman Catholic	3	3	-	3	35.1	1.1	0
551	1975	Evangelii Nuntiandi	Paul VI	-	3	3	Vatican	Roman Catholic	3	3	-	3	35.1	1.1	3
552	1975	Total World Evangelization Vision	L. Southwick	NLI-TWEV	6	14	USA	Charismatic	1	4	-	2	35.1	1.1	5
553	1975	Genesis Project: New Media Bible	J. Heyman	NMB-GP/CCCI	8	6	USA	Nondenominational	1	3	-	4	35.1	1.1	9
554	1975	World Evangelical Fellowship Missions Commission	Theodore Williams	MC-WEF	8	13	Korea	Conservative Evang	2	3	-	5	35.1	1.1	9
555	1976	Bold Mission Thrust	W. Hultgren	BMT-SBC	10	7	USA	Baptist	3	6	2000	6	34.4	1.1	9
556	1976	Gabriel Olasoji World Evangelism	Gabriel K. Olasoji	GOWE	8	8	Nigeria	Pentecostal	3	4	-	4	34.4	1.1	8
557	1976	US Center for World Mission	R.D. Winter	USCWM	10	7	USA	Conservative Evang	2	4	-	3	34.4	1.1	9
558	1976	Lausanne Strategy Working Group	C.P. Wagner	SWG-LCWE	8	3	USA	Conservative Evang	3	4	-	3	34.4	1.1	4
559	1976	Congress on World Missions and Evangelism	A.J. Dain	-	1	7	Australia	Evangelical	3	1	-	3	34.4	1.1	4
560	1976	American Military Evangelizing Nations	Ira North	AMEN-CCCC	7	3	USA	Disciples	2	4	-	4	34.4	1.1	4
561	1976	Church Growth International Seminars	P. Yonggi Cho	AoG	5	10	Korea	Pentecostal	3	4	-	2	34.4	1.1	9
562	1976	1st Chinese Congress on World Evangelization	Thomas Wang	CCOWE	4	7	Hong Kong	Evangelical	3	4	2000	2	34.4	1.1	8
563	1976	EFMA People Groups Tally	Wade Coggins	EFMA	3	3	USA	Conservative Evang	3	1	1990	1	34.4	1.1	4
564	1976	Lausanne Intercession Advisory Group	Vonette Bright	LCWE/CCCI	7	2	USA	Nondenominational	3	4	-	2	34.4	1.1	0
565	1976	Habitat for Humanity International	M.D. Fuller	HHI	8	4	USA	Evangelical	1	4	-	3	34.4	1.1	3
566	1976	Fellowship of World Christians	Bruce Graham	FOW/AWE/USCWM	1	4	USA	Evangelical	1	4	-	3	34.4	1.1	6
567	1977	Charismatic Renewal in the Christian Churches	K. Ranaghan	-	1	7	USA	Evangelical	2	1	-	2	34.4	1.1	0
568	1977	"Catechetics in our time"	Paul VI	-	3	13	USA	Pentecostal/Charismtc	3	3	-	3	33.7	1.0	9
569	1977	World Conference on Audio-Visuals and Evangelization	C. Hemelink	-	4	6	Vatican	Roman Catholic	1	3	-	3	33.7	1.0	3
570	1977	Here's Life, World	Bill Bright	CCCI-HLW	10	7	Germany	Ecumenical	2	5	1980	3	33.7	1.0	0
571	1978	World Mission 1978-1981	Alan Walker	WMC	9	7	USA	Nondenominational	1	2	1981	5	33.7	1.0	8
572	1978	Internatnl Conference on the Catholic Charismatic Renewal	L.-J. Suenens	ICCRO	4	2	Australia	Methodist	2	2	-	3	33.0	1.0	0
573	1978	Danvik National Conferences on World Evangelization	Sigurd Aske	-	1	4	Ireland	Roman Catholic	2	3	-	2	33.0	1.0	0
574	1978	Maryknoll "Statement of Mission Vision"	Raymond A. Hill	MM	4	4	Norway	Evangelical	1	5	-	1	33.0	1.0	3
575	1978	The Battle for World Evangelism	A.P. Johnston	-	3	7	USA	Roman Catholic	2	3	-	-	33.0	1.0	0

No. 1	Year 2	Brief name for plan 3	Author 4	Init 5	Type 6	Min 7	Origin 8	Tradition 9	Coop 10	P 11	Dline 12	Reso 13	Unev 14	Ratio 15	Status 16
576	1978	Systems, Hardware & Research for Evangelizatm (SHARE)	S. Wilson	SHARE-MARC-WVI	9	3	USA	Nondenominational	3	4	-	3	33.0	1.0	0
577	1978	Great Commission Strategy Resource Network	Larry Poland	GCSRN-CCCI	9	3	USA	Nondenominational	2	5	1980	3	33.0	1.0	0
578	1978	"The unfinished task of world mission"	J. Verkuyl	-	3	3	Costa Rica	Reformed	3	2	-	3	32.3	1.0	0
579	1979	Sharing of Ministries Abroad (SOMA)	Michael C. Harper	SOMA	9	8	Britain	Anglican	3	4	-	4	32.3	1.0	8
580	1979	Conference on Unreached Peoples	H. Marquardt	WEF	4	4	Germany	Conservative Evang	3	1	-	2	32.3	1.0	0
581	1979	National Missionary Congress: "A New Missionary Era"	Dermot J. Ryan	IMU	4	4	Ireland	Roman Catholic	1	2	-	3	32.3	1.0	0
582	1979	Pan-Orthodox Consultation on Monastic Life & Witness	Shenouda III	GOC/ROC/COC/&c	4	2	Egypt	Orthodox	2	2	-	3	32.3	1.0	8
583	1979	Foursquare Missions International	L. Edwards	ICFG-FMI	8	6	USA	Pentecostal	1	5	-	4	32.3	1.0	9
584	1979	International Charismatic Pilgrimage to Lourdes	L.-J. Suenens	ICCRO	5	8	France	Roman Catholic	3	2	-	2	32.3	1.0	9
585	1979	12th Pentecostal World Conference	E. Dando	PWC	1	2	Canada	Pentecostal	2	3	-	2	32.3	1.0	0
586	1979	Canadian Congress on World Evangelization	L.F.S. Ford	CCWE	1	3	Canada	Evangelical	3	3	-	4	32.3	1.0	0
587	1979	"Towards a New Age in Mission"	Jaime L. Sin	FABC	1	4	Philippines	Roman Catholic	1	4	-	3	32.3	1.0	0
588	1979	The Jesus Project ("Jesus" Film)	P. Eshleman	CCCI	10	4	USA	Nondenominational	3	5	2000	6	32.3	1.0	9
589	1979	"120,000 Missionaries by the Year 2000"	Billy Graham	BGEA/IVCF	6	7	USA	Evangelical	3	2	2000	3	32.3	1.0	0
590	1979	Angel-I/Angel-II/Angel-III Project	B. Armstrong	NRB/WEF	8	6	USA	Nondenominational	3	3	-	3	32.3	1.0	0
591	1979	PTL Ministries	-	PTL/AoG	6	6	USA	Pentecostal	1	4	-	1	32.3	1.0	0
592	1979	World Christian Magazine	G. Aeschliman	ISLCFM	4	14	USA	Evangelical	2	4	-	5	32.3	1.0	4
593	1979	Lutherans for World Evangelization	B. Day	LWE	6	3	USA	Lutheran	1	4	-	2	32.3	1.0	4
594	1979	Caleb Project/Joshua Project teams	S. Hawthorne	USCWM	9	3	USA	Evangelical	2	4	-	1	32.3	1.0	6
595	1979	Unreached Peoples series	C.P. Wagner	LCWE/MARC	5	3	USA	Evangelical	3	3	-	3	32.3	1.0	6
596	1979	"World evangelism by 2000 AD: can it be done?"	R.D. Winter	USCWM	3	10	USA	Conservative Evang	2	4	2000	2	32.3	1.0	6
597	1979	Global papal apostolic travels	John Paul II	-	10	7	Vatican	Roman Catholic	2	5	-	5	31.6	1.0	7
598	1980	International Consultation on Simple Life-Style	Harvie Conn	LCWE	1	5	Britain	Evangelical	3	3	-	3	31.6	1.0	1
599	1980	Stuttgart Congress on World Evangelization	P. Beyerhaus	-	1	7	Germany	Evangelical	3	4	-	2	31.6	1.0	1
600	1980	Operation World Begin From Here	Peter P.O. Alliu	WECCM-WCC	6	8	Nigeria	Charismatic	1	0	-	1	31.6	1.0	0
601	1980	"Your Kingdom Come"	Emilio Castro	CWME-WCC	4	8	Australia	Ecumenical	4	4	-	3	31.6	1.0	3
602	1980	Consultation on World Evangelization	G. Osei-Mensah	COWE-LCWE	4	7	Thailand	Conservative Evang	3	4	-	4	31.6	1.0	3
603	1980	"World Evangelization Today"	G.H. Anderson	ASM	3	3	USA	Nondenominational	2	2	-	1	31.6	1.0	0
604	1980	10th United Bible Societies Council Meeting	Ulrich Fick	UBS	10	14	USA	Ecumenical	4	3	-	3	31.6	1.0	0
605	1980	World Evangelization Crusade	P. Yonggi Cho	CCCI	1	8	Korea	Evang/Charismatic	2	4	-	5	31.6	1.0	0
606	1980	US Festival of World Evangelization	Billy Graham	-	1	7	USA	Interdenominational	3	3	1990	5	31.6	1.0	0
607	1980	Pan-Orthodox Consultation on Preaching & Teachg Today	A. Yannoulatos	GOC/ROC/COC/&c	4	7	Yugoslavia	Orthodox	2	4	-	5	31.6	1.0	8
608	1980	International Congress on Evangelization and Atheism	Karl Rahner	PUU/SJ	4	4	Italy	Roman Catholic	1	3	-	4	31.6	1.0	0
609	1980	"A Church for Every People by the Year 2000" (Edinburgh 1980)	R.D. Winter	USCWM	1	10	Britain	Conservative Evang	3	5	2000	4	31.6	1.0	5
610	1980	Third-Wave Renewal in the Holy Spirit: Power Evangelism	C.P. Wagner	MARC-WVI	5	8	USA	Evang/Charismatic	2	3	-	5	31.6	1.0	8
611	1980	Planning Strategies for World Evangelization	D.A. Fraser	-	8	3	USA	Conservative Evang	3	3	-	5	31.6	1.0	8
612	1981	Christian broadcasting worldwide	Paul Freed	-	10	6	Netherlands	Nondenominational	2	5	-	5	31.6	1.0	8
613	1981	Charismatic TV evangelists	Oral Roberts	CBN/PTL/&c	10	6	USA	Pentecost/Charismtc	1	5	-	5	31.6	1.0	5
614	1981	It Is Harvest Time	P. Beyerhaus	-	3	3	Germany	Conservative Evang	3	5	-	5	31.6	1.0	0
615	1981	Evangelize the World by Computer Dialing	Bill Bright	CCCI	7	6	USA	Nondenominational	0	0	-	0	31.6	1.0	0
616	1981	2nd Chinese Congress on World Evangelization	Thomas Wang	CCCOWE	6	7	Singapore	Evangelical	3	3	-	3	31.6	1.0	0
617	1981	World Evangelization Strategy Work Group	Imotemjen Aier	BWA	4	3	USA	Baptist	1	2	-	2	30.9	1.0	4
618	1981	Decade of Evangelism, World Evangelism Committee	Alan Walker	WE-WMC	10	8	USA	Methodist	2	2	1990	5	30.9	1.0	8
619	1981	World Evangelization and the Simple Life-style	Harvie Conn	-	3	3	USA	Presbyterian	3	3	-	3	30.9	1.0	1
620	1981	"Reaching Unreached Peoples"	Patrick J. Johnstone	EMA/WEC	4	3	Britain	Evangelical	3	2	-	2	30.9	1.0	0

No. 1	Year 2	Brief name for plan 3	Author 4	Init 5	Type 6	Min 7	Origin 8	Tradition 9	Coop 10	P 11	Dline 12	Reso 13	Unev 14	Ratio 15	Status 16
621	1981	Mission to Unreached Peoples (Goodseeds)	D.D. Martin	MUP	6	9	USA	Nondenominational	1	4	-	2	30.9	1.0	5
622	1981	Dominion Network/Video Satellite	R.W. Johnson	DVS-DBS	10	8	USA	Charismatic	3	5	-	3	30.9	1.0	5
623	1982	Project 223	Floyd McClung	YWAM	10	8	USA	Charismatic	2	5	2011	6	30.1	0.9	8
624	1982	Harvest Vision: 1990	L. Edwards	ICFG-FMI	9	8	USA	Pentecostal	1	5	1990	4	30.1	0.9	9
625	1982	International Association for Mission Studies	F. Verstraelen	IAMS	6	13	India	Nondenominational	2	3	-	4	30.1	0.9	5
626	1982	"The Unevangelized," *World Christian Encyclopedia, AD 1900-2000*	D.B. Barrett	WERC/CMS				Ecumenical		5	2000	2	30.1	0.9	1
627	1982	Beachhead Peoples and Bridge People Groups	R.D. Winter	LCWE/USCWM	3	3	Kenya	Conservative Evang	3	5	2000	2	30.1	0.9	8
628	1982	World Satellite Evangelism	P.I. McClendon	WSE/WSC/ORU	8	3	USA	Charismatic	3	2	2000	3	30.1	0.9	8
629	1982	1st Korean World Mission Congress	Yong Chik Han	-	8	6	Korea	Evangelical	2	5	-	4	30.1	0.9	8
630	1982	*Mission and Evangelism: An Ecumenical Affirmation*	Emilio Castro	CWME-WCC	3	7	Switzerland	Ecumenical	3	3	-	4	30.1	0.9	6
631	1982	Institute for World Evangelism	George Morris	IWE-WMC	9	7	USA	Methodist	1	2	1991	4	30.1	0.9	9
632	1982	*Panta ta ethni* (To All Peoples)	A. Yannoulatos	GOC-AD	3	14	Greece	Eastern Orthodox	1	1	-	2	30.1	0.9	5
633	1982	Frontier Peoples Committee	Larry Allman	IFMA-FPC	7	3	USA	Fundamentalist	2	1	-	2	30.1	0.9	4
634	1982	"The Challenge of Our Task"	Wade Coggins	EFMA	4	4	USA	Conservative Evang	4	3	2000	3	29.4	0.9	4
635	1983	World Baptist Congress on Urban Evangelism	Nilson Fanini	BWA	9	7	Brazil	Baptist	1	3	-	4	29.4	0.9	1
636	1983	"A global strategy for world evangelization: 105 steps"	D.B. Barrett	WERC-CSWE	9	3	Kenya	Anglican	5	4	2000	4	29.4	0.9	0
637	1983	1st International Conference for Itinerant Evangelists	Werner Burklin	BGEA	3	7	Netherlands	Conservative Evang	2	4	-	4	29.4	0.9	0
638	1983	"Jesus Christ the Life of the World"	Ted Scott	WCC	10	4	Canada	Ecumenical	4	3	-	5	29.4	0.9	3
639	1983	Global Mapping Project	R.H. Waymire	GMP	9	6	USA	Conservative Evang	2	5	2000	4	29.4	0.9	3
640	1983	Lumen 2000	Bobby Cavnar	L-2000/CTV	6	3	USA	Roman Catholic	1	4	-	4	29.4	0.9	8
641	1983	Committee on the Holy Spirit and Frontier Missions	G. Adkins	CHSFM/USCWM	7	8	Brazil	Charismatic	2	3	2000	1	29.4	0.9	1
642	1983	Third World mission societies: *The Last Age of Missions*	Larry D. Pate	OCM/TWMA	5	6	USA	Nondenominational	2	5	2000	5	29.4	0.9	9
643	1983	New Focus	R.K. Drollinger	ICCRO	7	2	Vatican	Roman Catholic	3	3	2000	4	28.6	0.9	8
644	1984	Worldwide Priests Retreat	Tom Forrest	-	8	2	Korea	Roman Catholic	2	3	-	4	28.6	0.9	3
645	1984	International Prayer Assembly for World Evangelization	Vonette Bright	LCWE/CCCI	8	4	USA	Evangelical	2	3	-	4	28.6	0.9	3
646	1984	Ethnic Chinese Congress on World Evangelization	Thomas Wang	ECCOWE	4	7	USA	Evangelical	3	4	-	2	28.6	0.9	3
647	1984	*International Journal of Frontier Missions*	Darrell Dorr	IJFM	3	3	USA	Conservative Evang	3	2	2000	4	28.6	0.9	5
648	1984	National and Regional LCWE Conferences	L.F.S. Ford	ICOWE-2	8	13	Hungary	Conservative Evang	3	1	-	4	28.6	0.9	6
649	1984	"In Christ—Hope for the World"	Zoltan Kaldy	LWF	1	4	Britain	Lutheran	2	5	-	3	28.6	0.9	1
650	1984	STEP-Programme (Strategy to Every People)	Patrick J. Johnstone	STEP-WEC	10	3	India	Nondenominational	1	3	1990	3	28.6	0.9	9
651	1984	World Catholic Federation for the Biblical Apostolate	Alberto Ablondi	WCFBA	1	14	Venezuela	Roman Catholic	2	3	-	4	28.6	0.9	9
652	1984	Baptist World Discipleship Movement	F. Aular	IVCF	7	9	USA	Baptist	1	1	-	2	28.6	0.9	1
653	1984	*The Unfinished Task*	J.E. Kyle	SWG-LWE	3	9	USA	Nondenominational	3	1	-	1	28.6	0.9	1
654	1984	Twenty-one Strategies for Lausanne	Bradford Smith	FEDEMEC/WEGO	8	13	Costa Rica	Conservative Evang	2	2	-	2	28.6	0.9	1
655	1984	"Unidos en Cristo Evangelizando las Naciones"	R.H. Sperger	SWM/USCWM	8	10	USA	Evangelical	3	0	-	3	28.6	0.9	6
656	1985	Mission 2000	D.A. McGavran	PUU	1	4	Italy	Conservative Evang	3	4	2000	3	27.9	0.9	0
657	1985	Internatnl Missionary Congress: "Bringing Christ to Man"	R. Pellegrino	-	10	8	Korea	Roman Catholic	3	3	-	3	27.9	0.9	0
658	1985	Korean Churches' Plan for Entering Every Country	Han Man	MM(CFMSA)/ASM	1	5	Germany	Interdenominational	1	1	2000	5	27.9	0.9	9
659	1985	Youth Congress on World Evangelization	H. Marquardt	LCWE/WEF	5	8	USA	Evangelical	3	1	-	2	27.9	0.9	9
660	1985	Future Trends in Christian World Mission	W. Knipe	LCWE/WEF	3	4	Norway	Roman Catholic	2	3	-	1	27.9	0.9	0
661	1985	*God the Evangelist*	David F. Wells	-	3	8	USA	Evang/Charismatic	0	3	-	2	27.9	0.9	0
662	1985	Integrity Keepers Conventions	F.W. Franz	IBSA-JWs	10	5	USA	Witnesses	1	6	1995	6	27.9	0.9	3
663	1985	Global Evangelization Strategy Consultation	R.K. Parks	FMB-SBC	6	7	USA	Baptist	1	1	2000	2	27.9	0.9	9
664	1985	World Conference of Baptist Evangelists	Perry Ellis	BWA/SBC	1	7	USA	Baptist	1	1	-	2	27.9	0.8	4
665	1985	"God calls: choose life: the hour is late!"	Pimen I	ACPA/CPC	1	13	Czechoslov	Ecumenical	4	2	-	2	27.9	0.9	5

No. 1	Year 2	Brief name for plan 3	Author 4	Init 5	Type 6	Min 7	Origin 8	Tradition 9	Coop 10	P 11	Dline 12	Reso 13	Unev 14	Ratio 15	Status 16
666	1985	5th West Malaysia Chinese Congress on World Evangzn	Gideon Chong	CCCOWE	1	7	Malaysia	Evangelical	3	2	-	3	27.9	0.9	0
667	1985	"Mobilizing Indigenous Missions for the Final Harvest"/ICOM			1	7			3	2		3	27.9	0.9	0
668	1985	Global Simultaneous Evangelistic Missions	Panya Baba	NEMA/ECWA/SIM	7	7	Nigeria	Evangelical	2	2	2000	4	27.9	0.9	4
669	1985	Asia Committee for World Evangelization	Alan Walker	WMC	4	13	Indonesia	Methodist	3	1		5	27.9	0.9	8
670	1985	Global Strategy Committee, Seventh-day Adventists	Fred Magpanua	LCWE	10	7	Hong Kong	Evangelical	3	1	2000	2	27.9	0.9	8
671	1985	God's Global Envoys: Nonresidential Missionaries	Neal C. Wilson	GSC-SDA	8	3	USA	Adventist	5	5	2000	6	27.9	0.9	8
672	1985	International Catholic Programme of Evangelization	D.B. Barrett	WERC/FMB	8	8	USA	Interdenominational	1	6		2	27.9	0.9	8
673	1985	The World by 2000	Mario Capello	ICPE	9	9	Malta	Roman Catholic	1	2	2000	5	27.9	0.9	5
674	1985	World Ambassadors	Paul E. Freed	TWR/FEBC/HCJB	7	7	USA	Nondenominational	1	5		5	27.9	0.9	5
675	1985	World Consultation on Evangelism	Mark A. Kyle	MCMI	4	8	USA	Charismatic	3	4	1991	3	27.9	0.9	6
676	1985	1st Venezuelan Congress of World Missions	Dwight Loder	WE-WMC	7	7	Venezuela	Methodist	1	1	2000	3	27.9	0.9	6
677	1985	CWME Orthodox Advisory Group	Calixto Patricio		7	7	Bulgaria	Evangelical	3	3		4	27.9	0.9	4
678	1985	Global Network of Centers for World Mission	A. Yannoulatos	CWME-WCC	4	7	USA	Orthodox	3	5	2000	3	27.9	0.9	9
679	1985	Amsterdam Prayer Conference for World Evangelization	Darrell Dorr	USCWM	9	2	Netherlands	Nondenominational	3	4		4	27.9	0.9	6
680	1985	EXPLO-85 Global Christian Training Teleconference	David Bryant	LCWE/YWAM	10	13	USA	Evang/Charismatic	3	5		5	27.9	0.9	3
681	1985	Association of International Mission Services	Bailey Marks	CCCI	8	10	USA	Evang/Charismatic	3	4	2000	4	27.9	0.9	6
682	1985	"Emergency call for United Global Evangelism"	Howard Foltz	AIMS	1	7	Korea	Charismatic	3	2		0	27.9	0.9	1
683	1985	*Power Evangelism, Power Healing, and Power Encounters*	D.A. McGavran	SWM/CGI	9	8	USA	Interdenominational	2	3	2000	2	27.1	0.8	8
684	1985	Reaching the World's Cities by AD 2000	John Wimber	AoG(USA)-DFM	9	8	USA	Charismatic	1	4	2000	5	27.1	0.8	8
685	1986	Consultation on Evangelizing World-Class Cities	J.P. Hogan	MBI	8	7	USA	Pentecostal	3	3		2	27.1	0.8	4
686	1986	*Touch the World Through Prayer*	R. Bakke	OMS	4	2	USA	Conservative Evang	1	3		1	27.1	0.8	6
687	1986	Worldwide Student NetWork	W.L. Duewel	WSNW/CCCI	8	7	USA	Holiness	2	5	2000	2	27.1	0.8	1
688	1986	International Prophetic Ministry Convention	David English		9	2	USA	Evangelical	3	4		5	27.1	0.8	8
689	1986	Latin American Evangelical Confraternity	B. Maoz	CONELA	4	7	Israel	Pentecst/Charismatic	1	4		3	27.1	0.8	8
690	1986	International Conference for Equipping Evangelists	M. Ortiz	CEI	7	1	Venezuela	Conservative Evang	2	4		3	27.1	0.8	5
691	1986	"Renew the Church—Reach the World"	Terry Edwards	WEF	6	13	USA	Charismatic	3	5	2000	5	27.1	0.8	9
692	1986	2nd International Conference for Itinerant Evangelists	David M. Howard	ICIE/BGEA	4	13	Singapore	Conservative Evang	3	3		5	27.1	0.8	9
693	1986	3rd Chinese Congress on World Evangelization	Werner Burklin	CCCOWE	4	13	Netherlands	Evangelical	3	5		4	27.1	0.8	8
694	1986	24th International Old Catholic Congress	Thomas Wang	IOCBC	6	13	Taiwan	Evangelical	6	1		3	27.1	0.8	3
695	1986	Asia Missions Association: "Thy Will be Done on Earth"	G.A. van Kleef	AMA/KIM	6	14	Germany	Old Catholic	3	2		4	27.1	0.8	0
696	1986	Good News World/Mass Scripture Distribution	David J. Cho	BSSB-SBC	7	13	Korea	Evangelical	0	4	1995	1	27.1	0.8	0
697	1986	"Toward 2000" (Issachar Frontier Missions Research)	J. Godwin	IFMR	8	7	USA	Baptist	5	0	2000	3	27.1	0.8	1
698	1986	*To the Ends of the Earth*	G.K. Otis III	NCCB/USCMA	7	7	USA	Conservative Evang	2	5		3	27.1	0.8	8
699	1986	Mandate '86	Joseph L. Bernadin	IVCF	7	13	USA	Roman Catholic	3	3		4	27.1	0.8	9
700	1986	Presbyterian Decade of Evangelism	J.E. Kyle	PC(USA)	7	7	USA	Evangelical	4	4	2000	3	27.1	0.8	9
701	1986	Leaders' Congress on the Holy Spirit & World Evangzn	C. Kirkpatrick	NARSC	7	8	USA	Presbyterian	1	4		4	27.1	0.8	9
702	1986	Society for Frontier Missiology	H. Vinson Synan	USSFM-SFM	6	3	USA	Pentecst/Charismatic	3	2	2000	2	27.1	0.8	3
703	1986	Intercontinental Broadcasting Network	R.D. Winter	IBN	6	9	Norway	Conservative Evang	1	4	2000	2	27.1	0.8	4
704	1986	Global Strategy Group	J. Martin	FMB-GSG	6	9	USA	Charismatic	2	1	2000	3	27.1	0.8	7
705	1986	One Million Native Missionaries	R.K. Parks	GFA	9	3	India	Baptist	2	3		4	27.1	0.8	6
706	1986	*Wanted: World Christians*	K.P. Yohannan		3	3	USA	Nondenominational	2	3		1	27.1	0.8	6
707	1986	Televised Evangelism for All	J.H. Kane	CBN	9	9	USA	Conservative Evang	0	0		3	27.1	0.8	9
708	1987	Evangelization 2000/*New Evangelization 2000*	N. Van Hamm	E-2000	10	6	Vatican	Charismatic	2	4	2000	6	26.4	0.8	9
709	1987	"Communicating Christ to the Nations"	Tom Forrest	NRB	1	6	USA	Roman Catholic	1	1	-	3	26.4	0.8	1

No.	Year	Brief name for plan	Author	Init	Type	Min	Origin	Tradition	Coop	P	Dline	Reso	Unev	Ratio	Status
1	2 3		4	5	6	7	8	9	10	11	12	13	14	15	16
710	1987	Consultation on World Evangelization	Larry Christenson	CCC/NARSC/SOMA	6	8	Singapore	Pentecstl/Charismatic	4	1	2000	3	26.4	0.8	6
711	1987	International Conference of Evangelical Bible Societies	J.R. Powell	ICEBS/IBS	8	14	USA	Nondenominational	4	1		3	26.4	0.8	8
712	1987	"By the Year 2000: Is God telling us something?"	Thomas Wang	LCWE	3	13	Singapore	Interdenominational	2	2	2000	1	26.4	0.8	8
713	1987	World Evangelization Strategy Committee	Gary Clark	WESC-NARSC	9	3	Britain	Pentecstl/Charismatic	5	3	2000	1	26.4	0.8	8
714	1987	Every Nation by 2000—Every Home for Christ	D.W. Kietzman	WLC-EHC	8	14	USA	Conservative Evang	1	1	2000	4	26.4	0.8	6
715	1987	"Countdown to the Year 2000"	R.D. Winter	USCWM	7	9	USA	Conservative Evang	3	1	2000	1	26.4	0.8	8
716	1987	Global-Village Evangelism	Rochunga Pudaite	BFTW-GVE	7	14	India	Conservative Evang	0	4		3	26.4	0.8	8
717	1987	LCWE Younger Leaders' Conference/Singapore '87	B. Stiller	LCWE	4	13	Singapore	Evangelical	3	1		3	26.4	0.8	6
718	1987	Global Rosary for World Peace	John Paul II	L-2000/CTV	8	2	Vatican	Roman Catholic	4	4		3	26.4	0.8	3
719	1987	*AD 2000 Together*	H. Vinson Synan	NARSC	8	8	USA	Pentecstl/Charismatic	4	1	2000	5	26.4	0.8	3
720	1987	Community Satellite Corporation	R.W. Johnson	CSC/DBS	9	6	USA	Charismatic	1	4		4	26.4	0.8	9
721	1987	Global Share Network	R.H. Waymire	GMI	9	6	USA	Nondenominational	4	4		1	26.4	0.8	9
722	1987	God's 100,000 New Envoys	T. Yamamori	FFH	3	5	USA	Evangelical	3	3		2	26.4	0.8	8
723	1987	The Future of the Christian World Mission	D.B. Barrett	FCWM/ASM	7	3	Britain	Anglican	5	2		1	26.4	0.8	1
724	1987	Mission World '89 (International Satellite Mission)	Billy Graham	BGEA	7	7	USA	Evangelical	2	1		3	26.4	0.8	5
725	1987	Global Broadcasting System (Top Hat platform network)	Paul F. Crouch	GBS	8	6	USA	Evangelical	3	4	2000	3	26.4	0.8	5
726	1987	Adopt-a-People	W. Tullis	USCWM	9	13	USA	Evang/Charismatic	0	5	2000	3	26.4	0.8	0
727	1987	Christian Communication Technology	J.O. Crawford	CCT-AV/CAPI	8	14	USA	Conservative Evang	2	4		3	26.4	0.8	1
728	1987	Worldwide Prayer Crusade	Sheila Beatty	E-2000/CTV	8	2	USA	Evangelical	4	4		2	26.4	0.8	6
729	1987	Project 2000: Helping Nationals focus on the Unreached	A. Finley	CNEC-PI	7	7	USA	Roman Catholic	2	2		4	26.4	0.8	8
730	1987	Destiny '87: Here's Life, Black America	Crawford Loritts	CCCI/IVCF	6	7	USA	Conservative Evang	4	4	2000	2	26.4	0.8	8
731	1987	New Life 2000: A Revolutionary Plan (Here's Life World)	C. Osterberg	CCCI	10	7	USA	Evangelical	1	1	2000	6	26.4	0.8	6
732	1987	*Towards 2000: Reaching the World's Billions*	Benjamin George	CFC/YFC	3	5	Malaysia	Nondenominational	2	5		0	26.4	0.8	1
733	1987	Interdenominational Global Missions Conferences	R.K. Parks	WMT (WMC)	9	13	USA	Conservative Evang	3	4		2	26.4	0.8	9
734	1987	*Status Report on the Great Commission*	C.D. Hutchins	AoG(USA)	10	6	USA	Interdenominational	5	1	2000	3	26.4	0.8	8
735	1987	Decade of Harvest	J.P. Hogan	AABF/BWA	4	8	USA	Nondenominational	5	6	2000	6	26.4	0.8	8
736	1987	Ibadan Declaratn on Holistic Evangelization of the World	S. Akande	ALCOWE II	4	13	Nigeria	Pentecostal	1	4		3	26.4	0.8	5
737	1987	2nd Asia Leadership Congress on World Evangelization	John Cho	COMIBAM	4	13	Singapore	Baptist	3	2		3	26.4	0.8	8
738	1987	COMIBAM 87/Ibero-American Missions Congress	Luis Bush	CoGWM	4	8	Brazil	Evangelical	4	1	2000	5	26.4	0.8	9
739	1987	Decade of Destiny for Church of God World Missions	C. Moree	-	8	8	USA	Evang/Charismatic	0	3	2000	5	26.4	0.8	1
740	1987	Advance Ministries: Reaching the Unreached	Steve Shank		6	8	USA	Pentecostal	3	3		2	26.4	0.8	8
741	1987	"The Missing Key to World Evangelization"	D. Shibley		3	3	USA	Charismatic	2	1		3	26.4	0.8	9
742	1987	World Evangelism World Plan 1987-1991	Maxie D. Dunnam	WE-WMC	10	7	USA	Methodist	1	3	1991	5	26.4	0.8	9
743	1988	5,300 conferences on evangelization	G.H. Anderson	OMSC/WCC/&c	4	13	Jamaica	Interdenominational	3	2		5	25.6	0.8	8
744	1988	"Great Commission Deadline: the Year 2000"	James W. Reapsome	CT/EMIS/EMQ	3	3	Switzerland	Evangelical	3	2	2000	1	25.6	0.8	8
745	1988	*The Church Triumphant at the End of the Age*	Nate Krupp		3	3	USA	Nondenominational	2	3	c2000	5	25.6	0.8	9
746	1988	Churches of the Poor	Julio de Santo Ano		5	5	Mexico	Interdenominational	2	1		3	25.6	0.8	4
747	1988	2nd All-India Congress on Missions & Evangelism	Ebenezer Sunder Raj	AICOME/IMA/EFI	9	3	India	Nondenominational	3	3		3	25.6	0.8	6
748	1988	World Evangelization Expert System/Database	D.B. Barrett	WEES/WED/WERC	9	3	USA	Interdenominational	5	5	2000	5	25.6	0.8	8
749	1988	10,000 new books/articles a yr. on mission & evangeliztn	W. Henkel	BM	7	2	Germany	Nondenominational	5	5		2	25.6	0.8	8
750	1988	World Prayer Force (to enroll 165 million Christians)	John Gibson	WPF-WMT(WTF)	8	3	USA	Nondenominational	2	2	2000	2	25.6	0.8	8
751	1988	Inter-Agency Consultation on Reaching the Unreached	E.R. Dayton	FMB/WVI/&c	7	3	USA	Nondenominational	5	1		1	25.6	0.8	8
752	1988	Evangelistic mass campaigns: Christ For All Nations	Reinhard Bonnke	CFAN/LPEA/&c	8	3	Argentina	Interdenominational	3	1	2000	5	25.6	0.8	6
753	1988	Charismatics United for World Evangelization	Larry Christenson	CUWE/CCC/NARSC	8	8	Singapore	Pentecstl/Charismatic	4	5	2000	5	25.6	0.8	9

No. 1	Year 2	Brief name for plan 3	Author 4	Init 5	Type 6	Min 7	Origin 8	Tradition 9	Coop 10	P 11	Dline 12	Reso 13	Unev 14	Ratio 15	Status 16
754	1988	Christian prophetic utterances	A. Woldben	-	1	1	Israel	Interdenominational	0	3	-	0	25.6	0.8	6
755	1988	Third World Missions Advance	David J. Cho	TWMA/AMA/PI	4	1	Brazil	Conservative Evang	4	1	2000	5	25.6	0.8	9
756	1988	Video churches and missions	K. Charoenwongsak	CSM	5	6	Thailand	Charismatic	2	1	2000	5	25.6	0.8	8
757	1988	Leadership '88: LCWE emerging leaders conference	Glandion Carney	LCWE	4	13	USA	Evangelical	3	4	-	3	25.6	0.8	8
758	1988	North American African World Missions Congress	Ekpo Ekpo	NACAC	4	7	Nigeria	Conservative Evang	3	4	-	3	25.6	0.8	8
759	1988	International Association for Mission Studies	J. Wietzke	IAMS	4	3	Italy	Nondenominational	3	3	2000	4	25.6	0.8	3
760	1988	International Evangelical Bible Consultation	Billy Graham	BGEA/LCWE	1	13	Jordan	Conservative Evang	2	1	-	2	25.6	0.8	3
761	1988	World Wesleyan Conference on Witness & Evangelism	Maxie D. Dunnam	WMC	4	7	Britain	Methodist	1	4	1991	3	25.6	0.8	3
762	1988	'88 World Evangelization Crusade	P. Yonggi Cho	-	7	8	Korea	Charismatic	3	4	2000	3	25.6	0.8	8
763	1989	Global Consultation on AD 2000 and Beyond	Thomas Wang	LCWE/TWMA/FMB	9	13	Singapore	Evang/Ecumenical	5	5	2000	5	25.6	0.8	8
764	1988	2nd World Consultation on Frontier Missions	L. Chen	WCFM	4	7	USA	Conservative Evang	2	2	2000	2	24.9	0.8	8
765	1989	2nd World Conference on Mission & Evangelism	Eugene Stockwell	CWME-WCC	4	7	Switzerland	Ecumenical	3	3	-	3	24.9	0.8	9
766	1989	International Bishops' Retreat 2000	Tom Forrest	E-2000	4	2	Vatican	Roman Catholic	1	5	2000	3	24.9	0.8	8
767	1989	World Evangelization Conference on Liberation Theology	Maxie D. Dunnam	WMC	4	4	Brazil	Methodist	3	4	-	4	24.9	0.8	8
768	1989	2nd International Congress on World Evangelization	Thomas Wang	ICOWE II	9	8	Singapore	Interdenominational	3	4	2000	4	24.9	0.8	9
769	1989	15th Pentecostal World Conference	Jakob Zopfi	PWC/AoG	4	8	Singapore	Pentecostal	2	2	2000	4	24.9	0.8	8
770	1989	Consultation on Dimensions of Christian Martyrdom	K.H. Ting	-	4	5	Korea	Nondenominational	3	5	-	1	24.9	0.8	9
771	1989	Jerusalem Charismatic Leaders Meeting	Michael C. Harper	GEM/LCWE	4	7	Israel	Charismatic	4	1	-	2	24.1	0.7	8
772	1990	Proliferation of denominational/agency AD 2000 plans	Paul E. McKaughan	E-2000	7	8	USA	Interdenominational	2	5	2000	4	24.1	0.7	8
773	1990	Decade of Universal Evangelization	John Paul II	JPIC-WCC/RCC	10	7	Vatican	Roman Catholic	2	5	2000	6	24.1	0.7	8
774	1990	Round the World Prayer Event	Maxie D. Dunnam	-	4	2	Australia	Methodist	2	4	-	4	24.1	0.7	9
775	1990	Peace Council/Convocation of Christians	Emilio Castro	CCCI-HLW	6	4	Britain	Ecumenical	3	4	-	3	24.1	0.7	8
776	1990	Joint IFMA/EFMA Conference on Countdown Thinking	Wade Coggins	IFMA/EFMA	4	8	USA	Conservative Evang	4	5	2000	5	24.1	0.7	8
777	1990	World Congress on the Holy Spirit & World Evangelization	H. Vinson Synan	JPIC-WCC/RCC	6	8	USA	Pentecstl/Charismatic	4	5	2000	5	24.1	0.7	8
778	1990	EXPLO '90 Worldwide Satellite Strategy	Bill Bright	CCCI-HLW	9	6	USA	Nondenominational	1	5	2000	5	24.1	0.7	8
779	1990	Asia Regional Missions Congress on AD 2000	David J. Cho	AMA/TWMA	4	4	Korea	Evangelical	3	4	2000	4	24.1	0.7	9
780	1990	Africa Regional Missions Congress on AD 2000	Panya Baba	LCWE/EMS/&c	4	7	Nigeria	Evangelical	3	4	2000	4	24.1	0.7	9
781	1990	AD 2000 National Consultations	Luis Bush	LCWE/TWMA	4	7	Argentina	Evangelical	3	2	2000	4	24.1	0.7	9
782	1991	Global Congress of Charismatic Leaders for World Evangelization	Michael C. Harper	CUWE/CCRO	6	8	Britain	Pentecstl/Charismatic	4	4	2000	6	23.3	0.7	9
783	1991	7th Assembly, World Council of Churches	Emilio Castro	WCC	4	7	Australia	Ecumenical	3	4	-	5	23.3	0.7	9
784	1991	4th Chinese Congress on World Evangelization	Hay-Him Chan	CCCOWE	4	7	Hong Kong	Evangelical	3	4	-	3	23.3	0.7	8
785	1991	Charismatic youth churches	Benson Idahosa	-	5	5	Nigeria	Charismatic	2	1	-	4	23.3	0.7	8
786	1991	WMC Conference on World Evangelization	Joe Hale	WE-WMC	4	7	Singapore	Methodist	1	3	2000	3	23.3	0.7	8
787	1991	AD 2000 Regional Consultations	Luis Bush	LCWE/TWMA	8	7	Philippines	Evangelical	4	5	-	4	23.3	0.7	9
788	1991	Great & Holy Council of the Orthodox Church	Demetrios I	EPC	6	5	Greece	Eastern Orthodox	2	5	-	4	23.3	0.7	8

Possible future scenarios with plans

No. 1	Year 2	Brief name for plan 3	Author 4	Init 5	Type 6	Min 7	Origin 8	Tradition 9	Coop 10	P 11	Dline 12	Reso 13	Unev 14	Ratio 15	Status 16
789	1994	Signs, Wonders, Miracles, and Evangelization	-	-	5	8	-	Pentecstl/Charismatic	-	-	-	5	21.1	0.6	9
790	1995	World Christian Congress on AD 2000 and Beyond	-	LCWE/TWMA/&c	9	8	-	Evang/Ecumenical	-	-	2000	5	20.3	0.6	9
791	1995	3rd World Consultation on Frontier Missions	-	-	4	7	-	Conservative Evang	-	-	2000	2	20.3	0.6	9
792	1996	Armageddonist Millennium	-	-	0	1	-	Fundamentalist	-	-	2000	0	19.6	0.6	9
793	1997	Conversion of Jewish race	-	-	5	7	Israel	Messianic Jewish	-	-	-	5	19.6	0.6	9
794	1999	Eve of Millennium Conference	-	-	4	7	-	Interdenominational	-	-	-	5	17.3	0.5	9
795	1999	AD 2000 Jubilee Year	-	RCC	10	13	Vatican	Roman Catholic	-	-	2000	5	17.3	0.5	9
796	2000	Celebration 2000	-	-	9	13	-	Pan-Christian	-	-	2000	5	16.6	0.5	9

No. 1	Year 2 3	Brief name for plan	Author 4	Init 5	Type 6	Min 7	Origin 8	Tradition 9	Coop 10	P 11	Dline 12	Reso 13	Unev 14	Ratio 15	Status 16
797	2000	Respect for Christ	-	-	1	1	-	-	-	-	-	5	16.6	0.5	9
798	2000	Entire World finally reached for Christ	-	-	1	1	-	-	-	-	-	5	16.6	0.5	9
799	2000	Global church-planting	-	-	0	13	-	-	-	-	-	6	16.6	0.5	-
800	2004	Pentecostal-charismatic Latter-Rain revival	-	-	10	10	-	Pentecstl/Charismatic	-	-	2000	6	15.1	0.4	-
801	2006	Itinerant tourist churches	-	-	0	8	-	-	-	-	2000	4	14.3	0.4	-
802	2008	Global church research project "The Past"	-	-	10	10	-	-	-	-	-	1	13.5	0.4	-
803	2009	Global holographic worship	-	-	9	3	-	-	-	-	-	6	13.1	0.4	-
804	2011	Itinerant pilgrim churches	-	-	9	2	-	-	-	-	-	4	12.4	0.4	-
805	2027	Broadcasting in 3,000 languages	-	-	10	10	-	-	-	-	-	6	6.5	0.2	-
806	2030	Church of Point Omega	-	-	0	6	-	-	-	-	2050	6	5.8	0.2	-
807	2030	Chinese global evangelization	-	-	0	0	China	-	-	-	-	5	5.8	0.2	-
808	2045	Global scripture distribution	-	-	10	8	-	-	-	-	2030	5	2.2	0.1	-
809	2050	Self-replicating media churches	-	-	10	14	-	-	-	-	2050	5	1.0	0.0	-
810	2080	Chinese/Arab global conversion mission	-	-	10	10	China	-	-	-	2080	5	0.7	0.0	-
811	2090	Church of the Martyrs	-	-	0	9	-	-	-	-	2090	5	0.6	0.0	-

788 GLOBAL PLANS ARRANGED BY CURRENT STATUS

Code	Status	Plans	%	Sub-totals
0	Fizzled out, dead, forgotten	297	37.7	
1	Defunct because no interest	41	5.2	51% fizzled
2	Defunct because completion claimed	14	1.8	out, dead
3	Implemented but not achieved	49	6.2	
4	Alive but fizzling out	31	3.9	17% fizzling
5	Alive but in decline	38	4.8	out, dying
6	Alive but static	39	4.9	
7	Alive but redefined	25	3.2	32% alive
8	Alive and making progress	134	17.0	and making
9	Alive and being massively implemented	120	15.2	progress
	Total Plans	788	100.0	

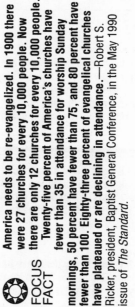

FOCUS FACT

America needs to be re-evangelized. In 1900 there were 27 churches for every 10,000 people. Now there are only 12 churches for every 10,000 people. Twenty-five percent of America's churches have fewer than 35 in attendance for worship Sunday mornings, 50 percent have fewer than 75, and 80 percent have fewer than 100. Eighty-three percent of evangelical churches have plateaued or are declining in attendance. —Robert S. Ricker, president, Baptist General Conference, in the May 1990 issue of *The Standard*.

FOCUS FACT

Not more than 10 percent of evangelical churches in North America are involved significantly in world evangelization.

“ ”
FOCUS
QUOTE   One day a lady criticized D. L. Moody for his methods of evangelism in attempting to win people to the Lord.
Moody's reply was, "I agree with you. I don't like the way I do it either. Tell me, how do you do it?"
The lady replied, "I don't do it."
Moody retorted, "Then I like my way of doing it better than your way of not doing it."

“ ”
FOCUS
QUOTE   While women weep, as they do now, I'll fight; while little children go hungry, I'll fight; while men go to prison, in and out, in and out, as they do now, I'll fight; while there is a drunkard left, while there is a poor, lost girl upon the streets, where there remains one dark soul without the light of God—I'll fight! I'll fight to the very end!—William Booth, the founding general of the Salvation Army.

FOCUS
FACT   25% of Americans say they have had a powerful religious experience
77% pray to God at least occasionally
72% say they believe Jesus is God or the Son of God
Source: *The Unchurched American—10 Years Later.* Published by The Princeton Religious Research Center, 1988.

WHO WATCHES TV EVANGELISTS?

20 Cities with the Highest Viewing Levels	20 Cities with the Lowest Viewing Levels
1. Washington, DC	1. Salt Lake City, UT
2. Dallas, TX	2. Albuquerque–Santa Fe, NM
3. Atlanta, GA	3. El Paso, TX
4. Houston, TX	4. Flint–Bay City, MI
5. Sioux Falls, SD	5. San Diego, CA
6. Birmingham, AL	6. Pittsburgh, PA
7. Nashville, TN	7. Phoenix, AZ
8. Chattanooga, TN	8. Las Vegas, NV
9. Jackson, MS	9. Waco, TX
10. Detroit, MI	10. Hartford–New Haven, CT
11. Philadelphia, PA	11. Austin, TX
12. Johnstown–Altoona, PA	12. Providence–New Bedford, RI
13. Greensboro, NC	13. Raleigh–Durham, NC
14. Indianapolis, IN	14. Milwaukee, WI
15. Charleston–Huntington, WV	15. West Palm Beach–Ft. Pierce, FL
16. Charlotte, NC	16. Cleveland, OH
17. Greenville–New Bern, NC	17. Omaha, NE
18. South Bend, IN	18. San Antonio, TX
19. Columbia, SC	19. Tampa, FL
20. Richmond, VA	20. Albany, NY

Source: Stephen Winzenburg, Grand View College, Des Moines, IA.

MOST WATCHED TV EVANGELISTS
(Number of Households)

PROGRAM	May 1991	May 1990	May 1988	May 1987	Feb 1987
Hour of Power/Robert Schuller	1,181,000	1,251,000	1,145,000	1,158,000	1,256,000
The World Tomorrow	717,000	1,025,000	632,000	588,000	653,000
Kenneth Copeland	495,000	502,000	354,000	334,000	379,000
Oral Roberts	430,000	542,000	539,000	707,000	881,000
In Touch/Charles Stanley	417,000	409,000	191,000	177,000	230,000
Jimmy Swaggart	348,000	359,000	565,000	819,000	1,091,000
D. James Kennedy	324,000	488,000	367,000	385,000	363,000
700 Club	198,000	217,000	164,000	254,000	313,000
Jerry Falwell	*	303,000	331,000	482,000	435,000
PTL Club	—	—	76,000	208,000	215,000

*Temporarily off syndicated airings: October 1990 to October 1991.
Sources: 1987-1988, A.C. Nielsen Co.; 1990, Arbitron Ratings are for syndicated airings and do not include cable broadcasts.

EVANGELISM FOCUSWORDS

Altar call—A request issued during an evangelistic sermon that people move to the front of the meeting hall if they want to inquire about Christianity or express a commitment to follow Christ. Used informally to refer to any direct invitation for people to become Christians.

Commitment—Becoming a Christian requires more than mental assent that God exists. "Making a commitment" to Christ means one is willing to change as he or she learns what it means to follow him.

Contact evangelism—Meeting people for the specific purpose of talking with them about the gospel.

Conversion—A popular expression marking the beginning of the Christian life describing both a person's response to the gospel and God's regenerating work in him or her. A person responds in faith and repentance to the grace of God and the activity of the Holy Spirit in his or her life.

Conviction—The act of the Holy Spirit in which a person recognizes his or her sinfulness before God and need for salvation.

Decision—A commitment to repent of one's sins, especially self-love, and to follow Christ.

Discipleship—A disciple is a learner. Discipleship is the process of following the Lord Jesus Christ in relationships of accountability with other believers, ideally in a local church. It involves discovering and practicing what it means to follow Christ.

Eternal Life—The quality of life that comes from living in relationship with God, which Christians experience now and for all eternity.

Evangelism—Spreading the good news that Jesus Christ is Savior and Lord and persuading people to come and follow him. "The results of evangelism," as summarized in the Lausanne Covenant, "include obedience to Christ, incorporation into his church, and responsible service in the world."

Evangelist—While all Christians are to share their faith, evangelists are especially gifted and active in doing evangelism.

Evangelistic talk—A sermon or lecture presented with the specific intent to explain the gospel and invite people to become Christians. It usually includes an invitation first to make a commitment and second to express that commitment, often in the form of an altar call.

Evangelization—Direct or indirect activity that contributes to people coming to a saving knowledge of Christ. This term is sometimes used as a synonym for evangelism, but it usually has a wider focus, as in "world evangelization."

Evangelized—People who have an intellectual and emotional understanding of the gospel along with some understanding of its personal application, and who have chosen to accept or reject Christ's claim on their life. Mission strategists also use this term to refer to a population segment which has a viable church.

Faith—Trust based on what God has revealed about his character and intentions. This includes depending on Christ as the Son of God and Savior of humankind, which is necessary for salvation.

Gospel—From the Anglo-Saxon "god-spell," meaning "God-story." This is a translation for the Greek *euangelion* or "good news." In addition, a "gospel" is an account of Jesus' life and teaching; the Bible contains four such accounts. See also *evangelism.*

Inquirers—People who respond to an evangelistic invitation. Some people respond in order to rededicate their lives to God or to seek counsel and prayer; others wish to begin following Christ.

Invitation—The climax of an evangelistic event in which people are asked to make a decision to follow Christ.

Life-style evangelism—An intentional orientation to life in which Christians consciously build relationships with non-Christians in order to develop true friendships and share the most important part of their lives, that is, their relationship with God through Christ. Sometimes called relational or friendship evangelism.

Lost, the—Non-Christians, who face eternity apart from God in hell.

Plan of Salvation—A summary of the basic truths of the gospel and steps necessary to become a Christian, which includes turning from sin and turning to Christ. Popular plans include the Four Spiritual Laws, the Bridge Illustration, the Romans Road, and the Evangelism Explosion presentation. See also Salvation.

Preevangelism—Efforts to cultivate a positive attitude toward Christianity in nonbelievers or communicate the basics of a Christian worldview. In today's secular world, this can mean simply cultivating a willingness to believe there is a spiritual dimension to life.

Relevancy—The gospel is relevant to all people in all ages because we are all sinners. The challenge in evangelism is to communicate the relevance of the gospel to non-Christians in word and deed.

Revival—A work of God in a particular time and place in which an unusually large number of people turn to Christ and Christians are renewed in their commitment, holiness, and evangelistic zeal.

Salvation—God's work in saving people from the power and effects of sin. This is possible through the sacrificial life and death of Jesus Christ. God saves people when they come to him in faith, saving them from eternal death and slavery to sin and its habits and adopting them as his people.

Saved—The condition of every Christian: free from slavery to sin and eternal death, and living in relationship with God.

Seekers—People who are interested in learning more about Christ and Christianity but who have not yet become Christians.

Sinner—A person who sins; a person who lives in a state of sin; a person who still lives under the curse of original sin and is alienated from God.

Tract—A small pamphlet that instructs or challenges its readers to change. Evangelistic tracts, the most common kind of Christian tract, challenge readers to become Christians.

Witnessing—Sharing the content of the gospel and one's faith experience with non-Christians.

Source: Daniel Moul, Research and Technical Resources Coordinator, Institute of Evangelism, Billy Graham Center.

FOCUS FACT

Eighty-five percent of the people who make a commitment to Christ do so by the time they are eighteen.

Source: *The Unchurched American—10 Years Later.* Published by The Princeton Religious Research Center, 1988.

BOOKLIST: SIGNIFICANT BOOKS ON EVANGELISM

Abraham, William J. *The Logic of Evangelism.* Grand Rapids: Eerdmans, 1989.

The author argues that evangelism should focus on initiation into the kingdom of God, not on proclamation or church growth, and he examines the implications of this change of focus.

Aldrich, Joseph C. *Life-Style Evangelism: Crossing Traditional Boundaries to Reach the Unbelieving World.* Portland, Oreg.: Multnomah Press, 1983.

Excellent practical guide for developing a natural Christian witness.

Bayly, Joseph. *The Gospel Blimp.* Elgin, Ill.: David C. Cook Publishing Company, 1960.

A satire of misdirected evangelism in story form. Entertains while addressing problems we face in doing evangelism.

Bright, Bill. *Witnessing without Fear.* Here's Life Publishers, Inc., 1987.

The founder of Campus Crusade for Christ shares how personal evangelism has become a way of life.

Calver, Clive, Derek Copley, Bob Moffett, and Jim Smith. *A Guide to Evangelism.* Basingstoke, Hanks, UK: Marshall Morgan & Scott, 1984. Available through Zondervan in the United States.

This book covers theory and practice in evangelism, highlighting evangelistic insights for a whole range of societal groupings, from the retired to work colleagues to the PTA. Written for Great Britain, but applicable almost everywhere.

Cocoris, G. Michael. *Evangelism: A Biblical Approach.* Chicago: Moody Press, 1984.

A sensible look at evangelism through the words and practices recorded in Scripture.

Coleman, Robert E. *The Master Plan of Evangelism.* Old Tappan, N.J.: Fleming H. Revell Company, 1963.

The author examines the Scriptures to uncover Jesus' plan for making disciples. Popular around the world.

Douglas, J. D., ed. *The Calling of an Evangelist.* Minneapolis: World Wide Publications, 1987.

A compendium of addresses from the Second International Congress for Itinerant Evangelists held in Amsterdam, the Netherlands, in 1986. An international array of contributors provide theological and practical guidance in evangelism for pastors and evangelists.

———*Let the Earth Hear His Voice.* Minneapolis: World Wide Publications, 1975.

A compendium of addresses from the historic International Conference on World Evangelism, Lausanne, Switzerland, in 1974. Provides a widely comprehensive and representative look at evangelism from leaders around the world.

Engel, James F., and H. Wilbert Norton. *What's Gone Wrong with the Harvest? A Communications Strategy for the Church and World Evangelism.* Grand Rapids: Zondervan Publishing House, 1975.

A good introduction to ways that communication and persuasion strategy can make our evangelism more effective.

Fish, Roy. *Every Member Evangelism for Today.* San Francisco: Harper Religious Books, 1976.

An update of J. E. Connant's classic *Every Member Evangelism.* A strong challenge for every Christian to witness for Christ.

Ford, Leighton. *Good News Is for Sharing.* Elgin, Ill.: David C. Cook Publishing, 1977.

Good introduction to what evangelism is and how every Christian can do it.

Graham, Billy. *How to Be Born Again.* Waco, Tex.: Word Books, 1977.

This book, along with *World Aflame* and *Peace with God,* presents Jesus Christ as the only way to God and only hope of the world.

Green, Michael. *Evangelism in the Early Church.* Grand Rapids: Eerdmans, 1970.

Well-researched look at the principles of evangelism as practiced by the early church. These principles are applied in *Evangelism: Now and Then* (InterVarsity Press, 1979).

Kennedy, James. *Evangelism Explosion.* Rev. ed. Wheaton, Ill.: Tyndale House Publishers, 1983.

Popular manual for practical training in evangelism. Good presentation of principles and methods for reproducing disciples in the local church.

Kunz, Marilyn, and Catherine Schell. *How to Start a Neighborhood Bible Study.* Rev. ed. Dobbs Ferry, N.Y.: Neighborhood Bible Studies, 1981.

This little booklet offers helpful advice on how to use investigative Bible studies as an evangelistic tool with the non-Christians in your everyday life.

Little, Paul. *How to Give Away Your Faith.* Downers Grove, Ill.: InterVarsity Press, 1966.

Helpful guide in learning to share your faith.

Packer, James I. *Evangelism and the Sovereignty of God.* Downers Grove, Ill.: InterVarsity Press, 1961.

A concise, readable argument for Christians to energize their evangelistic witness with a proper understanding of God's role in the evangelistic process.

Pippert, Rebecca M. *Out of the Saltshaker and into the World: Evangelism as a Way of Life.* Downers Grove, Ill.: InterVarsity Press, 1979.

Popular down-to-earth look at life-style evangelism.

Veerman, David R. *Youth Evangelism: When They're in Your Neighborhood But Not in the Fold.* Wheaton, Ill.: Victor Books, 1988.

Helpful for adults who want to build relationships and share the gospel with junior and senior high young people.

Wimber, John, and Kevin Springer. *Power Evangelism.* San Francisco: Harper & Row, 1986.

Examines the role of "signs and wonders" in evangelism.

Source: Compiled and annotated by Daniel Moul, Research and Technical Resources Coordinator, Institute of Evangelism, Billy Graham Center.

How People View Friendship Evangelism Responsibility

Do you agree that you have a responsibility to explain your religious beliefs to others who may believe differently?

		Agree Strongly	Agree Somewhat	Disagree Somewhat	Disagree Strongly	Don't Know
Total Population		28%	25%	20%	25%	2%
Age:	18 to 25	29	29	23	19	1
	26–44	26	26	20	26	2
	45–54	29	22	18	30	2
	55–64	28	32	21	19	1
	65 or older	40	15	22	21	2
Education:	High school or less	35	26	20	18	2
	Some college	26	27	21	24	2
	College graduate	19	23	20	36	1
Gender:	Male	28	24	20	26	2
	Female	28	27	20	23	2
Region:	Northeast	18	27	18	35	3
	Midwest	27	26	21	23	4
	South	32	29	18	20	1
	Mountain	43	20	19	17	
	Pacific	23	22	26	27	1
Born Again:	Yes	43	33	13	11	1
	No	20	21	24	32	2
Church Attender:	Yes	34	30	19	15	1
	No	16	14	27	42	2

Source: *What Americans Believe* by George Barna. Copyright © 1991. Published by Regal Books. Used by permission.

SAY YES! AMERICA CAMPAIGNS

Luis Palau has spoken to 9.3 million people in nearly 60 countries. He has held evangelistic campaigns and rallies in Central and South America, North America, Europe, the South Pacific, Asia, and Africa.

In 1989, at the encouragement of Billy Graham and other Christian leaders, Luis Palau embarked on a decade-long Say Yes! America campaign. The Palau Association plans to hold evangelistic campaigns in as many as 40 of the 50 U.S. metropolitan areas by the year 2000.

For information on upcoming campaigns, write to: Luis Palau Evangelistic Association, P.O. Box 1173, Portland, OR 97207-1173.

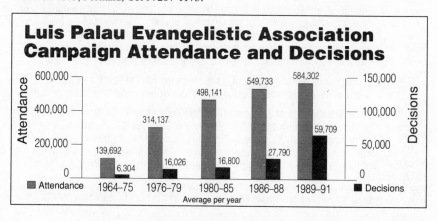

Luis Palau Evangelistic Association Campaign Attendance and Decisions

A CHRONOLOGY OF MODERN REVIVAL MOVEMENTS
Richard Owen Roberts

1517ff   The Great Protestant Reformation under John Calvin, John Knox, Martin
            Luther, Ulrich Zwingli, and a host of others marks the beginning of a
            marvelous series of modern revival movements.

1560ff   The Puritan age, continuing for more than a century following the first years of
            the reign of Elizabeth I, was one of the most blessed seasons of revival in all
            the history of the church. Men like Richard Baxter in England and Vavasor
            Powell and Walter Craddock in Wales were used extensively by God at this
            time.

1596   The Revival of the General Assembly of the Church of Scotland. This began in
            a Solemn Assembly in Edinburgh during the General Assembly of the church.
            John Davidson of Prestonpans was a chief leader.

1620–1630   An awakening occurred in Wales in connection with the publication of the first
            popular edition of the Welsh Bible by Vicar Prichard.

1623–1641   Revival in Ulster, North Ireland, principally among the Presbyterians.

1625   Revival at Stewarton, Scotland.

1630   The Revival of the Kirk of Shotts, Scotland. John Livingstone was greatly used
            of God in this movement.

1639ff   The spirit of revival affecting New England was so general at this time that a
            son born to Richard and Catharine Mather was named Increase in appreciation
            for what God was doing. Among those ministering during this season of
            awakening were John Cotton, Richard Mather, and John Wilson.

**Most of the great denominations in America grew to strength because of the
19th-century awakenings.**

FOCUS
FACT

1647–1670   John Eliot, apostle to the American Indians, was one of the first evangelists in
            America. Although pastor of the church in Roxbury, Massachusetts, from
            1631 until his death in 1690, Eliot spent a great portion of his time itinerating
            among the tribes in Massachusetts and Plymouth Colonies. In this work he
            met with those extraordinary results which must be described as revival.

1669–1729   During the nearly sixty years of his pastoral ministry at Northampton,
            Massachusetts, Solomon Stoddard saw four or five distinct seasons of revival.

1720ff   Under the ministry of Theodorus Jacobus Frelinghuysen, a Dutch Reformed
            minister at New Brunswick, New Jersey, the Great Awakening had its
            beginnings. A fearless preacher, Frelinghuysen did not restrict his ministry to
            the Raritan Valley but itinerated in New York, New Jersey, and Pennsylvania.
            Gilbert Tennent was among the later revival leaders greatly affected by him.

1721   A remarkable revival of religion occurred at Windham, Connecticut, under the pas-
            toral leadership of Samuel Whiting, pastor of the First Congregational Church.

1727ff   A powerful movement began in Germany under the leadership of Count
          Nicholas Ludwig-Graf von Zinzendorf that resulted in a major missionary
          thrust and powerfully influenced the Wesleys in the early years of their labors.
          The movement was variously known as the Unitas Fratrum or the Moravian
          church. Peter Boehler and August Gottlieb Spangenberg were among the
          leaders who worked with Zinzendorf.

1727   A major earthquake shook New England, and one of the results was a series of
          brief but potent revivals in widely scattered places. Among those whom God
          used at this time were James Allen, John Brown, William Cooper, John Cotton
          III, Thomas Foxcroft, and Thomas Prince.

1734–1735 The Congregational church at Northampton, Massachusetts, had experienced
          revival under Solomon Stoddard's ministry, but things were at a rather low
          ebb spiritually for the first several years of Jonathan Edwards's labors there.
          The major quickening that began in 1734 was one of the streams that
          contributed to the Great Awakening that followed.

1734   The First Congregational Church at Washington, Connecticut, experienced the
          first of several awakenings.

1735–1770 George Whitefield was converted in 1735 and very soon thereafter was
          preaching with great power and effectiveness. In the United Kingdom, the
          quickening that began under his ministry is generally referred to as the
          Evangelical Revival. Whitefield was the dominant figure in the movement
          that lasted, with several ebbs and flows, until his death in 1770. Charles
          Wesley was converted in 1738 and itinerated widely until his marriage in
          1749. His older brother John was converted in the same year as Charles
          and was soon the major figure in the non-Calvinistic branch of the work.
          Other major participants in the English movement included John Berridge,
          John Cennick, Risdom Darracott, John William Fletcher, John Gambold,
          William Grimshaw, James Hervey, Martin Madan, and William Romaine. In
          addition to the well-known Methodist church that emerged out of the
          awakening, the Countess of Huntingdon's Connexion was, for many years,
          a beneficial influence in Britain.

1735–1770 Howell Harris of Wales was brought to a vital relationship with Christ at
          approximately the same time as Whitefield. He too began itinerating almost
          immediately thereafter and quickly the beginnings of a mighty awakening
          were felt in various parts of the principality. Griffith Jones had started the
          Welsh Circulating Charity School movement in 1730 and this became a
          contributory to the revival. Other principle figures in the Welsh awakening
          include Howell Davies, Daniel Rowland, and William Williams. The Welsh
          Calvinistic Methodist church became the principle vehicle through which
          this movement expanded.

1738–1770 The powerful movement in America, led principally by Whitefield, became
          known as the Great Awakening. Whitefield's first ministry in the United
          States was in Georgia where profound effects were felt as the result of a
          three- to four-month ministry. By 1740 a significant portion of the colonies
          was ablaze with revival fires. God chose to use dozens of men in this
          awakening, including Isaac Backus, Joseph Bellamy, John Blair, Samuel
          Blair, David Brainerd, Samuel Buell, James Davenport, Samuel Davies,
          Jonathan Dickinson, Jonathan Edwards, Samuel Finley, Samuel Hopkins,
          Daniel Marshall, Jonathan Parsons, Ebenezer Pemberton, Benjamin
          Pomeroy, John Rowland, Shubal Stearns, Gilbert Tennent, John Tennent,
          William Tennent, Sr., William Tennent, Jr., and Eleazer Wheelock.

A CHRONOLOGY OF MODERN REVIVAL MOVEMENTS cont.

1742ff   Whitefield's ministry at Cambuslang and Kilsyth was especially powerful and led to major revivals in these centers as well as widely scattered parts of Scotland.

1749–1752 Revival in Holland.

1774   Revival in the church in Somers, Connecticut, under the pastoral leadership of Charles Backus, at Brown University in Providence, Rhode Island, and in several other places in America.

1776–1809 Under the leadership of Henry Alline, an extensive movement of the Spirit affected Nova Scotia.

1779–1789 Revival at Hampden-Sidney College and in numerous places in Virginia and North Carolina.

1781   Revival at Dartmouth College in Hanover, New Hampshire, the institution founded by Eleazer Wheelock.

1783   Revivals at both Princeton College in New Jersey and Yale College in Connecticut.

1784   Franklin, Massachusetts, experienced a revival under the ministry of Nathaniel Emmons. The First Presbyterian Church in Newark, New Jersey, was also stirred at this time.

1786   Revival at Trecastle, Wales.

1788   The Allgauer revival among the Bavarian Catholics led by Martin Boos, Michael Feneberg, Johannes Goszner, Ignatius Lund, and Johann Sailer.

1788   Revival at Dartmouth, Massachusetts, under Daniel Hix.

1789–1790 Revival in several parts of America.

1791   Revival at Bala, Wales, under the ministry of Thomas Charles, who became the founder of the British and Foreign Bible Society.

1792ff   A powerful series of revivals gripped the Congregational church in Lee, Massachusetts, in 1792, 1800, 1806, 1813, 1821, 1827, and 1831.

1792–1820? The Second Great Awakening in America. This was a wide scale movement affecting nearly every section of the nation. For instance, extensive revivals affected New Salem, Connecticut, 1793; Boston, 1803–1805; Freeport, Maine, 1811; Concord, New Hampshire, 1816, etc.

1795ff   Several extensive revivals gripped and altered Yale College under the Presidency of Timothy Dwight, including the revivals of 1801, 1808, and 1810.

1796ff   An awakening in Norway persisted for some time under the ministry of Hans Nielsen Hauge.

1797   Revival at Walthem Abbey School, Essex, England.

1798   Revival at Auburn Theological Seminary, Auburn, New York.

1798–1800 Revival at Moulin, Scotland.

1798–1799 Typical of the period, the Congregational church of West Simsbury, Connecticut, experienced revival under the leadership of its pastor, Jeremiah Hallock, in 1798–1799, 1805, 1812–1813, 1816, and 1821.

1799–1848 Revival was occurring in some part of western New York State every year during this long period.

1800   The southern camp-meeting revival deeply affected Kentucky, Tennessee, and the Carolinas. Alexander and Thomas Campbell, Peter Cartwright, James McGready, Richard McNemar, David Purviance, David Rice, and Barton Warren Stone were among the leaders. Both the Cumberland Presbyterian Church and some branches of the Churches of Christ and Disciples of Christ churches grew out of this awakening. This movement probably had its origins in touches of the Holy Spirit on the area as early as 1787.

1800   Movements in Scotland including Harris, Lewis, and Perthshire.

1800ff   Revival in several places in Canada.

1804   Revival on the Island of Arran, Scotland.

1804–1806   Revival at Williams College, Williamstown, Massachusetts.

1805   Revival at Aberystwyth, Wales.

1806   Revival at Darwen in the County of Lancaster, England.

1806–1814   A powerful movement largely under the leadership of John Elias profoundly affected the children of Wales and its Sunday schools.

1807   In England, there were movements particularly among the Independent and Primitive Methodists with a strong focus on camp meetings and revivals. Hugh Bourne, William Clowes, and Lorenzo Dow were among the leaders.

1807–1827   Almost continuous revival occurred in Portland, Maine, under the pastoral ministry of Edward Payson.

1810–1815   Llangeitho and many other places in Wales were affected in a movement similar to the southern revival of 1800 in America. Both Christmas Evans and John Elias were much used of God during this period.

1810   A revival in the Russian Orthodox church led to the formation of the Russian Bible Society in 1813. There were also revivals in Switzerland, parts of Germany, and other places on the continent that were partially under the leadership of the Haldane brothers.

1810   Revivals at Andover Seminary and Williams College in Massachusetts.

1812–1814   Revival occurred at Arran and in Skye, Scotland.

1814   Revival in Cornwall, England.

1814   Revival at Yale College in Connecticut.

1815   Revival at Princeton University in New Jersey. Numerous areas of Vermont also experienced revival including Chazy and Montpelier.

1815–1848   Several revivals touched parts of Germany during this period.

1816   Under the leadership of James Patterson, a revival moved the First Presbyterian Church of Philadelphia toward Christ.

1817   The Town of Northeast, Dutchess County, New York, experienced a movement of the Spirit.

1817–1822   The Beddgelert revival was mostly restricted to the Mt. Snowden area of North Wales. William Williams (Williams of Wern) was the principal human agent.

1818   A second wave of revival affected the Auburn Theological Seminary.

1818ff   Revival in Chillicothe, Ohio, under John Collins.

1819   Revival at Hamilton College in New York State.

1820   Revival in Pomerania, Germany.

1820ff   Revival at St. Helena during the last years of Napoleon's exile.

A CHRONOLOGY OF MODERN REVIVAL MOVEMENTS cont.

1820   Revival in Homer, New York, as well as other places in the western regions of the state. The Albany Presbytery also experienced a great work of the Holy Spirit at this time. Union College in Schenectady was wonderfully affected under the ministry of Asahel Nettleton.

1821–1843 A remarkable series of revivals took place at Williams College in Williamstown, Massachusetts, during the time Edward Dorr Griffin was president (1821–1836) and thereafter under the leadership of Prof. Albert Hopkins, who was the major tool God used in 1832 and at least every four years for the rest of his time at the college.

1823–1833 Revivals at Park Street Church, Boston, under the leadership of Edward Dorr Griffin.

1824–1835 The revival on the Island of Lewis in the north of Scotland.

1826   Revival at the Female Seminary in Beverly, Massachusetts.

1826–1827 Revival in Troy, New York, under the leadership of Charles G. Finney. Also in Oneida and Ithaca, New York.

1827   Revivals at Yale College, New Haven, Connecticut, and Dartmouth College, Hanover, New Hampshire.

1828–1830 The revival at Carmarthenshire, Wales, sometimes described as The Great Rejoicing Revival.

1830ff   Widespread movements of revival affected many parts of the United States from 1830 onward until the powerful prayer meeting revival of 1857–1858. Especially active during the thirties were Jedediah Burchard, Daniel Baker, James Caughey, Charles G. Finney, Emerson Andrews, Edward Dorr Griffin, James Inskip, Jacob Knapp, John Newland Maffitt, Asahel Nettleton, and Jabez Swan.

1830   Another wave of revival under the Haldane brothers touched Switzerland. Louis Gaussen, Ceasar Malan, and J. H. Merle D'Aubigne were among the leaders.

1830   A movement of the Spirit under the Monods touched France.

1831   A major revival affected much of the American East Coast as well as such far reaching places as Iowa, where God used the ministry of Reuben Gaylord.

1831   Revival in Ceylon.

1831–1832 Another revival under the leadership of John Elias occurred principally in Caernarvonshire, Wales. It was both very sudden and wonderfully deep.

1833–1836 Revivals at Albany, Hamilton, Homer, Saratoga, Schenectady, Utica, and many other places in New York State and adjacent regions.

1834–1835 A season of general revival touched numerous places in Canada.

1837–1838 Another general season of revival affected America at this time, affecting many communities and institutions including Cazenovia Seminary in upper New York State, Rutgers University in New Jersey, and the Portland area in Oregon.

1837–1843 A very powerful movement, led by the missionaries under the American Board of Commissioners, brought large numbers of Hawaiians to Christ. Records indicate that as much as 20 percent of the population was converted. Titus Coan was among the most largely used at this time.

1838–1843 Revival in Columbus, Ohio.

1839–1842 A fairly widespread movement under John Jones of Talsarn affected Wales.

1839–1843 A general season of revival touched Scotland and was especially powerful in the highlands. Included in the many places visited were Aberdeen, Dundee, Glasgow, Kilsyth, Perth, and Strathay. William Chalmers Burns and Robert Murray McCheyne were among the choice instruments.

1841 The revival in Cardiganshire, Wales, that powerfully impacted David Morgan of 1858-1859 fame.

1841–1842 Revival in the Channel Islands of Britain.

1842 Revival at Charlinch, Somersetshire, England.

1842 The revival in Richmond, Virginia, in which Cornelius Walker was a participant.

1842 The Boston revival under Jacob Knapp, Charles G. Finney, and Edward Norris Kirk.

1842 Norwegian revival.

1843 The Hermannsburg revival in western Germany.

1844–1846 Revivals in Canada under the powerful preaching of William Chalmers Burns.

1844–1850 Another movement, in which missionaries of the American Board of Commissioners were vitally used, occurred among the Nestorians in Persia.

c.1845ff Revival in Denmark under such men as Søren Kierkegaard and Nikolai Grundtvig.

1847ff Extensive revivals began in China under William Chalmers Burns and continued under J. Hudson Taylor.

1849–1850 A movement spoken of as the cholera revival gripped Wales, especially in the south.

1857–1858 The Third Great Awakening, sometimes called the Prayer-Meeting Revival, began at the Old Dutch Reformed Church, Fulton Street, in New York City. Before many months had passed, almost every major population center in America was deeply touched as well as many small town and rural areas. A city missionary, Jeremiah Lanphier, was the initial agent God used in this revival. Upwards of a million converts were reported in two years in America and another million in the movement that followed in the United Kingdom.

1858–1862 The movement that began in New York the previous year reached the United Kingdom soon thereafter and had an especially powerful impact upon Wales (under the leadership of David Morgan and Humphrey Jones) and Ireland (under many leaders including William Arthur, Andrew and Horatius Bonar, H. Grattan Guinness, Edward Payson Hammond, etc.) and affected to a lesser extent both England (Brownlow North and Charles Spurgeon were active participants) and Scotland (Reginald Radcliffe and Brownlow North were chief instruments). Sweden and Canada were among the other nations touched at this time.

1860 Revival in the Tinnavelly District of south India.

1860 Revival in the Ukraine.

1860 A major move of the Holy Spirit swept the churches of South Africa. Andrew Murray was a chief instrument.

1860 The Netherlands experienced the hand of God at work with G. Van Prinsterer and Abraham Kuyper as the human agents.

A CHRONOLOGY OF MODERN REVIVAL MOVEMENTS cont.

1861   The movement that began in America in 1857 touched Jamaica and resulted in a major spread of Christianity among the natives.

1861–1862   Cornish revivals in England.

1861–1865   A very powerful revival occurred in the southern army during the Civil War conflict. Large numbers of fighting men were converted on the front lines. Such Christian generals as Robert E. Lee and Stonewall Jackson played a very significant part in this amazing movement of the Spirit.

1866   Revival at Lafayette Avenue Church in New York City. This movement reappeared in 1872.

1869ff   Several revivals affected the Clarendon Street Church in Boston under the ministry of Adoniram Judson Gordon.

1870   Revival at Newport, Monmouthshire, England.

1870–1912   Under the Presbyterian mission, a large scale movement greatly affected the Hindu Chuhras in the Punjab. At the same time a work among Baptists, Lutherans, and Methodists brought in almost a million converts among the Telugu.

1871   Revival in south Wales.

1872   A wide spread movement affected Japan.

1873–1875   Dwight L. Moody's campaigns in England and Scotland were powerfully used of the Holy Spirit in revival.

1875–1877   A somewhat localized movement under Richard Owen and John Richard Hughes blessed Wales.

1876   A movement under the leadership of Skogsbergh and Paul Peter Waldenstrom affected the state church in Sweden.

1879   Revival at Banza, Manteke.

1880–1910   Scattered seasons of revival touched many in Germany and resulted in 100,000 conversions in the state churches.

1881   Revival in Cincinnati, Ohio, during under the leadership of Thomas Harrison.

1882–1884   A second movement under the leadership of Richard Owen reached many hearts in Wales.

1884   Another wave of revival moved Norway toward Christ.

1883–1890   Revivals blazed in several parts of Japan.

1887–1894ff   A long lasting revival occurred among Lutheran and London Missionary Society churches in Madagascar.

1889   Revival at Rothesay in the Island of Bute.

1892   An evangelistic crusade in Cincinnati and Covington, Ohio, resulted in clear evidences of genuine revival.

1893   A revival was experienced in St. Paul, Minnesota, under the ministry of B. Fay Mills.

1895   Revival in Lisbon, New Hampshire.

1896   Uganda revival.

1902–1904   Reuben A. Torrey and Charles M. Alexander made a worldwide tour during part of this period and saw revival in several places including Australia.

1903–1905	A deep spiritual movement began quietly in several places in Wales in 1903 and then became very public under the leadership of Evan Roberts in 1904, resulting in 100,000 conversions within six months. The movement spread rapidly to other parts of the world including America, China, Denmark, Finland, Germany, India, Korea, Madagascar, Russia, and Sweden. Pandita Ramabai became an outstanding leader in India as did "Praying" John Hyde.
1904	While ministering in Pittsburgh, Pennsylvania, J. Wilbur Chapman saw a deep stirring of the Holy Spirit throughout Allegheny County.
1905	An awakening took place in St. Paul, Minnesota, also under the preaching of J. Wilbur Chapman.
1906–1909	The Azusa Street meeting in Los Angeles marked the beginnings of the modern Pentecostal movement.
1907–1990	The Korean revival began and continues to some extent even to this day.
1908	Largely under the ministry of Jonathan Goforth, a marvelous revival began in Manchuria.
1909	Under the leadership of J. Wilbur Chapman, an extensive movement of the Spirit affected the City of Boston during the simultaneous crusade.
1921	A very considerable movement, affecting large portions of the Lower Congo, began under the preaching of Simon Kimbangu.
1925	A charismatic movement within the Anglican churches of Nigeria led to many conversions and the establishment of several indigenous churches.
1927–1937	Revival in China.
1927–1935	The East African revival movement appears to have started in Ruanda and quickly affected vast numbers of people. It spread rapidly across Uganda, Zaire, Malawi, and numerous other places. Revival conventions drew as many as 50,000 persons.
1930–1933	The Shantung revival in China was principally among those under the leadership of the Southern Baptist Convention. C. L. Culpepper was one of the leaders.
1932	A charismatic revival in the American Methodist churches of Southern Rhodesia under the leadership of Johane Maranke led to the formation of the massive African Apostolic church that has spread across much of Africa.
1936	Powerful revival at Wheaton College, Wheaton, Illinois.
1936–1948	Revival in Ethiopia, especially among the Wallamo tribe.
1938ff	Revival in South Africa under Nicholas Bhekinkosi Bhengu.
1941	Revivals touched many of the Orthodox churches in German-occupied Russia.
1943	Another revival at Wheaton College, Wheaton, Illinois.
1949–1953	Revival in the highlands and islands of Scotland under the leadership of Duncan Campbell.
1950	Revivals at Wheaton College, Wheaton, Illinois; Asbury College, Wilmore, Kentucky; and other Christian schools.
1953	Revival in the Congo.
1953–1971	Revival in Indonesia and in the Solomon Islands.
1954	Revival in Buenos Aries, Argentina, under Tommy Hicks.

A CHRONOLOGY OF MODERN REVIVAL MOVEMENTS cont.

1955–1957 Palavan revival.

1958 Revival at Asbury College.

1970 Another brief but potent revival affected Asbury College and Seminary in Wilmore, Kentucky, and spread swiftly to numerous other campuses.

1970–1972 The Jesus People revival among American young people affected principally the hippies on the West Coast.

1971ff Revival in Viet Nam.

1971–1972 The Canadian revival centered in Saskatchewan and affected principally the western parts of the nation. Ralph and Lou Sutera were among the chief instruments.

For extensive bibliographic details on the revivals listed see "Revival Literature: An Annotated Bibliography with Biographical and Historical Notices," Wheaton, Illinois, 1987, and "Whitefield in Print: A Bibliographic Record of Works by, for and against George Whitefield. With Annotations, Biographical and Historical Notices and Bibliographies of his Associates and Contemporaries," Wheaton, Illinois, 1988. Available from Richard Owen Roberts, Publishers, Box 21, Wheaton, Illinois 60189.

FOCUS FACT

There have been more martyrs produced in the 20th century than in all the other centuries combined since the time of Christ. Many have come out of Russia. In the 1930s and the 1940s tens of thousands of Christians lost their lives to the state authorities. Out of 47,000 Russian Orthodox churches which existed in 1917, by 1939 there may have been as few as 100 left open.—Kent Hill, executive director, The Institute on Religion and Democracy in Washington, D.C.

FOCUS FACT

American missionary work started in a haystack during a thunderstorm! In 1860, during an awakening at Williams College in western Massachusetts, Samuel Mills and four other students hid themselves in a haystack to avoid a summer thunderstorm. While there they united in prayer and pledged themselves to go as missionaries wherever God might lead them. Out of this group went the first American missionaries.

Source: *Christian History* magazine, Issue 23. Copyright © 1989, Christianity Today, Inc. Used by permission.

BOOKLIST: SIGNIFICANT BOOKS ON REVIVAL

The Spiritual Awakeners: American Revivalists from Solomon Stoddard to Dwight L. Moody by Keith Hardman. Moody Press, 1983.

Charles Grandison Finney 1792-1875, Revivalist and Reformer by Keith Hardman. Syracuse University Press, 1987.

An Endless Line of Splendor by Earle E. Cairns. Tyndale House Publishers, 1988.

Memoirs of C. G. Finney by Garth Rosell and A. G. Dupuis. Zondervan Publ. House, 1989.

The Sense of His Presence: Experiencing Spiritual Regenesis by David R. Mains.

Word, Inc., 1988.

Dynamics of Spiritual Life: An Evangelical Theology of Renewal by Richard Lovelace. InterVarsity Press, 1979.

The Journal of George Whitefield. Banner of Truth, 1960.

Jonathan Edwards, A New Biography by Iain Murray. Banner of Truth, 1987.

Revivals, Awakenings, and Reform by William G. McLoughlin. Univ. of Chicago, 1978.

Source: Compiled by Dr. Keith J. Hardman for *Christian History* magazine, Issue 23. Copyright © 1989 Christianity Today, Inc. Used by permission.

Evangelization through Martyrdom

The term *martyr* on this page refers exclusively to Christian martyrs (except for the seven non-Christian lines in the table at top left). Martyrs are defined here as believers in Christ who lose their lives prematurely, in situations of witness, as a result of human hostility.

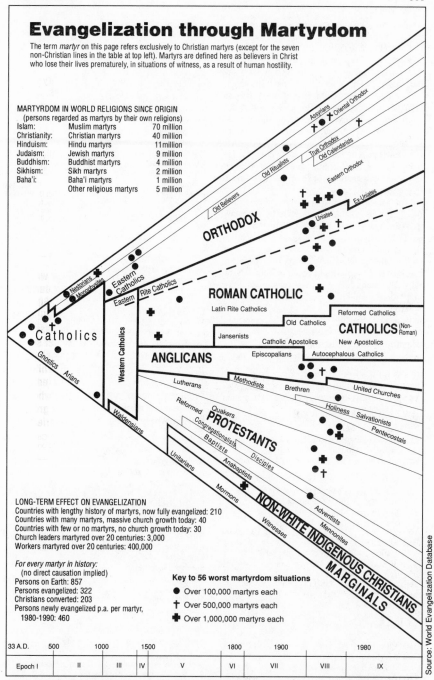

MARTYRDOM IN WORLD RELIGIONS SINCE ORIGIN
(persons regarded as martyrs by their own religions)

Islam:	Muslim martyrs	70 million
Christianity:	Christian martyrs	40 million
Hinduism:	Hindu martyrs	11 million
Judaism:	Jewish martyrs	9 million
Buddhism:	Buddhist martyrs	4 million
Sikhism:	Sikh martyrs	2 million
Baha'i:	Baha'i martyrs	1 million
	Other religious martyrs	5 million

Assyrians · Oriental Orthodox
Old Ritualists · True Orthodox · Old Calendarists
Old Believers
ORTHODOX
Eastern Orthodox
Uniates · Ex-Uniates

Nestorians · Monophysites
Eastern Catholics · Eastern Rite Catholics

ROMAN CATHOLIC

Catholics
Gnostics · Arians

Western Catholics
Latin Rite Catholics
Jansenists
Old Catholics
Catholic Apostolics
Reformed Catholics
CATHOLICS (Non-Roman)
New Apostolics
Episcopalians · Autocephalous Catholics

ANGLICANS

Lutherans · Methodists · Brethren · United Churches
Reformed
Quakers
PROTESTANTS
Congregationalists
Baptists · Disciples
Holiness · Salvationists
Pentecostals
Waldensians
Unitarians · Anabaptists
Mormons
Adventists
Witnesses · Mennonites
NON-WHITE INDIGENOUS CHRISTIANS
MARGINALS

LONG-TERM EFFECT ON EVANGELIZATION
Countries with lengthy history of martyrs, now fully evangelized: 210
Countries with many martyrs, massive church growth today: 40
Countries with few or no martyrs, no church growth today: 30
Church leaders martyred over 20 centuries: 3,000
Workers martyred over 20 centuries: 400,000

For every martyr in history:
(no direct causation implied)
Persons on Earth: 857
Persons evangelized: 322
Christians converted: 203
Persons newly evangelized p.a. per martyr,
1980-1990: 460

Key to 56 worst martyrdom situations

● Over 100,000 martyrs each
† Over 500,000 martyrs each
✚ Over 1,000,000 martyrs each

33 A.D.	500	1000	1500		1800	1900		1980
Epoch I	II	III	IV	V	VI	VII	VIII	IX

Source: World Evangelization Database

40 MILLION CHRISTIANS KILLED FOR THEIR FAITH IN 220 COUNTRIES ACROSS 20 CENTURIES

At the heart of the Great Commission is the command "Witness!" Because living as a witness to Christ (NT Greek *martyrs*) often resulted in persecution and death, by the end of the first century AD, *martyrs* had taken on today's connotations of the "martyr" who witnesses to Christ by his death.

The diagram sets descriptive data on the phenomenon of martyrdom onto a background diagram showing the expansion of Christianity in all its traditions over 20 centuries. History's 56 worst situations of mass martyrdom (over 100,000 each) are then shown as black crosses or dots, the last being Amin's Uganda massacres in 1971. Since then no major situations have arisen (too dangerous for persecutors).

This table puts Christian martyrs in the context of all persons regarded as martyrs by their own non-Christian religions. All such martyrs share with Christian martyrs in this greatest of deprivations of human rights.

The effect of Christian martyrdom on evangelization over the centuries has been profound. Naturally, Christians have almost always insisted that martyrdom should not be deliberately sought for; but when it happens, the news spreads widely, and unbelievers, including persecutors, are converted. Martyrdom can be termed the final witness, the complete personal statement of faith in Christ, the ultimate proclamation of the gospel.

TOTAL PERSONS, AD 33-1990

All persons born since AD 33: 34,903 million
All persons evangelized since AD 33: 13,116 million (38% of human race)
All Christians since AD 33: 8,286 million (24% of human race)
All martyrs killed since AD 33: 40,725,000
Martyrs as % all Christians ever: 0.49%
Martyrs among all Christian leaders ever: 2.0%

HISTORICAL OVERVIEW, AD 33-1990

420 major martyrdom situations over 20 centuries
    56 with over 100,000 martyrs each
    20 with over 500,000 martyrs each
    12 with over 1 million martyrs each
Average martyrs per martyrdom situation: 100,000
Martyrdom loci: 220 countries
Ecclesiastical traditions involved: all 160
Denominations with own martyrs: 4,000

CONFESSIONS OF VICTIMS, AD 33-1990

(total martyrs of each tradition)

Eastern Orthodox	8,524,000
Roman Catholics	6,850,700
East Syrians (Nestorians)	3,723,900
Protestants	2,694,700
Quasi-Christians	1,000,000
Catholics (before AD 1000)	926,550
Gregorians (Armenian Apostolic)	925,000
Ethiopian Orthodox	625,000
West Syrians (Jacobites)	425,700
Coptic Orthodox	406,900
Masonites	128,200
Anglicans	124,000
Non-White Indigenous Christians	117,000
Total all martyrs	40,725,000

PERSECUTORS AND THEIR VICTIMS, AD 33-1990

Persecutors responsible	*Martyrs*
Secular governments	24,402,200
Atheists (overlap with above)	12,400,800
Muslims	5,821,200
Roman Catholics	4,534,100
Quasi-Christians	2,591,000
Buddhists (Mahayana)	1,608,100
Shamanists	1,083,700
Eastern Orthodox	527,000
Hindus	411,400
Zoroastrians (Parsis)	397,000
Pagans (animists)	225,600
Other non-Christians	202,100
Other Christians	165,500
Subtotals:	
Non-Christian persecutors	32,900,000
Christian persecutors	7,825,000
Total all martyrs	40,725,000

SITUATION BY 1990

Martyrs in 20th century (1900-1990): 26,625,000
Martyrs since 1950: 9,965,000
Average annual martyrs since 1950: 249,100 per year
Recent annual martyrs: 300,000 per year
Current annual martyrs: 290,000 per year
Countries heavily involved in 1990: 50

CONFESSIONS OF VICTIMS, 1990

(average annual martydom rates)

Roman Catholics	180,000
Protestants	60,000
Orthodox	25,000
Non-White Indigenous Christians	14,000
Marginal Protestants	10,000
Anglicans and Old Catholics	1,000
Total martyrs per year	290,000

LIKELIHOOD OF BEING MARTYRED

(at current rates)

Full-time workers	*%*	*per year*
Bishops	5.0	15
Evangelists	4.0	133
Catechists	3.5	175
Foreign missionaries	3.0	131
Clergy	2.0	303
All Christian workers	2.0	1,700
Monks, brothers	1.9	63
Sisters, nuns	1.8	300
Other Christians		
Great Commission Christians	1.6	133,000
Christians (all kinds)	1.0	290,000

Source: Reproduced with permission from *Our Globe and How to Reach It* by David B. Barrett and Todd M. Johnson. Copyright © 1990 by the Foreign Mission Board of the Southern Baptist Convention. Published by New Hope, Birmingham, Ala. Data source: World Evangelization Database

Family

VALUES IN THE HOME
Dr. James C. Dobson

In a Focus on the Family radio interview with Bob Biehl, president of Masterplanning Associates, a creative suggestion was offered to parents that I now strongly endorse. It related to the process by which values can be transmitted from one generation to the next. All mothers and fathers know it is their responsibility to teach their beliefs and concepts to their children, but this task is usually approached in a haphazard and casual manner. Mr. Biehl designed a procedure by which parents can instill their most highly valued principles and then reinforce them by the technique of repetition.

The first step in this system is to list the values which parents consider most critical. They should be designed and written for a particular child at his current age and level of understanding. Children are then offered money for memorizing the concepts in sets of five, paying them what they could earn for physical labor. When the entire list has been learned, approximately 75 percent of the original payment could be earned for memorizing it again. The reward would drop to 50 percent the third time through, and 25 the fourth. By this repetitive process, the individual items begin to "live" in the mind of the child, being recalled when a violation of the principle is observed in everyday life.

While each parent should create his own list of values and concepts, I am providing herewith the set we are using in our home. Please feel free to modify it, adapt it to a younger or older age child, or eliminate the statements with which you disagree. (If you would be willing to share your list with me, I would enjoy reading and perhaps adopting some of the items you have created.)

Appreciation is expressed to Mr. Biehl for his suggestion of this creative approach to parental instruction. He would agree that we are most likely to "shoot straight" when we have clear, well-defined targets at which we aim. His system identifies the targets—the values—which we hope to hit on behalf of our children.

1. "Seek ye first the Kingdom of God, and his righteousness, and all these things shall be added unto you" (Matthew 6:33). This is the fundamental principle of life on which all others rest.
2. Overcommitment and time pressure are the greatest destroyers of marriages and families. It takes time to develop any friendship . . . whether with a loved one or with God himself.
3. The overwhelming feeling of being "in love" is not a very reliable emotion during the early years (or at any age!). This intense affection can evaporate in a matter of days, leaving the person confused (and perhaps unhappily married). The only way to know you are in love with another person is to give yourselves plenty of time to get acquainted. Once the decision is made and marriage occurs, then your *commitment* to one another will be much more important than the feelings, which come and go.
4. The universe and everything in it will someday pass away and be made new by the Creator. Therefore, the events of *today* that seem so important are not really very

significant, except for those matters that will survive the end of the universe (such as securing your own salvation and doing the work of the Lord).

5. God is like a Father to his children. He loves them more than they can understand, but he also expects them to be obedient to his will. And he has said, "The wages of sin is death" (Romans 6:23). It is still true.

6. This is the way to be successful in life: Treat every person as you want to be treated; look for ways to meet the physical, emotional and spiritual needs of those around you. Suppress your desire to be selfish and to seek unfair advantage over others. Try to turn *every* encounter with another person into a new or stronger friendship. Then when this confidence with people is combined with hard work, your future success is assured.

7. Human worth does not depend on beauty or intelligence or accomplishments. We are all more valuable than the possessions of the entire world, simply because God gave us that value. This fact remains true, even if every other person on earth treats us like losers.

8. Strong desire is like a river. As long as it flows within the banks of God's will—be the current strong or weak—all is well. But when it floods over those boundaries and seeks its own channels, then disaster lurks in the rampage below (James Dobson, Sr.).

9. The killing of unborn children through medical abortions is one of the most evil occurrences of our time, with 1.5 million babies sacrificed in America each year and 55 million worldwide.

10. Comparison is the root of all feelings of inferiority. The moment you begin examining other people's strengths against your most obvious weaknesses, your self-esteem starts to crumble!

11. Never risk that which you can't afford to lose.

12. There will come a day, much quicker than we as your parents would wish, when you will no longer be comfortable living at home. You will want to move out and establish a home of your own. After that time, we will be more like your friends than your parents. Although we have enjoyed every phase of your life to this moment, we also look forward to the time when you will be an adult and assume responsibility for your own life.

13. If you're going through difficult times today, hold steady. It will change soon. If you are experiencing smooth sailing and easy times now, brace yourself. It will change soon. The only thing you can be certain of is change.

14. God created *two* sexes, male and female. They are equal in worth, although each is unique and different. It is not only impossible to blend maleness and femaleness into a single sex (unisex), it is dangerous to even attempt it.

15. The *love* of money is the root of all evil (1 Timothy 6:10). That's why Jesus issues more warnings about materialism and wealth than any other sin. It takes a steady hand to hold a full cup.

16. Christians should never consult astrologers, psychics or those who practice witchcraft (Isaiah 47:13, 14). They are usually phonies who only pretend to have extrasensory powers. But in some cases, they are working in cooperation with Satan. Rather than tamper with this evil world, the one true God wants us to bring our needs and problems and decisions to him. He has promised to lead us into all truth (John 8:32).

17. One of the secrets of successful living is found in the word *balance,* referring to the avoidance of harmful extremes. We need food, but we should not overeat. We should work, but not make work our only activity. We should play, but not let play rule us. Throughout life, it will be important to find the safety of the middle ground, rather than the imbalance of the extremes.

18. Your life is before you. Be careful of the choices you make now that you could regret later. This regret is the subject of an old poem whose author has been forgotten. I hope you'll never have reason to apply it to yourself.

Across the fields of yesterday,
He sometimes comes to me
A little lad just back from play—
the boy I used to be
He looks at me so wistfully
When once he's crept within
It is as if he hoped to see
the man I might have been.

19. Those who are the happiest are not necessarily those for whom life has been easiest. Emotional stability is an *attitude*. It is refusing to yield to depression and fear, even when black clouds float overhead. It is improving that which can be improved and accepting that which is inevitable.

20. Communism and socialism are economic systems whereby the government assumes responsibility to see that each person's needs are met and that no one individual earns more than the state feels is fair. Capitalism, such as we have in America, is based on free enterprise, whereby a person can achieve a better income for himself and his family by working and sweating and saving and investing. To compare these systems, think of yourself about to take a history test. Suppose you studied very hard and earned an "A" grade, but the teacher gave you a "C" so he could share some of your correct answers with a failing student who didn't study at all. Obviously this would destroy your motivation to study in the future. This need for personal incentives explains why capitalism produces more energetic people than communism and socialism, and why America is the richest nation on earth.

21. Take in a great breath of air and then blow it out. Contained in that single breath were at least three nitrogen atoms that were breathed by every human being who ever lived, including Jesus Christ, William Shakespeare, Winston Churchill and every president of the United States. This illustrates the fact that *everything* we do affects other people, positively or negatively. That's why it is foolish to say, "Do your own thing if it doesn't hurt anybody else."

22. Faith in God is like believing a man can walk over Niagara Falls on a tightrope while pushing a wheelbarrow. Trust in God is like getting in the wheelbarrow! To believe God can do something miraculous is one thing; to risk his willingness to do it in your life is another.

23. With God, even when nothing is happening . . . something is happening.

24. The first five minutes are vitally important, especially to:

A new friendship
A pastor's sermon
A family during the early morning hours
A dad who has just come home from work
A television program
A salesman's presentation
A visit to the doctor

Those first few moments of any human activity set the stage for everything that follows. If we accomplish our purpose quickly, we will probably be successful over the long haul. Therefore, spend more time preparing the first five minutes than any comparable period of time.

25. Whenever two human beings spend time together, sooner or later they will probably irritate one another. This is true of best friends, married couples, parents and children, or teachers and students. The question is: How do they respond when friction occurs?

There are four basic ways they can react:

    a. They can internalize the anger and send it downward into a memory bank that never forgets. This creates great pressure within and can even result in disease and other problems.

    b. They can pout and be rude without discussing the issues. This further irritates the other person and leaves him to draw his own conclusions about what the problem may be.

    c. They can blow up and try to hurt the other person. This causes the death of friendships, marriages, homes and businesses.

    d. Or, they can talk to one another about their feelings, being very careful not to attack the dignity and worth of the other person. This approach leads to permanent and healthy human relationships.

26. Don't marry someone with intolerable characteristics in the hope of changing him or her. If you can't live with someone who drinks, or someone who isn't a Christian, or someone who isn't clean, then don't marry that kind of person. The chances for miraculous improvements are slim. What you see is what you get!

27. "Except the Lord build a house, they labor in vain which build it" (Psalms 127:1).

28. Feelings are neither right nor wrong. It's what you do with them that causes the problems.

29. Most loneliness results from *insulation* rather than *isolation*. In other words, we are lonely because we insulate ourselves, not because others isolate us.

30. Some men watch so many sporting events on television that they wouldn't even know of their wives' decision to divorce them unless it was announced on Wide World of Sports! Remember, balance and moderation are needed in television watching, too.

31. The human body seems indestructible when we are young. However, it is incredibly fragile and must be cared for if it is to serve us for a lifetime. Too often, the abuse it takes during early years (from drugs, improper nutrition, sporting injuries, etc.) becomes painful handicaps during later years. One eighty-year-old man said it best: "If I'd known I was gonna live so long, I'd have taken better care of myself."

32. Before you criticize your parents for their failures and mistakes, ask yourself: "Will I *really* do that much better with my own children?" The job is tougher than it looks, and mistakes are *inevitable!*

33. Remember this about bragging and self-centeredness: Conceit is a weird disease—it makes everybody sick except the guy who has it. Or like the mother whale told her baby, "When you get to the surface and start to blow, that's when you get harpooned!"

34. Satan will attempt to offer you *whatever* you hunger for, whether it be money, power, sex or prestige. But Jesus said, "Blessed are those who hunger and thirst after righteousness" (Matthew 5:6).

35. Sexual contact between a boy and a girl is a progressive thing. In other words, the amount of touching and caressing and kissing that occurs in the early days tends to increase as they become more familiar and at ease with one another. Likewise, the amount of contact necessary to excite one another increases day by day, leading in many cases to an ultimate act of sin and its inevitable consequences. This progression must be consciously resisted by Christian young people who want to serve God and live by his standards. They can resist this trend by placing deliberate controls on the physical aspect of their relationship, right from the first date.

36. God is entitled to a portion of our income. Not because he needs it, but because we need to give it.

37. "For what shall it profit a man if he shall gain the whole world and lose his own soul?" (Jesus Christ, Mark 8:36).

38. It is better to be single and unhappy than unhappily married.

39. In order to find a satisfactory life's work, it is necessary to answer five vitally important questions:
What do I like to do?
What do I have an opportunity to do?
What do I have an ability to do?
What can I earn a living doing?
What can I do that will bring respect from society?
   Unfortunately, all five of these questions must lead to the same answer if job satisfaction is to be found. Any one that is missing will create a certain degree of frustration. This explains why so many people have trouble getting started in adult life. It also makes clear why divine assistance is needed in choosing a profession or occupation.
40. "A wet bird never flies at night." (My grandfather said that to me when I was a child, and warned me not to forget it. I remember his words but never did figure out what he meant!)

FAMILY ACTIVITIES FOR EACH SEASON OF THE YEAR

Winter
CHRISTMAS TRADITIONS

Yuletide Family Fun. Start a tradition of viewing family photographs, slides, and movies at Christmastime. It's fun to see how everyone has changed and to reminisce about past holidays together.

On December 1, set up a jigsaw puzzle with a winter or Christmas scene on a card table. As guests visit your home throughout the holidays, encourage them to work on the puzzle. Challenge your family to complete it by Christmas Day, perhaps saving the final piece for then.

Go caroling with another family and invite them over for refreshments.

Cover a large Styrofoam ball with sprigs of mistletoe, and hang it in a doorway as a reason for family hugs and kisses. (Be sure to pick up any berries that fall from this ornament, since they are poisonous and may be swallowed by small children.)

Make large letters out of newspaper or construction paper to spell the words "Happy Birthday, Jesus" on a large, front window of your home.

Growing Christmas Collections. Every year, give each child an ornament of his or her own. As the children grow up, they will have their own ornaments to cherish and eventually take with them into their families' homes. Give a different kind each year. Here are some suggestions: crystal; straw; wood; metal; cloth.

These ornaments should be collections of special memories, to be treasured throughout the years.

WINTER ACTIVITIES

Family Fun for the New Year. Materials needed: decorated coffee can; colored construction paper; 3″x3″ cardboard patterns, one for each family member; scissors; pencils.

During the first week of the New Year, place a colorfully decorated coffee can near the kitchen table. Label it "Family Fun Throughout the Year."

Give each member of the family a different colored piece of construction paper, scissors, a pencil and a 3″x3″ cardboard pattern.

Have each person trace the square pattern five times on his construction paper, and cut out the shapes.

Everyone should then write on each of their squares a family activity which they would like to do on "Family Fun" night, and drop the slips of paper into the container.

Each week, draw one activity from the can. The person whose color was selected one week does not get another turn until all other colors have been chosen. This gives each family member a fair chance to choose an activity.

FAMILY ACTIVITIES FOR EACH SEASON OF THE YEAR cont.

Replenish the coffee can with new cards as needed.

Celebration of the First Snow. Make up a simple song or cheer for the sight of the first snowflake.

Decorate your home with paper snowflakes. Make them by folding a piece of white paper in half, then half again three more times. Cut snips randomly from the corners and edges. Use your imagination, so no two will be alike. Unfold the papers and hang the snowflakes by black thread in doorways and from ceiling fixtures.

Build "snowmen" and "snow forts" from marshmallows and toothpicks. Set them on a mirror, and use the display for a table centerpiece!

Birdseed Pretzels. Birdseed pretzels are sure to draw a winter crowd of feathered guests. Explain to your children how difficult it is for birds to find food during these months, and how they can help by providing attractive nourishment for the birds in your neighborhood:

Lay a 12-inch piece of waxed paper on a protected surface. (The corners may have to be taped down to keep the paper from curling.)

Squirt wide lines of Elmer's Glue on the waxed paper to form a pretzel-like design in which all lines meet another.

Sprinkle birdseed or sunflower seeds onto the glue, and allow the project to dry overnight.

Turn the designs upside down on a flat surface. Carefully peel away the waxed paper.

Hang the "pretzels" from tree limbs or fences using strands of thread.

A VALENTINE'S DAY TREAT

How Mom and Dad Met. With the family gathered around, Mom and Dad can tell the story of their first date and courtship. They may want to include: How and where they met; activities and places they enjoyed while dating; when they "fell in love"; what qualities attracted them to one another; humorous stories about their courtship and engagement.

Everyone will enjoy pictures of Dad and Mom when they were young. And, as a nice touch, they can show the family how they kissed the very first time!

Winter Gardens. While nothing is growing outside, you can start a garden inside your home by planting vegetables and placing them in your kitchen window:

a. Beans. Fill small paper cups or sections of an egg carton with potting soil. Soak bean seeds or dried beans such as navy, pinto or butter beans in water overnight. Push two beans into the soil in each cup until they are just below the surface, and cover them. Water daily.

b. Carrots. Cut off the tops of several carrots, leaving about one inch of carrot attached to each top. Place the carrot tops in a saucer or pie pan and add enough water to keep the bottom of each piece in water. Do not allow them to dry out. Before long, roots will form and new tops will grow.

c. Sweet potatoes. Cut sweet potatoes in the same way as carrots, and use the same method to grow green tops. Toothpicks can be used to suspend the potato from the rim of a small glass. Keep enough water in the glass so that the bottom of the vegetable cutting stays totally submerged.

d. Alfalfa or bean sprouts. Fold several paper towels and place them in the bottom of a flat bowl or large saucer. Soak the towels with water and sprinkle alfalfa seeds or beans on them. Keep the towels wet. In a few days the seeds will sprout, and can be used in salads or on sandwiches. (Sprouts can also be grown in a sealed jar. Put just enough water in a jar to partially cover the seeds. As the water inside the jar evaporates, moisture eventually condenses on the underside of the lid and "rains" down on the seeds. You will have sprouts within a few days.)

Spring
SIGNS OF SPRING

Spring First. Use a bulletin board or chalkboard in your home to record special signs of spring. Print the title "Spring Firsts" at the top of the board.

As a family, discuss things that remind each person of a typical spring sight. Then decide which things everyone should notice, and list them on the board. The first person to spot a sign of spring can put his or her name on the board beside the "Spring First," and paste on a picture of what was observed.

First Robin Contest After a cold winter, welcome spring by having a "first robin" contest. The first member of the family to see and report a robin is the winner. This contest can continue even after children are grown. No matter where they live, they can call home with "first robin" and claim victory. This tradition celebrates the triumphant return of spring.

SPRINGTIME FUN

The following activity is especially good for elementary and preschool-age children. But be prepared for their older brothers and sisters to participate as well!

Spring Penny Walk. When the flowers and trees begin to bloom, take a "Spring Penny Walk" and enjoy the beautiful sights of spring. Toss a penny at each intersection to determine what path will be taken. ("Heads" indicates a right turn and "tails" specifies a left turn.) After returning home, have each member of the family color a picture of what he or she liked best about the springtime walk. Share the results after dinner.

FAMILY EASTER SUNRISE SERVICE

Ahead of time . . . Choose a special, quiet place from which the sunrise can be seen.

Prepare a simple, carry-along breakfast of boiled eggs, rolls, juice, etc. (Each person's breakfast can be packed in a colorful Easter basket, with surprises hidden in the bottom.)

The week before Easter, read from the Bible or a Bible storybook about the events leading up to the Resurrection, and discuss them together.

The night before Easter Sunday, talk about how the disciples must have felt on the Saturday night before the Resurrection; how Jesus' mother must have felt; what Mary Magdalene and those who had known Jesus might have felt.

On Easter morning. . . . Rise early enough to get to your special place before the sun does! Wear casual clothes (you can get ready for church later), and take warm jackets and blankets.

Sit together on a blanket, and read the Easter story from the Bible.

As the sun comes peeping over the horizon, sing a victorious song about our risen Lord. Then, with your eyes wide open, thank God for the Resurrection and what it means to your family.

Celebrate by sharing the simple breakfast you prepared.

FRUIT BLOSSOM FESTIVAL

Decorate windows and bulletin boards with pictures cut from magazines or seed catalogs of the fruit most commonly grown in your area.

Bring dead limbs into the house and decorate them with mock blossoms made from tissue or crepe paper. Make ice cream using frozen fruit from last year's crop.

Celebrate the bees. Explain how without them, there would be no fruit. Ask one of your children to find out why and report on the subject at supper.

Tie "welcome ribbons" around each budding tree. Match the ribbons to the colors of the fruit that each tree will bear.

Plant a seedling. If your yard is small, a dwarf tree is best. You may want to use this idea in the fall, so the seedling can develop a root system during the dormant winter months.

MAY DAY SURPRISE

On May 1, rise early in the morning and pick a bouquet of spring flowers. Place the flowers in a pretty basket that can hang on a doorknob. (You can make your own basket from construction paper.)

Hang the May basket on the knob of the front door at a friend's house. Ring the doorbell, and hide. When someone comes to the door, jump out and shout, "May Day!"

Summer

SUMMER MEMORY BOOK

At the beginning of summer, record dates and descriptions of special outings, family activities and unusual events. Paste or tape ticket stubs, programs, place cards and other

FAMILY ACTIVITIES FOR EACH SEASON OF THE YEAR cont.

souvenirs into a "summer memory book" for your family.

Review the notebook with family members at the end of the summer, and enjoy the memories you have created!

SUMMER LOLLIPOP COOKIES

Use a favorite crispy cookie recipe:

Roll out the dough (not too thin) and cut into round shapes with a cookie cutter or a glass.

Place the cookies on a baking sheet, insert a wooden Popsicle stick one or two inches into the base of each one, and bake.

After cookies have cooled, frost them with a sunshine-yellow icing.

Candies or raisins can be used to decorate the "suns" with faces!

JULY 4TH PATRIOT PARADE

Ahead of time . . . Invite family and friends to join in the parade.

Decorate bikes, trikes, wagons, "Big Wheels," and doll buggies with red, white or blue paper stars, crepe-paper streamers and ribbons.

Have each participant choose a patriot to represent. Make suitable costumes from crepe paper, construction paper and old clothes. (Some possible characters: George Washington, Betsy Ross, Uncle Sam, Abraham Lincoln, Daniel Boone, Davy Crockett, Paul Revere, Martha Washington, a bugler, a drummer.)

Get family pets into the act. Tie bright ribbons, bows or strips of paper to leashes, collars, cages or pet boxes. (Be careful to separate pets who don't like each other.)

At the scheduled time . . . Have observers sit in lawn chairs where they can see the "parade route."

Announce the beginning of the parade with a bugle call, and signal the drummer(s) to lead the procession.

Have an announcer introduce each patriot or parade entry as that "act" passes by.

After the parade, have the announcer invite everyone to sing "America the Beautiful" together. Serve cold slices of watermelon.

PATRIOTIC GIFTS

A Present for Our Land. Give a living and growing present to our land by planting a tree or bush. Determine what kind of plant should be selected and where it would grow best.

Talk with your children about the environmental reasons for giving such a gift. (It releases oxygen into the atmosphere, gives shelter to birds, provides shade, etc.) Plant the tree or bush in your yard, or ask the city or park service to select an appropriate spot for it in the community.

July 4th "We Love You, America" Dinner. Plan an all-American dinner:

Include traditional foods such as hot dogs, hamburgers, apple pie and ice cream.

Decorate the table with a patriotic theme, using red, white and blue napkins, tablecloths and flowers.

If a globe is available, show young children where the United States is located in relation to other countries. Talk about the customs of peoples in other countries and our own, and reasons why people love their native lands.

Look in an encyclopedia for further information concerning Independence Day, and share it with everyone. After you have discussed the article, ask each child to remember one important fact or idea he or she learned from it.

NEIGHBORHOOD ART SHOW

Ahead of time . . . With other families in the neighborhood, agree on a place, time and date for the art show. Give two or three weeks' notice.

Make colorful signs about the event and post them in places where they will attract attention.

While the children make art pieces for the show, mothers and fathers can plan simple refreshments.

On the day of the show . . . Collect all entries at an early hour (which should be announced in advance) such as 9 a.m.

Make sure each item is clearly marked with the name of the artist and the price.

Separate entries into categories, such as paintings, sculptures and drawings.

Set up displays, keeping categories together and arranging entries so they may be easily seen.

At show time . . . Serve refreshments while parents and friends browse.

Provide a cashier's table where art may be purchased. If the money is to return to the individual artists, have the cashier keep track of the items sold.

After the event . . . Make each artist responsible for picking up unsold items and taking them home.

Have a clean-up committee put away tables and chairs, pick up trash and take care of leftover refreshments.

Autumn
LEAF CRAFTS

Crayon-Leaf Transfers. Materials needed: white or light-colored construction paper; crayons; an iron and an ironing board.

Collect strong leaves without holes or flaws. (Green leaves are usually strong and not easily torn.)

With bright crayons, carefully color the outer side of each leaf.

Lay the construction paper on an ironing board. Arrange the leaves on top of it, with the colored sides face down on the paper.

Iron the leaves with a medium-to-hot iron. (You can iron through a sheet of waxed paper if you prefer not to iron directly onto the leaves.)

Peel the waxed paper (if you used any) and the leaves from the paper. A crayoned print will be left on the construction paper.

Have fun decorating a wall, bulletin board or bedroom door with these natural art pieces—or turn them into note paper or attractive gift wrap!

Stained-Glass Leaves. Materials needed: waxed paper, construction paper, glue, scissors, an iron and an ironing board.

Collect brightly colored leaves of different sizes or shapes.

Make identical picture frames from two sheets of construction paper. Cut a rectangle, square, oval, circle or more ornate design from the center of each sheet. Trim the outer edges to whatever shape you desire.

Cut a piece of waxed paper large enough so that, when folded double, it is larger than the cut-out center of the construction paper frame.

Place one or two leaves inside the folded waxed paper.

Iron with a medium-to-hot iron until the waxed paper layers are sealed to each other around the leaves.

Insert the sealed sheet between the two paper frames, and glue the edges of the frames together.

Tape the completed "stained-glass leaves" to your windows, or hang them in a selected place in your home.

HALLOWEEN FUN

The Night before Halloween. Place a candle and a small amount of dry ice inside a carved-out pumpkin. (The ice will release a spooky vapor.) An adult should handle these to avoid the danger of a child burning himself from the ice or the candle. Also, set an eerie atmosphere with decorations and lighting effects. Let the children dress up in their Halloween costumes and masks. Discuss the characters they are pretending to be. Also, talk about the different kinds of invisible "masks" we sometimes wear, and why people wear them.

In addition, encourage each member of the family to share some of their fears—real and imaginary. Discuss how these might be diminished or dispelled.

For refreshments, serve Halloween cupcakes and orange soda.

THANKSGIVING TRADITIONS

Invite a few guests to dinner who otherwise would spend Thanksgiving Day alone. A few days before the dinner, ask each guest to recall several of his or her favorite dishes from previous Thanksgivings or other holidays. Serve one of each guest's favorite dishes with your turkey dinner. They will be delighted by your thoughtfulness!

Create a Centerpiece. As a family project, create a traditional centerpiece to be used each year on your Thanksgiving table.

FAMILY ACTIVITIES FOR EACH SEASON OF THE YEAR cont.

It can be as simple or as complex as you choose, but family participation is important. Be creative!

Some suggestions: Pilgrim salt and pepper shakers, a *papier-maché* turkey, a horn o' plenty filled with fresh fruits and vegetables, or a dried flower arrangement.

"Thank You" Place Cards. Fold 3"x5" cards in half to make place cards for every person at the Thanksgiving table.

Decorate the cards in a Thanksgiving theme, writing each person's name on the front of a card.

On the inside, write a thank-you message. Make each message personal, honest and specific.

Larger cards may be used so that every member of the family can write a message to each person. That way, all receive an expression of gratitude from several people.

"I'm Thankful For . . ." Play the "20 Questions" game, and base it on things for which each person is thankful. The person who is "it" thinks of one thing for which he or she is thankful, and the others try to guess what it is by asking questions which can only be answered yes or no. If the group cannot guess the answer in 20 questions or less, the person who is "it" is the winner.

Any Season
THE FIRST TO SHARE

Celebrate the arrival of nature's first fruits by sharing as a family:

a. The first rosebud. Place it in a prominent place and enjoy its beauty together.

b. The first apple from the tree. Divide it and make every bite count!

c. The first cider. Buy it as a family. Make a tradition by always serving it in a special way; with popcorn, hot with cinnamon sticks and honey, or straight from the jug.

d. The first pumpkin pie. Make a tradition of inviting the same guest(s) to share it— such as a grandparent, friend, neighbor or relative.

THE GIFT OF WORK

To help your children appreciate the gift of work, make arrangements to take them to your place of employment on a regular workday. If that is impossible, share pictures and materials with them that demonstrate the work you do.

Talk about how work is a gift to us and about the joy we find in contributing to other person's lives through the use of our skills.

Take an outing to your place of employment. (If both parents work, include both jobs.) Help the children learn about the end result of your specific job.

Show them the entire facility, especially your work area, and introduce them to some of your coworkers.

Eat together in the plant cafeteria, an office snack shop or a nearby restaurant where you often go for lunch. If you usually take your lunch, pack one for each member of the family.

At the end of the day, discuss how each person in your family does specific jobs to make your home run smoothly. Thank God together for the health, strength and intelligence to work.

THE GIFT OF WHO YOU ARE

This gift is very special for a family member away at college or in the service, and makes a thoughtful birthday present. It is great medicine for countering discouragement all year long!

Buy large, empty capsules from a drugstore or pharmacy.

On strips of bright-colored paper, have each member of the family write, "I love you because. . ." and sign his or her name on the back. Each person may contribute many words of encouragement!

Roll the strips tightly and insert one in each capsule.

Put the capsules into a small box, and wrap or decorate the package. Then send it to the person you are honoring. He or she can read the slips of paper now, or save them as bolsters for their self-esteem in the future!

Source: Gloria Gaither and Shirley Dobson in *Let's Make A Memory.* Published by Word, Incorporated, Dallas, TX. Copyright © 1983. Used by permission.

CHRISTIAN LEADERS TELL HOW THEY
LIKE TO SPEND LEISURE TIME

"What do you most like to do in your leisure moments?"

Steve Green, soloist: I like to read, work in the yard, and play games with my children.

Josh McDowell, president of Josh McDowell Ministries, author, speaker, and promoter of "Why Wait" campaign: One of the greatest privileges in the world is to be married to my wife and to be father of our four children. In spite of my heavy traveling schedule, one of my favorite things to do is to have creative and intimate dates with each of my children and wife. Every moment I invest with them will reap temporal fulfillment and eternal dividends.

Lloyd Ogilvie, pastor, First Presbyterian Church of Hollywood: I enjoy golf, fishing and my grandchildren. I enjoy traveling and studying Scottish history and customs. Each summer I spend my study leave at the University of Edinburgh in Scotland.

Anne Ortlund, author, speaker: I like to be with my husband . . . running on the beach . . . walking around Balboa Island . . . watching clean movies while sharing popcorn and Diet Coke.

R. C. Sproul, president of Ligonier Ministries, author, speaker: I read, golf, play jazz piano, and play Nintendo with my grandchildren.

Kenneth N. Taylor, chairman of the board, Tyndale House Publishers, author, translator of *The Living Bible*: My leisure time is spent writing, with grandchildren, reading, and worrying.

THIRTY IDEAS FOR HUSBANDS AND FATHERS

1. Old sayings. After dinner tonight, quiz your children on how many old sayings they know and understand. Write out the first half of the adage and ask them to fill in the rest. Sayings such as: "Don't put all your eggs in . . . ," "All is fair in love and . . . ," and "Children should be seen and. . . ." You'll be amazed at what answers turn up and the discussion that follows. Then try giving the first half of Bible proverbs, such as: "The getting of treasures by a lying tongue is . . ." (Proverbs 21:6). Let them look up the answers, then talk about them.

2. How teachable are you? Surprise your children tonight by asking them to tell you about something they're currently studying in school—some new mathematical or chemical formula, a new psychological or sociological study, a current trend in English literature, etc. Select a topic you know little about, and really get into it.

3. Instant motorcycle. Remember how you used to turn your bike into a motorcycle by fastening cardboard squares to the frame with clothespins so that they rapped against the spokes? Maybe it's time your child discovered the trick.

4. Motivation plus. To spark interest, let your kids choose and lead the family devotions for a week. Tell them they can be as creative and imaginative as they want, as long as you approve their plan. Motivation and responsibility grow through this experience. Use it frequently.

5. Call your wife at 10:30 A.M. sometime this week and say in these words, or others more natural to you, "I was just thinking of you and wanted to say that I'm immensely pleased that you are my wife. . . . You're wonderful!"

6. Chores, children, and character. The chores we did as a child are a fond memory for most of us. Sadly, children today are missing the valuable character qualities that regular chores build. They've become lost in our quest for leisure and labor-saving

516 *The Almanac of the Christian World*

devices. But assigning chores is a most productive way of teaching responsibility and accountability to your children.

a. **Start early.** Even 3-year-olds can set tables, though it may take three times as long.

b. **Don't discourage volunteers.** Between the ages of 8 and 12, children go through an especially helpful age when they want to model their parents.

c. When possible, cooperate with the interests and abilities of the child in assigning chores. Children take a lot of pride in getting good at something they want to do.

d. Divide and rotate both the less desirable and the most popular tasks equally among all the family members.

e. Spell out each task in writing and make clear what the standard of performance is for a job well done. Leaving this up to individual interpretation creates problems.

f. Create and display a chart where assignments and performance are logged.

g. Don't spare the praise. If you spend more time criticizing a poorly done job than praising a good one, you're actually rewarding the negative behavior more than the positive performance. Lavish compliments are fun to give and never hurt anyone.

7. **Picture memories.** Tonight after dinner, haul out the family photo albums or slides for an hour of reminiscing. It's lots of fun, great for reinforcing family unity and recognizing growth. Follow it up with a short planning session for your next outing. Add a little popcorn and make an evening of it. (By the way, is your youngest child getting shortchanged in the photo department? It happens in most every family, so keep working at it!)

8. **Take a moment** to jot a note to your child's schoolteacher. Thank him or her for the interest poured into your child and express your appreciation. A similar note to a Sunday school teacher, scout leader, or anyone else involved regularly with your child can really make his or her day. Everyone needs sincere praise and encouragement.

9. **The observation game.** This is excellent for teaching children of any age to observe details (yourself, too). After you've been to a place or event together, test each other on memory of details that were there, i.e. "Did you see the man wearing tennis shoes and a suit?" With older children, test for things like inner qualities, personality traits, and nationalities. "Did you see the married couple that wasn't happy?" "Did you see the German, the Italian, and the Englishman?"

10. **Library search.** If you haven't been to the library with your kids recently, go for an hour this Saturday. Help them find one good historical fiction and one hobby or craft resource they can absorb in the next four weeks. If the library has a recording, filmstrip, video, or film department, check one out for your next family night at home. (The library, your church, club, or business may have a projector or VCR you can borrow.)

11. **The story factory.** Try some "add on" stories with your family after dinner or when you're driving somewhere. One person begins ("Once upon a time. . ." will do), and the next person adds a phrase, character, or action. Keep on going till it draws to a natural close or you're all on the floor with laughter.

12. **Magnified fun.** If you don't already have one, pick up a large, high-powered magnifying glass at a stationery store on the way home from work tonight. Spend a half-hour with your children, rediscovering your backyard, their hair and skin, food and clothing, insects . . . just about everything.

13. **To better love her.** If your wife hasn't said it recently, certainly a book or marriage counselor has: "It's the little things that count!" And it's true. One *Dads Only* reader put it this way: "Your wife doesn't really want a dozen roses every day. Just one rose a month will do." It's the small but consistent remembrances—the little touches—that fan the flame of romance in marriage, that say as nothing else can: "I love you," "You're beautiful!" "You're the only one in the world for me." Surveys indicate that the absence of romance and love ranks high as a source of depression in women. First Peter

3:7 instructs us, "Husbands . . . live with your wives in an understanding way. . . ." Certainly part of such "understanding" is to know her so well that you sense just what special expressions, gifts or touches will be the "little things" she'll cherish and thrive on. Become a student of your wife. Watch and listen for the important clues.

For starters, consider some "little things" like these:

a. Send her a Mailgram in which you express your love and invite her out to dinner with you.

b. Drop by a bookstore, library, or newsstand and bring her a book or magazine on home decorating, cooking, sewing, tennis, or anything that may be a special hobby or interest of hers.

c. Leave a note for her on the bathroom mirror, in the cupboard, in the dresser drawer, on her pillow . . . anywhere!

d. Turn off the TV in the middle of a program just because you'd rather visit with her and know about her day.

e. Buy her a gift she wouldn't buy for herself, like a music box or a special teacup and give it to her on an "unspecial" day.

14. Frisbee golf. Grab a frisbee or two, some bath towels, your family, and head for the backyard or your local park. Lay out a golf course as large as space will allow, using the towels spread on the ground as "holes." (The frisbee scores upon landing if any part is touching the towel.) The person with the fewest throws in completing the course wins. You can team little folks with older ones to make the competition more even.

15. A sense of specialness is one of the great gifts we can give our children. In Psalms 139:13-18 God describes how special we are to him. Use the passage as a springboard for some family sharing about each other. Ask each member to think of two special qualities about each of the others and then share them. Watch out; it could be an emotional evening.

16. Love letters shouldn't be the sole domain of the young. If you haven't written one to your wife recently, take 20 minutes

and do it right now. Talk about her most endearing quality and thank her for being your wife.

17. Imagination. Get inside your child's imagination with a "Pretend that you're a . . ." game. Select an object and ask your son or daughter to tell you how it feels to be that object. For starters try: a swimming pool, a tall building, a car, a tree, a bus, a church building, or a doormat. Concentrate on feelings and emotions.

18. Bedtimes. Maybe you've never thought of yourself as a bedtime storyteller. But it's one of the best and most entertaining ways to pass along values to your children. The tales you spin become treasured memories to both you and your child.

Storytelling is quite easy if you keep these simple concepts and ideas in mind:

a. Nature stories are a natural. They can be about animals, trees, or phenomena such as brooks, volcanoes, even thunder and lightning. For example, an "I met a frog . . ." story could be approached this way: (1) Look up frogs in an encyclopedia and discover some facts—things like size, unique features, kinds of noises they make, how they are hatched, misconceptions about them and special abilities. (2) Decide what facts to use and give at least one of them personal significance to your child. (3) Make up the story by imagining that a frog you met is talking to you. Try it out. The more you tell it, the more interesting it will get. Then write it down for your children to read or illustrate with drawings.

b. "Look at that over there" stories can be about man-made things like bridges, paintings, pianos, airplanes, clocks, or medicine.

c. "Give me three words" stories begin by letting the children pick three words like "little girl, grandma, vacations," then you weave a story from them.

d. "Do you remember the story of . . . " stories take the characters from a familiar children's tale and give them a new adventure of your own making.

As you launch into your story, concentrate on describing the people, places and objects in detail (color, movement, size, and shape), include some humor, choose a moral that the child can apply and let it come to a natural conclusion.

So, suppress your fears and give storytelling a try. You'll look forward to bedtimes as much as your children will.

19. Exploring. Remember that side street or back road you always wondered about . . . that quaint shop you've never checked out? Your wife and children probably have such places too. So, set some limits (such as mileage, time, and expense) and let each family member choose where he or she wants to take the family "exploring." Go each Saturday morning until everyone has led an adventure.

20. Instead of TV tonight, invest an hour after dinner "reminiscing" about when each family member: 1) had the most fun; 2) felt the most embarrassed; 3) cried the hardest; 4) was so tired that; 5) never worked harder; and 6) felt the closest to God. The family scrapbook or photo albums can embellish the sharing or jog your memories. And close by thanking God for the privileges and protection he has given each family member.

21. Last thoughts of the day. Remain active in your child's subconscious all night—certainly a prime reason for resolving any tensions in your relationship before your child falls asleep. Turn the "last thoughts" principle to your advantage each evening this week by expressing to your child (1) one specific character strength he or she has, and (2) recalling an action your child did that day that made you proud. Bedtimes are not the moment for punishment or criticism.

22. Ping-Pong baseball. Grab a Ping-Pong ball, roll up a newspaper for a bat, and try a little game of "Work-up" in the living room. There are no strikes, and the ball must be hit or you're out. Adjust rules to fit your children's ages and skills.

23. Meals are a great learning environment for younger children. They can practice the alphabet, multiplication tables, or spelling words. Vocabulary can be increased by naming animals, historical dates, famous people . . . even places and geography. If you have a teenager who is studying a foreign language, let him lead a meal devoted only to speaking that language. The possibilities are endless.

24. Table sentences. One person starts and each person around the table adds a word till the sentence is finished. There's no penalty for completing the sentence. The next person starts a new one.

25. A little squeeze can communicate a lot of love. When you bow to say the blessing, join hands and give the person on your right a little "love" squeeze. The important point is clear: A little love given brings some in return.

26. Creative analogies can sharpen verbal skills and bring out thoughts and feelings sometimes hard to express. Start with everyone stating the relationship between a personal characteristic or feeling and some other familiar phenomenon. For example: "I'm as thin as a stick" or "I'm as happy as a lark."

27. The return. After dinner tonight, suggest that your family go again on a favorite vacation or outing—this time by memory. With everybody contributing, try to recall all the steps and events that happened, beginning with packing suitcases and the car, incidents en route, and the chronology of each day's events until you returned. Get out your photos taken on the trip. You'll discover this "walk through" will trigger lots of warm memories, and this time the trip won't cost a cent.

28. Grace at meals can easily lapse into a lifeless routine. You can enliven these important prayers by adding variety: 1) Slow down the prayer so each thought is emphasized. 2) Discuss the prayer's key ideas during the first moments of the meal. 3) Pray at the end of the meal. 4) Have each family member offer a short portion of the prayer. 5) Start eating without prayer and when someone notices, lead a discussion about why a prayer of thanksgiving is important, what should be included in the prayer, how specific it can or should be and what causes grace at mealtime to lose its significance. 6) Try singing grace and holding hands for variety.

29. Precede breakfast with some physical exercise together. Have each member of the family lead one "waker-upper."

30. Practical prayers. It's difficult for children, even adults, to see prayer as a direct course of action in meeting needs and solving problems. Concentrate this month on guiding your child to pray for specific circumstances in his life and the lives of others in your family and his circle of friends. Keep a simple log next to the bed, with requests and God's answers. Watch their enthusiasm about prayer grow!

Source: Paul Lewis in *Dads Only*. Published by Corporate Family Resources, Julian, CA. Copyright © 1982. Used by permission.

Dads Only, edited by Paul Lewis, is a bimonthly newsletter with tips, research, and ideas for fathers. For subscription information write P.O. Box 340, Julian, CA 92036 or call 1-800-HELP-DAD. Additional resources are available from National Center for Fathering, 217 Southwind Place, Manhattan, KS 66502.

66 99
FOCUS
QUOTE
In 1991 parents spent 40% less time with their children than in 1965.—John Robinson, University of Maryland.

CHECKLIST FOR SPIRITUAL TRAINING
Dr. James C. Dobson

Listed below is a checklist for parents—a set of targets at which to aim. Many of the items require maturity that children lack, and we should not try to make adult Christians out of our immature youngsters. But we can gently urge them toward these goals—these targets— during the impressionable years of childhood.

Essentially, the six scriptural concepts that follow should be consciously taught, providing the foundation on which all future doctrine and faith will rest. I encourage every Christian parent to evaluate his child's understanding of these six areas:

Concept I— "And thou shalt love the Lord thy God will all thy heart" (Mark 12:30).
1. Is your child learning of the love of God through the love, tenderness and mercy of his parents? (most important)
2. Is he learning to talk about the Lord, and to include him in his thoughts and plans?
3. Is he learning to turn to Jesus for help whenever he is frightened or anxious or lonely?
4. Is he learning to read the Bible?
5. Is he learning to pray?
6. Is he learning the meaning of faith and trust?
7. Is he learning the joy of the Christian way of life?
8. Is he learning the beauty of Jesus' birth and death?

Concept II— "Thou shalt love thy neighbor as thyself" (Mark 12:31).
1. Is he learning to understand and empathize with the feelings of others?
2. Is he learning not to be selfish and demanding?
3. Is he learning to share?
4. Is he learning not to gossip and criticize others?
5. Is he learning to accept himself?

Concept III— "Teach me to do thy will; for thou art my God" (Psalm 143:10).
1. Is he learning to obey his parents as preparation for later obedience to God? (most important)
2. Is he learning to behave properly in church—God's house?

3. Is he learning a healthy appreciation for both aspects of God's nature: love and justice?
4. Is he learning that there are many forms of benevolent authority outside himself to which he must submit?
5. Is he learning the meaning of sin and its inevitable consequences?

Concept IV— "Fear God, and keep his commandments: for this is the whole duty of man" (Ecclesiastes 12:13).
1. Is he learning to be truthful and honest?
2. Is he learning to keep the Sabbath day holy?
3. Is he learning the relative insignificance of materialism?
4. Is he learning the meaning of the Christian family and the faithfulness to it which God intends?
5. Is he learning to follow the dictates of his own conscience?

Concept V— "But the fruit of the Spirit is . . . self-control" (Galatians 5:22, 23, RSV).
1. Is he learning to give a portion of his allowance (and other money) to God?
2. Is he learning to control his impulses?
3. Is he learning to work and carry responsibility?
4. Is he learning to tolerate minor frustration?
5. Is he learning to memorize and quote Scripture?

Concept VI— " . . . he that humbleth himself shall be exalted" (Luke 14:11).
1. Is he learning a sense of appreciation?
2. Is he learning to thank God for the good things in life?
3. Is he learning to forgive and forget?
4. Is he learning the vast difference between self-worth and egotistical pride?
5. Is he learning to bow in reverence before the God of the universe?

Source: James C. Dobson in *Straight Talk to Men and Their Wives.* Published by Word, Incorporated, Dallas, TX. Copyright © 1980. Used by permission.

SEVEN REASONS FAMILY DEVOTIONS ARE IMPORTANT

1. It unifies the home life, and puts faith in the place of friction.

2. It brings to the family group a sense of God's presence.

3. It shows the children that God is relevant to everyday living, and not just a Being to be worshiped on Sunday.

4. It gives members of the family an opportunity for self-examination and confession of sin.

5. It strengthens the members of the household for the tasks and responsibilities they are to face during the day.

6. It insulates us against the hurts and misunderstandings which come our way.

7. It supplements the work of the church, and makes of our homes a sanctuary where Christ is honored.

Source: Billy Graham in *My Answer.* Published by Doubleday and Company. Copyright © 1960.

TOP 10 BEST-SELLING CHILDREN'S BOOKS OF 1991

1. *The Beginner's Bible,* by Karyn Henley, Questar Publishers, c
2. *Wee Sing Bible Songs,* by Wee Sing, Price Stern Sloan (Tyndale), p/cassette
3. *My First Bible in Pictures,* by Kenneth Taylor, Tyndale House Publishers, c
4. *Rock-a-Bye Bible,* by Marjorie Ainsborough Decker, World Bible Publishers, c
5. *Love You Forever,* by Robert Munsch, Firefly Books Ltd., p
6. *The Door in the Dragon's Throat,* by Frank Peretti, Crossway Books, p
7. *Mandi and the Secret Tunnel,* by Lois Gladys Leppard, Bethany House Publishers, p
8. *What Would Jesus Do?* by Mack Thomas, Questar Publishers, c
9. *Precious Moments Stories From the Bible,* by Sheri Haan, Baker Book House, c
10. *Escape From the Island of Aquarius,* by Frank Peretti, Crossway Books, p

This list is based on actual sales in Christian retail stores in the United States and Canada during 1991. All rights reserved. Copyright 1992 CBA Service Corp. and Spring Arbor Distributors. Distributed by Evangelical Christian Publishers Association. Reprinted by permission from the February 1992 issue of *Bookstore Journal,* official trade publication of the Christian Booksellers Association.

A YEAR'S READING PROGRAM FOR AGES 0–3

January   *My Book of Bible Rhymes* by John Knapp II, illustrated by Dianne Turner Deckart, David C. Cook Publishing Company

February   *Good Night Moon* by Margaret Wise Brown, illustrated by Clement Hurd, Harper & Row, Publishers

March   *Read Aloud Bible Stories, Volumes 1 and 2* by Ella K. Lindvall, Moody Press

April   *A to Z Picture Book* by Gyo Fujikawa, Grosset & Dunlap

May   *God Made It All* by Mary Thornton Blanton, Scripture Press, SonFlower Books

June   *Colors* by John J. Reiss, Bradbury Press

July   *Animals on the Farm* by Feodor Rojankovsky, Alfred A. Knopf

August   *Mother Goose* by Michael Hauge, Holt, Rinehart & Winston

September   *Pat the Bunny* by Dorothy Kunhardt, Golden Books

October   *God Made All the Colors* by Linden Evans, Lion Publishing Corporation

November   *Brown Bear, Brown Bear, What Do You See?* by Bill Martin, Jr., Holt, Rinehart & Winston

December   *Poems to Read to the Very Young* by Josette Frank, illustrated by Eloise Wilkins, Random House

Source: All books selected by Elaine K. McEwan. Further information about these and other books are included in *How to Raise a Reader* by Elaine K. McEwan, available at your local Christian bookstore. Copyright © 1987. Published by David C. Cook Publishing Company. Used by permission.

* Books from Christian publishers are indicated with an asterisk.

When Mother Teresa received her Nobel Prize she was asked, "What can we do to help promote world peace?" "Go home and love your family," she replied.

FOCUS FACT

A YEAR'S READING PROGRAM FOR AGES 4–7

January   *A Child's Book of Prayers* by Christine Harder Tangvald, David C. Cook Publishing Company

February   *The Very Hungry Caterpillar* by Eric Carle, Puffin

March   *Big Thoughts for Little People* by Kenneth Taylor, Tyndale House Publishers

April   *Who's a Friend of the Water Spurting Whale?* by Sanna Anderson Baker, Illustrated by Tomie dePaola, David C. Cook Publishing Company

May   *Bread and Jam for Frances* by Russell Hoban, illustrated by Lillian Hoban, Harper & Row, Publishers

June   *Mike Mulligan and His Steam Shovel* by Virginia Lee Burton, Houghton Mifflin Company

July   *The Five Hundred Hats of Bartholomew Cubbins* by Dr. Seuss, Vanguard Press

August   *Animal Alphabet* by Bert Kitchen, Dial

September   *The Helen Oxenbury Nursery Story Book* by Helen Oxenbury, Alfred A. Knopf

October   *Now You Can Read Stories from the Bible* by Elaine Ife and Rosalind Sutton,
              Thomas Nelson, Inc., Publishers
November   *The Mitten* by Alvin Tresselt, Lothrop, Lee & Shepard
December   *The Christmas Pageant* by Tomie DePaola, Winston Press

A book your child will enjoy year-round: *Egermeier's Bible Story Book* by Elsie
        Egermeier, Warner Press

Source: All books selected by Elaine K. McEwan. Further information about these and other books are included in *How to Raise a Reader* by Elaine K. McEwan, available at your local Christian bookstore. Copyright © 1987. Published by David C. Cook Publishing Company. Used by permission.

* Books from Christian publishers are indicated with an asterisk.

A YEAR'S READING PROGRAM FOR AGES 8–10

January   *Homer Price* by Robert McCloskey, Viking
February   *The Lion, the Witch, and the Wardrobe* by C. S. Lewis, The Macmillan Company
March   *Charlotte's Web* by E. B. White, Harper & Row, Publishers
April   *Little House in the Big Woods* by Laura Ingalls Wilder, Harper & Row,
              Publishers
May   *A Wrinkle in Time* by Madeleine L'Engle, Farrar, Straus, & Giroux
June   *The Secret Garden* by Frances Hodgson Burnett, illustrated by Tasha Tudor, J.
              B. Lippincott
July   *Tales of the Kingdom* by David and Karen Mains, illustrated by Jack
              Stockman, David C. Cook Publishing Company
August   *The Princess and the Goblin* by George MacDonald, illustrated by Linda Hill
              Griffith, David C. Cook Publishing Company
September   *The Great Brain* by John D. Fitzgerald, Dial
October   *The Incredible Journey* by Shelia Burnford, Little Brown
November   *Where the Red Fern Grows* by Wilson Rawls, Bantam Books
December   *The Best Christmas Pageant Ever* by Barbara Robinson, Avon

A book your child will enjoy year-round: *The Children's Bible In 365 Stories* by Mary
        Batchelor, Lion Publishing Corporation

Source: All books selected by Elaine K. McEwan. Further information about these and other books are included in *How to Raise a Reader* by Elaine K. McEwan, available at your local Christian bookstore. Copyright © 1987. Published by David C. Cook Publishing Company. Used by permission.

* Books from Christian publishers are indicated with an asterisk.

A YEAR'S READING PROGRAM FOR AGES 10–12

January   *The Book of Three* by Lloyd Alexander, Holt, Rinehart & Winston
February   *The Wind in the Door* by Madeleine L'Engle, Farrar, Straus, and Giroux
March   *Tales of the Resistance* by David & Karen Mains, David C. Cook Publishing Co.
April   *Island of the Blue Dolphins* by Scott O'Dell, Houghton
May   *Sarah, Plain and Tall* by Patricia MacLachlan, Harper & Row, Publishers
June   *Dangerous Journey: The Story of Pilgrim's Progress* by Oliver Hunkin,
              editor. Illustrated by Alan Parry, Wm. B. Eerdmans Publishing Company
July   *Bridge to Terabithia* by Katherine Paterson, Thomas Y. Crowell
August   *In Search of Perlas Grandes* by Timothy C. Davis, Accent Books

September   *Potter* by Walter Wangerin, Jr., David C. Cook Publishing Company
October   *The Yearling* by Marjorie Kinnan Rawlings, illustrated by N. C. Wyeth,
             Charles Scribner's Sons
November   *Treasure Island* by Robert Louis Stevenson, illustrated by N. C. Wyeth,
             Charles Scribner's Sons
December   *Classics to Read Aloud to Your Children* by William F. Russell, Crown
             Publishers

A book your child will enjoy year-round: *The Illustrated Bible,* Living Values Edition,
David C. Cook Publishing Company

Source: All books selected by Elaine K. McEwan. Further information about these and other books are included in *How to Raise a Reader* by Elaine K. McEwan, available at your local Christian bookstore. Copyright © 1987. Published by David C. Cook Publishing Company. Used by permission.

* Books from Christian publishers are indicated with an asterisk.

A YEAR'S READING PROGRAM FOR PARENTS WITH CHILDREN 0–3

January   *The First Three Years of Life* by Burton L. White, Prentice-Hall, Inc.
February   *Infants and Mothers: Differences in Development* by T. Berry Brazelton,
            Delacorte Press
March   **The Complete Book of Baby and Child Care* by Grace H. Ketterman, Fleming
            H. Revell
April   **A Hug and a Kiss and a Kick in the Pants* by Kay Kuzma, David C. Cook
            Publishing Company
May   **Heart and Home: A Reaffirmation of Traditional Mothering* by Debra Evans,
            Crossway Books
June   **The Christian Family* by Larry Christenson, Bethany House Publishers
July   **Seven Things Children Need* by John M. Drescher, Herald Press
August   **Dare to Discipline* by James Dobson, Tyndale House Publishers
September   **The Encyclopedia of Christian Parenting* by Leslie Keylock, editor, Fleming
            H. Revell
October   **What Happens When Your Children Grow* by Margaret Bailey Jacobsen,
            Victor Books/Scripture Press
November   **Building Your Child's Faith* by Alice Chapin, Here's Life Publishers
December   *How to Play with Your Children* by Brian and Shirley Sutton-Smith, Hawthorn
            Books

Source: All books selected by Elaine K. McEwan. Further information about these and other books are included in *Super Kid? Raising Balanced Children in a Super Kid World* by Elaine McEwan, available at your local Christian bookstore. Copyright © 1988. Published by David C. Cook Publishing Company. Used by permission.

* Books from Christian publishers are indicated with an asterisk.

A YEAR'S READING PROGRAM FOR PARENTS WITH CHILDREN 4–7

| January | *Christian Child-Rearing and Personality Development* by Paul D. Meier, Baker Book House |

January   *Christian Child-Rearing and Personality Development* by Paul D. Meier, Baker Book House

February   *Hide or Seek* by James Dobson, Fleming H. Revell

March   *How to Talk with Your Children about God* by Frances Loftiss Carroll, Prentice-Hall, Inc.

April   Traits of a Healthy Family by Dolores Curran, Ballantine/Epiphany Books

May   How to Make Your Child a Winner by Victor Cline, Walker and Company

June   The Quality Time Almanac: A Source Book of Ideas and Activities for Parents and Kids by S. Adams Sullivan, Doubleday Company

July   *Dr. Dobson Answers Your Questions* by James Dobson, Tyndale House

August   *From the Inside Out* by Kay Kuzma, David C. Cook Publishing Company

September   Self-Esteem: The Key to Your Child's Well-Being by Harris Clemes and Reynold Beam, G. Putnam's Sons

October   The Parents Book of Physical Fitness for Children by Martin I. Lorin, Atheneum

November   Kids and Play by Joanne F. Oppenheim, Ballantine Books

December   Bringing Up a Moral Child by Michael Shulman and Eva Mekler, Addison-Wesley Publishing Company, Inc.

Source: All books selected by Elaine K. McEwan. Further information about these and other books are included in *Super Kid? Raising Balanced Children in a Super Kid World* by Elaine McEwan, available at your local Christian bookstore. Copyright © 1988. Published by David C. Cook Publishing Company. Used by permission.

* Books from Christian publishers are indicated with an asterisk.

❝❞ FOCUS QUOTE If parents took the responsibility that should rightfully be theirs, we wouldn't have 99% of the problems we have in the schools in America. —Guy Doud, in the Focus on the Family film, *Molder of Dreams.*

A YEAR'S READING PROGRAM FOR PARENTS WITH CHILDREN 8–10

January   The Challenge of Friendship: Helping Your Child Become a Friend by Shirley Gould, Dutton Publishing

February   *Discovering Your Child's Design* by Ralph Matson and Thom Black, David C. Cook Publishing Company

March   *Rights, Wrongs, and In-Betweens* by Jim Larson, Augsburg Publishing House

April   Raising Good Children by Thomas Lickona, Bantam Books

May   *Parents, Take Charge!* by Perry L. Draper, Tyndale House Publishers

June   *Parenting Isn't for Cowards* by James Dobson, Word Inc.

July	*Working and Caring* by T. Berry Brazelton, Addison-Wesley

July   *Working and Caring* by T. Berry Brazelton, Addison-Wesley

August   **Should You Be the Working Mom?* by Bee-Lan C. Wang and Richard J. Stellway, David C. Cook Publishing Company

September   **The Intimate Family* by Marlee Alex, Questar Publishers, Inc.

October   **Preparing Your Child for Success at School* by Cheri Fuller, Honor Books/ Harrison House

November   **Parents' Most-Asked Questions about Kids and Schools* by Cliff Schimmels, Victor Books/Scripture Press

December   *The Difficult Child* by Stanley Turecki and Leslie Tonner, Bantam Books

Source: All books selected by Elaine K. McEwan. Further information about these and other books are included in *Super Kid? Raising Balanced Children in a Super Kid World* by Elaine McEwan, available at your local Christian bookstore. Copyright © 1988. Published by David C. Cook Publishing Company. Used by permission.

* Books from Christian publishers are indicated with an asterisk.

---

66 99
FOCUS QUOTE
Sometimes we're so concerned about giving our children what we never had growing up, we neglect to give them what we *did* have growing up.
—Dr. James Dobson

A YEAR'S READING PROGRAM FOR PARENTS WITH CHILDREN 10–12

January   **Why Wait? What You Need to Know about the Teen Sexuality Crisis* by Josh McDowell and Dick Day, Here's Life Publishers

February   **Keeping Your Teen in Touch with God* by Robert Laurent, David C. Cook Publishing Company

March   **How to Keep Your Kids on Your Team* by Charles Stanley, Oliver Nelson Books

April   **Raising Positive Kids in a Negative World* by Zig Ziglar, Oliver Nelson Books

May   *Growing with Sports: A Parents' Guide to the Young Athlete* by Ernest M. Vandeweghe and George L. Flynn, Prentice-Hall, Inc.

June   **How to Motivate Your Child toward Success* by William Steuart McBirnie, Tyndale House Publishers

July   **Home: Where Life Makes Up Its Mind* by Charles R. Swindoll, Multnomah Press

August   **How to Enjoy a Family Fight* by Will Cunningham, Questar Publishers, Inc.

September   **Kids Who Have Too Much* by Ralph E. Minear and William Proctor, Thomas Nelson, Inc., Publishers

October   **40 Ways to Teach Your Child Values* by Paul Lewis, Tyndale House Publishers

November   *The Birth Order Book* by Kevin Leman, Dell Publishing Company

December   **Parents and Teenagers* by Jay Kesler, Victor Books/Scripture Press

Source: All books selected by Elaine K. McEwan. Further information about these and other books are included in *Super Kid? Raising Balanced Children in a Super Kid World* by Elaine McEwan, available at your local Christian bookstore. Copyright © 1988. Published by David C. Cook Publishing Company. Used by permission.

* Books from Christian publishers are indicated with an asterisk.

100 BEST-SELLING CHILDREN'S BOOKS

This list was compiled from information supplied by publishers. The first sales figure shown for each entry represents the number of copies sold during 1991, the second figure is the total number sold in that book's history with that publisher.

We requested that publishers submit figures for sales through retail outlets only, but some (marked by an asterisk) were unable to separate the numbers, so their sales figures probably include distribution via ministries, book clubs, etc.

Although books are ranked according to the total sold in the past year, not all publishers granted permission to release these figures. Unreleased or unavailable figures are designated by "n.a.," but the books are ranked in their correct order.

Of the top 100 books, category totals (according to publishers' grading) are: preschool, 20; primary, 6; junior, 12; young teen, 6; preschool-primary, 34; preschool-junior, 1; primary-junior, 14; and junior-young teen, 7.

1. **Love You Forever,** Robert Munsch, Firefly Books Ltd. ©1982 (preschool), n.a. A little boy is assured that whatever he does, his mother will love him forever.

2. **The Beginner's Bible,** Karyn Henley and illus. by Dennas Davis, Questar ©1989 (preschool-primary), 349,286 / 721,192. Ninety-five Bible stories are told in large type and colorful illustrations.

3. **The Lion, the Witch and the Wardrobe,** C.S. Lewis, Macmillan ©1970 (junior-young teen), 200,047 / n.a.* This book in "The Chronicles of Narnia" series tells how Aslan, the noble lion, frees Narnia from the spell of the White Witch.

4. **The Littlest Angel,** Charles Tazewell and illus. by Paul Micich, Ideals ©1991 (preschool-primary), 141,800 / 141,800.* Heaven's smallest angel finds a role to play at Christmas.

5. **Precious Moments Bedtime Stories,** Samuel Butcher, Baker ©1989 (preschool), n.a. Illustrated by Butcher, these stories focus on honesty, sharing, giving, and God's love and care. A section of favorite bedtime prayers is included.

6. **The Chronicles of Narnia** (boxed set), C.S. Lewis, Macmillan ©1970 (junior-young teen), 116,997 / n.a.* This set comprises Lewis' seven classic "Narnia" tales.

7. **The Picture Bible,** Iva Hoth, illus. by Andre LeBlanc, and Bible editing by Elvan Olmstead, Chariot (Cook) ©1988, 1989, 1990 (primary), n.a. This full-color, picture-strip version of the Bible includes brief captions.

8. **Precious Moments Stories From the Bible,** Sheri Haan, Baker ©1987 (preschool), n.a. Bible stories illustrated by Samuel Butcher's Precious Moments drawings are grouped by theme, including Creation, faith, obedience, and humility.

9. **The Children's Bible in 365 Stories,** Mary Batchelor, Lion ©1985 (preschool-primary), 98,383 / 338,210. This collection spans the scope of the Bible with stories for daily reading.

10. **The Story of Easter for Children,** Beverly Charette and illus. by Lorraine Wells, Ideals ©1987 (preschool-primary), 91,600 / n.a.* This book tells the story of Easter in easy-to-read rhyme.

11. **Precious Moments Through-the-Day Stories,** V. Gilbert Beers, Baker ©1991 (preschool), n.a. These 58 stories illustrated by Samuel Butcher allow parents and kids to relive the sounds, smells, and wonders of daily events.

12. **What Would Jesus Do?** Mack Thomas, Questar ©1991 (primary), 83,969 / 83,969. Charles Sheldon's classic novel is told for children.

13. **Rock-a-Bye Bible,** Marjorie Ainsborough Decker, World Bible ©1987 (preschool), n.a. This 96-page volume offers selected Scripture that relates to favorite Christian Mother Goose rhymes.

14. **The Door in the Dragon's Throat,** Frank Peretti, Crossway ©1985 (young teen), 70,464 / 159,469. Archaeologist Cooper and his children accept the challenge to solve a desert mystery.

15. **My Little Bible,** Mary Hollingsworth and illus. by Stephanie McFetridge Britt, Word ©1991 (preschool), n.a. Each of the 44 Bible stories in this book has a color illustration, Scripture reference, and an interactive statement or question.

16. **Escape From the Island of Aquarius,** Frank Peretti, Crossway ©1986 (young teen), 55,549 / 134,286. Searching for missing missionaries, the Coopers face insects, earthquakes, and a tyrannical island king.

17. **The Christmas Story,** Carol Heyer, Ideals ©1991 (preschool-primary), 54,200 / 54,200. This retelling of Christ's birth encourages children to notice and honor the true meaning of Christmas.

18. **Mandie and the Singing Chalet,** Lois Gladys Leppard, Bethany ©1991 (junior), 53,453 / 53,479. Mandie discovers strange melodies coming from a European chalet.

19. **The Story of Christmas for Children,** Beverly Charette and illus. by Lorraine Wells, Ideals ©1988 (preschool-primary), 51,600 / n.a.* This book tells the story of Christ's birth in easy-to-read rhyme.

20. **Mandie and the Secret Tunnel,** Lois Gladys Leppard, Bethany ©1983 (primary-junior), 50,660 / 300,965. Almost a teenager, Mandie is certain God no longer loves her. She watches her father being buried and her mother remarry. It seems Uncle Ned is her only friend.

21. **Trapped at the Bottom of the Sea,** Frank Peretti, Crossway ©1988 (young teen), 47,962 / 129,500. Lila's flight to the States is hijacked, and now she's prisoner in a top-secret weapons pod.

22. **Prince Caspian,** C.S. Lewis, Macmillan ©1970 (junior-young teen), 47,437 / n.a.* This book in "The Chronicles of Narnia" series tells how Prince Caspian and his army of Talking Beasts conquer the Telemarines.

23. **The Tombs of Anak,** Frank Peretti, Crossway ©1987 (young teen), 46,507 / 120,748. The Coopers are looking for a missing co-worker, but they find a new mystery that endangers them all.

24. **The Bible in Pictures for Little Eyes,** Ken Taylor, Moody ©1979, 1991 (preschool), 44,836 / n.a. Taylor makes Bible stories understandable to children through simple words. The book includes 190 color pictures.

25. **A Very Special Birthday,** Chariot (Cook) ©1986 (preschool-primary), n.a. This 3 x 4-inch title in the "My Jesus Pocketbook" series focuses on Christ's birth.

26. **The Amazing Book, Vol. 1,** John Kohlenberger III and Noel Wescombe, Multnomah ©1991 (preschool-primary), 40,833 / 40,833.* Video characters Doc, Rikki, Revver, and Dewey guide children through 72 Scripture-based readings.

27. **My Little Bible Picture Book,** Chariot (Cook) ©1988 (preschool), n.a. Each brief Bible story includes a prayer and a Bible verse to remember.

28. **Mandie and the Cherokee Legend,** Lois Gladys Leppard, Bethany ©1983 (primary-junior), 36,060 / 223,050. Mandie discovers her ancestry and learns of a mysterious Indian legend.

29. **A Child's Book of Manners,** Ruth Odor, Standard ©1990 (preschool), 34,699 / n.a. This "Happy Day" book teaches kids manners that are appropriate at home, school, play, and church.

30. **Would You Like to Know Jesus?,** Eira Reeves, Chariot (Cook) ©1989 (preschool-primary), n.a. This book explains how

100 BEST-SELLING CHILDREN'S BOOKS cont.

children can find Jesus as their friend
Who offers salvation.

31. **The Littlest Angel,** Charles Tazewell
and illus. by Sergio Leone, Ideals
©1946 (preschool-primary), 32,700 /
n.a.* Heaven's smallest angel finds a
role to play at Christmas.

32. **Twenty-Third Psalm,** Chariot (Cook)
©1986 (preschool-primary), n.a. This 3
x 4-inch title in the "My Jesus Pocketbook" series teaches kids about trust.

33. **Mandie and the Forbidden Attic,** Lois
Gladys Leppard, Bethany ©1985 (primary-junior), 31,726 / 196,607. Mandie
and her friend investigate noises in their
boarding school's attic and break school
rules in the process.

34. **The Great Bible Adventure,** Sandy
Silverthorne, Harvest House ©1990
(preschool-junior), 30,987 / 44,147.
Each of the 14 Bible stories in this book
is illustrated, with items to find in each
scene.

35. **The Silver Chair,** C.S. Lewis, Macmillan ©1970 (junior-young teen), 30,609 /
n.a.* Prince Rilian escapes from the Em-
erald Witch's underground kingdom.

36. **Mandie and the Ghost Bandits,** Lois
Gladys Leppard, Bethany ©1984
(primary-junior), 30,264 / 182,869.
Mandie and her friends discover the
value of their Christian faith while solving a mystery involving a missing gold
shipment and a train wreck.

37. **ABC's,** Chariot (Cook) ©1986 (preschool-primary), n.a. This 3 x 4-inch title
in the "My Jesus Pocketbook" series
teaches youngsters about praise.

38. **The Ten Commandments,** Chariot
(Cook) ©1987 (preschool-primary), n.a.
This 3 x 4-inch title in the "My Jesus
Pocketbook" series teaches youngsters
about obedience.

39. **The Easter Story,** Carol Heyer, Ideals
©1990 (preschool-primary), 29,400 /
77,600.* This story recounts Jesus' birth,
life, and sacrifice and explains Easter
rituals, symbols, and traditions.

40. **Nursery Rhymes,** Chariot (Cook)
©1986 (preschool-primary), n.a. This 3
x 4-inch title in the "My Jesus Pocketbook" series discusses discipleship.

41. **Lord's Prayer,** Chariot (Cook) ©1986
(preschool-primary), n.a. This 3 x 4-inch
title in the "My Jesus Pocketbook" series
teaches youngsters about prayer.

42. **Bedtime Hugs for Little Ones,**
Debby Boone, Harvest House ©1988
(preschool-primary), 28,977 /
193,332. This book provides children
and parents an opportunity to discuss
growing up, the dark, dreams, shooting stars, and being loved.

43. **Sleep Sound in Jesus,** Michael Card,
Harvest House ©1990 (preschool),
28,282 / 72,728. Sixteen illustrated lullabies in this book are a companion to
Card's record of the same name.

44. **Mandie and the Trunk's Secret,**
Lois Gladys Leppard, Bethany ©1985
(primary-junior), 28,192 / 172,361.
Mandie and her friends find old letters in a trunk that leads to a mystery
involving hidden diamonds, an enemy, and a secret cabin.

45. **Every Day With God,** Word ©1990
(primary), n.a. This kids' devotional features passages from the *International
Children's Bible,* memory verses, prayers, and color illustrations.

46. **International Children's Story Bible,**
Word ©1990 (preschool), n.a. Kids from
around the world illustrated the 115
Bible stories included in this book.

47. **Mandie and the Foreign Spies,** Lois
Gladys Leppard, Bethany ©1990
(junior), 26,923 / 78,159. Mandie's European trip takes an interesting turn.

48. **The Tale of Three Trees,** Angela
Elwell Hunt, Lion ©1989 (primary-
junior), 26,640 / 83,300.* Three trees
dream of achieving greatness and play
roles in Jesus' life.

49. **The Picture Bible—New Testament,**
Iva Hoth, illus. by Andre LeBlanc, and
Bible editing by Elvan Olmstead,

Chariot (Cook) ©1991 (primary), n.a. This full-color, picture-strip version of the New Testament includes brief captions.

50. **Manners,** Chariot (Cook) ©1986 (preschool-primary), n.a. This 3 x 4-inch title in the "My Jesus Pocketbook" series discusses relationships.

51. **The Vanishing Footprints,** Lois Walfrid Johnson, Bethany ©1991 (junior), 25,699 / 25,699. In Book 4 of the "Adventures of the Northwoods" series, Kate, Anders, and Erik's discovery of stolen money puts them in danger.

52. **My First Book of Bible Devotions,** Chariot (Cook) ©1991 (preschool), n.a. A sequel to *My Little Bible Picture Book,* this volume features stories about Jesus and contemporary life to teach faith.

53. **The Magician's Nephew,** C.S. Lewis, Macmillan ©1970 (junior-young teen), 25,192 / n.a.* Aslan creates Narnia and gives the gift of speech to its animals.

54. **The Horse and His Boy**, C.S. Lewis, Macmillan ©1970. (junior-young teen), 25,145 / n.a.* A talking horse and a boy prince save Narnia from invasion.

55. **My Little Box of Prayers,** Felicity Henderson, Lion ©1988 (preschool), 25,100 / 62,500.* Four 32-page books offer contemporary and traditional prayers arranged by theme.

56. **The Last Battle,** C.S. Lewis, Macmillan ©1970 (junior-young teen), 24,984 / n.a.* Evil comes to Narnia, and Aslan leads his people to a glorious new paradise.

57. **Stories From the Growing Years,** Arleta Richardson, Chariot (Cook) ©1991 (junior), n.a. Grandma, now in her 90s, looks back at the significant years of her life.

58. **God Made Me,** Linda Boyer, Standard ©1990 (preschool), 24,192 / n.a. This "Happy Day" book teaches kids shapes and why God made them the way they are.

59. **God's Greatest Day,** Chariot (Cook) ©1986 (preschool-primary), n.a. This 3 x 4-inch title in the "My Jesus Pocketbook" series focuses on Easter.

60. **Something Old, Something New,** Judy Baer, Bethany ©1991 (young teen), 23,119 / 23,119. In Book 11 of the "Cedar River Daydreams" series, Peggy returns to Cedar River after having her baby, and she and Lexi begin an ecological campaign.

61. **Good News for Little People,** Kenneth Taylor, Tyndale ©1991 (preschool), 23,082 / 23,082. Fourth in the "Little People" series, this book introduces youngsters to the Lord with poems, stories, and prayers.

62. **Scripture Pictures,** Chariot (Cook) ©1986 (preschool-primary), n.a. This 3 x 4-inch title in the "My Jesus Pocketbook" series teaches readers Bible skills.

63. **Bible Promises,** Chariot (Cook) ©1988 (preschool-primary), n.a. This 3 x 4-inch title in the "My Jesus Pocketbook" series teaches faith and trust.

64. **Mandie and the Holiday Surprise,** Lois Gladys Leppard, Bethany ©1988 (primary-junior), 22,746 / 114,625. Mandie can't wait to see family and friends. Will she have a special present waiting when she arrives home for Christmas?

65. **The Race,** Lauraine Snelling, Bethany ©1991 (junior), 22,710 / 22,710. In Book 1 of the "Golden Filly" series, 16-year-old Tricia must overcome setbacks to get into the big race that can help her family.

66. **Vanishing Star,** Judy Baer, Bethany ©1991 (junior), 22,487 / 22,487. In Book 12 of the "Cedar River Daydreams" series, Lexi's friends get hooked on horror movies until something more alarming happens.

67. **Mandie and the Shipboard Mystery,** Lois Gladys Leppard, Bethany ©1990 (junior), 22,216 / 83,475. While on board a ship for Europe, Mandie and her

100 BEST-SELLING CHILDREN'S BOOKS cont.

friends track down a mystery.

68. **God's Fruit,** Chariot (Cook) ©1986 (preschool-primary), n.a. This 3 x 4-inch title in the "My Jesus Pocketbook" series teaches kids about love.

69. **I Know Why We Have Easter,** Chariot (Cook) ©1990 (preschool), n.a. A girl who lived when Jesus did tells the story of His death and resurrection.

70. **New Girl in Town,** Judy Baer, Bethany ©1988 (junior), 20,544 / 81,038. In Book 1 of the "Cedar River Daydreams" series, Lexi Leighton decides whether to compromise her values to gain new friends.

71. **If God Loves Me, Why Can't I Get My Locker Open?** Lorraine Peterson, Bethany ©1980 (young teen), 20,423 / 591,658. Ninety-one short readings explore teen problems with questions and Scriptures.

72. **Mandie and the Silent Catacombs,** Lois Gladys Leppard, Bethany ©1990 (junior), 20,162 / 65,532. Mandie and her friends track down a dark secret in the mysterious catacombs.

73. **Mandie and the Midnight Journey,** Lois Gladys Leppard, Bethany ©1989 (primary-junior), 20,041 / 99,325. The school year is over, and Mandie anticipates going home—to share her mother with a new baby.

74. **Mandie and the Medicine Man,** Lois Gladys Leppard, Bethany ©1986 (primary-junior), 20,038 / 129,423. Someone is tearing down the walls of the new hospital as quickly as they are built. Is a Cherokee superstition responsible?

75. **Mandie and the Abandoned Mine,** Lois Gladys Leppard, Bethany ©1987 (primary-junior), 19,857 / 124,534. Exploring a deserted farmhouse, Mandie and Joe discover a fancy dress that later disappears. Is it in the mine?

76. **Li'l Critters,** Chariot (Cook) ©1986 (preschool-primary), n.a. This 3 x 4-inch title in the "My Jesus Pocketbook" series

focuses on faith.

77. **Mandie and the Mysterious Bells,** Lois Gladys Leppard, Bethany ©1988 (primary-junior), 19,731 / 115,993. When church bells ring at midnight and bizarre writing appears on a wall, Mandie and friends must investigate.

78. **Praise,** Chariot (Cook) ©1987 (preschool-primary), n.a. This 3 x 4-inch title in the "My Jesus Pocketbook" series teaches how to praise God.

79. **Mandie and the Washington Nightmare,** Lois Gladys Leppard, Bethany ©1989 (primary-junior), 19,304 / 95,235. Mandie is invited to the White House. While there, she hears strange noises at night and thinks she sees George Washington.

80. **The Beginning,** Chariot (Cook) ©1986 (preschool-primary), n.a. This 3 x 4-inch title in the "My Jesus Pocketbook" series teaches about Creation.

81. **Mandie and the Charleston Phantom,** Lois Gladys Leppard, Bethany ©1986 (primary-junior), 19,248 / 127,612. Mandie learns about friendship and jealousy while investigating an oceanfront phantom.

82. **Tomorrow Is a Brand New Day,** Debby Boone and illus. by Gabriel Ferrer, Harvest ©1989 (preschool), 19,137 / 74,009. This picture book helps kids imagine about God's gift of a brand-new day.

83. **Mandie and the Hidden Treasure,** Lois Gladys Leppard, Bethany ©1987 (primary-junior), 19,034 / 117,371. Mandie and her friends search for an elusive treasure. Nearly forgotten history and an angry man threaten their search.

84. **Noah and the Floating Zoo,** Chariot (Cook) ©1986 (preschool-primary), n.a. This 3 x 4-inch title in the "My Jesus Pocketbook" series teaches trust.

85. **The New Testament in Pictures for Little Eyes,** Kenneth Taylor, Moody ©1989 (preschool-primary), 18,433 /

96,970. This title comprises New Testament stories from the classic *The Bible in Pictures for Little Eyes.*

86. **What I Like Best About Christmas**, Julie Cassat, Chariot (Cook) ©1989. (preschool), n.a. A little girl recounts how her family prepares to celebrate Christmas.

87. **Lent Is for Children**, Julie Kelemen, Liguori ©1987 (primary), 18,143 / 94,164. This book teaches kids Lenten basics through stories, activities, and prayers.

88. **Little Visits With God**, Allan Jahsmann and M.P. Simon, Concordia ©1957 (preschool-primary), 18,123 / 1 million+. The title includes 200 devotions with Scripture texts, stories, questions, adult Bible readings, and family prayers.

89. **Now You Can Read Stories From the Bible**, Elaine Ife and Rosalind Sutton, Nelson ©1983 (preschool-primary), n.a. Colorful art accompanies Bible stories for beginning readers.

90. **The First Christmas**, Penny Frank, Lion ©1986 (preschool-primary), 17,000 / 115,260.* Part of the "Lion Story Bible" series, this 24-page book offers an illustrated story of Christ's birth.

91. **Rock-a-Bye Christmas**, Marjorie Ainsborough Decker, World Bible ©1991 (preschool), n.a. Christian Mother Goose and other characters honor the true meaning of Christmas with this 96-page collection of new rhymes.

92. **Trouble With a Capital "T"**, Judy Baer, Bethany ©1988 (junior), 16,357 / 67,259. Lexi becomes the target of Minda's anger. Will she be able to respond with love?

93. **A Special Time of Year**, Chariot (Cook) ©1990 (preschool), n.a. Beginning with the joys of spring, this book reveals what makes spring so happy: Easter.

94. **A Donkey for Jesus**, Chariot (Cook) ©1990 (preschool-primary), n.a. This 3 x 4-inch title in the "My Jesus Pocketbook" series. teaches about Easter.

95. **Jonah and the Big Fish**, John and Kim Walton, Chariot (Cook) ©1986 (preschool-primary), n.a. This 3 x 4-inch title in the "My Jesus Pocketbook" series teaches obedience to God.

96. **Learning to Count**, Chariot (Cook) ©1986 (preschool-primary) n.a. This 3 x 4-inch title in the "My Jesus Pocketbook" series teaches kids to trust God.

97. **Daniel in the Lion's Den**, Chariot (Cook) ©1986 (preschool-primary), n.a. This 3 x 4-inch title in the "My Jesus Pocketbook" series focuses on trust.

98. **The Portal**, Bill Myers, Bethany ©1991 (junior), 15,768 / 15,768. First in the "Journeys to Fayrah" series, this fantasy takes Denise and Nathan on a journey to an unknown land and adventures.

99. **Adventures in the Big Thicket**, Ken Gire, Focus on the Family ©1990 (primary), 15,482 / 24,596. Fables about animals with Southern personas illustrate Proverbs.

100. **The Disappearing Stranger**, Lois Walfrid Johnson, Bethany ©1990 (junior), 15,297 / 48,115. First in the "Adventures of the Northwoods" series, this story introduces Kate O'Connell and her stepbrother Anders, who work together to solve a mystery.

The family circle is the supreme conductor of Christianity.
—Henry Drummond
FOCUS QUOTE

ADOPTION AGENCIES

Most of the agencies listed provide intercountry adoption placements. Religious organizations are noted with an asterisk. Service areas and requirements will differ with agency. Some agencies are more efficient than others so check with other clients who have adopted from the agency before applying.

Agency Name   *Address/City/Zip*

Alabama
*Wales Goebel Ministry .... 2908 Pump House Road, Birmingham 35243
Adoptions International of Alabama, Inc. .... 1538 Wellington View Road, Birmingham 35209

Arizona
*Globe International Adoption, Inc. .... 6334 West Villa Theresa Drive, Glendale 85308
Dillon Southwest .... P.O. Box 3535, Scottsdale 85257

California
*Catholic Charities San Francisco .... 2045 Lawton Street, San Francisco 94122
AASK America/Aid to Adoption of Special Kids .... 1540 Market, San Francisco 94102
Adoption Horizons .... P.O. Box 247, Arcata 95521
Adoption Services International .... 4737 Ortega Drive, Ventura 93003
Bal Jagat—Children's World, Inc. .... 9311 Farralone Avenue, Chatsworth 91311
Bay Area Adoption Services .... P.O. Box 2617, Sunnyvale 94087
Family Connections .... 1528 Oakdale Road, Modesto 95355
Life Adoption Services .... 440 West Main Street, Tustin 92680

Colorado
*Hand in Hand International .... 4695 Barnes Road, Colorado Springs 80917
Friends of Children of Various Nations, Inc. .... 600 Gilpin Street, Denver 80218
Universal Family .... 315 South Clay, Denver 80219

Connecticut
Family Service, Inc. .... 92 Vine Street, New Britain 06052
Heal the Children Northeast, Inc. .... Box 129, New Milford 06776
International Alliance for Children .... 23 South Main Street, New Milford 06776

District of Columbia
ASIA .... 7720 Alaska Avenue N.W., Washington 20012
The American Adoption Agency .... 1228 M Street N.W., Washington 20005
The Barker Foundation .... 114 River Road N.W., Washington 20016
World Child .... 121 Colorado Avenue N.W., Washington 20011

Florida
*Shepherd Care Ministries, Inc. .... 5935 Taft Street. Suite B, Hollywood 33021
Adoption Center, Inc. .... 500 N. Maitland Avenue, Maitland 32751
Suncoast International Adoptions .... P.O. Box 332, Indian Rocks Beach 34635
Universal Aid for Children .... P.O. Box 610246, North Miami 33162

Georgia
Children's Services International .... 1819 Peachtree Road #318, Atlanta 30309
Homes for Children International .... 1655 Peachtree Street NE, #1109, Atlanta 30309
Illien Adoptions, International .... 1254 Piedmont Avenue NE, Atlanta 30309

Agency Name	Address/City/Zip

Open Door Adoption Agency . . . . P.O. Box 4, Thomasville 31799

Idaho
Adoptions In Idaho . . . . P.O. Box 729, Post Falls 83854

Illinois
*Bensenville Home Society . . . . 331 South York Road, Bensenville 60106
*Evangelical Child and Family Agency . . . . 1530 N. Main Street, Wheaton 60187
*Sunny Ridge Family Center . . . . 2S426 Orchard Road, Wheaton 60187
Adoption World . . . . One E. Erie, #235, Chicago 60611
Children's Home and Aid Society of Illinois . . . . 730 N. Main street, Rockford 61103
Travelers and Immigrants Aid of Chicago . . . . 327 LaSalle Street, Chicago 60604

Iowa
Hillcrest Family Services . . . . 1727 1st Avenue SE, Cedar Rapids 52402

Kansas
*Gentle Shepherd Child Placement Services . . . . P.O. Box 1172, Olathe 66061

Maine
*International Christian Adoption Agency . . . . 60 W. River Road, Waterville 04901
Growing thru Adoption . . . . P.O. Box 7082, Lewiston 04240

Maryland
*Associated Catholic Charities of Baltimore, Inc. . . . . . . 320 Cathedral Street, Baltimore 21201
ACORN . . . . 10784A Hickory Ridge Road, Columbia 21043

Massachusetts
Aliance for Children, Inc. . . . . 110 Cedar Street, Wellesley 02181
Cambridge Adoption and Counseling Associates, Inc. . . Box 190, Cambridge 02142
International Adoptions, Inc. 282 Moody Street, Waltham 02154
World Adoption Services, Inc. . . . . 161 Auburn Street, Newton 02166

Michigan
*Bethany Christian Services . . . . 901 Eastern Avenue NE, Grand Rapids 49503
Americans for International Aid and Adoption . . . . 877 S. Adams, Birmingham 48011
Children's Hope Adoption Services . . . . 7823 South Whiteville Road, Shepherd 48883
Foreign Adoption Consultants . . . . P.O. Box 489, Kalamazoo 49005

Minnesota
*Catholic Charities Archdiocese, St. Paul/Minneapolis . . 215 Old 6th Street, St. Paul 55102
*Lutheran Social Services . . . . 2414 Park Avenue South, Minneapolis 55404
Building Families Through Adoption . . . . Box 550, Dawson 56232
Children's Home Society of Minnesota . . . . 2230 Como Avenue, St. Paul 55108
Crossroads, Inc. . . . . 4940 Viking Drive, #388, Edina 55435
HOPE International Family Services Inc. . . . . 421 Main Street, Stillwater 55082

Missouri
*Highlands Child Placement Services . . . . 1445 Boonville Avenue, Springfield 65802
*Love Basket, Inc. . . . . 8965 Old Lemay Ferry Road, Hillsboro 63050
Adoption Resource Center, R&R Health Services . . . . . . 2207 Park Avenue, St. Louis 63104
Family Adoption and Counseling Services, Inc. . . . . 9378 Olive Street Road, #320, St. Louis 63132
Worldwide Love for Children . . . . 1221 E. Republic Road, Springfield 65807

Montana
Adoptions in Montana . . . . 554 W. Broadway, #557A, Missoula 59802
Montana Intercountry Adoption, Inc. . . . . 109 S. 8th Avenue, Bozeman 59715

New Jersey
Children of the World .... 855 Bloomfield Avenue, Glen Ridge 07028
Children's Services International, Inc. .... P.O. Box 688, Long Valley 07853
Golden Cradle Adoption Agency .... 2201 Route 38, Cherry Hill 08002

New Mexico
Rainbow House International .... 19676 Highway 85, Belen 87002

New York
*Evangelical Adoption and Family Service, Inc. .... 119 Church Street, North Syracuse 13212
Adoption and Counseling Service, Inc. .... 1 Fayette Park, Syracuse 13202
Family Focus Adoption Agency .... P.O. Box 388, Glen Oaks 11004
Family Resources .... 226 N. Highland Avenue, Ossining 10562
Family Service of Westchester, Inc................. 470 Mamaroneck Avenue, White Plains 10605
Parsons Child and Family Center .... 845 Central Avenue, Albany 12206

North Dakota
*Covenant Children .... P.O. Box 2344, Bismark 58502
New Horizons Foreign Adoption Services, Inc. .... 2876 Woodland Place, Bismark 58501

Ohio
*Lutheran Social Services of Central Ohio .... 57 E. Main Street, Columbus 43215
Spaulding for Children—Beech Brook .... 3737 Lander Road, Cleveland 44124

Oklahoma
*Deaconess Home .... 5401 N. Portland Avenue, Oklahoma City
                                              73112
*Dillon's Children's Services, Inc. .... 7615 E. 63rd Place South #215, Tulsa 74133
Project Adopt .... 1613 N. Broadway, Oklahoma City 73103
Small Miracles International, Inc. .... 7430 SE 15th, #220, Midwest City 73110

Oregon
*Give Us This Day, Inc. .... 2207B Portland Road, P.O. Box 796, Newberg
                                              97132
*Holt International Children's Services .... P.O. Box 2880, Eugene 97402
Plan Loving Adoptions Now, Inc. .... P.O. Box 667, McMinnville 97128

Pennsylvania
*Catholic Social Services .... 222 N. 17th Street, Room 329, Philadelphia
                                              19103
*Tressler Lutheran Service Associates .... 25 W. Springettsbury avenue, York 17403
Adoptions International Inc. .... Benson Manor, #101, Jenkintown 19046
Children and Home Study Associates .... 31 E. Franklin Street, Media 19063
Love the Children .... 221 W. Broad Street, Quakertown 18951
The Adoption Agency .... 63 W. Lancaster Avenue, Ardmore 19003
Welcome House .... P.O. Box 836, Doylestown 18901

South Carolina
*Love Life Adoption Agency .... P.O. Box 247, Florence 29503

Tennessee
*Catholic Charities of Tennessee, Inc. .... 30 White Bridge Road, Nashville 37205
*Holston United Methodist Home for Children .... P.O. Box 188, Greenville 37744

Texas
*Agape Social Services, Inc. .... 3200 Maple, #400, Dallas 75201
Adoption Resource Consultants of North Texas .... P.O. Box 1224, Richardson 75083
Child Placement of Texas .... 615 N. 2nd Street, Killeen 76541
The Care Connection, Inc. .... 400 Harvey Street, San Marcos 78666

| Agency Name | Address/City/Zip |

Vermont
Rootwings Ministries, Inc. . . . . .P.O. Box 614, Barre 05641

Virginia
*Catholic Family Services . . . . .4206 Chamberlayne Avenue, Richmond
                                                                 23227
*Family Life Services, Inc. . . . . .520 Eldon Street, Lynchburg 24501
Family Services of Tidewater, Inc. . . . . .222 19th Street, West Norfolk 23517
Pan American Adoption Agency, Inc. . . . . .12604 Kahns Road, Manassas 22111

Washington
*Catholic Community Services . . . . .1715 E. Cherry, P.O. Box 22608, Seattle
                                                                 98122
*New Hope of Washington . . . . .1100 Lake City Way NE, Seattle 98125
*Open Arms . . . . .16429 NE 133rd Court, Redmond 98052
*Regular Baptist Child Placement Agency . . . . .Box 16353, Seattle 98116
Adoption Advocates International . . . . .658 Black Diamond Road, Port Angeles
                                                                 98362
Western Assoc of Concerned Adoptive Parents
  (WACAP) . . . . .P.O. Box 88948, Seattle 98138

Wisconsin
*Evangelical Child and Family Agency . . . . .2401 N. Mayfair Road, Milwaukee 53226
*Lutheran Soc Services, Wisconsin and Upper Michigan .3200 W. Highland Boulevard, Milwaukee
                                                                 53208
Adoption Option, Inc. . . . . .1804 Chapman Drive, Waukesha 53186
Pauquette Children's Service . . . . .325 W. Connant, P.O. Box 162, Portage
                                                                 53901

Source: *The Adoption Option* by Angela Elwell Hunt. Published by Victor Books. Copyright © 1989 by SP Publications, Inc.
Used by permission.

GALLUP SURVEY INDICATES TEENAGERS ARE SPIRITUALLY RESPONSIVE

Psychological studies and survey results show deep interest in spiritual matters before the years of young adulthood when preoccupation with other matters may result in young adults temporarily losing their faith. The findings below are based on telephone interviews with 513 teenagers, 13–17, from June 26 to July 2, 1991.

Do you believe that God loves you?

Yes	93%
No	2%
Do not believe in God	2%
Not sure	3%

Do you think Jesus Christ was God or the Son of God, another religious leader like Muhammad or Buddha, or do you think Jesus Christ never actually lived?

God or Son of God	86%
Just another religious leader	6%
Never actually lived	3%
Not sure	5%

How often do you pray (read the Bible) alone?

	Pray when alone	Read the Bible when alone
Frequently	42%	13%
Occasionally	32%	31%
Hardly ever	17%	32%
Never	9%	24%

Source: Princeton Religion Research Center. Copyright © 1991. Used by permission.

10 MISTAKES PARENTS MAKE WITH TEENAGERS

1. Do as I say, not as I do
2. I'm the adult. I'm right
3. Because I said so, that's why
4. You want to be what?
5. This room's a pigsty
6. Can't you do anything right?
7. Where did you find him?
8. You did what?
9. Do you mind if we talk about something else?
10. I'm kind of busy right now. Could you come back later?

Source: Jay Kesler in *Ten Mistakes Parents Make with Teenagers (and How to Avoid Them)*. Published by Wolgemuth & Hyatt Publishers, Inc. Copyright © 1988. Used by permission.

WHAT DO PARENTS WORRY ABOUT MOST?

That their children won't remain
  true to their faith 56%
That their teens will abuse drugs,
  alcohol or smoking 41%
About their children's safety 34%
About the quality of friends in
  whom their teens confide 32%
About their teens' dating
  habits 20%
About peer pressure affecting
  their children 15%

Source: *Teach* magazine.

WHAT DOES FOCUS ON THE FAMILY DO?

Focus on the Family is familiar to most people. But few realize the total scope of the organization. A team of 750 people work together in more than 52 separate ministries. Included among them are:

* *Focus on the Family* magazine, going to nearly 1.7 million households monthly
* *Citizen* magazine, going to 210,000 households monthly
* *Physician* magazine, going to 22,000 doctors bimonthly
* *Clubhouse and Clubhouse Jr.* magazines for children, going to 80,000 and 85,000 households monthly, respectively
* *Breakaway* (for boys) and *Brio* (for girls) magazines for junior highers, going to 70,000 and 100,000 households monthly, respectively
* Book publishing, such as *Prodigals and Those Who Love Them* by Ruth Bell Graham
* Films and videos, such as *Twice Pardoned, A Man Called Norman,* and *Molder of Dreams*
* A church bulletin read by more than 3 million people each month
* Basketball camps, mostly for boys of single mothers
* "Adventures in Odyssey" dramatic

broadcast for children, heard on 1150 radio facilities each week
* "Family News in Focus" broadcast, heard on 766 radio facilities each week
* Armed Forces Radio Network broadcast, heard around the world on military bases and ships at sea
* Family Research Council, defending family values in Washington, D.C.
* Support for 2,000 Crisis Pregnancy centers in North America
* "Enfoque a la Familia," the Spanish-language broadcast heard on 522 radio facilities in the U.S. and across Latin America
* Videos, such as "Adventures in Odyssey"
* "Focus on the Family" broadcast on 1600 radio stations in U.S. and Canada
* International outreach, broadcast on 25 state-owned radio stations in Russia; weekly column by Dr. Dobson in Moscow newspaper, reaching 5.5 million readers

Source: Focus on the Family. Statistics current as of November 1991.

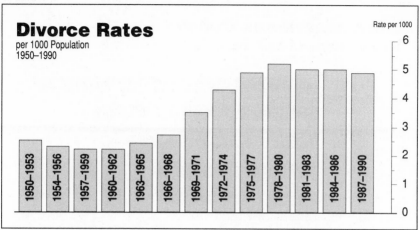

Divorce Rates
per 1000 Population
1950–1990

Source: *The American Family under Siege*. Published by Family Research Council, Washington, D.C.

Age at Time of First Marriage Increases

■ Men   □ Women

Source: U.S. Census Bureau

66 99
FOCUS
QUOTE
A good marriage is not one where perfection reigns; it is a relationship where a healthy perspective overlooks a multitude of "unresolvables."
—Dr. James C. Dobson

66 99
FOCUS
QUOTE
Husbands, wives, children are not getting enough family life. Nobody is. People are hurting-- both in the suburbs and the inner city.—Arlie Hochschild in *The Second Shift.*

COUPLES MOST LIKELY TO GET A DIVORCE

1. Those who marry young.
2. Those who have had more than one sexual partner prior to marriage.
3. Those with either less than a high-school education or two or more years of graduate school. (Least likely to divorce are four-year college graduates.)
4. Women who earn $50,000 or more annually.
5. Childless couples.
6. Among couples with children, those with daughters are more likely to divorce than those with sons.
7. Those who have been married before (50% divorce, 80% remarry).
8. Those whose parents were divorced.
9. Those who lived together before getting married.

Source: *Single Adult Passages* by Carolyn A. Koons and Michael J. Anthony. Copyright © 1991. Published by Baker Book House. Used by permission.

What Americans Consider Very Important in Life

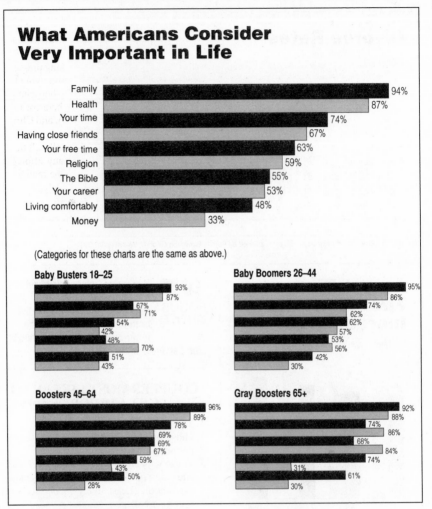

Family 94%
Health 87%
Your time 74%
Having close friends 67%
Your free time 63%
Religion 59%
The Bible 55%
Your career 53%
Living comfortably 48%
Money 33%

(Categories for these charts are the same as above.)

Baby Busters 18–25
93%
87%
67%
71%
54%
42%
48%
70%
51%
43%

Baby Boomers 26–44
95%
86%
74%
62%
62%
57%
53%
56%
42%
30%

Boosters 45–64
96%
89%
78%
69%
69%
67%
59%
43%
50%
28%

Gray Boosters 65+
92%
88%
74%
86%
68%
84%
74%
31%
61%
30%

Source: Barna Research Group. Used by permission.

WHO ARE THE BUSTERS, BOOMERS, AND BOOSTERS?

	Born	#/millions	Characteristics
Baby Busters	1965–1983	66	Both indulged and neglected; range from affluent to latchkey.
Baby Boomers	1946–1964	77	Individualistic; status/success important; likes involvement
Boosters	1927–1945	49	Institutional; loyal and patriotic; stability and security important
Gray Boosters	AD33–1926	30	Blazing new trails, shattering stereotype expectations

REDEFINING THE FAMILY

We seem to be headed for a fundamental redefinition of the family. The Census Bureau currently defines the family as "two or more persons related by birth, marriage, or adoption who reside in the same household." In the future, however, there will be increasing pressure to redefine families as "a group of people who love and care for each other." And vying for the title of "family" will be a number of living arrangements: single-parent households (including those of women who had children through artificial insemination), heterosexual and homosexual couples living together without marriage (some with children), and Christians living in family-like residential communities.

However we define family, most churches I work with are targeting virtually all their ministries to the intact nuclear family. It is the unusual church that makes any effort to address the special needs of single-parent and stepparent families, recognizes the reality of "alternate living arrangements," or ministers to those living together cooperatively.

Tom Sine in *Wild Hope*. Published by Word, Inc. Used by permission.

A Look at America's 41.9 Million Households

The percentage of traditional families—married couples with or without children—is at its lowest rate in at least 200 years, the 1990 census found.

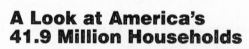

1960	75%
1980	60%
1990	55.2%
Projected 2000	53%

Highest: Utah	64.8%
USA average	55.2%
Lowest: District of Columbia	25.3%

Headed by Single Mothers
Single mothers make up more than 60% of female-headed households. The rest are women with whom other relatives live.

Highest: District of Columbia	19.5%
USA average	11.6%
Lowest: North Dakota	7.3%

Headed by Single Fathers
Single fathers make up about 40% of male-headed households. The rest are men with whom other relatives live.

Highest: California	4.6%
USA average	3.4%
Lowest: Iowa	2.4%

Non–Family Households
Almost 30% of households were non-family households—the highest rate ever—made up mainly of people living alone. Other non-family households include unmarried heterosexual partners, gay couples, and roommates.

1960	15%
1980	27%
1990	30%

Living Alone
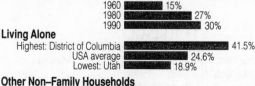

Highest: District of Columbia	41.5%
USA average	24.6%
Lowest: Utah	18.9%

Other Non–Family Households

Highest: District of Columbia	9.6%
USA average	5.3%
Lowest: Mississippi	2.6%

Source: Census Bureau

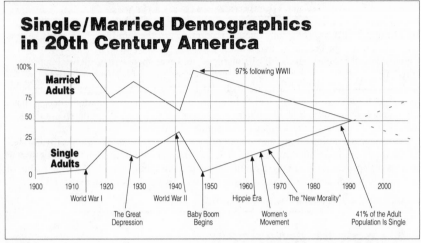

Single/Married Demographics in 20th Century America

Married Adults

97% following WWII

Single Adults

1900 1910 1920 1930 1940 1950 1960 1970 1980 1990 2000

World War I   World War II   Hippie Era   The "New Morality"

The Great Depression   Baby Boom Begins   Women's Movement   41% of the Adult Population Is Single

Source: *Single Adult Passages* by Carolyn A. Koons and Michael J. Anthony. Copyright © 1991. Published by Baker Book House. Used by permission.

FOCUS BOOKS

National Single Adult Ministries Resource Directory 1991/92 edited by Jerry Jones. The complete "yellow pages" directory for single adults. Useful information for effective ministry and networking with singles ministry people and resources. Published by Single Adults Ministry Resources/NavPress.

Single Adult Passages by Carolyn A. Koons and Michael J. Anthony. The first significant study specifically on singleness as a phenomenon among Christian adults. Based on a survey of more than 1300 single adult Christians across the U.S. and Canada. Published by Baker Book House.

What Singles Look for in Friends

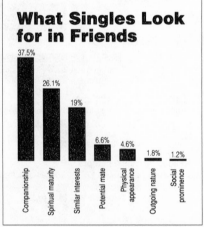

37.5% Companionship
26.1% Spiritual maturity
19%   Similar interests
6.6%   Potential mate
4.6%   Physical appearance
1.8%   Outgoing nature
1.2%   Social prominence

Source: *Single Adult Passages* by Carolyn A. Koons and Michael J. Anthony. Copyright © 1991. Published by Baker Book House. Used by permission.

MAGAZINES FOR SINGLES

Christian Single, 127 Ninth Avenue North, #140, Nashville, TN 37234. Monthly.
Single Impact, 7245 College Street, Lima, NY 14485. Phone: 716-582-2790. Quarterly.
Singles News, Christian Singles International, Box 543, Harrison, OH 45030. Monthly.
Singles Scene, P.O. Box 310, Allardt, TN 38504. Phone: 615-879-4625. Monthly.
Today's Singles, 1933 W. Wisconsin, Milwaukee, WI 53233. Phone: 414-344-7300. Quarterly.

Growth of Single Adult Population

in U.S. since 1970

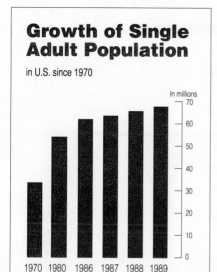

Source: *National Single Adult Ministries Resource Directory, 1991/92.* Jerry D. Jones, editor. Copyright © 1991. Published by Singles Ministry Resources/NavPress. Used by permission.

PEOPLE LIVING ALONE

American Demographics magazine projects a 17.7% increase from 1990 to 2000 in the number of householders who live alone.

The most dramatic growth in people living alone will be among those aged 45 to 64, as baby boomers become middle-aged.

Those living alone who are expected to show the largest increase over the next decade are:

	Percent Change 1990–2000
Men ages 45–64	50.5
Women ages 45–64	35.2
Men 65 and older	19.4
Women 65 and older	13.0
Women ages 25–44	9.8
Men ages 25–44	6.1

Reprinted from *National Single Adult Ministries Resource Directory 1991/92.* Jerry D. Jones, editor. Copyright © 1991. Published by Singles Ministry Resources/NavPress. Used by permission. Sources: *American Demographics* magazine and U.S. Bureau of the Census.

Religious Attitudes of Singles

■ Never- marrieds
■ Divorced, separated, widowed
□ Married

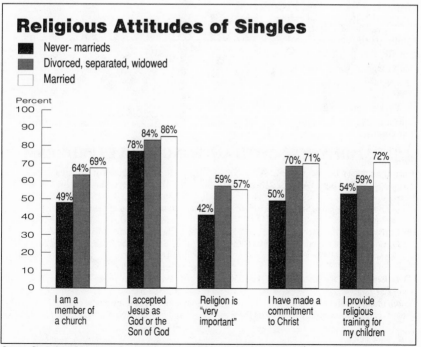

Source: *Single Adult Passages* by Carolyn A. Koons and Michael J. Anthony. Copyright © 1991. Published by Baker Book House. Used by permission.

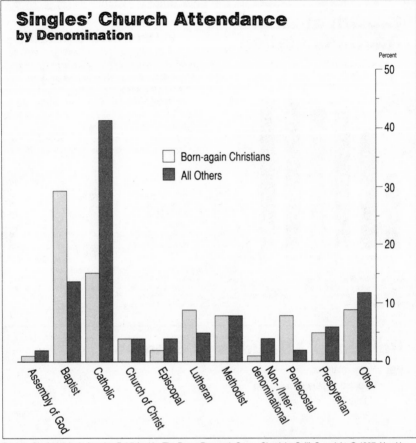

Singles' Church Attendance
by Denomination

☐ Born-again Christians
■ All Others

Source: *Single Adults in America*. Published by The Barna Research Group, Glendale, Calif. Copyright © 1987. Used by permission.

DENOMINATIONS WITH A STRONG SINGLES PROGRAM

American Baptist Churches in the USA
  Box 851, Valley Forge, PA 19482 215-768-2271
Assemblies of God
  1445 Boonville Avenue, Springfield, MO 65807
  417-862-2781
The Christian and Missionary Alliance
  P.O. Box 35000, Colorado Springs, CO 80935-
  3500 719-599-5999
Church of God
  P.O. Box 2430, Cleveland, TN 37311 615-478-
  7229
Church of the Nazarene
  6401 The Paseo, Kansas City, MO 64131 816-
  333-7000
Episcopal Church
  P.O. Box 12385, Dallas, TX 214-363-5471

Evangelical Free Church of America
  1515 E. 66th Street, Minneapolis, MN 55423
  612-866-3343
International Church of the Foursquare Gospel
  1910 Sunset Blvd., Los Angeles, CA 90026
The Lutheran Church—Missouri Synod
  1333 S. Kirkwood Road, St. Louis, MO 63122
  314-965-9000
Presbyterian Church (USA)
  100 Witherspoon Street, Louisville, KY 40202
  502-569-5487
Southern Baptist Convention
  127 9th Avenue North, Nashville, TN 37234
  615-251-2575

Source: *National single Adults Resource Directory*

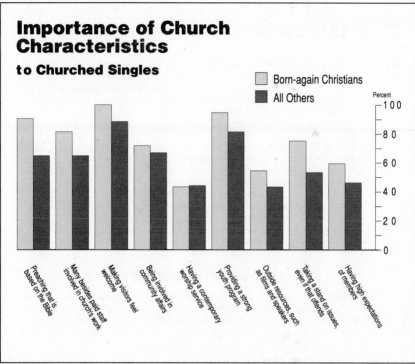

Importance of Church Characteristics

to Churched Singles

Source: *Single Adults in America.* Published by The Barna Research Group, Glendale, CA. Copyright © 1987. Used by permission.

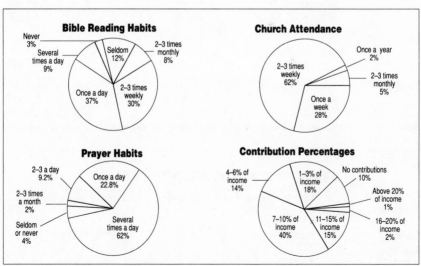

Source: *Single Adult Passages* by Carolyn A. Koons and Michael J. Anthony. Copyright © 1991. Published by Baker Book House, Used by permission.

A YEAR'S READING PROGRAM FOR SINGLES

January	*God's Call to the Single Adult* by Michael Cavanaugh, Whitaker/Oasis House
February	*Remarriage and God's Renewing Grace: A Positive, Biblical Ethic for Divorced Christians* by Dwight Hervey Small, Baker Books or *The Blessing* by Gary Smalley and John Trent, Thomas Nelson, Inc.
March	*Intimacy* by Terry Hershey, Harvest House
April	*Singles Ask* by Harold Ivan Smith, Augsburg
May	*Celebration of Discipline* by Richard Foster, Harper and Row
June	*Healing for Damaged Emotions* by David Seamands, Victor Books
July	*Too Close Too Soon* by Jim Talley and Bobbie Reed, Thomas Nelson
August	*Growing Through Divorce* by Jim Smoke, Harvest House or *Wide My World, Narrow My Bed* by Luci Swindoll, Multnomah Press
September	*Positively Single* by Harold Ivan Smith, Victor Books
October	*Ordering Your Private World* by Gordon McDonald, Thomas Nelson
November	*Becoming a Friend and Lover* by Dick Purnell, Here's Life
December	*Inside Out* by Larry Crabb, NavPress

WHAT TO SAVE FOR RETIREMENT

To live a comfortable, nonworking life, you'll need at least 75 percent of your preretirement income. Part of that money will come from social security and maybe a pension. For the rest, you'll have to save. Here's what a typical working couple should be putting aside each year, assuming 5 percent wage inflation and retirement at the age of 65.

Current salary	Current age	Needed to invest annually*: With a company pension	With a double IRA but no pension+
$35,000	30	$ 3,660	$ 4,000
	40	$ 4,360	$ 5,990
	50	$ 6,000	$ 9,970
$50,000	30	$ 7,590	$ 8,350
	40	$ 8,940	$11,790
	50	$12,280	$17,950
$75,000	30	$15,270	$18,050
	40	$17,890	$23,220
	50	$24,730	$33,700

*At 6 percent, taxed in a state and federal bracket of 30 percent. +Including $6,000 for the IRAs. Source: Ernst & Young.

CHURCH-RELATED RETIREMENT CENTERS

Retirement centers listed below have a population of 100 or more and offer independent living units.

Name	Address/Phone	Affiliation
Alabama		
Episcopal Place	1112 S. 26th Street, Birmingham 35205/205-939-0085	Episcopal
Fair Haven Retirement Comm	1424 Montclair Road, Birmingham 35210/205-956-4150	Methodist
John Knox Manor Ret Tower	4401 Narrow Lane Road, Montgomery 36116/205-288-6462	Presbyterian

Name	Address/Phone	Affiliation
New Pilgrim Towers	3416 7th Avenue S., Birmingham 35222/205-323-3940	Baptist
Princeton Towers	909 Princeton Avenue, SW, Birmingham 35211/205-326-9197	Baptist
Wesley Acres	700 Cedar Lake Road, Decatur 35603/205-355-8281	Methodist
Wesley Manor	210 Honeysuckle Road, Dothan 36301/205-792-0921	Methodist
Wesley Terrace	1365 Gatewood Drive, Auburn 36830/205-826-7200	Methodist
Westminster Village	500 Spanish Fort Boulevard, Spanish Fort 36527/205-626-7007	Presbyterian

Arizona

Baptist Village	11315 W. Peoria Avenue, Youngtown 85363/602-972-2371	Baptist
Beatitudes Campus of Care	1616 W. Glendale Avenue, Phoenix 85021/602-995-2611	United Church of Christ
Christian Care	11812 N. 19th Avenue, Phoenix 85029/602-861-3241	Christian Churches
Glencroft Retirement Comm	8611 N. 67th Avenue, Glendale 85302/602-939-9475	Mennonite, Apostolic, Christian, Friends
Good Shepherd Ret Center	10323 W. Olive Avenue, Peoria 85345/602-974-2555	Lutheran
Orangewood	7550 N. 16th Street, Phoenix 85020/602-944-4455	American Baptist
Paradise Valley Estates	11645 N. 25th Place, Phoenix 85028/602-482-7100	Baptist
Tanner Gardens Apartments	4420 S. 18th Place, Phoenix 85040/602-268-8866	African Methodist/Episcopal
Waymark Gardens	5325 W. Butler Drive, Glendale 85302/602-931-7002	Christian Church
Wooddale Retirement Comm	18616 N. 99th Avenue, Sun City 85373/602-933-0022	Lutheran Brethren

Arkansas

Good Samaritan Cedar Lodge	5 Cortez Road, Hot Springs Village 71909/501-922-2000	Lutheran
Good Shepherd Ecumenical Retirement Center	2701 Aldersgate Road, Little Rock 72205/501-224-7200	Ecumenical Ret Board
Parkway Village	14300 Rock Creek Parkway, Little Rock 72211/501-227-2036	Baptist

California

Alhambra	2400 S. Fremont Avenue, Alhambra 91803/213-289-6211	Lutheran
Atherton Baptist Homes	214 S. Atlantic Boulevard, Alhambra 91801/818-289-4178	Baptist
Auburn Ravine Terrace	750 Auburn Ravine Road, Auburn 95603/916-823-6131	Congregational
Baptist Gardens	1011 Pine Avenue, Long Beach 90813/213-432-4454	Baptist
Bellflower Friendship Manor	9550 E. Oak Street, Bellflower 90706/213-867-9550	Baptist
Bethany Center	580 Capp Street, San Francisco 94110/415-821-4515	United Methodist
Bethany Towers	1745 N. Gramercy Place, Hollywood 90028/213-467-3121	Christian Church/DCC
Bethlehem Towers, Inc.	801 Tupper Street, Santa Rosa 95404/707-544-5560	Lutheran
Brethren Hillcrest Homes	2705 Mountain View Drive, La Verne 91750/714-593-4917	Church of the Brethren
Buttes Christian Manor	223 F Street, Marysville 95901/916-742-2421	Christian Church/DCC
California Christian Home	8417 E. Mission Drive, Rosemead 91770/818-287-0438	Christian Church/DCC
Canterbury Woods	651 Sinex Avenue, Pacific Grove 93950/408-373-3111	Episcopal
Carlotta	41505 Carlotta Drive, Palm Desert 92260/619-346-5420	Lutheran
Carlsbad by the Sea	2855 Carlsbad Boulevard, Carlsbad 92008/619-729-2377	Lutheran
Carmel Valley Manor	8545 Carmel Valley Road, Carmel 93923/408-624-1281	Congregational
Casa de la Paloma	133 S. Kenwood Street, Glendale 91205/818-243-0337	Presbyterian
Casa De Verdugo (Verdugo Home, Inc.)	155 0 175 N. Girard Street, Hemet 92344/714-658-2274	Baptist
Covenant Village of Turlock	2125 N. Olive Avenue, Turlock 95380/209-632-9976	Evangelical Covenant
El Bethel Arms	1234 McAllister Street, San Francisco 94115/415-567-3950	Christian Church
El Bethel Terrace	1099 Fillmore Street, San Francisco 94115/415-931-4496	Baptist
Fairhaven Retirement Center	4360 63rd Street, Sacramento 95820/916-452-2100	World Gospel Mission
Fellowship Manor	1201 Golden Gate Avenue, San Francisco 94115/415-922-0154	Bethel AME Church
Fickett Towers	14801 Sherman Way, Van Nuys 91405/818-988-8628	Baptist
Forest Hill Manor	551 Gibson, Pacific Grove 93950/408-375-5125	Methodist
Good Shepherd Manor	4411-11th Avenue, Los Angeles 90043/213-299-5735	Episcopal
Grand Lake Garden	401 Santa Clara Avenue, Oakland 94610/415-893-8897	Baptist
Inland Christian Home	1950 S. Mountain Avenue, Ontario 91761/714-983-0084	Christian Reformed
Judson Terrace Homes	3000 Augusta Street, San Luis Obispo 93401/805-544-1600	Baptist
Kern Crest Manor	250 E. Tulare Street, Shafter 93263/805-746-6521	Mennonite Brethren
Lake Park Ret Residence	1850 Alice Street, Oakland 94612/415-835-5511	United Methodist
Life's Garden	450 Old San Francisco Road, Sunnyvale 94086/408-245-5433	Presbyterian
Lincoln Glen Manor	2671 Plummer Avenue, San Jose 95125/408-265-3222	Mennonite Brethren
Long Beach Brethren Manor	3333 Pacific Place, Long Beach 90806/213-426-6547	Church of the Brethren
Los Gatos Meadows	110 Wood Road, Los Gatos 95030/408-354-0211	Episcopal
Luther Tower	1455 Second Avenue, San Diego 92101/619-234-1271	Lutheran

Name	Address/Phone	Affiliation
Lytton Gardens and Health Care Center	656 Lytton Avenue, Palo Alto 94301/415-328-3300	Presbyterian/Methodist
Martin Luther Tower, Inc.	1001 Franklin Street, San Francisco 94109/415-771-9931	Lutheran
Mennonite Brethren Homes, Inc.	856 S. Reed Avenue, Reedley 93654/209-638-3615	Brethren
Monte Vista Grove Homes	2889 San Pasqual Street, Pasadena 91107/818-796-6135	Presbyterian
Mount Miguel Covenant Vil	325 Kempton Street, Spring Valley 92077/619-479-4790	Evangelical Covenant
Mount Rubidoux Manor	3993 Tenth Street, Riverside 92501/714-684-3154	Baptist
Mount San Antonio Gardens	900 E. Harrison Avenue, Pomona 91767/714-624-5061	United Church of Christ
Neighborhood Manor, Inc.	1200 Woodrow Avenue, Modesto 95350/209-526-0308	Assembly of God
Oak Center Towers	1515 Market Street, Oakland 94607/415-465-1166	Episcopal
Piedmont Gardens	110-41st Street, Oakland 94611/415-654-7172	Baptist
Pilgrim Haven	373 Pine Lane, Los Altos 94022/415-948-8291	Baptist
Pilgrim Tower for the Deaf	1207 S. Vermont Avenue, Los Angeles 90006/213-387-6541	Lutheran
Plymouth Square	1319 N. Madison Street, Stockton 95202/209-466-4341	Congregational
Plymouth Tower	3401 Lemon Street, Riverside 92501/714-686-8202	Congregational
Plymouth Village of Redlands	900 Salem Drive, Redlands 92373/714-793-1233	Baptist
Presidio Gate Apartments	2770 Lombard Street, San Francisco 94123/415-567-1050	Episcopal
Quaker Gardens	12151 Dale Street, Stanton 90680/714-530-9100	Friends
Redwoods	40 Camino Alto, Mill Valley 94941/415-383-2741	Community Church
Regents Point	19191 Harvard Avenue, Irvine 82715/714-854-9500	Presbyterian
Rohlff's Memorial Manor, Inc.	2400 Fair Drive, Napa 94558/707-255-9555	Lutheran
Rosewood Retirement Comm	1301 New Stine Road, Bakersfield 93309/805-834-0620	Baptist
Royal Oaks Manor	1763 Royal Oaks Drive, Duarte 91010/818-359-9371	Presbyterian
Saint John's Retirement Vil	135 Woodland Avenue, Woodland 95695/916-662-1290	United Church of Christ
Salem Lutheran Home	2361 E. 29th Street, Oakland 94606/415-534-3637	Lutheran
Samarkand of Santa Barbara	2550 Treasure Drive, Santa Barbara 93105/805-687-0701	Covenant
San Joaquin Gardens	5555 N. Fresno Street, Fresno 93710/209-439-4770	Baptist
Seaview Lutheran Plaza	2800 Pacific View Drive, Corona Del Mar 92112/714-720-0888	Lutheran
Sequoias-Portola Valley	501 Portola Road, Portola Valley 94028/415-851-1501	Presbyterian
Sequoias-San Francisco	1400 Geary Boulevard, San Francisco 94109/415-922-9700	Presbyterian
Solheim Lutheran Home	2236 Merton Avenue, Los Angeles 90041/213-257-7518	Lutheran
Spring Lake Village	5555 Montgomery Drive, Santa Rosa 95405/707-538-8400	Episcopal
St. Paul's Manor and Health Care Center	P.O. Box 128048, San Diego 92112/619-239-2097	Episcopal
St. Paul's Towers	100 Bay Place, Oakland 94610/415-835-4700	Episcopal
Summerfield Plaza East & West	2624 Traction Avenue, Sacramento 95815/916-924-0961	National Church Residences
Sunny View Lutheran Home	22445 Cupertino Road, Cupertino 95014/408-253-4300	Lutheran
Town and Country Manor	555 E. Memory Lane, Santa Ana 92706/714-547-7581	Christian and Missionary Alliance
Town Park Towers	60 N. Third Street, San Jose 95112/408-288-8750	Presbyterian
Upland Manor	1125 W. Arrow Highway, Upland 91786/714-985-1215	Brethren
Valle Verde Ret Center	900 Calle de Los Amigos, Santa Barbara 93105/805-687-1571	Baptist
Valley Village	390 N. Winchester Blvd, Santa Clara 95050/408-241-7750	United Church of Christ
Vista Towers	3000 Leeward Avenue, Los Angeles 90005/213-386-2786	Baptist
Walnut Manor	891 S. Walnut Street, Anaheim 92802/714-776-7150	Lutheran
Wesley Manor	1655 S. Winchester Blvd, Campbell 95008/408-374-9511	Methodist
Western Park Apartments	1280 Laguna Street, San Francisco 94115/415-922-5436	Presbyterian
Westlake Christian Terrace	275-28th Street, Oakland 94611/415-893-2998	Christian Church
White Sands of La Jolla	7450 Olivetas Avenue, La Jolla 92037/619-454-4201	Presbyterian
Windsor Manor	1230 E. Windsor Road, Glendale 91205/818-244-7219	Presbyterian
Wysong Plaza	111 N. Chapel Avenue, Alhambra 91801/818-284-3956	National Church Residences

Colorado

Name	Address/Phone	Affiliation
Bonell Good Samaritan Ctr	708-22nd Street, Greeley 80631/303-352-6082	Lutheran
Christian Living Center at University Hills	2479 S. Clermont Street, Denver 80222/303-758-3682	Christian Reformed
Eaton Terrace Residences	333 S. Eaton Street, Lakewood 80226/303-937-3000	Baptist
First Christian Manor/dba Golden West Manor	1055 Adams Circle, Boulder 80303/303-444-3967	Christian Church
Frasier Meadows Manor	350 Ponca Place, Boulder 80303/303-499-4888	United Methodist
Liggins Tower	5150 E. 34th Avenue, Denver 80207/303-321-3891	Baptist

Name	*Address/Phone*	*Affiliation*
Loveland Good Samaritan	2101 S. Garfield, Loveland 80537/303-669-3100	Lutheran
Rocky Mountain Residences	1535 Franklin Street, Denver 80218/303-832-4859	Baptist
Senior Homes of Colorado	4901 E. Kentucky Circle, Denver 80222/303-756-5218	Congregational, Presbyterian, American Baptist

Connecticut

Covenant Village and Pilgrim Manor	Missionary Road, Cromwell 06416/203-635-5511	Evangelical Covenant
Elim Park Baptist Home, Inc.	140 Cook Hill Road, Cheshire 06410/203-272-3547	Baptist
Immanuel House	15 Woodland Street, Hartford 06195/203-525-4228	Immanuel Church Housing Corp.
Noble Horizons	Lower Cobble Road, Salisbury 06068/203-435-9851	Church Homes, Inc.
Pierce Memorial Baptist Home	44 Canterbury Road, Brooklyn 06234/203-774-9050	Baptist
United Methodist Home of Connecticut, Inc.	584 Long Hill Avenue, Shelton 06484/203-929-5321	United Methodist

Delaware

Cokesbury Village	Lancaster Pike & Loveville Rd, Hockessin 19707/302-239-2371	United Methodist
Lutheran Senior Services	1201 N. Harrison Street, Wilmington 19806/302-652-3737	Lutheran
Lutheran Senior Services of Dover, Inc.	430 Kings Highway, Dover 19901/302-674-1408	Lutheran
Methodist Country House	4830 Kennett Pike, Wilmington 19807/302-654-5101	Methodist
Methodist Manor House	1001 Middleford Road, Seaford 19973/302-629-4593	Methodist

District of Columbia

Friendship Terrace	4201 Butterworth Place, Washington 20016/202-244-7400	Episcopal
Presbyterian Home of the Distr. of Columbia	3050 Military Road, NW, Washington 20015/202-363-8310	Presbyterian
Thomas House	1330 Massachusetts Avenue, NW, Washington 20005/ 202-628-3844	Baptist

Florida

Alliance Retirement Center of Deland, Inc.	600 S. Florida Avenue, Deland 32720/904-734-3481	Christian & Missionary Alliance
Asbury Arms, Inc.	1430 Dixon Boulevard, Cocoa 32922/305-632-4943	Methodist
Asbury Towers	1533 4th Avenue West, Bradenton 33505/813-747-1881	Methodist
Baptist Towers of Jacksonville	1400 La Baron, Jacksonville 32207/904-398-3406	Baptist
Bay Village of Sarasota	8400 Vamo Road, Sarasota 33581/813-966-5611	Presbyterian
Bradenton Manor	1700-21st Avenue West, Bradenton 34205/813-748-4161	Presbyterian
Central Manor	136 Fairview Avenue, Daytona Beach 32014/904-255-2622	Baptist
Christian Manor, Inc.	325 Executive Ctr. Drive, West Palm Beach 32014/904-255-2622	Baptist
Covenant Village of Florida	9201 W. Broward Boulevard, Plantation 33324/305-472-2860	Evangelical Covenant
Epworth Village West, Inc.	5300 W. 16th Avenue, Hialeah 33012/305-556-3500	Methodist
Florida Christian Center Residential Center	1071 S. Edgewood Avenue, Jacksonville 32205/904-389-3123	Christian Church
Florida Lutheran Ret Ctr, Inc.	431 N. Kansas Avenue, Deland 32724/904-734-0603	Lutheran
Florida Presbyterian Homes, Inc.	16 Lake Hunter Drive, Lakeland 33803/813-688-5521	Presbyterian
Heritage Apartments	10200-122nd Avenue North, Largo 34643/813-393-3477	Presbyterian
Kissimmee Good Samaritan Vil	1550 Aldersgate Drive, Kissimmee 32741/407-933-3200	Lutheran
Lake Worth Towers, Inc.	1500 Lucerne Avenue, Lake Worth 33460/305-585-7591	Nazarene
Morris Manor	9050 Norfolk Boulevard, Jacksonville 32208/904-764-3252	Episcopal
Orlando Lutheran Towers	300 E. Church Street, Orlando 32801/407-425-1033	Lutheran
Palm Shores of St. Petersburg	830 N. Shore Drive, St. Petersburg 33701/813-894-2102	Baptist
Plymouth Harbor, Inc.	700 John Ringling Boulevard, Sarasota 34236/813-365-2600	United Church of Christ
Riverside Presbyterian Apartments, Inc.	1045 Oak Street, Jacksonville 32204/904-353-6111	Presbyterian
Riverside Presbyterian House, Inc.	2020 Park Street, Jacksonville 32204/904-388-9376	Presbyterian
Saint James' Residence of the Palm Beaches	208 Fern Street, West Palm Beach 33401/305-655-1504	Episcopal
Shell Point Village	15000 Shell Point Boulevard, Fort Myers 33908/813-454-2155	Christian and Missionary Alliance

Name	Address/Phone	Affiliation
Southwest Florida Ret Center	950 Tamiami Trail South, Venice 34285/813-484-9753	Lutheran
St. Mark Village	2655 Nebraska Avenue, Palm Harbor 34684/813-785-2577	Lutheran
Sunnyside Village	5201 Bahia Vista Street, Sarasota 34232/813-371-2729	Mennonite
Tampa Baptist Manor, Inc.	214 W. Grand Central Avenue, Tampa 33606/813-253-2868	Baptist
Wesleyan Village	8225 Wesley Drive, Brooksville 34601/904-799-1644	Methodist
Westminster Oaks	4449 Meandering Way, Tallahassee 32308/904-878-1136	Presbyterian
Westminster Towers	70 W. Lucerne Circle, Orlando 32801/407-841-1310	Presbyterian
William Booth Towers	633 Lake Dot Circle, Orlando 32801/407-843-5533	Salvation Army
Winter Park Towers and Vil	1111 S. Lakemont Avenue, Winter Park 32792/407-647-4083	Presbyterian

Georgia

Name	Address/Phone	Affiliation
Asbury Harris Epworth Towers/ Wesley Homes	3033 Continental Colony, Parkway Southwest, Atlanta 30331/ 404-344-9400	Methodist
Branan Lodge/Wesley Homes, Inc.	Box 140, Clairsville 30512/404-745-5565	Methodist
Branan Towers/Wesley Homes, Inc.	1200 Glenwood Avenue, SE, Atlanta 30316/404-622-5471	Methodist
Briarcliff Oaks	2982 Briarcliff Road, NE, Atlanta 30329/404-634-3263	Baptist
Calvin Court Apartments	479 E. Paces Ferry Road, Atlanta 30305/404-261-1223	Presbyterian
Campbell-Stone Apts, Inc.	2911 Pharr Court South, NW, Atlanta 30305/404-261-4132	Christian Church/DCC
Campbell-Stone North Apts	350 Carpenter Drive, NE, Atlanta 30328/404-256-2612	Christian Church
Canterbury Court	3750 Peachtree Road, NE, Atlanta 30319/404-261-6611	Episcopal
Christian City Ret Homes	7340 Lester Road, Atlanta 30349/404-964-3301	Christian Churches/ Churches of Christ
Clairmont Oaks	441 Clairmont Avenue, Decatur 30030/404-378-8887	Baptist
Gwinnett Christian Terrace	414 Berkmar Way, Lilburn 30247/404-925-3300	Church of Christ
Lanier Gardens/Wesley Homes, Inc.	801 Riverhill Drive, Athens 30610/404-546-1480	Methodist
Lutheran Towers	717 Juniper Street, Atlanta 30308/404-873-6087	Lutheran
Magnolia Manor Methodist Retirement Home	S. Lee Street, Americus 31709/912-924-9352	Methodist
Philips Presbyterian Tower	218 E. Trinity Place, Decatur 30030/404-373-4361	Presbyterian
Saint Anne's Terrace,Inc.	3100 Northside Parkway, NW, Atlanta 30327/404-238-9200	Episcopal
St. George's Court, Inc.	110 N. 10th Street, Griffin 30223/404-229-5405	Episcopal
St. John Towers/Wesley Homes, Inc.	724 Greene Street, Augusta 30901/404-722-2096	Methodist
St. Mark's Towers	One Towers Plaza, Brunswick 31520/912-267-7125	Episcopal
St. Paul Apartments	1330 Forsyth Street, Macon 31201/912-745-0829	Episcopal
Trinity Towers	2611 Springdale Road, SW, Atlanta 30315/404-763-4044	Episcopal
Vineville Christian Towers, Inc.	2394 Vineville Avenue, Macon 31204/912-743-4661	Christian Church
Wesley Woods Towers/ Wesley Homes, Inc.	1825 Clifton Road, NE, Atlanta 30329/404-728-6683	Methodist

Illinois

Name	Address/Phone	Affiliation
Brementowne Manor of Tinley Park	16130 S. Oak Park Ave, Tinley Park 60477/708-429-4088	Mennonite
Carefree Village	P.O. Box 508, Woodstock 60098/815-338-2110	Woodstock Christian Care, Inc.
Christian Life Retirement Ctr	2750 N. Mulford Road, Rockford 61111/815-633-5544	Assembly of God
Covenant Vil of Northbrook	2625 Technology Road, Northbrook 60062/708-480-6380	Evangelical Covenant
Englewood Cooperative/ aka Bethel Terrace	900 W. 63rd Parkway, Chicago 60621/312-873-8703	Lutheran
Fairhaven Christian Home, Inc.	3470 N. Alpine Road, Rockford 61111/815-877-1441	Evangelical Free
Fairview Baptist Home	7 S. 241 Fairview Avenue, Downers Grove 60516/ 708-852-4350	Baptist
Faith Countryside Homes	P.O. Box 220, Highland 62249/618-654-2393	Evangelical United Church of Christ
Friendship Village of Schaumburg	350 W. Schaumburg Road, Schaumburg 60194/708-844-5000	Evangelical Ret Homes
Holmstad	700 W. Fabyan Parkway, Batavia 60510/708-879-4000	Evangelical Covenant
Maple Lawn Homes	700 N. Main, Eureka 61530/309-467-2337	Mennonite
Moorings	811 E. Central Rd, Arlington Heights 60005/708-437-6700	Lutheran
Plymouth Place	315 N. La Grange Rd, La Grange Park 60525/708-354-0340	United Church of Christ

Name	Address/Phone	Affiliation
Presbyterian Home	3200 Grant Street, Evanston 60201/708-492-2900	Presbyterian
Rest Haven Christian Services	13259 S. Central Avenue, Palos Heights 60463/708-597-1000	Christian Reformed
Salem Village	1314 Rowell Avenue, Joliet 60433/815-727-5451	Lutheran
Spoon River Towers	401 N. Illinois Street, Lewistown 61542/309-547-7274	Christian Church
Sunset Home	418 Washington Street, Quincy 62301/217-223-2636	Methodist
Sunset Manor	920 N. Seminary Road, P.O. Box 508, Woodstock 60098/ 815-338-1749	Woodstock Christian Care, Inc.
United Methodist Village, Inc.	1616 Cedar Street, Lawrenceville 62439/618-943-3347	United Methodist
Wesley Village Retirement/ Health Care Center	1200 E. Grant, Macomb 61455/309-833-2123	Methodist
Windsor Park Manor	124 Windsor Park Drive, Carol Stream 60188/708-682-4377	Interdenominational

Indiana

Brethren Care (St. Paul's Retirement Comm)	Inwood Road, South Bend 46614/219-291-8205	Brethren
Brethren's Home of Indiana, Inc.	Route 2, P.O. Box 97, Flora 46929/219-967-4571	Brethren
Colonial Oaks Retirement Ctr	4725 Colonial Oaks Drive, Marion 46953/317-674-9791	Methodist
Concord Village	6723 S. Anthony Blvd., Fort Wayne 46816/219-447-1591	Lutheran
Crawford Manor	5340 W. 96th Street, Indianapolis 46268/317-873-6510	Baptist
Friendship Haven Ret Comm	2600 W. Jefferson Street, Kokomo 46901/317-459-9343	Mennonite
Golden Years Homestead	8300 Maysville Road, Fort Wayne 46815/219-749-9655	Churches of Christ/ Christian Churches
Grace Village	Wooster Rd, P.O. Box 337, Winona Lake 46590/219-372-6100	Brethren
Greencroft Court Apts, Inc.	1820 Greencroft Boulevard, P.O. Box 819, Goshen 46526/ 219-534-1546	Mennonite
Hubbard Hill Estates Ret Comm	28070 C.R. 24 W., Elkhart 46517/219-295-6260	Missionary Church
Ken-Mar Apartments	210 W. Pike Street, P.O. Box 1412, Martinsville 46151/ 317-342-5671	Christian Church
Peabody Retirement Comm	400 W. 7th Street, North Manchester 46962/219-982-8616	Presbyterian
Swiss Village, Inc.	Berne 46711/219-589-3173	Mennonite
Timbercrest-Church of the Brethren Home	P.O. Box 501, North Manchester 46962/219-982-2118	Brethren
Village Christian Parke	675 S. Ford Road, Zionsville 46077/317-873-5205	Christian Homes
Yellowood Terrace	2100 Greentree N., Clarksville 47130/812-282-7761	United Church of Christ

Iowa

Calvin Manor	4210 Hickman Road, Des Moines 50310/515-277-6141	Presbyterian
Elsie Mason Manor	430 Grand Avenue, Des Moines 503209/515-243-8759	Baptist
Evangelical Free Church Home	112 W. 4th Street, Boone 50036/515-432-1393	Evangelical Free
Eventide Lutheran Home for the Aged	20th Street & 1st Ave. South, Denison 51442/712-263-3114	Lutheran
Friendship Haven,Inc.	S. Kenyon Road, Fort Dodge 50501/515-573-2121	Methodist
Halcyon House	1015 S. Iowa Avenue, Washington 52353/319-653-7264	Methodist
Heritage House	1200 Brookridge Circle, Atlantic 50022/712-243-1850	Methodist
Luther Park Apartments	2824 E. 16th Street, Des Moines 50316/515-262-1153	Lutheran
Mayflower Homes, Inc.	616 Broad Street, Grinnell 50112/515-236-6151	United Church of Christ
Meth-Wick Retirement Comm	1224-13th Street, NW, Cedar Rapids 52405/319-365-9171	Methodist
Oaknoll Retirement Residence	701 Oaknoll Drive, Iowa City 52246/319-351-1720	Christian Ret Services
Ridgecrest Village	4130 Northwest Boulevard, Davenport 52806/319-391-3430	Christian Ret Homes, Inc.
Stone Crest Apartments	3330 E. 25th Street, Des Moines 50317/515-265-2172	Christian Church
United Presbyterian Home	1203 E. Washington Street, Washington 52353/319-653-5473	Presbyterian
Valley View Village	2571 Guthrie Avenue, Des Moines 50317/515-265-2571	Interdenominational
Wesley Acres Ret Community	3520 Grand Avenue, Des Moines 50312/515-271-6500	Methodist

Kansas

Aldersgate Village	7220 Asbury Drive, Topeka 66614/913-478-9440	Methodist
Arkansas City Presbyterian Manor	1711 N. Fourth Street, Arkansas City 67005/316-442-8700	Presbyterian
Brewster Place	1205 W. 29th Street, Topeka 66611/913-267-1666	United Church of Christ Congregational
Buhler Sunshine Home	412 W. C Street, Buhler 67522/316-543-2251	Mennonite Brethren
Emporia Presbyterian Manor	2300 Industrial Road, Emporia 66801/316-343-2613	Presbyterian
First Christian Church Apts	3805 W. 18th Street, Topeka 66604/913-272-6700	Christian Church

Name	Address/Phone	Affiliation
Friends Village	628 S. Hiram, Wichita 67213/316-267-8811	Evangelical Friends Alliance
Garden Valley Ret Village Inc.	1505 E. Spruce, Garden City 67846/316-276-7879	Mennonite Brethren
Lakeview Village, Inc.	9100 Park Street, Lenexa 66215/913-888-1900	Interdenominational
Lawrence Presbyterian Manor	1429 Kasold Drive, Lawrence 66049/913-841-4262	Presbyterian
Memorial Home for the Aged	P.O. Box 29, Moundridge 67107/316-345-2901	Mennonite, Methodist
Newton Presbyterian Manor	1200 E. 7th Street, Newton 67114/316-283-5400	Presbyterian
Parkside Homes, Inc.	200 Willow Road, Hillsboro 67063/316-947-2301	N/A
Pleasant View Home	108 N. Walnut, Inman 67546/316-585-6411	N/A
Salem Home	701 S. Main, Hillsboro 67063/316-947-2272	N/A
Salina Presbyterian Manor	2601 E. Crawford, Salina 67401/913-825-1366	Presbyterian
Schowalter Villa	200 W. Cedar, P.O. Box 5000, Hesston 67062/316-327-4261	Mennonite
Sunset Home	620 Second Avenue, Concordia 66901/913-243-2720	Baptist
Topeka Presbyterian Manor	4712 W. 6th Street, Topeka 66606/913-272-6510	Presbyterian
United Methodist Homes	1135 College, Topeka 66607/913-234-0421	Methodist
Wesley Towers, Inc.	700 Monterey Place, Hutchinson 67502/316-663-9175	Methodist
Wichita Presbyterian Manor	4700 W. 13th Street, Wichita 67212/316-942-7456	Presbyterian

Kentucky

Name	Address/Phone	Affiliation
Baptist Towers, Inc.	1014 S. Second, Louisville 40203/502-587-6632	Baptist
Chapel House	945 S. 5th Street, Louisville 40203/502-584-5178	Christian Church
Florence Christian Center	100 Christian Drive, Florence 41042/606-525-9233	Christian Church
Friendship House	960 S. 4th Street, Louisville 40203/502-589-5747	Christian Church
Helmwood Village Ret Comm	106 Diecks Drive, Elizabethtown 42701/502-737-2738	Presbyterian
Wesley Manor Ret Comm	5012 E. Manslick Road, P.O. Box 19258, Louisville 40219/ 502-969-3277	Methodist
Westminster Terrace	2116 Buechel Bank Road, Louisville 40218/502-499-9383	Presbyterian

Louisiana

Name	Address/Phone	Affiliation
Cedar Hill Apartments	7401 Saint Vincent, Shreveport 71106/318-861-6915	Baptist
St. James Place of Baton Rouge, Inc.	333 Lee Drive, Baton Rouge 70808/504-769-1407	Episcopal

Maryland

Name	Address/Phone	Affiliation
Asbury Methodist Village	201 Russell Avenue, Gaithersburg 20877/301-330-3000	Methodist
Carroll Lutheran Village	205 Saint Mark Way, Westminster 21157/301-848-0090	Lutheran
Collington Episcopal Life Care Community	10450 Lottsford Road, Mitchellville 20716/301-925-9610	Episcopal
Fahrney-Keedy Memorial Home, Inc.	Boonesboro 21713/301-733-6284	Brethren
Fairhaven	7200 Third Avenue, Sykesville 21784/301-795-8800	Episcopal
Friends House Ret Comm	17340 Quaker Lane, Sandy Spring 20860/301-924-5100	Quaker
Homewood Retirement Ctr	2750 Virginia Avenue, Williamsport 21795/301-582-1750	United Church of Christ
National Lutheran Home for the Aged	9701 Viers Drive, Rockville 20850/301-424-9560	Lutheran
New Towne Village	RR 2, Box 1, Leonardtown 20650/301-475-3161	Natl Church Residences
Ravenwood Lutheran Village	1183 Luther Drive, Hagerstown 21740/301-790-1000	Lutheran
Springvale Terrace	8505 Springvale Road, Silver Spring 20910/301-587-0190	United Church of Christ
Wesley Home, Inc.	2211 W. Rogers Avenue, Baltimore 21209/301-664-4006	Methodist

Massachusetts

Name	Address/Phone	Affiliation
Turtle Creek Residential Comm	401 Essex Street, Beverly 01915/617-922-1112	Baptist

Michigan

Name	Address/Phone	Affiliation
Au Sable Valley Apartments	1441 Maple Drive, Fairview 48621/517-848-5630	Mennonite
Boulevard Temple United Methodist Ret Home	2567 W. Grand Boulevard, Detroit 48208/313-895-5340	United Methodist
Canton Place	44505 Ford Road, Canton 48187/313-981-6420	Natl Church Residences
Cathedral Terrace	80 E. Hancock, Detroit 48201/313-832-1020	Episcopal
Chelsea United Methodist Retirement Home	805 W. Middle Street, Chelsea 48118/313-475-8633	United Methodist
Clawson Manor-New Life, Inc.	255 W. Fourteen-Mile Rd., Clawson 48017/313-435-5650	Methodist
Columbia Court	275 W. Columbia Avenue, Belleville 48111/313-697-8200	Natl Church Residences
Danish Village	2566 Walton Boulevard, Rochester Hills 48309/313-375-1810	Lutheran
Detroit Baptist Manor	30301 W. 13 Mile Rd., Farmington Hills 48018/313-626-6100	Baptist

Name	Address/Phone	Affiliation
Evangelical Homes of Mich	6700 W. Outer Drive, Detroit 48235/313-836-1700	United Church of Christ
Grand Ravine Apartments	725 Grand Street, Allegan 49010/616-673-7155	Lutheran
Lakeside Towers	15000 Shoreline Drive, Sterling Heights 48078/313-247-7411	Natl Church Residences
Luther Haven	464 E. Grand Boulevard, Detroit 48207/313-579-2255	Lutheran
Luther Village Community	2000-32nd Street, SE, Grand Rapids 49508/616-452-6084	Lutheran
M. J. Clark Memorial Home	1546 Sherman, SE, Grand Rapids 49506/616-452-1568	Methodist
Park Place of Harper Woods	19460 Park Drive, Harper Woods 48225/313-884-2122	Natl Church Residences
Park Village Pines	2920 Crystal Lane, Kalamazoo 49009/616-372-1928	Christian Retirement Associates, Inc.
Pilgrim Manor, Inc.	2000 Leonard, NE, Grand Rapids 49505/616-458-1133	United Church of Christ
Porter Hills Presbyterian Vil, Inc.	3600 E. Fulton, Grand Rapids 49546/616-949-4971	Presbyterian
Presbyterian Village E.ast	33875 Kiely Drive, New Baltimore 48047/313-725-6030	Presbyterian
Presbyterian Village North	420 S. Opdyke Road, Pontiac 48057/313-334-4379	Presbyterian
Presbyterian Vil of Detroit, Inc.	17383 Garfield Avenue, Redford 48240/313-531-6874	Presbyterian

Minnesota

Name	Address/Phone	Affiliation
Augustana Home of Minneapolis	1007 E. 14th Street, Minneapolis 55404/612-333-1551	Lutheran
Augustana Lutheran Homes, Inc.	600 S. Davis, Litchfield 55355/612-693-2430	Lutheran
Bethesda Lutheran Care Ctr	558 Capitol Boulevard, St. Paul 55103/612-221-2347	Lutheran
Chapel View Care Center	615 Minnetonka Mills Road, Hopkins 55343/612-938-2761	Methodist
Covenant Manor	5800 Saint Croix Avenue, Minneapolis 55422/612-546-6125	Evangelical Covenant
Crest View Lutheran Home	4444 Reservoir Blvd, Columbia Heights 55421/612-788-1678	Lutheran
Elim Home	101 S. 7th Avenue, Princeton 55371/612-389-1171	Evangelical Free
Elim Home	409 Jefferson Avenue, S.W., Watertown 55388/612-955-2691	Evangelical free
Elim Home	730-2nd Street, SE, Milaca 56353/612-983-2185	Evangelical Free
Glenwood Retirement Homes	719 SE Second Street, Glenwood 56334/612-634-5131	Lutheran
Grandview Christian Home	800 Second Avenue, NW, Cambridge 55008/612-689-1474	Baptist
Lutheran Retirement Home of Southern Minnesota	400 N. 4th Avenue, East, Truman 56088/507-776-2031	Lutheran
Lynblomsten Center	1415 Almond Avenue, St. Paul 55108/612-646-2941	Lutheran
Mankato Lutheran Home	718 Mound Avenue, Mankato 56001/507-345-4576	Lutheran
Margaret S. Parmly Residence	28210 Old Towne Road, Chisago City 55013/612-257-5620	Lutheran
Martin Luther Manor	1401 E. 100th Street, Bloomington 55425/612-888-7751	Lutheran
Mount Olivet-Careview Homes	5517 Lyndale Avenue S., Minneapolis 55419/612-827-5677	Lutheran
Presbyterian Homes of Minnesota, Inc.	3220 Lake Johanna Boulevard, St. Paul 55112/612-631-6100	Presbyterian
Seminary Memorial Home	906 College Avenue, Red Wing 55066/612-388-1591	Lutheran
Thorne Crest Retirement Ctr	1201 Garfield Avenue, Albert Lea 56007/507-373-2311	Baptist
Walker Methodist Residences/ Health Services	3737 Bryant Avenue S., Minneapolis 55409/612-827-8301	Methodist

Mississippi

Name	Address/Phone	Affiliation
Aldersgate Retirement Center	P.O. Box 3846, Meridian 39303/601-482-5561	Methodist
Boardtown Village	905 N. Montgomery Street, Starkville 39759/601-323-3461	Natl Church Residences
Methodist Retirement Comm	1450 Beach Boulevard, Biloxi 39530/601-435-3861	Methodist
Traceway Manor	2800 W. Main Street, Tupelo 38801/601-844-1441	Methodist
Trinity Place	300 Airline Road, Columbus 39702/601-327-6716	Methodist
Wesley Manor Ret Comm	P.O. Box 16298, Hattiesburg 39402/601-264-8847	Methodist

Missouri

Name	Address/Phone	Affiliation
Armour Home	8100 Wornall Road, Kansas City 64114/816-363-1510	Women's Christian Association
Beautiful Savior Home	Route 2, Box 306, Belton 64012/816-331-0781	Lutheran
Foxwood Springs Living Ctr	P.O. Box 1400, Raymore 64083/816-331-3111	Christian Church
Friendship Village of West County	15201 Olive Street, Chesterfield 63017/314-532-1515	Evangelical Ret Homes
Gambrill Gardens, Inc.	One Strecker Road, Ellisville 63011/314-394-2992	Methodist
Good Samaritan Home	5200 S. Broadway, St. Louis 63111/314-352-2400	Church of Christ
Jaycee Fairgrounds Village	1355 Fairgrounds Road, St. Charles 63301/314-947-1324	Natl Church Residences
Kingswood Manor	10000 Wornall Road, Kansas City 64114/816-942-0994	Methodist
Laclede Oaks Manor	701 S. Laclede Station Rd., St. Louis 63119/314-968-9200	Lutheran
Lenoir Health Care Center	3300 New Haven Road, Columbia 65201/314-443-2478	Christian Church
Lenoir Retirement Center	3612 Lenoir Street, Columbia 65201/314-876-5800	Christian Church

Name	Address/Phone	Affiliation
Maranatha Village	233 E. Norton Road, Springfield 65803/417-833-0016	N/A
Ozarks Methodist Manor	205 S. College Street, P.O. Box C, Marionville 65705/ 417-463-2573	Methodist
Presbyterian Manor at Farmington	Manor Court, Farmington 63640/314-756-6768	Presbyterian
Tower Grove Manor	2710 S. Grand Boulevard, St. Louis 63118/314-773-2800	Episcopal, Presbyterian

Montana

Downtowner	100 Central Avenue, Great Falls 59401/406-761-1444	Methodist
Saint John's Lutheran Home	3940 Rimrock Road, Billings 59102/406-656-2710	Lutheran

Nebraska

Christian Homes, Inc.	Holdrege 68949/308-995-4493	Evangelical Free
Maple Crest Retirement Ctr	2824 N. 66th Avenue, Omaha 68104/402-551-2110	Baptist
Methodist Memorial Homes, Inc. Retirement Center	1320-11th Avenue, Holdrege 68949/308-995-8631	Methodist
Skyline Manor, Inc.	7300 Graceland Drive, Omaha 68134/402-572-5750	Nondenominational

New Hampshire

Havenwood Ret Community	33 Christian Avenue, Concord 03301/603-225-5363	United Church of Christ
Heritage Heights	149 E. Side Drive, Concord 03301/603-225-6999	United Church of Christ

New Jersey

Asbury Tower	1701 Ocean Avenue, Asbury Park 07712/201-988-9090	Presbyterian
Cadbury	2150 Route 38, Cherry Hill 08002/609-667-4550	Quaker
Clymer Village	211 Red School Lane, Phillipsburg 08865/201-454-4661	Natl Church Residences
Evergreens	309 Bridgeboro Road, Moorestown 08057/609-235-2503	Episcopal
Francis Asbury Manor	70 Stockton Avenue, Ocean Grove 07756/201-774-1316	Methodist
Friends Home at Woodstown, Inc.	Friends Drive, P.O. Box 457, Woodstown 08098/609-769-1500	Friends
Harvest Village	114 Hayes Mill Road, Atco 08004/609-753-2000	Presbyterian
Heath Village	Schooleys Mountain Rd., Hackettstown 07840/201-852-4801	Episcopal
Kinder Towers	400 Hoover Road, Bloomfield 07003/201-748-0982	Natl Church Residences
Luther Arms	323 S. Broad Street, Trenton 08618/609-392-5628	Lutheran
Luther Towers	489 W. State Street, Trenton 08618/609-695-7755	Lutheran
Medford Leas Continuing Care Retirement Center	Route 70, Medford 08055/609-654-3000	Friends
Monroe Village	117 Hale Acre Road, Jamesburg 08831/201-521-6400	Presbyterian
Muhlenberg Gardens	1065 Summit Avenue, Jersey City 07307/201-792-4475	Lutheran
Navesink House	40 Riverside Avenue, Red Bank 07701/201-842-3400	Baptist
Pitman Manor	535 N. Oak Avenue, Pitman 08071/609-589-7800	Methodist
Plainfield Tower West	601 W. 7th Street, Plainfield 07060/201-668-1963	Presbyterian
Presbyterian Home at Meadow Lakes	Etra Road, P.O. Box 70, Hightstown 08520/609-426-6805	Presbyterian
Wesley Homestead	805 E. 8th Street, Ocean City 08226/609-394-1608	Methodist
Wiley Christian Ret Comm	99 E. Main Street, Marlton 08053/609-983-0411	Wiley Mission Society
Woodmere Senior Citizens Housing Corporation	250 Crescent Avenue, Spotswood 08884/201-251-3242	Reformed Church

New Mexico

Encino House Midtown	609 Encino Place, NE, Albuquerque 87102/505-247-4185	New Mexico Conference of Churches
Landsun Homes, Inc.	2002 Westridge Road, Carlsbad 88220/505-887-2894	Methodist
University Terrace Good Samaritan Village	3025 Terrace Drive, Las Cruces Drive 88001/505-526-1362	Lutheran

New York

Bethel Springvale Inn	500 Albany Post Road, Croton-on-Hudson 10520/914-739-4404	Methodist
Clinton Manor Apts, Inc.	50 Franklin Avenue, P.O. Box 100, Clinton 13323/315-853-3698	Lutheran
Embury Apartments, Inc.	Lawrence Street, Saratoga Springs 12866/518-587-3300	Methodist
Episcopal Church Home	24 Rhode Island Street, Buffalo 14213/716-884-6500	Episcopal
Fairport Baptist Home	4646 Nine Mile Point Road, Fairport 14450/716-377-0350	Baptist
Flushing House	38-20 Bowne Street, Flushing 11354/718-762-3198	Presbyterian
Fort Schuyler House, Inc.	3077 Cross Bronx Expressway, Bronx 10465/212-597-4100	Presbyterian
Good Shepherd-Fairview Home, Inc.	80 Fairview Avenue, Binghamton 13904/607-724-2477	Episcopal, Presbyterian

Name	Address/Phone	Affiliation
Heritage Village	Route 60, Gerry 14740/716-985-4612	Free Methodist
Hilltop Retirement Center	285 Deyo Hill Road, Johnson City 13790/607-798-7818	Methodist
Saint Margaret's House	49 Fulton Street, New York 10038/212-766-8122	Episcopal
Valley Manor	1570 E. Avenue, Rochester 14610/716-442-6450	Presbyterian
Village of Saint John	2000 Bishop's Road, Smithtown 11787/516-724-2226	Episcopal
Wheatfield Tower	6849 Plaza Drive, Niagara Falls 14304/716-731-4600	Natl Church Residences

North Carolina

Albemarle	200 Trade Street, Tarboro 27886/919-823-2799	Presbyterian
Brookridge Retirement Comm	1199 Hayes Forest Dr., P.O. Box 11024, Winston-Salem 27116/ 919-759-1044	Baptist
Brooks-Howell Home	29 Spears Avenue, Asheville 28801/704-253-6712	Methodist
Capital Towers	4812 Six Forks Road, Raleigh 27609/919-787-1231	Presbyterian
Cypress Glen	100 Hickory Street, Greenville 27858/919-830-0036	Methodist
Deerfield Episcopal Ret Comm	1617 Hendersonville Road, Asheville 28803/704-274-1531	Episcopal
Episcopal Home for Aging	East Thode Island Ave. Exten., P.O. Box 2001, Southern Pines 28387/919-692-0300	Episcopal
Epworth Place	3420 Shamrock Drive, Charlotte 28215/704-532-7000	Methodist
Friends Homes, Inc.	925 New Garden Road, Greensboro 27410/919-292-8187	Friends
Givens Estates United Methodist Ret Comm	Sweeten Creek Road, Asheville 28803/704-274-4800	Methodist
Golden Years Home	P.O. Box 39, Falcon 28342/919-892-6048	Pentecostal Holiness
J.W. Abernathy Center United Church Homes	100 Leonard Avenue, Newton 28658/704-464-8260	United Church of Christ
Methodist Retirement Comm	2616 Durham Road, Durham 27705/919-383-2567	Methodist
Moravian Home, Inc.	5401 Indiana Avenue, Winston-Salem 27106/919-767-8130	Moravian Church
Presbyterian Home at Charlotte, Inc.	5100 Sharon Road, Charlotte 28210/704-553-1670	Presbyterian
Presbyterian Home of High Point	2001 Greensboro Road, P.O. Box 2007, High Point 27261/ 919-883-9111	Presbyterian
Scotia Village Ret Comm	2200 Elm Avenue, Laurinburg 28352/919-277-2000	Presbyterian
Triad United Methodist Home	1240 Arbor Road, Winston-Salem 27104/919-724-7921	Methodist
Twin Lakes Center	100 Wade Coble Drive, Burlington 27215/919-538-1400	Lutheran
Wesley Pines	100 Wesley Pines Road, Lumberton 28358/919-738-9691	Methodist
Wesleyan Arms Ret Center	1901 N. Centennial Street, High Point 27260/919-884-2222	Methodist

North Dakota

Bethany Homes, Inc.	201 S. University Drive, Fargo 58103/701-237-0720	Lutheran
Elim Home	3534 S. University Drive, Fargo 58103/701-237-4392	Evangelical Free

Ohio

Bethany Lutheran Village	6451 Far Hills Avenue, Dayton 45459/513-433-2110	Lutheran
Booth Residence, c/o The Salvation Army	6000 Townevista Drive, Cincinnati 45224/513-242-4482	The Salvation Army
Breckenridge Village	36855 Rodge Road, Willoughby 44094/216-942-4342	Presbyterian
Brethren Care, Inc.	2000 Center Street, Ashland 44805/419-289-1585	Brethren
Brethren's Home	750 Chestnut Street, Greenville 45331/513-547-8000	Brethren
Bristol Village	111 Wendy Lane, Waverly 45690/614-947-2118	Natl Church Residences
Canterbury Court	450 N. Elm Street, West Carrollton 45449/513-859-1106	Episcopal
Canton Christian Home	2550 Cleveland Avenue, NW, Canton 44709/216-456-0004	Christian and Churches of Christ
Copeland Oaks	800 S. 15th Street, Sebring 44672/216-938-6126	Methodist
Covenant House, Inc.	702 N. Erie Street, Toledo 43604/419-243-2334	Lutheran
Dorothy Love Ret Community	3003 W. Cisco Road, Sidney 45365/513-498-2391	Presbyterian
Elyria United Methodist Home	807 W. Avenue, Elyria 44035/216-323-3395	United Methodist
Fairlawn Haven	407 E. Lutz Road, Archbold 43502/419-445-3075	Mennonite
First Community Village	1800 Riverside Drive, Columbus 43212/614-486-9511	First Community Church
Hilty Memorial Home	P.O. Box 265, Pandora 45877/419-384-3218	Missionary Church
Hopeton Village	153 University Drive, Chillicothe 45601/614-773-5220	Natl Church Residences
Lincoln Garden	98 Sturbridge Road, Columbus 43228/614-878-4394	Natl Church Residences
Llanfair Retirement Comm	1701 Llanfair Avenue, Cincinnati 45224/513-681-4230	Presbyterian
Luther Pines	805 Mumaugh Road, Lima 45804/419-225-9045	Lutheran
Lutheran Senior City	935 N. Cassady Avenue, Columbus 43219/614-252-4987	Lutheran
Marjorie P. Lee Ret Comm	3550 Shaw Avenue, Cincinnati 45208/513-871-2090	Episcopal

Name	*Address/Phone*	*Affiliation*
Mount Pleasant Village	225 Britton Lane, Monroe 45050/513-539-7391	Presbyterian
Otterbein-Lebanon	585 N. State, Route 741, Lebanon 45036/513-932-2020	Methodist
Park Vista Retirement Comm	1216 5th Avenue, Youngstown 44504/216-746-2944	Presbyterian
Portage Trail Village	45 Cathedral Lane, Cuyahoga Falls 44223/216-929-4227	Natl Church Residences
Rockynol Retirement Comm	1150 W. Market Street, Akron 44313/216-867-2150	Presbyterian
Stygler Village	140 Imperial Drive, Gahanna 43230/614-475-2255	Natl Church Residences
Twin Towers	5343 Hamilton Avenue, Cincinnati 45224/513-853-2000	Methodist
Wesley Glen, Inc.	5155 N. High Street, Columbus 43214/614-888-7492	Methodist
West View Manor Ret Center	1715 Mechanicsburg Road, Wooster 44691/216-264-8640	Brethren
Worthington Christian Vil, Inc.	165 Highbluffs Boulevard, Worthington 43085/614-846-6076	Church of Christ

Oklahoma

Carmen Home	P.O. Box 10, Carmen 73726/405-987-2577	Pentecostal Holiness
Corn Heritage Village	Corn 73024/405-343-2295	Mennonite Brethren
Fairview Fellowship Home	605 E. State Street, Fairview 73737/405-227-3784	Mennonite Brethren
Oklahoma Christian Apts, Inc.	325 Enz Drive, Edmond 73034/405-340-0311	Christian Church

Oregon

Cascade Manor, Inc.	65 W. 30th Street, Eugene 97405/503-342-5901	Methodist, Congregational, Presbyterian
Fairlawn Towne	1280 NE Kane Road, Gresham 97030/503-667-1965	Lutheran
Friendsview Manor	1301 E. Fulton Street, Newberg 97132/503-538-3144	Quaker
Holladay Park Plaza	1300 NE 16th Avenue, Portland 97232/503-288-6671	Presbyterian
Mennonite Home	5353 SE Columbus, Albany 97321/503-928-7232	Mennonite
Olive Plaza	1133 Olive Street, Eugene 97401/503-683-3247	Christian Church
Oregon Baptist Ret Home	2545 NE Flanders Street, Portland 97232/503-232-5055	Baptist
Presbyterian Comm Care Ctr	1085 N. Oregon Street, Ontario 97914/503-889-9133	Presbyterian
Rogue Valley Manor	1200 Mira Mar Avenue, Medford 97504/503-776-5212	Episcopal, Presbyterian, Methodist
Village Retirement Ctr, The	310 W. Ellendale Avenue, Dallas 97338/503-623-9211	Brethren
Weidler Retirement Center	1825 NE 108th Avenue, Portland 97220/503-255-7160	Baptist
Willamette Lutheran Homes, Inc.	7693 Wheatland Rd. N, P.O. Box 169, Salem 97308/503-371-2696	Lutheran

Pennsylvania

Alliance Home, The,	770 S. Hanover Street, Carlisle 17013/717-249-1363	Christian and Missionary Alliance
Asbury Heights	700 Bower Hill Road, Pittsburgh 15243/412-341-1030	Methodist
Bethany Towers	335 Wesley Drive, Mechanicsburg 17055/717-766-7698	Bethany Development Corporation
Bethany Village Ret Center	325 Wesley Drive, Mechanicsburg 17055/417-766-0279	Methodist
Brethren Home	2990 Carlisle Pike, P.O. Box 128, New Oxford 17350/ 717-624-2161	Brethren
Brethren Village	3001 Lititz Pike, P.O. Box 5093, Lancaster 17601/717-569-2657	Brethren
Calvary Fellowship Homes, Inc.	502 Elizabeth Drive, Lancaster 17601/717-393-0711	Nondenominational
Cathedral Village	600 E. Cathedral Road, Philadelphia 19128/215-487-1300	Episcopal
Cornwall Manor	P.O. Box 125, Cornwall 17016/717-273-2647	Methodist
Dock Woods Community, Inc.	275 Dock Drive, Lansdale 19446/215-368-4438	Mennonite
Elm Terrace Gardens, Inc.	660 N. Broad Street, Lansdale 19446/215-362-6087	Baptist
Evangelical Congregational Church Retirement Village	S. Railroad Street, Myerstown 17067/717-866-6541	Congregational
Evangelical Manor	8401 Roosevelt Boulevard, Philadelphia 19152/215-624-5800	Methodist
Foulkeways at Gwynedd	Meeting House Road, Gwynedd 19436/215-643-2200	Friends
Frederick Mennonite Comm	Route 73, Frederick 19435/215-754-7878	Mennonite
G.D.L. Manor Corporation	570 Welsh Road, Huntingdon Valley 19006/215-947-7362	Lutheran
Germantown Home	6950 Germantown Avenue, Philadelphia 19119/215-848-3306	Lutheran
Gettysburg Lutheran Retirement Village	1075 Old Harrisburg Road, Gettysburg 17325/717-334-6204	Lutheran
Green Ridge Village	Big Spring Road, Newville 17241/717-776-3192	Presbyterian
Jefferson Apartments/ Christian Concern, Inc.	1514 W. Marshall Street, Norristown 19403/215-539-4844	United Church of Christ
Kendal At Longwood	P.O. Box 100, Kennett Square 19348/215-388-7001	Friends
Landis Homes Ret Comm	1001 E. Oregon Road, Lititz 17543/717-569-3271	Mennonite
Lebanon Valley Brethren Home	1200 Grubb Street, Palmyra 17078/717-838-5406	Brethren

Name	Address/Phone	Affiliation
Lewisburg United Methodist Homes	Lewisburg 17837/717-524-2271	United Methodist
Luther Crest	800 Hausman Road, Allentown 18103/215-398-8011	Lutheran
Lutheran Home at Topton	Home Avenue, Topton 19562/215-682-1225	Lutheran
Lutheran Manor Apartments	2085 Westgate Drive, Bethlehem 18018/215-866-6010	Lutheran
Menno-Haven, Inc.	2075 Scotland Avenue, Chambersburg 17201/717-263-8545	Mennonite
Messiah Village	100 Mount Allen Drive, Mechanicsburg 17055/717-697-4666	Brethren
Moravian Hall Square Retirement Community	175 W. North Street, Nazareth 18064/215-746-1000	Moravian Church
Moravian Manor	300 W. Lemon Street, Lititz 17543/717-626-0214	Moravian Church
Parkview Towers	111 Caroline Street, Munhall 15120/412-461-2993	Methodist
Passavant Retirement and Health Center	401 S. Main Street, Zelienople 16063/412-452-5400	Lutheran
Paul's Run Retirement Comm	9896 Bustleton Avenue, Philadelphia 19115/215-934-3000	Lutheran
Penn Lutheran Village	800 Broad Street, Selinsgrove 17870/717-374-8181	Lutheran
Pennswood Village	Route 413, Newtown 18940/215-968-9110	Quaker
Peter Becker Community	Maple Avenue and Yoder Road, Harleysville 19438/215-256-9501	Brethren
Phoebe Home, Inc.	1925 Turner Street, Allentown 18104/215-435-9037	United Church of Christ
Phoebe Terrace, Inc.	1940 Turner Street, Allentown 18104/215-820-9081	United Church of Christ
Presbyterian Apartments, Inc.	322 N. 2nd Street, Harrisburg 17101/717-233-5114	Presbyterian
Presbyterian Medical Center, Westminster Pl	1215 Hulton Road, Oakmont 15139/412-828-5600	Presbyterian
Presbyterian Senior Care	825 S. Main St., P.O. Box 677, Washington 15301/412-222-4300	Presbyterian
Quarryville Presbyterian Retirement Community	625 Robert Fulton Highway, Quarryville 17566/717-786-7321	Presbyterian
Quincy United Methodist Home	P.O. Box 217, Quincy 17247/717-749-3151	United Methodist
Riverside Presbyterian Tower	158 N. 23rd Street, Philadelphia 19103/215-563-6200	Presbyterian
Rockhill Mennonite Comm	Box 21, Route 152, Sellersville 18960/215-257-2751	Mennonite
Rosemont Presbyterian Vil	404 Cheswick Place, Rosemont 19010/215-527-6500	Presbyterian
Rydal Park	1515 On the Fairway, Rydal 19046/215-885-6800	Presbyterian
Saint Andrew's Village	1155 Indian Springs Road, Indiana 15701/412-349-4870	Presbyterian
Sharpsburg Tower	601 Main Street, Sharpsburg 15215/412-784-0600	Natl Church Residences
Shrewsbury Lutheran Retirement Village	200 Luther Road, Shrewsbury 17361/717-235-6895	Lutheran
Simpson House	Belmont and Monument Avenues, Philadelphia 19131/ 215-878-3600	Methodist
Souderton Mennonite Homes	207 W. Summit Street, Souderton 18964/215-723-9881	Mennonite
Tel Hai Retirement Comm	P.O. Box 190, Honey Brook 19344/215-273-3149	Mennonite
Thomas Campbell Christian Ctr	850 Beech Street, Washington 15301/412-225-2290	Christian Church
Wesbury United Methodist Community	31 N. Park Avenue, Meadville 16335/814-724-8000	United Methodist
Wesley Village	Laflin Road, Pittston 18640/717-655-2891	Methodist

Rhode Island

Beneficent House	One Chestnut Street, Providence 02903/401-331-4755	Congregational
United Methodist Ret Center	40 Irving Avenue, East Providence 02914/401-438-4456	United Methodist

South Carolina

Greenwood Methodist Home	1110 Marshall Road, Greenwood 29646/803-227-1220	Methodist
Martha Franks Baptist Ret Ctr	1 Martha Franks Drive, Laurens 29360/803-984-4541	Baptist
Methodist Home	1000 Live Oaks Drive, SW, P.O. Drawer 327, Orangeburg 29116/ 803-534-1212	Methodist
Presbyterian Home of South Carolina	C M R Box 140, Summerville 29483/803-873-2550	Presbyterian
Westminster Towers	P.O. Box 2894, Rock Hill 29731/803-329-5121	Presbyterian

South Dakota

Dow-Rummel Village	1000 N. Lake Avenue, Sioux Falls 57104/605-336-1490	United Church of Christ, Episcopal

Tennessee

Appalachian Christian Village	2021 Sherwood Drive, Johnson City 37601/615-928-3168	Christian Churches and Churches of Christ
Ascension Towers	3910 Stuart Road, Memphis 38111/901-454-1108	Lutheran
Christian Towers of Gallatin	138 E. Franklin Street, Gallatin 37066/615-452-9363	Church of Christ

Name	Address/Phone	Affiliation
Luther Towers	274 S. Highland, Memphis 38111/901-323-3639	Lutheran
McKendree Village, Inc.	4347 Lebanon Road, Hermitage 37076/615-889-6990	Methodist
Park Manor	115 Woodmont Boulevard, Nashville 37205/615-383-7303	Presbyterian
Parkview	1914 Poplar Avenue, Memphis 38104/901-725-4606	Presbyterian
Trezevant Manor and Allen Morgan Nursing Center	177 N. Highland at Waynoka, Memphis 38111/901-325-4000	Episcopal

Texas

Name	Address/Phone	Affiliation
Amarillo Good Samaritan Retirement Center	2200 W. 7th, Amarillo 79106/806-374-6896	Lutheran
Bayou Manor	4141 S. Braeswood Blvd, Houston 77025/713-666-2651	Presbyterian
Buckner Baptist Village	4800 Samuell Boulevard, Dallas 75228/214-381-2171	Baptist
Crestview Methodist Retirement Community	2501 Villa Maria Rd., P.O. Box 4008, Bryan 77805/409-776-4778	Methodist
Denton Good Samaritan Vil	2500 Hinkle Drive, Denton 76201/817-383-2651	Evangelical Good Samaritan Society
Edgewater Methodist Retirement Community	2228 Seawall Boulevard, Galveston 77550/409-763-6437	Methodist
Golden Palms Retirement and Health Center	2101 Treasure Hills Blvd, Harlingen 78550/512-421-4653	Baptist
Grace Presbyterian Village Ministries	550 E. Ann Arbor, Dallas 75216/214-376-1701	Presbyterian
Lake Forest Good Samaritan Vil	3901 Montecito Drive, Denton 76205/817-383-1541	Lutheran
Lakewood Village Ret Center	5100 Randol Mill Road, Fort Worth 76112/817-451-8001	Christian Care Centers
Meadows	730 Babcock Street, San Antonio 78201/512-734-1155	Morningside Ministries
Park Place Towers	1300 S. Harrison, Amarillo 79101/806-376-1177	Baptist
Presbyterian Manor, Inc.	4600 Taft Boulevard, Wichita Falls 76308/817-691-1710	Presbyterian
Presbyterian Village North	8600 Skyline Drive, Dallas 75243/214-349-3960	Presbyterian
Trinity Towers Manor Park	2208 N. Loop 250 W., Midland 79707/915-689-9898	Presbyterian
Trinity Towers Retirement Ctr	2800 W. Illinois, Midland 79701/915-694-1691	Presbyterian
Village Christian Apartments	7925 Rockwood Lane, Austin 78758/512-459-9550	Christian Services, Inc.
White Acres Good Samaritan Retirement Village	7304 Good Samaritan Court, El Paso 79912/915-581-4683	Lutheran

Virginia

Name	Address/Phone	Affiliation
Burke Lake Gardens	9608 Old Keene Mill Road, Burke 22015/703-644-0061	Assembly of God
Culpeper Baptist Ret Comm	P.O. Box 191, Culpeper 22701/703-825-2411	Baptist
Goodwin House, Inc.	4800 Fillmore Avenue, Alexandria 22311/703-824-1185	Episcopal
Heritage Haven Ret Housing	1501 Virginia Avenue, Harrisonburg 22801/703-433-8900	Mennonite
Hermitage	1600 Westwood Avenue, Richmond 23227/804-355-5721	United Methodist
Hermitage in Northern Virginia	5000 Fairbanks Avenue, Alexandria 22311/703-820-2434	Methodist
Hermitage on the Eastern Shore	North Street Extended, Onancock 23417/804-787-4343	Methodist
Hunters Woods Fellowship House	2231 Colts Neck Road, Reston 22091/703-620-4450	Fellowship Square Fndn
Lake Anne Fellowship House	11450 N. Shore Drive, Reston 22090/703-471-6474	Fellowship Square Fndn
Lake Ridge Fellowship House	12800 Harbor Drive, Woodbridge 22192/703-494-4455	Fellowship Square Fndn
Lakewood Manor Baptist Retirement Community	1900 Lauderdale Drive, Richmond 23233/804-740-2900	Baptist
Luther Manor	350 Malibu Drive, Virginia Beach 23452/804-463-3510	Lutheran
Newport News Baptist Retirement Community	955 Harpersville Road, P.O. Box 6010, Newport News 23606/ 804-599-4376	Baptist
Rappahannock Westminster— Canterbury	10 Lancaster Drive, Irvington 22480/804-438-4000	Episcopal, Presbyterian
Retirement Village Ltd.	315 N. Second Street, Bridgewater 22812/703-828-3223	Brethren
Sunnyside Presbyterian Retirement Community	P.O. Box 928, Harrisonburg 22801/703-568-8200	Presbyterian
Westminster-Canterbury House	1600 Westbrook Avenue, Richmond 23227/804-264-6000	Episcopal, Presbyterian
Westminster-Canterbury of Lynchburg, Inc.	501 V.E.S. Road, Lynchburg 24503/804-386-3500	Episcopal, Presbyterian
Westminster-Canterbury of Winchester, Inc.	956 Westminster-Canterbury Drive, Winchester 22601/ 703-665-0156	Episcopal, Presbyterian

Washington

Name	Address/Phone	Affiliation
Bayview Manor	11 W. Aloha Street, Seattle 98119/206-284-7330	Methodist

Name	Address/Phone	Affiliation
Campus Towers Ret Residence	1767-20th Avenue, Longview 98632/206-423-6200	Baptist
Covenant Shores	9150 N. Mercer Way, Mercer Island 98040/206-236-0600	Evangelical Covenant
Exeter House	720 Seneca Street, Seattle 98101/206-622-1300	Presbyterian
Fred Lind Manor	1802-17th Avenue, Seattle 98122/206-324-1632	Baptist
Hearthstone	6720 E. Green Lake Way N., Seattle 98103/206-525-9666	Lutheran
Hilltop House	1005 Terrace Street, Seattle 98104/206-624-5704	Baptist
Horizon House	900 University Street, Seattle 98101/206-624-3700	United Church of Christ
Judson Park Ret Residence	23600 Marine View Dr. S., Des Moines 98198/206-824-4000	Baptist
Life Manor	1601 S. Puget Sound, Tacoma 98405/206-383-3363	Assembly of God
Lilac Plaza	North 7007 Wiscomb Street, Spokane 99208/509-489-7612	Baptist
Northaven, Inc.	11045 8th Avenue, NE, Seattle 98125/206-365-3020	Olympic View Community Church
Rockwood Retirement Comm	2903 E. 25th Avenue, Spokane 99223/509-536-6650	Methodist
Tacoma Lutheran Home and Retirement Comm	1301 Highland Parkway, Tacoma 98406/206-752-7112	Lutheran
Warm Beach Senior Comm	20420 Marine Drive N.W., Stanwood 98292/206-652-7585	Methodist
Wesley Homes	815 S. 216th Street, Des Moines 98198/206-824-5000	Methodist
Yakima First Baptist Homes	6 N. 6th Street, Yakima 98901/509-248-3191	Baptist

West Virginia

Ceredo Manor	P.O. Box 608, Ceredo 25507/304-453-4544	Natl Church Residences

Wisconsin

Cedar Crest, Inc.	1700 S. River Road, Janesville 53546/608-756-0344	United Methodist
Cedar Lake Home Campus of the Benevolent Corp	5595 Highway Z, West Bend 53095/414-334-9487	United Church of Christ
Evergreen Retirement Community, Inc.	1130 N. Westfield Street, P.O. Box 1720, Oshkosh 54902/ 414-233-2340	United Methodist
Fairhaven Corporation	435 Starin Road, Whitewater 53190/414-473-2140	United Church of Christ
Grace Lutheran Foundation, Inc.	816 Porter Avenue, Eau Claire 54701/715-832-3003	Lutheran
Luther Manor	4545 N. 92nd Street, Wauwatosa 53225/414-464-3880	Lutheran
Marquardt Memorial Manor, Inc.	1020 Hill Street, Watertown 53094/414-261-0400	Moravian Church
Northland Lutheran Retirement Community, Inc.	831 Pine Beach Road, Marinette 54143/715-732-0155	Lutheran
Oakwood Village	6201-09 Mineral Point Road, Madison 53705/608-231-3451	Lutheran
Tudor Oaks Retirement Comm	S77, W12929 McShane Rd., P.O. Box 901, Hales Corners 53130/ 414-529-0100	Baptist

Wyoming

Heritage Towers	428 N. Jefferson Street, Sheridan 82801/307-674-8825	Christian Church

Source: Selected from *1990 American Association of Homes for the Aging Directory of Members.*

65 AND GROWING

Year	Population	Percent
1900	3,100,000	4.0
1955	9,000,000	6.8
1985	28,500,000	12.0
2030	64,600,000	21.0

Source: US Bureau of the Census

FOCUS QUOTE 66 99 The family was established long before the church. My duty is to my family first. —D. L. Moody

85 AND STILL GROWING

Year	Population	Percent
1900	125,000	4.0
1985	2,700,000	9.5
2030	8,600,000	13.0

Source: US Bureau of the Census

LIVING GOES ON: LIFE EXPECTANCY

Year	Men	Women
1900	46.3	48.3
1985	71.2	78.2
2030	81.8	87.1

Source: US Bureau of the Census

Coming Soon: Age of the Aged

As the old get older, the percentage of young gets dramatically smaller.

Age distribution of total U.S. population

1960	1990	2030	Age:
9.3%	12.7%	20.7%	65 and older
8.6	8.4		
11.4	10.2	8.4	55–64
13.4	15.2	12.1	45–54
12.7	17.4	13.0	35–44
8.9		12.3	25–34
	10.3	11.6	18–24
35.7	25.8	21.9	Under 18

Source: U.S. Census Bureau

Ever Grayer, Ever Greater

Percent of total male and female populations age 75 and older

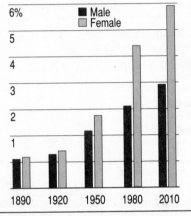

Source: U.S. Census Bureau

When to Retire?

Most people say they'll retire before they're 65 years old.

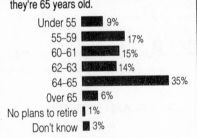

Under 55 — 9%
55–59 — 17%
60–61 — 15%
62–63 — 14%
64–65 — 35%
Over 65 — 6%
No plans to retire — 1%
Don't know — 3%

Source: Towers Perrin survey of 1,000 adults working for companies with 750 or more employees

ORGANIZATIONS OFFERING RETIREMENT PLANNING SERVICES

Write for retirement planning packet:
American Association of Retired Persons, 215 Long Beach Blvd., Long Beach, CA 90801
U.S. Government Printing Office, Washington, DC 20402
American Council on Life Insurance, 1850 K Street NW, Washington, DC 20006
Action for Independent Maturity, 1909 K Street NW, Washington DC 20049

A CHILD'S VIEW OF A RETIREMENT PARK

After Christmas break, the teacher asked her small pupils how they spent their holidays. One small boy's reply went like this:

We always spent Christmas with Grandma and Grandpa in their big brick home, but Grandpa got retarded and they moved to Florida.

They live in a place with lots of retarded people; they live in tin huts; they ride three-wheeled tricycles.

They go to a big building called a wrecked hall, but if it was wrecked, it is fixed up now. They play games there and do exercises, but they don't do them very well.

There is a swimming pool, and they go to it and just stand there in the water with their hats on. I guess they don't know how to swim.

My Grandma used to make cookies and stuff, but I guess she forgot how; nobody cooks there—they all go to the fast food restaurants.

As you come into the Park, there is a doll house with a man sitting in it. He watches all day, so they can't get out without him seeing them.

They all wear badges with their names on them. I guess they don't know who they are.

My Grandma said Grandpa worked hard all his life and earned his retardment. I wish they would move back home, but I guess the man in the doll house won't let them out.

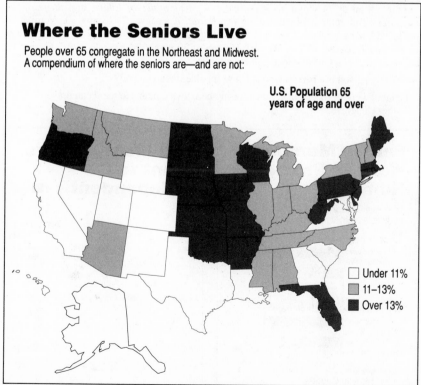

Where the Seniors Live

People over 65 congregate in the Northeast and Midwest.
A compendium of where the seniors are—and are not:

U.S. Population 65 years of age and over

☐ Under 11%
▨ 11–13%
■ Over 13%

Source: U.S. Census Bureau

REFLECTIONS ON AGING

One thing about getting old is that you can sing in the bathroom while brushing your teeth.

The older the fiddle, the sweeter the tune.
—English Proverb

There is more danger of rusting out than wearing out.
—Humphrey Davy Rolleston

We must both, I'm afraid, recognize that, as we grow older, we become like old cars—more and more repairs and replacements are necessary. We must just look forward to the fine new machines (latest resurrection model) which are waiting for us, we hope, in the divine garage.
—C. S. Lewis

What matter if one chapter nears the end?
What matter if the silver deck the brow?
Chanting I go.
—Ralph Spaulding Cushman

Winter is on my head, but eternal spring is in my heart.
—Victor Hugo

Between the ages of 70 and 83 Commodore Vanderbilt added about $100 million to his fortune. Kant at 74 wrote his *Anthropology, Metaphysics of Ethics,* and *Strife of the Faculties.* Tintoretto at 74 painted the vast *Paradise,* a canvas 74 feet by 30. Verdi at 74 produced his masterpiece, *Otello*; at 80, *Falstaff*; and at 85, the famous *Ave Maria, Stabat Mater,* and *Te Deum.* Oliver Wendell Holmes at 79 wrote *Over the Teacups.* Cato at 80 began the study of Greek. Goethe at 80 completed *Faust.*

An elderly person is a person who is ten years older than you are!

If I cannot work or rise from my chair or my bed, love remains to me; I can pray.
—Father Congreve

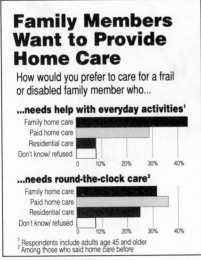

Family Members Want to Provide Home Care

How would you prefer to care for a frail or disabled family member who...

...needs help with everyday activities[1]

Family home care
Paid home care
Residential care
Don't know/ refused

0   10%   20%   30%   40%

...needs round-the-clock care[2]

Family home care
Paid home care
Residential care
Don't know/ refused

0   10%   20%   30%   40%

[1] Respondents include adults age 45 and older
[2] Among those who said home care before

Source: AARP/ICR EXCEL

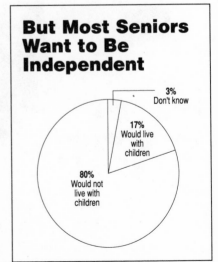

But Most Seniors Want to Be Independent

3% Don't know

17% Would live with children

80% Would not live with children

Source: Marriott Seniors' Attitudes Survey

Leisure Time

1993 CRUISES

Jan	1-4	Caribbean	SS Dolphin IV	$445-$860	New Creation Cruises
	3-8	Mexico	SS Britanis	$770-$1590	
	3-10	Caribbean/Virgin Islands	SS Seabreeze	$875-$1745	
	4-8	Caribbean/Bible Study Cruise		$595-$995	Templeton Tours
	4-8	Caribbean	SS Dolphin IV	$545-$1220	New Creation Cruises
	5-18	Caribbean	SS Dolphin IV	$445-$860	
	8-11	Caribbean	SS Dolphin IV	$445-$860	
	10-15	Mexico	SS Britanis	$770-$1590	
	10-17	Cayman/Jamaica/Mexico	SS Seabreeze	$875-$1745	
	11-15	Caribbean	SS Dolphin IV	$545-$1220	
	17-22	Mexico	SS Britanis	$770-$1590	
	17-24	Caribbean/Virgin Islands	SS Seabreeze	$875-$1745	
	18-22	Caribbean	SS Dolphin IV	$545-$1220	
	22-25	Caribbean	SS Dolphin IV	$445-$860	
	24-29	Mexico	SS Britanis	$770-$1590	
	24-31	Cayman/Jamaica/Mexico	SS Seabreeze	$875-$1745	
	25-29	Caribbean	SS Dolphin IV	$545-$1220	
	29-Feb 1	Caribbean	SS Dolphin IV	$445-$860	
	31-Feb 5	Mexico	SS Britanis	$770-$1590	
	31-Feb 7	Caribbean/Virgin Islands	SS Seabreeze	$875-$1745	
Feb	1-5	Caribbean	SS Dolphin IV	$545-$1220	
	5-8	Caribbean	SS Dolphin IV	$445-$860	
	7-12	Mexico	SS Britanis	$770-$1590	
	7-14	Caribbean/Virgin Islands	SS Seabreeze	$875-$1745	
	8-12	Caribbean	SS Dolphin IV	$545-$1220	
	12-15	Caribbean	SS Dolphin IV	$445-$860	
	14-19	Mexico	SS Britanis	$770-$1590	
	14-21	Cayman/Jamaica/Mexico	SS Seabreeze	$875-$1745	
	15-19	Caribbean	SS Dolphin IV	$545-$1220	
	19-22	Caribbean	SS Dolphin IV	$445-$860	
	21-26	Mexico	SS Britanis	$770-$1590	
	21-28	Caribbean/Virgin Islands	SS Seabreeze	$875-$1745	
	22-26	Caribbean	SS Dolphin IV	$545-$1220	
	26-Mar 1	Caribbean	SS Dolphin IV	$445-$860	
	28-Mar 5	Mexico	SS Britanis	$770-$1590	
	28-Mar 7	Cayman/Jamaica/Mexico	SS Seabreeze	$875-$1745	
	*	Caribbean/Coral Ridge Island Adventure/ James Kennedy			Templeton Tours
	*	Caribbean/Jubilee at Sea Cruise			
Mar	1-5	Caribbean	SS Dolphin IV	$545-$1220	New Creation Cruises
	5-8	Caribbean	SS Dolphin IV	$445-$860	
	7-12	Mexico	SS Britanis	$770-$1590	
	7-14	Caribbean/Virgin Islands	SS Seabreeze	$875-$1745	
	8-12	Caribbean	SS Dolphin IV	$545-$1220	
	12-15	Caribbean	SS Dolphin IV	$445-$860	
	14-19	Mexico	SS Britanis	$770-$1590	
	14-21	Cayman/Jamaica/Mexico	SS Seabreeze	$875-$1745	
	15-19	Caribbean	SS Dolphin IV	$545-$1220	
	19-22	Caribbean	SS Dolphin IV	$445-$860	

1993 CRUISES cont.

Mar	21-26	Mexico	SS Britanis	$770-$1590	New Creation Cruises
	21-28	Caribbean/Virgin Islands	SS Seabreeze	$875-$1745	
	22-26	Caribbean	SS Dolphin IV	$545-$1220	
	26-29	Caribbean	SS Dolphin IV	$445-$860	
	28-Apr 2	Mexico	SS Britanis	$770-$1590	
	28-Apr 4	Cayman/Jamaica/Mexico	SS Seabreeze	$875-$1745	
	29-Apr 2	Caribbean	SS Dolphin IV	$545-$1220	
	*	Caribbean/Good News Bible Cruise			Templeton Tours
Apr	2-5	Caribbean	SS Dolphin IV	$445-$860	New Creation Cruises
	4-9	Mexico	SS Britanis	$770-$1590	
	4-11	Caribbean/Virgin Islands	SS Seabreeze	$875-$1745	
	5-9	Caribbean	SS Dolphin IV	$545-$1220	
	9-12	Caribbean	SS Dolphin IV	$445-$860	
	11-16	Mexico	SS Britanis	$770-$1590	
	11-18	Cayman/Jamaica/Mexico	SS Seabreeze	$875-$1745	
	12-16	Caribbean	SS Dolphin IV	$545-$1220	
	16-19	Caribbean	SS Dolphin IV	$445-$860	
	18-23	Mexico	SS Britanis	$770-$1590	
	18-25	Caribbean/Virgin Islands	SS Seabreeze	$875-$1745	
	19-23	Caribbean	SS Dolphin IV	$545-$1220	
	23-26	Caribbean	SS Dolphin IV	$445-$860	
	25-30	Mexico	SS Britanis	$770-$1590	
	25-May 2	Cayman/Jamaica/Mexico	SS Seabreeze	$875-$1745	
	26-30	Caribbean	SS Dolphin IV	$545-$1220	
	30-May 3	Caribbean	SS Dolphin IV	$445-$860	
May	2-9	Caribbean/Virgin Islands	SS Seabreeze	$875-$1745	
	3-7	Caribbean	SS Dolphin IV	$545-$1220	
	7-10	Caribbean	SS Dolphin IV	$445-$860	
	9-14	Mexico	SS Britanis	$770-$1590	
	9-16	Cayman/Jamaica/Mexico	SS Seabreeze	$875-$1745	
	10-14	Caribbean	SS Dolphin IV	$545-$1220	
	14-17	Caribbean	SS Dolphin IV	$445-$860	
	16-21	Mexico	SS Britanis	$770-$1590	
	16-23	Caribbean/Virgin Islands	SS Seabreeze	$875-$1745	
	17-21	Caribbean	SS Dolphin IV	$545-$1220	
	21-24	Caribbean	SS Dolphin IV	$445-$860	
	23-28	Mexico	SS Britanis	$770-$1590	
	23-30	Cayman/Jamaica/Mexico	SS Seabreeze	$875-$1745	
	24-28	Caribbean	SS Dolphin IV	$545-$1220	
	28-31	Caribbean	SS Dolphin IV	$445-$860	
	30-June 4	Mexico	SS Britanis	$770-$1590	
	30-June 6	Caribbean/Virgin Islands	SS Seabreeze	$875-$1745	
	31-June 4	Caribbean	SS Dolphin IV	$545-$1220	
June	4-7	Caribbean	SS Dolphin IV	$445-$860	
	5-12	Alaska	MS Westerdam	$1920-$2220	
	6-11	Mexico	SS Britanis	$770-$1590	
	6-13	Caribbean/Virgin Islands	SS Seabreeze	$875-$1745	
	7-11	Caribbean	SS Dolphin IV	$545-$1220	
	11-14	Caribbean	SS Dolphin IV	$445-$860	
	12-18	Alaska	MS Westerdam	$1920-$2220	
	13-18	Mexico	SS Britanis	$770-$1590	
	13-20	Cayman/Jamaica/Mexico	SS Seabreeze	$875-$1745	
	14-18	Caribbean	SS Dolphin IV	$545-$1220	
	18-21	Caribbean	SS Dolphin IV	$445-$860	
	19-25	Alaska	MS Westerdam	$1920-$2220	
	20-25	Mexico	SS Britanis	$770-$1590	
	20-27	Caribbean/Virgin Islands	SS Seabreeze	$875-$1745	
	21-25	Caribbean	SS Dolphin IV	$545-$1220	
	25-28	Caribbean	SS Dolphin IV	$445-$860	
	26-July 2	Alaska	MS Westerdam	$1920-$2220	

June	27-July 2	Mexico	SS Britanis	$770-$1590	New Creation Cruises
	27-July 4	Cayman/Jamaica/Mexico	SS Seabreeze	$875-$1745	
	28-July 2	Caribbean	SS Dolphin IV	$545-$1220	
	*	Alaska/In Touch/Charles Stanley		Templeton Tours	
	*	Caribbean/Singing at Sea Cruise			
July	2-5	Caribbean	SS Dolphin IV	$445-$860	New Creation Cruises
	3-9	Alaska	MS Westerdam	$1920-$2220	
	4-9	Mexico	SS Britanis	$770-$1590	
	4-11	Caribbean/Virgin Islands	SS Seabreeze	$875-$1745	
	5-9	Caribbean	SS Dolphin IV	$545-$1220	
	9-12	Caribbean	SS Dolphin IV	$445-$860	
	10-16	Alaska	MS Westerdam	$1920-$2220	
	11-16	Mexico	SS Britanis	$770-$1590	
	11-18	Cayman/Jamaica/Mexico	SS Seabreeze	$875-$1745	
	12-16	Caribbean	SS Dolphin IV	$545-$1220	
	16-19	Caribbean	SS Dolphin IV	$445-$860	
	17-23	Alaska	MS Westerdam	$1920-$2220	
	18-23	Mexico	SS Britanis	$770-$1590	
	18-25	Caribbean/Virgin Islands	SS Seabreeze	$875-$1745	
	19-23	Caribbean	SS Dolphin IV	$545-$1220	
	23-26	Caribbean	SS Dolphin IV	$445-$860	
	25-30	Mexico	SS Britanis	$770-$1590	
	25-Aug 1	Cayman/Jamaica/Mexico	SS Seabreeze	$875-$1745	
	26-30	Caribbean	SS Dolphin IV	$545-$1220	
	30-Aug 2	Caribbean	SS Dolphin IV	$445-$860	
	31-Aug 6	Alaska	MS Westerdam	$1920-$2220	
Aug	1-6	Mexico	SS Britanis	$770-$1590	
	1-8	Caribbean/Virgin Islands	SS Seabreeze	$875-$1745	
	2-6	Caribbean	SS Dolphin IV	$545-$1220	
	6-9	Caribbean	SS Dolphin IV	$445-$860	
	7-13	Alaska	MS Westerdam	$1920-$2220	
	8-13	Mexico	SS Britanis	$770-$1590	
	8-15	Cayman/Jamaica/Mexico	SS Seabreeze	$875-$1745	
	9-13	Caribbean	SS Dolphin IV	$545-$1220	
	13-16	Caribbean	SS Dolphin IV	$445-$860	
	14-20	Alaska	MS Westerdam	$1920-$2220	
	15-20	Mexico	SS Britanis	$770-$1590	
	15-22	Caribbean/Virgin Islands	SS Seabreeze	$875-$1745	
	16-20	Caribbean	SS Dolphin IV	$545-$1220	
	20-23	Caribbean	SS Dolphin IV	$445-$860	
	21-27	Alaska	MS Westerdam	$1920-$2220	
	22-27	Mexico	SS Britanis	$770-$1590	
	22-29	Cayman/Jamaica/Mexico	SS Seabreeze	$875-$1745	
	23-27	Caribbean	SS Dolphin IV	$545-$1220	
	27-30	Caribbean	SS Dolphin IV	$445-$860	
	28-Sept 4	Alaska	MS Westerdam	$1920-$2220	
	29-Sept 3	Mexico	SS Britanis	$770-$1590	
	29-Sept 5	Caribbean/Virgin Islands	SS Seabreeze	$875-$1745	
	30-Sept 3	Caribbean	SS Dolphin IV	$545-$1220	
Sept	3-6	Caribbean	SS Dolphin IV	$445-$860	
	5-12	Caribbean/Virgin Islands	SS Seabreeze	$875-$1745	
	6-10	Caribbean	SS Dolphin IV	$545-$1220	
	10-13	Caribbean	SS Dolphin IV	$445-$860	
	12-19	Cayman/Jamaica/Mexico	SS Seabreeze	$875-$1745	
	13-17	Caribbean	SS Dolphin IV	$545-$1220	
	17-20	Caribbean	SS Dolphin IV	$445-$860	
	19-26	Caribbean/Virgin Islands	SS Seabreeze	$875-$1745	
	20-24	Caribbean	SS Dolphin IV	$545-$1220	
	24-27	Caribbean	SS Dolphin IV	$445-$860	
	26-Oct 3	Cayman/Jamaica/Mexico	SS Seabreeze	$875-$1745	
	27-Oct 1	Caribbean	SS Dolphin IV	$545-$1220	

1993 CRUISES cont.

Oct	1-4	Caribbean	SS Dolphin IV	$445-$860	New Creation Cruises
	3-10	Caribbean/Virgin Islands	SS Seabreeze	$875-$1745	
	4-8	Caribbean	SS Dolphin IV	$545-$1220	
	8-11	Caribbean	SS Dolphin IV	$445-$860	
	10-17	Cayman/Jamaica/Mexico	SS Seabreeze	$875-$1745	
	11-15	Caribbean	SS Dolphin IV	$545-$1220	
	15-18	Caribbean	SS Dolphin IV	$445-$860	
	17-24	Caribbean/Virgin Islands	SS Seabreeze	$875-$1745	
	18-22	Caribbean	SS Dolphin IV	$545-$1220	
	22-25	Caribbean	SS Dolphin IV	$445-$860	
	24-31	Cayman/Jamaica/Mexico	SS Seabreeze	$875-$1745	
	25-29	Caribbean	SS Dolphin IV	$545-$1220	
	29-Nov 1	Caribbean	SS Dolphin IV	$445-$860	
	31-Nov 5	Mexico	SS Britanis	$770-$1590	
	31-Nov 7	Caribbean/Virgin Islands	SS Seabreeze	$875-$1745	
	*	Mediterranean/Journeys of Paul Cruise			Templeton Tours
Nov	1-5	Caribbean	SS Dolphin IV	$545-$1220	New Creation Cruises
	5-8	Caribbean	SS Dolphin IV	$445-$860	
	7-12	Mexico	SS Britanis	$770-$1590	
	7-14	Caribbean/Virgin Islands	SS Seabreeze	$875-$1745	
	8-12	Caribbean	SS Dolphin IV	$545-$1220	
	12-15	Caribbean	SS Dolphin IV	$445-$860	
	14-19	Mexico	SS Britanis	$770-$1590	
	14-21	Cayman/Jamaica/Mexico	SS Seabreeze	$875-$1745	
	15-19	Caribbean	SS Dolphin IV	$545-$1220	
	19-22	Caribbean	SS Dolphin IV	$445-$860	
	21-26	Mexico	SS Britanis	$770-$1590	
	21-28	Caribbean/Virgin Islands	SS Seabreeze	$875-$1745	
	22-26	Caribbean	SS Dolphin IV	$545-$1220	
	26-29	Caribbean	SS Dolphin IV	$445-$860	
	28-Dec 3	Mexico	SS Britanis	$770-$1590	
	28-Dec 5	Cayman/Jamaica/Mexico	SS Seabreeze	$875-$1745	
	29-Dec 3	Caribbean	SS Dolphin IV	$545-$1220	
Dec	3-6	Caribbean	SS Dolphin IV	$445-$860	
	5-10	Mexico	SS Britanis	$770-$1590	
	5-12	Caribbean/Virgin Islands	SS Seabreeze	$875-$1745	
	6-10	Caribbean	SS Dolphin IV	$545-$1220	
	10-13	Caribbean	SS Dolphin IV	$445-$860	
	12-17	Mexico	SS Britanis	$770-$1590	
	12-19	Cayman/Jamaica/Mexico	SS Seabreeze	$875-$1745	
	13-17	Caribbean	SS Dolphin IV	$545-$1220	
	17-20	Caribbean	SS Dolphin IV	$445-$860	
	19-24	Mexico	SS Britanis	$770-$1590	
	19-26	Caribbean/Virgin Islands	SS Seabreeze	$875-$1745	
	20-24	Caribbean	SS Dolphin IV	$545-$1220	
	24-27	Caribbean	SS Dolphin IV	$445-$860	
	26-31	Mexico	SS Britanis	$770-$1590	
	26-Jan 3	Cayman/Jamaica/Mexico	SS Seabreeze	$875-$1745	
	27-31	Caribbean	SS Dolphin IV	$545-$1220	
	31-Jan 3	Caribbean	SS Dolphin IV	$445-$860	

*For more information and specific dates on 1993–1994 cruises contact:

ACTS (American Christian Tours)
102 South St.
Rice Lake, WI 54868
1-800-367-4484

Specialty Tours
1443 Del Prado Blvd., Suites A & B
Cape Coral, FL 33990
1-800-458-8281

New Creation Cruises and Vacations
Box 574837
Orlando, FL 32857-4837
1-800-554-5454

Templeton Tours
P.O. Box 2630
Boone, NC 28607
1-800-334-2630

VACATION SPOTS WORTH SEEING

Arizona

Flagstaff, *Oak Creek Canyon*
Scenic route. Spectacular 3,000 foot drop
from rim. U.S. 89A between Flagstaff and
Sedona 602-774-4505

Grand Canyon National Park
Sheer cliffs drop more than a mile to the
floor of the Canyon and the Colorado
River; width varies from one to 18 miles.
Look for plaques with inscriptions from
Mother Basilea Schlink at the Watch
Tower at Desert View, at the head of
Bright-Angel Trail, and outside Hermit's
Rest Gift Ship. Admission fee. North rim
(closed during winter) is off AZ Hwy. 67;
South rim is off AZ Hwy. 64/U.S. 180
602-638-7888

Phoenix, *Desert Botanical Gardens*
10,000 varieties of desert plants from all
over the world. Admission fee. 1201 N.
Galvin Pkwy., Papago Park 602-252-8848

Arkansas

Eureka Springs, *The Bible Museum*
Collection of Bibles include handwritten
volumes from pre-printing press days.
Contains 7,000 volumes of old Bibles and
3,000 primitive manuscripts. Dr. Fred Mc-
Graw, Library of Congress, considers this
the greatest collection anywhere. Admission fee. Daily May through October 9
A.M. to 8 P.M. except Monday and Thursday, 9 A.M. to 5 P.M. P.O. Box 471, Eureka Springs, AR 72632 501-253-8781

Eureka Springs, *Christ of the Ozarks*
Seven-story concrete sculpture of Christ.
Span of the outstretched arms is 65 feet,
weight is more than one million pounds.
Magnetic Mountain.

Eureka Springs, *Eureka Springs Passion
Play*
The drama portrays the story of Jesus,
using a cast of more than 200 people.
Stage effects include a replica of the street
of Jerusalem. Admission fee. Daily May
through October, except Monday and

Thursday, at 8:30 P.M.; 7:30 P.M. after
Labor Day. Off U.S. 62, three miles east of
Eureka Springs 501-253-9200

Eureka Springs, *Walls of Jerusalem*
Life-size replica of Old Jerusalem.

California

Anaheim, *Disneyland*
Main Street U.S.A. fantasy. Experience
the land of yesterday and the land of tomorrow. Admission fee. 1313 S. Harbor
Blvd. 714-999-4000

Garden Grove, *The Crystal Cathedral*
The 120-feet-high, $18 million glass
church houses the congregation of
televangelist Dr. Robert Schuller. "Hour
of Power" telecasts originate here. South
of Disneyland off the Santa Ana Frwy.
12141 Lewis St. 714-971-4000

Glendale, *Forest Lawn Memorial Park*
Outstanding trilogy of huge paintings por-
traying the three most dramatic moments
in the life of Christ: The Crucifixion, the
Resurrection, and the Ascension. Forest
Lawn also contains reproductions of Mi-
chelangelo's greatest sculptural works.
Brief program of narration, special light-
ing and sound effects. 1712 S. Glendale
Ave. 213-241-4151

Monrovia, *World Vision*
International network of Asian orphanages.
Also actively involved in disaster relief and
community development projects overseas.
Two tours a day at 9:30 A.M. and 1:30 P.M.
Tours last about two hours and include an
audiovisual presentation. Off U.S. 210. 919
W. Huntington Dr. 818-357-7979

Rancho Palos Verdes, *Marineland*
More than 1,000 fish. The only swim-
through coral reef in U.S. Admission fee.
6610 Palos Verdes Dr. South 213-377-1571

San Bernardino, *Arrowhead Springs Christian Conference Center*
Home of Campus Crusade. Spacious
grounds. Group tours can be arranged.
From Interstate 15E take state highway 18

VACATION SPOTS WORTH SEEING cont.

to Waterman Canyon. Watch for entrance sign into the Conference complex. Campus Crusade, Arrowhead Springs, San Bernardino, CA 92414 714-886-5224

San Bernardino, *Missionary Aviation Fellowship*

Air support agency serving missionaries around the world. Tours are available during work hours. If possible, call in advance. Off I-10, southeast of San Bernardino. 1849 N. Wabash, Redlands Municipal Airport 714-794-1151

San Diego, *Museum of Creation and Earth History*

Opened in 1977 by the Institute of Creation Research, the museum presents evidence that refutes evolution. Associated with Christian Heritage College. Guides are on hand from 1-4 P.M. weekdays. Group tours conducted by appointment. In El Cajon, off U.S. Hwy. 8, east of San Diego 714-440-2443

San Diego, *Sea World*

Killer whales, sharks, great variety of fish, daily marine-life shows. Admission fee. 1720 S. Shores Rd. 619-226-3845

Universal City, *Universal Studios*

Here you can see (and experience) the parting of the Red Sea! An "electronic miracle" creates the illusion. A tour tram waits for the waters to part, then drives through. Five-hour tours through movie/television studios available. Admission fee. Junction Hollywood and Ventura Frwys. 818-508-5444

Victorville, *Roy Rogers/Dale Evans Museum*

Souvenirs of their personal and professional lives. You will see, Roy's famous horse, Trigger, in stuffed form, his gun collection and other displays. Dale's books are on sale in the museum gift ship. On the edge of the Mohave Desert at Victorville on I-15. Near Apple Valley Ranch.

Yosemite Village, *Yosemite National Park*

Half Dome and El Capitan tower above Yosemite Valley. Admission fee. 200 miles northwest of San Francisco off CA Hwy. 140 209-372-0264

Colorado

Colorado Springs, *Air Force Academy Chapel*

The chapel with 150 feet high spires is visible for miles. An aeronautical motif is prominent—the end of each pew in the Protestant chapel is sculptured to resemble an airplane propeller. Open 9 A.M. to 5 P.M. Monday through Saturday and 1 to 5 P.M. Sundays. Worship services at 9 and 11 A.M. are open to the public. 4.5 miles north of Colorado Springs, off I-25 719-472-2555

Colorado Springs, *Garden of the Gods*

1500 acres of towering red sandstone formations. Off I-25 or U.S. 24. 3500 Ridge Rd. 719-578-6933

Colorado Springs, *The Navigators' Glen Eyrie*

Conference center, although visitors are welcome to stop in for a visit. A 67-room sandstone tudor-style castle is the focal point of the 750-acre scenic grounds. The castle's red tiled roof was shipped, each tile individually wrapped, from England. Exit 146 off I-25. P.O. Box 20, Colorado Springs, CO 80901 303-598-1212

Colorado Springs, *Pike's Peak*

Drive, walk or take cog railway to summit. N. off CO 67 719-635-7506

Golden, *Golden Gate Canyon State Park*

Panorama views of Continental Divide. 2 miles north on CO 93, 14 miles west 303-592-1502

Connecticut

Hartford, *Harriet Beecher Stowe Home*

Harriet Beecher Stowe is author of Uncle Tom's Cabin, a powerful antislavery novel that rocked the nation. Next door is the home where Mark Twain once lived. Admission fee. 351 Farmington Ave. 203-527-6984

New Haven, *Yale University*

Concerned Christians launched this Ivy League school in 1701 as an alternative to Harvard. Jonathan Edwards was one of Yale's early graduates.

West Hartford, *Noah Webster House and Museum*

Birthplace of Noah Webster who spent 36 years developing his American Dictionary. Converted at age 40, he studied the Scriptures as diligently as the information which made up his enduring work. 18th century furnishings. Admission fee. North of Rt. 84. 227 S. Main St. 203-521-5262

Woodbury, *Glebe House*
Birthplace of American Episcopacy. Site of Samuel Seabury's election as the first bishop of the Episcopal Church in America. The first floor is an authentically restored home; the second floor is a church museum. Saturday through Wednesday, 1-5 P.M.

D.C.

Washington, *Library of Congress*
340 miles of bookshelves. Exhibits a three-volume, 1455 edition of the Gutenberg Bible. You will see a number of Bible quotations inside this library of libraries. Open daily except on Christmas and New Year's Day. Certain exhibit areas are open from 8:30 A.M. to 9:30 P.M. Monday through Friday; to 6:00 P.M. Saturdays. Closed Sundays and holidays. At the Thomas Jefferson Building, free 45-minute tours begin Monday through Friday, 9 A.M. through 4 P.M., and the 15-minute multi-media show before every hour starts at 8:45 A.M. Southeast of the Capitol. First St. and Independence Ave. 202-287-5000; James Madison Memorial Bldg. is 287-5111

Washington, *Lincoln Memorial*
Daniel Chester French marble statue of Lincoln. Erected in honor of Lincoln's greatness. Some of his more memorable words are inscribed in the walls, including his second inaugural address. West Potomac Park at 23rd St., NW 202-426-6895

Washington, *National Archives*
On view are the three foundational documents that underlie our national government: The Declaration of Independence, the United States Constitution, the Bill of Rights. Open daily. Constitution Ave. between 7th and 9th Streets, NW 202-523-3000

Washington, *National Presbyterian Church and Center*
Contains The Chapel of the Presidents, ded-icated to Dwight D. Eisenhower, whose pew is marked. Seventeen presidents have worshiped here.

Washington, *National Shrine of the Immaculate Conception*
Largest Roman Catholic church in the United States. Headquarters for the Roman Catholic church in the United States. Michigan Ave. and 4th St., NW.

Washington, *St. John's Church*
Built in 1816, it is often called the "Church of the Presidents." Every president since James Madison has attended it. Lower Manhattan's Lafayette Square.

Washington, *Thomas Jefferson Memorial*
19-foot bronze statue of Jefferson. Quotes inscribed in the walls will remind you of basic truths on which our country was founded. South bank of Washington's Tidal Basin, SW 202-426-6822

Washington, *United States Capitol*
A gallery pass from your Congressman will allow you to watch proceedings if Congress is in session. Each session opens in prayer, a tradition that began in 1774 when Rev. Jacob Duche offered the first prayer in the Continental Congress. Open 9 A.M. to 4:30 P.M. daily from November through April; until 10 P.M. the rest of the year. Capitol Hill, First St.

Washington, *United States Supreme Court*
Classical building built in 1935. A tableau of the Ten Commandments is one of the emblems above the Bench. Moses is included among the great lawgivers in Herman A. MacNeil's marble sculpture group on the east front. Open 9 A.M. to 4:30 P.M. Monday through Friday; closed on Saturday, Sunday and holidays. First St. and Maryland Ave. NE 202-479-3000

Washington, *Vietnam Veteran Memorial*
Black granite wall. Names of those who gave their lives for freedom in Vietnam inscribed on wall. West end of the Mall 202-357-2700

Washington, *Washington Bible College*
Offers a limited number of guest accommodations during the school year. Is a 20-minute drive into the heart of the Capitol. Special rates for people in full-time

VACATION SPOTS WORTH SEEING cont.

Christian work. 6511 Princess Garden Pkwy., Lanham, MD 20801 301-552-1400

Washington, *Washington Monument*
Towering 555 feet into the air, the Washington Monument is Washington D.C.'s most prominent landmark. Elevator takes visitors to top. Admission fee. On the Mall near 15th St. NW 202-426-6839

Washington, *Washington National Cathedral*
Situated on the highest point of land in D.C.—Mount St. Alban. Famous men are buried here. Every year, more than 500,000 visit—to mourn a leader, to tour the Cathedral, to worship.

Washington, *The White House*
Tours of public rooms available 10 A.M. to noon, Tuesday through Saturday. During summer Saturday hours extended to 2 P.M. Closed Sunday, Monday and some holidays. No admission fee. E. Executive Ave. and 15th St., 202-456-2200

Delaware

Wilmington, *Old Swedes Church*
Oldest church in the United States standing as originally built and regularly used for church services. Built and dedicated in 1698 as Helga Trefaldighet Kyrcka (Holy Trinity Church) by Swedish settlers. Heart of Wilmington's industrial district.

Florida

Boca Raton, *Bibletown*
Winter Bible conference and sacred concert complex. Winter concerts run January through March. 2,000-seat auditorium. P.O. Box A, Boca Raton, FL 33432 305-391-7800

Florida City, *Everglades National Park*
Largest subtropical wilderness in U.S. Admission fee. 10 miles SW on FL 997 305-247-6211

Ft. Myers, *Shell Point Village*
Christian and Missionary Alliance retirement community. 75-acre village with more than 1,000 residents. McGregor Blvd., 15 miles south of Ft. Myers on Rt. 867, Ft. Myers, FL 33901 813-481-3737

Ft. Myers, *Thomas A. Edison Winter Home*
Home, gardens, laboratory. Admission fee. 2350 McGregor Blvd. 813-334-3614

Lake Buena Vista, *Walt Disney World*
Magic Kingdom, Epcot Center, MGM Studios Theme Park. Admission fee. 22 miles SW of Orlando, north on I-4. 305-824-2222

Orlando, *Sea World*
Marine shows, water-ski shows, fish. Admission fee. 7007 Sea World Dr. 305-351-0021

St. Petersburg, *Moody Keswick Bible Conference*
Largest winter Christian conference grounds on Florida's west coast. Sacred music concerts on Saturday nights from January to April. 7500 100th Way North, St. Petersburg, FL 33708 813-391-2998

Tampa, *Busch Gardens*
African theme; 3,000 animals. Allow a full day for this one. Admission fee. 3000 Busch Blvd. 813-971-8282

West Palm Beach, *Lion Country Safari*
Experience jungle life. Drive through this 320-acre preserve to see animals in their natural environment. 18 miles west of I-95 on FL 80 305-793-1084

Winter Haven, *Cypress Gardens*
Boat trips through the Gardens. Daily water-skiing shows. Admission fee. SE off U.S. 27 on FL 540 813-324-2111

Georgia

Atlanta, *Jimmy Carter Library*
Exhibits on the Carter presidency. 1 Copen Hill, east of State Capitol 404-331-0296

Atlanta, *Martin Luther King, Jr., District*
Includes tomb and birthplace of Martin Luther King, Jr., as well as the Ebenezer Baptist Church where he was pastor. Open daily 9:30 A.M. to 5:30 P.M. Tours: Monday–Saturday at 10 A.M. to 4 P.M. 522 Auburn Ave., NE 404-331-3919

Columbus, *Callaway Gardens*
Resort, sports, and leisure education facilities on acres of gorgeously landscaped scenery. Approximately 15 miles north of Columbus off I-185.

St. Simons Island, *Christ Church*
Founded by Wesley Brothers in 1736.
Island is setting of Eugenia Price best-
selling novels.

Savannah, *Christ Episcopal Church*
John Wesley founded what is believed to
be the world's first Sunday school at
Christ Episcopal Church. 28 Bull St.

Savannah, *First African Baptist Church*
Organized in 1788, the first black church
in the United States. 403 W. Bryan St.

Toccoa Falls, *Toccoa Falls Park*
At 186 feet the falls are 17 feet higher than
Niagara Falls. Toccoa Falls College is
nearby. Open daily until sundown.

Hawaii

Honolulu, Oahu, *Kawaiahao Church*
Honolulu's oldest church, the Westminster Abbey of Hawaii. The setting for
royal inaugurations, weddings, funerals
and other pageantry. Sunday services at
10:30 A.M. are in both Hawaiian and
English. Open daily. 957 Punchbowl St.
808-538-6267

Honolulu, Oahu, *Pearl Harbor*
National historic landmark. The USS *Arizona* Memorial of the December 7, 1941
Japanese attack. Free tour of the USS *Arizona*. Daily except Mondays from Halawa
Landing. 1 Arizona Memorial Place 808-
422-2771

Lahaina, Maui, *Historic Lahaina Experience*
Begins at the onetime home of medical
missionary Dr. Dwight Baldwin. Largest
Banyan tree in the islands was planted in
1873 to commemorate the 50th anniversary of the first missionaries to arrive on
the island. The tree spreads over two-
thirds acre. Daily 10 A.M. to 4 P.M.

Illinois

Carbondale, *Bald Knob Cross*
Lighted white marble cross, visible day and
night; Bald Knob Mountain, Illinois' second highest peak. Shawnee National Forest.

Charleston, *Lincoln Log Cabin State Park*
Final Illinois home of the Lincolns.

Chicago, *Moody Bible Institute*
Half-hour multimedia show. Moodyana
Museum houses D. L. Moody's old arti-

facts. Tours begin at 10 A.M. and 1 P.M. 820
N. LaSalle St.

Chicago, *Moody Church*
Founded by D. L. Moody. Sunday services at 10:45 A.M. and 7 P.M. Across
from Lincoln Park, at North Ave. and
Clark St.

Chicago, *Pacific Garden Mission*
Granddaddy of U.S. rescue missions. The
site was once an old-time beer garden. Evening services at 7 P.M. Open daily, 24 hours.
Late afternoon and early evening visits recommended. 646 S. State St. 312-922-1462

Chicago, *Rockefeller Chapel*
One of the outstanding examples of
Gothic architecture in the United States.
Completed in 1928 at a cost of nearly
$2,000,000. University of Chicago cam-
pus, 57th and Woodlawn Sts.

Decatur, *Lincoln Trail Homestead State Park*
First log cabin built by the Lincolns.

Salem, *William Jennings Bryan Birthplace*
White frame house of his birth contains
many of his personal possessions—family
pictures, Bibles, law books, walking cane.
Open daily from 1 to 5 P.M., except Thurs-
days. 618-548-1236

Springfield, *Lincoln Depot*
Here Lincoln's Springfield days ended
with a farewell speech: "I now leave, not
knowing when or whether ever I may return, with a task before me greater than
that which rested upon Washington." On
Monroe between 9th and 10th Sts.

Springfield, *Lincoln's Springfield Home*
It was in this modest clapboard home that
Lincoln received the announcement of his
nomination for the presidency in 1860.
426 S. 7th St. 217-492-4150

Springfield, *Lincoln's Tomb*
178 feet high granite spire marks the tomb
of Lincoln and his family. Monument Ave.
217-782-2717

Wheaton, *Wheaton College*
Houses the Marion E. Wade Collection of
books and papers by C. S. Lewis, J.R.R.
Tolkien, Dorothy Sayers, and other writers
of faith. Tours conducted three times daily
at 11:15 A.M., 1:30 and 3:00 P.M. 25
miles east of Chicago.

VACATION SPOTS WORTH SEEING cont.

Wheaton, *Billy Graham Center*
Panorama view of American evangelism from early church leaders to the present-day Billy Graham Evangelistic Association. Open 9:30 A.M. to 5:30 P.M. Tuesday, Wednesday, Thursday and Saturday; 1 to 9 P.M. Friday; 1 to 5 P.M. Sunday. 25 miles west of Chicago 708-260-5909

Indiana

Hammond, *First Baptist Church*
One of the largest Sunday schools/churches in the United States. Sunday school hour on Sundays at 9:30 A.M. 523 Sibley Blvd.

Nappanee, *Amish Acres*
Complex depicts the religious beliefs and customs of a people who still hold to the life-style of 17th century Europe. Outstanding Amish family style restaurant. Open daily 9 A.M. to 8 P.M. May through October; weekends only from November through April. 1 mile west of Nappanee on U.S. 6.

Valparaiso, *Chapel of the Resurrection*
Seating 3,000, one of the largest houses of worship on a college chapel. Valparaiso University campus, off U.S. 30.

Iowa

Amana, *Amana Colonies*
Iowa's most popular tourist attraction, the seven colonies blend the Old World with the new. Shops, factories and restaurants. Six museums within the 27,000-acre grounds. Take exit 225 between Des Moines and Davenport off I-80. Amana Colonies Travel Council, Amana, IA 52203 319-622-3828

Dubuque, *Mississippi River*
Mississippi River boat rides. Woodward Riverboat Museum—exhibits cover 300 years of riverboat history. Admission fee. 2nd St. Harbor 319-557-9545

Nashua, *Little Brown Church in the Vale*
Draws nearly 150,000 visitors a year. A popular wedding chapel. Couples come from all over the world. About forty miles northeast of Waterloo. Two miles northeast of Nashua on U.S. Hwy. 218.

West Branch, *Herbert Hoover's National Historical Site*
Birthplace and gravesite of former U.S. President Herbert Hoover. Schoolhouse Hoover attended, his father's blacksmith shop, and the Herbert Hoover Presidential Library-Museum. Admission fee. One-half mile north of Exit 254, off I-80 319-643-2541

Kansas

Abilene, *Eisenhower Center*
Family home, museum and library, chapel, and gravesites. Open 9 A.M. to 5 P.M. daily, year-round. 201 SE 4th St. 913-263-4751

Cedar Vale, *Wee Kirk of the Valley*
Perhaps the smallest church in U.S. The six pews seat two persons each—symbolic of the twelve disciples. In south central Kansas, 6 miles south of Cedar Vale.

Medicine Lodge, *Carry Nation Home*
Carry Nation, temperance crusader during the late 1800s and early 1900s, made use of her hatchet, Bible and loud-voiced prayers to break up or put out of business many liquor establishments. Today her home is a museum. U.S. Hwys. 160 and 281.

Kentucky

Bardstown, *My Old Kentucky Home State Park*
Stephen Foster outdoor drama. Mansion built 1793-1818 by Judge J. Rowan. Admission fee. 502-348-5971

Harrodsburg, *Shakertown*
The Shaker Village of Pleasant Hill, situated on more than two thousand acres, has been restored as a rural Shaker community in the early nineteenth century. Pleasant Hill Shakertown, Rt. 4, Harrodsburg, KY 40330 606-734-5411

Park City, *Mammoth Cave National Park*
Kentucky cave area. 300 miles of caverns. The Diamond Caverns are the gem of Kentucky caves with flowstone formations. Take Park City exit 48 off I-65 502-749-2891

Park City, *Mammoth Cave Wax Museum*
129 lifelike figures of famous Americans. Includes Leonardo da Vinci's "Last Supper," Moses receiving the Ten Commandments, and Billy Graham. Take Park City exit 48 off I-65.

Park City, *Wondering Woods*
Reconstructed 1900s town. Crafts and other skills are demonstrated. Sunday morning worship services in Old Community Meeting House. Take Park City exit 48 off I-65 to the junction of Hwys. 70 and 255. Chamber of Commerce, Rt. 1, Box 149, Wondering Woods, KY 42160 502-749-5221

Louisiana

Monroe, *Bible Research Center*
Very old and rare manuscripts, Bibles, engravings, maps, portraits and musical instruments are on display. Open Monday through Thursday. Closed in August. 2004 Riverside Dr.

Maryland

Annapolis, *U.S. Naval Academy*
Impressive ceremony of noon formation on Tecumseh Court at 12:05 P.M. weekdays, at 12:10 on Saturdays, and 12:30 on Sundays and holidays, weather permitting. The museum has one of the world's finest displays of sailing ship models. Open daily. Visitors Center, Ricketts Hall 301-263-6933

Baltimore, *Fort McHenry*
It was here on September 14, 1814, that lawyer Francis Scott Key jotted down the words to the Star Spangled Banner on the back of an old letter. Key was one of the founders of the American Sunday School Union. Admission fee. Three miles from Baltimore on East Fort Ave. Open 9 A.M. to 5 P.M. seven days a week 301-962-4290

Baltimore, *Lovely Lane Methodist Church*
Collection of Methodist historical materials. Contains John Wesley's personal copy of *Imitation of Christ*, a fragment from the diary of Susanna Wesley, possibly the first pulpit used by a Methodist preacher in America. Open weekdays 9 A.M. to 4 P.M. and Sundays after church. St. Paul and 22nd Sts. 301-889-1512

Massachusetts

Boston, *The Boston Tea Party Ship and Museum*
From Boston Harbor on the Freedom Trail a courtesy bus will take you there for a tour of a full-scale replica of the brig Beaver, one of the invaded British vessels. Tea-tossing. Congress St. Bridge 617-338-1773

Boston, *Freedom Trail*
The three-mile long trail is a walking tour of 16 sites and structures in downtown Boston and Charlestown. A red line on the sidewalk directs you from site to site. Originates at Information Center, Boston Common 800-858-0200

Boston, *Park Street Church*
An evangelical bastion, the church stands on Boston Common. In 1831 "America" was first sung here. In 1942 the National Association of Evangelicals was organized in this church. Sunday services at 10:30 A.M. and 7:30 P.M. Boston Common.

Pittsfield, *Hancock Shaker Village*
The third Shaker settlement, Hancock, "the City of Peace" was established in 1790. The Village recaptures the Shaker legacy of fine craftsmanship, love and simplicity. Admission fee. Open daily, June 1 to October 31. 5 miles west of Pittsfield at Rts. U.S. 20 and MA 41 413-443-0188

Plymouth, *Burial Hill*
Up a stone stairway where the first Pilgrim Fort was located and where Governor William Bradford is believed to be buried near his son. In back of the First Church in Town Square.

Plymouth, *The Mayflower Experience*
Three electronic theaters allow you to experience the voyage on the Mayflower during its historic crossing. Next to the Governor Bradford Motel. 114 Water St.

Plymouth, *Mayflower II*
Replica of the original Mayflower. "Crewman and passengers" will tell you about their experiences on the 1620 voyage. Anchored at the State Pier next to Plymouth Rock 508-746-1622

Plymouth, *Pilgrim Hall Museum*
The oldest historical museum in America. Contains the most complete collection of

VACATION SPOTS WORTH SEEING cont.

Pilgrim possessions and lore. Open daily. 75 Court St. at Chilton St. 508-746-1620

Plymouth, *Plimoth Plantation*

A re-creation of life in Plymouth Colony as it was in the early 1800s. 3 miles south of Plymouth Rock on Rt. 3A 508-746-1622

Plymouth, *Plymouth Rock*

The rock is small and under cover, yet it is symbolic of the inscription on the Plymouth Rock monument which reads: "They laid the foundation wherein every man through countless ages should have liberty." On the waterfront overlooking Plymouth Harbor.

Provincetown, *The Pilgrim Monument*

It is here on November 21, 1620, that the Pilgrims first touched shore. The tallest granite structure in the USA, the 255-foot monument dominates the town and is a landmark for fishermen, sailors and tourists. Daily throughout the summer. Town Hill, off Bradford St. 508-487-1310

Stockbridge, *Mission House*

In Stockton, Jonathan Edwards spent the final 8 years of his life among the Indians, while writing his famous theological treatises. Main and Sergeant Sts.

Stockbridge, *Norman Rockwell Museum*

18th century Georgian House. Exhibits many of Norman Rockwell's paintings. The famous Americana painter spent the final years of his life in Stockbridge. Admission fee. Main St. 413-298-3822

Williamstown, *Haystack Monument*

The Monument commemorates the historic haystack prayer meeting which resulted in the beginning of the foreign missions movement.

Michigan

Albion, *Birthplace of "The Old Rugged Cross"*

A bronze marker indicates where the Rev. George Bennard wrote what has become one of the most beloved hymns of all time. He once served in the Salvation Army but later became an itinerant evangelist. He died in 1958, relatively unknown. College Ct. and Michigan Ave.

Dearborn, *Greenfield Village/Henry Ford Museum*

300 years of Americana. Colonial homes and Motor House. Admission fee. 20900 Oakwood Blvd. 313-271-1620

Frankenmuth, *Christmas Village*

It's Christmas any time of the year in this Bavarian town where you can always shop for Christmas decorations and ornaments. A German missionary, August Craemer, led 15 immigrants from Bavaria to Frankemuth in 1845 to establish a home base for mission outposts. 517-652-6106

Holland, *Holland Tulip Festival*

Here you can see one of the largest tulip plantings in the country, visit a wooden shoe factory, tour a Netherlands museum, enjoy folk dances and a "Festival Musicale," a mix of hymns, anthems and spirituals. Write Tulip Time Office, Civic Center, 8th and Pine, Holland, MI 49423 616-396-4221

Minnesota

Minneapolis, *Bethany Fellowship*

The complex has a Christian school, factory, church, mission society and publishing house. Tours available upon request on weekdays at 10 A.M. and 3 P.M. Write 6820 Auto Club Rd., Minneapolis, MN 55438 612-944-2121

St. Cloud, *Shekinah Bible Gardens*

This $3.8 million project includes gardens and waterfalls, re-creations of the Garden Tomb and Golgotha, and a 400-seat amphitheater. The exhibit center includes walk-in replicas of the Temple, Solomon's House, & Herod's Palace. Adjacent to St. Cloud off I-94. P.O. Box 823, St. Cloud, MN 56301 612-253-2811

Mississippi

Lucedale, *Palestinian Gardens*

Authentic scale model of the Holy Land at the time of Christ. Twenty acres scaled one yard to a mile. A walk through the gardens will acquaint you with Holy Land geography. Excellent preparation for a trip to Israel. 12 miles north of Lucedale, 6.5 miles east of U.S. Hwy. 98. Rt. 9, Box 792, Lucedale, MS 39492

Missouri

Diamond, *George Washington Carver Monument*

Birthplace of a slave who rose to fame as a godly educator and agriculturalist. The Visitor Center traces Carver's career and achievements. Carver once said, "I love to think of nature as an unlimited broadcasting system through which God speaks to us." From Neosho or Carthage, take U.S. 71 Alternate to Diamond, then go west 2 miles on County Hwy. V and south 1 mile.

Kansas City, *Hallmark Visitor's Center*

Presents history of Hallmark's growth. Crown Center Complex 816-274-3613

Independence, *Harry S. Truman Library and Museum*

Presidential Library of America's 33rd president and gravesite. Admission fee. U.S. 24 and Delaware St. 816-833-1400

Montana

West Glacier, *Glacier National Park*

Glacier adjoins Waterton Lakes National Park in Canada and the two parks comprise the Waterton/Glacier International Peace Park. 10,000 foot peaks, more than 50 glaciers. Worship services can be found on Sundays at more than a dozen locations. Admission fee. On U.S. Hwy. 2 406-888-5441

Nebraska

Omaha, *Boys Town*

Now internationally known, Father Edward J. Flanagan in 1917 opened a facility for homeless boys. Tours of the 400-acre facility include the dairy farm and the Music Hall where the world-famous Boys Town Choir rehearses. Open daily from 8 A.M. to 4:30 P.M. 134th and W. Dodge Rds. 402-498-1111

New Hampshire

Hanover, *Dartmouth College*

Like other famous Ivy League schools, Dartmouth College was one of the results of the First Great Awakening. Its royal charter, signed by King George III, specified the school's intent to reach the Indian tribes and to educate English youth.

New Jersey

Princeton, *Princeton University*

Originally called "The College of New Jersey," Princeton was another outcome of the First Great Awakening. Jonathan Edwards and John Witherspoon, signer of the Declaration of Independence, were among Princeton's first presidents. Off Rts. 1 and 206 609-921-6748

New Mexico

Santa Fe, *The capital city of New Mexico*

The nation's most unusual capital. A full decade before the Pilgrims landed at Plymouth Rock, Don Pedro de Peralta established it. The Indians still hold open-air markets as they have for centuries. It is the nation's oldest city (1610) and its highest (7,000 feet). 800-777-CITY

Santa Fe, *Old Mission Churches*

The ancient city has several historic mission churches including St. Francis Cathedral, Loretto Chapel—with its mysterious spiral staircase—and San Miguel Mission, the oldest mission church in the United States.

Taos, *Mission of St. Francis of Assisi*

One of the most beautiful Spanish churches in the southwest. Contains the mysterious painting, "The Shadow of the Cross" by Henri Ault. In daylight it portrays the barefoot Christ. In darkness, the portrait becomes luminescent, outlining the figure while clouds over Jesus' left shoulder form into a cross.

New York

New York City, *Historic New York City churches*

Visit: Trinity Church on Wall St., St. Paul's Chapel at Broadway and Fulton Sts., St. Patrick's Cathedral at 5th Ave. and 50th St., Cathedral of St. John the Divine at Amsterdam Ave. and 112th St., Riverside Church at Riverside Dr. and 122nd St., and Marble Collegiate Church at 29th

VACATION SPOTS WORTH SEEING cont.

St. and 5th Ave. Tours available. Check with each church for details.

New York City, *Salvation Army Headquarters*

Most Friday evenings from October through May the Salvation Army presents an inspirational program at its Centennial Memorial Temple. Tours of the territorial headquarters on the same site may be arranged in advance. 120 W. 14th St., between 6th and 7th Aves. 212-620-4968

New York City, *Statue of Liberty*

For more than a century the Statue of Liberty has been holding high the torch of freedom. The Statue of Liberty was given by the people of France to the people of the United States in recognition of ties forged during the American revolution. Open daily from 9 A.M. to 5 P.M. Extended hours in effect on weekends during the spring season; seven days a week during the summer. The Statue of Liberty Ferry leaves every hour on the hour from Battery Park, in lower Manhattan, to take you to Liberty Island where you follow the broad mall to the statue. 212-363-3200

West Point, *Cadet Chapel*

The Chapel dominates the entire Academy. This classic edifice of Gothic architecture contains the world's largest church organ. Sunday morning services are open to the public. Sunday evening concerts by the Military Academy Band, July and August. NY Hwy. 218 at New South Post 914-938-2638

North Carolina

Blue Ridge Parkway

469 miles of magnificent scenery on the Blue Ridge crest. Many natural and historic attractions. Runs between Great Smoky National Park and Shenandoah National Park in Virginia.

Murphy, *The Ten Commandments, Large Print edition*

At Field of the Wood, the Ten Commandments can be read in letters five feet high and four feet wide, all carved in stone. One mile away stands a 2,210-foot All Nations Cross, largest of its kind in the world. Open daily. West of Murphy and east of Turtletown off Hwy. 294.

Ohio

Canton, *Christian Hall of Fame*

Canton Baptist Temple contains 100 original oil portraits of Christian leaders from New Testament times to the present day. The 260 feet of corridors include paintings of Tertullian, Luther, Calvin, Knox, Carey, Hudson Taylor, and Billy Sunday. Off U.S. Rt. 30. 515 Whipple, NW.

Cincinnati, *Harriet Beecher Stowe House*

In this house, Harriet Beecher Stowe researched what would become a classic best-seller, *Uncle Tom's Cabin*. The book, released in 1852, soon sold more than 300,000 copies. Stowe memorabilia, exhibits on black history. Open Tuesdays through Sundays. 2950 Gilbert Ave. 513-632-5120

Mentor, *Home of President James A. Garfield*

Lawnfield, home of the 20th president of the USA and the only president who was also an ordained preacher, is furnished with Garfield's personal possessions. Garfield preached frequently and once baptized 40 converts during an evangelistic campaign. Open daily except Mondays from mid-April to November. On U.S. 20. 8095 Mentor Ave. 216-255-8722

Oklahoma

Tulsa, *Oral Roberts University*

The University which evangelist Oral Roberts founded in 1963 has become Tulsa's top tourist attraction drawing about 180,000 visitors a year. All visits begin in the Prayer Tower at the heart of the campus. Tours are usually self-guided. Media presentations available on a continuous basis from 8:30 A.M. to 5:30 P.M. 2-1/2 miles south of the Skelly Bypass (I-44 and U.S. 66) on Lewis Ave.

Pennsylvania

Bethlehem, *Historic Bethlehem*

In 1741 a small group of Moravians from

Germany settled in Bethlehem to minister to the Indians and the German settlers of Pennsylvania. The original Bethlehem has been restored, and to visit is to step back into three centuries of history. 11 W. Market St., Bethlehem, PA 18018 215-867-3788

Fallsington, *Historic Fallsington*

Fallsington's first houses were built by friends and followers of William Penn. This untouched village mirrors 300 years of American architectural history, from a primitive log cabin to the Victorian extravaganzas of the 19th century. Admission fee. Open March 15 to November 15, Wednesday through Sunday, 1 to 5 P.M.

Gettysburg, *Prince of Peace Museum*

Artist Paul Cunningham has re-created the life of Christ in a series of colorful, life-like three-dimensional scenes. South of Gettysburg Sq. on Rt. 15.

Hershey, *Hershey Gardens*

Theme gardens. 25,000 rose plants. Spring flowers. Admission fee. Park Blvd. 717-534-3005

Kennett Square, *Longwood Gardens*

One of the most beautiful gardens in the east. 350 acres, 20 indoor gardens. Former estate of Pierre S. Du Pont. U.S. 1 215-388-6741

Lancaster, *Pennsylvania Dutch Country*

Ride an Amish buggy, tour an Amish kitchen, watch Swiss cheese being made, shop at farmers markets and factory outlets. Explore both antiques and boutiques. Live as guests in a private Amish home. Lancaster County. Pennsylvania Dutch Visitors Bureau provides a tour guide and map, and a 72-page booklet "Pennsylvania Dutch Country Sampler." 1799 Hempstead Rd., Lancaster, PA 17601 717-299-8901

Philadephia, *Freedoms Foundation at Valley Forge*

Patriots Hall of Fame, a walk-through exhibit honoring famous Americans. "Forge of Freedom" and a multimedia presentation in the visitor center theatre. Faith of Our Fathers Chapel features Washington at prayer. Open air concerts during summer. For concert schedule write Freedoms Foundation, Valley Forge, PA 19481 215-933-8825

Philadelphia, *Independence Hall*

"The most historic square mile in America" where delegates to the Second Continental Congress debated whether or not to declare independence from Great Britain. Visitors may view the chamber in which the Constitution was framed. Independence National Historical Park 215-597-8974

Philadelphia, *The Liberty Bell*

July 8, 1776, the Liberty Bell heralded the news of liberty to the land. By coincidence, Leviticus 25:10 was inscribed on the bell: "Proclaim liberty throughout the land unto all the inhabitants thereof." Now in a glass and steel pavilion. Behind Independence Hall.

Philadephia, *University of Pennsylvania*

When Philadelphia churches denied George Whitefield access to their pulpits, some of his supporters, including Benjamin Franklin, erected a building to accommodate the crowds that wanted to hear him. This became the University's first building.

Philadelphia, *Valley Forge*

This 2500-acre park includes Washington's winter camp 1777-78, an old house owned by Quaker preacher Isaac Potts, a collection of Revolutionary arms and the original tent Washington used in the field, and Washington Memorial Chapel. N. Gulph Rd. and PA Hwy. 23 215-783-7700

Scranton, *Steamtown, USA*

World's largest collection of steam locomotives and steam era rolling stock, including the massive Union Pacific "Big Boy," the largest steam locomotive ever built. Train excursions available. Open May through October. 700 Lackawanna Rd.

Rhode Island

Providence, *Brown University*

Brown was one of the five colonial universities organized as a result of the First Great Awakening. Art galleries, Rockefeller Library and the Annmary Brown Memorial housing rare Renaissance books. At edge of city on Prospect Ave. 401-863-1000

Providence, *The First Baptist Church in America*

The first Baptist church in America, First Baptist in Providence has maintained

VACATION SPOTS WORTH SEEING cont.

continuous services for more than 350 years. From this first group came the largest Protestant movement in America. The present church dates back to 1775. Tours available 10 A.M. to 3 P.M. weekdays and 10 A.M. to noon on Saturdays, April through October.

South Carolina

Greenville, *Bob Jones University*
Houses one of the most important art collections in the Southeast. Its gallery of Sacred Art and Bible Lands Museum contains 30 rooms displaying the art of Europe from the thirteenth through the nineteenth centuries also includes works of major artists. Open from 2 to 5 P.M. throughout the year except Mondays.

South Dakota

Keystone, *Mount Rushmore National Monument*
Black Hills. Heads of four American presidents carved from the face of granite: George Washington, Thomas Jefferson, Abraham Lincoln and Theodore Roosevelt. The project took 14 years to complete. Off U.S. Hwy. 16A 605-574-2523

Rapid City, *Norwegian Chapel-in-the-Hills*
Exact copy of the famous 800-year-old Borgund Church in Norway. More than a half million have visited the church with its intricate wood carvings, dragon heads and ingenious construction. Vesper services at 8 P.M. during summer months. Southeast of Rapid City off Hwy. 44.

Spearfish, *Black Hills Passion Play*
More than 200 actors and actresses dramatize the World's Greatest Story three times a week. The play depicts the Roman domination over Palestine, the devotion of the disciples and friends, and the supreme sacrifice of Christ. Mid-June through late August, every Sunday, Tuesday and Thursday. For best choice of seats, order tickets in advance. Black Hills Passion Play, Box 469, Spearfish, SD 57783 605-642-2646

Tennessee

Gatlinburg, *Christus Gardens*
Of special interest to children, life-size beeswax scenes include the Nativity, the Sermon on the Mount, "Suffer the Little Children to Come unto Me," and the Last Supper. The rotunda houses the nation's most complete collection of coins of biblical times. A half block from the center of Gatlinburg on River Rd. 615-436-5155

Gatlinburg, *National Bible Museum*
300 rare volumes of the Bible in 120 languages are on display. Artifacts date back to 1500 B.C., including a lamp believed to be from the time of Abraham. Admission fee. Open most of the year except Sundays. Between Christus Gardens and Aerial Tramway.

Nashville, *Baptist Sunday School Board*
Huge complex in downtown Nashville covers several blocks and employs about 1500 people. Largest postal customer in Nashville and responsible for Nashville being second only to Washington, D.C., in volume of second-class mail shipped. One hour tours with audiovisual presentations weekdays from 8 A.M. to 3 P.M. 127 9th Ave., N., Nashville, TN 615-251-2796

Nashville, *Grand Ole Opry*
Live radio program featuring country music. 1804 Opryland Dr. 615-889-7502

Nashville, *Methodist Publishing House*
Presses roll out approximately 100 Abingdon book titles a year, church school material and millions of *The Upper Room* magazine each month. Tours daily Monday through Friday at 10 A.M. and 2 P.M. 201 8th Ave., S.

Nashville, *The Parthenon*
Replica of the Greek Parthenon. Exact size of the original although materials are different. 9 A.M. to 4:30 P.M. Tuesday through Saturday, 1 to 4:30 P.M. Sundays. Centennial Park, West End Ave. 615-259-6358

Texas

Dallas, *Biblical Arts Center*
Exhibit centers around a 124 feet long and 20 feet high painting depicting the Miracle

at Pentecost. Dramatic 30-minute sound and light presentation every hour at half past the hour. Admission fee. Open Tuesday through Saturday, 10 A.M. to 5 P.M. 7500 Park Ln. at Boedeker 214-691-4661

San Marcos, *Aquarena Springs*
Features Ralph, the diving pig, who does a swine dive into 71-degree Spring Lake. Underwater aquatic show, alligator exhibit and an old West Texas town are other attractions. Admission fee. Open daily except Christmas from 9 A.M. to 5:30 P.M. Take Exit 30 off I-35 for half a mile.

Utah

Salt Lake City, *Temple Square*
Symbolic heart of Mormonism. The Square is dominated by the Mormon Temple on the east, the Tabernacle on the west and a visitor's center filled with Mormon history. Noon recitals and Thursday Tabernacle choir rehearsals are open to the public. N., S., and W. Temple Sts. and Main St. 801-531-2534

Virginia

Virginia Beach, *The 700 Club*
View the filming of "The 700 Club" and the total operation of the Christian Broadcasting Network. Weekday tours every half hour from 10:30 A.M. to 2:30 P.M. For tickets write The 700 Club, "Tickets," CBN Center, Virginia Beach, VA 23465 804-424-7777

Williamsburg, *Colonial Williamsburg*
Relive the 18th century in this mile-long colonial city, restored by John D. Rockefeller, Jr., "that the future may learn from the past." 100 original buildings. Admission fee. Take Colonial Williamsburg exit off I-64 804-229-1000

Wisconsin

New Glarus, *Little Switzerland*
Relive Swiss history—visit a reconstructed blacksmith shop, schoolhouse, store, cabin, cheese factory and a replica of the first Swiss log church built for worship in 1849. U.S. Rts. 39 and 69.

Wyoming

Grand Teton National Park, *Church of the Transfiguration*
One of Wyoming's most photographed scenes. A wall of glass behind the altar permits a broad view of the towering sawtooth Teton range. The park itself has more than 200 miles of trails. 4 miles west of Jackson on U.S. 26/89/191 307-733-2880

STATE TOURISM OFFICES

Write or phone for helpful information.

Alabama Bureau of Tourism & Travel, 532 S. Perry St., Montgomery, AL 36104 1-800-Alabama

Alaska Alaska Division of Tourism, P.O. Box E, Juneau, AK 99811 907-465-2010

Arizona Office of Tourism, 1100 W. Washington, Phoenix, AR 85007 602-542-Tour

Arkansas Department of Parks and Tourism, 1 Capitol Mall, Little Rock, AR 72201 1-800-482-8999 (within state), 1-800-643-8383 (outside state)

California Office of Tourism, 1121 L Street, Suite 103, Sacramento, CA 95814 1-800-862-2543; X 100 (outside state)

Colorado Tourism Board, 1625 Broadway, Suite 1700, Denver, CO 80202 1-800-433-2656

Connecticut Tourism Promotion Service, 865 Brook St., Rocky Hill, CT 06067 203-566-3948 (within state), 1-800-CT BOUND (outside state)

Delaware Tourism Office, 99 Kings Highway, P.O. Box 1401, Dover, DE 19903 1-800-441-8846

District of Columbia Washington Convention and Visitors Association, 1212 New York Ave., NW, Washington, D.C. 20005 202-789-7000

Florida Department of Commerce Visitors Inquiry, 126 Van Buren St., Tallahassee, FL 32399 904-487-1462

Georgia Tourist Division, P.O. Box 1776, Atlanta, GA 30301 404-656-3590

Hawaii Visitors Bureau, 2270 Kalakaua Ave., Suite 901, Honolulu, HI 96815 808-923-1811

Idaho Department of Commerce, 700 W. State St., Boise, ID 83720 1-800-635-7820

Illinois Bureau of Tourism, 620 East Adams St., Springfield, IL 62701 217-782-7139

Indiana Tourism Division, 1 North Capitol, Suite 700, Indianapolis, IN 46204 317-232-8860

Iowa Bureau of Tourism, 200 E. Grand Ave., Des Moines, IA 50309 515-281-3100

Kansas Travel & Tourism Development, 400 W. 8th St., 5th Floor, Topeka, KS 66603 913-296-2009

Kentucky Department of Travel Development, Capital Plaza Tower, Frankfort, KY 40601 1-800-225-TRIP

Louisiana Office of Tourism, P.O. Box 94291, Baton Rouge, LA 70804 1-800-334-8626

Maine Publicity Bureau, 97 Winthrop St., P.O. Box 2300, Hallowell, ME 04347 207-289-2423

Maryland Office of Tourism Development, 217 E. Redwood St., Baltimore, MD 21202 301-333-6611

Massachusetts Office of Travel and Tourism, 100 Cambridge St., 13th Floor, Boston, MA 02202 617-727-3201

Michigan Travel Bureau P.O. Box 30226, Lansing, MI 48909 1-800-543-2937

Minnesota Minnesota Office of Tourism, 375 Jackson St., 250 Skyway Level, St. Paul, MN 55101 1-800-652-9747 (within state), 1-800-328-1461 (outside state)

Mississippi Division of Tourism, P.O. Box 849, Jackson, MS 39205 1-800-647-2290

Missouri Division of Tourism, 301 W. High St., P.O. Box 1055, Jefferson City, MO 65102 314-751-4133

Montana Travel Montana, 1424 9th Ave., Helena, MT 59620 1-800-541-1447

Nebraska Division of Travel and Tourism, 301 Centennial Mall South, P.O. Box 94666, Lincoln, NE 68509 1-800-742-7595 (within state), 1-800-228-4307 (outside state)

Nevada Commission on Tourism, Capitol Complex, Carson City, NV 89710 1-800-NEVADA-8

New Hampshire Office of Vacation Travel, P.O.Box 856, Concord, NH 03301 603-271-2666

New Jersey Division of Travel and Tourism, CN-826, Trenton, NJ 08625 609-292-2470

New Mexico New Mexico Tourism & Travel Division, Room 119, 1100 St. Francis Dr., Santa Fe, NM 87503 1-800-545-2040

New York Division of Tourism, 1 Commerce Plaza, Albany, NY 12245 1-800-225-5697

North Carolina Travel and Tourism Division, 430 North Salisbury St., Raleigh, NC 27611 1-800-VISIT NC

North Dakota North Dakota Tourism, Liberty Memorial Building, Capitol Grounds, Bismarck, ND 58505 701-224-2525 (within state), 1-800-437-2077 (outside state)

Ohio Ohio Division of Travel and Tourism, P.O. Box 1001, Columbus, OH 43266 1-800-BUCKEYE

Oklahoma Oklahoma Tourism and Recreation Dept., P.O. Box 60000, Oklahoma City, OK 73146 1-800-652-6552

Oregon Tourism Division, 595 Cottage St., NE, Salem, OR 97310 1-800-543-8838 (within state), 1-800-547-7842 (outside state)

Pennsylvania Bureau of Travel Development, 453 Forum Building, Harrisburg, PA 17120 1-800-VISIT PA, X 275

Rhode Island Rhode Island Tourism Division, 7 Jackson Walkway, Providence, RI 02903 401-277-2601

South Carolina South Carolina Division of Tourism, Box 71, Columbia, SC 29202 803-734-0235

South Dakota Department of Tourism, Capitol Lake Plaza, Pierre, SD 57501 1-800-952-2217 (within state), 1-800-843-1930 (outside state)

Tennessee Department of Tourist Development, P.O. Box 23170, Nashville, TN 37202 615-741-2158

Texas Travel Information Services, P.O. Box 5064, Austin, TX 78763 512-463-8971

Utah Utah Travel Council, Council Hall, Capitol Hill, Salt Lake City, UT 84114 801-538-1030

Vermont Travel Division, 134 State St., Montpelier, VT 05602 802-828-3236

Virginia Division of Tourism, 202 N. 9th St., Suite 500, Richmond, VA 23219 804-786-4484

Washington Washington State Dept. of Trade and Economic Development, 101 General Administration Bldg., Olympia, WA 98504 206-753-5630

West Virginia Department of Commerce, State Capitol Complex, Charleston, WV 25305 1-800-225-5981

Wisconsin Division of Tourism, Box 7606, Madison, WI 53707 1-800-432-TRIP

Wyoming Wyoming Travel Commission, 1-25 at College Drive, Cheyenne, WY 82002 1-800-225-5996

FAVORITE VACATION SPOTS

ACW asked: "What is your favorite vacation spot?" The replies:

Jim Dobson: Mammoth Lake, CA. This is where we have made our warmest memories for our family.

Bill and Gloria Gaither: We've celebrated the childhood of Suzanne, Amy and Benji on the Nantucket, Massachusetts, beaches. Each year we've watched their little footprints grow bigger. And now we make the island our welcome mat for grown-up days.

Tim Hansel: Elk Canyon Ranch, a few miles out of Bozeman, MT. It must be one of the most beautiful places on planet earth. "Exquisite " is almost an understatement. Nestled in the mountains of Montana's big sky country, it is a western resort that has everything—horseback riding, tennis, swimming and some of the finest fly-fishing in the country. The accommodations are elegant and the food is four-star. I asked my family recently what was the most fun place they had ever been. And in unison they all cried, "Elk Canyon Ranch."

Billy Melvin: Chesapeake Bay, VA, because the fishing is good and I like the peace and tranquility.

Norman Vincent Peale: Either St. Moritz or Interlaken, Switzerland. Mrs. Peale and I like to walk on high mountain paths—good for body, good for soul. You're among mountain peaks and deep valleys. Gives physical exercise and spiritual inspiration.

Eugenia Price: Almost anywhere IF the place is small or so large I'm not likely to be recognized. Vacation for me—at least my favorite times—are those when a novel is really rolling. My own home is my favorite spot! But, now and then, Joyce Blackburn, with whom I live and work, and I need to get away from the mailbox and the telephone, so we select either a tiny town with a comfortable motel and some history to explore or a huge city—New York, Atlanta, etc.—in which I can, if I keep my trip a secret, "get lost" in a good hotel with dependable room service! We often rent a condo at Fernandina Beach, FL, or on Sanibel Island, FL. I seek no tennis, no golf, NO fishing nor boating! What I seek is nothing to do but read someone else's books.

Chuck Swindoll: My favorite vacation spot is not limited to a particular place but is a setting where certain ingredients are present. First, my wife and all those in our family. Next, a broad mixture of pleasurable delights: early morning quietness and the solitude of uninterrupted silence, a variety of activites throughout the day that may include exercise, a boat ride, water-skiing, fishing for the ultimate wide-mouth bass, laughter, meals, conversation, a hot cup of coffee by a campfire, a great book, and watching the sun set in all its colorful splendor. Ideally, those days provide time to reflect on where I've been—the lessons learned, the goals accomplished, the struggles endured, the blessing enjoyed—and to entertain a few random thoughts on where I'm going. Making such settings complete includes the moving strains of magnificent music, refreshing and unguarded discussions with my grown children and my sister, walks in the woods or along a seashore, fun stuff, plus hugs and kisses from my grandkids, and certainly mean-' ingful moments all alone with Cynthia as we deliberately give ourselves permission to take time to sift the essentials from the incidentals.

TIPS FOR HAPPY VACATIONS

1. **Have reasonable expectations** rather than impossible ones that invariably lead to disappointment. A vacation will not necessarily make you a new person or salvage a troubled marriage.
2. **Examine your past vacations.** Be objective, but be compassionate. Don't vilify yourself, no matter how your past trips have turned out. Think of ways they could be improved.
3. **Relax.** Don't hurry past the beauty. Joy is a gentle and delicate living thing. Let it happen.
4. **Don't take yourself too seriously.** Expect some obstacles. Embrace them. Laugh at them if you can. Convert them into part of your vacation. Make an adventure out of your inevitable mishaps. Murphy's Law—which says that if anything can possibly go wrong, it will not only do so, but at the worst possible time—still has a habit of inviting itself on a lot of vacations. Don't let it ruin yours.
5. **Be creative.** Put a little variety into your celebrations. Don't let someone from a travel agency plan your happiness. Let your imaginative juices flow. Make each vacation a once-in-a-lifetime experience.
6. **Take all of you on vacation.** Use all of your senses. This is a time when you can be whole, when you can use your smeller for something more than just to hang your glasses on, and those funny-looking contraptions on the side of your head for something more than just to keep your hat off your shoulders. Don't just eat; taste your food. Let your vacation be a five-sense event.
7. **Plan a strategy for vacation diet.** Enjoy your food, but don't make it the whole purpose of your vacation. Resistance is usually a little lower during vacations. Fatigue, frustration, or even boredom sometimes stimulate indulgence. Have a plan. Overeating can ruin a vacation. Take low-calorie snacks for those long rides in the car.
8. **Get regular exercise.** A good balance between rest and activity is best.
9. **Take short vacations if long ones make you homesick,** especially if you are taking one of those special getaways without the kids. But give yourself enough time to unwind fully.
10. **Forget such maxims as "Hard work deserves a rest."** Don't spend all your time justifying your vacation.
11. **Break your routine.** Get up at a different time than you usually do during the year. If you never get to read—read. If you read as part of your job—put down the books for a few weeks.
12. **Do something unusual.** Be an experimenter. Meet new people, try new experiences. Let people think you're loony. Wear a funny hat or put your shirt on backwards for a day. Roller-skate down a shopping mall. Climb a mountain, or a tree. Don't wear a watch for a week. Hug a tree, fly a kite, wear a button, jog in triangles. Fool somebody. Fool two somebodies. Go for a long walk in your bare feet. Poke some holes in your rigidity. This is not a time to be timid. Take a chance. It's worth it.
13. **Do something a little extravagant.** Buy something you've always wanted. Let go a little bit. Don't be so reasonable all the time.
14. **Learn something new** on your vacation. Teach yourself to play chess, or learn to needlepoint. Learn calligraphy and send fancy postcards to all your friends.
15. **Learn to look for the best and laugh at the worst.** You will usually see what you are looking for. Choose to see the good,

the best, the beautiful. Also choose to laugh at the crazy things that always want to go on vacation with you—flat tires, flat hair, flat spirits, flat experiences.

16. **Give yourself permission to be happy.** Practice it. Work hard to eliminate that free-floating guilt that says you should be working or doing something more useful, and that you shouldn't be having such a good time.

17. **Let the hero out in you.** Live each day and each vacation as if it were your last opportunity. Rejoice and crack the skies with laughter. Let your passion for being alive and being one of God's people encourage you to be the very best you can be.

Source: Tim Hansel in *When I Relax, I Feel Guilty*. Published by David C. Cook Publishing Company. Copyright © 1979. Used by permission.

VACATION IDEAS

1. **Health vacations.** If you're feeling a little sluggish, maybe you need to spend some time focusing on yourself and your health. Develop some solid health patterns. It may be a tennis vacation, a jogging vacation on the coast, a cycling vacation to some friends, or a hiking vacation in the mountains. Work on filling your lungs with a lot of oxygen, your mind with a lot of good thoughts, and your body with a lot of good food.

2. **Educational vacations.** Learn something new: how to fix a car, do woodwork, or rock-climb. Go somewhere to learn how to paint or cook, or set aside special time at home to take classes at a local college.

3. **Back-roads vacations.** Use only back roads. Enjoy all the serendipitous events that naturally happen on such a trip.

4. **Children's vacations.** Let your children plan and, as much as possible, implement a short vacation. It might be very exciting seeing the world from their eyes. Stay flexible, and plan on a lot of surprises.

5. **Cheap vacations.** Discover how much you can do with as little money as possible. How many things can you do for twenty-five cents? One dollar? What can your whole family do for five dollars? Look in the newspapers for all the free films and exhibits you can go to. List all the places you can explore for nothing. How creative are you at eating for a day on $1.12?

6. **Sunset Magazine vacations.** Many of us want our houses to look like Better Homes and Gardens. But we need time to develop ideas that will fit our particular home. Take the time! Leave the children home and go see different kinds of architecture, color patterns, fences, and porch designs. Take a sketch pad and talk of all the wild possibilities over dinner.

7. **Reinventory vacations.** Take time to remember what is special to you. Redefine your values. What are some of your lifetime dreams? Your priorities? How could you improve? Be specific. Take whatever resources along with you that you might need (Bible, writing material, tapes, other books, etc.), but don't forget that unhurried and uncrowded time will be your most important resource.

8. **Memory lane vacations.** Revisit some of those special places that have been hallmarks in your life. Take the time to see old friends. Spend some evenings remembering, laughing, telling stories, and maybe even going through some of the old annuals. Relish the nostalgia for a while.

9. **Evangelistic vacations.** Make your distinct purpose to share your faith in Jesus Christ. Revitalize not only the lives of other people but your own as well.

10. **Just being vacations.** Take off your watch for a while. Forget what time it is. Eat when you're hungry instead of at noon. Reestablish your relationship with God, with your lifetime companion, and with yourself on the basis of who you are rather than what you do. Travel very light, plan very little, lead with your heart, and let life surprise you around every corner.

11. **Vacations you train for.** It may be a bike

trip. Select a purpose and make a vacation out of getting ready for it.

12. **Seeing vacations**. Deliberately spend some days (either at home or traveling) to discover the magic of seeing. See color, for example. Follow one color for the whole day. You will be amazed at how much you've been blind to. Sit quietly on the grass and allow your eyes to marvel at the world around you. A bush, a cloud, or a leaf might become an unforgettable experience. Take along a camera, and photograph the splendor you see. If you like, choose to focus on seeing and photographing faces for a day.

13. **A wonder trip**. Explore the magnificence of life with all your senses. There is so much more there than normally meets the eye. Take time to ask questions rather than seek answers. How does grass grow up through cement? How does a bird fly? How do grunion know to ride the high tide?

14. **Gourmet vacations**. Turn an evening into a mini vacation by immersing yourself without inhibition into the life of a gourmet. Dress in your fanciest. Eat very slowly, tasting every morsel. Feast on the candlelight atmosphere. Take a menu home for memories.

15. **Change of life-style or service vacations**. Take your family to the midwest to work on a farm, or to help friends build a house. What about arranging a long trip with a truck driver you know? Volunteering your services at a hospital or a convalescent home?

16. **Exploration vacations**. Your only limit here is creativity. Explore a friendship through traveling together on a vacation. Explore a book or an idea.

17. **Once-in-a-lifetime specials**. Design a day around going for a ride in a helicopter, or going to a horse race. Find a bookbinder and find out how books are bound. Go skydiving or shoot the rapids. Go to an umbrella factory or follow the whole process behind the making of toilet paper.

18. **One parent, one child occasions**. Spend quality time with one of your children. It can just be dinner together, or it can be a whole weekend trip. You might participate in an event together or explore an idea together.

19. **Rest vacations**. Go somewhere where no one can find you, take the phone off the hook, and spend most of the days horizontal. Give yourself permission to get recharged.

Source: Tim Hansel in *When I Relax I Feel Guilty*. Published by David C. Cook Publishing Company. Copyright © 1979. Used by permission.

SERVICE VACATIONS AT HOME AND ABROAD

This directory introduces you to a range of short-term mission opportunities you may not know about. The directory contains a wide selection of jobs, places, and agencies. You can find a way to use a two-week vacation, a summer, or up to three years of your life.

ABMJ/Chosen People Ministries

1300 Cross Beam Drive
Charlotte, NC 28217
704-257-9000
Galen Banashak
Program. Summer Training and Evangelism (STEP), 4 wks. training, 2 wks. outreach.
Agency Background. Founded 1894 by Rabbi Leopold Cohn. ABMJ/CPM pioneered the biblical evangelistic methods still used in Jewish missions around the world.
Requirements and Costs. 18 yrs. and older, desire to reach Jewish people with the gospel. $995 for training, outreach covered by participating churches.
Training Provided. Scripture study, understanding and handling Jewish objections to Jesus. Evangelism experience during outreach.
Work Description. Visitation and door-to-door evangelism. Also help conduct Jewish evangelism seminars at participating churches.

Countries Served. U.S. cities, Israel, Argentina, Canada

Action International
P.O. Box 490
Bothell, WA 98041
206-485-1967
Pearl Kallio
Program. Summer of Service (SOS), 8 wks; misc. short-term projects, 2 wks.–2 yrs.
Agency Background. Founded 1974, Interdenom. agency doing evangelism, Bible distribution, church planting, social work, support of nationals.
Requirements and Costs. 19 yrs. and older; prof. skills useful for longer term commitments. Raise own funds. SOS: approx. $2300. Other short terms: vary according to location and commitment.
Training Provided. SOS: 1-wk. orientation. Other short terms: depends on length of commitment.
Work Description. Discipleship, evangelism, counseling, youth work, Bible studies, music, drama, administration, literature distribution, social work, prison work, church planting. With SOS, live in homes of nationals.
Country Served. Philippines

Africa Inland Mission Int'l
P.O.Box 178
Pearl River, NY 10965
914-735-4014
Mr. Warren H. Day, Short/Full Term Program (STP) (FTP)
Mr. Wade Ewing, Volunteer Program (VP)
Program. FTP: 4 yrs. STP: 1–3 yrs. VP: 10 wks.–12 mos.
Agency Background. Founded 1895. Interdenom. missions agency serving 14 countries.
Requirements and Costs. 19 yrs. and older. Agree with doctrinal statement, French required in Zaire and Comoro Islands. Raise own funds. STP: cost varies according to location. VP: approx. $2500–$2800 for 3 mos.
Training Provided. STP: required orientation offered twice yearly. VP: orientation

materials sent through mail (incl. reading), pre-field orientation of 1–2 days; 3 days for those going to Kenya.
Work Description. STP: development work, evangelism, medical work, Bible teaching, church planting, education. VP: clerical, teaching, construction, youth work, evangelism, general support ministries.
Countries Served. Africa and the surrounding islands

AIMS: World Christian Expeditions
P.O. Box 64534
Virginia Beach, VA 33464
804-424-6333
Pat Foltz
Program. World Christian Expeditions (WCE) Participants are linked with existing programs of other short-term agencies. Variety of opportunities offered. About 200/calendar year.
Agency Background. Project of Association of International Mission Service (AIMS), which networks with individuals, churches, agencies and training institutions.
Requirements and Costs. Vary according to the agency selected.
Training Provided. Training materials available for purchase.
Work Description. Construction, medical, drama, evangelism, Bible distribution, musical, helps.
Countries Served. Varies according to the agency selected. Europe, the Commonwealth of Independent States (formerly the USSR), Africa, South America, LA/Central America, Far East, South East Asia, Middle East

Baptist General Conference (BGC) World Mission
2002 S. Arlington Hts. Rd.
Arlington Hts., IL 60005
1-800-323-4215
John Marrs
Program. 6 mos.–2 yrs. Special ministries may be less than 6 mos.
Agency Background. Founded 1850s. Multi-ethnic denom. with cross-cultural witness in North America and 11 foreign countries.
Requirements and Costs. Must be a member

SERVICE VACATIONS AT HOME AND ABROAD cont.

of a BGC church. Prefer a minimum of 2 yrs. of college or equivalent experience, and technical skill. Raise own funds: varies with position and country. Single: $7800–$14,000/yr.

Training Provided. Orientation on the field.

Work Description. English teaching, puppetry, medicine, youth ministry, famine relief, and agricultural extension. Short-termers also serve in theological and MK schools, as well as in a guest house and child care.

Countries Served. Eastern Europe, Mexico, Far East, Eastern & Western Africa, Middle East, Latin America, urban areas of United States

Caleb Project
P.O. Box 101239
Denver, CO 80250-1239
303-347-1044
Shane Bennett

Program. Joshua Project, fall and spring (5–6 mos.)

Agency Background. Interdenom. service agency, seeking to encourage and equip Christians to commit themselves to world evangelization.

Requirements and Costs. Complete "Perspectives on the World Christian Movement" course. Basic spiritual maturity and relational fitness. Raise own funds: $4500–$5000.

Training Provided. Advance reading and counsel. 5-week pre-field training before departure. Follow-up of 3 weeks.

Work Description. Teams conduct relationally-based sociological research in large cities to identify unreached peoples and encourage Christian workers.

Countries Served. Asia, Middle East, North Africa

Camp-of-the-Woods
Gilmantown Road
Speculator, NY 12164
518-548-4311
C. Robert Purdy

Program. Cross-cultural exchange camps, 4–10 wks.

Agency Background. International camping

ministry to families & youth; non-denominational. Founded 1900.

Requirements and Costs. College-age and older. Serve whole/part summer in USA as part of project. Raise own funds. $1000–$2500 (incl. airfare).

Training Provided. Personal spiritual growth, development of leadership potential, living and learning in a cross-cultural environment.

Work Description. Christian education (ages 3–12); teen activity leaders; camp and staff counselors, small group leaders. General maintenance and service projects.

Countries Served. Hong Kong, South Africa

Campus Crusade for Christ
100 Sunport Lane
Orlando, FL 32809
407-826-2104
Penny Poppinga

Program. U.S. summer projects, 10–13 wks.

Agency Background. Founded 1951. Campus Crusade helps to fulfill the Great Commission by actively communicating the message of Jesus Christ to college students throughout the world.

Requirements and Costs. College student; $600–$1500, depending on project. Job also required while on project.

Training Provided. Training throughout the program.

Work Description. Train others in evangelism and discipleship.

Countries Served. United States, urban and other areas

Campus Crusade for Christ Int'l
(U.S. Campus Ministries)
100 Sunport Lane
Orlando, FL 32809
407-826-2104
Randy Pierfelice

Program. Worldwide Student Network (WSN), overseas summer opportunities, 6–8 wks.

Agency Background. In addition to the emphasis of Campus Crusade, WSN helps students of the world reach the world.

Requirements and Costs. Christian with teachable attitude, willing to share his or her faith. $1500–$3300, varies with location.

Training Provided. 1-wk. orientation in cross-cultural sensitivity, personal evangelism and follow-up. Support development materials provided.

Work Description. Show *Jesus* film to unreached peoples, personal evangelism, train national Christians, use of some vocational skills (especially medical).

Countries Served. East Africa, Southeast Asia, South America, Western Europe, Far East

Christian Camping International/USA
P.O. Box 646
Wheaton, IL 60189
708-462-0300

Program. Summer staff and year-round positions at more than 1000 camps in the USA and hundreds of camps overseas.

Agency Background. CCI/USA is an association of Christian camps and conference centers with 11 sister associations around the world.

Requirements and Costs. Each individual camp determines their own transportation, salary, and benefits package.

Training Provided. Varies with each camp.

Work Description. Counselors, lifeguards, wranglers, teachers, nurses, food service workers, maintenance workers, etc.

Countries Served. Worldwide

A Christian Ministry in the National Parks
222 1/2 E. 49th Street
New York, NY 10017
212-758-3450
Warren Ost

Program. Program staff in parks, 3–15 mos., year-round.

Agency Background. Founded 1952. Interdenom. ministry started by student working at Yellowstone Nat'l Park.

Requirements and Costs. College-age, flexible, contagious faith, disciplined work habits. Raise own transportation costs to/from park. Pay own rm/brd.

Training Provided. 2-day orientation.

Work Description. Work at secular job in the park (i.e., desk clerks, bellhops, waitressing, etc.), friendship evangelism.

Countries Served. In 65 U.S. national parks

Christian Missionary Fellowship (CMF)
P.O. Box 8537
Ft. Collins, CO 80524
303-225-9949
Joe Varela

Program. 1–3 mos.

Agency Background. Founded 1969. Nondenom.

Requirements and Costs. Agree with doctrinal statement. Raise own funds: $300/mo. plus airfare.

Training Provided. 2-week class for linguistic and support raising assistance for those who can travel to Colorado.

Work Description. Construction, evangelism, discipleship, or prison work.

Countries Served. West Africa

Christian Outreach Int'l
12480 Wayzata Boulevard
Minnetonka, MN 55343
612-541-5344
Jack Isleib

Program. Evangelizing through the medium of music and sports. Trips are about 25 days or can be longer.

Agency Background. C.O.I. is an interdenom. sending agency, organizing teams and lay people for short/long term mission work overseas. Founded in 1984.

Requirements and Costs. Personal commitment to Christ. Good music/sports ability. Application procedure. Desire to win souls to the Lord. Cost: $1150–$3500—short-term.

Training Provided. Training and orientation camp is held in the U.S. prior to departure, emphasizing practical evangelism and skill development.

Work Description. Evangelism using music/sports as a tool, reaching out to a wide variety of people in and out of churches. Ministry takes place in public squares, schools, athletic events, concerts. Wonderful opportunity to travel and minister the gospel, and experience great personal growth. Daily Bible studies and group meetings.

SERVICE VACATIONS AT HOME AND ABROAD cont.

Countries Served. U.K., Sweden, Finland, Norway, Germany, Switzerland, Italy, France, Holland, Germany, Austria and the Commonwealth of Independent States (formerly the USSR).

Conservative Baptist Foreign Mission Society
P.O. Box 5
Wheaton, IL 60189
708-665-1200
Raymond Buker, Jr.
Program. Missionary Assistant Corps (MAC), 10 wks.–2 yrs.
Agency Background. A denom. sending agency engaged in evangelism, establishing churches and serving national churches. Also involved in education, literature, linguistics, medicine, radio and national support.
Requirements and Costs. Good health, fully trained for the position, single or married, able to sign CBFMS evangelical doctrinal statement. Raise own funds: $400/mo–$1000/mo. plus airfare.
Training Provided. Brief pre-field orientation and on-site training.
Work Description. Evangelism, church planting, home Bible studies, literature distribution, camp counseling, teaching, house-parenting, maintenance, construction, secretarial work, bookkeeping, and farming.
Countries Served. South America, Africa, Asia, Europe, Far East

Destination SUMMIT
New Tribes Mission
Sanford, FL 32771
407-321-6196
Program. Assist, summer (8 wks.) and winter (4 wks.)
Agency Background. Founded 1979. Nondenom. division of New Tribes Mission. Emphasis on work in tribal regions.
Requirements and Costs. 15 yrs. and older. Raise own funds, costs vary with location and program.
Training Provided. 4-day orientation, follow-up.
Work Description. Missionary support, maintenance, construction and other manual labor.
Countries Served. East Asia, West Africa, Latin America, Greenland

Destination SUMMIT
New Tribes Mission
Sanford, FL 32771
407-321-6196
Program. INTERFACE summer (9 wks.)
Agency Background. Founded 1989. Nondenom. Division of New Tribes Mission. Emphasis on study in tribal regions.
Requirements and Costs. 17 yrs. thru retirement. Raise own funds: $2981.
Training Provided. Brief pre-field orientation continued on-site.
Work Description. On-site college-level missions course, includes language and culture study with tribal people for teachers!
Countries Served. Papua New Guinea—Highlands Province

Eastern European Bible Mission (EEBM)
P.O. Box 110
Colorado Springs, CO 80901
303-577-4450
Bill Baker, Margaret Sims
Program. Summer mission program, 1 mo. min., 2 mos. aver.
Agency Background. Nondenom. agency working to strengthen the church in Eastern Europe.
Requirements and Costs. Age range: 22–70. Sometimes families, good health, agree with doctrinal statement. German is helpful. Raise own funds: $32/day (Eastern Europe), $16/day (Holland); plus airfare.
Training Provided. Pre-field training manual to study; support-raising ideas and materials; in Europe, 30 hrs. of classroom training.
Work Description. Serve as teachers and encouragers in camps and seminars; work with children, teens and adults.
Countries Served. Eastern Europe

Eastern Mennonite Board of Missions
Oak Lane and Brandt Blvd.
Salunga, PA 17538-0628
717-898-2251
Dan Gehman

Program. Youth Evangelism Service (YES) 7–11 mos.

Agency Background. Founded 1914. Denom. agency of Mennonite tradition with emphasis on community development, evangelism, support of national churches.

Requirements and Costs. Personal commitment to Christ and desire to share faith through word and deed. Raise own funds: $4000–$5000.

Training Provided. 1-day orientation; 3 mos. training in discipleship, evangelism, and hands-on experience; 1 mo. on-location language study for most teams.

Work Description. The team lives together and is involved in street (drama/mime), youth and other evangelism ministries.

Countries Served. Latin America, Central/ Northern Europe, Far East, United States, Caribbean

Eastern Mennonite Board of Missions
Oak Lane and Brandt Blvd.
Salunga, PA 17538-0628
Dan Hoellwarth

Program. Summer TRAINING ACTION Teams (STAT). 2 mos.

Agency Background. Founded 1914. Denom. agency of Mennonite tradition with emphasis on community development, evangelism, support of national churches.

Requirements and Costs. Personal commitment to Christ and desire to share faith through word and deed. Raise own funds: $2300.

Training Provided. 1-day orientation; 1 mo. training in discipleship.

Work Description. Team lives together and is involved in construction and other manual labor.

Countries Served. Latin America, Central/ Northern Europe, Far East, United States, Caribbean

Emmaus Road International
7150 Tanner Court
San Diego, CA 92111
619-292-7020
Neal Pirolo

Program. Team Orientation, 1 day; Acts Boot Camp, 1 wk.; Acts Training Course, 12 wks.

Agency Background. Founded 1983. ERI helps churches mobilize, train and network individuals in cross-cultural outreach ministry.

Requirements and Costs. Church: Team desiring to do cross-cultural outreach. Individual: Ministry experience, church or agency sponsor, Scripture study skills, call to ministry. Costs: Team Orientation—offering; Acts Boot Camp—$165; Acts Training Course—$1200.

Training Provided. 12-wk. course: cultural adaptation, language learning, spiritual warfare, interpersonal relationships, orientation, Bible study. Team and 1-wk. curriculum adapted from 12-wk. course.

Work Description. Classroom training and experience living and working with a Mexican family in Tijuana. Teams and individuals network with established ministries.

Countries Served. Network of agency opportunities available worldwide

Evangelical Free Church of America
Board of Overseas Missions
1515 E. 66th St.
Minneapolis, MN 55423
612-866-3343
Lloyd Childs

Program. Summer Overseas (SOS) 4–8 wks.; Apprentice in Missions (AIM) 3 yrs.; Mission Associate (MA) 2 wks. to 2 yrs.

Agency Background. Founded 1887. Evangelical Free Church denom. Main thrust is church planting.

Requirements and Costs. Denom. member, college/sem. students, 20 yrs. and older. Raise own funds. SOS: $400–$650/mo. plus airfare; AIM/MA: $1000–$2000/mo. per adult.

Training Provided. 2-wk. orientation and candidate school. Follow-up on field.

Work Description. SOS: maintenance, secretarial, literature distribution, camp ministry, evangelism, teaching. AIM: evangelism, church planting, discipling, teaching. MA: medical, secretarial, accounting, teaching, mechanics, maintenance, construction.

Countries Served. Southeast Asia, East Asia, Europe, Africa, South America

SERVICE VACATIONS AT HOME AND ABROAD cont.

FACE (Fellowship of Artists for Cultural Evangelism)
1605 E. Elizabeth Street
Pasadena, CA 91104
818-398-2445
Mary Lou Totten
Program. FACE Summer Institute, 8 wks. (4 wks. classroom training); China Interface, 3–4 wks.
Agency Background. Founded 1976. Evangelical, interdenom., emphasis on bringing creative expression and cross-cultural missions together.
Requirements and Costs. 21 yrs. and older. Professional artists for workshops and for performances. Raise own funds. FACE Summer Institute: approx. $1300. China Interface: approx. $3000.
Training Provided. FACE Summer Institute: 4 wks. classroom; China Interface: 6 wks. rehearsal and orientation. Follow-up on field; sponsors M.A. degree in Arts/Cross-cultural Communication, Wm. Carey University, Pasadena.
Work Description. Painting, music, mime, drama, dance, puppets, poetry, literature (work with all ages).
Countries Served. FACE Summer Inst.: Pasadena, CA, Arizona Navajo Indian Reserv. China Interface: China.

The Fold, Inc.
P.O. Box 1188
Lyndonville, VT 05851
802-626-5620
Fred Tomaselli
Tim Whiting
Program. Summer program, 10–12 wks.; Internships, 3–6 mos.
Agency Background. Founded 1967. Nondenom., family-style living.
Requirements and Costs. 20 yrs. and older. Rm/brd provided. Raise personal and trans. money plus small salary.
Training Provided. 1-wk. orientation plus weekly meetings. Follow-up.
Work Description. Work with troubled youth, discipling, Bible studies, recreational activities.

Countries Served. United States, rural and inner-city areas

Food for the Hungry
7729 E. Greenway Road
Scottsdale, AZ 85252
602-998-3100 or
800-2-Hunger
Gary Womelsduff
Program. Hunger Corps Projects (HCP) 1–3 wks., geared for church/school teams; Hunger Corps Volunteer (HCV) 2-yr. min. commitment.
Agency Background. Founded 1971. Nondenom., evangelical, involved in relief/community development, development of human resources and self-help projects.
Requirements and Costs. HCP: Terms—15 yrs. and older. Individuals—19 yrs. and older. HCV: 21 yrs. and older. No families with children. Cost varies. HCP: approx. $800 and up. HCV: approx. $950/mo.
Training Provided. Orientation, on-field training. Follow-up.
Work Description. HCP: Building projects. HCV: development and refugee/relief work.
Countries Served. Caribbean, Africa, Southeast Asia, So. Asia, Europe, Latin America

Foreign Mission Board,
Southern Baptist Convention
P.O. Box 6767
Richmond, VA 23230
804-353-0151
Mike Barnett
Glenn Prescott
Program. International Service Corps, 4 mos.–2 yrs.; Tentmakers & Baptists Living Abroad, open-ended terms.
Agency Background. A denom. sending agency. Establishes churches, engaged in aid and/or relief, development of human resources, radio and TV broadcasting and medicine.
Requirements and Costs. Good health, member in good standing of an active SBC church. Cost varies. Both paid and support-raising positions.
Training Provided. Cross-cultural training, technical skills, evangelism, and many other

orientation, learning situations provided.
Work Description. Engineer, TESL, agricultural; teachers at all levels and in many categories.
Countries Served. Opportunities throughout the world

Forward Edge Int'l
P.O. Box 65238
Vancouver, WA 98665
206-693-3343
Joseph Anfuso
Program. Forward Edge Teams (FET), 10 days–3 wks.; 1-yr. internship in Europe or Latin America.
Agency Background. A nondenom. church-planting ministry.
Requirements and Costs. 14 yrs. and older. Should not be opposed to charismatic orientation, though need not be charismatic. Raise own funds: $199–$1995.
Training Provided. Audio cassette tapes, reading materials, plus a 3-day intensive training session and 1-day re-entry session. Fund-raising kit provided.
Work Description. Evangelism, medical, construction, backpacking.
Countries Served. Far East, United States, Europe, Central America

Global Outreach Mission
P.O. Box 711
Buffalo, NY 14240
716-842-2220
Bill James
Program. Prince of Peace Corps (POPC), Summer, 7–8 wks.; Encounter Assignment (EA), 1–3 yrs.
Agency Background. Founded 1943. Interdenom., involved primarily in church planting, radio, camps, evangelism, literature distribution.
Requirements and Costs. POPC: 1 yr. of college. EA: 18 yrs. and older. Raise own funds. POPC: approx. $2000, trans. inc. EA: varies with commitment and location.
Training Provided. 1-wk orientation for POPC and EA in New York.
Work Description. POPC: evangelism, music, drama, literature distribution, children's ministry, church planting, construction, pas-

toral internships. EA: evangelism, church planting, maintenance, construction.
Countries Served. Europe, Latin America, South Asia, Caribbean

Gospel Missionary Union
10000 N. Oak
Kansas City, MO 64155
816-734-8500
Rex Sandiford
Program. Summer programs, 2–10 wks.
Agency Background. Founded 1892. Nondenom., evangelical, involved in evangelism, church planting, educational ministries, radio, literature distribution.
Requirements and Costs. 1 yr. of college, (Bible college and foreign language beneficial). Raise own funds: costs vary with location and commitment.
Training Provided. On the field.
Work Description. Work with missionaries, youth, camp work, VBS, literature distribution, evangelism, maintenance.
Countries Served. Europe, Alaska, Caribbean, Africa, Latin America

Greater Europe Mission
P.O. Box 668
Wheaton, IL 60189
708-462-8050
Personnel Dept.
Program. Eurocorps "91," 9 wks. and 4 wks.
Agency Background. Emphasis on training Europeans to reach their own in one of ten Bible institutes or three seminaries and in church planting locations.
Requirements and Costs. At least 1 yr. out of high school. Good health, language ability, couples with no children. Raise own funds: approx. $2600 for 9 wks. and $1800 for 4 wks.
Training Provided. Training manual provided. Orientation at Wheaton College before departure. Ongoing orientation after arrival on field.
Work Description. Open-air evangelism, door-to-door surveys, literature distribution, construction, and conference ministries.
Countries Served. Most of the Western European countries and expanding in the East.

SERVICE VACATIONS AT HOME AND ABROAD cont.

Habitat for Humanity
Habitat and Church Streets
Americus, GA 31709
912-924-6935
FAX 912-924-6541
Amy Parsons

Program. Domestic programs (headquarters and worksites), 3 mos. or longer; Int'l programs, 3 yrs.

Agency Background. Founded 1976. Ecumenical Christian housing ministry that works together with the poor to build low-cost housing for their purchase at no profit and no interest.

Requirements and Costs. Domestic: 18 yrs. and older; housing, food, insurance available. Construction and office experience welcomed. Int'l: 23 yrs. and older; housing, food, insurance, and fund-raising help provided. Some administration, construction, or community organizing experience required; international experience and language ability preferred.

Training Provided. Domestic: on-site training. Int'l: 11-wk. training at HQ in construction, procedures, intercultural awareness, community organizing, and development issues. Language training overseas, debriefing upon return.

Work Description. Headquarters: work in accounting, administration, construction, computers, graphic arts, hospitality, personnel, child care, photography, printing, public relations, translation. North American sites: project supervision, construction, personnel, office work. Int'l: community organizing, construction, administration, training, sharing life in another culture.

Countries Served. Africa, Latin America, Caribbean, Asia, Pacific Islands, North America

Harvesting in Spanish (HIS)
245 S. Benton Street
Lakewood, CO 80226
303-232-3030
FAX 303-232-3561
Don Benner

Program. Indefinite length of term.

Agency Background. Founded 1976. Interdenom. missionary agency working in 8 countries.

Requirements and Costs. Spanish helpful, doctrinally hold to Lausanne Convention. Raise own funds: singles, $600/month; couples, $1000/mo.

Training Provided. Training manual provided.

Work Description. Work in orphanage, construction, medical and dental work, street, school and market evangelism.

Countries Served. Guatemala, El Salvador, Mexico, Panama, Costa Rica, Argentina, Peru, Colombia

Helps International Ministries, Inc.
Rt. 1, Box 171D
Harlem, GA 30814-1071
404-556-3408
David DeJong

Program. Short-term, 1 wk.–2 yrs.

Agency Background. Founded 1976. Interdenom. technical sending agency serving other mission agencies and churches.

Requirements and Costs. 16 yrs. and older, good health. Raise own funds for trans. to/from location. Rm/brd may be provided.

Training Provided. On-the-field training.

Work Description. Construction, architecture, engineering, accounting, computer.

Countries Served. Africa, United States, Southeast Asia, Europe

Inner City Impact (ICI)
2704 W. North Avenue
Chicago, IL 60647
312-384-4200
Kerri Johnson

Program. Summer in Chicago (SIC), June 8–Aug. 17, 1991.

Agency Background. Primary goals are evangelism, discipleship, and church planting.

Requirements and Costs. Post high school, a desire to share Christ with others, teachable spirit, good attitude, flexible. Raise own funds: Singles, $1400–$1800, plus trans. Couples, $2200–$3100, plus trans.

Training Provided. Orientation provided before the program, follow-up provided during support raising.

Work Description. One-on-one model involvement with team discipleship. Could also be a Bible, music or crafts teacher, drama team, block club or recreation leader.

Country Served. United States (Chicago)

International Christian Assistance
P.O. Box 583
Neenah, WI 54956
414-722-3731
Jean Hoppe
Program. 21–60 days.
Agency Background. Founded 1974. Involved in agriculture, medical, trade schools; train native pastors.
Requirements and Costs. Mature leader. Raise own funds: $2500.
Work Description. Construction, agriculture, teaching, nursing, health, evangelism, church planting.
Countries Served. Ghana, Kenya, Uganda, Liberia, Mexico, U.S.

International Messengers
1600 Oakhills Road, SW
Bemidji, MN 56601
218-751-0388
Robert Rasmusson
Program. Group Action Projects (GAP), 3–6 wks.; Mission Project Planning Service (MPPS), 1–4 wks.
Agency Background. Evangelical, interdenom. missions organization comprised of an international staff team. Committed to the evangelization and discipleship of people of all nations; and to the motivation and training of members of the body of Christ for active involvement in world missions.
Requirements and Costs. 18 yrs. and older, committed Christian with a desire to serve. Raise own funds: ranges from $1000–$2500.
Training Provided. 2–7 days.
Work Description. Evangelistic English camps (teach English), work projects, other camp work.
Countries Served. Varies. Mainly Austria,

Poland, Hong Kong, Czechoslovakia, Yugoslavia, Romania

International STEP
P.O. Box 10305
Jacksonville, FL 32247-0305
904-398-6559
Tony Portell
Program. Short-term evangelistic projects, 2–3 wks. (depending on location).
Agency Background. Founded 1985. Provides young people and adults an opportunity to see and experience firsthand ministry in a foreign country.
Requirements and Costs. 15 yrs. and older. Raise own funds: $650–$1500 (scholarships available).
Training Provided. Home training provided through correspondence and videos for individuals and church groups: 2-day orientation and debriefing.
Work Description. One-to-one evangelism, preaching in churches, street ministry, mime, drama, music, puppets, clown ministry, medical teams, relief work.
Countries Served. Jamaica, Haiti, Philippines, England, France, Kenya, South Africa, Ecuador, Costa Rica, Guatemala, South Korea, China, Eastern Europe, Commonwealth of Independent States (formerly the USSR)

International Teams
P.O. Box 203
Prospect Heights, IL 60070
708-870-3800 or
1-800-323-0428
Glenn Schuman
Program. Two-Year Program (TYP); Summer Servants Program (SSP), 6 weeks.
Agency Background. Evangelical, nondenom. mission agency that trains and sends teams overseas for 2 yrs. or for a summer (since 1961).
Requirements and Costs. TYP: 20 yrs. and older. SSP: min. 18 yrs. old, foreign language helpful. Raise own funds. TYP: $975-$1200/mo., varies upon location. SSP: $2000-$2500 (Chicago to field and return).
Training Provided. TYP: 4 mos. training in language, culture, interpersonal relations,

SERVICE VACATIONS AT HOME AND ABROAD cont.

evangelism, discipleship, church planting, support raising and other. SSP: 4-day pre-field orientation.

Work Description. TYP: church planting and community development. SSP: evangelism, open-air meetings, drama, puppets, etc., work alongside two-year and career teams.

Countries Served. France, Italy, Spain, Philippines, Portugal, Austria, Poland, East Germany, Czechoslovakia, Romania, Hungary, Bulgaria, Yugoslavia, Commonwealth of Independent States (formerly the USSR)

LIFE Ministries
P.O. Box 200
San Dimas, CA 91773
714-599-8491
Todd McCollum

Program. Directions 1–3 yrs.; Scrum Dendo, 10 wks., summer; career

Agency Background. Interdenom., ministries in teaching English as an opportunity for evangelism, church planting, national leadership training, and music.

Requirements and Costs. Directions: at least 21 yrs., min. 2 yrs. college. Scrum Dendo: at least 19 yrs., 1 yr. college. Raise own funds; varies with program.

Training Provided. Orientation, conversational English training, introduction to Japanese language and culture. Re-entry.

Work Description. Teaching conversational English in conjunction with a Japanese church, friendship evangelism. Also opportunities in administration, church planting, music, and national leadership training.

Country Served. Japan

Mennonite Board of Missions
P.O. Box 370
Elkhart, IN 46515-0370
219-294-7523
Nancy Thiessen

Program. Mennonite Service Venture, 3 wks. in the summer for individuals; 2 days–2 wks. year-round for groups.

Agency Background. Founded 1882. Seeks to lead and enable the Mennonite church to be involved in programs of Christian ministry in North America and overseas.

Requirements and Costs. 14–18 yrs. Exceptions for youth and young adult groups. Raise own funds; varies, depending on travel.

Training Provided. Pre-field orientation. Study and orientation materials available for groups before and after experience.

Work Description. Painting, home repair, clean-up, construction, children's recreation programs, VBS.

Countries Served. Israel, United States, Canada, Ireland

Mercy Ships
P.O. Box 2020
Lindale, TX 75771-2020
214-963-8341
Cindy Ryan

Program. Volunteer program, 2 wks.–3 mos. year-round.

Agency Background. Interdenom., division of Youth With A Mission, started in 1978 on the YWAM ship, *Anastasis.* Now also on the *Good Samaritan.* Both ships aid in relief and development and medical needs to nationals.

Requirements and Costs. 18 yrs. and older, good health. Raise own funds: $150/mo. plus trans. to/from, and personal money.

Training Provided. Minimum orientation. Follow-up upon request.

Work Description. Varies. Carpentry, waitressing, electrical and plumbing work, etc., on ships. Also literature distribution, evangelism, hospitality, translation, medical/ dental work, construction, etc., on land.

Countries Served. *Anastasis* and *Good Samaritan* ships to United States, Canada, Mexico, Caribbean, Dominican Republic

MK Educational Center
(A branch of New Tribes Mission)
P.O. Box 1200
Camdenton, MO 65020
314-346-6053
David A. Lotz

Program. Teachers for 1990–1991 school yr. (10 mos.)

Agency Background. Interdenom., with

objective to reach tribal peoples through evangelism, translation, tutoring, church planting. Also help maintain schools for MKs.

Requirements and Costs. Qualified teacher, min. 1 yr. classroom experience, conservative life-style. Raise own funds: varies with location.

Training Provided. 10-day pre-field orientation.

Work Description. Teaching elementary/secondary children.

Countries Served. 20 countries

NAIM Ministries
P.O. Box 151
Point Roberts, WA 98281
604-946-1227
Jim Hamilton

Program. Summer Missionary Institute, 8 weeks

Agency Background. Founded 1949. Interdenom. mission agency reaching Native Indian and Sikh and Hindu people by personal evangelism and church planting in villages and urban centers.

Requirements and Costs. 1 yr. of college, English speaker. Raise own funds: $625 per individual or $1035 per couple, plus trans. cost to/from Vancouver, BC.

Training Provided. 5 days of intensive cross-cultural training. Regular supervision and midsummer refresher course.

Work Description. Live in an Indian village or community. Engage in evangelism and personal relationships, organizing activities, and community services.

Country Served. Primarily in British Columbia, Canada

OC International
(formerly Overseas Crusades)
P.O. Box 36900
Colorado Springs, CO 80936-6900
719-592-9292
Judy Shewy (STEP)
Robin Cook, Sports Ambassadors (SA)

Program. STEP (Summer Team Evang. Program), 2–6 mos.; SA, 2–6 wks. or 4–6 mos.

Agency Background. Founded 1950. Interdenom., assisting in discipling nations and equipping nationals.

Requirements and Costs. Good health, Christian, 18 yrs. old. STEP: Summer $1400–$3000 SA: $2000–$3400 depending on location.

Training Provided. STEP: Pre-field manual, 5 day on-field orientation. SA: Pre-field manual, training camp on-field.

Work Description. STEP: Evangelism, Bible studies, discipleship. SA: Play games against national clubs, share testimony, distribute literature, evangelism.

Countries Served. Canada, Mexico, Philippines, Argentina, Taiwan, Zimbabwe, Kenya

OMS International
P.O. Box A
Greenwood, IN 46142
317-881-6751
O. Kemp Edwards

Program. NOW Corps, 2–5 mos. (usually summer).

Agency Background. Nondenom., based on Wesleyan Armenian theological tradition.

Requirements and Costs. 19 yrs. and older, good health. Raise own funds: varies with location.

Training Provided. Orientation stateside and abroad, manual provided covering cross-cultural principles, logistics, etc.

Work Description. Administrative, youth work, maintenance, arts/crafts, sports, evangelism, teaching English, Sunday school, camp counseling, discipling, secretarial.

Countries Served. South America, Europe, Asia, Caribbean

Operation Mobilization
P.O. Box 444
Tyrone, GA 30290-0444
404-631-0432
Chip Kirk

Program. Summer program: Mexico, 2 months; Quebec, 1–2 months; Europe, 1–2 months. Also 1- and 2-yr. programs.

Agency Background. Founded 1957. Also known as Send the Light. Interdenom., with emphasis on short-term youth training, evangelism, literature distribution, discipling.

Requirements and Costs. Belong to local

SERVICE VACATIONS AT HOME AND ABROAD cont.

church, willingness to learn. Europe: 2 mos., approx. $1900. Mexico: 2 mos., approx. $1200. Canada: 2 mos., approx. $900. 1–2 yr. programs: approx. $500/mo.

Training Provided. Attend a 1-wk. training conference, read books, listen to tapes; additional 1-wk. conference if going to Europe. Follow-up.

Work Description. Evangelism, literature distribution, open-air meetings, drama, mime, puppets, local church work, concerts, administration, bookkeeping, accounting.

Countries Served. Europe, Middle East, MV *Logos II* and *Doulos* ships, South Asia, Canada

Outreach Canada
#16—12240 Horseshoe Way
Richmond, B.C. V7A4X9
Gerry Kraft

Program. STEP, 8 wks.

Agency Background. Nondenom. Equips people for ministry through research, motivational models, training and mobilization by direct involvement.

Requirements and Costs. 18 yrs., 2 yrs. born-again Christian, cross-cultural experience, service in and endorsement of home church. Spanish required for Mexico. Mexico, $1500; Philippines, $2400; Zimbabwe, $3200.

Training Provided. Pre-field manual with language tapes, 3-day orientation in United States; training on field with supervisory guidance.

Work Description. Training and mobilizing local Christians in evangelism, small group Bible studies, discipleship.

Countries Served. Canada, Mexico, Philippines

Outreach for Christ International
6585 Eden Vale Blvd.
Suite #110
Eden Prairie, MN 55346
612-934-5651
1-800-541-SONG

Program. The Reach Out Singers: 3- and 9-wk. tours.

Agency Background. Founded 1973. Sponsoring organization for Reach Out Singers, works in partnership with Northern and Eastern Europe.

Requirements and Costs. 16–30 yrs., good health. Raise own funds: $2249–$4686.

Training Provided. Orientation combines evangelism training and music coaching with nationally known vocal coaches.

Work Description. Evangelism through music.

Countries Served. Commonwealth of Independent States (formerly the USSR), Europe, Scandinavian countries, Eastern Europe, Canada, United States, Australia, Southeast Asia, Middle East, Tanzania, Zimbabwe, New Guinea

Overseas Christian Servicemen's Center
P.O. Box 1268
Englewood, CO 80150
303-762-1400
Dotty Hash

Program. Summer ministries, 6 wks.–3 mos. (could go to 2 yrs.); Hospitality House and Malachi youth programs; internships during year or summer.

Agency Background. Founded 1954. Ministry to American military worldwide.

Requirements and Costs. College-age, Christian walk, flexible, local church recommendation, prefer 1 yr. Bible training and ability to teach. Raise own funds: varies with commitment.

Training Provided. Orientation, on-the-field supervision. Evaluation at end of term.

Work Description. Malachi: ministry to military youth. Also Bible teaching, maintenance, evangelism, discipleship.

Countries Served. United States, Panama, Philippines, Korea, Japan, Germany, England, Italy, Spain

Pioneers
P.O. Box 527
Sterling, VA 22170
703-478-0004
Ruth Wright

Program. Pioneers Active in Cross-Cultural Evangelism (PACE), 7–8 wks.; Pioneers short-term, 1–2 yrs.

Agency Background. Founded 1979. Concerned with reaching the unreached with the gospel.

Requirements and Cost. Out of high school, conservative evangelical doctrine. Raise own funds. PACE: $2000–$3000. Short-term 1–2 yrs: varies.

Training Provided. Orientation manual provided. PACE: 3 days spent at Pioneers annual Candidate School for Specialized Training.

Work Description. PACE: evangelism, tutoring English, language/culture learning, children's ministry, literature distribution. PA: language/culture learning, participate as a team member with career missionary.

Countries Served. PACE: China, Papua New Guinea, S. America, India, Indonesia, Thailand, Mali, Guyana, Egypt

Presbyterian Church in America
Mission to the World/SIMA
P.O. Box 29765
Atlanta, GA 30359
404-320-3373
Dan Camp

Program. Servants in Missions Abroad (SIMA), 2 yrs.; summer, 2 mo.; two-week exposure trips.

Agency Background. Founded 1974. Conservative evangelical Presbyterian church.

Requirements and Costs. Should be familiar with Westminster Confession of Faith. Raise own funds. 2 yr.: $1500/mo. plus $6000 one time. Summer: $1500–$3000. Two-week trips: $500–$1500.

Training Provided. Support-raising and cross-cultural training for 2-mo. and 2-yr. candidates.

Work Description. Evangelism, discipling, church construction, conversational English, teaching MKs, children's ministry.

Countries Served. Europe, Africa, Latin America, Asia, Caribbean, Australia

RBMU International
8102 Elberon Avenue
Philadelphia, PA 19111
215-745-0680

Program. Project Timothy, 4–8 wks.

Agency Background. Founded 1873. Devoted

to church planting among unreached people groups.

Requirements and Costs. Conservative evangelical Raise own funds: $1500–$2500, depending on field.

Work Description. Evangelism, puppet shows, music, testimony giving, light labor.

Countries Served. Indonesia, Philippines, Chile, Peru, Cameroon, United States

Reciprocal Ministries Int'l
10720 Caribbean Blvd., Suite 450
Miami, FL 33189
305-251-8308
Herb Shoemaker

Program. Short-term Overseas Assignment (SOA), 2 wks.–2 yrs.; Ministry Teams (MT), 8–10 days; Work Teams (WT), 8–10 days; Sister Church Program (SCP), ongoing.

Agency Background. Interdenom., emphasis on lay ministries. Unique cross-cultural Sister Church Program, 10 yrs.

Requirements and Costs. 18 yrs. and older, some exceptions. Raise own funds. SOA: approx. $1000–$1500 for 4–6 wks. WT: $200–$300, plus trans. MT: $200–$300, plus trans.

Training Provided. SCP and SOA: 10 wk. training by tape.

Work Description. SOA: local church, VBS, administration, teaching, evangelism. MT: evangelism, music, drama, retreats. WT: construction, maintenance, local church work. SCP: adopt a church in Third-World country.

Countries Served. Caribbean, Europe

The Rocky Mountain Center for World Mission
P.O. Box 458
Pasadena, CA 91102
818-796-5425
Jim Proud

Program. Short term, 2–8 wks.

Agency Background. Begun 1988. A mission center on the pattern of and affiliated with the U.S. Center for World Mission.

Requirements and Cost. 18 yrs. and older. Under 18 must be accomp. by parent or guardian. Good health, a growing Christian

SERVICE VACATIONS AT HOME AND ABROAD cont.

for at least 1 year. Raise own funds. 2 weeks: plus airfare. 4 weeks: depends on trip. $600–$800.

Training Provided. Orientation in Europe. Training manual provided.

Work Description. Deliver Bibles, food, medical and relief supplies; fellowship with other believers; evangelism, construction work, teaching in youth camps, teaching English.

Countries Served. Poland, Hungary, Commonwealth of Independent States (formerly the USSR), Costa Rica, Middle East

Send International
P.O. Box 513
Farmington, MI 48332
313-477-4210, ext. 110
Verona Dutton

Program. Summer program, 10 wks.; short terms of 6 mo.–2 yrs.

Agency Background. Founded 1947. Nondenom., evangelical with Baptist tradition. Formerly Far Eastern Gospel Crusade.

Requirements and Costs. College-age. Raise own funds. Summer prog.: $1200–$3300. Short term: approx. $1300/mo.

Training Provided. Mainly on-field orientation. Follow-up.

Work Description. Summer Prog.: evangelism, discipleship, teaching, camp, VBS, administration, radio, maintenance. Short-term: professional skills (e.g., teaching, medical, administration), TESL, construction, evangelism.

Countries Served. United States, Southeast Asia

S.I.M. USA
P.O. Box 7900
Charlotte, NC 28241-8819
704-588-4300
Les Unruh

Program. 8 wks.–2 yrs.

Agency Background. Founded 1893. Interdenom. Main goal is evangelism.

Requirements and Costs. Good health, solid character references. Raise own funds: $11–$17/ day. Varies with location.

Work Description. Logistical and support to

pilot programs in church planting.

Countries Served. Liberia, Niger, Benin, Ethiopia, Kenya, Ghana, Nigeria, Bolivia

South America Mission, Inc.
P.O. Box 6560
Lake Worth, FL 33466
407-965-1833
Evie Opitz

Program. Short-Term (ST), 3 mos.–3 yrs.; Summer Team Program (STP), 4–8 wks.

Agency Background. Founded 1914. Interdenom., with objective to reach the unreached people throughout Latin America.

Requirements and Costs. ST: 21 yrs. STP: 1 yr. of college. Good health. ST: $1400/mo., inc. travel depending on location and length of time. STP: $1590, 1 mo.; $2050, 2 mos.

Work Description. ST: teaching, work with handicapped. STP: films, street meetings, camps, music, literature distribution.

Countries Served. Bolivia, Brazil, Peru, Colombia

Special Projects in the Tribes (SPRINT)
c/o World Outreach Fellowship
P.O. Box 585603
Orlando, FL 32858
407-425-5552
Howard Lisech

Program SPRINT Ministries, summer (7–8 wks.) and winter (1–3 wks.)

Agency Background. Nondenom. Assist missions and Third-World churches with needed projects.

Requirements and Costs. 15 yrs. and older, good health. Raise own funds. Summer: $1300–$3000. Winter: $980–$1400.

Training Provided. 5 days of pre-field training, includes cross-cultural, language, building group skills.

Work Description. Balanced ministry and work projects that are realistic yet leave a visible reminder of our love in action.

Countries Served. Papua New Guinea, Indonesia, Peru, Ecuador, Belize, Nepal, Philippines, Argentina, Bolivia, Alaska, Liberia

Stem Ministries
P.O. Box 290066
Minneapolis, MN 55429
612-535-2944
Jan, Pat, or Kathy
Program. 15 days.
Agency Background. Founded 1984. Independ. Christian organization placing short-termers overseas in 3 different countries.
Requirements and Costs. All ages (parental approval for youth 16 and under). Raise own funds: $300 plus round-trip airfare.
Training Provided. 4–8 hrs., pre-field; 8 hrs. on location; preparation manual given.
Work Description. Evangelism, construction, mercy, service, and creative ministries.
Countries Served. Haiti, Jamaica, Trinidad

The Evangelical Alliance Mission (TEAM)
P.O. Box 969
Wheaton, IL 60189-0969
708-653-5300
800-343-3144
Barry Hancock
Program. Summer Program, June 10–Aug. 15, 1991; SST Program, 3–12 mos.; Assoc. Program, 1–4 yrs.
Agency Background. Founded 1890. Nondenom. Principal focus on planting churches. Involved in education and health care on many fields.
Requirements and Costs. Summer: 20 yrs./2 yrs. college. SST: 20 yrs. up, skill to match a need. Assoc.: training appropriate to particular assignment. Summer: Raise own funds, $1900–$3200. SST: Costs vary.
Training Provided. Summer: 1-wk pre-field orientation. SST: On-field orientation only. Assoc.: 3-wk. candidate school.
Work Description. Summer: Evangelism, music, children's work, construction, etc. SST: Teaching, clerical, health care, etc. Assoc.: 127 openings in various areas.
Countries Served. 30 world areas in Europe, Africa, Latin America, East and West Asia

Teen World Outreach
7245 College Street
Lima, NY 14485

716-582-2790
Jim Porter
Program. Summer: 4 and 7 wk. Adult fall teams: 2 wks.
Agency Background. Founded 1982. Interdenom. charismatic tradition in service with other agencies with short-term programs.
Requirements and Costs. 13 yrs. and older. Raise own funds. Summer: $995–$2895. Adult fall: 21 yrs. and older, $795–$1995.
Training Provided. Support-raising training, technical skills, minimal language, evangelism, and drama.
Work Description. Building projects, repair and renovation programs, evangelism through drama and mime.
Countries Served. Amsterdam, Brazil, Costa Rica, France, India, Kenya, Mexico, Miami FL, New Guinea, New York City, Peru, Scotland, Egypt, South Africa

Trans World Radio
P.O. Box 700
Cary, NC 27512
919-460-3700
Cliff Floyd
Program. Summer program, 10-week minimum. Short-term of 6 months to 1 year, plus.
Agency Background. A superpower missionary network broadcasting the gospel in 85 languages from 7 stations and 25 transmitters strategically located worldwide by an international staff of over 750 using technical, administrative, and radio production skills.
Requirements and costs. All workers must have at least 2 years experience or training beyond high school. Summer program— $2000–$2500; short-term—$650–$800 per month.
Work Description. Work right alongside career missionary staff in administrative, technical and production skills.
Countries served. Europe, South America, Asia and Africa.

United World Mission
P.O. Box 250
Union Mills, NC 28167
704-287-8996

SERVICE VACATIONS AT HOME AND ABROAD cont.

Betty Sadler
Program. Summer, 6–7 wks.; MK school,
1–2 yrs. (grades 1–12).
Agency Background. Founded 1946;
nondenom.; engaged primarily in church
planting, targeting urban centers and
unreached peoples groups.
Requirements and Costs. Summer: 18 yrs.
and older raise own funds, $1600 and up.
MK school: certified, raise partial support.
Training Provided. Pre-field orientation;
further orientation on field.
Work Description. Summer: evangelism,
music, children's/youth work, sports, drama,
camping, etc. MK school: teaching one's
grade or subject, Bible, assist in activities.
Countries Served. Summer: Europe, other
countries MK school: Senegal

WorldTeam, Inc.
P.O. Box 143038
Coral Gables, FL 33114
305-446-0861
David Melick
Program. Summer teams, 1–8 wks.; minis-
try, camps, evangelism, Bible clubs.
Agency Background. Founded 1928. Inter-
denom., evangelical sending agency en-
gaged primarily in church planting and
evangelism.
Requirements and Costs. 20 yrs. and older.
Raise own funds. YHM: $2000, inc.
trans. STP: varies with location.
Training Provided. 1 week U.S. work with
missionary or national pastors on the field.
Work Description. STP: VBS, evangelism,
music, camp work, missionary support in
church planting, seminars.
Countries Served. Caribbean, Europe,
South America

Wycliffe Associates
202 S. Prospect St.
Orange, CA 92669
714-639-9950
Program. Construction length varies with
project. Generally 2–3 wks.
Agency Background. A support ministry of
lay people to Wycliffe Bible Translators
and The Summer Institute of Linguistics.

Requirements and Costs. Willingness to
serve and learn in a cross-cultural setting.
Raise own funds: $7-10/day rm/brd. Trans.
and visas can be handled through WA.
Training Provided. Fact sheet on location,
culture, currency, climate and what to
bring provided. Orientation on work site.
Follow-up provided.
Work Description. WA home ministry:
hospitality for missionaries traveling
through the U.S., prayer ministry, local
chapters. Missions Alive: construction
and helpers. Utilities: skilled people for
well drilling, electrical, etc.
Countries Served. Wycliffe fields worldwide and U.S. facilities

Youth in Mission
6401 The Paseo
Kansas City, MO 64131
816-333-7000
Dale Fallon
Program. Youth in Missions Prog. (YIM).
Summer (8 wks.): Advance, 1–2 yrs.
Agency Background. Founded late '60s. Inter-
denom., part of Nazarene Youth Int'l Min-
istry: purpose to provide hands-on exper-
ience in evangelism/discipleship ministries.
Requirements and Costs. 18 yrs. and older.
Raise own funds. YIM: approx. $750–
$1500 (partial subsidy). Advance: varies.
Training Provided. Training camp for 10 days.
Work Description. Youth work, puppetry,
Bible studies, teaching Sunday school,
evangelism, mime, drama, music.
Countries Served. United States (mainly
urban areas), Caribbean, Europe, Latin
America, Southeast Asia

YUGO Ministries
P.O. Box 25
San Dimas, CA 91773
714-592-6621
Dennis Mohler
Program. Week-long outreach trips to Mexico.
Agency Background. Founded 1964. Non-
profit evangelical organization dedicated
to ministry in Mexico.
Requirements and Costs. Most weeks are
planned for high school/college age.

Two weeks are for junior-highers. $130–$150.

Training Provided. Training materials provided in culture preparation and personal spiritual growth.

Work Description. Children's VBS, films, sports, drama, puppets, women's Bible studies, evangelistic services.

Country Served. Mexico

Source: *Stepping Out.* Published by Short-Term Missions Advocates, Inc. Copyright © 1987. Used by permission. Updated by ACW staff.

---

66 99
FOCUS QUOTE
Nothing in Scripture suggests we have to work forty hours a week for income. If we can find creative ways to reduce our economic needs, become economically self-reliant, and retire early, then we can more fully take charge of our lives. We don't have to be chronically dependent on an employer, working at jobs that are often irrelevant to the new order that God is birthing. And we can make the best hours of the day available to advance God's kingdom.—Tom Sine in *Wild Hope.* Published by Word Publishing.

SHOULD I GO OR NOT?

Below is a list of reasons why many people go on a short-term mission. Read through the entire list and mark ten items which reflect most closely your hopes and desires. Then return to those ten items and assign each one a numerical value:

3: most powerful motivator
2: strong motivator
1: not so strong a motivator

I want to go on a short-term . . .

Personal
___ for the excitement and fun of travel.
___ to see if I want to be a missionary.
___ to experience another culture.
___ to get away from home.
___ to get experience in a certain skill.
___ to get training as a Christian worker.
___ to buy duty-free electronics.
___ to add to my list of countries visited.
___ to see and experience real poverty.
___ as a way to spend a summer growing.
___ to find a mate with interests like mine.
___ other: _____

Spiritual
___ to know God as never before.
___ to show God that I'm serious about following him.
___ because I have a missionary call.
___ because God has told me specifically to go.
___ to gain favor with God.

___ to use my gifts for God.
___ other:_____

External
___ to help finish the task of world evangelization.
___ to better mobilize my church.
___ to help establish God's kingdom.
___ because it's strategic to help nationals.
___ to help rebuild a world with God's justice.
___ because Jesus commands it of us all.
___ other:_____

Needs-related
___ to help hungry children.
___ to give overworked missionaries a break.
___ because people are going to hell without the gospel.
___ because I feel compassion for poverty-stricken people.
___ other:_____

Within each of the five categories, add up the numbers that you have assigned to the ten most important motivating factors you have selected. There are no "correct" answers. You may have 15 or 20 points in a category, or none at all. The important thing is to recognize your motives and to work on balancing your reasons for going. There really is no "ideal" or "correct" balance of motives.

Source: *Stepping Out.* Published by Short-Term Missions Advocates, Inc. Copyright © 1987. Used by permission.

WHAT TO ASK AN AGENCY

Every agency is different, and every opportunity that an agency offers is unique. Use the chart below to learn what you can about each agency or opportunity that interests you.

Name of Agency:_____

	What I want	OK by me	Not what I want
Length of stay:			
Type of work:			
Amount of work:			
Location:			
Training:			
in support-raising:			
in the culture:			
in teamwork:			
debriefing:			
Contact with other culture:			
Cost:			
Team atmosphere:			
Doctrine:			
Living environment:			
Leadership, authority structure:			
Potential for career:			
Others' counsel about it:			

Source: *Stepping Out*. Published by Short-Term Missions Advocates, Inc. Copyright © 1987. Used by permission.

VACATIONS YOU NEVER THOUGHT TO TAKE

1. **Vacation from words**. We speak more than five thousand words in a day. A quiet revolution might occur if we didn't speak for a day.

2. **Vacation from food**. It's commonly called a fast, rather than a vacation—but make it a celebration rather than an endurance contest. It will change not only your weight but also your life-style.

3. **Vacation from seeing or hearing**. Years ago I taped my eyes for a good part of a week so that I was totally blind. That time probably taught me more about my senses than any five books could have done. Since then I've intentionally limited other senses in order to isolate and experience them. They have been priceless life investments.

4. **Vacation from complaining**. Trying it is poignant, painful, and enlightening.

Source: Tim Hansel in *When I Relax, I Feel Guilty*. Published by David C. Cook Publishing Company. Copyright © 1979. Used by permission.

CAMPS, CONFERENCES, RETREAT CENTERS

Let *The Almanac of the Christian World* help you find the right camp for your family vacation. The following camps, conference, and retreat centers are members of Christian Camping International/USA (CCI/USA), an association of Christian camps and conference centers and their leaders. Further information is available from:
Christian Camping International/USA
P.O. Box 646
Wheaton, IL 60189
Phone 708-462-0300 FAX 708-462-0499

State/Camp	Address	Phone
Alabama		
Alpine Camp for Boys	Rt. 1, Box 216, Mentone, AL 35984	205-634-4404
Camp Alamisco	Rt. 3, Box 221, Dadeville, AL 36853	
Camp Chula Vista	Rt. 6, Box 1720, Pell City, AL 35125	205-338-2940
Camp Desoto	P.O. Box 432, Mentone, AL 35984	205-634-3411
Camp Skyline Ranch	P.O. Box 287, Mentone, AL 35984	205-634-3201
Camp Victory	Rt. 3, Box 212, Samson, AL 36477	205-898-7948
Marannook, Inc.	P.O. Box 581, Lafayette, AL 36862	205-864-7504
Ponderosa Bible Camp	P.O. Box 285, Mentone, AL 35984	205-634-3795
Shocco Springs Conference Ctr.	Route 1, Box 17A, Talladega, AL 35160	205-362-4151
Alaska		
Camp Challenge	P.O. Box 1833, Palmer, AK 99645	907-745-3731
Camp Li-Wa (Living Water)	590 Wigwam Way, Fairbanks, AK 99701	907-457-6059
Camp Maranatha	P.O. Box 521038, Big Lake, AK 99652	
Coal Bay Camp & Retreat	P.O. Box 7400, Ketchikan, AK 99901	907-225-2893
Covenant Bible Camp	Box 209, Unalakueet, AK 99684	907-543-3225
Echo Ranch	Box 210608, Auke Bay, AK 99821	907-789-9463
LaVerne Griffin Youth Rec Camp	1131 E.76th Avenue 201, P.O. Box 110670, Anchorage, AK 99511-0670	907-337-6076
North Star Bible Camp	Mile 36.5 Hatcher Pass, Willow, AK 99688	907-495-6378
Solid Rock Bible Camp	P.O. Box 489, Soldotna, AK 99669	907-262-4741
The Salvation Army–Alaska Div.	143 E. Ninth Avenue, P.O. Box 101459, Anchorage, AK 99510-1459	907-276-2515
Victory Bible Camp	HCO3 Box 8392, Palmer, AK 99645-9405	907-745-4203
Arizona		
Camp Grace & Grace Lodge	Rt. 3, Box 2568, Lakeside, AZ 85929	602-537-2080
Emmanuel Pines Camp	5095 Iron Springs Rd., Prescott, AZ 86301	602-445-1509
LOMONA	601 E. Highway 260, Payson, AZ 85541	
Living Water Retreat Ctr.	P.O. Box 529, Cornville, AZ 86325	
Mountain Meadow Ranch	Star Route Box 144, Payson, AZ 85541	602-478-4435
New Chance Camp	Signal Road, 1115 E. Van Buren, Phoenix, AZ 85006	602-258-2639
Pine Summit Bible Camp & Conf.	HC 32, Box 293, Prescott, AZ 86303	
Pinerock Christian Camp & Conf.	1400 Pine Drive, Prescott, AZ 86301	602-445-8357
Prescott Pines Bapt. Camp	P.O. Box 12921, Prescott, AZ 86304-2921	602-445-5225
Tonto Rim American Bapt. Camp	HCR 95-P, Payson, AZ 85541	602-478-4630
United Christian Youth Camp	1600 Linden Road, Prescott, AZ 86301	
Victory Heights Bible Camp	HC 31, Box 161, Show Low, AZ 85901	602-253-0200
Arkansas		
Camp Wyldewood	P.O. Box 1255, Searcy, AR 72143	501-268-6809

State/Camp	Address	Phone
Ozark Conferences, Inc.	1300 Westpark Dr., Suite 5A, Little Rock, AR 72204	501-666-3266
Ozark-Lithia Camp	Star Rt. 10, Box 97, Hot Springs, AR 71909	501-568-2194
Park Hill Baptist Church	P.O. Box 4064, North Little Rock, AR 72116	501-753-3412

California

State/Camp	Address	Phone
Agape Christian Retreat & Conf.	21651 Yucca Road, Perris, CA 92370	213-232-8790
Alliance Redwoods	6250 Bohemian Hwy., Occidental, CA 95465	707-874-3507
Alpine Covenant Conf. Ctr.	P.O. Box 155, Blue Jay, CA 92317	714-337-6287
Angeles Crest Christian Camp	2500 E. Nutwood Ave., Fullerton, CA 92631	714-870-9190
Calif. Conference Free Meth.	504 Woodrow Ave., Modesto, CA 95350	
Calvary Chapel Youth Camp	32355 Green Valley Lake Rd., P.O. Box 8560, Green Valley Lake, CA 92341-8560	714-867-4444
Calvin Crest Conferences	45800 Calvin Crest Road, Oakhurst, CA 93644	209-683-4450
Camp Alandale	P.O. Box 35, Idyllwild, CA 92349	714-659-5253
Camp Alta	794 Power House Road, Alta, CA 95701	916-389-2277
Camp Cedar Crest	P.O. Box 179, Running Springs, CA 92382	714-867-2531
Camp Cherith/Sky Meadows	HC 01, Box 90, Angelus Oaks, CA 92305	714-828-7585
Camp Emmanuel	P.O. Box 309 8346 O'Donovan Rd., Creston, CA 93432.	805-238-3582
Camp Hammer	21401 Big Basin Hwy., Boulder Creek, CA 95006	408-338-3200
Camp Maranatha	P.O. Box CC, Idyllwild, CA 92549	714-659-2739
Camp Mattole	P.O. Box 86, Eureka, CA 95501	707-445-8602
Camp O-Ongo for Boys & Girls	P.O. Box 98 CC, Running Springs, CA 92382	714-867-7041
Camp Redwood Glen/Salv. Army	3100 Bean Creek Rd., Scotts Valley, CA 95066	415-553-3585
Camp Sugar Pine	48478 Mill Canyon Rd., Oakhurst, CA 93644	209-683-4938
Camp Wawona	P.O. Box 2055, Wawona, CA 95389	209-375-6231
Camp Yolijwa	39136 Harris Road, Yucaipa, CA 92399	818-367-8784
Campus by the Sea	P.O. Box 466, Avalon, CA 90704	213-510-0015
Canyon Meadows Conf. Ctr.	41600 Lake Hughes Rd., Lake Hughes, CA 93532	805-724-1225
Capital Mountain Christian Camp	P.O. Box 89, Weimar, CA 95736	916-346-8384
Captain Kids Daycamp	3590 Elm Ave., Long Beach, CA 90807	213-595-6881
Cedar Grove Bible Camp	3456 Triangle Rd., Mariposa, CA 95338	209-742-7369
Cedar Lake Christian Camp	P.O. Box 1568, Big Bear Lake, CA 92315	714-866-5714
Chinquapin Christian Conf. Ctr.	P.O. Box 1057, Pinecrest, CA 95364	209-521-0181
City Team Camp May-Mac	9115 E. Zayante Rd., Felton, CA 95018	408-335-3019
Diamond Arrow Conf. Grounds	15742 Bloomfield Rd., Nevada City, CA 95959	209-369-1094
Discovery Expeditions	17183 Retrac Way, Grass Valley, CA 95949	916-268-0877
El Camino Pines	13724 Fenton Ave., Sylmar, CA 91342	818-367-8784
Emerald Cove Camp	Box 449, Bass Lake, CA 93604	209-642-3512
Family Maintenance Ctr., Inc.	9250 Fruitridge Road, Sacramento, CA 95826	916-381-4380
Golden Valley Camp	P.O. Box 115, Volcano, CA 95689	209-296-4616
Harmony Pines Chrst. Ctr.	1720 W. 17th, Santa Ana, CA 92802	
Hartland Christian Camp	P.O. Box 25, Badger, CA 93603	209-337-2349
Hartstone Bible Conf. Inc.	17856 Van Arsdale Road, Potter Valley, CA 95469	707-743-1621
Heavenly Hills Chr. Camp	P.O. Box 1628, Twain Harte, CA 95383	209-586-1306
Hume Lake Christian Camps	64144 Hume Lake Road, Hume, CA 93628	209-251-6043
Idyllwild Pines Camp	26375 Hwy 243, Idyllwild, CA 92549	714-659-2605
Indian Hills Camp	15763 Lyons Valley Camp, Jamul, CA 91935	
J H Mountain Ranch	8525 Homestead Lane, Etna, CA 96027	916-467-3468
Kidder Creek Orchard Camps	2700 S. Kidder Creek Rd Box 208, Greenview, CA 96037	916-467-3265
Know Your Bible Camp	3462 E. Vista Way, Vista, CA 92084	619-724-4867

State/Camp	Address	Phone
Koinonia Conference Grds.	1473 Eureka Canyon Rd., Watsonville, CA 95076	408-722-1472
Laurel Pines Camp	P.O. Box 75, Redlands, CA 92373	714-793-3994
Let's Go Fishing	22 Del Rio Ct., Moraga, CA 94556	415-376-6283
Meteor Ranch Bible Conf.	2255 E. Hwy. 20, Upper Lake, CA 95485	707-275-2170
Mile High Pines Camp	12131 Harclare Drive, Moreno Valley, CA 92387	714-247-7577
Mission Springs	1050 Lockhart Gulch Road, Scotts Valley, CA 95066	408-335-9133
Missionary Athletes, Int'l.	P.O. Box 945, La Habra, CA 90633	213-690-4934
Mount Crags/Camp Gilmore	P.O. Box 15899 Del Valle Station, Los Angeles, CA 90015	818-347-6327
Mount Cross Camp & Retreat	P.O. Box 387, Felton, CA 95018	
Mount Gilead Bible Conference	13485 Green Valley Rd., Sebastopol, CA 95472	707-823-4508
Mount Hermon Association	P.O. Box 413, Mount Hermon, CA 95041	408-335-4466
Oak Glen Christian Conf. Ctr.	39364 Oak Glen Rd., Yucaipa, CA 92399	714-797-2570
Oakhurst Christian Conf. Ctr.	36616 Mudge Ranch Rd., Coarsegold, CA 93614	209-683-6563
Old Oak Ranch Conference Ctr.	15250 Old Oak Ranch Rd., Sonora, CA 95370	209-532-4295
Palomar Baptist Camp	Palomar Mountain, CA 92060	619-742-3438
Paradise Springs	P.O. Box 68, Valyermo, CA 93563	805-944-4500
Pine Springs Ranch	P.O. Box 37, Mt. Ctr., CA 92361	714-659-3173
Pine Summit	P.O. Box 2871, Big Bear Lake, CA 92315	714-866-5801
Pine Valley Bible Conference	P.O. Box 400, Pine Valley, CA 91962-0400	714-473-8879
Pinecrest Christian Conf. Ctr.	P.O. Box 409, Twin Peaks, CA 92391	714-338-4243
Ponderosa Pines	33484 Green Valley Lake Rd., Running Springs, CA 92382	714-867-7037
Quaker Meadow Camp	P.O. Box 1607, Whittier, CA 90609	213-947-2883
Rancho Agua Viva Ministries	724 Isthmus Court, San Diego, CA 92109	
Rancho Capistrano Renewal Ctr.	29251 Camino Capistrano, San Juan Capistrano, CA 92675	714-364-3023
Rancho Del Cielo	14488 Mussey Grade Rd., Ramona, CA 92065	619-789-1322
Rancho Del Rey Christian Ctr.	655 Burnham Rd., Oakview, CA 93022	805-643-5821
Rancho Ybarra	3150 Big Tujunga Cyn. Rd., Tujunga, CA 91042	818-353-2423
Rawhide Ranch	P.O. Box 216, Bonsall, CA 92003	714-758-0083
Redwood Christian Park	15000 Two Bar Rd., Boulder Creek, CA 95006	408-338-2134
Redwood Glen Baptist Camp	1430 Wurr Rd., Loma Mar, CA 94021	415-879-0320
Royal Family Kids' Camps, Inc.	1068 Salinas Avenue, Costa Mesa, CA 92626	714-556-1420
Sa Ha Le Lodge	39873 Crocus Drive, Big Bear Lake, CA 92315	714-866-4155
Sequoia Brigade Camp	2952 Euclid Ave., Concord, CA 94519	415-689-7618
Sierra Pines Baptist Camp	P.O. Box 7, Little Norway, CA 95721	916-659-7111
Silver Spur Chr Cmp & Conf Ctr.	P.O. Box 578, Tuolumne, CA 95379	209-928-4248
Sky Mountain Christian Camp	P.O. Box 79, Emigrant Gap, CA 95715	916-389-2118
Sonshine Camps	2599 Newport Blvd., Costa Mesa, CA 92627	714-966-0454
Summit Adventure	P.O. Box 498, Bass Lake, CA 93604	
Tahquitz Conf. Assoc., Inc.	55251 S. Circle Drive, Idyllwild, CA 92349	714-659-2934
The Lighthouse	313 Canvasback, Big Bear Lake, CA 92315	714-532-5241
The Neighborhood Church	20600 John Dr., Castro Valley, CA 94546	415-537-4690
The Oaks Christian Camp	P.O. Box 437, Lake Hughes, CA 93532	
Thousand Pines	POB 3288, Crestline, CA 92325	818-915-7641
Verdugo Pines Bible Camp	22400 Big Pines Hwy., Wrightwood, CA 92397	
Victory Ranch	123 Star Route, Moreno, CA 92360	714-654-7766
Westminster Woods	6510 Bohemian Hwy., Occidental, CA 95465	707-874-2426
Wolf Mountain Conference Assn	16555 Jericho Rd., Grass Valley, CA 95949	916-273-8709
Wynola Bible Conference	P.O. Box 278, Julian, CA 92036	619-765-0288
Young Life's Oakbridge Camp	27224 Highway 78, Ramona, CA 92065	714-789-6980

State/Camp	Address	Phone
Young Life's Woodleaf	P.O. Box 397, Challenge, CA 95925	916-675-2252
Zephaniah's Camp	648 Chelham Way, Santa Barbara, CA 93108	
Colorado		
Bear Trap Ranch	Box 1327, Colorado Springs, CO 80901	303-632-0740
Black Forest Camp & Conf. Ctr.	780 E. Baptist Road, Colorado Springs, CO 80921	719-488-3750
Camp Chief Ouray	P.O. Box 648, Granby, CO 80446	303-887-2152
Camp Eden	11583 Camp Eden Rd., Golden, CO 80403	303-642-3683
Camp Elim	5567 County Road 78, Woodland Park, CO 80863	719-687-2030
Camp Id-Ra-Ha-Je	571 County Rd. 43, Bailey, CO 80421	303-674-8442
Camp Id-Ra-Ha-Je West	27862 Co. Rd. 12, Somerset, CO 81434-9601	303-929-5221
Camp Redcloud	Box 130, Lake City, CO 81235	303-944-2625
Camp Santa Maria	P.O. Box 280003, Lakewood, CO 80228-0003	303-935-0035
Christian Wilderness Encounter	P.O. Box 28147, El Jebel, CO 81628	303-963-3215
Colorado Camp Cherith	c/o Quaker Ridge Camp, SR 1208, Woodland Park, CO 80863	303-353-3170
Colorado Chr. Service Camp	P.O. Box 36, Como, CO 80432	303-634-3318
Covenant Heights Conf. Ctr.	7400 S. St. Vrain Hwy. 7, Estes Park, CO 80517	303-586-2900
Deer Creek Christian Camp	228 S. Pine Drive, Bailey, CO 80421	303-838-5647
Eagle Lake Camp	P.O. Box 6000, Colorado Springs, CO 80934	719-472-1260
Estes Park Ctr./YMCA	P.O. Box 20800, Estes Park, CO 80511-2800	
Golden Bell Ranch	Box 380/Co. Rd. 512, Divide, CO 80814	303-687-9651
High Peak Camp & Conference	Long's Peak Route, Estes Park, CO 80517	
K-Life Summer Kamps	3651 S. Colorado, Englewood, CO 80110	303-781-0091
Living Rock Christian Retreat	P.O. Box 209, South Fork, CO 81154	719-873-5215
Meadowdale	5532 U.S. Highway 36, Longs Peake Route, Estes Park, CO 80517	303-586-4359
Noah's Ark Adventure Company	Box 850, Buena Vista, CO 81211	303-395-2158
Presby. Highlands Camp	P.O. Box 66, Allenspark, CO 80510	303-747-2451
Quaker Ridge Camp	30150 N. Hwy 67, Woodland Park, CO 80863	719-687-9012
Rocky Mountain Mennonite Cmp	Box 6, Divide, CO 80814	719-687-9506
Spring Canyon	26000 C.R. 344, P.O. Box 2047, Buena Vista, CO 81211	303-395-2328
Twin Peaks Bible Camp	Box 907, Grand Junction, CO 81502	303-242-9121
Woodbine Ranch	2584 N. Hwy. 67, Sedalia, CO 80135	303-688-3422
Young Life's Frontier Ranch	22150 Co. Rd. 322 POB 2025, Buena Vista, CO 81211	303-395-8696
Young Life's Trail West Lodge	Route 1, Buena Vista, CO 81211	719-395-2477
Young Life's Wilderness Ranch	General Delivery, Creede, CO 81130	303-473-4262
Connecticut		
Mountain Lake Bible Camp	64 Mountain Lake Road, New Preston, CT 06777	203-868-2048
Delaware		
Fenwick Island Surf & Beach Camp	10 S. Carolina Avenue, Fenwick Island, DE 19944	302-539-0248
District of Columbia		
Camp Dynamite	Box 166, Falling Waters, DC 20032	
Florida		
Camp Dovewood	P.O. Box 606, Branford, FL 32008	904-935-0863
Camp Gilead	P.O. Box 98, Polk City, FL 33868	813-984-1353
Camp Horizon	7369 Sunnyside Drive, Leesburg, FL 34748	904-728-5822

State/Camp	Address	Phone
Camp Keystone/Salv. Army	Route 3, Box 757, Starke, FL 32091	813-962-6611
Camp Kuluqua	Rt. 2, Box 110, High Springs, FL 32643	904-454-1351
Camp o' the Pines	Box 18000, Pensacola, FL 32523	904-478-8480
Camp Sonlight	P.O. Box 183, Summerfield, FL 32691	813-839-5186
Camp Sparta-RBCoF	5055 Camp Sparta Road, Sebring, FL 33872	813-382-8696
Camp Suwannee Retreat Ctr.	Rt. 6, Box 370, Live Oak, FL 32060	904-658-3333
Canaveral Christian Retreat	P.O. Box 1056, Merritt Island, FL 32952	305-453-0350
Church of God Youth Ctr.	P.O. Box 885100, Leesburg, FL 32788	904-742-2500
Florida Sheriffs Youth Camp	P.O. Box 1000, Barberville, FL 32105	904-749-9999
Gold Coast Christian Camp	7495 Parklane Rd., Lake Worth, FL 33467	407-968-3136
Lake Aurora Chrst. Assembly	237 Golden Bough Rd., Lake Wales, FL 33853	813-696-1102
Lake Placid Conference Ctr.	2665 Placid View Dr., Lake Placid, FL 33852	813-465-2197
Lake Swan Camp	Rt. 1, Box 1294, Melrose, FL 32666	904-475-2828
Land o' Sunshine Camp Cherith	8290 141st Street N., Seminole, FL 34646	708-615-0782
Life for Youth Ranch	1416 82nd Avenue, Vero Beach, FL 32966	
North Florida Christian Service Camp	6873 Camp Road, Keystone Heights, FL 32656	904-473-3281
The Lord's Barn	25001 S.W. 167th Ave., Homestead, FL 33031	305-248-6890
Young Life's Southwind	P.O. Box 550, Oklawaha, FL 32679	904-288-2500

Georgia

Believers' Bible Church Camp	3693 Cambellton Road, Atlanta, GA 30331	404-587-4171
Camp Agape	2601 Flat Shoals Road, College Park, GA 30349	404-996-0600
Camp Hope	P.O. Box 3581, Augusta, GA 30904	
Camp J.O.Y.	P.O. Box 1232, Hamilton, GA 31902	404-322-8267
Camp Westminster	2412 Lake Rockaway Rd., Conyers, GA 30207	404-483-2225
Camp Winshape	WinShape Centre, Box 9, Mt. Berry, GA 30149	404-235-8407
Cohutta Springs Adventist	Rt. 1, Box 17-A, Crandall, GA 30711	404-695-9093
Hi-Life Christian Camp	101 S. Spencer Street, Dalton, GA 30721-3122	404-278-9713
Toccoa Wilderness Min., Inc.	P.O. Box 1266, Blue Ridge, GA 30513	404-632-3554
Woodland Christian Camp	90 Woodland Camp Rd., Temple, GA 30179	404-562-3103

Hawaii

Camp Homelani	68-581 Crozier Dr., Waialua, HI 96791	808-988-2136

Idaho

ALACCA Bible Conference	HCR 67, Box 40, Grangeville, ID 83530	208-983-1188
Daystar Conference Ctr.	P.O. Box 455, Donnelly, ID 83615	208-325-8210
Quaker Hill Conf., Inc.	P.O. Box 1181, Mc Call, ID 83638	208-634-2083
Ross Point Baptist Camp	South 600 Ross Point Rd., Post Falls, ID 83854	208-773-1655
Timber Ridge Ranch	P.O. Box 285, Harrison, ID 83833	208-689-3209
Victory Cove	P.O. Box 971, Mc Call, ID 83638	208-888-0988

Illinois

Camp Good News	RR 1, Liberty Lane, Washington, IL 61571	309-444-3255
Camp Hickory	P.O. Box 400, Round Lake, IL 60073	708-546-2855
Camp Maranatha	RR 1, Box 143, Ramsey, IL 62080	217-235-1205
Camp One Way	RR 1, Box 245C, Mt. Auburn, IL 62547	217-676-2533
Dickson Valley Camp & Conf.	17K420 Finnie Road, Newark, IL 60541	312-553-6233
East Bay Camp	RR 2, Hudson, IL 61748	309-829-7531
Epworth Springs Camp	RR 4, Lewiston, IL 61542	309-547-2047
Great Oaks	P.O. Box 236, Lacon, IL 61540	309-246-4005
Green Valley Camp	501 E. Poplett's Hollow, Peoria, IL 61615	309-673-9176
Inner City Impact Camping Min.	2704 W. North Avenue, Chicago, IL 60647	312-384-4200
Jensen Woods Camp	1211 N. Park Street, P.O. Box 515, Bloomington, IL 61702-0515	

State/Camp	*Address*	*Phone*
Lake Williamson Christian Ctr.	P.O. Box 620, Carlinville, IL 62626	217-854-9686
Lamoine Christian Camp	Rt. 1, Box 46, Tennessee, IL 62374	217-654-2238
Land-o-Lincoln Camp Cherith	Route 1, Tiskilwa, IL 61368	312-741-6518
Little Galilee Chr. Assembly	RR 2, Box 266, Clinton, IL 61727	217-935-3809
Manitoqua Ministries	8122 W.Sauk Trail, Frankfort, IL 60423	815-469-2319
Menno Haven Camp & Retreat Ctr.	RR 1, Box 94, Tiskilwa, IL 61368	815-646-4344
Moody Bible Institute	820 N. LaSalle Dr., Chicago, IL 60610	312-329-4000
Reynoldswood Christian Camp	621 Reynoldswood Road, Dixon, IL 61021	815-284-6979
Riverwoods Christian Ctr.	35 W701 Riverwoods Lane, St. Charles, IL 60174	708-584-2222
Rock River Bible Camp	910 Bend Road, Dixon, IL 61021	815-652-4744
Rock River Christian Camp	16482 IL Rt. 64 W., Polo, IL 61064	815-493-6622

Indiana

Bear Lake Camp	RR 4, Box 125, Albion, IN 46701	
Bible Memory Program	Box 382, Goshen, IN 46526	219-533-5388
Brethren Retreat Ctr.	9095 W. 275 N., Shipshewana, IN 46565-9620	219-768-4519
Camp Alexander Mack, Inc.	P.O. Box 158, Milford, IN 46542	219-658-4831
Camp Allendale	Rt. 1, Box 72, Trafalgar, IN 46181	317-878-4400
Camp Challenge	Rt. 16, Box 530, Bedford, IN 47421	812-834-5159
Camp Good News	P.O. Box 344, N.Webster, IN 46555	219-834-2769
Camp Ray Bird	25765 W. Edison Rd., South Bend, IN 46628	219-232-8523
Camp Reveal	300 S.E. Seventh St., Evansville, IN 47713	812-867-2668
Camp Tecumseh YMCA	Route 2, Box 311, Brookstown, IN 47923	317-564-2898
Cedar Lake Bible Conference	P.O. Box 665, Cedar Lake, IN 46303	219-374-5941
Epworth Forest Conf. Ctr.	P.O. Box 16, N. Webster, IN 46555	219-834-2212
F.C.A. National Conf. Ctr.	Rt. 1, Box 81A, Marshall, IN 47859	317-597-2323
Higher Ground Camping/Retreat	Rt. 3, Box 320 A, W.Harrison, IN 47060	812-637-3777
Indiana Regular Baptist Camps	205 N. County Road 700 W., Warsaw, IN 46580	219-858-2451
Lake James Christian Assembly	Rt. 2, Box 581, Angola, IN 46703-9535	219-833-2786
Lake Placid Conference Ctr.	0397 S., 200 E, Harford City, IN 47348	317-348-3641
Outdoor Ministries	P.O. Box 5008, Bloomington, IN 47402	812-336-0186
Prairie Camp	28042 C.R. 24, W., Elkhart, IN 46517-9774	219-293-1332
Quaker Haven Camp	EMSD16C Lane, Syracuse, IN 46567	219-834-4193
Salvation Army Camp	RR 16, Box 180-1089, Bedford, IN 47421-9806	812-279-2495
Walnut Hills Retreat	10026 E. Northshore Dr., Unionville, IN 47468	812-988-4405

Iowa

Camp Quaker Heights	Rt. 3, Box 53, Eldora, IA 50627	515-858-5977
Central Iowa Bible Camp	P.O. Box 309, Earlham, IA 50072	515-265-8435
Clear Lake United Meth. Camp	RR 1, Box 210, Clear Lake, IA 50428	515-357-2085
Dayton Oaks Baptist Camp	RR 1, Dayton, IA 50530	515-547-2417
East Iowa Bible Conf.	RR 2, Deep River, IA 52222	319-655-7693
Episcopal Ctr.	RR 4, Boone, IA 50036	
Forest Lake Baptist Camp	RR 3, Bloomfield, IA 52537	515-684-8908
Inspiration Hill	Rt. 1, Box 168, Inwood, IA 51240	712-986-5193
Pine Lake Christian Ctr.	Box 535, Eldora, IA 50627	515-858-3284
Twin Lakes Bible Camp	Route 1, Box 194, Manson, IA 50563	712-297-7714
Village Creek Bible Camp	RR 1, Box 191-A, Lansing, IA 52151	319-535-7320
Willowbrook Bible Camp	4375 N.E. 38th Street, Des Moines, IA 50317	515-262-5026

Kansas

Camp Daniel	Route 2, Box 64, Bonner Springs, KS 66012	913-441-3407
Camp Quaker Haven	RR 4, Box 323, Arkansas City, KS 67005	316-442-1228
Kansas Bible Camp	4508 W. 56th, Hutchinson, KS 67502	316-662-7791
The Shepherd's Staff Conf	Main & Kansas, Box 66, Rexford, KS 67753	913-687-3335

State/Camp	Address	Phone
Kentucky		
Bethel Mennonite Camp	2952 Bethel Church Road, Clayhole, KY 41317	606-666-4911
Camp Caleb	P.O. Box 670, Paintsville, KY 41240	606-789-3817
Eagle Ridge Ctr.	8744 Barren River Rd., Bowling Green, KY 42101	606-666-7138
Twin Rocks Bible Camp	RR 1, Box 26-H, Viper, KY 41774	606-436-6643
Louisiana		
Judson Baptist Retreat Ctr.	Rt. 1, Box 9-H, Jackson, LA 70748	504-634-7225
Okaloosa Baptist Encampment	1280 Okaloosa Road, Eros, LA 71238	318-249-4495
Tall Timbers Bapt. Conf.	Route 1, Box 134a, Forest Hill, LA 71430	318-445-6797
Maine		
Camp Berea	North Turner, ME 04266	207-224-7730
Camp Good News of Maine	778 Forest Ave, Portland, ME 04103	207-772-8642
Camp Lawroweld	RR 1, Box 27, Weld, ME 04285	207-797-3760
Fair Haven Camps	RR 2, Box 1180, Brooks, ME 04921	207-722-3456
New England Camp Cherith	P.O. Box 154, Alfred, ME 04002	207-247-5251
New England Frontier Camp	RR 1, Box 220, Lovell, ME 04051	207-925-6735
Maryland		
Cedar Ridge Ministries	Rt. 2, Box 325, Williamsport, MD 21795	301-582-0282
SDA Youth Camp	Rt. 1, Box 283, Hagerstown, MD 21740	301-995-1910
Sandy Cove Bible Conference	Sandy Cove Road, North East, MD 21901	
Summit Lake Camp	7610 Hampton Valley Rd., Emmitsburg, MD 21727	301-770-5338
Massachusetts		
American Bapt. Camp/Conf. Ctr.	Prescott St., Groton, MA 01450	617-448-5763
Camp Wonderland	186 Massapoag Ave., Sharon, MA 02067	617-784-5934
Chilaven Camp	P.O. Box 152, E. Douglas, MA 01516	508-476-7766
Focus Study Ctr.	RFD Box 459, Vineyard Haven, MA 02568	617-693-1359
Lakeside Christian Camp	195 Cloverdale St., Pittsfield, MA 01201	413-447-8930
New England Keswick	Chestnut Hill Rd., Monterey, MA 01245	413-528-3604
Michigan		
Bair Lake Bible Camp	12500 Prang Street, Jones, MI 49061	616-244-5193
Bay Shore Camp	450 N. Miller, Sebewaing, MI 48759	517-883-2501
Brook Cherith Camp	4050 County Line, Pierson, MI 49339	616-937-5305
Camp Amigo	26455 Banker St. Rd., Sturgis, MI 49091-9355	616-651-2811
Camp Ao-Wa-Kiya	8415 Glen Drive, Shelby, MI 49455	616-693-2145
Camp Arcadia	P.O. Box 229, Arcadia, MI 49613	616-889-4361
Camp Au Sable	P.O. Box 546, Grayling, MI 49738	517-348-5491
Camp Barakel	P.O. Box 157, Fairview, MI 48621	517-848-2279
Camp Beechpoint	3212 125th Avenue, Allegan, MI 49010	616-673-5767
Camp Calvary	7500 Pettit Dr., Newaygo, MI 49508	
Camp Friedenswald	15406 Watercress Dr., Cassopolis, MI 49031	616-476-2426
Camp Kaskitowa	3799 108th Ave., Rt. 4, Allegan, MI 49010	313-468-4970
Camp Lakeview	5868 Tody Rd., Goodrich, MI 48438	313-627-2530
Camp Living Waters	Route 1, Luther, MI 49656	616-797-5107
Camp Mel Tro Mi	6644 Lincoln Lake Ave., Belding, MI 48809	616-691-8008
Camp Michawana	5800 Head Lake Road, Hastings, MI 49058	616-948-2981
Camp Selah	3600 Long Lake Rd., Reading, MI 49274	517-283-2527
Carolyn Darch Ministries	154 E. Lovell Avenue, Troy, MI 48098	313-879-6917
Cedar Campus	Cedarville, MI 49719	616-538-6300
Ctr. Lake Bible Camp	4200 W. 20 Mile Road, Tustin, MI 49688	616-829-3441
Circle Y Ranch	Rt. 2, Box 150, Bangor, MI 49013	616-427-7127

State/Camp	Address	Phone
Cran-Hill Ranch	14444 17 Mile Road, Rodney, MI 49342	616-796-7669
Eagle Village Camps	RR 1, Box 300, Hersey, MI 49639	616-832-2234
Echo Grove Camp	1101 Camp Rd., Leonard, MI 48038	
Fa-Ho-Lo Park	3000 Mt. Hope Rd., Grass Lake, MI 49240	517-522-4510
Five Pines Chr. Family Ctr.	6613 Smith Road, Berrien Ctr., MI 49102	616-471-1396
Geneva Camp & Conference Ctr.	3990 Lakeshore Drive, Holland, MI 49424	616 399-3150
Gitche Gumee Bible Camp	Box 30, Eagle River, MI 49924	906-337-0527
Good News Camp	3613 N. M-30, Gladwin, MI 48624	517-426-9074
Grace Youth Camp	Box 392, Mears, MI 49436	616-873-3662
Gull Lake Bible Conference	1988 Midlake Drive, Hickory Corners, MI 49060	616-671-5155
Hiawatha Youth Camp	P.O. Box 1456, Southgate, MI 48195	313-284-0200
Huron Forest Camp Cherith	Star Rt. River Rd., Oscoda, MI 48750	313-374-2288
Lael Baptist Camp	2062 Ferns Road, Lapeer, MI 48446	313-664-6795
Lake Ann Baptist Camp Inc.	P.O. Box 109, Lake Ann, MI 49650	616-275-7329
Lake Ellen Baptist Camp	212 Baptist Camp Rd., Crystal Falls, MI 49920	906-542-3529
Lake Louise Baptist Camp	10750 Stafford Road, Boyne Falls, MI 49713	616-549-2889
Legendary Lodge	HC 31, Box 900 S, Seeley Lake, MI 59868	
Life Action Ranch	Clear Lake Road, Buchanan, MI 49107	616-695-2191
Mahn-Go-Tah-See	P.O. Box 126, Hale, MI 48739	517-728-2495
Manton Youth Camp	218 N Simons, Cadillac, MI 49601	
Michiana Christian Serv. Cmp	1619 Steinbauer Road, Niles, MI 49120	616-683-4403
Michindoh	4545 E. Bacon Rd., Hillsdale, MI 49242	517-523-3331
Miracle Camp	25281 80th Ave., Lawton, MI 49065	616-624-6161
New Life Camp	701 E. Mayhew, Rose City, MI 48654	517-685-2949
Pine Ridge Bible Camp & Conf.	8415 - 17 Mile Rd., Cedar Springs, MI 49319	616-866-1071
Pine Trail Camp	P.O. Box 35, Saugatuck, MI 49453	616-857-2564
Rock Lake Christian Assembly	7384 Vestaburg Road, Vestaburg, MI 48891	
Simpson Park Camp	70199 Campground Rd., Romeo, MI 48065	313-752-3202
Somerset Beach Campground	POB 307, 930 Brooklawn Drive, Somerset Ctr., MI 49282	517-688-3783
Son-Life Camps	189-126th Avenue, Wayland, MI 49438	616-792-2081
Spring Hill Camps	Box 100, Evart, MI 49631	616-734-2616
Warner Memorial Camp	P.O. Box 140, (55th St.), Grand Junction, MI 49056	616-434-6844
Wildwood Ranch	4909 Brophy Rd., Howell, MI 48843	313-965-3224
Willow Creek/Camp Paradise	P.O. Box 657, Newberry, MI 49868	708-382-6200
Wisdom Valley Ranch & Camps	P.O. Box 3601, Grand Rapids, MI 49501-3601	616-243-6954
YMCA Storer Camps	7260 S. Stony Lake Road, Jackson, MI 49201	517-536-4922
Youth Haven Ranch	3796 Perrine Rd., Box 97, Rives Junction, MI 49277	517-569-3328

Minnesota

Adventurous Christians	HC 64, Box 300, Grand Marais, MN 55604	218-388-2286
Big Sandy Camp	HCR 3, Box 567, Mc Gregor, MN 55760	218-426-3389
Camp Joy Bible Camp	R 2, Box 302, Dent, MN 56528	218-758-2924
Camp Lebanon	Box 370, Upsala, MN 56384	612-573-2125
Camp Shamineau	Route 1, Motley, MN 56466	218-575-2240
Covenant Park Bible Camp	1572 County Road 7, Mahtowa, MN 55762	218-722-2934
Covenant Pines Bible Camp	HCR 4, Box 440, Mc Gregor, MN 55760	218-768-2610
Lake Beauty Bible Camp	Rt. 1, Box 149, Long Prairie, MN 56347	612-732-3218
Lake Geneva Bible Camp	Rt. 8 Box 769, Alexandria, MN 56308	612-332-2409
Lake Koronis Assembly Grounds	15752 County Rd. 181, Paynesville, MN 56362	612-243-4544
Mink Lake Camp	P.O. Box 1000, Grand Marais, MN 55112	218-543-4565
North Central Camp Cherith Inc	Rt. 4, Box 295, Frazee, MN 56544	612-754-1878
Plymouth Point Bible Camp	HCR 1, Box 991, Hackensack, MN 56452	218-682-2714

State/Camp	Address	Phone
Shalom House	HCR 77, Box 145, Pine River, MN 56474	218-543-4565
Silver Lake Camp & Conf. Ctr.	2950 County Road E.W., Minneapolis, MN 55421	612-788-9048
Trout Lake Camp	HCR 77, Box 145, Pine River, MN 56474	218-543-4565
Young Life's Castaway Club	Route 5, Box 374, Detroit Lakes, MN 56501	218-532-2662
Youth Investment Foundation	HCR 67, Box 382, Onamia, MN 56359	612-532-3200

Mississippi

Camp Garaywa	P.O. Box 1014, Clinton, MS 39056	601-968-3800
Camp Hidden Lake	Rt. 2, Box 21-B, Lexington, MS 39095	601-834-2149
Camp of the Rising Son	French Camp Academy, French Camp, MS 39745	601-547-6892
Camp Pioneer, Inc.	P.O. Box 6182, Jackson, MS 39288-6182	601-939-3659
Central Hills Bapt. Ret.	Rt. 2, Box 51-X, W., MS 39192-9508	601-289-9730
Lake Forest Ranch	Rt. 4, Box 189, Macon, MS 39341	601-726-5052
Pine Lake Fellowship Camp	Rt. 14, Box 272, Meridian, MS 39305	601-483-2267
Twin Lakes Conference Ctr.	Route 2, Box 148 B, Florence, MS 39073	601-845-6858

Missouri

Camp Allen	Rt. 1, Box 45, Greenville, MO 63944	314-224-3826
Camp Bended Knee	P.O. Box 250, Van Buren, MO 63965	314-323-4347
Camp Mihaska	S.R. 23, Bourbon, MO 65441	314-732-5239
Camp Penuel	Lake Killarney, P.O. Box 367, Ironton, MO 36350-0367	314-546-3020
Camp Pinecrest	HCR 71, Box 576, Fredericktown, MO 63645	314-783-3534
Camp Soaring Hawk	Rt. 2, Box 131, Purdy, MO 65734	417-476-2565
Dayspring Bible Camp	P.O. Box 4, Ironton, MO 63650	
Echo Valley Bible Camp	P.O. Box 68, Rolla, MO 65401	314-364-7708
Heritage Crossing	HC 65, Box 208-C, Sullivan, MO 63080	314-629-0607
Kanakuk Kanakomo Kamps	HCR 4, Box 2124, Branson, MO 65616	417-334-2432
Logan Valley Christian Retreat	Route 3, Box 255, Ellington, MO 63638	314-663-2735
MO State Free Will Bapt. Camp	HCR-83, Niangua, MO 65713	314-431-2533
Miracle Hills Ranch	P.O. Box 73, Bethany, MO 64424	816-425-2277
Ne-Ka-Mo Camp Cherith	Route 1, Warsaw, MO 65355	913-687-3335
Turkey Hill Ranch Bible Camp	Route 71, Box 190, Vienna, MO 65582	314-744-5843
Windermere Baptist Assembly	P.O. Box 458, Roach, MO 65787	314-346-2205

Montana

Big Sky Bible Camp	501 McCaffery Rd., Bigfork, MT 59911	406-837-4864
Camp Bighorn	321 Highway 135 S., Plains, MT 59859	406-826-3144
Clydehurst Chrst. Ranch	802 N. 27th, Billings, MT 59101	406-252-3886
Glacier Kids	1702 Colton Blvd., Billings, MT 59102	
Trail's End Ranch	P.O. Box 271, Ekalaka, MT 59324	406-775-6401

Nebraska

Camp Calvin Crest	RR 2, Box 226, Fremont, NE 68025	402-628-6455
Camp Moses Merrill	Rt. 1, Box 170 A, Linwood, NE 68036	
Camp Rivercrest	RR 2, Box 224, Fremont, NE 68025	402-628-6465
Camp Rockhaven	Route 1, Box 26C, Gothenburg, NE 69138	308-537-3159
Covenant Cedars Bible Camp	P.O. Box 68, Hordville, NE 68846	402-757-3241
Manna Resort	RR 1, Box 32, Fairfield, NE 68938	402-262-2280
Maranatha Bible Camp & Conf.	P.O. Box 549, North Platte, NE 69103	308-582-4513
NE Dist. Assemblies of God	Star Rt. Box 2, Lexington, NE 68850	308-384-1234
NE Youth Leadership Dev. Ctr.	RR 2, Box 9A, Aurora, NE 68818	402-694-3934
Nat'l Camps/Blind Children	4444 S. 52nd St., Lincoln, NE 68506	402-488-0981

State/Camp	Address	Phone
Salvation Army Gene		
Eppley Camp	915 Allied Rd. RR 73, Omaha, NE 68123	
Timberlake Ranch Camp	Rt. 1, Box 86, Marquette, NE 68854	308-946-2148
Whispering Cedars Bapt. Camp	Rt. 1, Box 134, Genoa, NE 68640	402-483-4469

New Hampshire

Brookwoods/Deer Run	Chestnut Cove Rd., Alton, NH 03809	603-875-3600
Camp Advenchur	RT 11, Box 321, Alton Bay, NH 03810	215-233-5930
Camp Berea, Inc.	West Chore Rd., Bristol, NH 03222	203-572-8563
Camp Fireside	49 Pond Hill Rd., Rochester, NH 03867	603-332-1701
Camp Spofford	Route 9A, Spofford Lake, NH 03462	603-363-4788
Monadnock Bible Conf.	78 Dublin Road, P.O. Box 70, Jaffrey Ctr.,	
	NH 03452-0070	603-532-8321
Pilgrim Pines Conf. Ctr.	Box 40, W. Swanzey, NH 03469	603-352-0443
Rumney Bible Conference	P.O. Box 99, Rumney, NH 03266	603-786-9504
Singing Hills Chr. Fellowship	Stage Rd., Plainfield, NH 03781	603-469-3236
Trinity Christian Ctr.	740 Old Ashburnham Road, Rindge, NH 03461	
Windsor Hills Naz. Family Camp	RR 2, Box 157, Hillsboro, NH 03244	603-478-3363

New Jersey

America's Keswick	601 Route 530, Whiting, NJ 08759	201-350-1187
Baptist Camp & Conf. Ctr.	57 Blossum Hill Road, Lebanon, NJ 08833	201-236-2638
Christian Youth Camp Min.	P.O. Box 1872, Livingston, NJ 07039-1872	201-763-8371
Fellowship Conference	Center Valley Rd., Liberty Corner, NJ 07938	201-647-1777
Haluwasa	377 S. Ehrke Road, Hammonton,	
	NJ 08037-9540	609-561-3081
Harvey Cedars Bible Conf.	P.O. Box 1000, Harvey Cedars, NJ 08008	609 494-5689
Liebenzell Mission	Heath Lane, Schooley's Mtn., NJ 07870	908-852-3044
Pine Bush Bible Camp	1473 Whitty Road, Toms River, NJ 08753	
United Methodist Camps & Conf.	801 Mt. Misery Road, Browns Mills, NJ 08015	609-893-3354

New Mexico

Bonita Park Nazarene Camp	Alto Route, Capitan, NM 88316	
Broken Arrow Bible Ranch	Box 337, VanderWagen, NM 87326	505-778-5526
Camp Stoney	Route 7, Box 115, Santa Fe, NM 87505	505-983-5610
Fellowship Bible Church	10110 Constitution NE, Albuquerque, NM 87112	505-294-0571
Glorieta Baptist Conf. Ctr.	P.O. Box 8, Glorieta, NM 87535	505-757-6161
Lone Tree Bible Camp	Box 523 Capitan Gap Rd., Capitan, NM 88316	505-354-2523
Sacramento Methodist Assembly	188 Assembly Road, Sacramento, NM 88347	505-687-3414
Southwest Bible Camp, Inc.	P.O. Box 265, Glenwood, NM 88039	915-598-4660

New York

American Baptist Churches NYS	P.O. Box, Cooperstown, NY 13326	
Beaver Camp	Star Route, Box 221, Lowville, NY 13367	315-376-2640
Boys Jim Club of America	Box 58, Bemus Point, NY 14712	716-386-3806
Camp Asbury	Box 218, Silver Lake, NY 14549	716-237-5262
Camp Cherith/Adirondacks	R.D. 2, Box 309, Corinth, NY 12822	201-361-0797
Camp Comanche, Inc.	335 W. 51st, New York, NY 10019	
Camp Deerpark	Box 405, Westbrookville, NY 12785	914-754-8669
Camp Findley	RR 2, Box 212, Clymer, NY 14724	716-769-7146
Camp Hickory Hill	2970 Kohler Rd., Varysburg, NY 14167	716-741-9060
Camp Li-Lo-Li	P.O. Box 70, Salamanca, NY 14779	416-934-1027
Camp Pinnacle	RD 1, Box 200, Voorheesville, NY 12186	518-872-1053
Camp Taconic	R.D. 2, Box 255, Red Hook, NY 12571	914-758-8764
Camp Timberledge	PAR Road, Liberty, NY 12754	
Camp-of-the-Woods	Speculator, NY 12164	518-548-4311

State/Camp	Address	Phone
Catskill Christian Assembly	Rt. 1, Box 265, Prattsville, NY 12468	518-299-3611
Chambers Wesleyan Camp	RD 2 Box 26A, Beaver Dams, NY 14812	607-962-4292
Christian Youth Aflame	7245 College St., Lima, NY 14485	716-582-2790
Cortland Bible Club Camp	P.O. Box 100, Pitcher, NY 13136	607-863-4225
Covenant Acres Camp & Retreat	24 Albro Road, Pike, NY 14130	716-493-2220
Deerfoot Lodge	Rt. 30, Speculator, NY 12164	518-966-4115
Delta Lake Bible Conf. Ctr.	6374 Pillmore Dr., Rome, NY 13440	315-336-7210
Fowler Camp and Conf. Ctr.	Route 8, Speculator, NY 12164	518-374-4573
Good Tidings Bible Conf.	103 Sutton Rd., Cornwallville, NY 12418	518-239-4178
High Braes Refuge, Inc.	RR 1, Box 45B Waterbury Road, Redfield, NY 13437	315-599-7362
King's Campground	166 W. 92 Street, New York, NY 10025	
Lakeside Bible Conference	P.O. Box 670, Carmel, NY 10512	914-225-2005
LeTourneau Conference Ctr.	4950 County Road 11, Rushville, NY 14544	716-554-3400
Lighthouse Christian Camp	9574 Somerset Drive, Barker, NY 14012	716-688-9195
Living Waters Circle C Ranch	RR 2, Box 2303, Delevan, NY 14042	716-492-3687
Mission Meadows	Box 42, Dewittville, NY 14728	716-488-1555
New Horizons Ministries, Inc.	189 Allen Street, Hempstead, NY 11550	516-481-5769
Northern Frontier Camp	Route 28, North River, NY 12856	
Odosagih Bible Conference	Hazelmere Avenue, Machias, NY 14101	716-353-8555
Sacandaga Bible Conference	P.O. Box 247, Broadalbin, NY 12025	518-883-3713
Salvation Army Camp Long Point	200 Twin Oaks Drive, Syracuse, NY 13206	315-536-6301
Stony Brook School	Rt. 25 A, Stony Brook, NY 11790	516-751-1800
Sunshine Acres	887 Sportsman Rd., Napanoch, NY 12458	914-647-4230
White Lake Covenanter Camp	Mattison Road, P.O. Box 208, White Lake, NY 12786	914-583-4231
Wildwood Christian Camp	R.D. 1, E. Freetown, NY 13055	
Young Life's Lake Champion	P.O. Box 207, Glen Spey, NY 12737	914-856-6871
Young Life's Saranac Village	Star Route Box 88, Saranac Lake, NY 12983	518-891-3010

North Carolina

Ambassador Camp	Lakeshore Dr. (Box 200), Lake Waccamaw, NC 28450	919-642-2853
Appalachian Advent Christian	1942 N. Center St., Hickory, NC 28601	
Camp Cherith in the Carolinas	2937 Welcome Drive, Durham, NC 27705	919-489-9300
Camp Dayspring	Box 150, 7545 Hwy 29 S, Browns-Summit, NC 27214	919-656-7937
Camp Dixie, Inc.	Rt. 7, Box 247, Fayetteville, NC 28306	919-865-5180
Camp Hollmont for Girls	Lake Eden Road, Route 1, Box 254-A, Black Mountain, NC 28711	704-686-5343
Camp Joy	P.O. Box 41, Hickory, NC 28603	704-328-1541
Camp Lurecrest	P.O. Box 400, Lake Lure, NC 28746	704-568-7704
Camp Maranatha	P.O. Box 818, Dunn, NC 28334	
Camp Oak Hill & Retreat Ctr.	Route 7, Box 273, Oxford, NC 27565	919-782-2888
Camp Rockmont	Lake Eden Road, Black Mountain, NC 28711	704-686-3885
Camp Willow Run	Mangum Lane, Littleton, NC 27850	919 586-4665
Child Evan. Fell. of NC, Inc.	3700 Western Boulevard, P.O. Box 37667, Raleigh, NC 27627-7667	919-664-8877
Crusader Youth Camp	P.O. Box 1568, Dunn, NC 28334	919-892-4161
Falcon Youth Camp	P.O. Box 60, Falcon, NC 28342	919-892-6670
Hickory Cove Bible Camp	Route 6, Box 313, Taylorsville, NC 28681	704-632-6084
Maranatha Springs Camp & Conf.	Rt. 1, Box 450, Silver City, NC 27344	919-742-5617
Merriwood Christian Camp	9640 Ctr. Grove Church Road, Clemmons, NC 27012	919-766-5151
Mountain Top Youth Camp	Rt. 1, Box 258, Pinnacle, NC 27043	919-767-7158

State/Camp	Address	Phone
New Life Camp	Route 7, Box 251, Raleigh, NC 27614	919-847-0764
Nosoca Pines Ranch	P.O. Box 25848, Charlotte, NC 28229-5848	704-535-6720
Quaker Lake Camp	1503 NC Hwy 62, E, Climax, NC 27233	919-674-2321
Quiet Reflections Retreat, Inc.	500 Pond Road, Spruce Pine, NC 28777	
Ridgecrest Summer Camps	P.O. Box 278, Ridgecrest, NC 28770	704 669-8051
South Mtns. Chr.Youth Camp	Route 3, Box 345 A, Bostic, NC 28018	704-245-2622
Teen Valley Ranch	P.O. Box 25, Plumtree, NC 28664	704-765-7860
The Cove Camp	1 Porter's Cove Road, Asheville, NC 28805	
The Master's Mission, Inc.	P.O. Box 547, Robbinsville, NC 28771	704-479-3492
The Vineyard	Rt. 1, Box 131, Westfield, NC 27053	919-351-2070
Young Life's Windy Gap	120 Cole's Cove Rd., Weaverville, NC 28787	704-645-7187

North Dakota

Cooperstown Bible Camp	Rt. 2, Box 59 A, Cooperstown, ND 58425	701-797-2174
Cross Roads Range, Inc.	HCR 2, Box 36A, Saint John, ND 58369	701-244-5225
Crystal Springs Bapt. Camp	RR 1, Box 141, Medina, ND 58467	701-486-3467

Ohio

Beulah Beach Conference	6101 W. Lake Road, Vermilion, OH 44089	216-967-4861
Big Prairie Camp/Assemblies	P.O. Box 83, Holmes Co. Rd, Big Prairie, OH 44611	216-496-2381
Camp Burton	14282 Butternut Road, Burton, OH 44021	216-834-8984
Camp Carl	8054 Calvin Rd., Ravenna, OH 44266	
Camp Co-Tu-Bic	2158 Road 25 N, Bellefontaine, OH 43311	513-468-2519
Camp ECCO	5140 Pioneer Road, S.E., Carrollton, OH 44615	216-644-5616
Camp McPherson	21880 Shadley Valley Rd., Danville, OH 43014	
Camp Otyokwah	Route 1, Butler, OH 44822	419-883-3854
Church Of God Youth Camp	2474 Lebanon Rd., Lebanon, OH 45036	513-932-3003
College Hill Pres. Church	5742 Hamilton Ave., Cincinnati, OH 45224	513-541-5676
Evangelical Friends Church	1201 30th St. NW, Canton, OH 44709	216-493-1660
Faith Ranch	Box 384, Jewett, OH 43986	614-946-2255
Geneva Hills Ctr.	1380 Blue Valley Road, Lancaster, OH 43130	614-746-8434
Grand Valley Christian Ctr.	Route 1, Box 262, Rock Creek, OH 44084	216-563-3081
Greenwood Lake & Conf. Ctr.	340 Lake Street, Delaware, OH 43015	
Heart & Hand Kids Kamp	2570 Woodhill, Box 604209, Cleveland, OH 44104-0209	216-229-3400
Judson Hills Camp	3298 Township Rd. 629, Loudonville, OH 44842	419-994-4657
King's Domain Retreat & Conf.	5778 State Route 350, Oregonia, OH 45054	513-932-2223
Kirkwood Camp & Conf. Ctr.	5719 S.R. 73 W., Wilmington, OH 45177	513-382-3535
Koinonia Camp & Conf. Ctr.	6810 Cork-Cold Springs Rd, Geneva, OH 44041	216-466-1278
Marmon Valley Farm Camp	5807 Co. Rd. 153, Zanesfield, OH 43360	513-593-8051
Nazarene Youth Camps/C. Ohio	2708 Morse Road, Columbus, OH 43229	614-475-1728
Ohio Camp Cherith	Stony Glen Camp, Ford Rd., Madison, OH 44057	
Pleasant Vineyard Ministries	1191 Swan Beatty Rd., Camden, OH 45311	513-452-3347
Quaker Canyon Camp	P.O. Box 55, Damascus, OH 44619	216-537-2991
Salvation Army/Camp NEOSA	5037 Edgewood Rd., S.W., Carrollton, OH 44615	216-735-2671
Stony Glen C.S.B.	Ford Rd., Madison, OH 44057	614-871-9976
Stony Glen Camp	Ford Rd., Madison, OH 44057	216-298-3264
The King's Valley Ranch	Rt. 2, Box 147, Lower Salem, OH 45745	614-585-2325
Woodland Lakes Christian Camp	3054 Lindale - Mt. Holly Rd., Amelia, OH 45102	513-797-5268

Oklahoma

Camp Heart o' Hills	7816 Maehs Circle, Oklahoma City, OK 73162	405-840-0735
New Life Ranch	Rt. 1, Box 274, Colcord, OK 74338	918-422-5506

State/Camp	Address	Phone
Shepherd's Fold Ranch	P.O. Box 86, Avant, OK 74001	918-263-3622
Sunset Bible Camp	RR 2, Box 1032, Mannford, OK 74044	918-965-2246
Oregon		
Aldersgate Conference Ctr.	P.O. Box 16, Turner, OR 97392	503-743-2494
American Bapt. Churches/OR	24075 E. Arrah Wanna Blvd., Wemme, OR 97067	503-228-8394
Big Lake Youth Camp	Hwy 20, Box 13100, Sisters, OR 97759	503-652-2225
Camp Emerald Forest	26000 Pittsburg Rd., St. Helens, OR 97051	503-397-4226
Camp Harlow	3850 County Farm Road, Eugene, OR 97401	503-683-5416
Camp Kuratli-Trestle Glen	24751 S.E. Hwy. 224, Boring, OR 97009	503-658-3122
Camp Morrow Bible Conference	Rt. 1, Box 31CM, Wamic, OR 97063	503-544-2971
Camp Tadmor	43943 McDowell Cr. Dr., Lebanon, OR 97355	503-451-4270
Canby Grove Conference Ctr.	7501 Knight's Bridge Road, Canby, OR 97013	503-266-5176
Cannon Beach Conference Ctr.	289 N. Spruce, Cannon Beach, OR 97110	503 436-1501
Canyonview Camp	12730 Finlay Rd. N.E., Silverton, OR 97381	503-873-8296
Drift Creek Camp	POB 2186, Lincoln City, OR 97367	503-764-2854
Eagle Fern Camp	37680 S.E. Camp Rd., Estacada, OR 97023	503-255-7961
Evangelical Ctr. Conf. Grnds	18121 S.E. River Rd., Milwaukie, OR 97267	503-654-0436
Evans Creek Upward Bound Camp	36155 N. Fork Road, Lyons, OR 97358	503-897-2447
Molalla Retreat	36208 S. Molalla Forest Road, Molalla, OR 97038	503-829-9653
Mountain Lakes Bible Camp	2244 Wiard Street, Klamath Falls, OR 97603	503-883-2289
Oregon Camp Cherith	421 S. River, Newberg, OR 97132	503-266-5176
TAPAWINGO	22505 Black Rock Rd., Falls City, OR 97344	503-787-3828
Tilikum: Ctr. for Retreats	15321 N.E. North Valley Rd., Newberg, OR 97132	503-538-2763
Trout Creek Bible Camp	8815 N.E. Glisan, Portland, OR 97220	503-695-2948
Twin Rocks Friends Conference	18705 Highway 101n, Rockaway Beach, OR 97136	503-355-2284
White Branch Youth Camp	61500 Old McKenzie Hwy., McKenzie Bridge, OR 97413	503-822-3511
Wilderness Trails, Inc.	44 N. Front Street, Medford, OR 97501	503-779-7756
Pennsylvania		
Arrowhead Bible Camp	Arrowhead Rd., Brackney, PA 18812	717-663-2419
Black Rock Retreat	1345 Kirkwood Pike, Quarryville, PA 17566	717-786-1266
Blue Mountain Chr. Retreat	RD 2, Box 118a, New Ringgold, PA 17960	717-386-2154
Brush Valley Chr. Retreat	RD 3, Box 956, Rte 259, Homer City, PA 15748	412-824-8684
Camp Allegheny	RD 2, Box 212, Stoystown, PA 15563	814-754-5122
Camp Andrews	1226 Silver Spring Rd., Holtwood, PA 17532	717-284-2624
Camp Cherith in Pennsylvania	Tel Hai Camp, Honey Brook, PA 19344	302-731-1453
Camp Conquest	RD 2 Forest Rd., Denver, PA 17517	215-267-2006
Camp Hebron, Inc.	957 Camp Hebron Road, Halifax, PA 17032	717-896-3441
Camp Iroquoina	Rt. 1, Halsted, PA 18822	609-890-0450
Camp Joy-El	3741 Joy-El Drive, Greencastle, PA 17225	717-369-4539
Camp Kanesatake/CPCI	P.O. Box 11, Spruce Creek, PA 16683	814-632-6024
Camp Ladore/The Sal. Army	P.O. Box 99, Waymart, PA 18472	717-488-6121
Camp Mantowagan	Box 95, Saxton, PA 16678	814-658-3815
Camp Men-O-Lan	1415 Doerr Road, Quakertown, PA 18951	215 679-5144
Camp Orchard Hill	RD 3, Box 275, Dallas, PA 18612	717-333-4098
Camp Sankanac	RD 1, Box 372, Spring City, PA 19475	215-469-6320
Camp Sunrise Mountain	RD 1, Markleysburg, PA 15650	412-537-7298
Camp Susque, Inc.	Susque Road, Trout Run, PA 17771	717-998-2151
Christian Retreat Ctr.	Box 13A, RD 1, East Waterford, PA 17021	717-734-3627

State/Camp	Address	Phone
Covenant Village	Rt. 3, Box 70, Clearville, PA 15535	703-821-8844
Doorkeepers Chr. Outreach	Box 57, Spring Creek, PA 16436	814-664-8547
Doubling Gap Ctr.	1550 Doubling Gap Road, Newville, PA 17241	717-776-5281
Grace Brethren Retreat Ctr.	480 Forest Rd., Denver, PA 17517	215-267-2541
Greenwood Hills Bible Conf.	7062 Lincoln Way E., Fayetteville, PA 17222	717-352-2150
Gretna Glen Program Ctr.	87 Mine Rd., Lebanon, PA 17042	717-273-6525
Handi*Camp	237 Fairfield Ave., Upper Darby, PA 19082-2299	215-352-7177
Harmony Heart Camp	Rural Route 2, Box 246, Jermyn, PA 18433	717-254-6272
Haycock Camping Ministries	3100 School Road, Kintnersville, PA 18930	215-346-7155
His Thousand Hills	RD 6, Box 22, Wellsboro, PA 16901	717-724-2366
Innabah Program Ctr.	RD 1, Spring City, PA 19475	215-469-6111
Judson Baptist Camp & Retreat	398 Holiday Road, N.Springfield, PA 16430	814-922-3834
Jumonville	RR 2, Box 128, Hopwood, PA 15445	412-439-4912
Kenbrook Bible Camp	501 Pine Meadow Dr., Lebanon, PA 17042	717-865-4547
Laurel Lake Youth Camp	RD 1, Box 83A, Rossiter, PA 15772	215-814-9300
Laurelville Menn. Church Ctr.	Route 5, Box 145, Mt. Pleasant, PA 15666	412-423-2056
Miracle Mountain Ranch	RD 1, Box 95, Spring Creek, PA 16436	814-664-7673
Mont Lawn Camp/Paradise Lake	Sugar Mountain Road, Box 252, Bushkill, PA 18324	914-769-9000
Montrose Bible Conference	P.O. Box 159, Montrose, PA 18801	717-278-1001
Mountain View Bible Camp	Box 124, Snydertown, PA 17877	717-672-2296
Mt. Gilead Camp & Conf. Ctr.	RD 8, Box 8162, Stroudsburg, PA 18360	215-857-3727
Mt. Lou-San Bible Camp	2200 Blue Mt. Parkway, Harrisburg, PA 17112	717-545-2841
New Life Bible Camp, Inc.	RFD 1, Box 202, Buffalo Mills, PA 15534	814-842-3325
Oil City Conference	Box 229, Pleasantville, PA 16341	814-589-7330
Pa-De Conference Ctr.	430 Union Hall Road, Carlisle, PA 17013	717-243-7381
Penn York Camp	RD 1, Box 420, Ulysses, PA 16948	814-848-9811
Pine Springs Camp	P.O. Box 186, Jennerstown, PA 15547	814-629-9834
Pine Valley Bible Conf. & Camp	RD 2, Box 3595, Ellwood City, PA 16117	412-752-1661
Pinebrook Bible Conference	P.O. Box 1, Stroudsburg, PA 18360	717-424-1212
Pocono Mtn. Bible Conference	Star Route Box 87, Gouldsboro, PA 18424	717-842-9746
Pocono Plateau Program Ctr.	RR 2, Box 1002, Rt. 191, Cresco, PA 18326	717-676-3665
Refreshing Mountain Camp, Inc.	455 Camp Rd., Stevens, PA 17578	717-738-1490
Rhodes Grove Camp	7693 Brown's Mill Rd., Chambersburg, PA 17201	717-375-4162
Seneca Hills Bible Conference	Box 288, Franklin, PA 16323	814-432-3026
Sherman Acres Camp	RD 5, Box 220, New Castle, PA 16105	412-652-4300
Spruce Lake Retreat	RD 1, Box 605, Canadensis, PA 18325	717-595-7505
Streamside Camp & Conf. Ctr.	RD 3, Box 3306, Stroudsburg, PA 18360	717-629-1902
Summer's Best Two Weeks	RD 2, Box 299, Boswell, PA 15531	814-629-9744
Tel Hai Camp	RD 2, Box 126-1, Honey Brook, PA 19344	215-273-3969
Tuscarora Inn	RD 1, Box 1704, River Road, Mt. Bethel, PA 18343	717-897-6000
Twin Pines Camp	3000 Twin Pine Road, Stroudsburg, PA 18360	717-629-2411
Victory Valley Camp	7472 Sigmund Road, Zionsville, PA 18092-9736	215-966-5880
Wesley Woods, Inc.	Box 155A, RD 1, Grand Valley, PA 16420	814-436-7425
Westminster Highlands	RD 3, Box 338, Emlenton, PA 16373	412-662-4481
White Sulphur Springs	RD 1, Box 98, Manns Choice, PA 15550	814-623-5583
Whitehall Camp	RD 1, Box 31, Emlenton, PA 16373-9514	412-867-6861

South Carolina

Awanita Valley	125 Mtn. View Road, Marietta, SC 29661	803-836-3956
Ben Lippen Camp	P.O. Box 3999, Columbia, SC 29230	803-786-0766
Bethel Bible Camp	Route 7, Box 655, Columbia, SC 29223	803-788-1724
Longridge Camp & Retreat Ctr.	P.O. Box 460, Ridgeway, SC 29130	803-776-3570

State/Camp	Address	Phone
Look-Up Lodge Chr. Retreat Ctr.	100 Old Hwy 11, Travelers Rest, SC 29690	803-836-6392
New Heritage USA	3000 Heritage Parkway, Fort Mill, SC 29715	803-547-8301
The New Heritage USA	3000 Heritage Parkway, Fort Mill, SC 29715	803-548-7800

South Dakota

Byron Bible Camp	Box 211, Huron, SD 57350	605-352-7267

Tennessee

Ambassador Conference Ctr.	P.O. Box 358, Madison, TN 37116-0358	
Appalachian Chr. Serv. Camp	Route One, Box 323, Unicoi, TN 37692	
Bancroft Bible Camp	Rt. 1, Bancroft Rd., Kingsport, TN 37660	615-323-5191
Camp Ba Yo Ca	Rt. 7 Box 224 Happy Hollow, Sevierville, TN 37862	615-453-6274
Camp Garner Creek	P.O. Box 100924, Nashville, TN 37224	615-254-8343
Camp Glen Leven	3906 Franklin Road, Nashville, TN 37204	615-298-5549
Camp Hillmont	Route 1, Box 303, White Bluff, TN 37187	615-797-3616
Camp Joshua	Rt. 10, Box 318-A, Greeneville, TN 37743	615-639-2879
Camp Ta-Pa-Win-Go	POB 280, Elizabethton, TN 37643	615-543-2201
Camp Tsungani	6655 Winchester, Memphis, TN 38115	901-365-4648
Cedar Lake Camp	Rt. 3, Box 232, Livingston, TN 38570	615-823-5656
Cedar Tree Day Camp	645 Old Hickory Boulevard, Nashville, TN 37209	615-353-0018
Cedine Bible Camp & Conf. Ctr.	Rt. 1, Box 2390, Spring City, TN 37381	615-365-9565
Confrontation Point	Rt. 21, Box 3, Crossville, TN 38555	615-484-8483
Doe River Gorge Chr Cmp & Conf	P.O. Box 791, Elizabethton, TN 37644	615-928-8936
Grace Church Camp	P.O. Box 11021, Nashville, TN 37222	
Horton Haven Christian Camp	P.O. Box 276, Chapel Hill, TN 37034	615 352-1745
International Youth Camp	P.O. Box 2910, Cleveland, TN 37320-2910	615-479-8511
Mountain Lake Ranch	Route 5, Box 181, Dandridge, TN 37725	615-397-3853
Mountain T.O.P.	P.O. Box 128, Altamont, TN 37301	615-298-1575

Texas

Baylor Camp	BU Box 7187, Waco, TX 76798	817-755-3505
Blue Barn Christian Retreat	Route 2, Box 239 G, Alba, TX 75410	214-765-2354
Brookhaven Retreat	Rt. 2, Box 289, Hawkins, TX 75765	903-769-2811
Camp Arrowhead	Rt 9, Box 480, Cleburne, TX 76031	817-897-2323
Camp Buckner	Rt. 2, Box 25, Burnet, TX 78611	
Camp Cullen	Rt. 3, Box 135-D, Trinity, TX 75862	713-659-2733
Camp Deer Run	Route 2, Box 75, Winnsboro, TX 75494	903-629-7165
Camp El-Har	Rt. 1, Box 236, Dallas, TX 75211	214-298-3873
Camp Good News	P.O. Box 38062, Houston, TX 77238	713-524-0961
Camp Hoblitzelle/S. Army	587 Singleton Road, Midlothian, TX 76065	214-775-2387
Camp Manison	P.O. Box 148-C, Friendswood, TX 77546-0148	713-482-1521
Camp Peniel, Inc.	Rt. 4, Box 135, Marble Falls, TX 78654	713-667-9605
Camp Stewart for Boys	Guadalupe River, Hunt, TX 78024	512-238-4665
Camp Ta-Ku-La, Inc.	P.O. Box 7, Chester, TX 75936	409-969-2455
Camp Tejas	Rt. 2, Box 102A, Giddings, TX 78942	409-366-2422
Camp Thurman	2203 W. Park Row, Arlington, TX 76013	817-274-1315
Christian Camp/Living Word	Rt. 1, Box 107, Point, TX 75472	214-598-2497
Country Camp	P.O. Box 100, Columbus, TX 78934-0100	409-732-6218
Daniel Springs Bapt. Camp	P.O. Box 310, Gary, TX 75643	903-685-2433
Don Anderson Ministries	Station A, Box 6611, Tyler, TX 75711	214-597-3018
El Shaddai Ranch	Rt. 2, Box 232, Yorktown, TX 78164	512-564-3552
Evangelistic Temple	123 McClellan Road, Kingwood, TX 77339	
Forest Glen Chr. Camp & Conf.	P.O. Box 38062, Houston, TX 77238	713-847-0300
Frontier Camp	Rt. 1,Box 138, Grapeland, TX 75844	409-544-3206
H.E. Butt Foundation Camp	Route 1, Box 154, Leakey, TX 78873	512-896-2505

State/Camp	Address	Phone
Harambe Oaks Ranch	P.O. Box 645, Fischer, TX 78623	512-935-2557
Heart of Texas Bapt. Encamp.	Rt. 1, Box 280A, Brown Wood, TX 76801	915-784-5821
Hidden Acres, Inc.	Route 6, Box 442, Kaufman, TX 75142	214-932-2996
Hidden Falls Ranch, Inc.	P.O. Box 136, Wayside, TX 79094	806-764-3466
Highland Lakes Baptist Encamp.	Route 1 Box 33, Ranch Road 2322, Spicewood, TX 78669-0033	512-264-1777
Hus School Encampment	Route 2, Caldwell, TX 77836	713-272-8176
Impact Christian Youth Camp	3743 S. Texas Avenue, Bryan, TX 77801	
Iron Springs Christian Camp	Rt. 1, Box 148K, Whitney, TX 76692	817-694-2719
Jan-Kay Ranch	Rt. 1, Box 21, Detroit, TX 75436	214-674-3159
Mid South Covenant Camp	16155 Aspenglen, Houston, TX 77084	713-859-5683
Mountain View Camp	P.O. Box 2097, Jacksonville, TX 75766	214-586-5361
Pine Cove Conf. Ctr.	Rt. 8, Box 443, Tyler, TX 75703	903-299-6130
Piney Woods Camp Cherith	Rt. 7, Box 7193, Athens, TX 75751	713-937-9717
Plains Baptist Assembly	Route 3 Box 162, Floydada, TX 79235	806-983-3954
S.A. Christadelphian Church	P.O. Box 39181, San Antonio, TX 78232	512-494-2370
Sandy Creek Bible Camp	Route 1, Box 803, Washington, TX 77880	713-836-6817
Sky Ranches, Inc.	9330 LBJ Freeway, Suite 850, Dallas, TX 75243	214-222-2137
T Bar M Sports Camp	P.O. Box 310600, New Braunfels, TX 78131	512-625-2164
The Pines	5231 Meadowcreek, Dallas, TX 75248	214-867-4684
Timberline Bapt. Camp & Conf.	Rt. 1, Box 151, Lindale, TX 75771	903-882-3183
Trinity Pines Conf Ctr.	Route 3, Highway 356, P.O. Box 707, Trinity, TX 75862	409-594-5011
Wilderness Ridge	10115 Kerrwood, Houston, TX 77080	713-827-8018
Zephyr Baptist Encampment	HCR 2, Box 7200, Sandia, TX 78383	512-547-2448

Virginia

Camp Bethel	P.O. Box 390, Wise, VA 24293	703-328-6876
Camp Blue Ridge	P.O. Box 120, Montebello, VA 24464	703-886-0771
Camp Eagle	P.O. Box 7010, Roanoke, VA 24019	703-366-2431
Camp Happyland	P.O. Box 14, Richardsville, VA 22736	202-783-9085
Camp Lightfoot	Treasury Island Road, Williamsburg, VA 23185	202-387-8233
Camp Rudolph	P.O. Box 33, Yale, VA 23897	804-535-8147
Camp Shenandoah Springs	HC-6, Box 122, Madison, VA 22727	703-923-4300
Camp Tuk-A-Way	5512 Hollins Road, Roanke, VA 24019	703-362-0336
Circle C Ministries & Camp	11330 Danforth Road, Chesterfield, VA 23832	804-590-9024
Dogwood Lake Conference Ctr.	1317 Pleasant Valley Road, Winchester, VA 22601	703-667-9400
Eastern Mennnonite College	Harrisonburg, VA 22801	703-433-2771
Grace Bible Camp	Route 1, Goshen, VA 24439	703-997-9316
Highland Retreat Camp	Route 1, Box 121, Bergton, VA 22811	703-852-3226
Oak Hill Christian Svc. Camp	Rt. 1, Box 521, Mechanicsville, VA 23111	804-779-3050
SKYANCHOR	Box 7, Route 10, Spring Grove, VA 23881	804-866-8698
The Master's Inn	Rt. 2, Box 94A, Altavista, VA 24517	804-369-5053
Triple-R Ranch	3531 Bunch Walnut Rd., Chesapeake, VA 23322	804-421-2287
Upward Bound	P.O. Box 11883, Lynchburg, VA 24506	703-586-8974

Washington

ALPS	16210 SE 24th Street, Bellevue, WA 98008	206-878-7839
Black Lake Bible Camp & Conf.	6521 Fairview Drive SW, Olympia, WA 98502	206-357-8425
CRISTA Camps & Conferences	12500 Camp Court N.W., Poulsbo, WA 98370	206-697-1212
Camp Arnold at Timberlake	33712 Webster Rd. E, Eatonville, WA 98328	206-281-4600
Camp Berachah	19830 - S.E. 328 Pl., Auburn, WA 98002	206-854-3765
Camp Casey Conference Ctr.	1276 S. Fort Casey Road, Coupeville, WA 98239	206-775-0775

State/Camp	Address	Phone
Camp Ghormley	Star Route Box 190, Naches, WA 98937	509-672-4311
Camp Gilead	30919 NE Carnation Farm Road, Carnation, WA 98014	206-333-4311
Camp Harmony	P.O. Box 698, Stanwood, WA 98292	206-629-4536
Camp Lutherwood	1185 Roy Road, Bellingham, WA 98226	206-734-7652
Camp Mc Cullough	20665 S.E. 264th, Kent, WA 98031	206-927-7981
Camp Nooksack	Box 22256, Nooksack, WA 87276	206-322-6228
Camp Volasuca	617 1st St., Sultan, WA 98294	206-259-3191
Cascade Camp Cherith	2214 Bedal Lane, Everett, WA 98208	206-337-5930
Cascades Camp & Conf. Ctr.	22825 Peissner Road S.E., Yelm, WA 98597	206-451-7434
Cedar Springs Camp	4820 State Road 92, Lake Stevens, WA 98258	206-334-6215
Clear Lake Grace Brethren	Star Route, Box 221-G, Naches, WA 98933	509-848-2746
Double-K Ranch	P.O. Box 98, Easton, WA 98925	206-683-8516
Fourth Memorial Church	Rt. 2, Box 80, Usk, WA 99180	509-487-2786
Lake Retreat Camp & Conf. Ctr.	27850 Retreat Kanaskat Rd SE, Ravensdale, WA 98051	206-365-9890
Lakeside Bible Camp	S. 6443 W. DeerLake Rd., Clinton, WA 98236	206-221-3936
Mt. Baker Baptist Conf. Ctr.	8444 Mt. Baker Highway, Deming, WA 98244	206-599-2921
Pinelow Park Campground & Rtr	3806 N. Deerlake Road, Loon Lake, WA 99148	509-233-2367
Royal Ridges Retreat	P.O. Box 778, Battle Ground, WA 98604	206-686-3737
Sambica Camp & Conf. Ctr.	17700 W. Sammamish Rd. SE, Bellevue, WA 98008	206-746-9110
Shiloh Bible Camp	Box 524, Cosmopolis, WA 98537	206-533-5074
Sunset Lake Camp	P.O. Box D, Wilkeson, WA 98396	206-829-0311
Tall Timber Ranch	White River Star Route, Leavenworth, WA 98826	509-966-0481
The Dunes Bible Camp	Rt. 1, Box 332, Ocean Park, WA 98640	206-665-4055
The Firs Bible/Miss. Conf.	4605 Cable St., Bellingham, WA 98226	206-733-6840
Warm Beach Christian Camp	20800 Marine Dr. NW, Stanwood, WA 98292	206-652-7575
Wilderness Northwest	1903 Duckabush, Brinnon, WA 98320	206-796-4968

West Virginia

Camp Tomahawk	Rt. 2, Hedgesville, WV 25427	304-754-3849
Hemlock Wilderness Brigade Camp	General Delivery Trout Run Rd., Wardensville, WV 26851	304-367-6769
Mission Farms	R 6, Box 265, Fairmont, WV 26554	304-363-1790
Potomac Park Camp & Conf. Ctr.	P.O. Box 787, Falling Waters, WV 25419	304-274-2700
Salvation Army/Camp Joy	P.O. Box 818, Bluefield, WV 24701	304-327-7411
Valley Vista	1400 Liberty Street, Parkersburg, WV 26101	

Wisconsin

Army Lake Camp	1449 Army Lake Rd., East Troy, WI 53120	414-462-5226
Arrowhead Bible Camp	Rt. 3, New Auburn, WI 54757	715-967-2140
C.B.A. of Wisconsin	733 Coleman St., Chippewa Falls, WI 54729	715-723-0894
Camp Awana	9025 Camp Awana Rd., Fredonia, WI 53021	312-736-2792
Camp Forest Springs	N8890 Forest Lane, Westboro, WI 54490	715-427-5241
Camp Phillip	Rt. 3, Box 190-4, Wautoma, WI 54982	414-787-3202
Camp Zion	Door Bluff Road, Ellison Bay, WI 54210	312-746-1411
Church of God Prophecy Campground	6522 W. Fremont Place, Milwaukee, WI 53219	608-254-8903
Covenant Harbor Bible Camp	1724 Main St., Lake Geneva, WI 53147	414-248-3600
Fort Wilderness	6180 Spider Lake Rd., McNaughton, WI 54543	800-622-5571
Honey Rock/High Road	8660 Honey Rock Road, Three Lakes, WI 54562	708-260-5154
Inspiration Ctr.	P.O. Box 948, Walworth, WI 53184	414-275-5753
Lake Geneva Youth Camp	650 S. St., Lake Geneva, WI 53147	414-248-5500
Lake Helen Bible Camp	Route 3, Wausaukee, WI 54177	217-423-2022
Lake Lundgren Bible Camp	N18250 Lake Lane, Pembine, WI 54156	715-324-5457

State/Camp	Address	Phone
Lake Waubesa Bible Camp	2847 Crescent Drive, McFarland, WI 53558	608-838-3335
Living Waters Bible Camp	Route 1, Box 86a, Westby, WI 54667	608-634-4373
Northern Grace Youth Camp	RR 1, Gillett, WI 54124	414-855-2759
Phantom Ranch	W309 S10910 Hwy. I, Mukwanago, WI 53149	414-363-7291
Silver Birch Ranch	Star Route, White Lake, WI 54491	715-484-2742
Sky Lodge Chr. Camp	Route 3, Box 650, Montello, WI 53949	608-297-2566
Spencer Lake Bible Camp	N.1385 County Highway E, Waupaca, WI 54981	715-258-5707
The ARC	Rt. 1 Box 92, Osceola, WI 54020	715-294-2877
Timber-lee Christian Ctr.	2381 Scout Rd., East Troy, WI 53120	414-642-7345
Trail Ridge Camp Cherith	RR 1, Box 97, Hillsboro, WI 54634	
Wesley Woods Conference Ctr.	200 Stam Street, Williams Bay, WI 53191	414-245-6631
Wisconsin Conf. UMC Camp & Retreat	750 Windsor Street, PO Box 220, Sun Prairie, WI 53590	608-846-2938
Wonderland Camp & Conf. Ctr.	P.O. Box 222, Camp Lake, WI 53109	414-889-4305
Wood Lake Baptist Camp	Rt. 1, Box 451, Grantsburg, WI 54840	715-689-2418

Wyoming

Camp Bethel	Dayton, WY 82836	307-655-2490
Rocky Mountain Lodge	Star Route Box 373, Jackson, WY 83001	307-735-4517
Sky -n- Canyon Ranch	Star Route Box 489, Fort Laramie, WY 82212-9607	307-837-2858

A YEAR'S READING PROGRAM FOR YOUR LEISURE TIME
Selected by Dr. John F. Walvoord, Chancellor, Dallas Theological Seminary

January . . . . *Mere Christianity* by C. S. Lewis
February . . . . *Balancing the Christian Life* by Charles C. Ryrie
March . . . . *Growing Deep in the Christian Life* by Charles R. Swindoll
April . . . . *What We Believe: Discovering Biblical Truth* by John F. Walvoord
May . . . . *Failure: The Backdoor to Success* by Erwin Lutzer
June . . . . *Happiness Is a Choice* by Frank B. Minirth and Paul Meier
July . . . . *Emotions: Can You Trust Them?* by James Dobson
August . . . . *Little House on the Freeway* by Tim Kimmel
September . . . . *Hudson Taylor's Spiritual Secret* by Dr. and Mrs. Howard Taylor
October . . . . *The Knowledge of the Holy* by A.W. Tozer
November . . . . *Facing Death and the Life After* by Billy Graham
December . . . . *Sense and Nonsense about Prayer* by Lehman Strauss

FOCUS QUOTE

**Words are things; and a small drop of ink
Falling like dew upon a thought, produces
That which makes thousands, perhaps millions, think.
—George Byron**

NATIONAL PARKS

Park	ST	Features
Acadia	ME	Rugged seashore, 41,409 acres
Arches	UT	Unusual stone arches, 73,379 acres
Badlands	SD	Fossils, 243,244 acres
Big Bend	TX	Bordering the Rio Grande, 802,541 acres
Biscayne	FL	Coral reef, 173,039 acres
Bryce Canyon	UT	Erosion effects, 35,835 acres
Canyonlands	UT	Red-rock canyons, 337,570 acres
Capitol Reef	UT	Rock formation, 241,904 acres
Carlsbad Caverns	NM	Largest known caves, 46,755 acres
Channel Islands	CA	Marine mammals, 249,354 acres
Crater Lake	OR	Deep blue lake, 183,224 acres
Denali	AK	Mt. McKinley, North America's highest mountain (20,320 ft.), 4,716,726 acres
Everglades	FL	Subtropical area, 1,398,938 acres
Gates of the Arctic	AK	Wilderness, 7,523,888 acres
Glacier	MT	Glaciers, 1,013,572 acres
Glacier Bay	AK	Wildlife, 3,225,284 acres
Grand Canyon	AZ	Mile-deep gorge, 1,218,375 acres
Grand Teton	WY	Picturesque range of high mountain peaks, 309,994 acres
Great Basin	NV	Exceptional scenic, biologic, and geologic attractions, 77,109 acres
Great Smoky Mountains	NC-TN	Highest mountain range east of Black Hills; luxuriant plant life, 520,269 acres
Guadalupe Mountains	TX	Contains highest point in Texas: Guadalupe Peak (8,751 ft.), 86,416 acres
Haleakala	HI	10,023 ft. Haleakala volcano, 28,655 acres
Hawaii Volcanoes	HI	Volcanic area, 229,177 acres
Hot Springs	AR	Mineral hot springs, 5,839 acres
Isle Royale	MI	Wilderness island, 571,790 acres
Katmai	AK	Brown bear, fishing, 3,716,000 acres
Kenai Fjords	AK	Seacoast park, 669,541 acres
Kings Canyon	CA	Giant sequoias, 461,901 acres
Kobuk Valley	AK	Native culture, 1,750,421 acres
Lake Clark	AK	Wilderness, 2,636,839 acres
Lassen Volcanic	CA	Volcanic phenomena, 106,372 acres
Mammoth Cave	KY	Limestone, 52,419 acres
Mesa Verde	CO	Prehistoric cliff dwellings, 52,085 acres
Mount Rainier	WA	Glacial system, 235,404 acres
North Cascades	WA	Alpine landscape, 504,781 acres
Olympic	WA	Rain forest, 921,942 acres
Petrified Forest	AZ	Petrified wood, 93,532 acres
Redwood	CA	World's tallest known tree (369.2 ft.), 110,132 acres
Rocky Mountain	CO	More than a hundred peaks over 10,000 ft., 265,200 acres
Sequoia	CA	Giant sequoias, 402,482 acres
Shenandoah	VA	Skyline Drive, 195,382 acres
Theodore Roosevelt	ND	Wildlife, 70,416 acres
Voyageurs	MN	Wildlife, 218,036 acres
Wind Cave	SD	Limestone caverns, 28,292 acres
Wrangell-St. Elias	AK	Largest park system, 8,331,604 acres
Yellowstone	WY-MT-ID	Geyser area, 2,219,791 acres
Yosemite	CA	Giant sequoias, 761,170 acres
Zion	UT	Multicolored gorge, 146,598 acres

Media

TOP 10 BEST-SELLING BOOKS OF 1991

CLOTHBOUND

1. *Good Morning, Holy Spirit,* by Benny Hinn, Thomas Nelson Publishers
2. *The New World Order,* by Pat Robertson, Word Publishing
3. *The Coming Economic Earthquake,* by Larry Burkett, Moody Press
4. *My Utmost for His Highest,* by Oswald Chambers, Barbour & Co., Discovery House Publishers, G.R. Welch Co. Ltd.
5. *The Grace Awakening,* by Charles Swindoll, Word Publishing
6. *In the Eye of the Storm,* by Max Lucado, Word Publishing
7. *The Applause of Heaven,* by Max Lucado, Word Publishing
8. *Love for a Lifetime,* by James Dobson, Multnomah Press
9. *Under Fire,* by Oliver North with William Novak, Harper Collins Publishers and Zondervan Publishing House
10. *Love Must Be Tough,* by James Dobson, Word Publishing

PAPERBACK

1. *Armageddon, Oil and the Middle East Crisis,* by John Walvoord, Zondervan Publishing House
2. *Roses for Mama,* by Janette Oke, Bethany House Publishers
3. *This Present Darkness,* by Frank Peretti, Crossway Books
4. *The Rise of Babylon,* by Charles Dyer with Angela Elwell Hunt, Tyndale House Publishers
5. *A Woman Named Damaris,* by Janette Oke, Bethany House Publishers
6. *Piercing the Darkness,* by Frank Peretti, Crossway Books
7. *Stick a Geranium in Your Hat and Be Happy!* by Barbara Johnson, Word Publishing
8. *Joshua,* by Joseph Girzone, Macmillan Publishing Co.
9. *The Blessing,* by Gary Smalley and John Trent, Pocket Books
10. *Julia's Last Hope,* by Janette Oke, Bethany House Publishers

This list is based on actual sales in Christian retail stores in the United States and Canada during 1991. All rights reserved. Copyright © 1992 CBA Service Corp. and Spring Arbor Distributors. Distributed by Evangelical Christian Publishers Association. Reprinted by permission from the February 1992 issue of *Bookstore Journal,* official trade publication of the Christian Booksellers Association.

TOP 10 BEST-SELLING BOOKS OF THE 1980s

CLOTHBOUND

1. *Growing Strong in the Seasons of Life* by Charles Swindoll, Multnomah Press/ Walker and Company
2. *Love Must Be Tough* by James Dobson, Word, Inc.
3. *Improving Your Serve* by Charles Swindoll, Word, Inc.
4. *The Strong-Willed Child* by James Dobson, Tyndale House
5. *A Shepherd Looks at Psalm 23* by W. Phillip Keller, Zondervan Publishing House
6. *The Christian Mother Goose Book* (Volume 1 of Trilogy) by Marjorie Ainsborough Decker, World Bible Publishers Inc.
7. *Love for a Lifetime* by James Dobson, Multnomah Press
8. *Loving God* by Charles Colson, Zondervan Publishing House/Walker and Company

9. *Strengthening Your Grip* by Charles Swindoll, Word, Inc.
10. *Irregular People* by Joyce Landorf, Walker and Company / originally released by Word Publishing

PAPERBACK
1. *Hinds' Feet on High Places* by Hannah Hurnard, Tyndale House/Walker & Company/Barbour & Company
2. *Dare to Discipline* by James Dobson, Tyndale House/Bantam Books
3. *Free to Be Thin* by Marie Chapian and Neva Coyle, Bethany House
4. *Three Steps Forward, Two Steps Back* by Charles Swindoll, Thomas Nelson/ Bantam Books/Walker and Company
5. *The Seduction of Christianity* by Dave Hunt and T.A. McMahon, Harvest House Publishers
6. *The Late Great Planet Earth* by Hal Lindsey, Zondervan/Bantam Books
7. *The Act of Marriage* by Tim and Beverly LaHaye, Zondervan/Bantam Books
8. *Ordering Your Private World* by Gordon MacDonald, Oliver-Nelson
9. *Love Life for Every Married Couple* by Ed Wheat with Gloria Okes Perkins, Zondervan Publishing House
10. *The Pursuit of Holiness* by Jerry Bridges, NavPress/Walker and Company

100 BEST-SELLING CHRISTIAN ADULT BOOKS

The list was compiled from information supplied by publishers. To qualify as "backlist," the books had to have been published before July 1991.

The first sales figure shown for each entry is the number of copies sold during 1991, and the second figure is the total number sold in the title's history with the publisher.

We requested that publishers submit figures for sales through retail outlets only, but some (marked by an asterisk) were unable to separate the numbers, so their sales figures probably include distribution via ministries, book clubs, etc.

Although the books are ranked according to the total sold in the past year, not all publishers granted permission for sales totals to be published. Unreleased or unavailable figures are designated by "n.a.," but the books are ranked in their proper position. Some publishers chose to not submit figures.

1. **Armageddon, Oil and the Middle East Crisis**
   John Walvoord, Zondervan, Prophecy © 1991. n.a. Walvoord discusses what the Bible says about the future of the Middle East and the fulfillment of prophecy in the '90s.

2. **Good Morning, Holy Spirit**
   Benny Hinn, Nelson, Chr. Living © 1990. n.a. Hinn presents insights about the Godhead and how members of the Trinity interact with each other and humans.

3. **The Bible Promise Book, NIV**
   Toni Sortor, editor, Barbour, Inspirational © 1990. 313,937 / 313,937. This collection of more than 1,000 Bible promises is arranged alphabetically by topic.

4. **The Rise of Babylon**
   Charles Dyer with Angela Elwell Hunt, Tyndale, Prophecy © 1991. 301,262 / 301,262*. Dyer recounts personal experiences in Saddam Hussein's Iraq and discusses Bible prophecy relating to the region.

5. **The Bible Promise Book**
   Toni Sortor, editor, Barbour, Inspirational © 1985. 278,365 / 1,583,397. This collection of more than 1,000 Bible promises is arranged alphabetically by topic.

6. **Roses for Mama**
   Janette Oke, Bethany, Fiction © 1991. 277,216 / 277,216. A young girl must assume responsibility for raising her younger siblings.

7. **My Utmost for His Highest**
Oswald Chambers, Barbour, Devotional © 1935. 258,701 / 1,049,656. This is a classic devotional volume.

8. **Prison to Praise**
Merlin Carothers, Merlin R. Carothers Co., Biography © 1970. 205,400 / 5,422,900. The autobiographer shares his life from his rebellious youth to finding the Lord and becoming a chaplain.

9. **This Present Darkness**
Frank Peretti, Crossway Books, Fiction © 1986. 198,387 / 1,648,539. A small-town reporter and pastor find themselves fighting a New Age plot to subjugate the townspeople and, eventually, the entire human race.

10. **Handbook for Today's Catholic**
Redemptorist Pastoral Publication, Liguori, Chr. Education © 1977. 187,566 / 3,083,747. This volume discusses Catholic beliefs, practices, and prayers.

11. **Piercing the Darkness**
Frank Peretti, Crossway Books, Fiction © 1989. 156,631 / 1,168,436. A young loner is pursued by evil forces and her mysterious past in this sequel to *This Present Darkness.*

12. **Joshua**
Joseph Girzone, Macmillan, Fiction © 1987. 134,411* / n.a. Girzone imagines how Jesus might be treated if he lived on earth today.

13. **Your Baby's Baptism**
Redemptorist Pastoral Publication, Liguori, Chr. Education © 1985. 127,623 / 780,306. A gift book for parents, this title discusses aspects of infant baptism.

14. **Love Is a Choice**
Robert Hemfelt, Frank Minirth, and Paul Meier, Nelson, Self-Help © 1989. n.a. Subtitled "Recovery for Codependent Relationships," this title offers a 10-stage recovery process.

15. **Good Grief**
Granger Westberg, Fortress, Self-Help © 1962. 118,472 / 1,588,022. Subtitled "A Constructive Approach to the Problem of Loss," this title discusses many forms of grief and presents 10 stages of normal grieving.

16. **No Wonder They Call Him the Savior**
Max Lucado, Multnomah, Devotional © 1986, 1990. 116,945 / 288,313*. Focusing on Christ's crucifixion, this book discusses the sayings, people, and principles of the cross.

17. **More Than a Carpenter**
Josh McDowell, Tyndale, Apologetics © 1980. 116,898 / 818,897*. McDowell offers answers to people who are skeptical about Jesus' deity, his resurrection, and his claims on their lives.

18. **The New Birth**
Kenneth Hagin, Kenneth Hagin Ministries, Chr. Living © 1975. 115,140 / 2,443,400. This minibook explains what being "born again" means.

19. **Danzig Passage**
Bodie Thoene, Bethany, Fiction © 1991. 112,977 / 112,977. Jewish children must be evacuated as Nazi reprisals break out; Book 5 in the "Zion Covenant" series.

20. **Little House in the Ozarks**
Laura Ingalls Wilder and Steven Hines, editor, Nelson, Biography © 1991. n.a. This collection of rediscovered writings offers insight into an era past.

21. **Stick a Geranium in Your Hat and Be Happy!**
Barbara Johnson, Word, Chr. Living © 1990. n.a. You can't escape pain, but you can choose how to react, says Johnson in this book for women.

22. **Becoming a Woman of Excellence**
Cynthia Heald, NavPress, Chr. Living © 1986. 97,602 / 430,220. This study teaches readers how to become excellent in their daily lives.

23. **The Love Hunger Weight-Loss Workbook**
Frank Minirth, Paul Meier, Robert Hemfelt, and Sharon Sneed, Nelson, Self-Help © 1990. n.a. Based on *Love Hunger,* this stand-alone text helps readers work through their psychological, spiritual, and physical aspects of food addiction with interactive questions and self-tests.

24. **The Bondage Breaker**. Neil Anderson, Harvest House, Chr. Living © 1990.

100 BEST-SELLING CHRISTIAN ADULT BOOKS cont.

93,672 / 112,153. Anderson discusses how to understand Satan's strategies and gain freedom from negative thoughts, irrational feelings, and habitual sin.

25. **52 Simple Ways to Say "I Love You"** Stephen Arterburn and Carl Dreizler, Nelson, Love/Marriage © 1991. n.a. This collection of fun, fresh ways to express love helps readers show loved ones how much they care.

26. **Men & Women: Enjoying the Difference** Larry Crabb, Zondervan, Love/Marriage © 1991. n.a. The reason men and women don't get along is that they're self-centered and don't recognize the God-created differences between them.

27. **Dead Air** Bob Larson, Nelson, Fiction © 1991. n.a. A radio talk show host attempts to rescue a young girl from her satanic captors' evil plans.

28. **Why Tongues?** Kenneth Hagin, Kenneth Hagin Ministries, Chr. Living © 1975. 79,116 / 1,928,400. This minibook presents 10 scriptural benefits of being filled with the Holy Spirit and speaking in tongues.

29. **In Him** Kenneth Hagin, Kenneth Hagin Ministries, Chr. Living © 1975. 72,960 / 2,100,400. In this minibook, Hagin examines individuals' redemptive rights in Christ.

30. **Hinds' Feet on High Places**. Hannah Hurnard, Tyndale, Fiction © 1979. 72,527 / 1,005,723*. This allegory dramatizes the desire of God's children to be led to new heights of love, joy, and victory.

31. **Mere Christianity** C. S. Lewis, Macmillan, Apologetics © 1964. 72,380* / n.a. Lewis presents the common faith that unites believers.

32. **A Mother's Manual for Summer Survival** Kathy Peel and Joy Mahaffey, Focus on the Family, Parenting © 1989. 71,098 / 163,150. The authors suggest summer ideas and activities.

33. **Dare to Discipline** James Dobson, Tyndale, Parenting © 1987. 70,444 / 329,608*. Dobson discusses maintaining order, developing responsibility, and building character in children.

34. **Personality Plus** Florence Littauer, Revell, Self-Help © 1982. 67,724 / 305,000. Littauer discusses how to improve relationships through an understanding of the four personality temperaments.

35. **Our Sufficiency in Christ** John MacArthur, Word, Chr. Living © 1991. n.a. MacArthur discusses the sufficiency of Christ's grace and three influences that are undermining spiritual life.

36. **Escape the Coming Night** David Jeremiah and Carole Carlson, Word, Prophecy © 1991. n.a. The authors discuss evidence of fulfilled prophecy for the end times from Revelation.

37. **The Strong-Willed Child** James Dobson, Tyndale, Parenting © 1985. 64,646 / 778,437*. Dobson shares how to discipline the strong-willed child without breaking his or her spirit.

38. **A Touch of His Freedom** Charles Stanley, Zondervan, Inspirational © 1991. n.a. Stanley offers a collection of meditations about our freedom through Christ, poems, prayers, quotations, and photographs.

39. **Apples of Gold** Jo Petty, Gibson, Inspirational © 1962. 63,000 / 3,492,229. This gift book offers inspirational nuggets.

40. **Design for Discipleship 1: Your Life in Christ** The Navigators, NavPress, Bible Study © 1973, 1980. 62,912 / 1,056,525. Questions and answers with key Scripture verses direct readers through five one-hour lessons.

41. **Lessons on Assurance** The Navigators, NavPress, Bible Study © 1957, 1975, 1980. 62,038 / 920,459. This is a personal-response Bible study to affirm young Christians' trust in the Lord.

42. **Arabs, Oil and Armageddon**
Edgar James, Moody, Prophecy © 1991.
61,668 / 126,362. James discusses end-
time prophecies in light of current events
in the Middle East.

43. **Financial Planning Workbook**
Larry Burkett, Moody, Financial Management © 1990. 61,461 / 325,000. Burkett's workbook contains many personal
finance worksheets.

44. **Prayers That Avail Much, Vol. 1**
Word Ministries, Harrison, Inspirational
© 1980. 61,378 / 706,243. Scriptures
expressed as prayers allow readers to
have confidence and faith that they are
praying in God's will.

45. **His Needs, Her Needs**
Willard Harley, Jr., Revell, Marriage ©
1987. 60,891 / 187,000. Harley examines
male and female priorities and shows how
to improve relationships by understanding
and meeting each other's needs.

46. **This Incredible Century**
Norman Vincent Peale, Tyndale, Inspirational © 1991. 60,820 / 60,820*. Peale
mixes his own reminiscences with descriptions of the momentous events of this
century, stressing God's hand in it all.

47. **I'll Hold You in Heaven**
Jack Hayford, Regal Books, Family ©
1990. n.a. Hayford offers hope to parents
who have lost a child before or soon after
birth.

48. **Julia's Last Hope**
Janette Oke, Bethany , Fiction © 1990.
59,487 / 283,879. Julia must try to save her
town and home when hard times come.

49. **God's Creative Power**
Charles Capps, Harrison, Chr. Living ©
1976. 58,854 / 2,378,651. Capps shares
from experience how Christians can apply the Word to life's circumstances and
live victoriously.

50. **Disappointment with God**
Philip Yancey, Zondervan, Chr. Living
© 1988. n.a. Yancey offers comfort to
those who have suffered loss and explains why God allows such losses.

51. **Preparing for Adolescence**
James Dobson, Regal Books, Chr.

Living © 1978, 1989. n.a. In this updated edition, Dobson talks to teens
about the. challenges they're learning to
face.

52. **If Only He Knew**
Gary Smalley with Steve Scott, Zondervan, Love/Marriage © 1982, 1987. n.a.
Smalley clarifies for men the differences
between the sexes and how to build a
stronger marital relationship.

53. **A Shepherd Looks at Psalm 23**
W. Phillip Keller, Zondervan, Inspirational © 1970, 1991. n.a. Keller discusses this Psalm from the perspective
of a shepherd.

54. **For Better or for Best**
Gary Smalley with Steve Scott, Zondervan, Love/Marriage © 1987, 1991. n.a.
Smalley shows how wives can cultivate
better relationships with their spouses.

55. **On the Trail of the Truth**
Michael Phillips and Judith Pella, Bethany , Fiction © 1991. 53,503 / 53,503. In
Book 3 of "The Journals of Corrie Belle
Hollister" series, Corrie has a new
mother to care for her younger siblings
so is now free to consider her career.

56. **Living the New Life**
Andrew Murray, Whitaker, Chr. Living©
1982. 52,989 / 138,600. Murray guides
new Christians through the steps to Christian maturity.

57. **Love Must Be Tough**
James Dobson, Word, Love/Marriage ©
1983. n.a. Dobson outlines steps and
principles that can help a determined
spouse save a marriage when the other
partner seems unconcerned.

58. **Precious Bible Promises**
Nelson, Inspirational © 1983. n.a. This
collection of Bible promises is designed
to assist personal devotions.

59. **The Gates of Zion**
Bodie Thoene, Bethany, Fiction © 1986.
50,212 / 222,214. First in the "Zion
Chronicles" series, this book depicts the
rise of Israel from the ashes of the Holo-
caust.

60. **Medjugorje: The Message**
Wayne Weible, Paraclete, Chr. Living

100 BEST-SELLING CHRISTIAN ADULT BOOKS cont.

© 1989. n.a. This book explores the Yugoslavian apparition of Mary and its message.

61. **Secrets of Your Family Tree**
Dave Carder, et al., Moody, Family/ Psychology © 1991. 49,681 / 49,681. This book takes the complex task of correcting and preventing destructive behavior in the family and makes it understandable.

62. **The Act of Marriage**
Tim and Beverly LaHaye, Zondervan, Love/Marriage © 1976. n.a. This book outlines principles, goals, and guidelines for achieving a mutually satisfying sexual relationship within marriage.

63. **The Practice of the Presence of God**
Brother Lawrence, Whitaker, Inspirational © 1982. 48,965 / 208,165. Lawrence shares the secret of living moment by moment with a sense of God's presence.

64. **Gold Rush Prodigal**
Brock and Bodie Thoene, Bethany , Fiction © 1991. 48,936 / 48,936. In this "Saga of the Sierras" title, David Bollin seizes the promise of a glamorous future only to lose it all in the California gold fields.

65. **The Power of a Parent's Words**
H. Norman Wright, Regal Books, Parenting © 1991. n.a. Wright teaches parents to use the power of their words to help their children grow.

66. **The Calling of Emily Evans**. Janette Oke, Bethany, Fiction © 1990. 47,729 / 305,889. A young Bible college student feels God's call to open a new work on her own.

67. **Lord, Is It Warfare?**
Kay Arthur, Multnomah, Bible Study © 1991. 47,431 / 47,431*. This devotional study helps readers recognize and avoid Satan's snares.

68. **In His Steps**. Charles Sheldon, Barbour, Fiction © 1984. 47,165 / 281,478. A pastor challenges his parishioners to live as Christ would.

69. **Kara, the Lonely Falcon**
Joseph Girzone, Macmillan, Fiction © 1991. 47,039* / n.a. Kara, the most powerful falcon in the forest, is also the loneliest until he vows never to kill again.

70. **Toxic Faith**
Stephen Arterburn and Jack Felton, Nelson, Self-Help © 1991. n.a. The authors help readers distinguish between healthy faith and misguided religiosity.

71. **Classic Christianity**
Bob George, Harvest House, Chr. Living © 1989. 46,978 / 135,752. For burned-out Christians, George shows the way back to authentic Christianity.

72. **Vienna Prelude**
Bodie Thoene, Bethany, Fiction © 1989. 46,299 / 161,176. In Volume 1 of the "Zion Covenant" series, Elisa takes an Aryan stage name, but her father doesn't escape the Nazi snare.

73. **Love for a Lifetime**
James Dobson, Multnomah, Love/ Marriage © 1987. 46,211 / 526,737*. Dobson shares insights about courtship, fidelity, commitment, finances, the uniqueness of men and women, and ways to build solid. marriages.

74. **The Applause of Heaven**
Max Lucado, Word, Chr. Living © 1990. n.a. Inner peace that thrives despite life's hardships can be attained through faith in Jesus. The book is first in a three-volume series on the Sermon on the Mount.

75. **We Are Driven**
Robert Hemfelt, Frank Minirth, and Paul Meier, Nelson, Self-Help © 1991. n.a. The authors help readers who are susceptible to compulsions prevent positive behaviors from becoming addictions.

76. **Quiet Times for Couples**
H. Norman Wright, Harvest House, Devotional © 1990. 45,610 / 60,165. With 366 readings, this book is designed to stimulate open communication between spouses.

77. **The Pursuit of Holiness**
Jerry Bridges, NavPress, Chr. Living © 1978. 45,549 / 842,164. Bridges shows readers how to live to please God.

78. **Maximized Manhood**
Edwin Louis Cole, Whitaker, Chr.

Living © 1982. 45,276 / 764,423. Subtitled "A Guide to Family Survival," this book discusses how to live fully as a man in a challenging world.

79. **Gifted Hands**
Ben Carson with Cecil Murphey, Zondervan, Biography © 1990. n.a. Carson recalls his inner-city childhood and rise to the position of director of pediatric neurosurgery at Johns Hopkins University Hospital.

80. **Growing in Christ**
The Navigators, NavPress, Bible Study © 1980. 44,759 / 482,643. This is an unabridged combination of *Lessons on Assurance* and *Lessons on Christian Living*. Memory verse cards for each chapter are included.

81. **What Happens When Women Pray?**
Evelyn Christenson, Victor Books, Chr. Living © 1975. 44,455 / 1,657,083. This book shows what happens when prayer becomes a life-changing dynamic in the church.

82. **Design for Discipleship 2: The Spirit-Filled Christian**
The Navigators, NavPress, Bible Study © 1973, 1980. 44,310 / 819,389. Questions and answers with key Scripture verses direct readers through five one-hour lessons.

83. **God Calling**
A. J. Russell, editor, Revell, Inspirational © 1981. 44,098 / 1,567,000. This book presents Christianity's wisdom through the ears and the voices of two listeners.

84. **Victory over the Darkness**
Neil Anderson, Regal Books, Chr. Living © 1990. n.a. Anderson shows that we have the power to conquer the powers of darkness, once we know who we are in Christ.

85. **Quest for Character**
Charles Swindoll, Multnomah, Chr. Living © 1988. 43,282 / 256,496*. This devotional gift book urges readers to develop godly character traits.

86. **Day by Day Love Is a Choice**
Richard and Jerilyn Fowler and Brian and Deborah Newman, Nelson, Inspirational © 1991. n.a. Based on the 10-step recovery process of *Love Is a Choice,* this book features daily inspirational messages.

87. **Always Daddy's Girl**
H. Norman Wright, Regal Books, Parenting © 1989. n.a. Wright explores how fathers affect their daughters' personalities and lives.

88. **The Frog in the Kettle**
George Barna, Regal Books, Chr. Living © 1990. n.a. This book gives a projection of the future and how Christians need to respond.

89. **Why Am I Afraid to Tell You Who I Am?**
John Powell, Tabor, Self-Help © 1969. n.a. This book discusses communication, trust, and love and shows readers how to grow in self-esteem, confidence, and personal relationships.

90. **Hiding from Love**
John Townsend, NavPress, Self-Help © 1991. 42,684 / 42,684. Townsend explores why people shut themselves off from others and how they can learn to set healthy boundaries and achieve connected relationships with God and others.

91. **The Screwtape Letters**
C.S. Lewis, Macmillan, Fiction © 1982. 42,671 / n.a.* Screwtape advises his young nephew, Wormwood, in the fine art of tempting a human soul to hell.

92. **Your Child's First Communion**
Redemptorist Pastoral Publication, Liguori, Chr. Education © 1990. 42,600 / 61,605. This magazine-style book helps parents effectively interact with children about to take First Communion.

93. **Wisdom from the Bible**
Dan and Nancy Dick, Barbour, Inspirational © 1986. 42,331 / 278,612. This daily devotional is based on Proverbs.

94. **A Path through Scripture**
Mark Link, Tabor, Chr. Education © 1987. n.a. This high school text presents an introductory tour of the Old and New Testaments.

95. **Food for the Hungry Heart**

100 BEST-SELLING CHRISTIAN ADULT BOOKS cont.

Cynthia McClure, Nelson, Inspirational © 1991. n.a. This devotional offers daily inspirations for overeaters.

96. **Bringing Out the Best in People**
   Alan Loy McGinnis, Augsburg, Self-Help © 1985. 41,440 / 401,696. This book is subtitled "How to Enjoy Helping Others Excel."

97. **Global Peace and the Rise of Antichrist**
   Dave Hunt, Harvest House, Prophecy © 1990. 41,382 / 70,637. In this biblical analysis of how global events could be setting the stage for the final conflict, Hunt emphasizes that the study of prophecy is meant to revive our passion for Jesus as we wait for him.

98. **User Friendly Churches**
   George Barna, Regal Books, Church Growth © 1991. n.a. This book is subtitled "What Christians Need to Know about the Churches People Love to Go To."

99. **Giving Up Lately?**
   David Wilkerson, Revell, Chr. Living © 1983. 40,841 / 192,000. Wilkerson confronts Christians' inner struggles and maps the road to healing.

100. **How to Manage Your Money**
   Larry Burkett, Moody, Financial Management © 1975. 40,706 / 364,000. Burkett explores how to apply and share God's

principles about money and its proper use.

Bookstore Journal, Official Trade Publication of the Christian Booksellers Association. Copyright © 1992. Reprinted by permission.

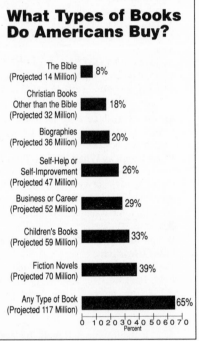

What Types of Books Do Americans Buy?

The Bible (Projected 14 Million)	8%
Christian Books Other than the Bible (Projected 32 Million)	18%
Biographies (Projected 36 Million)	20%
Self-Help or Self-Improvement (Projected 47 Million)	26%
Business or Career (Projected 52 Million)	29%
Children's Books (Projected 59 Million)	33%
Fiction Novels (Projected 70 Million)	39%
Any Type of Book (Projected 117 Million)	65%

Source: *What Americans Believe* by George Barna. Copyright © 1991. Published by Regal Books. Used by permission.

CHRISTIAN BOOK PUBLISHERS IN THE UNITED STATES

*Indicates Evangelical Christian Publishers Association membership

Abbey Press		St. Meinrad IN 47577
Abbott Loop Publications	2626 Abbott Road	Anchorage AK 99507
Abingdon Press	201 - 8th Avenue S.	Nashville TN 37202
Accent Books	P.O. Bx 15337, 12100 W. 6th Ave.	Denver CO 80215
Agape Ministries	P.O. Box 2959	Titusville FL 32781
Augsburg Publishing House	Box 1209, 426 S. 5th Street	Minneapolis MN 55440
Ave Maria Press		Notre Dame IN 46556
Baker Book House*	P.O. Box 6287	Grand Rapids MI 49506
Ballantine/Epiphany Books	201 East 50 Street	New York NY 10022
Bantam Books	666 - 5th Avenue	New York NY 10103
Baptist Publishing House	1319 Magnolia Street	Texarkana TX 75501
Baptist Spanish Publishing House	P.O. Box 4255, 7000 Alabama St.	El Paso TX 79914

Barbour and Company, Inc.*	P.O. Box 729	Uhrichsville OH 44683
Barclay Press*	600 E. Third Street	Newberg OR 97132
Bethany House Publishers*	6820 Auto Club Road	Minneapolis MN 55438
Bethel Publishing	1819 S. Main	Elkhart IN 46516
Bob Jones University Press		Greenville SC 29614
Brethren Press	1451 Dundee Avenue	Elgin IL 60120
Bridge Publishing, Inc.	2500 Hamilton Blvd.	South Plainfield NJ 07080
Bristol House Ltd.*	2201 Regency Road, Suite 302	Lexington KY 40503
Broadman/Holman/Genevox*	127 - 9th Avenue N.	Nashville TN 37234
Brownlow Publishing Co., Inc.*	6309 Airport Freeway	Fort Worth TX 76117
C & D International*	9029 Director Row	Dallas TX 75247
C. R. Gibson Company*	32 Knight Street	Norwalk CT 06856
Casa Editorial Nueva Albanza	P.O. Box 9944	El Paso TX 79990
Casa Nazarene de Publicaciones	6401 The Paseo	Kansas City MO 64131
Charles Scribner's Sons	866 Third Avenue	New York NY 10022
Christian Books Publishing House	P.O. Box 3368	Auburn ME 04210
Christian Classics Inc.	P.O. Box 30	Westminster MD 21157
Christian Education Publishers*	P.O. Box 2789	La Jolla CA 92038
Christian Heritage Publishing*	P.O. Box 5010	Lake Wylie SC 29710
Christian Publications, Inc.	3825 Hartzdale Drive	Camp Hill PA 17011
Clarion Books	52 Vanderbilt Avenue	New York NY 10017
Collier Books/Macmillan Company	866 Third Avenue	New York NY 10022
Concordia Publishing House	3558 S. Jefferson	St. Louis MO 63118
Cornerstone Publishing Company	Suite 326-320 6336 N. Oracle Rd	Tucson AZ 85704
Creation House	190 N. Westmonte Drive	Altamonte Springs FL 32714
Dake Bible Sales, Inc.	P.O. Box 1050	Lawrenceville GA 30246
David C. Cook Publishing Company*	850 N. Grove	Elgin IL 60120
Dayspring, Inc.	P.O. Box 201	Hazelwood MO 63042
Derek Prince Ministries	P.O. Box 300	Ft. Lauderdale FL 33302
Discovery House Publishers*	P.O. Box 3566	Grand Rapids MI 49501
Doubleday & Company	666 Fifth Avenue	New York NY 10103
Editorial Betania	5541 N.W. 82nd Avenue	Miami FL 33166
Editorial Caribe	3934 S.W. 8th Street, Suite 303	Miami FL 33134
Editorial Unilit	1360 N.W. 88 Avenue	Miami FL 33172
Eerdmans Publishing Co., Wm. B.	255 Jefferson, S.E.	Grand Rapids MI 49503
Emmanuel Press	5451 Moongate Road	Spring Hill FL 33526
Faith and Life Press	P.O. Box 347, 724 Main	Newton KS 67114
Fleming H. Revell Company*	120 White Plains Road	Tarrytown NY 10591
Focus on the Family Publishing*	420 N. Cascade Avenue	Colorado Springs CO 80903
Fortress Press	Box 1209, 426 South Fifth Street	Minneapolis MN 55440
Foundation Press	1121 N. Kraemer Place	Anaheim CA 92806
Good Family Publishing*	P.O. Box 850	Sisters OR 97759
Good News Publ./Crossway Books*	1300 Crescent Street	Wheaton IL 60187
Good Will Publishers*	1520 S. York Road	Gastonia NC 28052
Gospel Advocate Company*	1006 Elm Hill Pike	Nashville TN 37210
Gospel Light Publications/Regal Bks*	2300 Knoll Drive	Ventura CA 93003
Gospel Publishing House	1445 Boonville Avenue	Springfield MO 65802
Group Publishing, Inc*	P.O. Box 481	Loveland CO 80539
Guideposts Associates, Inc.*	757 Third Avenue	New York NY 10017
Hannibal Books*	921 Center Street, Suite A	Hannibal MO 63401
Harold Shaw Publishers	P.O. Box 567, 388 Gundersen Dr.	Wheaton IL 60189
HarperCollins, Evangelical Books*	151 Union St., Icehouse One—401	San Francisco CA 94111
Harrison House	P.O. Box 35035	Tulsa OK 74153
Harvest House Publishers*	1075 Arrowsmith	Eugene OR 97402
Hendrickson Publishers, Inc.*	137 Summit Street	Peabody MA 01961-3473
Herald Press	616 Walnut Avenue	Scottdale PA 15683

CHRISTIAN BOOK PUBLISHERS IN THE UNITED STATES cont.

Here's Life Publishers, Inc.*	P.O. Box 1576, 2700 Little Mountain Drive, Bldg. F.	San Bernardino CA 92405
Houghton Mifflin Company	2 Park Street	Boston MA 02108
Huntington House, Inc.	P.O. Box 53788	Lafayette LA 70505
Ideals Publishing Corporation	P.O. Box 140300	Nashville TN 37214
Ignatius Press	15 Oakland Avenue	Harrison NY 10528
Impact Books, Inc.	137 W. Jefferson	Kirkwood MO 63122
InterVarsity Press*	P.O. Box 1400, 5206 Main Street	Downers Grove IL 60515
John Knox Press	341 Ponce De Leon Avenue, NE	Atlanta GA 30308
Judson Press	P.O. Box 851	Valley Forge PA 19482
Keats Publishing, Inc.	P.O. Box 876	New Canaan CT 06840
B. B. Kirkbride Company, Inc.*	P.O. Box 606	Indianapolis IN 46206
Kregel Publications*	P.O. Box 2607, 733 Wealthy St. SE	Grand Rapids MI 49501
Life Publishers Interntl/Vida Editorial	3360 NW 110th Street	Miami FL 33167
Light and Life Press	999 College Avenue	Winona Lake IN 46590
Lillenas Publishing Company	P.O. Box 419527	Kansas City MO 64141
Lion Publishing Corporation	1705 Hubbard Avenue	Batavia IL 60510
Loizeaux Brothers, Inc.*	P.O. Box 277, 1238 Corlies Ave.	Neptune NJ 07753
Lutheran Publishing House	3547 Indiana Ave.	St. Louis MO 63118
Macmillan Company	866 - 3rd Avenue	New York NY 10022
Maranatha Publications	P.O. Box 1799	Gainesville FL 32602
Master Books	P.O. Box 1606	El Cajon CA 92022
Moody Press*	820 North LaSalle Drive	Chicago IL 60610
Multnomah Press*	10209 S.E. Division St.	Portland OR 97266
National Publishing Company*	P.O. Box 8386, 24th & Locust Sts.	Philadelphia PA 19101
NavPress*	7899 Lexington Center Drive	Colorado Springs CO 80920
New Hope Publishing Company	9123 Lorene - 106	San Antonio TX 78216
New Leaf Press	P.O. Box 311	Green Forest AR 72638
Oliver-Nelson	Nelson Place at Elm Hill Pike	Nashville TN 37214
Omega Publications	P.O. Box 4130	Medford OR 97501
Our Sunday Visitor, Inc.	200 Noll Plaza	Huntington IN 46750
Oxford University Press	200 Madison Avenue	New York NY10016
Paulist Press	997 Macarthur Blvd.	Mahwah NJ 07430
Pocket Books - Washington Sq. Press	1230 Avenue of the Americas	New York NY 10020
Praise Publications	P.O. Box 710231	San Jose CA 95171
Presbyterian & Reformed Publishing	P.O. Box 817	Phillipsburg NJ 08865
Publishing Directions, Inc.*	5301 Wisconsin Ave. NW, Suite 720	Washington DC 20015
Questar Publishers, Inc.*	P.O. Box 1720	Sisters OR 97759
Riverside/World Book and Bible House*	1500 Riverview Drive	Iowa Falls IA 50126
Roper Press*	4737-A Gretna	Dallas TX 75207
Scripture Press Publ./Victor Books*	1825 College Avenue	Wheaton IL 60187
Serendipity House, Inc.	2550 West Main Street	Littleton CO 80120
Servant Publications/Vine Books*	P.O. Box 8617, 840 Airport Blvd.	Ann Arbor MI 48107
Spire Books	184 Central Avenue	Old Tappan NJ 07675
Standard Publishing*	8121 Hamilton Avenue	Cincinnati OH 45231
STL Books	#2 Industrial Park Road	Waynesboro GA 30830
Strang Communications Company*	600 Rinehart Road	Lake Mary FL 32746
Sweet Publishing Company*	3950 Fossil Creek Blvd., Suite 201	Fort Worth TX 76137
Sword of the Lord Publishers	224 Bridge Avenue	Murfreesboro TN 37130
Thomas Nelson, Inc. Publishers*	P.O. Box 141000, Nelson Place at Elm Hill Park	Nashville TN 37214-1000
Tyndale House Publishers, Inc.*	Box 80, 351 Executive Drive	Wheaton IL 60189
Upper Room*	P.O. Box 189	Nashville TN 37202-0189
V. Countryman Publishers	P.O. Box 90776	Houston TX 77290
Victory House, Inc.	P.O. Box 700238	Tulsa OK 74170

Walk Thru The Bible Ministries*	P.O. Box 80587, 61 Perimeter Park, NE	Atlanta GA 30366
Warner Press, Inc.*	P.O. Box 2499, 1200 East 5th St.	Anderson IN 46018
Wellspring Books	Rt. 1, Box 27	Groton VT 05046
Wesley Press	8050 Castaway Drive	Indianapolis IN 46250
Western Publ. Co., Inc./Golden Books	1220 Mound Avenue	Racine WI 53404
Westminster Press	925 Chestnut Street	Philadelphia PA 19107
Whitaker House	580 Pittsburgh Street	Springdale PA 15144
William Carey Library Publishers	P.O. Bx 40129, 1705 N. Sierra Bonita	Pasadena CA 91104
Winston Seabury Press	151 Union Street	San Francisco CA 94111
Wolgemuth & Hyatt Publishers, Inc.*	1749 Mallory Lane, Suite 110	Brentwood TN 37027
Word, Inc.*	5221 N. O'Connor, Suite 1000	Irving TX 75039
World Bible Publishers, Inc.	P.O. Box 370, 1500 Riverside Drive	Iowa Falls IA 50126
World Wide Publications	1303 Hennepin Avenue	Minneapolis MN 55403
Worthy Publishing	3950 Fossil Creek Blvd., Suite 203	Fort Worth TX 76137
Youth Specialties, Inc.	1224 Greenfield Drive	El Cajon CA 92021
Zondervan Corporation*	5300 Patterson Ave., SE	Grand Rapids MI 49530

CHRISTIAN BOOKS PUBLISHED WORLDWIDE

	1900	1970	1980	1992	2000
New commercial book titles per year	2,200	17,100	18,800	22,870	25,000
New titles including devotional	3,100	52,000	60,000	67,440	75,000
Christian periodicals	3,500	23,000	22,500	26,000	35,000
New books/articles on evangelization per year	300	3,100	7,500	12,000	16,000

Adapted from David B. Barrett, World Evangelization database. Copyright © 1992 by the International Bulletin of Missionary Research. Reprinted by permission.

CAMPUS LIFE BOOK OF THE YEAR AWARDS

Campus Life readers review and rate a wide range of newly released books from Christian publishers. *Campus Life* editors select the winners from reader evaluations.

Award of Excellence/Biography

1981	*The Catch Me Killer*	Bob Erler with John C. Souter	Tyndale House Publishers
1982	*Lord of the Second Advent*	Steve Kemperman	Regal Books/Gospel Light Publ.
1983	*The Flames Shall Not Consume You*	Mary Ellen Ton	David C. Cook Publishing Co.
1985	*Empty Sleeves*	Phillip Rushing	Zondervan Publishing House
1986	*Sandy*	Leighton Ford	InterVarsity Press
1987	*Choices . . . Changes*	Joni Eareckson Tada	Zondervan Publishing Company
1990	*A Man Called Norman*	Mike Adkins	Focus on the Family Publishing

Award of Excellence/Fiction

1986	*Empyrion: The Search for Fierra*	Stephen R. Lawhead	Crossway Books/Good News Publ.
1987	*No Other Choice*	Lissa Halls Johnson	Fleming H. Revell
1989	*Two Worlds*	Lorry Lutz	Tyndale House Publishers
1991	*Jerusalem Interlude*	Bodie Thoene	Bethany House

Award of Excellence/General Interest

1981	*Too Old to Cry, Too Young to Die*	Edith Pendleton	Thomas Nelson, Inc., Publishers
1982	*Abortion: The Silent Holocaust*	John Powell	Argus Communications
1983	*Irregular People*	Joyce Landorf	Word, Inc.
1984	*Choices*	Stacy and Paula Rinehart	Navpress
1985	*Beating the Break-up Habit*	Dick Purnell with Jerry Jones	Here's Life Publishers
1986	*Beyond Choice*	Don Baker	Multnomah Press
1987	*Doorposts*	Timothy Botts	Tyndale House Publishers
1988	*A View from the Zoo*	Gary Richmond	Word, Inc.

CAMPUS LIFE BOOK OF THE YEAR AWARDS cont.

1989	*Being a Friend*	Donald Bubna with Al Janssen	Tyndale House Publishers
1990	*If God Is So Good, Why Do I Hurt So Bad?*	David B. Biebel	NavPress

Award of Excellence/Personal Growth

1981	*Living with Unfulfilled Desires*	Walter Trobisch	InterVarsity Press
1983	*How to Be Your Own Selfish Pig*	Susan Schaeffer Macaulay	Chariot Bks/David C. Cook Publ. Co.
1984	*Loving God*	Charles Colson	Zondervan Publishing House
1985	*When the Pieces Don't Fit— God Makes the Difference*	Glaphre Gilliland	Zondervan Publishing House
1986	*Dating, Sex & Friendship*	Joyce Huggett	InterVarsity Press
1987	*A Place to Stand When Life Throws You Off Balance*	Mark R. Littleton	Multnomah Press

Award of Excellence/Poetry and Fiction

1981	*Alpha Centauri*	Robert Siegel	Cornerstone Books
1982	*Surprised by Light*	Ulrich Schaffer	Harper & Row, Publishers
1983	*The Valiant Papers*	Calvin Miller	Zondervan Publishing House
1984	*Dream Thief*	Stephen R. Lawhead	Crossway Bks/Good News Publrs
1988	*Heaven*	Joseph Bayly	David C. Cook Publishing Co.

Award of Merit

1981	*Joseph*	Joyce Landorf	Fleming H. Revell
1981	*The Choice*	Harold Myra	Tyndale House Publishers
1982	*May's Boy*	Shirlee Monty	Thomas Nelson, Inc., Publishers
1984	*Dropping Your Guard*	Charles R. Swindoll	Word, Inc.
1984	*Finders Keepers*	Dee Brestin	Harold Shaw Publishers
1984	*Should I Keep My Baby?*	Martha Zimmerman	Bethany House Publishers
1985	*A House Divided*	Katherine Edwards	Zondervan Publishing House
1985	*Forgive and Forget*	Lewis B. Smedes	Harper & Row, Publishers
1985	*Growing into the Blue*	Ulrich Schaffer	Harper & Row, Publishers
1985	*Johnny Come Home*	R.C. Sproul	Regal Books/Gospel Light Publtns
1985	*The Sword and the Flame*	Stephen R. Lawhead	Crossway Bks/Gospel Light Publtns
1986	*Getting Along with Each Other*	Richard Strauss	Here's Life Publishers
1986	*Ordering Your Private World*	Gordon MacDonald	Oliver-Nelson Books
1987	*The Gates of Zion*	Bodie Thoene	Zondervan Publishing House

Award of Merit/Biography

1988	*Cry Freedom*	Lida Vaschenko with Cecil Murphy	Vine Books/Servant Publications
1988	*I Never Sang You Happy Birthday*	Judi Seifried	Chosen Books/Fleming H. Revell
1990	*A Gift of Hope*	Tony Melendez with Mel White	Harper and Row, Publishers
1990	*One Step at a Time*	Bob Wieland as told to Sarah Nichols	Zondervan Publishing House
1991	*Deadly Secrets*	Karen Scalf Linamen and Keith A. Wall	NavPress

Award of Merit/Fiction

1983	*In the Hall of the Dragon King*	Stephen R. Lawhead	Crossway Bks/Good News Publrs
1987	*Row This Boat Ashore*	Nancy Rue	Crossway Bks/Good News Publrs
1991	*Tales of the Neverending*	Mark Littleton	Moody Press

Award of Merit/General Interest

1988	*Will I Cry Tomorrow?*	Susan M. Stanford	Fleming H. Revell
1990	*Pregnant & Alone*	Henrietta VanDerMolen	Harold Shaw Publishers

Award of Merit/Issues

1991	*A Safe Place: Beyond Sexual Abuse*	Jan Morrison	Harold Shaw Publishers

Award of Merit/Personal Growth

1988	*The Complete Campus Companion*	Robert Kachur	InterVarsity Press
1989	*No Answers*	Bill Hybels	InterVarsity Press

1989	*Sharing Your Faith without Losing Your Friends*	Joseph Aldrich	Multnomah Press
1990	*Falling into the Big L*	Karen J. Sandvig	Gospel Light/Regal Books
1990	*Sex: It's Worth Waiting For*	Greg Speck	Moody Press
1991	*I Don't Remember Dropping the Skunk, But I Do Remember Trying to Breathe*	Ken Davis	Zondervan Publishing House

Award of Merit/Poetry

| 1983 | *With Open Eyes* | Ulrich Schaffer | Harper & Row, Publishers |

Award of Merit/Poetry and Fiction

1990	*A Requiem for Love*	Calvin Miller	Word, Inc.
1990	*Piercing the Darkness*	Frank E. Peretti	Crossway Books
1990	*Vienna Prelude*	Bodie Thoene	Bethany House Publishers

Biography

1973	*The Ghost in My Life*	Susan B. Anthony II	Chosen Books
1979	*Home Where I Belong*	B.J. Thomas with Jerry B. Jenkins	Word, Inc.
1980	*Kathy*	Barbara Miller and Charles Paul Conn	Fleming H. Revell

Book of the Year

1973	*The Hiding Place*	Corrie ten Boom with John and Elizabeth Sherrill	Chosen Books
1974	*Cry, the Beloved Country*	Alan Paton	Charles Scribner's Sons
1976	*If I Die at Thirty*	Meg Woodson	Zondervan Publishing House

Book of the Year/General Interest

| 1977 | *Joni* | Joni Eareckson and Joe Musser | Zondervan Publishing House |

Editor's Choice

1981	*Addicted to Mediocrity*	Franky Schaeffer	Cornerstone Books
1981	*Caring Enough to Forgive/ Caring Enough to Not Forgive*	David Augsburger	Regal Books/Gospel Light Publ.
1981	*Decision Making and the Will of God*	Garry Friesen with J. Robin Maxson	Multnomah Press
1982	*The Valiant Papers*	Calvin Miller	Zondervan Publishing House
1982	*With Wandering Steps and Slow*	Joy Hoffman	InterVarsity Press
1987	*Making Friends & Making Them Count*	Em Griffin	InterVarsity Press
1987	*Taliesin*	Stephen R. Lawhead	Crossway Books/Good News Publ.
1987	*The Amazing Body Human*	Mark P. Cosgrove	Baker Book House

General Interest

1973	*Tough Love*	Bill Milliken	Fleming H. Revell
1974	*How to Be a Christian without Being Religious*	Fritz Ridenour	Gospel Light Publications
1974	*The End of Youngblood Johnson*	Aaron Johnson and Jamie Buckingham	Chosen Books
1975	*Tramp for the Lord*	Corrie ten Boom and Jamie Buckingham	Fleming H. Revell
1978	*The Acorn People*	Ron Jones	Abingdon Press
1979	*A Face for Me*	Debbie Diane Fox with Jean Libman Block	Fleming H. Revell
1980	*The Friendship Factor*	Alan Loy McGinnis	Augsburg Publishing House

Mark of Excellence

1979	*If You Haven't Got a Prayer*	Stephen Crotts	InterVarsity Press
1979	*Lust: The Other Side of Love*	Mel White	Fleming H. Revell
1979	*Return from Tomorrow*	George Ritchie	Chosen Books

Personal Growth

1973	*I Married You*	Walter Trobisch	Harper & Row, Publishers
1975	*Born to Grow*	Larry Richards	Victor Books/Scripture Press
1976	*How to Talk to God*	Stephen Winward	Harold Shaw Publishers
1977	*I Love the Word Impossible*	Ann Kiemel	Tyndale House Publishers
1978	*Winter Past*	Nancy Smith	InterVarsity Press
1979	*My Friend the Bible*	John Sherrill	Chosen Books

CAMPUS LIFE BOOK OF THE YEAR AWARDS cont.

1980 *Out of the Salt Shaker and*
      into the World   Rebecca Manley Pippert   InterVarsity Press

Poetry/Fiction
1973 *For Mature Adults Only*   Norman C. Habel   Fortress Press
1974 *Hope for the Flowers*   Trina Paulus   Paulist Press
1975 *I'm Out to Change My World* Ann Kiemel   Impact
1976 *The Singer*   Calvin Miller   InterVarsity Press
1977 *The Secret Trees*   Luci Shaw   Harold Shaw Publishers
1978 *I Came to Love You Late*   Joyce Landorf   Fleming H. Revell
1980 *The Seven Last Years*   Carol Balizet   Chosen Books

Special Category
1973 *The Way*   Tyndale House Publishers

CORNERSTONE BOOK OF THE YEAR AWARDS

Christian Ethics
1990   *Witch Hunt* by Bob and Gretchen Passantino, Thomas Nelson Publishing

Cults & New Religions
1990   *Crystal Clear* by Dean Halverson, NavPress

Anthologies
1990   *A Testament to Freedom: The Essential Writings of Dietrich Bonhoeffer* edited by Geffrey
                Kelly and F. Burton Nelson, Harper San Francisco

First Person
1990   *Comeback* by Dave Dravecky with Tim Stafford, Zondervan Publishing House and Harper
                San Francisco

Bible Study Aids
1990   *The NIV Exhaustive Concordance* edited by Edward Goodrick and John Kohlenberger III,
                Zondervan Publishing House

Personal Growth
1990   *Intimate Deception: Escaping the Trap of Sexual Impurity* by P. Roger Hillstrom, Multnomah
                Press

Counseling
1990   *Before Burnout: Balanced Living for Busy People* by Frank Minirth, Paul Meier, Don Hawkins,
                and Chris Thurman, Moody Press

Social Issues
1990   *Against the Night* by Charles Colson with Ellen Santilli Vaughn, Servant Publications

Apologetics
1990   *Apologetics in the New Age: A Christian Critique of Pantheism* by David Clark and Norman
                Geisler, Baker Book House

Worst Book of the Year
1990   *Rescuing the Bible from Fundamentalism: A Bishop Rethinks the Meaning of Scripture* by
                John Shelby Spong, Harper San Francisco

CRITICS' CHOICE AWARDS

Sponsored by *Christianity Today* magazine. Selected by professionals in each field.

Biography and History
1990   *Christian Doctrine and Modern Culture (since 1700)* by Jaroslav Pelikan, University of Chicago
                Altered Landscapes edited by David Lotz, Wm. B. Eerdmans Publishing Co.
1991   *The Democratization of American Christianity* by Nathan Hatch, Yale University Press

Christian Living and Spirituality
1990   *Disappointment with God* by Philip Yancey, Zondervan Publishing House
                In the Name of Jesus by Henri Nouwen, The Crossroad Publishing Co.
1991   *In Search of Happiness* by James Houston, Lion Publishing
                A Quest for Godliness by J. I. Packer, Crossway Books

Commentaries
1990   *The Book of Ruth* by Robert Hubbard, Jr., Wm. B. Eerdmans Publishing Co.
1991   *The First Epistle of Peter* by Peter Davids, Wm. B. Eerdmans Publishing Co.

Contemporary Issues
1990   *Battered into Submission* by James and Phyllis Alsdurf, InterVarsity Press
1991   *Gender and Grace* by Mary Stewart Van Leeuwen, InterVarsity Press

Fiction
1990   *Piercing the Darkness* by Frank Peretti, Crossway
1991   *The Breaking of Ezra Riley* by John Moore, Lion Publishing

Reference and Textbooks
1990   *Dictionary of Pentecostal and Charismatic Movements* edited by Stanley Burgess and
               Gary McGee, Zondervan Publishing House
1991   *Dictionary of Christianity in America* edited by Daniel G. Reid, Robert D. Linder,
               Bruce L. Shelley, Harry S. Stout, InterVarsity Press

Theology and Biblical Studies
1990   *The Canon of Scripture* by F. F. Bruce, InterVarsity Press
1991   *After Modernity . . . What?* by Thomas Oden, Zondervan Publishing House

GOLD MEDALLION BOOK AWARDS

Evangelical Christian Publishers Association Awards

Bibles
1988	*Life Application Bible*		Tyndale House Publishers
1989	*Life Application Bible*		Tyndale House Publishers
1990	*Life Application Bible*	King James Version	Tyndale House Publishers
1991	*Life Application Bible*	New Revised Standard Version	World Bible Publishers/ Tyndale House Publishers

Biography/Autobiography
1978	*A Severe Mercy*	Sheldon Vanauken	Harper and Row, Publishers
1979	*Paul: Apostle of the Heart Set Free*	F. F. Bruce	Wm. B. Eerdmans Publishing Co.
1980	*By Their Blood*	James and Marti Hefley	Mott Media
1981	*Faith Despite the KGB*	Harmann Hartfeld	Diane Books Publishing, Inc.
1982	*The Tapestry*	Edith Schaeffer	Word, Inc.
1983	*It's My Turn*	Ruth Bell Graham	Fleming H. Revell
1984	*Guest of the Revolution*	Kathryn Koob	Thomas Nelson, Inc., Publishers
1985	*A Time for Remembering*	Patricia Daniels Cornwell	Harper and Row, Publishers
1986	*Letters of Francis A. Schaeffer*	Ed. Lane T. Dennis	Crossway Books/Good News Publ.
1987	*C. S. Lewis Through the Shadowlands*	Brian Sibley	Fleming H. Revell
1988	*Heir to a Dream*	Pete Maravich	Thomas Nelson, Inc., Publishers
1989	*First Ladies of the Parish*	Ruth A. Tucker	Zondervan Publishing House
1990	*Dr. Dobson: Turning Hearts toward Home*	Rolf Zettersten	Word, Inc.
1991	*Comeback*	Dave Dravecky with Tim Stafford	Zondervan Publishing House

Children's Books
1978	*Jesus, Friend of Children*		David C. Cook Publishing Co.
1979	*Family Bible Encyclopedia*	Berkeley and Alvera Mickelsen	David C. Cook Publishing Co.
1980	*Our Family Got a Divorce*	Carolyn E. Phillips	Gospel Light Publications
1981	*Who, What, When, Where Book about the Bible*	William R. Coleman	David C. Cook Publishing Co.
1982	*Leading Little Ones to God*	Marian M. Schoolland, Illustrated by Paul Stoub	Wm. B. Eerdmans Publishing Co.
1982	*What Happens When We Die?*	Carolyn Nystrom, Illus. by Wayne A. Hanna	Moody Press
1983	*Read-Aloud Bible Stories*	Ella K. Lindvall and Kent Puckett	Moody Press

GOLD MEDALLION BOOK AWARDS cont.

1984	Tales of the Kingdom	David and Karen Mains, Illus-trated by Jack Stockman	David C. Cook Publishing Co.
1985	Marvelous Me	Anne Townsend, Illus-trated by Saroj Vaghela	Lion Publishing Corp.
1986	Potter	Walter Wangerin, Jr.	David C. Cook Publishing Co.
1986	Talking Together about Love and Sexuality	Mildred Tengbom	Bethany House Publishers
1987	The International Children's Bible Handbook	Lawrence Richards	Sweet Publishing Co.
1987	What the Bible Is All About for Young Explorers	Frances Blankenbaker	Regal Bks/Gospel Light Publ.

Christian Education

1982	Answers to the Cultist at Your Door	Robert and Gretchen Passantino and Raymond Schafer	Harvest House Publishers
1983	Early Childhood Kit	Pat Holt and Robyn Vander Weide	Fleming H. Revell
1984	Int'l Children's Vers., NT		Sweet Publishing Co.
1984	Youth Leader's Sourcebook	Ed. Gary Dausey	Zondervan Publishing House
1985	Sing to the Lord	Connie Fortunato	David C. Cook Publishing Co.
1986	Discipling the Young Person	Ed. Paul Fleischmann	Here's Life Publishers
1987	Group Magazine's Best Youth Group Programs, Vol. 1	Cindy S. Hansen	Group Bks/Group Publishing, Inc.
1987	The Big Book of Home Learning	Mary Pride	Crossway Books/Good News Publ.
1988	It Couldn't Just Happen	Lawrence O. Richards	Worthy Publishing
1989	What'cha Gonna Do with What'cha Got: A Study in Christianomics	James W. Jackson	David C. Cook Publishing Co.
1990	Up Close & Personal	Wayne Rice	Zondervan Publishing House
1991	Developing the Teacher in You	Wesley R. Willis	Victor Books

Christian Living

1988	Living above the Level of Mediocrity	Charles R. Swindoll	Word, Inc.
1988	Understanding People	Lawrence J. Crabb, Jr.	Zondervan Publishing House
1989	Inside Out	Larry Crabb	NavPress
1990	The Man in the Mirror	Patrick M. Morley	Wolgemuth & Hyatt, Publishers
1991	A Path Through Suffering	Elisabeth Elliot	Vine Books/Servant Publications

Christian Ministry

1983	Between Two Worlds: The Art of Preaching in the 20th Century	John R. W. Stott	Wm. B. Eerdmans Publishing Co.
1984	Management: A Biblical Approach	Myron Rush	Victor Books/Scripture Press Publ.
1985	Counseling Teenagers	G. Keith Olson	Group Books
1986	Baker Encycl. of Psychology	Ed. David G. Benner	Baker Book House
1987	Christian Countermoves in a Decadent Culture	Carl F. H. Henry	Multnomah Press
1988	Encyclopedia of Biblical and Christian Ethics	Ed. R. K. Harrison	Thomas Nelson, Inc., Publishers
1989	The Youth Builder	Jim Burns	Harvest House Publishers
1990	The Fine Art of Mentoring	Dr. Ted W. Engstrom with Norman B. Rohrer	Wolgemuth & Hyatt, Publishers
1991	Mastering Ministry Series		Co-published by Multnomah Press and Christianity Today

Christianity and Society

1980	Whatever Happened to the Human Race	Francis Schaeffer and C. Everett Koop	Fleming H. Revell
1981	Life Sentence	Charles Colson	Chosen Books
1982	Freedom of Simplicity	Richard J. Foster	Harper & Row, Publishers

1983	*The Mustard Seed Conspiracy*	Tom Sine	Word, Inc.
1984	*Approaching Hoofbeats: The Four Horsemen of the Apocalypse*	Billy Graham	Word, Inc.
1985	*The Least of These*	Curt Young	Moody Press
1986	*Involvement:* Vols. I & II	John R. W. Stott	Fleming H. Revell
1987	*Crime and Its Victims*	Daniel W. Van Ness	InterVarsity Press
1988	*Kingdoms In Conflict*	Charles W. Colson	Zondervan Publishing House
1989	*Grand Illusions*	George Grant	Wolgemuth & Hyatt, Publ., Inc.
1990	*Against the Night*	Charles Colson	Vine Books/Servant Publications
1991	*Love Hunger: Recovery from Food Addiction*	Dr. Frank Minirth, Dr. Paul Meier, Dr. Robert Hemfelt, Dr. Sharon Sneed	Thomas Nelson/Janet Thoma Book

Classics

1983	*Real Christianity*	Ed. William Wilberforce and James Houston	Multnomah Press
1984	*Sermons of Martin Luther*	Martin Luther	Baker Book House
1985	*Religious Affections: How Man's Will Affects His Character before God*	Ed. James M. Houston	Multnomah Press
1986	*The Princess and the Goblin*	George MacDonald; illus. Linda Hill Griffith	David C. Cook Publishing Co.
1987	*Spiritual Awakening*	Ed. Sherwood Eliot Wirt	Crossway Books/Good News Publ.
1987	*The Works of Arminius: The London Edition*	James Arminius	Baker Book House
1988	*Oswald Chambers—The Best from All His Books*	Oswald Chambers; comp. Harry Verploegh	Oliver Nelson Books
1989	*Josephus: The Essential Writings*	Paul L. Maier	Kregel Publications
1990	*Oswald Chambers: The Best from All His Books.* Vol. II	Ed. Harry Verploegh	Oliver Nelson Books
1991	*The Complete Works of E. M. Bounds on Prayer*	E. M. Bounds	Baker Book House

Commentaries

1982	*Romans*	William Hendriksen	Baker Book House
1983	*Commentary on Galatians*	F. F. Bruce	Wm. B. Eerdmans Publishing Co.
1983	*The Expositor's Bible Commentary.* Vol. 12	Ed. Frank E. Gaebelein	Zondervan Publishing House
1984	*Word Biblical Commentary.* Vol. 50, Jude, 2 Peter.	Richard J. Bauckham	Word, Inc.
1985	*The Epistles to the Colossians, to Philemon, and to the Ephesians*	F. F. Bruce	Wm. B. Eerdmans Publishing Co.
1986	*NIV Study Bible*		Zondervan Publishing House
1986	*The Bible Knowledge Commentary OT*	Ed. John F. Walvoord and Roy B. Zuck	Victor Bks/Scripture Press Publ.
1987	*The International Bible Commentary, NIV*	Ed. F. F. Bruce	Marshall Pickering/Zondervan Publ.
1988	*First Epistle to the Corinthians.* New International Commentary on the NT	Gordon D. Fee	Wm. B. Eerdmans Publishing Co.
1989	*The Epistle to the Romans*	Leon Morris	Wm. B. Eerdmans Publishing Co.
1990	*Mark 1*	R. Kent Hughes	Good News Publ./Crossway Books
1990	*Mark 2*	R. Kent Hughes	Good News Publ./Crossway Books
1991	*Expositor's Bible Commentary.* Vol. 2, Genesis, Exodus, Leviticus, Numbers	Ed. Frank E. Gaebelein	Zondervan Publishing House

Devotional

1984	*Loving God*	Charles Colson	Zondervan Publishing House
1985	*In His Image*	Paul Brand and Phillip Yancey	Zondervan Publishing House

GOLD MEDALLION BOOK AWARDS cont.

1986	*Ordering Your Private World*	Gordon MacDonald	Oliver Nelson Books
1987	*A Closer Walk*	Catherine Marshall;	
		ed. Leonard E. LeSourd	Chosen Books/Fleming H. Revell
1988	*With My Whole Heart*	Karen Burton Mains	Multnomah Press
1989	*A Musician Looks at the*		
	Psalms: A Journal of		
	Daily Devotions	Don Wyrtzen	Zondervan Publishing House
1990	*Glorious Intruder*	Joni Eareckson Tada	Multnomah Press
1991	*Incredible Moments with*		
	the Savior	Ken Gire	Zondervan Publishing House

Elementary Children
1988	*Catherine Marshall's*		
	Storybook for Children	Cath. Marshall LeSourd	Chosen Books
1989	*Let's-Talk-about-It-Series*	Lois Johnson	NavPress
1990	*Destination: Moon*	Astronaut James Irwin	Multnomah Press
1991	*Treasure in an Oatmeal Box*	Ken Gire	NavPress

Fiction
1978	*I Came to Love You Late*	Joyce Landorf	Fleming H. Revell
1979	*The Kiowa*	Elgin Groseclose	David C. Cook Publishing Co.
1980	*Caught in the Cross Fire*	Levi Keidel	Herald Press
1981	*Alpha Centuri*	Robert Siegel	Crossway Books/Good News Publ.
1982	*The Iron Sceptre*	John White; illus. Elmar Bell	InterVarsity Press
1983	*Love's Long Journey*	Janette Oke	Bethany House Publishers
1984	*MacIntosh Mountain*	Victor J. Kelly	Zondervan Publishing House
1985	*Johnny Come Home*	R. C. Sproul	Regal Bks/Gospel Light Publ.
1985	*The Water Is Wide*	Elizabeth Gibson	Zondervan Publishing House
1986	*More Than Seven Watchmen*	Helen Norris	Zondervan Publishing House
1987	*The Gates of Zion*	Bodie Thoene	Bethany House Publishers
1988	*Taliesin*	Stephen R. Lawhead	Crossway Books/Good News Publ.
1989	*The Key to Zion*	Bodie Thoene	Bethany House Publishers
1990	*Piercing the Darkness*	Frank E. Peretti	Good News Publ./Crossway Books
1991	*Munich Signature*	Bodie Thoene	Bethany House Publishers

Gift Books/Poetry
1982	*Surprised by Light*	Ulrich Schaffer	Harper & Row, Publishers
1983	*Eerdmans' Book of Christian*		
	Poetry	Pat Alexander, editor	Wm. B. Eerdmans Publishing Co.
1984	*A Prophetical Walk Through*		
	the Holy Land	Hal Lindsey	Harvest House Publishers
1985	*The Miracles of Our Lord*	Charles Caldwell Ryrie	Thomas Nelson, Inc., Publishers
1986	*Come Before Winter . . . and*		
	Share My Hope	Charles R. Swindoll	Multnomah Press
1987	*Doorposts*	Timothy R. Botts	Tyndale House Publishers
1988	*Love for a Lifetime*	James C. Dobson	Multnomah Press
1988	*Psalms of My Life*	Joseph Bayly	David C. Cook Publishing Co.
1989	*The American Character*	Norman Vincent Peale	Fleming H. Revell
1990	*Windsongs*	Timothy R. Botts	Tyndale House Publishers
1991	*The Gospel of Mark Illuminated*	Patrick Vaughan and	
		Rex Nicholls	Lion Publishing Corporation

Inspirational
1978	*Where Is God When It Hurts*	Philip Yancy	Zondervan Publishing House
1979	*A Step Further*	Joni Eareckson	Zondervan Publishing House
1980	*Love Has a Price Tag*	Elisabeth Elliot	Servant Publications
1981	*Fearfully and Wonderfully Made*	Paul Brand and	
		Philip Yancey	Zondervan Publishing House
1982	*Gaining Through Losing*	Evelyn Christenson	Victor Books/Scripture Press Publ.
1983	*Giant Steps*	Ed. Warren W. Wiersbe	Baker Book House
1983	*Strengthening Your Grip*	Charles Swindoll	Word, Inc.
1988	*The Quest for Character*	Charles R. Swindoll	Multnomah Press
1989	*Disappointment with God*	Philip Yancey	Zondervan Publishing House

| 1990 | Six Hours One Friday | Max Lucado | Multnomah Press |
| 1991 | Honest to God? | Bill Hybels | Zondervan Publishing House |

Marriage and Family

1982	How to Really Love Your Teenager	Ross Campbell	Victor Books/Scripture Press Publ.
1983	Seasons of a Marriage	H. Norman Wright	Regal Bks/Gospel Light Publ.
1984	Love Must Be Tough	James C. Dobson	Word, Inc.
1985	Parents and Teenagers	Ed. Jay Kesler	Victor Books/Scripture Press Publ.
1986	The Mystery of Marriage	Mike Mason	Multnomah Press
1987	The Blessing	Gary Smalley and John Trent	Thomas Nelson, Inc., Publishers
1988	As for Me and My House	Walter Wangerin, Jr.	Thomas Nelson, Inc., Publishers
1989	Growing Wise in Family Life	Charles R. Swindoll	Multnomah Press
1990	Lonely Husbands/ Lonely Wives	Dennis Rainey	Word, Inc.
1991	Two Sides of Love	Gary Smalley and John Trent	Focus on the Family

Missions/Evangelism

1982	World of Difference	Thom Hopler	InterVarsity Press
1983	Eerdmans' Handbook to the World's Religions	Ed. R. Pierce Beaver	Wm. B. Eerdmans Publishing Co.
1984	From Jerusalem to Irian Jaya	Ruth A. Tucker	Zondervan Publishing House
1985	Eternal Word and Changing Worlds	Harvie M. Conn	Zondervan Publishing House
1986	Beyond Hunger: A Biblical Mandate for Social Responsibility	Art Beals with Larry Libby	Multnomah Press
1986	The Church in China	Carl Lawrence	Bethany House Publishers
1987	Wanted: World Christians	J. Herbert Kane	Baker Book House
1988	Witnessing without Fear	Bill Bright	Here's Life Publishers
1989	Youth Evangelism	David Veerman	Victor Books/Scripture Press Publ.
1990	Disarming the Secular Gods	Peter C. Moore	InterVarsity Press
1991	A Ready Defense	Josh McDowell	Here's Life Publishers

Personal/Group Bible Study

1989	Living Beyond the Daily Grind	Charles R. Swindoll	Word, Inc.
1990	Life Application Bible Study Guide: Romans		Tyndale House Publishers
1991	Lord, I Need Grace to Make It	Kay Arthur	Multnomah Press

Preschool Children

1988	What Does God Do?	Illus. Hans Wilhelm	Worthy Publishing
1989	Katie's Adventure at Blueberry Pond	Josh and Dottie McDowell	David C. Cook Publishing Co.
1990	Do You See Me, God?	Elspeth Campbell Murphy	David C. Cook Publishing Co.
1991	The Kidderminster Kingdom Series—King Leonard's Celebration	Christopher Lane	Victor Books

Reference/Text

1982	New American Standard Exhaustive Concordance of the Bible	Ed. Robert L. Thomas	Holman Bible Publishers
1983	General Revelation	Bruce Demarest	Zondervan Publishing House
1983	International Standard Bible Encyclopedia. Vol. 2	Ed. Geoffrey W. Bromiley	Wm. B. Eerdmans Publishing Co.
1983	Old Testament Survey	William S. LaSor, David Allan Hubbard, Frederic W. Bush	Wm. B. Eerdmans Publishing Co.
1984	Eerdmans' Handbook to Christianity in America	Mark Noll, Nathan Hatch, George Marsden, David Wells, John Woodbridge	Wm. B. Eerdmans Publishing Co.
1985	Evangelical Dict. of Theology	Ed. Walter A. Elwell	Baker Book House
1986	Theological Dict. of the NT. Abridged in 1 Vol.	Geoffrey W. Bromiley	Wm. B. Eerdmans Publishing Co.

GOLD MEDALLION BOOK AWARDS cont.

1987	*The International Standard Bible Encyclopedia.* Vol. 3	Ed. Geoffrey W. Bromiley	Wm. B. Eerdmans Publishing Co.
1988	*Eerdmans' Bible Dict.*	Allen C. Myers	Wm. B. Eerdmans Publishing Co.
1989	*Great Leaders of the Christian Church*	Ed. John D. Woodbridge	Moody Press
1990	*The Zondervan NIV Atlas of the Bible*	Carl Rasmussen	Zondervan Publishing House
1991	*The NIV Exhaustive Concordance*	John R. Kohlenberger III and Edward W. Goodrick	Zondervan Publishing House

Special Judge's Award

1983	*The Complete Works of Francis A. Schaeffer*	Francis A. Schaeffer	Crossway Books/Good News Publ.

Theology/Doctrine

1978	*Eerdmans' Handbook to the History of Christianity*	Ed. Tim Dowley	Wm. B. Eerdmans Publishing Co.
1979	*Affliction*	Edith Schaeffer	Fleming H. Revell
1980	*International Standard Bible Encyclopedia.* Vol. I	Ed. Geoffrey Bromiley	Wm. B. Eerdmans Publishing Co.
1981	*The Bible Almanac*	J. I. Packer, Merrill C. Tenney, William White, Jr.	Thomas Nelson, Inc., Publishers
1982	*Testaments of Love*	Leon Morris	Wm. B. Eerdmans Publishing Co.
1983	*The Case for Christianity*	Colin Chapman	Wm. B. Eerdmans Publishing Co.
1984	*God, Revelation, and Authority.* Vol. VI	Carl F. H. Henry	Word, Inc.
1985	*Miracles and the Critical Mind*	Colin Brown	Wm. B. Eerdmans Publishing Co.
1986	*Christian Theology.* 3 Vols.	Millard J. Erickson	Baker Book House
1987	*Betrayal of the Church: Apostasy and Renewal in the Mainline Denom.*	Edmund W. Robb and Julia Robb	Crossway Books/Good News Publ.
1988	*The Cross of Christ*	John R. W. Stott	InterVarsity Press
1989	*The Canon of Scripture*	F. F. Bruce	InterVarsity Press
1990	*So Great Salvation*	Charles C. Ryrie	Victor Books/Scripture Press
1991	*The Grace Awakening*	Charles R. Swindoll	Word, Inc.

Youth

1983	*How to Be Your Own Selfish Pig*	Susan Schaeffer Macauley	David C. Cook Publishing Co.
1984	*Putting God First*	Jim Burns; illus. David Bundschuh	Harvest House Publishers
1984	*The Christian Kids Almanac*	Robert G. Flood; illus. Britt Taylor Collins	David C. Cook Publishing Co.
1984	*Why Isn't God Giving Cash Prizes?*	Lorraine Peterson	Bethany House Publishers
1985	*You Can Make a Difference*	Tony Campolo	Word, Inc.
1986	*Judge for Yourself*	Steve and Alice Lawhead	Victor Books/Scripture Press Publ.
1987	*Handling Your Hormones*	Jim Burns	Harvest House Publishers
1987	*The Student Bible,* NIV	Notes by Philip Yancey and Tim Stafford	Zondervan Publishing House
1988	*Am I the Only One Here with Faded Genes?*	Marie Chapian	Bethany House Publishers
1989	*Lifelines:* Getting a Hold on Life Series	Fran and Jill Sciacca	World Wide Publications
1990	*Lifelines Introductory Series* (Booklets 1-4)	Fran & Jill Sciacca	World Wide Publications
1991	*I Don't Remember Dropping the Skunk, But I Do Remember Trying to Breathe*	Ken Davis	Zondervan Publishing House

GOLD/PLATINUM BOOK AWARDS

The Evangelical Christian Publishers Association presents gold book awards when titles reach 500,000 copies sold and platinum book awards when titles reach sales of one million copies or more. At least 50 percent of sales totals for qualifying books must have occurred through normal trade distribution channels.

Publisher	Title	Author	No. Sold	Award
Barbour	The Bible Promise Book	n.a.	1,305,032	Platinum
	My Utmost for His Highest	Oswald Chambers	1,088,628	Platinum
Bethany	The Christian Family	Larry Christenson	1,382,137	Platinum
	Free to Be Thin	Neva Coyle & Marie Chapian	1,004,988	Platinum
	Love Comes Softly	Janette Oke	829,100	Gold
	Love's Enduring Promise	Janette Oke	663,800	Gold
	When Calls the Heart	Janette Oke	564,100	Gold
	Love's Long Journey	Janette Oke	557,700	Gold
	If God Loves Me, Why Can't I Get My Locker Open?	Lorraine Peterson	553,100	Gold
	The Kingdom of the Cults	Walter Martin	522,300	Gold
	Once upon a Summer	Janette Oke	517,700	Gold
	Love's Abiding Joy	Janette Oke	500,028	Gold
Christian Heritage	Precious Promise New Testament	Betty Hopper & Ross Stover Rhoads (study helps)	1,350,000	Platinum
David C. Cook Pub. Co. Chariot Family Products Division	The Picture Bible		1,102,200	Platinum
Crossway Books	This Present Darkness	Frank Peretti	1,345,754	Platinum
	Piercing the Darkness	Frank Peretti	1,048,356	Platinum
Gibson	Apples of Gold	Jo Petty	3,361,702	Platinum
	Wings of Silver	Jo Petty	1,673,337	Platinum
	The Greatest of These Is Love	Audrey McDaniel	822,765	Gold
Harvest House	There's a New World Coming	Hal Lindsey	1,000,000	Platinum
	Redi-Reference	Bob Phillips	797,144	Gold
	The Spirit-Controlled Woman	Beverly LaHaye	596,164	Gold
	The Seduction of Christianity	Dave Hunt	582,059	Gold
	Christian Charm Course Student Book	Emily & Wayne Hunger	512,774	Gold
Here's Life	Evidence That Demands a Verdict, Vol. 1	Josh McDowell	1,016,825	Platinum
InterVarsity	Quiet Time	n.a.	1,000,000	Platinum
	Knowing God	J. I. Packer	700,000	Gold
Loizeaux	Rightly Dividing the Word of Truth	C. I. Scofield	789,505	Gold
Moody	The Bible in Pictures for Little Eyes	Kenneth Taylor	1,369,592	Platinum
	Now That I Believe	Robert Cook	1,000,075	Platinum
	Unger's Bible Dictionary	Merrill Unger	600,000	Gold
	Unger's Bible Handbook	Merrill Unger	596,500	Gold
	The Abundant Life	Ray Baughman	538,291	Gold
Multnomah	Faith Is . . .	Pamela Reeve	1,038,708	Platinum
	Growing Strong in the Seasons of Life	Charles Swindoll	1,023,436	Platinum
	For Those Who Hurt	Charles Swindoll	699,240	Gold
	Strike the Original Match	Charles Swindoll	546,709	Gold
	Love for a Lifetime	James Dobson	512,680	Gold
Navpress	Lessons on Assurance	Navigator Staff	1,135,655	Platinum
	Pursuit of Holiness	Jerry Bridges	885,500	Gold
	Lessons on Christian Living	Navigator Staff	524,839	Gold
Questar Publishers	The Beginner's Bible	Karyn Henley	650,000	Gold
Regal Books	What the Bible Is All About	Henrietta Mears	3,163,593	Platinum
	Preparing for Adolescence	James Dobson	1,190,000	Platinum
Tyndale	Dare to Discipline	James Dobson	2,428,885	Platinum
	More Than a Carpenter	Josh McDowell	1,704,093	Platinum
	What Wives Wish Their Husbands Knew about Women	James Dobson	1,697,520	Platinum

	Hinds' Feet on High Places	Hannah Hurnard	1,531,400	Platinum
	The Strong Willed Child	James Dobson	1,289,856	Platinum
	How to Be Happy Though Married	Tim LaHaye	842,833	Gold
	Life Is Tremendous	Charlie Jones	651,978	Gold
	The Search for the Twelve Apostles	William Steuart McBirnie	555,041	Gold
	In Touch	Edythe Draper	538,207	Gold
Upper Room	Pocket Prayer Book	Ralph Cushman, compiler	2,000,000+	Platinum
Victor Books	What Happens When Women Pray	Evelyn Christenson	1,600,201	Platinum
	"Lord, Change Me!"	Evelyn Christenson	953,300	Gold
	You Can Be the Wife of a Happy Husband	Darien Cooper	829,827	Gold
	Healing for Damaged Emotions	David Seamands	712,686	Gold
	How to Really Love Your Child	Ross Campbell	506,914	Gold
Warner	Egermeier's Bible Story Book	Elsie Egermeier	1,635,471	Platinum
Word	Peace with God	Billy Graham	2,379,250	Platinum
	Angels	Billy Graham	2,202,050	Platinum
	Be Happy Attitudes	Robert H. Schuller	1,605,475	Platinum
	My Answer	Billy Graham	1,560,102	Platinum
	The Secret of Happiness	Billy Graham	1,551,475	Platinum
	How to Be Born Again	Billy Graham	1,404,000	Platinum
	Til Armageddon	Billy Graham	1,134,976	Platinum
	World Aflame	Billy Graham	1,085,000	Platinum
	Straight Talk to Men and Their Wives	James Dobson	1,074,130	Platinum
	Love Must Be Tough	James Dobson	1,050,746	Platinum
	Approaching Hoofbeats	Billy Graham	1,023,823	Platinum
	The Holy Spirit	Billy Graham	945,348	Gold
	Living on the Ragged Edge	Charles R. Swindoll	610,813	Gold
	Improving Your Serve	Charles R. Swindoll	587,516	Gold
	Self-Esteem	Robert H. Schuller	580,949	Gold
	Parenting Isn't for Cowards	Dr. James C. Dobson	580,415	Gold
	Dropping Your Guard	Charles R. Swindoll	546,380	Gold
Zondervan	Armageddon, Oil and the Middle East Crisis	John Walvoord	1,676,886	Platinum

READERS' CHOICE AWARDS

Selected by readers of *Christianity Today* magazine.

Book of the Year
1990   *Disappointment with God* by Philip Yancey, Zondervan Publishing House
1991   *Dictionary of Christianity in America* edited by Daniel Reid, Robert Linder, Bruce Shelley
                and Harry Stout, InterVarsity Press

Biography and History
1990   *Dr. Dobson* by Rolf Zettersten, Word, Inc.
                Great Leaders of the Christian Church edited by John Woodbridge, Moody Press
1991   *Comeback* by Dave Dravecky with Tim Stafford, Zondervan Publishing House

Christian Living and Spirituality
1990   *Disappointment with God* by Philip Yancey, Zondervan Publishing House
1991   *The Grace Awakening* by Charles Swindoll, Word Publishing

Commentaries
1990   *Hard Sayings of the Old Testament* by Walter Kaiser, InterVarsity Press
1991   *The Spirit, the Church and the World: The Message of Acts* by John Stott, InterVarsity Press

Contemporary Issues
1990   *Against the Night* by Charles Colson, Servant Publications
1991   *The Agony of Deceit* edited by Michael Horton, Moody Press
                The Frog in the Kettle by George Barna, Regal Books/Gospel Light Publications
                The God of Stones and Spiders by Charles Colson, Crossway Books

Fiction
1990   *Piercing the Darkness* by Frank Peretti, Crossway
1991   *A Symphony in Sand* by Calvin Miller, Word Publishing

Reference
1990   *Baker Encyclopedia of the Bible* edited by Walter Elwell, Baker Book House
1991   *Dictionary of Christianity in America* edited by Daniel Reid, Robert Linder, Bruce Shelley
              and Harry Stout, InterVarsity Press

Theology and Biblical Studies
1990   *The Gospel According to Jesus* by John F. MacArthur, Jr., Zondervan Publishing House
1991   *Rich Christians in an Age of Hunger,* Third Edition By Ronald Sider, Word Publishing

TODAY'S CHRISTIAN WOMAN BEST BOOKS AWARDS

Marriage
1990   *Opposites Attack* by Jack and Carole Mayhall, NavPress
              21 Myths That Can Wreck Your Marriage by Barbara Russell Chesser, Word Publishing

Parenting
1990   *The Focus on the Family Guide to Growing a Healthy Home* edited by Mike Yorkey,
              Wolgemuth & Hyatt, Publishers
              What Did I Do Wrong? What Can I Do Now? by William and Candace Backus,
              Bethany House Publishers

Self Help
1990   *Adult Children of Legal or Emotional Divorce* by Jim Conway, InterVarsity Press
              The Curious Waltz of the Working Woman by Karen Scalf Linamen and Linda Holland,
              Regal Books/Gospel Light

Spiritual Life
1990   *Friends and Strangers* by Karen Burton Mains, Word Publishing
              Secret Passions of the Christian Woman by Carol Kent, NavPress

Devotional
1990   *A Christmas Longing* by Joni Eareckson Tada, Multnomah Press
              Secrets from Ordinary Places by Ruth Senter, Zondervan Publishing House

CHRISTIAN BOOKSELLER ASSOCIATION AWARDS

CBA awards are selected annually by the voting members of the Christian Bookseller Association

Supplier of the Year
1976   Fleming H. Revell
1977   Fleming H. Revell
1978   Zondervan Publishing
1979   Fleming H. Revell
1980   Word, Inc.
1981   Word, Inc.
1982   Thomas Nelson Publishers
1983   Thomas Nelson Publishers
1984   Thomas Nelson Publishers
1985   Word, Inc.
1986   Thomas Nelson Publishers
1987   Word, Inc.
1988   Word, Inc.
1989   Spring Arbor, Inc.
1990   The Zondervan Corporation
1991   Thomas Nelson Publishers

Store of the Year
1980   Foothills Bible Book Store, La Mesa, CA
1981   Dightman's Bible Book Ctr, Tacoma, WA
1982   The Better Book Room, Wichita, KS
1983   Berean Christian Stores, Canton, OH
1984   The Christian Armory, Columbus, OH
1985   Better Books Christian Center, Tyler, TX

1986   Fresno Bible House, Fresno, CA
1987   Bender's Christn Sup., Williamsville, NY
1988   Christian Armory, Tucker, GA
1989   Berean Christian Bkstore, Phoenix, AZ
1990   The Shepherd's Shoppe, San Antonio, TX
1991   The Christian Book and Gift Shoppe, Olathe, KS

Sales Representative of the Year
1967   Bill Zondervan, Zondervan Publishing
1968   Sid Zullinger, Moody Press
1969   William Reynolds, Harper & Row
1970   Paul Van Duinen, Zondervan Publ.
1971   Jim Pletcher, Warner Press
1971   Lloyd Van Horn, Zondervan Publishing
1973   Gene Uber, Concordia
1974   Ernie Owen, Fleming H. Revell
1975   Lloyd Eshbach, Moody Press
1976   Milton Steinford, Harper & Row
1977   Bob Lossa, Fleming H. Revell
1978   Clarence Hageman, Thom. Nelson Publ.
1979   Lane Hostetter, Standard Publishing
1980   Dan Fetters, Warner Press
1981   Denny Bray
1982   Pat Burtch, Warner Press
1983   Jack Doyle, Dickson's

1984 Gordon Mohr, Thomas Nelson Publ.
1985 Judith White, Zondervan Publishing
1986 Vance Hooper, Thomas Nelson Publ.
1987 John Stoesz, Warner Press
1988 Wayne Adams, Word, Inc.
1989 David Lewis, Zondervan Publishing
1990 Mark Funderburg, Sparrow-Star Song
1991 No award given

Editor's Choice Award
1988 Moody Press
1989 Standard Publishing
1990 Word, Inc.
1991 Word/Bibles

Key Person Award
The Key Person Award is CBA's most presti-

gious individual recognition. This award is given to an individual whose unique contribution is so outstanding it is not feasible or likely to be duplicated by someone else.
1981 Paul Benson and Pat Zondervan
1985 Don Baughman and Paul Curry
1989 Peter Gunther and Lloyde Johnson
1990 No award given
1991 Sid Zullinger and Bill Reynolds

Hall of Honor
The Hall of Honor is an industry-wide honor, and recognizes exceptional service to the Christian bookselling/literature industry.
1986 John and Betty Bass
1989 Dr. Kenneth Taylor

CHRISTIAN MAGAZINE PUBLISHERS

Periodical, Address Category	Format	Circulation	Cost
Action magazine, PO Bx A, Greenwood, IN 46142	Missions	Quarterly	8500	Free
Actionline, PO Bx 203, Prospect Heights, IL 60070	Missions	Newsltr/6/yr	N/A	Free
AD 2000 & Beyond, 850 Wycliffe Dr., Colorado Springs, CO 80906	Missions	4/yr		Free
AFA Journal, PO Drawer 2440, Tupelo, MS 38803	Decency		375,000	15.00/yr
Again magazine, PO Bx 106, Mt. Herman, CA 95041	Christian Living	N/A	2,500	10.00/yr
Around the World, PO Bx 553000, Miami, FL 33055	Missions	Quarterly	48,000	Free
Asbury Herald, The, 204 N. Lexington Ave., Wilmore, KY 40390	Christian Living	Quarterly	33,000	Free
Asian Report, PO Bx 9000, Mission Viejo, CA 92690	Missions			
Back to the Bible Today, Bx 82808, Lincoln, NE 68501	Christian Living	N/A	N/A	Free
Bethany Choice, The, 901 Eastern, NE, Grand Rapids, MI 49508	Pro-Life	3/yr	7,200	Free
Beyond, PO Bx 248, Waxhaw, NC 28173	Missions	6/yr	20,000	Free
Bible Review, 3000 Connecticut Ave., NW, Suite 300, Washington, DC 20008	Bible	Bimonthly	40,000	14.95/yr
Bibles for the World News, Bx 805, Wheaton, IL 60189	Missions	Quarterly	35,000	Free
Biblical Archaeology Review, 3000 Connecticut Ave., NW, Suite 300, Washington, DC 20008	Archaeology	Bimonthly	115,000	19.95/yr
Bookstore Journal, 2620 Venetucci Blvd., Colorado Springs, CO 80906	Trade/Bookstore	12/yr	7087	43.00/yr
Bread magazine, 6401 The Paseo, Kansas City, MO 64131	Youth	12/yr	27,000	7.50/yr
Breakthrough, PO Bx 1122, Wheaton, IL, 60189	Missions	6/yr	65,000	Donation
Bridgebuilder magazine, 610 Rhode Island Ave., NE, Washington, DC 20002	Racial Unity	6/yr	5,000	12.97/yr
Businessgram, 14305 N. Dale Mabry, PO Bx 273390, Tampa, FL 33618	Trade/Career	Nwsltr/11/yr	500	25.00 Sugg. don.
Call to Prayer, PO Bx WGM, Marion, IN 46952	Missions	6/yr	30,000	Donation
Campus Life magazine, 465 Gundersen Dr., Carol Stream, IL 60188	Youth	10/yr	160,000	14.95/yr
CBMC Contact, PO Bx 3308, Chattanooga, TN 37404	Trade/Career	6/yr	14,000	12.95/yr
Central Texas Messenger, The, PO Bx 309, Del Valle, TX 78617		12/yr	5,000	8.00/yr
Charisma & Christian Life mag., 600 Rinehart Rd., Lake Mary, FL 32746	Christian Living	12/yr	200,000	19.95/yr
Childlife magazine, 919 W. Huntington Dr., Monrovia, CA 91016	Missions	Quarterly	550,000	Donation
Chosen People, The, 1300 Cross Beam Dr., Charlotte, NC 28217	Missions	11/yr	65,000	5.00/yr
Christ for the Nations, PO Bx 769000, Dallas, TX 75376	Evangelism	12/yr	35,000	Free
Christian Activities Calendar, PO Bx 730, Ojai, CA 93023	Singles	Mag./6/yr		14.95/2 yrs.

Periodical, Address	Category	Format	Circulation	Cost
Christian Century, The, 407 S. Dearborn St., Chicago, IL 60605	Christn Thought	Weekly	35,000	28.00/yr
Christian Communicator, The, 26131 Av. Aeropuerto, San Juan Capistrano, CA 92675	Communictns	12/yr	N/A	14.97/yr
Christian Conjurer, 1705 Barbara Ln, Connersville, IN 47331	Digest	6/year		12.00 membshp
Christian Ed. Journal, PO Bx 650, Glen Ellyn, IL 60138	Christian Ed.	Journal/3/yr	2,700	9.00/yr
Christian Ed. Today, PO Bx 15337, Denver, CO 80215	Christian Ed.	Quarterly	9,000	3.00/copy
Christian Educators Journal, Dordt College English Dept., Sioux Center, IA 51250	Christian Ed.	Quarterly	4,000	7.50/yr
Christian Herald, 40 Overlook Dr., Chappaqua, NY 10514	Christian Living	11/yr	150,000	15.97/yr
Christian History magazine, 465 Gundersen Dr., Carol Stream, IL 60188	Educational	Quarterly	15,000	16.00/yr
Christian Home and School, 3350 East Paris Ave., SE, Grand Rapids, MI 49508	Parents	8/yr	9,500	10.95/yr
Christian Leadership Letter, 919 W. Huntington Dr., Monrovia, CA 91016	Leadership	Newsltr		Free
Christian Librarian, The, PO Bx 4, Cedarville, OH 45314	Trade/Career	Quarterly	400	16.00/yr
Christian Living for Senior Highs, 850 N. Grove Ave., Elgin, IL 60120	Youth	Quarterly	N/A	7.25/yr
Christian Management Report, PO Bx 4638, Diamond Bar, CA 91765	Trade/Career	6/yr	6,500	Free to mem.; 50.00/yr non-mem.
Christian Medical & Dental Society Journal, PO Bx 830689, Richardson, TX 75083	Trade/Career	Quarterly	8,300	16.00/yr
Christian Ministry, The, 407 S. Dearborn St., Chicago, IL 60605	Ministry	Bimonthly	9500	10.00/yr
Christian Mission, PO Bx 4488, Charlottesville, VA 22901	Missions	6/yr	24,000	Donation
Christian Newspaper, The, 2820 Linkhorne Dr., Ste. 231, Lynchburg, VA 24503	News	12/yr	20,000	Free
Christian Outdoorsman, The, PO Bx 18489, Fort Worth, TX 76118-9983	Recreation	6/yr	4,500	25.00/yr
Christian Parenting, PO Bx 3850, Sisters, OR 97759	Parents	6/yr	130,000	14.97/yr
Christian Psychology for Today, 2100 N. Collins Blvd., Richardson, TX 75080	Christian Living	Quarterly	7,477	10.00/yr
Christian Reader, The, 465 Gundersen Dr., Carol Stream, IL 60188	Christian Living	Digest/6/yr	188,000	12.00/yr
Christian Research Journal, PO Bx 500, San Juan Capistrano, CA 92693	Christn Thought	Triannual	7,000	2.50/yr
Christian Retailing, 190 N. Westmonte Dr., Altamonte Springs, FL 32714	Trade/Bookstore	12/yr	9700	18.00/yr
Christian School, 1308 Santa Rosa, Wheaton, IL 60187	Trade/Career	5/yr	3,000	10.00/yr
Christian Single, 127 Ninth Ave. N., Nashville, TN 37234	Singles	12/yr		
Christn Standard, 8121 Hamilton Ave., Cincinnati, OH 45231	Christian Living	Weekly	70,000	15.75/yr
Christian Writers Newsltr, PO Bx 8220, Knoxville, TN 37996	Communicatns	Newsltr/6/yr	400	10.00/yr
Christianity Today, 465 Gundersen Dr., Carol Stream, IL 60188	Christn Thought	18/yr	170,000	24.95/yr
Church and Society, 100 Witherspoon St., Louisville, KY 40202	Soc Respnsblty	Bimonthly	2350	7.50/yr
Church Herald, The, 6157 28th St., SE, Grand Rapids, MI 49506	Christian Living	12/yr	48,000	11.25/yr
Citizen magazine, PO Bx 35500, Colorado Springs, CO 80935-3550	Soc Respnsblty	12/yr	274,000	Donation: 15.00
Closer Walk, PO Bx 80587, Atlanta, GA 30366	Devotional	Digest/12/yr	16,987	17.00/yr
CLS Quarterly, PO Bx 1492, Merrifield, VA 22193	Trade/Career	4/yr	6,000	20.00/yr
Command Magazine, PO Bx 1177, Englewood, CO 80150	Trade/Career	Quarterly	6,500	12.00/yr
Commission, The, PO Bx 6767, Richmond, VA 23230	Missions			
Compassion Update, PO Bx 7000, Colorado Springs, CO 80933	Missions	6/yr	100,000	Free
Confident Living, PO Bx 82808, Lincoln, NE 68501	Christian Living	11/yr	93,000	10.95/yr
Connexions, 101 W. Ridgely Rd., Ste. 5-A, Lutherville, MD 21093	Christian Living	6/yr	3,300	Free

Periodical, Address Category		Format	Circulation	Cost
Contemporary Christian Music, 25231 Paseo De Alicia, Ste. 201, Laguna Hills, CA 92653	Youth	12/yr	40,000	18.00/yr
Cornerstone magazine, 4747 N. Maiden, Chicago, IL 60640	Youth	6/yr	75,000	6.95/yr
Crusader, PO Bx 7259, Grand Rapids, MI 49510	Youth	7/yr	12,000	6.25/yr
Crux, 2130 Wesbrook Mall, Vancouver, B.C., V6T 1W6	Christn Thought	Quarterly	700	10.00/yr
Daily Walk, PO Bx 80587, Atlanta, GA 30366	Devotional	12/yr	34,560	17.00/yr
Decision, 1300 Harmon Place, Minneapolis, MN 55403	Christian Living	11/yr	1,750,000	5.00/yr
Discipleship Journal, PO Bx 6000, Colorado Springs, CO 80934	Christian Living	6/yr	88,000	14.97/yr
Discipleship magazine, One Merrill St., Woburn, MA 01801-4629	Christian Living	4/yr	18,000	$15.00/yr
Discovery Digest, PO Bx 22, Grand Rapids, MI 49555	Christian Living	Quarterly	400,000	Free
Door of Hope, PO Bx 303, Glendale, CA 91209	Missions	Quarterly	12,000	Free
Door, The, 1224 Greenfield Dr., El Cajon, CA 92021	Christian Living	6/yr	15,000	18.00/yr
Doorways, PO Bx C, Colorado Springs, CO 80901	Missions	4/yr	N/A	Free
Dreams and Visions, R.R. 1, Washago, ON, L0K-2B0	Fiction Writing			
East Asia's Millions, 10 W. Dry Creek Circle, Littleton, CO 80120-4427	Missions			
11 Chronicles magazine, PO Bx 42, Medford, OR 97501		Semimonthly	5,000	10.00/2 yrs
Enterprise, The, 7185 Millcreek Dr., Mississauga, ON L5N 5R4	Missions			
Equipping the Saints, PO Bx 65004, Anaheim, CA 92815	Christian Living	Quarterly	100,000	Free
Europe Report, The, PO Bx 668, Wheaton, IL 60187	Missions	Tabloid/4/yr	35,000	Free
Eurovision Advance, PO Bx 1136, Claremont, CA 91711	Missions	Newsltr/4/yr	7,000	1.00/yr
Evangelical Beacon, The, 1515 E. 66th St., Minneapolis, MN 55423	Missions	17/yr	39,000	12.00/yr
Evang. Missions Quarterly, PO Bx 794, Wheaton, IL 60189	Missions	Bulletin/4/yr	9,500	14.95/yr
Evangelical World, PO Bx WEF, Wheaton, IL 60189	Missions	Newsltr/12/yr		Free
Evangelism, 12800 N. Lake Shore Dr., Mequon, WI 53092	Evangelism	Quarterly	2,000	10.00/yr
Family Walk, PO Bx 80587, Atlanta, GA 30366	Devotional	12/yr	18,933	17.00/yr
FEBC News, PO Bx 1, La Mirada, CA 90637	Missions	Quarterly	35,000	Free
Feed the Children, Bx 36, Oklahoma City, OK 73101	Missions	6/yr	115,000	Free
Focus on the Family, PO Bx 35500, Colorado Springs, CO 80935-3550	Family	12/yr	1,800,000	Free
Food for the Hungry, 7729 E. Greenway Rd., Scottsdale, AZ 85260	Missions	Newsltr/12/yr	40,000	Free
Footprints, PO Bx 700, San Diego, CA 92138	Evangelism	12/yr	100,000	Free
For Dads Only, PO Bx 340, Julian, CA 92036	Parenting	Newsltr/12/yr		24.00/yr
Forum, PO Bx 370, Elkhart, IN 46515	Singles	12/yr		
Fulness Magazine, PO Bx 79350, Fort Worth, TX 76179	Leadership	6/yr	15,000	14.95/yr
Global Prayer Digest, 1605 Elizabeth St., Pasadena, CA 91104	Missions	12/yr		8.00/yr
God's World Publicatns, PO Bx 2330, Asheville, NC 28802	College	30/yr	202,000	9.50/yr
Guideposts, Seminary Hill Rd., Carmel, NY 10512	General	12/yr	4,239,396	8.95/yr
Helping Hand, The, PO Bx 12609, Oklahoma City, OK 73157	Women	6/yr	3,000	3.00/yr
High Adventure, 1445 Boonville Ave., Springfield, MO 65802	Youth Boys	Quarterly	86,000	1.75/yr
Horizon International World Reporter, 17041 Ruffner St., San Diego, CA 92111	Missions	Quarterly	6,000	Free
Horizons, PO Bx 969, Wheaton, IL 60189	Missions	6/yr	48,957	2.00/yr
Ideals, Nelson Place at Elm Hill Pike, PO Box 148000, Nashville, TN	General	8/yr	240,0000	17.95/yr
Image mag., 115 Warren Dr., Ste. D, W. Monroe, LA 71291	Christian Living	12/yr	8,000	15.00/yr
Image: A Journal of the Arts and Religion, 526 Ziela Ave., Front Royal, VA 22630				
In Other Words, PO Bx 2727, Huntington Beach, CA 92647	Missions	8/yr	220,000	Free
Increase Magazine, PO Bx 410, Hatfield, PA 19440	Missions	Quarterly	16,000	Free
Indian Life, PO Bx 3765 Station B, Winnipeg, MB, R2W 3R6	Missions	6/yr	65,000	5.00/yr
Internatl Bulletin of Missionary Research, PO Box 821, Farmingdale, NY 11737-9721	Missions	4/yr	7,000	18.00/yr
International Journal of Frontier Missions, 1539 E. Howard St., Pasadena, CA 91104	Missions	Quarterly	1,000	15.00/yr
Intervarsity magazine, PO Bx 7895, Madison, WI 53707	College Evanglsm	Quarterly	95,000	Free

Periodical, Address	Category	Format	Circulation	Cost
Journal of Christian Nursing, PO Bx 1650, Downers Grove, IL 60515	Trade/Career	Quarterly	12,000	14.95/yr
Journal of Christn Camping, PO Bx 646, Wheaton, IL 60189	Trade/Career	6/yr	6,000	19.95/yr
Journal of Pastoral Care, The, 1549 Clairmont Rd., Suite 103, Decatur, GA 30033	Pastoral	Quarterly	13,668	20.00/yr
Joyful Woman, The, 118 Shannon Lake Circle, Greenville, SC 29615	Women	6/yr	11,262	13.95/yr
Jubilee, PO Bx 17500, Washington, DC 20041	Christian Living, News	Newsltr/12/yr	175,000	Free
Jubilee International, PO Bx 17434, Washington, DC 20041	Evangelism	Quarterly	5,500	Free
Junior High Ministry magazine, 2890 N. Monroe, PO Box 481, Loveland, CO 80539		5/yr	32,001	19.50/yr
Just Between Us, 1529 Cesery Blvd., Jacksonville, FL 32211		Bimonthly	6,500	14.95/yr
Kids!, 820 N. LaSalle, Chicago, IL 60610	Youth	9/yr	43,000	19.95/yr
Kindred Spirit, 3909 Swiss Ave., Dallas, TX 75204	Christn Thought	Quarterly	200,000	Free
Latin Am. Evangelist, PO Bx 52-7900, Miami, FL 33152	Missions	Quarterly	33,000	Free
Lausanne Communique, 5970 Fairview Rd., Ste. 514, Charlotte, NC 28210-3196	Missions	Newsltr/6/yr		Free
Leadership, 465 Gundersen Dr., Carol Stream, IL 60188	Leadership	Journal/4/yr	70,000	22.00/yr
Librarians World, PO Bx 353, Glen Ellyn, IL 60138	Church Libraries	Quarterly	620	12.00/yr
Lifechangers, 50 Mitchell Blvd., Bx 13459, San Rafael, CA 94913	Christian Living	6/yr	5,500	Donation
Lighted Pathway, 1080 Montgomery Ave., Cleveland, TN 37311	Youth	12/yr	20,000	8.00/yr
LPEA Heartbeat, PO Bx 1173, Portland, OR 97207	Evangelism	Newsltr/10/yr	7,500	Free
Luke Society News, The, 1121 Grove St., Vicksburg, MS 39180	Missions	Organizatnl/2/yr	95,000	Free
Mag. for Christian Youth!, PO Bx 801, Nashville, TN 37202	Youth	12/yr	47,000	18.00/yr
Map Internatl Report, PO Bx 50, Brunswick, GA 31521	Missions	6/yr	15,000	Free
MARC News Letter, 919 W. Huntington Dr., Monrovia, CA 91016	Missions	Newsltr/6/yr		Free
Marketplace, The, 402-280 Smith St., Winnipeg, MB, R3C 1KC	Trade/Career	6/yr	5,000	10.00/yr
Marriage Partnership, 465 Gundersen Dr., Carol Stream, IL 60188	Marriage	Quarterly	65,000	19.95/yr
Mature Living, 127 Ninth Ave. N., Nashville, TN 37234	Seniors	12/yr	355,000	13.00/yr
Mature Years, 201 Eighth Ave. S., PO Bx 801, Nashville, TN 37202	Seniors		99,940	9.50/yr
Media Update, PO Bx 969, Cardiff by the Sea, CA 92007	Music	6/yr	12,000	10.00/yr
Mennonite, The, Bx 347, 722 Main St., Newton, KS 67114	Christian Living	Biweekly	11,260	18.00/yr
Message of the Cross, The, 6820 Auto Club Rd., Minneapolis, MN 55438	Christian Living	6/yr	16,500	Free
Ministries Today, 190 N. Westmonte Dr., Altamonte Springs, FL 32714	Leadership	6/yr	30,000	19.95/yr
Mission Frontiers, 1605 Elizabeth St., Pasadena, CA 91104	Missions	12/yr	60,000	4.00/yr
Missionary Monthly, 4517-A Broadmoor Ave., Grand Rapids, MI 49508	Missions	9/yr	4,000	10.00/yr
Missionary Tidings, The, 901 College, Winona Lake, IN 46590	Missions	9/yr	16,500	6.00/yr
Moments with God, 1 South 210 Summit Ave., Oakbrook Terrace, IL 60181	Devotional	Denom./4/yr	14,400	4.00/yr
Moody Monthly Magazine, 820 N. LaSalle Dr., Chicago, IL 60610	Christian Living	11/yr	175,000	19.95/yr
National and International Religion Report, PO Bx 21433, Roanoke, VA 24018	News	Newsltr/26/yr	4,800	78.00/yr
Native Reflections, Bx 891, Hot Springs, SD 57747	Missions	Quarterly	16,000	Free
Network, 627 South 34th St., Birmingham, AL 35222	Ecumenical	12/yr	15,000	12.00/yr
New England Church Life, 88 Tremont St., Suite 600, Boston, MA 02108	Church Life	12/yr	15,000	8.97/yr
News and Views, 1317 Weavers Way, Abilene, TX 79602	Singles			
Newswire, PO Bx 1122, Wheaton, IL 60189	Missions	Newsltr/6/yr	65,000	Donation

Periodical, Address	Category	Format	Circulation	Cost
OC International, PO Bx 35500, Colorado Springs, CO 80935-355025	Missions	Quarterly	25,000	Donation
OMS Outreach, Bx A, Greenwood, IN 46142	Missions	6/yr	48,000	Donation
One-to-One, PO Bx 6000, Colorado Springs, CO 80934	Evangelism	Quarterly	49,000	Donation
Open Doors News Brief, PO Bx 27001, Santa Ana, CA 92799	Missions	12/yr	90,000	12.00/yr
Other Side, The, 300 W. Apsley, Philadelphia, PA 19144	Christian Living	6/yr	12,000	21.75/yr
Overcomer, The, 2020 Bell Ave., Des Moines, IA 50315	Youth	Quarterly	2,200	5.00/yr
Overseas Cncl Newsltr, PO Bx 751, Greenwood, IN 46142	Missions	5/yr	4,000	Free
Parents of Teenagers, 2890 N. Monroe, PO Bx 481, Loveland, CO 80539	Parenting	Bimonthly	6,000	18.97/yr
Partnership Update, PO Bx WRC, Wheaton, IL 60189	Missions	12/yr	10,000	Free
Pastoral Renewal, PO Bx 8617, Ann Arbor, MI 48107	Leadership	Newsltr/6/yr	7,000	20.00 Donation
Pentecostal Minister, The, PO Bx 2430, Cleveland, TN 37320	Pastoral Ldrshp	Quarterly	5,500	15.00/yr
People of Destiny magazine, 7881-B Beechcraft Ave., Gaithersburg, MD 20879	Christian Living	6/yr	12,000	12.95/yr
Perspectives on Science and Christian Faith, PO Bx 668, Ipswich, MA 01938	Trade/Career	Quarterly	3,600	20.00Ind, 30.00Inst
Plough, The, Hutterian Brethren, Ulster Park, NY 12487	Christian Living	Quarterly	14,000	7.00/yr
Plus magazine, 66 E. Main St., Pawling, NY 12564	Christian Living	12/yr	888,000	8.00/yr
Possibilities, 1223 Potomac St. NW, Washington, DC 20007	Christian Living	6/yr	300,000	Free
Potential magazine, 9135 Guilford Rd., #170, Columbia, MD 21046	Evangelism	6/yr	30,000	8.50/yr
Prayer Line, The, PO Bx 55146, Seattle, WA 98155	Prayer	Quarterly	3,800	Free
Preacher's magazine, The, 6401 The Paseo, Kansas City, MO 64131	Leadership	4/yr	17,000	3.50/yr
Preaching magazine, 1529 Cesery Blvd., Jacksonville, FL 32211	Pastoral	Bimonthly	7,000	22.95/yr
Psychology for Living, 1409 N. Walnut Grove Ave., Bx 5000, Rosemead, CA 91770	Psychology	12/yr	15,000	N/A
Pulpit Helps, 6815 Shallowford Rd., Chattanooga, TN 37422	Pastoral	12/yr	200,000	15.00/yr
Quiet Miracle, The, 625 E. North Broadway, Columbus, OH 43214	Missions	Organizatn/5/yr	17,000	Donation
Quiet Revolution, A, 1655 St. Charles St., Jackson, MS 39209	Evangelism	Quarterly	4,000	Donation
Railroad Evangelist magazine, The, Route 4, Bx 97, Spencer, IN 47460	Trade/Career	6/yr	2,500	6.00/yr
Real Issue, The, 14679 Midway, Ste. 100, Dallas TX, 75244	Trade/Career	Quarterly	8,000	Free
Reformed Journal, The, 255 Jefferson Ave., SE, Grand Rapids, MI 49503	Christn Thought, News	12/yr	2,800	15.00/yr
Religious Broadcasting magazine, PO Bx 1926, Morristown, NJ 07962-1926	Trade/Career	12/yr	9,900	24.00/yr
Resource, 6401 The Paseo, Kansas City, MO 64131	Leadership	Quarterly	16,400	N/A
San Diego Christn Times, PO Bx 21009, El Cajon, CA 92021	News, comm.	12/yr	20,000	10.00/yr
Second Look magazine, PO Bx 3566, Grand Rapids, MI 49501-3566		Bimonthly	20,000	15.00/yr
Servant, Prairie Bible Institute, Three Hills, AB, TOM 2A0	Christian Living	6/yr	30,000	Free
Sharing the Victory, 8701 Leeds Rd., Kansas City, MO 64129	Youth	6/yr	45,000	9.00/yr
SIM Now, 10 Huntingdale Blvd., Scarborough, ON, M1W 2S5	Missions	6/yr	136,000	Free
Singing News magazine, PO Box 2810, Boone, NC 28607-2810	Music	12/yr	147,000	19.00/yr
Single Adult Ministries Journal, PO Bx 3010, Colorado Springs, CO 80934	Leadership	10/yr	4,500	21.00/yr
Single Minded, PO Bx 4933, Vancouver, BC, V6B 4A6	Singles	6/yr		
Singles Scene, PO Bx 454, Crossville, TN 38557	Singles	12/yr		
Singles/Young Adults Newsltr, 412 Sycamore St., Cincinnati, OH 45202	Singles			
Sojourners, Bx 29272, Washington, DC 20017	Political conscience	11/yr	46,000	24.00/yr
Soloing, Bx 15523, W. Palm Beach, FL 33416	Singles	Tabloid/6/yr		
Spiritual Counterfeits Project Newsltr, PO Bx 4308, Berkeley, CA 94704	Cults and Relig. Movements	Newsltr/4/yr	11,600	Free

Periodical, Address Category	Format	Circulation	Cost
Spiritual Fitness in Business, 1900 Firman Dr., Ste. 100, Richardson, TX 75081	Trade/Career Newsltr/12/yr	1,400	36.95/yr
Student Venture, 17150 Via del Campo, Ste. 200, San Diego, CA 92127	Youth Quarterly	46,000	N/A
Sunday to Sunday, 465 Gundersen Dr., Carol Stream, IL 60188	Women/ Pastor's Wives Quarterly	10,000	7.95/yr
Tabletalk, 270 So. North Lake Blvd., Ste. 1270, Altamonte Springs, FL 32701	Christn Thought Newsltr/12/yr	50,000	Free
Teenage magazine, 2890 N. Monroe, PO Bx 481, Loveland, CO 80539	Teens 10/yr	32,111	17.97/yr
Teen Missions Control, 885 East Hall Rd., Merritt Island, FL 32953	Missions N/A	60,000	Free
Teen Quest magazine, Bx 82808, Lincoln, NE 68501	Youth/Teenagers 11/yr	65,000	10.95/yr
Today's Better Life, PO Bx 141000, Nashville, TN 37214	Christian Living 4/yr	100,000	16.95/yr
Today's Christian Woman, 465 Gundersen Dr., Carol Stream, IL 60188	Women 6/yr	200,000	14.95/yr
Today's Singles, 1933 Wisconsin Ave., Milwaukee, WI 53233	Singles Tabloid/4/yr		Donation
Together, 919 W. Huntington Dr., Monrovia, CA 91019	Missions Journal/4/yr		25.00/yr
Together Again, PO Bx 136130, Fort Worth, TX 76136	Evangelism 6/yr	57,000	Free
Touch, Bx 7259, Grand Rapids, MI 49510	Youth Girls 10/yr	15,000	7.50/yr
Trans World Radio magazine, PO Bx 700, Cary, NC 27512	Missions		
Trim Tab, The, 136 Providence Rd., Fayetteville, GA 30214	Trade/Career 6/yr	9,000	Free
U.S. Singles Today, PO Bx 927, Bedford, TX 76095	Singles Tabloid		
United Evangelical Action, PO Bx 28, Wheaton, IL 60189	Christn Thought 6/yr	11,000	10.00/yr
Upper Room, The, 1908 Grand Ave., PO Bx 189, Nashville, TN 37202-0189	Devotional 12/yr	2,175,000	4.50/yr
Urban Missions, PO Bx 27009, Philadelphia, PA 19118	Missions 5/yr	1,200	10.00/yr
Venture magazine, PO Bx 150, Wheaton, IL 60189	Yth/Boys 10-15 6/yr	23,500	8.00/yr
Virtue magazine, PO Bx 850, Sisters, OR 97759	Women 6/yr	120,000	14.95/yr
Vision magazine, 3150 Bear St., Costa Mesa, CA 92626	Trade/Career Quarterly	85,000	Free
Voice magazine, 3150 Bear St., Costa Mesa, CA 92626	Evangelism to men Digest/12/yr	600,000	4.95/yr
Voice of Prophecy News, PO Bx 2525, Newbury Park, CA 91320	Evangelism 6/yr	74,000	Free
War Cry, The, 799 Bloomfield Ave., Verona, NJ 07044	Christian Living Biweekly	N/A	7.50/yr
Wesleyan Woman, The, PO Bx 50434, Indianapls, IN 46250	Women Quarterly	3,400	5.00/yr
Wherever, PO Bx 969, Carol Stream, IL 60189	Missions 3/yr	19,000	Free
Wider Look, The, 68 Summerleaze Rd., Maidenhead, England, SI6 8EP	Missions Digest/4/yr		10.00/yr
Women Alive, PO Bx 4683, Overland Park, KS 66204	Women 6/yr	5,000	7.95/yr
Word of Faith, The, PO Bx 50126, Tulsa, OK 74150	Christian Living 12/yr	200,000	Free
World, Bx 2330, Asheville, NC 28802	News Weekly	10,000	18.00/yr
World Christian mag., 21550 Oxnard St., Ste. 860, Woodland Hills, CA 91367	Missions 6/yr		13.00/yr
World Harvest mag., PO Bx 12, South Bend, IN 46624	Missions 6/yr	70,000	Free
World Vision magazine, 919 W. Huntington Dr., Monrovia, CA 91016	Missions 6/yr	160,000	Free
Worldorama, PO Bx 12609, Oklahoma City, OK 73157	Missions Quarterly	22,000	Free
Worldwide News, PO Bx 800, Lititz, PA 17543	Evangelism Newsltr/6/yr	15,000	Free
Worldwide Thrust, Bx 1707, Fort Washington, PA 19034	Missions Quarterly	8,800	Free
Your Church Magazine, 1418 Lake St., Evanston, IL 60201	Leadership 6/yr	200,000	12.00/yr
Youth and Christn Ed. Leadrshp, 922 Montgomery Ave., NE, Cleveland, TN 37311	Christian Ed. Quarterly	14,000	6.50/qtr
Youth Leader, The, 1445 Boonville Ave., Springfield, MO 65802	Christian Ed. 8/yr	4,000	13.50/yr
Youth Walk, PO Bx 80587, Atlanta, GA 30366	Devotional/Yth 12/yr	26,463	17.00/yr
Youthworker Jrnl, 1224 Greenfield Dr., El Cajon, CA 92021	Christian Ed. Quarterly	11,000	24.00/yr

DENOMINATIONAL MAGAZINES

Periodical	Address	Format	Circulation	Cost
Alliance Life	Christian and Missionary Alliance, PO Box 3500, Colorado Springs, CO 80935	24/yr	56,000	$9.50
American Baptist, The	American Baptist Churches USA, Box 850, Valley Forge PA 19482-0851	6/yr	61,000	$9.95
Banner, The	Christian Reformed Church in America, 2850 Kalamazoo Ave SE, Grand Rapids MI 49560	50/yr	46,000	$27.00
Baptist Herald	North American Baptist Conference, One S 210 Summit Avenue, Oakbrook Terrace IL 60181	10/yr	8,000	$8.00
Baptist Standard	Baptist Standard Publishing Company, PO Box 660267, Dallas TX 75266-0267	52/yr	285,119	$8.98
Brethren Evangelist, The	The Brethren Church, Inc., 524 College Avenue, Ashland OH 44805-3792	12/yr	3386	$12.00
Brethren Missionary Herald	Brethren Missionary Herald Company, Box 544, Winona Lake IN 46590	12/yr	8,000	$8.75
Church Advocate, The	Churches of God, General Conf., 700 E. Melrose Avenue, PO Box 926, Findlay OH 45839	12/yr	7600	$10.00
Church Herald, The	Reformed Church in America, The 6157 28th Street SE, Grand Rapids MI 49546-6999	12/yr	45,000	$13.00
Conservative Baptist	Conservative Baptist Association of America, PO Box 66, Wheaton IL 60189	4/yr	7,000	$4.00
Covenant Companion, The	Evangelical Covenant Ch/Covenant Publications, 5101 N. Francisco Avenue, Chicago IL 60625	12/yr	24,000	$22.00
Cumberland Presbyterian	1978 Union Avenue, Memphis TN 38104	12/yr	68,500	$9.00
Episcopal Life	Episcopal Church USA, 815 2nd Avenue, New York NY 10017	12/yr	244,000	$6.00
Evangelical Beacon, The	Evangelical Free Church of America, 1515 E. 66th Street, Minneapolis MN 55423	17/yr	37,500	$12.00
Evangelical Friend	Evangelical Friends Alliance, PO Box 232, Newberg OR 97132	10/yr	10,500	$10.95
Faith and Fellowship	Faith and Fellowship Press, Box 655, Fergus Falls MN 56537	20/yr	5,500	$8.00
Friends Journal	Religious Society of Friends, 1501 Cherry Street, Philadelphia PA 19102	12/yr	9,000	$18.00
International Pentecostal Holiness Advocate, The	International Pentecostal Holiness Church/ Advocate Press, PO Box 12609, Oklahoma City OK 73157	12/yr	44,000	$4.00
Light and Life	Free Methodist Church of North America, PO Box 535002, Indianapolis IN 46253-5002	12/yr	39,000	$13.50
Lutheran Journal	7317 Cahill Road, Minneapolis MN 55435	4/yr	136,000	$4.00
Lutheran Witness	Concordia Publishing House, 1333 S. Kirkwood Road, St. Louis MO 63122-7295	12/yr	385,000	$7.50
Lutheran, The	Evangelical Lutheran Church in America, 8865 W. Higgins Road, Chicago IL 60631	17/yr	1,200,000	$8.50
Mennonite, The	General Conference, Mennonite Church, Box 347 Newton KS 67114	24/yr	11,000	$18.00
Moravian	Moravian Church in America, PO Box 1245, Bethlehem PA 18016-1245	10/yr	26,000	$5.50
Pentecostal Evangel	Assembly of God, 1445 Boonville Avenue, Springfield MO 65802	52/yr	285,000	$11.95
Pentecostal Messenger, The	Pentecostal Church of God, 4901 Pennsylvania, PO Box 850, Joplin MO 64802-0850	11/yr	8500	$11.00
Presbyterian Layman, The	Presbyterian Lay Commitee, Inc., 1489 Baltimore Pike, Suite 301, Springfield PA 19064-3989	6/yr	635,000	Free
Presbyterian Survey	100 Witherspoon, Louisville KY 40202-1396	10/yr	136,000	$11.00
Quaker Life	Friends United Meeting, 101 Quaker Hill Drive, Richmond IN 47374	10/yr	9,600	$14.00
Reformed Journal, The	255 Jefferson Avenue SE, Grand Rapids MI 49503	10/yr	2686	$15.00
Standard, The	Baptist General Conference, 2002 S. Arlington Heights Road, Arlington Heights IL 60005	11/yr	23,000	$15.00
Wesleyan Advocate, The	Wesleyan Church/The Wesleyan Pub. House, PO Box 50434, Indianapolis IN 46250-0434	12/yr	18,500	$12.50

For information about Southern Baptist Convention state magazines write to: Southern Baptist Convention, 901 Commerce Street, Nashville, TN 37203

MEDIA AND CHRIST: 1900

What would happen if a big-city newspaper, instead of reporting the usual crime and violence, emphasized the good news and instituted a policy following the teachings of Jesus Christ? It happened once, with surprising results, when a Kansas daily took up a popular clergyman's challenge and appointed him editor in chief for one week in March 1900. The clergyman was Dr. Charles M. Sheldon, a Congregational minister whose series of sermons was published in 1896 as a novel titled *In His Steps or What Would Jesus Do?* The book sold as many as 30 million copies making it one of history's leading best-sellers.

It was a news event in itself when Dr. Sheldon moved into the hard-boiled city room of the *Topeka Daily Capital* to run the newspaper according to the dictates of Christ. Reporters from across the United States converged on Topeka to cover the story, and thousands of additional subscriptions were sold. Dr. Sheldon made some notable changes in company policy. He banned smoking, drinking, and profanity from the editorial offices and eliminated the paper's advertisements for patent medicines, corsets, and sporting events.

The *Topeka Daily Capital* was transformed. Signed editorials became front-page items, while crime, society events, and theatrical notices were played down. A page one story about a famine in India included an appeal for contributions; the paper collected more than $1 million in aid to send to Bombay.

As a result of the experiment, daily circulation jumped from 15,000 to 367,000. Critics of the minister's policies credited the increase to novelty and publicity. But Sheldon's supporters maintained that it proved how much people crave the inspiration of good news.

Significa by Irving Wallace, David Wallechensky, Amy Wallace. © 1983. Published by E. P. Dutton, Inc.

MEDIA AND CHRIST: 1990

A two-year research project, The Religious News Service-Lilly Foundation Study of Religion Reporting and Readership in the Daily Press, confirms that church members want to see more evidence in the newspapers they read that religion is an important part of daily life for many Americans.

"They see much that could fit in the newspaper that does not. The idea that religion is not of interest to journalism seemed inferentially to indicate that it is not of interest to its readers. This turned out not to be true," says Judy Weidman, editor of Religious News Service.

USA Today columnist Barbara Reynolds quotes Peggy Say, sister of former hostage Terry Anderson. Say, a Christian, comments, "I have often told reporters this, and I have almost given up on seeing it in print. They don't want to hear anything about faith."

Reynolds goes on to ask some pointed questions: "What does the press have against Jesus? Is there a bias against Christianity? Why are people who identify God . . . as responsible for changing world events not taken seriously by the media?"

WHO READS WHAT?

Church leaders identify top 10 magazine reading preferences

Conservatives	%	Moderates	%	Liberals	%
Christianity Today	59	Christian Century	48	Christian Century	54
Readers Digest	52	Newsweek	39	New York Times	40
Leadership	48	Time	34	Christianity & Crisis	36
Newsweek	41	New York Times	27	Newsweek	34
Decision	36	Sojourner	26	Sojourner	30
Time	30	Christianity & Crisis	24	Time	30
US News & World Report	30	Christianity Today	21	Action Information	21
Moody Monthly	21	Readers Digest	21	New Yorker	21
Clergy Journal	13	JSAC Grapevine	18	JSAC Grapevine	20
Parish Paper	13	Clergy Journal	18	NCCC Newsletter	17

Source: *1991 Yearbook of American and Canadian Churches.*

RELIGIOUS MAGAZINES HAVE STAYING POWER

Of the 25 oldest magazines in the U.S., 12 are church related.

		First Published
1	New England Journal of Medicine	1812
2	American Bible Society Record	1818
3	Pittsburgh Catholic	1844
4	Scientific American	1845
5	Town and Country	1846
6	United Methodist Reporter	1847
7	Journal of the Am. Medical Assoc.	1848
8	Adventist Review	1850
9	Harper's magazine	1850
10	Atlantic	1857
11	Lutheran	1860
12	Ye Olde Bastards Bulletin	1863
13	Harper's Bazaar	1867
14	Medical Times	1872
15	Popular Science	1872
16	Signs of the Times	1874
17	McCall's	1876
18	American Salon	1877
19	Baptist Record	1877
20	Christian Herald	1878
21	Presbyterian Survey	1879
22	Watchtower	1879
23	Science	1880
24	War Cry	1880
25	Carpenter	1881
26	Farmer/The Dakota Farmer	1881
27	Lutheran Witness	1882
28	AAUW Outlook	1882
29	Grit	1882

Data refer to magazines that report a circulation of 100,000 or more and are published more than once a year. *U.S. News and World Report*, 16 October 1989, and Ulnch's International Periodicals Directory, R. R. Bowler Company.

FREQUENCY OF READING NEWSPAPER RELIGION NEWS

	Evangelicals %	Non-Evangelicals %
Whenever it appears	11.3	30.7
Frequently	8.3	19.0
Occasionally	20.1	23.3
Infrequently	25.5	13.9
Just about never	34.3	12.4
Don't know	0.4	0.7

RNS-Lilly Study of Religion Reporting and Readership in the Daily Press, October 1989.

STUDY SHOWS LOW READER SATISFACTION WITH RELIGION COVERAGE BY NEWSPAPER "MOST OFTEN READ"

Sports	5.74
Business	5.29
Entertainment	5.18
Education	5.00
Food	4.99
Health	4.76
The Arts	4.67
Personal Advice	4.39
Religion	4.32

RNS-Lilly Study of Religion Reporting and Readership in the Daily Press, October 1989.

EVANGELICAL PRESS ASSOCIATION MAGAZINE AWARDS

EPA awards are selected by university journalism professors and national experts in each field.

Category/Publication	Editor	Art Dir./Designer	Publisher	Award
Christian Ministries				
1987 Jrnl of Christian Nursing	Ramona Cass	Kathy Lay Burrows	Nurses Christian Fellowship	Excellence
Interlit	Tim Bascom	Joe Ragont	David C. Cook Foundation	Merit
Leadership	Terry C. Muck	Jeff Carnehl	Christianity Today, Inc.	Merit
Youth Worker	Noel Becchetti	Mark Rayburn	Wayne Rice and Mike Yaconelli	Merit
1988 Leadership	Terry C. Muck	Joan Nickerson	Christianity Today, Inc.	Excel
Interlit	Tim Bascom	Joe Ragont	David C. Cook Foundation	Merit
Jrnl of Christian Nursing	Ramona Cass	Kathy Lay Burrows	InterVarsity Christian Fellowship	Merit
Youthworker Journal	Noel Becchetti	Jack Rogers	Youth Specialties	Merit.
1989 Jrnl of Christian Nursing	Ramona Cass	Kathy Lay Burrows	InterVarsity Christian Fellowship	Excel
Interlit	Tim Bascom	Joe Ragont	David C. Cook Foundation	Merit
Student Leadership	Robert M. Kachur	Krisy Maxey	InterVarsity Christian Fellowship	Excel
Youthworker Journal	Wayne Rice	Jack Rogers	Youth Specialties	Merit
1990 Leadership	Marshall Shelley	Joan Nickerson	Christianity Today	Excel
Illustrated Bible Life	Stephen M. Miller	Crandall Vail	WordAction Publications/ Nazarene Publishing House	Merit
Perspective	Rebecca Powell Parat	Cheryl Whelan	Pioneer Clubs	Merit
Ministries Today	Jamie Buckingham	Geoffry V. Sprague	Strang Communications	Merit
Denominational				
1987 Good News	James V. Heidinger II	Mark Laurenson	Forum for Scriptural Christianity	Excel.
Light and Life	Robert B. Haslam	Emiline Secaur	Free Meth. Church of North Am.	Merit

	Category/Publication	Editor	Art Dir./Designer	Publisher	Award
1987	Pentecostal Minister	Clyner W. Buxton	L. Travis Kirkland and Paul West	Church of God	Merit
	The Standard	Donald E. Anderson	Pamela Nelson	Baptist General Conference	Merit
1988	Pentecostal Evangel	Richard G. Champion	Randy Clute	Gospel Publishing House	Excel
	Church of God Evangel	Hoyt E. Stone	L. Travis Kirkland	Church of God	Merit
	The Banner	Andrew Kuyvenhoven	R. Wayne DeJonge	CRC Publications	Merit
	The Standard	Donald E. Anderson	Pamela Nelson	Baptist General Conference	Merit
1989	The Banner	Galen Meyer	R. Wayne DeJonge	Christian Reformed Church	Excel.
	Light and Life	Robert B. Haslam	Emiline Secaur	Free Meth. Church of North Am.	Merit
	The Christian Leader	Don Ratzlaf		U.S. Conference of Mennonite Brethren Churches	Merit
	The Church Herald	John Stapert	Carl Meinke	The Church Herald, Inc.	Merit
1990	The Christian Leader	Don Ratzlaf		U.S. Conference of Mennonite Brethren Churches	Excel
	The Church Herald	John C. Stapert	Carl F. Meinke	Reformed Church in America	Merit
	Messenger	Robert G. Sweet	G. Thomas Evans	Presby. Church in America	Merit
	Pentecostal Evangel	Richard G. Champion	Randy Clute	Gen'l Council of the Assemblies of God	Merit

General

	Category/Publication	Editor	Art Dir./Designer	Publisher	Award
1987	Moody Monthly	Robert Flood and Michael Umlandt	Kent Puckett Assoc.	Moody Bible Institute	Excel.
	Christian Reader	Dwight Hooten and Bonne Steffen	Tamara Burgh Norrgard	Kenneth N. Taylor	Merit
	Christianity Today	Terry C. Muck	Joan Nickerson	Christianity Today, Inc.	Merit
	Discipleship Journal	Susan Maycinik	Naomi Ann Trujillo	The Navigators	Merit
1988	Marriage Partnership	Harold L. Myra and Scott W. Bolinder	Gary Michael Gnidovic	Christianity Today, Inc.	Excel.
	Discipleship Journal	Susan Maycinik	Naomi Ann Trujillo	The Navigators	Merit
	The Christian Reader	Dwight Hooten	Rai Whitlock	Tyndale House Publishers, Inc.	Merit
	Today's Christian Woman	Dale Hanson Bourke	Gary Michael Gnidovic	Christianity Today, Inc.	Merit
1989	Today's Christian Woman	Dale Hanson Bourke	Gary Michael Gnidovic	Christianity Today, Inc.	Excel
	Aglow	Gwen Weising	Kathy Boice	Women's Aglow Fellowship	Merit
	Christn Psychlgy for Today	Jane Mack	Graphic & Ed. Svcs.	Minirth-Meier Clinic	Merit
	Marriage Partnership	Ron R. Lee	Gary Michael Gnidovic	Christianity Today, Inc.	Merit
1990	Discipleship Journal	Susan Maycinik	Naomi Ann Trujillo	The Navigators	Excel.
	Moody Magazine	Andrew Scheer	Kent Puckett Assoc.	Moody Bible Institute	Merit
	Christianity Today	George Brushaber	Joan Nickerson	Christianity Today, Inc.	Merit
	Christian History	Kevin A. Miller	Jeff Carnehl	Christianity Today, Inc.	Merit
	Worldwide Challenge	Philip A. DeJong	Greg Breeding	Campus Crusade for Christ, Inc.	Merit

Missionary

	Category/Publication	Editor	Art Dir./Designer	Publisher	Award
1987	Latin America Evangelist	John Maust and Paul E. Pretiz	Carlos Gordon	Clayton L. Berg, Jr.	Excel.
	In Other Words	Roger Garland	Ken Harris	Wycliffe Bible Translators	Merit
	The Chosen People	Jonathan Singer	Jonathan Singer	Am. Board of Missions to the Jews, Inc.	Merit
	World Vision	David Olson	Don Aylard	World Vision	Merit
1988	World Vision	Terry Madison	Don Aylard	World Vision	Excel.
	In Other Words	Roger Garland	Kathy McBride	Wycliffe Bible Translators	Merit
	Mountain Movers	Nick Henry	Mickey Flodin	Assemblies of God Division of Foreign Missions	Merit
	OMS Outreach	Eleanor Burr	Gene Bertolet	OMS International, Inc.	Merit
1989	World Vision	Terry Madison	Don Aylard	World Vision	Excel.
	Impact	Art Heerwagen		Conserv. Bapt. Foreign Missn Soc.	Merit
	In Other Words	Roger Garland	Kathy McBride	Wycliffe Bible Translators	Merit
	OMS Outreach	Eleanor Burr	Curt Buller and Dyann Brodie	OMS International, Inc.	Merit
1990	In Other Words	W. Terry Whalin	Kathy McBride	Wycliffe Bible Translators, Inc.	Excel
	The Chosen People	Jonathan Singer		Chosen People Ministries, Inc.	Merit
	World Vision	Terry Madison	Don Aylard	World Vision, Inc.	Merit
	Indian Life	Jim Uttley, Jr.	Don Monkman	Intertribal Christian Comm.	Merit

Newsletter

	Category/Publication	Editor	Art Dir./Designer	Publisher	Award
1987	Bulletin	Clyne W. Buxton		Church of God	Excel.
	Jubilee	Megs Singer	Mike Harper	Prison Fellowship Ministries	Merit
	Pastoral Renewal	John Blattner		Servant Ministries	Merit
	The Vineyard Newsletter	Suzanne N. Springer	Bob Payne	John Wimber	Merit
1988	Tabletalk	Ralph D. Veerman		Ligonier Ministries	Excel.

Category/Publication	Editor	Art Dir./Designer	Publisher	Award
1988 Jubilee	Megs Singer	Brenda Young	Prison Fellowship Ministries	Merit
Pastoral Renewal	John Blattner		Servant Ministries	Merit
Spiritual Fitness in Business	Steve Webb		Probe Ministries International	Merit
1989 Pastoral Renewal	John C. Blattner	Cynthia Parker	Servant Ministries	Excel.
Breakthrough	Wil Triggs	Edward Tabb	Slavic Gospel Mission	Merit
Brown Bulletin	Fred Lollar	David Andrus	John Brown University	Merit
One-to-One	Judith Couchman	Richard Slaton	The Navigators	Merit
1990 Jubilee	Megs Singer	Carol Cable/		
		Toni Lee Curry	Prison Fellowship Ministries	Excel
LPEA Heartbeat	Mike Umlandt	Jim Allison	Luis Palau Evangelistic Assoc.	Merit
Advocate	Kathleen Hayes		Evangelicals for Social Action	Merit

Organizational

Category/Publication	Editor	Art Dir./Designer	Publisher	Award
1987 Fundamentalist Journal	Deborah Wade Huff	Larry C. Bevins	Jerry Falwell	Excel.
Decision	Roger Palms	Gary Carlson	The Billy Graham Evang. Assoc.	Merit
Discovery Digest	Dave Branon and			
	Kurt DeHaan	Brian Fowler	Radio Bible Class	Merit
Possibilities	Jeanne A. Dunn	Publishing Directions	Dale Hanson Bourke	Merit
1988 Fundamentalist Journal	Deborah Wade Huff	Larry C. Bevins	Old-Time Gospel Hour	Excel.
Equipping the Saints	Kevin Springer	Bob Payne	Vineyard Ministries International	Merit
Possibilities	Jeanne A. Dunn	Publishing Directions	Robert Schuller Ministries	Merit
Response	Jennifer Johnson			
	Gilnett	Dale Kegley	Seattle Pacific University	Merit
1989 Contact	Robaert J. Tamasy	Linda Peppers	Christian Business Men's	
			Committee USA	Excel.
Equipping the Saints	Kevin Springer	Bob Payne	Vineyard Ministries International	Merit
Fundamentalist Journal	Deborah Wade Huff	Larry C. Bevins	Old-Time Gospel Hour	Merit
Possibilities	Jeanne A. Dunn	Publishing Directions	Robert Schuller Ministries	Merit
1990 Kindred Spirit	Michael Edwards	Keith D. Yates	Dallas Theological Seminary	Excel
Confident Living	Jan E. Reeser	Gary Goodding	Good News Broad. Assoc., Inc.	Merit
Faith	Deborah Provencher	Frank M. Laudo	International Bible Society	Merit
Christian Home and School	Gordon L. Bordewyk		Christian Schools International	Merit

Sunday School Take Home

Category/Publication	Editor	Art Dir./Designer	Publisher	Award
1987 Vista	Patsy Whittenberg		Wesley Press	Excel.
Bible-in-Life Friends	Rita West	Gregory E. Clark	David C. Cook Publishing Co.	Merit
Christian Living	Anne E. Dinnan	Marilyn Duddles		
		Earibon	David C. Cook Publishing Co.	Merit
In Touch	James Watkins		Wesley Press	Merit
1988 Sprint	Paul N. Woods		David C. Cook Publishing Co.	Excel.
Bible-in-Life Friends	Nancy Raney	Donna Nelson	David C. Cook Publishing Co.	Merit
Bible-in-Life Pix	Lois Keffer	Donna Nelson	David C. Cook Publishing Co.	Merit
Sunday Digest	Jeanette L. Pearson		David C. Cook Publishing Co.	Merit
1989 Teens Today	Karen De Sollar		Beacon Hill Press	Excel.
Bible-in-Life Pix	Charlene Hiebert		David C. Cook Publishing Co.	Merit
Sprint	Paul N. Woods	Kellie Richter	David C. Cook Publishing Co.	Merit
The Lookout	Mark A. Taylor		Standard Publishing	Merit
1990 Bible-in-Life Friends	Charlene Hiebert/			
	Jeanette Dall/	Scot McDonald/		
	Linda Washington	Kay Currie	David C. Cook Publishing Co.	Excel
Sunday Digest	Ronda Oosterhoff	Paul Segsworth	David C. Cook Publishing Co.	Merit
Bible-in-Life Pix	Charlene Hiebert/			
	Jeanette Dall/	Scot McDonald/		
	Lorraine Triggs	Jennifer McGuire	David C. Cook Publishing Co.	Merit

Youth

Category/Publication	Editor	Art Dir./Designer	Publisher	Award
1987 Venture	Steve P. Neideck	Lawrence Libby	Christian Service Brigade	Excel.
Campus Life	James Long	Jeff Carnehl	Christianity Today, Inc.	Merit
TQ	Roger S. Morrow and			
	Nancy Brumbaugh	Victoria Valentine	Back To The Bible	Merit
U	Verne Becker	Kathy Lay Burrows	InterVarsity Christn Fellowship	Merit
1988 Campus Life	Jim Long	Jeff Carnehl	Christianity Today, Inc.	Excel. (tie)
The Mag. for Christn Youth!	Christopher B. Hughes	Susan J. Scrugg	The United Meth. Publ. House	Excel. (tie)
Contemp. Christian Music	John W. Styll	Lynn Schrader	CCM Publications, Inc.	Merit
TQ	Barbara K. Comito	Victoria Valentine	Good News Broadcasting Assoc.	Merit
1989 Kids!	Bonnie Burnett	Killion McCabe &		
		Associates	Moody Bible Institute	Excel.
Campus Life	James Long	Jeff Carmehl	Christianity Today	Merit

Category/Publication	Editor	Art Dir./Designer	Publisher	Award
1989 Cornerstone	Dawn Herrin	Dick Randall	Jesus People USA	Merit
TQ	Roger S. Morrow	Victoria Valentine	Good News Broadcasting Assoc.	Merit
1990 Kids!	Bonnie Burnett	Larry Taylor	Moody Bible Institute	Excel
Sharing the Victory	John Dodderidge	Frank Grey	Fellowship of Christian Athletes	Merit
Touch	Joanne Ilbrink/			
	Carol Smith	Chris Cook	Calvinettes	Merit
TQ	Win Mumma	Victoria Valentine	Good News Broad. Assoc., Inc.	Merit

CHRISTIAN RADIO AND TELEVISION STATIONS IN THE UNITED STATES

Radio stations listed here are all full-time Christian radio stations. TV stations are designated as Christian if religious programming is 150 hours or more per week; family if religious programming is 35-150 hours per week. Stations with religious programming below 35 hours per week are not included.

State / Channel / Frequency	Address	City/Zip
Radio		
AK KATB 89.3 FM	PO Box 21089	Anchorage 99521
AL WAGG 1320 AM	PO Box 697	Birmingham 35201
WAPZ 1250 AM	PO Box 210339	Montgomery 36121
WASG 1140 AM	1210 S. Main Street	Atmore 36502
WAYD 1200 AM	PO Box 1331, Sam Lisenby Road	Ozark 36360
WAYE 1220 AM	4650 Avenue W, Suite K, PO Box 3800-E	Birmingham 35208
WBHY 840 AM	PO Box 1328, 102 Dauphin St., #1103	Mobile 36602
WBLX 550 AM	PO Box 1964	Mobile 36633
WBTG 106.3 FM	PO Box 518, HH21 Countryboy Lane	Sheffield 35660
WEBT 91.5 FM	PO Box 96	Valley 36864
WFRC 90.5 FM	1010 7th Place	Phenix City 36867
WJBU 930 AM Stereo	PO Box 930	Rainbow City 35902
WKWL 1230 AM	PO Box 158	Florala 36442
WLBF 89.1 FM	381 Mendel Parkway E., Box 17140	Montgomery 36117
WLPH 1480 AM	561 12 Ct.	Pleasant Grove 35127
WMBV 91.9 FM	PO Box 91.9	Dixon's Mills 36736
WMGY 800 AM	2305 Upper Wetumpka Road	Montgomery 36107
WMOB 1360 AM	Suite 206, 3943 Airport Blvd.	Mobile 36608
WNDA 95.1 FM	2407 9th Avenue	Huntsville 35805
WVRT 101.7 FM	RR 5, Box 70-A	Gordo 35466
WVSM 1500 AM	Box 339	Rainsville 35986
WWNT 1450 AM	226 N. Foster St., Suite 24, PO Box 1828	Dothan 36302
WYDE 850 AM	90 Bagby Drive, Suite 310	Birmingham 35209
AR KAAB 1130 AM	Box 2946	Batesville 72501
KAAY 1090 AM	7123 I-30, Suite 1	Little Rock 72209
KCGS 960 AM	PO Box 368	Marshall 72650
KCMH 91.5 FM	PO Box 93	Mountain Home 72653
KFDF 1580 AM	Suite 225, Central Mall	Fort Smith 72903
KITA 1440 AM	723 W. 14th Street	Little Rock 72202
KMTL 760 AM	PO Box 4360	North Little Rock 72116
KPHN 94.5 FM	1311 Fort St., PO Box 98	Barling 72923
KSBC 90.1 FM	PO Box 2771	Hot Springs 71914
AZ KFLR 90.3 FM	2345 W. Buckeye Road	Phoenix 85009
KFLT 830 AM	PO Box 3025	Tucson 85702
KHAC 1110 AM	PO Box F	Window Rock 86515
KHEP 1280 AM	3883 N. 38th Avenue	Phoenix 85019
KMLE 107.9 FM	500 W. Ray Road	Chandler 85224
KNLB 91.1 FM	PO Box V, 510 N. Acoma Blvd.	Lake Havasu City 86403
KVOI 690 AM	3425 E. Grant Road	Tucson 85716
KWFH 90.1 FM	PO Box 603, 401 15th Street	Parker 85344
KXEG 1010 AM	1817 N. 3rd St., Suite 202	Phoenix 85004
CA KAMB 101.5 FM	90 E. 16th Street	Merced 95340
KAVC 105.5 FM	PO Box 2069, 2997 Desert Street	Rosamond 93560
KBIF 900 AM	261 N. Broadway	Fresno 93701
KBRT 740 AM	3183 Airway Avenue	Costa Mesa 92626
KCJH 90.1 FM	PO Box 8744	Stockton 95208
KCLB 91.9 FM	50 Mark W. Springs Road No. 3	Santa Rosa 95403
KDAR 98.3 FM	500 Esplanade Dr., Suite 1510	Oxnard 93030
KDNO 98.5 FM	1305 Glenwood	Delano 93215
KEAR 106.9 FM	1234 Mariposa Street	San Francisco 94107
KEBR 100.5 FM	3108 Fulton Avenue	Sacramento 95821
KECR 93.3 FM	312 W. Douglas	El Cajon 92020
KEFR 89.9 FM	PO Box 52	Le Grand 95333
KERI 1180 AM	Box 3189	Bakersfield 93385

State / Channel / Frequency	Address	City/Zip
CA KFAX 1100 AM	3106 Diablo Avenue	Hayward 94545
KFIA 710 AM	5705 Marconi Avenue	Carmichael 95608
KFRN 1280 AM	105 Linden Avenue	Long Beach 90802
KFSG 96.3 FM	1100 Glendale Blvd.	Los Angeles 90026
KGBA 100.1/98.3 FM	Box 133, 605 State Street	El Centro 92243
KGDP 660 AM Stereo	2634 Ocotillo Street	Santa Maria 93455
KGER 1390 AM	3759 Atlantic Avenue, PO Box 7126	Long Beach 90807
KGFT 101.7 FM	5565 Carpinteria Avenue, Suite 23	Carpinteria 93013
KHIS 800 AM 96.5 FM	521 H Street	Bakersfield 93304
KKLA 99.5 FM	4640 Lankershim Blvd.	North Hollywood 91602
KKMC 880 AM	SE Allisal, Suite 501	Salinas 93901
KLFE 1240 AM	992 Inland Center Drive	San Bernardino 92408
KLRD 90.1 FM		Oak Glen 92399
KMJC 910 AM	500 Fesler Street, Suite 207	El Cajon 92020
KMRO 90.3 FM	2310 Ponderosa Dr., Suite 28	Camarillo 93010
KPRA 89.5 FM	25 Oak Knoll	Ukiah 95482
KPRO 1570 AM	7351 Lincoln Avenue	Riverside 92504
KPRZ 1210 AM	1635 S. Rancho Santa Fe Road	San Marcos 92069
KPZE 1190 AM	1190 E. Ball Road	Anaheim 92805
KRDU 1130 AM	597 N. Alta Avenue	Dinuba 93618
KSGN 89.7 FM	11498 Pierce Street	Riverside 92505
KSPD 790 AM	3636 N. First	Fresno 93726
KTSJ 1220 AM	1580 Clarmont Blvd. #202	Clarmont 91711
KTYM 1460 AM	6803 W. Boulevard	Inglewood 90302
KVIP 540 AM 98.1 FM	PO Box 1359	Redding 96099
KWVE 107.9 FM	1644 N. El Camino Real	San Clemente 92672
KYMS 106.3 FM	1748 W. Katella	Orange 92667
WGOR 650 AM	4610 Briarwood Drive	Sacramento 95821
CO KCIC 88.5 FM	3102 E Road	Grand Junction 81504
KLLV 550 AM	14780 State Highway 140, Breen-Hesperus	Breen 81326
KRKS 990 AM	6535 W. Jewell Avenue	Denver 80226
KWBI 91.1 FM	16075 W. Belleview Avenue	Morrison 80465
KWYD 105.5 FM 1580 AM	PO Box 5668	Colorado Springs 80931
CT WCTF 1170 AM	13 Park Street, PO Box 1170	Vernon 06066
WFIF 1500 AM	90 Kay Avenue	Milford 06460
DC WYCB 1340 AM	Natl Press Bldg., 529 14th St. NW, #228	Washington 20045
FL WAFG 90.3 FM	5555 N. Federal Highway	Ft. Lauderdale 33308
WAPG 1480 AM	PO Box 632, 201 W. Asbury Street	Arcadia 33821
WAPN 91.5 FM	1508 State Avenue	Holly Hill 32017
WAYJ 88.7 FM	1860 Boyscout Drive	Fort Myers 33907
WAYR 550 AM	2500 Russell Road	Green Cove Spgs 32043
WCIE 91.1 FM	777 Carpenters Way	Lakeland 33809
WCIF 106.3 FM	PO Box 366, 702 E. New Haven Avenue	Melbourne 32902
WCVC 1330 AM	117 1/2 S. Henderson Road	Tallahassee 32312
WEGS 91.7 FM	703 N. Stewart Street	Milton 32570
WEXY 1520 AM	3411 NW 9th Avenue #701	Ft. Lauderdale 33309
WGNB 1520 AM,	Box 8888	St. Petersburg 33738
WGTO 540 AM	PO Box 123	Cypress Gardens 33884
WGTX 1280 AM	PO Box 627	DeFuniak Springs 32433
WHGS 90.3 FM	124 N. 10th Street, PO Box 1909	Haines City 33844
WHYM 610 AM	PO Box 17446	Pensacola 32522
WJLU 89.7 FM	2596 State Road 44	New Smyrna Bch 32069
WKES 101.5 FM	Box 8888	St. Petersburg 33738
WKZM 105.5 FM	PO Box 7627	Sarasota 34278
WLJP 91.5 FM	8410 US 19, Suite 107-A	New Port Richey 34668
WLTG 1430 AM	PO Box 15635	Panama City 32406
WLVF 930 AM	110 W. Scenic Highway	Haines City 33844
WLVS 1380 AM	1939 7th Avenue N	Lake Worth 33461
WMCU 89.7 FM	2300 NW 135th Street	Miami 33167
WMFJ 1450 AM	340 S. Beach Street	Daytona Beach 32014
WMIE 91.5 FM	1150 W. King Street	Cocoa 32922
WNCM 88.1 FM	2361 Cortez Road	Jacksonville 32216
WNLE 91.7 FM	Rt. 2, Box 705-A	Yulee 32097
WPCF 1290 AM 100.1 FM	1111 Laurie Avenue	Panama City Bch 32407
WPCS 89.3 FM	Box 18000	Pensacola 32523
WPFA 790 AM	4151 N. Pace Blvd.	Pensacola 32505
WPIO 89.3 FM	505 Josephine Street	Titusville 32796
WPLA 910 AM	PO Drawer J	Plant City 34289
WPSM 91.1 FM	13 Kelly Avenue	Fort Walton Bch 32548
WSEB 91.3 FM	Suite 110, 2800 Placida Road	Englewood 33533

State / Channel / Frequency	Address	City/Zip
FL WSOR 95.3 FM	940 Tarpon Street	Ft. Myers 33901
WTBH 91.5 FM	Rt. 2, Box 497	Chiefland 32626
WTIS 1110 AM	311 12th Avenue NE	St. Petersburg 33716
WTLN 1520 AM	PO Box 607000	Orlando 32860
WTWB 1570 AM	PO Box 7	Auburndale 33823
WVCF 1480 AM	Box 15550	Orlando 32858
WVIJ 91.7 FM	3279 Sherwood Road	Port Charlotte 33980
WWBC 1510 AM	1150 W. King Street	Cocoa 32922
WWOL 91.1 FM	124 N. 10th Street, PO Box 1909	Haines City 33844
WYFB 90.5 FM	Rt. 2, Box 1012	Keystone Heights 32656
GA WACL 570 AM	Box 858	Waycross 31502
WAEC 860 AM	1465 Northside Drive NW, Suite 14	Atlanta 30318
WBPS 89.5 FM	Box N, Highway 29	Winder 30680
WCCV 91.7 FM	PO Box 708, #206 Cowan Bldg, E. Main St.	Cartersville 30120
WCOP 1350 AM	PO Box 2127	Warner Robins 31099
WECC 1190 AM	2101 Highway 40 E., PO Box 1171	St. Marys 31558
WFAM 1050 AM	552 Laney-Walker Ext.	Augusta 30901
WFDR 1370 AM	PO Box 510	Manchester 31816
WGEC 103.9 FM	Box 15267	Springfield 31329
WGIA 1350 AM	PO Drawer 619, 245 Main Street	Blackshear 31516
WHYD 1270 AM	1825 Buena Vista Road	Columbus 31906
WJEP 1020 AM	PO Box 90	Thomasville 31799
WKZK 1600 AM	PO Box 1454	Augusta 30903
WMAC 1360 AM	Box 238	Metter 30439
WNIV 970 AM	805 Peachtree Street NE, Suite 633	Atlanta 30308
WRAF 90.9 FM	PO Box 128	Toccoa Falls 30598
WTPO 1050 AM	954 S. Main Street	Conyers 30207
WWEV 91.5 FM	889 Buford Road, Highway 20	Cumming 30143
WXLL 1310 AM	419 W. Ponce de Leon Avenue	Decatur 30030
WYFA 100.9 FM	T. 1, Box 305	Waynesboro 30830
WYFK 89.5 FM	Rt. 1, Box 109	Cataula 31804
WYFS 89.5 FM	Rt. 1, Box 358	Bloomingdale 31302
WYNX 1550 AM	2460 Atlanta Road	Smyrna 30080
WZOT 107.1 FM	PO Box 192	Rockmart 30153
HI KAIM 870 AM 95.5 FM	3555 Harding Avenue, PO Box 375	Honolulu 96816
IA KBQC 93.5 FM	4855 Forest Grove Drive	Bettendorf 52722
KFGQ 1260 AM	924 W. 2nd Street	Boone 50036
KNWS 102 FM 1090 AM	4880 Texas Street	Waterloo 50702
KTFC 103.3 FM	RFD 2	Sioux City 51106
KTFJ 1250 AM	RFD 2	Sioux City 51106
KTOF 104.5 FM	1957 Blairs Ferry Road, NE	Cedar Rapids 52402
KYFR 920 AM	618 1/2 W. Sheridan Avenue	Shenandoah 51601
ID KBGN 1060 AM	3303 E. Chicago	Caldwell 83605
KCIR 90.7 FM	1446 Filer Avenue E.	Twin Falls 83301
KFXD 580 AM	PO Box 107	Boise 83701
IL KJOR 550 AM	613 S. La Grange Road	La Grange 60525
WCBW 104.9 FM	111 W. Locust Street	Columbia 62236
WCRM 103.9 FM	PO Box 249, 651 S. 8th Street	Dundee 60118
WDLM 89.3 FM	Box 149	East Moline 61244
WGCA 88.5	PO Box 467	Quincy 62306
WGGH 1150 AM	Box 340, Old Rte. 13 E.	Marion 62959
WIBI 91.1 FM	Box 126	Carlinville 62626
WJCH 91.9 FM	13 Fairlane Drive	Joliet 60435
WLUJ 97.7 FM	PO Box 500	Petersburg 62675
WMBI 1110 AM 90.1 FM	820 N. LaSalle Drive	Chicago 60610
WPEO 1020 AM	1708 Highview Road E.	Peoria 61611
WVEL 1140 AM	28 S. 4th Street	Pekin 61554
WVLJ 105.5 FM	RR 1, Box 1231	Monticello 61856
WWRJ 1200 AM	613 S. La Grange Road	La Grange 60525
WXAN 103.9 FM	Rt. 2, Box 213A	Ava 62907
IN WBRI 1500 AM	4802 E. 62nd Street	Indianapolis 46220
WFCV 1090 AM	909 Coliseum Blvd. N.	Fort Wayne 46805
WFRN 104.7 FM	25802 CR 26	Elkhart 46517
WMII AM	PO Box 1462	Jeffersonville 47131
WNTS 1590 AM	4800 E. Raymond Street	Indianapolis 46203
WRRD 940 AM	2711 Highway 62	Jeffersonville 47131
WVHI 1330 AM	PO Box 3636	Evansville 47735
WXIR 98.3 FM	4802 E. 62nd Street	Indianapolis 46220
WXLW 950 AM	Box 22300, 3003 Kessler Blvd., N. Drive	Indianapolis 46222
WYCA 92.3 FM	6336 Calumet Avenue	Hammond 46324

State / Channel / Frequency	Address	City/Zip
KS KCNW 1380 AM	4535 Metropolitan	Kansas City 66106
KGCR 107.7 FM	Box 948	Goodland 67735
KJTY 88.3 FM	2519 N. Topeka Blvd.	Topeka 66617
KVCY 101.7 FM	PO Box 191	Ft. Scott 66701
KY WBCE 1200 AM	PO Box 128	Wickliffe 42087
WBFI 91.5 FM	Box 2, Highway 2595	McDaniels 40152
WCVK 90.7 FM	PO Box 539, 313 State Street	Bowling Green 42102
WDFB 1170 AM	PO Box 106, State Route 300	Danville 40422
WFIA 900 AM	410 S. Third Street	Louisville 40202
WFJT 1590 AM	Box 410, Spring Branch Road	Inze 41224
WLCK 1250 AM	PO Box 158, 104 1/2 Public Square	Scottsville 42164
WLJC 102.3 FM	N. Rt. 11, Box 50	Beattyville 41311
WNKJ 89.3 FM	PO Box 1029	Hopkinsville 42240
WRSL 1520 AM	Box 237	Stanford 40484
WSOF 89.9 FM	PO Box 1246	Madisonville 42431
WVCT 91.5 FM	Rt. 11, Box 381	Keavy 40737
WWLK 900 AM	Box 90, Dale Avenue	Eddyville 42038
WWXL 103.5 FM 1450 AM	Route 50, Box 50	Manchester 40962
WXLN 103.9 FM	410 S. Third Street	Louisville 40202
LA KAJN 102.9 FM	Box 1469	Crowley 70527
KCIJ 980 AM	Box 197	Shreveport 71161
KCKW 1480 AM	PO Box 1340	Jena 71342
KCTO 103.1 FM	Box 1319	Columbia 71418
KDBS 1410 AM	1515 Jackson Street	Alexandria 71301
KHAA 106.7 FM	650 Poydras St., Suite 1020	New Orleans 70130
KPAE 91.5 FM	13028 US Highway 190 W.	Port Allen 70767
KVDP 89.1 FM	Box 214	Dry Prong 71423
KXLA 990 AM Stereo	PO Box 990, Highway 80 W.	Rayville 71269
WBIU 1210 AM	601 Hatchell Lane	Denham Springs 70726
WBSN 89.1 FM	3939 Gentilly Blvd.	New Orleans 70126
WQCK 92.7 FM	PO Box 7934	Clinton 70722
WSHO 800 AM	4900 Veterans Blvd.	Metairie 70006
MA WEZE 1260 AM	Milton PO Box 206	Boston 02186
WLVG 740 AM	1972 Massachusetts Avenue	Cambridge 02140
MD WBGR 860 AM	334 N. Charles Street	Baltimore 21201
WBZE 1030 AM Stereo	Box 3B, Montgomery Lane	Waldorf 20601
WCRH 90.5 FM	Route 2, Box 325	Williamsport 21795
WFSI 107.9 FM	918 Chesapeake Avenue	Annapolis 21403
WOEL 89.9 FM	PO Box 246	Elkton 21921
WOLC 102.5 FM	PO Box 130	Princess Anne 21853
WRBS 95.1 FM	3600 Georgetown Road	Baltimore 21227
ME WKTQ 1450 AM	PO Box 72	Norway 04268
WTME 1530 AM	PO Box 3128	Auburn 04210
MI WBCM 1440 AM	Davidson Bldg., Suite 301	Bay City 48708
WCLS 1500 AM	15704 Six and One-Half Mile Road	Battle Creek 49017
WCSG 91.3 FM	1159 Beltine NE	Grand Rapids 49505
WFLT 1420 AM	317 S. Averill	Flint 48506
WGNR 88.9 FM	1331 Franklin SE	Grand Rapids 49506
WKJR 1520 AM	6803 Martin Road, PO Box 839	Muskegon 49443
WMAX 1480 AM	3250 28th Street SE	Grand Rapids 49508
WMIV 1550 AM	PO Box 190, 517 N. Beebe Street	Fremont 49412
WMPC 1230 AM	1800 N. Lapeer Road	Lapeer 48446
WMUZ 103.5 FM	12300 Radio Place	Detroit 48228
WNLF 1390 AM	Box 338, 1613 W. Lawrence Highway	Charlotte 48813
WOLW 91.1 FM	PO Box 1066	Cadillac 49601
WPHN 90.5 FM	PO Box 1212, 1511 M-32 E.	Gaylord 49735
WPRJ 1020 AM Stereo	8201 E. Chippewa Trail	Mt. Pleasant 48858
WUFL 1030 AM	42669 Garfield, Suite 328	Mt. Clemens 48043
WUFN 96.7 FM	2255 N. Concord Road	Albion 49224
WUGN 99.7 FM	510 Isabella Road, PO Box 366	Midland 48640
WUNN 1110 AM	1571 Tomlinson Road	Mason 48854
WWCM 990 AM Stereo	17 N. Huron Street	Ypsilanti 48197
MN KBHL 103.9	5l5 Pike Street E., Box 247	Osakis 56360
KBHW 99.5 FM	PO Box 433	International Falls 56649
KCFB 91.5 FM	Box 1683	St. Cloud 56302
KJLY 100.9 FM	PO Box 72, Faribault County Road 6	Blue Earth 56013
KKCM 1530 AM	Box 357, 421 E. First Street	Minneapolis 55379
KNOF 95.3 FM	1347 Selby Avenue	St. Paul 55104
KTIG 100.1 FM	PO Box 409	Pequot Lakes 56472
KTIS 900 AM 98.5 FM	3003 N. Snelling	St. Paul 55113

State / Channel / Frequency	Address	City/Zip
MN KYCR 1570 AM	5730 Duluth Street	Golden Valley 55422
WCTS 100.3 FM	2105 Fremont Avenue N.	Minneapolis 55411
WWJC 850 AM	1120 E. McCuen Street	Duluth 55808
MO KCCV 1510 AM	10841 E. 28th Street	Independence 64052
KJAB 90.1 FM	PO Box 336, 310 N. Wade	Mexico 65256
KKLL 1100 AM	831 W. Daugherty, PO Box 1100	Webb City 64870
KLFJ 1550 AM	811 Boonville	Springfield 65802
KLJC 88.5 FM	15800 Calvary Road	Kansas City 64147
KMFC 92.1 FM	Box 998	Columbia 65205
KNEO 91.5 FM	PO Box 391	Neosho 64850
KSIV 1320 AM	1750 S. Brentwood Blvd., Suite 811	St. Louis 63144
KSTL 690 AM	814 N. Third Street	St. Louis 63102
MS WACR 1050 AM	1910 14th Avenue N., PO Box 1078	Columbus 39703
WCFB 1060 AM	PO Box 1626	Tupelo 38802
WFCA 107.8 FM	Rt. 1, Box 12	French Camp 39745
WJWF 1400 AM	702 2nd Avenue N., PO Box 707	Columbus 39703
WKCU 1350 AM	2192 Highway 72 E.	Corinth 38834
WMBC 103.1 FM	702 2nd Avenue N., PO Box 707	Columbus 39701
WMER 1390 AM	601 22nd Avenue, 15th floor	Meridian 39301
WTWZ 1120 AM	PO Box 31	Clinton 39056
MT KGVW 640 AM	2050 Amsterdam Road	Belgrade 59714
KURL 730 AM	Box 31038	Billings 59107
KXEI 95.1 FM	Box 2426, 315 First Street	Havre 59501
NC WAJA 1480 AM	251 Highlands Road	Franklin 28734
WBFJ 1550 AM	Suite A, 3066 Trenwest Drive	Winston-Salem 27103
WBZQ 1550 AM	918 Dickinson Avenue	Greenville 27834
WCIS 760 AM	PO Box 2798	Morgantown 28655
WEGG 710 AM	PO Box 608	Rose Hill 28458
WFGW 1010 AM	PO Box 158	Black Mountain 28711
WGAS 1420 AM	Box 250	Gastonia 28052
WGCR 720 AM	105 Mull Arcade	Brevard 28712
WGHB 1250 AM	Highway 121 N., PO Box 229	Farmville 27828
WHPE 95.5/238 FM	1714 Tower Avenue	High Point 27260
WHVN 1240 AM	5732 N. Tryon Street	Charlotte 28213
WMIT 106.9 FM	PO Box 158	Black Mountain 28711
WNOW 1030 AM	PO Box 23509	Charlotte 28212
WPET 950 AM	Box 16924	Greensboro 27415
WPGT 90.1 FM	515 Becker Drive	Roanoke Rapids 27870
WPJL 1240 AM Stereo	515 Bart Street, PO Box 27946	Raleigh 27611
WRTP 1530 AM	4411 Chapel Hill Blvd.	Durham 27707
WSGH 1040 AM	PO Box 25368	Winston Salem 27114
WSML 1200 AM	1040 Ivey Road, PO Box 900	Graham 27253
WSTS 96.5 FM	Box 529	Laurinburg 28352
WTSB 580 AM	PO Box 1123	Lumberton 28350
WVCB 1410 AM	Box 314	Shallotte 28459
WWGL 94.1 FM	PO Box 668	Lexington 27292
WWMO 830 AM	149 N. Fieldcrest Road	Eden 27288
WYCM 1080 AM	Drawer 38, Highway 158	Murfreesboro 27855
ND KFNW 1200 AM 97.9 FM	PO Box 6008	Fargo 58108
NE KGBI 100.7 FM	1515 S. 10th Street	Omaha 68108
KGRD 105.3 FM	Box 247	Orchard 68764
KJSK 900 AM	Box 99	Columbus 68601
KROA 95.7 FM	Box K	Doniphan 68832
NH WCRN 94.9 FM/67 KHZ	PO Box 6336	East Rochester 03867
WDER 1320 AM	8 Lawrence Road, Box 465	Derry 03038
NJ WAWZ 99.1 FM	Box 97	Zarephath 08890
WFME 94.7 FM	289 Mt. Pleasant Avenue	W. Orange 07052
WKDN 106.9 FM	2906 Mt. Ephraim Avenue	Camden 08104
WNNN 101.7 FM	Box 132	Salem 08079
WSJL 102.3 FM	Box 258	Rio Grande 08242
WWDJ 970 AM	167 Main Street, PO Box 970	Hackensack 07602
NM KDAZ 730 AM	Box 4338	Albuquerque 87106
KKIM 1000 AM	307 Los Ranchos Road, NW	Albuquerque 87107
KNMI 88.9 FM	PO Box 1230	Farmington 87499
NV KCRV 1340 AM	100 N. Arlington Avenue, Suite 240	Reno 89501
KILA 90.5 FM	2201 S. 6th Street	Las Vegas 89104
KNIS 94.7 FM	6363 Highway 50 E.	Carson City 89701
NY WCHP 760 AM	Rapid Road, PO Box 888	Champlain 12919
WCIK 103.1 FM	PO Box 506	Bath 14810
WDCX 99.5 FM	625 Delaware Avenue	Buffalo 14202

State / Channel / Frequency	Address	City/Zip
NY WFBR FM		W. Seneca 14224
WFRS 88.5 FM	3200 Expressway Drive	Central Islip 11722
WFRW 90.7 FM	555 Canal Place	Palmyra 14522
WJIV 101.9 FM	Victory Mountain, PO Box 507	Cherry Valley 13320
WJSL 90.3 FM	Houghton College	Houghton 14744
WLIX 540 AM	138 W. Main Street	Bay Shore 11706
WMHN 89.3	675 Holt Road	Webster 14580
WMHR 102.9 FM	4044 Makyes Road	Syracuse 13215
WNYM 1330 AM	60 W. Castor Place, #2	Staten Island 10312
WOIV 105.1 FM	7095 Meyers Road E.	Syracuse 13057
WRUN 1150 AM	Thomas Road	Oriskany 13424
WSIV 1540 AM	7095 Meyers Road E.	Syracuse 13057
WTHE 1520 AM	266 Maple Place	Mineola 11501
WWWG 1460 AM	1850 S. Winton Road	Rochester 14618
WXIK 600 AM	Box 746	Watertown 13601
OH WAKW 93.3 FM	6275 Collegevue Place	Cincinnati 45224
WCRF 103.3 FM	9756 Barr Road	Cleveland 44141
WCUE 1150 AM	1675 State Road	Cuyahoga Falls 44223
WCVJ 90.9 FM	4422 Lenon New Lymer, PO Box 112	Jefferson 44047
WCVO 105 FM	4400 Reynoldsburg	New Albany 43054
WCVZ 93 FM	2477 E. Pike	Zanesville 43701
WEEC 100.7 FM	2348 Troy Road	Springfield 45504
WFCJ 93.7 FM	PO Box 93.7	Dayton 45449
WGCF 830 AM	2909 Weymouth Road	Shaker Heights 44120
WGFT 1500 AM	131 W. Boardman Street	Youngstown 44503
WGGN 97.7 FM	3809 Maple Avenue	Castalia 44824
WGOJ 105.5 FM	Box 725	Conneaut 44030
WHLO 640 AM	3535 S. Smith Road	Akron 44313
WHVT 90.5 FM	144 Lemon Street	Clyde 43410
WJYM 730 AM	8761 Fremont Pike	Perrysburg 43351
WMMX 1110 AM	16 S. Broad Street, Suite 5	Fairborn 45324
WPOS 102.3 FM	7112 Angola Road	Holland 43528
WQRP 88.1 FM	1514 W. Dorothy Lane	Dayton 45449
WRFD 880 AM	PO Box 802, N. High St. & Powell Road	Columbus 43985
WTGN 97.7 FM	1600 Elida Road	Lima 45805
WTOF 98.1 FM	120 Cleveland Avenue, NW	Canton 44702
WTSJ 1050 AM	800 Compton Road, Unit 33	Cincinnati 45231
WVMC 90.7 FM	500 Logan Road	Mansfield 44907
WZLE 104.9 FM	42851 N. Ridge Road	Elyria 44035
OK KCFO 970 AM	3737 S 37 W Avenue	Tulsa 74107
KEOR 1590 AM	PO Box 608	Atoka 74525
KOKF 90.9 FM	Box 22000	Edmond 73123
KQCV 800 AM	1919 N. Broadway	Oklahoma City 73103
KTLV 1220 AM	3336 SE 67th Street	Oklahoma City 73135
KUTA 101.1 FM	Oral Roberts University	Tulsa 74171
KWJY 92.1 FM	PO Box 1600	Woodward 73802
OR KDOV 1230 AM	PO Box 520	Ashland 97520
KGRV 700 AM	PO Box 1598, 196 SE Main Street	Winston 97496
KLIQ 1290 AM	5410 SW Macadam, #240	Portland 97201
KLWJ 1090 AM	PO Box 1410	Umatilla 97882
KORE 1050 AM	2080 Laura Street	Springfield 97477
KPDQ 800 AM 93.7 FM	5110 SE Stark Street	Portland 97215
KYTT 98.7 FM	455 N. Broadway	Coos Bay 97420
PA WCHR 94.5 FM	Woodside Road	Yardley 19067
WCTL 106.3 FM	Old Lincolnville Road, R.D. 3	Union City 16438
WDAC 94.5 FM	Box 3022	Lancaster 17604
WFRJ 88.9 FM	PO Box 876	Johnstown 15907
WGCB 1440 AM 96.1 FM	Box 88, Windsor Road	Red Lion 17356
WGSI 103.1 FM	PO Box 434, Rt. 62 N.	Russell 16345
WJLY 1550 AM	1233 Braddock Avenue	Braddock 15104
WJSA 1600 AM 93.5 FM	262 Allegheny Street	Jersey Shore 17740
WJSM 1110 AM 92.7 FM	RD 2, Box 87	Martinsburg 16662
WJTL 90.3 FM	780 Eden Road	Lancaster 17601
WLIH 107.1 FM	Box 97	Wellsboro 16901
WNAP 1110 AM	2311 Old Arch Road	Norristown 19401
WQJU 107.1 FM	22 N. 4th Street	Mifflintown 17059
WRGN 88.1 FM	RD 3	Hunlock Creek 18621
WSCR 1320 AM	1520 N. Keyser Avenue	Scranton 18504
WTLR 89.9 FM	2020 Cato Avenue	State College 16801
WVCH 740 AM	Box A	Brookhaven 19015

State / Channel / Frequency	Address	City/Zip
PA WZZD 990 AM	PO Box 26098	Philadelphia 19128
WERR 104.1 FM	Box RR, 65 Infantry Station	Rio Piedras 00929
WIDA 1400 AM 90.5 FM	Box 188	Carolina 00628
WIVV 1370 AM	GPO Box A	San Juan 00936
WNRT 96.9 FM	PO Box 201	Manati 00701
WORO 92.5 FM	415 Carbonell Street	Hato Rey 00918
WRFE 105.5 FM	PO Box 847	Mayaquez 00709
WVID 90.3 FM	Box 3420, Marina Station	Mayaguez 00709
RI WARV 1590 AM	19 Luther Avenue	Warwick 92886
SC WAGP 88.7 FM	PO Box 119	Beaufort 29901
WBBR 1580 AM	PO Box 3886	Greenville 29608
WCKI 1300 AM	Box 709	Greer 29652
WFCH 88.5 FM	PO Box 1286	Mt. Pleasant 29464
WHPB 1390 AM	Box 490	Belton 29627
WLFJ 89.3 FM	2420 Wade Hampton Blvd.	Greenville 29614
WMCJ 950 AM	PO Box 67, 314 Remburt Dennis Blvd.	Moncks Corner 29461
WMHK 89.7 FM	PO Box 3122	Columbia 29230
WMUU 1260 AM	920 Wade Hampton Blvd.	Greenville 29609
WPSC 1510 AM	100 S. Arant Street, PO Box 305	Pageland 29728
WQXL 1470 AM	1303 Sunset Drive, Box 3277	Columbia 29230
WSSC 1340 AM	201 Oswego Road	Sumter 29151
WTGH 620 AM	1303 State Street	Columbia 29033
WXAX 1170 AM	PO Box 609	Lexington 29072
WYFG 91.1 FM	101 E. Overbrook Drive	Gaffney 29340
WYFH 90.7 FM	7796 Dorchester Road	North Charleston 29418
WZJY 1480 AM	PO Box 12039	Charleston 29412
SD KCGN 101.5 FM	PO Box 101, E. Highway 12 and Airport Road	Milbank 57252
KJIA 1520 AM	305 W. 14th Street	Sioux Falls 57102
KSLT 107.3 FM	PO Box 845, 745 5th Street	Spearfish 55783
KVCX 101.5	PO Box 101	Gregory 57533
KVSR 97.9 FM	4040 Tower Road	Rapid City 57702
TN KSUD 730 AM	PO Box 3696	Memphis 38103
KWAM 990 AM	80 N. Tillman Street	Memphis 38111
WBCV 1550 AM	Box 68, 26 1/2 6th Street	Bristol 37621
WBLC 1360 AM	PO Box 100	Lenoir City 37771
WDYN 1070 FM	1815 Union Avenue	Chattanooga 37404
WEAB 960 AM	106 Main Street, PO Box 559	Adamsville 38310
WENR 1090 AM	PO Drawer 670, Highway 39 E.	Englewood 37329
WGVT 980 AM	PO Box 989	Chattanooga 37401
WHGG 88.3 FM	PO Box 2061	Bristol 37621
WITA 1490 AM	7212 Kingston Pike	Knoxville 37919
WMBW 89 FM	PO Box 11127	Chattanooga 37401
WMCH 1260 AM	PO Box 128	Church Hill 37642
WMOC 1450 AM	4707 12th Avenue	Chattanooga 37407
WNAH 1360 AM	44 Music Square E.	Nashville 37203
WNAZ 89.1 FM	333 Murfreesboro Road	Nashville 37210
WNQM 1300 AM	3314 W. End Avenue	Nashville 37203
WOCV AM	Box 370	Oneida 37841
WQKZ 96.7 FM	Box 191, 115 E. Jackson Street	Bolivar 38008
WREA 1520 AM	Box 609	Dayton 37321
WRJZ 620 AM	1515 E. Magnolia Avenue	Knoxville 37917
WWGM 1560 AM	2003 Blair Blvd., PO Box 12040	Nashville 37212
TX KAGC 1510 AM	PO Box 3420	Bryan 77805
KAGN 91.3 FM	209 S. Danville, #132-A	Abilene 79605
KBJS 90.3 FM	Box 193	Jacksonville 75766
KCBI 90.9 FM	Box 1809	Dallas 75221
KCTA 1030 AM	PO Box 898	Corpus Christi 78403
KDFT 504 AM	PO Box 440	Ferris 75125
KDLF 1150 AM	3185 Merriman Avenue, PO Box 545	Port Neches 77651
KDRY 1100 AM	8100 Roughrider, Suite 202, Box 34478	San Antonio 78265
KDVE 1510 AM	PO Box 1716, 117 Nederland Avenue	Nederland 77627
KENT 920 AM	PO Box 3509	Odessa 79760
KGLY 91.3 FM	PO Box 8525	Tyler 75711
KHCB 105.7 FM	2424 S. Blvd.	Houston 77098
KHQS 98.3 FM	PO Box 918	Gatesville 76528
KHVN 970 AM	1229 Corporate Drive W.	Arlington 76006
KHYM 1060 AM	104 W. Cass Street	Gilmer 75644
KIJN 1060 AM 92.3 FM	PO Box 458	Farwell 79325
KIXL 970 AM	1018 W. 11th	Austin 78703
KJAK 92.7 FM	Box 3890	Lubbock 79452

State / Channel / Frequency	Address	City/Zip
TX KJIC 88.1 FM	2936 Oleander	Pasadena 77503
KJOJ 106.9 FM	I-45 N	Spring 77381
KKKK 99.1 FM	Box K	Midland 79711
KLLF 1290 AM	PO Box 4647	Wichita Falls 76308
KMOC 89.5	PO Box 41	Wichita Falls 76307
KNBO 1530 AM	PO Box 848	New Boston 75570
KNRB 1360 AM	3001 W. 5th Street	Fort Worth 76107
KPAS 103.1 FM	PO Box 370982	El Paso 79937
KPDR 90.5 FM	106 E. Texas Street, PO Box 469	Wheeler 79096
KSBJ 88.1 FM	PO Box 187	Humble 77347
KSKY 660 AM	2727 Inwood Road	Dallas 75235
KSLR 630 AM	5430 Fredericksburg Road, Suite 504	San Antonio 78229
KTDN 91.5 FM	PO Box 1518	Palestine 75802
KTFA 92.1 FM	PO Box 820, 200 Roundbunch	Bridge City 77611
KVNE 89.5 FM	PO Box 8525	Tyler 75711
KVOJ 1130 AM	Drawer HH	Edna 77957
KVTT 91.7 FM	11061 Shady Trail	Dallas 75229
KXOI 810 AM	PO Box 2344	Odessa 79760
UT KANN 1120 AM	2222 Washington Blvd.	Ogden 84401
KBBX 1600 AM	481 S. 400 E.	Bountiful 84010
KCGL 106 FM	481 S. 400 E.	Bountiful 84010
KEYY 1450 AM	PO Box KEYY	Provo 84603
VA WABS 780 AM	5545 Lee Highway	Arlington 22207
WBTX 1470 AM	PO Box 337	Broadway 22815
WDCT 1310 AM	PO Box 1310, 3909 Oak Street	Fairfax 22030
WDUF AM	Route 5, PO Box 391	Duffield 24244
WDYL 92.1 FM	10600 Jefferson Davis Highway	Richmond 23237
WFAX 1220 AM	161-B Hillwood Avenue	Falls Church 22046
WFTH 1590 AM	5021 Brook Road	Richmond 23227
WGGM 1410 AM	10600 Jefferson Davis Highway	Richmond 23237
WGTH 105.5 FM	PO Drawer 370	Richlands 24641
WIVE 1430 AM	PO Box 866	Ashland 23005
WJYJ 90.5 FM	PO Box 905, 830 Gunnery Hill Road	Spotsylvania 22553
WKBA 1550 AM	2043 10th Street NE	Roanoke 24012
WKGK 1600 AM	Box 910	Saltville 24370
WKGM 940 AM	PO Box 339	Smithfield 23430
WMYT 1180 AM	2043 10th Street NE	Roanoke 24012
WNLR 1150 AM	PO Box 400	Churchville 24482
WOKT 1040 AM	400 Alleghany Street	Blacksburg 24060
WPLZ 1240 AM	1012 N. Avenue	Petersburg 23803
WPRZ 1250 AM	PO Box 3220	Warrenton 22186
WRIS 1410 AM	PO Box 6099	Roanoke 24017
WRVL 88.3 FM	Box 25000	Lynchburg 24506
WTJZ 1270 AM	553 Michigan Drive	Hampton 23669
WTRM 91.3 FM	PO Box 2627	Winchester 22601
WVZN 1170 AM	PO Box 11343	Lynchburg 24506
WXRI 105.3 FM	1318 Spratley Street, PO Box 1338	Portsmouth 23704
WYFI 99.7 FM	PO Box 1818	Chesapeake 23320
WYFJ 100.1 FM	407 S. Washington Highway	Ashland 23005
WYFT 103.9 FM	598 5th Street	Luray 22835
WZAM 1110 AM	5520 Greenwich Road	Virginia Beach 23462
WZAP 690 AM	180 Wallace Pike, PO Box 369	Bristol 24203
VT WGLY 103.1 FM	PO Box 150, Route 2	Waterbury 05676
WA KARI 550 AM	4840 Lincoln Road	Blaine 98230
KARR 1460 AM	220 Kirkland Avenue	Kirkland 98033
KBBO 1390 AM	Box 9188, 2120 Riverside Road	Yakima 98909
KBLE 1050 AM	114 Lakeside Avenue	Seattle 98122
KCIS 630 AM	19303 Fremont Avenue N.	Seattle 98133
KCMS 105.3 FM	19303 Fremont Avenue N.	Seattle 98133
KGNW 820 AM	2815 Second Avenue, Suite 100	Seattle 98121
KJVH 89.5 FM	1130 14th Avenue	Longview 98632
KLYN 106.5 FM	1843 Front Street	Lynden 98264
KMBI 107.9 FM 1330 AM	S 5408 Freya	Spokane 99223
KRSS 1230 AM	N. 1306 Ash	Spokane 99201
KUDY 1280 AM	S 5106 Palouse Highway	Spokane 99203
KVSN 1500 AM	PO Box 4207	Tuymwater 98501
WI WEMI 100.1 FM	360 Chute Street	Menasha 54952
WGNV 88.5 FM	PO Box 88	Milladore 54454
WNWC 102.5 FM	5606 Medical Circle	Madison 53719
WRVM 102.7 FM	PO Box 212	Suring 54174
WVCX 98.9 FM	PO Box 187	Tomah 54660

State / Channel	Address	City/Zip
WI WVCY 107.7 FM	2712 W. Vliet Street	Milwaukee 53208
WWIB 103.7 FM	5558 Hallie Road	Chippewa Falls 54729
WV WBKW 99.5 FM	PO Box AB, 102 N. Kanawha Street	Beckley 25801
WEMM 107.9 FM	703 3rd Avenue	Huntington 25701
WMEJ 91.9 FM	PO Box 7575	Huntington 25777
WOAY 860 AM	PO Box 251	Oak Hill 25901
WSCW 1410 AM	PO Box 8718, 605 D Street	South Charles 25303
WVKV 1080 AM	PO Box 1080	Hurricane 25526
WVVW 630 AM	Box 374, Greens Run Road	St. Marys 26170
WXIT 1490 AM	136 High Street	Charleston 25311
WYJP 100.9 FM	PO Box 8718, 605 D Street	South Charles 25303
WY KUYO 830 AM	PO Box 90395	Casper 82905

Television

State / Channel	Address	City/Zip
AL WHBR-TV Chan. 33 (F)	2080 County Road 63	Robertsdale 36567
WMCF-TV Chan. 45 (F)	PO Box 45	Montgomery 36101
WMPV-TV Chan. 21 (F)	120 Zeigler Circle E	Mobile 36608
AR KVTN-TV Chan. 25 (C)	PO Box 22007	Little Rock 72221
AZ K25AL Chan. 25 (C)	510 N. Acoma Blvd.	Lake Havasu City 86403
KPAZ-TV Chan. 21 (C)	3551 E. McDowell	Phoenix 85008
CA Cable TV (C)	Redwood Chapel Community Church, 19300 Redwood Road	Castro Valley 94546
K62BT-TV Chan. 62 (C)	PO Box 1606	Placerville 95667
KAGL-TV Chan. 30 (C)	318 Mira Loma Avenue	Glendale 91204
KCBA-TV Chan. 35 (F)	PO Box 3560	Salinas 93912
KCSO-TV Chan. 19 (F)	PO Box 3689	Modesto 95352
KFCB-TB Chan. 42 (C)	PO Box 4242, 5101 Port Chicago Highway	Concord 94524
KLXV-TV Chan. 65 (C)	PO Box 2B	San Jose 95109
KMSG-TV Chan. 59 (F)	706 W. Herndon Avenue	Fresno 93650
KNXT-TV Chan. 49 (F)	1550 N. Fresno Street	Fresno 93704
KO7TA-TV Chan. 7 (F)	PO Box 172	Santa Marie 93456
KO9UF-TV Chan. 9 (F)	PO Box 172	Santa Maria 93546
KTBN-TV Chan. 40 (C)	2442 Michelle	Tustin 92680
KVEA-TV Chan. 52, 57 (F)	3075 Cohasset Road	Chico 95926
KWBB-TV Chan. 38 (F)	45 Franklin Street, Suite 205	San Francisco 94102
VPN-TV Chan. 3, 6, 14, 26 (F)	3075 Cohasset Road	Chico 95926
CO K47AQ-TV Chan. 47 (C)	455 S. Platte River Drive	Denver 80223
KWBI-TV (F)	16075 W. Belleview Avenue	Morrison 80465
FL Chan. 21 (C)	PO Box 6922	Clearwater 34618
Chan. 59 (C)	PO Box 6922	Clearwater 34618
Group W Cable (C)	1723 S. Bartow Highway	Lakeland 33801
W15AG (C)	1305 E. Helvenston, PO Box 6922	Clearwater 34618
W24AA (C)	2600 Pine Island Road	Cape Coral 33910
W53 H I Chan. 53 (C)	PO Box 6922	Clearwater 34618
W65BG-TV Chan. 65 (C)	300 N. Meridian Road	Tallahassee 32312
WACX SUPER Chan. 55 (C)	4520 Parkbreeze Court	Orlando 32808
WCLF-TV Chan. 22 (C)	PO Box 6922	Clearwater 34618
WHFT-TV Chan. 45 (C)	3324 Pembroke Road	Pembroke Park 33021
WPJX-TV Chan. 42 (F)	2104 SW 42nd Avenue	Ocala 32674
WSWS-TV Chan. 66 (F)	1800 Pepperell Parkway, PO Box 870	Opelika 36801
WTGL-TV Chan. 52 (C)	PO Box 1852	Cocoa 32923
HI K5OAP Chan. 50 (F)	1960 Kapiolani Blvd., Suite 113-327	Honolulu 96822
IA Cable Chan. 13 (C)	217 N. High Street	Keokuk 52632
Cable Team TV (C)	1000 E. 41st Street	Sioux Falls 57105
K60CL-TV Chan. 60 (C)	217 N. 4th Street	Keokuk 52632
IL W51AF-TV Chan. 51 (C)	1 N. Wacker Drive	Chicago 60606
W68BR-TV Chan. 68 (C)	1 N. Wacker Drive	Chicago 60606
WCFC-TV Chan. 38 (C)	38 S. Peoria	Chicago 60607
WFHL-TV Chan. 23 (C)	2510 Parkway Court	Decatur 62526
WTCT-TV Chan. 27 (C)	PO Box 1010, Route 37 N.	Marion 62959
WWTO-TV Chan. 35 (C)	E 1251 Road	Ottawa 61350
IN WHMB-TV Chan. 40 (F)	Box 50250	Indianapolis 46250
WHME-TV Chan. 46 (F)	61300 S. Ironwood Road	South Bend 46614
WINM-TV Chan. 63 (F)	PO Box 11925	Ft. Wayne 46861
WJRM-TV Chan. 17 (F)	Highway 56E	Salem 47167
WKOI-TV Chan. 43 (C)	1702 S. 9th Street	Richmond 47374
WO5BE-TV Chan. 5 (C)	PO Box 1462	Jeffersonville 47131
KS KYFC-TV Chan. 50 (F)	4715 Rainbow	Shawnee Mission 66205
KY WLCN-TV Chan. 19 (F)	Box 1087	Madisonville 42431
WLJC-TV Chan. 65 (C)	Route 36, Box 50	Beattyville 41311
WTSF-TV Chan. 61 (C)	3100 Bath Avenue	Ashland 41101
LA KMCT-TV Chan. 39 (C)	PO Box 2957	W. Monroe 71294

State / Channel	Address	City/Zip
MI Cable C.A.R.T.A. Chan. 29 (F)	PO Box 16296, 1441 E. Michigan Avenue	Lansing 48901
WAQP-TV Chan. 49 (C)	PO Box 2215, 707 Federal Street	Saginaw 48605
WGPR-TV Chan. 62 (F)	3140-6 E. Jefferson	Detroit 48207
WLLA-TV Chan. 64 (F)	PO Box 431, 207 E. Water Street	Kalamazoo 49005
WTLJ-TV Chan. 54 (C)	10290 48th Avenue	Allendale 49401
MN K22AE-TV Chan. 22 (C)	303 N. Minnesota Street	New Ulm 56073
K28AE-TV Chan. 28 (C)	64 Downtown Plaza	Fairmount 56031
MO KNLC-TV Chan. 24 (C)	PO Box 924	St. Louis 63188
MKNLJ-TV Chan. 25 (C)	Rt. 2, Box 72	New Bloomfield 65063
KTAJ-TV Chan. 16 (C)	RR 1, Box 403A	Agency 64401
MS W56BH-TV Chan. 64 (C)	PO Box 786	Jackson 39205
NC WEJC-TV Chan. 20 (F)	PO Box 2020	Lexington 27293
WRDG-TV Chan. 16 (C)	PO Box 16	Burlington 27216
NM K636D-TV Chan. 63 (F)	1017 N. Y. Avenue	Alamogordo 88310
KCHF-TV Chan. 11 (C)	216 Frontage Road, Highway 14	Santa Fe 87505
KNAT-TV Chan. 23 (C)	1510 Coors Road NW	Albuquerque 87105
KRPV-TV Chan. 27 (C)	Box 967	Roswell 88201
NV KREN-TV Chan. 27 (F)	PO Box 40127	Reno 89504
NY WTBY-TV Chan. 54 (C)	PO Box 534, Route 9 & Merritt Road	Fishkill 12524
OH WDLI-TV Chan. 17 (C)	6600 Atlantic Blvd. NE	Louisville 44641
WGGN-TV Chan. 52 (C)	3809 Maple Avenue, PO Box 2397	Sandusky 44870
WSFJ-TV Chan. 51 (C)	10077 Jacksontown Road, SE	Thornville 43076
WTJC-TV Chan. 26 (C)	PO Box 26	Dayton 45401
WTLW-TV Chan. 44 (F)	1844 Baty Road	Lima 45807
OK KTBO-TV Chan. 14 (C)	3705 NW 63rd Street	Oklahoma City 73116
KWHB-TV Chan. 47 (C)	PO Box 470047	Tulsa 74147
KDOR-TV	2120 N. Yellowood	Broken Arrow 74012
OR K61CC-TV Chan. 61 (C)	838 Commercial NE	Salem 93701
PA WFMZ-TV Chan. 69 (F)	E. Rock Road	Allentown 18103
WGCB-TV Chan. 49 (F)	Box 88, Windsor Road	Red Lion 17356
WKBS-TV Chan. 47 (C)	Rt. 48, Signal Hill Drive	Wall 15148
WPCB-TV Chan. 40 (C)	Rt. 48, Signal Hill Drive	Wall 15148
WPHL-TV Chan. 17 (F)	5001 Wynnefield Avenue	Philadelphia 19131
PR WECN-TV Chan. 64 (C)	Box 310, Road 167	Bayamon 00621
SC WCCT-TV Chan. 57 (F)	PO Box 5757	W. Columbia 29171
WGGS-TV Chan. 16 (F)	PO Box 1616, 3409 Rutherford Road	Greenville 29602
WGSE-TV Chan. 43 (F)	PO Box 1616	Greenville 29602
SD Team TV (C)	1000 E. 41st Street	Sioux Falls 57105
TN Chan. 67 (C)	4707 12th Avenue	Chattanooga 37407
W61AR-TV Chan. 61 (C)	200 Hill Avenue	Nashville 37210
WHTN-TV Chan. 39 (F)	5202 Lebanon Road	Old Hickory 37138
WPMC-TV Chan. 54 (C)	PO Box 847	Jellico 37762
TX GETV Cable TV (C)	18755 Stone Oak Parkway	San Antonio 78258
K31A1 Chan. 31 (C)	PO Box 73313	Houston 77273
K66CA Chan. 66 (C)	PO Box 73313	Houston 77273
K67DU Chan. 67 (C)	PO Box 73313	Houston 77273
KIIRT-TV (F)	PO Box 1712	Jacksonville 75766
KLTJ-TV Chan. 57 (C)	3737 Red Bluff	Pasadena 77503
KO2MQ Chan. 2 (C)	PO Box 73313	Houston 77273
KO5HX-TV Chan. 5 (C)	PO Box 73313	Houston 77273
KO51A Chan. 5 (C)	PO Box 73313	Houston 77273
WUJA-TV Chan. 58 (C)	1386 N. Reagan Street	San Benito 78586
VA WAZT-TV Chan. 10 (F)	123 E. Court Street	Woodstock 22664
WEFC-TV Chan. 38 (C)	612 Bullitt Avenue SE	Roanoke 24013
WJCB-TV Chan. 49 (F)	1930 E. Pembroke Avenue	Hampton 23663
WLBU-TV Chan. 11 (F)		Lynchburg 24506
WTKK-TV Chan. 66 (F)	9008 Center Street	Manassas 22110
WZXK-TV Chan. 65 (C)	10211 Staples Mill Road	Glen Allen 23060
WA KTBW-TV Chan. 20 (C)	1909 S. 341st Place	Federal Way 98003
WI WSCO-TV Chan. 14 (C)	3434 W. Kilbourn Avenue	Milwaukee 54174
WVCY-TV Chan. 30 (F)	2712 W. Vliet Street	Milwaukee 53208

International

6911-Switzerland Chan. 44/37/46	Via per Pugerna, No. 3,	Campione, D'Italia
Guatemala Chan. 21	Audio Video de Guatemala,	
	20 Calle 7-71, Zona 14	La Canada
Netherlands	Evangelische Omroep, PO Box 565,	1200 AN Hilversum
South Africa Chan. 24	The Ciskei Government, PO Box 81	Bisho, Rep. of Ciskei
Taiwan	Overseas Radio & Television, Inc., PO Box 37-3	Taipei
USA, MET-TV Chan. 12	CBN Center	Virginia Beach, VA 23463
West Indies, Chan. 13	Bath Plain	Charlestown, Nevis

CHURCH ATTENDANCE UNCHANGED BY RELIGIOUS TV

Has watching religious TV changed your involvement in your local church or synagogue? Has your involvement increased or decreased? (Based on total viewers.)

Has not changed involvement 90%
Has changed involvement 8%
  Increased 4%
  Decreased 2%
  Not sure 2%
Not sure 2%
                                             100%

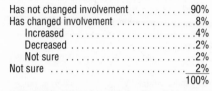

Gallup Poll, April 1987. From *100 Questions and Answers* by George Gallup, Jr., and Sarah Jones. Copyright © 1989. Princeton Research Center.

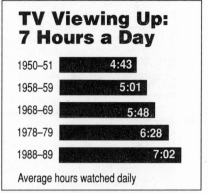

TV Viewing Up: 7 Hours a Day

1950–51	4:43
1958–59	5:01
1968–69	5:48
1978–79	6:28
1988–89	7:02

Average hours watched daily

Source: Nielson Television Index

CHRONOLOGY OF CHRISTIAN RADIO AND TELEVISION

1865   English physicist James Clerk Maxwell assumes existence of electromagnetic waves.
1885-1888   German physicist Heinrich Hertz verifies Maxwell's theories.
1895   Italian physicist Guglielmo Marconi improves and applies Hertz's inventions.
1901   Marconi transmits messages across the Atlantic from England to Newfoundland.
1920   First radio broadcasts begin in the U.S.
1921   U.S. Department of Commerce licenses 32 broadcasting stations.
1921   Origins of global electronic church: first broadcast of a church worship service—Calvary Episcopal Church, Pittsburgh, Pa.
First Baptist radio broadcast.
1922   First Pentecostal broadcast by Aimee S. McPherson.
1923   Ten churches now operate radio stations. By 1928, 60 stations, falling by 1933 to 30.
1930   "The Lutheran Hour" broadcast over station WHK in Cleveland, Ohio, begun by the Lutheran Church—Missouri Synod; 1931, heard by 5 million a week, 1943 15 million, 1965 30 million in 120 countries over more than 1,000 radio stations; 1940, foreign broadcasting now named "Bringing Christ to the Nations"; 1945, worldwide to 20 million a week; 1975, broadcast in over 50 languages, heard by 22 million a week; 1987, 40 million regular listeners in 34 languages around world.
1930   Radio is now second only to newspapers as a major form of communciation.
1931   Radio Vatican inaugurated in Rome by Pius XI (1857-1939); entrusted to Jesuits; daily announcement motto "Laudetur Jesus Christus" (Praised be Jesus Christ); 1975, broadcasts to 157 countries in 32 languages for 16 hours a day; 1982, John Paul II inaugurates Vatican Television; 1987, in 35 languages.
1933   Experimental television transmission begins from Empire State Building, New York, N.Y.
1939   Public television programming in U.S. begins with the televising of the New York World's Fair opening.
1943   National Religious Broadcasters of North America formed as official broadcasting arm of National Association of Evangelicals, with 50 organizations growing by 1979 to over 800; by 1986, annual convention attracts 4,000.
1946   World Literature Crusade begins in Canada for radio outreach.
1949   Sales of television sets in U.S. reach 250,000 a month.
1950   Evangelistic broadcasting spreads: 1950, Billy Graham begins on ABC radio, and 1951 on TV; 1953, Rex Humbard telecasts weekly.
1950   Rise of television overshadows radio.
"Hour of Decision" radio program with Billy Graham begins over 150 stations; 1951,

20 million listeners (200,000 letters received per year); by 1978, 900 radio/TV stations worldwide, and a million letters per year (with 70 million viewers in U.S.).

1953 World Committee for Christian Broadcasting constituted in Britain, then International Committee for Christian Broadcasting; 1961, founds World Association for Christian Broadcasting; 1968, merges with Coordinating Committee for Christian Broadcasting to form World Association for Christian Communication.

1955 World Conference on Missionary Radio begins in U.S.; 1963, joins with National Religious Broadcasters of North America to form International Christian Broadcasters, which disbands in 1968.

1961 First religious TV station opens in U.S.: WYAH (M. G. "Pat" Robertson, in Tidewater, Va.), later Christian Broadcasting Network; by 1980, almost every major metropolitan center in U.S. has its own religious TV stations; by 1987, CBN World Outreach involves "sharing the love of Jesus in more than 85 nations."

World Association for Christian Broadcasting founded, becoming by 1968 the World Association for Christian Communication.

World Radio Missionary Fellowship inaugurates HCJB-TV (Quito, Ecuador) as pioneer missionary telecaster; 1985, 218 overseas personnel in eight countries.

1963 U.S. evangelicals form International Christian Broadcasters; 1967, meets in Concordia, Milwaukee; fades out by 1968, displaced by National Religious Broadcasters.

1969 Pentecostal evangelist Jimmy L. Swaggart begins U.S. radio ministry "Camp Meeting Hour"; in 1972 television ministry begins; by 1987, Jimmy Swaggart Ministries airs telecasts over 3,200 TV stations in 15 languages viewed by 510 million in 145 countries weekly, receiving donations of $150 million a year and claiming that "the medium of television is the most expedient method of spreading the gospel the world has ever known. It is God's directive that the Great Commission be carried out by this means"; 1988, partial collapse due to sex scandal.

1973 Trinity Broadcasting Network, CA, launches Pentecostal television station "to get the gospel to every living human being on planet Earth" before Jesus comes; by 1986, TBN owns 55 TV stations in the U.S. with 26 affiliates, also stations in Guatemala, St. Kitts-Nevis, Italy, and Ciskei.

1974 Number of radios worldwide reaches 922 million.

1975 International Christian Broadcasters begins Project Look Up. Plans to reach world via NASA's ATS-6 geostational satellite to beam TV seminary teaching and lay institutes across world; 1977, begins broadcasts to Puerto Rico; satellite suddenly withdrawn by NASA; 1979, Project Look Up fizzles out due to inadequate funding, though committees go on meeting until after 1988.

1979 National Religious Broadcasters and World Evangelical Fellowship propose Angel-I/Angel-II/Angel-III Project to blanket earth with gospel broadcasts; three satellites in geostationary orbit filling roles of three angels of Revelation 14:6-11, each covering a third of earth's surface, fulfilling Matthew 24:14 "for a witness unto all nations"; by 1983, author realized project has been "committed to death," so proposal passes into oblivion, though use of satellites for U.S. Christian TV grows.

TV evangelist Jim Bakker of PTL Ministries announces plans to start PTL missions throughout the world; funds raised by plan fizzle out within a year; in 1987, PTL Ministries collapses in financial and sex scandal.

1981 Christian broadcasting expands from origin in 1921 to global force heard or seen regularly by 23% of world's population.

New generation of charismatic TV evangelists arises, including Oral Roberts (who began Pentecostal TV preaching in 1953) and son Richard, Pat Robertson, Rex Humbard, Jimmy Swaggart, Kenneth Copeland, Paul Crouch, Jim Bakker, et al.

Dominion Video Satellite (Dominion Network), FL, launched to provide Christian radio/TV programs over direct broadcast satellite systems, based on Great Commission; direct broadcast satellites fulfill roles of the angel of Revelation 14:6 and, using 30-inch portable dish receivers, bypass secular control over TV.

1982 World Satellite Evangelism (motto: Using Mass Media to Reach the Unreached of the World for Christ) begins in Tulsa, Okla., "mobilizing media to reach every person in every home with the gospel" especially in closed countries; forms a global media task force in 50 nations, starting Christian universities and other centers.

1983 Catholic global television evangelism agency launches Lumen 2000, based in Dallas and Vatican City, "to preach the gospel of Jesus to the uttermost parts of the earth, spreading the love of Jesus around the globe"; 1986, in 50 countries.

1985 Three major Christian broadcasting agencies, FEBC, HCJB/World Radio Missionary Fellowship, TWR (and later ELWA-SIM) announce "Project: The World by 2000" to be completed by AD 2000, giving everyone on earth the opportunity to hear the gospel of Christ by radio (September); 1987, target modified to be: all major trade languages with over one million speakers each by AD 2000, then all minor trade languages, and finally changed to the world's 6,500 "heart" languages.

1986 Intercontinental Broadcasting Network begins in Virginia Beach, Va., by independent charismatics linking up with European counterparts.

Televised Evangelism for All, a project proposed by Christian Broadcasting Network vice-president N. Van Hamm: 6 million 10-inch flat liquid-screen printed-circuit solar-cell television units, costing $1 each, dumped out of aircraft across world, glide to earth over unevangelized peoples, pretuned to 18-language transmissions over three or four geostationary satellites.

1987 Global Rosary for World Peace and world evangelization prayed by John Paul II in St. Peter's basilica, Vatican; 16 Marian shrines across the world linked by 18 satellites and 75 TV cameras, with TV audience of 1.5 billion in over 30 countries in 35 languages; most complex and ambitious television program of all times.

Community Satellite Corporation, U.S., launches Dominion Network (satellites to homes) into orbit by utilizing direct broadcast satellites.

Global Broadcasting System launched for Christian radio and TV broadcasting to any place on earth through "Top Hat" system of super-pressure platform network of 800 high-tech balloons at 120,000 feet altitude covering the whole world.

1988 Regular listeners/viewers for Christian programs number 1.2 billion (14% of the world).

Possible Future Scenario

2000 Entire world finally reached with Christian gospel for first time in history, in the sense that everyone everywhere has heard or hears the gospel in depth with understanding and has access to Scripture, churches, missions, Christians, Christian broadcasting (with 4,000 Christian radio and TV stations worldwide), movies, literature, and other means of grace.

Source: Extracted from "788 Global Plans" in *Seven Hundred Plans to Evangelize the World* by David B. Barrett and James W. Reapsome. Copyright © by Foreign Mission Board of the Southern Baptist Convention. Published by New Hope. Used by permission.

66 99
FOCUS
QUOTE
The more children watch violent television, the more likely they are to be violent.
—Dr. William H. Deitz, pediatrician

FOCUS
FACT
As many as 50 million adults look to religious television as a major input to their faith.

NATIONAL RELIGIOUS BROADCASTING AWARDS

Distinguished Service Award Presented to an individual or organization for outstanding contributions to the field of broadcasting
Milestone Award Presented to an individual or organization for 50 years of continuous service in the field of religious broadcasting
Broadcasting Hall of Fame Presented to a Christian broadcaster who has achieved wide recognition in religious media communication with the highest standards

Award of Merit

	1959	Hour of Decision, Billy Graham
	1960	Old Fashioned Revival Hour, Charles E. Fuller
	1961	Lutheran Hour, Oswald C. J. Hoffmann
	1962	Light and Life Hour, Myron Boyd
	1963	Back to the Bible Broadcast, Theodore Epp
	1964	Revivaltime, C. M. Ward
		The Far East Broadcasting Company, Robert Bowman
	1965	Radio Station HCJB, Clarence Jones
		Showers of Blessing, T. W. Willingham
	1966	Christian Brotherhood Hour, W. Dale Oldham
		TEAM, Tom Watson
	1967	Moody Radio Network, James E. Draper
		Trans World Radio, Paul Freed
	1968	Radio Station ELWA, Raymond Davis
		This Is the Life, Martin Neeb, Jr.
	1969	Christian Broadcasting System, E. Otto DeCamp
		Morning Chapel Hour, Wilbur Nelson
	1970	Bible Fellowship Hour, Celia Webb
	1970	Chapel of the Air, John D. Jess
	1971	Family Stations, Inc., Harold Camping
		Mennonite Broadcast, Inc., Kenneth Weaver
	1972	Haven of Rest, Paul Evans
	1973	Cornelius Keur, Paul Ramseyer
		Northwestern College Radio, KTIS AM-FM
	1974	Christian Broadcasting Network, M. G. 'Pat' Robertson
		Radio Bible Class, Richard DeHaan
	1975	John Brown University, John E. Brown, Jr.
		Southern Baptist Radio-TV Commission, Paul M. Stevens
	1976	Grand Old Gospel Hour, B. Sam Hart
		KRDU, David Hofer
		Unshackled! Harry G. Saulnier
		WRVM, Ken Hettinga
	1977	Inspirational Broadcasting Corp., KPDQ, Robert W. Ball
		The Back to God Hour, Joel Nederhood
	1979	Day of Discovery, Richard DeHaan
		KHEP, Jack Willis
	1980	At Home with the Bible, Frank Pollard
		Hour of Freedom, Howard O. Jones
		WCFC-TV, Jerry Rose
		WKDH/WIVE, James Birkett
	1981	Trinity Broadcasting Network, Paul Crouch
		WDAC, Paul Hollinger
		WFGW, Edna Edwards
	1982	Focus on the Family
		Rex Humbard Television Ministry
	1983	In Touch
		Insight for Living
		Le Sea Broadcasting Co., Lester Sumrall
		WRBS/Baltimore, Maryland
	1984	100 Huntley Street
		Family Life Broadcasting

Grace to You
The First Estate, WNBC-TV
Tips for Teens
Wesleyan Hour
WTLW-TV/Lima Ohio
1985 A Visit with Mrs. G.
Afterglow
KCFO/Tulsa, Oklahoma
The Grace Worship Hour
WPCB-TV 40/Wall, Pennsylvania
1986 Continente '85 Campaign—Luis Palau
CTN Magazine—Glenn Plummer
Explo '85—Bill Bright
Inside Russia—Billy Graham
KFCB Chan. 42/Concord, California
KGNW/Seattle, Washington
KIRV/Fresno, California
Moody Presents
Point of View—Marlin Maddoux
The Pat Boone Show—Pat Boone
Un Mensaje a la Conciencia—Herman Pablo
WBCL/Fort Wayne, Indiana
WGCB/Red Lion, Pennsylvania
1987 Al Sanders—Ambassador Advertising Agency
Ben Haden—Changed Lives
Dan Matthews—Christian Lifestyles Magazine
Jane Dickerson—The Filling Station
Jimmy and Joanne Thompson—Nite Line
John Helder—Coral Ridge Ministries
Juan Boonstra—La Hora de la Reforma
Nathan Travis Middleton—Sanctity of Human Life Week
Stephen Brown—Key Life
Lou Velker—WWCM
1988 The 700 Club
Prime Time America
Salem Communications Corp.

Award of Merit for Management	1989	Jon Campbell, President, Ambassador Advertising Agency, Fullerton, Calif.
Award of Merit for Program Production	1989	Ron Hutchcraft, Saturday Night Alive, Moody Broadcasting Network, Chicago, Ill.
Black Ministry Award	1988	Anthony Evans
	1989	Clay Evans, What a Fellowship Hour, Chicago, Ill.
	1990	Dr. B. Sam Hart, Grand Old Gospel Fellowship, Philadelphia, Pa.
Board of Directors Award	1988	Richard E. Wiley
	1989	Senator Bill Armstrong, (R) Colorado
	1991	Paul Harvey
Broadcast Facility of the Year Award	1988	KFIA/Carmichael, Calif. KJNP/North Pole, Alaska KTBN, TBN/Santa Ana, Calif. WCFC-TV/Chicago, Ill.
Broadcast Facility of the Year for Radio— Large Market	1989	KKLA-FM, Salem Communications Corp, Dennis Worden, General Mgr., Los Angeles
Broadcast Facility of the Year for Radio— Small Market	1989	KURL-AM, Enterprise Network, Billings, Mont., Bruce Erickson
Broadcast Facility of the Year for Television	1989	WPCB-TV/Ch. 40, Russell and Norma Bixler, Pittsburgh, Pa.

NATIONAL RELIGIOUS BROADCASTING AWARDS cont.

Christian Broadcaster of the Year	1989	Pat Robertson, Christian Broadcasting Network, Virginia Beach, Va.
Direct Response and/ or Magazine Award	1988	Christian Management Review
	1989	Fund Raising Managament Magazine, Hoke Communications, Garden City, N.Y., William Olcott, Editor
Distinguished Service Award	1972	Stanley N. Whitcanack, Showers of Blessing
	1973	Thomas F. Zimmerman, Assemblies of God
	1974	Dean Burch, FCC Chairman
		Eugene R. Bertermann, President of NRB
		Pamela Ilott, CBS News
	1977	Richard E. Wiley, FCC Chairman
		Sol Taishoff, Broadcasting Magazine
	1979	C. M. Ward, Revivaltime
	1980	Wendell Loveless
	1981	J. Vernon McGee, Thru the Bible
	1982	W. Dale Oldham, Christian Brotherhood Hour
	1983	Theodore Epp, Back to the Bible
	1984	Carl Smith, Consulting Engineer
		Herrmann Braunlin, Hawthorne Gospel Church
		Mary Dorr, Religion in Media
	1985	Clay Evans, What a Fellowship Hour
		Mark Fowler, FCC Chairman
		Neal Doty and Sherman Williams, Redwood Chapel
		Orva Koenigsburg, Domain Communications
	1986	Bishop Samuel L. Green, Jr.
		Patrick Buchanan
		Paul Bearfield
	1987	John D. Jess
		Joseph Barbera
		Luis Palau
		Paul Freed
		Ralph Montanus, Sr.
		Stephen Olford
		Steve Allen
		Ted Engstrom
	1988	George Sweeting, Moody Presents
		Robert A. Cook, The Kings Hour
	1989	Oswald C. J. Hoffmann
	1990	Dr. E. Brandt Gustavson, Trans World Radio, Chatham, N.J.
		Dr. Robert Cook, The King's Hour, Tannersville, Pa.
		Tom Zimmerman, Lausanne Committee for World Evangelization, Springfield, Mo.
	1991	Ralph Carmichael
Headquarters and NRB Staff Award	1988	Esther DiGiovanni
	1989	Anne Dunlap, Administrative Assistant, National Religious Broadcasters, N.J.
Hispanic Ministry Award	1988	Jose Reyes
	1989	Radio Vision Cristiana, Staten Island, N.Y.
	1990	Alberto Mottesi, Alberto Mottesi Evangelistic Association, Midway City, Calif.
International Award	1991	Robert Carlton Savage (posthumously), HCJB
Milestone Award	1976	Moody Bible Institute
	1977	This Is the Life
	1978	Theodore Elsner
	1979	Dale Crowley
	1980	Glenn Tingley
	1981	Celia Webb, Bible Fellowship Hour
		Charles Leaming, Faith Gospel Broadcast

Clarence Jones, HCJB
Dr. Oswald C. J. Hoffmann, The Lutheran Hour
Howard Ferrin, Mountaintop Hour
1982 Gordon K. Powell, Radio Revival Hour
KFSG/Los Angeles, Calif.
Manford George Gutzke, The Bible for You
Pillar of Fire Radio Stations
1983 David Webber, Southwest Radio Church of the Air
KPPC/Pasadena, Calif.
Quinton Everest, Your Worship Hour
Rev. Donald Baughey
Rex Humbard, Sr.
Russell Killman, Heaven and Home Hour
WMPC/Michigan
1984 Berean Bible Society
Family Altar
KDRY/San Antonio, Tex.
Sunday Evening Club, Chicago, Ill.
Union Rescue Mission, Los Angeles, Calif.
1985 Nation's Family Prayer Period
1986 Celia Webb
Norman Vincent Peale
William and Anne Schafer, The Lifeline Hour
1987 Ernest C. Manning
Noah Edward McCoy
Samuel Kelsey
Sunday School of the Air
The Biola Hour
The Calvary Hour
Wealthy Street Baptist Church
1988 Park Street Church
1989 Back to the Bible Broadcast, Lincoln, Nebr.
Chapel of the Air, Wheaton, Ill.
Haven of Rest, Hollywood, Calif.
Radio Bible Class, Grand Rapids, Mich.
1990 Chaplain Ray Hoekstra, International Prison, Dallas, Tex.
Dr. Jack MacArthur, Voice of Calvary, Seattle, Wash.
Dr. Jack Wyrtzen, Word of Life Fellowship, Schroon Lake, N.Y.
Dr. James Boice, The Bible Study Hour, Philadelphia, Pa.
John D. Jess, Family Life Radio, Tucson, Ariz.
Mel Johnson, Northwestern College & Radio, Roseville, Minn.
Mrs. Robert Fraser, Fraser Gospel Hour, Philadelphia, Pa.
1991 The Baptist Hour
Constantine & Elizabeth Lewshenia
Neil C. Macaulay
J. Vernon McGee (posthumously)
Slavic Gospel Association

Ministry of the Year Award	1988	Focus on the Family International Media Services There's Hope
New Ministry Award	1988	Minirth-Meier Clinic
NRB Chapter Award	1988 1989	Caribbean Chapter Midwest Chapter, Minneapolis, Minn.
President's Award	1988 1989 1991	Charles Colson Billy Graham Maranatha! Music
Radio Broadcast Facility of the Year	1989 1990 1991	Hope for the Heart, Dallas, Tex. WIHS, Alfred C. Thyberg, Connecticut Radio Fellowship, Middletown, Conn. WFGW-AM/WMIT-FM, Black Mountain, N.C.

NATIONAL RELIGIOUS BROADCASTING AWARDS cont.

Radio Program	1990	Larry Burkett, Money Matters, Christian Financial Concepts,
Producer		Dahlonega, Ga.
	1991	Family News in Focus
Religious	1975	Clarence W. Jones, HCJB
Broadcasting		John Zoller, Christ for Everyone
Hall of Fame		Walter A. Maier, The Lutheran Hour
	1976	George Palmer, Morning Cheer Broadcast
		Paul Rader, Radio evangelist
		R. R. Brown, Radio Chapel Service
	1977	"First Mate Bob" Paul Myers, Haven of Rest
		Miss Lois Crawford, KFGQ
	1978	Donald Grey Barnhouse, Bible Study Hour
		William Ward Ayer, First President of NRB
	1979	Herman Gockel, This Is the Life
	1980	Myron Boyd, Light and Life Hour
	1981	Billy Graham, Hour of Decision
	1982	Percy Crawford, Radio-TV Pioneer
	1983	Richard M. DeHaan, Radio Bible Class
	1984	Eugene R. Bertermann
	1985	Jerry Falwell, The Old Time Gospel Hour
	1986	M. G. (Pat) Robertson, Christian Broadcasting Network
		Theodore H. Epp, Back to the Bible (posthumously)
	1987	Thomas F. Zimmerman
	1988	Charles Stanley, In Touch Ministry
	1989	J. Vernon McGee, Thru the Bible Broadcast
	1991	James Dobson, Focus on the Family
		Rex Humbard, Humbard Evangelistic Assoc.
Technical Achievement	1988	United Video (Tulsa, Okla.)
Award	1989	Joseph Flaherty, Chief Engineer, CBS
	1990	Adventures in Odyssey, Focus on the Family, Dr. James Dobson
	1991	Skylight Satellite Network
Television Broadcast	1989	Love Worth Finding, Bellevue Baptist Church, Memphis, Tenn.
Facility	1990	Super Channel 55, WACX-TV, Claud Bowers, Orlando, Fla.
of the Year	1991	WCLF-TV, Sweetwater, Fla.
Television Program	1990	Dr. Billy Graham, Billy Graham Evangelistic Association,
Producer		Minneapolis, Minn.
	1991	The Family Channel, CBN, Virginia Beach, Va.
William Ward Ayer	1989	Oswald C.J. Hoffmann, The Lutheran Hour, Lutheran Layman's
Distinguished Service		League, St. Louis, Mo.
Award	1991	Ralph Carmichael
Youth Achievement	1988	Heidi Russell
Award	1989	Matthew Mighell, Northwestern College, Minneapolis, Minn.

Missions

MISSION AGENCIES

The following directory includes mission agencies with 25 or more full-time employees who are directly engaged in ministries outside of North America or who support those who are.

Action International Ministries. P.O. Box 490, Bothell, WA 98041-0490. 206-485-1967 (1974). *Ministry:* Church planting, street children ministry, literature distribution and support of national churches and workers. *Countries:* Philippines, Mexico, Colombia, Brazil, India, and Guatemala.

Advent Christian World Missions. P.O. Box 23152, Charlotte, NC 28212. 704-545-6161 (1880). *Ministry:* Church planting, theological education, evangelism and support of national workers. *Countries:* India, Japan, Philippines

Africa Evangelical Fellowship. P.O. Box 2896, Boone, NC 28607. 704-264-6036 (1906). *Ministry:* Evangelism, church planting, theological education, correspondence courses, TEE and agricultural assistance. *Countries:* Angola, Botswana, Gabon, Malawi, Mauritius, Mozambique, Namibia, Reunion South Africa, Swaziland, United Kingdom, Zambia, Zimbabwe

Africa Inland Mission International, Inc. P.O. Box 178, Pearl River, NY 10965. 914-735-4014 (1895). *Ministry:* Evangelism, church planting, development and training of national leadership, theological education, TEE, literature production/distribution, medical work and support of national churches. *Countries:* Central Africa Rep, Chad, Comoros Islands, Kenya, Lesotho, Madagascar, Mozambique, Namibia, Seychelles, Sudan, Tanzania, Uganda, United Kingdom, Zaire

Africa Inter-Mennonite Mission, Inc. P.O. Box 518, Elkhart, IN 46515. 219-295-3711 (1911). *Ministry:* Agricultural assistance, church planting, theological education, evangelism, community development and medical work. *Countries:* Botswana, Burkina Faso, Lesotho, Transkei, Zaire

African Methodist Episcopal Church, Inc. 475 Riverside Drive, Room 1926, New York, NY 10115. 212-870-2258 (1844). *Ministry:* Christian education, literature distribution and support of national workers. *Countries:* Lesotho, Liberia, Mozambique, Namibia, Nigeria, South Africa, Swaziland, Zambia

Allegheny Wesleyan Methodist Missions. P.O. Box 357, Salem, OH 44460. 216-332-0696 (1969). *Ministry:* Agricultural assistance,

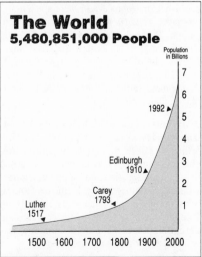

The World
5,480,851,000 People

Population in Billions

Source: *Perspectives on the World Christian Movement,* by Ralph D. Winter and Steven Hawthorne. Published by William Carey Library.

MISSION AGENCIES cont.

relief aid, church planting, Christian education, evangelism and self-help projects. *Countries:* Haiti, Peru

American Baptist Association Missionary Committee. P.O. Box 1050, Texarkana, TX 75504. 214-792-2783 (1924). *Ministry:* Church planting, evangelism, theological education and literature distribution. *Countries:* American Samoa, Australia, Colombia, Costa Rica, France, India, Israel, Japan, South Korea, Mexico, New Zealand, Nicaragua, Nigeria, Peru, Philippines, Solomon Islands

American Baptist Churches in the U.S.A. P.O. Box 851, Valley Forge, PA 19482. 215-768-2200 (1814). *Ministry:* Evangelism, church planting, human resource development, theological education, medical work and support of national churches. *Countries:* Burma, Costa Rica, Dominican Rep, El Salvador, Europe-General, Haiti, Hong Kong, India, Japan, Mexico, Nicaragua, Philippines, Thailand, Zaire

American Leprosy Missions, Inc. 1 Alm Way, Greenville, SC 29601. 803-271-7040 (1906). *Ministry:* Medical, social rehabilitation and spiritual assistance to leprosy victims, public health, technical assistance and training programs. *Countries:* Angola, Benin, Brazil, Burma, Burundi, Cameroon, Central Africa Rep, China (PRC), Comoros Islands, Congo, Ethiopia, India, Indonesia, South Korea, Liberia, Malawi, Mozambique, Nepal, Paraguay, Philippines, Somalia, Taiwan (ROC), Tanzania, Thailand, Zaire

AMG International. P.O. Box 21000, Chattanooga, TN 37422. 615-894-6060 (1942). *Ministry:* Bible distribution, child care, church planting, correspondence courses, theological education and support of national workers. *Countries:* Brazil, Burma, Colombia, Cyprus, Greece, Guatemala, Haiti, Hong Kong, India, Israel, Japan, Mexico, Pakistan, Peru, Philippines, Sri Lanka, Suriname, Taiwan (ROC), Thailand, Zaire

Arab World Ministries. P.O. Box 96, Upper Darby, PA 19082. 215-352-2003 (1952).

Ministry: Radio broadcasting, church planting, correspondence courses, evangelism and literature distribution/production. *Countries:* Algeria, Egypt, France, West Germany, Jordan, Mauritania, Morocco, Spain, Tunisia, United Kingdom, United Arab Emr

Assemblies of God. 1445 Boonville Avenue, Springfield, MO 65802. 417-862-2781 (1914). *Ministry:* Evangelism, church planting, relief aid, child-care programs, correspondence courses and support of national churches. *Countries:* Active in 109 countries

Associate Reformed Presbyterian Church. 1 Cleveland Street, Greenville, SC 29601. 803-233-5226 (1839). *Ministry:* Church planting, theological education, evangelism, literacy work, medical work and support of national churches. *Countries:* Asia-Mid East, Liberia, Mexico, Pakistan, Tanzania

Association of Baptists for World Evangelism, Inc. P.O. Box 5000, Cherry Hill, NJ 08034. 609-424-4606 (1927). *Ministry:* Church planting, theological education, evangelism, medical work and Bible translation. *Countries:* Argentina, Australia, Bangladesh, Brazil, Chile, Colombia, France, Gambia, Hong Kong, Italy, Japan, Kenya, Norway, Papua New Guinea, Paraguay, Peru, Philippines, Portugal, South Africa, Spain, Togo, United Kingdom

Baptist Bible Fellowship. P.O. Box 191, Springfield, MO 65801. 417-862-5001 (1950). *Ministry:* Evangelism, church planting, church construction and theological education. *Countries:* Active in 58 countries

Baptist Faith Missions. 1009 Balsam Drive, Lexington, KY 40504. 606-277-4947 (1923). *Ministry:* Church planting, Christian education, theological education, evangelism and furloughed missionary support. *Countries:* Brazil, Honduras, Peru, Philippines, South Korea

Baptist General Conference Board of World Missions. 2002 S. Arlington Heights Road, Arlington Heights, IL 60005. 708-228-0200 (1944). *Ministry:* Evangelism, church planting, development of human resources,

Major World Religions

	Where	Supreme Being	Founder/ Founded	Historical Leaders	Leadership	Sacred Writings	Holy Places	Typical Holy Days	Symbols
Christianity	Western Europe Western Hemisphere	God	Jesus A.D. 30	John the Baptist 12 disciples 4 Gospel writers Writers of Epistles	Varied Priests Ministers Lay people	Bible Old Testament New Testament	Bethlehem Jerusalem Rome Nazareth	Christmas Good Friday Easter	Protestant Catholic and Eastern Orthodox
Islam	Arabia Middle East Northern Africa	Allah	Muhammad A.D. 570–632	Muhammad Husein (grandson) Abu Bakr, Omar, Othman, Ali	None	Koran	Mecca Jerusalem	Ramadan (Sacred Month)	The crescent (New Moon)
Hinduism	India Sri Lanka (Ceylon)	Brahman All Reality	No founder 3200 B.C.	Mahatma Gandhi Ramakrishna	Sannyasis (holy men) Gurus (preachers)	Vedas Brahmanas Upanishads Great Epics	Benares Ganges River	The Mela Holi Festival Dasera Divuli	8-fold law cycle of birth and rebirth 8-spoked wheel
Confucianism	China Japan Korea	Confucius Shang-Ti	Confucius 557 B.C.	Yang Chu Moh Tih	None	NuChing Ssu Shu	None	None	None
Buddhism	China Japan India Burma	108 different names	Gautama 560–480 B.C.	Gautama Amitabha	Bhikkhus Monks Nuns Lamas	Dharma (Sutta) Vinaya Abhidhamma	Sarnath Lumbini Buddh-Gaya Kusinara	Perahera Festival in Ceylon Wesak (Kason) in May	Lotus blossom
Shintoism	Japan	Izanagi (Sky Father) Izanami (Earth Mother)	No founder A.D. 6th Cent.	None	None	Nihongi Kojiki	Mt. Fujiyama	New Year Bon (Festival of Dead) Temri-Kyo (January)	Torii Mirror
Taoism	China	Jade emperor Many folk gods	Lao-Tzu (or Lao-Tse) 604 B.C.	Lao-Tse Chuang-Tse 350–275 B.C.	None	Tao-Te-Ching	Kiangsi and many holy mountains	Birthdays of Gods Festival of Souls Autumn Festival	Yin—female, dark Yang—male, light
Judaism	Israel Europe Western Hemisphere	Yahweh (Jehovah or God)	Abraham 1900 B.C.	Moses Amos Micah	Rabbis Laymen	Torah Talmud	Jerusalem	Rosh Hashanah Yom Kippur Hanukkah Purim Passover	Star of David Tablets of Law Menorah

MISSION AGENCIES cont.

theological education, TEE and medical work. *Countries:* Argentina, Asia-Mid East, Brazil, Cameroon, Cote d'Ivoire, Europe-Eastern, Ethiopia, France, India, Japan, Mexico, Philippines

Baptist International Missions, Inc. P.O. Box 9215, Chattanooga, TN 37412. 615-698-1523 (1960). *Ministry:* Radio/TV broadcasting, church planting, Christian education, evangelism, handicapped programs and armed services ministry. *Countries:* Active in 53 countries

Baptist Mid-Missions. P.O. Box 308011, Cleveland, OH 44130. 216-826-3930 (1920). *Ministry:* Evangelism, church planting, theological education, medical work and Bible translation. *Countries:* Argentina, Australia, Austria, Bangladesh, Brazil, Central Africa Rep, Chad, Cote d'Ivoire, Dominican Rep, Ecuador, Finland, France, Germany, Ghana, Haiti, Honduras, Hong Kong, India, Ireland, Italy, Jamaica, Japan, Liberia, Mexico, Netherlands, New Zealand, Peru, Puerto Rico, Spain, St. Lucia, St. Vincent, Taiwan (ROC), United Kingdom, Venezuela

Baptist Missionary Association of America. 721 Main Street, Little Rock, AR 72201. 501-376-6788 (1950). *Ministry:* Planting churches, evangelism, Bible distribution and theological education. *Countries:* Australia, Bahamas, Bolivia, Brazil, Cape Verde Isls, Costa Rica, Honduras, India, Italy, Japan, South Korea, Mexico, Philippines, Taiwan (ROC), Uruguay

Baptist World Mission. P.O. Box 1463, Decatur, AL 35602. 205-353-2221 (1962). *Ministry:* Evangelism, church planting and Christian education. *Countries:* Argentina, Australia, Brazil, Colombia, Costa Rica, Dominican Rep, France, Germany, Haiti, India, Israel, Italy, Japan, South Korea, Malaysia, Mexico, Papua New Guinea, Portugal, Puerto Rico, Singapore, South Africa, Spain, Thailand, United Kingdom, Uruguay

BCM International, Inc. 237 Fairfield Avenue, Upper Darby, PA 19028. 215-352-7177

(1936). *Ministry:* Camping programs, church planting, correspondence courses, evangelism, handicapped and youth ministry and literature production. *Countries:* Austria, Brazil, Cuba, France, Germany, Ghana, Haiti, India, Ireland, Italy, Japan, Kenya, Mexico, Netherlands, Philippines, Spain, Sri Lanka, Suriname, Swaziland, Tanzania, United Kingdom, Zimbabwe

Berean Mission, Inc. 3536 Russell Blvd., St. Louis, MO 63104. 314-773-0110 (1937). *Ministry:* Church planting, theological education, TEE, evangelism, medical work and Bible translation. *Countries:* Barbados, Brazil, Dominica, Ecuador, Kenya, Liberia, Micronesia, New Zealand, Philippines, United Kingdom, Zaire

Bethany Fellowship Missions. 6820 Auto Club Rd., Minneapolis, MN 55438. 612-944-2121 (1945). *Ministry:* Church planting, evangelism, theological education, literature distribution and missionary orientation. *Countries:* Brazil, Chile, Dominican Rep, France, Germany, Indonesia, Japan, Mexico, Philippines, Puerto Rico, Singapore, Virgin Islands

Bible and Literacy League. 8955 Old Le-May Ferry Road, Hillsboro, MO 63050. 314-789-4368 (1973). *Ministry:* Child care, church planting, Christian education, evangelism, support of national churches and support of national workers. *Countries:* Colombia, Germany, Haiti, India, Kenya, Philippines, Tanzania, Uganda, Venezuela

Bible Christian Union, Inc. P.O. Box 410, Hatfield, PA 19440. 215-361-0500 (1904). *Ministry:* Church planting, radio/TV broadcasting, evangelism, missionary orientation and support of national churches. *Countries:* Austria, France, Germany, Greece, Ireland, Italy, Netherlands, Portugal, Spain, Sweden, United Kingdom

The Bible League. 16801 Van Dam Road, South Holland, IL 60473. 708-331-2094 (1938). *Ministry:* Bible distribution, correspondence courses, evangelism, and literature distribution.

Bible Missionary Church, Foreign Missions Department. P.O. Box 2030, Homedale, ID 83628. 208-337-3873 (1977). *Ministry:* Bible distribution, church planting, evangelism, literacy work, literature distribution and training. *Country:* India

Biblical Ministries Worldwide. P.O. Box 464-250, Lawrenceville, GA 30246. 404-339-3500 (1948). *Ministry:* Evangelism, church planting, correspondence courses, handicapped programs, literature production and armed services ministry. *Countries:* Antigua, Argentina, Australia, Austria, Belgium, Cyprus, Germany, Guam, Honduras, Hong Kong, Ireland, Italy, Japan, Luxembourg, Mexico, Netherlands, New Zealand, Puerto Rico, Western Samoa, South Africa, Spain, United Kingdom, Uruguay

Billy Graham Evangelistic Association. P.O. Box 779, Minneapolis, MN 55440. 612-338-0500 (1950). *Ministry:* Evangelism, Christian education, radio/TV broadcasting, films and relief aid. *Countries:* France, Germany, Hong Kong, Japan, United Kingdom

Brazil Gospel Fellowship Mission. P.O. Box 355, Springfield, IL 62702. 217-523-7176 (1939). *Ministry:* Radio broadcasting, church planting, correspondence courses, theological education and evangelism. *Country:* Brazil

Bread for the World, Inc. 802 Rhode Island Avenue NE, Washington, DC 20018. 202-269-0200 (1974). *Ministry:* Seeks to help shape U.S. public policies that affect hungry people, at home and overseas. Also provides educational resources on hunger.

Brethren Assemblies. P.O. Box 13, Spring Lake, NJ 07762. 201-449-8880 (1921). *Ministry:* Assists missionaries through funds transmission and other service agencies. *Countries:* Active in 51 countries

Calvary Commission, Inc. P.O. Box 100, Lindale, TX 75771. 214-882-5501 (1985). *Ministry:* Evangelism, church planting, Bible distribution, Christian education, literature distribution and support of national workers. *Countries:* Belize, Germany, Mexico, Sweden, United Kingdom

Calvary Ministries International. P.O. Box 10305, Jacksonville, FL 32247. 904-398-6559 (1981). *Ministry:* Christian education, evangelism, funds transmission, missionary orientation, mobilization for mission and training. *Countries:* Bahamas, China (PRC), Costa Rica, Ecuador, France, Guatemala, Haiti, Israel, Jamaica, Kenya, Malawi, Netherlands, Nigeria, Philippines, Spain, Taiwan (ROC), United Kingdom

CAM International. 8625 La Prada Drive, Dallas, TX 75228. 214-327-8206 (1890). *Ministry:* Radio/TV broadcasting, church planting, theological education, evangelism and literature production/distribution. *Countries:* Costa Rica, El Salvador, Guatemala, Honduras, Mexico, Panama, Spain

Campus Crusade for Christ, International. 100 Sunport Lane, Orlando, FL 32809. 407-826-2000 (1951). *Ministry:* Christian education, evangelism, support of national workers, training and small group discipleship. *Countries:* Active in 95 countries

Child Evangelism Fellowship, Inc. P.O. Box 348, Warrenton, MO 63383. 314-456-4321 (1937). *Ministry:* Evangelism, camping programs, support of national workers, training and translation work. *Countries:* Active in 55 countries

Childcare International. P.O. Box W, Bellingham, WA 98227. 206-647-2283 (1981). *Ministry:* Relief aid, community development, child-care projects, church planting, self-help projects and providing medical supplies. *Countries:* Haiti, India, Kenya, Peru

China Ministries International. P.O. Box 40489, Pasadena, CA 91104. 818-398-0145 (1987). *Ministry:* Missionary and theological education, mission-related research and support of national workers. *Countries:* Hong Kong, Taiwan (ROC)

Chinese Christian Mission, Inc. P.O. Box 617, Petaluma, CA 94953. 707-762-1314 (1961). *Ministry:* Broadcasting, church

MISSION AGENCIES cont.

planting, evangelism, literature distribution and production and training. *Countries:* Costa Rica, Hong Kong, Panama, Philippines, Singapore, Taiwan (ROC)

Chosen People Ministries, Inc. 1300 Cross Beam Drive, Charlotte, NC 28217. 704-523-0523 (1894). *Ministry:* Church planting, evangelism, literature distribution, missionary orientation and video/film production. *Countries:* Argentina, France, Greece, Israel

Christ for India, Inc. P.O. Box 271086, Dallas, TX 75227. 214-388-7809 (1986). *Ministry:* Evangelism through support of national workers. *Country:* India

Christian Aid Mission. 3045 Ivy Road, Charlottesville, VA 22903. 804-977-5650 (1953). *Ministry:* Church planting, missionary education, funds transmission, mission-related research, serving other agencies and support of national workers. *Countries:* Active in 44 countries

Christian and Missionary Alliance. P.O. Box 35000, Colorado Springs, CO 80935. 719-599-5999 (1887). *Ministry:* Evangelism, church planting, radio/TV broadcasting, literature production/distribution, theological education and Bible translation. *Countries:* Active in 37 countries

Christian Blind Mission International (U.S.A.). P.O. Box 19000, Greenville, SC 29601-9000. 803-239-0065 (1975). *Ministry:* Ministering to the blind through programs of medicine, community development, evangelism, literacy, education, and other aid.

Christian Broadcasting Network. CBN Center, Virginia Beach, VA 23463. 804-424-7777 (1960). *Ministry:* Produces Christian programs for telecasting and radio broadcasting in the U.S. and parts of Asia, Europe, the Middle East, and Central America. *Countries:* Argentina, Chile, Colombia, Costa Rica, Cyprus, Dominican Rep, Ecuador, El Salvador, Guatemala, Israel, Lebanon, Panama, Peru, Philippines, Puerto Rico, Taiwan (ROC), Uruguay

Christian Catholic Church (Evangelical Protestant). Dowie Memorial Drive, Zion, IL 60099. 708-746-1411 (1896). *Ministry:* Church planting, evangelism, camping programs, literature production, support of national churches and youth ministry. *Countries:* Angola, Australia, Egypt, Guyana, Israel, Jamaica, Japan, Malawi, Philippines, South Africa, United Kingdom

Christian Church (Disciples of Christ). P.O. Box 1986, Indianapolis, IN 46206. 317-353-1491 (1920). *Ministry:* Church planting, support of national churches, agricultural assistance, community development, Christian education and medical work. *Countries:* Africa-General, Argentina, China (PRC), Cuba, Ecuador, Europe-General, Hong Kong, India, Indonesia, Jamaica, Japan, Kenya, South Korea, Lesotho, Mexico, Nepal, Nigeria, Paraguay, Philippines, Puerto Rico, Singapore, Swaziland, Taiwan (ROC), Thailand, Venezuela, Vietnam, Zaire, Zambia

Christian Church of North America Missions Department. P.O. Box 141-A, Transfer, PA 16154. 412-962-3501 (1927). *Ministry:* Radio/TV broadcasting, child care, church planting, evangelism, literature distribution and support of national workers. *Countries:* Argentina, Australia, Barbados, Belgium, Chile, Colombia, France, Germany, India, Italy, Luxembourg, Paraguay, Philippine, Switzerland, United Kingdom, Uruguay, Venezuela

Christian Churches/Churches of Christ. P.O. Box 2427, Knoxville, TN 37901. 615-577-9740 (1927). *Ministry:* Sends and supports missionaries directly from local congregations. *Countries:* Active in 74 countries

Christian Dynamics. 10878 N. 57th Avenue, Glendale, AZ 85304. 602-878-6892 (1976). *Ministry:* Agricultural assistance, child care, church planting, literacy work, support of national workers and training. *Countries:* Bhutan, India, Nepal

Christian Literature Crusade, Inc. P.O. Box 1449, Fort Washington, PA 19034. 215-542-1242 (1941). *Ministry:* Literature production,

Bible distribution and literature distribution. *Countries:* Colombia, France, Germany, Hong Kong, Italy, Liberia, Philippines

Christian Medical Dental Society. P.O. Box 830689, Richardson, TX 75083. 214-783-8384 (1931). *Ministry:* Medical doctors, dentists and students serving in short-term medical projects in underdeveloped areas. *Countries:* Africa-General, Belize, Dominican Rep, Ecuador, Guatemala, Honduras, Jamaica, Mexico, Nicaragua, Philippines

Christian Missionary Fellowship (Indiana). P.O. Box 26306, Indianapolis, IN 46226. 317-542-9256 (1949). *Ministry:* Evangelism, church planting and medical work. *Countries:* Brazil, Ethiopia, Indonesia, Kenya, Mexico, Tanzania

Christian Reformed World Missions. 2850 Kalamazoo Avenue SE, Grand Rapids, MI 49508. 616-246-0740 (1888). *Ministry:* Church planting, evangelism, theological education, TEE, literature distribution and extension education. *Countries:* Argentina, Bangladesh, Belize, Costa Rica, Dominican Rep, El Salvador, Guam, Guinea, Haiti, Honduras, Hong Kong, Japan, Kenya, Liberia, Mali, Mexico, New Zealand, Nigeria, Papua New Guinea, Philippines, Sierra Leona, Taiwan (ROC)

Christian Reformed World Relief Committee. 2850 Kalamazoo Avenue SE, Grand Rapids, MI 49560. 616-241-1691 (1962). *Ministry:* Relief aid, agricultural assistance, literacy work, medical work and management consulting. *Countries:* Bangladesh, Belize, Costa Rica, Dominican Rep, Ecuador, El Salvador, Guatemala, Guinea, Haiti, Honduras, India, Indonesia, Kenyz, Liberia, Mali, Mexico, Nicaragua, Nigeria, Panama, Philippines, Sierra Leone, Sri Lanka, Uganda

Christians in Action, Inc. P.O. Box 728, Woodlake, CA 93286. 209-564-3762 (1958). *Ministry:* Church planting, evangelism, armed services ministry and misssionary orientation. *Countries:* Brazil, Ecuador, Germany, Guatemala, Japan, Korea South, Macao, Mexico, Peru, Philippines, Sierra Leone, Switzerland, Taiwan (ROC), United Kingdom

Church of God (Anderson, Indiana) Missionary Board. P.O. Box 2498, Anderson, IN 46018. 317-642-0258 (1909). *Ministry:* Church planting, Christian education, evangelism, medical work, self-help projects and support of national workers. *Countries:* Bermuda, Bolivia, Brazil, Costa Rica, Egypt, Greece, Guam, Haiti, Hong Kong, Japan, Kenya, South Korea, Taiwan (ROC), Tanzania, Thailand, Uganda, Uruguay, Venezuela

Church of God in Christ, Mennonite General Mission. P.O. Box 230, Moundridge, KS 67107. 316-345-2533 (1933). *Ministry:* Evangelism, church planting, child-care programs, Christian education and medical work. *Countries:* Belize, Brazil, Dominican Rep, Germany, Guatemala, Haiti, India, Mexico, Nigeria, Philippines

Church of God of Prophecy, World Mission Committee. P.O. Box 2910, Cleveland, TN 37320. 615-479-8511 (1903). *Ministry:* Evangelism, church planting, missionary orientation, training and orphanage work. *Countries:* Active in 74 countries

Church of God World Missions. P.O. Box 2430, Cleveland, TN 37320. 615-472-3361 (1910). *Ministry:* Church planting, church construction, Christian education and support of national churches. *Countries:* Active in 94 countries

Church of the Nazarene. 6401 The Paseo, Kansas City, MO 64131. 816-333-7000 (1900). *Ministry:* Church planting, theological education, medical work, support of national churches and self-help projects. *Countries:* Active in 83 countries

Church of the United Brethren in Christ. 302 Lake Street, Huntington, IN 46750. 219-356-2312 (1853). *Ministry:* Church planting, Christian education, theological education, medical work, support of national churches and workers. *Countries:* Honduras, Hong Kong, India, Jamaica, Macao, Mexico, Nicaragua, Sierra Leone

Churches of Christ. P.O. Box 814565, Dallas, TX 75381. (1961). *Ministry:* Sends and supports missionaries from local congregations. *Countries:* Active in 73 countries

MISSION AGENCIES cont.

Churches of Christ in Christian Union.
P.O. Box 30, Circleville, OH 43113. 614-474-8856 (1909). *Ministry:* Church planting, Christian education, theological education, furloughed missionary support, support of national churches and Bible translation. *Countries:* Antigua, Barbados, Bolivia, Dominica, Honduras, Kenya, Mexico, Papua New Guinea, Spain, Trinidad & Tobago

Churches of God General Conference, Commission on World Missions. P.O. Box 926, Findlay, OH 45839. 419-424-1961 (1898). *Ministry:* Church planting, community development, extension education, handicapped programs, medical work and support of national churches. *Countries:* Bangladesh, Haiti, India

Compassion International, Inc. P.O. Box 7000, Colorado Springs, CO 80933. 719-594-9900 (1952). *Ministry:* Child care, community development, relief aid and self-help projects. *Countries:* Belize, Bolivia, Brazil, Burma, Burundi, Colombia, Dominican Rep, Ecuador, El Salvador, Fiji, Guatemala, Haiti, Honduras, Hong Kong, India, Indonesia, Jamaica, Kenya, South Korea, Malaysia, Mexico, Peru, Philippines, Rwanda, Singapore, Thailand, Tonga, Uganda, Zaire

Conservative Baptist Foreign Mission Society. P.O. Box 5, Wheaton, IL 60189. 708-665-1200 (1943). *Ministry:* Evangelism, church planting, theological education, TEE, medical work, literature production/distribution and Bible translation. *Countries:* Argentina, Austria, Brazil, Cote d'Ivoire, Europe-Western, France, Germany, Hong Kong, India, Indonesia, Italy, Japan, Jordan, Kenya, Macao, Madagascar, Netherlands, Pakistan, Philippines, Portugal, Rwanda, Senegal, Singapore, Spain, Taiwan (ROC), Uganda, Venezuela, Zaire

Conservative Baptist Home Mission Society. P.O. Box 828, Wheaton, IL 60189. 708-653-4900 (1950). *Ministry:* Evangelism, church planting, church construction, TEE, armed services ministry and support of national churches. *Countries:* Belize, Dominican

Rep, Guam, Honduras, Mexico, Puerto Rico

Conservative Mennonite Board of Missions and Charities. 9920 Rosedale Milford Center Road, Irwin, OH 43029. 614-857-1366 (1919). *Ministry:* Evangelism, church planting, relief aid, community development and medical work. *Countries:* Costa Rica, Ecuador, Germany, Nicaragua

Dayspring International. P.O. Box 3309, Virginia Beach, VA 23454. 804-428-1092 (1979). *Ministry:* Evangelism, church planting, child-care programs, literacy work, support of national workers and video/film production. *Country:* India

Derek Prince Ministries International. P.O. Box 300, Fort Lauderdale, FL 33302. 305-763-5202 (1963). *Ministry:* Audio recording/distribution, broadcasting, correspondence courses, literature distribution, translation work and video/film production

Eastern European Bible Mission. P.O. Box 110, Colorado Springs, CO 80901. 719-577-4450 (1972). *Ministry:* Bible distribution, camping programs, TEE, literature distribution, support of national churches and mission-related research. *Countries:* Bulgaria, Czechoslovakia, Germany, Hungary, Poland, Romania, Commonwealth of Independent States (formerly the USSR), Yugoslavia

Eastern Mennonite Board of Missions and Charities. P.O. Box 628, Salunga, PA 17538. 717-898-2251 (1914). *Ministry:* Evangelism, church planting, relief aid, community development, extension education and support of national churches. *Countries:* Australia, Belize, China (PRC), Dominican Rep, El Salvador, Ethiopia, France, Germany, Guatemala, Haiti, Honduras, Hong Kong, Indonesia, Jamaica, Kenya, Luxembourg, Peru, Philippines, Somalia, Swaziland, Sweden, Tanzania, Venezuela, Virgin Islands (USA), Yugoslavia

Elim Fellowship. 7245 College Street, Lima, NY 14485. 716-582-2790 (1947). *Ministry:* Church planting, broadcasting, camping programs, TEE support of national churches and youth programs. *Countries:* Argentina, Brazil, Colombia, Costa Rica, Germany, Haiti, Hong Kong, Israel, Japan, Kenya, Malaysia, Mexico, Nigeria, Peru, South Africa, Spain, Tanzania, Uganda, United Kingdom, Zaire

EMC Missions (Evangelical Mennonite Church). 1420 Kerrway Court, Fort Wayne, IN 46805. 219-423-3649 (1943). *Ministry:* Evangelism, church planting, TEE, literature distribution, medical work and Bible translation. *Countries:* Asia-Southeast, Burkina Faso, Dominican Rep, Germany, Indonesia, Japan, South Korea, Philippines, United Kingdom, Venezuela, Zaire, Zimbabwe

Episcopal Church, World Mission in Church and Society. 815 Second Avenue, New York, NY 10017. 212-867-8400 (1929). *Ministry:* Support of national churches, aid and relief, community development, medicine, training and support of national workers. *Countries:* Argentina, Brazil, China, Costa Rica, Dominican Rep, Ecuador, El Salvador, Guam, Guatemala, Haiti, Honduras, Israel, Japan, South Korea, Kenya, Lesotho, Malawi, Mexico, Namibia, Panama, Philippines, Puerto Rico, South Africa, Spain, Tanzania, Turks & Caicos islands, Uganda, United Kingdom, Vanuatu, Zaire, Zimbabwe

Evangelical Baptist Mission, Inc. P.O. Box 2225, Kokomo, IN 46904. 317-453-4488 (1928). *Ministry:* Evangelism, church planting, theological education, Bible translation and video/film production. *Countries:* Argentina, Australia, Benin, Cote d'Ivoire, France, French Guiana, Germany, Italy, Japan, Mali, Martinique, Niger, Nigeria, South Africa, Sweden, United Kingdom

Evangelical Bible Mission, Inc. P.O. Drawer 189, Summerfield, FL 32691. 904-245-2560 (1939). *Ministry:* Church planting and construction, Christian education, literacy work, technical assistance and training. *Countries:* Belize, Dominican Rep, Ghana, Haiti, Nigeria, Papua New Guinea

Evangelical Congregational Church Division of Missions. P.O. Box 186, Myerstown, PA 17067. 717-866-7581 (1922). *Ministry:*

Church planting, Christian education, support of national churches and workers, missionary education and Bible translation. *Countries:* India, Japan, Kenya, Liberia, Mexico

Evangelical Covenant Church. 5101 N. Francisco Avenue, Chicago, IL 60625. 312-784-3000 (1885). *Ministry:* Church planting, Christian education, TEE, medical work and support of national churches. *Countries:* Colombia, Ecuador, Japan, Mexico, Taiwan (ROC), Thailand, Zaire

Evangelical Free Church of America, Overseas Missions. 901 East 78th Street, Minneapolis, MN 55420-1300. 800-745-2202 (1887). *Ministry:* Evangelism, church planting, extension education, theological education, TEE and medical work. *Countries:* Austria, Belgium, Brazil, France, Germany, Hong Kong, Japan, Mexico, Peru, Philippines, Singapore, Venezuela, Zaire

Evangelical Friends Mission. P.O. Box 525, Arvada, CA 80001. 303-421-8100 (1978). *Ministry:* Evangelism, church planting, TEE, medical work, support of national churches and training. *Countries:* Bolivia, Burundi, Hong Kong, India, Mexico, Peru, Philippines, Rwanda, Taiwan (ROC)

Evangelical Lutheran Church in America. 8765 W. Higgins Road, Chicago, IL 60631. 312-380-2650 (1842). *Ministry:* Evangelism, church planting, theological education, human resource development, support of national churches and medical work. *Countries:* Active in 46 countries

Evangelism Explosion III International. P.O. Box 23820, Fort Lauderdale, FL 33307. 305-491-6100 (1970). *Ministry:* Training pastors and lay leaders to equip others for "lifestyle" evangelism. *Countries:* Australia, Belgium, Denmark, Germany, Malawi, Netherlands, New Zealand, Norway, Portugal, South Africa, Spain, United Kingdom, Zambia, Zimbabwe

Evangelism Resources. P.O. Box 8263, Lexington, KY 40533. 603-858-3334 (1976). *Ministry:* Evangelism and training. *Country:* Zaire

MISSION AGENCIES cont.

Every Home for Christ. P.O. Box 35930, Colorado Springs, CO 80935-3593. 719-260-8888 (1954). *Ministry:* Evangelism, correspondence courses, literature production, literature distribution and support of national workers. *Countries:* Active in 43 countries

Faith Christian Fellowship World Outreach. P.O. Box 50370, Tulsa, OK 74150. 918-428-3861 (1978). *Ministry:* Evangelism, church planting, Christian education and funds transmission. *Countries:* Australia, Botswana, Costa Rica, Finland, Germany, Guatemala, Hungary, India, Indonesia, Israel, Jamaica, Nigeria, Philippines, Poland, Sweden, United Kingdom, Zimbabwe

Far East Broadcasting Company, Inc. P.O. Box 1, La Mirada, CA 90637. 213-947-4651 (1945). *Ministry:* Radio broadcasting, correspondence courses and literature distribution. *Countries:* Burma, Hong Kong, Indonesia, Japan, South Korea, Neth Antilles, North Mariana Isls, Philippines, Singapore, Thailand

Fellowship of Evangelical Bible Churches. 5800 S. 14th Street, Omaha, NE 68107. 402-731-4780 (1936). *Ministry:* Church planting, Christian education, theological education, TEE, evangelism and medical work. *Countries:* Argentina, Bahamas, Belgium, Brazil, Colombia, Cuba, Ecuador, France, Germany, Guadeloupe, India, Italy, Japan, Kenya, Latin Amer-Gen, Malawi, Mali, Mexico, Netherlands, Nigeria, Panama, Paraguay, Peru, Philippines, Taiwan (ROC), Togo, Uruguay, Zaire

Fellowship Independent Mission. P.O. Box 72, Fairless Hills, PA 19030. 215-752-1170 (1950). *Ministry:* Evangelism, church planting, childcare programs, church construction, theological education and video/film production. *Countries:* Australia, Bahamas, Brazil, Ecuador, France, Germany, Japan, Mexico, Morocco, Niger, Nigeria, Suriname, Sweden, United Kingdom, Uruguay, Venezuela

Food for the Hungry. 7729 East Greenway Road, Scottsdale, AZ 85260. 602-998-3100 (1971). *Ministry:* Relief aid, community development, human resource development and self-help projects. *Countries:* Bangladesh, Bolivia, Dominican Rep, Ethiopia, Guatemala, Haiti, Japan, Kenya, Mexico, Peru, Philippines, Switzerland, Thailand

Foundation for His Ministry. P.O. Box 9803, North Hollywood, CA 91609. 818-766-6923 (1967). *Ministry:* Relief aid, child care, evangelism, medical work, support of national churches and training. *Countries:* United Kingdom, Kenya, Mexico

Foursquare Missions International. 1910 W. Sunset Blvd., Suite. 200, Los Angeles, CA 90026. 213-484-2400 (1923). *Ministry:* Church planting, theological education, literature production and training. *Countries:* Active in 57 countries

Free Gospel Church, Inc., Missions Department. P.O. Box 477, Export, PA 15632. 412-327-5454 (1982). *Ministry:* Evangelism and church planting with teams in the Muslim world

Free Methodist Church of North America, Department of World Missions. P.O. Box 535002, Indianapolis, IN 46253. 317-244-3660 (1885). *Ministry:* Church planting, theological education, child-care programs, community development, Christian education and medical work. *Countries:* Brazil, Burundi, Chile, Dominican Rep, Ecuador, Egypt, Haiti, Hong Kong, India, Japan, Malawi, Mexico, Mozambique, Paraguay, Philippines, Puerto Rico, Rwanda, South Africa, Taiwan (ROC), Venezuela, Zaire, Zimbabwe

Frontiers. P.O. Box 40159, Pasadena, CA 91104. 818-798-0807 (1982). *Ministry:* Evangelism and church planting with teams in the Muslim world

Global Outreach Mission. P.O. Box 711, Buffalo, NY 14240. 716-842-2220 (1943). *Ministry:* Evangelism, church planting, relief aid, broadcasting, community development and support of national workers.

Countries: Congo, Austria, Bangladesh, Bahamas, Brazil, Belgium, Guatemala, France, Germany, Haiti, India, Ireland, Netherlands, Portugal, Spain, United Kingdom

Global Outreach, Ltd. P.O. Box 1, Tupelo, MS 38802. 601-842-4615 (1970). *Ministry:* Community and human resource development, evangelism, medical work and self-help projects. *Countries:* Belize, Haiti, Honduras, India, Uganda

Globe Missionary Evangelism. P.O. Box 3138, Pensacola, FL 32516. 904-453-4318 (1973). *Ministry:* Evangelism, church planting, theological education, medical work and support of national churches. *Countries:* Austria, Cen Africa Rep, Costa Rica, Ecuador, France, Germany, Greece, Guatemala, Haiti, Indonesia, Japan, Kenya, Mexico, Philippines, United Kingdom, Spain, Thailand

Go-Ye Fellowship. P.O. Box 26405, Los Angeles, CA 90026. 213-250-5347 (1944). *Ministry:* Church planting, broadcasting, correspondence courses, theological education, funds transmission and support of national churches. *Countries:* Argentina, Brazil, France, Germany, Indonesia, Singapore, Taiwan (ROC), Thailand

Gospel for Asia, Inc. 1932 Walnut Plaza, Carrollton, TX 75006. 214-416-0340 (1979). *Ministry:* Evangelism, church planting, funds transmission, support of national churches and support of national workers in Asia.

Gospel Mission of South America, Inc. 1401 SW 21st Avenue, Ft. Lauderdale, FL 33312. 305-587-2975 (1923). *Ministry:* Evangelism, church planting, camping programs, correspondence courses, theological education and literature distribution. *Countries:* Argentina, Chile, Uruguay

Gospel Missionary Union. 10000 N. Oak, Kansas City, MO 64155. 816-734-8500 (1892). *Ministry:* Evangelism, church planting, Christian education, literature distribution, medical work and training. *Countries:* Argentina, Austria, Bahamas, Belgium, Belize, Bolivia, Brazil, Colombia, Ecuador, Europe-General, United Kingdom, France, Germany, Greece, Italy, Mali, Mexico, Morocco, Panama, Spain

Grace Brethren Foreign Missions. P.O. Box 588, Winona Lake, IN 46590. 219-267-5164 (1900). *Ministry:* Evangelism, church planting, theological education, support of national churches and training. *Countries:* Argentina, Brazil, Cen Africa Rep, Chad, France, Germany, Japan, Mexico, Philippines, Spain, United Kingdom

Grace Ministries International, Inc. P.O. Box 9405, Grand Rapids, MI 49509. 616-241-5666 (1939). *Ministry:* Church planting, theological education, literature production and medical supplies. *Countries:* Australia, Bolivia, Brazil, Neth Antilles, Puerto Rico, Philippines, Tanzania, Uruguay, India, Zaire

Greater Europe Mission. P.O. Box 668, Wheaton, IL 60189. 708-462-8050 (1949). *Ministry:* Evangelism, church planting, camping programs, theological education and TEE. *Countries:* Austria, Belgium, Eastern Europe, France, Greece, Germany, Iceland, Ireland, Italy, Netherlands, Portugal, Spain, Sweden

Harvest Evangelism, Inc. P.O. Box 20310, San Jose, CA 95160. 408-248-5855 (1980). *Ministry:* Church planting, radio broadcasting, literature production, support of national churches and training. *Country:* Argentina

Have Christ Will Travel Ministries, Inc. 528 E. Church Lane, Philadelphia, PA 19144. 215-438-6308 (1965). *Ministry:* Church planting, Bible distribution, broadcasting, camping programs, Christian education, mobilization for mission and training. *Countries:* Haiti, Liberia, Philippines

Helps International Ministries, Inc. P.O. Box 1209, Harlem, GA 30814. 404-556-3408 (1976). *Ministry:* Serves other agencies, church construction, computer services, financial accounting and other technical assistance. *Countries:* Kenya, Taiwan (ROC)

High Adventure Ministries, Inc. P.O. Box 7466, Van Nuys, CA 91409. 818-701-5133 (1972). *Ministry:* Radio broadcasting

MISSION AGENCIES cont.

(short/medium wave) in 13 languages, evangelism, relief aid and literature distribution. *Countries:* Israel, Lebanon

Highland Christian Mission. P.O. Box 16528, Rochester, NY 14616. 716-227-0588 (1964). *Ministry:* Evangelism, church planting, Christian education, literacy work, technical assistance and youth programs. *Country:* Papua New Guinea

Holt International Children's Services, Inc. P.O. Box 2880, Eugene, OR 97402. 503-687-2202 (1956). *Ministry:* Serves the needs of homeless children and families at risk through child-care programs, adoption, medical work, camping programs and self-help projects. *Countries:* Bolivia, Brazil, Costa Rica, Guatemala, India, South Korea, Philippines, Thailand

Holy Land Christian Mission. 2000 E. Red Bridge Road, Kansas City, MO 64131. 816-942-2000 (1936). *Ministry:* Child-care sponsorship, relief aid, community development, Christian education, medical work and self-help projects. *Countries:* Chile, Colombia, Dominican Rep, Gaza, Guatemala, Honduras, India, Israel, Philippines, Thailand, West Bank

Impact Ministries, Inc. P.O. Box 2500, Redmond, WA 98073. 206-882-0761 (1981). *Ministry:* Bible distribution, church construction, literature distribution, supplying equipment and support of national workers. *Countries:* Bulgaria, Czechoslovakia, Germany, Hungary, Poland, Romania, Commonwealth of Independent States (formerly the USSR), Yugoslavia

Independent Board for Presbyterian Foreign Missions. 246 W. Walnut Lane, Philadelphia, PA 19144. 215-438-0511 (1933). *Ministry:* Evangelism, church planting, theological education, literature distribution and medical work. *Countries:* Australia, Brazil, Chile, Guatemala, Israel, Kenya, South Korea, Philippines, Taiwan (ROC), United Kingdom

Independent Faith Mission, Inc. P.O. Box 7791, Greensboro, NC 27407. 919-292-1255 (1950). *Ministry:* Serves local churches by servicing missionaries engaged in evangelism, church planting and theological education. *Countries:* Antigua, Italy, Kenya, Mexico, South Africa, Suriname, United Kingdom

India Evangelical Mission, Inc. P.O. Box 1633, Lakewood, CA 90716. 714-739-8068 (1966). *Ministry:* Evangelism, church planting, child-care programs, correspondence courses and literature distribution. *Country:* India

India Gospel Outreach. 10970 Arrow Route, #204, Rancho Cucamonga, CA 91730. 714-948-2404 (1984). *Ministry:* Church planting, theological education, medical work, church construction, support of national churches and missionary education. *Country:* India

International Children's Care, Inc. P.O. Box 4406, Vancouver, WA 98662. 206-254-5061 (1978). *Ministry:* Child-care programs, Christian education and relief aid. *Countries:* Colombia, Costa Rica, Dominican Rep, Guatemala

International Christian Aid. 5217 Verdugo Way, Unit B, Camarillo, CA 93012. 805-987-8888 (1960). *Ministry:* Relief aid, community development, literacy work, medical work, self-help projects and training

International Fellowship of Evangelical Students, USA. P.O. Box 7895, Madison, WI 53707. 608-274-9001 (1947). *Ministry:* Student evangelism, funds transmission, missions information service, mobilization for mission, serving other agencies and support of national workers. *Countries:* Africa-General, Austria, Belgium, Brazil, France, Germany, India, Italy, Latin America-Central, Puerto Rico, Spain, Sri Lanka, Switzerland, United Kingdom

International Lutheran Laymen's League. 2185 Hampton Avenue, St. Louis, MO 63139. 314-647-4900 (1917). *Ministry:* Radio/TV broadcasting and correspondence courses. *Countries:* Argentina, Australia, Brazil, France, Germany, Guatemala, Hong Kong, India, Indonesia, Japan, South Korea, Lebanon, New Zealand, Nigeria, Philippines, Portugal,

South Africa, Taiwan (ROC), Venezuela

International Missions, Inc. P.O. Box 14866, Reading, PA 19612. 215-375-0300 (1930). *Ministry:* Evangelism, church planting and literature distribution. *Countries:* Hong Kong, India, Kenya, Pakistan, Philippines, Suriname, United Kingdom, Japan, Australia

International Pentecostal Church of Christ, Global Missions Department. P.O. Box 18145, Atlanta, GA 30316. 404-627-2681 (1917). *Ministry:* Church planting, Christian education, child care, Bible distribution, literature distribution and providing medical supplies. *Countries:* India, Kenya, Mexico, United Kingdom

International Students, Inc. P.O. Box C, Colorado Springs, CO 80901. 719-576-2700 (1953). *Ministry:* Student evangelism, church planting, training and ministry among international student and trainees in the USA. *Countries:* Austria, France, Honduras, India, Japan, Jordan, Philippines, Portugal, Singapore, Sweden, Uganda, United Kingdom

International Teams. P.O. Box 203, Prospect Heights, IL 60070. 708-870-3800 (1960). *Ministry:* Evangelism, church planting, community development, literature distribution, missionary orientation and mobilization for mission. *Countries:* Austria, Europe-General, France, Italy, Philippines, United Kingdom

Interserve / USA (International Service Fellowship). P.O. Box 418, Upper Darby, PA 19082. 215-352-0581 (1964). *Ministry:* Extension education, medical work, theological education, agricultural assistance, technical assistance and serving other agencies. *Countries:* Asia-Mid East, Bangladesh, Bhutan, Egypt, India, Nepal, Pakistan

Japan-North American Commission on Cooperative Mission. 475 Riverside Drive, Room 618, New York, NY 10115. 212-870-2021 (1947). *Ministry:* Human resource development, Christian education, evangelism, support of national churches and serving other agencies. *Country:* Japan

Jews for Jesus. 60 Haight Street, San Francisco, CA 94102. 415-864-2600 (1973). *Ministry:* Evangelism, literature production, literature distribution and missionary orientation. *Countries:* Argentina, Israel, United Kingdom

Korea International Mission, Inc. P.O. Box 40288, Pasadena, CA 91104. 818-797-1260 (1968). *Ministry:* Evangelism, church planting, Christian education, theological education, missionary orientation and video/film production. *Countries:* Hong Kong, Indonesia, South Korea, Philippines, Thailand

Larry Jones International Ministries, Inc. P.O. Box 36, Oklahoma City, OK 73101. 405-942-0228 (1964). *Ministry:* Relief aid, agricultural assistance, child-care programs, evangelism and medical work. *Countries:* Bangladesh, Belize, Chad, Costa Rica, Dominican Rep, El Salvador, Ethiopia, Ghana, Guatemala, Haiti, Honduras, Jamaica, Kenya, Mexico, Mozambique, Nigeria, Panama, Philippines, Poland, Sierra Leone, Sri Lanka, Thailand, Uganda

Latin America Mission, Inc. P.O. Box 52-7900, Miami, FL 33152. 305-884-8400 (1921). *Ministry:* Evangelism, church planting, camping programs, child-care programs, Christian education and theological education. *Countries:* Argentina, Brazil, Colombia, Costa Rica, Ecuador, Honduras, Mexico, Panama, Peru

Liberty Baptist Mission. P.O. Box 20000, Lynchburg, VA 24506. 804-239-2036 (1978). *Ministry:* Evangelism, church planting, community development, Christian education and theological education. *Countries:* Australia, France, Germany, Kenya, South Korea, Mexico, Philippines, Trinidad & Tobago

Liebenzell Mission of USA, Inc. 1360 Hillside Drive, Tarpon Springs, FL 34689. 813-938-9995 (1941). *Ministry:* Evangelism, theological education, TEE, support of national churches, camping programs and youth programs. *Countries:* Guam, Japan, Micronesia, Papua New Guinea

Life Ministries. P.O. Box 200, San Dimas, CA 91773. 714-599-8491 (1965). *Ministry:*

MISSION AGENCIES cont.

Evangelism, support of national churches and training. Teaches conversational English to Japanese students. *Country:* Japan

Living Bibles International. P.O. Box 863, Wheaton, IL 60189-0863. 708-510-9500 (1968). *Ministry:* Bible distribution, broadcasting, literature production and Bible translation. *Countries:* Botswana, Brazil, Burma, Denmark, Egypt, Ethiopia, Finland, France, Germany, Ghana, Greece, Hong Kong, India, Indonesia, Italy, Kenya, Malawi, Malaysia, Mexico, Nepal, Netherlands, Nigeria, Norway, Philippines, Portugal, Sri Lanka, Sweden, Taiwan (ROC), Thailand, Uganda, United Kingdom, Yugoslavia, Zaire, Zambia, Zimbabwe

Living Water Teaching International. P.O. Box 3040, Broken Arrow, OK 74012. 918-455-8070 (1979). *Ministry:* Evangelism, correspondence courses, theological education, TEE, missionary orientation and youth programs. *Countries:* Australia, Colombia, El Salvador, Guatemala, Liberia, Nicaragua, Panama

Logoi, Inc. 13200 SW 128th Street, #D-1, Miami, FL 33186-5826. 305-232-5880 (1965). *Ministry:* Church planting, TEE, literature production and distribution, support of national workers and video/film production. *Countries:* Argentina, Belize, Chile, Colombia, Ecuador, El Salvador, Guatemala, Honduras, Mexico, Paraguay, Uruguay

Luis Palau Evangelistic Association. P.O. Box 1173, Portland, OR 97207. 503-643-0777 (1978). *Ministry:* Evangelism, broadcasting, literature distribution and training. *Countries:* Argentina, Australia, Finland, Guatemala, Mexico, United Kingdom

Luke Society. P.O. Box 349, Vicksburg, MS 39180. 601-638-1629 (1964). *Ministry:* Evangelism, church planting, community development, medical work and support of national workers. *Countries:* Dominican Rep, Ecuador, Ghana, Honduras, India, Mexico, Peru, Philippines, Uganda

Lutheran Bible Translators, Inc. P.O. Box 2050, Aurora, IL 60507. 708-897-0660

(1964). *Ministry:* Bible translation, linguistics, literacy and literature production. *Countries:* Cameroon, Ecuador, Liberia, Papua New Guinea, Sierra Leone

Lutheran Brethren World Missions. P.O. Box 655, Fergus Falls, MN 56538. 218-739-3336 (1901). *Ministry:* Medical work, church planting, theological education, literature production and distribution, Bible translation and agricultural assistance. *Countries:* Cameroon, Chad, Japan, Taiwan (ROC)

Lutheran Church—Missouri Synod, Board for Mission Services. 1333 South Kirkwood Road, St. Louis, MO 63122. 314-965-9000 (1945). *Ministry:* Relief aid, human resource development, providing medical supplies, medical work, self-help projects and technical assistance. *Countries:* Active in 45 countries

Maranatha Baptist Mission, Inc. P.O. Drawer 1425, Natchez, MS 39121. 601-442-0141 (1961). *Ministry:* Funds transmission and information service for missionaries. *Countries:* Antigua, Argentina, Australia, Austria, Bolivia, Brazil, Chile, Colombia, France, Germany, Grenada, Haiti, Israel, Japan, Mexico, Norway, Papua New Guinea, Peru, Puerto Rico, Spain, United Kingdom, Venezuela

Maranatha Campus Ministries. P.O. Box 1799, Gainesville, FL 32602. 904-375-6000 (1975). *Ministry:* Evangelism, church planting, training and youth programs. *Countries:* Australia, Brazil, France, Germany, Guatemala, Honduras, Indonesia, Ireland, Jamaica, Japan, South Korea, Mexico, New Zealand, Panama, Philippines, South Africa, Venezuela

Maranatha South Africa. 855 S. Newcombe Way, Denver, CO 80226. 303-980-9888 (1986). *Ministry:* Evangelism, church planting and construction, agricultural assistance, missionary education and support of national workers. *Countries:* South Africa

Medical Ambassadors International. P.O. Box 6645, Modesto, CA 95355. 209-524-0600 (1973). *Ministry:* Medical work, evangelism, church planting, Bible distribution, human resource development and support of national workers. *Countries:* China (PRC), Dominican Rep, El Salvador, Guatemala, Haiti, Hong Kong, Honduras, India, Kenya, South Korea, Nepal, Nicaragua, Philippines, Tanzania, Zaire

Mennonite Board of Missions. P.O. Box 370, Elkhart, IN 46515. 219-294-7523 (1906). *Ministry:* Evangelism, church planting, theological education, literature production and support of national churches. *Countries:* Argentina, Belgium, Benin, Bolivia, Brazil, China (PRC), Cote d'Ivoire, France, Ghana, India, Ireland, Israel, Japan, Nepal, Peru, Spain, Suriname, Sweden, United Kingdom, Uruguay, Zaire

Mennonite Brethren Missions/Services. P.O. Box V, Hillsboro, KS 67063. 316-947-3151 (1878). *Ministry:* Church planting, agricultural assistance, community development, theological education and providing medical supplies. *Countries:* Afghanistan, Angola, Austria, Botswana, Brazil, Colombia, Ecuador, Germany, India, Indonesia, Japan, Mexico, Nepal, Nigeria, Pakistan, Panama, Paraguay, Peru, Portugal, Spain, Uruguay, Zaire

Mennonite Central Committee. 21 South 12th Street, Akron, PA 17501. 717-859-1151 (1920). *Ministry:* Agricultural assistance, relief aid, community development, human resource development and self-help projects. *Countries:* Active in 51 countries

Mennonite Economic Development Associates. 12 Greenfield Road, Lancaster, PA 17602-3312. 717-399-9440 (1953). *Ministry:* Programs of economic development in less-developed areas of the world. *Countries:* Bolivia, Haiti, Jamaica, Paraguay, Tanzania, Uruguay

Mexican Mission Ministries, Inc. P.O. Box 636, Pharr, TX 78577. 512-787-3543 (1954). *Ministry:* Church planting, correspondence courses, theological education, TEE, literature distribution and youth programs. *Country:* Mexico

Middle East Media. P.O. Box 359, Lynnwood, WA 98046. 206-778-0752 (1976). *Ministry:* Broadcasting, correspondence courses, literature production and distribution, evangelism and video/film production. *Country:* Egypt

Ministries in Action, Inc. P.O. Box 140325, Coral Gables, FL 33114. 305-642-3113 (1961). *Ministry:* Evangelism, community development, extension education, support of national churches and training. *Countries:* Grenada, Haiti, Jamaica, St. Lucia, St. Vincent

Mission Aviation Fellowship (MAF). P.O. Box 3202, Redlands, CA 92373. 714-794-1151 (1945). *Ministry:* Aviation, community development, providing medical supplies, technical assistance, support of national workers and serving other agencies. *Countries:* Australia, Bangladesh, Botswana, Brazil, Ecuador, Ethiopia, Guatemala, Haiti, Honduras, Indonesia, Kenya, Lat A-Caribbean, Lesotho, Mali, Mexico, Suriname, Venezuela, Zaire, Zimbabwe

Mission Mailbag, Inc. P.O. Box 15237, Del City, OK 73155. 405-672-4989 (1962). *Ministry:* Broadcasting, evangelism, funds transmission and serving other agencies.

Mission Possible, Inc. P.O. Box 1596, Ft. Pierce, FL 34954. 305-465-0373 (1978). *Ministry:* Evangelism, relief aid, Christian education, medical work, missionary orientation and serving other agencies. *Countries:* Bahamas, Dominican Rep, Haiti, Honduras, Jamaica

Mission Society for United Methodists, The. P.O. Box 1103, Decatur, GA 30031. 404-378-8746 (1984). *Ministry:* Evangelism, church planting, training, support of national churches, medical work, education, and agricultural assistance. *Countries:* Costa Rica, Ghana, Guatemala, Hong Kong, Indonesia, Philippines, Solomon Islands, Spain

Mission to Unreached Peoples. 19303 West Valley Hwy., #R 102, Kent, WA 98032. 206-251-9601 (1981). *Ministry:* Evangelism, church planting, community development, missionary orientation and mobilization for mission. *Countries:* Hong Kong, India,

MISSION AGENCIES cont.

Indonesia, Nepal, Pakistan, Philippines, Taiwan (ROC), Thailand

Missionary Church—World Partners. 3901 S. Wayne Avenue, Fort Wayne, IN 46807. 219-456-4502 (1969). *Ministry:* Evangelism, church planting, theological education, TEE, medical work and support of national workers. *Countries:* Brazil, Dominican Rep, Ecuador, France, Haiti, India, Jamaica, Mexico, Nigeria, Sierra Leone, Spain

Missionary Revival Crusade. 102 E. Lyon Street, Laredo, TX 78040. 512-722-2646 (1959). *Ministry:* Broadcasting, church planting, correspondence courses, evangelism and literature distribution. *Countries:* Colombia, France, Guatemala, Germany, Mexico, Spain, Sri Lanka, Yugoslavia

Moravian Church in North America, Board of World Missions. P.O. Box 1245, Bethlehem, PA 18016. 215-868-1732 (1949). *Ministry:* Support of national churches and workers, theological education, Bible translation, medical work and missions information services. *Countries:* Dominican Rep, Guyana, Honduras, Nicaragua, Tanzania, Virgin Islands

National Association of Free Will Baptists. P.O. Box 1088, Nashville, TN 37202. 615-361-1010 (1935). *Ministry:* Church planting, theological education, linguistics, literature production/distribution and medical work. *Countries:* Brazil, France, India, Cote d'Ivoire, Japan, Panama, Spain, Uruguay

National Council of the Churches of Christ in the U.S.A. 475 Riverside Drive, New York, NY 10115. 212-870-2257 (1946). *Ministry:* Agricultural and relief aid, community and human resource development, funds transmission, purchasing services, support of national churches and workers, mobilization for missions, self-help projects and technical assistance. *Countries:* Active in 57 countries

Navigators. P.O. Box 6000, Colorado Springs, CO 80934. 719-589-1212 (1933). *Ministry:* Evangelism, training and discipleship. *Countries:* Active in 41 countries

New England and World Missions. P.O. Box 2880, Worcester, MA 01613. 508-752-7352 (1983). *Ministry:* Evangelism, church planting, child-care programs, Christian education, medical work and self-help projects. *Country:* Haiti

New Life League. P.O. Box 7623, Waco, TX 76714. 817-772-0021 (1954). *Ministry:* Church planting, broadcasting, child-care programs, theological education, literature production, medical work and support of national workers. *Countries:* Brazil, Costa Rica, Guatemala, Haiti, Hong Kong, India, Japan, Mexico, Nepal, Papua New Guinea, Sri Lanka, Norway, Thailand, United Kingdom

New Tribes Mission. 1000 E. First Street, Sanford, FL 32771. 407-323-3430 (1942). *Ministry:* Evangelism, church planting, Bible translation, linguistics, literacy work, missionary orientation and aviation. *Countries:* Australia, Bolivia, Brazil, Colombia, Cote d'Ivoire, Greenland, Guinea, Guinea-Bissau, India, Indonesia, Japan, South Korea, Liberia, Mexico, Panama, Papua New Guinea, Paraguay, Philippines, Senegal, Thailand, United Kingdom, Venezuela

North American Baptist Conference. 1 South 210 Summit Avenue, Oakbrook Terrace, IL 60181. 708-495-2000 (1883). *Ministry:* Church planting, theological education, relief aid, medical work and support of national churches. *Countries:* Brazil, Cameroon, Japan, Nigeria, Philippines

O.C. International. P.O. Box 36900, Colorado Springs, CO 80936-6900. 719-592-9292 (1951). *Ministry:* Evangelism, church planting, support of national churches, mission-related research and training. *Countries:* Argentina, Brazil, Colombia, France, Germany, Greece, Guatemala, India, Indonesia, Japan, Kenya, Mexico, Philippines, Singapore, Swaziland, Taiwan (ROC)

OMS International, Inc. P.O. Box A, Greenwood, IN 46142. 317-881-6751 (1901). *Ministry:* Evangelism, church planting, broadcasting, theological education, literature distribution and training. *Countries:* Brazil, Colombia, Ecuador, France, Greece, Haiti, Hong Kong, India, Indonesia, Japan, South Korea, Philippines, Spain, Taiwan (ROC)

Open Air Campaigners, U.S., Inc. P.O. Box 26, Lincroft, NJ 07738-0026. 201-757-8427 (1956). *Ministry:* Evangelism, literature distribution and training. *Countries:* Argentina, Germany, India, Italy, Jamaica

Open Bible Standard Missions, Inc. 2020 Bell Avenue, Des Moines, IA 50315. 515-288-6761 (1935). *Ministry:* Evangelism, church planting, theological education, TEE, literature distribution and self-help projects. *Countries:* Argentina, Brazil, Chile, Cuba, Dominican Rep, El Salvador, Ghana, Grenada, Guatemala, Guinea, Jamaica, Japan, Kenya, Liberia, Mexico, Papua New Guinea, Peru, Philippines, Puerto Rico, Trinidad & Tobago, Uganda, Uruguay, Paraguay, Spain, St. Vincent

Open Doors with Brother Andrew. P.O. Box 27001, Santa Ana, CA 92799. 714-531-6000 (1955). *Ministry:* Bible distribution in limited access or closed countries. *Countries:* Australia, Brazil, Europe-General, Hong Kong, Kenya, New Zealand, Netherlands, Philippines, Singapore

Operation Mobilization—U.S.A. P.O. Box 2277, Peachtree City, GA 30269. 404-631-0432 (1957). *Ministry:* Evangelism, church planting, literature distribution, missionary orientation and support of national workers. *Countries:* Argentina, Asia-Mid East, Austria, Bangladesh, Belgium, Brazil, Finland, France, Germany, India, Ireland, Israel, Italy, Mexico, Nepal, Netherlands, Pakistan, Singapore, Spain, Sweden, Turkey, United Kingdom

Orthodox Presbyterian Church, Committee on Foreign Missions. 303 Horsham Road, Suite G, Horsham, PA 19044-2029. 215-782-1690 (1937). *Ministry:* Evangelism, church planting, theological education, literature distribution and support of national churches. *Countries:* Cyprus, Japan, Kenya, South Korea, Philippines, Suriname, Taiwan (ROC)

Overseas Christian Servicemen's Centers. P.O. Box 1268, Englewood, CO 80150. 303-762-1400 (1954). *Ministry:* Evangelism, literature distribution, armed forces ministry. *Countries:* Germany, Italy, Japan, South Korea, Panama, Philippines, Spain, United Kingdom

Overseas Missionary Fellowship U.S.A. P.O. Box 101208, Denver, CO 80250-1208. 303-797-6160 (1865). *Ministry:* Evangelism, church planting, theological education, Christian education, support of national churches and training. *Countries:* Hong Kong, Indonesia, Japan, South Korea, Malaysia, Philippines, Singapore, Taiwan (ROC), Thailand

Partners International. P.O. Box 15025, San Jose, CA 95115. 408-453-3800 (1943). *Ministry:* Support of national workers involved in evangelism, church planting and theological education. *Countries:* Active in 37 countries

Pentecostal Church of God. P.O. Box 2248, Joplin, MO 64803. 417-624-7050 (1919). *Ministry:* Church planting, Bible distribution, agricultural assistance, relief aid, church construction, literature distribution and furloughed missionary support. *Countries:* Antigua, Belize, Brazil, Cote d'Ivoire, Cuba, Ghana, Guatemala, Haiti, Honduras, Hong Kong, India, Indonesia, Jamaica, Japan, Macao, Malawi, Mexico, Philippines, Portugal, Tanzania, Trinidad & Tobago, United Kingdom, Zaire, Zambia

Pentecostal Holiness Church. P.O. Box 12609, Oklahoma City, OK 73157. 405-787-7110 (1904). *Ministry:* Evangelism, church planting, TEE, missionary orientation, support of national churches and mobilization for mission. *Countries:* Argentina, Botswana, Chile, Costa Rica, France, Germany, Haiti, Hong Kong, India, Israel, Italy, Jamaica, Kenya, Malawi, Mexico, Nigeria, Philippines, Singapore, South Africa, Spain, United Kingdom, Venezuela, Zambia, Zimbabwe

Pioneer Bible Translators. P.O. Box 381030, Duncanville, TX 75138. 214-296-4843 (1974). *Ministry:* Bible translation, linguistics,

MISSION AGENCIES cont.

training, literacy work and support of national churches. *Countries:* Liberia, Papua New Guinea, Zaire

Pioneers. P.O. Box 527, Sterling, VA 22170. 703-478-0004 (1979). *Ministry:* Evangelism, church planting, linguistics, literacy work, support of national workers and Bible translation. *Countries:* China (PRC), France, Guyana, Indonesia, Japan, Kenya, Mongolia, Nepal, North Mariana I, Papua New Guinea, South Africa, Thailand

Pocket Testament League, Inc., The. P.O. Box 800, Lititz, PA 17543 (1908). *Ministry:* Scripture distribution, evangelism and discipleship. *Countries:* Austria, Belgium, Brazil, Czechoslovakia, France, Germany, India, Indonesia, Italy, South Korea, Mexico, Philippines, Portugal, Spain, Taiwan (ROC), United Kingdom, Yugoslavia

Prakash Association, U.S.A. 99 Airport Blvd., Freedom, CA 95019. 408-722-2244 (1969). *Ministry:* Self-help projects, support of nationals and training. *Country:* India

Presbyterian Church (U.S.A.). 100 Witherspoon Street, Louisville, KY 40202. 502-569-5000 (1837). *Ministry:* Relief aid, church planting, theological education, evangelism, support of national churches and workers. *Countries:* Active in 45 countries

Presbyterian Church in America Mission to the World. P.O. Box 29765, Atlanta, GA 30359. 404-320-3373 (1973). *Ministry:* Church planting, theological education, Bible translation, aviation, medical work and technical assistance. *Countries:* Active in 39 countries

PRM International. 760 Waverly Road, Holland, MI 49423. 616-396-5291 (1967). *Ministry:* Audio recording/distribution, cassette Bible distribution and evangelism, supplying equipment, technical assistance and training. *Countries:* Bangladesh, India, Kenya, Singapore, Sudan

RBMU International. 8102 Elberon Avenue, Philadelphia, PA 19111. 215-745-0680 (1948). *Ministry:* Evangelism, church plant-

ing, theological education, TEE and Bible translation. *Countries:* Cameroon, Chile, Indonesia, Peru, Philippines

R.E.A.P. (Reinforcing Evangelists and Aiding Pastors). P.O. Box 488, La Mirada, CA 90637. 213-802-2159 (1951). *Ministry:* Evangelism, church planting, literature production and support of national workers. *Countries:* Indonesia, Japan

Reformed Church in America. 475 Riverside Drive, New York, NY 10115. 212-870-2265 (1857). *Ministry:* Church planting, Christian education, agricultural assistance, medical work and serving other agencies. Countries: Bahrain, Egypt, Ethiopia, Honduras, India, Indonesia, Japan, Kenya, Kuwait, Mexico, Oman, Pakistan, Philippines, Singapore, Sudan, Taiwan (ROC), Zambia

Rio Grande Bible Institute, Inc. 4300 South Business #281, Edinburg, TX 78539 (1946). *Ministry:* Theological education, broadcasting and training. *Country:* Mexico

Salvation Army, U.S.A. 799 Bloomfield Avenue, Verona, NJ 07044. 201-239-0606 (1865). *Ministry:* Evangelism, literature distribution and production, medical work and support of national workers. *Countries:* Argentina, Bahamas, Brazil, Chile, Colombia, Congo, Costa Rica, Germany, Guatemala, Guyana, Hong Kong, India, Indonesia, Jamaica, Japan, Kenya, South Korea, Mexico, Philippines, Singapore, South Africa, Spain, Sri Lanka, Suriname, Taiwan (ROC), Tanzania, Uganda, Uruguay, Venezuela, Zaire, Zambia, Zimbabwe

Samaritan's Purse. P.O. Box 3000, Boone, NC 28607. 704-262-1980 (1970). *Ministry:* Relief aid, evangelism and support of national workers.

Send International. P.O. Box 513, Farmington, MI 48332. 313-477-4210 (1947). *Ministry:* Evangelism, church planting, theological education, TEE, camping programs and support of national churches. *Countries:* Hong Kong, Japan, Philippines, Spain, Taiwan (ROC)

Seventh Day Adventists General Conference. 12501 Old Columbia Pike, Silver Spring, MD 20904. 301-680-6000 (1863). *Ministry:* Evangelism, church planting, mobilization for mission, missionary orientation, medical work, theological education, literature production and Christian education. *Countries:* Active in 67 countries

Shield of Faith Mission International. P.O. Box 29207, San Antonio, TX 78229. 512-733-9045 (1953). *Ministry:* Evangelism, church planting, missionary orientation and education, serving other agencies and training. *Countries:* Australia, Brazil, Mexico, Nigeria, Pakistan

SIM International. P.O. Box 7900, Charlotte, NC 28241. 704-588-6100 (1893). *Ministry:* Church planting, community development, broadcasting, theological education, medical work and support of national workers. *Countries:* Benin, Bolivia, Burkina Faso, Central African Rep, Cote d'Ivoire, Ethiopia, Ghana, Guinea, Haiti, Italy, Kenya, Liberia, Niger, Nigeria, Peru, Sudan

Slavic Gospel Association, Inc. P.O. Box 1122, Wheaton, IL 60189. 708-690-8900 (1934). *Ministry:* Radio broadcasting, literature production, Bible distribution, TEE and evangelism with a focus on Slavic peoples. *Countries:* Argentina, Ecuador, France, Germany, Italy, Monaco, Commonwealth of Independent States (formerly the USSR), Spain

Son Shine Ministries International, Inc. Route 5, Box 289, Azle, TX 76020. 817-444-3777 (1977). *Ministry:* Evangelism, correspondence courses, missionary training and armed forces ministry. *Countries:* Australia, Germany, Guam, United Kingdom

Source of Light Ministries International, Inc. 1011 Mission Road, Madison, GA 30650. 404-342-0397 (1953). *Ministry:* Church planting, correspondence courses, literature translation, production and distribution. *Countries:* Brazil, Chile, Guyana, India, Jamaica, South Korea, Liberia, Mexico, Peru, Philippines

South America Mission, Inc. P.O. Box 6560, Lake Worth, FL 33466. 407-965-1833 (1914). *Ministry:* Evangelism, church planting, theological education, TEE, aviation, programs for the handicapped. *Countries:* Bolivia, Brazil, Colombia, Peru

South American Missionary Society of the Episcopal Church. P.O. Box, 99 Ambridge, PA 15003. 412-266-0669 (1976). *Ministry:* Evangelism, church planting, Christian education, missionary education, theological education and medical work. *Countries:* Chile, Colombia, Costa Rica, Dominican Rep, Honduras, Peru

Southern Baptist Convention. P.O. Box 6767, Richmond, VA 23230. 804-353-0151 (1845). *Ministry:* Evangelism, church planting, relief aid, radio/TV broadcasting, theological education, literature production/ distribution. *Countries:* Active in 113 countries

Team Expansion, Inc. P.O. Box 4100, Cincinnati, OH 45204. 513-244-81 49 (1978). *Ministry:* Evangelism, church planting, missionary orientation, mobilization for mission, mission-related research and training. *Countries:* Argentina, Ireland, Senegal, Uruguay, Venezuela

Tele-Missions International, Inc. P.O. Box 563, Valley Cottage, NY 10989. 914-268-9222 (1954). *Ministry:* Broadcasting, evangelism and literature distribution. *Countries:* Africa-General, Ecuador, Kenya, Sierra Leone, Zaire

The Evangelical Alliance Mission (TEAM). P.O. Box 969, Wheaton, IL 60189. 708-653-5300 (1890). *Ministry:* Evangelism, church planting, linguistics, medical work, broadcasting. *Countries:* Austria, Brazil, Chad, Colombia, France, Hong Kong, India, Indonesia, Italy, Japan, South Korea, Mexico, Mozambique, Nepal, Neth Antilles, Pakistan, Peru, Philippines, Portugal, South Africa, Spain, Sri Lanka, Taiwan (ROC), Trinidad & Tobago, Turkey, United Arab Emr, Venezuela, Zimbabwe

Things to Come Mission, Inc. 2200 English Avenue, Indianapolis, IN 46201-4017. 317-262-8806 (1955). *Ministry:* Evangelism, church planting, broadcasting, theological

MISSION AGENCIES cont.

education, literature production and support of national workers. *Countries:* Brazil, India, Indonesia, Kenya, Nigeria, Philippines, United Kingdom

Trans World Missions. P.O. Box 10, Glendale, CA 91209. 213-663-1176 (1949). *Ministry:* Evangelism, church planting, radio broadcasting, childcare programs, mobilization for mission and support of national workers. *Countries:* Brazil, Costa Rica, Guatemala, Mexico, Nicaragua

Trans World Radio. P.O. Box 700, Cary, NC 27512-0700. 919-460-3700 (1952). *Ministry:* Medium and shortwave radio broadcasting from overseas facilities in over 70 languages, correspondence courses. *Countries:* Cyprus, Dominican Rep, Guam, Hong Kong, India, Malawi, Monaco, Netherlands, Neth Antilles, South Africa, Spain, Sri Lanka, Swaziland, United Kingdom, Uruguay, Venezuela

UFM International. P.O. Box 306, Bala-Cynwyd, PA 19004. 215-667-7660 (1931). *Ministry:* Evangelism, church planting, theological education, TEE, literature production and distribution, medical work and Bible translation. *Countries:* Austria, Brazil, Dominican Rep, France, Germany, Guyana, Haiti, Indonesia, Ireland, Italy, Mexico, Philippines, Puerto Rico, South Africa, Sweden

UIM International (United Indian Missions). P.O. Box 3600 Flagstaff, AZ 86003. 602-774-0651 (1956). *Ministry:* Evangelism, church planting, camping programs, aviation support, literature production and youth programs. *Country:* Mexico

United Church Board for World Ministries. 700 Prospect Avenue East, 6th Floor, Cleveland, OH 44115. 216-736-3202 (1810). *Ministry:* Nurture of national churches and leaders, relief aid, community development, Christian education, theological education and medical work. *Countries:* Active in 58 countries

United Methodist Church, Board of Global Ministries. 475 Riverside Drive,

#1370, New York, NY 10115. 212-870-3720 (1940). *Ministry:* Evangelism, church planting, Christian education, theological education, support of national churches and training. *Countries:* Active in 66 countries

United Pentecostal Church International. 8855 Dunn Road, Hazelwood, MO. 314-837-7300 (1924). *Ministry:* Evangelism, church planting, relief aid, Bible distribution, theological education and training. *Countries:* Active in 64 countries

United States Center for World Mission. 1605 Elizabeth Street, Pasadena, CA 91104. 818-797-1111 (1976). *Ministry:* Missionary orientation and education, mission information services, mobilization for mission, mission-related research and serving other agencies

United World Mission. P.O. Box 250, Union Mills, NC 28167. 704-287-8996 (1946). *Ministry:* Church planting, Christian education, theological education, programs for the handicapped and support of national churches. *Countries:* Belgium, Bolivia, Brazil, Congo, Guatemala, South Korea, Mali, Philippines, Senegal, Venezuela, Spain, United Kingdom

Voice of China and Asia Missionary Society, Inc. P.O. Box 15-M, Pasadena, CA 91102. 818-796-3117 (1946). *Ministry:* Radio broadcasting, Christian education, missionary education, programs for the handicapped, support of national churches and workers. *Countries:* Hong Kong, India, South Korea, Philippines, Taiwan (ROC)

WEC International. P.O. Box 1707, Fort Washington, PA 19034. 215-646-2322 (1922). *Ministry:* Evangelism, church planting, theological education, literacy work, medical work and Bible translation. *Countries:* Asia-General, Asia-Mid East, Australia, Austria, Brazil, Burkina Faso, Chad, Colombia, Cote d'Ivoire, Cyprus, France, Gambia, Germany, Guinea-Bissau, Indonesia, Italy, Japan, Kenya, Liberia, Nepal, Pakistan, Philippines, Senegal, Spain, Sri Lanka, Taiwan (ROC), Thailand, United Kingdom, Venezuela, Zaire

WEGO, Inc. (World Encounter Gospel Organization). P.O. Box 763187, Dallas, TX 75376. 214-943-6365 (1974). *Ministry:* Evangelism, church planting, relief aid, theological education, support of national workers. *Countries:* Australia, Belgium, Belize, Chile, Colombia, Germany, Ghana, India, Israel, Japan, Kenya, Lebanon, Mexico, New Zealand, Nigeria, Pakistan, Philippines, South Africa, Sri Lanka, United Kingdom, Zimbabwe

Wesleyan Church. P.O. Box 50434, Indianapolis, IN 46250. 317-576-8160 (1968). *Ministry:* Evangelism, church planting, theological education, TEE, medical work and Christian education. *Countries:* Australia, Brazil, Colombia, Guyana, Haiti, Honduras, India, Indonesia, Japan, South Korea, Liberia, Mexico, Nepal, Papua New Guinea, Peru, Philippines, Puerto Rico, Sierra Leone, South Africa, Sri Lanka, Suriname, Swaziland, Zambia, Zimbabwe

Wisconsin Evangelical Lutheran Synod. 2929 N. Mayfair Road, Milwaukee, WI 53222. 414-771-9357 (1955). *Ministry:* Church planting, broadcasting, theological education, literature production, support of national churches and workers. *Countries:* Brazil, Cameroon, Colombia, Hong Kong, Indonesia, Japan, Malawi, Mexico, Nigeria, Puerto Rico, Taiwan (ROC), Zambia

Word of Life Fellowship, Inc. P.O. Box 278, Schroon Lake, NY 12870. 518-532-7111 (1940). *Ministry:* Camping programs, broadcasting and youth programs. *Countries:* Argentina, Australia, Brazil, Chile, Ecuador, Germany, Israel, Kenya, New Zealand, Portugal, Spain, United Kingdom

World Baptist Fellowship Mission Agency, Inc. P.O. Box 13459, Arlington, TX 76094. 817-274-7161 (1928). *Ministry:* Evangelism, church planting, TEE, funds transmission, literature distribution and missionary orientation. *Countries:* Brazil, Colombia, Ecuador, Fiji, France, Ghana, Guatemala, Honduras, Indonesia, Ireland, Mexico, New Zealand, Peru, Philippines, Portugal, Singapore, Spain, Sri Lanka, Thailand

World Concern. P.O. Box 33000, Seattle, WA 98133. 206-546-7201 (1973). *Ministry:* Community development, medical work, agricultural assistance, providing medical supplies and training. *Countries:* Afghanistan, Bangladesh, Bolivia, Burkina Faso, Chad, Costa Rica, El Salvador, Ethiopia, Haiti, Kenya, Laos, Malaysia, Nepal, Pakistan, Philippines, Somalia, Sudan, Thailand, Uganda

World Gospel Mission. P.O. Box WGM, Marion, IN 46952. 317-664-7331 (1910). *Ministry:* Evangelism, church planting, Christian education, TEE and medical work. *Countries:* Argentina, Bangladesh, Barbados, Bolivia, Brazil, Burundi, Haiti, Honduras, India, Japan, Kenya, Mexico, Tanzania

World Indigenous Missions, Inc. P.O. Box 310627, New Braunfels, TX 78131. 512-629-0863 (1985). *Ministry:* Evangelism, church planting, Christian education and support of national workers. *Countries:* Dominican Rep, France, Germany, Mexico, Philippines, Spain

World Mission Prayer League. 232 Clifton Avenue South, Minneapolis, MN 55403. 612-871-6843 (1937). *Ministry:* Evangelism, church planting, TEE, community development, medical work and support of national churches. *Countries:* Bangladesh, Bolivia, Ecuador, India, Kenya, Mexico, Nepal, Pakistan, Peru, Philippines

World Missions Far Corners, Inc. P.O. Box 2611, Long Beach, CA 90801. 213-427-9885 (1958). *Ministry:* Evangelism, church planting, radio broadcasting, correspondence courses, literature distribution and support of national workers. *Countries:* Bolivia, Ecuador, Ghana, Hong Kong, India, Jamaica, South Korea, Mexico, Peru, Philippines, South Africa, United Kingdom

World Neighbors, Inc. 4127 NW 122nd Street, Oklahoma City, OK 73120-8869. 405-946-3333 (1951). *Ministry:* Community development, agricultural assistance, self-help projects and training. *Countries:* Bolivia, Burkina Faso, Chad, Ghana, Haiti, Honduras, India, Indonesia, Kenya, Mali, Mexico, Nepal, Peru, Philippines, Tanzania, Togo, Uganda

World Outreach Fellowship. P.O. Box 585603, Orlando, FL 32858. 407-425-5552

MISSION AGENCIES cont.

(1981). *Ministry:* Missionary orientation and training, mobilization for mission, mission-related research and serving other agencies. *Countries:* Belize, Bolivia

World Radio Missionary Fellowship, Inc. P.O. Box 39800, Colorado Springs, CO 80949-9800. 719-590-9800 (1931). *Ministry:* Radio broadcasting, evangelism, technical assistance, community development, medical work and training. *Countries:* Ecuador, Panama

World Reach, Inc. P.O. Box 26155, Birmingham, AL 35226. 205-979-2400 (1982). *Ministry:* Evangelism, church planting, relief aid, Bible distribution, literature distribution and medical work. *Countries:* Guatemala, Honduras, Kenya, Somalia, Tanzania, Uganda, Zambia

World Relief Corporation. P.O. Box WRC, Wheaton, IL 60189. 708-665-0235 (1944). *Ministry:* Relief aid, community development, support of national churches, self-help projects, technical assistance and training. *Countries:* Afghanistan, Bangladesh, Burkina Faso, El Salvador, Ethiopia, Guatemala, Haiti, Honduras, Hong Kong, India, Indonesia, Kenya, Malawi, Mali, Morocco, Mozambique, Philippines, Senegal, Sri Lanka, Swaziland, Thailand, Zaire

World Salt Foundation, Inc. P.O. Box 1929, Newnan, GA 30264. 404-253-8451 (1978). *Ministry:* Evangelism, church planting and Bible distribution. *Countries:* Belize, Brazil, Cameroon, Chile, Costa Rica, Guatemala, Haiti, Hong Kong, India, Ireland, Israel, Mexico, Philippines, Puerto Rico, Thailand

World Servants. 8233 Gator Lane, #6, West Palm Beach, FL 33411. 407-790-0800 (1985). *Ministry:* Community development, childcare programs, mobilization for mission, medical work and missionary orientation.

World Vision. P.O. Box O, Pasadena, CA 91109. 818-357-7979 (1950). *Ministry:* Child care programs, community development, relief aid, evangelism, leadership development and public health.

World Vision International. 919 W. Huntington Drive, Monrovia, CA 91016. 818-303-8811 (1978). *Ministry:* Child-care programs, relief aid, community development, evangelism, medical work and training. *Countries:* Active in 64 countries

Worldteam, Inc. P.O. Box 14308, Coral Gables, FL 33114-3038. 305-446-0861 (1928). *Ministry:* Evangelism, church planting, TEE and training. *Countries:* Brazil, Cuba, Dominican Rep, France, Grenada, Guadeloupe, Haiti, Italy, Spain, St. Lucia, St. Vincent, Suriname, Trinidad & Tobago, United Kingdom

Worldwide Discipleship Association, Inc. 110 Carnegie Place, Suite 100, Fayetteville, GA 30214. 404-460-1337 (1974). *Ministry:* Evangelism, church planting, training national leaders, youth programs and TEE. *Countries:* Japan, Kenya, South Korea

Wycliffe Bible Translators, International. 7500 W. Camp Wisdom Road, Dallas, TX 75236. 214-709-2400 (1934). *Ministry:* Bible translation, linguistics, literacy and missionary training. *Countries:* Africa-General, Asia-South, Australia, Austria, Brazil, Cameroon, Colombia, Cote d'Ivoire, Ecuador, Germany, Indonesia, Kenya, Latin America-Central, Malaysia, Mexico, Netherlands, Panama, Papua New Guinea, Peru, Philippines, Senegal, Singapore, Suriname, Sudan, Thailand, Togo, United Kingdom

Young Life, Inc. P.O. Box 520, Colorado Springs, CO 80901. 719-473-4262 (1941). *Ministry:* Evangelism—primarily to young people through youth and camping programs. *Countries:* Algeria, Australia, Austria, Belgium, Burma, Brazil, China (PRC), Costa Rica, Denmark, Dominican Rep, France, Germany, India, Japan, Kenya, South Korea, Malawi, Mexico, Peru, Philippines, Singapore, South Africa, Switzerland, Uganda, United Kingdom, Virgin Islands (USA), Zimbabwe

Youth Enterprises, Inc. P.O. Box 777, Chula Vista, CA 92012. 619-421-9828 (1960). *Ministry:* Evangelism and literature distribution through sports programs. *Countries:* Bolivia, Brazil, Costa Rica, France, Guatemala, South Korea, Mexico, New Zealand, United Kingdom

Youth for Christ/USA. P.O. Box 228822, Denver, CO 80222. 303-843-9000 (1944). *Ministry:* Evangelism, mobilization for mission, youth ministries and camping programs. *Countries:* American Samoa, Austria, Brazil, Burma, Colombia, Ecuador, France,

Germany, Guatemala, Kenya, Lebanon, Liberia, Netherlands, Panama, Portugal, Singapore, South Africa, Spain, Sweden, Switzerland, United Kingdom

Youth with a Mission (YWAM). P.O. Box 55309, Seattle, WA 98155. 206-283-1071 (1960). *Ministry:* Evangelism, relief aid and training. *Countries:* Active in 75 countries.

Source: *Mission Handbook, 14th Edition.* W. Dayton Roberts and John A. Siewert, editors. Copublished by MARC (Missions Advanced Research and Communications Center), a division of World Vision, and Zondervan Publishing House. Copyright © 1989. Used by permission. Agency names, addresses and telephone numbers updated October 1991.

FOCUS FACT

The most significant missiological fact of the last part of this century is the enormous upsurge of the Pentecostal/charismatic movement. Pentecostal/ charismatic churches worldwide
- have 382 million menbers, or one of every five Christians
- gain 19 million members each year
- donate $34 billion every year

—L. Grant McLung in *International Bulletin of Missionary Research.* October 1990.

USA MISSION AGENCY STATISTICS

Overseas personnel sent from the U.S.A.	1985	1988
Total personnel (career and short-term)	58,700	70,969
Person/year equivalent index	48,300	52,208
Career personnel	37,500	40,221
Short-term personnel	21,200	30,748
Percentage of total personnel that is career	64%	57%
Percentage of total personnel that is short-term	36%	43%
Number of "tentmakers" sponsored or supervised	NA	873
Mission agencies based in the U.S.A.		
Number of agencies with career personnel	371	395
Percentage of agencies with career personnel	56%	57%
Median number of career personnel for an agency	16	13
Average number of career personnel for an agency	101	101
Number of agencies with short-term personnel	209	208
Percentage of agencies with short-term personnel	32%	30%
Mission funding in millions of U.S.A. dollars		
Total income for overseas ministries	1,320	1,728.1
Median amount of income for overseas in an agency	NA	.33
Average amount of income for overseas in an agency	NA	2.50
Overseas missions activity from the U.S.A.		
Number of countries with U.S.A. personnel or projects	187	186
Number of countries with U.S.A. personnel	175	177

Source: *Mission Handbook, 14th Edition.* W. Dayton Roberts and John A. Siewert, editors. Copublished by MARC (Missions Advanced Research and Communications Center), a division of World Vision, and Zondervan Publishing House. Copyright © 1989. Used by permission.

FIFTEEN LARGEST MISSION AGENCIES
Ranked according to overseas career personnel

Rank / Agency	Career Personnel	Short-term 1 yr or more	2-11 months
1. Southern Baptist Conv. Foreign Missions	3,839	200	7,350
2. Youth with a Mission (YWAM)	2,506	0	13,954
3. Wycliffe Bible Translators International	2,269	316	0
4. New Tribes Mission	1,807	0	250
5. Christian Churches/Churches of Christ	1,717	NA	NA
6. Assemblies of God Foreign Missions	1,530	0	402
7. Churches of Christ	982	NA	NA
8. Christian and Missionary Alliance	917	54	134
9. The Evangelical Alliance Mission (TEAM)	872	69	148
10. General Conference Seventh-Day Adventist	842	59	46
11. Baptist Bible Fellowship International	734	NA	NA
12. Baptist Mid-Missions	636	NA	NA
13. Church of the Nazarene World Missions	629	0	35
14. Baptist International Missions	620	0	9
15. Association of Baptists for World Evangelism	618	16	33

Source: *Mission Handbook, 14th Edition.* W. Dayton Roberts and John A. Siewert, editors. Copublished by MARC (Missions Advanced Research and Communications Center) and Zondervan Publishing House. Copyright © 1989. Used by permission.

HOPEFUL TRENDS / ONGOING CONCERNS

Hopeful Trends

1. Mushrooming of Third-World missionary sending agencies. There may be more than 1,000 of them, fielding at least 35,000 workers. They represent a whole new wave of evangelistic vitality in the church.

2. Renewal in the Roman Catholic church. In many places there are as many renewed Catholic Christians as there are evangelicals. Despite Pope John Paul II's efforts to control the charismatic movement, it still carries much momentum.

3. Multiplication of "tentmakers" among evangelicals. As "professional" missionaries find it increasingly difficult to gain access to inhospitable nations, the number and caliber of "intentional laypersons" in these areas is growing sharply.

4. Christian responses to world hunger. An acute shortage of food—particularly in Africa—has evoked massive waves of compassion and continues to force upon the church a healthy, holistic agenda.

5. Spectacular technological advances. The strategic advantages of modern research and communications to speed up the acquisition of basic knowledge and to foster unity and cooperation are dramatic, to say the least.

Ongoing Concerns

1. World hunger and environmental abuse. Sin and poverty are leaving their tragic trail across the face of society. As Christians we need not only to respond with compassion but also to grapple with the causes of famine.

2. *Barriers preventing access to the gospel.* By AD 2000, more than half the world will live in cities (with their social isolation) and 80 percent in countries that bar traditional missions.

3. *The rise of Muslim fanaticism.* The Shi'ite form of Islam in some places, as well as the Sunni activism in others, is militant in its attempts to control society. Strong anti-Christian sentiments may well require innovative—and no doubt costly—evangelism.

4. *Oppression of women, children, castes, and racial minorities.* Women are the key to Christian development, as well as evangelism, and children are always the most vulnerable to opposing forces. Discrimination and the gospel are in strong contradiction.

5. *Deep-rooted disunity in the Christian community.* Many feel that as per John 17:21, the world will not be able to believe until the followers of Christ can become one, "as the Father is in me, and I in Him."

Source: *Mission Handbook, 14th Edition.* W. Dayton Roberts and John A. Siewert, editors. Copublished by MARC (Missions Advanced Research and Communications Center), a division of World Vision, and Zondervan Publishing House. Copyright © 1989. Used by permission.

Future Outlook:
What Still Needs to Be Done

as measured by Specialized Ministries, USCWM

The Tools	The Goals	Progress as of December 1991	Still to Be Accomplished
Satellite, TV	7 "world" languages	One language now (English)	6 languages to be on satellite
Major missionary radio	307 major languages	144 languages now broadcast	163 languages to be broadcast
Film ministry (Campus Crusade JESUS Film)	271 language groups	210 translations	61 translations to go
Scripture in print (Wycliffe and others)	6,442 "visual" languages	2,729 (at least one portion in print)	3,713 (need Scripture in print)
Audio cassettes (Gospel recordings and others)	12,398 "audio" languages	4,453 (now on cassettes)	7,945 (to be put on cassettes)
Church planting (in unreached peoples, 15% of missionaries directly involved)	24,000 "church movements" needed	13,000 (now with church movements)	11,000 (need a church movement)

Source: U.S. Center for World Mission, Pasadena, CA.

The Finishable Task

Year (A.D.)	Total World Population (Millions) 1	People Who Do Not Claim to Be Christians (Millions) 2	People Who Call Themselves Christians (Millions) 3	Evangelical Christians (Out of Col. 3) (Millions) 4	Ratio of Non-Christians to Evangelical Christians (Col. 2 : Col. 4) 5	Unreached People Groups 6	Ratio of Congregations to Unreached People Groups (Col. 4÷100 : Col. 6) 7
100	181	180	1	0.5	360 to 1	60,000	1 to 12
1000	270	220	50	1	220 to 1	50,000	1 to 5
1500	425	344	81	5	69 to 1	44,000	1 to 1
1900	1,620	1,062	558	40	27 to 1	40,000	10 to 1
1950	2,504	1,650	854	80	21 to 1	24,000	33 to 1
1980	4,458	3,025	1,433	275	11 to 1	17,000	162 to 1
1992	5,480	3,647	1,833	540	6.8 to 1	11,000	600 to 1
2000	6,260	?	?	?	?	?	?

Whence These Amazing Numbers?
The first three columns are published figures in the World Christian Encyclopedia, plus recent estimates by *Mission Frontiers* magazine.

Source: *Mission Frontiers* magazine. Used by permission.

THE STATISTICS ARE...

- 3,500 new churches are opening every week worldwide.
- 28,000 additional Christians every day in the People's Republic of China. In 1950, when China closed to foreign missionaries, there were one million Christians. Today, conservative estimates say there are 40 to 50 million.
- 20,000 additional Christians every day in Africa; that continent was 3 percent Christian in 1900 and is now more than 40 percent Christian.
- 70,000 additional Christians every day in the world.
- In 1900, Korea had no Protestant church; it was thought "impossible to penetrate." In 1991 Korea was 30 percent Christian with 4,000 churches in Seoul alone.
- In Indonesia, the percentage of Christians is so high the government won't print the statistic—which is probably nearing 25 percent of the population.
- After 70 years of oppression in the Soviet Union, Christians number at least 100 million—five times the number in the Communist party and 36 percent of the population.
- More Muslims in Iran have come to Christ since 1980 than in the previous 1000 years combined.
- In AD 100, there were 360 non-Christians per evangelical Christian. Today the ratio is seven to every evangelical Christian.
- In AD 100 there were 12 unreached people groups per church congregation. In 1991, with 5 million churches worldwide, there are at least 500 congregations for every unreached people group.
- Of the 70 million evangelicals in America, 17.5 million are age 18 to 35. The 100,000 new missionaries needed are only half of one percent of these young adults in the U.S.
- American evangelicals have a disposable annual income of about $850 billion. About one-fifth of one percent of that income—$1.5 billion—would support the needed 12,000 church-planting teams.
- According to survey results, the prayer necessary would take only 2 percent of the time evangelical Christians spend daily watching TV and shopping.

Source: *Frontiers* magazine. January/February 1990 issue. Used by permission.

BOOKLIST: A MISSIONS READING PROGRAM
Selected by Edwin L. (Jack) Frizen, Jr., Consulting Director, IFMA

January *From Jerusalem to Irian Jaya* by Ruth A. Tucker, Zondervan Publ. House.

February *What in the World is God Doing?* by C. Gordon Olson, Global Gospel Publishers.

March *The Fall of Tyrants* by Laszlo Tokes, Crossway Books

April *Touch the World through Prayer* by Wesley L. Duewel, Zondervan Publishing House.

May *Gold Fears No Fire* by Ralph Toliver, OMF Books.

June *Priority One* by Norm Lewis, Promise Publishing.

July *J. Hudson Taylor: A Man in Christ* by Roger Steer, OMF Books.

August *Countdown to AD 2000,* Edited by Thomas Wang, The AD 2000 Movement.

September *Guardians of the Great Commission* by Ruth A. Tucker, Zondervan Publishing House.

October *Today's Choices for Tomorrow's Mission* by David J. Hesselgrave, Zondervan Publishing House.

November *Bold as a Lamb* by Ken Anderson, Zondervan Publishing House

December *Dawn 2000: 7 Million Churches to Go* by Jim Montgomery, William Carey Library.

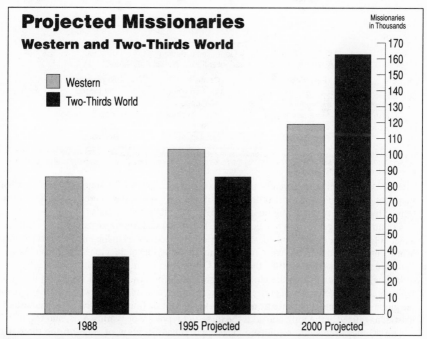

Projected Missionaries

Missionaries in Thousands

Western and Two-Thirds World

Western
Two-Thirds World

1988   1995 Projected   2000 Projected

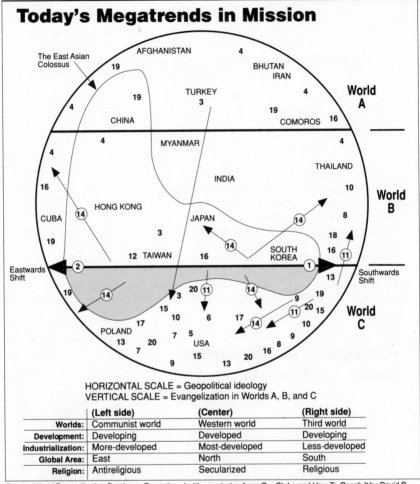

Today's Megatrends in Mission

HORIZONTAL SCALE = Geopolitical ideology
VERTICAL SCALE = Evangelization in Worlds A, B, and C

	(Left side)	(Center)	(Right side)
Worlds:	Communist world	Western world	Third world
Development:	Developing	Developed	Developing
Industrialization:	More-developed	Most-developed	Less-developed
Global Area:	East	North	South
Religion:	Antireligious	Secularized	Religious

Source: World Evangelization Database. Reproduced with permission from *Our Globe and How To Reach It* by David B. Barrett and Todd M. Johnson. Copyright © 1990 by the Foreign Mission Board of the Southern Baptist Convention. Published by New Hope, Birmingham, AL.

The globe portrays schematically the approximate locations of 20 major Christian global megatrends that have come into prominence since 1980. At first they were seen as short-term trends; by 1990 they are taking on all the attributes of long-term trends.

Countries are located by two scales. (a) The horizontal scale refers to geopolitical ideology, as set out below the globe. This locates countries and populations in the First World (Western World, also referred to as the West, or the North) in the middle of the globe, the Second World (Communist world, or since 1989 the former Communist world, or the Communist sphere of influence) on the left within the globe, and the Third World (nonaligned world) on the right within it. (b) The vertical scale refers to evangelization, as explained in words to the right of the globe. This locates countries by degree of evangelization (most-evangelized at the bottom, least-evangelized at the top), and adds the three-tier typology of Worlds A, B, and C.

The 20 megatrends are numbered. The approximate location of each on the three-tier globe is then shown by using the same numbers on the globe.

CHRISTIAN GLOBAL MEGATRENDS

1. Southward shift of Christian center of gravity from North to Third World (47%).
2. Eastward shift of Christian center of gravity from West to Communist world (21%).
3. Migrations of 1,000 Third-World peoples to Christian West.
4. Countries restricting access by foreign missions: 119 (43 closed countries).
5. Rise of 56 global ministry networks with 54 million computers.
6. Massive global growth of electronic radio/TV Christianity to 26% of world.
7. Mushrooming of literature on evangelization (11,000 items a year).
8. Proliferation of 400 conferences on evangelization each year.
9. 50 new global plans for world evangelization each year.
10. 2,500 evangelistic mass campaigns a year.
11. Emergence of 1,000 Third-World mission agencies.
12. Rise of the East Asian colossus with 80 million Christians.
13. 3 waves of worldwide Pentecostal/charismatic renewal, to 372 million.
14. Power Christianity by osmosis across the world: signs and wonders.
15. Retrograde or negative Christian activities hindering world mission.
16. Pluralism: proliferation of 23,500 denominations and 30,000 religions across world.
17. Spread of Christian activism worldwide opposing injustice and human rights abuses.
18. New ministries to 1.3 billion urban poor in exploding "planet of slums."
19. Escalating martyrdoms reach 300,000 a year in 50 countries and in all Christian branches.
20. Emergence of the AD 2000 megamagnet throughout the world.

VERTICAL SCALE:
Evangelization in Worlds A, B, C

A. THE UNEVANGELIZED WORLD

133 million newly-evangelized each year, but offset by 142 million new births a year.

30 closed countries increasing by 2 a year.

Sizable numbers from 200 large unreached peoples migrate to Christian West.

B. THE EVANGELIZED NON-CHRISTIAN WORLD

Emergence of 1,000 Third-World mission agencies.

31 partially-closed countries increasing each year.

Reaction to social injustice and abuses in Third World.

Rapid spread of Christian activism in 30 World B countries (150 countries worldwide).

Escalating martyrdoms of Christian workers.

Vast numbers from 800 non-Christian peoples migrate to Christian West.

Numerous ministries escalate among 520 million slumdwellers.

C. THE CHRISTIAN WORLD

Eastward and southward shift of Christian center of gravity.

Christians now 32% in West, 21% in Communist world, 47% in Third World.

East Asian colossus: 80 million Christians (shaded gray) among 1.2 billion population.

Pluralism: over 10,000 new religions spread across West.

❝❞ FOCUS QUOTE There is not a home church and a foreign church. It is all one great work.
—Oswald Chambers

Retrograde Christian activities, with ecclesiastical crime $1.1 billion p.a., mainly in West.

Massive global growth of electronic radio/TV Christianity, used by 26% of world.

AD 2000 plans launched by most major churches and agencies.

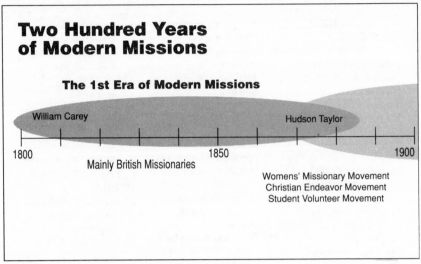

Two Hundred Years of Modern Missions

The 1st Era of Modern Missions

William Carey   Hudson Taylor

1800   1850   1900

Mainly British Missionaries

Womens' Missionary Movement
Christian Endeavor Movement
Student Volunteer Movement

Source: *Mission Frontiers* Magazine. Used by permission.

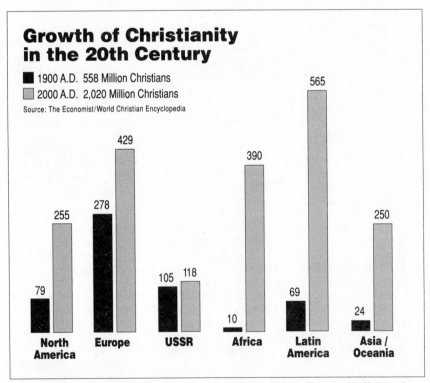

Growth of Christianity in the 20th Century

■ 1900 A.D. 558 Million Christians
☐ 2000 A.D. 2,020 Million Christians

Source: The Economist/World Christian Encyclopedia

	North America	Europe	USSR	Africa	Latin America	Asia / Oceania
1900	79	278	105	10	69	24
2000	255	429	118	390	565	250

Source: *Target Earth*, edited by Frank Kaleb Jansen. Copyright © 1989. Copublished by University of the Nations and Global Mapping International. Used by permission.

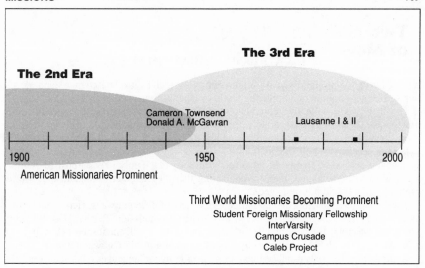

WHAT IS THE AD 2000 MOVEMENT?

**The Mobilization of God's people to reach the unreached by AD 2000.
It can be done, it ought to be done, it must be done.**

The purpose of the AD 2000 Movement is to motivate and network men and women church leaders by inspiring visions through consultations, prayer efforts, and written materials. The intention is to encourage cooperation among existing movements and structures to work together toward this same vision. The expected result is the establishment of a mission-minded church-planting movement within every unreached people and city by AD 2000 so that all peoples might have a valid opportunity to experience the love, truth, and saving power of Jesus Christ.

—Thomas Wang, Chairman, AD 2000 Movement, 1605 Elizabeth Street, Pasadena, CA 91104

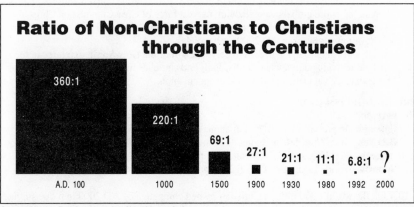

Source: *Mission Frontiers* magazine. Used by permission.

168 AD 2000 GLOBAL GOALS

A selection of 168 proposed Great Commission goals, each by itself based on a stand-alone, self-sufficient definition of completing world evangelization.

The listing is a collective compilation of final goals put forward by agencies and protagonists, in most cases separately. Each one is considered to be a final closure goal to complete an aspect of world evangelization by AD 2000.

It is not necessary for all 168 goals to be achieved—by most people's definition, only one such goal is necessary. To be safe, however, we can say that if only 10 or at most 20 of these goals were to be achieved, then (remembering that they interact synergistically) world evangelization would be completed.

These goals can be listed and classified in a variety of different ways. Here, we classify them broadly by the Seven Mandates of Christ's Great Commission: Receive! Go! Witness! Proclaim! Disciple! Baptize! and Train! These mandates are distinguished below in bold type, and further subdivided by various generic types of ministry (shown in italics).

A number of the goals produced here originated in major languages other than English. Goals were sent in Bahasa Indonesian, Bengali, Chinese, French, German, Japanese, Korean, Malayalam, Portuguese, Sango, Spanish, Telugu, et al.

Individual Christians, groups, churches, organizations, or agencies are encouraged to select one or more of the goals to concentrate on implementing in collaboration with other Great Commission Christians and agencies which have similar goals.

PRAYER EVANGELISM (RECEIVE!)

1. Establish 15,000 prayer movements by 1995 in every city over 50,000 and on all 15,000 university campuses, evangelizing the urban and academic worlds by 2000.
2. Enlist by AD 2000, 30 million Christians to pray full time every day for world evangelization through a globally organized network of young pacesetter intercessors to cover all countries, cities, peoples, topics, needs, and persons.
3. Enroll 170 million Christians (10% of world total) in a world prayer force promising to pray daily for successful closure of world evangelization by 2000.
4. Enthuse all prayer-oriented or contemplative brothers and sisters, monks and nuns, to regain past monastic enthusiasm for world evangelization and to rededicate monasteries and convents worldwide by 2000 to prayer support for the Great Commission task.
5. Prepare the entire global evangelization harvest force of Great Commission Christians to be ready and waiting at any time for Christ's parousia and second advent, whether today, or tomorrow, or in AD 2000, or beyond.
6. Preach and emphasize the need to receive the gift of the Holy Spirit, to intercede for spiritual revival and renewal of individuals and churches by 2000, and to promote the thesis that revival is the key to world evangelization.

PRE-EVANGELISM (GO!)

Preparation

7. Increase the proportion of Christian annual finance expended on World A, the Unevangelized World, from today's 1% to 4% by 2000.
8. Increase World A's share of Christian computers from today's 0% to 5% by 2000.
9. Increase World A's share of Christian computer specialists from today's 0% to 5% by 2000.
10. Link the world's 350 million Christian-owned computers by AD 2000 into one single global giganetwork to facilitate Great Commission information exchange.

11. Circulate by AD 2000, as a service to apologetes and evangelists, a computerized Great Commission glossary-dictionary, listing (a) definitions of all the major English terms in use related to global mission and world evangelization, and (b) listings of the major wider Christian terms, words, and concepts (God, Christ, gospel, sin, disciple, etc.) with their equivalents in all languages of the world (2,500 languages with Scripture translation, 9,500 without).

12. Systematically place, by AD 2000, the best Christian apologetic and evangelistic literature and materials (including the Bible) in any language at all strategic points in all strata of the modern information/knowledge/computer/artificial intelligence explosion and revolution: in public-access databases, knowledge bases, OCLC (library retrieval), DIALOG (with 100 databases), Religion One, and all other similar secular services.

13. Translate by AD 2000 the most influential, effective, and persuasive works of Christian apologetics in any language into the top 20 non-Christian languages of the world, and publish and disseminate them widely through all varieties of print and electronic media.

14. Pursue systematic region-by-region dialogue with the world's organized atheists, agnostics, nonbelievers, and nonreligious, as well as with the great non-Christian world religions and newer cults and religious movements, so that all may genuinely understand each other's position and the full message of Christ may be fully understood in all these contexts by 2000.

15. Place into operation a Great Commission expert system to guide the prioritization of all proposed or suggested AD 2000 programs and ministries in any part of the world.

16. Have an electronic Great Commission global network and expert system to guide the actual accomplishment of all corporate and individual AD 2000 goals, both at intermediate years (1990, 1995) and also by the AD 2000 deadline.

17. Translate into 100 Christian megalanguages the major AD 2000 strategic planning documents and methods, including Great Commission expert systems, and the Kaleidoscopic Global Plan.

18. Encourage AD 2000 global and nonglobal plans to develop corporate plans and consequently achieve major collective goals for AD 2000.

19. Redistribute the great majority of Christian resources of manpower, money, and methods across the world's unevangelized peoples and cities strictly according to need, by 2000.

Development

20. Monitor and encourage a final massive attempt by AD 2000 at the promotion of human development in all its forms worldwide as an integral part of world evangelization.

21. Support FAO goal for eradication of human hunger by 2000, and then beyond.

22. Feed and nourish the world's 600 million persons on the verge of starvation during the year 2000, and see that they continue to live nourished lives thereafter.

23. Support WHO goal of safe drinking water for every soul on earth by 2000 and beyond.

24. Minister in the name of Jesus to all the world's poor, destitute, sick, and dying, bringing Jesus to the poorest of the poor in every country and city on earth by 2000.

25. Abolish the global state of absolute poverty (per capita daily income of under US $1) by AD 2000 through massive redistribution everywhere of national and international wealth, certainly by all Christian denominations and agencies, also by secular organizations persuaded by Christian activists.

26. Raise physical quality of life of all disadvantaged peoples of earth to a livable level by 2000, and even higher levels beyond.

27. Develop creative approaches for total ministry directed to the world's 2.4 billion children by AD 2000, through evangelism, education, aid and relief, in all languages and in all 15,000 population segments.

168 AD 2000 GLOBAL GOALS cont.

28. Support UNICEF goal to halve child deaths (38,000 a day in 1988) by 1997, then continuing to decrease by 2000 and beyond.
29. Support WHO goal to halt child diarrhea deaths by giving all parents of children under five access to ORT (oral rehydration therapy) and a trained health worker, the world proportion of children so covered to increase from 3% (1980) to 50% (1988) to 100% by AD 2000.
30. Support WHO goal of rise of worldwide immunization coverage from 9% (1980) to 50% (1987) to 100% by 1990, staying there through 2000, and beyond.
31. Increase annual medical consultations in Christian hospitals, dispensaries, centers, clinics, and mobile clinics, to 20 million a year worldwide by 2000.
32. Insist on a final negotiated settlement and end to the stateless or homeless status of 60 million refugees on earth, half of whom are children, by the symbolic 2,000th anniversary of the birth of the child Jesus, a refugee from political evil.
33. Eliminate poverty housing throughout the world in the name of Jesus Christ by AD 2000, and build adequate urban housing in its place in the cities of the world.
34. Extend adequate aid, assistance, care, and ministry to the world's entire 1.8 billion disabled persons (33% being children) in AD 2000.
35. Set in place by 2000, a network of fully trained, financed and prepared disaster-relief teams (and other Christian emergency structures) ready to minister anywhere in the world at an hour's notice.
36. Reduce the level of human suffering in 50 highly-disturbed countries to a minimum level by 2000, then eradicate it beyond.
37. Support UNESCO goal to increase adult literacy from the present 45% to 100% by 2000.
38. Increase pupils and students in all types of Christian schools and colleges to 30 million worldwide by 2000.
39. Monitor the status of human rights in every country and work with specializing agencies to see all abuses rectified by AD 2000.
40. Raise to an acceptable level by 2000 the level of human rights experienced by all populations who have been and still are severely discriminated against.
41. Monitor, with Amnesty International, the status of state-sanctified police/military torture in all countries, and see it abolished universally by 2000, and never recur beyond.
42. Monitor religious liberty or persecution in every country, have it reported regularly by Amnesty International, and see that action for liberty results by 2000.
43. Place into action by AD 2000 a massive worldwide Christian movement adamantly opposing and outlawing all war, warfare, mass-destruction weapons, militarization, paramilitarization, arms sales, arms traders, death squads, and all indiscriminate mass killings.
44. Curtail by AD 2000 the worst manifestations of the world's "structures of sin" through determined Christian publication and activism.
45. Support UTU goal of universal telephone access for every population on earth by 2000 and beyond.

PERSONAL EVANGELISM (WITNESS!)
Witness
46. Evangelize the unevangelized World of 3,030 peoples, metropolises, and countries by 2000.
47. Establish a witness in every unreached people on earth by 2000.
48. Establish a witness in every unreached minipeople (people group) on earth by 2000.
49. Establish a witness in every unreached ethnos (micropeople) on earth by 2000.
50. Establish a witness in every unreached metropolis on earth by 2000.
51. Establish ongoing mission and ministry by 2000 in every one of the world's 120 closed

or closing countries, its 500 closed or closing metropolises, and its 2,000 closed or closing peoples.

52. Put in place by 2000 adequate ministry, witness, and diakonia, including structures, among the world's 10,000 urban slum populations.

53. See all 15,000 population segments on earth by AD 2000 either entered (with resident missionaries) or engaged (with other deliberate but nonresidential modes) by at least one denomination or agency but preferably several different yet cooperating denominations or agencies.

54. Engage, with foreign missionary presence and ministry, every closed country, unreached people, and unevangelized metropolis in the world by 2000.

55. Assign one worker or couple to work exclusively with each of the 3,030 unevangelized population segments by 2000.

56. Locate 100,000 bivocational Christian lay tentmakers in secular work in 120 closed or closing countries by 2000.

57. See at least two tentmakers become resident in every unevangelized people on earth by 2000.

58. See at least two tentmakers become resident in every unevangelized minipeople (people group) on earth by 2000.

59. See at least two tentmakers become resident in every unevangelized ethnos (micropeople) on earth by 2000.

60. See at least two tentmakers become resident in every unevangelized metropolis on earth by 2000.

61. Establish awareness of Christ and his gospel among all the world's populations by 2000.

62. Bring half the human race (50%, or 3.1 billion) face-to-face with Christ by AD 2000 by means of radio/TV, Scriptures, missions, personal witness, etc.

63. Direct evangelization by AD 2000 primarily to *panta ta ethne,* all nations and peoples and cities and populations, thus giving every individual in them adequate (but not necessarily a customized, personalized, individualized) opportunity to respond to Christ.

64. Visit every home on earth, leaving at least two gospel leaflets in each's language, by 2000.

65. Establish by AD 2000 a system for visiting each year the world's 30 million new homes (families) begun that year, leaving at least two gospel leaflets in each's languages.

66. Train and develop the world's 2.1 billion lay persons in the mystical body of Christ by AD 2000 in the apostolate of daily witness by word and deed, engaging non-Christians directly in conversation about Christ's message of redemption and liberation.

67. After a 10-year emphasis (1990-2000) on the perils of affluence, aim to see a majority of Great Commission Christians, leaders, churches, and agencies embracing and adopting the basic, simple, biblical, Christian life-style (including self-denial, fasting, tithing) and to see them implementing life-style evangelism worldwide by the beginning of the new millennium.

68. Enable by AD 2000 one million youths as short-term missionaries every year to serve abroad for 2 weeks to a year as foreign missionaries especially witnessing in closed or closing territories and cities.

69. Emphasize to the entire Christian world by AD 2000 that martyrdom is a major form of evangelization, that the world's anticipated 500,000 annual Christian martyrs are major players in God's global plan, and that Christians suffering for their faith should realize they are playing a vital role in world evangelization.

Broadcasting

70. Record and make available a gospel message in every language on earth by 2000.

71. Expand broadcast Christian programs, now in 2,000 languages, to 3,000 languages by 2000.

72. Extend radiophonic schools (radio broadcasting plus local classes, phone-in, talk-back,

168 AD 2000 GLOBAL GOALS cont.

write-back, or other feedback) to every country in the world by 2000.

73. Ensure that regular television evangelism proceeds weekly in the world's 300 largest languages by 2000.
74. Ensure that regular radio evangelism proceeds weekly in the world's 1,000 largest languages by 2000.
75. Increase global audience listening regularly to Christian radio/TV from the present 25% to 50% (3.1 billion) by AD 2000.
76. Increase World A's (the Unevangelized World's) share of Christian broadcast hours from today's 0% to 20% by 2000.
77. Reach the entire world with the Christian gospel for the first time ever by AD 2000, in the sense that everyone everywhere has heard or hears the gospel in depth with understanding and has access to Holy Scripture, churches, mission, Christians, Christian broadcasting (through both secular stations and 4,000 Christian radio and TV stations worldwide), videos, movies, literature, and other means of grace.
78. Prepare or dub films on the Bible or life of Christ, specifically the *Jesus* film, in 500 languages and show to the world's entire population by 2000.
79. Produce and distribute by AD 2000 a thousand different Christian or biblical films, in 200 major languages, with 25,000 prints in circulation resulting in 500,000 showings a year, with 500 million viewers and 25 million decisions or converts.

PREACHING EVANGELISM (PROCLAIM!)
Proclamation
80. Present the gospel message to all 6.2 billion people by AD 2000.
81. Proclaim the gospel to every population segment on earth by 2000.
82. Proclaim the gospel to every culture on every continent by the year 2000.
83. Proclaim the gospel to every unevangelized people on earth by 2000.
84. Proclaim the gospel to every unevangelized minipeople (people group) on earth by 2000.
85. Proclaim the gospel to every unevangelized ethnos (micropeople) on earth by 2000.
86. Proclaim the gospel to every unevangelized metropolis on earth by 2000.
87. Provide every people and population on earth with a valid opportunity to hear the gospel in a language they can understand by 2000.
88. Establish by AD 2000 a system for directing evangelistic resources specifically towards the annual increase in the world's unevangelized population—new, first-time, unevangelized populations (children and youths reaching ages of decision, averaging 15 years old).
89. Send out one million native evangelists from among the thousands of native missionary movements in the Third World, to produce by 2000 a massive revolutionary Third Wave of missions across the world.
90. Have the three or four top leaders of the world's 2.1 billion Christians preach on live 30-satellite TV in 50 languages directly to the entire world of 6 billion souls on 25 December 2000, appealing to all to welcome and receive Jesus Christ as Lord and Savior on his 2,000th birthday.
91. Conduct by AD 2000 some 500 annual organized citywide multidenominational evangelistic campaigns, some 3,000 citywide denominational campaigns, and hundreds of evangelistic megameetings (each with over 100,000 attenders at once).
92. Conduct global citywide evangelistic campaigns simultaneously by AD 2000, in hundreds of metropolises worldwide, based on an originating campaign in a major Third-World city, beamed by satellite to participating cities.
93. Increase persons attending or reached by organized evangelistic campaigns to 100 million per year by 2000.

94. Increase World A's, the Unevangelized World's, share of citywide campaigns from today's nil to at least 100 (3% of total) by 2000.

Power Evangelism

95. See the decade of 1990-2000 close as greatest decade in Christian history for signs and wonders, miracles, conversion, evangelism and evangelization, with the greatest sign or wonder being Christians loving one another and gathering in unity everywhere.
96. Enable 300,000 itinerant charismatic evangelists to target unevangelized cities, countries, and peoples by 2000.
97. Train 50,000 three-man evangelistic teams of Third World evangelists by 2000, who will itinerate through unreached peoples and cities, evangelizing.
98. Deliberately exercise power evangelism in the world's least evangelized and most hostile environments so that by AD 2000 power Christianity (gifted ministries of signs and wonders) is not enjoyed solely in Christian lands.

PERSUASION EVANGELISM (DISCIPLE!)
Conversion

99. Bring the majority of the human race to Jesus Christ by the end of the century.
100. See at least half of humanity (51%) profess some form of allegiance to Christ by 2000.
101. See one billion people receive Christ as Savior and Lord or rededicate their lives to him and be incorporated into local congregations in the decade culminating in 2000.
102. See recorded inquirers or decisions for Christ (all types of campaigns, missions, correspondence course, decisions cards) reach 60 million a year by 2000.
103. See local church converts/baptisms/confirmation/receptions/new members reach 30 million a year for all churches by 2000.
104. Launch a movement on all 3,000 major university campuses in the world to help fulfill the Great Commission among the 60 million college students in the world's 30,000 tertiary-level universities and colleges by the year 2000.
105. Generate by AD 2000 thousands of converts worldwide as "God's key representatives" in key positions in the entire global range of secular worlds, which representatives will then bring about closure in world evangelization.
106. Make disciples of all nations by AD 2000 through the multiplication method "each one teach and reach one," in which one disciple wins one other within one month, both win one more each in the next month, these four win four, then eight win eight, etc., until the world is fully discipled after 32 months.
107. Finish the Worldwide Decade of Universal Evangelization (1990-2000) with all its major goals accomplished, with Christ and his gospel universally known and respected, with all Christians united as never before since the Apostolic era, and with over 50% of the world professing some sort of allegiance to Christ as Lord and Savior.

PLANTING EVANGELISM (BAPTIZE!)
Church Planting

108. Make at least a handful of disciples, and plant a beachhead church, within every unevangelized population segment on earth (country, people, metropolis) by 2000.
109. Establish a bridgehead church in every unreached ethnolinguistic people on earth by 2000.
110. Establish a bridgehead church in every unreached minipeople (people group) on earth by 2000.
111. Establish a bridgehead church in every unreached ethnos (micropeople) on earth by 2000.
112. Establish a bridgehead church in every unreached metropolis on earth by 2000.
113. Establish a church-planting movement in every people on earth by 2000.
114. See global church-planting goal completed, with at least one fellowship or church or congregation or nucleus of disciples planted as an ongoing indigenous witness in each

168 AD 2000 GLOBAL GOALS cont.

of the world's 11,500 ethnolinguistic peoples and 7,000 metropolises of over 50,000
population each in AD 2000.

115. See full emergence by AD 2000 of a vast worldwide rash of spontaneous house-church
video networks spreading like wildfire across all countries with large denominations.

116. Have in place by AD 2000 a worldwide network of self-replicating media churches
(self-propagating youth-led video/radio/TV house-church networks), with well-
worked-out autospread procedures and optional low-key full logistical support from
older churches and agencies.

117. Begin 3.5 million new churches or house worship centers over the period 1988-1999
resulting in a global total of 6 million churches and, on average, one church by AD
2000 for every 1,000 persons including peoples still unreached in 1988.

118. See 5 million small-group base ecclesial communities (comunidades de base, CEBes)
mushroom among the world of the desperately poor by 2000, enabling the poor (46%
of the world) to be world evangelizers in their own right.

119. See AD 2000 rapidly-multiplying self-replicating networks of (a) itinerant tourist
churches ceaselessly circulating around the world, and (b) itinerant pilgrim churches
circumambulating continually across the globe.

120. Mobilize the entire world's 6 million local churches and congregations to complete by
AD 2000 the task of world evangelization in their localities and beyond.

PASTORAL EVANGELISM (TRAIN!)
Training

121. Increase World A's, the Unevangelized World's, share of full-time Christian workers
from today's 0.7% to 5% by 2000.

122. Increase World A's share of foreign missionaries received from today's 0% to 40% by 2000.

123. Increase World A's share of foreign mission money received from today's 1.3% to 40%
by 2000.

124. See that every one of the 7,000 metropolises on earth has several varieties of urban-
industrial mission and ongoing ministry begun by AD 2000.

125. Have a system in place by AD 2000 to regularly extend family ministries, of at least
rudimentary form, to all 30 million new families begun on earth each year, within one
year of each family being begun.

126. Train 800,000 evangelists to equip 600,000,000 Christians to reach 4,000,000,000 unbelievers by the year 2000.

127. Have 600,000 career foreign missionaries of all nationalities serving abroad by 2000.

128. Have 200,000 Third-World citizens serving abroad as foreign missionaries by 2000.

129. Have the world's 22,000 denominations mobilized in such a way that by 2000 each is
actively pursuing closure and contributing toward it.

130. See 20,000 foreign missionaries, at present working with Christians in Christian lands,
redeployed to work with unevangelized non-Christian populations by 2000.

131. Have 10,000 trained pilgrim evangelizers in closed or closing populations by 2000,
traveling around with all the largest religious pilgrimages and pilgrim movements.

132. Harness by AD 2000 the Christian world's one million professional theologians and
10,000 missiologists (including biblical scholars and teachers, church historians, etc.)
so that they not only support the global evangelization movement but actively lead
and guide it in all parts of the world.

133. Develop a foolproof, inexpensive, Christian communications network available to and
usable by all Christians everywhere by 2000.

134. Get, by AD 2000, substantial Great-Commission-content messages (news stories about

Christianity, Christ, and the gospel) circulating every day in the world's 20 major languages of telecommunication, in three modes: (a) across the world's secular news services (wire services, teletype services, audio services, video services, film services, global telecommunication networks), (b) throughout the world's satellite networks (broadcasting, telephone, communication links), and (c) in the world's professional computer networks (academics, librarians, scholars, financiers, aid & relief, church executives, research & development, military/armed forces, police/INTERPOL, espionage, government, diplomacy, UN agencies, etc.).

135. Inaugurate numerous series of leadership spiritual renewal seminars to renew all the world's church leaders who will then bring fundamental change within all nations, and so bring about worldwide evangelization by 2000.

136. Plan an interactive series of local, national, regional, continental, confessional, and global consultations on world evangelization climaxing in AD 2000.

137. Celebrate the millennial year with Celebration 2000, a massive global event on the part of all Great Commission Christians, in myriads of locations across the world.

Literature

138. Increase World A's, the Unevangelized World's, share of annual Scripture distribution from today's 1% to 25% by 2000.

139. Increase World A's share of annual tract distribution from today's 4% to 20% by 2000.

140. Increase World A's share of Scripture languages from todays 3% to 10% by 2000.

141. Increase World A's share of annual Christian literature circulation from today's 0.2% to 10% by 2000.

142. Increase World A's share of Christian periodicals from today's 1% to 10% by 2000.

143. See annual distribution of Christian literature (tracts, leaflets, books, Scriptures) reach 2 billion pieces per year, evenly distributed worldwide by 2000.

144. Have adequate access to Holy Scripture by 2000 for every population segment on earth, through written or spoken translations either in its mother tongue, or a closely-related language or idiom, or a market language, or trade language, or lingua franca.

145. Publish a printed Gospel in every language on earth by 2000.

146. Translate and publish Scriptures (at least one Gospel) in 4,000 languages by AD 2000.

147. Complete media versions of the whole Bible (on audio cassette, tape, record, computer disk, hypertext, video, film) in the 6 major Christian languages by 2000.

148. Expand total languages possessing a basic list of printed essential Christian literature (Holy Scripture, commentaries, daily readings, daily living) from the present 500 to 3,000 by AD 2000.

149. Coordinate a whole series of megaministries (ministries each reaching over one million different people a day)—Scripture circulation, literature, broadcasting, tract distribution, house-to-house visiting, citywide evangelistic campaigns, nationwide crusades, etc.—to the point where cumulative evangelization far outstrips the birth rate and the whole world is reached by these methods by the end of this century.

150. Hand a tract with a gospel message or picture to every individual in the world by 2000.

151. Distribute a Scripture selection to every soul on earth, in his or her own language, by 2000.

152. Give a Gospel or portion to every literate person on earth by 2000.

153. Give a Gospel selection or leaflet, in pictorial or comic form with minimum words, to every preliterate soul on earth, in his or her own language, by 2000.

154. Help every literate Christian on earth to own his or her own copy of the New Testament by 2000.

155. Mail a New Testament to every telephone subscriber on earth by 2000.

156. Place a Bible in the hands of every family on earth by 2000.

157. Teach every capable man, woman, and child on earth, by the year 2000, to read the

168 AD 2000 GLOBAL GOALS cont.

Bible in their own language, using computer/laser technology.
158. Enroll 500 million non-Christians in Bible correspondence courses by 2000.
159. See Bible correspondence course graduates reach 50 million each year by 2000.

CLOSURE: SOME FUTURIST MEGAGOALS
160. Assist today's megacomplex of "2000 plans toward AD 2000" to achieve, collectively as well as individually, their AD 2000 goals.
161. Assist the Kaleidoscopic Global Plans view of today's 2,000 plans for AD 2000 to achieve their numerous goals.
162. See an enormous synergistic cross fertilizing effect evolve in which the "2,000 plans toward AD 2000" all interact and assist each other resulting in closure on most of their goals by 2000.
163. See individual goals of all 2,000 global and nonglobal AD 2000 plans fulfilled by the turn of the century.
164. Accomplish by AD 2000 definitive fulfillment of the 20 top global megapriorities as seen by Great Commission Christians.
165. See major features of future scenarios for world evangelization by 2000 actually take place.
166. Fulfill positive goals set out in alternate scenarios for world evangelization by AD 2000 and beyond.
167. See to it that all achievements by AD 2000, especially provision of concrete resources or totals, have provision for annual upgrading to take care of (a) attrition among human resources due to illnesses, resignation, retirements, departures, deaths, (b) replacement of concrete items due to wear and tear (15% of all Bibles, film prints, etc., disintegrate annually), and (c) the world's population explosion with 14 million new souls arriving on earth in the year 2000 itself; this overall provision then being extended for each successive year beyond.
168. Attain total world evangelization for first time ever by 31 December 2000 but regard that milestone date not primarily as the end of the 20th century but as the beginning of the 21st with its years beyond.

Source: *Countdown to AD 2000: The Official Compendium of the Global Consultation on World Evangelism by AD 2000 and Beyond.* Edited by Thomas Wang. Copyright © 1989 by AD 2000 Movement, Inc. Used by permission.

HOW YOU CAN BECOME INVOLVED IN THE AD 2000 MOVEMENT

Select one of the interest groups listed below. Write or phone the group coordinator for specific information on goals and action plans.

Group	Chairperson	Coordinator
Saturation Church Planting	Dr. Chris Marantika Indonesia	Dr. Jim Montgomery, Dawn Ministries, P.O. Box 40969, Pasadena, CA 91114. FAX: 818-398-2379 PH: 818-398-2300
Mobilization of Local Church	Mr. Roger Forster England	Dr. Ramesh Richard, RREACH International, 16250 Dallas Parkway, Suite 110, Dallas, TX 75248. FAX: 214-931-2169 PH: 214-841-3675
Unreached Peoples	Patrick Johnstone England	Mr. John Robb, MARC, 919 W. Huntington Drive, Monrovia, CA 91016. FAX: 818-301-7786 PH: 818-301-7713
Women	Mrs. Judy Mbugua Kenya	Mrs. Lorry Lutz, Partners International, 1470 North Fourth Street, San Jose, CA 95112

Group	Chairperson	Coordinator
		FAX: 408-437-9708 PH: 408-453-3800
Young People	Rev. Floyd McClung Netherlands	Rev. Paul Borthwick, Grace Chapel, 59 Worthen Road, Lexington, MA 02173. FAX: Use Sir Speedy 617-863-1081 Have them call Grace Chapel PH: 617-862-6499
Nonresidential Missionaries & Tentmakers to the Unevangelized World	George Houssney USA	Mr. David Garrison, Foreign Mission Board, Southern Baptist Convention, Box 6767, Richmond, VA 23230. FAX: 804-358-0504 PH: 804-353-0151
Cross-Cultural Mission Training	Rev. Reuben E. Ezemadu Nigeria	Dr. William D. Taylor, WEF Missions Commission, 29 Simpson Avenue, Cedar Creek, TX 78612. FAX: 512-321-0535 PH: 512-321-7618
Unevangelized Cities	Dr. Sam Kamaleson USA	Mr. Viv Grigg, Urban Leadership Foundation, 727 South Brady, East Los Angeles, CA 90022. FAX: 213-726-1735 PH: 213-726-2817
Theological Issues	Dr. Peter Kuzmic Yugoslavia	Dr. Bong-Rin Ro, WEF Theological Commission, P. O. Box 94 Choong Jongno, Seoul, Korea 120-650. FAX: 82-2-393-8462 PH: 82-2-393-9895
Mobilization of National Research	Rev. Niyi Gbade Nigeria	Mr. Bob Waymire, Light International, Box 368, Etna, CA 96027. FAX: 916-467-3686 PH: Same
Prayer	Dr. Kim Joon-Gon Korea	Dr. C. Peter Wagner, Fuller Theological Seminary, School of World Missions, 135 No. Oakland Avenue, Pasadena, CA 91182. FAX: 818-449-5073 PH: 818-584-5285
Radio/TV Media	H. Ricardo Glaser Brazil	Mr. Ron Cline, HCJB World Radio, Box 553000, Opa Locka, FL 33055, FAX: 305-621-2333 PH: 305-624-4252
Spiritual Mapping	Ted Yamamori USA	Mr. George Otis, Jr., Sentinel, P. O. Box 6334, Lynnwood, WA 98036. FAX: 206-672-3028 PH: 206-672-2989

MISSIONS MAGAZINES

Action Magazine, P.O. Box A, Greenwood, IN 46142. Quarterly, free.

Actionline, P.O. Box 203, Prospect Heights, IL 60070. Organizational, bimonthly, free.

AD2000 and Beyond, 850 Wycliffe Drive, Colorado Springs, CO 80906. Bimonthly, free.

Around the World, P.O. Box 553000, Miami, FL 33055. Quarterly, free.

Asian Report, P.O. Box 9000, Mission Viejo, CA 92690.

Beyond, P.O. Box 248, Waxhaw, NC 28173. Organizational, bimonthly, free.

Bibles for the World News, Box 805, Wheaton, IL 60189. Organizational, quarterly, free.

Breakthrough, P.O. Box 1122, Wheaton, IL 60189. Soviet Union and Eastern Europe, bimonthly, donation.

Call to Prayer, P.O. Box WGM, Marion, IN 46952. Organizational, bimonthly, donation.

Childlife Magazine, 919 W. Huntington Drive, Monrovia, CA 91016. Organizational, quarterly, donation.

Chosen People, The, 1300 Cross Beam Drive, Charlotte, NC 28217. Jewish evangelism, 11/yr, $5.00/yr.

Christian Mission, 3045 Ivy Road, Charlottesville, VA 22903. Support national workers, bimonthly, donation.

Compassion Update, P.O. Box 7000, Colorado Springs, CO 80933. Child aid, bimonthly, free.

MISSIONS MAGAZINES, con't

Door of Hope, P.O. Box 303, Glendale, CA 91209. Quarterly, free.

Doorways, P.O. Box C, Colorado Springs, CO 80901. Organizational, 4/yr, free.

East Asia's Millions, 10 W. Dry Creek Circle, Littleton, CO 80120-4427.

Eastern Challenge, Box 14866, Reading, PA 19612-4866. Quarterly, free.

Europe Report, The, P.O. Box 668, Wheaton, IL 60187. Organizational, 4/yr, free.

Eurovision Advance, P.O. Box 1136, Claremont, CA 91711. Eastern bloc countries, quarterly, $1.00/yr.

Evangelical Missions Quarterly, P.O. Box 794, Wheaton, IL 60189. News, quarterly, $14.95/yr.

Evangelical World, P.O. Box WEF, Wheaton, IL 60189. Monthly, free.

FEBC News, P.O. Box 1, La Mirada, CA 90637. Organizational, quarterly, free.

Feed the Children, Box 36, Oklahoma City, OK 73101. Child aid, bimonthly, free.

Food for the Hungry, 7729 E. Greenway Road, Scottsdale, AZ 85260. Poverty, monthly, free.

Global Prayer Digest, 1605 Elizabeth Street, Pasadena, CA 91104. Monthly, $9.00/yr.

Horizon International World Reporter, 17041 Ruffner Street, San Diego, CA 92111. Organizational, quarterly, free.

Horizons, P.O. Box 969, Wheaton, IL 60189. Bimonthly, $2.00/yr.

In Other Words, P.O. Box 2727, Huntington Beach, CA 92647. Organizational, 8/yr, free.

Increase Magazine, P.O. Box 410, Hatfield, PA 19440. Organizational.

Indian Life, P.O. Box 3765 Station B, Winnipeg, MB, R2W 3R6. North American Indians, bimonthly, 5.00/yr.

International Bulletin of Missionary Research, P.O. Box 821, Farmingdale, NY 11737-9721. Research/scholarly issues, quarterly, $18.00/yr.

International Journal of Frontier Missions, 1539 E. Howard St., Pasadena, CA 91104. Frontier missions, quarterly, $15.00/yr.

Latin America Evangelist, P.O. Box 52-7900, Miami, FL 33152. Latin America, quarterly, free.

Lausanne Communique, 5970 Fairview Road, Suite 514, Charlotte, NC 28210-3196. Bimonthly, free.

Luke Society News, The, 1121 Grove Street, Vicksburg, MS 39180. Biannual, free.

Map International Report, P.O. Box 50, Brunswick, GA 31521. Organizational, 6/yr, free.

MARC News Letter, 919 W Huntington Dr., Monrovia, CA 91016. Research, bimonthly, free.

Mission Frontiers, 1605 Elizabeth Street, Pasadena, CA 91104. Monthly, $4.00/yr.

Missionary Monthly, 4517-A Broadmoor Avenue, Grand Rapids, MI 49508. Reformed and Presbyterian churches, 9/yr, $10.00/yr.

Missionary Tidings, The, 901 College, Winona Lake, IN 46590. Women's missionary group news, 9/yr, $6.00/yr.

Native Reflections, Box 891, Hot Springs, SD 57747. Native Americans, quarterly, free.

Newswire, P.O. Box 1122, Wheaton, IL 60189. Eastern bloc countries, bimonthly, donation.

OC International, P.O. Box 36900, Colorado Springs, CO 80936-6900. Organizational, quarterly, donation.

OMS Outreach, Box A, Greenwood, IN 46142. Organizational, bimonthly, donation.

Open Doors News Brief, P.O. Box 27001, Santa Ana, CA 92799. Eastern bloc, monthly, $12.00/yr.

Overseas Council Newsletter, P.O. Box 751, Greenwood, IN 46142. Training nationals, 5/yr, free.

Partnership Update, P.O. Box WRC, Wheaton, IL 60189. Organizational, monthly, free.

Quiet Miracle, The, 625 E. No. Broadway, Columbus, OH 43214. Missions, 5/yr, donation.

SIM Now, 10 Huntingdale Blvd., Scarborough, ON, M1W 2S5. Organizational, bimonthly, free.

Teen Missions Control, 885 East Hall Road, Merritt Island, FL 32953. Youth ministries, n/a, free.

The Commission, P.O. Box 6767, Richmond, VA 23230.

The Enterprise, 7185 Millcreek Drive, Mississauga, ON, L5N 5R4.

The Wider Look, 68 Summerleaze Road, Maidenhead, England, Sl6 8EP. World evangelization news, quarterly, $10.00/yr.

Together, 919 W. Huntington Drive, Monrovia, CA 91019. Ministry to two-thirds world poor, quarterly, $25.00/yr.

Trans World Radio Magazine, P.O. Box 700, Cary, NC 27512. International broadcasting ministry news, quarterly, free.

Urban Missions, P.O. Box 27009, Philadelphia, PA 19118. 5/yr, $10.00/yr.

Wherever, P.O. Box 969, Carol Stream, IL 60189. 3/yr, free.

World Christian Magazine, 21550 Oxnard Street, Suite 860, Woodland Hills, CA 91367. Bimonthly, $13.00/yr.

World Evangelization, 2531 Nina Street, Pasadena, CA 91107. News, monthly, donation.

World Harvest Magazine, P.O. Box 12, South Bend, IN 46624. Bimonthly, free.

World Vision Magazine, 919 W. Huntington Drive, Monrovia, CA 91016. Bimonthly, free.

Worldorama, P.O. Box 12609, Oklahoma City, OK 73157. Quarterly, free.

Worldwide Thrust, Box 1707, Fort Washington, PA 19034. Quarterly, free.

---

66 99
FOCUS
QUOTE

The spirit of Christ is the spirit of missions, and the nearer we get to him the more intensely missionary we must become. —Henry Martyn

---

GUIDELINES FOR A MISSIONS CONFERENCE

The Planning

1. Set the date for the best time of the year— when the weather is good, few people will be away, and there are few conflicts with school activities and other events. Should be held at the same time every year.
2. Determine the duration of the conference; the eight-day conference is the most effective.
3. One year is needed to prepare adequately. Schedule speakers and musicians; other conference personnel.
4. Form subcommittees. Involvement of people is the key to interest and success.
5. Establish a work schedule.
6. Select a short, catchy conference theme; also a Scripture verse that expresses the theme.
7. Select a missionary display area.
8. Choose your conference participants: appointees, missionaries, main speakers, musicians, nationals.

EXPENSE REIMBURSEMENT AND HONORARIA

1. Pay travel, lodging, and meal expenses.
2. Determine honorarium. Range: from $50 to $200 per day.
3. Encourage volunteers to house and feed participants.

UTILIZATION

1. Appointees: one to two minutes.
2. Missionary report: five to six minutes.
3. Main speakers: 25 minutes.
4. Musicians: two or three numbers.
5. National report: five to seven minutes.

The Program
SUNDAY SCHOOL

1. Schedule missionaries in as many classes as possible.
2. Determine missionaries best suited for various age groups.
3. Print schedules two weeks in advance.

MAIN SERVICES

1. Determine number and times of services.

2. Print and distribute order of services to participants.
3. No dead spots or wasted time.
4. Keep introductions to a minimum.
5. Variety is an asset; interview a national or well-known missions leader for five to eight minutes; phone a missionary out on the field—install a phone in the sanctuary and amplify through the sound system; eight to ten minute skits; don't follow the same order of service every night; if your church has multiple choirs, have a combined choir leading the worship; utilize a small orchestra; schedule a "missionary choir" of 15 or more missionaries.

Special Events
1. Orientation dinner for participants on the Saturday evening prior to the conference.
2. A children's conference for children, grades one through five or six. A full-time children's worker should be brought in to conduct this conference.
3. Focus on the young people. Promote one night of the main conference as Youth Night. Plan an extravaganza after the service: the world's largest pizza; the world's largest noodle; missionary scavenger hunt.
4. Flashes from the field—slide/tape or video presentation of your own missionaries 15 minutes prior to the evening service.
5. Ladies' luncheon midweek at an attractive restaurant. Keep cost low, provide missionaries with complimentary tickets.
6. Mens' breakfast Saturday morning before the closing Sunday of the conference. Select a speaker appealing to men (could be a woman). Schedule the conference musician to sing (doesn't matter if he's a she). Begin at 8:00 A.M. and finish by 9:30 A.M.
7. Missions banquet Saturday evening just before the final Sunday at 6:30 P.M. Make it a dress-up affair. Allow high school and college-age young people to attend at half price. Ask the conference musician to do a 20–25 minute mini-concert.

The Promotion
INTERNAL PUBLICITY
1. Put promotional covers on hymnbooks.

2. Meet with Sunday school workers six weeks before the conference and ask them to promote it every Sunday in their classes.
3. Pulpit announcement: play a two-minute taped portion of a message by one of your speakers or play one minute of a song by your musician. Begin announcements eight weeks prior to the conference.
4. Begin prayer emphasis at mid-week services eight weeks prior to the conference. Each week devote increasing amount of prayer time; the week before opening day, devote the entire mid-week service to the conference.
5. Friday evening before the conference, schedule home prayer meetings.

DIRECT MAIL
1. Two mailings will be sufficient.
2. Letter one week prior with a brochure, faith-promise envelope, and prayer card.
3. Letter at mid-conference reminding people to pray for the conference, their faith-promise offering, and to attend the "Great Final Day."

PUBLIC ADVERTISING
1. Newspaper: regular, weekly ad for four weeks giving conference dates, speakers, and musicians.
2. Radio: both pay and free opportunities are frequently available. Send announcements to all stations, secular and Christian. Purchase spot announcements. Try for "drive times" (7 A.M. to 9 A.M. and 4 P.M. to 6 P.M.).
3. Television: try to get an interview the week before the conference; also try scheduling interviews for your conference guests. Many TV stations have a community calendar each week. Send the same information to them as you would to the radio stations.

Source: *The Big Event* by Dr. Kenneth Moon, minister at large, Greater Europe Mission. Used by permission. A more comprehensive treatment with sample exhibits and helpful sample promotional material is available for $5 from Greater Europe Mission, P.O. Box 668, Wheaton, IL 60189-0668. Send check with order and ask for *The Big Event: Planning Your Missions Conference.*

MISSIONARY CONFERENCE THEMES

A Church for Every People by AD 2000 ● A Light to the Nations ● Anywhere, Provided It Be Forward (David Livingstone) ● Beyond My World ● Building Our World Vision ● Challenge of the 90s ● Countdown to the Year 2000 ● Decade of Decision—Reaching Out for Christ in the 90s ● Expect Great Things from God, Attempt Great Things for God (William Carey) ● His Last Command—Our First Concern ● His Plan—Our Purpose ● If Not Me, Who? If Not Now, When? If Not Here, Where? ● If Jesus Christ be God and died for me, then no sacrifice can be too great for me to make for him (C. T. Studd) ● Jesus Christ: Lord of the Earth, Hope of the World ● Let the Earth Hear His Voice ● Light My Fire (with candles in all services) ● Love This World Through Me ● Missions: Around the Community, Around the World ● Missions: God's Heart for the World ● Missions: A Family Affair ● Now Let Me Burn Out for Christ (Henry Martyn) ● Oh for a hundred thousand lives to be spent in the service of Christ (George Whitfield) ● Operation Opportunity ● Our Church a Mission Station—Our Congregation a Missionary Team ● Our Mission—(name of town) and the World for Christ ● Our Best for Our Master ● Pass It On—Across the Street; Reach Out—Across the Sea ● People Who Change the World; Will You Be One of Them? ● Putting Wings to Missions (Isaiah 40:31) ● Reaching Out: Around the World, Across the Street ● Tell the nations that the Lord reigns (Psalm 96:10) ● So Send I You ● The Unfinished Task—The Unchanging Task ● The Word to a World in Revolution ● The Glory of the Impossible ● The World Is Changing . . . the Need Remains ● The World Is Waiting ● The supreme task of the Church is the evangelization of the world ● The light that shines farthest shines brightest nearest home ● The prospects Are as Bright as the Promises of God (Adoniram Judson) ● The Mission of the Church Is Missions ● To See As God Sees ● Toward AD 2000 ● Untold Millions Still Untold ● Why should anyone hear the Gospel twice before everyone has heard it once? (Oswald J. Smith) ● World Evangelism until Christ Returns ● World Crisis—My Involvement ● World Christians ● World Changers ● World in Review

ADOPT-A-PEOPLE PROGRAM

The world is too big for any one church to tackle, and many pastors despair from the constant barrage of requests for funds and prayers. In this program, each church, depending on its size, adopts one or more 12,000 unreached people groups and its mission team. When a church adopts a people, it commits to pray for, financially support, and become acquainted with their adopted people. In this practical way a church can fulfill a part of its mission stewardship.

1. The adopt-a-people program provides a way for churches to become involved in reaching an unevangelized group.
2. Churches work through a chosen mission agency, providing informed, concerned, dedicated prayer and financial support.
3. It does not mean giving up current mission support, but taking on a new, more intimate commitment of responsibility for their unreached group.
4. It means hanging in there until a small, growing church is established which can begin evangelizing its own people.
5. It means the joy and excitement of being part of a worldwide cooperative effort involving thousands of churches and hundreds of mission agencies—each taking a small, bite-sized piece.

What can your church do?

1. Contact your denominational mission agency or select a mission agency from the list below. The "adoption list" of the groups not yet evangelized might look something like this:

Adopt-a-People

#9,320	☑	Teda	(Chad)	Adopted by First Presbyterian
#9,321	☐	Teimurtash	(Iran)	Not yet adopted
#9,322	☑	Tharu	(Nepal)	Adopted by Calvary Baptist
#9,323	☐	Totis	(India)	Not yet adopted
#9,324	☐	Tuareg	(Niger)	Not yet adopted
#9,325	☑	Turkomans	(Iran)	Adopted by Trinity Assembly

2. Determine which group to adopt.
3. Ask the agency you select to send you information on this group and to put you on the mailing list of the team working with them.
4. Begin to receive special offerings or save your loose change and send it to the agency supervising the efforts. Designate this money for outreach to your adopted people group.
5. Give reports and pray corporately during your church missionary activities.

Agencies Participating in the Adopt-A-People Program

(For addresses, refer to mission agencies list.)
Africa Inland Mission International
Assemblies of God/USA, Div. of Foreign Mission
Associate Reformed Presbyterian Church, Board of Foreign Missions
Baptist General Conference, Board of World Missions
Bethany Fellowship Missions
Bible Christian Union
The Bible League
Christian and Missionary Alliance
Christian Missionary Fellowship
Conservative Baptist Foreign Mission Society
Evangelical Free Church of America, Board of Overseas Missions
Evangelical Friends Mission
Every Home for Christ
Free Methodist World Missions
Frontiers
General Baptist Foreign Mission Society
Gospel Missionary Union
Greater Europe Mission
International Missions
International Students

InterServe
LIFE Ministries
Mennonite Brethren Missions/Services
Mission Society for United Methodists
Mission to Unreached Peoples
Operation Mobilization
Overseas Missionary Fellowship USA
Partners International
Pentecostal Holiness Church, World Missions Dept.
Pioneer Bible Translators
Pioneers
Presbyterian Frontier Fellowship (PCUSA)
RBMU International
SEND International
SIM International
South America Mission
Team Expansion
The Evangelical Alliance Mission
WEC International
World Concern
World Mission Prayer League
World Radio Missionary Fellowship

For more information on the Adopt-A-People program write: U.S. Center for World Mission, Mobilization Division, 1605 Elizabeth Street, Pasadena, CA 91104.

❝❞
FOCUS
QUOTE
If you educate, you get what education can do; if you organize, you get what organization can do; but when you pray, you get what God can do!
—Dr. Robert Lee

20 SIGNIFICANT MISSIONARY LEADERS

Selected by Dr. Earle E. Cairns, author and historian.

Ulfilas (c.311–381). Apostle to the Goths, born perhaps in the region of the Lower Danube, which, according to some historians, had become the home of his Cappadocian parents, who in 246 had been taken captive by the Goths in one of their raids in Asia Minor. When about twenty he was taken by the king of the Goths on an embassage to Constantinople, where he remained for ten years. There became a Christian and received a good education. In Constantinople became acquainted with the Arian bishop, Eusebius of Nicomedia, who with other bishops consecrated him to the episcopate in 341. He then returned as a missionary to the Goths. It is said that the whole tribe of the Visigoths were won to the Christian faith. For the first seven years (341–348), he labored in his native land beyond the Danube, until persecution compelled him and his fellow Christians to seek refuge on Roman soil. From here he continued work among the Goths. By force of circumstances Ulfilas had been won to Arian Christianity. As an Arian, he preached to the Goths and led them to the same doctrinal views of Christianity. Greatly enhanced missionary labors by inventing an alphabet for the Goths, and then by giving them most of the Bible in their own language.

Patrick or **Patricius** (c.389–461). Celtic missionary to Ireland. His father, Calpurnius, seems to have been a deacon in the local Celtic church, his grandfather a priest. When sixteen years old he was taken captive in one of the Irish pirate raids and was sold as a slave to a herdsman in North Ireland, where he was held for six years. He escaped and somehow found his way to Gaul, where he spent some time in a monastic school. After returning home he saw a vision and heard voices from the Irish coast, crying, "We beseech thee, child of God, come and walk again among us." Answering the call, he set out for Ireland. About 432 he gathered people about him in the open fields and preached Christ to them. His burning zeal, deep sincerity, and gen-

tleness of manner won peasants and nobility alike. Planted scores of churches and baptized over 100,000 converts. At Armagh he founded a monastery which was to become important and historic in the annals of the Christian church. His preaching made a strong impact, not only upon the Ireland of his day, but upon all medieval missions and church life of Ireland, of Great Britain, and of Continental Europe. Both Catholics and Protestants like to claim Patrick, but he was neither. He was a Celtic missionary in the British Isles before the time of either Protestants or Roman Catholics. Chief writing and our chief source of information concerning his life is his *Confessions*.

Columba or **Columkille** (c.521–597). Irish Celtic missionary, "Apostle of Caledonia," born of Royal stock at Gartan, a wild district in Donegal county, Ireland; son of an Ulster chief. Given an excellent education and in the Christian faith, early distinguishing himself for piety and zeal. Dedicated himself to monastic zeal. Ordained deacon and priest, about 551. In 563, at the age of forty-two, he left Ireland with twelve companions and landed on the small island of Iona off the coast of Scotland. There founded his monastery from which center he and companions evangelized the Picts and more carefully taught the Scots who had already professed Christianity. He made Iona his chief abode and a great school and missionary training center. He made frequent visits to Scotland, where he founded many churches, and maintained a close connection with Ireland, making frequent visits there in behalf of his monasteries. Soon smaller societies had to be formed and other monasteries founded. Accounted one of the poets of Ireland, being the author of three hymns. Finished his missionary career, dying beside the altar in the church while engaged in his midnight devotions. Columba was a product of the Celtic church of the Isles, whereas Augustine was from Rome and represented the Catholic church.

Augustine, Archbishop of Canterbury (d.c.604). Missionary to England and prior of St. Andrews monastery in Rome. In AD

20 SIGNIFICANT MISSIONARY LEADERS cont.

596 Pope Gregory I sent him and several companions as missionaries from Rome to England. They were kindly received by King Ethelbert and permitted to worship in the Church of St. Martin where the Christian queen Bertha worshiped. In 597 the king was baptized. Later many of his subjects likewise were baptized. Augustine then went to Arles, France (597), to be consecrated as first archbishop of Canterbury. Gregory then made Augustine metropolitan bishop of England, which made England independent of the French see. He was successful in winning Kent and Essex to the Roman church.

Boniface or **Winfrid** or **Wilfrith** (680–755). English Benedictine missionary—"The Apostle to the Germans." An Anglo-Saxon, born in Devonshire, England. He entered monastic life early and at thirty was ordained. Seemingly had before him an assured place in his church in England but preferred to be a missionary. About 716 he sailed with a few companions for Frisia, a group of small islands off the Dutch coast, to help Willibrord in his difficult task. Meeting strong opposition from the local Frisian king, he returned to England. Soon he was back on the continent, going first to Rome from 718–719, there receiving from Pope Gregory II a commission to Germany. Began work in Thuringia; but before many months, hearing of the death of the hostile Frisian king, he went back to Frisia to help Willibrord establish the church in Frisia. From 719–722 he worked with Willibrord, then went to Germany and entered upon the main work of his life. He first went to Hesse, and then later back to Thuringia. His ten years' work in these two provinces was highly successful. Great numbers of pagans were converted; the Irish or Celtic monks were brought largely into obedience to Rome. In 732 Pope Gregory III made Boniface an archbishop with authority to establish new sees in Germany. In 738, after his third and last trip to Rome, he organized the church in Bavaria and later in Thuringia. About 744 he helped to establish the important and influential monastery of Fulda. A year or two later he was made archbishop of Mainz.

He also worked among the Franks, trying to reform the Frankish church. Everywhere Boniface went, it was with papal sanction and authority. In 739 the pope named him apostolic vicar or papal legate. His authority and influence were tremendous. In 742 he assembled the first German council, and organized churches, schools, and monasteries according to the Roman pattern. He trained and sent missionaries from the German churches and did more than any other to instill in the hearts of the bishops and clergy of Central Europe permanent obedience to the pope; he did much to lay the foundation for the medieval papacy. In 753 he went back to preach to the Frisians with a company of monks and priests, spending about two years traveling among them, preaching to them, baptizing thousands of converts, destroying pagan temples, and building churches. In 755 a body of hostile pagans fell upon the group, and Boniface was slain. He died with a copy of the Gospels in his hands.

Cyril or **Cyrillus**, original name **Constantinus** (c.826–869). Missionary to the Slavs, born in Thessalonica; studied at Constantinople. He and brother Methodius (c.815–885), both monks and priests in the Eastern Catholic church, in 860 went to the Khazars, a Tartar tribe on the northeast shore of the Black Sea, and planted a church. For a while they worked among the Bulgars whose king was Boris or Bogaris. About 862, in answer to an invitation from Duke Ratislav of Moravia, Emperor Michael III sent Cyril and his brother to Moravia, where they labored with great success. Cyril invented an alphabet and translated the Bible into the Slavic language. In 868 he and Methodius went to Rome and effected an agreement with Pope Adrian II for the use of the Slavic language; their work thus came under the supervision of the Roman church. In 869 Cyril died while in Rome. His brother returned to Moravia having been consecrated archbishop.

Methodius (d.885). "Apostle to the Slavs," born in Thessalonica, son of a military officer, educated in Constantinople. In 860 with his brother Cyril (d.869) he began mission work on the northeast shore of the Black Sea. Later, at the invitation of Duke Ratislav, they were sent to the Moravians. Great success attended their labors. In 868 the brothers, representatives of the Eastern church, went to Rome to effect an agreement with Pope Adrian II relative to their work. Cyril died in Rome the next year, and Methodius returned to Moravia. After the death of Ratislav of Moravia and of Pope Adrian II of Rome, the attitude of both Rome and the people of Moravia changed. In 879 he was again summoned to Rome, and though the independence of the Slavic church was confirmed, the status of the church became insecure. After the death of Methodius, Latin replaced the Slavic language, the church deteriorated, and paganism again became dominant.

Lull, Raymond (c.1235–1315). Missionary to the Muslims, born at Palma, capital of Majorca, one of the Baleric Islands. He lived a worldly life in the court of King James of Aragon until he was about thirty when he turned to the ascetic life and became a Franciscan tertiary. Began zealous preparation for missionary work among the Muslims, first learning Arabic from a Moorish slave, then starting the College of Miramar to teach the Arabic and Chaldean tongues. For several years lectured in Paris and Montpellier. Wrote a book of diagrams and arguments to prove the truth and superiority of Christianity. In 1291, when about fifty-five, he made first missionary trip to the Muslims. In Tunis, North Africa, he challenged the fanatical Muslims to a public disputation, which resulted in banishment. Back home spent several years lecturing and writing. In 1305 or 1306 made a second attempt to convert the Muslims of Tunis, but was again banished. Back in Europe succeeded in securing a council decree to establish professorships of oriental languages at Avignon, Paris, Bologna, Oxford, and Salamanca. In 1315 at age eighty made third attempt to penetrate the Muslim lines of North Africa. The Muslim population rose against him and drove him from the city with sticks and stones. The next day, on his way back to Majorca, he died. Lull had introduced some new principles into the missionary enterprise by studying the Arabic language at home, writing and lecturing on missions, seeking to establish schools of oriental languages, and substituting love for force in missionary labors. His theologico-philosophical works were many, reaching perhaps the number of three hundred.

FOCUS QUOTE

66 99 Rewards God gives; reward God is. —Ralph D. Winter

Las Casas, Bartolome de (1474–1566). Spanish priest and missionary to the American Indians of the West Indies. Born at Seville, Spain, he studied the humanities and law at the universities of Seville and Salamanca and entered the Dominican order in 1523. He and father were companions of Columbus on the latter's second voyage to America in 1498. Bartolome made his second trip to the New World when he came with Columbus to Haiti in 1502. As a planter, he owned Indian slaves as did the other colonists. In 1510 ordained a priest, the first to be ordained in the New World. Soon saw the evil of enslaving the Indians and released his slaves. Las Casas then returned to Spain to seek amelioration for the ill-treated Indians. Cardinal Ximenes appointed him Protector General of the Indians, and he returned with this commission to the New World. Spent most of his long life preaching to the American Indians and defending them against the cruelties of their conquerors. Nine times he traveled between America and Spain seeking respite for the horrible miseries that the Spaniards were inflicting upon the Indians. Efforts were made in behalf of the Indians, not only in Haiti, but in Cuba, Peru, Guatemala, Nicaragua, St. Domingo, and Mexico. In 1544 at age seventy became bishop of Chiapa, Mexico. In 1547 returned to Spain and completed *Historia General de las Indias,*

20 SIGNIFICANT MISSIONARY LEADERS cont.

the source of much valuable information on the Spanish discoveries and conquests in the New World.

Xavier, Francis (1506–1552). Jesuit missionary, born in an aristocratic family in Navarre, northern Spain. As a student in the University of Paris distinguished himself in philosophical studies. Came under the influence of Ignatius Loyola, who persuaded him in 1534 to become a charter member of what was later to become the Society of Jesus, popularly known as the Jesuit Order. Ordained a priest in 1537. In 1540, at the request of King John III of Portugal, Loyola appointed Xavier to go to India as papal legate. Sailing from Lisbon, Portugal, the next year, he landed in the Portuguese colony of Goa in west India in 1542. He had the Creed, the Lord's Prayer, the Ave Maria, and the Decalogue translated into the vernacular and committed them to memory. Dissatisfied with the results he was achieving in India, in 1545 he turned to the East Indies, where he worked for three years, returning to India in 1548. During seven years in India and the Indies, he baptized people by the thousands, both adults and infants. Founded a missionary school at Goa. Having been made a missionary bishop of the entire East, he felt he must go to other lands too. He left to others his work in southern Asia and proceeded to Japan in 1549. Spent two years preaching through interpreters and baptizing. Then leaving to others this mission also, he proceeded toward China to build a church, making a visit to Goa on the way in 1552. But he died of a fever off the coast of the mainland of south China, near Canton. Work was superficial, an exploration rather than a structure. He was canonized in 1622.

Carey, William (1761–1834). "The father of modern missions," born in the home of a poor Northamptonshire weaver and schoolmaster in Paulersbury, England. Elementary schooling received under father's teaching in the village school. At fourteen apprenticed to a shoemaker and cobbler. Applied himself so diligently to study while working that he early learned Latin, Greek, Hebrew, French, and Dutch, and in his teens could read the Bible in six languages. This bent toward language was a great asset in his missionary life. In 1783 he joined the Baptist church and shortly after began preaching. Along with his cobbling, teaching, and preaching, he continued his study of languages, followed the missionary activities of John Eliot and David Brainerd, and read with avidity the *Voyages* of Captain James Cook. As pastor at Moulton he preached missions and urged his neighboring ministers to do likewise. Wrote a treatise on "An Enquiry into the Obligations of Christians to Use Means for the Conversion of the Heathen." In 1792 he preached a memorable sermon on "Expect Great Things from God; Attempt Great Things for God." In that year helped organize the English Baptist Missionary society; the next year went to India as one of its first missionaries. His first plan had been to go to Tahiti. During his first years on the field many hardships and disappointments developed for him. Financial reverses due to Dr. Thomas's mismanagement, illness, and death among his children, and the serious mental illness of his wife until her death in 1807 made his work difficult. Soon after arriving in India he became superintendent of an indigo factory from 1794–1799. In 1799, purchased a small indigo plantation and started a mission. Because of opposition from East India Company, in 1800 he moved to Serampore in Danish territory a short distance from Calcutta. William Ward and Joshua Marshman joined him to form the famous Serampore Trio; teaching, preaching, and printing provided the chief missionary activity and also provided much of the fund for carrying on the mission. In 1800 Carey baptized first converts, among them his oldest son, Felix. From 1831, he was professor of Oriental languages in the newly founded Fort William College in Calcutta, a position held for thirty years. He and Marsham did much translating of the Scriptures. The Bible or portions of it were issued by the Serampore press in about thirty-six languages and dialects. Besides preaching and translating the Scriptures, they translated Indian classics into English, prepared grammars and dictionaries in various languages, opened many mission stations in India, Burma and East Indies, and established schools out of which in 1818 came Serampore College. Did much for the advancement of horticulture and agriculture in India. He advocated two important missionary principles: (1) equality of missionaries and natives, and (2) self-sustaining missions. Forty-one years of missionary life in India were crowded full. He was an indefatigable worker, even to death at age seventy-three. The labors of few missionaries have been more fruitful. The Serampore Press under his direction rendered the Bible accessible to more than 300 million people. Helped end the burning of child widows in 1829.

Morrison, Robert (1782–1834). First Protestant missionary to China, born in Morpeth, Northumbria, England, of a Scottish father and English mother. In childhood an industrious student, as a man a learned scholar. In preparation for life work gave special attention to the study of theology, medicine, astronomy, and the Chinese language, the latter learned from a Chinese scholar who was living in London, and from some Chinese manuscripts in the British museum. In 1807 the London Missionary Society ordained and sent Morrison to Canton, China, as the first Protestant missionary to that land. The East India Company refused him passage; he went to Canton by way of New York. In China he lived in a cellar and was rarely seen in public. He made such good progress in his mastery of the language that in 1809 he was employed by the British East India Company as an interpreter, a position held for the next twenty-five years. He worked assiduously for the mission, but labors were confined largely to literary activities, writing a Chinese grammar, preparing the standard Anglo-Chinese dictionary and encyclopedia, writing tracts and books, preparing a hymnbook, translating morning and evening prayers from the *Book of Common Prayer,* and translating the entire Bible by 1823. Work was that of foundation laying, a very necessary part of the work of introducing missions in China. The number of converts as a result of twenty-seven years of labor perhaps did not exceed three or four, the first of which was not until after he had been seven years in China. Activities other than serving as interpreter for the East India Company, and translating and writing for the mission,

consisted in treating the sick in his dispensary and the founding of an Anglo-Chinese school at Malacca to train missionaries for the Far East. Made a trip to England in 1824, at which time he was made a fellow of the Royal Society. Promoted the cause of missions in China. In 1826 returned to China. As interpreter for the East India Company, he was forced to become negotiator in the Anglo-Chinese War that had broken out about that time.

Mills, Samuel John (1783–1818). Promoter of foreign missions, born in Torringford, Connecticut. Graduated from Williams College and Andover Theological Seminary, and spent a short time at Yale. While in college, he was a member of the famous haystack prayer group. During a brief stay at Yale, he met and befriended young Henry Obookiah from the Sandwich Islands, who found a home and a genial fellowship with Samuel and his parents. In the seminary he became a part of the prayer meeting and mission study group that resulted in the organization of the American Board of Commissioners for Foreign Missions in 1810, and in the sending of Judson, Rice, Nott, Hall, and Newell to India in 1812. He also helped start a mission to the Sandwich Islands. Licensed to preach in 1812, he made two missionary tours through the midwestern and southern states between 1812 and 1815, distributing Bibles and visiting sick soldiers. In 1815 he was ordained. The next year he became an agent for the School for Educating Colored Men. He was influential in the founding of the United Foreign Missionary Society for the Presbyterian and Reformed Churches, in the organization of the American Bible Society in 1816, and in starting an African school near Newark. In 1817 he went as an agent of the colonization society to Western Africa, which led to the formulation of the Republic of Liberia.

Moffat, Robert (1795–1883). Pioneer translator and missionary, born at Ormiston, Scotland. At fourteen apprenticed as a gardener; formal education meager. Soon after conversion became interested in missions and applied to the

20 SIGNIFICANT MISSIONARY LEADERS cont.

London Missionary Society. After some special instruction, he accepted and went to Cape Town, South Africa, arriving there in 1817. He was thrust into the center of several cannibalistic tribes in this colony, which had just, three years before, come under the British. The next year, 1817, he set out for Namaqualand, the home of the notorious outlaw, Afrikaner. To the surprise and marvel of everyone, won the dreaded outlaw to Christ. In 1817 brought him to Cape Town. Moffat next went to Lattakoo in 1820. Mary Smith came from London to become Moffat's wife, and the couple settled at Kuruman in Bechuanaland in 1825, where a mission was soon established. Later, with much hard work and many obstacles, he organized a mission station at Inyati among the Matabele. The Moffats spent the years 1839–1843 in England furthering the cause of missions in Africa. It was at this time that Livingstone was inspired by Moffat to go to Africa. After arriving on the field, Livingstone married Moffat's daughter, Mary. In 1870 the aged missionaries returned to England. During last years in England, he labored untiringly for the cause to which he had devoted his earlier life and talents. While on the field, he translated the Bible into Sechvana by 1859, authored a hymnbook, and wrote two missionary books on South Africa: *Labors and Scenes in South Africa* and *Rivers of Water in a Dry Place.*

❝❞ **God had an only Son and he was a missionary and a physician.** —David Livingstone
FOCUS
QUOTE

Livingstone, David (1813–1873). Missionary and explorer. Born near Glasgow, Scotland, in poor family. With first wages bought a Latin grammar. By studying while at work and at home he secured an early education. In 1830 at age seventeen he entered the University of Glasgow and began the study of medicine and theology. His goal was to be missionary in China. In 1838 he was accepted by the London Missionary Society.

The Opium War in China was on, and the society sent him to Africa in 1840. Went to Robert Moffat's station in South Africa, but soon pushed on to the tribes farther north. In 1843 started a mission at Mabotsa, two hundred miles north of Moffat. In 1845 married Mary Moffat and built a home. The next year found it necessary to move forty miles farther north; built second home and established a station. Because of a long, continued drought, they soon had to move again. Went forty miles farther north to Kolebeng and built third and last house for himself and family. When Boers sacked this house, he built no more. Began great work of missionary and colonial exploration, saying, "The end of the geographical feat is the beginning of the missionary enterprise." He discovered Lake N'gami in 1849 and the Victoria Falls in 1853. Sent his family to England; then made hazardous fourteen hundred mile trip to Loanda and back. In 1856 returned to England with high acclaim as a world-renowned explorer. Opened Africa both to missions and to civilization. In 1857 he resigned from the London Missionary Society and returned to Africa under the British government with the threefold goal: (1) to make Christ known to Africa; (2) to find the source of the Nile and open Africa to the West; and (3) to eradicate pernicious slave traffic. In 1858 he discovered great lakes of East Africa. In 1864 he was back in England; but in 1865 returned to Africa to spend his last eight years. On this trip in 1871, Stanley found him when lost to the world. In 1873 his native helpers found him on his knees in the posture of prayer, his spirit having departed from the body. His body was taken to England and buried in Westminster Abbey.

Nevius, John Livingston (1829–1893). American Presbyterian missionary to China, born near Ovid, New York, educated at Ovid Academy, Union College, Schenectady, and Princeton Theological Seminary. In 1849 taught school in Georgia for a year and became a Christian. Upon conversion decided to prepare for the ministry; while in the seminary decided to be a missionary. In 1853 he completed his seminary course and was ordained. He married, was appointed by the Presbyterian Mission Board, and assigned to Ningpo, China. They arrived in China when the Tai Ping Rebellion was in progress and found much difficulty in establishing work. Nevius was at Ningpo, Chekiang Province from 1854–1859; in Japan from 1859–1861, preparing a *Compendium of Theology.* for Chinese students; at Tungchow, Shantung Province from 1861–1864; in America from 1864–1868; and at Chefoo, Shantung from 1871–1893, where he spent his last days in Bible translation. He wrote *China and the Chinese* and *Demon Possession and Allied Themes.* He was noted especially for the "Nevius Method," which places strong emphasis on the training of the Chinese Christians to carry on their own work, with their own resources, and from their own homes. He built churches in native style and trained ablest nationals in Bible and prayer to be leaders. In 1890 Dr. Nevius met in conference with the Korean missionaries to explain the plan, following which time it was effectively applied in that country. Also introduced into China Western fruits and vegetables, Jersey cows for milk, and tires for the wheels on their carts.

Taylor, James Hudson (1832–1905). Founder of China Inland Mission, born in Barnsley, Yorkshire, England. After spending time in the study of medicine and theology, he went to China under the newly formed China Evangelization Society, arriving in Shanghai in 1854. He stressed prayer and faith only in money raising and adopted Chinese dress. For six months he lived in the home of Dr. Medhurst of the London Missionary Society, whose book *China* had helped stir him to go to China. Spent years 1854–1860 working in Shanghai, Swatow, and Ningpo. Before long retired from the society that had sent him out and continued as an independent worker. At Ningpo he had charge of a hospital and in 1858 married Maria Dyer, the daughter of a missionary in China. In 1860 he returned

home, spending the next five years translating the New Testament into the Ningpo dialect, writing a book on China, and praying for missionaries for inland China. His definite planning in 1865 at Brighton to establish a society for the evangelization of inland China and return to China in 1866 with his wife and children and sixteen new missionaries was the beginning of the China Inland Mission. Became the director of the mission, traveled widely in China and Europe in its interest. Returned to China in 1872. At his death in 1905 at Changsha, there were 205 stations with 849 missionaries and 125,000 Chinese Christians in the China Inland Mission.

Slessor, Mary (1848–1915). Scottish missionary to Africa, born near Aberdeen, Scotland. Her father died when she was a child, and she became the main means of support for the family. The appeal of David Livingstone for missionaries to Africa intensified her desire to serve. With her mother's approval she sailed for Nigeria in 1876. For three years she labored so self-sacrificingly and strenuously that her health gave way. She had to return to Scotland and, when in 1880 she returned to Africa, she was assigned to Old Town and worked hard as before. In 1891 the British government appointed her vice-consul for Okoyong. She knew the mind of the African well. In later years she chose to remain in Africa.

---

66 99
FOCUS QUOTE
Some wish to live within the sound of church and chapel bell. I wish to run a rescue mission within a yard of hell.
—C. T. Studd

Studd, Charles T. (1862–1931). Missionary pioneer, born in England. C. T. Studd's father, Edward, had been converted in the Moody-Sankey campaign in 1877. His father then became deeply concerned about the spiritual welfare of his three sons. By the time CT was sixteen, he had become an expert cricket player; when nineteen captain of his team at Eton. After finishing Eton College,

20 SIGNIFICANT MISSIONARY LEADERS cont.

he attended Cambridge University (1880–1883), and here, too, was an outstanding cricketer. In 1883, while still at Cambridge, he heard Moody and Sankey and was converted, dedicating life and inherited wealth to Christ. He gave away about $150,000 while in China. He and six others, the famous "Cambridge Seven," offered themselves to Hudson Taylor for missionary service in the China Inland Mission and in 1885 sailed for China. They at once began the study of the language, donned Chinese garb, and ate with the Chinese, trying to substitute Chinese for Western ways and to identify themselves with the natives. Three years later Studd married a young Irish missionary from Ulster. By 1894 the Studds were broken in health and had to return to England. Unable to return to China they severed their connection with the China Inland Mission and turned their property over to the mission. In 1896–97 Mr. Studd toured the universities of America in behalf of the newly formed Student Volunteer movement. In 1900 the family went to south India in search of a climate more conducive to Mr. Studd's health and for a place to serve. For six years C. T. Studd was pastor of the Union Church at Ootacamund. After their return to England in 1906, he began to plan with Dr. Karl Kumm on a scheme of opening Africa from the Nile to the Niger for Christian missions. In 1910, leaving his wife and four daughters in England to care for the secretarial responsibilities for both the home base and the field, he started on his journey to penetrate the heart of Africa. On a part of the trip he was accompanied by Alfred Buxton, a young man who later became his son-in-law. The Heart of Africa Mission was organized in 1912. A mission was established at Niangara in 1913; in June 1915 twelve converts were baptized. Late in 1914 Studd returned to England for more missionaries, and in 1916 to Africa with a party of missionaries. In 1919 Gilbert Barclay, another son-in-law, joined the mission which was named the Worldwide Evangelization Crusade. Studd died in Africa two and a half years after Mrs. Studd, who had died in Malaga.

Zwemer, Samuel Marinus (1867–1952). American Dutch Reformed missionary to the Muslims, born at Vriesland, Michigan, and educated at Hope College, Holland, Michigan, and New Brunswick Theological Seminary in New Jersey. In college came under the influence of Robert Wilder and became one of the first members of the Student Volunteer movement and one of its leaders. In 1888–1889 Zwemer and others formed a new missionary organization, The Arabian Mission. In 1889 James Cantine went to Arabia. The next year Zwemer was ordained and followed. In 1894 the regular board of the Dutch Reformed Church in America took over the mission. Between 1890 and 1905 Zwemer worked at Busrah, Bahrein Islands, and Muscat; later with headquarters at Cairo, Egypt, he traveled over the most of the Islamic world, arousing in Europe and America interest in bringing the Christian faith to Muslims and in training missionaries. In spite of the firm hold of Islam on these lands a few converts were made. In 1906 he organized and was chairman of the Conference on Islam at Cairo but maintained his residence in the United States from 1905–1910 while promoting missions in his denomination. In 1910 returned to missionary field on the Arabian Gulf. Visited many missions over the Muslim world, making notable contributions to the cause in South Africa and the Netherlands Indies, where he preached in Dutch, English, and Arabic. Also visited India and China several times. In 1911 started the *Moslem World,* and was its editor for about forty years. For nearly a decade after returning from the mission field, he was professor of missions and comparative religions at Princeton Theological Seminary. He authored about fifty volumes in English and a number in Arabic. A few of his works: *Arabia the Cradle of Islam, Moslem Doctrine of God, Islam a Challenge to Faith, The Unoccupied Mission Fields of Africa and Asia, The Moslem World,* and *Mohammed or Christ.*

Scudder, Ida (1870–1960). Medical missionary to south India. Born at Ranipet near Madras. Educated in Moody's girls' school at Northfield. Back in India to help her mother, she was "called" to be a medical missionary. Studied medicine at Women's Medical College in Philadelphia and Cornell University Medical School. Returned to India in 1900. Founded Schall Hospital at Vellore, a nursing school, school of pharmacy, and a medical college in 1915 for women and one for men in 1947.

Source: *Wycliffe Biographical Dictionary of the Church.* Elgin Moyer, revised and enlarged by Earle E. Cairns. Published by Moody Press. Copyright © 1982. Used by permission.

ROBERT W. PIERCE AWARD FOR OUTSTANDING CHRISTIAN SERVICE

Sponsored by World Vision. Recipients are selected based on effectiveness of ministry, length of time devoted to ministry, number of people helped through the ministry, difficulty of situation, and quality of the ministry program.

Year	Name	Ministry	Location
1980	Dr. Kenneth A. Elliott	medical missionary	Upper Volta, West Africa
1981	Dr. Eleanor Soltau	World Presbyterian medical missionary	Middle East
1982	Fritz Urschitz	Liebenzell (Germany) missionary	Papua New Guinea
1983	Miriam Krantz	Mennonite missionary nutritionist	Nepal
1984	Molly Lou Holt	public health nurse	Korea
1985	Dr. Mary Varghese	doctor to the disabled	India
1986	Elfrieda Toews	C&MA missionary nurse	Irian Jaya, Indonesia
1987	Rev. Hedley J. Sleath	Methodist pastor	South Africa
1988	Dr. Bob Foster	Africa Evang. Fellowship med. missionary	Zambia
1989	Maria Das	lay pastor	Bangladesh
1990	Odessa Nesfield	Salvation Army volunteer	Panama
	Ram Sharan	Superintendent, Four Square Churches	Nepal
1991	Jessie Stevens	Children's ministry	Costa Rica
	Simon Agusto	Church planter	Mozambique

THE 10/40 WINDOW

One of the more recent mission concepts is the 10/40 Window, a rectangular area of the world that represents acute spiritual and physical need. It is a belt that extends from West Africa across Asia, between ten degrees north to forty degrees north of the equator. The area has often been referred to as the resistant belt.

We need to become acquainted with the 10/40 Window for many reasons. One is the historical and biblical significance of this part of the world. So much of God's dealings with humanity took place on this piece of earth. Ancient empires came and went. Here Christ was born, lived his life, died on the cross, and rose again. It was not until the second missionary journey of the Apostle Paul toward the end of the biblical record that events of divine history occurred outside of the 10/40 Window area.

Today, most of the unevangelized peoples are here. It is the heart of Muslim, Hindu, and Buddhist beliefs. It is where the majority of the world's people live, and included among them are 82% of the poorest of the poor. The six maps that follow graphically portray these reasons why committed Christians everywhere should focus their prayers and resources on this needy area of our world.

The focus of the concerned Christian community 200 years ago was for the coastlands, followed by a focus 100 years ago on the interiors of the continents, and then, within the last century, the unreached peoples. In the next ten years—the decade of the '90s—perhaps it is the 10/40 Window that needs our focus.

Source: Luis Bush in *AD 2000 and Beyond* magazine, September-October 1990 issue. Statistical data from Global Research Data Base, provided by Global Mapping International. Map design by Pete Holzmann of Strategic Mapping.

THE 10/40

THE POOREST COUNTRIES

82% of the poorest of the poor live in the 10/40 Window

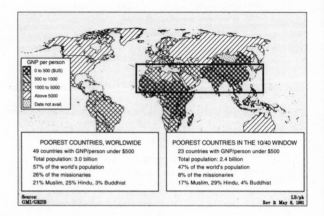

GNP per person
0 to 500 ($US)
500 to 1000
1000 to 5000
Above 5000
Data not avail.

POOREST COUNTRIES, WORLDWIDE
49 countries with GNP/person under $500
Total population: 3.0 billion
57% of the world's population
26% of the missionaries
21% Muslim, 25% Hindu, 3% Buddhist

POOREST COUNTRIES IN THE 10/40 WINDOW
23 countries with GNP/person under $500
Total population: 2.4 billion
47% of the world's population
8% of the missionaries
17% Muslim, 29% Hindu, 4% Buddhist

Source:
GMI/GRDB
LB/ph
Rev 2: May 9, 1991

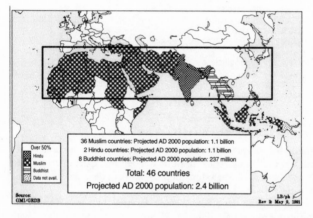

Over 50%
Hindu
Muslim
Buddhist
Data not avail.

36 Muslim countries: Projected AD 2000 population: 1.1 billion
2 Hindu countries: Projected AD 2000 population: 1.1 billion
8 Buddhist countries: Projected AD 2000 population: 237 million

Total: 46 countries
Projected AD 2000 population: 2.4 billion

Source:
GMI/GRDB
LB/ph
Rev 2: May 9, 1991

THE THREE RELIGIOUS BLOCKS

Countries with Muslim, Hindu, Buddhist majority

THE 55 LEAST EVANGELIZED COUNTRIES

97% of the people in the least evangelized countries live here

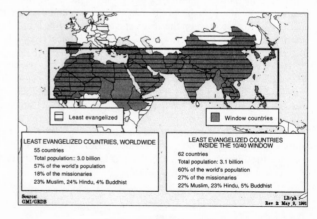

Least evangelized   Window countries

LEAST EVANGELIZED COUNTRIES, WORLDWIDE
55 countries
Total population: 3.0 billion
57% of the world's population
18% of the missionaries
23% Muslim, 24% Hindu, 4% Buddhist

LEAST EVANGELIZED COUNTRIES
INSIDE THE 10/40 WINDOW
62 countries
Total population: 3.1 billion
60% of the world's population
27% of the missionaries
22% Muslim, 23% Hindu, 5% Buddhist

Source:
GMI/GRDB
LB/ph
Rev 2: May 9, 1991

WINDOW

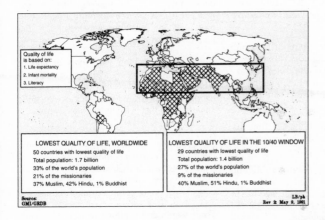

QUALITY
OF LIFE

84% of the people
with lowest quality
of life live in the
10/40 Window

ISLAM

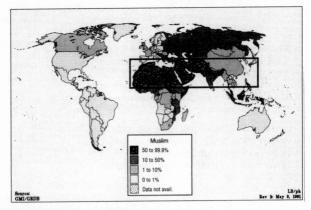

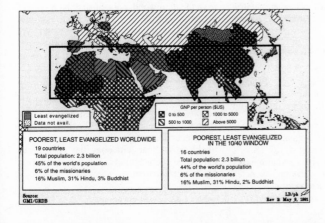

POOR AND
UNEVANGELIZED

99% of the least
evangelized poorest
people live in the
10/40 Window

FOCUSWORDS

Closure: Finishing the one task Christ gave his church to do, go into all the world to disciple all the nations.

Contextualize: putting the truths of God into the context of the local culture. This involves seeing how one's own culture colors understanding of biblical truths, and then taking the unvarnished truth and applying it in another culture.

Development: a process enabling a community to provide for its own needs, beyond former levels, with dignity and justice.

EFMA: Evangelical Fellowship of Mission Agencies. A department of the National Association of Evangelicals that began meeting in 1945. Comprises both interdenominational and denominational mission agencies.

Great Commission Christians: believers who take the Great Commission seriously.

IFMA: Interdenominational Foreign Mission Association of North America. An association of faith mission agencies. Founded in 1917, it is the oldest North American association of mission agencies. No denominational mission belongs to this group.

Incarnational: living as much like and with the people to whom you're ministering as you are able. Just as Christ took on our flesh (incarnate means to en-flesh) and culture to serve us, so cross-cultural missionaries often aspire to enter the culture and struggles of the people they serve.

Indigenous: native; originating in and having characteristics of a certain place or country. "Indigenous music" is usually created by nationals in their local style.

International: what we call a national when he comes to our country.

ISFM: International Society for Frontier Missiology. A missiological think-tank association founded in 1986 to focus interest on unreached peoples.

Mission agency: a Christian organization helping to further God's work in the world. There's an amazing variety of activities and emphases among the hundreds of mission agencies throughout the world. *Mission board* and *sending agency* are virtually the same thing. *Para-*

church refers to a Christian organization independent of any church denominational structures. Many mission agencies are also para-church structures.

National: any person who lives in another country. The *national leaders* are local people who are leading the church or mission. Many national leaders are also missionaries. A *national church* is one that is led by national leaders.

People group: a significantly large sociological grouping of individuals who perceive themselves to have a common affinity for one another because of their shared language, religion, ethnicity, residence, occupation, class or caste, situation, or combination of these.

Tentmaker: a cross-cultural witness who works at a paying, usually secular, job overseas. Often they are able to gain entry into *closed countries* that severely restrict traditional mission efforts. Tentmakers rarely make tents for a living, like the apostle Paul did, but they all should have the intention to further God's work in the world.

Third World: Years ago, the United States and "free" Europe came to be called "the West." Eastern bloc countries, such as the Commonwealth of Independent States (formerly the USSR) and other communist nations, formed a second world. A good chunk of the lands formerly colonized by European powers came to be dubbed as the "third world." Third-world countries are typically "underdeveloped" economically by Western standards. Recently, someone from the third world, not realizing the history of the term, said, "Wait a minute, we're not even second. We don't want to be a 'third world.' We want to be called the 'two-thirds world' since two-thirds of the world's population lives in these countries." The third world is now sometimes referred to as the two-thirds world.

Unreached peoples: essentially "unchurched" peoples lacking an indigenous, evangelizing, church-planting movement. Without such a movement, the people within these groups will likely never hear and obey the gospel. An unreached people group is less than 20 percent practicing Christian.

Sources: *Stepping Out* published by Short-Term Missions Advocate, Inc. and *Mission Frontier* magazine.

Organizations & Foundations

EVANGELICAL COUNCIL FOR
FINANCIAL ACCOUNTABILITY MEMBERS

ECFA exists to increase the public's confidence in the business affairs of evangelical organizations by establishing standards, helping organizations meet the standards, certifying compliance, communicating with the public. The following organizations are ECFA members as of September 1991.

ACMC, Inc., P.O. Box ACMC, Wheaton, IL 60189 708-260-1660. Mobilizes local churches for world missions through consultation services, seminars, and communication ministries.

Advent Christian General Conference of America, P.O. Box 23152, Charlotte, NC 28212 704-545-6161. Serves denominational church by providing resources and training opportunities, legal entities, communications, funding plans, and becoming a catalyst for evangelism and edification.

Advent Christian Village, Inc., P.O. Box 4305, Dowling Park, FL 32060 904-658-3333. Services to children, individuals, retired adults, and families with special needs.

Africa Evangelical Fellowship, P.O. Box 2896, Boone, NC 28607-2896 704-264-6036. Sending councils in the United States, Canada, Great Britain, South Africa, and Australia/New Zealand. Missionaries serve in 13 countries of Africa and in adjacent islands in evangelism, church planting, medical and educational work.

Africa Inland Mission International, Inc., P.O. Box 178, Pearl River, NY 10965 914-735-4014. Evangelizes unreached peoples, develops Christian leadership, encourages local evangelism and cross-cultural missionary outreach by churches.

African Bible Colleges, Inc., P.O. Box 103, Clinton, MS 39060 601-352-1791. Establishes and funds Bible colleges in Africa.

African Children's Welfare Foundation, 2630 S. Manhattan Place, Suite 1, Los Angeles, CA 90018 213-735-6570. An indigenous organization, formed by native Africans in the United States to complement the efforts of other organizations working or sending

aid to Africa. Sets up clinics, provides nutritional feeding, medical and school supplies, helps in community projects, and responds to emergencies.

African Enterprise, Inc., P.O. Box 727, Monrovia, CA 91017 818-357-8811. Serves the church in Africa through African evangelists, leadership training, reconciliation ministry, and human need programs. Emphasis on urban complexes.

AGAPE Counseling Associates, Inc., 2530 Browncroft Blvd., Rochester, NY 14625 716-385-6030. Christian counseling, including support groups for pastors.

Akron Pregnancy Services, 105 E. Market St., Akron, OH 44308 216-434-2221. Provides support to women in the area of sexual responsibility, pregnancy, and abortion.

All Nations, Inc., P.O. Box 41540, Pasadena, CA 91114 818-398-2473. Literacy program in ethnic languages, produces Christian literature in various languages and missions awareness materials for all age levels.

Allentown Rescue Mission, P.O. Box 748, Allentown, PA 18105 215-437-3529. Works with alcoholics, drug addicts, and homeless men with problems.

Alpha Center Inc., P.O. Box 604, Placentia, CA 92670-0604 714-993-4400. Professional counseling services, parenting program for barrio parents.

Alpha/Omega Ministries, 1742 S. Cliff Ave., Sioux Falls, SD 57105 605-335-0739. Provides alternatives to abortion, offers a 24-hour hotline, qualified referrals.

Ambassadors for Christ International, Inc., 1355 Terrel Mill Rd., Bldg. 1484, Marietta, GA 30067 404-980-2020. National evangelistic teams.

ECFA MEMBERS cont.

Ambassadors For Christ, Inc., P.O. Box 0280, Paradise, PA 17562 717-687-8564. Ministers to Chinese students and professionals in the U.S.

America's Keswick, Keswick Grove, Whiting, NJ 08759 201-350-1187. Drug and alcohol rehabilitation program, Bible conference and retreat center.

American Association of Bible Colleges, P.O. Box 1523, Fayetteville, AR 72702 501-521-8164. Provides accreditation services, research, seminars, information services.

The American Council of the Ramabai Mukti Mission, P.O. Box 4912, Clinton, NJ 08809 908-735-8770. Ministries include orphanage, schools, medicine, homes for the blind, handicapped and destitute women, evangelism, agriculture, church planting in India.

American Family Association, P.O. Drawer 2440, Tupelo, MS 38803 601-844-5036. Promotes biblical ethic of decency.

American Institute for Teen AIDS Prevention, P.O. Box 136116, Fort Worth, TX 76136 817-237-0230. Puts HIV/AIDS into a biblical context. Provides educational material for schools and presents assemblies, seminars, and classes focusing on prevention.

American Leprosy Missions, Inc., 1 Alm Way, Greenville, SC 29601 803-271-7040. Leprosy medical treatment, rehabilitation, research, public and patient education.

American Missionary Fellowship, P.O. Box 368, Villanova, PA 19085 215-527-4439. Plants and develops churches, prison ministries, and mailbox clubs in rural and urban America.

American Tract Society, P.O. Box 462008, Garland, TX 75046 214-276-9408. Prints and circulates religious tracts.

AMG International, 6815 Shallowford Rd., Chattanooga, TN 37421 615-894-6060. Worldwide ministry through newspaper evangelism, support of national workers, radio and church planting. Supports orphanages, schools, day-care centers, hospitals, food and clothing centers, leprosariums, and clinic ministries. Publishes *Pulpit Helps,* maintains Expositors Microfilm library and AMG Publishers.

Appalachian Bible College, Box ABC, Bradley, WV 25818 304-877-6428. Collegiate-level biblical instruction.

The Art of Family Living, P.O. Box 2000, Dallas, TX 75221 214-437-4377. Teaches through radio broadcasts, audio cassette tapes, books.

Asbury Theological Seminary, 204 N. Lexington Ave., Wilmore, KY 40390 606-858-3581. Provides graduate, professional and continuing studies for ordained and lay ministries. Resource center for World Wesleyan Leadership.

Aslan, Inc., P.O. Box 270, Red Bank, NJ 07701 908-741-7824. Serves disadvantaged, low-income youth and families with predominant emphasis in the African-American community.

Association for Christian Conferences, Teaching & Service, P.O. Box 27239, Denver, CO 80227-0239 303-985-8808. Assists military Christians to evangelize, disciple, and develop strong fellowship groups within their national Armed Forces.

Association of International Mission Services, P.O. Box 64534, Virginia Beach, VA 23464 804-523-7979. Provides framework for unity and fellowship among churches, mission agencies, and training institutions. Involved in world evangelization.

Athletic Ministries International, Inc., P.O. Box 241076, Memphis, TN 38124 901-345-0258. Utilizes basketball to share the gospel.

Atlanta Care Center, Inc., 3960 Peachtree Rd., Suite 547, Atlanta, GA 30319 404-261-2736. Helps women deal with unexpected pregnancy.

Atlanta Union Mission, P.O. Box 1807, Atlanta, GA 30301 404-588-4000. Provides shelter and care, activities, counseling, and religious instruction.

Atlantic City Rescue Mission, P.O. Box 5358, Atlantic City, NJ 08404 609-345-5517. Provides meals, shelter, food baskets, furniture, counseling. Residential rehabilitation/discipleship program.

Azusa Pacific University, P.O. Box A.P.U. Azusa, CA 91702-7000 818-969-3434. Fully accredited, coeducational, Christian university.

Bachman Memorial Home, Inc., P.O. Box 849, Cleveland, TN 37364-0849 615-479-4523. Provides emotional, spiritual, and developmental treatment to young men ages 13 to 19.

Back to God Hour of the Christian Reformed Church, 6555 W. College Dr., Palos Heights, IL 60463 708-371-8700. Radio and television ministry of the Christian Reformed church. Produces radio and television programs.

Back to the Bible, P.O. Box 82808, Lincoln, NE 68501 402-474-4567. Teaches the Word of God through the media.

Bakersfield Rescue Mission, P.O. Box 2222, Bakersfield, CA 93303 805-325-0863. Evangelistic gospel services, meals, clothing, shelter. Live-in discipleship programs.

BALL World Missions, 8955 Old Lemay Ferry Rd., Hillsboro, MO 63050 314-789-4368. Provides spiritual help, shelter and care; trains national leaders.

The Baptist Foundation of Oklahoma, 3800 N. May, Oklahoma City, OK 73112 405-949-9500. Receives and administers endowment gifts for Baptist causes, offers estate planning services to individuals.

Baptist General Conference, 2002 S. Arlington Heights Rd., Arlington Heights, IL 60005 708-228-0200. Fellowship of Baptist churches in the U.S. and Caribbean Islands.

Barry Moore Ministries, Inc., P.O. Box 611529, Port Huron, MI 48060 313-982-6584. Conducts evangelistic crusades.

BCM International, Inc., 237 Fairfield Ave., Upper Darby, PA 19082 215-352-7177. Strengthens the local church, leading children, teenagers, and adults to faith in Jesus Christ, encouraging them to attend local Bible-believing churches.

Ben Haden Evangelical Association, Inc., 554 McCallie Ave., Chattanooga, TN 37402 615-267-7959. Produces a worldwide weekly TV and radio program.

The Berean League, 2875 Snelling Ave., N., St. Paul, MN 55113 612-633-0654. A coalition of Christians in Minnesota providing concise, credible information of current state, political, social, and moral issues, including relevant biblical principles.

Berean Mission, Inc., 3536 Russell Blvd., St. Louis, MO 63104 314-773-0110. Establishes and assists local churches in foreign countries and the U.S.

Bethany Bible Church, 6060 N. 7th Ave., Phoenix, AZ 85013 602-246-9788. Major emphasis is study of God's Word. Not affiliated with any denomination.

Bethany Christian Services, 901 Eastern Ave., NE, Grand Rapids, MI 49503 616-459-6273. Private child welfare/child placement agency.

Bethany College of the Assemblies of God, 800 Bethany Drive, Scotts Valley, CA 95066 408-438-3800. Prepares students for ministry in the church and for effective lay and professional ministry and church-related vocations.

Bethel Bible Village, P.O. Box 5000, Hixson, TN 37343 615-842-5757. Family-style care for children from broken homes where one or both parents are in prison.

Bethel Ministries, P.O. Box 390, Wise, VA 24293 703-328-6876. Released time classes, Bible clubs, camping program, correspondence school, senior citizens, and jail ministry.

Bethel Temple of Evansville, Inc., 4400 Lincoln Ave., Evansville, IN 47714-0650 812-477-8888. Interdenominational church, Christian school, television ministry, unwed mothers' home, food and clothing bank.

Bethesda Mission, P.O. Box 3041, Harrisburg, PA 17105 717-257-4440. A missionary arm of the local church. Provides the poor and homeless with shelter, food, and clothing.

Bethesda Outreach Ministries, 1465 Kelly Johnson Blvd., Suite 210, Colorado Springs, CO 80920 719-593-0099. Bible school and Bible college training, a Christian day school, medical outreach ministries and training, feeding programs for the needy in any part of the world.

Bible Basics International, P.O. Box 340508, Tampa, FL 33694 813-920-2264. Teaching ministry to believers in China, India and Third World countries through literature and cassettes. Conducts seminars and conferences in churches, camps, and retreats in the U.S.

Bible Christian Union, Inc., P.O. Box 410, Hatfield, PA 19440-0410 215-361-0500. Establishes and strengthens local churches with emphasis in Europe, evangelism, discipleship, and leadership training.

The Bible League, 16801 S. Van Dam Rd., South Holland, IL 60473 708-331-2094. Scripture placement agency through local churches in Third World countries.

Bible Literature International, Inc., P.O. Box 477, Columbus, OH 43214 614-267-3116. Provides Bibles and literature through missions and national ministries worldwide.

Bible Study Fellowship, 19001 Blanco Rd., San Antonio, TX 78258 512-492-4676. Helps people better understand the Bible through a five-year course of study.

ECFA MEMBERS cont.

Bible Translations on Tape, Inc., P.O. Box
2500, Cedar Hill, TX 75104 214-291-1555.
Records, programs, and distributes the Scriptures on cassettes predominately for people
who are illiterate.
Bibles for the World, Inc., P.O. Box 805, Wheaton, IL 60189 708-668-7733. Prints and distributes Bibles worldwide, supports and trains
national missionary workers, supports and educates needy children in India under the Partnership Parents program.
Bibletown Community Church, Inc., P.O.
Box A, Boca Raton, FL 33429-9000 407-
367-6827. Church services.
Biblical Theological Seminary, 200 N. Main
Street, Hatfield, PA 19440 215-368-5000.
Independent, interdenominational graduate school of theology. Offers the Master of
Arts degree, the Master of Divinity degree
and the Master of Sacred Theology degree.
Bill Glass Evangelistic Association, P.O. Box
1105, Cedar Hill, TX 75104 214-291-7895.
Interdenominational crusades, "Total Per-
son Weekends" in prisons.
Billy Graham Evangelistic Association,
1300 Harmon Pl., Minneapolis, MN 55403
612-338-0500. Evangelistic crusades,
Schools of Evangelism, "Hour of Decision,"
Decision magazine, literature distribution,
and films.
Biola University, Inc., 13800 Biola Ave., La
Mirada, CA 90639 213-903-4760. Offers un-
dergraduate, masters, and doctoral programs.
Blessings International, Inc., 5881 S. Garnett
Road, Tulsa, OK 74146 918-250-8101. Fa-
cilitates medical missions by being a source
of pharmaceuticals and medical supplies for
ministries primarily in developing nations.
Bob Cryder Team Ministries, Inc., P.O. Box
14845, Portland, OR 97214-0845 503-238-
4728. Revival, discipleship, evangelistic cru-
sades.
Boise Bible College, Inc., 8695 Marigold
Street, Boise, ID 83714-1220 208-376-7731.
Biblical and general education programs.
Bowery Mission Ministries, 40 Overlook
Drive, Chappaqua, NY 10514 914-769-
9000. Gospel services, live-in discipleship
program, soup kitchen, free clothing, bathing
facilities, medical care, and overnight shelter.
Christian Herald Children and *Christian
Herald* magazine.
Breakthrough, Inc., P.O. Box 121, Lincoln,
VA 22078 703-338-4131. Intercessory

prayer ministry, annual prayer conference.
Brinkhaven Homes for Youth, Inc., P.O. Box
210, North Lawrence, OH 44666 216-854-
4521. Provides homes for troubled and
needy youth with a scriptural climate of living to stimulate the resident to accept the
teachings of the Word of God as the basis for
life.
Bryan College, P.O. Box 7000, Dayton, TN
37321 615-775-2041. Four-year, Christian
liberal arts college.
Caleb Project, P.O. Box 101239, Denver, CO
80250-1239 303-347-1044. Mobilizes the
church for involvement in missions.
Calvary Bible College, 15800 Calvary Road,
Kansas City, MO 64147-1341 816-322-
0110. Offers certified Associate of Arts,
Bachelor of Arts, Bachelor of Science, and
Bachelor of Music (B. Mus.) degrees.
Calvary Church, 5801 Pineville Matthews
Rd., Charlotte, NC 28226 704-543-1200.
Nondenominational, 4,000-member church.
Calvary Community Church, 31293 Via
Colinas, Westlake Village, CA 91363 818-
991-8040. Christ-centered, biblically
based, culturally relevant and outreach oriented group of believers. The church exists
to celebrate the life of God, cultivate personal growth in Christ, care about one another in Christ, and communicate Christ to
the world.
CAM International, 8625 La Prada Drive,
Dallas, TX 75228 214-327-8206. Establishes
indigenous churches, assists existing
churches in Spanish-speaking areas.
Campus Crusade for Christ International,
100 Sunport Lane, Orlando, FL 32809 407-
826-2104. Evangelistic and discipling ministry.
Cannon Beach Conference Center, P.O. Box
398, Cannon Beach, OR 97110 503-436-
1501. Beach resort conference facility.
Capitol Hill Crisis Pregnancy Center, 323 8th
Street, NE, Washington, DC 20002 202-546-
1018. Helps women who face crisis pregnancies to see their ultimate worth in the eyes of
God and to see the same worth of their unborn children. Provides free services including pregnancy testing, alternatives to
abortion, baby clothes, referrals. Affiliated
with the Christian Action Council.
Carriage Town Mission, P.O. Box 318, Flint,
MI 48506 313-233-8787. Provides food,
lodging, and assistance to the needy and

unfortunate; gospel services and youth program for inner city children.

Cedar Ridge Children's Home & School, Inc., P.O. Box 439, Williamsport, MD 21795 301-582-0282. Boys' home and school, radio station, counseling services, and an outdoor adventure program.

Center for Christian Study, 128 Chancellor St., Charlottesville, VA 22903 804-295-2471. Outreach ministry in the university community; encourages people to think seriously about their Christian faith. Provides a regular slate of evening lectures, a nine month diploma in Christian studies, Saturday seminars, summer study program.

Central Church, Inc., P.O. Box 751950, Memphis, TN 38175-1950 901-365-4673. A New Testament church.

Challenger Films, Inc., 2951 Flowers Road, S., Suite 243, Atlanta, GA 30341 404-458-6632. Produces media material through television broadcasting as well as the video cassette market. Primary target is youth, ages 12-22.

The Chapel, 895 N. Forest Rd., Williamsville, NY 14221 716-634-2636. Interdenominational church, daily radio broadcasts, television program, Christian Central Academy.

The Chapel of the Air, P.O. Box 30, Wheaton, IL 60189 708-668-7292. Radio broadcast ministry.

Chaplaincy Ministries, Inc., 7777 Forest Lane, Suite B211, Dallas, TX 75230 214-661-7584. Provides pastoral care to health care facilities without a chaplaincy program.

Chattanooga Bible Institute, 1001 McCallie Ave., Chattanooga, TN 37403 615-266-4574. Resource center for laity or clergy.

Chattanooga Prison Ministries, Inc., P.O. Box 3026, Chattanooga, TN 37404 615-622-5768. Ministers to inmates and their families within a 30-mile radius of Chattanooga.

Cherry Hills Community Church, 3651 S. Colorado Blvd., Englewood, CO 80110 303-781-0091. Seeks to help Christians in their knowledge of Scripture, Christlike character, skills for ministry; Christian school.

Chicago Bible Society, 104 S. Michigan Ave., #520, Chicago, IL 60603 312-236-2169. Promotes serious reading of the Scriptures and their distribution throughout the greater Chicago area. Provides Bible materials without charge to the disadvantaged, prison-

ers, the poor, the elderly, the blind, the handicapped, and those in shelters and rescue missions.

Child Evangelism Fellowship, Inc., P.O. Box 348, Warrenton, MO 63383 314-456-4321. Reaches multitudes of children with God's Word. Encourages them in daily devotions, witnessing, church attendance, missions.

Childcare International, P.O. Box W, Bellingham, WA 98225 206-647-2283. Meets the needs of the poor with emphasis on children. Works in Haiti, Kenya, Uganda, Peru, India, Tonga, Mexico, and southern California with clinics, schools, feeding programs, evangelism, food for work programs, nutrition centers, trade schools, agricultural projects, eye care and surgery, and child sponsorship.

Children's Ministries, Inc., 250 N. Highland Ave., Pittsburgh, PA 15206 412-363-0425. Aids the church through evangelism to children and young people. Encourages Bible reading. Offers services to churches and organizations.

China Ministries International, P.O. Box 40489, Pasadena, CA 91104-7489 818-398-0145. Evangelization of the Chinese people, particularly those living in Mainland China. Gathers and disseminates information on the church in China, trains Chinese evangelists via radio and literature. Provides seminary training in Hong Kong and Taiwan.

Chinese Christian Mission, Inc., P.O. Box 617, Petaluma, CA 94953 707-762-1314. Missionary-sending agency to the Chinese people.

Chinese Overseas Christian Mission, Inc., P.O. Box 310, Fairfax, VA 22030 703-273-3500. Seeks to reach the people of China by (1) sponsorship of daily broadcasts to China; (2) support of persons on campus contacting Chinese students; (3) tour-guided entertainment program; (4) recruitment and placing of campus workers; (5) missions conference and seminars.

Choices, Inc., 775 Second Street Pike, Southampton, PA 18966 215-322-8520. Ministry to women in crisis pregnancy situations; provides alternatives to women seeking abortions.

Chop Point, Inc., R.F.D. 1, Box 715, Woolwich, ME 04579 207-443-6860. Interdenominational youth agency. Encourages youth to spend time in Bible reading and meditation.

ECFA MEMBERS cont.

Chosen People Ministries, 1300 Cross Beam Drive, Charlotte, NC 28217-2800 704-357-9000. Arm of the local churches with specific emphasis on the Jews.

Christ in Youth, Inc., Box B, Joplin, MO 64802 417-781-7770. Offers programs and resources for young people to help them understand and accept their responsibilities as Christians.

Christ for the Island World, P.O. Box 18962, Greensboro, NC 27410 919-855-0656. Supports national evangelists. Helps them purchase transportation, such as outboard motors and motorbikes.

Christ for the Nations, Inc., P.O. Box 769000, Dallas, TX 75376-9000 214-376-1711. Religious, educational, and missionary organization, two-year Bible school.

Christ Truth Radio Crusade, P.O. Box 610, Upland, CA 91786 714-981-2838. Prison ministry, distributing Bibles to prisoners and offering them a correspondence course.

The Christian & Missionary Alliance, P.O. Box 35000, Colorado Springs, CO 80935-3500 719-599-5999. Church denomination committed to world missions.

Christian Action Council Education and Ministries Fund, 101 W. Broad Street, #500, Falls Church, VA 22046 703-237-2100. Campaigns against abortion, infanticide, and euthanasia.

Christian Aid Ministries, P.O. Box 360, Berlin, OH 44610 216-893-2428. Provides spiritual and material aid to needy Christians. Currently working in Romania, Nicaragua, the Commonwealth of Independent States (formerly the Soviet Union), and Haiti.

Christian Blind Mission International, P.O. Box 19000, Greenville, SC 29601 803-239-0065. Ministers to blind and handicapped people of the Third World.

Christian Business Men's Committee International, P.O. Box 3239, Chattanooga, TN 37404 615-622-8200. Coordinates the CBMC ministry around the world.

Christian Business Men's Committee of U.S.A., P.O. Box 3308, Chattanooga, TN 37404 615-698-4444. Ministers to business and professional men.

Christian Camping International/USA, P.O. Box 646, Wheaton, IL 60189 708-462-0300. An association of Christian camps and conference centers.

Christian Camps, Inc., R.D. 2, Box 159B, Greenville, NY 12083 518-966-4115. Camping program for boys 8-16 in the Adirondack wilderness.

Christian Chaplain Services, Inc., P.O. Box 860307, Los Angeles, CA 90086-0307 213-974-8085. Provides chaplains and chaplaincy services to jails, prisons, juvenile detention centers, homes for abused children, and drug and alcohol rehabilitation centers worldwide.

The Christian Church Extension Foundation, P.O. Box 260758, Lakewood, CO 80226 800-843-2233. Financial ministry to independent Christian Churches and Churches of Christ, offers interdenominational church data survey and consultant-guided analysis.

Christian College Coalition, 329 8th Street, N.E., Washington, DC 20002-6158 202-546-8713. An association of approximately 80 liberal arts colleges in the U.S. and Canada. Sponsors professional development activities for faculty and administrators.

Christian Communications of Chicagoland, Inc., 38 S. Peoria St., Chicago, IL 60607 312-433-3838. Utilizes mass media as an arm of the church.

Christian Counseling & Enrichment, Inc., 14581 E. Tufts Ave., Aurora, CO 80015 303-693-3954. Biblical counseling, consultation, and conferences to help leaders, boards, and staffs.

Christian Counseling Services, Inc., P.O. Box 60383, Nashville, TN 37206 615-254-8341. Marriage, family, and individual counseling, maternity, and adoption services. Individual and family counseling for homosexuality.

Christian Educators Association International, P.O. Box 50025, Pasadena, CA 91115 818-795-1983. Promotes Judeo-Christian values in our schools through magazine, newsletters, prayer groups, seminars, and national convention.

Christian Encounter Ministries, P.O. Box 1022, Grass Valley, CA 95945 916-268-0877. Residential and community counseling center; seminars, retreats, on-property camps, and wilderness camps.

Christian Eye Ministry, P.O. Box 3721, San Dimas, CA 91773 714-599-8955. Overseas medical mission organization to help eradicate blindness in less developed countries.

Christian Family Care Agency, 1121 E. Missouri, Phoenix, AZ 85014 602-234-1935. Helps children and families in crisis: pregnancy assistance, foster care, adoption, and family counseling.

Christian Fellowship Church, 4100 Millersburg Rd., Evansville, IN 47711 812-867-6464. Nondenominational evangelical church, adult Bible Lay Institute.

Christian Financial Concepts, 601 Broad Street, SE, Gainesville, GA 30501 404-534-1000. Teaches principles of finance and money management.

Christian Herald Association, 40 Overlook Drive, Chappaqua, NY 10514 914-769-9000. Publishes *Christian Herald* magazine. Related ministries: Family Bookshelf, The Bowery Mission of New York City, camping/counseling program for New York City youth.

Christian Homes, Inc., 200 N. Postville Dr., Lincoln, IL 62656 217-732-9651. Provides a ministry of the Christian Churches and Churches of Christ for the aging and infirm requiring special long-term care and retirement living. Reduces and waives fees based on the applicant's ability to pay.

Christian Homes for Children, Inc., 275 State Street, Hackensack, NJ 07601-5512 201-342-4235. Adoption services, counseling, food and clothing, educational training, and foster care.

Christian Hope Indian Eskimo Fellowship (CHIEF), 1644 E. Campo Bello Drive, Phoenix, AZ 85022 602-482-0828. Ministers to the 36 million Native Americans in the 1,200 tribes of the Western Hemisphere.

Christian Lay Ministries, P.O. Box 1027, Lake Junaluska, NC 28745 704-456-3960. Disciples laity. Sponsors developmental projects in Zaire, Africa.

Christian Laymen's Association of Will County, P.O. Box 2454, Joliet, IL 60434 815-723-6837. Summer day camp for ages 5-12. Youth activities.

Christian Leadership Concepts, Inc., P.O. Box 24274, Nashville, TN 37202 615-726-1717. Trains Christians to use their leadership abilities.

Christian League for the Handicapped, Inc., P.O. Box 948, Walworth, WI 53184 414-275-6131. Encourages disabled persons toward maximum independence.

Christian Legal Society, 4208 Evergreen Lane, Suite 222, Annandale, VA 22003 703-642-1070. Fellowship of lawyers, judges, law professors, and law students. Promotes the constitutional right of free exercise of religion, resolving conflicts among Christians.

Christian Life Missions, 388 E. Gundersen Drive, Wheaton, IL 60188 708-653-4200. Works through other established missions. Operates the Christian Writers Institute; sponsors writing seminars.

Christian Management Association, P.O. Box 4638, Diamond Bar, CA 91765 714-861-8861. Professional association for those involved in the management of Christian organizations.

Christian Medical & Dental Society, P.O. Box 830689, Richardson, TX 75083-0689 214-783-8384. Encourages Christian students and doctors to apply a Christian mind-set in the fields of medicine and dentistry.

Christian Military Fellowship, P.O. Box 1207, Englewood, CO 80150 303-761-1959. Works within the military society with emphasis toward the enlisted ranks.

Christian Mission for the United Nations Community, P.O. Box 159, Monroe, CT 06468 203-261-1277. Ministry based at the United Nations and from there to leaders throughout the world.

Christian Missionary Fellowship, P.O. Box 26306, Indianapolis, IN 46226 317-542-9256. Assists the local church in world evangelism. Recruits, equips, and sends missionaries to unreached peoples.

Christian Renewal Ministries, Inc., 200 N. Main St., Milltown, NJ 08850 908-828-4545. Interdenominational, para-church organization dedicated to preaching, discipleship training, and mass-media ministries, especially literature to the Chinese.

Christian Research Institute, Inc., P.O. Box 500, San Juan Capistrano, CA 92693 714-855-9926. Studies cults, the world of the occult, and Christian apologetics. Expertise spans 300 areas of biblical research and data.

Christian Service Brigade, P.O. Box 150, Wheaton, IL 60189 708-665-0630. Provides programs, training, and counsel in leadership of children.

Christian Service Foundation, Inc., P.O. Box 41, Wichita Falls, TX 76307 817-767-3303.

ECFA MEMBERS cont.

Ministers to military personnel in the Wichita Falls area.

Christian Solidarity International, Inc., P.O. Box 70563, Washington, DC 20024 301-989-0298. Works in Communist, Islamic, Hindu, and totalitarian-ruled countries where Christians are persecuted for their faith.

Christian Stewardship Association, 13 S. 13th St., Minneapolis, MN 55403 612-338-0500. An association of evangelical IRS Section 501 (c) (3) organizations. Promotes Christian stewardship.

Christian Television Network, P.O. Box 6922, Clearwater, FL 34618 813-535-5622. A nationwide 24-hour Christian network.

Christian Television of Ohio, Inc., P.O. Box 770, Thornville, OH 43076 614-833-0771; 24-hour Christian programming in 145 counties in central Ohio.

Christian Witness Support Team, P.O. Box 1226, Reedley, CA 93654 209-591-7508. Serves national ministries in the Third World.

Christianity Today, Inc., 465 Gundersen Drive, Carol Stream, IL 60188 708-260-6200. Promotes the fundamental truths of the Scriptures through the publication of *Christianity Today, Leadership, Partnership, Today's Christian Woman, Campus Life,* and *Christian History.*

Christians in Action, Inc., P.O. Box 728, Woodlake, CA 93286 209-564-3762. Specializes in personal evangelism and indigenous church planting.

Church Extension Plan, P.O. Box 12629, Salem, OR 97309-0629 503-399-0552. Provides capital loans to churches across the country for new construction, building purchases, remodeling, refinancing, etc.

Church of the Saviour, 480 Fry Rd., Wooster, OH 44691 216-264-5233. Independent Bible church. Theme is "making more and better disciples."

Church of the Saviour, 651 N. Wayne Ave., Wayne, PA 19087 215-687-6453. Exists to exalt the living God, equip God's people, and evangelize the nations.

Church Resource Ministries, P.O. Box 5189, Fullerton, CA 92635 714-879-5540. Trains church leaders with the focus on church growth, renewal, and the establishment of new churches.

Churches Alive International, P.O. Box 3800, San Bernardino, CA 92413 714-886-5361. Helps local churches establish and multiply discipling ministries.

Cincinnati Bible College & Seminary, P.O. Box 043200, Cincinnati, OH 45204-3200 513-244-8100. Special-purpose institution to prepare people for Christian service.

Circle Urban Ministries, 118 N. Central Ave., Chicago, IL 60644 312-921-1446. Aids disadvantaged residents in the Austin neighborhood of Chicago.

The City Mission of Schenectady, Inc., P.O. Box 760, Schenectady, NY 12301 518-346-2275. Mission work to those not reached by regular church organizations.

City Mission Society, Inc., P.O. Box 496, Buffalo, NY 14205 716-854-8181. Full- service gospel rescue mission in western New York. Open 24 hours a day. Serves over 300 meals daily. Chapel services and Bible studies.

City Rescue Mission of Muskegon, 400 W. Laketon Ave., Muskegon, MI 49441 616-722-2313. Provides shelter, food, clothing to men, women, and children who are in need.

City Union Mission, Inc., 1108 E. 10th Street, Kansas City, MO 64106 816-474-9380. Provides material relief: food, clothing, shelter. Counseling. Transition to housing stability and useful job skills.

City Team Ministries, P.O. Box 143, San Jose, CA 95103 408-998-4770. Serves disadvantaged people of cities through rescue missions. Family outreach, youth outreach, cross-cultural ministries.

CMJ/U.S.A. (A Christian ministry among Jewish people), P.O. Box 429, Ambridge, PA 15003 412-266-5991. Ministers to Jewish people. Educates Christians, especially Episcopalians, as to the Jewish origins of the church, and their continuing obligations to the Jewish people.

Coalition for Christian Outreach, 6740 5th Ave., Pittsburgh, PA 15208 412-363-3303. Works with tomorrow's leaders on college and university campuses in western Pennsylvania, eastern Ohio, northern West Virginia.

Colorado Christian University, 180 S. Garrison Street, Lakewood, CO 80226 303-238-5386. Equips for Christian ministry.

Columbia Bible College and Seminary, P.O. Box 3122, Columbia, SC 29230 803-754-4100. Nondenominational Bible college with a seminary, extension school, secondary boarding school (Ben Lippen School), and an FM radio station (WMHK).

Community Chaplain Service, Inc., P.O. Box E-734, New Bedford, MA 02742 508-997-3174. Career missionary chaplains minister in nursing homes.

Compassion International, Inc., P.O. Box 7000, Colorado Springs, CO 80933 719-594-9900. Increases awareness and builds understanding concerning the problems facing needy children.

Concerts of Prayer International, Pentagon Towers, Box 36008, Minneapolis, MN 55435 612-835-2553. A ministry to the church-at-large. Helps to mobilize, train, and equip Christians to seek God in united prayer for spiritual awakening and world evangelization.

Conservative Congregational Christian Conference, 7582 Currell Blvd., Suite 108, St. Paul, MN 55125 612-729-1474. Promotes fellowship and cooperative endeavor among Congregational churches of the historic biblical persuasion.

Coral Ridge Ministries, Inc., 5555 N. Federal Highway, Fort Lauderdale, FL 33308 305-771-8840. Coral Ridge Presbyterian Church. Westminster Academy, a K–12 school with 950 students. TV and radio broadcasts.

Cornerstone Church, 6930 Wood Haven Rd., Roanoke, VA 24019 703-362-2187. Family-oriented, charismatic church.

Cornerstone Pregnancy Services, 800 Middle Ave., Elyria, OH 44035 216-284-1010. Provides education, emotional and material support to any women experiencing a crisis pregnancy.

Covenant Theological Seminary, 12330 Conway Rd., St. Louis, MO 63141 314-434-4044. Trains ministers, particularly for the Presbyterian Church in America.

Crichton College, P.O. Box 757830, Memphis, TN 38175-7830 901-367-9800. Four-year college offering eight programs of study: Bible and theology, natural sciences, music, psychology, elementary education, church ministries, and secondary education.

Crisis Pregnancy Center, 1124 N. Third Ave., Tucson, AZ 85705 602-622-5774. Provides support to assist pregnant women during pregnancy and after birth.

Educates youth regarding their sexuality and offers post abortion counseling. All services free.

Crisis Pregnancy Center of Cleveland, Inc., Williamsport Plaza, 398 Bagley, Suite 13, Berea, OH 44017 216-243-2520. Offers alternatives to abortion by providing assistance, positive services, and creative choices to women and girls faced with unwanted or otherwise distressful pregnancies.

The Crisis Pregnancy Center of Greater Toledo, 4427 Talmadge Rd., Suite R, Toledo, OH 43623 419-472-8223. Provides Christian alternatives to abortion. Helps individuals and families experiencing crisis or difficulties as a result of a pregnancy. The Center believes that from the moment of conception, no one is a mistake.

Crisis Pregnancy Center of the Lehigh Valley, 29 S. 8th St., Allentown, PA 18101-2430 215-821-0943. Outreach to women in the Greater Lehigh Valley Community with crisis pregnancies. Offers alternatives to abortion.

Crisis Pregnancy Clinic, 2991 Shattuck Ave., #201, Berkeley, CA 94705 415-849-9916. Provides counseling and care for women and their families in the East Bay area who are experiencing pregnancy-related crises.

Crisis Pregnancy Support Center 1915 1/2 Church Street, Nashville, TN 37203 615-321-0005. Network of support for women facing unexpected pregnancies.

CRISTA Ministries, 19303 Fremont Ave., N., Seattle, WA 98133 206-546-7200. Seven distinct ministries: CRISTA schools, World Concern, CRISTA Senior Community, Intercristo, CRISTA Broadcasting, CRISTA Camps, and CRISTA Counseling Service.

Criswell Center for Biblical Studies, 4010 Gaston Ave., Dallas, TX 75246 214-821-5433. Educates and trains laymen and full-time Christian workers in biblical, theological, and professional studies. The school's stance is conservative, it's endeavor is evangelistic.

Crown Ministries, Inc., 530 Crown Oak Centre Drive, Longwood, FL 32750 407-331-6000. Trains people to be financially faithful. Scriptural financial principles are taught in a small group study.

ECFA MEMBERS cont.

Dad the Family Shepherd, Inc., P.O. Box 21445, Little Rock, AR 72212 501-221-1102. Exists to equip men to become more effective family shepherds. Trains them to model and practice biblical family life principles. Provides evaluation services, live and video conferences, small group discipleship.

Dallas Theological Seminary, 3909 Swiss Ave., Dallas, TX 75204 214-824-3626. An institutional organization of higher education. Consists of seven programs of study, five master level programs, and two doctoral programs.

Dawn Ministries, P.O. Box 40969, Pasadena, CA 91114 818-398-2300. Teaches national leaders how to develop a DAWN (Discipling A Whole Nation) project. Desires to establish a strong evangelical congregation in every group of 500 to 1,000 citizens in every village.

Dayspring Enterprises International, P.O. Box 3309, Virginia Beach, VA 23454 804-428-1092. Innovative use of media in the two-thirds world by means of the publication, production, distribution, broadcast, and exhibition of educational and dramatic programs on motion picture films, slides, video and audio tapes, records, and by printed materials.

Daystar Communications, P.O. Box 150, Winfield, IL 60190 708-653-8586. U.S.-based support organization of Daystar University College in Nairobi, Kenya.

Denver Area Youth for Christ, Inc., P.O. Box 101600, Denver, CO 80250 303-843-9000. Campus Life. High school and junior high campuses, youth guidance, incarcerated kids, and urban ministries reaching youth through the probation and court system.

Denver Conservative Baptist Seminary, P.O. Box 10,000, Denver, CO 80250 303-761-2482. Graduate theological school.

Denver Rescue Mission, P.O. Box 5206, Denver, CO 80205 303-294-0157. Oldest full-time evangelical service provider to the poor and homeless in the Rocky Mountain West. Includes emergency shelter and meals, free clothing distribution, and medical services. Maintains a 100-acre working farm in northeastern Colorado and a transitional housing program for single mothers with dependent children.

Detroit Metro Youth for Christ, 24331 W. Eight Mile Rd., Detroit, MI 48219 313-533-3900. Four major ministry divisions: Campus Life, Youth Guidance, Urban, and Quizzing and Music.

Detroit Rescue Mission Ministries, P.O. Box 2087, Detroit, MI 48231 313-993-4700. Provides emergency shelter, food, substance abuse counseling, and work training in the Detroit metropolitan area.

Disciple Renewal, Inc., P.O. Box 106, Lovington, IL 61937 217-873-5126. Promotes spiritual renewal with the Christian Church (DOC), primarily through the publication *Disciple Renewal.* Sponsors renewal conferences.

Discipleship Counseling Services, 2300 Valley View Lane, Suite 200, Dallas, TX 75234 214-620-1755. Radio and teaching ministry that concentrates on effectiveness in biblical counseling and discipleship.

Don Anderson Ministries, Inc., P.O. Box 6611, Tyler, TX 75711 903-597-3018. Communication, camping, and counseling.

Eastern European Bible Mission, P.O. Box 110, Colorado Springs, CO 80901-0110 719-577-4450. Strengthens the church in Eastern Europe.

Eastern European Seminary, Inc., 6730 LBJ Freeway, #2195, Dallas, TX 75240 214-404-8077. Seminary-level curriculum in six Eastern European languages.

Echoing Hills Village, Inc., 36272 CR 79, Warsaw, OH 43844 614-327-2311. Services developmentally disabled.

ECL/Door of Hope International, P.O. Box 303, Glendale, CA 91209 818-840-8677. Prints and distributes Bibles and Christian literature, supports national Christian workers and pastors in the Commonwealth of Independent States (formerly the Soviet Union.)

Ed Robb Evangelistic Association, P.O. Box 1945, Marshall, TX 75671 214-938-8305. Evangelism, reform, and renewal. Publishes *The Challenge.*

Edgewood Children's Ranch, Inc., 1451 Edgewood Ranch Rd., Orlando, FL 32811 407-295-2464. Christian boarding school; children are accepted on the basis of need.

The Eleventh Hour Mission, Inc., P.O. Box 7, Alamo, TX 78516 512-787-2024. Establishes churches in Mexico by teaching students at the Bible Institute in Monterrey, Mexico, a four-year night school program.

Elim Bible Institute, 7245 College Street, Lima, NY 14485 716-582-1230. Preparation for ministry.

Elim Fellowship, Inc., 7245 College Street, Lima, NY 14485 716-582-2790. Establishes and maintains churches and missions in the U.S. and abroad; licenses and ordains Christian ministries; buys, handles, and sells property; establishes and maintains orphanages, schools (parochial and Bible), and maintains homes for the aged.

Emmanuel International Mission, P.O. Box 8082, Port Huron, MI 48061-8082 313-985-8730. Recruits, trains, and prepares Christian personnel for disaster relief, emergency relief, and community development programs.

Emmaus Bible College, 2570 Asbury Rd., Dubuque, IA 52001-3096 319-588-8000. Associated with Plymouth or Christian Brethren; undergraduate and graduate programs; correspondence school.

Encounter Ministries, Inc., P.O. Box 757800, Memphis, TN 38175 901-757-7977. Radio ministry, distribution of tapes and literature; Institute for Biblical Preaching.

English Language Institute/China, P.O. Box 265, San Dimas, CA 91773 714-599-6773. Recruits, selects, trains, and helps place qualified teachers in Chinese universities.

Eternal Truth Ministries, Inc., P.O. Box 1853, Huntington Beach, CA 92647 714-847-1710. Teaching and writing ministry; conferences and retreats. Support for the preparation of Bible study material.

Evangelical Assoc. for the Promotion of Education, P.O. Box 238, St. Davids, PA 19087 215-341-1722. Christian development organization in inner-city neighborhoods.

Evangelical Child and Family Agency, 1530 N. Main Street, Wheaton, IL 60187 708-653-6400. Adoption, foster family care, services to unmarried parents, and family counseling.

Evangelical Ministries, Inc., 1716 Spruce Street, Philadelphia, PA 19103 215-546-3696. "The Bible Study Hour," a weekly radio broadcast on 189 stations in the U.S., Canada, the Caribbean, and China. James M. Boice is speaker; *Bible Study* magazine, Bible study seminars, and study books.

Evangelical Presbyterian Church, 26049 Five Mile Rd., Detroit, MI 48239 313-532-9555. Denomination of Reformed tradition. Nine presbyteries and 135 churches with membership of over 40,000 nationwide and in Argentina.

Evangelism Explosion III International, Inc., P.O. Box 23820, Fort Lauderdale, FL 33307 305-491-6100. Lay evangelism.

Evangelistic Association of New England, 279 Cambridge Street, Burlington, MA 01803 617-229-1990. Resource agency to help churches reach and serve their communities.

Evansville Rescue Mission, Inc., 300 SE M.L. King Blvd., Evansville, IN 47713 812-421-3800. Ministers to the homeless and needy.

EvanTell, Inc., 9212 Markville Drive, Dallas, TX 75243 214-690-3624. Evangelistic crusades, evangelism seminars, and development of materials to equip Christians to evangelize.

Every Child Ministries, Inc., P.O. Box 715, Crown Point, IN 46307 219-996-4201. Equips African churches in evangelistic, missionary, and church planting programs.

Every Home for Christ/World Literature Crusade, P.O. Box 7139, Canoga Park, CA 91304 818-341-7870. Mobilizes and trains the church to participate in the systematic personal presentation of the gospel to every home.

Exodus World Service, P.O. Box 7000, West Chicago, IL 60185 708-665-0004. A refugee ministry to help those who can't go home. Encourages Christians to welcome and serve refugees each step of the way.

Faith Haven CFLYO, 7824 W. Hollow Rd., Naples, NY 14512 716-374-5659. Provides temporary Christian environment for young unmarried women going through a crisis pregnancy.

Faith Venture Visuals, Inc., P.O. Box 423, Lititz, PA 17543 717-626-8503. Conducts seminars on making and using overhead transparencies. Distribution, consultation, and custom transparency making/designing.

Family Hope Services, Inc., 3315 Fernbrook Lane, N., Plymouth, MN 55447 612-557-8670. Supports youth and their families during difficult times.

Family Life Broadcasting System, P.O. Box 35300, Tucson, AZ 85740 602-742-6976. Radio ministry.

Far East Broadcasting Co., Inc., P.O. Box 1, La Mirada, CA 90637 213-947-4651. Operates 32 broadcasting stations in the Philippines, South Korea, Seychelles, Saipan, and San Francisco in over 100 languages.

ECFA MEMBERS cont.

Fellowship Bible Church, 12601 Hinson Rd., Little Rock, AR 72212 501-224-7171. Independent evangelical church.

Fellowship of Christian Athletes, 8701 Leeds Rd., Kansas City, MO 64129 816-921-0909. Ministers to athletes and coaches.

Fellowship of Christians in Univ. and Schools, 139 E. Putnam Ave., Greenwich, CT 06830 203-622-0430. Nondenominational organization of alumni, teachers, administrators, parents, and friends of independent secondary schools for the purpose of conveying the traditional Christian message to students.

Fellowship of Companies for Christ, 2920 Brandywine Rd., #150, Atlanta, GA 30341 404-457-9700. Equips and encourages Christian chief executive officers to operate their businesses and conduct their personal lives according to biblical principles.

Fellowship Independent Mission, P.O. Box 72, Fairless Hills, PA 19030 215-752-1170. FIM meets the need of each missionary or mission, allowing each to serve with individuality and creativity, while providing the adhesive quality and discipline of an effective organization. Missionaries are responsible to the FIM Board.

Fellowship Urban Outreach, 200 Plymouth Ave., San Francisco, CA 94112 415-585-6002. Fellowship Academy, Fellowship Bible Institute, and community projects such as a preschool, prison visits, and food and clothing distribution to needy families.

The Firs Bible & Missionary Conference, 4605 Cable St., Bellingham, WA 98226 206-733-6840. Bible-centered conferences and camp programs.

First Assembly of God of Fremont, 4760 Thornton Ave., Fremont, CA 94536 415-793-8687. Exists for the purpose of knowing God and properly responding to him in such a way that others will come to know him and properly respond to him.

The First Baptist Church of Modesto, California, P.O. Box 4309, Modesto, CA 95352 209-521-0181. Unaffiliated local Baptist church with a regional and world outreach.

First Evangelical Free Church, 2801 N. Brea Blvd., Fullerton, CA 92635 714-529-5544. Worship, instruction, fellowship, and expression.

Floresta USA, 1015 Chesnut Ave., Suite F2, Carlsbad, CA 92008 619-434-6311. Addresses the rural farmers' economic problems. Seeks to attack the causes of deforestation and bring some long term relief to the rural poor. Includes a revolving loan program to provide loans and training to farmers to help them convert to tree crops.

Focus on the Family, 420 N. Cascade, Colorado Springs, CO 80903 719-531-3400. Dedicated to preserving Christian values for the home. Daily radio broadcast.

Follow-Up Ministries, Inc., P.O. Box 2514, Castro Valley, CA 94546 415-881-1178. Works with the local church and other Christian ministries in discipling prisoners. Recruits Christian volunteers, trains them in prison chaplaincy skill, leads discipleship seminars for prisoners, conducts after-care for exiting felons, provides correspondence Bible studies.

Food for the Hungry, Inc., 7729 E. Greenway Rd., Scottsdale, AZ 85260 602-998-3100. Provides food and material aid for disaster relief, conducts ongoing relief and rehabilitation programs. Initiates integrated community development projects. Hunger Corps, Child Sponsorship Program.

Ford Philpot Evangelistic Association, Inc., P.O. Box 3000, Lexington, KY 40533 606-276-1479. TV program that includes interviews, music, and a Christian message. Citywide and areawide evangelistic crusades.

Forest Home, Inc., 40000 Valley of the Falls Drive, Forest Falls, CA 92339 714-794-1127. Conferences for all ages.

The Forum for Scriptural Christianity, Inc., P.O. Box 150, Wilmore, KY 40390 606-858-4661. Committed to renewal within the United Methodist church. Bimonthly *Good News* magazine, renewal groups, political strategy.

Free Methodist Church of North America, P.O. Box 535002, Indianapolis, IN 46253-5002 317-244-3660. Denomination with support ministries for local churches, missions, and child support programs in other countries; coordination of denominational higher education institutions.

The Free Methodist Foundation, P.O. Box 580, Spring Arbor, MI 49283 517-750-2727. Provides support to the people and ministries of the Free Methodist church through giving assistance, investments in pension and trust funds, loan assistance, trustee for charitable trusts and counsel in fund-raising endeavors.

French Camp Academy, School Street, French Camp, MS 39745 601-547-6482. Provides Christian school and home for young people with family problems.

Fresno Christian Schools, Inc., 7280 N. Cedar, Fresno, CA 93720 209-299-1695. Christian day school sponsored by eight evangelical churches in Fresno.

Fresno Pacific College, 1717 S. Chestnut Ave., Fresno, CA 93702 209-453-2000. Christian higher education.

The Friends of Israel Gospel Ministry, P.O. Box 908, Bellmawr, NJ 08099 609-853-5590. Evangelical faith mission to Jewish people and their Gentile neighbors. A staff of 97 serve in seven countries on four continents.

Friendship Crisis Pregnancy Center, Inc., P.O. Box 1491, Morristown, NJ 07962 201-538-0967. Provides information and support to women facing unplanned or crisis pregnancies.

Friendship Village of Schaumburg, 350 W. Schaumburg Rd., Schaumburg, IL 60194 708-884-5000. Provides quality living arrangements and services to persons of retirement age.

Frontiers-MIO, Inc., P.O. Box 40159, Pasadena, CA 91104 818-798-0807. Plants churches among the Muslim people.

Frontline Ministries, Inc., P.O. Box 548, Newburyport, MA 01950 508-462-3538. A ministry of spiritual refreshment and renewal to local churches, ministers, and missionaries, both in the United States and abroad.

Fuller Theological Seminary, 135 N. Oakland Ave., Pasadena, CA 91182 818-584-5200. Schools of Theology, Psychology, and World Mission.

Gary Case Evangelistic Ministries, Inc., P.O. Box 70-114, Louisville, KY 40270 812-969-2888. Local church revivals, camp meetings, area crusades, evangelism on the foreign fields, mission conferences, and youth conferences.

Gateway Rescue Mission, Inc., P.O. Box 3763, Jackson, MS 39207-9987 601-353-5864. Provides bathing facilities, lodging, hot meals, clothing, and a daily evangelistic service for homeless street people.

The Gathering/USA, Inc., 106 E. Church Street, Orlando, FL 32801 407-422-9200. Citywide outreach breakfasts or lunch gatherings, Bible study groups, and individual discipleship. Also sponsors social and mission outreach projects.

General Baptist Foreign Mission Society, Inc., 100 Stinson Drive, Poplar Bluff, MO 63901 314-785-7746. Evangelism, church planting, child care, schools, health care, support of national ministries in the Philippines and Jamaica, a camping ministry in Jamaica, and missions education to U.S. constituency.

General Synod, Assoc. Reformed Presbyterian Church, One Cleveland Street, Greenville, SC 29601 803-232-8297. 180 churches located in 16 states and the District of Columbia; missionaries in three countries. Erskine College and Erskine Theological Seminary, Bonclarken Conference Center.

Generation Ministries, Inc., 10124 N. Tatum Blvd., B-300, Phoenix, AZ 85028 602-948-2545. Research, speaking, and writing ministry focusing on teenagers, parents, and youth workers.

Globe Missionary Evangelism, P.O. Box 3040, Pensacola, FL 32516-3040 904-453-4318. Charismatic sending agency; more than 200 missionaries in over 19 countries.

Glory to God Ministries, P.O. Box 4167, Palm Springs, CA 92263 619-321-5222. Purpose is to sow the Word of God, be a "servant to the servants," motivate believers and let God move in power.

God's World Publications, Inc., P.O. Box 2330, Asheville, NC 28802 704-253-8063. Publishes *World* magazine to provide current news and practical commentary on issues.

Good News Mission, 1036 S. Highland Street, Arlington, VA 22204 703-979-2200. Largest supplier of civil jail and prison chaplains in the U.S. Ministers to prisoners, ex-offenders, correctional staff, and their families.

Goodwill Home & Missions, Inc., P.O. Box 7026, Newark, NJ 07102 201-621-9560. Exists to minister to the spiritual and material needs of the poor and disadvantaged; reestablish clients in society, encourage church membership for long-term nurturing, support, and fellowship.

Good Samaritan Mission Services, Inc., 8323 Sand Lake Rd., Orlando, FL 32819-5099 407-896-3900. Distributes Scripture through Bible text greeting cards. Chapel ministry and mission outreach program.

ECFA MEMBERS cont.

Gordon College, 255 Grapevine Rd., Wenham, MA 01984 508-927-2300. College education in the liberal arts and sciences; Bible.

Gordon-Conwell Theological Seminary, 130 Essex Street, South Hamilton, MA 01982 508-468-7111. Graduate school offering: Doctor of Ministry, Master of Divinity, Master of Religious Education, and Master of Arts in Theological Studies.

Gospel Center, P.O. Box 816, Stockton, CA 95201 209-466-2138. Ministers basically to the poor, down trodden, and wayward. Christian education, Bible college, and parenting classes are a proven means in which responsibility and stability are obtained.

Gospel Films, Inc., P.O. Box 455, Muskegon, MI 49443 616-773-3361. Produces and/or distributes, without profit, religious and educational films.

Gospel for Asia, Inc., 1932 Walnut Plaza, Carrollton, TX 75006 214-416-0340. Educates Christians and enlists prayer and financial support for native missions.

Gospel Literature International, P.O. Box 488, Rosemead, CA 91770 818-288-2812. Provides copyrighted English Christian education curriculum materials and books for translation and adaptation into other languages. Provides support to Christian publishers in more than 60 nations.

Gospel Missionary Union, 10000 N. Oak, Kansas City, MO 64155 816-734-8500. An interdenominational foreign missions agency with ministries in 21 countries on four continents. Plants and develops churches. Emphases include ministry to North American Hispanics, Muslims in England, Chinese in Brazil, and East/Central Europeans.

Gospel Missions of India, P.O. Box 1043, Warren, MI 48090 313-577-8298. Assists the work of the gospel within the nation of India.

Gospel Volunteers, Inc., Camp-of-the-Woods, Speculator, NY 12164 518-548-4311. Operates Camp-of-the-Woods, Woodlands Conference Center, Tapawingo Island Camp for girls.

Gospel-Rescue Mission, P.O. Box 1371, Grants Pass, OR 97526 503-479-8869. Ministers to men, women, and children, helping them to help themselves.

Grace College of the Bible, Inc., 1515 S. 10th Street, Omaha, NE 68108 402-449-2800. Curriculum consists of biblical/theological studies, as well as co-curricular experiences; provides education for nonvocational Christian ministries.

Grace Community Church, 13248 Roscoe Blvd., Sun Valley, CA 91352 818-782-5920. Independent, evangelical, Protestant church.

Grace Community Church of the Valley, P.O. Box 26967, Tempe, AZ 85285-6967 602-894-2201. Membership: 3,600; average Sunday school attendance of 3,200. Operates a school of 650 students.

Grace Schools, Inc., 200 Seminary Drive, Winona Lake, IN 46590 219-372-5100. Grace College and Grace Theological Seminary is affiliated with the fellowship of Grace Brethren churches.

The Greater Baltimore Crisis Pregnancy Center, 12 E. 21st St., Baltimore, MD 21218 301-625-0102. Provides emotional support, practical assistance to women with crisis pregnancies.

Greater Europe Mission, P.O. Box 668, Wheaton, IL 60189 708-462-8050. Ministers to the people of greater Europe.

Greater Minneapolis Association of Evangelicals, 3361 Republic Ave., Minneapolis, MN 55426 612-920-8147. Social concerns outreach extension of over 150 member churches and Christian organizations in the Minneapolis area.

H.O.P.E. Bible Mission, Inc., P.O. Box 161, Morristown, NJ 07963-0161 201-543-4492. Works in New York City from a center called the Voyager. Summer camp in Brookside, NJ.

Haluwasa, Inc., 377 Erhke Rd., Hammonton, NJ 08037 609-561-3081. Bible camp and church activity center.

Harvest Evangelism, Inc., P.O. Box 20310, San Jose, CA 95160-0310 408-927-9052. Motivates, trains, and mobilizes national leaders in evangelism and church planting.

Harvesting In Spanish (HIS), 245 S. Benton Street, Suite 100, Lakewood, CO 80226 303-232-3030. Distributes Spanish Bibles and Christian literature. Child care. Ministers to Indians as well as prostitutes and derelicts.

Hasten International, Inc., 1611 W. First Street, Winston-Salem, NC 27104-4320 919-721-1075. Provides physical relief whenever possible. Trains the national to help his own people.

Haven of Rest Ministries, 2410 Hyperion Ave., Los Angeles, CA 90027 213-664-2103. Daily half-hour radio program on more than

350 radio stations. Publishes *Anchor* and *The Log.*

Haven of Rest Ministries, Inc., P.O. Box 1758, Akron, OH 44309-1758 216-535-1563. Provides emergency and residential care to disadvantaged people.

Help for Christian Nationals, Inc., P.O. Box 381006, Duncanville, TX 75138 214-780-5909. Serves Christian national workers throughout the world.

High Adventure Ministries Inc., 990 Enchanted Way, Suite 101, Simi Valley, CA 93065 805-520-9460. International radio broadcasting. Owns and operates facilities in the Middle East and North America.

Highland Christian Mission Foundation, 900 S. Washington St., Suite 202, Falls Church, VA 22046 703-536-5103. Provides Bible instruction, general academic education, and vocational training to the people of the Highlands area of Papua New Guinea. Operates high school and five elementary schools.

His Branches, Inc., 344 Arnett Blvd., Rochester, NY 14619 716-235-9000. Coordinates and facilitates the work of groups serving the inner-city areas of Rochester.

His Mansion Ministries, P.O. Box 40, Hillsboro, NH 03244 603-464-5555 and **His Mansion Midwest,** P.O. Box 186, Prospect Hts., IL 60070 708-870-1576. Residential care facilities for emotionally and behaviorally hurting young people; special program for pregnant women.

Hobe Sound Bible College, Inc., P.O. Box 1065, Hobe Sound, FL 33475 407-546-5534. Four-year Bible college providing degrees in ministry, missions, music, and education.

Holt International Children's Services, Inc., P.O. Box 2880, Eugene, OR 97402 503-687-2202. International adoption and child care agency serving homeless children in Asia and Latin America.

Holy Innocents Ministry, Inc., at Dayspring, P.O. Box 399, Chelsea, AL 35043 205-678-8331. An ecumenical Christian ministry to abused/multiple-needs children, ages 6-14. Where possible, ministers to the whole family unit in hopes for eventual reunification.

Home Sweet Home Mission, Inc., 300 Mission Drive, Bloomington, IL 61701 309-828-7356. Provides food, clothing, shelter, counseling, spiritual nurture to people in need in McLean and contiguous counties of Illinois.

Honey Creek Christian Homes, P.O. Box 208, Lowell, MI 49331-9241 616-897-8461. Child care and family service organizations; works with pregnant teens and multihandicapped young adults.

Hope for the Hungry, P.O. Box 786, Belton, TX 76513 817-939-0124. Shares the Bread of Life with a starving world.

Hospitality House, Inc., 1220 Logan Ave., N., Minneapolis, MN 55411 612-522-4485. Seeks to repair the family unit through a network of referrals, counseling, and relationship building.

Houghton College, P.O. Box 128, Houghton, NY 14744 716-567-9200. Liberal arts institution with a rural main campus and a suburban campus near Buffalo, NY. Owned and operated by the Wesleyan church.

House of Ichthus, Turning Point, P.O. Box 10357, Pompano Beach, FL 33061 305-781-1400. Rehabilitation center for men 18 years or older.

House of New Beginnings, 13 Arch St., High Bridge, NJ 08853 201-638-5052. A ministry to unwed, pregnant girls. Each girl receives biblical counseling to overcome problem areas and plan for the future.

House of Samuel, Inc., 2430 N. Sycamore Blvd., Tucson, AZ 85712 602-325-2662. Foster placement and adoption agency throughout Arizona. Also provides services for children in Central and South America.

Hume Lake Christian Camps, Inc., 256 N. Maple, Fresno, CA 93702 209-251-6043. Camping center divided into four major areas: Ponderosa Camp for high schoolers, Meadow Ranch Camp for junior highs, Wagon Train Camp for juniors, and the Lakeview adult program.

Huntington College, 2303 College Ave., Huntington, IN 46750 219-356-6000. Liberal arts college affiliated with the Church of the United Brethren in Christ.

In Touch Ministries, 777 West Peachtree Street, NE, Atlanta, GA 30308 404-347-8500. A television and radio broadcast ministry that presents the teaching ministry of Dr. Charles F. Stanley. Supported by a discipling follow-up program.

In Touch Mission International, Inc., P.O. Box 28240, Tempe, AZ 85281 602-968-4100. Ministry of evangelism and support to Christians living in Eastern Bloc and other countries.

ECFA MEMBERS cont.

India Gospel Outreach, 10970 Arrow Route, Suite 204, Rancho Cucamonga, CA 91730 714-948-2404. Plans to plant dynamic churches in each of India's castes and tribes by the year 2000.

India National Inland Mission, P.O. Box 652, Verdugo City, CA 91046-0652 818-241-4010. Headquartered in New Delhi, India, with outreach concentrated in the northern states of India. Includes Grace Bible College, children's home for orphans, and evangelistic services.

India Rural Evangelical Fellowship, Inc., 8915A Robin Drive, Des Plaines, IL 60016 708-297-6414. An independent evangelistic ministry in south India with national evangelists, orphanage, school, and medical work.

Indiana Wesleyan University, 4201 S. Washington Street, Marion, IN 46953 317-674-6901. Liberal arts coeducational college related to the Wesleyan church.

Inner City Impact, 2704 W. North Ave., Chicago, IL 60647 312-384-4200. Works with young people in multiethnic, inner- city communities.

Inner-City Ministries, P.O. Box 6265, Chattanooga, TN 37401 615-756-4825. Helps meet the spiritual, physical, and social needs of the poor of Chattanooga.

Insight for Living, 1065 Pacific Center Dr., Suite 400, Anaheim, CA 92806-2126 714-575-5000. Daily "Insight for Living" broadcast heard on five continents; cassette tapes, Bible study guides, seminars.

Institute for Advanced Christian Studies, P.O. Box 241, Wheaton, IL 60189 708-665-3417. Fosters the development and articulation of Christian perspectives through conferences, research, and writing by evangelical scholars. Provides grants for scholars with an earned doctorate in the forefront of their field of study.

Institute for Creation Research, P.O. Box 2667, El Cajon, CA 92021 619-448-0900. Research, education, and speaking in the areas of biblical and scientific creationism.

Institute in Basic Life Principles, Inc., Box One, Oak Brook, IL 60522-3001 708-323-9800. Seminars to define biblical principles and train others to implement these principles.

Inter Serv, USA, P.O. Box 418, Upper Darby, PA 19082 215-352-0581. Ministers in South Asia and the Middle East. Provides medical, educa-

tional, professional, and technical personnel.

Inter-Varsity Christian Fellowship, P.O. Box 7895, Madison, WI 53719 608-274-9001. Establishes and assists Christian groups on college and university campuses, nursing schools, and seminaries.

Intercessors for America, P.O. Box 2639, Reston, VA 22090 703-471-0913. Encourages effective prayer and fasting for the church, our nation, and their leaders. Prayer helps include a monthly *First Friday* newsletter, which focuses prayer on national issues, and *Church Pray,* a monthly Sunday bulletin insert.

INTERDEV, P.O. Box 30945, Seattle, WA 98103 206-789-8330. Identifies major language groups where there is little or no church. Brings resource agencies together for development of long-term strategy evangelism and development of the church.

Interest Ministries, 218 W. Willow, Wheaton, IL 60187 708-653-6573. Serves approximately 1,200 congregations with a Christian Brethren identity.

International Aid, Inc., 17011 W. Hickory, Spring Lake, MI 49456 616-846-7490. Relief and mission service organization. Provides health and medical supplies, home care products. Receives donations of hospital equipment, drugs, and medical supplies.

International Bible Society, 1820 Jet Stream Dr., Colorado Springs, CO 80921-3696 719-488-9200. Translates, publishes, and distributes God's Word. Sponsor of New International Version of the Bible. Outreach includes below-cost Scripture sales and worldwide granting of Scripture.

International Chaplain's Ministry, P.O. Box 476, Edmonds, WA 98020 206-774-9544. Provides a holistic Christian ministry to officers, personnel, and families of emergency service organizations and to victims and families these organizations serve during moments of crisis.

International Child Care (U.S.A.), Inc., P.O. Box 2645, Toledo, OH 43606 419-472-7470. Program objective is to enable Haitian health service personnel to control tuberculosis in Haiti.

International Christian Media Commission, P.O. Box 70632, Seattle, WA 98107 206-781-0461. Facilitates ongoing flow of ideas, information, news, and continued dialogue among Christian media people and church leaders.

International Christian Outreach and Relief Group, 5685 Mutiny Bay Blvd., Freeland, WA 98249 206-321-1989. Helps Filopino people meet their spiritual, physical, material and emotional needs. Focuses on children.

International Friendship Ministries, Inc., P.O. Box 12504, Columbia, SC 29211 803-799-3452. Shares the gospel of Jesus Christ with international students studying in U.S. colleges and universities through friendship and hospitality.

International Institute for Christian Studies, P.O. Box 13157, Overland Park, KS 66212 913-339-6530. Assists people of the Third World as they lead their countries in education, economic, political, and spiritual development. Assists Third World universities in establishing departments of Christian studies.

International Leadership Group, 11590 W. Bernardo Court, Suite 230, San Diego, CA 92127 619-487-2766. Exists to help marketplace leaders maximize their strategic impact for Christ. Provides networking/connecting individuals, projects, and resources.

International Lifeline, Inc., P.O. Box 32714, Oklahoma City, OK 73123 405-728-2828. Provides medical assistance, volunteer personnel, food, and education to underdeveloped countries.

International Ministries to Israel, 3323 N. Ridge Ave., Arlington Heights, IL 60004 708-394-4405. Ministers the gospel to Jewish people.

International Missions, Inc., P.O. Box 14866, Reading, PA 19612-4866 215-375-0300. Establishes local, indigenous churches among Chinese, Hindus, Muslims, and Oriental people.

International Needs, Inc., P.O. Box 889, Scranton, PA 18501 717-346-0455. Helps nationals serve God by building prayer partnership teams, leadership training, short-term mission teams, and financial assistance.

International Services of Hope, Inc., 905 Farnsworth Rd., Toledo, OH 43566 419-878-8546. Gathers medical equipment and supplies, food, clothing, books, furnishings, generators, vehicles, building components of use to the poor or institutions anywhere in the world.

International Society of Christian Endeavor, P.O. Box 1110, Columbus, OH 43216 614-258-8545. Promotes Christianity among young people.

International Students Incorporated, P.O. Box C, Colorado Springs, CO 80901 719-576-2700. A cross-cultural outreach program to befriend, evangelize, and disciple international students.

International Teams, P.O. Box 203, Prospect Heights, IL 60070 708-870-3800. Trains and sends summer, two-year, and career missionaries to Europe and Asia for evangelism, discipling, and church planting. Promotes community development among the urban poor, assists refugees from Eastern Europe.

International Union of Gospel Missions, 1045 Swift, N. Kansas City, MO 64116-4127 816-436-6334. An association of rescue ministries. Provides services to members; promotes and establishes new rescue ministries.

Iranian Christians International, Inc., P.O. Box 25607, Colorado Springs, CO 80936 719-596-0010. Reaches and disciples Iranians for Jesus Christ. Trains Iranian believers to return to Iran as church leaders and as cross-cultural missionaries to other unreached peoples.

Isaiah 61 Prison and Mercy Ministries, 164 Chelsea Ave., North Babylon, NY 11704 516-661-6398. Seeks to build self-esteem through discipleship and evangelism in New York City, Long Island, NY, and upstate prisons and hospitals.

Issachar, P.O. Box 6788, Lynwood, WA 98036 206-744-0400. Provides consulting, planning, educational materials, and services to local churches, denominations, parachurch groups, and lay leaders who desire to take advantage of the resources God has given them for world evangelization. Particular attention is paid to nations where innovative and nontraditional methods are essential for success.

Italy for Christ, P.O. Box 941653, Atlanta, GA 30341 404-263-9003. Assists the evangelical churches of Italy in evangelistic outreach to the 99 percent of the people of Italy who do not have a personal relationship with Jesus Christ.

Iwa, Inc., 128 East Palm Ave., Suite 103, Monrovia, CA 91016-2851 818-358-8077. Works with Christian leaders and churches to develop needed resources among Japanese Americans and Asian Americans. Develops culturally

ECFA MEMBERS cont.

appropriate and biblically sound ministry practices effective with target audience.

J. Gordon Henry Ministries, 2114 Arrow Court, Murfreesboro, TN 37130 615-890-8384. Provides prayer seminars, church growth seminars, leadership seminars, and Christian tours to local churches and/or colleges, camps, and conferences.

JAARS, Inc. (Jungle Aviation and Radio Service), Box 248, Waxhaw, NC 28173 704-843-6250. Training and support center for Wycliffe Bible translators.

Jack Shaw Ministries, Inc., P.O. Box 3778, Johnstown, PA 15904 814-269-3377. Christian hospital in Kenya, East Africa.

Jews for Jesus, 60 Haight Street, San Francisco, CA 94102 415-864-2600. An outreach by Jewish Christian evangelists. Personal visitation, tract distribution, media ads in secular newspapers and magazines.

John Abraham Memorial Christian Relief Fund, P.O. Box 30007, Amarillo, TX 79120 806-383-7631. Funds and manages Christian children's homes in India, Honduras, and the Dominican Republic. Family feeding project in Honduras and the Dominican, medical clinic in India, schools for underprivileged children in Africa and the Dominican Republic.

John Brown University, 2000 W. University, Siloam Springs, AR 72761 501-524-3131. Bachelor degree programs including distinctive programs in broadcasting, journalism, business administration, education, and construction.

John Guest Evangelistic Team, 3366 Burton Street, SE, Grand Rapids, MI 49546 616-942-5600. Organizes citywide, evangelistic–renewal crusades; provides materials and training for pastors.

John M. Perkins Foundation, 1581 Navarro Ave., Pasadena, CA 91103 818-791-7439. Supports churches and other Christian organizations; grants aid to the needy; assists minorities in bettering their lives. Attempts to lessen racial tensions in a spirit of Christian harmony.

Joni and Friends, P.O. Box 3333, Agoura Hills, CA 91301 818-707-5664. Brings together the church and disabled people through evangelism, encouragement, inspiration, and practical services. Assists persons with disabilities toward independence and fulfillment.

Joy of Jesus, Inc., 12255 Camden, Detroit, MI 48213 313-839-4747. Summer camp with community follow-up provides Christian growth and fellowship opportunities to the total family on a year-round basis.

Joy Ranch, Inc., P.O. Box 727, Hillsville, VA 24343 703-236-5578. Residential facility providing care to dependent, neglected children. Operates Christian school.

Kansas City Youth for Christ, Inc., 4715 Rainbow Blvd., Shawnee Mission, KS 66205 913-262-1700. Teen evangelism and discipleship through weekly Saturday night rallies, campus ministries, and summer and winter teen ranch programs. Other ministries include: KYFC TV50, a Bible institute, crisis pregnancy center and *Conquest* monthly magazine.

Kenmore New Covenant Tabernacle, 1 World Ministry Center, Buffalo, NY 14223 716-877-9882. One of the fastest growing and most progressive churches in the northeastern United States. A Jewish-Christian fellowship with more than 50 departments of ministry.

Kenya Children's Fund, 6913 Gleason Rd., Edina, MN 55439 612-941-7209. Ministry to children living in the slums of Nairobi, Kenya. Program provides pre-primary schooling, a daily hot lunch program and basic health care.

Key Life Network, Inc., P.O. Box 499002, Key Biscayne, FL 33149 305-854-8444. Daily 15-minute radio broadcasts by the Rev. Stephen Brown. "Key Life Tapes" available free of charge.

Kids Alive International, 2507 Cumberland Drive, Valparaiso, IN 46383 219-464-9035. Dedicated to meeting the spiritual, physical, and emotional needs of children in Beirut, Lebanon, Ramallah (West Bank), Jordan, Hong Kong, and Taiwan.

The King's College, 150 Lodge Rd., Briarcliff Manor, NY 10598 914-941-7200. Christian liberal arts college. Bachelor of arts or bachelor of science degree in over 20 areas of concentration.

Knox Area Rescue Mission, Inc., P.O. Box 3352, Knoxville, TN 37927 615-673-6540. Provides food, clothing, and shelter for the homeless.

Lamb & Lion Ministries, P.O. Box K, McKinney, TX 75069 214-736-3567. Daily radio program, cassettes, books, seminars, and monthly prophetic newsletter.

Lamb's Players, Inc., P.O. Box 26, National City, CA 92050 619-474-3385. Presents the historic Christian worldview through a varied use of the dramatic arts. International touring company performs on campuses, in theaters, churches, prisons, and military installations.

The Langham Foundation, 2336 Lawndale Ave., Evanston, IL 60201 708-864-0490. Supports the worldwide ministry of John Stott—author and Rector Emeritus of All Souls Church, London—in evangelism, preaching, and seminary teaching. Provides scholarships to Third World students, helps laymen integrate biblical faith and contemporary issues. Supplies significant Christian books to Third World pastors, scholars, and students.

Latin America Mission, Inc., P.O. Box 52-7900, Miami, FL 33152-7900 305-884-8400. Works with and under the direction of Latin organizations to train and further the outreach of national churches and ministries. Emphasis on large cities in Latin America.

Lausanne Committee for World Evangelization—U.S., 5970 Fairview Rd., Suite 514, Charlotte, NC 28210 704-554-6803. Brings Christian leaders together to develop vision, leadership, and strategies for world evangelization.

Lay Renewal Ministries, Inc., 3101 Bartold, St. Louis, MO 63143 314-647-0717. Conducts renewal events, leadership development, and church consultation. Researches trends and resources.

Leadership Resources International, P.O. Box 413, New Lenox, IL 60451-0413 815-485-4900. Discipleship resource to build the local church through Bible study conferences and teaching materials. Primary focus is on North America, Latin America, and Asia.

Lebanon Rescue Mission, Inc., P.O. Box 5, Lebanon, PA 17042 717-273-2301. Gives board and lodging to transients; distributes clothing and food to the needy; temporary shelter to families in need.

Leighton Ford Ministries, 6230 Fairview Rd., #300, Charlotte, NC 28210 704-366-8020. A fellowship of associates committed to world evangelism.

LeTourneau Ministries International, P.O. Box 26200, Colorado Springs, CO 80936-6200 719-528-6000. Assists organizations and national churches with a unique strategy of concentrated evangelism and church planting techniques; assists with necessary resources to construct the kind of church facilities needed to carry on this kind of work.

LeTourneau University, P.O. Box 7001, Longview, TX 75607-7001 903-753-0231. Four-year programs in the liberal arts and sciences, engineering and technology, and business administration.

Liberty Christian College, P.O. Box 3138, Pensacola, FL 32506 904-453-3451. Offers associate, bachelor's, and master's degrees.

Liebenzell Mission of USA, Inc., P.O. Box 66, Schooley's Mountain, NJ 07870 908-852-3044. Camp and guest house for conferences and retreats. Recruits and sends missionaries to the Micronesian Islands, Japan, Africa, and New Guinea.

Life Action Ministries, 2000 Morris Drive, Niles, MI 49120 616-684-5905. Revival crusades, multimedia musical productions, high school assemblies, revival publications, camp program.

Life Challenge of Tennessee, Inc., P.O. Box 60362, Nashville, TN 37206 615-226-6857. Outreach and educational programs; counseling; residential training in Christian discipleship for young adults (17–36) with life-controlling problems (primarily chemical dependency).

LIFE Ministries, P.O. Box 200, San Dimas, CA 91773 714-599-8491. Missionary organization in Japan involved in church planting, national leadership training, and student evangelism through teaching conversational English. Career missionaries, short-termers, and summer workers.

Lifewater International, P.O. Box 3336, S. El Monte, CA 91733 818-443-1787. Consortium of water resource specialists. Combines training, experience, and faith in assisting relief/development organizations to plan, implement, and maintain water projects.

Light of Life Rescue Mission, Inc., P.O. Box 6823, Pittsburgh, PA 15212 412-321-4716. Rescue mission in inner-city Pittsburgh; gospel services, counseling, meals, lodging, and rehabilitation program.

Lighthouse Mission of Indianapolis, 520 E. Market, Indianapolis, IN 46204 317-636-0209. Assists and cares for needy persons. Assists in obtaining employment and rehabilitation.

ECFA MEMBERS cont.

Ligonier Ministries, Inc., P.O. Box 547500, Orlando, FL 32854 407-834-1633. Teaching fellowship of Dr. R. C. Sproul. Video and audio cassette tapes, curriculum, and regional conferences.

Lincoln Christian College and Seminary, 100 Campus View Dr., Lincoln, IL 62656 217-732-3168. Undergraduate and graduate educational ministry.

Little Galilee Christian Assembly, Inc., R.R. 2, Box 266, Clinton, IL 61727 217-935-3809. Conducts camps, conferences, and rallies.

Living Bibles International, P.O. Box 725, Wheaton, IL 60189 708-510-9500. Worldwide Scripture translation and distribution.

Lloyd Ogilvie Ministries, Inc., 6037 Hollywood Blvd., Hollywood, CA 90028 213-464-7690. "Let God Love You" television and radio ministry. The television program is a 30-minute format airing on Sundays. The radio program is a 25-minute daily broadcast. Programs are comprised of messages by Dr. Lloyd Ogilvie.

LOGOI, Inc., 13200 S.W. 128th St., Suite D-1, Miami, FL 33186 305-232-5880. Provides biblical, theological, and ministerial training to Spanish-speaking Christians. Target audiences are those already in service living in outlying areas with no access to theological training.

Long Beach Rescue Mission, P.O. Box 1969, Long Beach, CA 90801 213-591-1292. Provides gospel services, emergency and long-term shelter, meals, counseling, and rehabilitation to the needy.

Loop Crisis Pregnancy Center, 104 S. Michigan Ave., #832, Chicago, IL 60603 312-263-1576. Provides alternatives to abortion for women facing unwanted pregnancies.

Los Angeles Mission, P.O. Box 5749, Los Angeles, CA 90055 213-629-1227. Relief and rehabilitation agency that provides food, shelter, clothing, shaves and showers, counseling, and rehabilitation programs for destitute and homeless people.

Lost and Found, Inc., 9189 S. Turkey Creek Rd., Morrison, CO 80465 303-697-5049. Treats people caught in an addictive process. Offers primary and secondary residential care, outpatient counseling, wilderness experiences, DUI/DWAI classes, cult/occult interventions, community education, etc.

Love & Action, 3 Church Circle, Annapolis, MD 21401 301-268-3442. Ministers to individuals who are HIV positive or who have AIDS, their families, friends and churches.

Love Basket, Inc., 4472 Goldman Rd., Hillsboro, MO 63050 314-789-4100. An international adoption ministry placing destitute children from foreign countries with Christian families. Also has domestic adoptive placement program.

Loving Grace Ministries, Inc., P.O. Box 500, Lafayette, NJ 07848 201-729-6203. Live syndicated one-hour call-in radio program, "Let's Talk about Jesus," crusades, seminars, retreats, Holy Land pilgrimages, home-study Bible courses.

Luis Palau Evangelistic Association, P.O. Box 1173, Portland, OR 97207 503-643-0777. Seeks to stimulate, revive, and mobilize the church to effective evangelism.

The Luke Society, Inc., P.O. Box 349, Vicksburg, MS 39180 601-638-1629. Christian physicians and dentists helping the poor in the United States and Third-World countries through community health and the gospel.

Lumiere Medical Ministries, Inc., P.O. Box 3707, Gastonia, NC 28054-0020 704-868-3703. Medical services of the national church (MEBSH) in Haiti.

Lutheran Bible Institute in California, 641 S. Western Ave., Anaheim, CA 92804 714-827-1940. Two-year college of biblical studies, serves the Lutheran church as a movement which fosters renewal and promotes evangelism and missions.

Lutheran Bible Institute of Seattle, 4221 228th Ave., SE, Issaquah, WA 98027 206-392-0400. College-level school offering in-depth biblical and related courses preparing for lay ministries and church-related vocations.

Lutheran Bible Translators, P.O. Box 2050, Aurora, IL 60507 708-897-0660. Analyzes unwritten languages and translates the Bible into the vernacular.

Macedonian Ministries, Inc. P.O. Box 210304, Bedford, TX 76095 817-540-2770. Provides practical ministry training; primary focus overseas is in Third-World countries assisting native evangelists, pastors, and their congregations through intensive Bible training seminars. Committed to the local church at home as well.

Malcolm Smith Ministries, Inc., Box 29747,

San Antonio, TX 78229-0747 512-558-3838. Audio and video teaching tapes, books, a daily radio program "Covenant Love," bimonthly teaching journal *Living Word*, and seminars.

Manna International Relief and Development, P.O. Box 3507, Redwood City, CA 94064 415-365-3663. International relief and development organization. Short-term disaster relief and long-term projects designed to promote self-sufficiency and self-direction. Existing programs stress public health, agricultural development, water development.

MAP International, P.O. Box 50, Brunswick, GA 31521-0050 912-265-6010. Global health organization that provides donated medicines and supplies to Africa, Asia, and Latin America. Works in community health development, coordinating projects to improve water supplies, food production, and health education.

Market Street Mission, Inc., 9 Market Street, Morristown, NJ 07960 201-538-0431. Provides for the needs of homeless, indigent, troubled, and alcoholic and/or drug addicted people.

Marketplace Ministries, Inc., P.O. Box 27813, San Diego, CA 92198-1813 619-673-8544. Equips business people for a workplace ministry and spiritual leadership in the marketplace. CrossTalk groups cultivate biblical thinking; Marketplace workshops teach relational skills; Marketplace Roundtable develops spiritual leaders.

Mars Hill Broadcasting Co., Inc., 4044 Makyes Rd., Syracuse, NY 13215 315-469-5051. Operates radio stations WMHR-FM 102.9 Syracuse, NY, and WMHN-FM 89.3 Webster, N.Y. Delivers service to 13 translator stations and WJSL-FM, Houghton College, Houghton, N.Y.

The Master's College and Seminary, P.O. Box 878, Newhall, CA 91322 805-259-3540. Offers 32 fields of study in 17 departments and a one-year diploma in Bible. The seminary offers a master of divinity degree.

The Master's Communication, P.O. Box 4000, Panorama City, CA 91412 805-295-5777. Communication branch of John MacArthur's ministry which includes "Grace to You" daily radio program, tapes, and books.

Mastermedia International, Inc., 409 E. Palm Ave., Suite E, Redlands, Ca 92373-6135 714-335-7353. Evangelism and discipleship to leaders in the film and television industries by one-on-one appointments and small-group meetings and retreats. Seeks to create an awareness of the impact of media on society through publications, radio, TV, and speaking events.

Match-Two (M-2) Prisoner Outreach, P.O. Box 447, San Quentin, CA 94964 415-457-8701. Prison visitation ministry.

Media Associates International, Inc., P.O. Box 218, Bloomingdale, IL 60108 708-893-1141. Assists Third-World Christian nationals in becoming effective creators, producers, distributors, and users of the media.

Medical Teams International, Inc., P.O. Box 231177, Portland, OR 97223 503-624-0229. Relief and development agency.

Mel Trotter Ministries, 225 Commerce, SW, Grand Rapids, MI 49503 616-454-8249. Rehabilitation program for men and women. Youth camp for children.

Al Menconi Ministries, P.O. Box 5008, San Marcos, CA 92069-1050 619-591-4696. Challenges Christians to evaluate the effect of entertainment on their spiritual lives.

The Mendenhall Ministries, P.O. Box 368, Mendenhall, MS 39114 601-847-3421. Ministers to the poor, rural areas of Mississippi; develops models that can be replicated in other communities and countries.

Mennonite Brethren Homes, 856 S. Reed, Reedley, CA 93654 209-638-3615. Operates a nonprofit retirement community.

Mercy Corps International, 3030 S.W. First Ave., Portland, OR 97201 503-242-1032. Emergency relief, self-help development projects, and development education.

Mercy Medical Airlift, P.O. Box 1940, Manassas, VA 22110 703-361-1191. Provides medical air transportation for patients who cannot afford commercial air ambulance and offers cost-effective air transportation for staff and volunteers of churches and nonprofit Christian organizations.

Messiah Village, P.O. Box 2015, Mechanicsburg, PA 17055-2015 717-697-4666. Brethren in Christ retirement village. Independent living, health care, and related services.

The Messianic Vision, 9057 B Gaither Rd., Gaithersburg, MD 20877 301-963-4400. Dedicated to reaching Jewish people

ECFA MEMBERS cont.

through radio, seminars, and evangelistic meetings.

Mexican Medical Inc., 13910 Lyons Valley Rd., #C, Jamul, CA 91935 619-669-1409. Medical outreach, cross-cultural ministries, evangelism, and relief assistance.

Miami Rescue Mission, Inc., P.O. Box 420-620, Miami, FL 33127 305-571-2273. Ministry to the homeless. Offers a six-month Christian Regeneration Program for those who choose a new way of life.

Miami Valley Christian Television, Inc., P.O. Box 26, Dayton, OH 45401 513-323-0026. Produces and distributes programs, materials, and helps through its television stations to encourage Christian faith; coordinates projects to assist the needy.

Michigan Christian Home Association, 1845 Boston Street, SE, Grand Rapids, MI 49506 616-245-9179. An approved social agency of the GARBC. Offers three types of housing and health services.

Mid-America Reformed Seminary, Box 163, R.R. 2, Orange City, IA 51041 712-737-3446. An academic institution to prepare men for the ministry.

Mid-America Teen Challenge Training Center, Inc., P.O. Box 1089, Cape Girardeau, MO 63701 314-334-3643. Residential care program for men with life-controlling problems.

Middle East Media, P.O. Box 359, Lynnwood, WA 98046 206-778-0752. Uses the mass media to communicate the gospel to Muslims of the Middle East, North Africa, and elsewhere.

Midwest Challenge, Inc., P.O. Box 7364, Minneapolis, MN 55407 612-825-6871. Counsels people to apply biblical principles to overcome life-dominating problems, particularly substance abuse and prostitution.

Ministries in Action, P.O. Box 140325, Miami, FL 33114 305-642-3113. Works with churches throughout the Caribbean. Utilizes church growth strategies; trains national leaders (Iona Center for Theological Study); serves as a facilitating agency that enables churches in the U.S., Canada, and Caribbean countries to become directly involved in a Caribbean missions ministry.

Ministry to Men Foundation, Inc., 860 Ridgelake Blvd., Suite 384, Memphis, TN. 38120 901-761-7865. Encourages men to a Christian life-style in the marketplace. Programs include "Maximum Man" confer-

ences, "Executive Outreach" dinners, "Applying God's Principles" seminars, Bible studies, and prayer breakfasts.

Mission Aviation Fellowship, P.O. Box 3202, Redlands, CA 92373-0998 714-794-1151. Aviation and related ministries.

Mission Safety International, Inc., P.O. Box 1632, Elizabethton, TN 37644 615-543-3534. Assists missionary/Christian oriented aviation organizations in aviation safety.

The Mission Society for United Methodists, Inc., P.O. Box 1103, Decatur, GA 30331 404-378-8746. Voluntary association of United Methodists and other Wesleyan related groups, congregations, pastors, and laypersons seeking to expand missionary outreach.

Mission to the World, P.O. Box 29765, Atlanta, GA 30359-0765 404-320-3373. Affiliated with The Presbyterian Church in America. Places and supervises personnel on the foreign mission field.

Mission to Unreached Peoples, 19309 W. Valley Hwy., Suite R102, Kent, WA 98032 206-251-9601. Plants churches among unreached people groups. Recruits and sends teams of committed Christian lay people, including tentmakers.

Missionary Athletes International, Inc., P.O. Box 945, La Habra, CA 90633 213-690-4934. Soccer sports evangelism ministry: soccer camps, tours, and local teams.

Missionary Internship, Inc., P.O. Box 457, Farmington, MI 48332 313-474-9110. Cross-cultural orientation and training organization serving IFMA & EFMA mission agencies.

Missionary World Service and Evangelism, P.O. Box 123, Wilmore, KY 40390 606-858-3171. Assists mission organizations with volunteer work and witness crusades; also local congregations in evangelism, missions, and discipleship with crusades, missionary conferences, seminars, and discipleship training.

Missions Unlimited, P.O. Box 929, Jasper, AL 35501 205-221-5515. Presents underdeveloped nations with opportunities to improve life standards. Brings Third-World crafts to the American consumer.

Monroeville Crisis Pregnancy Center, P.O. Box 633, Monroeville, PA 15146 412-373-2775. Provides counseling in crisis pregnancy situations and postabortion crises.

Montgomery Christian Educational Radio, Inc., P.O. Box 17140, Montgomery, AL 36117 205-271-8900. Listener-supported FM station, affiliated with the Moody Broadcasting Network of Chicago.

The Montrose Broadcasting Corporation, P.O. Box 248, Montrose, PA 18801 717-278-2811. Owns and operates noncommercial radio stations WPEL-AM-FM in Montrose and WPGM-AM-FM in Danville, Pa.

The Moody Bible Institute of Chicago, 820 N. LaSalle Street, Chicago, IL 60610 312-329-4123. Bible institute; correspondence school; missionary aviation; radio stations; publication and distribution of books; films.

Mount Hermon Association, Inc., P.O. Box 413, Mount Hermon, CA 95041 408-335-4466. Christian camp and conference programming.

Mount Vernon Christian Academy, 4449 Northside Drive, NW, Atlanta, GA 30327 404-256-4057. Christian college preparatory education.

Multimedia Ministries International, 18221 Torrence Ave., Lansing, IL 60438 708-895-7000. Assists Christian organizations in promoting their cause through mass media.

Multnomah School of the Bible, 8435 NE Glisan, Portland, OR 97220 503-255-0332. Education and literature (Multnomah Press and the Christian Supply Center stores).

Narramore Christian Foundation, P.O. Box 5000, Rosemead, CA 91770-0950 818-288-7000. Counseling ministry, monthly magazine, radio and TV programs, films, and personal enrichment groups.

Nashville Union Mission, Inc., P.O. Box 22157, Nashville, TN 37202 615-255-2475. Reaches out to those who need to rebuild their lives.

National Assoc. of Christian Physical Therapists, P.O. Box 100, Port Gibson, NY 14537-0100 315-331-4318. Christian physical therapy association. Sending agent for mission organizations who need a Christian physical therapist.

National Association of Evangelicals, 450 Gundersen Drive, Carol Stream, IL 60188 708-665-0500. Provides a united voice, fellowship, and services through national programs and the work of its commissions and affiliates.

National Christian Fellowship, P.O. Box 516, Carlsbad, CA 92008 619-431-9890.

"Friendship evangelism" ministry to federal, state, and local public officials across America; Bible/prayer fellowship groups, governors' and mayors' prayer breakfasts. CERT International, a ministry of NCF, provides short-term lay missionary opportunities through medical assistance and humanitarian programs in response to emergency needs.

National Coalition Against Pornography, 800 Compton Rd., #9224, Cincinnati, OH 45231 513-521-6227. Denominations and organizations united to eliminate illegal, dangerous, hard-core pornography from our society.

The National Network of Youth Ministries, 17150 Via del Campo, #102, San Diego, CA 92127 619-451-1111. Teaches and disciples high school students.

National Religious Broadcasters, Inc., 1777 Ashton Avenue, Manassos, VA 22110. An association of organizations engaged in religious programming for radio and television and the operation of religious radio and TV.

Navajo Gospel Mission, Inc., P.O. Box 3717, Flagstaff, AZ 86003 602-526-0875. Evangelization of North American Indian tribes.

Navajo Missions, Inc., P.O. Box 1230, Farmington, NM 87401 505-325-0255. Interdenominational mission outreach. Care of dependent Navajo children, Christian radio station, evangelism, printshop, and bookstore.

The Navigators, P.O. Box 6000, Colorado Springs, CO 80934 719-598-1212. Teaches people to take the gospel to non-Christians and to disciple new believers in the faith.

Need, Inc., P.O. Box 54541, Phoenix, AZ 85078 602-992-1321. International Christian agency providing assistance to the displaced, disenfranchised, and needy people of the world.

Neues Leben International, 14819 N. Cave Creek Rd., Phoenix, AZ 85032 602-482-2366. Biblical counseling and training ministry.

The New Directions Ministries, Inc., P.O. Box 2347, Burlington, NC 27215 919-227-1273. Interracial ministry committed to evangelism and discipleship. Particular orientation toward reconciliation in USA and cross-cultural ministry abroad. Catalyst between churches in America and the Third World.

New Horizons Youth Ministries, Inc., Roads

ECFA MEMBERS cont.

100 S. at 350 E., Marion, IN 46953 317-668-4009. Christian program for youth who are underachieving.

New Life Ranch, Inc., Rt. 1, Box 274, Colcord, OK 74338 918-422-5506. Summer camps and short retreats during the school year.

New Life, Inc., 10901 Lake Ridge Rd., Knoxville, TN 37922 615-675-4420. Adult friendship evangelism, discipling, leadership training.

New Mexico Boys Ranch, Inc., 203 Rio Communities Blvd., Belen, NM 87002 505-864-2177. New Mexico Boys Ranch, New Mexico Girls Ranch, and Hart Youth Ranch are residential child-care centers for children from troubled backgrounds. Families for Children is an adoption and foster care agency.

New Moms, Inc., 3600 W. Fullerton, Chicago, IL 60647 312-252-3253. Ministers to single, teen mothers. Provides support through home visits, Bible studies, drop-ins, emergency services, student job training program, and the Cooperative Living program.

Niños de Mexico, P.O. Box 309, Union, MO 63084 314-583-2000. Missionary project of the Christian churches and Churches of Christ. Involved in the evangelism of Mexico and care of homeless children.

North Central Bible College, 910 Elliot Ave., S., Minneapolis, MN 55404 612-332-3491. Offers academic programs in 16 major fields. Owned and operated by 10 Assemblies of God church districts: IA, MN, SD, IL, WI/N. IN, MI, NE, N.MO and ND.

Northern Christian Radio, Inc., P.O. Box 695, Gaylord, MI 49735 517-732-6274. Radio ministry operating two noncommercial educational FM radio stations in northern Michigan; an affiliate of the Moody Broadcasting Network.

Northern Pines of Minnesota, Inc., 6701 Penn Ave., S., Minneapolis, MN 55423 612-861-5100. Operates week-long family conferences at Lake Geneva, WI.

Northwest Conservative Baptist Association, Inc., P.O. Box 30029, Portland, OR 97230-0029 503-669-1515. Missions agency operating in Idaho, Oregon and Washington to establish new churches and provide services for existing churches.

Northwestern College, 3003 N. Snelling Ave., St. Paul, MN 55113 612-631-5100. Educational programs from one-year certificates to bachelor degree programs. Noncommercial, Christian satellite network of radio stations. Seminars and conferences.

O.C. International, P.O. Box 36900, Colorado Springs, CO 80936-6900 719-592-9292. Overseas Crusades equips national Christians to reach their nation for Christ.

Oak Hills Fellowship, 1600 Oak Hills Rd., SW, Bemidji, MN 56601 218-751-8670. Home mission organization with several divisions: Oak Hills Bible College, International Messengers, Camp Oak Hills, Oak Hills Bible Conference, and Oak Hills Church Ministries.

Officers' Christian Fellowship of the U.S.A., P.O. Box 1177, Englewood, CO 80150-1177 303-761-1984. Ministry to cadets and midshipmen at service academies and ROTC schools and to officers located at bases throughout the world; Bible studies, newsletters, *Command* magazine, and retreats.

Okinawa Christian School, P.O. Box 90031, Gainesville, FL 32607 904-371-6012. Ministers to Asian, Asian-American, American missionary dependents and American military dependents from its mission school facility in Okinawa, Japan.

Olive Branch Mission, 1047 W. Madison St., Chicago, IL 60607 312-243-3373. Provides a soup kitchen, day shelter, and emergency housing. The Wesleyan Urban Coalition provides learning and service experiences for college and seminary students.

Olive Crest Treatment Centers, Inc., 1300 N. Kellogg Drive, #D, Anaheim, CA 92807 714-777-4999. Provides an alternative to institutional care of abused/neglected/abandoned children: a small surrogate family setting that is structured, safe, and nurturing. Also offers a foster family program for children.

OMS International, Inc., P.O. Box A, Greenwood, IN 46142 317-881-6751. Establishes and maintains schools for the training of missionaries, pastors, evangelists, and their children. Publications, radio, social welfare, and relief work.

Open Doors with Brother Andrew, Inc., P.O. Box 27001, Santa Ana, CA 92799 714-531-6000. Delivery of Bibles and other aids to the church in the restricted countries of the world. Mobilizes and trains the church in the free world to identify with and become involved in assisting the suffering church.

Operation Love, P.O. Box 4040, Woodbridge,

VA 22191 703-690-0040. Cares for the homeless and the poor. Distributes food that would otherwise go to waste.

Operation Mobilization, P.O. Box 444, Tyrone, GA 30290-0444 404-631-0432. Biblical teaching and life-style, cross-cultural discipleship training teams and long-term workers. Widely known for the international outreach of the ships *Doulos* and *Logos*.

The Orange County Rescue Mission, P.O. Box 4007, Santa Ana, CA 92702 714-835-0499. Provides temporary shelter, live-in rehabilitation program, job search assistance.

Outreach, Incorporated, P.O. Box 1000, Grand Rapids, MI 49501 616-363-7817. Evangelism and Christian education through radio, television, and distribution of biblical literature; scholarships for Christian leaders within their own countries; theological training. .

Overseas Christian Servicemen's Centers, P.O. Box 1268, Englewood, CO 80150 303-762-1400. Ministry to the U.S. military community. A special division, Malachi Ministries, ministers to youth.

Overseas Council, Theological Education & Missions, P.O. Box 751, Greenwood, IN 46142 317-882-4174. Assists evangelical theological institutions in developing churches in the Third World.

Ozark Christian College, 1111 N. Main, Joplin, MO 64801 417-624-2518. Coeducational Christian college.

Ozark Conference Center, 1300 W. Park Drive, #5A, Little Rock, AR 72204 501-666-3266. Bible conferences for adults, pastors, lay leaders, and families.

P.R.O. Missions, Inc., P.O. Box 11448, Memphis, TN 38111 901-458-0325. Supports missionary activities, projects, and establishments.

Pacific Coast Study Center, P.O. Box 4374, San Clemente, CA 92672 714-498-4418. Offers specialized training required to identify and deal with the complexities of teenagers' problems.

Pacific Island Ministries, 701 Welch Rd., A-2215, Palo Alto, CA 94304 415-328-8203. Development of indigenous Christian leadership for church growth in the Pacific Ocean area, particularly Papua New Guinea. Pioneers in remote areas.

Pacific Missionary Aviation, P.O. Box 3209,

Agana, GU 96910 671-646-6464. Evangelism, discipleship, leadership, training, church planting, and support.

Paraclete Social Outreach, Inc., 302 1/2 Conant St., Suite A, Maumee, OH 43537 419-893-4187. Networks Christian homes for foster care to troubled, dependent, and neglected youth. Helps older teens to become independent and coordinates counseling services to troubled families and youth.

Partners in Christ International, P.O. Box 1715, Chandler, AZ 85244-1715 602-821-9321. Trains indigenous pastors and leaders; operates a children's home in Mexico. Provides opportunities for U.S. churches to participate in cross-cultural ministry/ projects in Mexico.

Partners International, P.O. Box 15025, San Jose, CA 95112 408-453-3800. Works in partnership with nationals in over 40 countries. All ministries are under national boards that set their goals, design their policies, and implement their programs.

Pennsylvania State Sunday School Association, 5915 Fox St., Harrisburg, PA 17112 717-652-1930. Serves the needs of local Sunday schools throughout Pennsylvania through teacher training schools, service awards and recognitions, enlargement campaigns, information and publications, media services, and a state Sunday school convention.

People of Destiny International, 7881-B Beechcraft Ave., Gaithersburg, MD 20879 301-926-2200. Church planting, leadership development, conferences.

Persecuted Church Commission, Inc., P.O. Box 1340, Kingston, NY 12401 914-382-1275. Ministers to Christians of all denominations in the Commonwealth of Independent States (formerly the USSR) through prayer and letters of encouragement.

Pine Cove, Inc., P.O. Box 9055, Tyler, TX 75711 214-561-0231. Interdenominational camp and conference center.

Pioneer Bible Translators, P.O. Box 381030, Duncanville, TX 75138-1030 214-296-4843. Translates God's Word into languages in which there is no written language or Bible. Team includes not only translators and literacy specialists but also teachers, evangelists, buyer-shippers, builders, mechanics, accountants, and computer specialists.

Pioneer Clubs, P.O. Box 788, Wheaton, IL

ECFA MEMBERS cont.

60189 708-293-1600. Helps children and youth put Christ in every phase of life, to nurture healthy relationships, and to develop a positive self-image. Assists adults in understanding children and their development.

Pioneers, P.O. Box 527, Sterling, VA 22170 703-478-0004. Sends missionaries to the five blocks of unreached people groups in the world: Chinese, Hindu, Buddhist, Muslim, tribal. Tentmaking missionaries as well as national workers are used to penetrate "closed" restricted-access countries.

The Pocket Testament League, P.O. Box 800, Lititz, PA 17543-7026 717-626-1919. Combines Scripture distribution with worldwide evangelism. Encourages daily reading of the Bible by Christians; correspondence courses designed to lead people to Christ.

Portland Rescue Mission Ministries, P.O. Box 3713, Portland, OR 97208-3713 503-227-0421. Provides food, lodging, clothing, and a drug and alcohol recovery program; family and individual counseling.

Prakash Association, U.S.A., 99 Airport Blvd., Freedom, CA 95019 408-722-2244. Develops self-supporting, educational institutes and churches in India. Trains nationals to become Christian businessmen and spiritual leaders in their local areas.

Precept Ministries of Reach Out, Inc., P.O. Box 182218, Chattanooga, TN 37422 615-892-6814. Bible study and conference center.

Presbyterians for Renewal, 8134 New LaGrange Rd., Louisville, KY 40222 505-425-4630. Youth and adult conferences, officer training, and lay renewal ministry to encourage renewal in the Presbyterian Church (USA).

Priority Living, Inc., 17240 E. 17th St., Suite 200, Tustin, CA 92680 714-544-8903. Evangelical ministry serving business and professional men and women. Directs the unchurched to local, Bible-teaching churches. Emphasizes biblical principles for practical living.

Prison Fellowship Ministries, P.O. Box 17500, Washington, DC 20041 703-478-0100. Assists prisoners, ex-prisoners, and their families through outreach programs. Involved in national criminal justice reform. Seeks to mobilize churches and volunteers for involvement in prison ministry.

Probe Ministries International, 1900 Firman Drive, #100, Richardson, TX 75081 214-480-0240. Bible study and conference center.

Project Partner with Christ, Inc., P.O. Box 1054, Middletown, OH 45042 513-425-0938. Supports the national church in the Third World to evangelize, disciple, and plant churches.

Racerunners, Inc., P.O. Box 59230, Birmingham, AL 35259 205-870-1188. Big-brother, big-sister program where young adults act as role models to high school students.

Radio Bible Class, Inc., P.O. Box 22, Grand Rapids, MI 49555 616-942-6770. Teaches the Word of God through audio, video, and correspondence media.

Radio Voice of Christ, Inc., P.O. Box 7145, Beaverton, OR 97007 503-649-0717. Farsi-language broadcast outreach to Iran and to Iranians in some Persian Gulf countries.

Rainbow Acres, Inc., P.O. Box 1326, Camp Verde, AZ 86322 602-567-5231. Residential/vocational ranch communities for mentally handicapped adults.

The Raleigh Rescue Mission, Inc., P.O. Box 27391, Raleigh, NC 27611 919-828-2003. Work therapy, counseling, and job training.

Ramesh Richard Evangelism and Church Helps—RREACH, 16250 Dallas Parkway, Suite 110, Dallas, TX 75248 214-841-3675. Provides resources to facilitate transfer of skills, tools, and resources to national leaders in and from poor countries; links Christian funding resources with urban-area local church needs in economically deprived lands.

Ravi Zacharias International Ministries, Inc., 4725 Peachtree Corners Circle, #250, Norcross, GA 30092 404-449-6766. Resource centers, seminars, open forums in churches and the "hotbeds of intellectualism."

Reap International, Inc., 972 W. 9th Street, Upland, CA 91786 714-981-5777. Serves medical missions by providing rebuilt medical equipment; on-site technical service; training and maintenance of medical equipment.

Reformed Theological Seminary, 5422 Clinton Blvd., Jackson, MS 39209 601-922-4988. An institute of theological studies committed to the Reformed faith.

Regent College Foundation, 12600 SE 38th St., Bellevue, WA 98006 206-649-9118. Conducts and promotes seminars, lectures, and extension classes on issues of theological education; participates in fund-raising for specific programs and provides some scholarship funds for students who want to obtain a theological education.

Regent University, 1000 Centerville Turnpike, Virginia Beach, VA 23464-9800 804-523-7405. Includes five colleges: education and human services, communication and the arts, law and government, administration and management, and theology and ministry.

Reign Ministries, Inc., 5517 Warwick Pl., Minneapolis, MN 55436 612-925-3519. Supplements the efforts of churches and organizations in becoming more effective centers and more aggressive witnesses to God's redeeming power.

Rescue Mission of the Mahoning Valley, P.O. Box 298, Youngstown, OH 44501 216-744-5485. Provides emergency shelter, clothing, furniture, referrals, and counseling. Residential facility for crisis pregnancy.

Rescue Mission Alliance of Syracuse, New York, 120 Gifford Street, Syracuse, NY 13202 315-472-6251. Serves people whose needs go unfulfilled. Seeks to develop the whole person in physical, mental, and spiritual areas.

Richmond Rescue Mission, P.O. Box 1112, Richmond, CA 94803 415-233-5333. Provides emergency shelter and meals, food boxes for needy families, and clothing and furniture as available.

Rio Grande Bible Institute, Inc., 4300 S. Business 281, Edinburg, TX 78539 512-380-8100. Prepares Spanish-speaking Christian leaders to minister. Provides Spanish language program for those interested in missionary service in Spanish areas; Spanish broadcasts.

Riverside Christian Ministries, Inc., 968 NW 2nd Street, Miami, FL 33128 305-545-8841. Reentry and support programs for prisoners and their families.

Riverwoods Christian Center, 35 W 701 Riverwoods Lane, St. Charles, IL 60174 708-584-2222. Ministers to the economically disadvantaged people of the Fox River Valley through camp and community ministries.

Rochester Youth for Christ, Inc., P.O. Box 69, Rochester, NY 14601 716-442-0330. Seeks to aid in the moral and mental improvement of teenagers through social gatherings and entertainments that are instructive and inspirational, helping them to realize the importance of balance in mental, spiritual, social, and physical development.

Roever Evangelistic Association, Inc., P.O. Box 136130, Ft. Worth, TX 76136 817-238-2000. Supports the ministry of evangelist Dave Roever as he conducts assemblies in public high schools and speaks in crusades, churches, youth rallies, men's retreats, etc. Distributes audio and video tapes, books, newsletters. Weekly television program.

Romanian Missionary Society, P.O. Box 527, Wheaton, IL 60189-0527 708-665-6503. Translation of biblical literature into the Romanian language; radio broadcasts; other humanitarian aid to Romanian refugees.

Rural Home Missionary Association, P.O. Box 300, Morton, IL 61550 309-263-2350. Plants and establishes independent Bible churches in rural America.

Samaritan's Purse, Inc., P.O. Box 3000, Boone, NC 28607 704-262-1980. Responds to emergency needs in crisis areas of the world through missionaries and national churches. World Medical Mission, its medical arm, recruits Christian physicians for voluntary short-term service in evangelical mission hospitals overseas.

San Diego Rescue Mission, Inc., P.O. Box 80427, San Diego, CA 92138 619-234-2109. Provides shelter, medical services, and spiritual advice to homeless men. These men perform the day-to-day tasks needed to maintain the facility—a unique program wherein the "homeless" care for the homeless.

Scripture Press Ministries, P.O. Box 650, Glen Ellyn, IL 60137 708-668-6000. Provides leadership training programs, support materials and literature programs to foster spiritual growth. These programs are carried out in U.S. churches, correctional institutions, hospitals, mission organizations, overseas Christian schools, seminars, and translation of Sunday school curriculum and Bible reference books.

Scripture Union, Inc., 7000 Ludlow Street, Upper Darby, PA 19082 215-352-5400. Seeks to open God's Word creatively with people, using programs like "Operation Quiet Time," a congregation-wide daily Bible study and prayer effort.

Search Ministries, Inc., 5038 Dorsey Hall Dr., Ellicott City, MD 21042 301-740-5300. Life-style evangelism helps Christians pro-

ECFA MEMBERS cont.

vide friends with a comfortable, natural opportunity to think through their beliefs.

Seattle Pacific University, 3307 3rd Ave., W., Seattle, WA 98119 206-281-2222. An evangelical Christian university; undergraduate and graduate disciplines.

SEND International, P.O. Box 513, Farmington, MI 48332 313-477-4210. Missionary agency serving the Philippines, Hong Kong, Taiwan, Japan, Spain, Alaska, and northwest Canada.

Serve International, 120 Interstate N. Parkway, E., #404, Atlanta, GA 30339 404-952-3434. Interdenominational relational evangelism equipping ministry. Serve's Friendly Witness Building Process helps believers grow from profession of faith to responsible evangelistic reproduction.

Shalom International Outreach, Inc., P.O. Box 4400, Costa Mesa, CA 92628 714-966-1377. Challenges the church to confront anti-semitism and other racial bigotry.

The Sheepfold, Inc., P.O. Box 3948, Tustin, CA 92680 714-669-9569. Shelter for homeless women with children.

Shepherd's Gate, P.O. Box 894, Livermore, CA 94551 415-449-0163. Emergency shelter for homeless women and children.

SIM USA, Inc., P.O. Box 7900, Charlotte, NC 28241 704-588-4300. Interdenominational mission agency working primarily in South America, Africa, and southern Asia.

Sky Ranches, Inc., 9330 LBJ Freeway, #850, Dallas, TX 75243 214-437-9505. Christian camping and related activities.

Skyline Wesleyan Church, 1345 Skyline Drive, Lemon Grove, CA 91945 619-460-5000. Ministers to the greater San Diego, CA area.

Slavic Gospel Association, Inc., P.O. Box 1122, Wheaton, IL 60189 708-690-8900. Russian radio broadcasts; Bible and Christian literature translation, production, and distribution; and personal evangelism to Russian- and other Slavic-speaking people.

Songtime Inc., P.O. Box 350, Boston, MA 02101 617-848-7787. National radio ministry.

SonScape Re-Creation Ministries, Inc., P.O. Box 7777, Pagosa Springs, CO 81147 303-264-4777. Retreat center for pastors, professional staff, missionaries, and their families.

Sound Words Communications, Inc., 1000 S.

84th Street, Lincoln, NE 68510 402-488-5949. Provides systematic study of the Bible using various media.

South America Mission, Inc., P.O. Box 6560, Lake Worth, FL 33466 407-965-1833. Establishes self-supporting, self-governing, and self-propagating churches in Bolivia, Brazil, Colombia, and Peru.

South America Missionary Society, P.O. Box 399, Ambridge, PA 15003 412-266-0669. An Episcopal/Anglican church society that recruits, supports, trains, and sends Episcopalians as missionaries to Latin America.

South Dade Crisis Pregnancy Center, 7575 SW 62nd Ave., Miami, FL 33143 305-665-7201. Ministers to women in crisis pregnancies.

South Evangelical Presbyterian Fellowship, 3780 S. Broadway, Englewood, CO 80110 303-761-8780. Ministers to those in need, supplying both physical and spiritual aid.

South Hills Community Church, 6601 Camden Ave., San Jose, CA 95120 408-268-1676. Nondenominational evangelical church in San Jose's Silicon Valley.

South Side Mission of Peoria, Inc., P.O. Box 5579, Peoria, IL 61601 309-676-4604. To evangelize and disciple the youth of the Peoria inner city. New Promise Center (a women's and children's shelter), King's Kids Nursery School, Camp Kearney, Break Out, Youth Ministries, and Second Touch Clothing store.

Southeastern Bible College, 3001 Highway 280, E., Birmingham, AL 35243-4181 205-269-0880. Offers Christian higher education.

Spanish Evangelical Enterprises, P.O. Box 452424, Miami, FL 33245 305-358-9207. Promotes and establishes the Christian faith throughout Spanish-speaking countries.

Spiritual Counterfeits Project, Inc., P.O. Box 4308, Berkeley, CA 94704 415-540-0300. Researches various religious groups from a Christian perspective; publishes and distributes literature and maintains research files and a library; educates Christians about current religious trends in Western society.

Spiritual Overseers Service International, P.O. Box 2756, Vacaville, CA 95696 707-451-9830. Sends experienced men and women overseas for two to three weeks to teach and train national Christian ministers and leaders.

Sports World Ministries, Inc., P.O. Box 500,

New Tazewell, TN 37825 615-626-8291. Trains and sends the professional football player to reach young America with a call to "Say no to drugs forever and yes to God."

Spring Arbor College, P.O. Box 219, Spring Arbor, MI 49283 517-750-1200. In addition to a strong liberal arts program, the college provides nontraditional delivery of degree completion programs for adult learners.

Spring Hill Camps, P.O. Box 100, Evart, MI 49631 616-734-2616. Youth camps, family camps, retreats, conferences.

Springfield Rescue Mission, P.O. Box 2424, Springfield, MA 01101 413-732-0808. A Christian rehabilitation center for the homeless, the addicted, and the poor of Greater Springfield and the surrounding areas.

Star of Hope Mission, P.O. Box 4052, Houston, TX 77210 713-748-0700. Assists the homeless of Houston. Includes a variety of ministries.

STEER, Inc., P.O. Box 1236, Bismarck, ND 58502 701-258-4911. Evangelical, agricultural, fund-raising organization for missions worldwide. A farmer/rancher buys livestock or plants a crop. The profit is sent to missions.

Steve Wingfield Ministries, Inc., P.O. Box 1464, Harrisonburg, VA 22801 703-828-4747. Supports the local church in evangelism and discipleship.

Student Ministries, Inc., P.O. Box 22212, Milwaukie, OR 97220 503-653-8800. Contracts with graduate students to serve in Christian ministries. Functions as a mission agency for seminarians who develop support through donors and receive it in monthly payments from SMI.

Student Mobilization, P.O. Box 24805, Little Rock, AR 72221-4805 501-225-4488. Evangelizes and equips college students for lifelong ministry. Works on small college campuses in the south central U.S. Ministries include Campus Outreach, The Kaleo Summer Project, The Graduate Training Center and Pioneer Missions.

The Suffering Church Ministries, P.O. Box 930937, Norcross, GA 30093 404-921-0630. Prints and distributes Bibles and Christian literature to Romania and other lands. Provides help, relief, medicine, tools of evangelism for persecuted and suffering pastors and Christians. Informs Christians in the free world about their brothers in other lands.

Summit Chaplain Services, P.O. Box 728, Akron, OH 44309 216-376-7388. Evangelizes and disciples those in prisons, their families, and staff serving in correctional facilities.

Summit Christian College, 1025 W. Rudisill Blvd., Fort Wayne, IN 46807 219-456-2111. Coeducational institution of higher education in the Bible college tradition.

Summit Ministries, P.O. Box 207, Manitou Springs, CO 80829 719-685-9103. Training ministry for young adults, helping high school and college age students develop a Christian philosophy of life. Arms them with facts about what Christians are to stand for and why, as well as what we stand against.

Sunday Breakfast Association, Inc., P.O. Box 296, Philadelphia, PA 19105 215-922-6400. Shelters and counsels needy men, women, and children; distributes Bibles and other Christian literature; conducts a Sunday school and a summer camp for children.

Taylor University, Reade Ave., Upland, IN 46989 317-998-5198. Offers liberal arts and professional training.

TCM International, Inc., P.O. Box 24560, Indianapolis, IN 46224 317-299-0333. Missionaries, short-term workers, and specialized volunteers minister in Eastern Europe.

Teen Challenge of Arizona, Inc., P.O. Box 5966, Tucson, AZ 85703 602-322-0981. Drug and alcohol rehabilitation program.

Teen Challenge of Chattanooga, Inc., P.O. Box 2280, Chattanooga, TN 37409-0280 615-756-5558. Ministers to people who have drug, alcohol, and other life-controlling problems.

Teen Challenge of New Mexico, Inc., P.O. Box 20610, Albuquerque, NM 87154 505-281-8467. Ministers to people who have life-controlling problems.

Teen Challenge of Southern California, Inc., P.O. Box 5039, Riverside, CA 92517 714-682-8990. Ministers to people who have life-controlling problems.

Teen Challenge Training Center, Inc., P.O. Box 98, Rehrersburg, PA 19550 717-933-4181. Center for men who have life-controlling problems with drugs, alcohol, and crime.

Teen Challenge, Inc., 444 Clinton Ave., Brooklyn, NY 11238-1602 718-789-1414. Ministers to people with life-controlling

ECFA MEMBERS cont.

problems.

Teen Ranch, Inc., 2861 Main, Marlette, MI 48453 517-635-7511. Works with troubled boys, 11–17 years of age, helping them to build a respect for self, others, academic achievement, the home, and to return to society as productive, confident young men.

Tele-Missions International, Inc., P.O. Drawer J, Valley Cottage, NY 10989 914-268-9222. Mass-media, crusades, literature, counseling, seminars, and scholarships to aid students preparing for Christian service.

TENTMAKERS Youth Ministry, 500 Blake Road, S., Hopkins, MN 55343 612-935-3147. A relational skills training organization for youth directors that focuses heavily on management, communication, motivation, decision-making and ministry skills.

Timber-lee Christian Center, 2381 Scout Rd., East Troy, WI 53120 414-642-7345. Year-round facility for seminars and retreats, recreation activities, and educational opportunities.

TITUS International Institute, P.O. Box 3074, Chattanooga, TN 37404 615-629-5514. Assists in upgrading the quality of instruction in Bible Institutes worldwide. Produces video-based educational materials that can supplement the curricular program for training nationals as well as U.S. students.

Toccoa Falls College, P.O. Box 800068, Toccoa Falls, GA 30598 404-886-5235. Prepares men and women for service.

Today's Family, P.O. Box 22111, Phoenix, AZ 85028 602-867-2999. Conferences, film series, audio cassettes, radio and television programs.

Total Outreach for Christ Ministries, Inc., 3300 Asher Ave., Little Rock, AR 72204 501-663-0300. Utilizes street evangelism, tent crusades, conferences, and media ministry throughout the U.S. and abroad. Includes a church fellowship, Christian academy, and Missions Institute.

Town and Country Manor, 555 E. Memory Lane, Santa Ana, CA 92706 714-547-7581. Retirement center with skilled and intermediate care. Affiliated with The Christian and Missionary Alliance.

Trans World Missions, P.O. Box 10, Glendale, CA 91209 213-663-1176. Focuses on indigenous church planting and training national

leaders in Mexico, Central America, South America, and the Caribbean.

Trans World Radio, P.O. Box 700, Cary, NC 27512-0700 919-460-3700. Radio evangelistic ministry to more than 80 percent of the world's population.

Transformation International Enterprises, 1730 N. Lynn St., Suite 500, Arlington, VA 22209 703-243-9500. Enables the unemployed and underemployed poor in developing countries to become productive, self-supporting citizens. Provides micro-economic development training and capital access.

Transport for Christ International, P.O. Box 303, Denver, PA 17517 215-267-2444. An interdenominational organization to win truck drivers to Jesus Christ and establish them in their faith. Eighteen-wheel tractor-trailer trucks are converted into chapels and deployed permanently at key truck stops throughout North America.

Tri-City Union Gospel Mission, P.O. Box 1443, Pasco, WA 99301 509-547-2112. Provides food, shelter, clothing, and spiritual guidance to unwed mothers, homeless families, and runaways.

Trinity Bible College, 50 S. 6th Ave., Ellendale, ND 58436 701-349-3621. Provides Bible-centered courses of training to prepare for ministry at home and abroad.

Trinity Christian Academy, 17001 Addison Rd., Addison, TX 75248 214-931-8325. Provides quality alternative to secular school education for children from families who want their own biblical values, corresponding moral emphases, and Christian worldview reinforced by the school. Kindergarten through grade twelve.

Trinity Christian Community, 1619 Prytania Street, New Orleans, LA 70130 504-581-6541. Ministers to the urban poor in New Orleans and other urban areas.

Trinity Episcopal School for Ministry, 311 Eleventh Street, Ambridge, PA 15003 412-266-3838. Trains men and women called to lay and ordained ministry in the Episcopal church, in the wider Anglican Communion, and in the church of Christ throughout the world.

Trinity School of Cape Cod, 10 Carter Rd., S. Yarmouth, MA 02664 508-394-4118. Christian day school, pre-kindergarten through ninth grade.

Union Gospel Mission Association of Seattle,

P.O. Box 202, Seattle, WA 98111 206-723-0767. Rescue ministry of Seattle area churches involved in emergency services, rehabilitation, youth programs, senior services, jail and prison ministry.

Union Gospel Mission of St. Paul, 435 E. University Ave., St. Paul, MN 55101-4495 612-292-1721. Provides services to the community. Free and low-income housing; medical clinics, secondhand store.

Union Mission Settlement, Inc., P.O. Box 112, Charleston, WV 25321 304-925-0366. Rescue mission with a transient hostel, adult personal care home with nursing services, recovery program for men.

Union Rescue Mission, P.O. Box 629, Los Angeles, CA 90053 213-628-6103. A community-designed mission to communicate principles of Christian living and relieve suffering. Specialized help for jobs, education and recreation, alcoholics.

United World Mission Incorporated, P.O. Box 250, Union Mills, NC 28167 704-287-8996. Evangelism and church planting. Major strategies are urban evangelism, training nationals to work among unreached people groups.

Utah Institute for Biblical Studies, P.O. Box 2096, Salt Lake City, UT 84110 801-581-1900. College level courses for people interested in pursuing biblical studies.

Vennard College, P.O. Box 29, University Park, IA 52595 515-673-8391. Bible college with a Wesleyan-Arminian theological tradition.

Ventura County Rescue Mission, P.O. Box 5545, Oxnard, CA 93030 805-487-8252. Feeds, clothes, and shelters poor and homeless men, administers a drug and alcohol program entitled "Breakthrough."

Vietnam Ministries, Inc., P.O. Box 4568, Anaheim, CA 92803 714-758-8767. Publishes and distributes Christian literature, provides leadership and training to Vietnamese-speaking individuals and churches.

Voice of Calvary Ministries, P.O. Box 10562, Jackson, MS 39209 601-353-1635. Black-led ministry of Christians seeking to express the love of Christ in the poor communities of Jackson, Mississippi.

Voice of Hope Ministries, P.O. Box 224845, Dallas, TX 75222-4845 214-631-7027. Ministers to the community using principles of self-help, evangelism, and renewal. Activities for all age groups.

Walk Thru the Bible Ministries, Inc., P.O. Box 80587, Atlanta, GA 30366 404-458-9300. Seminars; devotional guides (*The Daily Walk, Closer Walk, Youth Walk,* and *Family Walk*); study tours.

The Walter Hoving Home, Inc., P.O. Box 194, Garrison, NY 10524 914-424-3674. Drug and alcohol rehabilitation center focusing on women aged 17 to 50.

Washington Bible College, 6511 Princess Garden Parkway, Lanham, MD 20706 301-552-1400. Undergraduate and graduate biblical and professional education; resource center for Christian laymen and the continuing education of pastors, missionaries, and other Christian workers.

Water Street Rescue Mission, 210 S. Prince Street, Lancaster, PA 17603 717-393-7709. Emergency services, rehabilitation, prevention programs.

Waterfront Rescue Mission, Inc., P.O. Box 854, Pensacola, FL 32594 904-438-4027. Facilities for transients, Bargain Center Store, rehabilitation and discipleship programs, youth Bible clubs.

Wesley Biblical Seminary, P.O. Box 9938, Jackson, MS 39286 601-957-1314. Graduate school of theology.

The Wesleyan Church Corporation, P.O. Box 50434, Indianapolis, IN 46250 317-842-0444. Receives, holds, and manages assets of the Wesleyan church.

Western Conservative Baptist Seminary, 5511 SE Hawthorne Blvd., Portland, OR 97215 503-233-8561. Trains men and women for Christian leadership.

Western Indian Ministries, P.O. Drawer F, Window Rock, AZ 86515 505-371-5749. Trains Navajo leadership. Ministry includes church growth, radio, crisis ministries, counseling, and day school for Navajo children.

Westminster Theological Seminary, P.O. Box 27009, Philadelphia, PA 19118 215-887-5511. Trains men for the gospel ministry as pastors, evangelists, and teachers as set forth in the Westminster Confession of Faith and Catechisms and the fundamental principles of Presbyterian church government.

Westmont College, 955 La Paz Rd., Santa Barbara, CA 93108 805-565-6000. Undergraduate liberal arts program.

Wheaton College, 501 E. College Ave., Whea-

ECFA MEMBERS cont.

ton, IL 60187 708-752-5000. Independent, liberal arts college.

Wheeler Mission Ministries, 245 N. Delaware Street, Indianapolis, IN 46204 317-635-3575. Housing, clothing, counseling for men.

Whosoever Gospel Mission & Rescue Home, 101 E. Chelten Ave., Philadelphia, PA 19144 215-438-3094. A six-month Christ-centered rehabilitation program designed to help homeless men become productive citizens.

William Taylor Foundation, Taylor University, Reade Ave., Upland, IN 46989 317-998-5239. Support organization for Taylor University. Works with alumni and friends on estate plans and deferred gifts.

Wilson Family Living, P.O. Box 3400, Orange, CA 92665 714-637-7900. Facilitates good family relationships through seminars, and radio.

Windsent, Inc., P.O. Box 101, Madison, MN 56256 612-598-3330. Supports the proclamation of the gospel through the media; encourages Christian believers to stand for the truths and moral principles of historic Christianity.

Winebrenner Theological Seminary, P.O. Box 478, Findlay, OH 45839 419-422-4824. Provides theological education for ministerial candidates in the Churches of God, General Conference.

Women for Christ, P.O. Box 517, Winnetka, IL 60093 708-446-9295. Non-affiliated women's ministry. Seminars and conferences with special emphasis on strengthening family relationships, supporting working women, and ministering to women in leadership positions.

Words of Hope, Inc., P.O. Box 1706, Grand Rapids, MI 49503 616-459-6181. Worldwide radio and media ministry of the Reformed Church in America.

World Emergency Relief, P.O. Box 1518, Carlsbad, CA 92008 619-434-4900. Short- and long-term relief assistance to victims of natural disasters. Assists in long-term development projects such as orphanages, schools, hospitals, and vocational programs internationally and in the U.S. Also sponsors several feeding programs.

World Evangelical Fellowship, P.O. Box WEF, Wheaton, IL 60189 708-668-0440. Provides the structure and forum for evangelicals worldwide to identify together, de-

fend the faith together, and cooperate forcefully in advancing the gospel.

World Evangelistic Enterprise Corporation, 2348 Troy Rd., Springfield, OH 45504 513-399-7837. Principal ministry is noncommercial radio station WEEC; supports two radio missionary families in Brazil and Korea.

World Gospel Crusades, Inc., P.O. Box 3, Upland, CA 91785 714-982-1564. Trains nationals in South and Central America to reach every home with a witness, a Gospel of John, Bible correspondence courses, and follow-up.

World Gospel Mission, P.O. Box 948, Marion, IN 46952 317-664-7331. Cross-cultural ministries such as church planting, biblical training centers, education, medical, literature, radio, agricultural.

World Impact, Inc., 2001 S. Vermont Ave., Los Angeles, CA 90007 213-735-1137. Bible studies, worship services, schools, medical/dental clinic, housing in inner- city communities.

World Medical Mission, Inc., P.O. Box 3000, Boone, NC 28607 704-262-1980. Recruits physicians for short-term service in mission hospitals.

World Messianic Fellowships, Inc., P.O. Box 449, Lynbrook, NY 11563 516-593-1724. Outreach to Jews; trains missionaries for Jewish work.

World Mission Prayer League, Inc., 232 Clifton Ave., Minneapolis, MN 55403 612-871-6843. Independent Lutheran mission society.

World Missionary Press, Inc., P.O. Box 120, New Paris, IN 46553 219-831-2111. Produces and mails millions of free Scripture-by-subject booklets in over 235 languages.

World Opportunities International, 1415 N. Cahuenga Blvd., Hollywood, CA 90028 213-466-7187. Missions outreach to some 51 countries; relief distribution including food, clothing, and medical supplies.

World Radio Missionary Fellowship, Inc., P.O. Box 39800, Colorado Springs, CO 80949-9800 719-590-9800. In South America, HCJB broadcasts from Ecuador in key languages to major world areas by shortwave radio; local radio in Latin America. In Panama, WRMF assists in operating HOXO's Spanish/English station. In Europe, it assists local groups in developing radio ministries. In the USA, WRMF assists World Radio Network, Inc. to operate five stations along the Mexican border.

World Relief Corporation, P.O. Box WRC, Wheaton, IL 60189 708-665-0235. Aids victims of war and natural disaster—specializing in helping people to help themselves.

World Servants, 8233 Gator Lane, #6, West Palm Beach, FL 33411 407-790-0800. Seeks to expand the mission vision of the church through training seminars and short-term missions familiarization trips.

World Thrust, Inc., P.O. Box 405105, Atlanta, GA 30345-0105 404-939-5215. Serves as a mobilizing force for world evangelization. It is a catalytic and multiplication ministry focusing primarily on senior pastors and key church leaders. Provides seminars, consultation, foreign mission exposure trips and overseas work projects.

World Vision, Inc., 919 W. Huntington Drive, Monrovia, CA 91016 818-357-7979. Relief and development organization in more than 80 countries.

World-Wide Christian Schools, P.O. Box 851, Grandville, MI 49468-0851 616-531-9102. Helps Christian organizations in Third-World countries to develop schools.

World Wide Pictures, Inc., 1201 Hennepin Ave., Minneapolis, MN 55403 612-338-3335. Producer and distributor of Billy Graham evangelistic films.

World Witness, One Cleveland Street, Greenville, SC 29601 803-233-5226. Board of Foreign Missions of the Associate Reformed Presbyterian Church.

World-Wide Missions, P.O. Box 7125, Pasadena, CA 91109-7125 818-355-9495. Ministers to needy peoples in 32 underdeveloped countries.

Worldteam Associates, Inc., P.O. Box 902, Morton, IL 61550 309-266-6080. Exists to involve lay people with missions in general and with Worldteam specifically. Encourages lay people to get involved with missionaries, go to mission fields with its seminar/observation tours or work/ministry teams.

Worldteam USA, 1607 Ponce de Leon Blvd., Coral Gables, FL 33134 305-446-0861. Church-planting teams in unreached cities and people groups.

Worldwide Discipleship Association, Inc., 110 Carnegie Pl., #100, Fayetteville, GA 30214 404-460-1337. Works with college students and pastors in training laymen in the churches.

Worldwide Friendship, Inc., P.O. Box 8809, Minneapolis, MN 55408 612-827-5197. Seeks to reach internationals for Christ who have come to the Twin City area to study. Provides free services, programs, and activities; outreach ministry in Egypt.

WRVM, Inc., P.O. Box 212, Suring, WI 54174 414-842-2839. Christian radio station broadcasting 24 hours a day to northeast Wisconsin and south central Upper Michigan.

Wycliffe Associates, Inc., P.O. Box 2000, Orange, CA 92669 714-639-9950. Service ministry for lay participation in Wycliffe Bible Translators. Encourages and allows lay people to become directly involved in projects for Bible translation. Projects include building and/or funding of translation centers, missionary housing, equipment, new country start-ups, vehicles, and other needs.

Wycliffe Bible Translators, Inc., P.O. Box 2727, Huntington Beach, CA 92647 714-969-4600. Provides translation of the Scriptures for the 3,000 languages that do not have them.

Young Life, P.O. Box 520, Colorado Springs, CO 80901 719-473-4262. Ministry with adolescents. Ministry starts when trained staff and volunteers befriend teenagers. Nationwide camps offer young people an opportunity to learn about themselves and their Creator.

Youth Challenge International Bible Institute, R.D. 2, Box 33, Sunbury, PA 17801 717-286-6442. A three-year, college-level educational community that provides specialized training for the Youth Challenge conceptual approach in rehabilitating troubled youth.

Youth for Christ International Council, 6890 S. Tucson Way #205, Englewood, CO 80112 303-790-4477. One of six worldwide offices that coordinates YFC mission in more than 100 countries. Provides support services for nationals raising funds in the USA and liaisons with other mission organizations in North America.

Youth for Christ/USA, Inc., P.O. Box 228822, Denver, CO 80222 303-843-9000.

ECFA MEMBERS cont.

Youth evangelism and the discipleship of young people in the church: Campus Life Clubs, Youth Guidance for delinquent teens, Minority/Urban for the unique needs of urban centers, World Outreach in 53 countries.
Youth Guidance, Inc., R.D. 2, Duff Rd., Sewickley, PA 15143 412-741-8550. Brings troubled young people together with Christian adults in a long-term one-to-one friendship. Trains the volunteer to be a friend and spiritual guide.
Youth Haven, Inc., P.O. Box 97, Rives Junction, MI 49277 517-569-3328. Year round ministry to underprivileged children.
Youth Investment Foundation, 15306 Minnetonka Industrial Rd., Minnetonka, MN

55343 612-938-6123. Works with alienated suburban and small-town youth.
YUGO Ministries, P.O. Box 25, San Dimas, CA 91773 714-592-6621. Missionary outreach to the border areas of Mexico. Short-term ministry program.
Zwemer Institute of Muslim Studies, P.O. Box 365, Altadena, CA 91003-0365 818-794-1121. Brings opportunities for ministry to Muslims into focus. Weekend Muslim Awareness seminars and publications, research, church-planting strategies. Field teams coordinate Muslim evangelism in strategic urban centers.

Source: Evangelical Council for Financial Accountability September 1991 Member Profile Directory.

CHRISTIAN FOUNDATIONS WITH NATIONAL INTERESTS

Artevel Foundation, Well's Fargo Center, 333 S. Grand Avenue, Suite 4150, Los Angeles, CA 90071-3164 213-680-9212
Recipient Types: Aged, Bible societies, Bible translation, child welfare, colleges & universities, community services, counseling, emergency relief, family services, food distribution, homeless, hospitals, inner-city populations, international relief, missionaries, missions, nursing homes, pastoral counseling, religious education, right-to-life issues, seminaries, shelters, stewardship, substance abuse, women's affairs, and youth ministry.

Believers Foundation, 1570 Dutch Hollow Road, P.O. Box 3175, Elida, OH 45807 419-339-4441
Recipient Types: Bible societies, churches, missions, and religious education.

Ash Family Foundation, 84 Lake Padgett Drive, Land O'Lakes, FL 33539 813-996-4313
Recipient Types: Athletics, campus crusades, churches, colleges and universities, prison work, religious broadcasting, religious centers, religious organizations, religious welfare, youth ministry, and youth organizations.

Atkinson, Myrtle L., Foundation, 101 Alma Street, #1207, Palo Alto, CA 94301 415-321-6430
Recipient Types: Athletics, Bible societies, Bible study, Bible translation, campus crusades, churches, colleges and universities, distribution of religious materials, disabled, divinity schools, emergency relief, ministries, minority education, missionaries, missions, prison work, refugee services, religious broadcasting, religious education, religious organizations, seminaries, youth ministries, and youth organizations.

Christian Workers Foundation, 3038 Bankhead Avenue, Montgomery, AL 36106 205-263-5571
Recipient Types: Bible study, campus crusades, colleges and universities, parochial education—secondary, religious education, youth ministry, youth organizations, and youth welfare.

Aurora Foundation, P.O. Box 1848, Bradenton, FL 34206 813-748-4100
Recipient Types: Bible societies, Bible study, Bible translation, campus ministries, child welfare, churches, colleges and universities, distribution of religious materials, ministries, missionaries, missions, religious broadcasting, religious education, religious

organizations, religious welfare, youth ministries, and youth organizations.

Berry, Lowell, Foundation, 315 Washington Avenue, Waco, TX 76701 817-752-5551
Recipient Types: Campus crusades, churches, colleges and universities, community services, missions, prison work, religious education, religious higher education, religious organizations, religious welfare, seminaries, and youth organizations.

Caddock Foundation, Inc., 1717 Chicago Avenue, Riverside, CA 92507 714-788-1700
Recipient Types: Aged, Bible societies, Bible study, Bible translation, campus crusades, campus ministries, child welfare, Christian centers, churches, colleges and universities, counseling, distribution of religious materials, family services, ministries, missionaries, missions, nursing homes, prison work, religious broadcasting, religious centers, religious organizations, religious welfare, and youth organizations.

Chatlos Foundation, Inc, 122 E. 42nd Street, New York, NY 10168 212-867-9630
Recipient Types: Aged, Bible study, Bible translation, campus crusades, campus ministries, colleges & universities, community centers, disabled, emergency relief, international relief, ministries, missions, prison work, religious centers, religious education, religious broadcasting, religious organizations, seminaries, shelters, youth ministry, and youth organizations.

C.I.O.S., 4 Orinda Way, #140B, Orinda, CA 94563-2513 415-254-1944
Recipient Types: Bible societies, Bible study, Bible translation, campus crusades, child welfare, churches, colleges and universities, distribution of religious materials, divinity schools, family services, international relief, ministries, missionaries, minority education, missions, parochial education-secondary, prison work, religious broadcasting, religious education, religious organizations, seminaries, youth ministry, and youth organizations.

Crowell, Henry P. and Susan C., Trust, Lock Box 442, Chicago, IL 60690 312-372-5202
Recipient Types: Aged, Bible societies, Bible study, churches, colleges and universities, disabled, family services, inner-city populations, international relief, ministries, missions, parochial education-secondary, prison work, religious broadcasting, religious education, religious higher education, religious organizations, religious welfare, seminaries, youth ministry, youth organizations, and youth welfare.

DeMoss, Arthur S., Foundation, St. Davids Center, Suite A-300, St. Davids, PA 19087 215-254-5500
Recipient Types: Campus crusades, child welfare, churches, colleges and universities, community services, distribution of religious materials, disabled, ministries, missions, prison work, religious broadcasting, religious centers, religious education, religious higher education, religious organizations, religious welfare, right-to-life issues, seminaries, and youth welfare.

Firestone, Harvey S., Trust No. 1 Fund, c/o Bank One Akron, 50 S. Main Street, Akron, OH 44308 216-375-1865
Recipient Types: Bible societies, churches, homeless, international relief, and ministries.

First Fruit, Inc., 7400 W. 20th Avenue, Lakewood, CO 80215 303-232-4084
Recipient Types: Bible societies, Bible study, Bible translation, child welfare, clinics, community development, community services, counseling, distribution of religious materials, emergency relief, family services, food distribution, health care in-home, hospitals, international development, international health care, international relief, medical assistance, ministries, missionaries, missions, prison work, refugee services, religious broadcasting, religious welfare, rural populations, and substance abuse.

Helms Foundation, Inc., 25765 Quilla Road, P.O. Box 55827, Valencia, CA 91355 805-253-3485

CHRISTIAN FOUNDATIONS . . . cont.

Recipient Types: Churches, colleges and universities, hospitals, ministries, prison work, religious education, religious higher education, religious organizations, religious welfare, seminaries, youth ministry, and youth welfare.

Huston Foundation, P.O. Box 139, Gladwyne, PA 19035 215-527-4371

Recipient Types: Athletics, Bible study, Bible translation, campus crusades, campus ministries, child welfare, churches, colleges and universities, family services, medical assistance, ministries, missions, parochial education-secondary, religious broadcasting, religious education, religious organizations, religious welfare, youth ministries, and youth organizations.

Johnson Foundation, 225 Merrill Street, Birmingham, MI 48011 313-646-7500

Recipient Types: Athletics, Bible study, campus crusades, Christian centers, churches, clothes distribution, colleges and universities, counseling, emergency relief, food distribution, homeless, inner-city populations, medical assistance, minority education, missionaries, missions, religious broadcasting, religious organizations, right-to-life issues, seminaries, substance abuse, youth ministry, and youth organizations.

Jubilee Foundation, 175 W. Jackson, Suite 800, Chicago, IL 60604 312-922-2494

Recipient Types: Campus crusades, campus ministries, Christian centers, churches, clothes distribution, colleges and universities, counseling, distribution of religious materials, emergency relief, family services, food distribution, inner-city populations, medical assistance, ministries, minority education, missionaries, missions, religious broadcasting, religious education, religious higher education, religious organizations, youth ministry, and youth organizations.

Kejr Foundation, Inc., 6500 Xerxes Avenue, S., Minneapolis, MN 55423 612-920-0574

Recipient Types: Bible societies, campus ministries, churches, distribution of religious materials, ministries, missions, religious education, religious higher education, religious organizations, and youth ministries.

Kresge Foundation, P.O. Box 3151, Troy, MI 48007 313-643-9630

Recipient Types: Colleges and universities, hospitals, nursing homes, religious centers, religious higher education, religious organizations, and religious welfare.

Lamb, Kirkland S. and Rena B., Foundation, 1312 Eckles Drive, Tampa, FL 33612

Recipient Types: Churches, international relief, missionaries, missions, religious broadcasting, religious organizations, seminaries, and youth ministry.

Luce, Henry, Foundation, 111 W. 50th Street, New York, NY 10020 212-489-7700

Recipient Types: Colleges and universities, divinity schools, religious education, and seminaries.

Maclellan Foundation, Provident Building, Suite 501, Chattanooga, TN 37402 615-755-1366

Recipient Types: Missions, prison work, religious broadcasting, religious education, religious higher education, religious organizations, seminaries, youth ministries, youth organizations, and youth welfare.

Mostyn Foundation, Inc., c/o James C. Edwards and Company, Inc., 805 Third Avenue, New York, NY 10022 212-319-8490

Recipient Types: Churches, ministries, religious education, and religious organizations.

Oldham Little Church Foundation, 5177 Richmond Avenue, Suite 1068, Houston, TX 77056 713-621-4190

Recipient Types: Churches and missions.

Rainbow Fund, P.O. Box 937, Fort Valley, GA 31030 912-825-2021

Recipient Types: Athletics, campus crusades, churches, colleges and universities, ministries, missions, parochial education-secondary, religious broadcasting, religious education, religious higher education, religious organizations, religious welfare, seminaries, and youth organizations.

Stewardship Foundation, P.O. Box 1278, Tacoma, WA 98401 206-272-8336

Recipient Types: Aged, athletics, Bible societies, Bible study, Bible translation, campus crusades, child welfare, Christian centers, churches, civil rights, clinics, clothes distribution, colleges and universities, community development, community services, counseling, disabled, distribution of religious materials, emergency relief, employment, family services, food distribution, health care in-home, homeless, hospitals, human rights, inner-city populations, international development, medical assistance, ministries, minority education, missionaries, missions, parochial education-elementary, parochial education-secondary, pastoral counseling, prison work, religious broadcasting, religious centers, religious education, religious higher education, religious organizations, right-to-life issues, rural populations, seminaries, substance abuse, youth ministry, youth organizations, and youth welfare.

Storehouse Foundation, P.O. Box 1532, Camden, SC 29020 803-432-8677

Recipient Types: Bible study, Bible translation, campus crusades, campus ministries, churches, ministries, distribution of religious materials, missionaries, missions, religious broadcasting, and religious welfare.

Tell Foundation, 4010 N. 38th Avenue, Phoenix, AZ 85019 602-278-6209

Recipient Types: Bible study, campus crusades, campus ministries, churches, colleges and universities, community services, distribution of religious materials, family services, hospitals, international relief, medical assistance, ministries, missions, parochial education-elementary, parochial education-secondary, prison work, religious broadcasting, religious education, religious organizations, religious welfare, youth ministries, and youth welfare.

Tell, Paul P., Foundation, Inc., 1105 Trans Ohio Building, 7 W. Bowery Street, Akron, OH 44308 216-434-8355

Recipient Types: Bible societies, Bible study, Bible translation, campus crusades, child welfare, churches, colleges and universities, disabled, distribution of religious materials, emergency relief, international relief, ministries, missionaries, missions, parochial education-secondary, prison work, religious broadcasting, religious communities, seminaries, youth ministry, and youth organizations.

Vermeer Foundation, c/o Vermeer Manufacturing Company, Box 200, Pella, IA 50219 515-628-3141

Recipient Types: Athletics, Bible societies, Bible study, Bible translation, child welfare, Christian centers, churches, colleges and universities, counseling, distribution of religious materials, family services, medical assistance, ministries, missionaries, missions, parochial education-elementary, parochial education-secondary, pastoral counseling, prison work, religious broadcasting, religious higher education, right-to-life issues, stewardship, youth ministry, and youth organizations.

Ware Foundation, 147 Alhambra Cir., #215, Coral Gables, FL 33134 305-443-8728

Recipient Types: Bible societies, campus crusades, churches, colleges and universities, distribution of religious materials, hospices, medical assistance, ministries, missions, religious broadcasting, religious education, religious organizations, religious welfare, youth ministries, and youth organizations.

CHRISTIAN MANAGEMENT AWARDS

Awarded by Christian Management Association to an individual or an organization who has made a significant contribution to the development and advancement of Christian management and practice.

Year	Recipient	Affiliation	Location
1981	Richard Schmidt	Foursquare Missions International	Los Angeles, CA
1982	George Martinez	Good Shepherd Church	Deming, NM
1983	Arthur C. Borden	Evangl. Cncl for Financial Accountability	Washington, DC
1984	No award given		
1985	Richard Capin	OMS International	Greenwood, IN
1986	Ted Engstrom	World Vision	Monrovia, CA
1987	Lorne Sanny	The Navigators	Colorado Springs, CO
1988	George Wilson	Billy Graham Evangelistic Association	Minneapolis, MN
	Harold Beaty	Wycliffe Bible Translators	Huntington Beach, CA
1989	Eugene Habecker	American Bible Society	New York, NY
1990	Peter Drucker	Claremont College	Claremont, CA
1991	Stephen Douglass	Campus Crusade for Christ International	Orlando, FL
1992	Steve Holbrook	Princeton Management Assoc. Inc.	Belle Mead, NJ

ON WRITING MEMOS

Put it before them
briefly, so they will read it
clearly, so they will appreciate it
picturesquely, so they will remember it
accurately, so they will be guided
by its light.
—Joseph Pulitzer

Social and Political Concerns

MOST IMPORTANT PROBLEM FACING THE NATION
What Adults Think

	1991 %	1989 %	1987 %	1985 %	1983 %
Economy in general	16	7	10	6	8
Drugs, drug abuse	12	27	11	2	—
Poverty, homeless, hunger	12	8	5	6	—
Unemployment	11	2	13	20	53
Quality of education	8	1	—	—	—
Federal budget deficit	7	6	11	18	5
Crime	4	3	3	4	2
Health care	3	3	—	—	—
Ethics, moral decline	2	3	5	2	4
Recession/depression	2	*	—	—	—
Environment, pollution	1	6	—	—	—
Fear of war, international tensions	1	4	23	27	2
High cost of living, inflation	1	3	5	11	18
Dissatisfaction with government	1	2	5	—	2
Other economic problems	1	12	21	16	6
None, don't know	7	8	4	3	—
Trade deficit	—	2	3	—	—
Abortion	—	2	—	—	—
Interest rates	—	*	—	—	2

* Less than one-half of one percent. Source: The Gallup Organization, Inc., poll. September 1991. Used by permission.

ONE DAY IN THE LIVES OF AMERICA'S CHILDREN
Every day in the USA:

- 2,756 teens get pregnant
- 372 teens miscarry
- 1,106 teens have abortions
- 1,340 teens give birth
- 638 babies are born to women who have had inadequate prenatal care
- 742 babies are born at low birthweight (less than 5 lbs., 8 oz.)
- 129 babies are born at very low birthweight (less than 3 lbs., 5 oz.)
- 2,685 babies are born into poverty
- 67 babies die before one month of life
- 107 babies die before their first birthday
- 27 children die from poverty
- 10 children are killed by guns
- 30 children are wounded by guns
- 6 teenagers commit suicide
- 135,000 children bring a gun to school

- 8,441 teenagers become sexually active
- 623 teenagers get syphilis or gonorrhea
- 176 children are arrested for drug abuse
- 427 children are arrested for drinking or drunken driving
- 248 children are arrested for violent crime
- 2,250 teenagers drop out of school

- 10,988 students are suspended from school
- 2,739 children are abused or neglected
- 3,288 children run away from home
- 1,629 children are in adult jails
- 2,754 children are born out of wedlock
- 2,989 children see their parents divorced
- 100,000 children go to sleep homeless

Source: Children's Defense Fund

For every 10,000 children in day care centers, about 5.5 are abused each year. Less than 6% of all child molestations are reported.

FOCUS
FACT

ASSAULTS AGAINST WOMEN REACH ALL-TIME HIGH

- Every hour 16 women confront rapists; a woman is raped every six minutes. More women were raped in 1990 than in any year in U.S. history.
- 1990 continued a three-year trend of increases in the number of rapes. The 1990 increase was nearly three times greater than the 1989 increase.
- 3 to 4 million women are battered each year; every 18 seconds a woman is beaten.
- 3 out of 4 women will be victims of at least one violent crime during their lifetime.
- More than one million women seek medical assistance for injuries caused by battering each year.
- A woman in the United States is 20 times more likely to be raped than in Japan; 13 times more likely than in England; and 4 times more likely than in Germany.
- The five states with the greatest number of rapes in 1990 were: California, Texas, Michigan, Florida, and New York.

Source: Senate Judiciary Committee

---

66 99 American culture is no longer a paradigm of Christian values. Isn't it a fascinating paradox that while Russian children are studying Bibles in their FOCUS classrooms, American kids are being sequestered from them? . . . Perhaps QUOTE someday America will become a target. Not for missiles, but for Russian missionaries. —Rolf Zettersten, senior vice president, *Focus on the Family* magazine, March 1990 issue.

---

66 99 If I straighten the pictures on the walls of your home, I am committing no sin, am I? But suppose that your house were afire, and I still went calmly FOCUS about straightening pictures, what would you say? Would you think me QUOTE merely stupid or very wicked? . . . The world today is on fire. What are you doing to extinguish the fire? —Corrie ten Boom in *Amazing Love.*

THE FACTS ABOUT ABORTION

How many there are
- There are 1.6 million abortions in the U.S. each year
- 30% of pregnancies each year end in induced abortion
- Abortions end more than 4 in 10 pregnancies to both teenagers and women over 40

The reasons women give
- Three-fourth say having a baby would interfere with work, school, or other responsibilities
- Two-thirds say they cannot afford to have a child
- Half say they do not want to be a single parent or have partnership relationship problems

Where they are done
- 87% are performed in nonhospital facilities
- Free-standing abortion centers constitute only 15% of all providers but are responsible for 60% of all abortions

Source: Studies in Family Planning (*The Population Council*), Vol. 21, No. 1, January/February 1990.

FOCUS FACT

More than 10,000 babies were aborted in the USA during the 58 hours it took to rescue Jessica McClure from an abandoned well in Midland, Texas, October 14–16, 1987.

TRENDS IN ABORTION VIEWS

Do you think abortions should be legal under any circumstances, legal only under certain circumstances, or illegal in all circumstances?

	Always legal	Legal depending on circumstances	Never legal
1991	32%	50%	17%
1990	31	53	12
1989	29	51	17
1988	24	57	17
1983	23	58	16
1981	23	52	21
1980	25	53	18
1979	22	54	19
1977	22	55	19
1975	21	54	22

NOTE: "No opinion" omitted
Source: The Gallop Organization Poll, June 1991.

The Who, When, and Where of Abortion

Each year, three out of every 100 American women age 15 to 44 choose to end unwanted pregnancies— 1.6 million abortions in all.

Age	% in category
Under 15 years	1
15-17 years	11
18-19 years	13
20-24 years	33
25-29 years	22
30-34 years	12
35-39 years	6
40 and over	2

Race	Rate per 1,000
White	23.0
Nonwhite	52.6

Family Income	% in category
Under $11,000	33
$11,000-$24,999	34
$25,000 and over	33

Length of Pregnancy*	1983	1973
8 weeks and under	50.3%	38.2%
9-10 weeks	26.9%	29.8%
11-12 weeks	13.3%	17.5%
13-15 weeks	5.3%	6.0%
16-20 weeks	3.4%	7.2%
21 weeks and over	0.8%	1.4%

*Time since last menstrual period

Locations*	
Hospitals	13%
Abortion clinics	60%
Other clinics	23%
M.D.'s offices	4%

*1985 figures

Source: The Alan Guttmacher Institute and *USA Today*, June 3, 1991, issue.

WHAT AMERICANS THINK ABOUT GOVERNMENT RESTRICTIONS

Some people feel that if the government helps pay for family planning services, it has the right to prohibit any discussion of abortion as a family planning option. What is your view?

Government has right to prohibit discussion	19%
Health care professionals have right to discuss	74%
No opinion	7%

Would you favor or oppose Congress passing a law that would allow federally-funded clinics to provide information about abortion?

Favor	66%
Oppose	28%
No opinion	6%

Source: The Gallup Organization poll, June 1991.

❝❞
FOCUS QUOTE

How would you like to be that baby inside the womb of a woman who isn't sure she wants you to live any longer?—Charles R. Swindoll

❝❞
FOCUS QUOTE

Read the Yellow Pages. Look under *abortion.* They're full of advertisements if a woman wants to exterminate her child.—Rep. Henry Hyde (R-IL)

FOCUS FACT

One out of every six women who have an abortion describes herself as an evangelical Christian.—Alan Guttmacher Institute study

RELIGIOUS AFFILIATION OF POSTABORTION WOMEN

Agnostic/no faith	3.1%
Catholic	11.0%
Evangelical	35.6%
Baptist	4.7%
Pentecostal	4.7%
Evangelical Free	3.1%
Assemblies of God	3.1%
Nondenominational	7.8%
Covenant	1.6%
Full Gospel	1.6%
Nonspecific	9.0%
Lutheran	25.0%
Episcopal	1.6%
Methodist	1.6%
Christian (denomination not noted)	14.0%

Source: 1990 study of 68 postabortion women. Reported in *Post-Abortion Trauma* by Jeanette Vought. Published by Zondervan Publishing House.

THE EARLY CHURCH AND ABORTION

Abortion as a socially acceptable practice is nothing new under the sun. Pagans from antiquity on regarded killing the fetus and "exposure of children" after birth as entirely permissible options in family planning.

Fact is, several ancient philosophers, Plato and Aristotle included, advocated abortions. Men and women above the ideal age, according to Plato's thinking, should not have children. Aristotle advised couples who already had children in excess to "let abortion be procured before sense and life have begun."

The voice of the Greek physician Hippocrates was one of the few raised in those ancient times against abortion. He even wrote it into the Hippocratic oath, which declares, "I will not give to a woman a pessary to produce abortion."

This oath influenced many early doctors against counseling abortion. The practice nonetheless continued rampant down to the Christian era. Then, as great numbers of pagans converted to the new faith and heard in church frequent sermons on the sanctity of life, public opinion against the practice grew.

The early church minced no words about abortion and exposure of children as family-planning options. It labeled both as murder. Ministers, reading from *The Teaching of the Twelve Apostles* (written about A.D. 60), warned church members: "A further commandment of the Teaching: Do not murder; do not commit adultery; do not practice pederasty; do not fornicate; do not steal; do not deal in magic; do not practice sorcery; do not kill a fetus by abortion, or commit infanticide."

Churchgoers of that era heard the same message from *The Epistle of Barnabas*. About a century later, Tertullian stated the church's position on abortion in these words: "In our case, murder being once for all forbidden, we may not destroy even the fetus in the womb. . . . To hinder a birth is merely a speedier man-killing, nor does it matter whether you take away a life that is born, or destroy one that is coming to the birth."

Thanks mainly to the church's influence, abortion eventually became a socially unacceptable practice—until *Roe vs. Wade*.

Source: Charles DeLoach in *USA Today*, July 16, 1991.

PRO-LIFE ORGANIZATIONS

Arizona
Crisis Pregnancy Center, Inc.
1124 N. 3rd Avenue
Tucson, AZ 85705
602-622-5774

PACE (Postabortion Counseling and Education)
P.O. Box 35032
Tucson, AZ 85740

Washington, D.C.
Ad Hoc Committee in Defense of Life, Inc.
1187 National Press Bldg.
Washington, DC 20045
202-347-8686

Christian Defense Coalition
P.O. Box 48070
Washington, DC 20002
202-547-1735

National Right to Life Committee, Inc.
419 7th St. NW, Suite 500
Washington, DC 20004
202-626-8800

Florida
Legal Action for Women
1145 Candlewood Circle
Pensacola, FL 32514
904-474-1091

Georgia
Operation Rescue
2359 Windy Hill Road, Suite 207-D
Marietta, GA 30067
404-421-9552

Illinois
Americans United for Life
343 S. Dearborn St., Suite 1804
Chicago, IL 60604
312-786-9494

Pro-Life Action League
6160 N. Cicero Aveenue, Suite 600
Chicago, IL 60646
312-777-2900

Minnesota
New Beginnings
40 25th Avenue, North
St. Cloud, MN 56303
612-255-1252

Missouri
Open Arms
P.O. Box 1056
Columbia, MO 65205
314-449-7672

Pro-Life Direct Action League
P.O. Box 11881
St. Louis, MO 63105
314-863-1022

PRO-LIFE ORGANIZATIONS cont.

New Hampshire
His Mansion
P.O. Box 40
Hillsboro, NH 03244
603-464-5555

New York
Operation Rescue
P.O. Box 1180
Binghamton, NY 13902
607-723-4012

Pennsylvania
Loving and Caring Inc.
1905 Olde Homestead
  Lane
Lancaster, PA 17601
717-293-3230

Tennessee
American Rights Coalition
P.O. Box 487
Chattanooga, TN 37405
1-800-634-2224

Texas
Americans Against
  Abortion
Box 70
Lindale, TX 75771
214-963-8671

Women Exploited
  by Abortion (WEBA)
Route 1, Box 821
Venus, TX 76084
214-366-3600

Virginia
American Life League Inc.
P.O. Box 1350
Stafford, VA 22554
703-659-4171

Christian Action Council
101 W. Broad St., Suite 500
Falls Church, VA 22046
703-237-2100

Liberty Godparent
  Ministries
P.O. Box 27000
Lynchburg, VA 24506
1-800-54CHILD
804-384-3043 (office)

National Pro-Life Political
  Action Committee
2525 Wilson Blvd.
Arlington, VA 22201
703-528-1515

Women of Ramah
701 W. Broad Street,
Suite 405
Falls Church, VA 22046

The Least of These: What Everyone Should Know about Abortion by Curt Young. Moody Press.

ABORTION   **Who Broke the Baby?** by Jean Garton. Bethany House Publishers.
FOCUS
BOOKS   **Abortion: Questions and Answers** by Dr. and Mrs. J. C. Wilke. Haynes and Associates Publishing Inc.

Mom, I'm Pregnant by Bev O'Brien. Tyndale House Publishers.

Post-Abortion Trauma by Jeanette Vought. Zondervan Publishing House.

When Does Life Begin? by John Ankerberg and John Weldon. Wolgemuth & Hyatt.

The Scarlet Lady by Carol Everett with Jack Shaw. Wolgemuth & Hyatt.

Should I Keep My Baby? by Martha Zimmerman. Bethany House Publishers.

❝❞
FOCUS
QUOTE
The AIDS epidemic is far from over. It's not even under control. The worldwide situation is deteriorating. We are facing a decade in the 1990s that will be far more difficult than anything we saw in the 1980s. The World Health Organization estimates that 700,000 people have developed AIDS worldwide and 8 million to 10 million have contracted the virus that causes it. By the end of the decade, an estimated 5 million to 6 million will be sick, and the total number infected may approached 20 million. Worse still, the situation isn't expected to stabilize for several more decades.—Dr. Jonathan Mann, former director of the World Health Organization's Global Program on AIDS.

Global Epidemic

Most of the 1 million infected in the United States will be sick by the year 2000; worldwide, six times that many.

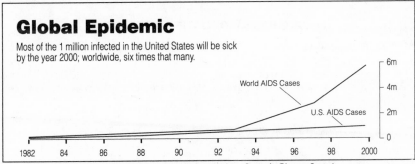

World AIDS Cases

U.S. AIDS Cases

6m
4m
2m
0

1982   84   86   88   90   92   94   96   98   2000

Source: World projections: World Health Organization; U.S. projections: Center for Disease Control.

DEATHS FROM AIDS

Year	Number of Deaths
1993	53,000–76,000
1992	49,000–64,000
1991	43,000–52,000
1990	37,000–42,000
1989	20,422
1988	18,488
1987	14,796
1986	11,108
1985	6,505

National AIDS Information Clearinghouse and the U.S. Centers for Disease Control

The Changing Profile of AIDS

Most AIDS patients are still gay men and IV drug users. But the rate of increase among heterosexuals and newborns proves that the virus knows no boundaries

Number of AIDS cases 1989

Gay or bisexual men   19,652

IV drug users   7,970

Heterosexuals   1,562

Newborns   547

Percent Increase 1988–1989

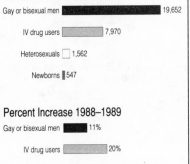

Gay or bisexual men   11%

IV drug users   20%

Heterosexuals   36%

Newborns   38%

AIDS Hits Close to Home

Percentage of people who know someone who has the AIDS virus

16 of every 100 people — 1989

22 of every 100 people — 1991

Source: American Association of Blood Bank polls

Source: Center for Disease Control.

66 99
FOCUS QUOTE
AIDS is the leading cause of death among men 25–44 in San Francisco, Los Angeles, and New York City and is the leading cause of death among black women ages 15–44 in New York State and New Jersey.—Associated Press, January 25, 1991

AIDS patients are afraid to talk. Their image of God is what they receive from the church as a whole, and so often, because the church has rejected them for being homosexuals or drug users or prostitutes, they think God hates them too. —Jeff Collins, director of Love & Action, about AIDS patients he works with, in *Christianity Today*.

PEOPLE RESPOND TO THE AIDS EPIDEMIC

As I read off some statements about AIDS, tell me whether you agree or disagree?

	Agree	Disagree	No opinion		Agree	Disagree	No opinion
AIDS sufferers should be treated with compassion				*I would refuse to work alongside someone who has AIDS*			
1991 May	91%	6%	3%	1991 May	16	80	4
1987 Oct	87	8	5	1987 Oct	25	65	10
1987 Jul	78	7	15	*People with AIDS should be isolated from the rest of society*			
The government is not doing enough about the problem of AIDS				1991 May	10	86	4
1991 May	60	32	8	1987 Oct	21	71	8
1987 Oct	53	37	10	*Landlords should have the right to evict a tenant from an apartment because that person has AIDS*			
People with the AIDS virus should be made to carry a card to this effect				1991 May	10	87	3
1991 May	59	37	4	1987 Oct	17	75	8
1987 Oct	54	38	8				
1987 Jul	60	24	16				

Source: The Gallup Organization. Telephone interviews with 1014 adults, 18 and older, May 2-5, 1991.

Everyone should have a blood test to see if they have AIDS

	Agree	Disagree	No opinion
1991 May	58	39	3
1987 Oct	48	46	6

I sometimes think that AIDS is a punishment for the decline in moral standards

	Agree	Disagree	No opinion
1991 May	34	62	4
1987 Oct	43	50	7
1987 Jul	42	43	15

In general, it's people's own fault if they get AIDS

	Agree	Disagree	No opinion
1991 May	33	63	4
1987 Oct	51	44	5
1987 Jul	45	13	42

Employers should have the right to dismiss an employee because that person has AIDS

	Agree	Disagree	No opinion
1991 May	21	71	8
1987 Oct	25	64	11
1987 Jul	33	43	24

AIDS
FOCUS
BOOKS

AIDS and Young People by Robert Redfield and Wanda Franz. Regnery Gateway, Inc.

Gays, AIDS and You by Enrique Rueda and Michael Schwartz. Devin Adair Co.

Christians in the Age of AIDS by Shepherd and Anita Moreland Smith. Victor Books.

AIDS ORGANIZATIONS

AIDS Clinical Trials Information Service
1-800-TRIALS-A

National AIDS Network (DC) 202-293-2437

National HIV and AIDS Information
Service Hotline 1-800-342-AIDS

People with AIDS Coalition Hotline (NY)
1-800-828-3280

Public Health Service Hotline
1-800-342-AIDS

National AIDS Prevention Institute,
P.O. Box 2500, Culpeper, VA 22701
703-825-4040

Walter Reed Army Institute of Research,
Department of Virus Diseases,
Washington, DC 20307
301-427-5176

Americans for a Sound AIDS Policy, P.O.
Box 17433, Washington, DC 20041
703-471-7350

Love and Action, 3 Church Circle, Annapolis, MD 21401
301-268-3442

The Bridge: Living with AIDS, 1759 Oak
Street, San Francisco, CA 94117
415-552-AIDS

DRUG USE DECLINING

Nearly a third of all people in the USA—7.4 million people—have used marijuana, cocaine or other illegal drugs at least once, according to the National Institute on Drug Abuse. Other statistics:

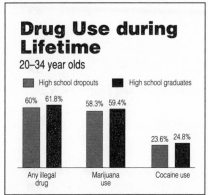

Drug Use during Lifetime

20–34 year olds

■ High school dropouts   ■ High school graduates

	Any illegal drug	Marijuana use	Cocaine use
High school dropouts	60%	58.3%	23.6%
High school graduates	61.8%	59.4%	24.8%

Source: National Institute of Drug Abuse survey based on interviews with 9,259 people, age 12 and older.

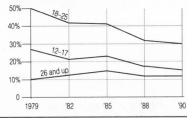

Drug Use in Past Years by Age Groups

18–25

12–17

26 and up

1979   '82   '85   '88   '90

Source: National Institute of Drug Abuse survey based on interviews with 9,259 people, age 12 and older.

FOCUS FACT

The United States has the highest rate of teen alcohol and drug use of any industrialized nation. The drug problem in this country is 10 times greater than in Japan.

WHO DOES, DOESN'T DO DRUGS

Drug abuse is more common among the affluent and the poor than in middle-income groups, according to a survey conducted by the Media-Advertising Partnership for a Drug-Free America. Other findings of the survey of 4,737 adults:

- 20% consider cocaine use a status symbol
- 11% feel that occasional use of cocaine is not risky
- 29% think cigarettes are worse than marijuana
- 26% think it's OK to smoke marijuana in private
- Women today are nearly identical to men in their use of marijuana and cocaine
- Blacks and Hispanics are more likely to be drug abusers than the general public
- About 30% of those 18 to 35 have used cocaine at least once
- Regular church attendance is strongly related to much lower levels of drug abuse among all populations

Source: *USA Today*, December 6, 1989.

TEENAGERS CONTINUE TO SAY SUBSTANCE ABUSE IS THEIR BIGGEST PROBLEM

Teenagers were asked: What do you feel is the biggest problem facing people your age?

	1991 %	1987 %	1983 %	1977 %
Drug abuse	49	54	35	27
Peer pressures	13	10	8	5
Alcohol abuse	11	12	10	7
Teenage pregnancy	10	11	-	-
Teenage gangs, crime	9	-	-	-
AIDS	6	5	-	-
Sex	4	-	-	-
School problems	3	1	5	3
College acceptance and financing	3	3	-	-
Unemployment	2	2	16	6
Getting along with parents	2	2	5	20
Economic problems	2	1	2	3
Problems in growing up	1	2	1	6
Teenage suicide	1	2	-	-
Career uncertainties	1	-	3	3
Fear of war	*	1	4	-
Miscellaneous	8	5	5	12
Don't know	12	8	18	14

*Less than one-half of one percent. Source: The George H. Gallup International Institute poll. July 1991. Used by permission.

What People Say about Drugs

A USA TODAY poll on illegal drugs reveals widespread concern.

Fear of drug violence tops list of concerns

Those who say they are concerned "a great deal" about:

Becoming a victim of drug-related violence	71%
Someone close becoming exposed to drugs	70%
Someone close becoming a drug user	66%
Drug use leading to the decline of the USA	58%
Bribes and threats corrupting the government	53%

Large majority thinks drug problems are worse than most people think...

It's worse

Men	86%
Women	91%

It's overblown

Men	11%
Women	5%

...But half think the battle can be won

U.S. can win drug war	51%
Drug problem won't be solved	39%

What we see as key to drug war victory

Stiffer penalties for drug dealers	45%
More education	34%
Legalize drugs	8%
Other	25%
Don't know	8%

Percentage who view drug addicts as

Victims	56%
Criminals	19%
Neither	6%
Both	16%

Hours per week people would be willing to volunteer to work in the drug war

- 6% don't know, refused
- 14% would work 10 hours
- 21% would work 5 hours
- 19% would work none
- 40% would work 1 hour

How much people would pay in new anti-drug taxes

- 11% don't know, refused
- 11% would pay $500
- 10% would pay $300
- 36% would pay none
- 32% would pay $100

Source: An Oct. 15-16, 1989 USA TODAY telephone poll of 814 people by Gordon S. Black Associates. Sampling error is plus or minus 3.5 percent.

EFFECTIVE ANTI-DRUG CAMPAIGNERS: TEENS TELL WHOM THEY WOULD LISTEN TO

	Teens %
Former drug addicts	71
Sports figures	55
Rock stars	47
Physicians	33
Policemen	32
Ministers, priests, or rabbis	24
Scientists	22
Teachers	16
Congressmen	16

Source: The Gallup Organization, Inc., poll. July 1989. Used by permission.

SUB-STANCE ABUSE FOCUS BOOKS

Drugs and Drinking by Jay Strack. Thomas Nelson, Inc.

Dying for a Drink by Anderson Spickard and Barbara R. Thompson. Word, Inc.

Smart Kids, Stupid Choices by Kevin Leman. Regal Books/Gospel Light Publications.

A Secret Hell by Claire Costales and Priscilla Barak. Regal Books/ Gospel Light Publications.

Staying Dry by Claire Costales and Jo Berry. Regal Books/Gospel Light Publications.

Understanding Alcoholism by Carolyn Johnson. Zondervan Publishing House.

❝❞ FOCUS QUOTE We're seeing a lot of 9 and 10 year olds—they're not all getting caught (for drugs), but they tell us they are dealing.
—Melinda Mills, supervising probation officer, San Francisco Juvenile Court

Use of Alcoholic Beverages Declines

Do you have occasion to use alcoholic beverages such as liquor, wine, beer?

	Yes	No
1990	57%	43%
1987	65	35
1981	70	30
1974	68	32
1960	62	38
1950	60	40
1945	67	33
1939	58	42

Has drinking ever been a cause of trouble in your family?

	Yes	No
1990	23%	76%
1987	24	76
1981	22	78
1974	12	88
1966	12	88
1950	14	86

When did you last take a drink of any kind of alcoholic beverage?

	1987	1990
Within last 24 hours	38%	29%
Over one day to one week ago	30	23
Over 1 week ago	31	47
No opinion	1	1

Source: The Gallup Organization. Poll of 1,007 adults, 18 and older, December 6-9, 1990.

FOCUS FACT How can you know whom to contact about your social and political concerns, what to say, and when to say it? Keep in touch with an organization providing "inside Washington" information. The Family Research Council's publication, *Washington Watch,* will keep you on target with the latest reports from the nation's capitol—free of charge. To receive *Washington Watch,* telephone or write: The Family Research Council, 700 Thirteenth Street NW, Suite 500, Washington, DC 20005. 202-393-2100. Request it by name.

Why Teenagers Drink

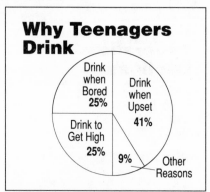

Source: National Council on Alcoholism and Drug Dependence, Surgeon General survey.

Drunk Driving Deaths Decline

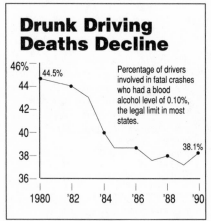

Percentage of drivers involved in fatal crashes who had a blood alcohol level of 0.10%, the legal limit in most states.

Source: National Highway Traffic Safety Administration.

TOP FIVE PROBLEMS IN PUBLIC SCHOOLS—THEN AND NOW

1940	1991*
1. Talking	1. Alcohol abuse
2. Chewing gum	2. Apathy
3. Making noise	3. Drug abuse
4. Running in the halls	4. Discipline
5. Getting out of line	5. Poor Teachers

*Survey of 1,237 student delegates to the National Association of Student Councils June 1991.

FOCUS FACT

Even if you never use alcohol, drunk driving is still *your* problem--because you share the road with others. **Every year more than 25,000 people are killed in alcohol-related accidents, and more than $5 million worth of property is destroyed. At least a million people are injured, maimed, or crippled for life.**—Mothers Against Drunk Driving (MADD).

FOCUS BOOK

Wake Up, America! **by Tony Campolo. A challenge in involvement in grass roots ministries.** Published by Crossway Books.

HOW TO SAY NO TO SUBSTANCE ABUSE: THE RIMSHOT APPROACH

Here are some snappy answers to the question: Want some alcohol or other drugs?

No, thanks, I'd rather walk my pet python.

No way, I'm in a skateboarding contest today.

No, thanks, I'm saving my bad breath for pepperoni pizza.

You must be kidding! If I'm going to ruin my body, I'd rather do it with a hot fudge sundae.

No, thank you. I need all my brain cells, so I'd rather have noodle soup.

I'd rather not. I'm too special.

No, thanks, I don't like the taste.

No, thanks, I'm all-American. I'll stick to milk.

Source: Flier distributed by the Department of Health and Human Services Office for Substance Abuse Prevention. Copies of the flier are available for conferences, workshops, or youth events.

SUBSTANCE ABUSE RECOVERY ORGANIZATIONS

Adcare Referral (drug and alcohol problems)
1-800-252-6465

Nat'l Fed. of Parents for Drug-Free Youth
1-800-535-8196

National Referral Hotline
1-800-COCAINE

Parents Resource for Drug Education (PRIDE)
1-800-241-9746

Arizona
Calvary Rehabilitation Center
329 N. Third Avenue
Phoenix, AZ 85003
602-254-7092

California
New Life Treatment Centers
570 Glenneyre, Suite 107
Laguna Beach, CA 92651
1-800-227-LIFE

Overcomers Outreach, Inc.
2290 W. Whittier Blvd., Suite D
La Habra, CA 90631
213-697-3994

Schick Shadel Hospitals for Alcoholism
Treatment*
1901 Avenue of the Stars, Suite 1530
Los Angeles, CA 90067

Victory Outreach
454 Cobera Avenue
LaPuente, CA 91746
818-961-4910

Illinois
Alcoholics Victorious
123 S. Green Street
Chicago, IL 60607

Kentucky
Possibilities Unlimited, Inc.
4514 Briar Hill Road
Lexington, KY 40516
606-229-0445

Maryland
Nat'l. Inst. on Alcohol Abuse and Alcoholism
5600 Fishers Lane
Rockville, MD 20852

Michigan
Alcoholics for Christ
1316 N. Campbell Road
Royal Oak, MI 48067
1-800-441-7877

New Mexico
Support
3812 Central SE
Albuquerque, NM 87108
505-265-6417

New Jersey
Salvation Army
799 Bloomfield Avenue
Verona, NJ 07044
201-239-0606

New York
Alcoholics Anonymous*
P.O. Box 459, Grand Central Station
New York, NY 10163

Al-anon* or Alateen*
(for relatives & friends)
One Park Avenue
New York, NY 10016

National Council on Alcoholism
12 W. 21st Street
New York, NY 10010

Walter Hoving Home for Women
P.O. Box 194
Garrison, NY 10524
914-424-3674

Pennsylvania
New Life for Girls
RD 3, Box D700
Dover, PA 17315
717-266-5614

Toughlove
P.O. Box 1069
Doylestown, PA 18901
215-348-7090

Texas
Mothers Against Drunk Driving (MADD)
P.O. Box 541688
Dallas, TX 75354-1688
214-744-MADD

*These organizations have regional offices. Look in the telephone book for the one nearest you.

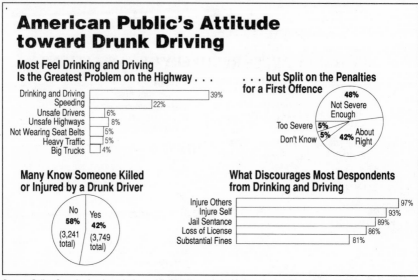

American Public's Attitude toward Drunk Driving

Most Feel Drinking and Driving Is the Greatest Problem on the Highway . . .

Drinking and Driving	39%
Speeding	22%
Unsafe Drivers	6%
Unsafe Highways	8%
Not Wearing Seat Belts	5%
Heavy Traffic	5%
Big Trucks	4%

. . . but Split on the Penalties for a First Offence

48% Not Severe Enough
Too Severe 5%
Don't Know 5%
About Right 42%

Many Know Someone Killed or Injured by a Drunk Driver

No 58% (3,241 total)
Yes 42% (3,749 total)

What Discourages Most Despondents from Drinking and Driving

Injure Others	97%
Injure Self	93%
Jail Sentance	89%
Loss of License	86%
Substantial Fines	81%

Source: Gallup Organization, Inc. telephone poll of 9,028 people for Mothers Against Drunk Driving (MADD), September 1990–August 1991.

PUBLIC OPINION ON HOMOSEXUALITY

Do you think homosexual relations between consenting adults should or should not be legal?

	1989	1987	1986	1985	1982	1977
	%	%	%	%	%	%
Legal	47	33	33	44	45	43
Not legal	36	55	54	47	39	43
Don't know/ No opinion	17	12	13	9	16	14

There has been considerable discussion in the news regarding the rights of homosexual men and women. In general, do you think homosexuals should or should not have equal rights in terms of job opportunities?

	1989	1982	1977
	%	%	%
Yes, should	71	59	56
No, should not	18	28	33
No opinion	11	13	11

Percent saying homosexuals should be hired for each occupation.

	1989	1987	1985	1982	1977
	%	%	%	%	%
Salespersons	79	72	71	70	68
Armed forces	60	55	55	52	51
Doctors	56	49	52	50	44
Clergy	44	42	41	38	36
Elementary school teachers	42	33	36	32	27

Source: The Gallup Poll, October 12-15, 1989.

❝❞ FOCUS QUOTE People with homosexual desires need the church's concern. Many desperately want help from a church, but they are afraid to identify themselves for fear of being ostracized.—Tim Stafford in *Christianity Today,* August 18, 1989, issue.

HOMOSEXUAL RECOVERY ORGANIZATIONS

California
Desert Stream
  12488 Venice Blvd.
  Los Angeles, CA 90066 / 213-572-0140

Exodus International
  P.O. Box 2121
  San Rafael, CA 94912 / 415-454-1017

Love in Action
  P.O. Box 2655
  San Rafael, CA 94912 / 415-454-0960

New Life Treatment Center Inc.
  570 Glenneyre Avenue, Suite 107
  Laguna Beach, CA 92651 / 1-800-227-LIFE
  714-494-8383

Spatula Ministries (for parents)
  P.O. Box 444
  LaHabra, CA 90631 / 213-691-7369

Florida
Victory House
  719 SW 4th Court
  Fort Lauderdale, FL 33312 /
  305-680-3538

Minnesota
Outpost
  3044 Chicago Avenue S., P.O. Box 7067
  Minneapolis, MN 55407
  612-827-1419

Pennsylvania
Homosexuals Anonymous Fellowship
  Services
  Box 7881
  Reading, PA 19603 / 1-800-253-3000

HOMO-SEXUAL RECOVERY FOCUS BOOKS

Growing Up Straight: What Every Family Should Know about Homosexuality by George A. Rekers. Moody Press.

How Will I Tell My Mother? by Jerry Arteburn. Oliver Nelson Books.

Where Does a Mother Go to Resign? by Barbara Johnson. Bethany House Publishers.

The Broken Image by Leanne Payne. Crossway Books/Good News Publishers.

The Return of Love by Alex Davidson. InterVarsity Press.

RESPONSE TO THE PORNOGRAPHY ARGUMENTS

1. **Pornography is harmless. A 1970 Presidential Commission Report said so.** The Majority Report of the 1970 Presidential Commission on Obscenity and Pornography was called a "scientific scandal" by many in the scientific community. It was rejected by the U.S. Senate by a vote of 60 to 5. The Hill-Link Minority Report of that Commission was read into the record in both Houses of Congress as a "responsible position on the issues." The Hill-Link Report cited numerous instances where evidence was suppressed when it went counter to the pre-determined "findings" of the majority report. The Hill-Link Report and the chapters by Dr. Victor B. Cline in *Where Do You Draw the Line?* expose the majority report for what it was. In addition, studies in the Hill-Link Report show linkages between exposure to obscene material and sexual deviancy, promiscuity, affiliation with criminal

RESPONSE TO THE PORNOGRAPHY ARGUMENTS cont.

groups, and more. However, extremists who want obscenity laws repealed as the majority report recommended began a campaign in early 1977 to have the report resurrected and considered a reputable document.

2.**You can't legislate morality.** On its face this cliché is absurd because every law legislates morality. Every law sets some standard for its citizens, and every citizen must ultimately make the moral decision to obey and disobey.

Private morals are private. Public morals are the business of the entire community and the officers empowered by the community to defend the welfare of the community against the willful minority. Commercial obscenity is public business. It is public morality that obscenity laws are designed to safeguard, not private morality.

FOCUS FACT

Porn is an $8-billion-a-year business in the United States, which includes:
- **more than 450 different pornographic magazines**
- **nearly 20,000 adult bookstores**
- **800 adult movie theaters**
- **2 million pornographic video casettes**
- **more than 165,000 purveyors of pornography including producers, publishers, distributors, retailers, writers, and photographers.**

Source: Jerry R. Kirk in *The Winnable War*.

---

3. **Obscenity is in the eye of the beholder. What is obscene to you may not be obscene to me.** This implies that obscenity is subjective. It is not. It is the description or depiction of specific sexual activity, the description or depiction of which is prohibited by law, to protect the common good. It is as objective as stealing or murder. This statement also denies the existence of evil.

4. **I'd rather see people make love than make violence.** There is no love in pornography. It is totally loveless, debasing women, children, and humanity generally. In addition, violence is inherent in pornography.

5. **War, poverty, hunger, violence are the real obscenities. Sex is not obscene.** The extension of the word *obscenity* to cover all kinds of social evils is a recent development in our language. It is a well-known technique to confuse and blunt the force of obscenity law.

Of course sex is not obscene. It is the design and creation of God. It is the debasing abuse of sex that is obscene. And, as in the past, so now all over the country, legislatures and the judiciary definitely specify certain abuses of sex as obscene.

6. **If you don't like porn films and books, you don't have to see them or buy them, but don't interfere with my rights to see or buy them.** I don't see or buy pornography, but it is there polluting the environment in which I am trying to raise my children. Society says it does not want it there and has enacted laws against it.

The United States Supreme Court has said that what you do in the privacy of your home is your own business, but your privacy right does not extend to the marketplace. It is against the law for anyone to sell or exhibit obscenity to you.

7. **Well, the Supreme Court has said a lot of things, but it still can't define obscenity.** This statement is incorrect. The Supreme Court defined obscenity in June of 1973 to the satisfaction of the majority of the American people.

8. **Freedom of expression is protected by the First Amendment.** It most certainly is. But the Supreme Court has said, and has always held, that obscenity is not protected by the

First Amendment. It is not protected expression, any more than libel or slander are. Obscenity is not a First Amendment issue. It is a crime, and 90 percent of the traffic in hard-core pornography in the country is controlled by organized crime.

9. **Who are you to tell me what I can see or read? You are imposing your morality on me.** Nobody can tell you what to see or to read, but the community can tell you what commercial spectacles and literature cannot be sold or distributed to you—if you choose to live in that community. The community sets up standards for itself and has a right to legislate to protect those standards.

Nobody is imposing his morality on anybody. It is only the consensus of the community that determines the standards of public decency. When that consensus is properly manifested in public law, that is community or public morality, not "ours."

This implies there should be no law regulating the traffic in pornography.

10. **Obscenity is a victimless crime.** There is no such thing as a victimless crime. In every crime there is a seller or seducer, and the person who purchases, or the seduced. That person is the immediate victim, and society is the ultimate victim, for with each seduction the moral fabric of society is diminished. The victimless crimes theory is an active and insidious attack on almost all laws dealing with public morality, maintaining there is no victim when consenting adults indulge in drugs, prostitution, obscenity, homosexuality, adultery, incest, gambling, etc.

A glaring instance of victimization in obscenity are the children used in child pornography.

For centuries civil communities have maintained laws against such behavior as detrimental to the public health, morals, and welfare.

Denmark and the Boston Combat Zone have recently and vividly proved that increase in commercial pornography causes concentration of violent prostitution and organized crime.

11. **When "consenting adults" go to see a dirty movie, no one is being harmed.** Regarding so-called "consenting adults." The United States Supreme Court said in Paris Theatre in June of 1973: "We categorically disapprove the theory that obscene films acquire constitutional immunity from state regulation simply because they are exhibited for consenting adults only. Rights and interests other than those of the advocates are involved. These include the interest of the public in the quality of life, the total community environment, the tone of commerce, and, possibly, the public safety itself."

12. **If you'd let pornography flow freely, people would get bored and the problem would take care of itself.** This boredom or satiation theory is invalid. (See *Where Do You Draw the Line?* by Dr. Victor B. Cline). Heavy users of pornography do not get bored. They go deeper and deeper into more and more bizarre forms of it.

Professor Irving Kristol said in the same volume, "I would like to go along with this theory [boredom] but I cannot. I think it is false. The sexual pleasure one gets from pornography is autoerotic and infantile; put bluntly, it is a masturbatory exercise of the imagination when it is not masturbation pure and simple. Now, people who masturbate do not get tired of masturbation, just as sadists don't get bored with voyeurism. In other words, infantile sexuality is not only a permanent temptation—it can easily become a self-reinforcing neurosis."

Denmark is often brought up when the boredom theory is espoused. Denmark legalized pornography, the argument goes, and porn profits dropped because people got bored. Denmark's porn profits are falling, but not because of boredom. Underworld infiltration of the porn industry, gangland violence, and tie-ins with traffic in narcotics forced the Copenhagen police to close down dozens of smut dens, and all live sex shows have been outlawed (Associated Press Reports, 1972-76).

Remember, every day children are seeing pornography for the first time. Pornography strikes at children in the mail, at newsstands, etc.

RESPONSE TO THE PORNOGRAPHY ARGUMENTS cont.

13. **How do you define obscenity?** How I define obscenity is not the issue. The Supreme Court has defined obscenity to the satisfaction of most. The test for obscenity is: materials which "taken as a whole appeal to the prurient interest in sex, which portray sexual conduct in a patently offensive way, and which, taken as a whole, do not have serious literary, artistic, political or scientific value."

14. **But the Supreme Court left it to communities to decide what is obscene.** This is an oversimplification and a misleading one. Community standards is not the test for obscenity, but a part of the test for obscenity, and has been part of the test for obscenity since 1957. In 1973 the Court said: "The basic guidelines for the trier of the fact must be: a) whether the average person, applying contemporary community standards, would find that the work taken as a whole appeals to the prurient interest, b) whether the work depicts or describes, in a patently offensive way, sexual conduct specifically defined by the applicable state law, etc." It is the "trier of the fact," a jury or a judge who decides what is obscene under the guidelines.

15. **How is a producer or publisher to know his material is obscene when the court can't even decide what is obscene?** The Court has decided what is obscene, and it is up to a person who traffics in pornography to be alert to and know what the Supreme Court decisions are. The Court said in its landmark Miller decision when it defined obscenity. "We are satisfied that these prerequisites (the three-part test) will provide fair notice to a dealer in such materials that his public and commercial activities may bring prosecution."

PORNO-GRAPHY FOCUS BOOKS

Pornography: The Human Tragedy edited by Tom Minnery. Tyndale House Publishers.

The Mind Polluters by Jerry R. Kirk. Thomas Nelson, Inc.

Out of the Shadows by Patrick Carnes. CompCare Publications.

The Case Against Pornography by Donald Wildmon. Victor Books.

The Seduction of Society by William Stanmeyer. Servant Books.

---

16. **Why be concerned about obscenity when there is so much violent crime?** They're related. Pornography outlets breed and attract violent crime.

17. **The porno industry is flourishing and growing, so the American people must want it or simply don't care.** Certainly there are some who want it. That's what makes it so profitable. And obviously there are some who don't care. But all surveys show that the majority of Americans are vehemently opposed to the traffic in pornography and want it stopped. The majority do care, but they are confused and discouraged in the face of a highly organized industry and the loud prophets of false freedom. One of the major factors in the growth of the pornography traffic is the lack of vigorous enforcement of obscenity laws, particularly at the federal level.

18. **Why bother enforcing the law? The "adult" bookstores and porno movie houses keep operating while their owners are in the courts.** Continuous, vigorous enforcement of the law is the answer. When arrests and prosecutions begin, the sex industry is put on warning. Prison sentences, fines, and legal fees will put the pornographers out of business. Atlanta, Jacksonville, and Cincinnati are clean cities because of vigorous, continuous enforcement of the law. And experts say that with aggressive enforcement of federal law, the back of the porno industry would be broken in 18 months.

TEN THINGS YOU CAN DO TO COMBAT PORNOGRAPHY

1. Become knowledgeable about the issues.

2. Call and write those who are responsible for enforcing laws against crime.

3. Call and write those who hold elected positions in city or county government, such as your mayor and the members of your city and county councils.

4. Write your governor and state legislators and ask them to seek revision of state anti-obscenity laws so that they are as strong as allowed by the state and federal constitutions.

5. Write the president, attorney general, your congressman, and U.S. senators. Ask them to strengthen federal laws against pornography.

6. Write representatives of the news media and "letters to the editor" about your views against pornography.

7. Initiate a petition to public officials, stating your concern and disapproval of the public display and sale of pornography—films, video cassettes, books, and magazines.

8. Use this step-by-step procedure and strategy in contacting neighborhood stores that display and sell pornographic materials:

   a. Courteously speak to the store manager and tell him that his display and sale of pornographic magazines and materials is offensive to you. Ask him to: (1) put these out of sight, and (2) seek a change in business policy that will discontinue the sale of this material.

   b. After a short time, if he still continues to display and sell these products, again speak to the store manager and tell him of your concern.

   c. If the merchant persists in openly promoting and selling these materials, write a letter to the headquarters office of the store telling them of your concern; send a copy of your letter to the store manager.

   d. If there is no change in store practices, stop buying at this store. Write the local store and headquarters office and tell them you will no longer patronize their business.

9. Contact National Coalition Against Pornography for the names and addresses of organizations that may be able to help you.

10. Join with others in all of your efforts. Be persistent.

Source: National Coalition Against Pornography.

ORGANIZATIONS THAT FIGHT
THE SPREAD OF PORNOGRAPHY

Arizona
Children's Legal Foundation
P.O. Box 10050
Phoenix, AZ 85064-0050
602-381-1322

Mississippi
American Family Association
P.O. Drawer 2440
Tupelo, MS 38803
601-844-5036 1-800-FAMILIE

New York
Morality in Media, Inc.
475 Riverside Drive, Suite 239,
New York, NY 10115
212-870-3222

Ohio
National Coalition Against
   Pornography
P.O. Box 7777
Cincinnati, OH 45231
513-521-6227

National Consultation on
   Pornography, Inc.
5742 Hamilton Avenue
Cincinnati, OH 45224

FOCUS
FACT

- • Rape rates are highest in states that have high sales of sexually explicit materials and lax restrictions and enforcement of pornography.
- • Rapists are 15 times as likely as nonoffenders to have had exposure to hard-core pornography before the age of 10.
- • A crackdown on adult bookstores, X-rated movie theaters, and massage parlors in Cincinnati resulted in a 42 percent decrease in assaults, prostitution, and drug trafficking, and an 83 percent drop in rapes, robberies, and aggravated assaults.

- • A study by Michigan State Police Department Lieutenant Darrell Pope showed that 41 percent of the 38,000 sexual assault cases on file in Michigan involved some use of pornographic materials during or just prior to the act.
- • Adult bookstores outnumber McDonald's restaurants in the United States by a margin of at least three to one.

Source: Leigh Ann Metzger in *Understanding the Problem of Pornography*. Published by Family Research Council.

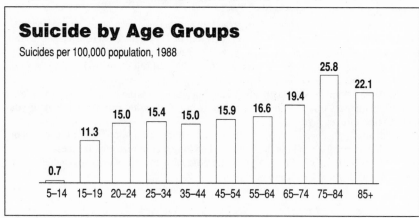

Source: National Center for Health Statistics; National Institute of Mental Health.

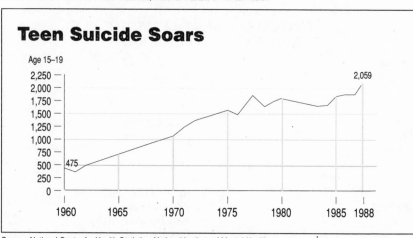

Source: National Center for Health Statistics; National Institute of Mental Health.

WHY TEENS BECOME SUICIDAL

A third of U.S. teenagers say they have considered suicide, 15% have thought seriously about it, and 6% have actually tried to kill themselves, a Gallup poll says.

According to the Center for Disease Control, among teens who tried or thought seriously about suicide:

47% cite family problems;

23% say they were depressed;

22% had problems with friends/peer pressure.

Biggest problems teens say they have: school, 33%; career, 25%; growing up, 18%

SIX TYPES OF SUICIDE

1. Rational (figured out a way to escape further pain)
2. Reaction (following loss)
3. Vengeful (to punish someone)
4. Manipulative (to thwart someone's plan)
5. Psychotic (to fulfill a delusion)
   6. Accidental (spontaneous decision reconsidered too late)

Source: Edwin Shneidman in *Definition of Suicide*. Published by John Wiley & Sons, New York, N.Y.

SIGNS OF SUICIDAL TENDENCIES

1. Changes in eating and sleeping habits
2. Withdrawal from friends, family, activities
3. Violent or rebellious behavior, running away
4. Drug, alcohol abuse
5. Changes in hygiene
6. Persistent boredom, difficulty concentrating, decline in schoolwork.
7. Frequent stomachaches, headaches, fatigue
8. Loss of interest in pleasurable activities
9. Inability to accept praise
10. Feeling "rotten inside"
11. Giving away favorite possessions
12. Verbal hints, such as "I won't see you again."

Source: American Academy of Child and Adolescent Psychiatry.

 FOCUS FACT **Suicide is the second leading cause of death for adolescents following accidents (of which many are suspected as suicide related). By the year 2000, projections are that 250,000–500,000 young people will attempt suicide each year.**

UNDERSTANDING HOW A SUICIDAL PERSON FEELS

1. Unendurable psychic pain. It builds until at last one says, "Too far. No farther."

2. Unmet needs accumulate with growing frustration. Every suicide is logical to the one who decides. It is faulty logic, to be sure, but it constricts finally to only one opinion.

3. A solution is sought to stop consciousness. Getting very upset even over trivia is critical at this point, especially if there is something lethal available.

4. Helpless and hopeless. It is an utter loneliness. There is nothing I can do and no one can help me.

5. Ambivalence. One wants escape but wants life as well. That is why one cries for help; 80 percent of suicide victims communicate their intention.

6. Constriction. A tunnel-visioning narrows until the focus can no longer even include loved ones who nurture. It is not simply that they are disregarded, they are not even within the range of what is in the mind.

7. Egression is the point where one takes leave from the mind which mediates the intolerable pain. Usually the high death wish is transient. A short while later, this person will be glad it did not happen.

Source: B. D. Garfinkel and H. Golombek, editors in *The Adolescent and Mood Disturbances.* Published by International Press, New York, N.Y.

HOW TEENAGERS BELIEVE THE CHURCH SHOULD RESPOND

What activities should the church offer to prevent teenagers from considering suicide?

Hot Line 92%
Counseling 89%
Drop-in centers 88%

Alternative activities 83%
Family counseling 80%
Teen shelter 64%
Counselor training 62%

Source: The Gallup Organization poll of 1,152 teenagers, aged 13-19, from November 1990 to January 1991.

SUICIDE CRISIS ORGANIZATIONS

Emergency 911

Suicide Prevention Hotline
1-800-333-4444

Suicide Prevention Hotline
1-800-882-3386

American Association of Suicidology
2459 S. Ash
Denver, CO 80222
303-692-0985

Life Line International
Box 224
Old Greenwich, CT 06870
203-324-1010

National Institute of Mental Health
Public Inquiries Section

5600 Fisher's Lane
Rockville, MD 20857
301-443-4515

National Suicide Help Center
P.O. Box 34
Rochester, MN 55903
507-282-2723

Teen Suicide Prevention Task Force
P.O. Box 76463
Washington, DC 20013
301-627-1595

Youth Suicide National Center
West Coast Office
1811 Trousdale Drive
Burlingame, CA 94010
415-877-5605

SUICIDE FOCUS BOOKS

When Someone Wants to Die **by S. J. Anderson. Relates the author's account of her struggle with suicide. InterVarsity Press.**

Suicide: Knowing When Your Teen Is At Risk **by T. Mitchel Anthony. Regal Books.**

A Reason to Live, **Melody Beattie, general editor. Explores reasons to live and contains suggestions for life-affirming actions. Tyndale House Publishers.**

FOCUS FACT

To die in America is no longer simple. Before the 1950s, most patients died at home. Now they may spend their final days (or months or years) in a hospital or nursing home, often attached to sophisticated machinery that can extend even the most fragile life. "Doctors have always been in control, but now it's not just doctors and patients," Ruth Macklin, professor of bioethics at Albert Einstein College of Medicine in New York City, says. "There are hospital administrators, in-house attorneys, and risk managers. . . . These are the people who are *really* in control." To circumvent that tangled bureaucracy, to avoid the crushing burden of extended illness, many people now consider the possibility of taking life—and death—into their own hands.—*Newsweek* magazine, August 26, 1991, issue.

Euthanasia: What Americans Believe Is Acceptable

What people say are circumstances in which a person has a moral right to end his or her life:

66%

In pain, no improvement

58%

Incurable disease

33%

Heavy burden on the family

16%

Under any circumstances

When a person has a disease that cannot be cured, do you think doctors should be allowed by law to end the patient's life by some painless means if the patient and his family request it?

Yes	65%
No	31
No opinion	4

If you were on life support systems and there was no hope of recovering, would you like to remain on the life support system or would you like treatment withheld so that you could end your life?

Kept on life support system	9%
Treatment withheld	84
No opinion	7

Suppose a terminally ill person wants treatment withheld so that he or she may die. Do you agree with each of the following statements:

The patient has the right to stop treatment . . .

	Agree	Disagree	No opinion
If the doctor agrees	75%	22%	3%
If he or she is in great pain	78	18	4
If his or her family agrees	76	22	2
Under any circumstances	59	40	3
Under no circumstances	11	87	2

Do you fear death?

	Yes	No	No opinion
Total	23%	75%	2%
Age:			
18–29	33	66	1
30–49	25	74	1
50 & older	16	83	1

Source: 1990 Gallup poll of 1,018 adults, November 15-18, 1990.

66 99 **FOCUS QUOTE** What our aging mothers and fathers need most is a reaffirmation of what the church has always taught: Life—even with suffering and pain—has meaning. It is not something to be discarded when it does not work properly or does not seem to be valued. Our Lord's love for us does not dim with age.... Sentiment favoring "assisted death" will increase as long as the elderly are left alone. That is exactly what the church should never do.
—Lyn Cryderman, in *Christianity Today* magazine.

MAJOR 19TH-CENTURY EVANGELICAL
SOCIAL REFORM MOVEMENTS

Reform Movement	Key Evangelical Leaders	Reform Organizations	Results Achieved
Abolition of Slavery	Samuel Hopkins (1721–1803) Lyman Beecher (1775–1863) Charles G. Finney (1792–1875) John Brown (1800–1859) Theodore Weld (1803–1895) Jonathan Blanchard (1811–1892) Harriet Beecher Stowe (1811–1896)	1807—Friends of Humanity Association 1817—Colonization Society 1818—American Conventions for Promoting the Abolition of Slavery and Improving the Condition of the African Race 1833—American Anti-Slavery Society 1840—Liberty Party 1848—Free Soil Party	1861–1865—Civil War 1863—Emancipation Proclamation 1865—Thirteenth Amendment 1866—Fourteenth Amendment
Prohibition of Alcoholic Beverages	Lyman Beecher (1775–1863) Frances Willard (1839–1898) Billy Sunday (1862–1935)	1813—Massachusetts Society for the Suppression of Intemperance 1826—American Society for the Promotion of Temperance 1836—American Temperance Union 1840—Washingtonians 1869—National Prohibition Party 1874—Women's Christian Temperance Union 1893—Anti-Saloon League	1846—Maine passed Prohibition Ordinance 1847–1855—Thirteen other states followed 1919–1932—Prohibition Amendment in force
Women's Rights	Emma Willard (1787–1870) Matthew Vassar (1792–1868) Angelina Grimke (1792–1873) Mary Lyon (1797–1849)	1848—Women's Rights Convention 1869—National Woman Suffrage Association 1869—American Woman Suffrage Association 1892—Federal Woman Suffrage Association	1821—"Female Seminary" founded in Troy, New York 1836—Mt. Holyoke College founded 1861—Vassar College founded 1917—Suffrage to women granted by New York 1918—Fourteen other states followed 1920—Woman Suffrage Amendment

Taken from *Chronological and Background Charts of Church History* by Robert Walton. Copyright © 1986 by The Zondervan Corporation. Used by permission.

WHAT TO WATCH FOR ON CAPITOL HILL IN 1993-1994
by Gary L. Bauer, President, Family Research Council

When the 104th Congress convenes in January 1993, we expect to see increased attention to domestic issues. This attention is long overdue, and we must be concerned about the ways in which domestic issues will be defined. One threat to the family is the definition of the family itself. Christians have historically viewed the family as a group of people bound by ties of blood, marriage, or adoption. Civil laws have incorporated this view.

But beginning in the 1960s, and with a quickening pace since, change has marched through our land. An insidious threat to defining the family comes through "domestic partnership" laws adopted by many localities. Under these laws, any couple, homosexual or heterosexual, can register with the city clerk their intent to remain in a close, meaningful, and enduring relationship. They can then claim the same benefits as married persons—sick leave, survivor benefits like pensions, and bereavement leave when one member dies. Through such tolerant and "compassionate" means, the family as an institution is undone. San Francisco and Minneapolis voters declined to repeal domestic partnership ordinances in 1991, perhaps without thinking through future costs. City taxpayers will see municipal budgets buckle under the strain of skyrocketing health care costs.

We expect to see the federal government come under increasing pressure to rescue the cities as social and financial costs of redefining the family strain budgets. We already have a model for how this has occurred in the example of Aid to Families with Dependent Children. When first conceived, this program was a modest one. It was intended to help small children of widows and abandoned mothers. But, as the program developed over time, AFDC payments began to go to the children of never-married mothers. Today, more than 90% of the recipients of AFDC payments have never married. Prominent social scientists say that the way the program operates discourages people from marrying.

A collapsing definition of family will bring increased pressures on the traditional family. Families who seek to raise their children without unwarranted government intrusion will be called upon to pay an increasing share of the costs of social breakdown. If it is true, as the old maxim says, that "what you tax you destroy, and what you do not tax, you cause to flourish," then nontraditional families will proliferate and traditional families will wither. Dr. James Dobson reports that in Australia the government actually penalizes couples for getting married; they collect more benefits if they stay single.

Taxes

The ballooning federal budget deficit means that the next generation will inherit the costs of governing this generation.

We must not only be aware of direct ways in which government taxes away the family paycheck, but we also must be alert to indirect taxes upon the family. For example, when environmentalists press government to legislate car size to achieve greater fuel economy, they are taxing family-size cars. Large cars are safer in crash tests. They are also the most economical means for a family with two or more children to get around. Government mandated standards for Corporate Average Fuel Economy (CAFE) thus becomes a hidden tax on families, discouraging them from making their own choices about the number of children to have and kind of car to buy.

Time is money, we know. The government can take away our money in the form of taxes, or our time in the form of bureaucratic regulation. Requiring in-home child-care providers to fill out extensive forms and endless reports burdens care-givers, reduces the satisfaction they derive from their calling, and renders them state employees rather than

WHAT TO WATCH FOR ON CAPITOL HILL IN 1993–1994 cont.

employees of the parents who trust them to provide good care for their children. It makes in-home child care a less attractive option for the mother who wants to supplement her family's income by caring for the children of her friends and neighbors. Increased regulation favors the *institutional* child care centers. Government bureaucracy can tax home-based providers out of the day-care picture. Expect increasing demands in the '90s for public subsidy of institutional care.

Crime

Crime is a hidden tax. As more families move out of inner cities to seek safety in the suburbs, they must buy or rent the larger homes that zoning laws so often require in suburban communities. As criminals follow their victims out of the cities, the cost of protecting families in the suburbs goes up. This seemingly unending spiral is set in motion by the failure of government to apprehend, try, convict, and lock up dangerous criminals. The impact of violent crime on families will be an important issue of the '90s.

Crime prevents businesses from locating within many parts of our cities. Suburban communities have similar problems. The need to hire security guards in the local supermarket drives up the price of groceries. The fear of crime requires businesses and colleges to schedule classes in daylight hours or to arrange protection for people who must walk down dark parking lots.

Failure to punish crime swiftly and surely encourages more people to believe they can get away with lawlessness. Families who find it difficult to put a roof over their own family are increasingly taxed by government to put a roof over the heads of criminals.

Health Care

Polls increasingly show health care is becoming a major concern of Americans. Some relief may be on the horizon. Proposals advanced in 1991 by Congressman William Dannemeyer (R-CA) would offer Americans a tax rebate provided they furnish proof of health care insurance. This proposal addresses the need millions of Americans have

for health insurance, while letting individual citizens make choices about where to purchase it. It also preserves competition—the surest guarantee of lower costs.

National health insurance often becomes an acute issue in times of economic downturn. A word of warning is in order. A nationalized health care system becomes dangerous when combined with a quality of life ethic. Washington state in 1991 voted down a proposal to allow doctors to kill their patients if the patients were within six months of dying and requested it. The vote of 46% of Washington voters for such a proposal is a chilling reminder of the threat of linking peoples' lives to their burden on the public tax rolls. Much of the propaganda in the Washington state referendum will be repeated over and over throughout the country as medical costs swell state and national budget deficits. And when people who are gravely ill are also tenacious, the cry will go up to help them die. Dr. Everett Koop, former surgeon general, has stated that the death toll from euthanasia—or mercy killing—may one day dwarf the terrible toll from abortion.

Abortion

Abortion will continue to divide our country throughout the decade of the '90s. Abortion-on-demand and abortion as a means of birth control trouble Americans, but they do not yet have enough information upon which to make reasoned judgments. Reliable polls show that most Americans do not know that abortion is legal throughout the nine months of pregnancy. Press reports routinely misstate the *Roe v. Wade* and *Doe v. Bolton* decisions and tell people that abortion was made legal by the Supreme Court for the first three months of pregnancy. That is like telling the American people Saddam Hussein invaded a 20-mile strip of the Kuwaiti border. It is true he did that. But he went on to take the whole country!

The Supreme Court decisions in *Webster v. Reproductive Health Services* (1989) and *Rust v. Sullivan* (1991) represented victories for the pro-life movement. Efforts by pro-life political activists to keep the Republican Platform plank on abortion solidified grassroots support but did not enlist immediate endorsement from the president.

While presidential vetoes fend off pro-abortion drives in Congress, it is important to find new areas for positive action. The campaign by the Christian Action Council (CAC) to identify the major corporations that give to Planned Parenthood is one example of citizen action. Because of CAC's truth-telling campaign, Americans demonstrated that they do not want their charity dollars going to Planned Parenthood. More than 50% who use a "donor choice" option that allows them to make "negative designations" on their local United Way forms, choose not to have money go to the abortion-providing Planned Parenthood. This is an amazing vote of no confidence!

With much of the action on abortion back in the states, it will be important for Christians to take an active interest in state government. There are signs of encouragement here. State legislative elections repeatedly show that the threatened strength of pro-abortion groups did not happen. Candidates who waffled or who tried to run from previously pro-life voting records often got trounced. Pro-life candidates who took the time to develop well-articulated positions on a host of important issues generally found their pro-life convictions helped them.

Several issues related to abortion will continue to trouble our country. RU-486, the French abortion pill, is being primed for launch. Despite deaths from this pill, pressure will be applied to find legitimate uses for the abortion pill.

Experimentation on tissues taken from intentionally aborted children continues to be an issue few Americans understand. Press reports have greeted unproven speculation about the efficacy of fetal-cell transplants as fact. The secular press seldom examines critically the claims made for using such tissues and accepts without question assurances that ethical safeguards will be applied. The simple fact is, abortion is one of the most unregulated procedures, and we have little reason to think that taking tissues from aborted children will be more ethical.

Pornography and Censorship
Despite years of wrangling over federal grants for obscene art, the governing class in Washington continues to confuse censorship with subsidy. Moves in Congress to restrict funding of obscene art—especially so-called performance art—have been continually rebuffed by powerful committee chairmen and majorities indebted to the fund-raising ability of the arts community. Occasionally, word comes of sincere efforts within that community to stem abuses. But too often these bear little fruit. The National Endowment for the Arts seems trapped between an increasingly radical, homosexual artist clique and American taxpayers who regard these grants as not only patently offensive, but a terrible waste of money. Instead of being the uplifting and unifying project art should be, it has become increasingly offensive. Too many artists justify their very existence by their ability to provoke revulsion in decent people.

The storm of controversy over federal funding of the arts will continue as a battlefield in what some call civil war over values until one or the other side wins. With a staggering national debt, it ought to be obvious that whatever its enthusiasts think of this questionable adventure in the arts, the United States cannot afford it. The inability of the National Endowment for the Arts to draw any lines between art and obscenity reminds me of an quotation from pop artist Andy Warhol: "Art is anything you can get away with."

Homosexuality
On November 11, 1991, Veterans Day, a crowd of fewer than 100 chanting, howling, leering demonstrators gathered outside the Pentagon to demand that the Department of Defense drop its historic ban on homosexuals serving in the military. The media covered the demonstration by the group that styled itself "Queer Storm" but did not report the obscenities of the speakers or the lewd chants of the

WHAT TO WATCH FOR ON CAPITOL HILL IN 1993–1994 cont.

mob that included filthy slogans about the sexual organs of the secretary of defense. Few people realize the lewdness and viciousness of militant homosexuals.

In the '90s we can expect an escalated use of violence and intimidation to force American society to accept homosexual conduct as the norm. It will not be enough for Americans to tolerate private conduct that remains private. Americans will be exposed to homosexual themes on television, in movies, on the stage, and in every national celebration and parade.

Resistance will build. The national tragedy of AIDS will prove the folly of treating a disease politically instead of medically. Americans will recoil at the repulsive antics of the militants, especially as they force their way of life on children in school programs. The cost of homosexual promiscuity will be borne by our entire society.

Despite the incessant propaganda for an elusive safe sex, the death toll from AIDS will continue to rise with dread certainty. The saddest part of the whole episode is that the spread of AIDS could be largely controlled by abstinence and the avoidance of intravenous drugs. Yet these two lifesaving messages are not the centerpiece for AIDS strategy. Leadership has been lacking from the White House, and also from the Congress. Constant, petulant demands for more money for AIDS research cannot shout down the quiet fliff-fliff of paper as every month the Centers for Disease Control sends out its new report on people infected with the deadly disease.

For millions of people, the argument is one of compassion, of civil rights for homosexuals. It is a strange compassion that tells the alcoholic he can continue drinking until we find the cure for cirrhosis of the liver. It is a strange compassion that fails to reach out to the homosexual with a message of lifesaving self-restraint.

Supreme Court

Liberals have relied on the Supreme Court because they are seldom able to carry their agenda into the representative branches of government. Their unpopular stands often result in lost presidential elections. The Supreme Court in the past has been convenient for liberals to hide behind the black robes of the justices and say: "The High Court has spoken. No more debate."

In the '90s the increasingly conservative shift of the Supreme Court to the right will make this impossible. Those who have never complained of an "ideological tilt" to the left in 30 years suddenly became alarmed when the Court turned conservative.

Americans who value religious freedom will watch the new Court warily as even strict construction justices reach unanticipated decisions. A freer, more tolerant stance toward free exercise can be expected. Swifter, sterner justice for the criminals who terrorize towns and cities will be a welcome reward for our efforts. The Court can be expected to end the concept of abortion rights. Homosexuals will need to fight their fights through legislature rather than expecting the Court to create new privacy rights. Divorce law may come under scrutiny as the Court deliberates on "no fault" divorce. Parents, finally, may receive from the Court recognition of their right to choose their children's schools and the right to retain a portion of their own earnings to do so. The Court doesn't "follow the iliction returns," as the fictitious Mr. Dooley said it. However, election returns often determine the membership of the Court. A possible benefit of the series of divisive campaigns against conservative nominees for the High Court is that Americans are now thoroughly schooled on how a person gets onto the bench. These have been harrowing civics lessons, but I hope they will motivate more Americans to get involved to make sure elected government representatives reflect their beliefs and values.

What You Can Do

The most effective grass-roots pressure is to be informed, accurate, and timely. I encourage Christian citizens to keep up on the issues. Find a way to stay up to the minute on information.

Second, the target of your letter or phone call must be precise. If your congressman has already voted on a bill, and it is now on the president's desk, the White House is the proper point of contact. Sometimes it is a federal agency that needs to hear from you, and not your representative on Capitol Hill.

Third, the timing of your action is crucial to its success. Congress and the White House consider thousands of issues each year, and this week's crisis is next week's forgotten business. The important thing to know is when to call or write.

GUIDE TO POLITICAL ACTION

The following step-by-step instructions for sending persuasive messages to congressmen and other leaders has been prepared by Richard Cizik, policy analyst for the National Association of Evangelicals. He gives some basic rules for composing effective letters that will get a representative's attention and tells how even a phone call can be successful.

A complete congressional directory with Senate and House committee assignments and a list of Cabinet members follows for your convenience in knowing who and where to write.

The Letter

One of the most frequently asked questions is, Do contacts with legislators make a difference? A government official, a veteran of about 20 years on Capitol Hill, once said: "If the average member of Congress received as many as half a dozen letters scrawled in pencil on brown wrapping paper, it would be enough to change his vote on most issues." Perhaps he has exaggerated, but his remarks indicate that members of Congress want to know what their constituents are thinking.

A 1983 survey of 219 top congressional staffers conducted by *The Washingtonian* magazine confirms this. According to the survey, the most influential factors in the decision-making process of members of Congress were (in order of priority): (1) a member's political philosophy, (2) constituent opinion, (3) office mail, (4) the White House position, (5) party leaders, (6) press back home, (7) Washington lobbies, (8) the national media.

These results reveal the importance placed on constituent thinking. Aside from a member's political philosophy, constituent opinion and office mail are more likely to determine his position on issues than even the position held by the White House or party leaders—proof that constituents are thus some of the most important people in a legislator's life.

The most important influence upon a congressman's voting behavior remains his ideological predisposition. His convictions will determine how he votes on a host of issues. Like anyone else, members of Congress indulge in selective perception and recall of what they hear. Most messages that a congressman hears or reads raise the prominence of a particular issue as much as they change attitudes on a subject. Letters force a member to think more about an issue and to become more prone to express whatever bias he has regarding it.

Messages from constituents serve more as triggers than as persuaders, unless the member's opinion is not yet formed. In that case, letters and phone calls from constituents become more influential in making the decision. Most congressional staffers agree that even one well-written letter on a subject can start the staff thinking about that issue. These aides see each letter as representing the opinions of many people who do not write. A number of letters on the same topic may prompt the assignment of a staff member to draft a position-paper for the congressman. In some cases, a letter may actually change a legislator's mind, particularly when a member is wavering on an issue.

But whether or not a communication from a constituent is the determining factor in a

GUIDE TO POLITICAL ACTION cont.

member's voting behavior, it is not ignored. Members of Congress and administration officials—at least those who want to remain in Washington—are sensitive to the feelings and opinions of their constituents. The pros and cons are counted and the administrative assistant to a member of Congress regularly reports on the mail received. Telegrams sometimes go directly to the legislator's desk. Phone calls are also tallied and reported.

Communication with elected officials, therefore, should be regarded not only as a privilege of citizenship but also as a responsibility. Members of Congress respect and appreciate that communication. Even a letter disagreeing with an elected official's stated position is worthwhile because it can help your representative to understand the other side of that issue. Do not become discouraged, however, if, following your literary effort, the member's vote is still unfavorable to your position. It is important to remember that other persuasive people have also contacted the member, and the next time the vote may go your way.

It is critical, though, that your message be presented as effectively as possible. On the first occasion, writing a letter to your congressman may seem difficult. But it can be done and done well. You do not need to be an expert on an issue to get attention. Neither do you need to be a literary wizard. Here are some basic rules to follow:

1. Concentrate on your own delegation. Your two senators and your representative have an obligation to consider your view. Generally, as a courtesy, letters from outside a congressman's district are forwarded to the congressman from whose district it was sent. Of course, if a staffer doesn't have the time to do this, the letter will end up in the wastebasket.

2. Confine your letter to one specific legislative subject. This ensures that it will be seen by the right staff member. To do otherwise is to decrease the force of your argument and complicate any response to it. Also, tell the legislator exactly what you want done.

3. Ask the legislator to tell you his position on the matter. Will he support or oppose this legislation? He has a responsibility to inform you as to where he stands.

4. Write in your own words. Mass-produced letters that are part of a mail campaign or petition drive are of little influence. Form letters usually receive form replies. In other words, your congressman or his staff assistants will measure your interest in an issue by the amount of time you take to inform him of your beliefs. If you are willing to take only 30 seconds (the time it takes to sign a petition, postcard or form letter) to protest your representative's action or inaction, he will conclude that you are really not serious about your concern. A two- or three-sentence personal letter has more impact that a preprinted postcard. This kind of seriousness is a measurement of your capacity to elect another representative.

5. Be brief. Letters that are more than one page are saved for another day. Completeness and clarity are both possible on one page. It will take more effort to condense your ideas into a single page, but it's worth it if you want to be read. Letters need not be typed, but they must be legible.

6. Give your reasons for taking a stand. But avoid emotional arguments or language that is demanding or threatening. While the subject may be emotion-laden, use facts and illustrations to make your point. Statements like "Vote against HR 100, I'm bitterly opposed" do not help much. But a letter which says, "I'm a small hardware dealer, and HR 100 will put me out of business for the following reasons . . ." says much more. If you disagree with your legislator, say so but do not berate him. Try to keep the dialogue open. Your attitude will inevitably come through and it should be polite and positive. Displaying anger or resentment in a letter only makes it easier to ignore. Your legislator will only assume that you wouldn't vote for him even if he did what you ask, and you want him to think of you as a potential supporter.

7. Do not assume that your member is well informed about a given issue. A member can't stay on top of everything. Treat him with respect, but do explain the situation.

8. Be constructive. Indicate how a bill is counter-productive. Letters should, whenever possible, include the bill number or the popular title since there can be many bills concerning any given topic.

9. Ask for a response. Request an answer to a specific question. A well-formulated question will often get a more personal response. Write a letter that cannot be answered by a computer.

10. Be timely. Read the newspaper or institutional newsletters for dates of scheduled floor votes or committee action. Obviously, your letter should come as early as possible before decisions are made. By doing so it's possible to encourage the legislator to take the right position before the opposition gets to him. The best time to write is when you first learn that Congress is going to consider the issue.

11. Be accurate and courteous. Be certain that your name and address are on both the envelope and letter. Write legibly and spell names accurately. Use proper etiquette. Any legislator is called "Honorable" on the envelope and inside address. The salutation, however, treats senators and representatives differently. A representative is addressed as "Mr.," "Ms." or "Mrs.," while a senator is called "Senator."

12. Point out the moral issues involved. Explain why you are for a particular position. Since legislators get so much mail from special interest groups, they need to hear from citizens who are primarily concerned with what seems right to them on moral grounds.

13. If you have expert knowledge, share it. Of all letters pouring into a congressman's office, perhaps one in a hundred comes from a constituent who is a real expert in that subject. All opinions expressed are important, but those from someone with real experience are a gold mine to conscientious members.

14. Say "well done" when deserved. Your members of Congress are human, too, and appreciate a word of thanks from people who believe they have done the right thing. Thank your legislator if he voted for your position on an issue. Very few constituents bother to do this. It will be appreciated! Also, do this while the vote is still fresh in the congressman's mind. If possible, phone after a vote and leave a message of thanks.

15. Avoid becoming a constant "pen pal." Quality, not quantity, is what counts. Write when you feel like it, but don't try to instruct your congressman on every issue that comes up. Writing only once a month is a good rule. One of the pet peeves on Capitol Hill is the "pen pal" who weighs down the mail every few days with long tomes on every conceivable subject.

16. Always keep copies of correspondence. Retain and file a copy of your letter and the reply from your representative. They are especially useful should you arrange an interview to discuss your concerns.

17. Try to get together with others. Join with others, if possible, and write your own individual letters in a group. There is motivation and support in numbers. If you've never written a letter to a legislator, hearing of someone else's experience can encourage you to try your own hand at it. If you receive a negative response, it helps to have others with whom to talk it over.

Correct Forms of Address, Salutation, and Closing
Note: Except for the president, the following items are closed with "Sincerely yours."

President
The President
The White House
Washington, DC 20500
Dear Mr. President:
Very respectfully yours,

Vice President
The Vice President
The White House
Washington, DC 20500
Dear Mr. Vice President:

GUIDE TO POLITICAL ACTION cont.

Members of the Cabinet
The Honorable James A. Baker III
The Secretary of State
Washington, DC 20301
Dear Mr. Baker:

Senators
The Honorable Robert Dole
United States Senate
Washington, DC 20510
Dear Senator Dole:

Representative
The Honorable Nancy Pelosi

House of Representatives
Washington, DC 20515
Dear Ms. Pelosi:

Judiciary
The Honorable Sandra Day O'Connor
Associate Justice
(or Chief Justice, as appropriate)
United States Supreme Court
Washington, DC 20543
My dear Justice O'Connor:
or
My dear Mr. (Miss or Mrs.) Chief Justice:
(when addressing this officer)

The Follow-Up Letter
Whatever the response, write a follow-up letter. If your congressman cannot comply with your request for legislative support, he may send back a letter agreeing with you on some other area of interest. Ignore this kind of flattery.

But if your legislator does disagree with you, write back promptly, refuting his arguments and once more asking him to take the position you favor. If you fail to follow up, the legislator and his staff will have little reason to reconsider his position. They will get the impression that either his letter persuaded you or that you didn't care strongly enough about the issue to pursue it further.

When follow-up letters arrive in a congressional office, the picture can change. These letters will communicate that the legislator's position is raising serious objections from constituents. Make these letters thoughtful and courteous, but insistent. This will require the staff to draft answers to your points.

Cover at least three elements in follow-up letters:

1. Express thanks for the legislator's candidness in stating his position.

2. Tell him you disagree and proceed to refute his arguments. Make new points if you can.

3. Ask a question or two, so the staff will have to think about the issue and respond. Some suggested questions include: Have you consulted . . .? Did you know . . .?

Above all, do not get discouraged. Remember, your legislator needs your help in casting votes. The "ballot box" is not far away. It's painted red, white, and blue, and it reads "U.S. Mail."

Telegrams
There is only one use for a telegram or mailgram and that is when it is too late for a letter. They are especially helpful to reemphasize your position just before the vote on a critical issue.

Telegrams are fast, but costly. Western Union will deliver a telegram of 10 words or less within two to five hours for $13.95; delivery by a messenger costs $25.90. Mailgrams have almost made telegrams obsolete. They provide next-day service by mail for a message of 50 words or less for about $13.95. Western Union also has available the "opinion gram." It provides same-day service to members of Congress using a telex system. A message of 20 words or less costs approximately $8.95.

Telephone Calls
You can also register your opinion by telephone call, although this is usually only effective if the issue you are calling about is well known to your legislator. If you've not written a

letter, a phone call will at least get you on the record. Many constituents incorrectly assume that they must call the legislator's Washington office to register a viewpoint or talk about an issue. A call to the congressional district office is just as effective, especially if you can generate a large volume of calls. When you call the local office, indicate that you want to register a citizen opinion or talk briefly with a staff member who is handling a particular issue. Briefly state your position and ask for a reply from the congressman.

When calls come into the local office, the Washington office is informed. Since most people are too apathetic to make a call, a dozen or more calls to the local offices can really make a difference. Staff in the district office are usually more politically oriented and very sensitive to what constituents are thinking.

A number of cautions about phone usage are in order. If you do use the phone to talk to staffers about an issue, avoid overdoing it. The constituent who calls once or twice a week to chat about issues can become annoying to staffers who are trying to handle their normally heavy work load.

Naturally, not every letter you send to an elected official will have the desired effect. Don't be discouraged. Many other people are clamoring for your congressman's attention, including some very persuasive lobbyists. He may also have received thousands of letters with an opposing perspective. But your views are important, too. They're just as worthy of your congressman's consideration as anyone's. Don't forget: *Your communication counts!*

Cabinet Directory
Vice President: Dan Quayle, 20501
Agriculture: Edward Madigan, 20250
Attorney General: William Barr, 20530
CIA Director: Robert Gates, 20505
Commerce: Barbara H. Franklin, 20230
Defense: Dick Cheney, 20301
Education: Lamar Alexander, 20202
Energy: James D. Watkins, 20585
Health and Human Services: Dr. Louis W. Sullivan, 20201
Housing and Urban Development: Jack Kemp, 20410
Interior: Manual Lujan, Jr., 20240
Labor: Lynn Martin, 20210
National Drug Policy Director: Robert Martinez, 20500
State: James A. Baker III, 20520

Transportation: James Busey, 20590
Treasury: Nicholas Brady, 20220
UN Ambassador: Thomas R. Pickering, 799 United Nations Plaza, New York, NY 10017
Veterans' Affairs: Edward J. Derwinski
* Not official cabinet status

Supreme Court Justices
Chief Justice: William H. Rehnquist
Associate Justices:
Byron R. White
Clarence Thomas
Harry A. Blackmun
Antonin Scalia
Sandra Day O'Connor
Anthony Kennedy
John Paul Stevens
David Souter

A Note about Addresses
Most agencies and departments of the government have their own zip codes. In order to write to them you need only the name of the person and the department, Washington, D.C. plus zip code.

Phone Numbers in Washington
Federal Information Center: (Operators can direct you to the agency or department you wish to call.) 202-655-4000
Capitol: (Call this number for all House and Senate offices.) 202-224-3121
White House: 202-456-1414 (switchboard), or 202-456-7639 (public opinion expressions).

GUIDE TO POLITICAL ACTION cont.

Congressional Directory, 103rd Congress

Numbers in the left-hand column indicate the congressional district; numbers following the name indicate committees. Committee code numbers correspond to the numbers given the committees in the list following. Senate committees are numbered 1–16. House committees are numbered 17–38.

Alabama

Senators:
  Howell Heflin (D) - 1, 12
  Richard C. Shelby (D) - 3, 4
Representatives:
  1 Sonny Callahan (R) - 24
  2 William L. Dickinson (R) - 19, 27
  3 Glen Browder (D) - 19, 34
  4 Tom Bevill (D) - 18
  5 Ronnie G. Flippo (D) - 38
  6 Ben Erdreich (D) - 20, 26
  7 Claude Harris (D) - 17, 37

Alaska

Senators:
  Frank H. Murkowski (R) - 7, 10, 16
  Ted Stevens (R) - 2, 6, 11, 14
Representative:
  Don Young (R) - 28, 30, 31

Arizona

Senators:
  Dennis DeConcini (D) - 2, 12, 16
  John McCain (R) - 3, 6
Representatives:
  1 John J. Rhodes III (R) - 28, 35
  2 Morris K. Udall (D) - 25, 28, 31
  3 Bob Stump (R) - 19, 37
  4 John Kyl (R) - 19, 26
  5 Jim Kolbe (R) - 18

Arkansas

Senators:
  Dale Bumpers (D) - 2, 7, 15
  David Pryor (D) - 1, 9, 11
Representatives:
  1 Bill Alexander (D) - 18
  2 Tommy F. Robinson (D) - 19, 23, 37
  3 John Paul Hammerschmidt (R) - 32, 37
  4 Beryl F. Anthony, Jr. (D) - 38

California

Senators:
  Alan Cranston (D) - 4, 10, 16
  John Seymour (R) - 1, 7

Representatives:
  1 Frank Riggs (R) - 20, 32
  2 Wally Herger (R) - 17, 30
  3 Robert T. Matsui (D) - 38
  4 Vic Fazio (D) - 18, 21, 36
  5 Nancy Pelosi (D) - 20, 26
  6 Barbara Boxer (D) - 19, 21
  7 George Miller (D) - 21, 28
  8 Ronald V. Dellums (D) - 19, 22
  9 Pete Stark (D) - 22, 38
  10 Don Edwards (D) - 29, 37
  11 Tom Lantos (D) - 25, 26
  12 Tom Campbell (R) - 34, 35
  13 Norman Y. Mineta (D) - 32, 34
  14 Norman D. Shumway (R) - 20, 30
  15 Gary Condit (D) - 17, 26
  16 Leon E. Panetta (D) 17, 27
  17 Calvin Dooley (D) - 17, 35
  18 Richard H. Lehman (D) - 20, 28
  19 Robert J. Lagomarsino (R) - 25, 28
  20 William Thomas (R) - 21, 27, 38
  21 Elton Gallegly (R) - 28, 35
  22 Carlos J. Moorhead (R) - 24, 29
  23 Anthony C. Beilenson (D) - 33
  24 Henry A. Waxman (D) - 24, 26
  25 Edward R. Roybal (D) - 18
  26 Howard L. Berman (D) - 25, 29
  27 Mel E. Levine (D) - 25, 28
  28 Julian C. Dixon (D) - 18, 36
  29 Maxine Waters (D) - 20, 37
  30 Matthew G. Martinez (D) - 23, 26, 35
  31 Mervyn M. Dymally (D) - 22, 25, 31
  32 Glenn M. Anderson (D) - 30, 32
  33 David Dreier (R) - 20, 35
  34 Esteban Torres (D) - 20, 35
  35 Jerry Lewis (R) - 18
  36 George E. Brown, Jr. (D) - 17, 34
  37 Al McCandless (R) - 26, 20
  38 Robert Dornan (R) - 25, 37
  39 William E. Dannemeyer (R) - 24, 29
  40 C. Christopher Cox (R) - 26, 32
  41 Bill Lowery (R) - 18
  42 Dana Rohrabacher (R) - 22, 34

43 Ronald C. Packard (R) - 32, 34
44 Randy Cunningham (R) - 19, 30
45 Duncan L. Hunter (R) - 19

Colorado
Senators:
Timothy E. Wirth (D) - 3, 4, 5, 7
Hank Brown (R) - 5, 10, 12
Representatives:
1 Patricia Schroeder (D) - 19, 29, 31
2 David Skaggs (D) - 32, 34
3 Ben N. Campbell (D) - 17, 28
4 Wayne Allard (R) - 17, 28, 35
5 Joel Hefley (R) - 34, 35
6 Dan Schaefer (R) - 24

Connecticut
Senators:
Christopher J. Dodd (D) - 4, 5, 10, 13, 14
J. I. Lieberman (D) - 8, 11, 15
Representatives:
1 Barbara B. Kennelly (D) - 38
2 Samuel Gejdenson (D) - 25, 27, 28
3 Rosa DeLauro (D) - 32, 26
4 Christopher Shays (R) - 26, 34
5 Gary Franks (R) - 19, 35
6 Nancy L. Johnson (R) - 21, 32

Delaware
Senators:
Joseph R. Biden, Jr. (D) - 10, 12
William V. Roth, Jr. (R) - 9, 11
Representative:
Thomas R. Carper (D) - 20, 30

Florida
Senators:
Connie Mack III (R) - 4, 10
Bob Graham (D) - 4, 8, 16
Representatives:
1 Earl Hutto (D) - 19, 30
2 Pete Peterson (D) - 32, 37
3 Charles E. Bennett (D) - 19, 30
4 Craig T. James (R) - 29, 37
5 Bill McCollum (R) - 20, 29
6 Clifford B. Stearns (R) - 20, 37
7 Sam M. Gibbons (D) - 38
8 C. W. (Bill) Young (R) - 18
9 Michael Bilirakis (R) - 24, 37
10 Andy Ireland (R) - 19, 35
11 Jim Bacchus (D) - 20, 34
12 Tom Lewis (R) - 17, 34
13 Porter J. Goss (R) - 25, 30

14 Harry A. Johnston II (D) - 25, 34
15 E. Clay Shaw, Jr. (R) - 29, 32
16 Lawrence J. Smith (D) - 25, 29
17 William Lehman (D) - 18
18 Ileana Ros-Lehtinen (R) - 25, 26
19 Dante B. Fascell (D) - 25

Georgia
Senators:
Sam Nunn (D) - 3, 11, 15
Wyche Fowler, Jr. (D) - 1, 5, 7
Representatives:
1 Lindsay Thomas (D) - 18
2 Charles F. Hatcher (D) - 17, 35
3 Richard Ray (D) - 19, 35
4 Ben Jones (D) - 32, 37
5 John Lewis (D) - 28, 32
6 Newt Gingrich (R) - 27, 32
7 George Darden (D) - 19, 28
8 J. Roy Rowland (D) - 32, 37
9 Ed Jenkins (D) - 21, 38
10 Doug Barnard, Jr. (D) - 20, 26

Hawaii
Senators:
Daniel K. Inouye (D) - 2, 6, 14
Spark M. Matsunaga (D) - 9, 13, 16
Representatives:
1 Neil Abercrombie (D) - 19, 30
2 Daniel K. Akaka (D) - 18

Idaho
Senators:
Larry Craig (R) - 1, 7
Steven D. Symms (R) - 3, 5, 8
Representatives:
1 Larry LaRocco (D) - 20, 28
2 Richard H. Stallings (D) - 17, 34

Illinois
Senators:
Alan J. Dixon (D) - 3, 4, 15
Paul Simon (D) - 5, 10, 12, 13
Representatives:
1 Charles A. Hayes (D) - 23, 35
2 Gus Savage (D) - 32, 35
3 Marty Russo (D) - 21, 38
4 George Sangmeister (D) - 29, 37
5 William O. Lipinski (D) - 30, 32
6 Henry J. Hyde (R) - 25, 29
7 Cardiss Collins (D) - 24, 26
8 Dan Rostenkowski (D) - 38
9 Sidney R. Yates (D) - 18

GUIDE TO POLITICAL ACTION cont.

10 John E. Porter (R) - 18
11 Frank Annunzio (D) - 20, 27
12 Phillip M. Crane (R) - 38
13 Harris Fawell (R) - 23, 34
14 Dennis Hastert (R) - 26, 32
15 Thomas Ewing (R) - 17, 32
16 John Cox (D) - 20, 26
17 Lane Evans (D) - 17, 37
18 Robert H. Michel (R)
19 Terry Bruce (D) - 24, 34
20 Richard J. Durbin (D) - 18, 21
21 Jerry Costello (D)
22 Glenn Poshard (D) - 23, 35

Indiana
Senators:
Richard G. Lugar (R) - 1, 10
Daniel R. Coats (R) - 3, 13
Representatives:
1 Peter Visclosky (D) - 23, 28, 32
2 Philip R. Sharp (D) - 24, 28
3 Tim Roemer (D) - 23, 34
4 Jill Long (D) - 17, 37
5 James Jontz (D) - 17, 23, 37
6 Danny L. Burton (R) - 25, 31, 37
7 John T. Myers (R) - 18, 31, 36
8 Frank McCloskey (D) - 19, 31
9 Lee H. Hamilton (D) - 25, 34
10 Andy Jacobs, Jr. (D) - 38

Iowa
Senators:
Charles E. Grassley (R) - 2, 5, 12
Tom Harkin (D) - 1, 2, 13, 15
Representatives:
1 Jim Leach (R) - 20, 25
2 Jim Nussle (R) - 17, 20
3 David R. Nagle (D) - 17, 34
4 Neal Smith (D) - 18, 35
5 Jim Ross Lightfoot (R) - 26, 32
6 Fred Grandy (R) - 17, 23

Kansas
Senators:
Robert Dole (R) - 1, 9, 14
Nancy Landon Kassebaum (R) - 5, 6, 10
Representatives:
1 Pat Roberts (R) - 17, 27
2 Jim Slattery (D) - 21, 24
3 Jan Meyers (R) - 25, 35
4 Dan Glickman (D) - 17, 29, 34

5 Dick Nichols (R) - 32, 37

Kentucky
Senators:
Wendell H. Ford (D) - 6, 7, 14
Mitch McConnell (R) - 1, 10
Representatives:
1 Carroll Hubbard Jr. (D) - 20, 30
2 William H. Natcher (D) - 18
3 Romano L. Mazzoli (D) - 22, 29, 35
4 Jim Bunning (R) - 20, 30
5 Harold Rogers (R) - 18, 21
6 Larry J. Hopkins (R) - 17, 19
7 Carl C. Perkins (D) - 23, 32, 34

Louisiana
Senators:
J. Bennett Johnston Jr. (D) - 2, 5, 7
John B. Breaux (D) - 1, 6, 8
Representatives:
1 Robert L. Livingston (R) - 18
2 William Jefferson (D) - 23, 30
3 W. J. Tauzin (D) - 24, 30
4 Jim McCrery (R)
5 Jerry Huckaby (D) - 17, 28
6 Richard H. Baker (R) - 28, 35
7 Jimmy Hayes (D) - 32, 34
8 Clyde C. Holloway (R) - 17, 35

Maine
Senators:
William S. Cohen (R) - 3, 11
George J. Mitchell (D) - 8, 9, 11, 16
Representatives:
1 Thomas Andrews (D) - 19, 35
2 Olympia J. Snowe (R) - 25

Maryland
Senators:
Barbara A. Mikulski (D) - 2, 8, 13, 15
Paul S. Sarbanes (D) - 4, 10
Representatives:
1 Wayne Gilchrest (R) - 34, 30
2 Helen Bentley (R) - 30, 32
3 Benjamin L. Cardin (D) - 29, 32
4 Thomas McMillen (D) - 20, 34
5 Steny H. Hoyer (D) - 18
6 Beverly B. Byron (D) - 19, 28
7 Kweisi Mfume (D) - 20, 35
8 Constance A. Morella (R) - 31, 34

Massachusetts
Senators:
  Edward M. Kennedy (D) - 3, 12, 13
  John F. Kerry (D) - 6, 10, 15
Representatives:
  1 Silvioi O. Conte (R) - 18, 35
  2 Richard E. Neal (D) - 20, 35
  3 Joseph D. Early (D) - 18
  4 Barney Frank (D) - 20, 26, 29
  5 Chester G. Atkins (D) - 21, 23, 25, 36
  6 Nicholas Mavroules (D) - 19, 35
  7 Edward J. Markey (D) - 24, 28
  8 Joseph P. Kennedy II (D) - 20, 37
  9 Joe Moakley (D) - 33
  10 Gerry E. Studds (D) - 25, 30
  11 Brian J. Donnelly (D) - 38

Michigan
Senators:
  Carl Levin (D) - 3, 11, 15
  Donald W. Riegle, Jr. (D) - 4, 5, 6, 9
Representatives:
  1 John Conyers Jr. (D) - 26, 29, 35
  2 Carl D. Pursell (R) - 18
  3 Howard Wolpe (D) - 21, 25
  4 Fred Upton (R) - 32, 35
  5 Paul B. Henry (R) - 23, 34
  6 Bob Carr (D) - 18
  7 Dale E. Kildee (D) - 23, 28
  8 Bob Traxler (D) - 18
  9 Guy Vander Jagt (R) - 38
  10 Dave Camp (R) - 17, 35
  11 Robert W. Davis (R) - 19, 30
  12 David E. Bonior (D) - 33
  13 Barbara Rose Collins (D) - 32, 34
  14 Dennis M. Hertel (D) - 19, 30
  15 William D. Ford (D) - 23, 31
  16 John D. Dingell (D) - 24
  17 Sander M. Levin (D) - 38
  18 William S. Broomfield (R) - 25, 35

Minnesota
Senators:
  Paul Wellstone (D) - 7, 13
  David Durenberger (R) - 8, 9
Representatives:
  1 Timothy J. Penny (D) - 17, 23, 37
  2 Vin Weber (R) - 18
  3 Jim Ramstad (R) - 29, 35
  4 Bruce F. Vento (D) - 20, 28
  5 Martin Olav Sabo (D) - 18
  6 Gerry Sikorski (D) - 24, 31

  7 Collin C. Peterson (D) - 17, 26
  9 James L. Oberstar (D) - 21, 32

Mississippi
Senators:
  Trent Lott (R) - 3, 6, 15
  Thad Cochran (R) - 1, 2, 13
Representatives:
  1 Jamie L. Whitten (D) - 18
  2 Mike Espy (D) - 17, 21
  3 G. V. (Sonny) Montgomery (D) - 19, 37
  4 Mike Parker (D) - 32, 37
  5 Gene Taylor (D) - 18, 30

Missouri
Senators:
  John C. Danforth (R) - 5, 6, 9
  Christopher (Kit) Bond (R) - 1, 4, 15
Representatives:
  1 William (Bill) Clay (D) - 23, 27, 31
  2 Joan Kelly Horn (D) - 34, 32
  3 Richard A. Gephardt (D) - 38
  4 Ike Skelton (D) - 19, 35
  5 Alan Wheat (D) - 22, 33
  6 E. Thomas Coleman (R) - 17, 23
  7 Mel Hancock (R) - 32, 35
  8 Bill Emerson (R) - 17, 28
  9 Harold L. Volkmer (D) - 17, 34

Montana
Senators:
  Max Baucus (D) - 8, 9, 15
  Conrad Burns (R) - 6, 7, 15
Representatives:
  1 Pat Williams (D) - 21, 23
  2 Ron Marlenee (R) - 17, 28

Nebraska
Senators:
  J. James Exon (D) - 3, 5, 6
  Robert Kerrey (D) - 1, 2
Representatives:
  1 Douglas K. Bereuter (R) - 20, 25
  2 Peter Hoagland (D) - 20, 35
  3 Bill Barrett (R) - 17, 23, 27

Nevada
Senators:
  Richard H. Bryan (D) - 4, 6
  Harry Reid (D) - 2, 8
Representatives:
  1 James A. Bilbray (D) - 25, 35
  2 Barbara Vucanovich (R) - 27, 28

GUIDE TO POLITICAL ACTION cont.

New Hampshire
Senators:
    Robert C. Smith (R) - 3, 8
    Warren Rudman (R) - 2, 5, 11, 15
Representatives:
    1 Bill Zeliff (R) - 26, 32
    2 Dick Swett (D) - 32, 34

New Jersey
Senators:
    Bill Bradley (D) - 7, 9
    Frank R. Lautenberg (D) - 2, 5, 8
Representatives:
    1 Robert Andrews (D) - 23, 35
    2 William J. Hughes (D) - 29, 30
    3 Frank Pallone, Jr. (D) - 30, 32
    4 Christopher H. Smith (R) - 25, 37
    5 Marge Roukema (R) - 20, 23
    6 Bernard J. Dwyer (D) - 18, 36
    7 Matthew J. Rinaldo (R) - 24
    8 Robert A. Roe (D) - 32, 34
    9 Robert G. Torricelli (D) - 25, 34
    10 Donald Payne (D) - 23, 26
    11 Dean A. Gallo (R) - 32, 35
    12 Dick Zimmer (R) - 26, 34
    13 James Saxton (R) - 20, 30
    14 Frank J. Guarini (D) - 21, 38

New Mexico
Senators:
    Pete V. Domenici (R) - 2, 5, 7
    Jeff Bingaman (D) - 3, 7, 11
Representatives:
    1 Steven H. Schiff (R) - 26, 34
    2 Joe Skeen (R) - 18
    3 William B. Richardson (D) - 23, 24, 28

New York
Senators:
    Daniel P. Moynihan (D) - 8, 9, 10, 14
    Alfonse M. D'Amato (R) - 2, 4, 15
Representatives:
    1 George J. Hochbrueckner (D) - 19, 30, 34
    2 Thomas J. Downey (D) - 38
    3 Robert J. Mrazek (D) - 18
    4 Norman F. Lent (R) - 24, 30
    5 Raymond J. McGrath (R) - 38
    6 Floyd H. Flake (D) - 20, 35
    7 Gary L. Ackerman (D) - 25, 31
    8 James J. Scheuer (D) - 24, 34
    9 Thomas J. Manton (D) - 20, 30
    10 Charles E. Schumer (D) - 20, 21, 29
    11 Edolphus Towns (D) - 26, 32
    12 Major R. Owens (D) - 23, 26
    13 Stephen J. Solarz (D) - 23, 25, 31
    14 Guy V. Molinari (R) - 32
    15 S. William Green (R) - 18
    16 Charles B. Rangel (D) - 38
    17 Ted Weiss (D) - 25, 26
    18 Robert Garcia (D) - 20, 31
    19 Eliot L. Engel (D) - 25
    20 Nita M. Lowey (D) - 23, 30
    21 Hamilton Fish Jr. (R) - 29
    22 Benjamin A. Gilman (R) - 25, 31
    23 Michael R. McNulty (D) - 19, 35
    24 Gerald B. Solomon (R) - 25, 37
    25 Sherwood L. Boehlert (R) - 32, 34
    26 David O'Brian Martin (R) - 19
    27 James T. Walsh (R) - 17
    28 Matthew F. McHugh (D) - 18
    29 Frank Horton (R) - 26, 31
    30 Louise M. Slaughter (D) - 26, 32
    31 William Paxon (R) - 20
    32 John J. LaFalce (D) - 20, 35
    33 Henry J. Nowak (D) - 32, 34
    34 Amo Houghton, Jr. (R) - 21, 26

North Carolina
Senators:
    Terry Sanford (D) - 4, 5, 10
    Jesse Helms (R) - 1, 10, 14
Representatives:
    1 Walter B. Jones (D) - 17, 30
    2 I. T. Valentine, Jr. (D) - 32, 34
    3 Martin Lancaster (D) - 17, 32, 35
    4 David E. Price (D) - 20, 34
    5 Stephen L. Neal (D) - 20, 26
    6 Howard Coble (R) - 29, 30
    7 Charles Rose (D) - 17, 27
    8 W. G. (Bill) Hefner (D) - 18
    9 J. Alex McMillan (R) - 20, 35
    10 Cass Ballenger (R) - 23, 32
    11 Charles H. Taylor (R) - 28, 32

North Dakota
Senators:
    Kent Conrad (D) - 1, 5, 7
    Quentin N. Burdick (D) - 2, 8
Representative:
    Bryon L. Dorgan (D) - 38

Ohio
Senators:
  John H. Glenn, Jr. (D) - 3, 11
  Howard M. Metzenbaum (D) - 7, 12, 13
Representatives:
  1 Charles Luken (D) - 20, 26
  2 Willis D. (Bill) Gradison, Jr. (R) - 21, 38
  3 Tony P. Hall (D) - 33
  4 Michael G. Oxley (R) - 24
  5 Paul E. Gillmor (R) - 20, 27
  6 Bob McEwen (R) - 32, 37
  7 David Hobson (R) - 26, 32
  8 John Boehner (R) - 17, 23, 35
  9 Marcy Kaptur (D) - 20, 37
  10 Clarence E. Miller (R) - 18
  11 Dennis E. Eckart (D) - 24, 35
  12 John R. Kasich (R) - 19
  13 Don J. Pease (D) - 38
  14 Thomas C. Sawyer (D) - 23, 26
  15 Chalmers P. Wylie (R) - 20, 37
  16 Ralph S. Regula (R) - 18
  17 James Traficant, Jr. (D) - 32, 34
  18 Douglas Applegate (D) - 32, 37
  19 Edward F. Feighan (D) - 25, 29
  20 Mary Rose Oakar (D) - 20, 27, 31
  21 Louis Stokes (D) - 18

Oklahoma
Senators:
  David L. Boren (D) - 1, 9, 15
  Don Nickles (R) - 2, 5, 7
Representatives:
  1 James M. Inhofe (R) - 26, 32
  2 Mike Synar (D) - 24, 26, 29
  3 Bill Brewster (D) - 32, 37
  4 Dave McCurdy (D) - 19, 34
  5 Mickey Edwards (R) - 18, 21
  6 Glenn English (D) - 17, 26

Oregon
Senators:
  Mark O Hatfield (R) - 2, 7, 14
  Robert W. Packwood (R) - 6, 9
Representatives:
  1 Les AuCoin (D) - 18
  2 Robert F. (Bob) Smith (R) - 17
  3 Ron Wyden (D) - 24, 35
  4 Peter A. DeFazio (D) - 28, 32, 35
  5 Mike Kopetski (D) - 17, 29, 34

Pennsylvania
Senators:
  H. John Heinz III (R) - 4, 9, 11

  Arlen Specter (R) - 2, 12, 16
Representatives:
  1 Thomas M. Foglietta (D) - 19, 30
  2 Lucien Blackwell (D)
  3 Robert A. Borski (D) - 30, 32
  4 Joseph P. Kolter (D) - 26, 27, 32
  5 Richard T. Schulze (R) - 38
  6 Gus Yatron (D) - 25, 31
  7 Curt Weldon (R) - 19, 30
  8 Peter Kostmayer (D) - 25, 28
  9 Bud Shuster (R) - 32
  10 Joseph M. McDade (R) - 18, 35
  11 Paul E. Kanjorski (D) - 20, 34, 37
  12 John P. Murtha (D) - 18
  13 Lawrence Coughlin (R) - 18
  14 William J. Coyne (D) - 38
  15 Donald L. Ritter (R) - 24, 34
  16 Robert S. Walker (R) - 26, 34
  17 George W. Gekas (R) - 29
  18 Rick Santorum (R) - 21, 32, 37
  19 William F. Goodling (R) - 21, 23
  20 Joseph M. Gaydos (D) - 23, 27, 36
  21 Thomas J. Ridge (R) - 20, 37
  22 Austin J. Murphy (D) - 23, 28
  23 William F. Clinger, Jr. (R) - 26, 32

Rhode Island
Senators:
  John H. Chafee (R) - 4, 8, 9
  Claiborne Pell (D) - 10, 13, 14
Representatives:
  1 Ronald K. Machtley (R) - 19
  2 John Reed (D) - 23, 29, 30

South Carolina
Senators:
  Ernest F. Hollings (D) - 2, 5, 6
  Strom Thurmond (R) - 3, 12, 13, 16
Representatives:
  1 Arthur Ravenel Jr. (R) - 19
  2 Floyd Spence (R) - 19, 36
  3 Butler Derrick (D) - 21, 33
  4 Liz J. Patterson (D) - 20, 37
  5 John M. Spratt, Jr. (D) - 19, 26
  6 Robin Tallon, Jr. (D) - 17, 30

South Dakota
Senators:
  Thomas A. Daschle (D) - 1, 9
  Larry Pressler (R) - 6, 8, 10, 15
Representative:
  Tim Johnson (D) - 17, 37

GUIDE TO POLITICAL ACTION cont.

Tennessee
Senators:
  Albert Gore, Jr. (D) - 3, 6, 14
  James R. Sasser (D) - 2, 4, 5, 11, 15
Representatives:
  1 James H. Quillen (R) - 33
  2 John J. Duncan (R) - 32
  3 Marilyn Lloyd (D) - 19, 34
  4 James H. Cooper (D) - 24, 35
  5 Bob Clement (D)
  6 Bart Gordon (D) - 33
  7 Don K. Sundquist (R) - 32, 37
  8 John S. Tanner (D) - 19, 34
  9 Harold E. Ford (D) - 38

Texas
Senators:
  Lloyd Bentsen (D) - 6, 9
  Phil Gramm (R) - 3, 4
Representatives:
  1 Jim Chapman (D) - 32, 34
  2 Charles Wilson (D) - 18
  3 Sam Johnson (R) - 20, 34, 35
  4 Ralph M. Hall (D) - 24, 34
  5 John Bryant (D) - 24, 29, 37
  6 Joe L. Barton (R) - 24
  7 Bill Archer (R) - 38
  8 Jack Fields (R) - 24, 30
  9 Jack Brooks (D) - 26, 29
  10 J. J. Pickle (D) - 38
  11 Chet Edwards (D) - 37, 19, 27
  12 Peter Geren (D) - 32, 37
  13 Bill Sarpalius (D) - 17, 35
  14 Greg Laughlin (D) - 30, 32
  15 E. (Kika) de la Garza (D) - 17
  16 Ronald D. Coleman (D) - 18
  17 Charles W. Stenholm (D) - 17, 37
  18 Craig Washington (D)
  19 Larry Combest (R) - 17, 22
  20 Henry B. Gonzalez (D) - 20, 35
  21 Lamar Smith (R) - 29, 34
  22 Tom DeLay (R) - 18
  23 Albert G. Bustamante (D) - 19, 26
  24 Martin Frost (D) - 21, 33
  25 Mike A. Andrews (D) - 38
  26 Richard K. Armey (R) - 21, 23
  27 Solomon P. Ortiz (D) - 19, 30

Utah
Senators:
  Jake Garn (R) - 2, 4, 14
  Orrin G. Hatch (R) - 12, 13
Representatives:
  1 James V. Hansen (R) - 19, 28, 36
  2 Wayne Owens (D) - 25, 28
  3 Bill Orton (D) - 20, 25, 35

Vermont
Senators:
  Patrick J. Leahy (D) - 1, 2, 12
  James M. Jeffords (R) - 8, 13, 16
Representative:
  Bernard Sanders (IND) - 20, 26

Virginia
Senators:
  Charles S. Robb (D) - 5, 6, 10
  John W. Warner (R) - 3, 8, 14
Representatives:
  1 Herbert S. Bateman (R) - 19, 30
  2 Owen B. Pickett (D) - 19, 30
  3 Thomas J. Bliley Jr. (R) - 22, 24
  4 Norman Sisisky (D) - 19, 35
  5 Lewis F. Payne Jr. (D)
  6 James R. Olin (D) - 17, 35
  7 George Allen (R) - 29, 34, 35
  8 James P. Moran (D) - 20, 31
  9 Frederick C. Boucher (D) - 24, 29, 34
  10 Frank R. Wolf (R) - 18

Washington
Senators:
  Slade Gorton (R) - 1, 3, 6
  Brock Adams (D) - 6, 10, 13, 14
Representatives:
  1 John Miller (R) - 25, 30
  2 Allan Swift (D) - 24, 27
  3 Jolene Unsoeld (D) - 23, 30
  4 Sid Morrison (R) - 17, 34
  5 Thomas S. Foley (D) - 21
  6 Norman D. Dicks (D) - 18
  7 Jim McDermott (D) - 20, 28
  8 Rodney Chandler (R) - 38

West Virginia
Senators:
  Robert C. Byrd (D) - 2, 12, 14
  John D. (Jay) Rockefeller IV (D) - 6, 9, 16
Representatives:
  1 Alan B. Mollohan (D) - 18, 36
  2 Harley O. Staggers, Jr. (D) - 17, 29, 37
  3 Robert E. Wise, Jr. (D) - 23, 26, 32
  4 Nick (Joe) Rahall II (D) - 28, 32

Wisconsin
Senators:
  Robert W. Kasten Jr. (R) - 2, 5, 6, 15
  Herbert Kohl (D) - 11, 12
Representatives:
  1 Les Aspin (D) - 19
  2 Scott Klug (R) - 23, 26
  3 Steve Gunderson (R) - 17, 23
  4 Gerald Kleczka (D) - 20, 26
  5 Jim Moody (D) - 38
  6 Thomas E. Petri (R) - 23, 32, 36
  7 David R. Obey (D) - 18
  8 Toby Roth (R) - 20, 25
  9 F. James Sensenbrenner, Jr. (R) - 29, 34

Wyoming
Senators:
  Alan K. Simpson (R) - 8, 12, 16
  Malcolm Wallop (R) - 7, 9, 15
Representative:
  Craig Thomas - 26, 28

District of Columbia
Delegate:
  Eleanor Holmes Norton (D)

American Samoa
Delegate:
  Eni F. H. Faleomavaega (D) - 25, 28

Puerto Rico
Resident Commissioner:
  Jaime B. Fuster (D) - 25, 28

Virgin Islands
Delegate:
  Ron de Lugo (D) - 28, 31, 32

Guam
Delegate:
  Ben Blaz (R) - 19, 25, 28

Senate Committees
  1. Agriculture, Nutrition & Forestry
     202-224-2035
  2. Appropriations 202-224-3471
  3. Armed Services 202-224-3871
  4. Banking, Housing & Urban Affairs
     202-224-7391
  5. Budget 202-224-0642
  6. Commerce, Science &
     Transportation 202-224-5115

  7. Energy & Natural Resources
     202-224-4971
  8. Environment & Public Works
     202-224-6176
  9. Finance 202-224-4515
  10. Foreign Relations 202-224-4651
  11. Governmental Affairs
     202-224-4751
  12. Judiciary 202-224-5225
  13. Labor & Human Resources
     202-224-5375
  14. Rules and Administration
     202-224-6352
  15. Small Business 202-224-5175
  16. Veterans' Affairs 202-224-9126

House Committees
  17. Agriculture 202-225-2171
  18. Appropriations 202-225-2771
  19. Armed Services 202-225-4151
  20. Banking, Finance & Urban Affairs
     202-225-4247
  21. Budget 202-226-7200
  22. District of Columbia 202-225-4457
  23. Education & Labor 202-225-4527
  24. Energy & Commerce 202-225-2927
  25. Foreign Affairs 202-225-5021
  26. Government Operations
     202-225-5051
  27. House Administration 202-225-2061
  28. Interior & Insular Affairs
     202-225-2761
  29. Judiciary 202-225-3951
  30. Merchant Marine & Fisheries
     202-225-4047
  31. Post Office & Civil Service
     202-225-4054
  32. Public Works & Transportation
     202-225-4472
  33. Rules 202-225-9486
  34. Science, Space & Technology
     202-225-6371
  35. Small Business 202-225-5821
  36. Standards of Official Conduct
     202-225-7103
  37. Veterans' Affairs 202-225-3527
  38. Ways & Means 202-225-3625

Powers and Composition of the Congress
The legislative powers and organization of Congress are defined in Article I of the Constitution. A Senate and a House of Representatives are chosen by direct election.

GUIDE TO POLITICAL ACTION cont.

There are two senators from each state. One-third of them are elected every two years for six-year terms.

The federal census determines each state's portion of 435 representative seats. State legislatures determine Congressional district boundaries. Every state has at least one representative. Representatives are elected for two-year terms.

Requirements A senator must be at least 30 years old, a U.S. citizen for at least nine years, and a resident of the state in which he/she is elected.

Responsibilities In addition to writing federal laws, the Congress has the power to conduct investigations, monitor federal agencies, impeach federal officials including the president, declare war, approve treaties, raise or lower taxes, appropriate money, approve top federal agency and judicial appointments and all armed forces officer appointments.

A two-thirds majority in each chamber will override a presidential veto.

Benefits The annual salary of a member of Congress in 1991 is $125,000. A retirement system offers liberal pension benefits.

In addition, a member of Congress receives free office space, complete with furnishings, machines and supplies. Funds are provided for staff salaries, phone bills, trips home, and operation of home offices.

Printing and radio-television broadcast taping facilities are provided. Banking facilities are available in the Capitol and free parking is provided. Office complexes have gymnasium facilities, dining facilities, and post offices. An attending physician is in the Capitol, and congresspersons can take advantage of a complete laboratory, x-rays, pharmacy, physiotherapy and electro-cardiographic service. Along with a health insurance plan, medical care is available at Walter Reed Army and Bethesda Naval Hospitals.

Committee Membership Members usually try to get membership on committees related to their personal interests and background and to economic interests of their district and state. However, if given the opportunity early in their careers, many members will seek membership in the powerful appropriations committees that control the flow of money to programs authorized by other committees.

Other powerful committees to which many members seek to obtain membership are the Senate Finance Committee and the House Ways and Means Committee; these committees consider tax legislation. The House and Senate budget committees, which now allow Congress to compete with the White House in establishing national priorities through a national budget, also are desirable assignments.

Committee assignments in the House and Senate are determined by special committes of Democrats and Republicans in each chamber. A party caucus in each chamber makes the final approval of assignments.

Congressional Party Leaders

SENATE
President of the Senate: Dan Quayle
President Pro-Tempore: Robert C. Byrd (D-WV)
Majority Leader: George J. Mitchell (D-ME)
Majority Whip: Wendell H. Ford (D-KY)
Minority Leader: Robert Dole (R-KS)
Minority Whip: Alan Simpson (R-WY)

HOUSE
Speaker: Thomas S. Foley (D-WA)
Majority Leader: Richard A. Gephardt (D-MO)
Majority Whip: David E. Bonior (D-MI)
Minority Leader: Robert H. Michel (R-IL)
Minority Whip: Newt Gingrich (R-GA)

Source: *The High Cost of Indifference,* edited by Richard Cizik. Copyright © 1984 by Regal Books, Ventura, CA 93006. Used by permission. Update by Richard Cizik.

Sports

SPOTLIGHT ON CHRISTIAN ATHLETES

Dave Dravecky
Former Pitcher
San Francisco Giants

I was certainly scared while I waited for the results of my biopsy. The possibility of losing my life seemed very real. I might lose Janice, Tiffany, Jonathan. They might lose me. But we could never lose the love of God. He was watching over me and my family. I was conscious of his eyes on me, his loving eyes. He was my audience.

You always wonder how it will be to go through a difficult time. You talk about the love of God, yet you can't help wondering: When tough times come will you really be able to live it? We found that we could. We found that faith carried us through our troubles, day by day.

I don't want people to think I've been able to handle this with no problem at all. I struggled like crazy.

The day after the surgery, I got up and walked into the bathroom with my gown on and I didn't want to look in the mirror. But I knew I had to. And when I did, it was a shock what I saw because it looked like the entire left side of my body was gone.

As I stood there and stared I just said to God, "OK, this is what you've given me to deal with; this is what you've given me to live with; now let me go forward from here.

Without Christ, I couldn't have endured all this. Not that I was holding unto him, but he was holding onto me.

I've learned to put my life in God's hands. The hardest part has been the uncertainty. I had to learn to do what was within my grasp, one day at a time, and leave control of the rest trustingly to God. Such are the lessons that come when a man faces adversity. I don't think I could have gained them in any other way.

Reality hasn't totally sunk in. I'll sometimes check the arm for a tan, and it's not there. We realize the arm is gone, but sometimes I look and it's hard to believe.

We're here on this earth for just a short period of time. Then I'll go to a glorified body. All this is temporary.

There's been a purpose to all this. I've had the opportunity to share the gospel with so many people, and the speaking invitations just keep coming.

—Selected from: *Comeback* by Dave Dravecky with Tim Stafford. Published by Zondervan Publishing House and Harper & Row, Publishers. Copyright © 1990 by Dave Dravecky and various other sources.

Dave Dravecky's emotional comeback August 10, 1989, after cancer surgery brought 34,810 fans at Candlestick Park to their feet to cheer him on with 8 standing ovations. Said Giants manager Roger Craig about the event, "I've seen a lot in baseball . . . but I've never seen such drama as this one." Doctors had told Dave he would never pitch again. Dravecky's seven-inning, one-hit performance that day earned a 4-3 win over the Cincinnati Reds. *USA Today*'s Rod Beaton said Dravecky's miracle comeback "could rank among the comeback stories of the decade." Dave Dravecky announced his retirement from baseball November 13, 1989, after learning the cancer had reappeared and he would need to undergo more surgery.

June 18, 1991 the left arm was amputated. Dravecky returned to Candlestick Park October 5, 1991 for Dave Dravecky Day and a final good-bye to baseball—the atmosphere swirling around the park a repeat of the August 1989 comeback.

Dravecky sorts through hundreds of speaking invitations, accepting only two a month. It is important to him to spend time with his family. A feature-length documentary film, *Dravecky: A Story of Courage and Grace*, and a second book, *When You Can't Comeback*, by Dave and his wife, Jan, compensate for the limited speaking engagements. Both film and book are Zondervan releases.

Dravecky has received numerous personal awards including the American Cancer Society Courage Award for 1990 and the Silvio O. Conte Award for Courage from the Vince Lombardi Foundation. February 1992 the American Cancer Society presented him with its first Humanitarian of the Year Award. He has set up the Dave Dravecky Foundation to help people facing adversity.

His health is excellent—February 19, 1992, he played 18 holes in the Pro-Am Event of the Buick Invitational of California at Torrey Pines Golf Club, San Diego, CA.

Nickname: Neck
Born: February 14, 1956, in Youngstown, OH. Grew up in Boardman, OH.
Personal status: 6', 215 lbs. Wife, Janice; two children, Tiffany Marie and Jonathan David.
Home: Boardman, OH.
Church affiliation: Word of Grace (Non-denominational).
Career highlights/awards: Played for San Diego Padres 1982-1987 and San Francisco Giants 1987-1989. Pitched two shutout innings in 1983 All-Star Game; had five strikeouts in 4 2/3 innings in 1984 World Series. Lowest ERA was 1.99. Was Giant's Opening Day starter, hurling a three-hitter at Los Angeles April 4, 1989, to win 5-1 over Fernando Valenzuela. Received American Cancer Society Courage Award from President George Bush on March 22, 1990.
Likes: Spending time with my wife and family.
Dislikes: Lima beans.
Hobbies/leisure time activities: Reading, golf, swimming.
Favorite Bible verse: We do not lose heart. Though outwardly we are wasting away, yet inwardly we are being renewed day by day. For our light and momentary troubles are achieving for us an eternal glory that far outweighs them all. So we fix our eyes not on what is seen, but on what is unseen. For what is seen is temporary, but what is unseen is eternal (2 Corinthians 4:16-18, NIV).
The best thing about baseball is: The challenge as a pitcher being one on one against the batter.
The best thing about life is: Serving God and being with my wife and kids.
What I want my children to learn from me: That Jesus Christ is the most important thing in my life and in their lives. My whole purpose here on earth is to do all I can to see them on the other side, in heaven.

A.C. Green
Forward
Los Angeles Lakers

A. C. Green was selected by the Lakers in the first round of the 1985 college draft (23rd overall). During the 1988-1989 season A.C. averaged career highs in points (13.3) and rebounds (9.0) as he has every season he's been in the league. The initials A.C., like his father's, do not stand for full names—his name is simply A.C. Green, Jr.

Born: October 4, 1963. Grew up in Portland, OR.
Personal status: 6' 9", 224 lbs. Wears size 15 shoes.
  Single. Two older brothers.
Home: Portland, OR.
Church affiliation: Non-denominational.

Career highlights/awards: During the 1988-1989 season led Lakers in rebounds for the third year in a row averaging 9.0, the most by a Laker since Earvin Johnson took 9.6 in 1981-1982. Selected by NBA coaches to the league's All-Defensive second team, the only Laker so honored. Career high 33 points at Seattle April 4, 1989. Was selected as Pac-10 Player of the Year as a junior. Voted by fans as a starter for the 1990 NBA All Star game.

Likes: Tennis, bowling, baseball, golf and eating frozen yogurt.
Dislikes: Gossip, disloyalty, compromise, pro-choice rulings.
Hobbies/leisure time activities: Frequently speaks to youth groups, bowling, sampling new yogurt flavors.
Favorite book: This Present Darkness and *Piercing the Darkness* by Frank E. Peretti. Published by Crossway Books.
Favorite Bible verse: Seek first his kingdom and his righteousness, and all these things will be given to you as well (Matthew 6:33 NIV). I am the way and the truth and the life. No one comes to the Father except through me (John 14:6 NIV).
The best thing about basketball is: The friendships you make and having a job you enjoy.
The best thing about life is: Knowing that my best relationship is with Jesus Christ.

Orel Hershiser IV
Pitcher
Los Angeles Dodgers

The average fan, unless he played at a fairly high level, would not be able to catch—let alone hit—a major league pitch.

It's my faith that lifts me up when I've failed. It's my faith that reminds me of my true insignificance when the world has been laid at my feet because of my success throwing a ball.

Our marriage had, and has, the usual rough spots that most couples endure, but a truly Christian marriage is different. The marriage with Christ at its head consists of a man

and a woman who are unwaveringly committed to each other, regardless what might be said or done in anger or a weak moment. While we might express ourselves bluntly in frustration, separation or divorce is not even part of our vocabulary. That's a bedrock security that both of us know and enjoy. It allows us to be honest with each other, working through our problems without fear of losing each other.

My faith has been a balancing agent in my life. Christ thrills me with who I am in him, and reminds me gently who I am not.

Selected from: *Out of the Blue* by Orel Hershiser with Jerry B. Jenkins. Published by Wolgemuth & Hyatt, Publishers. Copyright © 1989 by Orel Leonard Hershiser, IV. *Out of the Blue* reached the *New York Times* best-seller list for nine weeks in 1989.

April 27, 1990 Orel Hershiser underwent rotator cuff surgery bringing an early end to his 1990 season, the second year of a three-year, $7.9 million contract. His first start after rehabilitation was May 29, 1991 vs. the Astros. During the 1991 season, he moved up to 7th place on the all-time LA Dodger strikeout list with 1,100 strikeouts, recorded his 100th win, started his 200th career game, and recorded his 1,500th career inning. He finished the season with a 3.46 ERA.

Nickname: Bulldog. My manager, Tommy Lasorda, gave me the nickname because he thought I needed it. I never thought I needed it, so I don't personally use it, but he sure does. My teammates and a lot of my friends call me "O."

Born: September 16, 1958, in Buffalo, NY. Grew up in Southfield, MI and Cherry Hill, NJ.

Personal status: 6′ 3″, 190 lbs. Wife, Jamie; two sons, Orel Leonard V born November 24, 1984, whom we call Quinton, and Jordan Douglas born September 15, 1988.

Home: Pasadena, CA during the baseball season; Vero Beach, FL during the off-season and spring training.

Church affiliation: Lake Avenue Congregational Church, Pasadena, CA.

Career highlights/awards: In 1988, set major league record for most consecutive scoreless innings pitched—59. Named Most Valuable Player of the 1988 National League Championship series; Most Valuable Player of the 1988 World Series. National League Cy Young Award winner (best pitcher) for 1988. *Sports Illustrated* Sportsman of the Year, 1988. *The Sporting News* Major League Player of the Year, 1988. Associated Press Professional Athlete of the Year, 1988.

Likes: Competition, golf, lots of family time.

Dislikes: Being away from Jamie and the boys so much during the season.

Hobbies/leisure time activities: Golf, tennis, playing with the kids.

Favorite Bible verse: God so loved the world that he gave his one and only Son, that whoever believes in him shall not perish but have eternal life (John 3:16, NIV).

The best thing about baseball is: Its combination of complexity and simplicity. It is easy to understand and easy to play, but at the major league level, the competition is incredible, the strategy complicated, and the level of ability staggering. I love going against the percentages, having to think all the time, and competing at such an intense level.

The best thing about life is: Knowing Jesus Christ, getting your priorities in order, and sharing your faith and your abundance with others.

What I want my children to learn from me: Priorities—God, your wife, your children, others, and then your job.

---

66 99
FOCUS
QUOTE

The way in which you endure that which you must endure is more important than the crisis itself.—Sam Rutigliano

Parker Johnstone
Racer

Imagine sitting in a cramped cockpit that reaches 160 degrees—for two grueling hours!
Your body feels like it's going to explode under your three layers of protective clothing. Sweat rolls down your back. Your feet and legs burn from the heat, and your ears are numb from the deafening roar of the engine.
I've gotten blisters and first and second-degree burns on my feet. During one race, crews were pulling drivers from their cars because of heat exhaustion. Dehydration is a racer's biggest enemy.
How do I train to be a champion Christian? My friends at Motor Sports Ministries help me stay on the right track. I've learned to avoid using church as a service station . . . a place you stop by once a week to get a "spiritual dose." Jesus is the real guiding force in my life.
I pray before I race . . . right up to the point where we're scrubbing the tires. And once the green flag drops, I literally become part of the machine.
Music comes in many forms. To me, it is the revving sound of a race car engine.
Source: *Breakaway* magazine, May 1991 issue.

Parker Johnstone was chosen for three consecutive years as "America's Choice" by *On Track* magazine and in 1987 by *Sports Car* magazine as one of the upcoming young racing stars to watch. His achievements include 1991 and 1992 International Motor Sports Association (IMSA) Light class Daytona 24 Hour Winner, 1991 IMSA GTP/L Champion, 1991 Exxon Camel GT Outstanding Driver, 1991 All Time Point Record Scorer: IMSA GT, 1987 Formula Atlantic Most Improved Driver, 1984 IMSA Renault Cup Rookie of the Year.

Born: March 27, 1961, in Georgia. Raised in Salinas, CA, and San Francisco Bay area.
Personal status: 5'10", 160 lbs. Married high school sweetheart, Sharon. One daughter, Caitlin Hope.
Home: Redmond, OR.
Church affiliation: Forest Avenue Baptist Church.
Career highlights/awards: Five national championships. Holds more than 100 track records. Numerous Outstanding Driver Awards.
Likes: Travel. Being with energetic, highly motivated individuals who enjoy sharing philosophies and ideas with others.
Dislikes: Destructive forces in the world.
Hobbies/leisure time activities: Flying, golf, skiing, sailing, running, racquetball, reading, spending time with family.
Favorite book: Sum of All Fears by Tom Clancy.
Favorite Bible verse: I am the light of the world. Whoever follows me will never walk in darkness, but will have the light of life (John 8:12, NIV).
The best thing about racing is: The exhilaration of speed. The combination of science and art. It's thoroughly understanding the track, the chassis, your role as a driver, and together

with the team, trying to accomplish the job at hand. I want to use my racing position to share God's love with teenagers, show them God has purpose and fulfillment for their lives.

The best thing about life is: To each day enjoy the world God has provided.

What I want my children to learn from me: The Golden Rule, to cherish nature, to make the most out of the life God has given them.

FOCUS FACT

Quest Atlanta '96 has been developed to provide a platform for establishing a unique global witness for Christ during the grand sporting events that are coming to Atlanta: the 1994 World Cup, the 1994 Super Bowl and the 1996 Centennial Olympic Games.

For more information write to: *Quest Atlanta '96*, 579 Peachtree Street, NE, Atlanta, GA.

Betsy King
LPGA Tour

It's nice to be named 1989 Player of the Year. But I'd rather have respect as a person than as a player.

In my pre-Christian days I didn't feel any special commitment to charity and to the church. The use of my time and money to help others has been a big change. My commitment of a week each fall to work with other LPGA golfers to help build houses for poor families in Appalachia is an outgrowth of my Christian commitment.

I learned an important principle: I could be 100% committed to Christ and at the same time fully committed to my occupation. It had a great releasing power on me and gave me a new perspective for my career. The principle is found in Colossians 3:23: "Whatever you do, work at it with all your heart, as working for the Lord, not for men" (NIV).

Selected from: "What Betsy King has said about . . . " by Jim Adair in *The Christian Reader,* July/August 1990. Published by Tyndale House Publishers.

In 1991 Betsy King was one of six multiple winners. Of her 26 tournament starts, she had nine top-10 finishes. 1989 continues to be her most successful season, a year in which she shattered many LPGA all-time records. She won the LPGA's 1989 Rolex Player of the Year for the second time in her career. King earned 76 points in Rolex Player of the Year competition, 10 points more than runners-up Nancy Lopez and Beth Daniel. She won six tournaments, including the Women's U.S. Open and the LPGA World Championship titles. Since 1984 she has won 25 victories. She ranks third in total career earnings: $3,355,322.

Born: August 13, 1955, in Reading, PA.
Personal Status: 5' 6", blue eyes, blonde hair. Single. One brother, Lee.
Home: Limekiln, PA.
Church affiliation: Praise Cathedral, Phoenix, AZ.

Career highlights/awards: 1984 and 1989 Rolex Player of the Year. Received *Golf Digest*'s Most Improved Player Award in 1984. Named South Carolina's 1985 Professional Athlete of the Year. Received LPGA Good Samaritan Award in 1987 that acknowledges humanitarian, charitable efforts to improve health or alleviate physical suffering. Received *Golf Magazine*'s and *Golf Illustrated*'s Player of the Year Awards in 1987. 1989 awards included *Golf Digest*'s Mickey Wright Award, Founder's Cup, *Golf World*'s Player of the Year, Golf Writer's Association of America's Female Player of the Year.

Likes: The friendships made with the people of the LPGA Tour, theatre, concerts, and all sports.

Dislikes: Living out of a suitcase 40 weeks a year.

Hobbies/leisure time activities: Enjoy working out, reading, relaxing, watching TV. I spend a week each year with other LPGA players in the Tennessee mountains helping to build homes with Appalachia Habitat for Humanity.

Favorite book: Loving God by Charles Colson. Published by Zondervan Publishing House.

Favorite Bible verse: He who began a good work in you will carry it on to completion until the day of Christ Jesus (Philippians 1:6 NIV).

The best thing about golf is: The opportunity to compete and strive to be better.

The best thing about life is: My relationships with family, friends, God.

David Robinson
Center
San Antonio Spurs

Basketball is a vehicle to bring glory to God for what he's done for me. That's really my purpose for coming out here and wanting to be the best player. I used to play for myself, but now I have a different motivation.

I've been trying to be more emotional on the court because I am having fun, and I'm trying to show it more and get the other guys more excited. But spiritual things get me up. I've been reading, attending Bible studies, and I get excited about the Lord trying to reveal things. That's something that pumps me up, to see other people's lives changing, growing, and learning.

There are so many people who need to be touched, to be helped. The Lord says, "Serve." Jesus came down and he was a servant. Basketball is my vehicle to reach people and touch people's lives. But I have to spend my time with basketball to excel, as long as I keep my mind on where I'm headed in the long run.

Source: San Antonio *ExpressNews* and San Antonio *Light.*

David Robinson stands tall these days in more than one way. During the summer of 1991, his life began to move in new directions when he invited Jesus Christ to be his Lord and Savior. Today, he routinely includes Bible scriptures when signing autographs. A few months later, he married his longtime girlfriend Valerie along with continuing to add award after award to an exciting basketball career. He finished third in the 1992 NBA All-Star MVP voting behind Magic Johnson and Michael Jordan. He's already embodied everything anyone could want:

all-star, Olympian, military officer, role model, loving son, responsible brother, TV celebrity, pianist, math whiz, and multimillionaire.

Nickname: The Admiral

Born: August 6, 1965, in Key West, FL.

Personal status: 7′ 1″, 235 lbs. Wife, Valerie.

Home: San Antonio, TX.

Church affiliation: Tried Stone Baptist Church, San Antonio.

Career highlights/awards: Won several awards during the 1990-1991 season including, All-NBA First Team, NBA All-Defensive First Team, The Schick Award, All-NBA Interview Second Team, was voted onto the starting line-up for the 41st annual NBA All-Star game. Was the only player in the NBA to rank in the top 10 in four different categories, was 1st in rebounding, 2nd in blocks, 9th in scoring, and 9th in field goal percentage. Drafted by the Spurs with the first overall pick in the 1987 NBA draft, the unanimous choice for NBA Rookie of the Year after the 1989-1990 season.

Likes: Fellowship, sharing with good friends in a heartfelt way. Favorite meals are fettuccine or lasagna (if the cheese is right), peach cobbler, and ice cream.

Dislikes: Situations where people won't listen to logic. (Has a math degree from Navy, scored 1,320 on the SAT College Board Exams.) Wearing socks tucked in or rolled down. Is turned off when people want to do things they know are wrong. For example, a drug addict who knows better, but does what he really doesn't want to do and doesn't even make an effort not to.

Hobbies/leisure time activities: Bowling, golfing, playing and listening to music.

Favorite book: The Believer's Authority by Kenneth Hagen.

Favorite Bible verse: Be joyful always; pray continually; give thanks in all circumstances, for this is God's will for you in Christ Jesus (1 Thessalonians 5:16-18, NIV).

The best thing about basketball is: I get a chance to touch so many people's lives. I want the Lord to use me where he puts me. So many guys come in young and are overwhelmed by the money and the fame. I want to help others see right from wrong.

The best thing about life is: Paul said, "To live is Christ," and that's the best thing by far for me. So many things are depressing in life, it's great to know the answer is Jesus.

What I want my friends to learn from me: What life is all about, to see that God is worth fearing.

Ted Schulz
PGA Tour

1991 was a storybook year for Ted Schulz. His 1991 earnings were $508,058, more than $116,000 better than his previous high, placing him 29th overall on the money list. He ranks among statistical leaders in total driving (3rd) and all-around (15th).

Born: October 29, 1959, in Louisville, KY.

Personal status: 6′ 2″, 195 lbs. Wife, Diane.

Home: Louisville, KY.

Church affiliation: Southeast Christian Church, Louisville, KY.

Career highlights/awards: Won 1991 Nissan Los Angeles Open, 1989 Southern Open, 1983 Kentucky State Amateur, 1984 and 1988 Kentucky State Open, 1989 Southern Open. Named Rookie of the Year.

Likes: All sports, games.

Dislikes: Traffic jams, travel, sin.

Hobbies/leisure time activities: Bible study, games.

Favorite book: The Man In the Mirror by Patrick Morley. Published by Wolgemuth and Hyatt.

Favorite Bible verse: Ask and it will be given to you; seek and you will find; knock and the door will be opened to you (Matthew 7:7 NIV).

The best thing about golf is: I can make a living and enjoy it at the same time.

The best thing about life is: Knowing someday I'll be with God. This gives me peace.

What I want people to learn from me: I want people to learn biblical principles and to love the Lord.

Mike Singletary
Linebacker
Chicago Bears

I believe in work. I take tremendous pride in it. Whatever I do, I want to do it to the utmost. I believe I can never fail as long as I try, and I'm not afraid to fail. I'm persistent. I got that from my dad. I'll jump in and say, let me try that. Bet I can do it. And if I fail, hey, I'll get it next time. If I want to do something and I put my mind to it, it's going to take an awful lot to stop me.

Know what you want. Find out what it takes. Study, learn, set goals, go after it. Focus. Don't be defeated by one defeat. Don't be discouraged. Don't let anyone talk you out of it. Be willing to accept criticism and to put up with people who make fun of you or who don't understand.

If you think it will be easy, you won't succeed. If you need things to fall in place for you, you'll fail. If you're counting on luck or breaks or fortune, it won't happen. If you think you can get something for nothing, you're mistaken. No, it isn't easy. It isn't common. But the prize is right there on the shelf. The price tag is on it. The requirement is all of yourself.

The true Christian is not concerned about what he looks like in society. He measures himself by Christ and knows that he always falls short of that standard. We need to humble ourselves, to commit to doing things right . . . That's the only way to be used of God.

Source: *Singletary on Singletary* with Jerry Jenkins. Published by Thomas Nelson Publishers. Copyright © 1991 by Mike Singletary and Jerry B. Jenkins.

Mike Singletary ended the 1991 season with his 9th consecutive trip to the Pro Bowl. He led the Bears with 124 tackles, the 10th straight season he has finished first or second. Singletary is active in community services, speaking to youth groups in Chicago and Houston. He donates time to the Better Hearing Institute, Hemophilia Foundation of Illinois, Drug and Substance Abuse.

Nickname: Samurai. I scream when I hit someone—loud, karate-like yells. When I get excited, I scream and throw my arms around the way the late John Belushi did on "Saturday Night Live" a few years ago.

Born: October 9, 1958, in Houston, TX.

Personal status: 6', 228 lbs. Wife, Kim; three children, Kristen, Matthew, and Jill.

Home: Lake Forest, IL.

Church affiliation: Willow Creek Community Church, South Barrington, IL.

Career highlights/awards: Named 1988 NFL Defensive Player of the Year by Associated Press and *Pro Football Weekly.* Named NFC Defensive Player of Year by UPI and *Football News.* Named to virtually every All Pro team. Conference "Player of the Year" final two seasons at Baylor University.

Likes: To be at home with my family. Southern meal with smothered chicken, red beans, rice and corn bread. Music.

Dislikes: To see young kids drop out of school without a purpose or goal. Eating in a place that is not clean.

Hobbies/leisure time activities: Reading.

Favorite book: The Amazing Results of Positive Thinking by Norman Vincent Peale.

Favorite Bible verse: Blessed is the man who perseveres under trial, because when he has stood the test, he will receive the crown of life that God has promised to those who love him (James 1:12, NIV).

The best thing about football is: When I step onto the field I'm playing for the glory of God, and I won't settle for second best. I won't leave one ounce of energy in the locker room.

My bottom-line philosophy about life is: Whatever you have, take it, multiply it as much as you can, and then give, whether it's on the field, the office, or at home.

Henry Soles, Jr.
Senior Chaplain
Chicago Bulls

Sometimes all you have to do is listen because that's what they want. They don't know who to trust. Even though you're surrounded by a whole lot of people, it can be very lonely.

They're pro athletes, they're on the road a lot. Their families are hurting sometimes. We've prayed for families and have done family counseling and marital counseling because that's a problem in professional sports. The wife sometimes feels like she's left out of the whole picture. For instance, her husband goes away for a long period of time, he comes home, he wants some home cooking. Well, she wants to go out because she's been home all the time. The children might feel sometimes that Daddy is a stranger because they haven't seen him.

How does one deal with sudden fame without getting a big head? It's very difficult. That's where religious values come into play. It puts things into perspective. We let them know that sports is just a slice of life, not all of life.

Henry Soles wears many hats. He is a pastor, executive, award-winning editor, musician and community activist. He is president of Intersports Associates, Inc., a ministry to professional athletes and their families and sponsor of Bible studies for the Chicago Bulls and other professional teams. He serves on numerous local community boards as well as the Pro Basketball Fellowship board. Both Henry and his wife, Effie, are ordained ministers with the African Methodist Episcopal Church.

Nickname: Hank or Junior.

Born: August 17, 1935, in Anniston, AL. Grew up in Plainfield, NJ.

Personal status: 6′ 4″, 195 lbs. Wife, Effie.

Home: Wheaton, IL.

Church affiliation: Associate minister of DuPage A.M.E. Church, Wheaton, IL. Wife, Effie, is also associate minister.

Career highlights/awards: Trip to Kenya for missionary work and basketball clinics. Meeting and conversing with a member of the British Royal Family. Leading a group of ministers and their wives on a tour of Israel. Being nominated for two television Emmy awards. Compiling *Soul Food New Testament,* published by Tyndale House Publishers.

Likes: My wife's infectious smile and hearty laugh. Sharing the Good News of the Gospel. Travelling.

Dislikes: Injustices against the poor and disadvantaged.

Hobbies/leisure time activities: Playing the piano, singing, volunteer activities, sports, writing.

Favorite book: The Great Classics, books on Christian topics, social issues, and business.

Favorite Bible verse: Trust in the Lord will all your heart and lean not on your own understanding; in all your ways acknowledge him and he will make your paths straight (Proverbs 3: 5-6, NIV).

The best thing about sports is: It promotes teamwork, discipline, setting goals, physical and mental conditioning.

The best thing about life is: Jesus Christ.

What I want people to learn from me: That God loves them. And that when they allow him to control their lives, they'll experience abundant life.

Reggie White
Defensive End
Philadelphia Eagles

Vocalizing my relationship with Jesus Christ is as natural as breathing for me. And I use the word *relationship,* because it's a day-by-day, night-by-night, ongoing communication between Jesus and me. We talk about the blessings as well as the unanswered questions that occur daily in my life.

I want to live and breathe Jesus Christ so much that when people come into contact with me, they see Jesus. I still mess up and fall far short of imitating him in my life, but he always forgives me and encourages me in my daily walk with him. When I'm working and when I'm relaxing, with my teammates and with my family, I want my relationship with Jesus to be obvious.

God has given me an incredible platform as an NFL professional football player. The reason I'm in Philadelphia today is that that's exactly where God wants me to serve him right now. And any time I have a chance to proclaim Jesus Christ as Lord, I'm going to do it. Period!

Source: *Reggie White: Minister of Defense* with Terry Hall. Published by Wolgemuth & Hyatt. Copyright © 1991 by Reggie White and Terry Hall.

Reggie White, football's premier defensive lineman, is on his way to the Hall of Fame. Dick Vermeil, ABC-TV analyst, describes Reggie White as the Rolls-Royce of defensive lineman. During the 1991 season, he surpassed the century mark in career sacks. Selected as starter for the 1991 Pro Bowl for a 5th consecutive season. Has built a second home called "Hope Palace" in Knoxville, TN, where he and his wife, Sara, plan to house unwed mothers.

Nickname: Minister of Defense

Born: December 12, 1961, in Chattanooga, TN.

Personal status: 6'6", 290 lbs. Wife, Sara; son, Jeremy; daughter, Jecolia.

Home: Maryville, TN.

Church affiliation: Inner City Ministries.

Career highlights/awards: Recovering a fumble against Washington Redskins during the 1987 season and running a 70 yard touchdown. Lombardi finalist, All American-consensus during college. During USFL career was USFL Man of the Year; Rookie of the Year; Defensive Player of the Year. During NFL career, 4 times, defensive player of the year; 5 times Pro Bowl selection; 1987 MVP, All Madden team, 4 times MacKey Award.

Likes: To ride my Harley Davidson motorcycle. Wrestling with my children. Going on family trips. Going to the movies with my wife, Sara.

Dislikes: Seeing people contradict or compromise their convictions. The phone ringing more than three times (especially when the kids and I are napping).

Hobbies/leisure time activities: Model trains, remote boats, airplanes, and trucks.

Favorite book: This Present Darkness and *Piercing the Darkness* by Frank Peretti.

Favorite Bible verse: Yet now I am happy, not because you were made sorry, but because your sorrow led you to repentance. For you became sorrowful as God intended and so were not harmed in any way by us. Godly sorrow brings repentance that leads to salvation and leaves no regret, but worldly sorrow brings death. See what this godly sorrow has produced in you: what earnestness, what eagerness to clear yourselves, what indignation, what alarm, what longing, what concern, what readiness to see justice done. (2 Corinthians 7:9-11 NIV).

The best thing about football is: Being able to use my platform to get opportunities to share Christ.

The best thing about life is: Sharing it with my wife and best friend, Sara. Watching my children love the Lord, imitating the way Sara and I live and act.

What I want my children to learn from me: To always be faithful to Christ, their future spouses, and children. To work hard at whatever they do. To become a role model for their children. To love the Lord with all their heart, soul, and mind.

Bob Wieland
Weightlifter, Marathon Runner

After being denied the National Power Lifting Championships' bantamweight title: I'm not bitter. Who would ever have anticipated someone with no legs breaking the world record?

. . . God was mapping out in my mind a bigger project. I remembered Canadian Terry Fox's walk, and the Lord was giving me a new twist. I said to Harry, "I want to walk all the way across the country and share my testimony. We could use it as a fund-raising event, encouraging corporations and individuals to pledge money to charity and relief organizations—you know, so many dollars for each mile walked. While in Vietnam, I had wanted to feed hungry kids who were begging for food. Now since I've been back home, I've seen that people here are starving spiritually. I want to introduce them to Jesus. I want to do anything I can to stop both physical and spiritual hunger."

The Lord Jesus Christ . . . is my power source. And whether the finish line is at the end of a cinder track or at the gates of heaven, the race is only run one step at a time.

Selected from: *One Step At a Time* by Bob Wieland as told to Sarah Nichols. Published by Zondervan Publishing House. Copyright © 1989 by Bob Wieland and Sarah Nichols. *One Step At a Time* received *Campus Life* Magazine's 1990 Award of Merit/Biography.

Bob Wieland has been credited with "the greatest physical accomplishment ever in the history of sports." A star athlete in college, he was close to signing a contract to pitch for the Philadelphia Phillies when he went to Vietnam to serve his country as a combat medic. June 14, 1969, while on a search and destroy mission with his platoon, Wieland stepped on a 82-millimeter mortar round powerful enough to put a tank out of commission. He went flying one way, his legs went flying another. He went to Vietnam a 6′ 3 ″, 200-pound athlete and returned home a 3′ 5 ″, 87-pound double amputee.

Eight years later he broke the official world record in the bench press, lifting 303 pounds at the Senior National Power Lifting Championships in competition against able-bodied opponents in the bantamweight division only to be refused the world record-holder because of a technical rule that shoes must be worn during competition.

Born: February 19, 1946
Personal status: Wife, Jackey, a former fashion designer and interior decorator. Family includes three dogs.
Home: Arcadia, CA.
Church affiliation: Crenshaw Christian Center, Los Angeles, CA.
Career highlights/awards: Former 4-time world record holder in the bench press competition against able-bodied individuals. Walked 4,900,016 steps across America on my hands in 3 years, 8 months and 6 days. Competed in the 1986 and 1987 New York City Marathon; the 1987 and 1988 Los Angeles Marathon and 1989 Marine Corp Marathon. The only amputee to complete the grueling Iron Man Triathalon course in Kona, HI—2.4 mile swim, 112 mile bike ride, 26 mile marathon. In 1988 named the USA Track Athlete of the Year. In 1989 set a world record 35 day, 5 minute bike race across America using arm power. Appointed to the President's Council on Physical Fitness and Sports.
Likes: All sports, dining out, travel.
Hobbies/leisure time activities: Weightlifting.
Favorite Bible verse: Nothing is impossible with God (Luke 1:37, NIV).
The best thing about sports is: Crossing the finish line.
The best thing about life is: Living.

FOCUS QUOTE I have more treasure here on earth than most people, but I know where my true treasure lies. My teasure is in what I give away in obedience to the Lord, not in what I accumulate.—Reggie White, DE, Philadelphia Eagles

CHRISTIAN ATHLETIC ORGANIZATIONS

Athletes for Kids
P.O. Box 40945, Washington, DC 20016
Trains athletes to speak to the issues of drugs
and pornography.

Athletes in Action International
7899 Lexington Drive #220, Colorado Springs,
CO 80920
To proclaim the gospel to the four billion
people that are influenced by sports.

Athletes in Action, USA
9815 Mason-Montgomery Road, Mason, OH
45040
To proclaim the gospel to the four billion
people that are influenced by sports.

Athletes International Ministries
13613 N. Cave Creek Road, Phoenix, AZ
85022
Ministers to athletes from every sport.

Athletic Ministries Intl., Inc.
P.O. Box 241076, Memphis, TN 38124
Basketball ministry, primarily through half
time events and other speaking opportunities.

Baseball Chapel, Inc.
P.O. Box 300, Bloomingdale, NJ 07403
Chapel services for professional ball players—
all major league teams and most minor league
cities. Newsletter available at no cost.

Beyond Victory Ministries
P.O. Box 12475, Portland, OR 97212
To serve God through the medium of athletics
and to share the gospel of Jesus Christ and the
joy of living Spirit-controlled lives with athletes and coaches.

Champions for Christ
P.O. 1799, Gainesville, FL 32602
Champions for Christ chapters on major uni-
versity campuses and professional teams.

Christian College Sports News Network
111 Assembly Drive, P.O. Box 250, Montreat,
NC 28757
Radio coverage of Christian college sports.

Christian Motorcylists Association
P.O. Box 1265, Loveland, TX 79336
Winning motorcyclists for Jesus.

Christian Motor Sports, International
433 W. Allen Avenue #105, San Dimas, CA
91773
Bringing spiritual inspiration to the world of
motorsports.

Christian Sports Outreach, Intl.
12480 Wayzata Blvd., Minnetonka, MN 55343
Sports evangelism worldwide.

Christian Surfing Association, Inc.
P.O. Box 11296, Costa Mesa, CA 92627
To share Christ with amateur surfers and the
surf industry—at the same time to improve
the amateur competition structure.

Christian Team Ministries, Inc.
1025 Grange Road, Meadow Vista, CA 95722
Ministers to the running and fitness population. Newsletter. Christian Runner's Association (CRA) chapters.

Christian Youth Athletics
1607 Cromwell Bridge Road, P.O. Box 10294,
Baltimore, MD 21234
Ministers to youth by instruction in sports:
baseball, T-ball, soccer and basketball.

Christlike Living Ministries
P.O. Box 627, Branson, MO 65616
Produces materials and conducts seminars that
help Christian athletes and coaches represent
Christ in athletic competition.

Fellowship of Christian Anglers Society
P.O. Box 434, Moraga, CA 94556
Helps develop sense of balance and Christian
leisure ethic in today's stress filled world
through teaching fishing skills. Newsletter.
Conferences.

Fellowship of Christian Athletes
8701 Leeds Road, Kansas City, MO 64129
Strives to strengthen moral, mental and spiritual fiber of the athletes and coaches of America. Fellowship evangelism.

Four Winds Christian Athletics
P.O. Box 29331, Minneapolis, MN 55429
Evangelistic outreach at major world competi-
tions and U.S. meets. Predominately track and
field.

Friendship Sports International
P.O. Box 221, Upland, IN 46989
Sends collegiate and college athletes and
coaches overseas for short term coaching clinic
ministry.

Golf Fellowship
P.O. Box 1911, Maitland, FL 32751
Network of Christian golfers throughout the
world. Training videos. Manual for sponsoring
a fund raising golf tournament. Conducts

"Kids 'N Dads Golf Days." Family golf clinics.

Hockey Ministries International
P.O. Box 36, Beaconsfield, PQ H9W 5T6
Hockey camps and evangelism

International Sports Coalition
579 Peachtree Street, NE., Atlanta, GA 30308
A coalition of churches and ministries internationally working together to use the venue of sports and recreation to win others for Christ.

Kanakuk-Kanakoma Kamps, Inc.
Route 4, Box 2124, Bronson, MO 64616
Evangelistic and discipleship of youth in a sports camping ministry that trains athletes in 30 sports on land and water.

Lay Witnesses for Christ, Int.
P.O. Box 127, Hurst, TX 76053
Chapel services for athletes. Olympic outreach. "Evening With the Stars" evangelistic meeting with testimonies of athletes. Offers sports evangelism training.

Lightrider, Inc.
P.O. Box 178, Upland, IN 46989
Provides opportunity to travel and experience God's creation. Physical involvement is limited to skiing, swimming, hiking, climbing, rubber rafting. Takes groups of 30 adults or teenagers from any location within a five-hour driving radius of Upland, IN to any destination on the North American Continent north of the Rio Grande.

Lo Debar Race Track Ministry
P.O. Box 4822, Hollywood, FL 33083
Ministers to personnel within the race track industry.

The Mike Barber Ministry
P.O. Box 949, Huntsville, TX 77342
To use the testimonies of professional athletes to reach prison inmates, prison administrative staff, and young people in inner cities for Christ.

Ministry to Golfers
1904 North Adams Street, Arlington, VA 22201
Fellowship and Bible study among Tour Pros. Publishes Links Letter. Conducts Executive Golf Seminars.

Missionary Athletes International, Inc.
P.O. Box 945, LaHabra, CA 90633
Soccer evangelism.

Morning Star Christian Fellowship
P.O. Box 2022, Napa, CA 94558
Works with local churches in developing a sports fellowship.

Motor Racing Outreach
Smith Suite 336, Highway 29 North, Harrisburg, NC 28075
Witnesses Jesus Christ to active and retired motor racing professionals—drivers, crew members, business people related to motor racing sports, and their spouses.

Motorsports Ministries
P.O. Box 2737, Rohnert Park, CA 94927
Motorsports chapel ministry at the professional racing level, including I.M.S.A. Camel GT, C.A.R.T. Indy cars, and Trans-Am, Pikes Peak, Sports Cam Club of America. Has bimonthly newsletter.

N.B.C. Camps
N. 21808 Panorama Road, Colbert, WA 99005
Sports evangelism through basketball, volleyball, track and soccer camps. Sends tour teams overseas. Staff available to speak at functions throughout the Northwest.

News Release Basketball
1949 Lake Whatcom Blvd., Bellingham, WA 98226
Basketball sports evangelism tours to Europe.

Overwhelming Victory Ministries
2130 31st Street, N.W., Canton, OH 44709
To help lead coaches and athletes into an initial relationship with Christ. To help coaches and athletes deepen their walk with Christ. To help churches understand how a sports ministry can be used to evangelize and disciple for church growth.

Pass Ministry
9 Meadowrue Drive, Mt. Laurel, NJ 08054
PASS (Pro Athletes Spiritual Service) is a division of the Association of Baptists for World Evangelism (ABWE). Offers assistance and services to pro athletes and to those who minister to them. Informs and encourages those associated with ABWE on how to use a sports ministry.

Pro Athletes for Christ
P.O. Box 271073, Tampa, FL 33688
Offers counsel to those called to serve in an athletic ministry. Pro Athlete Speakers Bureau. Organizes outreach opportunities.

Pro Athletes Outreach
P.O. Box 1044, Issaquah, WA 98027
Leadership training ministry for pro athletes and their spouses. Publishes "Sportspage" tabloid quarterly. Conducts tennis, baseball and football conferences.

Pro Basketball Fellowship
P.O. Box 792, Salida, CA 95368
Provides regular chapel services for NBA
teams and mission opportunities for Christian
ball players.

Professional Skiers Fellowship
401 Ute Lane, Gunnison, CO 81230
Fellowship groups and Bible studies at ski
areas. Evangelistic outreach to ski racers. Ski
instructor conferences.

Racers for Christ, International
(see Christian Motor Sports, International)

RLM Athletics
31 Rainbow Drive, Hauppauge, NY 11788
To glorify God through the medium of athletics, using Christian principles in order to show
the community a difference in attitudes toward
competition.

Sports Ambassadors
25 Corning Avenue, Milpitas, CA 95035
Establishes indigenous sports ministries overseas as an ongoing missionary effort.

Sports Outreach America
290 N. D Street, Suite 202, San Bernardino,
CA 92401
A coalition formed for the purpose of bringing
together churches and other Christian organizations and individual leaders of these organizations, with a common desire to carry out Christian
evangelistic service and discipleship activities
throughout the United States, focusing primarily
on sports and recreation-related activities.

Sports Outreach Institute
P.O. Box 119, Monroe, VA 24574
Develops models of sports outreach that can be
used by churches. Provides research and training.

Sports World Ministries, Inc.
P.O. Box 500, New Tazewell, TN 27825
Sports evangelism by ex-pro football athletes
to collegiate and college campuses.

The Tennis Ministry
135 Fir Hill, Akron, OH 44304
Fellowship and evangelistic outreach on the
pro tour. Puts together tennis mission trips to
other countries.

Unlimited Potential, Inc.
P.O. Box 1355, Warsaw, IN 46580
Baseball clinics worldwide, taught by profes-
sional baseball athletes and collegiate coaches.

Victory Ministry
7420 Stone Creek Avenue, Anaheim, CA
92808
Chapel services and Bible studies for the California Major League football and baseball
clubs.

Winning Women
1010 Eckles Drive, Tampa, FL 33612
To encourage and equip athletes and coaches
worldwide to see themselves as ministers in
their sports.

Women's Tennis Ministry
3417 Worth Hills Drive, Fort Worth, TX 76109
Offers fellowship and outreach opportunities
to the women on the international professional
tennis circuit.

World Sports
160 Harbor Drive, Key Biscayne, FL 33149
Encourages worldwide sharing of information
and working relationships between athletes,
churches, denominations and mission agencies. Offers educational and sports skill evangelism videos, conferences, and development
of new sports ministries.

**Youth Enterprises Sports & Cultural Ex-
change, International**
P.O. Box 777, Chula Vista, CA 92010
Spreading the good news to all lands through
athletes and sports people.

CATCH THE SUPERBOWL OPPORTUNITY!

Each year a special Super Bowl issue of *Sports Spectrum*, a Christian sports magazine
published by Discovery House Publishers and Radio Bible Class, is produced. Copies are
available in increments of 50 at minimum cost as an evangelistic tool. Possibilities: ●Give to
students to distribute to school sports teams. ●Encourage church members to host neighborhood Super Bowl parties and distribute copies of the magazine to neighbors. ●Distribute at
sports bars and other public places where people gather to watch the Super Bowl.
For more information and a free preview copy write to:
Tom Felton, Sports Spectrum magazine, Box 3566, Grand Rapids, MI 49501-3566,
Phone: 616-942-9218, Fax: 616-957-5741

Writers' Guide

CHRISTIAN WRITERS' CONFERENCES AND WORKSHOPS

Write to the conference for additional information.

Arizona

Arizona Christian Writers Conference. Phoenix. Usually held in November. Contact: Reg A. Forder, Box 5169, Phoenix, AZ 85010. 602-838-4919. Attendance: 200.

Christian Writers Conference. Living Water Worship and Teaching Center, Cornville. Usually held in May. Contact: Lee Brownson, Box 529, Cornville, AZ 86325. 602-634-4421. Attendance: 35.

Mini Writing Workshops. Held in various U.S. locations, April 15 to end of year. Contact: Donna Goodrich, 648 S. Pima St., Mesa, AZ 85210. 602-962-6694. Two-hour to day-long workshops on various topics. Attendance: 10-20.

Prescott Christian Writers Seminar. Prescott. Usually held in September. Contact: Barbara Spangler, Box 26449, Prescott Valley, AZ 86312. 602-772-6263. Pauline Dunn, 1840 Iron Springs Rd., #A2F, Prescott AZ 86301. 601-778-7342.

Sweetwater Christian Writers' Workshop. Glendale/Phoenix area. Date to be announced. Contact: Carla Bruce, Box 5640, Glendale, AZ 85312.

California

Biola University Writer's Institute. La Mirada. Usually held in July. Contact: Susan Titus, 13800 Biola Ave., La Mirada, CA 90639. 310-903-4805; 800-75-WORDS (messages). Attendance: 400. Also offers manuscript critique service, writing classes, private tutoring, and video correspondence course.

Christian Writers Fellowship of Orange County. Huntington Beach. Usually held March and October. Contact: Marian Bray, 1017-C N. Baker, Santa Ana, CA 92703. Attendance: 60.

Christian Leaders and Speakers Seminars (C.L.A.S.S.). Various locations nationwide, various dates (send for schedule). Contact: Florence Littauer, 1645 S. Rancho Santa Fe, #102, San Marcos, CA 92069. (619)471-1722. Attendance 100.

Independent Writers of Southern California/Christian Caucus. One-day seminars, various dates, Pasadena. Contact: Pat DeVorss, IWOSC, 13856 Bora Bora Way, #2260, Marina Del Rey, CA 90292-6885.

Inland Empire Christian Writers Seminars. Moreno Valley. Usually held February and September. Contact: Bill Page, Box 8154, Moreno Valley, CA 92552. (714)924-0610.

Lodi All-Day Writers Seminar. San Joaquin Delta College. Date to be announced. Contact: Dee Porter, 103 Koni Court, Lodi, CA 95290.

Mount Hermon Christian Writers Conference. Mount Hermon (near Santa Cruz). Usually held in April. Contact: David R. Talbott, Box 413, Mount Hermon, CA 95041. (408)335-4466. Attendance 200.

Narramore Christian Writers Conference. Narramore Christian Foundation/Rosemead. Usually held in April. Contact: Dr. Clyde M. Narramore, 1409 N. Walnut Grove Ave., Rosemead, CA 91770. 818-288-7000. Attendance: 30.

San Diego Christian Writers Guild One-Day Seminar. Horizon Christian Fellowship campus/San Diego. Usually held in September. Contact Dr. Sherwood Wirt, 14140 Mazatlan Ct., Poway, CA 92064. 619-748-0565.

Santa Clara Valley Christian Writers Seminar. San Jose. Usually held in October.

CHRISTIAN WRITERS' CONFERENCES AND WORKSHOPS cont.

Contact: Pamela Erickson, 71 Park Village Ave., San Jose, CA 95136. 408-226-2064. Attendance: 125.

San Diego State University Writers Conference. San Diego campus. Usually held in January. Contact: Jan Wahl, SDSU, 5630 Hardy St., San Diego, CA 92182. 619-594-2514. Attendance: 350.

West Contra Costa County Christian Writers Conference. Oakland. Usually held in September. Contact: Tammy Nichols, 4839 State Ct., Richmond, CA 94804. 510-237-9890.

"Write to be Read" Workshop. Hume Lake. Usually held in July. Contact: Norman B. Rohrer, 260 Fern Ln., Hume, CA 93628. 209-335-2333. Attendance: 80.

YWAM Christian Writers Seminars. Various locations, various dates. Contact: Registrar, YWAM Writer's Seminars, Box 3464, Orange, CA 92665. 714-637-1733.

Colorado

Christian Writers Conference—Pikes Peak Area. Colorado Springs. Usually held in Fall. Contact: Lynn Dyatt, 3506 Brady Blvd., Colorado Springs, CO 80909. 719-574-2164.

Colorado Christian Communicators Writers Conference. Colorado Springs. Usually held in September. Contact: Shannon R. Sperte, 1294 Amsterdam Dr., Colorado Springs, CO 80907. 719-589-1939. Conference attendance: 50–125.

Colorado Christian Writers Conference. Denver. March 5-6, 1993. Contact: Debbie Barker, Box 3303, Lyons, CO 80540. 303-823-5718. Attendance: 200.

Glen Eyrie Writers' Workshops. Glen Eyrie Conference Center, Colorado Springs. Various dates throughout the year. Contact: Joab Owinyo, Box 6000, Colorado Springs, CO 80934. 719-598-1212, ext. 466.

Writing for the Local Church . . . and Sometimes Beyond. Nazarene Bible College. Held every three years, usually in Spring. Instructor: Betty R. Robertson. Contact: Verla Lambert, NBC, Box 15749, Colorado Springs, CO 80935. 719-596-5110.

Connecticut

Wesleyan Writers Conference. Middletown. Usually held in June. Contact: Anne Greene, c/o Wesleyan University, Middletown, CT 06457. 203-347-9411, ext. 2448.

Florida

Charisma/Florida Christian Writers Conference. Orlando. Usually held in February. Contact: Florida Christian Writers Conference, 600 Rinehart Rd, Lake Mary, FL 32746. 407-333-6000.

Florida Christian Writers Conference. Park Avenue Retreat Center/Titusville. January 14-18, 1993. Contact: Billie Wilson, 2600 Park Avenue, Titusville, FL 32780. 407-269-6702 or 5831. Attendance: 100–150.

Georgia

Northeast Georgia Writers Conference. Gainesville. Biennial, usually held in October. Contact: Elouise Whitten, 660 Crestview Terrace, Gainesville, GA 30501. 404-532-3007.

Hawaii

Frontline Communications/YWAM. Kona. Usually held in June. Contact: Writer's Seminars, 1621 Baldwin Ave., Orange, CA 92665. 714-637-1733.

YWAM Writers School. Hawaii (Big Island). June–August. Contact: Merry Puff, 75-5851 Kuakini Hwy., Kailua-Kona HI 96740. Three month school.

Idaho

Beginners Writing Seminars. Idaho and Washington. January, March, and October. Contact: Linda Hutton, Box 1870, Hayden, ID 83835. 208-772-6184. Attendance: 25 maximum.

Christian Writers Conference of Idaho. Post Falls. Usually held in October. Contact: Sheri Stone, Box 97, Post Falls, ID 83854. 208-667-9730.

Illinois

Christian Writers Institute Conference. Wheaton, June 1-4, 1993. Contact: Christian Writers Institute, 388 E. Gundersen Dr., Carol Stream IL 60188. 708-653-4200. Attendance: 250.

Mississippi Valley Writers Conference. Augustana College/Rock Island. Usually held in June. Contact: David R. Collins, 3403 45th St., Moline, IL 61265. 309-762-8985. Attendance: 90.

Moody Write-to-Publish Conference. Chicago. Usually held in June. Contact: Lin Johnson, Moody Bible Institute, 820 N. LaSalle, Chicago, IL 60610. 312-329-4020. Attendance: 225.

Indiana

Charlene Farris Christian Writers Retreats. Various locations, various dates. Contact: Charlene Farris, 9524 Guilford Dr., #A, Indianapolis, IN 46440. 317-848-2634.

Midwest Writers Conference. Muncie. Usually held in July. Contact: Dr. Earl Conn, Dept. of Journalism, Ball State University, Muncie, IN 47306. 317-285-8200. Attendance: 125.

The Writing Academy Seminar. New Harmony, IN. Usually held in August. Contact: Ann Poppen, 6512 Colby, Des Moines, IA 50311. 515-274-5026. Attendance: 50–60.

Iowa

Writing that Makes a Difference. Cedar Rapids. Usually held in October. Contact: Rev. Marvin Ceynar, 300 Cherry Hill Rd. NW, Cedar Rapids, IA 52405. 319-396-2732. Attendance: 15–25.

Kansas

BCCC Creative Writing Workshop. Butler County Community College, El Dorado. Usually held in Fall. Contact: Vivien Minshull-Ford, 901 S. Haverhill Rd., El Dorado, KS 67042. 316-321-5083, ext. 233. Attendance: 200.

National Lamplighters Inspirational Writers Conference. Bethel College/North Newton. Usually held in July. Contact: Sharon Stanhope, Box 415, Benton, KS 67017. 316-778-1043. Attendance: 50–150. Quarterly newsletter $10.

Louisiana

Louisiana Baptist Christian Writers Conference. Tall Timbers. Usually held in April. Contact: Louisiana Baptist Convention, Box 311, Alexandria, LA 71309.

Maryland

Sandy Cove Christian Writers Conference. Sandy Cove/North East. Usually held in October. Retreat on President's Weekend in February. Contact: Gayle Roper, RD 6, Box 112, Coatesville, PA 19320. 215-384-8125. Attendance: 50.

Review and Herald Writers' Workshop. Review & Herald Publishing Assn., Hagerstown. Usually held in July. Contact: Penny E. Wheeler, 55 W. Oak Ridge Dr., Hagerstown, MD 21740. 301-791-7000, ext. 2595. Attendance: 70.

Massachusetts

Cape Cod Writers' Conference. Craigsville Conference Center. Usually held in August. Contact: Marion Vuilleumier, c/o Cape Cod Conservatory, Rt. 132, West Barnstable, MA 02668. 508-775-4811. Attendance: 130. Also offers Cape Literary Workshops: 6 week-long workshops, July–August. Limited to 10 in each workshop.

Christian Writers Conference. Orleans (Cape Cod), MA. Usually held in October. Contact: Lee Brownson, Box 529, Cornville, AZ 86325. 602-634-4421. Attendance: 40.

Michigan

International Christian Writers Workshop. Berrien Springs. Usually held in June. Contact: Dr. Ron Bowes, ICWW Lifelong Learning, Andrews University, Berrien Springs, MI 49104. 616-471-3125. Attendance: 70.

Maranatha Christian Writers Seminar. Maranatha Bible & Missionary conference/Muskegon. Usually held in August. Contact: Leona Hertel, 4759 Lake Harbor Rd., Muskegon, MI 49441. 616-798-2161. Attendance: 50.

Michigan Northwoods Writers Conference. Glen Arbor. Usually held in July. Contact: Robert Karner, 1 Old Homestead Rd., Glen Arbor, MI 49636. 616-334-3072.

"Speak Up With Confidence" Seminars. Hillsdale. Usually held in July. Contact: Carol Kent, 4184 Quaker Hill Dr., Port Huron, MI 48060. 313-982-0898. Speaking seminar. Attendance 125.

CHRISTIAN WRITERS' CONFERENCES AND WORKSHOPS cont.

Spring Arbor Summer Institute for Christian Writers. Spring Arbor. Usually held in June. Contact: Wally Metts, 112 Main St., Spring Arbor, MI 49283. 507-750-1200, ext. 368. Attendance: Limited to 30.

Minnesota

Minnesota Guild Freelance Writing Seminars. Minneapolis/St. Paul. Usually held in April and October. Contact: Sharron D. McCann, Box 354, Grand Marais, MN 55604.

Missouri

Central Missouri Writer's Retreat. Warrensburg. Usually held in July. Contact: Central Missouri State University, Office of Extended Campus, 402 Humphreys Bldg., Warrensburg, MO 64093. 1-800-SAY-CMSU. Secular.

Right Writing Christian Writers' Workshop. Columbia. Usually held in October. Contact: Teresa Parker/Linda Ordway/Mike Kateman, 237 E. Clearview Dr., Columbia, MO 65202. 314-875-1141/449-2465. Attendance: 100.

Greater St. Louis Inspirational Writers Workshop. St. Louis metro area. Contact: Lila Wold Shelburne, 23 Blackberry, St. Charles, MO 63301. 314-946-8533.

Mark Twain Writers Conference. Hannibal-LaGrange College. Usually held in June. Contact: Dr. James C. Hefley, 921 Center St., Hannibal, MO 63401. 314-221-2462. Attendance: 50–75.

New Mexico

Southwest Christian Writers Seminar. Farmington. Usually held in September. Contact: Patricia Burke, Box 2635, Farmington, NM 87499. 505-327-1962. Attendance: 30.

New York

Artsfest Writers' Workshop. New York. Usually held in May. Contact: Lisa Ledlow, 123 W. 57th St., New York, NY 10019. 212-975-0170, ext. 53. Attendance: 50–100.

Greater Syracuse Christian Writer's Conference. Liverpool. Usually held in May. Contact: Jeri Doner, RR Box 471, Whiting Rd., Jordan, NY 13080. 315-689-6389. Attendance: 60–75.

North Carolina

Blue Ridge Writers Conference. Montreat (NC) Conference Center. Usually held in June. Contact: Yvonne Lehman, Box 188, Black Mountain, NC 28711. 704-669-8421. Attendance: 75.

Evangelical Press Association Convention. St. Paul, MN, May 1993 (held in different location each year). Contact: Gary Warner, Box 4550, Overland Park, KS 66204. 913-381-2017. Attendance: 300–1400. Annual convention; free-lance communicators welcome.

Star Books Writers' Workshop. Aqueduct near Chapel Hill. Usually held in October. Contact: Irene Burk Harrell, 408 Pearson St., Wilson, NC 27893. 919-237-1591. Attendance: 20–30.

Ohio

Cincinnati Bible College Christian Writers Workshop. Cincinnati. Usually held in September. Contact: Dana Eynon, 2700 Gateway Ave., Cincinnati, OH 45204. 513-244-8181. Attendance: 100.

Columbus Christian Writers Workshop. Columbus. Usually held in October. Contact: Brenda Custodio, 3732 Shoreline Dr., Columbus, OH 43232. 614-837-8825. Attendance: 30.

Marion Area Christian Writers Seminar. Marion/Nazarene Church. Usually held in April. Contact: Marge Taylor, 16944 Th127, Harpster, OH 43323. 614-496-4565.

Northwest Ohio Christian Writers Seminar. Findlay. Usually held in September. Contact: Anne Williman, Box 52, Old Fort, OH 44861. 419-992-4756. Attendance: 50.

Writer's World Conference. Akron. Usually held in May. Contact: Tom Raber, Box 966, Cuyahoga Falls, OH 44223. Attendance: 100–200.

Oklahoma

Writing Workshops. Various locations and dates. Contact: Kathryn Fanning, 1016

NW 39th, Oklahoma City, OK 73118.

Professionalism in Writing School. Tulsa. Usually held in March. Contact: Myrna Marshall, 1320 N. 157 E. Ave., Tulsa, OK 74116. 918-437-2886. Attendance: 130.

Oregon

Cascade East Christian Writers Seminar. Redmond. Usually held April and September. Contact: Lois Brenchley, 4773 NE Vaughn, Terrebonne, OR 97760. 503-548-5773. Attendance: 35–50.

Oregon Assn of Christian Writers Coaching Conference. Aldersgate (near Salem). Usually held in July. Contact: Russ Pierson, 2672 Almaden, Eugene, OR 97405. 503-484-0410. Attendance: 125.

Pennsylvania

Christian Writers Workshop. Northeastern Christian Junior College, Villanova. Usually held in October. Contact: Eva Walker Myer, 1860 Montgomery Ave., Villanova, PA 19085. 215-525-6780. Attendance: 100.

Creative and Free-lance Writing Workshop. Royce Hotel/Coraopolis (near Pittsburgh airport). Usually held in April. Contact: Markle Enterprises, Box 209, Ambridge, PA 15003. 412-266-7110. Attendance: 150–200.

Writers' Workshops. Date not set; possibly Spring. Contact: Rita Atwell Holler, 100 Greenwood Rd., York, PA 16301. 717-792-0228.

Greater Philadelphia Christian Writers' Conference. Paoli. Usually held in May. Contact: Marlene Bagnull, 316 Blanchard Rd., Drexel Hill, PA 19026. 215-626-6833. Attendance: 250.

Writing for Publication. Pittsburgh Theological Seminary. Usually held in May. Contact: The Rev. Mary Lee Talbot, 616 N. Highland Ave., Pittsburgh, PA 15206. 412-362-5610. Attendance: 25.

St. Davids Christian Writers' Conference. St. Davids. Usually held in June. Contact: Shirley Eaby, 1775 Eden Rd., Lancaster, PA 17601. 717-394-6758. Attendance: 120.

Tennessee

Religious Communications Congress. Nashville. Usually held in April. Contact: RCC, Mail Stop 192, 127 Ninth Ave. N., Nashville, TN 37234.

Southern Baptist Writers Workshop. Nashville, July 19-22, 1993. Contact: Bob Dean, 127 Ninth Ave. N., Nashville, TN 37234. 615-251-2939. Attendance: 50.

Texas

Christian Booksellers Assn. Convention. Dallas, July 10-15, 1993 and July 16-21, 1994. Contact: CBA, Box 200, Colorado Springs, CO 80901. 719-576-7880. Entrance badges available through book publishers.

The Art of Writing, The Act of Writing. Longview. Usually held in March. Contact: Ernestine Finigan, Box 8513, Marshall, TX 75670. 214-935-3047 or 938-0756 (days). Attendance: 50+.

Frontiers in Writing. Amarillo College. Usually held in August. Contact: Doris R. Meredith, Box 19303, Amarillo, TX 79114. 806-352-3889. Attendance: 150.

Prestonwood Christian Writers Guild Conference. Dallas. Usually held in October. Contact: Debra Frazier, 1809 Waterford Ln., Richardson, TX 75082. 214-783-6319.

Washington

SDA Camp Meeting Writing Class. Auburn. Usually held in June. Contact: Marion Forschler, 18115-116th Ave. SE, Renton, WA 98058. 206-235-1435. Attendance: 60.

Northwest Christian Writers Assn. Seminars. Seattle area, date to be announced. Contact: Margaret Sampson, 8227 NE 115th Way, Kirkland, WA 98034.

Seattle Pacific Christian Writers Conference. Seattle. Usually held in June. Contact: Linda Wagner, Humanities Dept., Seattle Pacific University, Seattle, WA 98119. 206-281-2109. Attendance: 160.

Wenatchee Christian Writers Seminar. Wenatchee. Usually held in May. Contact: Elaine Wright Colvin, Box 11337, Bainbridge Island, WA 98110.

CHRISTIAN WRITERS CONFERENCES AND WORKSHOPS cont.

Word Artists Seminars/Retreats/Classes. Various dates and locations. Contact: Gloria Chisholm, 4915-168th St. SW, #C-201, Lynnwood, WA 98037. 206-743-1012.

Writers Information Network (W.I.N.) Seminars. Variety of one-day and weekend seminars across the country (Washington, DC, Texas, Ohio/Pennsylvania, and Washington/British Columbia). Contact: Elaine Colvin, Box 11337, Bainbridge Island, WA 98110. 206-842-9103. Attendance: 75–150.

Green Lake Christian Writer's Conference Green Lake, July 10-17, 1993. Contact: Dr. Arlo R. Reichter, American Baptist Assembly, Green Lake, WI 54941. 800-558-8898. Attendance: 80.

The Salvation Army Christian Writers' Conference. Camp Lake. Held every two years, usually in April. Contact: Mrs. Major Charles Moffitt, 860 N. Dearborn St., Chicago, IL 60610. 312-440-4653. Attendance: 65–70.

The Writer's Toughest Job—Marketing. University of Wisconsin Center—Fox Valley. Usually held May and November. Instructor: Margaret Houk. Contact: Eugene Gibas, Dir. of Continuing Education, 1478 Midway Rd., Menasha, WI 54952-8002. 414-832-2636.

Limit: 15–20.

Timber-Lee Christian Writer's Conference. Timber-Lee Christian Center/East Troy. Usually held in February. Contact: Gene Schroeppel, 2381 Scout Rd., East Troy, WI 53120. 414-642-7345. Attendance: 30–40.

Canada

Christian Writers of British Columbia. Contact: Beryl Henne, 541-56th St., Delta, BC V4L 1Z5 Canada (Box 1208, Roberts, WA 98291). 604-943-9676.

God Uses Ink Writers Conference. Ancaster, Ontario. Usually held in June. Contact: Audrey Dorsch, Faith Today, Box 8800, Sta. B, Willowdale, ON M2K 2R6 Canada. 416-479-5885. Attendance: 135.

Alberta Christian Writers Fellowship Conference. Usually held in October. Contact: Lela Ball, RR 3, Welaskiwin, AB T9A 1X1 Canada.

Foreign Countries

Frontline Communications. This division of Youth With a Mission sponsors writer's workshops in several foreign countries. Contact: Writer's Seminars, 1621 Baldwin Ave., Orange, CA 92665. 714-637-1733.

Source: Sally E. Stuart, free-lance writer, consultant, and publisher of *The Christian Writers' Market Guide.* For more information about these publications write to 17768 SW Point Forest Ct., Aloha, OR 97006 or phone 503-642-9844.

FOR WRITERS EVERYWHERE

When your vision is as flat as a monobleptic, you're as shilpit as a geophagous Januzary, and it seems like life is just a bowl of stale mundungus—remember to stop and smell the roselles.

—From *Friends of the Friends Newsletter*, June 1991 edition. Published by Friends of the Groom Christian Drama Group.

Inside Religious Publishing: A Look Behind the Scenes by Leonard George Goss and Don M. Aycock. Combines the wisdom and experience of many of the best-known people in religious publishing, each writing in his or her area of expertise. Published by Zondervan Publishing House.

FOCUS BOOK

1991 NEW WORD LIST

James Lowe, new words editor, Merriam-Webster, Inc., reads voraciously, looking for new words. When a word begins to appear over and over, it becomes a candidate for acceptance into Webster dictionaries and thus an established word in our language. Only 20 to 25 new words are selected for the *Collegiate Dictionary* each year.

African-American *n* : an American and esp. of Negroid descent

A-list *n* : a list or group of individuals of the highest level of society, excellence, or eminence

andouille *n* : a highly spiced smoked pork sausage

bodhran *n* : an Irish goatskin drum

camcorder *n* : a small portable combined video camera and recorder

cash cow *n* : a consistently profitable business, property, or product whose profits are used to finance a company's investments in other areas

CD-ROM *n* : a compact disc containing data that can be read by a computer

desktop publishing *n* : the production of printed matter by means of a desktop computer having a layout program that integrates text and graphics

homeboy *n* : a man from one's own hometown, community, or region

intrapreneur *n* : a corporate executive who develops new enterprises within the corporation

Kwanza *n* : an African-American festival held in late December

laser printer *n*: a high-resolution printer for computer output that xerographically prints an image formed by a laser

liposuction *n* : surgical removal of local fat deposits (as in the thighs) esp. for cosmetic purposes

local area network *n* : a network of personal computers in a small area (as an office) that are linked by cable, can communicate directly with other devices in the network, and can share resources

muesli *n* : a breakfast cereal of Swiss origin consisting of rolled oats, nuts, and fruit

porcino *n, pl* **porcini** : a wild edible mushroom of the genus *Boletus*

ultralight *n* : a very light recreational aircraft powered by a small gasoline engine

wanna-be *n* : a person who wants to be someone or something else

Source: From *Webster's Ninth New Collegiate Dictionary.* Copyright © 1991 by Merriam-Webster Inc., publisher of the Merriam-Webster ® dictionaries. Used by permission.

EVANGELICAL CLICHÉS

Christians have developed a vocabulary that may or may not be understandable to non-Christians. While many of these words and phrases are essential to clear writing, writers should be wary of Christian jargon. Unconsciously, some authors have allowed the rhetorical language of sermons, hymns, and devotional literature to shape their prose, resulting in indefiniteness, lack or originality, and at worst, insincerity. Here are a few clichés to avoid:

abundant life

after God's own heart

believe on (the name of the Lord)

born again

burden on my heart

carnal desires

Christian walk

daily walk

den of iniquity

depths of depravity

depths of despair

desires of the flesh

devout Catholic

epitome of evil

eternal refuge

eternal resting place

eternal reward

fervent prayer

forever and ever

from on high

EVANGELICAL CLICHÉS cont.

get into the Word
giant of the faith
God-fearing man (or woman)
God made known to me
God revealed to me
God-shaped vacuum
good Christian
groanings of the spirit
grounded in the faith
grounded in the Word
heart of the gospel
heavenly angels
heavenly anthems
hellfire and damnation
hopeless sinner
inspired Word of God
just pray (just ask)
laid upon my heart
let go and let God
life-changing experience
life everlasting
life of sin
lift up the Lord
lift (someone) up in
    prayer

lusts of the flesh
meet his (or her) Maker
moved by the Spirit
of old (as in "Abraham of
    old")
passions of the flesh
pearly gates
prayer warrior
precious blood of Jesus
prepare our hearts
primrose path
realms of glory
rooted in the faith
rooted in the Word
saving knowledge of
    Christ
seventh heaven
share a verse (of Scripture)
sins of the fathers
snares of the Devil
sorely tempted
soul of humility
soul-stirring message
spiritual high
spiritual state

spoke to my heart
stand before the judgment
    seat
stars in one's crown
storms (tempests) of life
straight and narrow
take it to the Lord
throughout eternity
time immemorial
traveling mercies
trials and tribulations
trophies of grace
trust and obey
unto eternity
unspoken needs
uphold in prayer
urgings of the Spirit
vale of tears
victorious living
walk with God
watch and pray
wicked ways
wiles of the devil
wondrous ways of God
word of prayer

Taken from the *Christian Writer's Manual of Style* by Bob Hudson and Shelley Townsend. Copyright © 1988 by The Zondervan Corporation. Used by permission.

BOOKLIST: A WRITER'S REFERENCE LIBRARY

Standard References

The Chicago Manual of Style. 13th ed. Chicago: University of Chicago Press, 1982.

The NIV Study Bible. Grand Rapids: Zondervan, 1985.

12,000 Words: A Supplement to Webster's Third New International Dictionary. Springfield, Mass.: Merriam-Webster, 1986.

Webster's Ninth New Collegiate Dictionary. Springfield, Mass.: Merriam-Webster, 1985.

English Usage, Style, and Grammar

Bernstein, Theodore M. *The Careful Writer: A Modern Guide to English Usage*. New York: Atheneum, 1965.

Dos, Don'ts & Maybes of English Usage. New York: Times Books, 1977.

Miss Thistlebottom's Hobgoblins: The Careful Writer's Guide to the Taboos, Bugbears and Outmoded Rules of English Usage. New York: Simon and Schuster, 1984.

Copperud, Roy H. *American Usage and Style: The Consensus*. New York: Van Nostrand Reinhold, 1979.

Curme, George O. *English Grammar*. New York: Barnes & Noble, 1967.

Fernald, James C. *English Grammar Simplified*. New York: Barnes & Noble, 1979.

Follet, Wilson. *Modern American Usage: A Guide*. Edited and completed by Jacques Barzun and others. New York: Hill and Wang, 1966.

Fowler, H. W. *A Dictionary of Modern English Usage.* 2d ed. London: Oxford University Press, 1983.

Gordon, Karen Elizabeth. *The Transitive Vampire: A Handbook of Grammar for the Innocent, the Eager, and the Doomed.* New York: Times Books, 1984.

————. *The Well-Tempered Sentence: A Punctuation Handbook for the Innocent, the Eager, and the Doomed.* New Haven: Ticknor and Fields, 1983.

Johnson, Edward D. *The Handbook of Good English.* New York: Facts on File, 1982.

Morris, William, and Mary Morris. *Harper Dictionary of Contemporary Usage.* 2d ed. New York: Harper & Row, 1985.

Opdycke, John B. *Harper's English Grammar.* New York: Warner Books, 1983.

Paxson, William C. *The Mentor Guide to Punctuation.* New York: Mentor Books/New American Library, 1986.

Shaw, Harry. *Punctuate It Right!* New York: Harper & Row, 1963.

————. *Errors in English and Ways to Correct Them.* 3d ed. New York: Harper & Row, 1986.

Shertzer, Margaret. *The Elements of Grammar.* New York: Macmillan, 1986.

Strunk, William, Jr., and E. B. White. *The Elements of Style.* 3d ed. New York: Macmillan, 1979.

Success with Words: A Guide to the American Language. Pleasantville, N.Y.: Reader's Digest Association, 1983.

Words into Type. 3d ed. Englewood Cliffs, NJ: Prentice-Hall, 1974.

Writing, Revising, and Editing

1. General

Appelbaum, Judith, and Nancy Evans. *How to Get Happily Published.* New York: Harper & Row, 1978.

Atchity, Kenneth. *A Writer's Time: A Guide to the Creative Process, From Vision Through Revision.* New York: W. W. Norton, 1986.

Barzun, Jacques. *On Writing, Editing and Publishing.* 2d ed. Chicago: University of Chicago Press, 1986.

Simple and Direct: A Rhetoric for Writers. Rev. ed. New York: Harper & Row, 1984.

Boston, Bruce O., ed. *STET! Tricks of the Trade for Writers and Editors.* Alexandria, VA.: Editorial Experts, 1986.

Boswell, John. *The Awful Truth about Publishing: Why They Always Reject Your Manuscript . . . and What You Can Do about It.* New York: Warner Books, 1986.

Cheney, Theodore A. Rees. *Getting the Words Right: How to Revise, Edit and Rewrite.* Cincinnati: Writer's Digest Books, 1983.

Flesch, Rudolf. *The Art of Readable Writing.* Rev. ed. New York: Harper & Row, 1974.

Graves, Robert, and Alan Hodge. *The Reader Over Your Shoulder: A Handbook for Writers of English Prose.* 2d ed. New York: Random House, 1979.

Gunning, Robert. *The Technique of Clear Writing.* Rev. ed. New York: McGraw-Hill, 1968.

Plotnik, Arthur. *The Elements of Editing: A Modern Guide for Editors and Journalists.* New York: Macmillan, 1982.

Read, Herbert. *English Prose Style.* New York: Pantheon Books, 1952.

Stainton, Elsie Myers. *Author and Editor at Work: Making a Better Book.* Toronto: University of Toronto Press, 1982.

Zinsser, William. *On Writing Well: An Informal Guide to Writing Nonfiction.* 3d ed. New York: Harper & Row, 1985.

2. Religious

Anderson, Margaret J. *The Christian Writers Handbook.* Rev. ed. New York: Harper & Row, 1983.

Aycock, Don M., and Leonard George Goss. *Writing Religiously: A Guide to Writing Nonfiction Religious Books.* Grand Rapids: Baker, 1984.

————. *Inside Religious Publishing.* Grand Rapids: Zondervan, 1989.

Gentz, William H. *The Religious Writer's Marketplace: The Definitive Sourcebook.* Rev. ed. Philadelphia: Running Press, 1985.

Gentz, William, et al. *Writing to Inspire: A Guide to Writing and Publishing for the Expanding Religious Market.* Cincinnati: Writers Digest Books, 1982.

Herr, Ethel. *An Introduction to Christian Writing.* Wheaton, IL: Tyndale House, 1983.

BOOKLIST: A WRITER'S REFERENCE LIBRARY cont.

McCarthy, David S. *Practical Guide for the Christian Writer.* Valley Forge, PA: Judson Press, 1983.

Schell, Mildred. *Wanted: Writers for the Christian Market.* Valley Forge, PA: Judson Press, 1975.

Spencer, Sue Nichols. *Words on Target: For Better Christian Communication.* Richmond: John Knox Press, 1964.

Wirt, Sherwood E. *Getting into Print.* Nashville: Nelson, 1977.

The Making of a Writer: A Christian Writers Guide. Minneapolis: Augsburg, 1987.

Special Aspects of Writing and Editing

1. Copyediting and proofreading

Butcher, Judith. *Copy-editing: The Cambridge Handbook.* New York: Cambridge University Press, 1975.

Judd, Karen. *Copyediting: A Practical Guide.* Los Altos, CA: William Kaufmann, 1982.

McNaughton, Harry H. *Proofreading and Copyediting.* New York: Hastings House, 1973.

Smith, Peggy. *Mark My Words: Instruction and Practice in Proofreading.* Alexandria, VA: Editorial Experts, 1987.

Simplified Proofreading. Alexandria, VA: Editorial Experts, 1984.

2. Gender-specific language

Equality in Print: A Guide for Editors and Publishers. Chicago: Chicago Women in Publishing, 1978.

Guidelines for Creating Positive Sexual and Racial Images in Educational Materials. New York: Macmillan, 1975.

Maggio, Rosalie. *The Nonsexist Word Finder: A Dictionary of Gender-Free Usage.* Phoenix: Oryx, 1987.

Miller, Casey, and Kate Swift. *The Handbook of Nonsexist Writing.* New York: Lippincott and Crowell, 1980.

Supplement to the Publication Manual of the American Psychological Association. 2d ed. Washington, DC: APA, 1974.

Wiley Guidelines on Sexism in Language. New York: John Wiley and Sons, 1977.

3. Indexing

Collison, Robert L. *Indexing Books.* Rev. ed. Tuckahoe, NY: John de Graff, 1967.

Spiker, Sina. *Indexing Your Book: A Practical Guide for Authors.* Madison: University of Wisconsin Press, 1954.

4. Writing and word processing

An Author's Primer to Word Processing. New York: Association of American Publishers, 1983.

Chicago Guide to Preparing Electronic Manuscripts. Chicago: University of Chicago Press, 1987.

McWilliams, Peter A. *The Word Processing Book: A Short Course in Computer Literacy.* New York: Ballantine/Prelude Press, 1982.

Zinsser, William. *Writing With a Word Processor.* New York: Harper & Row, 1983.

5. Copyright

Johnston, Donald F. *Copyright Handbook.* New York: R.R. Bowker, 1978.

Nimmer, Melville B. *Nimmer on Copyright: Literary, Musical, Artistic Property.* 4 vols. New York: Matthew Bender. Continually updated.

Strong, William S. *The Copyright Book: A Practical Guide.* Cambridge: MIT Press, 1984.

The Publishing Business

Adler, Bill. *Inside Publishing.* Indianapolis: Bobbs-Merrill, 1982.

Bailey, Herbert S., Jr. *The Art and Science of Book Publishing.* Austin: University of Texas Press, 1970.

Balkin, Richard. *A Writer's Guide to Book Publishing.* Revised and expanded edition. New York: Hawthorn/Dutton, 1981.

Brownstone, David M., and Irene M. Franck. *The Dictionary of Publishing.* New York: Van Nostrand Reinhold, 1982.

Current Christian Books. Colorado Springs: Christian Booksellers Association Service Corporation. Published annually.

Dessauer, John P. *Book Publishing: What It Is, What It Does.* 2d ed. New York: R.R. Bowker, 1981.

Duke, Judith S. *Religious Publishing and Communications.* White Plains, NY: Knowledge and Industry Publications, 1981.

Lee, Marshall. *Bookmaking: The Illustrated Guide to Design, Production, Editing.* Rev. ed. New York: R.R. Bowker, 1980.

Literary Market Place (LMP). New York: R.R. Bowker. Published annually.

Polking, Kirk, ed. *Writer's Encyclopedia.* Cincinnati: Writer's Digest Books, 1983.

Shatzkin, Leonard. *In Cold Type: Overcoming the Book Crisis.* Boston: Houghton Mifflin, 1982.

Journals for Writers and Editors

1. General trade magazines

The Editorial Eye. Newsletter on style, usage, and professional standards published by Editorial Experts, Inc., 85 S. Bragg St., Alexandria, VA 22312.

Publishers Weekly: The International News Magazine of Book Publishing. Published by the Cahners Publishing Company, 249 W. 17th St., New York, NY 10011.

Righting Words: The Journal of Language and Editing. Published by the Righting Words Corporation, 425 E. 65th St., New York, NY 10021.

Scholarly Publishing. Journal published quarterly by the University of Toronto Press, Toronto, Canada M52 1A6.

Small Press: The Magazine for Independent/In-House/Desktop Publishing. Published by the Meckler Corporation, P.O. Box 3000, Denville, NJ 07834.

2. For writers and editors of religious books

Books & Religion: A Quarterly Review. Trinity Church, 74 Trinity Place, New York, NY 10006.

Bookstore Journal. The official publication of the Christian Booksellers Association, 2620 Venetucci Blvd., P.O. Box 200, Colorado Springs, CO 80901.

The Inspirational Writer. Writer's Digest, 1507 Dana Ave., Cincinnati, OH 45207.

Christianity and Literature. Calvin College, Grand Rapids, MI 49506.

Suppliers of Books on Writing, Editing, and Publishing

Editorial Experts, Inc., 85 Bragg St., Alexandria, VA 22312. Supplies their own newsletter, *The Editorial Eye*, and their own publications for editors and proofreaders.

Mehitabels, P.O. Box 60357, Palo Alto, CA 94306. General books for writers and editors.

Ross Book Service, 3718 Seminary Rd., Seminary PO, Alexandria, VA 22304. General books for writers and editors.

WRITERS' MAGAZINES

Byline Magazine, Box 130596, Edmond, OK 73013. 405-348-5591. General publication for free-lance writers and poets. Kathryn Fanning, managing ed. To inform, instruct and encourage beginning free-lance writers; publishes new and professional writers. Monthly mag.; circ. 5,000. 80% free-lance. Complete ms. Pays $35-$50, on acceptance, for 1st rts. Articles 1,500-1,800 wds. (240/yr.); personal experiences 800 wds.; fiction 2,500-4,000 wds. (12/yr.). Reports in 2-4 wks. Seasonal 4 months ahead. Accepts simultaneous submissions. Guidelines; copy $3.

Poetry: Marcia Preston. Buys 120/yr. Any type; 2-32 lines/$5-$10. Writing themes. Submit maximum 3 poems.

Fillers: Buys 72/yr. Anecdotes, cartoons, facts, jokes, prose, short humor, word puzzles; 300-800 wds./$15-35.

Columns/Departments: End Piece (personal essay on writing theme), 800 wds.; First Sale (joy of selling first ms.), 300-800 wds.; Only When I Laugh (writing humor), 300-800 wds.; $15-$35.

WRITERS' MAGAZINES cont.

Tips: All our material, except fiction, must have a writing theme with the new free-lancer in mind. Most open to End Piece essay. Avoid: choosing a computer, waiting for the muse or the mailman, first writers' conference, how I got started, or rejection slips I'd like to send an editor.

Canadian Writer's Journal, Box 6618, Depot 1, Victoria, British Columbia V8P 5N7, Canada. 604-477-8807. Gordon M. Smart, ed. How-to articles for writers. Quarterly mag; circ. 250, 90% free-lance. Complete ms. Pays $5/published pg.; on publication; for 1st, one-time or reprint rts. Articles 250-1,200 wds. (70/yr.); book reviews 250-500 wds./$5. Reports in 4-6 wks. Seasonal 4 months ahead. Accepts simultaneous submissions. Guidelines; copy $4.

Poetry: Tradition, haiku: on writing.

Fillers: Anecdotes, cartoons, short humor; 100-250 wds.

Tips: Avoid overworked topics such as overcoming writer's block, rejection blues, finding time to write, etc.

Chips Off the Writer's Block, Box 83371, Los Angeles, CA 90083. Secular. Wanda Windham, ed. For beginning writers. Bimonthly newsletter; circ. 500+. 100% free lance. Complete ms. Pays in copies, for one-time or reprint rts. Articles and fiction to 1,200 wds.; book reviews (on writing books) 500 wds. Reports in 1-3 wks. Seasonal 6 months ahead. Accepts simultaneous submissions. Guidelines; copy $3.

Poetry: All forms (on writing only); 1-25 lines. Submit max. 5 poems.

Fillers: Anything on writing; any length.

Tips: Need articles on how to get published, how to get organized in your writing, etc. Also personal experience related to writing and publishing.

The Christian Communicator, Joy Publishing, Biola Writers Institute, LaMirada, CA 90639. 310-903-4805. Susan Titus, managing ed. For the Christian who wants to polish writing skills, develop public-speaking techniques, and glorify God with a writing ministry. Monthly mag.; circ. 1,500. 50% free lance. Query or complete ms. Pays in copies for one-time or reprint rts. All articles printed are eligible for "Article of the Month" contest. Monthly winners receive prizes and are eligible for cash prizes at the end of the year: 1st/$300, 2nd/$200, and 3rd/$100. Buys one-time & reprint rts. Articles 1,000-1,400 wds. (60/yr.); book reviews (on writing) 500 wds. Reports in 2-6 wks. Seasonal 3 months ahead. Accepts simultaneous submissions. Guidelines in each issue; copy for a 9x12 SAE/2 stamps.

Poetry: Uses 12/yr. Poems on writing; 4-24 lines. Submit maximum 6 poems.

Fillers: Uses 12/yr. Anecdotes, cartoons; 400-800 wds.

Special Needs: Celebrity pcs. on writers or editors; writing how-to articles.

Tips: Looking for nuts and bolts articles to help the reader improve writing skills. Most open to fillers and poetry on writing.

Christian Vision RR1, Washago, Ontario L0K 2B0, Canada. Skysong Press. Steve Stanton, ed. For Christian writers, editors, publishers, and artists. Quarterly newsletter; circ. 400. 50% free lance. Complete ms. Pays in copies for one-time rts. Articles 1-2 pgs. (8/yr.); book reviews 1 pg. Reports in 2-8 wks. Seasonal 3 months ahead. Accepts simultaneous submissions & reprints. Free copy.

Poetry: Accepts 4/yr. About writing or publishing. To 1 pg.

Cross & Quill, 590 W. Mercers Fernery Rd., DeLand, FL 32720. Christian Writers Fellowship Intl. Mary Sayler, ed. For Christian writers, editors, agents, conference directors. Bimonthly newsletter; circ. 1,000. 50% freelance. Complete ms. Pays $7.50-$25 in coupons (apply toward critique or CWFI membership), on acceptance, for 1st or reprint rts. Articles 250-500 wds. (12/yr.). Reports in 2-3 wks. Seasonal 6 months ahead. Guidelines; copy $2.

Poetry: Buys 6/yr. Free verse, haiku, light verse, traditional; 2-8 lines. Pays $5 in coupons. Submit maximum 2 poems. Must pertain to writing/publishing.

Fillers: Facts, ideas, short humor (for writers only); 25-100 wds. Pays $5 coupon.

Tips: Concisely written tips for writing professionals.

Explorer Magazine, Box 210, Notre Dame, IN 46556. 219-277-3465. Explorer Publishing Co. Ray Flory, ed. Short, inspirational material. Semiannual digest; circ. 200+. 95% free lance. Complete ms. Pays small cash prizes. Not copyrighted. Articles 100-400 wds. (2/yr.); fiction to 800 wds. (2/yr.). Reports in 2 wks. Seasonal 6 months ahead. Accepts simultaneous submissions. Guidelines; copy $3.

Poetry: Buys 20/yr. All types; to 16 lines.

Fillers: Buys 2/yr. Prose.

Tips: Overstocked.

Gotta Write Network Litbag, 612 Cobblestone Cir., Glenview, IL 60025. 708-296-7631. Secular. Denise Fleischer, ed/pub. A support system for new writers. Quarterly mag.; circ. 200. 50% free lance. Complete ms. (query for fiction). Pays $5 for assigned, pays in copies for unsolicited; between acceptance & publication; for 1st rts. Articles 250-750 wds. (20-30/yr.); fiction 5 pgs. (20-30/yr.); book reviews 3 pgs. Reports in 4-8 wks. Seasonal 3 months ahead. Guidelines; copy $3.75.

Poetry: Accepts 125/yr. Any type; 5-16 lines. Submit maximum 5 poems.

Columns/Departments: Life in General: Chronicle Entry; 3 pgs.

Tips: Ask what I'm looking for and send it. Become a qualified contributing writer and meet your deadline.

Housewife-Writer's Forum, Box 780, Lyman, WY 82937. 307-786-4513. Secular. Diane Wolverton, ed.; Linda Capel, articles ed.; Bob Haynie, fiction ed. Publishes the writings of housewife-writers. Bimonthly mag.; circ. 1,000. 90% free lance. Query (complete ms. for fiction). Pays 1¢-2¢/wd., on acceptance, for 1st rts. Articles (180/yr.) & fiction (6-12/yr.), 400-2,000 wds. Reports in 4-10 wks. Seasonal 6 months ahead. Accepts reprints. Guidelines/contest information; copy $4.

Poetry: Buys 50/yr. Free verse, light verse, traditional, humorous; to 36 lines; $1-$2. Submit maximum 6 poems.

Fillers: Buys 24/yr. Anecdotes, cartoons, facts, ideas, short humor, hints (on writing/running a home); to 200 wds.; $1-$4.

Columns/Departments: Buys 40/yr. Confessions of a Housewife-Writer or Domestic Humor, 400-1,000 wds.; 1¢/wd.

Lamplighters Family of Writers, 15503 Midland Dr., Shawnee, KS 66217. 913-268-4480. Aggie Villanueva, managing ed. To inform, educate, and unite the family of Christian writers. Quarterly newsletter; circ. 200. 30-40% free lance. Complete ms. Pays copies & subscription. Articles 300-1,500 wds. (20/yr.); book reviews 300-350 wds. Reports in 4-6 wks. Seasonal 5 months ahead. Accepts simultaneous submissions & reprints. Guidelines; copy $2.

Poetry: Accepts 4-10/yr. Avant-garde, free verse, light verse, traditional (all pertaining to writing); 5-20 lines. Submit maximum 5 poems.

Fillers: Accepts 40/yr. Anecdotes, cartoons, facts, ideas, newsbreaks, prose, short humor; 50-500 wds.

WRITERS' MAGAZINES cont.

Tips: We need lots of how-to & interview pcs. Also tips from writers, computer software, and book reviews.

Living Streams, Box 1321, Vincennes, IN 47591. 812-882-4289. Kevin Hrebik, founder/ed-in-chief. Inspirational and Christian literature written by writers for writers. Quarterly journal. 95% freelance. Complete ms. Pays in copies for now, for one-time rts. Articles (150-200/yr.), fiction (10/yr.), book reviews (25/yr.); 500-1,200 wds. Accepts simultaneous submissions & reprints. Guidelines; copy $3.75.

Poetry: Uses 100/yr. Free verse, haiku, light verse, traditional, special forms; 3-24 lines. Submit maximum 12 poems.

Tips: Only publishes subscribers. Be willing to rewrite.

Merlyn's Pen, The National Magazine of Student Writing, Box 1058, East Greenwich, RI 02818. Secular. R. James Stahl, ed. Written by students in grades 7-10 only. Mag. fiction to 2,500 wds.; reviews and travel pieces to 1,000 wds. Pays in copies. Not in topical listings. Students send for guidelines.

Poetry: To 100 lines.

The Poetry Connection, 301 E. 64th St. #6K (CWM), New York, NY 10021. 212-249-5494. Secular. Sylvia Shichman, ed./pub. Information on marketing poetry; contests. Bimonthly newsletter; circ. 200. No payment. Not copyrighted. Copy $5/4 stamps.

Poetry: All types.

Tips: Also available: Books on selling poetry; literary agent listing; books for purchase.

Teachers & Writers, 5 Union Square W, New York, NY 10003. 212-691-6590. Ron Padgett, ed. On teaching creative and imaginative writing. Mag. published 5 times/yr.; circ. 1,500-2,000. Query. Pays in copies. Articles 3,000-6,000 wds. Not in topical listings. Copy $2.50.

The Writer, 120 Boylston St., Boston, MA 02116. Secular. Sylvia K. Burack, ed-in-chief/pub. How-to for writers. Monthly mag. 20-25% free lance. Pays on acceptance, for 1st rts. Articles about 2,000 wds. Reports promptly. Not in topical listings. Copy $3.

Writers Anchor, 100 Greenwood Rd., York, PA 17404. 717-792-0228. York Writers, Rita Atwell Holler, ed. Secular. Quarterly newsletter; circ. 30. 80% free lance. Complete ms. Pays in copies for any rts. Not copyrighted. Articles 150-300 wds. (uses 10/yr.); book reviews 150 wds. Reports in 2-14 wks. Seasonal 3 months ahead. Deadlines are the 15th of March, June, September, and December. Accepts simultaneous submissions & reprints. Guidelines/copy for #10 SAE/1 stamp.

Poetry: Uses 4-6/yr. All types; 4-42 lines. Submit maximum 6 poems.

Fillers: Uses 15/yr. All except party ideas; 10-30 wds.

Columns/Departments: Uses 9/yr. Games (writing only), 150 wds.; Exhilaration (overcoming rejection), 75 wds.; Q & A (on writing), 35 wds.

Tips: Most open to poetry on writing.

Writers Connection, 1601 Saratoga-Sunnyvale Rd., Ste. 180, Cupertino, CA 95014. 408-973-0227. General newsletter with nuts and bolts information on writing and publishing in all fields. Jan Stiles, ed. Monthly newsletter; circ. 2,500. 60-70% free lance. Query or complete ms. Pays in copies, subscription, memberships or seminars, for 1st or reprint rts. Articles 1,000-2,000 wds. (25-35/yr.); book reviews 200 wds. Reports in 3 wks. Seasonal 8 months ahead. Not in topical listings. Free guidelines/copy.

Writer's Digest, 1507 Dana Ave., Cincinnati, OH 45207. 513-531-2222. Secular. Peter Blocksom, submissions ed. Information on writing and publishing. Monthly mag.; circ. 225,000. 90% free lance. Query or complete ms. Pays .10/wd. & up, on acceptance, for one-time rts. Articles 500-3,000 wds. (90-100/yr.). Reports in 2 wks. Seasonal 8 months ahead. Accepts reprints. Kill fee 20%. Guidelines; copy $3.
   Poetry: Buys 24-36 yr. Light verse on writing; 2-20 lines; $10-$50. Submit maximum 8 poems.
   Fillers: Buys 48/yr. Anecdotes and short humor on writing; 50-250 wds.; 10¢/wd.

Writer's Exchange, Box 394, Society Hill, SC 29593. Gene Boone, ed. Uses poetry of all types, including religious material. Quarterly newsletter; circ. 100+. 75% free lance. Complete ms. Pays in copies for one-time rts. Articles to 50-750 wds. (20/yr.). Reports in 3 wks. Seasonal 4-6 months ahead. Reports in 2-4 wks. Accepts reprints. Guidelines; copy $1/SASE.
   Poetry: Uses 35/yr. Any type; 3-20 lines. Submit maximum 10 poems.

Writer's Guidelines, RD #1, Ward Rd., Box 71, Mohawk, NY 13407. 315-866-7445. Secular. Carol Ann Vercz, ed. Informational, educational, and entertaining. Monthly mag; circ. 1,000. 100% free lance. Query. Pays 2¢/wd. (reprints 1¢/wd.), on publication, for one-time or reprint rts. Articles 500-1,200 wds. (200/yr.); fiction 1,500 wds. Reports in 6 wks. Seasonal 6 months ahead. Accepts simultaneous submissions. Guidelines; copy $3.
   Poetry: Buys 100/yr. Traditional; 6-25 lines; 25¢/line. Submit maximum 6 poems.
   Fillers: Buys 15/yr. Anecdotes, facts; $1-$5.
   Tips: Looking for ideas for new columns.

Writer's Info, Box 1870, Hayden, ID 83835. 208-772-6184. Hutton Publications. Linda Hutton, ed. Tips for free lancers writing for religious markets. Monthly newsletter; circ. 200. 90% free lance. Complete ms. Pays $1-$10; on acceptance; for 1st & reprint rts. Articles 300 wds. (50-75/yr.). Reports in 1 month. Seasonal 9 months ahead. Accepts simultaneous submissions. Guidelines; copy for #10 SAE/2 stamps.
   Poetry: Buys 40-50/yr. Free verse, light verse, traditional (no shaped poetry); 4-20 lines; $1-$10. Submit maximum 6 poems.
   Fillers: Buys 3-4/yr. Anecdotes, jokes, short humor; 10-100 wds.; $1-$10.

Writers Information Network, Box 11337, Bainbridge Island, WA 98110. 206-842-9103. Professional Assn. of Christian Writers. Elaine Wright Colvin, ed. Bimonthly newsletter; circ. 600+. 100% free lance. Complete ms. Variable pay rate, for 1st rts. Articles 350 wds. (20/yr.); book reviews 150 wds. Guidelines; copy for #10 SAE/2 stamps.

Writer's Journal, Minnesota Ink, Inc., 27 Empire Dr., St. Paul, MN 55103-1861. 612-225-1306. Secular. Valerie Hockert, ed. Monthly journal; circ. 37,000. 40% free lance. Complete ms. Pays to $50, on publication, for 1st rts. Articles 700-1,000 wds. (30-40/yr.). Reports in 4-6 wks. Seasonal 6 months ahead. Accepts simultaneous queries. Not in topical listings. Guidelines; copy $3.
   Poetry: Esther M. Leiper. Buys 20-30/yr. All types; to 25 lines; 25¢/line. Submit maximum 5 poems.
   Contest: Runs 2 poetry contests each year, spring & fall.

The Writer's Nook News, 38114 3rd St., #181, Willoughby, OH 44094. 216-975-8965. Secular. Eugene Ortiz, ed./pub. Dedicated to giving freelance writers specific information for their immediate practical use in getting published and staying published. Quarterly newsletter; circ. 1,000. 100% free lance. Complete ms. Pays $24, on acceptance, for 1st

WRITERS' MAGAZINES cont.

N.A. serial rts. Not copyrighted. Articles 400 wds. (75-80/yr.); book reviews 50-100 wds. (6¢/wd.). Reports in 2-16 wks. Guidelines; copy $5/9x12 SAE/2 stamps.

Fillers: Buys 20/yr. Cartoons, facts, newsbreaks; 6¢/wd.

Tips: Articles must be specific, terse, and contain information my readers can put to immediate practical use. Need articles on writer's rights.

ADDITIONAL PUBLICATIONS (Guidelines same as above)

The Nook News Review of Writers' Publications
The Nook News Contests & Awards Bulletin
The Nook News Conferences & Klatches Bulletin
The Nook News Market Bulletin

Writer's Resource Newsletter, Box 940335, Maitland, FL 32794. 407-260-5150. Jeffrey Atwood, ed. News and resources for writers. Bimonthly newsletter; circ 1500. 25% free lance. No payment. Articles 50-650 wds. (uses 10/yr.). Reports in 2 wks. Seasonal 3 months ahead. Accepts simultaneous submissions & reprints. Guidelines; free copy.

Fillers: Uses 10-15/yr. Anecdotes, facts, newsbreaks; 10-100 wds.

Tips: Straightforward, tight news, tips, techniques for writers—religious or otherwise. Especially tips and resources that help writers find ideas or write better.

Source: *The Christian Writers' Market Guide* by Sally E. Stuart. For more information about these publications write to 17768 SW Point Forest Ct., Aloha, OR 97006 or phone 503-642-9844.

MUTUALLY EXCLUSIVE

Real phony   —Gloria Schlesna
Strangely familiar   —Jacqueline Schiff
Light heavyweight   —C.P. Miscavish
Definite maybe   —Jon L. Runyan

Source: Reader's Digest.

Index

Page numbers in italics refer to charts or graphs.

Women
  assaults against 780
  equal to serve 21, 66-69
  ministry 3, 16, 20
  seminary, in *454*
Work ethic, lost 34
World Congress on Evangelism 465
World Council of Churches 11
World religions 81, 681
  population 75, 81
World Vision 567
Worldwide Evangelization Crusade 732
Writers, Christian

book suppliers 851
books for and about 846
journals and magazines for 851-856
conferences and workshops, Christian 841-846
reference, booklist for 848-851
words, new 847
words, worn-out 847-848
Wycliffe, John 350-351

X
Xavier, Francis 728

Y
Young Men's Christian Association (YMCA) 461, 463
Youth for Christ 465
Yugoslavia 29, 149-151

Z
Zaire 151-152
Zettersten, Rolf 780
Zinzendorf, Nicolaus Ludwig-Graf von, Count 353, 493
Zwemer, Samuel Marinus 732
Zwingli, Ulrich 351, 491